in the most ghastly disaster of the
whole war!

I wish to God it were
safely over.

June 6ᵗʰ

By 7.30. I began
to receive first news of the
invasion. The air-born landings
had been successful, the first
wave were reported as going in,
opposition not too serious, weather
dmg dmg fleunds, &c

Throughout the day information has
gone on coming in. On the British
front the landing has gone well
and the whole of 3 Division
are ashore. On the America
front the western landing was a
success but the East Corps (V)
has failed practically along its
whole front! They are now
asking to land on other western beaches

6 June 1944

WAR DIARIES
1939–1945

To Dad
even more to read
44 years later!
Christmas 2011
Love Jim

WAR DIARIES
1939–1945

Field Marshal Lord Alanbrooke

Edited by
Alex Danchev and Daniel Todman

Weidenfeld & Nicolson
LONDON

This edition first published in Great Britain in 2001 by
Weidenfeld & Nicolson
Second impression June 2001
Third impression June 2001
Fourth impression July 2001
Fifth impression October 2001
Sixth impression November 2001

A CIP catalogue record for this book is available
from the British Library.

ISBN 0 297 60731 6

Printed in Great Britain by Butler & Tanner Ltd,
Frome and London

Weidenfeld & Nicolson
The Orion Publishing Group
Orion House
5 Upper Saint Martin's Lane
London WC2H 9EA

'High rank can be very dangerous,' said Pangloss; 'all the philosophers say so.'

Voltaire, *Candide*

Dedicated to Benita Blanche Brooke,
first reader and safekeeper.

CONTENTS

ILLUSTRATIONS

The photographs of Benita Brooke and the children are reproduced by permission of her granddaughter, Benita Stoney. The other photographs, and Alanbrooke's drawing of Churchill on page lii, are reproduced by permission of the Trustees of the Liddell Hart Centre for Military Archives, King's College London.

The endpapers reproduce part of Alanbrooke's diary entries for 5 and 6 June 1944 (Liddell Hart Centre for Military Archives).

INTRODUCTION:
The Unhappy Warrior

Dedicated to Benita Blanche Brooke
Begun 28 September 1939
This book is not intended to be a diary of events, although it may contain references to my daily life. It is intended to be a record of my thoughts and impressions such as I would have discussed them with you had we been together.

   After living the last ten years with you and never being parted for more than a few weeks at a time, I should feel quite lost without an occasional opportunity of a talk with you although such a talk must necessarily be confined to writing: I therefore procured this book in Salisbury on purpose for such conversations with you. It was originally part of Smith's stock of books on the *Queen Mary*, but having failed to sell was reduced from 60/- to 15/-!

   The thoughts I express may contradict themselves as I wish to give full scope to free expression and do not care if I am forced to change my mind by events.

ON NO *ACCOUNT MUST THE CONTENTS OF THIS BOOK BE PUBLISHED.*[1]

For diarists as for other deviants, the fundamental question is the question of motive. Why? The natural supplementary is the question of audience. Who? To keep a diary is to posit a reader. Whether they recognize it or not, all diarists, especially dedicated diarists, hope to be read one day – read and understood – though not necessarily by anyone they know or identify.[2] 'I sometimes wonder why I keep a diary at all,' the Parliamentary socialite 'Chips' Channon recorded apostrophically. 'Is it to relieve my feelings? Console my old age? Or to dazzle my descendants?' Several volumes later he could feel that 'some day they may see the light of day and perhaps shock or divert posterity a little'. Channon kept a diary almost continuously for nearly forty years. His companionable contemporary Harold Nicolson performed a similar feat. When the idea of publication was first mooted – a version edited by his son Nigel – the venerable Nicolson was asked the 'why' question by Nigel and his brother Ben. He replied, 'Oh, because I thought I would.' 'Come,' they said, 'that's not good enough. You didn't write for publication?' 'No, that never entered my head.' 'You never showed it to anybody?' 'Never.' 'You never re-read it yourself?' 'Very, very rarely, when I wanted to check a name or a date.' 'Then why did you take such trouble?' 'Because I thought one day it might amuse you and Ben.' And that was all they could get out of him. Six months later, lunching alone with him at Sissinghurst, Nigel repeated the question. Nicolson responded that the diary had become a habit. 'Like brushing your teeth?' 'Exactly.'[3]

At some level, perhaps, motivation is always imponderable. Channon and Nicolson invoke in their different registers a selection of the most persuasive and evasive answers to these intransigent questions; or, if not answers exactly, then explanations of that solitary practice, 'a whole little secret life over and above the other', as Sartre said of his own war diaries – a practice expressly forbidden to the censored soldier, yet blithely flouted by the Chief of the Imperial General Staff.[4] Where, in this no man's land of persuasion and evasion, are the Alanbrooke diaries to be located?

Alanbrooke wrote initially out of love and loneliness. Characteristically, he had made provision for both, as the dedicatory note (reproduced above) in the first of the bargain books plainly states. In his case, apparently, the answer to the 'who' question is very clear. The diaries were destined for his second wife, Benita Brooke, née Pelly, widow of Sir Thomas Lees.[5] They were married in 1929, when he was forty-six, four years after his first wife had died, tragically, from an automobile accident with Alanbrooke at the wheel – a period shrouded in grief.[6] Benita brought life. They had two small children, Kathleen and Victor (Pooks and Ti in the diary), who joined two older ones, Tom and Rosemary, from his first marriage. He loved Benita with a passion: a Gascon-Edwardian passion, a compound of his upbringing and education in Pau in the French Pyrenees and his training and formation at 'The Shop' (the Royal Military Academy, Woolwich) and in the Royal Regiment of Artillery. Come September 1939, he wrote to his inamorata as he went to war (a military tradition in itself, but no less heartfelt for all that), to command one of the three Corps which made up the scratch British Expeditionary Force despatched to the over-familiar fields of France and Flanders when peace expired for a second time. Construed as a perpetual love letter in the guise of a journal, delivered personally but sporadically at Hitler's pleasure, the diary was a form of communion, an exigent outpouring, a beacon to Benita.

The communion was at once remote and intense. In the early years it is that combination which feeds the more sustained passages of the work, exciting it, and giving it a distinctive character: part entreaty, part release. Alanbrooke's unimpeachable reputation was founded on 'two qualities not readily interfusable', as Melville has it, 'prudence and rigour'.[7] As CIGS he could be prudent and rigorous all the long day – and it might seem, waltzing with Winston, all the long night – but not for ever. In the still small hour of duty to his diary, strong emotions welled up and spilled improvidently across the page: frustration, depression, betrayal, doubt. Keeping the diary may have begun as 'just a little daily intimate talk' with his truly beloved, a function of enforced separation, but it evolved, as diaries do, into something more instinctual.[8] It became a necessary therapy, even an offertory, for the diarist (no churchgoer) is prone to thanksgiving, and, *in extremis*, prayer.

> I pray God that the decisions we arrived at may be correct,
> and that they may bear fruit.

Reflecting on this entry after the war, the conclusion to a journey to the Western Desert to remake the command in August 1942, he wrote: 'one may be apt to overlook those ghastly moments of doubt which at times crowded in on me. Moments when one wondered whether one had weighed up situations correctly, arrived at the right conclusion, and taken suitable action. This little short prayer of 2 lines was not just a figure of speech, it was a very real, deep felt and agonized prayer written at a moment of considerable mental and physical exhaustion at the end of 3 most memorable weeks!'[9] Keeping the diary afforded some consolation, possibly, a measure of protection against 'the melancholies, the morosities and the sadnesses of war'.[10]

In a certain sense he had been trained to write – notwithstanding the embarrassment of his spelling and the incontinence of his script.[11] Punctilious in adoration from an early age, for nearly twenty years he wrote religiously to his valetudinarian mother Alice – his father, Sir Victor Brooke, 3rd Baronet of Colebrooke, County Fermanagh, Ulster, died when he was seven – who from her pedestal showered him with uncovenanted maternal blessings. 'She had that faculty, so rare amongst humans, to be able to enter entirely into one's actions, aspirations, disappointments, successes and failures and to throw herself wholeheartedly into one's life. She was consequently not only the most perfect mother but one of the very best of companions.'[12] Read in retrospect, his letters to her become rehearsals for a later production.[13] From the Royal Artillery Mess, Meerut, India, 7 January 1908:

I have just been adding up my game book, and find that my totals for the larger game work out most satisfactorily for my first year in India. They are as follows: 1 ovis ammon [wild sheep], 3 ibex [mountain goat], 4 bunhel, 1 sharpu, 2 bara sing[a] [swamp deer], 1 nilgai [antelope], 1 sambu[r] [large deer], 7 black buck, 2 para (one of them stuck, and more or less a record for the Kadir [country]), 9 pig (with a record tusk for the Kadir), 1 chinkara doe shot by mistake, 17 marmots.

Rather a nice assorted variety for the first year. Unfortunately I missed the Tibetan Gazelle and Red Bear last month, and failed to spear a hyena; these would have added 3 specimens to the above. So far, the carnivora have defeated me, but I intend to get level with them before I have done.

The Great War hardly dented his output. From 18th Division (Ivor Maxse) on the Somme, on the second day of the big push, 2 July 1916:

We have been busy at it since yesterday morning. At last our preliminary bombardment, which had been going on for several days, came to an end, and our infantry attacked at 7.30 am. It has been a continual war of guns for close on a week, both night and day, each gun with its special task and lines allotted to it throughout that period; slowly pounding away at the German trenches, some of them systematically hammering a way through the back wire entanglements, others pounding trenches to pieces, bombarding villages to demoralize supports, keeping up barrage on roads, to prevent the supplies, ammunition etc being brought up, whilst our counter batteries took on the German batteries. After an intense bombardment of 65 minutes, our infantry left their trenches and attacked the German trenches. We had a very careful timetable of lifts worked out, by which the artillery lifted off each system of trenches just before the infantry arrived there, and moved on in advance of the infantry the whole time.

The attack of our Division was a great success, and we took exactly what we intended to take. We advanced about 1500 yards on a 2000 yards front. Our casualties were pretty heavy, but not as heavy as they might have been, and up to the present we have taken 600 prisoners in this Division, and the whole countryside is covered with dead Germans.[14]

Whether Alice in her invalid bed fully appreciated this proud account of the first creeping barrage is a moot point, but she did preserve all her youngest son's letters. Loosely bound, for family and posterity, they made something very like a diary.[15]

'Little mother' hung on until 1920. By then her son was well married for the first time. For Alanbrooke there was always an audience, doting and devoted, in a safe place. He may have needed that: needed to adore as much as be adored; needed a 'you'. Conventionally repressed yet sentimentally advanced, at both ends of his career he was in some ways an isolate, 'not quite one of the herd', arrestingly insecure in youth – 'having learned French before English, and having spent the first 16 years of my life in France, I was in continual apprehension lest I should look like a Frenchman, speak as a Frenchman, and possibly earn the name of "Froggie"' – seemingly impregnable in maturity.[16] When he inherited the mantle of CIGS from his friend and confessor Dill, as 1941 drew to its ignominious end, he was 'temporarily staggered', not to say daunted, as his diary and notes movingly disclose. Except perhaps for Dill himself, no one would have known. By then the carapace was full-grown. As CIGS he appeared absolutely formidable. His overpowering presence has been brilliantly captured by the novelist Anthony Powell, who described:

… the hurricane-like imminence of a thickset general, obviously of high rank, wearing enormous horn-rimmed spectacles. He had just burst from a flagged staff-car almost before it had drawn up by the kerb. Now he tore up the steps of the building at the charge, exploding through the inner door into the hall. An extraordinary current of physical energy, almost of electricity, suddenly pervaded the place. I could feel it stabbing through me. This was the CIGS. His quite remarkable and palpable extension of personality, in its effect on others, I had noticed not long before, out in the open. Coming down Sackville Street, I had all at once been made aware of something that required attention on the far pavement and saw him pounding along. I saluted at admittedly longish range. The salute was returned. Turning my head to watch his progress, I then had proof of being not alone in acting as a kind of receiving-station for such rays –

which had, morally speaking, been observable, on his appointment to the top post, down as low as platoon commander. On this Sackville Street occasion, an officer a hundred yards or more ahead, had his nose glued to the window of a bookshop. As the CIGS passed (whom he might well have missed in his concentration on the contents of the window), this officer suddenly swivelled a complete about-turn, saluting too. No doubt he had seen the reflection in the plate glass. All the same, in its own particular genre, the incident gave the outward appearance of exceptional magnetic impact. That some such impact existed, was confirmed by this closer conjunction in the great hall. Vavassor, momentarily overawed – there could be no doubt of it – came to attention and saluted with much more empressement than usual. Having no cap, I merely came to attention. The CIGS glanced for a split second, as if summarizing all the facts of one's life.

'Good morning.'[17]

'In his demanding and abrupt efficiency', offered *The Economist* appreciatively, 'he knew when to scold, when to encourage, when to protect. Men admired, feared, and liked him: in that order, perhaps. He became, in peculiar, the conscience of the Army: a dark, incisive, round-shouldered, Irish eagle, the reluctant chairman of a council of war, frustrating, in selfless but far from patient service, those talents that could not otherwise but have forced him into the company of the great captains.'[18] Existentially reassuring, as Powell suggested, the CIGS presented a forbidding face to the world. His nickname in the War Cabinet Offices was an appropriate one: Colonel Shrapnel.[19] In debate his characteristic rejoinder was a bleak negative – 'I flatly disagree' – accompanied by the snapping of a pencil. Alanbrooke had mettle. It was for this very quality that he was selected by the Prime Minister, Winston Churchill, who invited him to Chequers, dined him royally, interrogated him pitilessly, passed him the chalice, and tenderly wished him luck – a *modus operandi* with which he was to become excessively familiar over the next few years.

The Prime Minister's selection was not unpremeditated. Churchill was tired of reverses and deadlocks, and tired too of the CIGS who had the misfortune to accompany them: Dilly-Dally, 'the dead hand of inanition'.[20] Ian Jacob appraised Churchill's strategic wanderlust from the spectator seats of the Cabinet Secretariat:

He was not a *calm* thinker, whose attention was naturally directed to grand strategy, a student of campaigns in their academic aspect, a Liddell Hart or a Clausewitz. He was a man who required to push away at some concrete project, not a cold, aloof strategist. He had studied battles, and by instinct tended to think of life as a series of conflicts with barriers to be overcome, opposition to be borne down. He hated those periods which are inevitable in a war when operations have come to a conclusion, and there must be a pause for planning and preparation, for regrouping and reorganization. His mind chafed, and he turned always to any project however minor, or however irrelevant to the main theme, in the hope that it would fill the gap. His frequent efforts to get the Chiefs of Staff and the planning staffs to work out an operation in Norway sprang not so much from a desire to free that country or to close German access to the oceans, but from his wish to have something happen before the next major operation was due to start. One of his favourite phrases was that the enemy must be made 'to bleed and burn', everywhere and all the time. ...[21]

Churchill had scrambled into supremacy in May 1940. His ambit was Elizabethan. 'I myself will be your General, Judge and Rewarder of every one of your virtues in the field.'[22] For some eighteen months he had been on short commons, unable to satisfy his craving. Finally, after wide inspection, he thought he had found his man. 'When I thump the table and push my face towards him what does he do? Thumps the table harder and glares back at me. I know these Brookes – stiff-necked Ulstermen and there's no one worse to deal with than that!'[23] What Churchill craved was disputation. Disputation is what he got: more, much more, than he bargained for. That is the tale told by the Alanbrooke diaries – one might almost say enacted in the Alanbrooke diaries – a tale of schism and self-control in the secret heart of the machine.

Churchill knew the Brookes of yesteryear – 'the friends of my early military life'.[24] How well he ever knew the one with whom he was yoked in harness for the greater part of the Second World War is a matter for speculation and scepticism. His doctor Sir Charles Wilson (Lord Moran) observed acutely that he was slow to recognize the merits of anyone who was not congenial to him. 'His judgements of men when he had to size up those around him – and it was a task he found not at all to his taste – were seldom impersonal. Efficiency in itself did not appear to influence his likes or dislikes. Beatty not Jellicoe, Mountbatten not Wavell, that was his form. Lloyd George, F. E. [Smith], Max Beaverbrook and Lord Cherwell, these men were his cronies, in their different ways all, mark you, men of violent thought; all men with a flamboyant streak. ...He would have been for the King, a Cavalier, disliking Puritans. Paget, Winant, Reith, he could make nothing of them, and the bloodless austerity of Stafford Cripps repelled him.'[25]

Was Alanbrooke in the other camp? He was Puritan enough: Churchill himself is said to have identified another Stafford Cripps. Beyond question, flamboyance was anathema to the CIGS. 'A meeting with Slim prior to his departure for India. I rubbed into him my dislike for "prima donna generals" and "film star generals", I hope he will take it to heart.'[26] Alanbrooke disapproved of cronyism; Beaverbrook, in particular, he abhorred. At his first *Alice in Wonderland* weekend at Chequers, he remembered, 'Beaverbrook was present; after dinner he sat at the writing table, pouring himself out one strong whisky after another, and I was revolted by his having monkey-like hands as they stretched out to grab ice cubes out of the bowl. The more I saw of him throughout the war, the more I disliked and mistrusted him. An evil genius who exercised the very worst of influence on Winston.'[27] His form was counterpoise: Bevin not Macmillan, Cunningham not Pound, Wilson not Alexander, Wavell, of course, not Mountbatten – the buddha rather than the principal boy. Dill first, last, and always. With Winant, the American Ambassador to London, he discovered real fellow-feeling. Moran was on hand to witness their encounter: 'Winant holds men, but that is as far as they get. He has wrestled with the world and has hidden, like Brooke, behind a curtain of his own making. It appeared to lift a little when the two men came together. There was Winant talking eagerly about [Grey's] *Fallodon Papers* and Brooke – a new Brooke to me – hardly able to wait his turn as he thought of some lines from *The Prelude*. When Winant had done, how his words cascaded!'[28]

Alanbrooke's curtain was a mask of command. High rank, he believed, carried a heavy obligation. The lacerations must not show. His performance of public impregnability was precisely that: a performance, for others, just as Churchill performed the indomitable chauvinist-in-chief, complete with gesture and growl, and more props. Apart from Dill (excommunicated to Washington), who knew at first hand the purgatory of a Chief of Staff, Alanbrooke's only outlet was his diary, as he is at pains to convey.[29] Ever since the publication of Sir Arthur Bryant's *The Turn of the Tide* (1957) and *Triumph in the West* (1959), artful confections of the diaries and Alanbrooke's autobiographical notes, sieved and selected by 'the Tacitus of our time', this is the accepted answer to the 'why' question: a kind of psychological safety-valve – the diary as diatribe.[30] It is also the plea entered in mitigation, by Alanbrooke and his apologists, for its worst excesses: that is to say, for its shocking candour about Winston, the greatest Englishman, deep in his black dog dotage; about Ike, the chateau general, and then, lo and behold, the chateau President; and, not least, about Colonel Shrapnel himself, the charnel house of his criticism, and his mental state.[31]

Doubtless the diaries are an inviting target for such an explanation. The entry for 6 July 1944, for example, an entry heavily (and silently) censored by Bryant, records one late-night, late-war passage of arms:

> At 10 pm we had a frightful meeting with Winston which lasted till 2 am!! It was quite the worst we have had with him. He was very tired as a result of his speech in the House concerning the flying bombs, he had tried to recuperate with drink. As a result he was in a maudlin, bad tempered, drunken mood, ready to take offence at anything, suspicious of everybody, and in a highly vindictive mood against the Americans. In fact so vindictive that his whole outlook on strategy was warped. I began by having a bad row with him. He began to abuse Monty because operations were not going faster, and apparently Eisenhower had said he was over cautious. I flared up and asked him if he could not trust his generals for 5 minutes instead of continuously abusing them and belittling them. He said that he never did such a thing. I then reminded him that during two whole Monday Cabinets in front of a large gathering of Ministers, he had torn Alexander to shreds for his lack of imagination and leadership in continually attacking at Cassino. He was furious with me, but I hope it may do some good in the future.

He then put forward a series of puerile proposals, such as raising a Home Guard in Egypt to provide a force to deal with the disturbances in the Middle East. It was not till after midnight that we got onto the subject we had come to discuss, the war in the Far East! Here we came up against all the old arguments that we have had put up by him over and over again. Attlee [Deputy Prime Minister], Eden [Foreign Secretary] and Lyttelton [Minister of Production] were there, fortunately they were at last siding with us [the Chiefs of Staff] against him. This infuriated him more than ever and he became ruder and ruder. Fortunately he finished by falling out with Attlee and having a real good row with him concerning the future of India! We withdrew under cover of this smokescreen just on 2 am, having accomplished nothing beyond losing our tempers and valuable sleep!![32]

Despite its absolutist phraseology, the flavour of this entry is not untypical of the diary of that period, excepting only that it omits Alanbrooke's intermittent speculation that the Prime Minister, surely, could not go on like this – that Winston might not make it after all.[33] The unspeakable corollary of the unspoken thought was that a swift death would be a several blessing, to his memory, to his coadjutants, and to the conduct of the war. Happily or otherwise, Churchill recovered, or was repaired, for a while, and so too was the professional relationship. Alanbrooke ruefully recanted. The old man of war was mightier than he thought. But the diarist had wished him dead, and something had dissolved in the process.

Alanbrooke was brought to such a pitch of aggravation by the cumulation of the war. After the alarums and excursions of 1942 and 1943 he was exhausted, as he frequently remarked. His diary fairly palpitates with exasperation at obtuse politicians, obstructive Americans, obstreperous Russians, obmutescent Chinese – to say nothing of the enemy – and, in a class of his own, Winston. The relationship between those two intimate adversaries changed over time. Churchill appointed Alanbrooke, in effect, as his minister-counsellor.[34] Taking the measure of his situation, Alanbrooke appointed himself Churchill's nanny, just as he appointed himself Montgomery's guardian. Uniquely, in each case, he was accepted in that role by both of these infantile tyrants, for his acumen, but above all for his rectitude. After two tempestuous years of it, however, Alanbrooke was sick of nannying. What sickened him was not so much that the spoiled child never learned grand strategy – Churchill's visionary *vagabondage* remained forever a mystery to the earthbound Alanbrooke – rather that, far from growing up, as nanny naively hoped, he appeared to regress, temperamentally, the longer the war went on.[35] For Alanbrooke, this was at bottom a moral issue. By the winter of 1943–44, fuelled by medicine and alcohol, Churchill's moral degradation was such that he seemed no longer master of himself. Here the two men parted company. Self-mastery was Alanbrooke's cardinal precept. It is no coincidence that the strongest language in his diaries (invariably censored by Bryant) relates to Churchill's laxity.[36]

To read the diary as a diatribe, a rage against the puerile and the pot-valiant, is very natural. But it is reductive. Alanbrooke's diary served a larger purpose. It was not simply an instrument of aggravation. Like Gide's journal, to which it bears a passing resemblance, it was essentially a tool for recovering possession of himself – a means of self-mastery and survival, a mode of moral life.[37] Like Gide, too, Alanbrooke furnishes only a 'mutilated me', a diary of telegrams and anger, the war of the outer world.[38] His children, especially the children of his first marriage, are mostly absent; even his wife, the ritual 'you', the witness of that life, becomes almost unmentionable, to be invoked only in the hushed tones of holy worship. Was Alanbrooke forbidding to his family too?[39] In this war diary their place is usurped by mewling ministers, the palimpsest of plans, and the high-wire act of Churchill's travelling circus.

In the final analysis, both Churchill and Alanbrooke were disposed to under-rate each other, Moran thought, on account of their own limitations. In council they were an indispensable complement and foil; but it was a carefully bounded cohabitation, a marriage of convenience for the duration of the war. The doctor once asked Churchill, '"Don't you think Brooke is pretty good at his job?" There was rather a long pause. "He has a flair for the business," he grunted. That was all he would concede.'[40] In his own notebooks the writer Elias Canetti points a distinction between *illuminating* and *ordering* minds.[41] That was the PM and the CIGS. Intellectually and affectively, they were out of phase. Certainly Churchill's war memoirs, that enigmatic touchstone of his feelings, are eloquently silent on the subject of his relationship with the Brooke who really counted. An elaborate footnote in Volume II contains an extraordinary excursus on 'his two gallant brothers', Victor (born 1873) and Ronnie (born 1866) – both much older than Alan (born 1883) – and incidentally on himself, gallant too:

> His brother Victor was a subaltern in the 9th Lancers when I joined the 4th Hussars, and I formed a warm friendship with him in 1895 and 1896. His horse reared up and fell over backwards, breaking his pelvis, and he was sorely stricken for the rest of his life. However, he continued to be able to serve and ride, and perished gloriously from sheer exhaustion whilst acting as liaison officer with the French Cavalry Corps in the retreat from Mons in 1914.
>
> General Brooke had another brother, Ronnie. He was older than Victor and several years older than me. In the years 1895–98 he was thought to be a rising star in the British Army. Not only did he serve with distinction in all the campaigns which occurred, but he shone at the Staff College among his contemporaries. In the Boer War he was Adjutant of the South African Light Horse, and I for some months during the relief of Ladysmith was Assistant Adjutant, the regiment having six squadrons. Together we went through the fighting at Spion Kop, Vaal Krantz, and the Tugela. I learned much about tactics from him. Together we galloped into Ladysmith on the night of its liberation. Later on, in 1903, although I was only a youthful Member of Parliament, I was able to help him to the Somaliland campaign, in which he added to his high reputation. He

was stricken down by arthritis at an early age, and could only command a reserve brigade at home during the first World War. Our friendship continued till his premature death in 1925.[42]

At which point chivalry gives out. The youngest of this gallant breed elicits no such admiration. On the contrary, Alanbrooke himself is something of a footnote throughout the next four volumes. He appears, if at all, as a stock character in a melodrama with one name above the title, bearing disappointments 'with soldierly dignity' and rendering services 'of the highest order'. His unexampled achievement is reduced to long service and good conduct, and despatched in a paragraph. He is not favoured with oratory or eulogy (unlike Admiral Pound, the parrot asleep on his perch). He is merely part of the retinue. It is evident that the pious motto of the work, 'in victory, magnanimity', did not extend to Churchill's most intimate adversary, the CIGS and chairman of the Chiefs of Staff committee.[43]

Churchill's memoirs appeared at regular intervals between the years 1948 and 1954. Alanbrooke read them carefully, and marked them well. He noted that Churchill put too much emphasis on the failure of the 1st Armoured Division in the Western Desert in 1941–42, rather than on the failure of the Commander-in-Chief, Auchinleck, to select well for his senior staff officers. He corrected the account of their inaugural altercation, on the telephone, adrift in France, in June 1940. He revisited his own crushing disappointment when, in August 1943, the Prime Minister summarily withdrew the proposal he had made on three occasions before, that Alanbrooke himself should have Supreme Command of Operation Overlord, and offered it instead to the Americans, for their gratification, and in cool anticipation of their preponderance. Churchill's exculpatory account of that inglorious episode was indeed as summary as the action itself, and it is clear that Alanbrooke was deeply wounded by it. 'Not for one moment did he realize what this meant to me. He offered no sympathy, no regrets at having had to change his mind, and dealt with the matter as if it were one of minor importance! The only reference to my feelings in his official history…is that I "bore the great disappointment with soldierly dignity".'[44] The involuntary deprivation hurt all the more, as Churchill well knew, because the CIGS had nobly foregone the offer of the Middle East Command a year earlier, feeling (rightly) that a substitute nanny for the Prime Minister would be hard to find.[45] In the interim the bells had tolled a famous victory. Did he ever practise signing Alanbrooke of Alamein on his blotter, as did Montgomery of that ilk? It would have made a pretty handle. His self-possession was sorely tried.

Keen as it was – keener than we think – disappointment was not the vital spark. Alanbrooke's basic objection to Winston and his works centred on deprivation of a different sort. This was the highly combustible matter of recognition. It had been smouldering for some time. A diary entry in September 1944 contains one outburst:

We had another meeting with Winston at 12 noon. He was again in a most unpleasant mood. Produced the most ridiculous arguments to prove that operations could be speeded up so as to leave us an option till December before having to withdraw any forces from Europe! He knows no details, has only got half the picture in his mind, talks absurdities and makes my blood boil to listen to his nonsense. I find it hard to remain civil. And the wonderful thing is that ¾ of the population of the world imagine that Winston Churchill is one of the Strategists of History, a second Marlborough, and the other ¼ have no conception what a public menace he is and has been throughout this war! It is far better that the world should never know, and never suspect the feet of clay of that otherwise superhuman being. Without him England was lost for a certainty, with him England has been on the verge of disaster time and again.

And with it all no recognition hardly at all for those who help him except the occasional crumb intended to prevent the dog from straying too far from the table. Never have I admired and despised a man simultaneously to the same extent. Never have such opposite extremes been combined in the same human being.[46]

An entry in January 1945 is less agitated and more specific: 'We had a fairly full COS [Chiefs of Staff] which completed our record week for the maximum number of items handled in one week since war started!!! It is a strange thing what a vast part the COS takes in the running of the war and how little it is known or its functions appreciated. The average man in the street has never heard of it. Any limelight for it could not fail to slightly diminish the PM's halo! This may perhaps account for the fact that he has never yet given it the slightest word of credit in public!'[47]

Diary entries, 'those vessels of discontent, are notoriously fickle', one authority has wisely said, 'subject to the torque of mutable feeling'.[48] How different it might have been if Churchill had delivered a more generous testament. As it was, to paraphrase Balfour's celebrated remark about his earlier memoirs, Winston wrote an enormous book about himself and called it *The Second World War*. The impact of that unscrupulously egocentric enterprise on his former CIGS was profound. 'Winston's books hardened Alan's heart considerably,' reflected Cynthia Brookeborough (wife of his nephew Basil), a shrewd and sympathetic witness, after putting the question to Alanbrooke himself, 'I think for their egoism and lack of praise for underlings or more, perhaps – his equals. Alan thought Winston very jealous towards equals.' He meant, above all, the much-neglected Dill, without honour in his own country, despite Alanbrooke's petitions on his behalf ('I shall never be able to forgive Winston for his attitude towards Dill'); but also, more surprisingly, the much-garlanded Montgomery; and of course the surviving Chiefs of Staff, Cunningham, Portal, and, naturally, himself.[49] 'Little ween the snug card players in the cabin of the responsibilities of the sleepless man on the bridge.'[50]

The torque, therefore, had been applied by Churchill himself. With appropriately tragedic irony for one whose whole life was triumph and tragedy, he was the agent of his own nemesis. The weight of post-war commentary, much of it instinctively Churchillian, is that Winston was shocked and distressed by the publication of Alanbrooke's diaries, even as emasculated by Bryant. He may well have been.[51] Winston was wronged, the Churchillians impute, and his turncoat table-thumper was the culprit.[52] It is less often remarked that Alanbrooke was baffled and pained by the publication of Churchill's memoirs. In fact, his feelings mirrored his reaction to their face-to-face encounters, writ large in the midnight hours. His response was the same. He glared back. Publication of the diaries was a continuation of disputation by other means. It was a courageous step, though the courage was only half-conscious. It added new meaning to the recovery of self-possession: it was in effect a recovery of history – his story – the diary as deposition. Churchill might have known what was coming; and perhaps he did. Moran was with him when he heard for the first time that Alanbrooke was going into print. 'Winston looked up quickly. "Is it a violent attack on me?"'[53]

A more subtle, not to say insidious, variant on the wronged Churchill was the injured Alanbrooke. 'The more I read *The Turn of the Tide*,' Lord Ismay wrote to his master a month after the book's publication, 'the more certain I am that Bryant has done Brookie an injury almost as grievous as Henry Wilson's widow did to her husband.'[54] The reference was to a previous CIGS (assassinated by the IRA) whose posthumously published diaries, edited and mediated in two reminiscent volumes, exposed the diarist as foolishly misguided and, worse still, actively disloyal.[55] Ismay peddled this line of self-injury assiduously, and there is a perceptible strain of it in contemporary reviews.[56] In the overheated atmosphere of the time, both variants were damaging.[57] When the book came out, Alanbrooke sought to mollify Churchill by sending him a copy personally inscribed, 'To Winston from Brookie,'

> With unbounded admiration, profound respect, and deep affection built up in our 5 years close association during the war. Some of the extracts from my diaries in this book may contain criticisms, and references to differences between us. I hope you will remember that these were written at the end of long and exhausting days, often in the small hours of the morning, and refer to momentary daily impressions. These casual day to day impressions bear no relation to the true feelings of deep-rooted friendship and admiration which bound me so closely to you throughout the war. I look upon the privilege of having served you in war as the greatest honour destiny has bestowed on me.

Churchill's reply was muted but unmistakable. 'Thank you for sending me a copy of your book. On the whole I think I am against publishing day to day diaries written under the stress of events so soon afterwards. However, I read it with great interest, and I am very much obliged to you for what you say in your inscription.' His darling Clementine was less restrained. 'Alanbrooke,' she exclaimed, 'wants to have it both ways.'[58]

Two years later Bryant returned to the fray with the effusive apologetics prefacing *Triumph in the West*:

> Some have questioned whether a diary so frank and revealing as Lord Alanbrooke's should have been published in the lifetime of its author. It was certainly not intended to be, for after his retirement he persistently refused to write his war memoirs or to allow any book to be written about him until after his death. Had others preserved the same silence the public would have had to wait many more years before his diaries saw the light of day or his part in the war became known. But during the first post-war decade a succession of widely read memoirs by American war leaders and Service chiefs appeared, presenting a very different view to Brooke's of the events which had brought about victory and reflecting on the judgement and competence both of himself and of the British commanders who served under him. During this period the six volumes of Sir Winston Churchill's *Second World War* also appeared, giving in great, though not always complete, detail Sir Winston's version of the events in which he and Alanbrooke were so intimately and, after 1941, inseparably associated. The latter's viewpoint and the extremely important story of what he sought to achieve, and how, were thus in danger of being obscured or forgotten.[59]

This was a rearguard action, plainly enough, and not entirely successful. Bryant had been warned. P.J. Grigg, the downright former Secretary of State for War, read *The Turn of the Tide* in manuscript. 'I don't suppose Winston or his toadies will like it very much but I hope that you will not make any major excisions or allow Norman Brook [the Cabinet Secretary] to frighten you with the Official Secrets Act, official etiquette and so forth.' Grigg was wise in the ways of the velvet throttle. The Cabinet Secretary's considered response was an admonition exquisite in sentience and syntax alike. 'I could have wished that the book was not to be published in Sir Winston Churchill's lifetime. And I cannot refrain from asking what steps are to be taken to prepare him for the kind of publicity which (if I am not mistaken) it will receive.'[60] The question was left hanging in the air. But not for long. Innocent or over-confident, neither Alanbrooke nor Bryant was prepared for the furore prompted by lurid serialization in the *Sunday Times* early in 1957.[61] Bryant, the arch butterer and shameless flatterer, should have known better.[62] Alanbrooke, a surprisingly simple man, was no doubt too passive for too long. For better or worse, he had placed himself in Bryant's hands. It was Bryant's book; that was the fiction or rationalization, and Alanbrooke, at once proud and infirm, ceded precedence to the professional author. Despite an undercurrent of nervy anticipation both men failed to comprehend what they had done.[63] By defacing a legend they had transgressed a norm. The legend, moreover, was still warm. Churchill's people were perplexed, and his friends were unforgiving. Alanbrooke may always have been beyond the Prime Ministerial pale. Now there was no way back.

But recognition did not evade him altogether. After the war, in time-honoured fashion, he was created first a Baron (under Churchill's dispensation) and then, in tacit acknowledgement of a certain parsimony, a Viscount (under Attlee's); and in the Birthday Honours List for 1946, His Majesty was pleased to confer upon him the Order of Merit. This last, royal and select, was especially gratifying. Elevation to the peerage, on the other hand, was not an unalloyed pleasure. 'We finished our COS with a private meeting discussing future of COS, our own successors and probable dates of our departures.... We then discussed the cost of becoming a Baron. Apparently I can't get out of it under £200 which appals me.'[64] He was ennobled but impoverished. The first Lord Alanbrooke had few means. His gratuity was a miserly £311 (Haig's was £100,000); his half-pay – a Field Marshal never retires – 'inconsiderable'. In the privacy of his diary, he coveted the Governor-Generalship of Canada, a position not merely dignified but remunerated, and was bitterly disappointed (once again) when it went instead to the effortless Alexander, at the behest of the King – so Churchill said. Correct to the end, Alanbrooke sported his stiff upper lip. 'Alexander came to lunch and I had a chance of asking him afterwards how he liked the idea of the Canadian Governorship. He was delighted with the thought of it, and well he might be.'[65] After a brief struggle he sold his house and moved into the converted gardener's cottage. '[I] am looking for some means of making money as I am broke (and forced to sell off bird books),' he wrote piteously to his confidante Cynthia Brookeborough in January 1946. 'I hope to find something in the line of a directorship which will help me along.'[66]

Apart from the precious bird books – a 45-volume set, realizing around £3,000 – he did have one under-capitalized asset: the Alanbrooke diaries.[67] How far he was aware of this, and how soon, it is difficult to be sure. Bryant spelt it out for him towards the beginning of their association, in 1954, when they were discussing the division of the spoils. 'One thing to bear in mind is that if the book [*The Turn of the Tide*] should prove a success on this major scale [some £60,000] – and Billy Collins [the publisher] feels that it well might – it would create a tremendous interest in the rest of your Diary and Notes and so increase their potential capital value, for in this volume we should only be using a very small proportion of the whole.'[68] There were cues to be picked up well before that, however, not only from the cold war of memoirs which broke out almost immediately open hostilities were concluded, but even as the hot war was being waged. As early as April 1944, for example, Alanbrooke's incorrigible charge Montgomery mentioned the existence of his own secret diary in an interview with the American journalist John Gunther. When Gunther remarked that it would surely be an essential source for historians, Montgomery asked whether it would therefore be worth money one day. Gunther suggested a figure of at least $100,000. Once this had been converted into pounds sterling for him, Montgomery is supposed to have grinned and said, 'Well, I guess I won't die in the poor house after all.'[69] The pecuniary answer to the 'why' question is perhaps too easily overlooked, even among the monks of war.

Brother Brooke, for his part, monkish in many ways – not least in his extreme self-containment – was happy to quit the monastery as often as he decently could. 'Throughout my life', he wrote in 1953, 'I have always held it as essential to cultivate some engrossing interest besides one's profession, to which one could turn for refreshment and rest whenever the exigencies of one's work admitted. In war the value of such a habit becomes more evident than ever. I sometimes doubt whether I should have retained my sanity through those long years of the last world war had I not had an interest capable of temporarily absorbing my thoughts, and of obliterating the war, even if only for short spells when circumstances permitted.'[70] In other words, unlike the monomaniac Montgomery, Alanbrooke had a hinterland. His diary is a dossier of that too.

Together with his wife, Alanbrooke's hinterland was populated with birds. 'In ornithology and in nature generally I had formed just such an interest', he continued, 'and I cannot describe its value better than by quoting the words which Viscount Grey [the former Foreign Secretary] had written in connection with the First World War in his *Fallodon Papers*: "In those dark days I found some support in the steady progress unchanged of the beauty of the seasons. Every year, as spring came back unfailing and unfaltering, the leaves came out with the same tender green, the birds sang, the flowers came up and opened, and I felt that a great power of Nature for beauty was not affected by the War. It was like a great sanctuary into which we could go and find refuge for a time from even the greatest trouble of the world, finding there not enervating ease, but something which gave optimism, confidence and security. The progress of the seasons unchecked, the continuance of the beauty of Nature, was a manifestation of something great and splendid which not all the crimes and follies and misfortunes of mankind can abolish or destroy."'[71]

This passage became something of a mantra for Alanbrooke immediately he was introduced to it by the sympathetic Winant ten years earlier.[72] He had come a long way since the avid bagging of the wild boar. Any salivary stocktaking had long since been confined to birds watched, logged, or filmed. Alanbrooke was one of the pioneers of wildlife photography, whose fine appreciation and sheer determination made admiring experts gape.[73] Throughout the war his search for bird books was unremitting – he seems to have been foiled on VE Day itself. His Director of Military Operations Sir John Kennedy (another initiate) remembered being asked to remain behind at the end of a long and difficult meeting at the War Office in 1943. When everyone had gone, the CIGS shut the door, opened a drawer in his desk, and took out a book. 'He handed it to me, and asked, "Have you read this? It is most remarkable." I looked at it. Its title was *The Truth About the Cuckoo*.'[74]

The quest for the birds themselves was similarly ceaseless. At sixty-eight, Alanbrooke stood for many hours knee-deep in water in the Camargue to film flamingoes. At seventy-four, he climbed a tall pylon hide on an expedition to the Coto Doñana to glimpse the Spanish Imperial Eagle. 'What form of mysterious pursuit caused me to get my feet wet like a child, to pant up a talus, to stare every dandelion in the face, to start at every coloured mote passing just beyond my field of vision? What was the dream sensation of having come empty-handed – without what? A gun? A wand?' Alanbrooke, strategist and ornithologist, would have understood the rapturous rhetoric of Vladimir Nabokov, novelist and lepidopterist, only too well.[75]

'Viscount Alanbrooke, I am quite sure, would prefer to be remembered as an ornithologist than as a soldier.' Raymond Fletcher's verdict may have been a mischievous one, yet he may not have been far wrong.[76] Nabokov declared that his pleasures were 'the most intense known to man: writing and butterfly hunting'.[77] Alanbrooke in his fashion shared Nabokov's dualism, and his intensity, but not his twofold pleasure. His only real fulfilment was his recreation – re-creation, as he said. In truth, he was an unhappy warrior. That was his merit. It is what separated him from Churchill, ultimately, and from so many of his peers. Alanbrooke was always a little foreign to his fellows in arms. Unlike Vigny, he did not suffer from the disease of military ardour. Nor do his diaries. That is their rarity, and their fascination. 'Let victory belong to those who made war without liking it.'[78]

NOTES

1 Dedication prefacing first wartime diary, begun 28 Sep. 1939. A similar dedication and a similar injunction against publication preface the second diary, begun 12 Apr. 1940. Thereafter each book simply records his wife's name and address, for safe return. The original handwritten diaries and the post-war typescript 'Notes on my life' are in the Alanbrooke Papers (5/1/1–12 and 5/2/13–31 respectively), Liddell Hart Centre for Military Archives, King's College, London [hereafter KCL]. All subsequent citations are from these papers unless otherwise indicated.

2 This is the conclusion of Thomas Mallon, *A Book of One's Own: People and their Diaries* (London: Pan, 1985), among others.

3 Robert Rhodes James (ed.), *Chips: The Diaries of Sir Henry Channon* (London: Weidenfeld & Nicolson, 1967), p. 7; Nigel Nicolson (ed.), *Harold Nicolson: Diaries and Letters 1930–1939* (London: Collins, 1966), pp. 13–14. In fact, as his son points out, Nicolson himself prepared one section of his diary for publication as early as 1941, but nothing came of this.

4 Jean-Paul Sartre, *War Diaries: Notebooks from a Phoney War, November 1939–March 1940*, trans. Quintin Hoare (London: Verso, 1984), p. xi.

5 The fullest portrait of the self-effacing Benita, refracted through her husband, is probably Marian Long's 'Notes on an interview with Lady Alanbrooke' (11/8). She is almost completely absent from David Fraser's biography, *Alanbrooke* (London: Collins, 1982).

6 Fragments of testimony in AB to Capt. F. W. Short, 30 Apr. 1927 (8/1/1); Marian Long's interview with Mrs Sandy Sinclair (11/3); and AB's notes on inter-war years, p. 73 (5/2/14). See also Fraser, *Alanbrooke*, pp. 92–93.

7 Herman Melville, *Billy Budd, Sailor* (Oxford: OUP, 1997), p. 335. In Churchill's euphonious parallel, wisdom and vigour. Churchill to Margesson, 17 Nov. 1941, in Martin Gilbert, *Finest Hour: Winston S. Churchill 1939–1941* (London: Heinemann, 1983), p. 1235.

8 And, from July 1940, there was less separation – at any rate less distance – as he took over successively Southern Command, Home Command, and then the whole show.

9 Dedication in second diary, begun 12 Apr. 1940; diary and notes, 24 Aug. 1942. Cf. notes to 16 Nov. 1941.

10 Jean-Paul Sartre, *Modern Times: Selected Non-Fiction*, trans. Robin Buss (London: Penguin, 2000), p. xxv.

11 'As regards the diaries...I am quite ready for the inside to be photographed provided you selected a page that was not too badly written, fair english, and no spelling mistakes! I may well be asking for the impossible!' AB to Arthur Bryant, 18 Oct. 1956.

12 Notes on early life, p. 2 (5/2/13). Cf. his sister Hylda's 'Notes about Alan's childhood and boyhood' (1/1). On his father, see Leslie Stephen, *Sir Victor Brooke, Sportsman and Naturalist* (London: Murray, 1894).

13 During the Second World War, in addition to the diary, he wrote a daily letter to his wife. See Fraser, *Alanbrooke*, p. 34.

14 AB to his mother, 7 Jan. 1908 and 2 July 1916 (2/1/1 and 2/1/9).

15 It seems he kept a diary too, at least for part of the time; the rest may have been lost. The extant portion, 1915, includes action around Neuve Chapelle and Festubert (1/5). It is briefer, more factual, less emotional – not as developed – as its Second World War successor.

16 Notes on early life, p. 3 (5/2/13).

17 Anthony Powell, *The Military Philosophers* (London: Fontana, 1971), pp. 57–58.

18 'Statesman and Soldier', *The Economist*, 23 Feb. 1957. 'The conscience of the Army' was borrowed later by Fraser, *Alanbrooke*, pp. 271ff.

19 Alex Danchev (ed.), *Establishing the Anglo-American Alliance: the Diaries of Brigadier Vivian Dykes* (London: Brassey's, 1990), p. 13.

20 See Alex Danchev, 'Dilly-Dally, Or, Having the Last Word: Field Marshal Sir John Dill and Prime Minister Winston Churchill', *Journal of Contemporary History* 22 (1987), pp. 21–44.

21 Gen. Sir Ian Jacob in Alex Danchev, 'Biffing: the Saga of the Second Front', in idem, *On Specialness: Essays in Anglo-American Relations* (London: Macmillan, 1998), pp. 42–43. See diary, e.g., 27 May and 5 June 1942. The Norway of the latter period of the war was Sumatra. See diary, e.g., 25 Feb. and 8 Mar. 1944.

22 Elizabeth I, speech to the troops at Tilbury on the approach of the Spanish Armada, 9 Aug. 1588, in Simon Schama, *A History of Britain* (London: BBC, 2000), p. 388. On Churchill unleashed, see Alex Danchev, 'Waltzing with Winston', *War in History* 2 (1995), pp. 202–30.

23 Nye note, n.d., in Anthony Harrison, *Archie Nye* (privately published, 1980), p. 12. For the inspection, see Winston S. Churchill, *The Second World War*, 6 vols (London: Cassell, 1948–54), vol. II, pp. 233–34; and diary, 17 July 1940. Churchill's Boswellian Private Secretary confirms that he had AB in mind as 'an alternative CIGS' well before he made the offer on 16 Nov. 1941. Colville diary, 28 Sep. 1941, in John Colville, *The Fringes of Power: Downing Street Diaries*, 2 vols (London: Sceptre, 1986 and 1987), vol. I, p. 530.

24 Churchill, *Second World War*, vol. II, p. 233.

25 Lord Moran, *Winston Churchill: The Struggle for Survival 1940–1965* (London: Constable, 1966), pp. 718–19.

26 Diary, 9 Aug. 1945. Slim, commander of the 'forgotten' 14th Army, was by no means the prime suspect for prima donna behaviour; he was taking command of Allied Land Forces, South East Asia.

27 Notes to 17 Aug. 1940. These asperities have hitherto gone unnamed or unpublished. Cf. Arthur Bryant, *The Turn of the Tide* (London: Collins, 1957), pp. 36–37, where the anonymously repulsive and greasy can now be identified as Pile and Hore-Belisha respectively (diary, 14 July 1942 and 24 Feb. 1943). With regard to cronyism, see his

reproof of Bedell Smith, diary and notes, 31 Dec. 1943. AB was often struck by the Alice in Wonderland war (diary, 8 Sep. 1941, 17 Mar. 1944; notes to 14 June 1940). He was not alone.

28 Moran diary, 16 Nov. 1943, in Moran, *Winston Churchill*, pp. 125–26. Cf. notes to 19 Nov. 1943. The Ambassador's account of his tenure is also curtained. J. G. Winant, *A Letter from Grosvenor Square* (London: Hodder & Stoughton, 1947).

29 See, e.g., diary and notes, 15 Sep. 1940, 29 July 1941, 29 Oct. 1942. The uninhibited exchanges with Dill are only patchily preserved, but see AB to Dill, 30 Mar. 1944, 'I have just about reached the end of my tether ...' (14/22); extracted in Arthur Bryant, *Triumph in the West* (London: Collins, 1959), pp. 170–71.

30 Bryant, *Triumph*, pp. 36–42; 'The Tacitus of our Time', *The Tatler*, 20 Feb. 1957.

31 See, e.g., AB to Bryant, 19 Feb. 1955; and the 'Preludes' to Bryant's volumes.

32 Diary, 6 July 1944. Cf. Bryant, *Triumph*, pp. 229–30. AB's account is corroborated by other participants. See Cunningham diary, in Martin Gilbert, *Road to Victory: Winston S. Churchill 1941–1945* (London: Heinemann, 1986), p. 844; Eden diary, in Earl of Avon, *The Eden Memoirs: The Reckoning* (London: Cassell, 1965), pp. 461–62.

33 See, e.g., 28 Mar., 8 and 9 Sep. 1944.

34 See 16 Nov. 1941.

35 The earthbound strategist is examined in Brian Bond, 'Alanbrooke and Britain's Mediterranean Strategy, 1942–1944', in Lawrence Freedman et al. (eds), *War, Strategy and International Politics* (Oxford: Clarendon, 1992), pp. 175–93; Alex Danchev, 'Great Britain: The Indirect Strategy', in David Reynolds et al. (eds), *Allies at War* (New York: St Martin's, 1994), pp. 1–26; Michael Howard, *The Mediterranean Strategy in the Second World War* [1968] (London: Greenhill, 1993).

36 See, e.g., 20 Dec. 1944 and 12 Apr. 1945.

37 Cf. André Gide, *Journals 1889–1949*, trans. Justin O'Brien (Harmondsworth: Penguin, 1967). 'Recover possession of oneself' is an expression of Gide's; the perception that his journal was a tool for doing so is Sartre's. *War Diaries*, pp. 90–91.

38 Gide journal, 26 Jan. 1939, in *Journals*, p. 637. 'Personal relations are the most important thing for ever and ever, and not this outer life of telegrams and anger.' (E. M. Forster)

39 His younger son (Mr Ti), also ritually invoked in the diaries, is always 'the small boy' in his correspondence with others, even with close friends like Maj. Nigel Aitken (11/7). The revealing Mrs Sinclair thought that 'by and large it would be true to say that Brooke had been disappointed by his children. His two sons ... were delicate, his eldest daughter's marriage he did not entirely approve of; the youngest daughter [Pooks] is his favourite ...' (11/3). There is perhaps a hint of such restrictions in the tendency of his official biography to cordon off the private sphere and stick resolutely to 'his professional dealings'. Fraser, *Alanbrooke*, e.g. p. 533.

40 Moran, *Winston Churchill*, pp. 712ff. Cf. the summations of Bryant, *Turn*, pp. 13–40, and *Triumph*, pp. 18–23; and Fraser, *Alanbrooke*, pp. 531–35.

41 Elias Canetti, *The Human Province*, trans. Joachim Neugroschel (New York: Seabury, 1978), p. 200. Canetti offers Heraclites and Aristotle as 'extreme cases'.

42 Churchill, *Second World War*, vol. II, pp. 233–34. In fact AB was the youngest of nine: six brothers and three sisters.

43 Churchill, *Second World War*, vol. II, p. 234; vol. V, p. 76. Cf. his 'true comrade' Pound: vol. I, p. 321; vol. V, pp. 145–46. For the parrot-like Pound, see diary, 3 Feb. 1942.

44 AB interview with Long (11/7); notes to 14 June 1940 and 15 Aug. 1943. Cf. Churchill, *Second World War*, vol. II, p. 171 and vol. V, p. 76.

45 Diary and notes, 6 Aug. 1942; Churchill, *Second World War*, vol. IV, p. 413.

46 Diary, 10 Sep. 1944, duly censored in Bryant, *Triumph*, pp. 270–71. An illustration perhaps of Colville's observation that AB was 'at once spellbound and exasperated' by Churchill (Colville diaries, biographical notes). Cf. notes to 24 Sep. 1942, 9 Nov. 1942, 7 May 1944.

47 Diary, 20 Jan. 1945, excised by Bryant.

48 Cynthia Ozick, 'The Buried Life', *New Yorker*, 2 Oct. 2000.

49 Lady Brookeborough to Marian Long, July 1954 (11/30); notes to 12 Oct. and 5 Nov. 1944; diary, 8 May 1945.

50 Melville, *Billy Budd*, p. 345.

51 The fullest first-hand account is in Moran, *Winston Churchill*, pp. 716–17; echoed, *inter alia*, in John Colville, *Footprints in Time* (Salisbury: Russell, 1984), p. 188.

52 Churchill's official biography contributes to this vein of commentary a notably partisan attack on the diaries and a gracenote on the wronged Winston, 'generous as usual'. Martin Gilbert, *Never Despair: Winston S. Churchill 1945–1965* (London: Heinemann, 1988), pp. 1232–33.

53 Moran, *Winston Churchill*, p. 716.

54 Ismay to Churchill, 5 Mar. 1957, in Gilbert, *Never Despair*, p. 1232. Part of a veritable flood. See also Ismay to AB and Bryant, 14 and 29 Mar. 1957 (12/8/8 and 12/9/17); and *The Memoirs of Lord Ismay* (London: Heinemann, 1960), pp. 317–18.

55 Maj. Gen. Sir C. E. Callwell, *Field Marshal Sir Henry Wilson* (London: Cassell, 1927). AB was, of course, familiar with the Wilson example. See diary, 10 July 1941.

56 See, e.g., 'At Churchill's Right Hand', *Times Literary Supplement*, 8 Mar. 1957; Michael Howard, 'Bryant or Alanbrooke?', *New Statesman*, 7 Nov. 1959; Alastair Buchan, 'The Over-sell', *Encounter* 78 (1960), pp. 86–88.

57 Looking back, Michael Howard noted that *The Turn of the Tide* appeared in the immediate aftermath of the Suez débâcle, amid a bitter debate about national decline, and 'winning the war but losing the peace'. *Mediterranean Strategy*, pp.vi–vii. Cf. Alastair Buchan's sardonic suggestion that interest in the diaries in particular and the Second World War in general was 'a sublimated form of anti-Americanism'. 'The Over-sell', p. 86.

58 Inscription and reply in Gilbert, *Never Despair*, pp. 1232–33; Clementine in Moran, *Winston Churchill*, p. 717.

59 Bryant, *Triumph*, pp. 25–26. AB died in 1963.

60 Grigg and Brook to Bryant, 16 and 18 Sep. 1956 (12/3); Bryant, Epilogue to Fraser, p. 558.

61 Serialization began on 3 Feb. 1957. There was a book launch at the Dorchester two days later. A first impression of 75,000 copies sold out within the month – a prelude to further vast sales in Britain and in the United States. Bryant to AB, 20 Feb. 1957 (12/4).

62 See Andrew Roberts, 'Patriotism: The Last Refuge of Sir Arthur Bryant', in his *Eminent Churchillians* (London: Weidenfeld & Nicolson, 1994), pp. 287–322.

63 There was an interesting contemporary parallel. Gen. Sir John Kennedy, AB's former DMO, was about to publish his own memoirs, also diary-based, edited by Brig. Bernard Fergusson (Lord Ballantrae). The book is brave and suave, but their correspondence betrays acute nervousenss about giving public offence to 'the greatest Englishman'. *The Business of War* (London: Hutchinson, 1957), Preface and Epilogue; Kennedy Papers, box 6, KCL.

64 Diary, 23 Aug. 1945; diary and notes, 10 Apr. 1946.

65 Diary, 4, 16 and 17 July 1945; Bryant, *Triumph*, pp. 536–37; Fraser, *Alanbrooke*, p. 514. The instructive contrast with Haig is not confined to finances. It would include Haig's specialities of political and especially monarchical intrigue – AB was not above the

former (see 15 Sep. 1942), but eschewed the latter absolutely (see 1–2 Mar. 1944) – to say nothing of the vexed question of diary doctoring, another charge levelled at Haig, of which AB was almost completely innocent (see Note on the Text).

66 AB to Lady Brookeborough, 16 Jan. 1946 (11/9).

67 On the purchase and sale of the bird books (a matter of no small consequence for AB) see diary and notes, 22 June 1943 and 11 Apr. 1946.

68 Bryant to AB, 24 Dec. 1954 (12/1).

69 *Sunday Chronicle*, 16 Apr. 1944; Introductory Note to Montgomery Papers, Imperial War Museum, London.

70 Foreword to David Armitage Bannerman, *The Birds of the British Isles* (Edinburgh: Oliver & Boyd, 1953), p. xiii.

71 Ibid., quoting from 'Recreation', in *Fallodon Papers* (London: Constable, 1928), p. 85.

72 Notes to 25 May 1941, 19 Nov. 1943.

73 David Bannerman, unpublished autobiography, pp. 132ff., Bannerman Papers, Natural History Museum [NHM], Tring; Eric Hosking, 'Field Marshal Viscount Alanbrooke', *Bird Notes* 30 (1963), pp. 247–48; Peter Scott testimony (11/48).

74 Diary, 8 May 1945; Kennedy, *Business of War*, pp. 290–91, corroborated by the DDMI, who had a similar experience. Kirkman testimony (11/48).

75 From *Look at the Harlequins!*, quoted in Brian Boyd, 'Nabokov, Literature, Lepidoptera', in *Nabokov's Butterflies* (London: Allen Lane, 2000), p. 16. AB himself reflects sensitively on the transition from gun to wand (or camera) in his notes on his early life, pp. 34–36 (5/2/13).

76 Raymond Fletcher, 'Books and People', *Tribune*, 6 Nov. 1959. Cf. 'On the way home in the car the CIGS said how he envied you having been able to spend your life in the way you have done. So do I!' Kennedy to Bannerman, 9 Nov. 1943, Bannerman Papers, NHM.

77 Nabokov, *Strong Opinions*, quoted in Boyd, 'Nabokov', p. 1.

78 André Malraux, quoted in Sartre, *Modern Times*, p. 293.

NOTE ON THE TEXT

The Alanbrooke diaries exist in several versions, selections or accretions, and subject to varying (sometimes dubious) editorial practices. It may be helpful to give a brief account of all of them.

There were really four versions before this one. First, the original handwritten diaries, kept nightly throughout the war, lodged with his wife, and preserved in his papers. Secondly, a kind of transcript with added commentary, 'Notes for my memoirs', made by Alanbrooke over the years 1951–56, in his own execrable hand, as an aide-mémoire for his eventual biographer (and perhaps for himself), and meanwhile for Sir Arthur Bryant in the preparation of the books based on the diaries, *The Turn of the Tide* (1957) and *Triumph in the West* (1959); some of these notes have not survived, including those on the period 1944–45. Thirdly, a typescript copy of the foregoing, confusingly known as 'Notes on my life', made by Marian C. Long, research assistant to the Royal Regiment of Artillery (who were commissioning the biography) and to Bryant, in 1954–56; this version is complete, but an unholy mix of guileless titivation and guiltless mistranscription means that it differs in detail from the 'Notes for my memoirs'. Fourthly, the jewel (as he said), cut and set by Bryant in the paste of his own prose; in other words, the selected and edited version that appears in those ubiquitous volumes. All of this material, including Bryant's, is now secure and available to researchers in the Liddell Hart Centre for Military Archives at King's College, London.

Surveying the plethora of documentation, it sometimes seems as if each successive version tried to improve upon its predecessor, artlessly and insignificantly in Alanbrooke's case, knowingly and egregiously in Bryant's.

Alanbrooke's improvements run to a confetti of additional punctuation (more commas especially), not always helpful; a certain modulation in the telegraphese of the original (more definite and indefinite articles); some variations in usage; and brief insertions of a contextual character (titles, appointments, physical or geographical detail). Interestingly, and honestly, he was almost never tempted to modify the tone or retouch the painting of his diary, at the time or in retrospect: that is the internal evidence of the texts. He had occasional qualms the morning after about his immoderate expression of the night before – his vituperation of the ailing Admiral Pound in 1942, his depression after the Quebec Conference in 1943 – but these were very much the exceptions that proved the rule (and were no more immoderate than so many other nights that troubled him not at all).[1] Considering his provenance and profession, in fact, Alanbrooke was astonishingly uninhibited in his diaries and notes, not only in the notorious invective so liberally applied and so seldom retracted, but also in ways which seem to cut closer to his unimpeachable persona. In the most secret matter of signals intelligence, for example, Alanbrooke was a good deal bolder than Bryant. Thirty years before the secret was out, the diary makes repeated and explicit reference to 'intercepts', not to mention 'the organization for breaking down ciphers' (Bletchley Park); and the notes call attention to the remarkably detailed intelligence being provided.[2] None of this survived Bryant's blue pencil. In his correspondence, too, Alanbrooke consistently broke the taboos of the time. 'Somehow the work has not decreased much', he wrote to a friend shortly after the war was won, 'but the responsibility is far less. I had some nasty moments wondering whether the Boche would forestall us with the Atomic Bomb and snatch victory from under our noses.'[3]

Bryant's improvements are another matter altogether. Bryant was a professional, as he did not shrink from reminding his public. 'In this volume even more than in its predecessor', he announced in *Triumph in the West*, 'I have based my book on the diary, quoting from it, wherever possible, in preference to Alanbrooke's post-war commentary or my own narrative. The latter has been used only to set his daily jottings into the general framework of a global war, many of whose events he took for granted and whose details the ordinary reader has probably forgotten.'

> Apart from providing this framework I have let the diary speak for itself. It has not been possible, of course, to print it in its entirety. Like all diaries it contains much that is repetitive or day-to-day routine of little general interest. It contains, too, as any diary must, material that might hurt personal feelings without adding anything essential to the record. Such passages, however, are less frequent than some reviewers of *The Turn of the Tide* assumed from the omission marks with which, out of a historian's habit, I indicated every omitted passage. I have therefore been less pedantic and have only used omission marks where substantial or important passages are missing.[4]

From this farrago two points only need detain us. In the first place, any author who claims to let his subject 'speak for himself' is claiming either too little or too much, usually for a purpose; and the usual purpose is the not-so-subtle aggrandizement of the subject.[5] In this instance there can be little doubt about Bryant's overall conception, which was of Alanbrooke as Happy Warrior in a sort of seafaring Elizabethan–Wellingtonian tradition. 'In one of my chapters in *The Age of Elegance*, I called Wellington "Neptune's General",' he wrote with typical address to his subject, 'and the title might apply as aptly to you.'[6] In the second place, Bryant's habits most definitely did not include pedantry – or, to give it another name, scrupulosity – as to omissions, excisions or alterations in Alanbrooke's text, which are legion, and silent, throughout both volumes.

There is one complaint against Bryant, however, which can be dropped as misleading, at least in part. He is traditionally held responsible for over-egging the pudding, as Portal put it privately; that is to say for presenting Alanbrooke as the unerring master strategist, uncannily following his star, with a blue-water blueprint for winning the war in the West. This takes us back to the injured Alanbrooke thesis (examined in the Introduction), which holds that the arch butterer did the Happy Warrior a disservice by making him appear almost omniscient, especially by pointed comparison with his American opposite number General Marshall, and the clueless claque that surrounded him. It is true that Bryant presented Alanbrooke so. But that was not his own idea. It was Alanbrooke's, as the unmediated diaries and notes serve to confirm. The vexatious presentation was in fact Alanbrooke's self-presentation, soused in Bryant's pickling panegyric. Bryant did prettify the record, as Gerhard Weinberg and others have charged.[7] Curiously enough, he had a certain authority from his subject so to do.

In documentary terms, Bryant's familiarity with the record was regrettably circumscribed. There is no evidence that he ever consulted the original diaries, or the handwritten 'Notes for my memoirs'. He appears to have worked solely from the typescript 'Notes on my life', unwittingly incorporating the corruptions of that version straight into his own, where they happily multiplied. Could it be that the awful truth about Arthur Bryant is not that he was tendentious or mendacious, but merely remiss?

This edition, then, is the fifth version thus far. As editors, we are not innocent either; but we do hope to be more transparent. For the wartime diary, we have cleaved to the handwritten original. For the post-war commentary, we have used the 'Notes on my life' as the point of departure, but we have also sought to collate different versions whenever there appeared to be discrepancy or doubt. We have done our level best to unscramble the various insertions and deletions of Sir Arthur Bryant. We have tried not to perpetrate any of our own.

The diary published here is complete and unexpurgated. But we too have felt the need to make some improvements. With a twinge of regret, we have silently corrected Alanbrooke's spelling (most proper names eluded him, including the site of his preferred strategy, 'Mediterranean'). We have reparagraphed extensively – as Bryant did, but differently – if the original can be said to be paragraphed at all, for Alanbrooke habitually began almost every sentence on a new line in his little diaries; to reproduce this in book form would be prohibitive, and in the end perhaps wearisome. On the other hand, we have preserved his scattergun punctuation – as Bryant did not – believing that the jagged feeling so displayed is intrinsic to the diaries' troubled composition, and that something important would be lost without it. The text of *The Turn of the Tide* and *Triumph in the West* is by comparison too smooth, we think, in this respect as in others. Exceptionally, we have punctuated for intelligibility. Alanbrooke's appreciation of the full-stop was wobbly, as Pooh Bear would have said; where we felt that the sentence could not be allowed to run on any further without doing violence to the sense, we added one. As for the trimmings, we have standardized the date of each entry, and of common abbreviations and designations (ranks, titles, formations). The interpolations in square brackets are ours; they are intended to give information or context, but [illegible] appears wherever we have failed to decipher his hieroglyphics. The rest – phrasing and paraphrasing, predicating and perorating, in all its fallible glory – is his.

Finally, the diary, like the sentence, runs on after the war until Alanbrooke eventually quits the field in June 1946. This long aftermath is a desultory anti-climax, we felt, unrelieved by a surprisingly tedious world tour from October to December 1945.[8] We decided to make an end with the entry of 31 August 1945. It closes on a characteristically downbeat note: 'In the evening I motored home.'

NOTES

1 See diary and notes, 31 Aug. 1942 and 25 Aug. 1943.
2 See, e.g., diary, 16, 17 and 24 Oct. 1940 and 16 Apr. 1942; notes to 18 Aug. 1942.
3 AB to Maj. Nigel Aitken, 26 Aug. 1945 (11/7). Cf. Fraser, *Alanbrooke*, p. 280. For more on his reaction to the bomb, see diary and notes, 23 July 1945.
4 Bryant, *Triumph*, pp. 15–16.
5 As, for example, in the parallel case of the official biography of Winston Churchill, where a similar claim lies at the very foundation of the work. See Alex Danchev, 'Dilly-Dally, Or, Having the Last Word', *Journal of Contemporary History* 22 (1987), pp. 21–44.
6 Bryant to AB, 30 Nov. 1954, quoted in Bryant, Epilogue to Fraser, *Alanbrooke*, p. 544. See also Bryant, Prologue, ibid., p. 27; and *Turn*, pp. 28ff. This view was trailed in 'Our Notebook', *Illustrated London News*, 30 July 1955.
7 Gerhard Weinberg, *A World at Arms* (Cambridge: CUP, 1994), p. 928.
8 Cf. Bryant, *Triumph*, pp. 493ff.; Fraser, *Alanbrooke*, pp. 503ff.

ABBREVIATIONS

A/A	Anti-Aircraft
AB	Alanbrooke
ABDA	American-British-Dutch-Australian Command
AC	Armoured Corps
ACI	Army Council Instruction
ADC	Aide de Camp
ADGB	Air Defence of Great Britain
AFV	Armoured Fighting Vehicle
AG	Adjutant-General
ANZAC	Australian and New Zealand Army Corps
AOC	Air Officer Commanding
AQMG	Assistant Quartermaster-General
A/T	Anti-Tank
ATS	Auxiliary Territorial Service (Women's)
ADC	Aide de Camp
Bde	Brigade
Bdr	Bombadier
BEF	British Expeditionary Force
BGS	Brigadier General Staff
Bn	Battalion
Can	Canadian
CAS	Chief of Air Staff
Cav	Cavalry
CB	Companion of the Order of the Bath
CCO	Chief of Combined Operations
CCRA	Corps Commander(s) Royal Artillery
CCS	Casualty Clearing Station/Combined Chiefs of Staff
CE	Chief Engineer
CGS	Chief of the General Staff
CIGS	Chief of the Imperial General Staff
C-in-C	Commander-in-Chief
CNS	Chief of the Naval Staff
CO	Commanding Officer
COS	Chief(s) of Staff
COSSAC	Chief of Staff, Supreme Allied Commander
Coy	Company
CRA	Commander Royal Artillery
DA	Director of Administration
DCGS	Deputy Chief of the General Staff

DCIGS	Deputy Chief of the Imperial General Staff
DCLI	Duke of Cornwall's Light Infantry
DDMI	Deputy Director of Military Intelligence
DDMS	Deputy Director of Medical Services
DG	Dragoon Guards
DGAE	Director-General Army Equipment
DGAMS	Director-General of Army Medical Services
Div	Division
DLI	Durham Light Infantry
DLM	Division Lourde Motorisée
DMI	Director of Military Intelligence
DMO	Director of Military Operations
DMT	Director of Military Training
DR	Despatch Rider
DSD	Director of Staff Duties
E-in-C	Engineer-in-Chief
FFI	French Forces of the Interior
FO	Foreign Office
GCB	Knight Grand Cross of the Order of the Bath
GHQ	General Headquarters
GI	General Branch Intelligence (Officer of Division)
GOC	General Officer Commanding
GQG	Grand Quartier Général (French/Belgian GHQ)
Gren	Grenadier
GSO	General Staff Officer
IB	Infantry Brigade
ICI	Imperial Chemical Industries
IDC	Imperial Defence College
Inf	Infantry
ITC	Infantry Training Centre
JIC	Joint Intelligence Committee (US)
JPS	Joint Planning Staff
JSM	Joint Staff Mission
KCL	King's College, London
KOSB	King's Own Scottish Borderers
KRR	King's Royal Rifles
KRRC	King's Royal Rifle Corps
LDV	Local Defence Volunteers
L of C	Lines of Communication
LO	Liaison Officer
LST	Landing Ship Tank
MA	Military Attaché/Assistant
ME	Middle East
MG	Machine Gun
MGAA	Major General Anti-Aircraft
MGO	Master General of the Ordnance

MGRA	Major General Royal Artillery
MI	Military Intelligence
ML	Motor Launch
MS	Military Secretary
MT	Motor Transport
NAAFI	Navy, Army and Air Force Institutes
NF	Northumberland Fusiliers
NHM	Natural History Museum, Tring
OC	Officer Commanding/Observer Corps
OCTU	Officer Cadet Training Unit
OM	Order of Merit
PUS	Permanent Under Secretary
Q	Quartermaster
QMG	Quartermaster-General
QMS	Quartermaster-Sergeant
RA	Royal Artillery
RAMC	Royal Army Medical Corps
RAOC	Royal Army Ordnance Corps
RAS	Royal Army Signals
RASC	Royal Army Service Corps
RE	Royal Engineers
Regt	Regiment
RHA	Royal Horse Artillery
RMC	Royal Military College, Sandhurst
SA	South Africa
SEAC	South East Asia Command
SIS	Secret Intelligence Service
SOE	Special Operations Executive
SOS	Senior Officers' School
S of S	Secretary of State*
SPA	Salisbury Plain Area
SSAFA	Soldiers', Sailors' and Airmen's Families Association
USS	Under Secretary of State
VCIGS	Vice Chief of the Imperial General Staff
WO	War Office

---

* Generally refers to Secretary of State for War, responsible for the Army and working out of the WO, one of three Service Secretaries under the Minister of Defence.

THE CAST

The family, comrades and friends

Alwyne Major Sir Harold Alwyne Pelly, Benita's brother.

Barney Capt. A.K. Charlesworth, AB's ADC 1940–45.

Basil Basil Brooke, Lord Brookeborough, PM of Northern Ireland, AB's nephew.

Bertie Lt Gen. Sir Bertram (Sergison)-Brooke, GOC London District (1939–42), British Red Cross Commissioner (1943–45), AB's cousin.

Budget Gen. Sir Henry Loyd, Commander 2nd Division (1939–40), CGS Home Forces (1941–42), GOC Southern Command (1942–43), GOC London District (1944–47).

Bulgy Gen. Sir Andrew Thorne, Comd 48th Division (1939–40), XII Corps (1940–41), GOC Scottish Command (1941–45).

Copper Gen. Sir Robert (Gordon)-Finlayson, AG (1939–40), GOC Western Command (1940–41).

Cynthia Cynthia Brooke, Lady Brookeborough, Basil's wife.

Evelyn Sir Evelyn Wrench, American Relations Officer to Government of India (1942–44).

Hylda AB's sister, Lady Wrench, wife of Evelyn.

Ivan Lt Col. Ivan Cobbold, ADC to Bertie, shooting companion, killed by V1 bomb which struck Guards Chapel, London, on 19 June 1944.

Madeline Madeline Lees (née Pelly), Benita's sister, wife of Col. Sir John (Jack) Lees.

Peter Col. Peter Dunphie, PA.

P.J. See **Grigg**.

Pongo Arthur Brooke, brother of Basil, AB's nephew.

Pooks Kathleen Stoney (née Brooke), AB's younger daughter (b. 1931).

Pug See **Ismay**.

Rex The dog.

Rollie Temp. Lt Col. (Brig) H.V.S. Charrington, ADC (1945–46), neighbour and comrade. Commanded 1st Armoured Bde in Greece 1941, invalided out of service, stepped into breach following Barney's death in plane crash.

Ronnie Capt. (later Lt Col.) R.T. Stanyforth, ADC (1939–40), of Eton, Christ Church and 21st Lancers. Author of *Wicketkeeping* (1935). Comptroller of the Royal Household (1939–40), GSO1 21st Army Group HQ (1941–45).

Rosemary Rosemary Macdonald (née Brooke), AB's elder daughter, b. 1918. Subaltern in ATS throughout war.

Sneezer Patricia Pelly, Benita's sister.

Ti Victor Brooke, AB's younger son, b. 1932.

Tom Tom Brooke, AB's elder son, b. 1921. Served Royal Artillery.

you Benita Brooke, née Pelly (1892–1968), AB's second wife (m. 1929), eldest daughter of Sir Harold Pelly, Bt., and widow of Sir Thomas Lees (killed in action, Gallipoli, 1915).

The Soldiers

Adam Gen. Sir Ronald F., 1885–1982

One of the lesser-known British military figures of WWII, Adam was an old comrade of AB's from his days with N Battery, Royal Horse Artillery, in India before WWI. He served in Europe 1914–18 and as a staff officer after the war, including GSO1 and DDMO at the War Office (1935–36), Commandant of the Staff College (1937), and DCIGS (1938–39). He was an outstanding Adjutant-General (1941–46), enlightened and effective. Precisely for those reasons, he was often open to criticism, not least by Churchill. In spite of this (perhaps partly because of it), AB's loyalty and friendship remained constant throughout.

Alexander Harold, Earl Alexander of Tunis, 1891–1969

'Alex' was a talented and enthusiastic small unit commander, who rose to command the 2nd Battalion Irish Guards on the Western Front in WWI, where he won the MC and DSO. During a two-year sojourn in Latvia as 'Relief Advisor' he commanded the Baltic Landswehr – German and Baltic soldiers – in battles against the Bolsheviks. AB encountered him as a student at the Staff College in 1926, where he first formed his opinion of Alexander as not being a 'big man'. He commanded a brigade on the North West Frontier before 1939. For the first years of WWII he specialized in rescuing the maximum possible number of British soldiers from the jaws of defeat, first in France where he commanded 1st Division and then I Corps at Dunkirk, and then in Burma.

He replaced Auchinleck as C-in-C ME in August 1942, and worked well with Montgomery, and then Eisenhower, in the ultimate defeat of Axis forces in North Africa. His campaigns in Sicily and the Italian mainland were less successful than they deserved to be, largely because of his inability to control independent-minded subordinates.

Intellectually he was unimpressive, although whether this stemmed from genuine stupidity or an Edwardian desire not to appear too keen is open to doubt. His amiability and desire to be agreeable to all often gave the impression that he lacked 'grip', but may on occasion have made him a suitable candidate for high command over an army which contained numerous and fractious allies. If his personality hindered victory, it prevented disintegration. It also made him an excellent lightning-rod to safeguard his subordinates from bolts of Churchillian invective.

Auchinleck   Field Marshal Claude, 1884–1981
The 'Auk' served throughout WWI in the 62nd Punjabis in Mesopotamia, and then as a Regimental and District Commander in India. He returned to England in January 1940 to take command of IV Corps, and was appointed GOC-in-C Northern Norway in April of that year. The débâcle that followed gave him little chance to show his generalship to good effect. After commanding V Corps and Southern Command, he took over from Wavell as C-in-C ME Command in June 1941. His first offensive, in late 1941, was a success, but the 8th Army was soon pushed back and Tobruk lost. Auchinleck dismissed its Commander, Ritchie, took over 8th Army himself, first checked and then pushed back Rommel's forces at the first Battle of Alamein. He was dismissed nonetheless. He was C-in-C India from 1943 until partition, and refused a peerage in 1947.

He had the misfortune to command during a period when Allied technological inferiority was insufficiently counterbalanced by numerical superiority. Churchill formed a negative opinion of him before the British command structure had developed sufficiently to protect its generals from the PM, and he was too honest and dutiful to play politics.

Dill   Field Marshal Sir John Greer, 1881–1944
After service in the Leinster Regiment in the Boer War, Dill went to the Staff College the year before the First World War broke out. During that conflict he served in a variety of Divisional and Corps Staff positions, rising to Brigadier General, General Staff (Operations) at GHQ France. Between the wars he was an instructor at the Imperial Defence College, Commandant of the Staff College, DMO and I at the War Office, and GOC Palestine and Transjordan and Home Command. He commanded I Corps BEF until April 1940, when he became VCIGS, and shortly afterwards AB's predecessor as CIGS.

Dill was forced to stand up to Churchill, but found the combination of Britain's desperate position and Churchill's confrontational style all but unbearable. Churchill dubbed him 'Dilly Dally'. The two were temperamentally unsuited to working together, but Dill in many ways constructed the mechanisms of the British High Command which were to function so well when he was replaced by AB. With America's entry into the war, Dill was saved from gentle retirement to the Governorship of Bombay when he was appointed Head of the Joint Staff Mission in Washington. There he did a masterly job of maintaining and coordinating the Alliance, fully deserving the praise AB heaps upon him. He was aided in this by the remarkably intimate friendship he enjoyed with Marshall. He died in harness, of aplastic anaemia, in Washington on 4 November 1944.

Montgomery   Field Marshal Viscount Montgomery of Alamein, 1887–1976
The only foretaste of Montgomery's future character and behaviour whilst he was at Sandhurst occurred when he set fire to the shirt tails of a fellow cadet, seriously burning him. For this crime he was held back a year, before being commissioned in the Royal Warwickshires. He served in India, returning to

Europe with his battalion at the outbreak of war in 1914. He was seriously wounded at 1st battle of Ypres, displaying great courage for which he received the DSO. After partial recovery he returned to the Western Front in a variety of staff roles. His experience of the last months of WWI was the basis of his belief in meticulous planning and all arms warfare. He was an Instructor at Camberley (1926–29), and Senior Instructor at Quetta (1934–37). The death of his wife, shortly after he returned to England to command a brigade, was a shattering event. His reaction was to throw himself even more fully into his job. AB's influence ensured that Montgomery accompanied him to France as Commander of the 3rd Division. After Dunkirk, as GOC V Corps, he demonstrated his excellence as a trainer and motivater of men – some of his most important skills in a newly-expanded civilian army. His subsequent career is charted in the diaries.

Montgomery had a remarkable ability to irritate his seniors with ill-considered remarks or actions. Yet the very self-centredness and self-advertisement which so annoyed them helped to make him popular with his troops. He remains Britain's best-known general of the Second World War. Doubts have been cast on his abilities as a general; and it is apparent that he was fortunate to take on high command at a point when the logistical position of the Allies tended to favour his mode of making war. He made many mistakes and errors and he was unable to work as part of a team. But he won battles, and he cared for the welfare and the lives of his soldiers, for which many of them respected him to the point of hero-worship.

Nye Sir Archibald Edward, 1895–1967
The son of a Regimental Sergeant Major, Nye was educated at the Duke of York's Military School after his father's death. He went to France as an NCO in 1914 and was selected for a commission in the Leinsters the following year. He was twice wounded in action and awarded the MC. He served in a variety of regimental posts with the Royal Warwickshires between the wars, including a spell at the Staff College (1924–25), where he was noted as a good prospect for the future. Without independent means, he was able to afford his mess bills because he abstained from alcohol, and from his winnings at billiards. In addition to his arduous regimental duties, he also managed to qualify as a barrister at the Inner Temple in 1932. Sent to India to raise a brigade in 1939, he was swiftly recalled on the outbreak of war, and became Director of Staff Duties at the War Office and a Major General. In 1941, he became VCIGS and a Lieutenant General. After the war he returned to India as Governor of Madras – a position he fulfilled so successfully that Nehru asked for him to stay on as High Commissioner.

Wavell Field Marshal Archibald Percival, Earl Wavell, 1883–1950
Another son of a soldier – albeit a General – who had his career set for him by his family background. Wavell was commissioned into the Black Watch in time to see service but little action in South Africa. He then served in India before attending the Staff College in England in 1908. He was obviously a high

flyer, at least in the context of the Edwardian Army. At the instigation of Robertson, the then Commandant, he travelled to Russia, learning the language and studying manoeuvres (he was to return as an observer again in 1936). On the outbreak of war in 1914 he was placed in command of the intelligence section at GHQ in France, a job which he escaped by engineering a post as a Brigade Major. In this role he was often in the trenches, and lost his left eye to a shell splinter in 1915. He subsequently took on a number of important staff and liaison jobs. After a period on half pay after the war – during which he supported himself by contributing articles to the *Encyclopaedia Britannica* – he eventually rose to command first a brigade and then a division. He served for a short while as GOC Palestine, and returned to England to take up the position of GOC Southern Command. In the brief period while he held this job before being made GOC ME in July 1939, Wavell delivered the Lees Knowles lectures on Military History at Cambridge University. In the Middle East he presided over the Libyan victory and the Greek débâcle. He proved unable to prevent Rommel's run of victories, and was dismissed in June 1941. His subsequent career is charted in the diaries.

An extremely, possibly overly, intelligent General, Wavell was in some ways unfortunate to be in command at the point when his initial successes almost inevitably turned sour as a result of British over-commitment and lack of means. He was badly served by his staff, but was not a good chooser of men. Above all, in his relationship with Churchill he was unlucky in that his character was unsuited to the highest level of command as it was exercised in Britain at the time. In terms of his taciturnity, Wavell was a commander in the Douglas Haig mould. In the political context of WWII, this was never an advantageous characteristic.

Weeks   Ronald Morce, Baron Weeks, 1890–1960
Weeks was the son of a mining engineer, educated at Charterhouse and Caius College, Cambridge (where he had the distinction of receiving a Third in Part I), before he joined Pilkington Brothers Ltd, a major UK glass manufacturer. As a Territorial officer, he was called up in 1915. He served until the end of the war, receiving a regular commission in the Rifle Brigade, a brevet majority, three mentions in despatches, an MC (1917), bar (1918), Croix de Guerre (1918) and DSO (1918). After the war he returned to Pilkingtons, where he showed his organizational ability and technical awareness, modernizing and internationalizing the family firm. He became Chairman of Executive Directors in 1938. He had remained in the Territorials, and in 1939 he was made GSO1 of 66th Division. In July of the following year he became BGS (Staff Duties) Home Forces HQ, with responsibility for Home Forces Equipment. In March 1941 he became Director General of Army Equipment. In June 1942, Weeks was appointed DCIGS, with the rank of Lieutenant General and a seat on the Army Council. The appointment recognized the need for the CIGS and VCIGS to work on operations, and for a centralized responsibility for equipment and organization. After leaving the DCIGS's post in June 1945, he spent two months as Deputy Military Governor in Germany before returning to Pilkingtons.

Weeks was industrious and decisive, but most importantly he adapted well to a changing global environment in which technology was increasingly important.

Wilson   Field Marshal Henry Maitland, 'Jumbo', Baron Wilson, 1881–1964
Wilson was one of Britain's most consistently successful generals of WWII, no matter what the complexities of the situation, but received the least public recognition. He served as a junior officer with the Rifle Brigade in the Boer War, and performed a number of staff jobs throughout WWI. He attended the Staff College in 1919, and returned there as Chief Instructor in 1930 after further regimental service. In 1939 he was appointed Commander British Troops in Egypt, with the rank of Lieutenant General. As such he laid the basis, through training and tactics, for the desert victories over the Italians in the early years of WWII. In 1941 he was appointed to command the British force in Greece. Placed in an impossible position, he extricated his troops with skill. He then served in difficult circumstances as Commander in Palestine and Trans-Jordan and then Syria and Palestine, which brought him into conflict with Vichy French troops. The diplomatic skills he showed here served him well when he became C-in-C Middle East (1943), and then Supreme Allied Commander in the Mediterranean (1944). Promoted Field Marshal in January 1945, he replaced Dill in Washington in the same month. 'Jumbo' referred to his size: more than six foot and of equivalent girth. Perhaps because of his greater age and experience, he showed better resilience to the slings and arrows of Churchill's interference than many of his colleagues.

The Chiefs of Staff Committee

Cunningham   Andrew Browne, Viscount Cunningham of Hyndhope, 1883–1963
Known as 'ABC' to his subordinates and friends, the CNS was not related to Sir John Cunningham, who succeeded him in the Mediterranean and as First Sea Lord; he was the elder brother of General Sir Alan Cunningham. He served in the Boer War (Naval Brigade), and in WWI at Gallipoli and Zeebrugge. In the Mediterranean in the early years of WWII, his audacious aggressiveness established a moral ascendancy over a powerful modern enemy fleet and air force. This allowed him to maintain a significant naval presence, despite growing shortages and adversity, and the necessity of supporting the army. During the evacuation of Crete his motto was: 'It takes the navy three years to build a ship but three hundred years to build a tradition.' Personally, he mixed human warmth and sympathy with an intolerance for fools or slackers and a drive for excellence, which made him an ideal colleague for AB.

Ismay   General Hastings, 'Pug', Baron Ismay, 1887–1965
Early on in his career, Ismay was marked out as a staff officer of distinction. After service in the Middle East and Africa during and after WWI, he went to

the Staff College at Quetta. From 1923, he was occupied solely in staff work. He toiled under Hankey at the Committee of Imperial Defence (1925–30), returned as his deputy in 1936, and replaced him in 1938. Ismay's combination of shrewdness, resilience and emollience meant that he fitted well into Whitehall. He was deaf in his left ear following a polo accident in 1933, the same year that his wife's inheritance made him independently wealthy. When Churchill became Minister of Defence, Ismay joined him as his Chief of Staff. He acted, generally successfully, as the lubricant in the sticky relationship between Churchill and the Chiefs of Staff Committee. 'Pug' was based on his appearance; although canine in his loyalty to his chief, his other characteristics were perhaps more feline. After the war he became the Secretary-General of NATO (1952).

Laycock   Sir Robert Edward, 1907–1968
Laycock joined the Royal Horse Guards in 1927, after being educated at Eton and the RMC, Sandhurst. He was appointed GSO2 with responsibility for Chemical Warfare to the BEF in 1939, largely because he had expressed some interest in scientific matters. He was in England during the retreat to Dunkirk, and his new job was as a trainer and leader of Commandos. Having led his troops on various jaunts around the Mediterranean through 1941, including the evacuation of Crete (where Evelyn Waugh was his intelligence officer), Laycock participated in the unsuccessful raid on Rommel's headquarters. Afterwards he was forced to hide in the desert behind enemy lines for two months. He claimed that he owed his survival to his knowledge of the behaviour of foxes. In return, he never hunted them again. In 1942, he returned to Britain and the raising of more Commandos. He led them in the vanguard of the invading forces at Sicily and Salerno, for which he was awarded the DSO. He replaced Mountbatten as CCO on the latter's departure for South East Asia in 1943. The second volume of Waugh's *Sword of Honour* trilogy, *Officers and Gentlemen*, was dedicated to Laycock, 'that every man in arms should wish to be'.

Mountbatten   Louis Francis Albert Victor Nicholas, Earl Mountbatten of Burma, 1900–79
Mountbatten's father, Prince Louis of Battenberg, First Sea Lord, was hounded from the Admiralty by the wave of anti-German sentiment at the start of WWI. His son, a great-grandson of Queen Victoria, saw service as a midshipman, and then spent the inter-war years working hard on his reputation as a playboy, and even harder at his chosen profession of naval signals expert. He rose to command his own ship (the appropriately named *Daring*) in 1934. The outbreak of war saw him captain of the *Kelly*. During eighteen months in command he almost capsized in high seas, collided with another destroyer, was mined once, torpedoed twice, and finally sunk by enemy aircraft. Many of these incidents were the result of Mountbatten's own bravado or carelessness. After surviving the ship's destruction off Crete in May 1941, he was sent to command the *Illustrious*, refitting in America, but before she could put to sea

was made Churchill's advisor on Combined Operations, and subsequently CCO (1942). Churchill told him: 'You are to give no thought to the defensive. Your whole attention is to be concentrated on the offensive.' For this role he must have seemed ideally suited. His time as CCO was marred by the wasteful disaster of the Dieppe raid, for which he must shoulder some of the blame. On the other hand, the enthusiasm for gadgetry and sponsorship of others' inventions which he had showed as a young naval officer in the 1930s stood him in good stead, and he encouraged construction of the vast array of specialized equipment necessary for amphibious invasion.

He was appointed to SEAC following the Quebec Conference of August 1943. There, thanks to a number of talented subordinates, he was able to preside over the eventual triumph of the Imperial Armies. The opposed seaborne invasion of the Malayan peninsula, which could have been the culmination of his career thus far – the invading troops sank to their waists in wet sand – was prevented by the end of the war. The second half of his career, spanning his time as last Viceroy of India, continued service as an admiral, NATO commander, First Sea Lord and CDS, was fully as controversial and dramatic as the first.

With the possible exception of Montgomery, he was the most talented self-publicist among the senior British commanders, with an instinctive grasp of how to enhance his popularity with those serving under him. This was most clearly seen in the film version of the sinking of the *Kelly, In Which We Serve*, featuring Noël Coward as Mountbatten, which he watched twelve times on its first release.

Portal   Charles Frederick Algernon, Viscount Portal of Hungerford, 1893–1971
Portal began military life as a despatch rider for the BEF during the retreat from Mons in 1914. He joined the RFC in July 1915, and was awarded MC, DSO and bar for his work on tactical reconnaissance and bombing and artillery observation. After a period as an instructor and squadron leader he attended the IDC in 1929, after which he pioneered an imperial policing role for the RAF in Aden. He returned to the IDC as a member of the directing staff, and then became Director of Organization at the Air Ministry. He was Chief of Bomber Command from April to October 1940, where he promoted efforts to carry the bombing war into Germany. After becoming CAS he continued to favour this policy, although he intended such efforts to make invasion of Europe possible rather than to win the war on their own. Highly intelligent, and a model of integrity, he was perhaps the most reserved of the COS.

Pound   Sir Alfred Dudley Pickman Rogers, 1877–1943
Entering the navy in 1891, Pound enjoyed the successful career of a promising naval officer. He specialized in torpedoes, and served at Jutland. He was responsible for the formation of the first naval staff at the Admiralty in 1917. He commanded in the Mediterranean (1936–39), and became First Sea Lord in June 1939. For three years he worked almost single-handed in that position. Pound was a generally successful naval strategist in adverse conditions, crucial-

ly gaining the measure of the submarine menace by the time of his death on Trafalgar Day, 21 October 1943. Though increasingly disabled by the illness which was to kill him, Pound belied a reputation for being reserved and unbending with his abilities as a raconteur and bon viveur in the company of those he found congenial. When it came to waltzing with Winston during the late-night drinking sessions at Chequers or the Admiralty, he had few equals.

The Politicians

Attlee   Clement Richard, Earl Attlee, 1883–1967
During a colourful military career in WWI, Major Attlee commanded the rear-guard at Suvla Bay, was badly wounded in Mesopotamia, served in the Tank Corps and was finally wounded again on the Western Front. He already had an interest in helping the poor and underprivileged, and had been a socialist since 1907. His war service marked him out from many of his Labour colleagues. He became an MP in 1922, and leader of the Labour Party in 1935. He served in Churchill's coalition government from May 1940, as Lord Privy Seal, Secretary of the Dominions, and then Lord President of the Council. He was Deputy Prime Minister in fact from the start, and in form from February 1942. He and Churchill worked well together despite vastly different characters and out-looks. This was partly the result of Attlee's loyalty and refusal to press socialist reforms too far, and partly because he concerned himself with civil matters, although he did chair the War Cabinet and Defence Committee in Churchill's absence. He became Prime Minister following Labour's election victory in 1945. A dedicated and honourable man, Attlee was shy and lacked small talk. As a result, he remained remote from many in his own party and the public at large.

Bevin   Ernest, 1881–1951
Bevin was leader of Britain's largest trade union, the Transport and General Workers, when Churchill made him Minister of Labour and National Service in May 1940. It was a brilliant appointment: the combination of his sweeping powers and popular response to his leadership led to the effective mobilization of the civil population. He was made a member of the War Cabinet in September 1940, and became Foreign Secretary in the 1945 Labour government.

Eden   Robert Anthony, Lord Avon, 1897–1977
Either a principled prince amongst men, the unluckiest but most handsome leader the Tory Party ever had, or a hysterical self-serving prima donna, depend-ing on one's point of view. Eden fought with great distinction in WWI, ending up as the youngest Brigade Major in the army. He became an MP in 1923, and his elegance and ability marked him out for success from the start. He was made Foreign Secretary in Baldwin's government in 1935, and continued in that posi-tion when Chamberlain became PM. His disagreements with the latter over the manner (though not the principle) of appeasement led him to resign in

February 1938, and to abstain from supporting the government over Munich. These acts were important in his subsequent recasting as a Churchillian ally, and vital in the mythological role as an anti-appeaser which he developed in his own mind, with disastrous results in 1956 at Suez. Eden became Secretary for the Dominions in 1939, without a cabinet seat, but was appointed Secretary for War by Churchill in May 1940. As such, Eden was influential even before he was raised to the position of Foreign Secretary in December of the same year, and he supported Dill, AB and Wavell when Churchill doubted their abilities. It was soon accepted that he was Churchill's understudy, a role he was destined to fulfil for many more years than he would have desired.

Grigg   Sir Percy James, 1890–1964
'P.J.' was first in his class in the exam for entry to the Civil Service. Like AB he was a gunner. Between the wars he served five Chancellors as PPS at the Treasury (1921–30), and was then Chair of the Board of the Inland Revenue and finance member of the Viceroy's executive council in India. He was PUS at the War Office (1939–42), and was then selected by Churchill to replace Margesson as Secretary of State for the Army. He became Nationalist MP for East Cardiff in 1942, losing his seat in the 1945 election. Grigg was hot-tempered and took no prisoners in his drive for efficiency – one of his colleagues remarked that he 'lacked human sympathy and was intolerant' – but he got things done, and was much approved of by the CIGS.

The Americans

Arnold   General of the Army Henry ('Hap'), 1886–1950
Arnold was taught to fly by the Wright brothers in 1911. He came to Europe too late to see service in WWI, but by 1918 was already Assistant Chief of the US Air Service and the youngest colonel in the army. 1938 saw him Chief of the Army Air Corps. He was a Deputy Chief of Staff from October 1940, and from March 1942 Commanding General of the USAAF which, under his drive and experienced enthusiasm, became the most powerful air force in the world. He worked himself incredibly hard, suffering four heart attacks during the war alone. Yet he was possessed of a sunny personality: 'Hap' was short for 'Happy'. He liked to consider himself something of a strong man, and when the CCS tested Mountbatten's ice-and-sawdust composite for the creation of iceberg aircraft carriers ('Habbakuk'), he attacked the material with an axe.

Eisenhower   General of the Army Dwight D., 1890–1969
Eisenhower ended WWI commanding 10,000 men, although he had been unable to obtain a posting to Europe. Instead he had remained in the United States and built the army's first tank corps from scratch. He passed out top of his year at Leavenworth, and then served on the staffs of Pershing and MacArthur. The period between 1939 and Pearl Harbor saw him rise rapidly to the rank of Brigadier General. Summoned to Washington by Marshall, he was

made deputy and then head of the War Plans Division (subsequently the Operations Division) until June 1942, when he became General commanding the European Theatre of Operations. Bearing in mind the difficulties of politics and alliances, let alone the inexperience of his troops and commanders, he did well to survive his first combat command in North Africa in early 1943. In doing so he displayed the skills and faults which characterized the rest of his war, as Commander of the Sicilian and Italian invasions, as Supreme Commander of the Mediterranean and then the Allied Expeditionary Forces in NW Europe. He was an able political general with a genius for managing intractable Allies and for making himself agreeable to all he met. He learned increasingly well how to take difficult decisions – seen best in the run-up to 'Overlord'. But he had an infuriating passion for consensus and compromise, and despite his intelligence his relative lack of experience may have denied him great strategic insight: he did not rein in Montgomery over Arnhem, and failed to predict the German counterstroke through the Ardennes during the winter of 1944.

Harriman   William Averell, 1891–1986
Beginning in 1934, Harriman's extensive career finally spanned four Democratic presidents and thirty-five years. The multimillionaire's son had known FDR since childhood. He served in the Defense Department before coming to Britain as Roosevelt's Special Envoy to administer Lend Lease. There he had more influence than the US Ambassador, Winant, not least because he was more personally congenial to Churchill. He was US Ambassador to Moscow, 1943–46.

King   Admiral Ernest Joseph, 1878–1956
King served in destroyers during WWI, and then on the staff of the Atlantic Fleet's Battleship Force. Keen to be a master of all aspects of maritime warfare, he became a naval aviator and a submariner between the wars. A temporary vice admiral in 1938, his career was revitalized by the European War, and he became an admiral when the Atlantic Squadron, which he was commanding, became a Fleet in February 1941. From then until America entered WWII, he fought an undeclared war against German submarines. In December 1941 he became C–in-C US Fleet (with the unfortunate acronym CINCUS), and from March 1942 combined this with the role of Chief of Naval Operations. As such he successfully commanded the largest fleet in history whilst at the same time serving on the JCS and the CCS in Washington: a testament to the qualities of his staff, and his own ability to concentrate on the broad principles of strategy. King was inflexible and ferocious. His own daughter said that he was 'the most even-tempered man in the Navy. He is always in a rage.' He reserved a special contempt for civilians, who he said should be told nothing of the war until it ended, and then only who had won.

Leahy   Admiral William D., 1875–1959
Whilst Roosevelt was assistant secretary of the navy during WWI, he made friends with William Leahy. By 1937, Leahy had reached the peak of his

profession, Chief of Naval Operations. He then retired, only to be recalled in 1941 to become FDR's ambassador to Vichy France. Recalled in April 1942, he became Chief of Staff to the President and Chairman of the Joint Chiefs in July of the same year. He was made the first Fleet Admiral in 1944. Leahy was a skilful and pragmatic bureaucrat, although his influence declined after Roosevelt's death.

Marshall   General of the Army George Catlett Jr., 1880–1959
The son of a failed hotelier, Marshall was a driven man right from his time as a cadet at the Virginia Military Institute. Ironically for one who saw himself as a man of action, he never saw combat. He arrived too late to fight in the Philippines Insurrection in 1902. He joined the US Army in France in 1917 and served with great distinction as Chief of Operations for the 1st Infantry Division. His inter-war service at the Infantry School, Fort Benning, put him in contact with many of America's future generals. He became chief of the War Plans Division in 1938, and Chief of Staff a year later. In pushing forward the restructuring, re-equipment and expansion of the army despite the resistance of Congress and the press, Marshall demonstrated the single-minded determination which was one of his great qualities. He ordered his life rigidly to ensure that his passion for work – he had already collapsed twice from overwork before WWI – did not interfere with his running of the war. That he was able to do this successfully was testament to his ability to block out whatever he was not thinking about at the time. As such he was never likely to be a close friend of the President, but he was a perfect counterpoint to FDR. The similarities to AB are remarkable. Marshall was the only Chief of Staff to serve through the entire war, and he retired at his own request. He has been called 'the epitome of the modern military manager'. He served subsequently as Truman's special representative to China, and Secretary of State, and was awarded the Nobel Peace Prize in 1953.

Smith   Lt-General Walter Bedell 'Beetle', 1895–1961
Smith began his military career as a private in the Indiana National Guard in 1910. He served in France during WWI, after which he gained a regular commission. But despite his formidable skills as an administrator, advancement was slow, and it was not until April 1941 that he became a lieutenant-colonel. After that promotion came rapidly, and he saw service as Eisenhower's Chief of Staff from 1942 until the end of the war. Abrupt and easily roused, he was also a brilliant chief of staff, on whose acumen and organization much of Eisenhower's success rested.

The Russians

Molotov   Vyacheslav, 1890–1986
Despite his well-to-do background, Molotov was a Bolshevik before 1917, and rose to prominence during the Civil War and the 1920s. His career took off

after Stalin's assumption of power. He was chairman of Sovnarkom from 1930. His total support of Stalin during the purges of the 1930s and enthusiastic endorsement of the victims' capital sentences confirmed his position. He was appointed People's Commissar of Foreign Affairs in 1939, and concluded the Nazi–Soviet Pact in August of the same year. By the time of the German invasion, he was the second most powerful man in the Soviet Union – and it was he who announced the news when Stalin was too shaken to do so. Molotov had a deserved reputation as a dour and harsh negotiator, which was a considerable weapon in its own right.

Shaposhnikov   Marshal Boris, 1882–1945
Commissioned in the Imperial Army, Shaposhnikov saw service as a staff officer on the Caucasian front in WWI. He joined the Red Army in 1918, but the Party only in 1930. He was highly influential in Soviet military planning and theory, arguing in *The Brain of the Army* (1927–29) for the integration of Party and military leadership. He was CGS in 1928–31 and 1937–40, and was recalled to the position again after the German invasion. His health failed him and he retired in May 1942. However, he retained considerable influence as Deputy Defence Commissar and head of the Military Academy.

Voroshilov   Marshal Kliment, 1881–1969
As AB records, Voroshilov was one of Stalin's earliest military acquaintances, which was the sole reason for his successful career. He was Soviet Defence Minister in 1925 and a Marshal in 1935, removed from the former post in 1940 when his incompetence led to embarrassing failure in the Finnish–Soviet War. He commanded the North West Front July–September 1941, was head of the partisan movement briefly in 1942, and was involved in planning operations in late 1943. At each stage and level he demonstrated his utter unsuitability for command. Nevertheless he remained a member of the Stavka throughout the war.

The Birds

Common Pheasant   *Phasianus colchicus*, known as pheasant or ring necked pheasant.
Continued releases of birds for hunting purposes means that there is a wide variation in colouring and size. The male has a distinctive crowing advertising call, a scraping 'ko-KOK', and both male and female give out 'kut-UK, kut-UK, kut-UK' when flushed – something which AB must have heard a lot, since his diaries record the killing of some 2,344 partridges, pheasants and quail (mainly the first) by shooting parties of which he was a member; and there were many days on which he shot and did not record tallies. He was too busy to do much shooting over the winter 1940–41: obviously frustrated, he took the opportunity of pursuing a pheasant with a prototype tank (see 10 May 1941).

Greater Scaup   *Aythya marila*, known simply as Scaup.
A medium-sized diving duck, chiefly marine outside the breeding season. Small numbers sometimes seen on inland freshwater lakes. Bulky appearance, with broad bill, and smoothly rounded crown shape. The female is dull brown with contrasting white at the bill. The male in summer has a black head, breast and behind, and grey upper parts with white at the bill. In winter the male plumage is duller and browner, without the white on the head.

Mistlethrush   *Turdus viscivorus.*
A very large thrush with an upright stance, deep chest, small head and long tail. Distinguished by grey upper parts, yellow legs, and conspicuous white underwing covets. The mistlethrush feeds in the open, never skulking like other thrushes, but is still shy and wary, although pugnacious during breeding season. Its song consists of very clear, fluting, far-carrying phrases with obvious pauses, rather like that of the blackbird.

Pallid harrier   *Circus macrourus.*
A slimly built harrier found mainly in South East Europe. Very often mistaken for the more common Montagu's harrier, but distinguishable by its outline and black wedge on more pointy wingtips. The pallid harrier likes open country and dry grassland.

Wryneck   *Jynx torquila.*
A remarkably unobtrusive bird, which is identifiable from a distance more by process of elimination (it looks like a large warbler or small thrush) than by distinctive markings, although up close it has beautiful, vermiculated, cryptic plumage. Although classified as a woodpecker, it does not clamber up trunks, and drums only very softly. It is shy, and sluggish, and often sits quietly for long periods of time. When threatened, it fans its tail, erects its crest, and twists its extended neck from side to side (whence the name). Its advertising call is a distinctive and plaintive 'quee-quee-quee-quee'. Once widespread in Britain, it is now only an irregular breeder there.

NOTE TO THE READER

The text in roman type (like this) constitutes the original diary, complete and unexpurgated, exactly as Alanbrooke wrote it, but for paragraphing and spelling.

The text in *italic type* constitutes a selection of his post-war reflections, written at leisure in the 1950s.

When he addresses 'you' directly, he is speaking to his wife, Benita Blanche Brooke.

For more on these textual matters, see Note on the Text.

Churchill by Alanbrooke, sketched on
10 Downing Street notepaper

28 September 1939 – 30 May 1940

28 September 1939

After seeing you off Michael [Fox, his ADC] and I left for Southampton. I found it quite impossible on that lovely morning as we drove along to realize that I was starting off for the war, and that we should not be meeting for some time. Even now surrounded by troops, on the Heysham-Belfast boat disguised under black paint, I find it impossible to realize. It is all too ghastly even to be a nightmare. The awful futility of it all, as proved by the last war! I am glad to say that it does not undermine my belief in an almighty and far seeing God, working towards one set purpose for the destiny of the human race. I suppose that conflicts between Right and Wrong are still necessary and that we have still got to be taught more fully the futility of war. Eventually we must come to ways of settling our difficulties without war. Evidently we are not yet sufficiently developed in the process of evolution for such methods.

We are now about due to sail down the Solent and shall cross over later in the night. With a two berth cabin I am far more comfortable than I had expected.

Later:

We have now moved out and are anchored close to those forts we watched the Schneider Trophy competitors fly round. It brought me back very vividly to that day we spent together, our dinner at the County Hotel which kept coming back to my mind again and again during the last few days without my daring to refer to it lest I might break down, and finally to our drive back to Thorngrove. The beginning of ten years of happiness such as I should never have thought would be possible on this earth. I cannot tell you what your example has been to me during those 10 years!

29 September   (Landed at Cherbourg)

On the whole a comfortable crossing though the ship rolled a bit and trying to sleep in a life belt is not easy! At any rate no submarines or mines which was a great deal to be thankful. Breakfast with the Base Commandant, Cherbourg, and then a 4½ hour drive to GHQ where I saw Maine and Lindsell [QMG BEF]. What I gathered from the former was not comforting. Both Corps to be put into defensive line on Belgium frontier forthwith, this is exactly what I have been trying to guard against in the case of II Corps, the Corps is at present unfit for war and requires at least one to one and a half months training. I told both Adam [III Corps] and [illegible] that this was the case and was assured by both of them that the early move of the Corps was a political gesture for the French and that I should be given time to finish training the Corps out here. So much for political promises!! I mentioned to Adam that in war the unexpected often happens, I was assured by him that it was quite impossible for the Germans to attack through Belgium before the winter sets in. I wonder if he was right?? Arrived in Corps HQ (Laval) about 6.30 pm very weary. Billet in an old chateau, quite a comfortable room.

30 September
Went to my office in the Schneider barracks: called on the French Cmdr of garrison (Colonel Marchal) and was asked to lunch with him and discovered he used to hunt at Pau, we found many mutual friends to talk about and lunch was a great success. French slovenliness, dirtyness and inefficiency are I think worse than ever; but no one could be kinder than they are. In afternoon I had visits from Duke of Gloucester accompanied by Munster and the AG (Brownrigg). Montgomery [3rd Division] and Hotblack also turned up. We seem to have collected a vast herd at GHQ – I wonder if they will all pull their weight??

1 October
The weather has broken, just as well as there was a serious shortage of water in these parts. I visited HLI [Highland Light Infantry] this afternoon, they had arrived yesterday evening and seem a good lot. Johnson [4th Division] arrived this afternoon and I explained the change of plans to him. Still no letters today and I am longing to hear from you, it is a horrid feeling to suddenly find yourself cut clean off from those you love and all that means everything to you in the world.

4 October
I was unable to write during the last 3 days as I went forward to look at the front we are to take over. I stopped with Dill [I Corps] in his temporary HQ for both nights, and had long talks with him. Found him still very depressed about the general state of unpreparedness for war. We condoled with each other on the lack of equipment and shortage of training of many components. I feel however that his disappointment at having missed both CIGS and C-in-C jobs has coloured his life, and that he is looking at his own situation possibly with slightly over pessimistic outlook. I feel desperately sorry for him as he is in the depths of gloom.

I have had the French liaison officer in my car for the 300 miles going up and 300 miles back to work up my French again, and it is now getting rather more fluent. Yesterday I visited the commander of the 51st French division in front of Lille and did a tour of the defences of the front we are to take up. On the way back looked up GHQ and saw both Gort [C-in-C BEF] and Pownall [CGS BEF] and discussed methods of holding the front, as I did not like the disposition I had been told to take up with the 4th Division. After much arguing I got Gort to come round to pretty well what I wanted. I feel that GHQ have made the mistake of being far too large for the force we have out here at present!

5 October

I was very weary last night after covering close on 900 miles in 3 days and slept like a log. Today I spent conferring with the Divisional Commanders on our method of occupation and defence of the line, and made plans for our move forward. In the evening established contact with Jules de Bonvouloir an old friend of Bagnères-de-Bigorre whom I had not seen for forty years! Tomorrow I am to lunch with him, and discuss old days of our youth. It will have the advantage of making me forget the present for a little.

I received two letters from you today, the first two, they transformed the whole day and seemed to make the sun shine brighter.

6 October

Went to inspect the 11th Inf Bde that I had been unable to see before starting. Then lunched with Jules de Bonvouloir at the Château de Saint-Jean-de-Bois par Noyen (Sarthe). He had asked Maric and Marth to lunch and we discussed old memories of Bagnères-de-Bigorre, and for an hour or so forgot the clouds of war that hung over us. And yet they were mostly somewhat sad memories as they were so closely linked with Victor, Kathleen, Mildred [older brother and sisters, all dead] and Mother. In the evening the owner of this chateau came to dine with us in her own dining room! She is rather pathetic, her husband has abandoned her and her only boy who is hidden from the world in the chateau is wanting.

7 October

Our last day at Laval. Paid an official call on the 'Préfet' and had Colonel Marchal (Garrison Commander) and his chief of staff to dine. Tomorrow we begin to move nearer to the frontier.

8 October

Left Laval this morning for good and motored to Amiens, 260 miles. Am putting up at the Hôtel de l'Universe. A bedroom with a bathroom and a treat to sleep between sheets again – first time since leaving Salisbury, and probably the last for some time.

9 October

After a very comfortable night in Amiens, left at 9 am and went first to GHQ where I saw Pownall about defence of the front. I am not happy about our general attitude, we are facing this war in a half hearted way. The forward area is still crammed with civilians that ought to be evacuated, and no real serious efforts seem to be made to organize civilian labour to prepare defences that are essential. Rear demolitions are not yet prepared, and there is still a serious shortage of barbed wire! I feel that the Germans would have been tackling the situation very differently.

Our new billets at Phalempin are good but congested by refugees from Lille who ought to have been evacuated much further west.

10 October

Did a reconnaissance of the front during this morning, and in the afternoon met Neame (the DCGS from GHQ) to discuss the employment of the 4th Res[erve] Division. I was not much edified by arguments put forward, I feel that it is a pity that GHQ was not kept smaller until such time as the BEF expanded beyond two corps. At present we suffer from 'too many cooks'. Looked up Dill on the way, he has been seedy with flu. Found Fagalde, who commands French Corps on our left, with him.

11 October

Had a Corps conference this morning to settle details of the defence of this front. Just as I was finishing Gort turned up with Holden [BGS, WO]. He gave us details as to present rate of production of various weapons and dates by which we might expect them. The prospects are not cheerful, but the most depressing part of the business is the apparent failure on the part of GHQ to realize how serious these difficulties are! Both the War Office and GHQ appear to be thinking in terms of the war in 6 months time. Our immediate danger in the event of an attack does not appear to be fully realized. Let us hope that he does not attack this year and gives us some time to complete our anti-tank, and anti air armament.

12 October

Spent the morning checking draft Corps Instructions for the occupation of our position amid continual interruption. Amongst others Lindsell (QMG) and the Duke of Gloucester, the latter very nice but not good at getting away. In the afternoon went to look at left portion of our present front.

13 October

I had a busy day with the French – I began by visiting General Gerrard of the 51st Div on our flank to settle matters of liaison with my 3rd Division. I then went to see General Pagézy who commands the [Lille] region. He was very interesting concerning the difficulties he is dealing with. His region contains over 3 million inhabitants. Big cloth industries near Lille essential to the army, the beetroot crop worth a 'milliard', and the coalfields – all short of labour and employing Belgians, Poles, inhabitants of the Saar and Italians! Consequently opportunities for spying unlimited. Also large Communist element to deal with. Belgium full of German spies and attitude of population not very satisfactory. German officers employed as caretakers of cemeteries evidently centres for collecting information. Went on with Pagézy to see the Prefect, explained to him that I had men of my Corps approached by Communists, he is only too ready to have them arrested if caught. Lunched with Pagézy and had to eat six oysters so as not to offend him, a very high test of 'l'entente cordiale'.

After lunch went to St-Omer to see General Fagalde commanding 16th Corps. He used to be Military Attaché in London. Had tea in Sir John French's old 1914 billet!

14 October

Worked in office in morning interrupted by visits. Dill came to lunch and we went on to GHQ to discuss their last order for defence of front which was quite unintelligible! While we were there Pagézy came to see Gort and we were called in to meet him and have tea with him. He had most recent intelligence from Belgium, not over comforting. Although this country is apparently all for resisting the Germans, the King, supported by his 4 principal advisors is for remaining neutral. One of those advisors is the C-in-C of the Belgian forces and is suspected of being distinctly pro-German. After the French departed Gort ran through a series of points. On leaving we heard that wireless had just announced the sinking of the *Royal Oak*!

15 October

Sunday – and the whole country dressed in their Sunday best, apparently oblivious that they may be sitting on a volcano! Very hard at present to realize that we are at war. In the morning visited the Div Cav[alry] Regiments in the back area, and in the afternoon discussed plans for a possible move forward with the Divisional Commanders. As I was going to bed telephone bell rang from GHQ and Neame informed me that Swayne (Liaison Officer with French GQG) reported that the French expected attack tomorrow morning, and that the attack might be expected to spread in our direction, and that the C-in-C wanted the commanders informed to that effect. I therefore telephoned through to Johnson and Montgomery to let them know.

16 October

Visited Supply and Ammunition railheads this morning. These not running properly yet. Rations coming up anyhow and proper pack trains not yet organized. Then lunched with Gort at the Château de la Cauroy to meet Gamelin [C-in-C French Army since 1935]. Billotte commanding our group of armies was also at lunch, I liked the look of him. Gamelin struck me as looking old and rather tired. After lunch a circular which had been chasing him came into action. During lunch we received information that the Germans had attacked on a 6,000 metre front and made some progress – as a result Gamelin altered his plans and went off to see General Georges instead of General Fagalde of 16 Corps as he had intended.

17 October

Spent the morning in the office. Amongst other jobs trying to write a letter to the King as Gort had told us he was rather hurt that we had not yet written to him. In the afternoon looked up Tom [AB's son, serving with Field Regiment Artillery in I Corps] whom I found very well and cheerful. His Colonel Henry Latham says he is doing well.

18 October

Most of the day wasted from the point of view of work requiring to be done. The Duke of Windsor was visiting the front, I had to meet him at I Corps HQ at 10.15 am and again at 12 noon on the southern part of my front to introduce Divisional Commanders to him, and to take him round a part of the front in my car. He was accompanied by Howard-Vyse who has instructions to guard against his endeavouring to stage any kind of 'come back' with the troops out here! He [Howard-Vyse] is acting as Liaison Officer at Gamelin's GQG. He appears to have aged but was full of go and of interest.

19 October

Spent the morning planning for our advance into Belgium in the event of the Germans violating her neutrality. In the afternoon attended a 2½ hour GHQ conference at I Corps HQ. Before the conference Dill and I got hold of Gort and tried to make him realize the serious aspect of the contemplated move. The danger of leaving our present prepared position for one totally unprepared, and the exposure of our left flank if Fagalde's 16th Corps does not come up on the left. He will assume a very light hearted aspect of the situation and is too inclined to under-estimate the strength and efficiency of the Germans. I sincerely hope that we shall not be forced to advance by a violation of Belgium.

20 October

Pouring rain again. Spent whole day 9 am to 6 pm with Monty going round his defences. Went round first of all the Divisional Reserve Line being prepared by Robb [9th Brigade]. Then right along the front, first 8th Inf Bde under Witts and then 7th Guards Div under Whitaker, finishing up with positions under Towell [CRA 3rd Division]. A lot of work has been done under very trying conditions, and defences are taking definite shape. Position would be strong except for desperate shortage of men in the long fronts held. With such a frontage serious resistance becomes impossible. There is no depth to the defence. Lunched with the 1st Gren[adier] Guards.

21 October

Fagalde, commanding 16th French Corps, was to come to lunch today but was unable to come. Started having Corps Staff Conference at 9 am in morning on specific dates to co-ordinate action. Gort, Pownall and Adam turned up at lunch time. Adam had come out from WO for a couple of days. According to him the Germans will not attack, and are themselves starting masses of their rumours about impending attacks, they will instead start another peace offensive with the hope that boredom with the present conditions of war will induce us to make peace. Personally I feel that if internal conditions become critical the Germans will be forced to start some form of offensive.

22 October

Fairly hard frost this morning. Went out with Johnson to look at the Reserve Line he is preparing. Started at 10 am and walked most of the day returning about 5.30 pm. They have been doing great work in spite of the very inclement weather, and the defences are making rapid strides. The position will soon be fairly strong but requires far more troops than we have got to hold it against a determined attack. Still very short of sandbags, when one remembers the lavish use made of sandbags at home in localities that will never see a bomb it makes one's blood boil to be so short of them out here.

23 October

Fagalde commanding 16th French Corps on my left came to lunch today. We discussed possible forward moves into Belgium and our mutual co-operation in this move. As he is some 30 miles behind us I shall have to hold a defensive flank until he comes up. He is a pleasant ruffian and an amusing companion but does not inspire one with unbounded confidence as far as his efficiency is concerned! Otto Lund [Deputy DMO] dropped in from the WO in the afternoon. In the morning went to look at the Army Tank Bde, commanded by Gatehouse. Unfortunately all Mk I tanks without any A/T guns.

24 October

Began the day with one of my Corps Staff Conferences at 9 am till 9.45. Then went out with Johnson to examine the Haute Deûle Canal defences. Spent a most interesting day. Each canal crossing presents a special problem, many of them not easy to solve. Got back about 5 pm – Duke of Gloucester came to my office shortly afterwards having been up to Squeak Curtis's front [3rd Infantry

Brigade] when he had seen Tom! Brought him round to tea and introduced him to Madame so as to 'sweeten' her up a bit. She is inclined to be pretty sour at times! I don't blame her with strange officers dumped down in her house.

25 October

Deluge of rain again, and may it damp the German ardour to commence any offensive operations. Had lunch with Dill and discussed with him a series of problems connected with our possible advance. In the end we decided that we must get GHQ to hold small conference to settle points they have left in the air. 17 Inf Bde joined up with the Corps. This evening dined at 2nd Div HQ in Orchies on Charles Finlay's invitation.

26 October

Went to see Essex Pioneer Bn at work and found them almost submerged after yesterday's rain. Both General Pagézy and the Prefect of Lille came to lunch with me. Both quite charming and easy to entertain but it meant some very hard work talking French like a machine gun from 12.30 to 2.30 pm! Much colder again, and some snow fell during the day.

27 October

Dill and I had asked Gort and Pownall to come to I Corps HQ for a conference to clear up matters as regards dispositions in the event of a move forward to avert a German violation of Belgium or Holland. It is hard to get Gort to realize the seriousness of the situation and what we may find ourselves up against. He refuses to really face the difficulties we may be up against and makes light of them all. Dill and I feel that the situation is not half as rosy as he tries to make out that it is. As the days pass the probability of a German advance this year lessens, but we are far from being out of the wood yet. If conditions in Germany are such as to render it inadvisable to wait, he [Hitler] might well still try a serious attempt through Belgium. Our main danger lies in being drawn into Belgium for political reasons to support the Belgians, instead of holding positions we have been preparing.

Review of situation on Nov 1st
I find that by mistake I have left these two pages out, I shall therefore use them to review the situation.

Here we are behind the Belgian frontier devoting all our efforts to creating a strong defensive line. And yet, should the Germans invade Belgium in all probability the Belgian army will defend its country. This is however uncertain, the King and his four principal advisors are known to have pro-German tendencies. Meanwhile we prepare for the possibility of moving forward into Belgium as soon as the Germans begin to invade that country. Our plans however only take us as far as the Scheldt River with delaying actions in advance. For political reasons this is desirable so as [to] free the industrial centre of Lille-Tourcoing-Roubaix from the threat of bombardment. But, and this is the great 'but', shall we even be allowed, again for political reasons, to sit on the Scheldt while the Belgians fight single handed in the east of their country? This seems highly improbable. Therefore, for political reasons we may well be forced to abandon what strategy dictates, and thus court disaster. Gamelin at all costs wishes to avoid an encounter battle in Belgium and wishes to meet the Germans in well-prepared positions. Will political considerations allow him to follow this wise course? I doubt it!!

28 October

After holding my periodic Corps Staff Conference, I toured back areas with Dawes [his DA and QMG]. Visited Corps Mobile Workshops, Field Ambulances, Supply Columns, and learned a good deal about units I am not familiar with. Was not at all pleased with the hospital established for Corps troops in a gloomy shed, and have ordered it to be moved. I wish my chief doctor had more energy and that old Dawes [b. 1884] was a bit younger (by the same token he is almost 6 months younger than I am, but I always feel that he is old enough to be my father!).

29 October

Ran a Divisional Commanders Conference on winter training from 10 to 12 noon. My Divisional Commanders [Johnson and Montgomery] amuse me, it would be hard to find two more different types, both most efficient in their own way. Afterwards had visit from Blunt, commanding RAF with Expeditionary Force, told him what I thought about paucity of aerodromes to operate Corps Squadrons from. Then Bridgeman [GSO1] in charge of GHQ came, and I bullied into him the necessity for anti-tank and A/A ranges. Finally, a tour of the front between our defences and the Belgian frontier, looking at our front from every point of view.

30 October

Began the day by inspecting in complete detail a man's daily ration and its various substitutes. Then spent the whole day walking round with Stopford visiting 17th Inf Brigade at work on the Reserve Line and meeting the COs of his battalions. A lovely day and a good walk in muddy fields which did me worlds of good.

31 October

A wasted day as far as work was concerned, but I hope that as a result of it all good relations with our allies were more closely knitted. I attended a large lunch party given by the Prefect de Lille. The guests were Gort, Prince Henry

[Duke of Gloucester], Dill, Pownall, Pagézy, General [illegible] of the French Mission, Mr and Mrs Gudgeon of the British Council in Lille and a lot of others. Champagne lunch consisting of oysters, lobster, chicken, pâté de foie gras, [illegible] cheese, and fruit coffee liqueurs etc. We sat down at 1 pm and got up about 3 pm! The ladies comprised Madame the Prefect, Madame the Sous Prefect, Mrs Gudgeon and the Prefect's daughter. Madame the Prefect worked very hard with 'Son Altesse', but did not get much response out of him. He told me that by the time he has thought of a good sentence and translated it into French inwardly it is too late and he has to start on a new one!

1 November

At last October is gone and with it the chances of a German violation of Belgium this winter have receded. We are not yet out of the woods but the probability of such an eventuality is distinctly less. Even should an attack materialize now we are in a much better situation to meet it than at the beginning of October. However we still require months of training with the necessary facilities, such as artillery and anti-tank ranges, before this Corps can be considered as fit for war. Spent the day touring round the artillery defences of the front, and am not satisfied with them. Positions are too far back and liaison between infantry and artillery inadequate. Shall see Monty about this tomorrow.

2 November

Went to see Monty to have his artillery dispositions improved and also to ensure that his parties visiting Lille were better turned out and more of a credit to our Corps than they are at present! While with him the Air Raid warning went and two German reconnaissance planes came over; in this evening's wireless report they are said to have been brought down.

Went to lunch with General Vouez, head of the French mission at GHQ. Prince Henry and Dill also lunching there. Again a heavy lunch with hors d'oeuvres, trout, duck and mushrooms, cheese, ices, fruit, coffee and liqueurs!! I hope this is the last of these lunches – they interfere with my work and my liver!

3 November

Was instructed to meet General Georges at 2.15 pm at Ulster Redoubt (one of the old Lille forts), and to bring Divisional Commanders to meet him. He arrived with [illegible] at 2.45, presumably having been delayed by Pagézy's good lunch at the 'Huîtrière' in Lille! I had a map ready with dispositions on it, and described them to him from the top of the fort. I like the look of him, quite charming to meet and inspires confidence. He then went on to I Corps front to meet Dill. When he left I took Monty and Johnson up to discuss defences of the Bachy switch which is at present being provided with an anti tank obstacle with the object of shortening the front and incorporating the high ground in front of my junction with I Corps.

4 November

Wet and dreary day again. Went up with Monty to 7th Gds Bde front to try out experiment of fumes in a closed pillbox. Eighteen of us got into pillbox, closed down all openings and then fired an anti-tank gun and a Bren gun through the apertures for five minutes to make certain that the fumes and gases from the firing would not be such as to affect the garrison of the pillbox. None of us felt any the worse, but it would have assisted promotion considerably if it had been otherwise as there were 1 Lt Gen, 1 Maj Gen, 2 Brigadiers, 1 Colonel and 3 Lt Colonels amongst those in the pillbox! Expensive 'white mice' for such a trial!

5 November

Instructed by Gort to attend Armistice Service with Commander of 9th French Army at the spot where Germans came out with a white flag in 1918. Left at 8 am to do 70 miles and arrive by 10.30. Took with me Johnson (GOC 4th Div) with his HQ officer, Cericz and Michael Fox. Met by General Martin commanding 11th French Army Corps. Shortly afterwards General Corap arrived, commander of French 9th Army. I accompanied him in his inspection of the guard of honour of infantry and cavalry, then stood facing the monument while British and French flags were unfurled in succession, and appropriate national anthems played. The monument has the following inscription: 'Ici triompha par sa ténacité, le Poilu' [Here French soldiers triumphed through tenacity]. Two speeches followed, then three prayers from a Catholic, a Protestant and a Jewish priest. Then flower wreaths, presented to Corap and me by ladies, which we proceeded to lay at the foot of the monument. We then reviewed the troops as they marched past the monument. Meanwhile a flight of fighters patrolled the sky to keep intruding Germans off, whilst AA guns were also ready to greet them. After the ceremony I went with Corap to see his anti tank obstacles in the Forest of St Michel. From then on to lunch with him.

The ceremony had been a simple one, lacking finish to every respect, almost comic at times in its lack of thoroughness, and yet there was something in it that gripped one mainly I think the past against the present. I could not help wondering whether the French are still a firm enough nation to again take their part in seeing this war through.

6 November

In the morning went to Vimy Ridge Memorial to arrange details of the Armistice ceremony next Saturday. Took the opportunity to visit foundations of monument and old trenches which are kept in a restored state. The monument is most impressive and must look very fine when flood lit on a black night. Then went on to Coumbain l'Abbé to see our old Canadian Corps HQ occupied during Battle of Vimy. I saw my old office, the window I used to look out of to see HQ staff playing baseball, Byng's room and that belonging to Bdr B Radcliffe, where our mess hut was and my bed room hut. It brought back floods of memories, and made me feel that the war had never stopped. It had only been interrupted by a happy dream of 20 years. And yet when I came away and thought of the last 10 years of paradise I felt that the last war and this war were only very trivial matters in my life as compared with the heavenly happiness which God had granted me by allowing me to share the last ten years with you.

7 November
Met Dill in front to coordinate junction of Bachy switch, pouring rain and a very exposed spot! After lunch attended GHQ Conference to decide about sending some of our inf Brigades in succession onto the active front opposite the Germans. Dill and I raised the point that a small British front of that kind would be liable to draw heavy fire from the Germans to prove their dislike for the British. As a result the casualties suffered might well out-weigh the advantages to be gained from the experience. This was overruled by Gort. We then discussed training instructions for winter months, it is pitiable how Gort cannot stick to the broader aspects of a subject and at once descends to the details!

8 November
Conference of Corps Staff in morning, then visit to Div Cav Regiments and after lunch inspected new types of pit for A/T gun. In the evening Neame [DCGS] came from GHQ to warn us of possible invasion of Holland by Germany, of French plans to frustrate them in south Holland by flying small force to hold isthmus and one division to hold island in south Holland. This will entail 2nd Corps taking over front on River Scheldt up to Oudenaarde, namely 28,000 yards for my two Divisions! In addition my left flank with Fagalde's 16th Corps as neighbour and pushed right forward gives me some anxiety. Hope to be left with both Div Cav Regiments to look after this flank.

9 November
The clouds are gathering fast on the horizon and an invasion of Holland, and possibly also Belgium, seems imminent. I do not relish the role of the 2nd Corps if we move into Belgium. We shall be forced to form 'front to a flank', thus throwing up my left flank in an exposed manner. If I felt certain that the French 16th Corps would be up on my left it would not be so bad, but I have

the gravest doubts on this account. I wonder if we shall still be in Phalempin tomorrow evening?!

10 November

Still here, and no move of the Germans yet, but the probability of an early invasion of Holland or Belgium or both seems most likely. All reports point to an early move, but it may well still be some form of bluff. The suspense is somewhat trying. I have made all plans for the move forward into Belgium with the 3rd Div on right and 4th Div on left. I don't like the exposure of the left flank of the 4th Division, and have grave doubts as to when I shall see Fagalde's 16th Army Corps on my left. Went to trials of gun tractors in a ploughed field in the morning, and in the afternoon, visited Anderson's 11th Infantry Brigade which is at present working for the 51st Division. The French appear to have done very little work on this front.

11 November   Armistice Day

The suspense continues, more threats to Belgium and Holland, but no further moves on the part of the Germans. This morning I took part in an Armistice ceremony at the Canadian Memorial at Vimy Ridge. We had two guards of honour, a French one formed by the 51st Division, and a British one from the Black Watch. General Pagézy came from Lille for the ceremony. He and I laid wreaths of poppies on the Memorial, the French guard then presented arms whilst their bugles sounded a 'Sonnerie', this was followed by the Black Watch guard presenting arms whilst their pipers played the 'Flowers of the Forest'. The ceremony ended with inspection of each other's guards, and by a march past of the guards.

   I felt throughout the ceremony as if I were in a dream. The white tall pillars of the monument standing out against the ashy grey sky seemed entirely detached from this earth, whilst the two red wreaths of poppies looked like two small drops of blood on that vast monument. They served as a vivid reminder of the floods of blood that had already been spilt on the very ground [on which] we were standing, and of the futility of again causing such bloodshed. I suppose that it is through such punishments that we shall eventually learn to 'love our neighbours as ourselves'.

12 November

A wire this evening from GHQ to say that the Germans are fairly certain to invade Holland and possibly Belgium between Nov 12th and Nov 15th!! I still have grave doubts as to the veracity of this forecast, and I don't believe that they really intend to go beyond a serious bluff with the object of intimidating those small nations and thus weakening the assistance they may give to Great Britain in blockade measures. In any case we are ready for such a move and have issued orders for the move into Belgium should it be required. I do *not* like the required manoeuvres to get onto the Scheldt, which entail forming front to a flank. In addition I am seriously hampered by the 51ˢᵗ French Division on my left, which is not moving and is being left on its present site.

Today I accompanied Anthony Eden and Dominion Representatives on a tour of my Corps front. Dill handed them over to me at 1 pm, and I toured them round till 4.15 pm. Harry Crerar was amongst them, and I hope may come out later commanding one of the Canadian Divisions.

13 November

We are still being kept in suspense – still no move of the Germans into Holland or Belgium! Went over to 16ᵗʰ Corps HQ to lunch with Fagalde and to discuss details of our forward move. A reserve French army the 7ᵗʰ has now been moved up onto our left and taken 16ᵗʰ Corps under its wing, the other Corps being the 1ˢᵗ. The mission of the 1ˢᵗ Corps appears to jump into South Holland as quickly as possible and to defend it against Germany. Fagalde's 16ᵗʰ Corps now reduced to 2 divisions moves up onto our left with the 9ᵗʰ Division on a 25 kilometre front to our immediate left! And its left depends for its protection on problematical Belgian cooperation. I only hope to God we do not have to hold the line of the Scheldt with such strung out forces against the Germans!! On returning Dill came to see me and to tell me results of his talk with Gort which he asked for to draw attention to our weakness on the proposed line. I gather that he failed to make Gort realize the risks he was taking with the BEF. I am afraid Dill feels the situation acutely, his astute military knowledge makes him see clearly that with such strung out forces, even behind a river, serious resistance is impossible. He feels it his duty to inform Gort who has not quite the same breadth of vision, and Dill feels that Gort has the impression that he suffers from 'cold feet' and is an alarmist. It is a very sad situation; he is torn between loyalty to his commander and loyalty to his Corps.

14 November

Still no invasion of Belgium or Holland, and the likelihood if it ever existed is decreasing. Went around the 10ᵗʰ Inf Brigade front with Barker during the morning, and had a good muddy walk. They have done a grand lot of work under most trying conditions. In the afternoon Neame came round and I discussed with him the difficulties connected with the moves they are asking us to carry out in the event of an invasion of Holland.

15 November

So this prediction of an invasion of Holland between Nov 12ᵗʰ and 15ᵗʰ has not come true. And I am heartily thankful that this should be the case. Our plans and preparations to meet such an eventuality did not inspire me with confidence! I only hope that such an invasion may now be deferred to the spring and that by then our plans and preparations have improved! It has been a somewhat nerve wracking week. This morning I inspected work of the 9ᵗʰ Inf

Brigade on the Div Reserve Line where they have done good work. In the afternoon went to Lens theatre to see Seymour Hicks with Gracie Fields and several others in a variety show organised by the NAAFI. A good show and much appreciated by the troops. Went to thank Seymour Hicks personally after the show.

16 November
Spent most of the day with Schreiber [45th Division] touring round artillery regiments. Visited first the 2nd RHA Regiment at La Bassée, then the Heavy Regiment, 2nd Survey Coy, followed by lunch in Lille at 'Chez André' and on to the 32nd Regiment. In every case interviewed all the officers and had a few words with them. While talking to them I always have the terrible feeling that I may at one time or another be instrumental towards the issue of orders that may mean death to them. It is I think one of the most trying sides of commanding in war, the haunting thought that you may at any time be forced to issue orders that mean probable death to your friends.

17 November
Spent the day with Hawkesworth commanding 12th Inf Brigade inspecting plans for defence of La Bassée Canal. In doing so visited old haunts at Festubert, Givenchy, Gorre etc all of which closely connected with winter of 1914/15 when I was with Indian Corps and commanding 'H' Ammunition Column. I felt very much as in a dream going over some of these places again, rather as if I had been there in another life.

18 November
Hore-Belisha [Secretary of State for War] came round the front today. Met him at 1 pm at Mons en Pevèle where we had lunch and then took him round to meet officers and men of 3rd and 4th Divisions. He looks tired and had not got as much life as usual. I drove him round in my car and he discussed the necessity of forming an 'Army Air Arm' similar to the 'Fleet Air Arm'. He said he was having difficulties with the Air Ministry on the matter.

On returning Dawes came to see me because he had received a letter from MS [Military Secretary] appointing him Base Commandant, Marseilles. We had a painful interview as he is very upset about it, and feels he has been a failure. I had to comfort him – tell him that he had been far from a failure but that his age (56) was too old to be able to do the job should we start active operations.

19 November
Sunday again, the one day that is hardest of all to bear being separated from you on! Received new orders from GHQ for yet another scheme of advance

into Belgium in the event of a violation of either Belgium or Holland. This time we plan to go forward to the line Louvain-Wavre with the French on our right and the Belgians on our left. If we can get there in time to organize ourselves properly to meet the German onrush it is without doubt the right strategy. It is the shortest line possible through Belgium, saves half that country, should give time for coordinated action between the three countries provided the Belgian advance guards on the Albert Canal, at Liège, and in the Ardennes can hold out sufficiently long. We must however resolutely resist being drawn in to try and save all Belgium by defending the line of the Albert Canal and Liège. By trying to save the whole of Belgium instead of half, not only would we lose the whole of Belgium but probably the war as well.

20 November
Went round the front with Monty examining A/T defences of this front and also discussing policy for the defence of A/T obstacles. Then went on to Lille to buy a new watch as my old one was broken. Received order this evening that we could reduce state of readiness for move into Belgium as threat to Holland appears to have temporarily decreased.

21 November
Went over to I Corps in the evening to discuss the new GHQ order with Dill. As usual he was most helpful, and his advice worth its weight in gold. I do wish he was C-in-C instead of Gort, he has twice the vision and ten times the ability. Gort's brain has lately been compared to that of a glorified boy scout! Perhaps unkind, but there is a great deal of truth in it.

22 November
GHQ Conference at I Corps HQ this morning to discuss order for advance into Belgium – should it be required. Dill and I having had previous conference yesterday had already settled what we wanted and we got it. Gort is queer mixture, perfectly charming, very definite personality, full of vitality, energy and joie de vivre, and gifted with great powers of leadership. But, he just fails to be able to see the big picture and is continually returning to those trivial details which counted a lot when commanding a battalion, but which should not be the main concern of a Commander-in-Chief. Poor old Dill finds it very hard to work under him, but is the very soul of loyalty and never shows anything on the surface. If he had not on several occasions given vent to his feelings to me I should never have realized what he was going through. He has risen higher than ever in my estimation since we have been out here.

23 November
Started the day by having to 'tell off' Monty for having issued a circular to his

troops on the prevention of venereal disease worded in such obscene language that both the C of E and RC senior chaplains had complained to the Adjutant General! The latter had shown this circular to Gort, who had instructed him to come and see me. I had already seen the circular and told Monty what I thought of it, namely that the issue of such a document he had inevitably undermined the respect and esteem of the division for him, and thus seriously affected his position as commander. The AG originally suggested that Monty should be made to withdraw the document he had issued. I was dead against such a procedure. Monty had already sufficiently undermined his position as a commander through the issue of the document; to make him withdraw it now would be a clear indication of superior authority disapproval which would remove any vestige of respect they might have for him. I told AG that instead I would have him up again, express the C-in-C's displeasure to him and impress on him again the magnitude of his blunder. I therefore pointed out to Monty that his position as the commander of a division had been seriously affected by this blunder and could certainly not withstand any further errors of this kind. I also informed him that I had a very high opinion of his military capabilities and an equally low one of his literary ones! He took it wonderfully well, and I think it ought to have done him good. It is a great pity that he spoils his very high military ability by a mad desire to talk or write nonsense.

24 November

Went around with Phipps (C[hief] E[ngineer]) to visit activities of Corps RE units. Looked at RE dumps, timber yards, workshops, CCS [Casualty Clearing Stations], station platforms and yards being rebuilt and roads widened. And all the while it poured with rain. Near Petrol Railhead we went down to Raudicourt Chateau, the old 1st Army HQ. The last time I had been there was when we moved out in 1918 to begin the final advance of the war! I felt a desperate longing to have reached the same stage of this war! This evening received instructions to prepare programme for a visit by the King to the 2nd Corps on Dec 6th. This programme is not easy to arrange as I must avoid taking him through industrial areas with communistic tendencies.

25 November

Held a conference of my staff and Div Commanders to arrange tour for King's visit. We had barely completed it when I received order for 4th Division to take over 51st French Div front on left of 3rd Div. This of course completely upset all we had done, and we had to start the programme afresh. A complicated business as the King is not to go into the industrial or mining areas for fear of communists. As the 4th Div front between Tourcoing and Roubaix and the Belgian frontier is just one vast mass of town and factory areas the matter is a little complicated!

26 November

Went to visit 4th Gordons (M[achine] G[un]) Bn which has recently been added to the Corps. It is totally unfit for war in every respect and will take at least 2 months to render it fit. It would be sheer massacre to commit it to action in its present state in addition to endangering the lives of others. I therefore consider that it is a very grave fault by those concerned in sending it out to this country in such a state. Hore-Belisha when he was out here asked me whether it would not be advisable to push units and formations out here to complete their training (mainly with the object of impressing people with the numbers he was dispatching). I told him that I considered that such a procedure was neither fair to the units, the BEF, or our allies the French.

27 November

Deluges of rain again today. Had Johnson up in the morning to settle details of relief of 51st Div by 4th Div with him. I am now to take over front as far as Armentières inclusive, a front of some 64 kilometres (40 miles). I am however to be given the 5th Division which is being formed out here, and the 2nd Corps will then consist of the 3rd, 4th and 5th Divisions. Brownrigg the AG then came to discuss details of programme of King's visit. French will not let him go near industrial areas so shall have to keep him south of Lille and Roubaix. Spent rest of day with CE going round concrete works under construction.

28 November

Called on Commander of French 51st Div to find out whether details of his relief by my 4th Division were working out according to his wishes. Found him quite happy and content. Then motored round our part of front between Armentières, Halluin, Tourcoing and Lille. A lovely day and had a very interesting time. French defences are to all intents and purposes non-existent on this front! When I see this state of affairs and think what might have happened if the Germans had attacked before the winter it makes me shudder!

It is a great relief and a load off my mind that the 2 Corps has not been subjected to active operations yet, and has had this additional time to complete its preparations and training. On arrival in this country and for the first 2 months the Corps was quite unfit for war, practically in every aspect. Even now our anti-tank gunners are untrained and a large proportion of our artillery have never fired either their equipment or type of smoke shell that they are armed with. To send untrained troops into modern war is courting disaster such as befell the Poles. I only hope that we may now be left in peace for the next 2 to 3 months to complete the required readiness for war of the 2nd Corps including its new division the 5th.

29 November

Went around gunner units with Schreiber and visited 91 and 88 [illegible]

Regiments and 53ʳᵈ, 51ˢᵗ, 2 Medium Regiments. A very good show all round. Country very badly flooded, water right over the road in some places, and Jones succeeded in getting the car stuck in a real wet spot! Heard this morning that Pope is to command the Heavy Armoured Brigade. Delighted for him, but very sorry to lose him.

30 November

Spent the day going round Corps Main Dressing Station, CCS, Petrol Railhead, and Petrol Dump. When I returned this evening Gort and Ironside [CIGS] came in. The latter informed me that when Hore-Belisha returned from his trip he informed both the Cabinet and the Privy Council that the BEF was doing no work and had left their front unprotected. That we were the laughing stock of the French on either flank and a few similar remarks! The true case is that the French have been doing practically nothing on our flanks, and that this was the reason why I asked Gort to relieve the 51ˢᵗ Div (French) by my 4ᵗʰ Div on my left flank so that I might prepare defences on this bit of the front and thus secure my flank. Tiny Ironside was very angry with HB for this accusation, told him that these were serious allegations that he was making, and that Tiny must at once come out to verify the situation for himself. He has therefore come out to look at our work so as to be able to go back and as the Irish say 'make a liar of him'!

1 December

Went to HQ 51ˢᵗ Division to meet Tiny Ironside and Gort. Here we had to listen to speech by Girard, the 51ˢᵗ Div commander, expressing his grief at leaving the BEF and his appreciation of the treatment he had received. Then Pagézy turned up with the British Ambassador in Brussels and the British Consul in Lille. I had some difficulty getting the CIGS away. We then went to Mont Halluin and showed him work north of Lille. Then went through Tourcoing and Roubaix to Laumoy where we met Monty and did front line, Brigade Reserve Line and Div Reserve Line. From there I took him to the Reserve position we were preparing. By 4 pm I think he was satisfied that we have done some work since we have been here. I wonder what the final upshot of this will be, and whether it will be the beginning of the downfall of HB? [See 6 January 1940.]

2 December

In the morning I held trials with the 4ᵗʰ Tank Bn in crossing obstacles, and confirmed my belief that the obstacle we are digging at present is neither deep nor wide enough. Dill came out to watch and we discussed Ironside's sudden rush out here. It rather reminds me in some ways of Kitchener's rush out in 1914 although the circumstances were very different. Yet it is one of those historical landmarks which may well lead to more sensational developments in the future.

Spent the afternoon reading a Polish account of the German operations in Poland. I think the invasion of Finland by Russia is sure to increase the differences between Hitler and his military leaders.

3 December
Had a lunch party for General Vouez (Head of the French Mission at GHQ), his Chief of Staff and his ADC. After lunch we sent 4 carrier pigeons with messages to General Fagalde of the 16th Corps. In the afternoon went to look for Tom but could not find him as his regiment had moved.

4 December
Bitter cold day and trying to snow. Spent morning going round King's tour and settling details of it. I only hope now that we may have a fine day for it. Otherwise it will be very trying for the King and for the troops. In the evening went to see Leslie Henson in Lens. A very good show. In 1918 I had seen him after the Armistice in the Lille Theatre, and hardly dreamed then that I should see him again in similar conditions in the same neighbourhood 20 years later!

5 December
Visited 7th Cheshire MG Bn, and Franklyn (Div Commander of 5th Div) came to lunch. He only arrived yesterday and will now have to assemble the various component parts of his division. Spent rest of day completing final arrangements for the King's visit tomorrow. Let us hope that it will be finer than today.

6 December
The King's visit is over and has been a great success. He arrived at 10.15 just outside Avelin, I met him and introduced him to my Corps Staff. He then saw the 4th R. Tank Bn, 14th Survey Regt, Corps RE, Corps Signals and the 12th Inf Bde. We then moved to north of Seclin where he was shown 7 Artillery Regiments. From then to the Lesquin aerodrome where the 8th Inf Bde, 15/19 Hussars, Gunners, Sappers, Signallers etc were awaiting him. He then saw two squadrons of fighters accompanied by Blunt. From then onward I took charge of him again and took him to Fort Ulster where he saw the 9th Inf Bde and the Middlesex Regt (MGs). Then on to Annapes Chateau where he was met by General Giraud, VII Army, Pagézy, 1st Region, Girard, 51st Division, Fagalde, 16 Corps and Colonel Berchti i/c defences of Lille. At the Chateau gates the King stood whilst the 7th Guards Brigade marched past 7 abreast with fixed bayonets. A very fine show.

We then went into lunch where the King sat between Girard and Pagézy. I sat next to Girard. After lunch I spent 5 minutes with a map showing King my dispositions. Then went out into Chateau grounds to see troops that had been assembled there during lunch. Mainly 11th Inf Bde, 5th Dgn [Dragoons], and representative attachments from rest of 4th Div and 13th and 17th Inf Bdes. Also NF [Northumberland Fusiliers], 7th Cheshires and 4th Gordons Machine [Gun] Battalions. The whole show was a first class turnout and all arrangements ran without a hitch. I felt very proud of the 2nd Corps. I then had to drive back to HQ with the King. Unfortunately he fell asleep for part of the way and things a bit awkward as all the villages were full of troops and civilians cheering and saluting. The King seemed very pleased with his day and thanked me very kindly. Gort was also very pleased and congratulated me on the day and on the turnout. I am issuing tomorrow a message of congratulation to the Corps.

7 December
Did a tour of the Bachy Switch with Monty in the morning and spent the afternoon squaring off work in the office.

8 December
Bulgy Thorne [48th Division] came to lunch with me, and it was a great joy to see him again. His face brought back memories of our shoot and a longing for days of peace! I had a long talk with him and gathered from him that fear of invasion by parachute armies had been very rampant at home! In the evening inspected my new Corps Junior Leader School at Béthune. Should be a good show I think.

9 December
A lovely day. Went out with Johnson around his new front doing the whole of the eastern side of Roubaix and Tourcoing close to the Belgian frontier. A very built over area, hard to organize, but which could be made very strong ultimately. It is astounding how little work the French 51st Division had done while it was in the line.

Received your letter this evening reminding me that the 7th was the anniversary of our wedding. I had forgotten the actual date, but knew that it was about this time in December. It is as well that 10 years ago we did not know that we should be at war again now, it would inevitably have cast a cloud over that sunlit plain of happiness which we have journeyed through together. But even had we known, the brightness of that sun of heavenly happiness would have greatly diminished the proportions of that black cloud. I never realized that such happiness could exist on this earth, and even now when its magnitude makes the parting all the harder to bear it has this compensation that the memory of such happiness is in itself an inspiration which eases the burden. Through you I have been able to realize better than any other time in my life the perfection of God's works. And I thank God from the bottom of my heart for having brought us together.

10 December

Wason [Maj Gen RA] came round in the morning to discuss the preparation of [illegible]. After lunch I visited Fources as a possible Corps HQ to be used in the event of moving out the present one. In the evening Pownall came round to discuss plans and orders already issued for the advance into Belgium.

11 December

Went to see Franklyn [5th Division] to discuss disposition of the defences on his front. He is longing to take over the defence of his front, but is still deficient of most of his staff, signallers and administrative units. On the way back bought two French books for Pooks and Ti [AB's children] for Xmas. After lunch went around with Schreiber to watch an artillery exercise that he is carrying out.

12 December

Very cold and trying to snow. Went to see 13th Inf Bde commanded by Dempsey and was introduced to the Commanding Officers of the Battalions. It forms part of the new 5th Div which we are building up. In the evening had a conference of the Divisional Commanders to settle details of the Prime Minister's visit next Saturday.

13 December

Bitterly cold weather. Spent most of the day watching Monty running an excellent exercise which represents the manoeuvres we should have to carry out if we moved into Belgium. A real useful exercise.

14 December

Went out in the morning to reconnoitre the value of the old Aubers-Fournelles ridge as a possible flank defence for the rear of this Corps front should it ever be required. On the way went through La Bassée and up to main road to Neuve Chapelle with all its memories of fighting in 1915. I also went past the first billet I ever occupied near the front in 1914 in the vicinity of Vieille Chapelle. I saw the old ditch into which the trench ambulance had fallen on that first night and out of which my Farrier extracted a silver communion set and a new pole for our water cart. The former we had to return to a French Priest who came to reclaim it, but the pole we kept! I also went past where the billet had been when the ration tobacco made us feel ill, another where we lost most of our horses to shellfire, and finally the one where my Colonel Asquith grumbled that the soup would never come up the stairs warm! It was just a mass of memories which were given a bitter tinge through the fact that I was back again starting again what I thought at the time I was finishing for good and all.

It gives me a lonely feeling also going back over these old grounds, so many of them that were with me then are now gone, and so many that are with me now were not born then! I then went back to look at the Aubers Ridge from where I was preparing an attack in 1915 that never came off, and then went over to the German side to see what we looked like from his side at that time.

15 December

Spent the day with Stopford going round his defences on Mont Halluin. An interesting part of the front. Mansergh (my new DA and QMG and Dawes's successor) has gone sick today, hope it is not serious as he is not very strong.

Just finished reading *Bouvines: Victoire Créatrice*, by Antoine Hadingue. It is a very interesting account of the battle fought in 1214 between Philippe Augustus of France and a coalition led by King John of England. The latter was heavily defeated and as a result made to sign the Magna Carta. The site where the battle was fought is just to the left of my Corps front and I had stood several times lately organizing the defences of a new line on the very spot where 100,000 men engaged in deadly combat in 1214!! The description in the book is excellent and with it it is possible to carry oneself back some 720 years and see in one's imagination the two armies drawn up facing each other only a few hundred yards apart, and to follow the whole combat right to the end of the dreadful carnage that resulted from it. The stained glass windows in the village of Bouvines give a complete pictorial record of the battle.

16 December

Today we were visited by the Prime Minister [Chamberlain]. He went to 1st Corps first, but arrived at 8th Inf Div HQ at 12.45 where he had his lunch in the old chateau occupied by Marlborough when besieging Lille. Or rather where the chateau stood, as the original was destroyed in the Revolution. I sat next to him at lunch and told him about the battle of Bouvines which he was very interested in. After lunch he met representatives of the 4th and 5th Divisions and then drove off in my car to the Lille aerodrome where he saw most of 3rd Division partly formed up and partly marching past him. The day was bitterly cold and I did not feel that he had enough clothes on, only a light waterproof over a shabby suit. I hope he did not catch a chill.

While we were with him a very sad tragedy occurred at my Junior Leaders Corps School. An engineer officer was demonstrating the use of the anti-tank mine when one blew up. It killed 3 officers outright, one more died shortly afterwards, three are very dangerously wounded and two badly wounded. It is very shattering that our anti-tank mines should be as unsafe to handle as that!

17 December

Two more young officers died during the night, bringing the total to 6 dead, and I fear one more of them may still fail to live. I have got a board sitting to try and get at the bottom of the matter, but it is not easy as most of those who were near were killed.

This afternoon I looked up Tom and had tea with him and found him very fit and happy. In the morning met Johnson and Monty on the boundary between the 3rd and 4th Divisions as I wanted to settle junction points of the various lines of defence. Bitterly cold and freezing hard.

18 December

A busy day. Office work, and interview with Camp Commandant to arrange distribution of comforts for Xmas. A visit by French general commanding Div on left of 5th Division. A visit to Lille to discuss concrete shelters and methods of closing the loopholes. A quarter of an hour for lunch and then to Becevy for funeral of 3 of the young officers killed by the mine. Then a visit to one of the survivors at the CCS. From there to Sainghin to see my new Corps MT [Motor Transport] maintenance school. And finally to have tea and a talk with Dill in which we poured our hearts out to each other over the shortcomings of GHQ!

19 December

Left Phalempin this morning at 9 am to come to Metz to visit the 12th Inf Bde of 4th Div which is at present under orders of 42nd French Division and facing the Germans on the front near the Moselle. Stopped for lunch in Rheims and came on to the HQ 3rd French army where I paid a call on General Condé who commands the army here. He was one of the instructors at Versailles when I did the Cycle d'Information which I reminded him of. Came on to Metz, where we arrived about 7 pm and where I met Gardiner who used to be with the HQ of the 18th Div Artillery with us in the last war. Johnson and Barker from 4th Div are also stopping in the hotel.

20 December

Spent a most interesting day. Left Metz at 7.45 am and went to call on the Div Comd of the 42nd [French] Div. Was very much impressed by him, a fine type of officer. From there motored to Kemplich where I met Johnson and Barker, and we went round one of the Maginot forts at Welshtenberg. The fort reminded me of a battleship built on land, a masterpiece in its way and there is no doubt that the whole conception of the Maginot line is a stroke of genius. And yet! It gave me but little feeling of security, and I consider that the French would have done better to invest the money in the shape of mobile defences such as more and better aircraft and more heavy armoured divisions than to sink all this money into the ground.

After visiting the fort I went up with Hawkesworth (commanding 12th Inf Bde) to see his Bns in the line. We first went to the Black Watch in the 'Ligne de Recueil', some 3,000 yards in front of the Maginot line. This line has no defence and a rotten anti-tank ditch. From there we went up to the PWV [Prince of Wales Volunteers] holding the outpost line some 6,000 yards further forward. A line with no power of resistance, a few isolated posts far apart and only lightly wired in. German patrols penetrate right in behind our posts at dusk and at night. A no-man's-land of some 1,500 to 2,000 yards exists between ill-defined fronts. But practically no activity on either side, a certain amount of shelling was going on on either side and an air battle in the afternoon, otherwise absolute peace. The defence does not inspire me with confidence.

21 December
Left Metz at 7.45 am on our way back to Phalempin. Lovely day but very cold. Stopped in Rheims on the way back and looked at the Cathedral. Unfortunately it was so heavily sandbagged up that it was impossible to see its full beauty. Lunched in Laon and we were back here by about 4 pm, when I put in two hours work in the office to square up work. Now I am about to pack up in anticipation of starting off on my journey home tomorrow! I cannot get to believe that it can be true and feel rather as if I was moving about in a dream, afraid that any sudden movement might bring the dream to an end.

22 December
Spent morning in office and after lunch started for Boulogne by car with Michael Fox. Dense fog and very cold. When we reached Arras decided that the fog was too bad and changed to the train. A six hours slow journey with many stops brought us to Boulogne by about 11 pm where we spent night.

23 December
Up early and caught 8 am leave boat. Calm crossing and foggy journey brought me here by about 5 pm where you met me at the station with the children.

An interval of 10 days absolute paradise with you and those two darling children. You know all about those happy days and there is no need to record them on paper as they are already engraved in our hearts.

2 January 1940
A New Year beginning and pray God that it may bring us Peace. After leaving you this morning I got into my carriage and tried to reassure myself that the bottom had not dropped out of the world! I comforted myself with the

thought of all the memories I am carrying away with me of those 10 heavenly days spent with you and those beloved small persons. Memories that I can call on during the next few months, like turning the leaves of a book, and relive those priceless moments with you again and again. They are moments so full of happiness that it is hard to assimilate their full beauty at this time and by reliving them again gradually the full beauty of what you can make of life dawns on one.

The journey back was cold but uneventful. Arrived Dover at 11 am, lunched, sailed at 2 pm and arrived at Boulogne at 4 pm. Then came a poisonously cold 4½ hours motor drive on roads covered with snow and ice. The climax was reached when we found the road completely blocked by a large six wheeled French lorry that had skidded. Luckily we were able to take an avoiding circuit. Finally reached Phalempin at 8.30 with frozen feet.

3 January

A hard day in the office catching up the threads and finding out what had been going on while I was away. Ritchie, my new BGS, seems to be turning out well and should, I think, be good. Bitter cold weather again freezing hard.

4 January

In the morning I went to inspect the new pill box mounting for A/T guns I have invented and was delighted with the result. Afterwards lunched with Gort who told me he wanted the Duke of Gloucester to do a tour with the 4th Division and I had to settle details, it is not a very easy visit to arrange from many points of view. In the evening Jack Collins (Cmdt Staff College) and Robin Money (Cmdt SOS [Senior Officers' School]) turned up to spend a few days with me.

5 January

Frost continues. Took Collins and Money round 3rd Division front. Concrete work all stopped by frost. Visited Bouvines Church and was very interested by the stained glass windows of the battle of Bouvines.

6 January

One cheerful bit of news this morning at any rate – Hore-Belisha has resigned and we have at last got a new S of S [Oliver Stanley]!

Took Collins up to 4th Division and left him with Johnson. I then had a haircut in Lille and selected a watch for the Pooks which Sykes will take home for me. In the afternoon went round to see Franklyn to discuss his dispositions with him, and to find out how he is getting on. Thaw has now set in and snow is going fast. Road pretty slippery this morning. Mansergh looking very ill, hope he will last out, leave should do him good.

7 January

Spent the day taking Jack Collins round. Went first of all to 17th Inf Bde and got Stopford to take us round the Halluin front. Then motored to near Béthune to interview Div Cav Commander. Finally came back by Loos to have a look at an Ordnance Workshop. Drizzled most of the day and snow going fast. Collins wonderfully young and full of go and energy. Hore-Belisha made a great mistake when he refused to promote him owing to him being over the age limit. But that is not the only mistake he made, and now he is certain to make himself most unpleasant.

8 January

Spent the whole day from 9 am to 6 pm in the office finishing up work I had neglected while Collins was there. Sidney Clive came to look me up in the afternoon, he is running Red Cross.

9 January

Hard frost again. Spent the day going round 18th Inf Bde front with Barker who is holding the ground just east of Tourcoing, a very interesting sector.

10 January

Bitterly cold day again. Spent most of the day inspecting the 53rd Light AA Regiment which is at present dispersed in protecting French electric power stations. I finished up having to drink champagne and eat biscuits at 3 pm with the manager of one of the stations.

On returning I had Mason-MacFarlane [DMI, GHQ] for an hour on security arrangements along the frontier. Followed by Pagézy for an interview on police and provost arrangements in Lille. I have now been told that I am to extend my front southwards towards Bailleul, taking over the 51st (Highland) Div when it comes out, and that I am to send one of my present divisions to III Corps. I propose sending the 5th Division away as they are the most recently added to the Corps and the least well known.

11 January

Bitterly cold weather again and never stopped freezing even in the sun. Spent the day going round 5th Div front with Franklyn and had most interesting time. Had to break the news to him that his division would be leaving the 2nd Corps. I am sorry he is going and should very much like to have retained the 5th Division. Franklyn is certainly a more attractive type of individual than Montgomery, but I felt that 3rd and 4th Divisions had formed part of 2nd Corps from the start and should go on doing so as long as possible.

12 January

The war of nerves starts again! A warning from GHQ that Belgium expects to be attacked during next few days, attack to extend through Holland and Luxembourg accompanied by heavy parachutist attacks. Div Commanders not to proceed on leave at present. How lucky I took my leave early. I expect this sort of continual scare will go on from now onwards. At present I cannot believe that the Germans would advance through Belgium at this time of year and with the heavy frost prevailing at present which will be followed by a period during which 'pavé' roads will stand no heavy traffic.

Started the day by officially 'reprimanding' a subaltern of the Sussex Regiment. Then inspected my patent mounting for anti-tank gun in pillboxes. It is making good progress. Back for lunch which General Fagalde commanding 16th Corps came to have with me. After lunch interviewed head NAAFI official to lodge many complaints. He did not impress me much! Finally visits of various members of the Staff and more work, before being able to get back to the one moment of the day that I live for, namely when I find your darling letter and later have my evening talk with you on paper.

13 January

Started early to see trial of MG against Berchti's bricks [pillboxes?] which proved successful. He has produced a simple method of closing up that part of the embrasure which is not in use. Then went on to see the Prefect of Lille to express my deep regrets for the murder of a French woman by a man of the 4th Div. He was very nice about it. Got back to find Prince Henry arriving at 12.30 pm and he stopped on for lunch. After lunch I looked up Monty who has been ill and came back in time to meet McNaughton and Crerar of the Canadian Corps who came to tea. Still bitterly cold!

14 January

The war of nerves continues! At 3.30 am I was woken by Ritchie (BGS) stating that an early invasion of Belgium was expected and that all preparations must be made for an early advance to meet them! This meant at once complicated plans with Auxiliary MT Companies to get Infantry Brigades out training back in their right places. At breakfast time I received orders to attend a conference of the C-in-C at GHQ at 11 am. It turned out to be an interesting conference. We were told that a German plane had made a false landing in Belgium containing 2 German officers and some plans which they tried to destroy by fire. They were stopped doing so, and the plans turned out to be a complete scheme for the invasion of Belgium and Holland by Germany to be carried out shortly. We discussed the whole evidence and came to the conclusion that the whole affair looked like a 'plant' on the part of Germany. It was not likely that officers would fly over Belgium with a plan of this kind in their possession. It seems probable that the whole affair was staged with the object of trying to induce Belgium to call on France and England for military support in the face of such a threat, and thus to provide Germany with an excuse for violating the frontier of Belgium and Holland. We may or may not have been right and so as to leave nothing to chance we are now at 4 hours notice to move. Within the next 24 hours or so we might be able to know how serious the threat is.

Whilst at GHQ Gort introduced Dill and me to a Mr X* who does a lot of travelling and was very interesting. After lunch I went to see Johnson and Monty to explain to them the situation and to find out whether they were recovering from their lumbago and sore throat respectively. They are better, but not really well enough to bear the full strain entailed by a move into Belgium. I wonder what the next 24 hours may bring for us!

15 January

24 hours have gone and the period of tension has again relaxed! This morning a liaison officer from GHQ came to inform me that a German invasion of Belgium no longer seemed imminent and that yesterday's scare was as we had thought a plant on the part of Germany. However events are now developing in another direction and Mr X's visits seem to be bearing some fruit. Apparently the King of the Belgians has now asked the British and French governments whether we should be prepared to come to his assistance to meet the possible German threat if invited by the Belgian government to do so. We are believed to have replied that on moral and military grounds we should be prepared to do so. This reply has gone back to the King of the Belgians and the answer is awaited.

The situation is an intensely interesting one – are we doing just what the Germans have been trying to make us do with the crashed aeroplane 'plant'? Is it to their advantage that we should enter Belgium at the request of the Belgian government? They would then be given an excuse for violating Belgium and Holland by stating that the attitude of these countries was no longer strictly neutral. They would also be provided with better opportunities for taking advantage of the considerable numerical superiority of forces which they enjoy at present by having a wide front of contact with greater facilities for circulation of forces. Finally an engagement between our forces in the middle of Belgium would be of the open warfare nature which would suit German forces. On the other hand – we should shorten our front by at least 100 kilometres, allowing us to pull some more divisions into reserve. We should also benefit from the addition of some 18 Belgian divisions to our forces, and finally we should be able to put all the work we are doing now into the defences which we are really likely to require. Since an invasion of Belgium by Germany will always necessitate our moving in. On the whole I think we should score by going in if invited to do so.

---

*Admiral of the Fleet Sir Roger Keyes, Special Liaison Officer to the King of the Belgians. A rare example of the use of some sort of code.

16 January
Still standing at 6 hours notice and I don't know what GHQ is up to as regards possible future plans, but I hope to hear soon. Went round the 5th Div Reserve Line with Franklyn, unpleasant as it was snowing most of the time. Then inspected the Indian Mule Coy to find they were badly housed, huts unfinished, no glass in windows, stove pipes missing and no palliasses to sleep on. Administered a few 'bites' and hope situation will improve shortly.

17 January
Bitterly cold wind with driving powdered snow, a most unpleasant day. Roger Evans visited me in the morning on his way to see his Regt the 5th Dgn [Dragoons]. He was most depressing about the progress made about the Armoured Division. Nobody at the WO seemed to provide the driving incentive and it looked to me as if Roger was not 'cutting much ice' and no one was listening to him. Shall have to try and get Gort to press for a Brigade at least to be sent out soon. Dill then came and stopped to lunch. We had a long talk together and comforted each other about the shortcomings of GHQ. He is still in a very depressed mood, but even more charming than ever.

18 January
A lovely cold day, bright sun but no thaw and powdery snow under foot. Walked the River Lys from Armentières to Comines with bits by car. Well worth the reconnaissance. There is no doubt that although it is a formidable tank obstacle, the Boche with their efficient bridging equipment would have little difficulty in negotiating it unless opposed by a strong defence. At present my defence is very weak owing to very wide fronts held by divisions.

19 January
Again bitter cold. Went round 12th Inf Bde front in the morning between Tourcoing and Mouscron, a desperately over-built up area. Back to lunch at 1.30 pm and a visit from Gort and Pownall at 2 pm. Both perfectly charming, but the points he [Gort] discussed were connected with [illegible] guns, bombing tactics, rifle fire by night and many more such minor details, whilst I had hoped that he would discuss the big alternatives connected with our possible advance into Belgium, and the larger points at issue connected with the extension of the BEF front. After they left I held a Div Conference concerning impending moves and changes within the Corps. After dinner Pownall called up to tell me that recent changes affected all decisions arrived at [at] my Conference this evening!!

20 January
Hard frost continues. I met Fagalde and his commander of the 53rd Division at

the bridge of the Lys north of Armentières at 9.30 am. We toured the whole of the front of this division in anticipation of the 51st Div taking over. And I then went for lunch with Fagalde at St-Omer. Now I hear that all plans are likely to be changed again. And that probably Adam with the III Corps will come in on my left and take over the 51st and 5th Divisions.

21 January

Spent the morning in my office. At 12.30 pm Davidson, who used to be in our shoot at Sandleford Priory, came to see me. He is by way of going to Brussels as the King's Messenger, at the same time looking at the country. I sent for him to tell him what I wanted him to look for from our point of view. After lunch I went out to 5th Div RE Park to see mock up of a pillbox with my patent mounting for the 25mm A/T gun. I then came back to see Martin, who used to command my 5th AA Div at Chester, and now commands all the AA of the BEF. We had a long talk on the organization of the AA defences of this country. Snowed most of the day, and was forced to postpone my visit to 8th Inf Bde on Saar front for which I was starting tomorrow.

22 January

Colder than ever and more snow in the night. Pownall came in the morning to discuss the new organization of the front. I had a satisfactory discussion with him and put all the II Corps points of view in front of him. Victor Fortune and Q. Martel also turned up, commanders of 51st and 50th Divisions. I have got to arrange about receiving them but am not certain which remains with me as a permanency. Probably 50th in any case, and this was the division I was GSO2 with for 3 years after the end of the last war with General Wilkinson.

23 January

No change, still bitterly cold. Visited my Cypriot Mule Company. A difficult unit to run, the men speak no English, only Greek or Turk. Only one officer talks Greek. This was a problem as most of them have never seen mules before. Heaven knows when, if ever, they will serve a useful purpose. Lunched with Dill and had a long conference with him on the subject of the expansion of our front when III Corps arrives, and necessity to [place] divisions in best positions for their forward advance into Belgium if required. The defence of the frontier must be a secondary consideration as the most unlikely of the two contingencies. Q. Martel returned to his division, Victor Fortune still here. I rather doubt if this latter is up to requirements.

24 January

No change in the weather. This evening dined with Pagézy at the Huîtrière in Lille in order to attend a gala performance of the film *The Lion has Wings*. The dinner was attended by the AG, QMG and E-in-C [Engineer-in-Chief]. Pagézy was in good form telling us about his efforts to learn English with a gramophone while he shaves. The gramophone says 'Why will you not dance with Helen? Because it is dangerous. And why is it dangerous? Because Helen will smoke cigarettes and I am wearing a cellulose collar!!!' At the cinema I sat between the Prefect and the Sous Prefect. Only returned home after midnight and to my surprise it was thawing!

25 January

Thaw did not last and cold as ever today. Went to inspect the 6th Argyll and Sutherland MG Bn just out from home, commanded by one Shaw Stewart who struck me as being no use at all. A good unit being spoilt by a bad CO. Shall arrange to have him changed.

26 January

Mild rain suddenly at 4 pm which froze as it fell and rendered roads impossible, followed by more falls of snow, and now bitter cold and freezing hard. Inspected HLI [Highland Light Infantry] in morning and did office work in the afternoon.

27 January

Thawing hard all day, but freezing again tonight. Bulgy Thorne came round at 10 am, and after about 1 hour's discussion we sallied forth and did a long tour of the front returning at 4 pm. His Division [48th] has various reinforcing jobs on the 2nd Corps front in event of our front being broken. I feel however that we are unlikely ever to defend the front we have spent so much work and thought in preparing. How can we avoid being drawn forward into Belgium? Our main difficulty will be not to be drawn beyond Antwerp-Namur line. Political consideration must NOT be allowed to override the strategical ones.

28 January

Hard frost again and roads a sheet of ice. Dewing DMO+I [Director of Military Operations and Intelligence] at WO, came out today for a tour of the front and we were out all day. I had an opportunity of pumping him as regards the WO view of the prosecution of the war. The feeling they give me is that whilst concentrating on ensuring that they are going to win the war in 3 years from now they neglect to realize the danger of losing it this year! Unless we get the Air Ministry and the War Office to realize that they are fighting the same war, and that their combined effort is required at the same spot, the same time and with the same object, we are courting disaster against an enemy who adheres to the doctrine of concentration of effort at the vital point at the right time. To contemplate bombing the Ruhr at a time when the Germans are using their combined army and air force effort in one mighty uniform attempt to crush the French and British forces to clear their way into France, is in my mind sheer folly. Two 'wrongs' will not make a 'right' in this case, and a misuse of our air force will not induce the Germans into a misuse of their own air force by diverting them from their proper task to that of bombing England. When the combined task of the German land and air forces is completed and northern France cleared of the Allies, then and only then, will the Germans turn their air might onto England.

29 January

Cold as ever. Spent the morning in the office, and in the afternoon attended cinema invitation of General Vouez to see French army film of King's visit, the decorating of Gort and Ironside, and other films of the French army. Mainly intended as propaganda, but left one with a feeling of depression as to the lack of real finish in the French army. A very amateur appearance which compares unfavourably with the utter efficiency of the Germans, even as exemplified by types of German prisoners in French hands. I only hope that they still possess the same fighting qualities which they showed in the last war.

30 January

Spent this morning in the office with a series of interruptions. Amongst others Martel (commanding 50th Div) and his staff came in. He was wondering why we were not more concerned with preparing offensive measures to attack the Siegfried Line; and seemed quite oblivious of the fact that instead of attacking this spring we are far more likely to be hanging on by our eye-lids in trying to check German attacks!

Went to the dentist at the CCS in the afternoon and had a tooth pulled out and my lower plate adjusted. On way home rain started, which froze as it fell and made the road almost impossible.

31 January

The first month of 1940 finished and I wish it was the last one of the year! Thawing hard all day, snow and ice going rapidly. Visited 1/7 Middlesex MG Bn this morning and decided that their commanding officer must go. It is sad the number of Territorial commanding officers who are proving quite unsuitable to command a unit out here. In the afternoon visited Johnson to fix up about his going on leave which he is urgently in need of. Neame came to tea to say goodbye before taking up command of a division in Egypt. Wilts succeeds him as DCGS and should be broader minded and better for the job.

1 February

The thaw continues. A nasty wet and foggy day. Went to inspect the 5th

Northamptons whom I had to exchange with my regular Oxford and Bucks Bn, in the present process of interchanges of units which we are carrying out. They seem a good lot. In the afternoon I went to see the mock up of the 25mm pillbox mounting which I am having made. It promises well.

No mail this evening, and consequently no letter from you, and as a result a colourless day! The receipt of your letter is the hub round which the day revolves. Without its hub the day turns with an aimless wobble!

2 February

Whilst out touring round gunner units near Armentières I received a telephone call saying Gort wanted to see me at 1 Corps HQ at 4 pm. I wondered if the Germans were again threatening an invasion of Holland and Belgium and started off at once on the long drive to Douai It was not the Germans that had stirred this time, but he wanted to tell us the results of his meetings whilst home on leave. They were not reassuring! Apparently various expeditions to other theatres of war are being considered by the highest, most of which would it strikes me lead to a dispersal of effort, and provide better chances than ever for our losing the war. History is repeating itself in an astonishing way. The same string-pulling as in the last war, the same differences between statesmen and soldiers, the same faults as regards changing key posts at the opening of hostilities, and now the same tendency to start subsidiary theatres of war, and to contemplate wild projects!! We shall apparently never apply the lessons of one war to the next.

3 February

The first feelings of spring. A lovely mild day which makes it harder than ever to realize that humanity can be so mad as to be at war again. I went for a walk in the woods and wished that I could wake up out of this nightmare of war and find myself at your side again with the world at peace!

4 February

Was just settling down to a quiet Sunday with a visit to Tom in the afternoon when Adam turned up at about 11 am. It was a great joy to see him and we had a tremendous talk and a tour of the front in the afternoon.

5 February

Metz. Left Phalempin this morning at 9 am with Ritchie and Ronnie [Stanyforth, his ADC]. Lunched at Rheims and arrived at 6 pm after a some-what foggy drive. Found Gort still here and dined with him and have just had long talk with him on his impressions of the day at the front. He is not pleased with what he saw in the Green Howards and has given me a whole list of points to put right. I think he had a terrible longing to stop up tonight and take a patrol out himself. His eyes were still twinkling with the excitement of it. He is the most inspiring person I have ever met when discussing questions related to the handling of a battalion in war. Tomorrow I visit the 15th Inf Bde of the 5th Division.

6 February

Up at 6.30 am and off at 7.45 first of all to see General Freydenberg who commands Colonial Corps on this front. A nice friendly old gentleman who gave me a feeling of quiet efficiency. Then a visit to the Div Commander of the 22nd Div. A fire eater with curled up moustaches constantly acting and I should think unreliable and useless! Then up to Barnett Hickling commanding 15th Inf Bde and a tour with him round front line posts which are as bad and inefficient as they were last December!

Whole country made snow and slush. Car then broke down by front wheel brakes seizing! Had to abandon it and borrow Barnett Hickling's as I was due at 2.30 pm to inspect Fort Hackenburg, one of the big Maginot forts and the one the King saw when he was over. Most interesting, garrison of over 1000 men, over 7 kilometres of passages, 4 vast great diesel engines, electric railway, electric kitchens, electric baths, automatic gun control and all round an astonishing engineering feat. But I am not convinced that it is a marvellous military accomplishment. Millions of money stuck in the ground for a purely static defence, and the total firepower developed by these works bears no relation to the time, work and money spent in their construction. Their most dangerous aspect is the psychological one, a sense of false security is engendered, a feeling of sitting behind an impregnable iron fence; and should the fence perchance be broken then French fighting spirit be brought down crumbling down with it! Owing to fog and car trouble it was only 7 pm when we returned to the hotel in Metz.

7 February

Left Metz at 9 am in Ritchie's car with him and Ronnie driving alternately. My car with two chauffeurs following as best they could slowly. Lunched in Rheims and back here by 5 pm. Found Adam still here. New ADC [Barney Charlesworth] also turned up. Car arrived back safely also.

8 February

Started the day with a busy hour in the office getting level with three days back work. Then took Martel out to go over the line which he is to prepare with his 50th Div. Got back about 3 pm and received a call almost at once from Munster [ADC to Gort] ordering me to attend a GHQ conference at I Corps HQ at 5 pm. When I arrived there Adam turned up with Gort, having been visited by Massy [DCIGS] who had been flown over from the WO. The plans which Gort had told us about after returning from leave are taking shape! The 42nd and 44th

Divisions are being held at home, also rest of Adam's [III] Corps HQ. We may also be called upon to send the 5th Division home.

The proposed plans fill me with gloom. They are based on the assumption that the Germans will not attack on this front during the spring. Personally I hold diametrically opposed views. Any forward move of the Germans on this front must necessarily bring operations in subsidiary theatres to a standstill, but unfortunately by then we shall have seriously reduced our strength on this front and will be less well able to meet any attack. We seem to be falling into all the errors that we committed in the last war by starting subsidiary theatres and frittering away our strength. However there is still hope that those we propose to help will select to be left alone, and may well decline our assistance. But meanwhile the least that we shall suffer from here will be delay and confusion.

9 February

Today the French President Monsieur Lebrun was visiting the BEF. I was asked to lunch at GHQ to meet him, many other guests, Dill, Adam, Prefect of Lille, Prefect of Arras, General Pagézy, General Vouez and several more. After lunch the usual photographs and cine-pictures and then a visit to I Corps front where Divisional Commanders were introduced to him. Afterwards tea at I Corps HQ, and then a move to Douai station to see him off on his way to Paris. British Ambassador in Paris (Sir Ronald Campbell) was also with him and Malise Graham, the new Military Attaché in Paris. Frost started again with cold north wind!

10 February

Hard frost again, and every indication of another spell of it. Spent the day in the office except for a trip to Lille to have my hair cut. We are still in a state of suspense as regards III Corps – no decision as to whether it is to stop here or go home. Meanwhile we are handling 5 divisions in the II Corps and are feeling the burden of it.

11 February

Sunday again, our day when we should be together. I went for a walk in the woods this afternoon and imagined you were with me and kept up an imaginary conversation with you. Life without your comradeship is just one long blank.

The situation in the Corps is getting more and more confused. Just as we were in the process of giving birth to the new III Corps the recent proposed diversions to other theatres have put everything into a state of suspense. The 5th Div is awaiting orders to be pulled into reserve, the 51st Division is in the middle of the relief of the 53rd French Division and the 50th Division is following on close behind. We are at present handling 5 divisions and in the middle of reliefs which have been partly counter-ordered, and can get no definite orders. I now discover that the last development is that Gamelin had never been informed that the British government proposed to withdraw the 5th Div and that he is objecting to this move! This will probably lead to Tiny Ironside dashing over, more cabinet meetings, more discussions and meanwhile we shall be left in uncertainty as to what reliefs should be carried out and when to put divisions which are in the process of arriving into the forward area. It is these uncertainties and counter-orders which are so killing and exhausting for the staffs, forcing them to prepare a multitude of alternative plans that are never carried out.

12 February

Another bitterly cold day, and snow again tonight. Visited the R Berks Bn which has come over from 48th Div to 3rd Div and then went for a tour of the front with Monty who wanted to show me all the new work he was starting.

13 February

The whole country under snow again this morning! The flu spreads. Adam still in bed, Ritchie and Schreiber both unwell today with the usual sore throat. Visited No 4 Workshops in the morning. Guy Williams, C-in-C Eastern Command arrived this evening on a 3 days visit.

14 February

Colder than ever. Cars refused to start and removed one burst water pipe! After much delay inspected 1st RHA [Royal Horse Artillery] Regt and 4th Medium Regt. Adam still in bed with fever, also Ritchie and Schreiber. Williams spent day with Monty.

15 February

Snowing hard all day, but melting as it falls. Took Williams on a tour of the front. Order came in for Adam to stop out here but the whole of his staff to go home again! Presumably Dill will be called on to command the new front, and Adam will replace him. 50th Div to remain leaving [illegible] behind. Relief of 53rd French Div by 51st Div now stopped. We shall eventually sort ourselves out.

16 February

Visit of the new Secretary of State for War [Stanley] and of Field Marshal Lord Milne. Met them at Wambrechies at the HQ of the 5th Division. Began by showing them mules and mule carts, then German pill boxes converted for our use, defence of the Lys, and lunch at 13th IB headquarters at La Montagu. After lunch a German [illegible] headquarters taken over by 13 Inf Bde and then onto 15th and 17th Inf Bde to see more defences on front between Halluin and Tourcoing.

Finally a visit to Pagézy and then with the Prefect. I had a long talk with the S of S in the car and explained to him how dangerous I thought any idea of reducing the strength of the BEF at the moment for any ventures in other theatres. He seemed inclined to agree. I told him that I considered this was the only front on which the war could be lost in 1940 if we were not careful, and might possibly win if we were fortunate. He expressed the view that he thought it very doubtful whether the Germans would attack on the Western Front this year. I told him I had no doubt about this matter whatsoever, and looked upon it as a certainty. I then had a talk with Lord Milne, whose mind is as clear as ever, he was very much of the same opinion as I was. He also expressed the view that from a military point of view he considered we were wrong to advance into Belgium.

17 February
Woke to find a snow blizzard raging and snow about 6 inches deep. Went to 4th Div to carry out reconnaissance of part of the Quesnoy Line, somewhat hampered by snow and roads very bad. In the evening had to turn out at 6pm to go and dine in Lille with General Pagézy to attend a charity performance for the benefit of AA gunners defending Lille of which I have been appointed patron. Madame Pagézy was there very charming and able to keep her husband in good order! The performance started at 8 pm and lasted till after 12.30!! I only got back here at 1.30 pm after a cold drive home. A very trying evening as the theatre was cold. The last time I had been in that theatre was in 1918 or '19 after the Armistice when I had driven over from Valenciennes to see Leslie Henson perform in *Aladdin and the Forty Thieves*. He was then running the 2nd Army entertainment company.

[No entry for 18 February 1940]

19 February 1940
Woke to find a heavy thaw set in. Took Adam out to show him front, but could not do much as whole country was under water and heavy fog as well. Chief Rabbi Gollop [?] and Rev Davidson came to lunch. After lunch interview with Wason from GHQ, Victor Fortune commanding 51st Div, and representative of *News Chronicle* for interview. Finally had to reprimand [illegible] for contravening censorship in a letter home.

20 February
Thaw continued. Country partially clear of snow and thaw precautions in full swing. Bob Haining turned up at lunch time from Western Command for his visit. Unfortunately broke my lower set of dentures at lunch and had to proceed to dentist at CCS this evening who is going to try and repair them.

21 February

Lovely spring day with warm sun. Took Adam and Haining for a tour of 3rd and 4th Division fronts. Excellent visibility. Concrete work going full swing. Collected my false teeth from CCS in the evening. I hope they will not go again.

22 February

Another lovely mild day, but the whole country under water and becoming a sea of mud. Spent the morning in the office, and the afternoon with 3rd Div who were carrying out an intelligence exercise. Sent Bob Haining to visit 5th Div, I Corps and GHQ. He leaves again tomorrow morning for Western Command.

23 February

Today Venning (QMG at the WO) came out for a tour. He is another example of those who consider that a state of stalemate prevails on this front and that no active operations are likely to take place. I did my best to convince him that the reverse was the case! We visited Supply Columns, Supply Railhead at Avion, Leave Camp, Mobile Baths, Billets etc. Finally lunch at the Huîtrière in Lille, and after lunch went to 9th Guards Bde HQ to meet Whitaker to examine plans for defence of Hempempont ridge. Adam came along with me.

24 February

Another lovely spring day. Took Adam off to see a GHQ demonstration of A/T pill boxes. Gort was there having been visited by Tiny Ironside yesterday, but he had little news. No decision has yet been reached as regards the proposed northern ventures. But between March 5th and 15th a decision is to be arrived at. Meanwhile life in the II Corps is somewhat complicated owing to the uncertainties of the future existence of the III Corps. In the afternoon took Adam and Schreiber up to roof of wool factory in Houilly and looked into Belgium as far as Tournai and beyond.

25 February

A morning in the office followed by a visit to Victor Fortune (Commanding 51st Div) in Béthune. All indications show that the WO now look upon this front as one of stalemate. They may well have a rude awakening! First day of summer time.

26 February

A visit of four Field Marshals: Birdwood, Jacob, Montgomery[-Massingberd] and Deverell. Started off from Armentières and took them round the front of the 5th, 4th and 3rd Divisions finishing up with a description of the battle of

Bouvines on the actual ground followed by a visit to the church windows. I was rather sad to see how Montgomery had aged, he was looking the oldest of the lot. Deverell just the same as ever, Birdwood full of reminiscences of old Victor and Ronnie and Douglas [AB's brothers]. I suppose this must be about the last of our visits. I had an opportunity of impressing on all of them the necessity for additional formations on this front.

27 February

Rainy weather has set in again. Visited 4th Div artillery and went round gun positions with them. In the evening Bertie Fisher [Southern Command] turned up with a very heavy cold on him.

28 February

Kirke [Inspector-General Home Forces] came in the morning for a short visit. After that I took Fisher for a tour of the 5th and 4th Div fronts. Adam also came along. The weather was beautiful and the visibility excellent. On the whole a very pleasant day. Winter seems at last to be going and pleasant spring weather setting in. Long may it last!

29 February

Another month gone, and ½ a year since the beginning of the war, and we seem further from finishing it than we were at the beginning! Spent the morning with Pagézy going round some of the AA defence of Lille, finally lunching with him in his billet. In the evening Rollie Charrington turned up [comrade and friend from Staff College], it was a great joy to see him again.

1 March

Bertie Fisher left this morning. I took Rollie Charrington round 3rd and 4th Div fronts. Cold bright day with good visibility. On returning had interview with Wilts on the availability of 5th Div in the event of an advance.

2 March

A good day's work. Started at 8.45 am with ¾ hour hard dealing with office work. Then ½ hour with Victor Fortune discussing Corps Reserve Line he is to prepare. Left at 10 am and walked most of the line starting from Attichy through Seclin and along Canal to Santes and on towards Armentières. Got back at 5.30 pm for tea with Dill who was touring [illegible] with Adam. Then office work and interviews until 7.30 pm. Finally a Sherry Party with 'B' Mess to celebrate the anniversary of the first 6 months existence of II Corps HQ. Back for dinner later, entertained Rollie Charrington till close on 11 pm. Then wrote your letter and finally sat down to learn my French speech for tomorrow!

3 March

Arrived in Lens at 10 am preceded by 2 Military police and 2 Gendarmes on motor cycles. As I descended from the car God Save the King was struck up followed by the Marseillaise. We then went to the buildings of the Miners' Federation where, in a large hall tables were decorated with champagne bottles and a large crowd of miners, officials and dignitaries of the town were assembled. The President of the Miners' Federation (aged 76), Prefect Cadot, began with a speech to which I had to reply (by a speech prepared by one of the French Liaison Officers!). Then a miner made a speech, and finally a British soldier. This was all punctuated with some champagne drinking and terminated with a flash photograph by press correspondent. We then formed a procession and marched to the war memorial where I had to lay a wreath on the memorial followed by the Last Post, Reveille, God Save the King and the Marseillaise. As we stood there in the main square I could not help looking back 20 years ago when I was busy writing orders to concentrate the maximum number of guns I could raise to shell this self same square! We then marched to the town hall where a banquet was ready to be followed by a football match and a tea (exclusively of champagne!). I escaped before the banquet to meet King, the Chief Engineer from GHQ to discuss the construction of pill boxes, and to visit Monty and discuss his exercise with him which takes place this week.

At dinner this evening I had the fun of hearing my own voice on the wireless on the evening news delivering a bit of my French speech, and I wondered whether you also were listening, and hoped you were. Tomorrow I start for another visit to the Saar. Rollie Charrington left for 1st Corps HQ this morning.

4 March

Left Phalempin at 9 am for the Saar accompanied by Adam, Schreiber and Stanyforth. Had a very good run down and lunched in Rheims on the way down. Called in to see General Condé who was out, but picked up message there that Adam was to return to England again. Spent a few minutes examining battlefield of Gravelotte (1870).

5 March

Left Hotel at 8 am, called on new French Div Commander and then on to meet Barker commanding 18th Inf Bde. He informed us that he had just had two men killed in a bombardment a couple of hours before. We went up to the forward battalion, the DCLI [Duke of Cornwall's Light Infantry], to find out details. In the battalion intelligence room we discovered that 2 posts had been raided, total damage unknown. While we were there one of the intelligence officers brought in a German uniform jacket and reported he had taken it off a dead German found near the post. We then went up to the post to find out what had happened. Apparently about 6.10 am the Germans put down heavy barrage on these posts and also enfiladed them by a Light Automatic [gun] pushed forward. Barrage was then lifted and the post assaulted. The Platoon

Sgt Major and one corporal were killed and also one German, but 16!! [illegible: ? prisoners]. There had been considerable fighting as there were a good few empty cartridges, and the shelling had been heavy, but the two section posts do not seem to have put up all the resistance that might have been expected.

I then did an inspection of several other posts and went down to Grindorf village to examine methods of holding it. A bad spot, very likely to be raided and hard to defend. Visited several other posts and then went to see the French gunners to obtain their version of the raid. Finally accompanied Barker to the commander of infantry of French Div to give him details of work done. Meanwhile Adam and Schreiber spent afternoon visiting Maginot Line.

6 March

Left Metz at 8 am and visited Douaumont fort near Verdun on the way back. Most impressive sight and one that brings home to one better than anything I have yet seen what the last war meant as regards devastation and destruction. Lunched Rheims and was back here about 4 pm. Then did one hour's work hard in the office, had tea and left for St-Pol where I was spending night to watch 3rd Div exercise. We had already done 250 miles from Metz and St-Pol meant another 60 miles and then a night's motoring in the dark watching night movements. I was out till about 1.45 am and came back to a very hard bed in the Hôtel de France to find a constant roar of traffic all night and any intervals then filled by a man snoring next door!

7 March

Attended a conference of Monty's at Fievert at 9 am and then spent the day till 4 pm watching the exercise which had represented an advance into Belgium and was most successfully carried out. While I was out I got a message from Gort he wanted to see me with reference to the raid on DCLI! I went to GHQ and was with him for a full hour, finally returning here about 8 pm feeling rather weary.

8 March

Left at 8.20 am to return to St-Pol for the remainder of 3rd Div exercise which was a great success. Then came back to Arras to lunch with Gort to meet Gamelin. Dill came also and we sat on either side of him. According to him Sweden is not prepared to allow passage of troops for relief of Finland in accordance with Article 16 of League of Nations, and on the contrary is bringing pressure to bear on Finland (egged on by Germany) to make peace with Russia. This seems to knock on the head any wild schemes of a northern theatre of operations. In addition apparently Italy is getting rather restless, but is unlikely to move until Germany is committed in one direction or another. Returned to do office work and to see Johnson to instruct him to ensure that Anderson [11 Inf Bde] takes the necessary measures to guard against being raided.

9 March

Spent the morning getting level again with the office work, and in the afternoon went round with Victor Fortune to look at the Corps Reserve Line he is preparing.

10 March

This morning attended a special service in Lille Cathedral held in honour of those who have died in the war, and to raise subscriptions for Madame Prefect's fund for knitting comforts. The Cardinal Lienart, Bishop of Lille, presided over the ceremony. The singing was by a special Lille choir and was very good. The Chanonine Detrez Curé of the Cathedral gave an excellent sermon. After the service the Prefect, General Pagézy and a few others were invited into the Cardinal's vestry to meet him, he was quite charming. Do so wish that you had been there with me to enjoy the service. Looked for Tom this evening but found him away on manoeuvres.

11 March

A lovely mild spring day at last! I attended Monty's conference on his exercise in the Salle de Fête of Seclin. An excellent conference very well run by him. Said a few words at the end. In the afternoon went to see Swinton's model for the 2 pdr gun in the pill box. A most enterprising bit of work made of scrap iron! We fired 5 rounds rapid with it and it worked admirably.

12 March

Went to see a morning exercise by 4th Division. Not up to the standard of the 3rd Div, and the artillery very weak. Shall have to take steps to change Franklyn, the CRA.

13 March

Spent the day with 5th Div artillery. Went to discuss with Franklyn the possibility of the withdrawal of 5th Div to go to Sweden. But this morning we heard of the Russo-Finnish peace. I had been expecting it and from the start I had laid 9 to 1 against any expedition ever setting out for Sweden. In my own view it is a god send that it should have fallen through. By getting ourselves implicated in the North we should have been in grave danger of being defeated in the West through shortage of troops. I wonder what wild schemes may be given birth next!

14 March

Carried out penetration trials with .5 machine gun, Boys Rifle, and 25 mm A/T gun against various types of defence such as sandbags, brick walls, shingle between boards, and concrete. I was very impressed with the results of the 25 mm gun penetration of concrete, passed through 2 feet of reinforced concrete easily! In afternoon visited Corps Survey Coy, the organization responsible for making maps for the Corps. Then had hair cut in Lille, followed by office work. Finally an early dinner and attendance in Lille of a gala performance of *The Four White Feathers* in French. Sat next to the Prefect. Dill also came. Heavy snow blizzard during afternoon!

15 March

The whole country covered with about an inch of snow, but gone by the evening. Gort came round the Corps gunners, who put up a very good show for him all round.

16 March

Spring again. Spent the day with Rowland Towell [CRA 3rd Div] going round artillery of the 3rd Division. The end of a rather trying week during which both lumbago and toothache did their best to embitter life! The lumbago I think I have defeated and the teeth I am preparing an attack on for Monday morning in the shape of the extraction of the last 3 remaining ones!

17 March

Poured rain again all day and I spent a Sunday in the office catching up office work I had neglected in the week. In the afternoon went to see Tom whom I found looking very well in spite of the fact that he had eaten something the previous evening which had disagreed with him. Orders have now been received for the III Corps to return to this country and take over the same front it should have taken over before we started contemplating wild ventures in Finland. The result is that we have lost a good six weeks in the preparations which we should be making for the defence of this country! What will be our next venture?

Tomorrow I have an unpleasant appointment with the dentist at 11 am to extract my 3 last remaining teeth! I shall not be sorry to see the last of them after the annoyance they have been causing me over the last 10 days!

18 March

Off to the CCS this morning to have my 3 teeth pulled out! He gave me a whiff of gas and they came out with little trouble. We took an impression straight away, and I hope to have the new dentures by the end of the week. After lunch went out to see the 4th Div exercise. Met Johnson in La Bassée and then followed up in advance of the 5th DGs [Dragoon Guards] towards Arras. Not a very good exercise, but the first that the 4th Div have had yet. There is a lot that wants putting right. Returned home 9 pm, had bath and dinner and am now off again to Lille to watch the 12th Inf Brigade filing past on their night march to take part in the exercise and attack cav and MGs on the River [illegible]. Lovely warm spring weather.

19 March

Got back at 2 am from watching the 1st RF and Black Watch Bns of 12 Inf Bde moving north of [illegible] in the dark. The latter were very ragged and will require a lot more. Left here at 8.15 to see remainder of 4th Div exercise and was very disappointed in what I saw, a great deal more training is required. Lunched at Montreuil where I had a look at Sir Douglas Haig's statue done by a French artist. I only wish it had been put in Whitehall instead of the existing atrocity. After lunch went on to Dannes, just north of Le Touquet, where we have got some mortar and field firing ranges. 51st Division was making use of it at the time, and putting up a very bad show. A pity as the ranges are excellent. In the evening came on to Boulogne where we stopped for the night.

20 March

Left for Oye-Plage, just north of Calais, where we have an anti-tank range. Attended a demonstration by 5th Division. A well run and interesting show. Stopped in St-Omer on the way back after lunch, another Hôtel de France, a poor hotel but quite fair mullet. Then went to try on my new dentures at the CCS near Arras and finally arrived back here at about 6 pm, and did 1½ hours office work. My leave has now been approved by Gort, and the cabin, Pullman and hotel all reserved, it only remains now to pray that the Germans may keep quiet for a little longer.

21 March

Went out to see the 4th Div exercise. A counter attack with tanks. Rather a better performance than what I had seen up to date. On the way home collected my new dentures, they are real 'soldiers' dentures' to look at, and a good mouthful. I cannot say whether they will be a success as my gums are still very tender from the extractions.

22 March

Up at 5.30 am to see the end of the 4th Div exercise. Watched Anstice handling the 5th DGs in a retirement, which he did very well. Rubbed in several of Johnson's mistakes into him and found that he was realizing them himself at last. Called at dentist on way home for further fitting of new dentures, and back to lunch at 1.30 pm. In the afternoon polished off work in the office, and prepared notes for 4th Div conference tomorrow morning. Weather getting more spring like, daffodils coming up, and bushes sprouting, which makes war even more objectionable.

Left out 23rd by mistake

24 March

Attended High mass at Lille Cathedral officiated by the Cardinal of Lille. A very impressive ceremony transporting one back to medieval days. It is astonishing how such ritual should have survived with the progress civilization has made. There was little in the whole ceremony to put one in harmony with God, except the lovely music. The cathedral itself is in an unfinished state having been started some 60 years ago. After the ceremony I was invited to visit the Cardinal in the vestry. In the afternoon I went to watch a rugger match between the II and I Corps in preparation for a match we are to play against the French. Then came back to meet Dewing, the G1 of 4th Div, to discuss with him his recent trip to Belgium as a civilian. Presented Madame and the children with Easter eggs which were appreciated.

25 March

Left for Metz shortly after 9 am and made a short diversion from Laon onwards so as to get up onto the Chemin des Dames road to show Ronnie [Stanyforth] and Barney [Charlesworth] where the BEF had come in 1914. We then dropped down into Rheims where we had lunch. Between Verdun and Metz we stopped to study the battlefields of Mars-la-Tour and Gravelotte from the war of 1870. Adam had procured a short history of these battles for us while he was home with very good diagrams. I had been reading them up over the last few days and found it most interesting going over the ground. I only wish I could have spared a little more time so as to go into it more thoroughly. We arrived here about 6 pm and found hotel fairly empty.

26 March

Left Metz at 8.45 and met Anderson at 9.30 am. Spent half an hour with him discussing the doings of the 11th Inf Bde during the last few days, and in obtaining from him details of the patrol encounter in which Hudson of the Lancs Fusiliers killed 5 Germans and captured one. It was a fine show as Hudson had only 5 men with him and there were 10 Germans in all, four of which escaped. I then went up to examine the front posts and the work that has been done on them lately. From a good point of observation we examined the village of Leuvage and Anderson explained to me his plans for an encirclement of the village by all his battalion battle patrols with the object of capturing Germans. It is to take place on Wednesday night. I had an interview with Hudson, a very nice boy who has spent most of his life shooting and poaching! He gave me a full and interesting account of his adventures. On the way home I went to call on the French general who commands the infantry of the division. While we were out an air combat took place over our heads. We could hear the machine guns firing and the roar of the planes but they were above the clouds. One plane was brought down but we could not see it nor could we discover its nationality. A perfectly lovely spring day, and very different from the freezing and snow visits of former occasions. Just as I was finishing writing the AA defence of Metz opened fire and has been hard at it, on and off, during the last half hour. I went out onto the balcony but could see nothing although the German planes were easily audible.

27 March

Left Metz at 8.30 am and on the way back spent another hour studying the battlefield of Gravelotte and that of St Privat, found it very interesting. As the Germans were buried practically where they fell it is easy to make out where their lines got to and where they suffered the heaviest casualties. We then went through Verdun to let Charlesworth see the ground that was fought over. Lunched in Rheims and were back here by 5.30 pm. Much colder again today, a nasty change after yesterday's spring like day!

28 March

Bulgy Thorne came at 9 am to discuss details concerning the defence of the Saar front. By 9.45 Martel arrived to discuss work he is to do now that 50th Div has rejoined the Corps and moved into billets of 51st Div, which has just taken over front from French up to Bailleul. By 10 am Warner had arrived, sent by GHQ instead of Hugh Elles to see front. Showed him billets etc and then went to Sainghin fort where I had trials of the new pill box mounting for the 25mm and 2 pdr guns. Pownall, Wason, King, Wood came as experts from GHQ. Then went to Bachy Switch and told Pownall about the battle of Bouvines. From then onto workshop in Loos and 5th DGs in Vimy. Finally visit to dentist and 2 hours in the office getting back here only just in time for dinner. Bitterly cold wind all day and snow blizzards!

29 March

Bitter cold weather again. Spent the morning catching up with office work. In afternoon visited my Corps Prisoner Detention Camp for malefactors. Found a very well run show, 110 malefactors there. I inspected them on parade before they went off on their route march. The staff are mainly prison warders, the whole place spotlessly clean. Men work from 6.30 am to 6.30 pm and only get ½ hour to read papers before lights out. Any giving trouble are put onto prison diet no. 1 which consists of 8 oz of bread for breakfast and 8 oz for dinner! Otherwise they receive ordinary rations. I then visited my Ordnance Field Park where spare vehicles, spare guns, rifles and repair engines and assemblies are kept to replace damaged ones. Dill came to tea, I gather that he is to command the 2nd Army in which the I and II Corps are to be, so that I will come under his orders. I am overjoyed at it, and had had fears of coming under Copper Finlayson [AG, then Western Command]! Left at 6.45 to watch Monty's exercise with 8th Inf Bde, got back here at 10 pm. A foul evening with cold wind and rain. A poor show, vehicles much too much closed up.

30 March

Auchinleck, commander of the IV Corps, came out with me today for a tour of the front. He is out here on a few days' visit. We had a long tour from Bouvines to Bailleul! Still very cold, but sun coming out at times! On returning found Adam back again having just arrived from the base. Looking much better and in very good form. Martin [MGAA] had also come up to discuss AA protection of this Corps HQs as he had rather skimped us in the number of guns to protect us. I succeeded in extracting additional protection out of him.

31 March

Adam came this morning at 11 am and we discussed details as regards his finally taking over his III Corps front from Bailleul to Mont Halluin. I hand him over the 5th and 51st Divisions, and one other division joins him a little later. I retain the 3rd, 4th and 50th Divisions. It will certainly lighten our load when the III Corps at last takes over. The Finland wild goose enterprise has meant unending work for the II Corps staff in handling formations intended for III Corps and carrying out a series of moves and counter moves. Adam and Wason stopped to lunch after which I took Neil Ritchie out to instruct him in the battle of Bouvines so that he should be able to relate the story to one of Gort's visitors whilst I am away. Clifton then arrived having come out to take command of the two Cav Regiments of this Corps.

1 April

Spent the morning visiting my Corps Junior Leader School in Lille and my Driving and Maintenance School in Sainghin. The former is situated in what was a young ladies' seminary and they are very comfortable with hot and cold water in every bedroom, and the old Lille exhibition ground for training in. The latter is not quite as well situated, but doing good work.

In the afternoon I went for one more visit to the dentist to collect my new set of upper dentures. They are a great success and much better than the lower ones. And in any case it is wrong to look a gift horse in the mouth as they cost me nothing!! In the evening both Monty and Martel came to visit me to discuss training matters. I am now going to start packing in anticipation of the hope of starting off tomorrow morning on 10 days leave. But I don't dare even now to start rejoicing at the thought.

2 April

Boulogne. This morning I did office work, finishing off odd jobs. Then into Lille to get my hair cut and to get something for the children. After lunch I finished packing and left Phalempin with Ronnie and Barney for Boulogne where we arrived after 2½ hours' run. Very different from my train journey of 6 hours in the dark last December! I have now had dinner and am off to bed. And yet I still don't dare let myself be carried away in a wild flood of joy at the thought of being on my way home, and at the prospect of perhaps being back with you within the next 24 hours!

It is the ghastly fear that something might yet crop up at the eleventh hour to stop me. It is rather a desperate feeling of having to almost conceal from oneself the fact that one may really be coming home at last. I feel that even as matters stand, and even with all the precautions I have taken I would feel as if the bottom of the world had dropped out if I was now stopped from coming back to you.

It is now more than 6 months since I started these notes for you, and looking back I feel that these pages have been filled with quite different accounts from what I had expected to have to enter. It is a very strange war, but I sometimes wonder whether if it lasts much longer in its present state we may not on both sides realize that there are better ways of settling our differences than by resorting to war. But this will require a change of mentality and outlook on both sides which are so very far from being reached at the present. However I am a firm believer that we can ultimately cease from war on this earth, but I am still doubtful whether we have yet reached this high standard of evolution in Europe.

12 April

The end of a week in the most perfect heaven with you came to an end this morning at 9.45 am just outside Waterloo platform as I drove away with [Ronnie] Stanyforth on the way to Dover. I felt a great tidal wave surging up in my throat which I had to gulp down hard, and a desperate flat feeling as if the bottom of the world had dropped out. After the last 6 months of it I know so well what it means being away from you, the awful longings to be back with you, and the incompleteness of everything in life when you are not there to share it with me. The thought of having to face it again is shattering.

When I am with you I hate to spoil a single minute of it by allowing the thoughts of impending departure to throw their shadows across the present. But when the parting does come, it just comes with a crash. If it was not for your wonderful courage and wonderful calm way of facing trials and difficulties I do not know what I should do. You are just a tower of strength to me.

We had a very good journey back. Ronnie Stanyforth motored us to Dover, Barney Charlesworth was there also. We lunched in Dover and sailed at 1.15 pm. Two leave boats had been withdrawn, presumably to move troops to Norway. Arrived Boulogne about 3.15 pm where the car met us, and by 5.30 pm we were back here.

So far there are only rumours of impending attacks through Belgium and Holland. Personally I feel that this is an unlikely eventuality as the Germans have their hands full with Norway for the present, where they require the bulk of their air force. Meanwhile negotiations are again taking place to try and induce the Belgians to invite us in to their assistance. So far these steps have not met with much success. Meanwhile we have been taking the necessary steps to concentrate troops forward in anticipation of possible moves.

13 April

A day spent entirely in the office picking up the threads and completing orders in readiness for a possible forward move into Belgium in the event of a German invasion. This evening GHQ reported that both French and the WO were reporting indications of a possible early move. On the other hand the Belgians are reported to have increased the wire obstacles on roads leading into their country. Possibly in an effort to prove to the Germans the sincerity of their neutrality! It does not look much like a Belgian invitation to come in prior to a German attack, though rumours have it that such an offer might be made conditional on our coming up to the Albert Canal defences.

14 April

Sunday, and such a very different Sunday from the last one spent with you! Went to see Monty in the morning to discuss the final arrangements for our race into Belgium if called on. All is now ready and he can start at short notice for Louvain and the vicinity with his division. I then came back to see Colin Jardine (MS) to discuss various appointments with him. He stopped to lunch. After lunch Martel turned up to discuss various points connected with his [50th] Division, including the desirability of changing his GSO1 and two of his Brigadiers! He does not quite agree with me in this respect, but I am certain that a change is very desirable. Gort then turned up and we had about an hour's talk discussing various officers in the Corps and their capabilities or otherwise.

Finally I slipped off for a short walk through the woods, which are now carpeted with wild anemones. I took you with me in spirit and we admired them together.

Throughout the day rumours have come in of Belgian preparations for a possible invasion by Germany. I still feel that such a move is unlikely until the Norwegian situation has been cleared up. This morning's victory by the *Warspite* [sinking German destroyers in Narvik Bay] was a nasty blow for them. However they may possibly extend the conflict. If so we are as ready as we can be.

15 April

So far we are still here and all the rumours of a German invasion of Holland or Belgium have not come to anything. Today was supposed to be one of the most critical days, and tonight may still see the start of operations. I still feel doubtful, however, and am inclined to think that these rumours and the Italian rattling of the sword in the scabbard are intended as a bluff to prevent troop withdrawals from France and naval withdrawals from the Mediterranean until the Germans have brought off their Norwegian 'coup' which is still very much in the balance.

I spent the day in deluge of rain going round the 150th Inf Bde of the 50th Div with Martel. This division is now definitely in II Corps which comprises 3rd, 4th and 50th. The other division which formed part of this Corps has now been taken over at last by III Corps.

16 April

Still no move on the part of Germany into either Holland or Belgium! This evening a move into Luxembourg seems more probable, though I fail to see why he should try such a move. Italy on the other hand is definitely looking more aggressive again, and likely to come in with Germany.

This morning I went to a demonstration of booby traps prepared by the 4th Div. Blunt (commanding RAF contingent with BEF) came to lunch. He is not very inspiring.

In the afternoon I went for a walk in the woods nearby and imagined you were at my side. We discussed the lovely carpet of anemones, and all the nice green young shoots. In the garden M. Rosette has found a blackbird's nest that I am watching. I wish I could take photographs of it.

17 April

Warmer weather. Spent most of the day with Martel going round the Corps Reserve position. In the evening Warner [Liaison Officer between GHQ and WO] came and gave me the most recent news as regards our expedition to Norway, and the general view of the war as appreciated in the War Office. Apparently, they consider that the Germans had intended to invade Holland shortly after Norway, but his failure in the latter expedition has upset his programme. They still expect him to walk into Holland shortly. It is not considered that Italy really means business.

18 April

Today the BEF sustained the most serious loss that it has had since the beginning of the war. Dill was ordered home to take up the appointment of DCIGS [strictly, VCIGS]. I only hope that this may be a preliminary step to his replacing Tiny [Ironside] as CIGS. That would be the wisest step we had taken since the start of hostilities. Meanwhile he leaves a terrible blank behind him, and I have a horrid lonely feeling knowing that he is gone. During those trying early months of October and November when an attack seemed imminent and there was little to meet it with, it was the greatest comfort to me to be able to discuss it with him and to obtain from him his valuable advice. Gort asked me to lunch with him at a farewell lunch party for Dill. Adam was there also. We then went to the aerodrome to see him off. He departed in a deluge of rain and was soon lost in a bank of black clouds. I felt very sad at seeing him go, he is quite one of the finest men I have ever known.

19 April

Met Monty at 9.30 am at Lesquin and spent the day going round some of his most modern defences. They have made tremendous progress, and he has some 90 pill boxes of various kinds all under construction. Returned at 4 pm. Did a short spell in the office, had tea and a bath and went off to join Prince Henry and Dudley Johnson to hear Gracie Fields in the Lille Theatre. She was as usual quite excellent and brought the house down. After the show we went to dine with Prince Henry at the Huîtrière in Lille and had an excellent dinner.

Ciriez, the French liaison officer at Corps HQ, has it on good information that the Germans are to overrun Holland within a fortnight! I wonder if he is right.

20 April

A lovely warm spring day. Spent the morning visiting two of my Ordnance Workshops and then went into Lille to visit the Church of England, and Scottish Institute, also the YMCA and Toc H. All of them very well established with tea rooms, reading rooms, games rooms and small chapels. In the afternoon examined GHQ new draft order for [illegible] possible moves into Belgium. I do not like this order and feel that they are on the wrong lines.

21 April

Another glorious spring day on which it is hard to realize that we are at war. Especially so owing to its being a Sunday, and all the French people in their best Sunday clothes out walking. Went to lunch with Adam in Béthune, afterwards discussed most recent GHQ orders with him and decided that we must get Pownall to hold a small conference as they are at present quite impossible to put satisfactorily into execution. We then went for a walk in Nieppe Forest. Carpets of cowslips, anemones and wild violets, the cuckoo singing and fresh tracks of roe deer. War under these surroundings seemed very far away. Then went on to GHQ to see Brownrigg, who was perturbed by an invitation from the Middlesex Regiment to the Duke of Windsor to watch a football match, which Ronnie Stanyforth had wired about to Metcalfe. This had led to a considerable flutter in the dovecot! Firstly because the Duke is no longer Colonel-in-Chief of the Middlesex Regt, and secondly because the invitation should have been sent by the C-in-C!! However I think that we have now smoothed the matter over.

22 April

I held a conference of Divisional Commanders in the morning to lay down the policy as regards the distribution of troops in billets to be able to ensure an early start at any moment. In the afternoon went round the front of the 8th Inf Bde with Woolner. This evening we dined Teddy Schreiber prior to his departure tomorrow. He is a very great loss to the II Corps.

23 April

General Georges [French C-in-C] came to visit the BEF today. He began with the III Corps and arrived on my front at 11 am, when I met him at Triez with Johnson and Martel whom I introduced to him. I then drove him past Riquoux-Tort and Purgaloes to Fleur where he was shown an A/T miniature range. I found him very nice and interesting. We then went over to Lille where GHQ stood lunch all round. Michael Barker, who replaced Dill [I Corps], turned up there. After lunch I went on to see a 4th Div exercise run by Johnson.

I got home by 5 pm to meet Mr Eves, the War Office Official Artist, engaged on similar lines to Orpen in the last war. He is to paint all the Corps Commanders' pictures, and also Gort's one. As he charges £1500 for a picture in private life he ought to be good. Unfortunately he does not present one with the picture when it is finished as it belongs to the state.

24 April

I spent most of the day with Jack Whitaker going round the 9th Inf Bde front and seeing the new concrete work he has been putting up. We lunched at the 2nd Grenadier Guards HQ, where I met Loyd who has just come out to replace Cornish in command, the latter having gone sick.

Came back to the office at 8 pm for a conference with Pownall, Adam and many others concerning the recent draft order for a move into Belgium which is quite impossible. I pointed out the concessions that GHQ had made to the 1st French Army by giving them road facilities in our area which now rendered it essential that the French should defend the northern divisional sector on the Escault which they were asking us to take over. I also showed them the impossibility of the II Corps carrying out the move that was intended for it. As a result of this conference there is a suggestion that the II Corps should take over the role of the I Corps in a move into Belgium, and that the III Corps should take over that at present allotted to II Corps. This would probably be the best solution.

Warner (Liaison Officer between GHQ and the WO) also came with Pownall, and gave us the most recent accounts of the Norwegian campaign. I don't much like our prospects there, and feel that matters are so very confused that we shall end by being pushed back into the sea with heavy losses.

25 April

Went to visit 50th Div in the morning and saw 9th DLI [Durham Light Infantry] and 2nd NF [Northumberland Fusiliers] digging anti tank ditch. Then visited Middlesex MG Battalion.

When I got back Ronnie told me that Mackie (Tom's Colonel) had written a note saying that Tom had been evacuated to No. 8 CCS at Rouvroy with acute appendicitis. Meanwhile Ronnie had called up the hospital and found out that Tom had arrived there at 3 am and had been operated on by 8 am. He was a very serious case as his appendix had burst, was gangrenous, and peritonitis had developed. I had an appointment with Eves, the painter, for 3 pm in Arras, so after sitting for my portrait went on to Rouvroy to find out how Tom was. I saw the surgeon, who said that the operation was quite successful, but in view of the peritonitis the next few days must necessarily be very critical.

26 April

Ronnie called up early to find out about Tom, told by Duty Officer that he was not so well this morning. Had to go to Sissonne artillery ranges near Laon today to see medium artillery shoot. On the way went to No. 8 CCS to look up Tom. Saw surgeon who was on the whole very pleased with his condition, but suggested that if I liked he would call in another surgeon for a consultation. I saw Tom, who was looking very ill and flat, only able to talk in a whisper and very little life in his eyes. But doctor said that in a case like his he might well have been practically unconscious for 2 or 3 days.

On returning this evening we tried to ring up to find out how he was, but unfortunately telephone was out of action. Luckily just about that time Munster called up on behalf of the C-in-C to find out how Tom was and offered to motor over as the hospital was not far from GHQ. Very kind of him. He saw the Sister who said he was no worse and was sleeping.

27 April

I held a Corps conference at HQ to discuss the suggestion that II Corps should advance on what has up to the present been I Corps front in the event of a move into Belgium. We are to have a GHQ conference on this matter on Sunday.

After lunch I went to see Tom. Surgeon said he was definitely not worse, and probably better. He had given him a blood transfusion in the morning and he had slept well at night.

This evening I went to see a demonstration of a trial pattern of searchlight for defensive purposes. The DCLI of 10th Inf Bde gave the demonstration. On the whole I was not impressed by the searchlights and consider that good Very lights are nearly as good.

28 April

Went to 50th Div HQ to attend Divine service with their Signals. A well run service in a RC Chapel with excellent singing by the men. After the service they marched past and I inspected their billets. Finally went to Martel's mess to hear his new divisional band. Adam and Barker came to lunch. I took Adam for a walk in the woods and then went to see Tom. I found him better and spent ½ hour with him. He seemed more cheerful, but the surgeon is still worried with the way his tummy is blown out and was preparing a system for draining his stomach.

29 April

This morning Tom was reported as not being so well. After office work I attended a GHQ conference at I Corps HQ. We spent a bare ½ hour discussing the important plans for an advance into Belgium, and their proposed changes, and followed it up with 2 hours of complete details on training matters of minor importance!! It is quite maddening not to be able to deal properly with the higher direction of this war without being drawn into minor details.

I then went on to Arras where I lunched and went to Eves for the second sitting for my portrait. He made what seemed to me an excellent oil paint sketch of my head from which he proposes to make the real portrait at home. I then went to see Tom whom I found desperately flat out and lifeless, but I was assured by the doctor that he was now, if anything, better than yesterday afternoon. I stopped with him about 20 minutes but he did not seem inclined to talk.

30 April

Tom is reported as being definitely better, and I found him quite different when I visited him this evening. Luckily I met Mitchiner [consulting surgeon] there also who said he thought that from now on he ought to go on well. This afternoon I had to accompany Mr Rogers, Canadian Defence Minister, Mr Massey, Canadian High Commissioner, and Harry Crerar in a tour around the First Corps front. Everything looks like Italy coming into the war against us in a very short time.

1 May

The news of Tom definitely better in the morning and when I went to see him this evening I found tremendous improvement. The surgeon very pleased with the way he was getting on. Went round the 12th Inf Bde units during the morning with Hawkesworth. This evening the order came in from GHQ changing the role of the Corps and giving the II Corps the task that the I Corps has had up to the present in the advance. This will entail a lot of work studying and preparing for a new line of advance.

2 May

Visited 9th Inf Bde and amongst other things inspected the Lezennes underground which I am going to have developed and which should prove most useful in the defence of the 3rd Div divisional reserve line. Needham came to lunch with me. He is at present in Lille awaiting the moment to advance into Belgium to establish a mission there. In the morning went to see Tom who is doing well and making real progress. Have just been listening to Chamberlain's statement as regards our withdrawal from the south of Trondheim. It is a sad blow and one which will I think have repercussions in the Mediterranean, as it is the first real conclusive proof we have had of the undermining of sea power by air power. However in the withdrawal and in the strategic logic of such action I already see evidence of Dill's hand on the tiller, and thank God for it.

3 May

In the morning I attended a debussing demonstration of Martel's given by the 50th Div. It was a good show and some useful lessons to be derived from it. General Odlum, commanding 2nd Canadian Div, came to lunch. I should classify him as a 'political general'. In the afternoon I went to Wambrechies to catch Gort at the 4th Div HQ to get him to withdraw certain instructions I had received from GHQ which interfered with my policy concerning preparation of defences on this front. Finally visited Tom who is making very good progress.

4 May

Spent the morning with Whitaker of 7th Guards Brigade and Johnson to go over defences with them. After lunch Adam came up for a discussion of the proposed D/E plan for a move into Belgium in the event of a German invasion. The GHQ order is unworkable and we had to work out some feasible plan of action. After tea I visited Tom who is getting on well.

5 May

Looked up Tom who is doing very well and will be moved off to the base next Wednesday. Lunched with Michael Barker at I Corps HQ, Adam there. We discussed recent GHQ order and proposed moves. These 'Corps Commanders Sunday Lunches' are a good institution and provide a good clearing house. This evening held a conference of Divisional Commanders to decide details on a new plan of advance.

6 May

Went out in the morning to watch an exercise I had set to exercise the light AA guns in an anti-tank role. It was a great success. In the afternoon went to Lille to have my hair cut. Sigs Osborne, commanding 44th Div, came to tea. He has grown very fat since I saw him last.

7 May

Left here at 8.30 am for Stella-Plage to see the 151st Inf Bde firing their AA guns.

Lunched at Le Touquet. On the way back, went to see Tom, thinking that it would be my last chance to see him before his leaving for the base. But instead I found the DDMS [Deputy Director Medical Services] and two other doctors just assembling for a consultation on him. Apparently last night he started complaining of acute pain and his temperature went up. They had to give him morphia. Today he was no better and they decided he must have an abscess forming. I left them to have their consultation. By 5 pm they called up to say that they considered an operation necessary. By 6 pm they called up to say that the operation had been successful and that he was doing as well as could be expected.

8 May

Went to see Tom in the morning and found him desperately ill. His voice is weak and distant sounding and his eyes are sunk into his head. But the worst part was that he seemed to be getting disheartened about his condition. After seeing him I had to go to a lunch in Lille followed by a visit to the Fives-Lille iron works. I did not feel a bit inclined to go, but the visit was interesting and helped to take my mind off poor old Tom. I went back to see Tom in the evening and found that they had reinserted the tube into his stomach through his mouth, and in addition he has a tube draining out his abscess. I had a long talk with the surgeon who considers that he has a good fighting chance of pulling through.

9 May

Tom much the same. Visited him twice. Doctor says he is certainly no worse and I thought possibly a little better this evening than he was yesterday morning. But very very weak. Visited my Corps Reception Camp in the morning, a very well run show. From then I went on to inspect my Cypriot Mule Column in anticipation of Saturday's visit by the Sec of State for the Colonies. They have come on very well since my last visit. This evening German planes came over about 10 pm. Our new searchlight layout opened up on them and AA engaged them, but I think without result.

10 May

The German planes returned early this morning between 3 and 4 am and an infernal bombardment of AA guns started. A little later Ritchie came to tell me that GHQ had rung up to place us at 6 hours notice. Shortly afterward he returned and said that the Germans had invaded Belgium and Holland at 3 am and that we were at last to put into effect our famous 'D' plan. This entails a rapid move forward to the River Dyle, east of Brussels. The II Corps goes onto a one divisional front with the 3rd Div forward and the 4th and 50th Divs back.

It was hard to believe on a most glorious spring day with all nature looking quite its best, that we were taking the first step towards what must become one of the greatest battles of history! All day long planes have been droning overhead and many have been brought down, one not very far from the Corps HQ. I spent the day checking over the orders for the move. Everything so far has been running like clockwork and with less interference from bombing than I had anticipated. Gort came to see us in the afternoon and discussed progress made. 3rd Div started off at 2.30 pm this afternoon, and by now its advance elements should be approaching the Dyle. It will however take some 8 days or so to assemble the whole Corps forward.

I move up tomorrow. Had time to look up Tom in the morning and found him holding his own well, I thought rather more cheerful about himself.

This finishes 7 months of war spent at Phalempin!

11 May Sotteghem

Left Phalempin at 12 noon after an early lunch. Gort and Pownall had been to see me in the morning. Called on Johnson for a final word before going forward. Then crossed frontier into the 'promised land' and motored to Sotteghem, my new Adv[ance] HQ. Here I dumped my kit and then visited my Road Control Centre under Massy to find out how forward movement was proceeding. Was informed that Alost had come in for a lot of bombing and that unfortunately Perkins my AQMG had been killed by a bomb whilst doing railhead reconnaissance. Went on to 3rd Div HQ in front of Brussels and found out from Monty that the 10th Belgian Div was already holding the front allotted to him. His men had been fired at by the Belgians, mistaking them for German parachutists and one man of the Middlesex had been seriously wounded! I then left Monty and proceeded to Brussels to look for Needham at the British Legation, but found Mason-MacFarlane (DMI) instead. He told me that the Belgian situation was bad and that the Germans had broken through at Maastricht. Asked him to let GHQ know of confusion with the 3rd Div front and sent officer to see Needham at Belgian GHQ. I was told that the King was especially keen for Belgians to hold Louvain, front allotted to 3rd Div.

Came back to Sotteghem to find order from GHQ to take up front between Belgian and I Corps. Quite impossible! With great difficulty got through to GHQ and was told by Pownall to double-bank the Belgian Div. Not a satisfactory solution. Belgians should be made to side step to their left. A day of ceaseless alarmist rumours of Belgians giving way!

12 May East of Sotteghem

Left Sotteghem by 7 am and motored to Brussels British Embassy. Here Duty Officer at Military Attaché's office informed me that Louvain had been captured by the Germans! Luckily this was incorrect. Rang up Needham at Belgian GQG to try and solve the problem of 3rd Div occupying front already held by Belgian 10th Div. Gathered from him that situation had been fairly jumpy all yesterday and he suggested I should come and see him.

I soon gathered from him that he had done nothing and was not likely to do anything!

He kept on telling me how upset the whole of the Staff were at the news from the front. He said that under these circumstances he did not think that he could approach them concerning the 10th Belgian Division being in the wrong place. I told him that we certainly had not got enough divisions to be able to afford double-banking them on the front. As I saw I was going to get little help from him, I decided to go over to the Belgian GQG myself.

I therefore motored to near Antwerp and found Roger Keyes in the office, who suggested I had better discuss the matter with the King. It was therefore fixed up that I should do so and I had a very pleasant interview with him, but his advisor Van Overstraeten would not let him give up the Louvain front!

… I was making progress in getting matters put right when I suddenly heard a voice speaking French from behind my right. On turning round I found an officer there who did not introduce himself to me, but went on speaking in French to the King. His contention was that the Belgian division could not be moved, that the whole of the BEF should be stopped further south and entirely clear of Brussels. I then turned on him in French and told him that he was not putting the whole case in front of the King… He then turned to me and said; 'Oh! Do you speak French?' I assured him that I did and that I happened to have been born in France. By that time he had interposed himself between me and the King. I therefore walked round him and resumed my conversation with the King in English. This individual then came round again and placed himself between me and the King, and the King then withdrew to the window. I could not very well force my presence a third time on the King, and I therefore discussed the matter with this individual who I assumed must be the Chief of Staff. I found that arguing with him was sheer waste of time, he was not familiar with the dispositions of the BEF and seemed to care little about them. Most of his suggestions were fantastic. I finally withdrew …

I then saw General Champon the French General Staff Liaison Officer and explained to him the full situation. As he was to attend a conference of General Georges' at Mons that afternoon with the King he said that he would raise the question. I then went to see 3rd Div and lunched with Monty and explained situation to him.

He [Monty] thereupon said that he had settled the matter for himself! I expressed surprise and asked him how he had settled the matter. He then told me: 'Well, I went to the Belgian Divisional Commander and said to him: "Mon Général, I place myself and my division unreservedly under your orders, and I propose to reinforce your front."' He said that the Belgian Commander was delighted with this relationship. I then asked Monty what he proposed to do if the Germans started attacking. He replied: 'Oh! I then place the Divisional Commander under arrest and I take command.'

At same time got message from GHQ suggesting that I should take over part of I Corps front. In view of the shaky state of Belgium I considered that it was more desirable to retain 3rd Div where they are. Then went up with Monty through Louvain to see front. Town had been heavily bombed and was burning near the station. Streams of refugees crowding the roads which provided queer contrasts of terrified refugees mixed with the normal Sunday church-going parties! Saw 15/19 Cav in their forward position. Then returned to Embassy to telephone back to Gort results of the morning, and reasons for leaving 3rd Div where they are. He asked me to let I Corps know. I therefore finished the trip by visiting I Corps just south of Brussels. Finally got back here at 7 pm to find Johnson and Clifton here.

Results of day are not satisfactory as regards resistance put up by Belgians, but panic is less. And our air [force] seems to be providing greater assistance.

13 May   North of Brussels

An indifferent night's sleep owing to AA gun fire. Ritchie came early to tell me that GHQ had wired to say that it was now fixed up for 3rd Div to relieve 10th Belgian Div! So all my work of yesterday did bear fruit! I was ordered to hold conference with 10th Div Commander to settle details of relief. Called at Embassy on way up and was given instructions concerning boundary which was to swing right south of Brussels and was quite hopeless. Called on Monty but found him out so took his G1 with me and went to HQ 10th Belgian Div. Found fat little Div Commander and settled all details of relief with him. Then went to look for 6th Belgian Corps HQ which I found with some difficulty. Here I found that a whole Belgian Corps, the 1st Corps, was re-forming after being broken up in front right in the area that the 4th Div was moving into and where my Corps HQ was to move to! I went to see Monty to ensure that relief for tonight was all right. Then to Embassy to try and telephone to Pownall (CGS). Could not get either him or C-in-C as they were moving to Renaix. I then found that the DMI Mason-MacFarlane was with the Ambassador so went round to him and explained situation of 1st Belgian Corps and necessity to move it out at once. He was going on to GHQ, and said he would fix it up. Called on 6th French Corps HQ on way back to establish liaison as they will be on our left area.

Came home and sent telegraph to Pownall and after dinner had talk with Gregson-Ellis [GSO1 Ops, GHQ] telling him how essential it was to move I Belgian Corps, and also arranged for conference with C-in-C or CGS tomorrow at the Embassy at 12 noon to settle future employment of 4th and 50th Divs. Belgian GQG ordered retirement of Belgian forces tonight onto the Antwerp, Louvain, Wavre line. So tomorrow we will be in contact with the Germans.

I do not think much of the Belgian Army and am very nervous as to my left flank.

14 May   Just North of Brussels

Left my HQ about 7 am after seeing Johnson who was on the move up, and proceeded to our new Corps HQ just north of Brussels. Left my kit there and reconnoitred a main line and a switch. Then went to 3rd Div HQ and from there on to the Embassy where I had an appointment with Gort. I met Admiral Keyes who asked me to try and influence Gort to go and see the King of the Belgians in the afternoon. He told me that he was having great difficulty keeping up the King's and Van Overstraeten's spirits. We then had a conference as Barker from I Corps had also been summoned to come. I found as I expected that Gort was not really in the picture as to the troubles and difficulties which I have been having with the Belgians. Nor did he realize their very poor fighting quality. I had to press on him the importance of insisting on the Belgians giving us sufficient room to deploy north of Brussels. We drew up plans for holding a main line along the Charleroi canal through Brussels, and for ways and means of withdrawal. News of the French at Dinant and at Sedan was not good as Germans had broken through at both these points. We are still short of fighters, but I understand that 3 more squadrons are coming out from home. The Ambassador came in while we were conferring to ask whether he should leave Brussels as he had been informed that the Belgian gov was leaving. I advised him to stop and told him that the fact of his leaving could only create a bad and depressing impression.

In the afternoon reconnoitred Charleroi Canal line through Brussels. 4th Div coming up well, 2 Bdes up now and one more by 6 am tomorrow. 50 Div coming up tomorrow. New billets very comfortable, a house evacuated by Italians this morning.

I received a telegram on that day and on the previous one that my boy [Tom] was 'just holding his own'; from then onwards I never heard another word until I returned home after the Dunkirk evacuation. It was an additional burden to bear throughout those very dark days.

15 May Just North of Brussels

A day filled with depressing news as to the fate which is befalling the French in the south! I began by being told that the Germans had got into Louvain on the 3rd Div front. This turned out to be false! and really consisted of a party of Belgians, 10 of whom were shot by the Grenadiers!! Later I was told that the 50th Div, which I had been counting on to hold the Charleroi Canal from Vilvoorde south through Brussels with the 4th Div as a reserve line, was being directed elsewhere. I then rang up Michael Barker and fixed up a meeting with him in the Embassy to coordinate our defences on this line. Later when talking to Pownall fixed up for him and C-in-C to come too. Gort gave us bad news that the 9th French Army and Corap (the General I went to for the Armistice ceremony on the 5th November) had broken on the front south of Dinant, also that Germans had penetrated at Sedan and Mezières. French 1st Army also heavily pressed on the Wavre-Namur gap. British I Corps expecting to be attacked.

On my left the Belgians are in a very shaky and jumpy condition and I would not trust them a yard. The conquest of Holland being completed frees additional forces for the attack on Antwerp.

The BEF is therefore likely to have both flanks turned and will have a very unpleasant time in extricating itself out of its current position! During the day several minor attacks took place on 3rd Div front with minor penetrations in each case, these were however restored in each case. But Coldstreams had some casualties. I have been busy drawing up plans for our withdrawal to the Charleroi Canal, and from there to the Dendre if necessary.

This is enough to make one feel gloomy. But I must say that I still have a firm conviction that Right must conquer over Wrong. Your letters which arrived this evening have been a great inspiration to me, and at present I feel prepared to face the next few days whatever may be in store. Whatever happens they can never take away from me our years of paradise.

16 May   West of Dendre

Germans pushed hard on French First Army front during yesterday afternoon and forced a retirement which involved the I Corps. I received orders to be prepared to retire from Louvain to the line of the Senne through Brussels. A bad night with continual interruptions followed by a very tiring day attending conferences which I fixed for the morning with I Corps and Gort. Then a visit to Monty to settle details of withdrawal of 3rd Div followed by a visit to the 6th Belgian Corps on my left to ensure that they were conforming with the movement. Finally another conference with Barker and Pownall.

Now I hope that withdrawal has started as it was to begin at 10 pm.

17 May   Terlinden [added later in pencil]

18 May   Renaix

I was too tired to write last night and now can barely remember what happened yesterday. The hours are so crowded and follow so fast on each other that life becomes a blur and fails to cut a groove on one's memory.

The 3rd Div withdrew successfully out of Louvain, and covered by Cav retired through Brussels and across the Charleroi Canal. Here the 4th Div were already in action. The 3rd Div then embussed and motored back to the Dendre which it began to reach early in the afternoon. When the Cav was withdrawn the bridges over the Canal through Brussels were blown, and the Germans gradually closed on to this front. I motored along the canal just after the blowing of the final bridge and then went back for a conference at I Corps HQ to settle details for withdrawal from Charleroi Canal through the Dendre. Finally came back to new command post just behind Dendre. Bombers paid some attention to us in the morning. After breakfast returned to I Corps HQ near Renaix for another GHQ conference.

Michael Barker in a very difficult state to deal with, he is so overwrought with work and the present situation that he sees dangers where they don't exist and cannot make up his mind on any points. He is quite impossible to cooperate with. He has been worse than ever today and whenever anything is fixed he changes his mind shortly afterwards.*

However after many changes I finally held a conference of divisional commanders and settled details of my withdrawal in the early hours of tomorrow from the Dendre to the Scheldt. I have taken over 1 Div and 50 Div and handed over 4 Div to III Corps for the present. The Germans unfortunately got into the 15/19 Regt today and I am afraid did in the HQ and at least 1 squadron.

19 May Wambrechies

Got up at 5 am after a short night and after examining reports started off to examine the new line of defence on the Scheldt. Found travelling difficult owing to masses of refugees but succeeded in covering the whole length of the line and in going up onto Mont-St-Aubert (near Tournai), to see to what extent it overlooks our new line. It is going to be a troublesome spot. I then motored on through [to] the new HQ of the 1st Div to try and find out how they were getting on. Then on to this new HQ which we reached in the middle of an air raid on the aerodrome which is unfortunately just along side of us! I had only just arrived when I was called to GHQ for a Corps Commanders conference. It was a momentous one!

The news of the French front was worse than ever, they were attempting one full counter attack to try and restore the situation. Should this fail it looked as if the Allies forces would be cut in the centre! The BEF communications to the sea would be completely exposed and so would our right flank. GHQ had a scheme for a move in such an eventuality towards Dunkirk, establishing a defended area around this place and embarking all we could of the personnel of the BEF, abandoning stores and equipment. I preferred pivoting on our left flank which is secure and in contact with the Belgians. To swing our right back onto the River Lys, up the new empty canal to Ypres and thence by Ypres Canal to the sea. By this means I feel that at any rate we can keep the BEF as a unity and not have it destroyed by bits. If we let go our hold of the Belgians now I feel certain they will stop fighting and both our flanks will be exposed, in which case there would be little hope. We are to meet again this evening for another conference if GHQ have any more news.

I have spent most of the afternoon in considerable anxiety trying to obtain information from 3rd and 1st Div as to whether they are back safe. It was not until about 7 pm that I began to get first reports of the arrivals of leading brigades during the afternoon, but it was not till after dinner that I got final confirmation of both 1st and 3rd Div being on their fronts. They are very tired and will require at least 24 hours to sort out vehicles and to put them in a real fit state again. The II Corps has now covered a good 150 miles in 9 days and in the process has

---

*Barker suffered a nervous breakdown, as did Budget Loyd in the same period. See David French, *Raising Churchill's Army* (Oxford: OUP, 2000), pp. 182–83.

occupied four successive defensive positions. It has entailed excessively hard work on the part of all ranks and has been exceptionally efficiently carried out.

20 May   Wambrechies

Went round in the morning to see Adam and discuss with him further moves, found him in agreement with me. Then visited Monty and discussed with him yesterday's withdrawal. He had had a difficult time and had been shelled, losing his car driver and some men of the anti-tank regt. He seemed now firmly established on his new front. I then visited 1st Div and saw Alexander and discussed his withdrawal, he apparently was subjected to flanking pressure owing to I Corps withdrawing too early. His 3rd Brigade I discovered later have lost a good deal of material, and the rear party finally had to abandon their vehicles and swim the canal owing to bridges being blown.

In the afternoon Gregson-Ellis came to give me the latest news from GHQ, which included German pressure on Arras!! Every possible measure is being taken to try and stop the advance of the tanks and armoured cars in the gap they have made, but the situation still remains very serious. CIGS has flown out from London to discuss future measures. Weygand appointed supreme commander. Pagézy has left Lille. The refugees are a desperate encumbrance on all roads.

If Arras was threatened, it was probable that Rouvroy had been overrun by the Germans, and I had no idea as to what had become of my son. I had had no further telegrams for the last few days, and I was uncertain as to whether he had survived, and if so, whether he had fallen into German hands.

After Gregson[-Ellis] left me I had a telephone call from Pagézy asking me where my Corps was. I told him where it was, whereupon he informed me that this was all wrong and that the Germans were in Roubaix. I told him that this was not the case, and that there were no Germans anywhere near Roubaix. He then said that he had been informed by the Mayor, that he knew where they were, and implied that I did not know what the situation was on my front! He was in a very worked up and excitable condition, and evidently losing control of his nerves. I told him fairly bluntly that I did not have to go to the Mayor of Roubaix to find out where the Germans were! Within the next 12 hours Pagézy was gone, and I have never seen him to this day. Nor do I wish to see him! He had been full of talk when the danger was non-existent, but now, at the moment when his services were most required, he disappeared into the blue....

21 May

Got up early to go round front and see divisions. First visited Monty and found 3rd Div well established but very thin on the ground, all 3 brigades up [in the line] and all 3 bns up in 2 bdes. In fact only 1 bn in reserve on whole Div front! Then went forward to look at front, visited OP [Observation Post] of 76th

Regiment, and then dropped in to HQ 1st Coldstreams to have a word with them as they had a bad time at Louvain, losing 5 officers and 160 men. Then visited 7th Guards Bde and had talk with Jack Whitaker on the fighting they had been through. While I was there a very heavy bombardment was going on just south on 1st Div front near Peck Bridge. I therefore went on to 1st Div to find out what was happening. I found out that Germans were across the river near Peck Bridge on 1 Guards Brigade front. I told Alexander that they must be pushed back.

Came here for lunch and was warned that Gort was coming to my HQ for a GHQ conference at 4.15 pm. He gave us an account of the situation which was very gloomy! Germans reported near Boulogne, these ports heavily mined, great ammunition and supply difficulties, little progress so far in closing the gap! Decided that we should have to come back to the line of the frontier defences tomorrow evening. Namely to occupy the defences we spent the winter preparing. Unfortunately we are too thin on the ground and forced to hold too wide a front.

22 May   Armentières

By yesterday evening the II Corps was back everywhere on the river, but penetrations of Germans still remained on I and III Corps fronts. I held a conference at 7 am at 1st Div HQ to settle details for withdrawal back to frontier defences. After lunch carried out a reconnaissance of canal line through Lille for the next withdrawal if necessary.

The refugee problem is very bad. The population of Lille, Roubaix and Tourcoing having left these places and found they could get no food outside are now beginning to crowd back in again! Tomorrow when we have completed our withdrawal they will all have to crowd back again. They are the most pathetic sight, with lame women suffering from sore feet, small children worn out with travelling but hugging their dolls, and all the old and maimed struggling along.

This evening we moved to Armentières in anticipation of the withdrawal of the front. The trouble is that our rear is now also threatened by German tanks! I have established a defence of Corps HQ of A/T and A/A guns plus an infantry platoon, all under one of the GSO2s. We heard on the wireless that General Giraud, commanding the 9th French Army, had been captured by the Germans. Also General Billotte who commanded this group of armies was badly damaged in a motor smash and is now in hospital in Ypres.

23 May   Armentières

Nothing but a miracle can save the BEF now and the end cannot be very far off!

We carried out our withdrawal successfully last night back to the old frontier defences, and by this evening were established in the defences we spent the winter preparing. But where the danger lies is on our right rear; the German armoured divisions have penetrated to the coast, Abbeville, Boulogne and Calais have been rendered useless. We are therefore cut off from our sea communications, beginning to be short of ammunition, supplies still all right for 3 days but after that scanty. This evening the Germans are reported to be pushing onto Béthune and on from St-Omer namely right in our rear. If only we now had the armoured division, and at least two of them, to clear our rear!

After visiting Div commanders in the morning I went to a conference at GHQ. I there discovered that I was to hand 1 Div back to I Corps and to take over 4th Div again, so that I am now back with my original divisions. In the afternoon I went to see 4th Div in anticipation of taking them over again, and found that the 11th Inf Bde had lost fairly heavily yesterday, the Northamptons losing 250 men, and 2 of the COs of the Bde being killed.

It is a fortnight since the German advance started and the success they have achieved is nothing short of phenomenal. There is no doubt that they are most wonderful soldiers.

24 May   Armentières

I attended a conference at GHQ at 9 am where we discussed proposed plans for an attack southwards, to join up with one to be carried out by the French from the south. Gort then left to meet Dill in Poperinghe, the latter being expected over by air. I then waited to discuss plans with Pownall and Adam when General Blanchard came in who commands the 1st French Army. Billotte had died from the motor accident so that there is no-one up here at present to coordinate the action of Belgians, British and French 1st Army. This is urgently required if we are to get out of our present position.

He [Blanchard] was standing studying the map as I looked at him carefully and I soon gathered the impression that he might as well have been staring at a blank wall for all the benefit he gained out of it! He gave me the impression of a man whose brain had ceased to function, he was merely existing and hardly aware of what was going on around him. The blows that had fallen on us in quick succession had left him 'punch drunk' and unable to register events. I was badly shaken and felt that if he was to take the tiller in the current storm it would not be long before we were on the rocks!

Visited 3rd and 4th Divisions who seemed quite happy.

Whilst at GHQ reports came in of German attacks on Hazebrouck. Wireless reports French advance to Bapaume, if this is true it is the best news I have heard since the beginning of the war!

Adam dropped in this evening having spent day discussing plans for attack, he informs me that Germans have stopped their advance on Hazebrouck. After tea Armentières was bombed, two bombs falling fairly near. A fire is now raging. Received a report this evening that the Germans had penetrated the Belgian front between Menin and Courtrai; I hope this is not correct, but feel very nervous about this flank, as I have no reserves to hand, should my flank be exposed.

25 May Lomme

During the night I received information at 2 am that German penetration through the Belgian front was growing rapidly and that the Belgians were not offering much resistance. I came to the conclusion that this was the beginning of a German offensive intended to push right through to our left rear and to join up with the armoured divisions which must have just about shot their bolt. Went to see GHQ to obtain reinforcement of a Brigade to hold the Ypres-Comines Canal. I had already sent our MG Bn from 3rd Div there. With great difficulty I finally extracted this Brigade. I was informed that the 'Rush for the Sea' plan was abandoned. Thank God for it, I have always hated this plan. The new plan is to try to break through to join the French forces south of the German penetration. It might be possible, but I should doubt it.

I then went round 4th and 3rd Div to discuss our break through plan with them. While I was with 4th Div a Liaison officer from Belgian 1st Div came in with very gloomy account of the fighting put up by the Belgians. Personally I am convinced that the Belgian Army is closing down and will have stopped fighting by this time tomorrow! This of course entirely exposes our left flank.

GHQ had another conference this evening at 7 pm. Found the atmosphere entirely changed and was at once presented with 5th Div to hold Ypres-Comines Canal. They have now realized the danger I warned them about this morning. The penetration scheme is temporarily abandoned. Armentières has been very badly bombed and we are well out of it, half the town is demolished, including the mad house, and its inmates are now wandering about the country.

The prospects were far from bright and I remember during the next few days seriously considering destroying my diary as I did not want it to fall into German hands, and this seemed quite a possible eventuality. ...

These lunatics let loose at that time were the last straw! With catastrophe on all sides, bombarded by rumours of every description, flooded by refugees and a demoralized French army, bombed from a low altitude, and now on top of it all lunatics in brown corduroy suits standing at the side of the road grinning at one with an inane smile, a flow of saliva running from the corner of their mouths, and dripping noses! Had it not been that by then one's senses were numbed with the magnitude of the catastrophe that surrounded one, the situation would have been unbearable.

Several years later, whilst dining at Chequers one weekend, Churchill said to me that the receptive capacity of a man's mind to register disaster is like a 3 inch pipe under a culvert. The 3 inch pipe will go on passing the water through under pressure, but when a flood comes the water flows over the culvert whilst the pipe goes on handling its 3 inches. Similarly the human brain will register emotions up to its '3 inch limit' and subsequently additional emotions flow past unregistered.

26 May   Lomme

Went early to see 5th Div in Plugstreet [Ploegsteert] Wood, found that they had been getting into position on Ypres-Comines Canal during the night. Motored on to Ypres to find out whether Belgians were defending this place. Found nothing on our left except the Postal Service of the 1st French Motorized Div!! Then examined canal and railway to see what defences were like. Only just escaped being locked out by the blowing of the bridge owing to the arrival of Germans. We then ran into German artillery fire which puzzled us as I thought it was bombs and could not see aeroplane.

Went back to GHQ to try and raise further troops for the defence of Ypres and secured one brigade of 50th Div. Then attended GHQ conference where we were informed of instructions received from home for evacuation of the BEF. We discussed plans for this operation and I spent the rest of the day in conferences finishing off plans for this withdrawal. It is going to be a very hazardous enterprise and we shall be lucky if we save 25% of the BEF! We are bound to suffer heavily from bombing. I have already been put into the ditch 3 times today to avoid bombing attacks. The Germans have carried out incessant air attacks on Armentières and surrounding towns.

Late that evening Corps HQ was suddenly disturbed by two rounds from a 25 pdr fired in quick succession! As these two shots came from the Corps HQ defence, I felt certain that we were receiving a visit from German tanks which were by then in Arras and the vicinity. However, on making enquiries I was informed that we had fired on a French tank, one of their heavier 'Char B', the shells had burst on the exterior, nobody had been hurt and after an exchange of salutations the French tank had gone on its way!

27 May   L'Alouette (near Plugstreet)

Held conference of Div Commanders of 3rd and 4th Divs at Bondues at 8 am to settle details of withdrawal. Called in on 1st Div to ensure that they stop sending traffic on 3rd Div road, which is required to move 3rd Div through back of 5th Div to extend defences northwards from Ypres for flank defence. Then proceeded to Plugstreet to see 5th Div commander and find out details of his front which was being shelled. From there to Ypres to see Martel commanding 50th Div and to arrange defence of Ypres. Placed him in command of his own 2 brigades, plus MG Bn of 4th Div, plus French 1st DLM [Division Lourde Motorisée]. Ypres being shelled on western approaches.

Motored back to GHQ south of Armentières to find that Germans had penetrated 5th Div front. Back to Lomme to my rear HQ to arrange for withdrawal of one brigade of 4th Div to go to assistance of 5th Div. Then proceeded to I Corps to secure assistance of 1st Div and secured 3 Bns which had already been withdrawn to rear of Plugstreet. On to GHQ where I secured 7 infantry tanks to be sent at once to help 5th Div. Back to HQ at Lomme and from there to HQ 1st Div at Wambrechies to find out their moves for next day, to know where to call on them for help if necessary. Back to Bondues to 3rd Div HQ to explain the situation to him. Returned to Lomme HQ and from there to GHQ to find they had left without saying where they were going.

I...returned to my HQ at Lomme to collect a few papers leaving Ronnie Stanyforth with the car at the gate of the house serving as our HQ. As I came back to the car he pointed to a body lying in the gutter on the opposite side of the road and said: 'They have just shot that chap!' When I said: 'Who shot him ?' he replied, 'Oh! Some of these retiring French soldiers, they said he was a spy, but I think the real reason was that he refused to give them any cognac!' This gives some idea of the lack of discipline in the French withdrawal, which at times looked more like a rout!

At 8 pm closed Lomme HQ and came to L'Alouette Command Post. From there proceeded to 5th Div to discuss results of day's fighting and plans for next day to ensure that road for retirement is kept open. It has been an anxious day. Bad congestion on roads due to French forces spreading over onto roads reserved for us.

Belgians have practically given up fighting so that security of eastern flank of retirements rests with II Corps.

There was little possibility of sleep that night, as the 3rd Division were moving past and I repeatedly went out to see how they were progressing....The whole movement seemed unbearably slow, the hours of darkness were slipping by; should daylight arrive with the road crammed with vehicles the casualties from bombing might well have been disastrous. Our own guns were firing from the vicinity of Mont Kemmel, the German artillery were answering back, and the Division was literally trundling slowly along in the darkness down a pergola of artillery fire, and within 4,000 yards of a battle front which had been fluctuating all day, somewhat to our disadvantage. It was an eerie sight which I shall never forget. Before dawn came, the last vehicles had disappeared northwards into the darkness, and I lay down for a few hours disturbed sleep. ...

28 May Vinchem (North of Furnes)

Visited 5th Div to find out situation which is not satisfactory at junction with 50th Div. Germans still pressing on. Gave verbal instructions for further withdrawal [tonight]. Then proceeded to 4th Div to instruct them to coordinate their further withdrawal with 5th Div, sending one brigade to covering position on line of railway Ypres-Poperinghe, remainder of division to go back to canal with 3rd Div.

Received instructions for organization of the [illegible] embarkation which Adam has been organizing. Proceeded north to see Martel who was covering Ypres and to find out what touch he had on his right south of Ypres with 5th Div. Saw Haydon commanding 150th Bde who said he had no contact on his right and that he had thrown back his right flank. Told Martel to send 4th NF to clear up this situation. Then proceeded further north to see whether Monty had reached his front along canal north of Ypres. Found he had as usual accomplished almost the impossible and had marched from Roubaix to north of Ypres, a flank march past front of attack, and was firmly established in the line with French DLM to his north.

Returned down south again to L'Alouette to see Ritchie who had gone to GHQ Conference where nothing was settled. Down again to 5th Div HQ to find situation of day's hard fighting. Division had held on by its eyelids, 17th and 13th Bdes greatly reduced by casualties, 10th and 11th Bdes [4th Division] supporting them. I Corps artillery which had been left behind to help had fired 5,000 rounds of medium artillery in 36 hours! Line had held thank God otherwise 5th and 4th Divisions were lost and II Corps would have been rolled up!

Moved HQ back to Vinchem just north of Furnes having settled final details for withdrawal of 4th and 5th Divisions and throwing back of flank of 50th Div to rest at Poperinghe whilst 3rd Div swung their right back slightly to Canal. 5th Div to move back to line of Yser, 4th Div to Dixmude and other crossings in vicinity. Went on to see Adam at La Panne and found Germans were already trying to force Nieuport. So had to alter orders to 4th Div to bring them into the perimeter defence to cover Furnes to Nieuport. Returned for dinner at 11 pm and had to wait till 1 am to see DLM commander.

I was not much impressed by him at that interview and my estimate of his value was not far out. Apparently his DLM had lost all its tanks and now consisted of a column of buses and workshops, with a certain number of men with rifles. The whole outfit was more of an encumbrance than anything else, its fighting value was practically nil, whilst its power of blocking roads with its huge vehicles was unlimited.

29 May   Adinberke

Received order from Gort that I was to proceed home and hand over Corps, so as to be available for task of reforming new armies. Went to see Gort to find out whether this was an order as I wanted to remain with Corps. Told it was an order which I must obey. Got him to agree that I could stop on until I had finished retiring Corps into perimeter defence covering embarkation.

Then went south to see Martel and Monty and find out how 3rd and 50th Divs were. Congestion on roads indescribable. French army become a rabble, and complete loss of discipline. Troops dejected and surly and refusing to clear road, panicking every time a Boche plane came over. Found that the 3rd and 50th Divs had drawn back right to Poperinghe most successfully. As a result Germans had attacked a village previously evacuated. Found right flank open at Poperinghe, I Corps not in line according to GHQ instructions! Told Martel to throw his 4th NF onto his flank and to use his cav, 13th/14th, to protect his right. Went back to Eisenberg to see 5th Div and to find out whether they had extricated themselves successfully. Found them on the Yser all well but with the 13th and 19th Brigades greatly reduced. Went back to La Panne to see how embarkation was proceeding and found arrangements quite inadequate and of a most Heath Robinson nature. Saw Gort and I asked him to get Admiralty to produce Marines and more landing craft. Went to see Johnson and discussed his dispositions. Finally returned to settle with Monty and Martel their dispositions for their withdrawal followed by 5th Div in perimeter defence. 2nd DLM to cover flank.

Then troubles started. 2nd DLM received orders from Blanchard to retire at once to La Panne to embark! I informed his Liaison Officer that if he did so he would uncover my left and cause hopeless road jam. Told Liaison Officer that if General disobeyed my order and I caught him I should have him shot! Then windy officer from 3rd Div came in to say that Germans had got in behind 5th Div on Yser! To complete troubles, the 32nd French Division cut in across from the west right across the lines of retreat of 50th, 5th and 3rd Divs!!

Utter confusion on roads and complete jam. However matters finally sorted themselves out and during night 3rd Div took over the centre portion of sector covering Furnes, 50th Div took over western sector and 5th Div went into reserve. The retirement from the Dyle east of Brussels to the perimeter round La Panne was completed!!

30 May **On destroyer**

Went round all 4 divs to ensure that defence of sectors was completed and to find what strength of Corps remained.

3rd Div at 13,000 strong,
4th Div at 12,000 strong,
very satisfactory considering what we had been through.
5th Div, only 2 brigades, 17th and 13th, both very weak, about 600 per brigade,
50th Div a little stronger with 2 brigades about 1200 each.

There is no doubt that the 5th Div in its fight on the Ypres-Comines Canal saved the II Corps and the BEF.

I can hardly believe that I have succeeded in pulling the 4 divisions out of the mess we were in, with allies giving way on all flanks. Now remains the task of embarking which will be a difficult one. Went to see how embarkation was proceeding and found the whole thing at a standstill owing to lack of boats!! Went to see Gort and got little satisfaction. Then found Sykes telephone to sec of 1st Sea Lord, returned to Gort to get him to telephone to 1st Sea Lord to press for marines, more ships and boats. Arranged for Monty to take over Corps, Anderson to replace him [3rd Division], and Horrocks to replace Anderson [11 Infantry Brigade]. Visited all Div Commanders to say goodbye. Went to see Gort and attended official Corps Conference at GHQ to discuss wire just received from S of S. Urged strongly for evacuation of II Corps complete and shortening of perimeter. Gort havered and would not make up his mind. Told him I would go and see Dill at once if I ever got back to put my suggestion.

Went down to beach at 7.15 pm, was carried out to open boat, and with Ronnie Stanyforth and Barney Charlesworth we paddled out to the destroyer and got aboard. There I found Adam, to my great joy. We have been waiting till 10 pm before starting, rather nerve wracking as the Germans are continually flying round and being shot at, and after seeing the ease with which a few bombs can sink a destroyer, it is an unpleasant feeling.

Later:

We never started until 12.15 am, at 3 am we were brought up short with a crash. I felt certain that we had hit a mine or been torpedoed. But she remained on an even keel and after some shuffling about proceeded on slowly. I heard later from the commander that he had 3 routes to select from, one was under gun fire from the coast, one had had a submarine and mines reported in it, and the other was very shallow at low water. He chose the latter and hit the bottom, damaging a propeller slightly. Finally arrived Dover at 7.15 am. Wonderful feeling of peace after the last 3 weeks!

I woke at home from a long sleep of well over 36 hours, and felt wonderfully refreshed, and on June 2ⁿᵈ set out for the War Office to find out what I was wanted for. I was still overcome by the wonderful transformation from war to peace. The awful load of responsibility had been laid aside, the nightmares of anxiety were gone, roads were free from refugees, demoralization no longer surrounded me on all sides, it was another glorious English spring day. From every point of view life had suddenly assumed a very rosy outlook, and I walked into Dill's room at the War Office with a light heart.

I sat in that chair next to the CIGS's table, which I was to know so well later on, and asked him what he now wished me to do. His reply was: 'Return to France to form a new BEF!' As I look back at the war, this was certainly one of my blackest moments. I knew only too well the state of affairs that would prevail in France from now onwards. I had seen my hope in the French army gradually shattered throughout those long winter months, I had witnessed the realization of my worst fears regarding its fighting value and morale, and now I had no false conceptions as to what its destiny must inevitably be. To be sent back again into that cauldron with a new force to participate in the final stages of French disintegration was indeed a dark prospect.

I asked Dill whether I could refit the 3ʳᵈ and 4ᵗʰ Divisions so as to bring out some seasoned troops. He told me that there was no time for this, that I should be given the 51ˢᵗ Division, the 52ⁿᵈ Division, the remnants of the Armoured Division, Beaumont's force, and the 1ˢᵗ Canadian Division. After some discussion he agreed to push on with the re-equipping of the 3ʳᵈ Division and to send them on as soon as possible. The 51ˢᵗ Highland Division met with its fate before I ever arrived in France, at St Valéry. All that I found on my return were the remnants of one brigade which had escaped capture, but were without much equipment and only fit for evacuation. My Corps Headquarters was dispersed all over England after its arrival back from Dunkirk. Chaos prevailed, and it was not an easy task in assembling personnel. Dill asked me who I should like as my Chief of Staff and I suggested Pownall as he had had experience. I found, however, that he could not be spared as Gort required him for the writing of despatches! I finally selected Eastwood, who was available, and also stipulated for Neil Ritchie to be with me again. After a long discussion with Dill about the preliminary details, I was told that Anthony Eden, who was then Secretary of State, wished to see me.

He was very charming and sympathetic as to all the difficulties that lay ahead of me, and finished by asking whether I was satisfied with what was being done for me. I think I astonished him by replying that I was far from satisfied. That the mission I was being sent on from a military point of view had no value and no possibility of accomplishing anything. Furthermore, that we had only just escaped a major disaster at Dunkirk and were now risking a second such disaster! I continued by stating that possibly this move had some political value and that was not for me to judge, but that I wanted him to be quite clear that the expedition I was starting on promised no chances of military success and every probability of disaster. It was for him to judge whether these risks were justified in the hope of gaining any political advantage that might exist. I left his room with the clear conviction that what I was starting on was based purely on political requirements, and from what I had seen of the French up to date I had very great doubts as to any political advantage to be gained. ...

I was informed that on arrival in France I should take command of all British forces in France, and that I should come under the orders of General Weygand. My role was to support the French. The situation in France as far as British command was concerned was slightly involved. In the first place there was General de Fonblanque who was in command of the Lines of Communication troops of the original Expeditionary Force. In addition, there were Generals Karslake and Marshall-Cornwall who had been sent out to assist in taking control. I was told that on my arrival I could either retain them out there or return them home, whichever suited me best.

On June 11th I was summoned to Buckingham Palace by the King and I was awarded the KCB as a reward for my services in France.

12 June 1940 – 30 November 1941

12 June 1940   Chateau near Cherbourg

After watching you disappear round the corner of Beaumont barracks, I turned back to make final arrangements before my departure.

At 11.30 am we motored off, Rusty Eastwood with me. By 1 pm we were at Southampton, but it took us some time to find the 'Duty Boat' by which we were to travel. When we did it turned out to be a dirty little Dutch steamer with 100 Frenchmen on board, and only capable of 12 knots! We sailed at 2 pm, no arrangements for food on board and I was very grateful for your excellent [illegible] sandwiches. At 9.30 pm we arrived at Cherbourg to be told that we should have to anchor out in the stream and could not land till 6 am tomorrow!! And these are the arrangements the WO has made after pushing me for the last week to get over as quickly as possible!! It's an absolute disgrace and I propose to let them know in no measured terms.

I had just laid myself down to sleep when I was told that a boat had come for us with Gervase Thorpe [Commander Cherbourg] on board! So I got up and in pitch dark, pouring rain and an air raid set out for the shore. It was not a pleasant return to France for a very unpleasant trip! Went to Thorpe's Chateau which we reached by 2 am.

13 June   GQG Mission HQ, East of Orléans

Left at 8 am for Le Mans which we did not reach until 2 pm, but was glad to arrive alive in spite of dangerous driver. Refugees again swarming everywhere, and heartbreaking to find oneself back amongst them. At Le Mans found de Fonblanque and Karslake and Swayne [British representative with Georges]. Told Karslake he could go home. Asked de Fonblanque for particulars of base organization.

As I walked into the drawing room I could at once feel a very tense atmosphere. The relations between Karlsake and de Fonblanque had not been as smooth as they might have been. After greeting Karslake I informed him that he need not wait any longer than he wanted. He told me he had a plane standing by and was off at once!

I then had lunch and discussed the base organization with de Fonblanque. To my consternation I found that there were still some 100,000 men from the BEF – L of C [Lines of Communication] troops! In addition, masses of dumps of clothes, equipment, vehicles, stores, petrol, etc etc. I instructed him to keep on evacuating home as many of these unarmed personnel as he could, only retaining personnel essential for maintenance of the four Divisions.

Then started off with Swayne to see Weygand. Another long drive of 170 miles, making some 340 miles in all for the day. Refugees round Orléans desperate.

Spending night with Howard-Vyse [British representative with Weygand] and am to see Weygand tomorrow. From all I can gather I can see no hope of the French holding out longer than the next few days.

14 June   L of C HQ, Le Mans

Went to see Weygand at 8.30 am. Found him looking very wizened and tired looking with a stiff neck from a car smash on previous evening. He said he would speak very frankly. That the French army had ceased to be able to offer organized resistance and was disintegrating into disconnected groups. That Paris had been given up and that he had no reserves whatever left. He then stated that at the Inter-Allied Council it had been decided to hold a position covering Brittany in front of Rennes. That consequently I could concentrate Canadian division in the vicinity of that place and that instructions would be issued to X Army Commander to manoeuvre British troops under his command during retirement so that I could collect them in the vicinity of Le Mans. He then suggested that I should go with him to Georges' HQ to draw up an agreement for this manoeuvre.

We then went to see Georges and finally drew up a statement confirming the above plan.

... as we were trundling along [Weygand] turned to me and said: 'This is a terrible predicament that I am in.' I was just preparing to answer that I could well understand how heavy the responsibility must be to be entrusted with the task of saving France in her distress. To my astonishment he continued with: 'Yes, I had finished my military career which had been a most successful one.' I remained dumb and unable to make any adequate remark, it seemed impossible that the man destined to minister to France in her death agonies should be thinking of his military career.

But both Weygand and Georges were in agreement with me that the Brittany Defence Scheme was quite impossible owing to lack of troops. I then sent a wire to the WO and instructed Howard-Vyse to fly home to explain situation to Dill.

Then motored back 170 miles to Le Mans through masses of refugees. Arrived back at 4 pm and called up Dill to explain situation and request that flow of troops out to this country (ie Can Div and Corps troops) should be stopped at once. He informed me that he had already done so. I then told him I considered Brittany Scheme a wild project which was quite impossible, and that there was only one course open to us namely to re-embark the Expeditionary Force as quickly as possible. He said he would see PM as he had not heard of Brittany Scheme, and would call up later. Later he informed me that Brittany Scheme was off and that I should proceed with embarkation of troops not under order of French X Army. I requested him to let Weygand know that I was still under his orders which he said he would do.

I then arranged for Canadian [troops] that had landed to retire to Brest at once, that 52nd Div (less Bde Group with French) to proceed as soon as possible to Cherbourg. For unserviceable and non-fighting elements of Armoured Div to move to Nantes. And for L of C troops (7,000 at Le Mans, 65,000 at Nantes, 20,000 at Rennes etc) to be despatched to various ports as quickly as possible. And I then sent for [Marshall-]Cornwall (Liaison Officer, X French Army) to come to me as soon as possible to discuss evacuation of troops with French as soon as they could be released.

Just before dinner (about 8 pm) called up by Dill who was at 10 Downing St and put PM onto me. I had a difficult discussion with him as regards the evacuation of the 2 bdes of 52nd Div. He considered they might be used to assist the French, or to fill the gap between X Army and army on its right (some 30 miles!). At last I got him to agree to what I was doing.

... I found myself speaking to Dill on that very indifferent line that had been kept going between Le Mans and London. I naturally thought that he was calling up from the War Office, but as a matter of fact he was with Churchill at 10 Downing Street. He asked me what I was doing with the 52nd Division, and I gave him an account of the dispositions which I have just described and which I had agreed with him on my previous talk. He replied: 'The Prime Minister does not want you to do that.' And I think I answered: 'What the hell does he want?' At any rate Dill's next reply was: 'He wants to speak to you': and he handed the receiver over to him! I found myself talking to Churchill on this very bad line of communication. I had never met him, I had never talked to him, but I had heard a good deal about him!

He asked me what I was doing with the 52nd Division, and after I had informed him, he told me that that was not what he wanted. I had been sent to France to make the French feel that we were supporting them. I replied that it was impossible to make a corpse feel, and that the French army was, to all intents and purposes, dead, and certainly incapable of registering what had been done for it. ...

Our talk lasted for close on half an hour, and on many occasions his arguments were so formed as to give me the impression that he considered that I was suffering from 'cold feet' because I did not wish to comply with his wishes. This was so infuriating that I was repeatedly on the verge of losing my temper. Fortunately while I was talking to him I was looking through the window at Drew and Kennedy sitting on a garden seat under a tree. Their presence there acted as a continual reminder of the human element of the 52nd Div and of the unwarranted decision to sacrifice them with no attainable object in view.

At last, when I was in an exhausted condition, he said: 'All right, I agree with you.'

It is interesting to note that in Volume II of Churchill's Second World War, *on page 171, he deals with this incident as under:*

*On the night of June 14, as I was thought to be obdurate, he [General Brooke], rang me up on a telephone line which by luck and effort was open, and pressed his view [up]on me. I could hear quite well, and after ten minutes I was convinced that he was right and we must go. Orders were given accordingly.**

---

*Strictly, Churchill's text runs 'and pressed *this* view' – that the position was hopeless and the remainder of the BEF should be re-embarked at once – but the point stands. Churchill, *The Second World War*, 6 vols (London: Cassell, 1948–54). Cf. David Fraser, *Alanbrooke* (London: Collins, 1982), pp. 167–69.

This interpretation of what happened is interesting. In the first place he states that I rang him up, this was hardly likely as I did not know him and had never spoken to him. All my communications were direct with the CIGS. His statement did not, however, disclose the fact that he was interfering with a commander in the field, and that without sufficient knowledge of conditions prevailing on that front at that time, he was endeavouring to carry out his wishes against that commander's better judgement. ... The strength of his power of persuasion had to be experienced to realize the strength that was required to counter it!

Saw Air representative, Vouez of French Mission, Warner from WO etc. Arranged for air support of evacuation and for evacuation of Air Force ground personnel. After dinner had another talk with Dill confirming all I was doing. And was informed by him that order had been sent by him placing me on my own and no longer under Weygand. Finally at midnight went to bed.

15 June   Vitre (West of Laval)

Woken at 3 am by arrival of Jimmy Cornwall. Told him that I wanted him to take command of the forces under French X Army as soon as they could be detached from him, and to then retire on Cherbourg. Gave him a written order to the effect that he was to take command of these troops, and whilst rendering all possible assistance to French X Army to direct his axis of retirement on Cherbourg. I had left an MT Column with the Infantry Brigade to make it mobile, as Beauman's force and the rest of the Armoured Div are all mobile. Jimmy should have a chance of moving back to Cherbourg and of covering his embarkation. Got up at 6.30 am after poor night's sleep and after early breakfast moved my HQ and that of L of C from Le Mans to Vitre. I considered the former too exposed owing to the absence of any French troops between this place and the Germans when the gap exists in which the German 4th Army is advancing with its left on Chartres.

   We are still very exposed here to raids from armoured cars or tanks and have practically no protection. We may consequently have to move further back before long. It is a desperate job being faced with over 150,000 men and masses of material, ammunition, petrol, supplies etc, to try and evacuate or dispose of, with nothing to cover this operation except the crumbling French army.

   Just before lunch the CIGS called up on a very bad telephone line to say that the 2 Brigades at Cherbourg were not to be embarked without orders from UK. This can achieve nothing but lead to chaos! It means that Jimmy Cornwall will probably arrive on the rest of the crowd before they have had time to be evacuated. After lunch I had another talk with Dill and was again told that for political reasons it is desirable that the two Brigades of the 52nd Div [Drew] should not be re-embarked for the present. In the evening I was told that shipping was available at Cherbourg to remove Drew's brigades, but that owing to WO instruction it could not be made use of! We are wasting shipping and valuable hours; at present bombing is not serious, at any moment it may become so. Received Liaison Officer from Jimmy Cornwall with his situation, and statement that he had not yet informed Altmayer of decision to re-embark BEF. Sent him reply not to disclose this fact for the present.

After dinner had another talk with Dill and Anthony Eden and pointed out to them that from a military point of view we were committing a grave error, we are wasting shipping, valuable time, and opportunities while hostile air interference is not serious. Subsequently was again called up by Dill and informed that I could embark some of the gunners of the 52nd Div and RE at Cherbourg, provided I retained the infantry of the two bdes. I am therefore trying to fill one ship with gunners etc at Cherbourg.

Modern developments, such as wireless and telephones, may constitute serious dangers for a commander in the field, if these systems are made use of by politicians to endeavour to influence operations without being conversant and familiar with the circumstances prevailing in that theatre of operations. Wellington was indeed fortunate!

Later Guy Rack commanding L of C troops at Rennes called up and said that 2 French generals were enquiring what all this movement towards the ports was implying!! I have replied that we are thinning out Base and L of C organization of BEF, originally intended for 12 Div but now much smaller. I hope this answer will satisfy them.*

16 June   Redon (North of St Nazaire)

Got to bed shortly after midnight and had good sleep till 6 am when I was called up by CIGS on very bad telephone line. Told [me] to prepare to carry on embarking 2 brigades of 52nd Div at Cherbourg confirmation to follow shortly. Also probably orders for Cornwall's force. At 8.45 had second message by telephone from Dill, telling me to fire ahead with 52nd Div, but to wait a little longer as regards Cornwall's force. Asked him whether Cornwall could agree to embarkation of French from Cherbourg for England if they desired, and told yes.

Called up Barratt (AOC-in-C) who is at Nantes to find out if there is anything more I can do for him as regards shipping his ground personnel. He stated all was well, and we both agreed that if we had to go we might do so suddenly. Told de Fonblanque to get in touch with Navy to ensure that [mine] sweeping of Brest is not left entirely in French naval hands, and that the Admiralty be prepared to do some sweeping in the event of an armistice putting a stop to all action on the part of French navy. Interviewed Naval Commodore at 10.15 am, asking him to get in touch with home, to procure sweeping facilities, large liners to work to big ports, and destroyer assistance in smaller ones. Instructed Eastwood to draw up orders for final evacuation making each Port Commander responsible for continuing embarkation of stores, equipment and personnel up

---

*Sections of the diary connected with misleading the French in this period are absent from both the 'Notes on my life' and from Arthur Bryant, *The Turn of the Tide* (London: Collins, 1957).

to the last moment. De Fonblanque as GOC LC to remain responsible for the whole as long as he can maintain his communications.

11.15 am. Interview with General Vouez who wanted to discuss situation and ensure that no misunderstanding existed between me and Weygand. He informed me as to situation on X Army front which is much as I thought, but he was inclined to take an over-rosy view of the situation and has now gone back to General Weygand to explain what the situation is as regards the BEF.

12.00. Called up WO to find out whether decision could be given for Jimmy Cornwall's withdrawal, but Dill still in conference in Downing St. Sent Ronnie off into the town to try and raise some food for lunch so as to save time and allow of our starting off for Redon (N of St Nazaire) as soon as I have received my message from Dill.

1.30 pm. Call from Dill confirming again removal of 2 brigades of Drew but not prepared yet to confirm withdrawal of Jimmy from X Army. As I had just received message from the latter stating that X Army still were working on Brittany Scheme and expecting British co-operation I told Dill and asked him to ensure that the French government knows.

Motored over to Redon where I arrived about 4.30 pm. Found that an error had been made as to the chateau that I was to go to. This entailed some loss of time. Then had great difficulty in getting through to WO. Finally found CIGS was still in a conference and was unable to get him.

At 6.25 pm I called up again and got Dill who informed me that the decision was that troops with X Army should remain there and continue fighting with the X Army as long as it remained intact. Should X Army begin to disintegrate they may retire on Cherbourg. This is an unsatisfactory arrangement, but possibly inevitable. At 6.30 pm Drew called up from Cherbourg to say that half his army there was embarked, the remainder to embark tomorrow. He asked about his brigade with X French Army and I told him he was not to wait for it but was to sail with his 2 brigades.

Dill in his last call said that Weygand was not satisfied that I should have departed from our signed agreement. But I reminded Dill that I had told him that this agreement was based [on] the supposition that the Allied governments had agreed on the Brittany Scheme. Dill had referred this matter to Winston Churchill who said that there was no such agreement between the governments. I had then specially asked Dill to let Weygand know as I was under an obligation of the document I had signed. I understood that this had been done and that the order taking me from under Weygand's orders included such information. However, I do not mind what accusations may be made against me. If I were faced with the same situation again I should act exactly in the same way, and am convinced that any other course of action could only result in throwing good money after bad.

I sent Neil Ritchie off home this evening as I did not feel that any useful purpose could be served by retaining him any longer. Barratt called up this evening stating that he did not consider that we were getting RAF personnel off quick enough. I assured him that they were getting their fair share of available shipping space, and were just as anxious as he was not to remain in this country an hour longer than necessary. Briggs, Jimmy Cornwall's GSO1 came this evening to give details of dispositions of force and to find out when 157th Bde could [illegible] rations, ammunition and petrol.

Midnight reports of embarkation are good. Some 45,000 have been embarked in last 24 hours, 12,000 previous 24 hours, giving total of just under 60,000 in 48 hours. Transportation hopeful of making 60,000 figure in next 24 hours which should complete evacuation.

17 June Aboard trawler *Cambridgeshire*

Received report in early morning that X French Army was in full retreat and that Jimmy Cornwall was retiring British forces under his command on Cherbourg. X French Army [illegible] on Laval and Rennes. Barratt's air reconnaissance reports Germans in Orléans and tanks advancing from there on north bank of Loire.

Had several conferences in place for the day. Settled that Fighter Squadron should move during the day from Dinant to the Channel Islands, to protect Cherbourg landings from there. Saw Naval Officer and instructed him to have destroyer ready for my HQ at St Nazaire this evening in case it should be necessary. Informed Naval Commodore and De Fonblanque of necessity to push on with all speed loadings today as this will probably be the last 24 hours clear for all ports.

At 10 am put call through to Dill to tell him of situation on X Army Front and of Jimmy Cornwall's move on Cherbourg. First reaction of Dill was that Jimmy should have remained with X French Army. However, as this army is in full retreat and as the forces of Jimmy Cornwall are based on Cherbourg, and further since Jimmy said that any pressure from Germans would result in disintegration of the X French Army, I cannot see that any other course was open to him. Dill then said that he hoped that if French wished they should be given opportunity of retiring in this direction. I assured him that Jimmy had already been instructed to that effect. I then gave him figures of embarkation and asked him what he wished me to do as I could not see that I was performing any useful function stopping on out here. He seemed to consider that my presence out here was important from a political point of view, which I fail to see as I am not in contact with any French forces nor under the command of any French formation. He then suggested that I should proceed by sea to Cherbourg to find out how evacuation was proceeding there. Finally informed me that he would call me up about 3 pm to let me know what I was to do. Telephone line to WO very bad and interrupted by bombing attack on Rennes.

At 10.30 am called up Barratt to fix up details with him as regards his final moves, and embarkation of party of RAF defending Nantes. Issued instructions to de Fonblanque as GOC L of C to remain here as long as he has signal communications and enemy situation admitted of his serving a useful purpose and then to proceed home. Individual port commanders at Cherbourg, St Malo, Brest, St Nazaire, Nantes and La Rochelle have already received orders to continue embarking men and matériel to the last moment.

11.30 am. Report brought in that Frenchman had reported German advance on Redon! I hope that this is the usual line of false rumour.

1.15 pm. Call from Dill saying that wireless reports French have stopped fighting. Agreed that we should now concentrate on personnel and that I could start with my HQ this evening. Agreed that I should call up once more if possible but if unable to call up should start off. In view of French stopping fighting advised that we should concentrate on personnel. As a result of above conversation instructed de Fonblanque to ensure that personnel were embarked with greatest speed, and also for L of C staff to proceed to Brest. Made further enquiries about the destroyer to pick us up at St Nazaire tonight.

2.30 pm. Have just seen Meric [French liaison officer] who told me he heard the French broadcast by Pétain telling French armies to cease hostilities, whilst he negotiates with Germans. This renders situation very critical lest negotiations should lead to internment of British troops in France! It is essential for us to get away early.

2.45 pm. Called up Barratt (AOC-in-C) to tell him GHQ was closing down and departing this evening and to make final arrangements for fighter protection up to the last moment.

2.45 pm. Called up WO but Dill was not back in WO.

3.30 pm. Called up again and was told that line to England had been cut and no longer possible to get through. Decided to leave for St Nazaire at 4 pm.

4.30 pm. We left Redon and motored to the vicinity of St Nazaire. There we parked in a lane hidden from aeroplanes and waited for the destroyer to arrive. We sent Allen the Naval officer on ahead to find out when the destroyer would arrive. He came back about an hour later saying that the *Lancastria* had been bombed with 6,000 on board as she was sailing out and sunk. The destroyer detailed for us had to be used to save the survivors and was no longer available! We had to choose between the *Ulster Sovereign*, not sailing till tomorrow, and an armoured trawler which would just take our HQ and could sail at once. We chose the latter, it can only sail at 9 knots per hour and will take some 30 hours to reach Plymouth!

When we arrived on board we found that she had just been saving 900 survivors from the *Lancastria*. She was in an indescribable mess, soaked in fuel oil and sea water with discarded wet clothes lying all over the place. Everything sticky with this beastly black fuel oil, all the walls, chairs, furniture etc. black with it. I have just spent ½ an hour clearing up what I have taken as my cabin. We are going to have a rough trip from most points of view. But I hope that we may look sufficiently small and insignificant as not to be worth bombing! I have got what is left of my HQ with me, and also de Fonblanque and part of his staff. It's going to be hard to keep clean here. But I have so far salvaged my whole kit!

18 June   Aboard trawler *Cambridgeshire*

After midnight there were 3 air raids on the port before we sailed. All AA guns, including the one on this trawler, firing furiously, but I did not hear any bombs being dropped. He may have been dropping magnetic mines. At 4 am we sailed instead of the previous evening as we had hoped. Did not get very much sleep owing to continued noise.

We were sleeping on deck and 'Rusty' Eastwood had his roll of bedding alongside of mine. ... Suddenly I heard a thump, followed by a grunt of discomfort from Eastwood. I asked him if he had been hit: he replied, 'Yes, by a Lewis gun drum thrown from the bridge, which landed on my stomach!' I was very glad to hear it was nothing worse.

Luckily the sea so far (2.30 pm) has been beautifully calm. The living conditions are fairly rough on the whole, but the food surprisingly good. This morning one of the crew went more or less mad and had to be held down on the deck. He had been assisting to save the drowning from the *Lancastria* and it had got on his nerves, and he kept shouting about wanting to save people. Rusty Eastwood filled him up with aspirin and he then went off to sleep. May be all right when he wakes up again. It is an extraordinary contrast to find oneself sailing along on a lovely day surrounded by a calm sea, with no refugees, no columns of troops, no problems, no decisions to make. A wonderful enforced rest.

The last week has been a very trying one, and I hope never to be entrusted with a similar task again! To try and relate political considerations, with which you are not fully informed, with military necessities, which stare one in the face, is a very difficult matter when these two considerations pull in diametrically opposed directions. Politically it may have been desirable to support our allies to the very last moment even to the extent of being involved in the final catastrophe and annihilation. Militarily it was self evident from the start that the very small forces at our disposal could do *nothing* towards restoring the military situation which would have required at least 2 complete armies to exercise any influence. Furthermore, it was clear that any additional forces landed in France, or existing forces retained in that country must inevitably be annihilated if left to fight the war to the last. The difficulty has been to extract the existing forces without giving the impression that we were abandoning our ally in its hour of need. Pétain's order to cease hostilities gave the ultimate necessary relief to this situation, but unless this situation had been anticipated in our preparations I doubt whether we should have saved much. It is a devastating process having to try to put the WO in the picture through a long and poor system of telephone communication with very indistinct speech.

19 June

Yesterday evening the sea became very choppy just about our high tea time! However, I put away the buttered toast and sardines and succeeded in keeping them stowed away, which is more than some of the others did!

From Ushant we took a very wide sweep out westwards to avoid minefields. We are in a bad way if we should strike a mine, bomb or torpedo, as the whole of the salvage gear is gone in the rescue of survivors of the *Lancastria*! We have no small boats, rafts, life belts, life buoys, or anything. We have now been told that we shall not get to Plymouth before 3 pm. We had been told that we should arrive at 9 am. But we have been moving with a convoy of 4 ships carrying 10,000 men and the destroyer escorting them has instructed the trawler to remain with the convoy to assist in protecting it. It has been quite amusing travelling on this trawler and getting a first hand idea of what the life on an armed trawler is like. The crew are a very good lot, very cheerful and have been very good in making us as comfortable as is possible. They come from Lewes, Lincoln and London but seem to mix together very well. The one that went queer yesterday is still in a bad way and suffering from a complete nervous breakdown continually shouting about saving people. At 6 pm we at last drew near to Plymouth and the Admiral's barge with Green (GOC Plymouth area) on board came out to meet me. I transferred into it with Eastwood and Ronnie. We sailed through Plymouth Bay, full of memories of our time there [with 8th Inf Bde in 1934–35]. The hotel we stopped at when house hunting, the Mount Edgecumbe tea party for American naval graduates, the steps we had come down before embarking in [Admiral] Drax's barge to see the big yachts racing etc, etc.

At last we set foot on British soil, and thanked God for again allowing us to come home. I also thanked God that the expedition which I had hated from the start was over.

We went up to the Admiralty House, where the Admiral gave us tea, and then provided us with baths and dinner. The luxury of Admiralty House after our trawler provided a pleasant change! I called up Dill and told him I was home and fixed up to see him at 9 am next day. After dinner the Admiral took us round the control office of 'Western Approaches'. Finally we caught the midnight train for London.

20 June

Train was late and I had to go direct from station to WO. Here I saw Dill and told him that if I had to start the whole trip again I should do exactly the same things again. Apparently the fact that we did not get off more stores from Brest is now looming far larger than the fact that if I had followed out the Gov wishes at the start they would have lost both the Canadian and 52nd Divisions besides all stores and L of C personnel!

Dill informed me that they were thinking of giving me Southern Command again. Met Jimmy Cornwall and discussed with him details of his withdrawal. After an early lunch motored back and at about 3 pm landed back at Ferney Close again.

20–26 June

Spent in resting, writing a report on recent operations and preparing to take over Southern Command.

During those few days I was invited up to lunch with Winston at 10 Downing Street. It was the first of many meals that we had together and left a very vivid impression on my mind. We lunched together at a small table for two and he cross-questioned me about my last trip to France, my impressions of the French, and details of my final evacuation. As we finished lunch he said he must now go and consult his two experts on France, and on my way down I ran into Duff Cooper [Minister of Information] and Spears [PM's Personal Representative with French PM]. I wondered whether these two were really the best advisors to consult about France.

26 June

Motored over to Salisbury where I spent rest of the day with Bertie Fisher taking over Southern Command. The main impression I had was that the Command had a long way to be put on a war footing and that a peace atmosphere was still prevailing. Put up at the White Hart Hotel while we hunt for a suitable billet. I have at present got the V Corps, and the 4th, 50th, and 48th Divs besides many heavy units and organization.

27 June

Spent day trying to pick up threads of this command. Must make some more troops available for an active defence of the area.

28 June

Went to Bulford and Tidewell to visit Salisbury Plain area and find out what was available in this portion of the command. In the afternoon was visited by Butler (Regional Commissioner at Reading), Allen, commanding 5th AA Div, Robb commanding SOS [Senior Officers' School]. Ciriez [II Corps Liaison Officer] who had been down for the night returned to London.

29 June

In the morning visited Australian contingent at Amesbury Abbey. It will take at least a month before any of them are ready for any active operation. In the afternoon attended a conference on the LDVs [Local Defence Volunteers] which lasted about 2 hours. Why do we in this country turn to all the old men when we require a new volunteer force? Old men spell delay and chaos! I wonder whether I have reached the age to stand clear and let younger men replace me!

30 June

Called up late last night and invited to lunch at Chequers with PM to see Paget [Chief of Staff to C-in-C Home Forces]! Suggested Paget should come here instead which he did. Had long talk with him telling him exactly what I wanted for the defence of Southern Command, namely another Corps HQ, another Div, some armoured units and a call on bomber squadrons. Some of these things I may get. At any rate I rubbed into him the nakedness of this command when taken in relation to the new situation in Western France. After lunch went home for the afternoon.

1 July

We have now moved Command HQ to Wilton House. Spent the whole day going round 4th Div with Eastwood. The more I see of conditions at home the more bewildered I am as to what has been going on in this country since the war started! It is now 10 months and yet the shortage of trained men and of equipment is appalling!! At present I fail to see how we can make this country safe against attack.

Two parachutists reported. One captured was a British prisoner paid 500 pounds for the job.

2 July

Spent the day with 50th Div going to Blandford, Bovington, Blandford, Dorchester, Yeovil and back. The more I see the nakedness of our defences the more appalled I am! Untrained men, no arms, no transport, and no equipment. And yet there are masses of men in uniform in this country but they are mostly untrained, why I cannot think after 10 months of war. The ghastly part of it is that I feel certain that we can only have a few more weeks left before the Boche attacks!

3 July

Spent a day in the office getting level with some of the work.

4 July

At 9.30 in the morning Germans carried out dive bombing attack on Portland and Weymouth with several casualties in the harbour. In the afternoon Bristol bombed again. During the day received reports of action taken by 2 bns of 4th Div in assisting the clearing of French crews from their ships. Visited Lumley at Sherborne.

[No entry for 5 July 1940.]

6 July

Spent the day going round Salisbury Plain Area Striking Force. A well run show organized by St Clair. We toured from 3 pm till 9.30 pm, going via Wilton, [illegible], Lavington, Swindon, Marlborough and Tidewell.

7 July

Attended exercises between SPA Striking Force and LDVs on Salisbury Race Course. Visited [illegible] in the afternoon. German air attacks intensified. Plymouth, Falmouth, and Purbeck Camp were all bombed and 16 killed at the latter place.

8 July

Visited Oxford to see my South Midland Area commanded by McMullen. A good show but not enough troops.

9 July

Ran Command Conference at 10.30 am attended by Divisional and Area Commanders. Visited MG and Art[illery] School.

10 July

Left here 9.15. Motored to Frome where I visited 144 Inf Bde, then lunched Honiton with Barney at Bloomfield's where we had as good a meal as usual. Met Green [SW Area] in Exeter at 2.30 pm and interviewed Fitzgerald concerning defence of Exeter sub-area. Not at all impressed by Fitzgerald. Then moved to Totnes where I saw 90th Inf Bde and looked at beach defence, much more work and drive required. Finally arrived Admiralty House at 8 pm and discussed defence problem with Admiral Nasmith [C-in-C Plymouth and Western Approaches] after dinner. From what I have seen I am not happy at the state of the defences in these parts, people have not yet realized the danger of attack.

11 July

Left Admiralty House 8.45. Met Green at Crownhill, discussed defence of Plymouth which seems very sketchy. Prior as Plymouth sub-area commander does not seem what is wanted and his plans of defence are very sketchy. Green must I am afraid go. He has not got the required qualities. Then proceed to Yelverton to see remainder of 48th Div. Saw 143rd Bde then lunched with Petre commanding 48th Div and finally on to Okehampton to see 145th Inf Bde, and then back.

12 July

This was supposed to be probable day of invasion! Spent the day in the office mainly occupied in writing a letter asking for Green to be relieved of the command of the South Western Area. He is too old and lacking in drive ever to make a job of the defence of Devon and Cornwall.

13 July

In the morning visited the Chemical Warfare Training Establishment near Andover to arrange about operational control of northern portion of Portsmouth Area. In afternoon did office work.

During the morning a German aircraft flew over Tidewell and Australia Camps, wounding 2 of them with MG fire. No further signs of impending attack. However I feel that I require a great deal more time to complete defensive arrangements within the Command. There is a mass of work to do and many officers to be replaced.

14 July

Took afternoon off to come and see you at Ferney Close. Such a complete rest to spend few hours of paradise with you.

15 July

Spent a long day going around beach defences from Bognor Regis to West Wittering. A lot of work still requires to be done, and we are painfully thin on the ground. Only got back at 7 pm. Pownall came to dine and to discuss LDVs.

16 July

Met Tiny Ironside [now C-in-C Home Forces] at Caversham and went round defences with him, then had him to lunch here and went on to see Australians after lunch.

17 July

Winston Churchill came to visit units of the V Corps. I lunched with Auchinleck at his Corps HQ (Melchett House). We then went to Gosport where we picked up the PM after his lunch with the Naval C-in-C. V Corps had prepared an excellent programme for his visit which was a great success, finishing off about 8 pm near Wool. He was in wonderful spirits and full of offensive plans for next summer.*

Heard this morning that Allfrey is to replace Green in South Western Area, a very good thing which should help in getting a move on. Also Franklyn appointed as commander of the Second Corps in Southern Command.

18 July

I spent the day with 50th Div going round beaches from Lulworth Cove, round Swanage, Studland Bay, Sandbank, Bournemouth up to mouth of Solent. All work going on well, but beaches very lightly held. On returning saw Monty

---

*The feeling was mutual. Cf. Churchill, *Second World War*, vol. II, pp. 233–34.

and arranged about his exercise. Then saw Paget who came to dine. After dinner explained to Charles Allfrey what he had to do in the SW Area.

19 July

Left at 8 am to pick up Auchinleck to visit Isle of Wight. In the middle of my visit received message to proceed to London to see S of S [Eden] at 7.30 pm. Left Island after lunch and motored up to London calling at Ferney Close on the way up. Unfortunately you were out. Arrived London about 7 pm and after waiting some 20 minutes saw Dill who told me he could not tell me anything until I had seen the S of S. Finally I went in to see him and was told that he wanted me to succeed Tiny Ironside as C-in-C Home Forces, the latter to be made a Field Marshal. Gort to be made Inspector of Training.

I find it hard to realize fully the responsibility that I am assuming. I only pray to God that I may be capable of carrying out the job. The idea of failure at this stage of the war is too ghastly to contemplate. I know that you will be with me in praying to God that he may give me the necessary strength and guidance.

The idea of failure was indeed appalling enough to render the load of responsibility almost unbearable. Perhaps the hardest part of it all being the absolute necessity to submerge all of one's innermost feelings and apprehension and maintain a confident exterior. To find yourself daily surrounded by your countrymen, who may at any moment find themselves entirely dependent for their security on your ability to defend them, to come into continuous contact with all the weakness of the defensive material at your disposal, to be periodically wracked with doubts as to the soundness of one's dispositions, and with it all to maintain a calm and confident exterior is a test of one's character, the bitterness of which must be experienced to be believed!

20 July

In the morning I finished off my short spell at Southern Command HQ by putting Auchinleck my successor into the picture and by installing Franklyn as an additional Corps HQ. I left at 1 pm and with Ronnie proceeded to Ferney Close where we lunched with you. I then went on to St Paul's School, Hammersmith. I was not impressed by the HQ! They are dirty and not very well equipped. However we can improve on that. As there was no furniture in my room I went to the Naval and Military Club for the night.

… when I arrived there Ironside had already gone! There was a note from him stating that he had arranged with the owner of the Rolls-Royce he had been using for me to take it over, and the best of wishes. That was all! Not a word concerning the defences or his policy of defence, etc., absolutely nothing!

21 July

Spent my first day as C-in-C Home Forces going round my staff. Meeting various members, had a long discussion with the Chief of Intelligence. Also the Naval Liaison Officer and the Chief Engineer. Had to suffer photographer and cine man during the morning. In the afternoon read up various papers connected with the defence of the country and tried to pick up the threads. Got back to club at 8 pm, and went for brisk walk around St James's Park after dinner. Was asked to go to Chequers but escaped out of it for this weekend.

22 July

In the morning went down to Hounslow where I had a long talk with Williams C-in-C Eastern Command. I went through his last appreciation of the situation of his front, and feel rather clearer about his problems now.

... much work and energy was being expended on an extensive system of rear defence, comprising anti-tank ditches and pill boxes, running roughly parallel to the coast and situated well inland. This static rear defence did not fall in with my conception of the defence of the country. ... To my mind our defence should be of a far more mobile and offensive nature. I visualized a light defence along the beaches, to hamper and delay landings to the maximum, and in the rear highly mobile forces trained to immediate aggressive action intended to concentrate and attack any landings before they had time to become too well established. I was also relying on heavy air attacks on the points of landing, and had every intention of using sprayed mustard gas on the beaches.

Lunched at St Paul's and went on to Horse Guards to see Bertie [Sergison-Brooke, London District] and to discuss with him problems of defence of London area. From there on to the Cabinet War Room where I may have to be near the PM if an invasion starts. It is well fitted up and should make a good HQ, except that I can only bring the heads of my departments up there. Back to St Paul's where I remained till 7 pm finishing off work.

I then drove to club and walked to 10 Downing Street to dine there with the PM. Just by ourselves at the end of a long day's work was rather trying! But he was very nice and I got a good insight into which way his brain is working. He is most interesting to listen to and full of the most marvellous courage, considering the burden he is bearing. He is full of offensive thoughts for the future, but I think he fully realizes the difficulties he is up against! He said he wondered if England had ever been in such straits since the Armada days. He refers to Hitler always as 'that man'!

I must say that it is very hard to see where we are heading for, but I have implicit faith in God that whatever happens it is for the good of mankind in the long (and perhaps distant) run.

23 July

Left Hendon by plane for York 9.30 am – arrived 10.30. Adam had both Corps Commanders Holmes and Alexander to meet me and we had a discussion lasting about 1 hour on the organization of defence. Then motored to Scarborough and inspected defences from there to Bridlington. A lot of good work has been done there. Motored back to York and after tea with Adam flew back, arriving Hendon 6.45 pm. Hylda and Evelyn [Wrench] came to dine with me at Club.

24 July

Flew to Chester, leaving 9.30 arriving 10.40. Copper [Finlayson, Western Command] met me at Sealand Airport. Discussed defences of Liverpool, Birkenhead etc. We then got into another plane and over area up to near Blackpool and Preston, inspecting possible landing grounds on sands. After lunch motored out to see Jimmy Cornwall at his [III] Corps HQ. Finally flew back, reaching Hendon at 9.45 pm.

25 July

Spent a day in the office. Had intended to start for Edinburgh tonight but had to put it off owing to Chiefs of Staff meeting tomorrow afternoon at 4 pm which I must attend. Have now moved over to the Army and Navy Club.

26 July

Worked in office during the morning. In afternoon went to see Dill at the WO at 3 pm and from there on to the Chiefs of Staff meeting. Main subject of discussion was the priority of use of fighters in the event of invasion. I came away feeling less confident as to our powers of meeting an invasion. The attitude of representatives of the Naval Command brought [out] very clearly the fact that the navy now realizes fully that its position has been seriously undermined by the advent of aircraft. Sea supremacy is no longer what it was, and in the face of strong bomber forces can no longer ensure the safety of this island against invasion. This throws a much heavier task on the army.

27 July

Caught night mail to Edinburgh. Had breakfast with Carrington [Scottish Command] and then went on to visit the 46th Div commanded by Anderson. Found it in a lamentably backward state of training, barely fit to do platoon training and deficient of officers. Lunched in a hotel where I met Alan Cunningham commanding 9th Div and Barnett Hickling, commanding 5th Div. Apparent 9th Div is in much the same state as 46th. Saw Wimberley's [152nd] Brigade of the 5th Div. I was much impressed by it. Returned to London by night mail.

28 July

Spent morning in the office. Lunched with you and unfortunately had to go to demonstration of methods of dealing with tanks. PM was present. Returned to have supper with you and then drove back to the Club.

29 July
Proceeded to my Cabinet War Room at 8 am for an exercise to test out the command organization. The exercise became rather too realistic in the morning as the Germans carried out intensive air attacks on Dover, sinking a destroyer but losing about 20 planes! During the morning Winston sent for me to attend part of the War Cabinet Meeting, which was interesting. Later on he came round our war room to find out how exercise was progressing. We have I think succeeded in acquiring the Office of Works building for our offices. This will make a very great difference and will make matters much easier to run.

There was, however, one point above all others which constituted a grave danger in the defensive organization of this country, there was no form of combined command over the three Services. And yet their roles were ultimately locked together. Who was deciding the claims between the employment of destroyers against hostile landing craft, as opposed to anti-submarine protection on the Western Approaches? Who would decide between conflicting calls of the Army for bombers to attack beaches, as opposed to Navy wanting them for attacks on hostile fleets? ... It was a highly dangerous organization; had an invasion developed I fear that Churchill would have attempted as Defence Minister to co-ordinate the actions of these various commands. This would have been wrong and highly dangerous, with his impulsive nature and tendency to arrive at decisions through a process of intuition, as opposed to 'logical' approach. Heaven knows where he might have led us!

30 July
Flew to the Wash where I met Osborne [44th Division] and Drew. Had a discussion with the latter as regards state of training etc of the 52nd Div. Then inspected beach defences from Wash to Yarmouth, visiting 18th Div and seeing Beckie Smith. Unfortunately weather was bad and had to motor back from Norwich instead of flying which took 3 hours instead of 40 mins!

31 July
Spent the day in the office with some interruptions. At 10.30 am the AG [Adjutant General] came to see me, at 11.30 am I had to go and see the King who was very nice and full of interest. He asked me to have the Duke of Gloucester taken onto my staff as Liaison Officer. Then called on Sikorski, the Polish PM and C-in-C to arrange about the employment of Polish troops. After lunch Somerset Maugham came to see me in anticipation of a propaganda tour of the USA. After him came an American sent out by Roosevelt to study conditions in England, and to discuss conscription problems.

1 August

July is now gone without the impending German attack commencing. It remains to be seen whether he will attack in August! Left Hendon at 9.30 by plane for Norwich where Massy (GOC XI Corps) met me. We started from Yarmouth and worked down southwards through the 55th Div commanded by Majendie. Fortifications getting on well and Division should be quite good with a bit of training. On way back saw Norman's Armoured Bde recently equipped with Beaverettes [see 10 August 1940], consisting of 12th, 13th/18th and 4th/9th.

2 August

After spending night with Massy, went on to Harwich and did front of 15th Div, commanded by Le Fanu. Do not think much of him, and doubtful whether he is good enough. Material in the division good but requires a great deal more training. Worked down to Southend and then motored back.

3 August

Spent most of the day in the office picking up the threads of the last two days. Dined with Evelyn [Wrench] to meet Geoffrey Dawson, Editor of *The Times*. In the afternoon went out to see Dowding [Fighter Command] at Stanmore to extract Bofors AA guns out of him.

4 August

Date of the beginning of the last war, but not used by Hitler to start his offensive on England! Spent the morning in the office and ran down to Ferney Close to spend the afternoon with you. I am just back and feel very refreshed after spending a few hours in paradise with you.

5 August

Attended Chiefs of Staff [illegible] Committee and made statement as to progress of defences. Lunched with Kirke and discussed guards for ICI. Then visited Admiralty War Room. Returned to St Paul's to finish off work. Finally went to WO at 6 pm to discuss points with Dill only returning to Club 8.15 pm. Spent most of my evening preparing for conference with C-in-Cs tomorrow.

6 August

Worked in the office during the morning. Dill gave lunch at the Senior to all Army commanders and the Army Council. This was followed by a conference at the War Office which Dill started and which I followed on with and settled many useful points at.

7 August

Left at 8.50 to spend 2 days with Bulgy [Thorne] going round his [XII] Corps. Started with 1st London Div at the Isle of Sheppey and worked round to Rye in 45th Div area. Ramsgate salient still requires more work on the sea defences. Intended for linear defence instead of active counter offensive. Dined with Bulgy. Auckland Geddes [Regional Commissioner for SE & NW] and Gen [illegible] came to dinner.

8 August

Met Schreiber at Hastings Pier and [illegible] his [45th] Division, finishing with Robin Money [15th Division] and visiting Tom at Eastbourne. Then went on to meet Brocas Burrows [9th Armoured Division] in Brighton and did rest of his front till beyond Shoreham. Also saw experiments in road mining for tanks and lighting up of roads with petrol. Got back at 8 pm.

9 August

Inspected Canadian Corps leaving here at 9 am. Went first of all to 1st Can Div, from there to 1st Army Tank Bde and from there to 1st Armoured Div. Discussed employment of Corps in its reserve role, and tried to counteract rather slow and sticky employment. Large lunch party of 50 to meet me. After lunch demonstrations of tanks attacking road obstacles and of McNaughton's secret A/T obstacle. I propose to push the latter as providing a good form of defence.

10 August

Attended two meetings with the S of S in the morning. The first connected with the employment of the LDV and their new charter of employment. The second was attended by Archie Wavell [C-in-C ME], back from Cairo for a few days, and concerned regiments of tanks to be given to him at once to proceed to Alexandria via the Mediterranean taking advantage of some reinforcements which are starting to be sent. I had, at this critical time, to agree to part with 1 Cruiser Rgt, 1 Lt Tank Regt and 1 Army Tank Regt!

This does not seem much when considered from the point of view of later years in the war, but in the early days even this small contribution constituted a large proportion of the total of my armoured forces. To make matters worse at this time, Beaverbrook, who was Minister of Aircraft Production, began to form an army of his own to protect aircraft factories in the event of invasion. He acquired large proportions of armour plating for the production of small armoured cars called 'Beaverettes', with which he equipped Home Guard personnel of factories for their protection. This was at a time when I was shouting for every armoured vehicle I could lay my hands on with which to equip regular forces. The whole thing was fantastic. How could individual factories have held out, and what part could they have played once the main battle for this country was lost?

In the afternoon I proceeded to Bomber Command to discuss with Portal the use of his bombers in war, and arranged a working agreement with him. Had Pope to lunch and discussed organization of armoured force with him, so as to decide what further changes would be necessary.

11 August

Budget Loyd [his CGS] came in this morning and we discussed the state of training of Divisions that he had seen, and the necessary steps required to remedy defects. Spent afternoon in paradise with you and the children.

12 August

Attended Chiefs of Staff Committee to discuss PM's paper on degree of threat to this country on various fronts. Also statement about ammunition supply. In the afternoon Prince Henry came to see me, and also Cyril Falls.

13 August

Swayne called up early to inform me that Admiralty had received accurate information that Germans in Norway had embarked on night of Aug 11th and that they expected an invasion in the north.

Left Hendon at 9.15. Flew to Old Sarum where I picked up Auchinleck and flew on to Exeter where I met Franklyn and Allfrey. Proceeded to inspect defences from Exmouth to Weymouth, meeting Monty and Martel, also Churchill and Haydon. All work proceeding well. Air fighting going on over Weymouth and we found German plane which had just come down. Pilot was all burned up, but as 500 lb bomb was in the debris which was burning we did not stop long. Finally flew back from Weymouth, arriving Hendon 6 pm. Went to St Paul's School to find out situation before going home.

14 August

Spent morning in the office. Lunched at Club, had hair cut and went to London Area HQ to discuss LDV problems with Bertie [Sergison-Brooke]. Back to St Paul's where Michael Barker came to discuss his new job of our war committee to check the endless vulnerable points requiring guards. Then Ugly Barratt came to discuss employment of bombers as experienced in France. He was followed by the head of the Home Office detectives. Finally Canadian Press Corps representative came to see me.

15 August

Left Hendon at 8.30 am and arrived at Sutton Bridge on the Wash at 9 am where I was met by Adam [Northern Command] and [Utterson-]Kelso. Proceeded to inspect western defences of the Wash up to Skegness. Then lunched with Archie Montgomery[-Massingberd] and proceeded up to the Humber doing Grimsby and Immingham docks. Picked up plane again at Grimsby aerodrome and flew over Humber estuary examining forts and Spurn Head defences. Then flew up coast to Hornsea before striking inland for York where we arrived at 8 pm. Stopped the night with Adam.

16 August

Left York 8.30 am by air for Middlesbrough where we picked up car and met Witts [59th Division]. We then went to Redcar which we did in detail crossing Tees by suspension bridge and working our way up the coast through Seaton and Sunderland which had been heavily bombed on previous day. Lunched South Shields, crossed Tyne by ferry to North Shields and worked up coast through Blyth to Amble. Finally picked up plane at Acklington aerodrome at 5.15 pm. Dropped Adam in York and was back in Hendon at 7 pm. Went to office before coming home.

17 August

Pownall [Inspector General Home Guard] came in this morning and gave me an account of his activities which did not impress me very much. Sholto Douglas came next and we finally fixed up details of Bomber Command co-operation in the event of an invasion. Dill [CIGS] also came about tea time and we had a long talk.

At 6.45 pm started off for Chequers where I was to dine with PM and spend the night. Party consisted of Beaverbrook, Portal (C-in-C Bomber Command), Pug Ismay [Deputy Secretary (Military) to War Cabinet], Sandys [Churchill's son-in-law]. After dinner long discussion between Beaverbrook and Portal on the training of pilots. In the middle of it I was taken for a walk by the PM in the moon light during which we discussed defensive dispositions. Got to bed about 1.45 am.

I cannot say that these weekends have left any happy memories. As I look back on them I remember best long drawn out evenings and a desperate longing for bed as these evenings extended well into the morning hours! There were no doubt times of intense interest, and one could be certain of boundless hospitality, but at the end of a very hard week's work, to be kept up to the early hours of the morning was, to put it mildly, a very trying procedure.

On this first occasion I remember well that Beaverbrook was present; after dinner he sat at the writing table, pouring himself out one strong whisky after another, and I was revolted by his having monkey-like hands as they stretched out to grab ice cubes out of the bowl. The more I saw of him throughout the war, the more I disliked and mistrusted him. An evil genius who exercised the very worst of influence on Winston.

18 August
Left Chequers at 9.30 am and motored back to St Paul's where I did almost 2 hours' work. Then at last came home to have lunch with you and to spend the afternoon in absolute paradise with you and those two beloved wee persons. Air raid warnings in the afternoon.

19 August
Worked in the office. Lunched with Anthony Eden to meet de Gaulle. Was not much impressed by him.

Whatever good qualities he may have had were marred by his overbearing manner, his 'megalomania' and his lack of co-operative spirit. ... In all discussions he assumed that the problem of the liberation of France was mine, whilst he was concentrating on how he would govern it, as its Dictator, as soon as it was liberated! Added to these disadvantages, his Headquarters were so completely lacking all sense of security that it became quite impossible to discuss any future plans with them.

In the afternoon Roger Evans came to see me to ask why he had been removed from the Armoured Division. This resulted in an unpleasant interview. Finally Selection Board meeting at WO at 6.30 pm, to select future Divisional Commanders. This resulted in a later return home.

20 August
Carried out another exercise to test out control of Home Defence. Found several minor defects. Visited our new offices in the Office of Works.

21 August
Left home 9 am. Proceeded by car to HQ, where I discussed employment of IV Corps with Nosworthy. Then went on to see Bn exercise carried out by 43rd Div, also met Young, commanding Inf Bde. Lunched with Pollock. After lunch proceeded to see the 2nd Armoured Division. Saw demonstration carried out by Rollie Charrington's Bde. Then inspected support group under Harry Latham. Also saw RHA Regiment including Eagle Troop. Finished up with tea with Scott [illegible] and his Armoured Brigade. Returned home at 8 pm.

22 August
Visited Aldershot Command. Discussed organization of defence with Johnson [Aldershot Command] and inspected defences. Lunched Gov[ernment] House. Returned to St Paul's and did office work.

23 August

Willoughby Norrie came at 10 am and I told him what I wanted done as regards handling of [1st] Armoured Division he takes over. At 11 went to see Anthony Eden who had sent for me with reference to number of TA officers who were being pushed out in proportion to Regular ones. Then to see Cave as regards production of 1st line vehicles and armoured forces. Lunched with Kirke at Carlton with ICI representatives to discuss WO reforms. At 4 pm, Princess Juliana of Holland's husband came to see me (Prince Bernhard). Seemed very nice. 5 pm: Admiral Bryce, who has been reporting on vulnerability of beaches. 6 pm: Pope to discuss organization of armoured forces, and to plan for the winter.

24 August

As I left town at 8.30 an air raid warning started. Motored through a deserted London with only Air Raid Wardens about. Arrived at Hendon aerodrome to find it deserted except for the defending troops. After some 11 minutes Fighter Command reported road safe, so I started off in my Flamingo, flying very low for Andover, which we reached at 9.45 am. Definite signs of bombing here. Motored to Tidworth, where I inspected Bns of 60th and RB [Rifle Brigade]. Then motored to West Lavington to inspect 1st Army Tank Bde. From there to Warminster where I saw 3rd Armoured Bde, including Bays, 9th L[ancers] and 10th H[ussars]. Finally to Chisledon to see QV [Queen Victoria's] Rifles which are just reforming after their Boulogne fight. Flew home from near there.

25 August

Sunday. After a night of air raid warnings went to the office in the morning and spent afternoon at home. As I write this we are again in the middle of an air raid warning.

26 August

More air raids during the night. Worked in the office all day and left by the 7.30 pm from Euston for Inverness. No dining car and an air raid warning of 2 hours which entailed going to bed in the dark made the journey less comfortable than usual.

27 August

Arrived in Inverness 2 hours late. Met by Alan Cunningham (commanding 51st Div) and Chalmers commanding Area. Flew to Wick where I inspected defence of aerodrome. Then examined neighbouring beaches. Next by car to Skitten aerodrome, Thurso and beaches close by and on to Castletown aerodrome. After discussing defences flew back to Evanton near Invergordon, there met battalion commander and discussed defence of aerodrome. Finally flew back to

Inverness. Visited ITC [Infantry Training Centre], met Admiral and ADC, and had discussion with Freddy Carrington after dinner.

28 August

Motored to Kenton aerodrome. After discussing defence onto Lossiemouth aerodrome. Also looked at beaches nearby. Then saw bn exercise by men of Stanley Clarke's bn. Stopped at House of Glenn's for lunch and was presented with 12 salmon by Dickie. On to Peterhead, visiting Graham's Bde HQ on the way where I met [Gen] Jock Burnett-Stuart. Looked at beaches and on to Dyce aerodrome, finishing off with Black Watch Bn in Aberdeen, Aberdeen Harbour, and beaches north of it. Caught 6.40 train back to London.

29 August

I arrived back in London at 8.15 am. Had breakfast at the club and then spent rest of the day in the office.

30 August

Left Hendon at 9 am and flew to Worcester where we arrived at 9.50 am. Motored on to 2 London Div HQ to see Signal Exercise. Met Copper [Finlayson] and Jimmy Cornwall there. Exercise took us right along valley of the R. Usk towards Pembroke. Finally picked up plane again at aerodrome west of Pwll. Had lovely fly back along the Bristol Channel passing over Cardiff, Bristol, Reading, Henley, Maidenhead. Took 1 hour and 5 minutes to return. On landing at Hendon was informed that they had just been watching an air battle over the aerodrome! We did not miss it by much.

31 August

Proceeded to Aldershot to inspect the New Zealand Division, and was very much impressed with the units I saw. They will be a great loss to Home Forces when they go and a great gain to the Middle East. Finished by lunching with Freyberg [NZ Forces] at [illegible] Place. Returned to St Paul's where I gave interview to General [illegible] of the USA Army. Weather very hot again.

1 September

Went to St Paul's School for the morning to do office work. Then spent afternoon in paradise with you and the children filling the tank in the garden for the Pooks and Ti to bathe in. It is very sad that our happy time in Cambridge House is drawing to a close.

2 September

Attended Chiefs of Staff meeting in the morning where we discussed defences of Scilly Isles, defence of Dover and Cornwall, and of aerodromes. In afternoon Michael Barker came to see me, and also head of secret service.

3 September

First day of the second year of the war! It is just a year ago that I drove over from Salisbury to Aldershot to see Dill to find out from him what the BEF would be required to do. I arrived just before 11 am and watched the war start with him! This evening instead I spent 1½ hours with him in the WO discussing how we are to run the 2nd year of the war, and how we are to meet the German invasion if it comes within the next few days.

Looking back it has been a year of heartbreaking partings from you which stand out for me above all else, a year of unending work and very heavy trials. I am quite convinced that if it had not been for the influence you have had in my life in confirming my belief in an Almighty and far seeing God that I should have found it hard to come through such trials and deficient of the grit to meet such ordeals. But it is quite impossible to live with you without seeing God's divine heaven radiating from you at all times. I do thank Him for having allowed me to meet you and through you to be able to get so much closer to Him.

I attended Lord Nathan of Churt at the Dorchester to hear Anthony Eden's address. I sat between the Chinese Ambassador and Vincent Massey the High Commissioner for Canada. This evening had long and useful interview with Dill.

4 September

Left Hendon at 9 am and flew to Yeovil where I landed 50 minutes later. Met by Gammell commanding 3rd Div. Proceeded to 7th Guards Div where I met Cazenove and watched ferrying by 1st Coldstreams. Went on to 1st Grenadiers where I saw Prescott. Then on to see Div Art, 8th and 9th Inf Bdes. Saw very good field firing by KOSBs [King's Own Scottish Borderers]. Finally flew back from near Cheltenham and went to office before retiring to Club. Indications of impending attack before Sept 15th are accumulating.

5 September

Spent the day with Bertie Brooke going around London defences. Piping hot day. Defences on NE, E and SE satisfactory, but in southern sector still behind hand. Dropped into office on way back.

6 September

Left at 9 am to visit 1st Armoured Division. Air raid warning on during run down – as a result roads were empty and we arrived 10 mins too early.

Discussed organization with Willoughby Norrie, then went round Evelyn Fanshawe's Brigade of Yeomanry Regts. A very good show. Lunched with Roddick (late of 10 H[ussars]). After lunch visited Morgan and his support group [Devon and Cornwall Division], also Crocker and his Brigade [6th Armoured Division]. Returned to office by 6 pm, put in ½ hour there, then back to Club to change and started at 7 pm for Chequers to spend night with PM.

Arrived there 8 pm. Found Mrs Churchill and Dill in hall. Told by her that PM had gone to rest – dinner to be at 8.45 pm. Finally sat down to dinner at 9 pm – Mrs Churchill did not come down. Party consisted of Dill, Ismay, Secretary, PM and self. PM warmed up and was most entertaining for rest of evening. First of all he placed himself in the position of Hitler and attacked these isles while I defended them. He then revised the whole of the Air Raid Warning system and gave us his proposals to criticize. Finally at 1.45 am we got off to bed!

7 September

All reports look like invasion getting nearer. Ships collecting, dive bombers being concentrated, parachutists captured, also 4 Dutchmen [spies] on the coast. Drove in from Chequers with Dill. On arriving in office was sent for to attend COS meeting to discuss latest intercepted message concerning German plans for putting down fog [screen in Channel]. Back to St Paul's to discuss expansion of armoured forces. Finally dined with Bertie [Brooke] after sending out orders for 'Cromwell' – ie state of readiness [exercise] in Eastern and Southern Commands.

After dinner I walked back from the Orleans [club] round St James's Square to the Army and Navy Club. Only a few yards to go, but that journey has never seemed longer, I had not even got a hat on, and there was a real inferno of a bomb raid, a continual roar of falling bombs and AA fire, and through the middle of it that unpleasant vicious hum of AA splinters as they came raining down.

8 September

Heavy bombing of London throughout the night, the whole sky being lit up by the glow of fires in London docks. Went to the office in the morning where I found further indications of impending invasion. Everything pointing to Kent and E. Anglia as the two main threatened points.

Went over to Ferney Close for lunch and spent the afternoon and evening in complete paradise with you and those two beloved small persons. It is so wonderful being able to get into such surroundings for a bit and to forget the war and all its horrors. Motored back at 8.30 with air raid on. Search lights working in all directions and a glowing red sky over London. It seemed so strange leaving you and all the wonderful peace and happiness connected with our combined lives to return here for what may well be the most eventful weeks in the history of the British Empire!

I called in at St Paul's School on the way back, and found that all reports still point to the probability of an invasion starting between the 8th and 10th of this month. The responsibility of feeling what any mistakes or even misappreciations may mean in the future of these isles and of the Empire is a colossal one! and one which rather staggers me at times. I wish I had more adequately trained formations under my orders. But for the present there is nothing to be done but to trust God and pray for his help and guidance.

This was certainly an understatement of the feelings which were tearing me to pieces daily! I do not think I can remember any time in the whole of my career when my responsibilities weighed heavier on me than they did during those days of the impending invasion. The full knowledge of all that depended on my preparations for, and conduct of, the battle to repel the invasion, combined with the unpleasant realization as to the deficiencies in equipment and training in the forces at my disposal, made the prospect of the impending conflict a burden that was almost unbearable at times. Added to it all was the necessity to maintain outward confident appearance, there was not a soul to whom one could disclose one's inward anxieties without risking the calamitous effects of lack of confidence, demoralization, doubts, and all those insidious workings which undermine the power of resistance.

9 September

Spent part of morning in office, then attended Chiefs of Staff meeting at 10.30 am. Returned to St Paul's School where I worked until lunch. I then lunched with Sir Findlater Stewart [PUS for India] to meet Sir John Anderson [Lord President of the Council] at the Athenaeum. After lunch went to War Office for Selection Board meeting. Returned to St Paul's School to see Pownall and continue with office work. Finally left office at 7.45 pm and returned to Club. Hope for a quieter night than the last one which was a continuous bombing of London. I counted over 60 bombs fall in vicinity in one hour! Two in St James's Park, 1 in Buckingham Palace, Madame Tussaud's destroyed, South Kensington Natural History Museum, many power stations, stations, hospitals etc.

10 September

Left Hendon at 10 am for Doncaster. Rather a bumpy journey. Met Adam [Northern Command], Alexander [Southern Command] and Percival [44th Division] at the aerodrome. Proceeded to watch an exercise between two Inf Bdes of 42nd Division. Finally left for Hendon again at 6.15 pm and landed just after an air raid warning at 7 pm. Last night again indiscriminate bombing of London. Still no invasion today. I wonder whether he will do anything during the next few days?

11 September

Called up early whilst shaving and told that Dill and Anthony Eden wanted to see me at 10 am. So went round to WO to be told that PM had been somewhat disturbed by Admiralty paper concerning security of guns mounted in vicinity of Dover. He proposed to visit that sector of the coast tomorrow. Returned to office and worked there rest of day. Evidence of impending invasion has been accumulating all day, more ships moving west down the Channel, intercepted cipher messages, etc. It is still possible that it may be a bluff to hide some other impending stroke. The next day or two are bound to be very critical.

12 September

Left the Rag [Club] shortly after 8 am and proceeded to pick up Dill and then on to Holborn Viaduct Station which we reached with some difficulty owing to results of night's bombing. Here we joined the PM's train for Shorncliffe. On the way had long talk with PM on the organization of defences for the Narrows.

Met by Bulgy Thorne and Massy at the station, proceeded to examine 9.2" railway guns, coast guns, defences to Dungeness. Then back to Dover for lunch in the castle with Bertie Ramsay. After lunch PM wanted to watch air fight but there was none to see. We then went on to see 12" howitzers and beach south of Ramsgate, finishing up at Ramsgate. Party consisted of PM, 1st Sea Lord Admiral Pound, 1st Lord of Admiralty [A.V. Alexander], Dill, Pug Ismay and self. PM was very pleasant and as usual most refreshing and entertaining. His popularity is astounding, everywhere crowds rush up and cheer him wildly, encouraging him with shouts of 'Stick it!'

13 September

Another night of bombing and AA fire, but a rainy morning and signs of break in the weather. Spent morning in the office studying increasing evidence of impending invasion. Lunched with the ICI at Nobel House where I found them all in the basement sheltering as Buckingham Palace had just been attacked by a dive bomber. After lunch returned to office where King-Hall came to see me about defence of aircraft industry. Finally returned to club at 8 pm. During dinner air raids started again and AA barrage is now going full blast. Today bombs have been dropped in Horse Guards, House of Lords, War Office etc. Everything looks like an invasion starting tomorrow from the Thames to Plymouth! I wonder whether we shall be hard at it by this time tomorrow?

14 September

A quieter night on the whole, but plenty of AA fire. Went to see the 3rd Independent Brigade commanded by Smyth. Got back to the Office about 5 pm. Ominous quiet!! German shipping reserves greatly reduced and air action too. Have the Germans completed their preparations for invasion? Are they giving their air force a last brush and wash up? Will he start tomorrow, or is it all a bluff to pin troops down in this country while he prepares to help Italy to invade Egypt etc??

15 September

Still no move on the part of the Germans! Everything remains keyed up for an early invasion, and the air war goes on unabated. The coming week must remain a critical one, and it is hard to see how Hitler can now retrace his steps and stop the invasion. The suspense of waiting is very trying especially when one is familiar with the weakness of our defence! Our exposed coastline is just twice the length of the front the French were holding in France with about 80 divisions and a Maginot Line! Here we have 22 divisions of which only about ½ can be looked upon as in any way fit for any form of mobile operation! Thank God the spirit is now good and the defeatist opinions expressed after Dunkirk are now no longer prevalent. But I wish I could have 6 months now to finish equipping and training the force under my command.

A responsibility such as that of the defence of this country under the existing conditions is one that weighs on one like a ton of bricks, and it is hard at times to retain the hopeful, confident exterior which is so essential to retain the confidence of those under one, and to guard against their having any doubts as regards final success.

... I considered the invasion a very real and probable threat and one for which the land forces at my disposal fell far short of what I felt was required to provide any degree of real confidence in our power to defend these shores. It should not be construed that I considered our position a helpless one in the case of an invasion. Far from it. We should certainly have a desperate struggle and the future might well have hung in the balance, but I certainly felt that given a fair share of the fortunes of war we should certainly succeed in finally defending these shores. It must be remembered that if my diary occasionally gave vent to some of the doubts which the heavy responsibility generated, this diary was the one and only outlet for such doubts.

Just back from an afternoon of blissful happiness with you and those two beloved wee things. Heavy air raid on at present and AA guns going full blast. Unfortunately the full moon remains uncovered by any clouds. Buckingham Palace was again hit today.

16 September

Still no invasion! Rumour has it that tonight is to be the night. He is certainly being infernally busy in the air tonight and 6 bombs have come whistling down fairly close to the Rag. Spent the morning in the office. Had Guy Williams [Eastern Command] to lunch to discuss winter reliefs with him and at 3.30 pm came up to War Office to discuss with Dill and Gort the reorganization of the divisions. Dined with Bertie at the Orleans and walked home in the middle of heavy air raid with sky lit up by burning houses in the direction of Charing Cross.

17 September

Still no invasion, and today a mild hurricane which should be stirring up the Channel well! Continual night raids last night with heavy anti-aircraft fire. Bombs dropped in Burlington Arcade, Bond St, Berkeley Square and Park Lane etc. Inspected 42nd Division with brigades in Maidenhead, Newbury and Oxford. A good division which will require a good deal more training. Returned to the office at 6.15 pm and put in 1½ hours in the office. Now back at the club after dinner and back again into our usual air raid with the droning of German planes, the crash of bombs and heavy roll of AA barrage. It is hard to believe that it is London!

18 September

Another day without invasion. Wind has dropped and weather unfortunately finer. Spent the day in the office with a series of interruptions. First Pope to settle future of Armoured Corps. Then Pownall to discuss Home Guard. Then Nosworthy to talk about methods of counter attack with IV Corps. Lunchtime – McHughes, Eastern Command [illegible] came to lunch. After lunch Lady Listowel for an interview for a book she is writing. Last night heavy bombing again, considerable damage in Oxford Street. Every indication continues to look [like] an invasion being staged, ready to be launched at any time. I wish the weather would really break up!

19 September

An unpleasant night with heavy bombing in the West End. In fact this morning when going to Hendon we found most roads closed, Piccadilly, Regent St, Bond St, North Audley St, Park Lane. Big craters round the Marble Arch, etc. Finally left Hendon at 10 am and in 20 minutes had covered the 70 miles to Mildenhall! Spent the day with James Drew going round the 52nd Division which I found in good form but still very short of transport. Got back to Hendon just before 9 pm and went to St Paul's for an hour in the office. At 8 pm air raid warning started again and has been on ever since. Heavy bomb has just fallen in the vicinity which shook the whole club building.

20 September

Another night of raids. Went to see Oliver Leese and his 29th Independent Brigade – a good show which will require a little more training in the case of 2 of the bns. After lunch returned to the office where I found Prince Henry. Finished by 8 pm and retired to club. All indications of impending invasion still remain, and unfortunately weather is improving!

21 September

Spent the day in the office. In the morning had an interview with the DMT

[Director Military Training] to settle details of the Command Company Commanders Courses. Then Freyberg came to say goodbye before starting again for the Middle East. In the evening came up to see Dill for a long talk. Air raids still going full blast again tonight. This evening PM sent me paper from [Ambassador] Sam Hoare in Spain giving details of talk with reliable American who had come from Germany. Speaking on the 7th of this month he said he was certain that Hitler would attack within a fortnight. Today, the 21st, must be the last day of that fortnight! Weather prophets predict a perfect sea.

22 September

After a night of almost continuous air raids, which did *not* prevent me having a very good night's sleep, I went to the office and finished work quickly. Then went home, where I found you all singing hymns in the drawing room. It was a wet day but it might have been brilliant sunshine for the joy of being back with you. In the evening gave Philip a lift back. The approach to London looked like approaching Dante's Inferno, continuous flashes of guns and sparks of bursting shells in the sky with haloes of searchlights.

23 September

Still no invasion! A day in the office with continuous work from 9 am to 8 pm without much let up. At present again our usual continuous night raid.

24 September

Proceeded to Aldershot to see the 2nd Canadian Division. Spent the day with Odlum going round what promises to be a very good show. Andy McNaughton came to lunch. On the way back came to Ferney Close to have tea with you. Finally put in 2 hours work in the office before coming back to the club.

25 September

Rather a worse night of 'bumps and crumps' than usual, with several unpleasantly close. The Savile Row, Burlington Gardens area was again receiving much attention. Spent a day in the office, and amongst other things reinforced the North Foreland-Dungeness front by an additional Brigade Group and machine gun battalion. It is that narrow neck of sea that constitutes a danger point now that he has all his shipping assembled on the French coast opposite to it. It is very hard to fathom what he intends to do and whether he still contemplates invasion. The conditions are still very good for it and the sea remains abominably calm! Spent the day in the office. After tea went round to Huntsman to order a new uniform jacket for the winter and found most of Savile Row in ruins! Also saw bad holes in Bond St including my beloved Dollond and Aitchison who have evacuated their premises.

26 September

Left the club at 8 am for Hendon. Delayed on the way owing to results of last night's air raids which included the Hendon underground station amongst others. The latter being completely demolished by a parachute bomb. Flew to Old Sarum where we picked up Auchinleck and Ritchie. From there we flew to St Ervan which we reached shortly after 10. Here Franklyn and Charles Allfrey met us and we proceeded towards Land's End, examining the defences of St Ives and Penzance beaches also Falmouth defences. Then back by air to St Ervan where we took off for Old Sarum at 5.30 pm and dropped Ritchie, going on to Hendon where we arrived just after 7 pm and just in time as it was getting dark and a ground mist was rising. Reached club about 7.30 pm having covered about 600 miles in the 12 hours!

27 September

Left Club at 8.30 am and, after many obstructions from last night's bombs, reached Hendon just as the air raid warning started. However we called up Fighter Command who reported Germans as attacking Biggin Hill, and that we could fly north safely. Flew to Liverpool taking 1 hour and 10 mins owing to head wind. Met by Copper [Finlayson] and Mansergh commanding Tank Bde. Then went to see exercise by Alston (Brig 118th Bde of 38th Div). From there on to see Lumsden and his Armoured Brigade. Then flew back to Hendon, and on to office to work till 8 pm.

Today is anniversary of my departure for France from Salisbury and our parting outside the County Hotel. I can see your car driving off now when I shut my eyes, and can again feel that ghastly desolation that froze into my heart at our having to part!

28 September

A day spent in the office which included several visits. Pownall came to say goodbye on going to Ireland, Rusty Eastwood coming to take over [Home Guard] from him. Budget Loyd came to discuss training. Holden [his BGS] to tell me about Beaverbrook's latest efforts at raising a special army of his own. Still always indications of impending invasion. And up to the present no signs that the Germans are proposing to give up the attempt. In fact the indications point towards working up to something definite.

29 September

After a short visit to the office, which was mainly taken up with a long talk to Dill, I went to spend the rest of the day with you. And a lovely peaceful and heavenly day we had, sawing wood and just basking in the sunshine of happiness spread by the presence of you and the wee ones. These Sunday afternoons with you are the most wonderful tonic after a hard week's work. When with you there I am able to forget everything connected with the war and its worries and come back refreshed for another week of this burden. This next week should I feel bring the matter of invasion to a head. If he intends to try it on I don't feel that he can leave it much later than this week. But I wish the weather would deteriorate more than it has up to the present.

30 September

Attended Chiefs of Staff Committee at 10.15. This organization works surprisingly slowly considering that there is a war on! We seem to meander along and there is no snap about it. I only wish that Dill was chairman of the Committee. Newall [CAS] is a better chairman than old Admiral Pound, but still leaves room for much improvement.

Returned to office. Chaplain General came to lunch. Gives one the feeling of a very human individual. Then Rusty Eastwood came to discuss the Home Guard, having just taken over. He was followed by Pope with whom I discussed organization of armoured force, things have been progressing satisfactorily and the organization I wanted has been adopted. We can now forge ahead. This evening at 9.15 pm I am due to attend meeting with Anthony Eden to discuss winter accommodation.

1 October

Left Hendon at 9 am and flew to Firbeech aerodrome (near Sheffield) where I met Adam and proceeded to meet No. 4 Group Special Battalions. A first class and most encouraging show. After sandwich lunch we looked at 1st Corps Junior Leader School, and from there to see 1st Derbyshire Yeomanry followed up by Command ammunition dump. Finally reaching York at 8 pm and spending night with Adam.

2 October

Left York 8.30 am, motored to Harrogate to see 24th Army Tank Bde. From there to Yeadon aerodrome where we embarked for Acklington. Foggy fly over, met by Holmes [Director of Movements] and Priestman. Proceeded to motor towards Berwick to see 2nd Motor Machine Gun Brigade and coast defences. Returned to Acklington by 4 and flew back, dropping Adam in York and arriving Hendon at 6 pm. Whilst at York had received messages from Anthony Eden asking me to come to WO at 6.30 pm. Was there till 8 pm discussing reinforcements to Archie Wavell [in ME], I am to lose the whole of 1st Armoured Div by 1st November! Worst part of the bargain is that all the cruiser tanks must be pulled back at once for overhaul. I shall therefore be short of 100 Cruisers from now onwards! Finally dined with Bertie Brooke at the Orleans Club.

3 October

Still no invasion! I am beginning to think that the Germans may after all not attempt it. And yet! I have the horrid thought that he may still bring off some surprise on us.

Had a long day in the office. First of all a long interview with Edward Grigg [Joint Parliamentary USS for War] and Rusty Eastwood on the future organization of the Home Guard. Then an interview with Finch [Chairman, WO Committees, soon retired], who proved himself to be an even more poisonous specimen than I thought he was! Then proceeded to Coastal Command to lunch with Bowhill and to look over his organization. Returned to the office to be attacked by Secretary of Jockey Club who wished to carry on with Newmarket race meetings as if no war existed. Finally retired to club at 8.30 pm.

4 October
Weather still unfortunately too bad to fly so had to go to Larkhill by road. There I joined McNaughton and we saw a demonstration of air burst ranging. Lunched in 'A' Mess, inspected Canadian Survey Regiment and then motored back here. Weather very foggy and overcast but unfortunately not much wind. On return to office had long interview with Guy Williams (C-in-C Eastern) as I did not like his winter dispositions. He was not getting divisions out to train and at the same time was giving inadequate protection to the Kent salient. I think we have now got a more satisfactory arrangement.

5 October
A day in the office. Auchinleck came in the morning and I discussed training matters with him. Did some shopping before lunch to try and catch shops open. Dined with Dill.

6 October
Spent an hour in the office and then came to spend the rest of the day in paradise with you and those two beloved wee ones.

7 October
Attended COS meeting in the morning, and did office work rest of the day. Got Pope to come up to discuss with him the running of an Armoured Force Conference during the winter. Heavy bombing again tonight after a fairly quiet night last night.

8 October
Left Hendon at 8.30 am having found the place in a sad plight after the night's bombing which had destroyed one hangar with some 27 machines in it! After 2 hours flight landed at Leuchars (near St Andrews) in Fifeshire. Here I

inspected units of one of the Brigades of the 46th Division having been met by Carrington, Anderson and Hudson (the Brigadier). Finally lunched with the latter, and then flew on to Grangemouth and from there visited units of Daley's Brigade and also some Yeomanry gunners. Finally returning to Carrington's house by about 7 pm. The Stopfords and Rolleston were there for dinner. Finally a very peaceful night with no bombs!

9 October

Left at 9 am and spent morning inspecting Inchkeith and Inchcolm islands in the Firth of Forth and their gun defences. A foul day with low cloud, driving rain and a strong wind. Lunched at the club in Edinburgh and went to see the last Brigade of Anderson's in the North Berwick area. Finally arrived at Drem aerodrome (near North Berwick) to embark for home. But blizzard of rain was blowing and impossible to see across aerodrome. So waited for rain to blow over and then got on board, but starboard engine refused to start. 'Booster Coil' was fused, this entailed more delay to replace it and was 4.10 by the time we got off. Very strong head wind and damnably rough. Pilot flew out to sea and skirted coast about 2 miles out until we reached Hartlepool and then struck inland. It was 6.45 pm by the time we reached Hendon and getting uncomfortably dark. However pilot made beautiful landing and I was glad to be on firm ground again. Two bombs have just rocked the club!

10 October

Spent day in the office catching up on two days' work. Dined at Berkeley with Joubert de la Ferté [Assistant CAS], while we were dining the Germans dropped a delay action fuse bomb in Piccadilly outside Rootes. We were asked to sit in an inner room in case bomb should explode.

11 October

After a night's heavy bombing with one or two fairly close to the Rag, started for Hendon. Much delayed by roads blocked with unexploded bombs. Flew to Old Sarum where Auchinleck met me and took me on to Monty's [V Corps] HQ where I attended part of his officers' week and said a few words. Received message whilst there asking me to dine and sleep Chequers. Flew back to London, changed and packed bag. Put in another hour in the office and then left for Chequers. There I found the PM, Mrs Churchill, Randolph C, Mr Sandys, Miss C, Pug Ismay, Tim Pile [AA Command], and Sec. Sat up till 2 am. PM in great form. Discussing probable course of war, likelihood of German move in Mediterranean, also reason for failure of Dakar expedition [the previous month]. He has a wonderful vitality and bears his heavy burden remarkably well. It would be impossible to find a man to fill his place at present.

12 October

After an early breakfast at Chequers motored back to office where I picked up Paget and Ronnie and we went to Hopkinson's intercommunications unit. A very good show. After lunch went to WO and spent 2 hours with Dill discussing various points.

13 October

Spent morning in the office. Left at 12.15 am with Barney for Windsor Castle where I was to lunch with the King. Was shown up into King's room on arrival and he discussed with me air defences of Windsor Castle and also possibility of his proceeding to Norfolk. I was then introduced to the Queen and the two small Princesses. We then moved on into a reception hall where the rest of the party was drawn up including Kattie (Hamilton that was) it was a great joy seeing her again and being able to talk over old Colebrooke days. At lunch I sat on the Queen's right, and found her quite charming and very easy to talk to. In fact, the whole lunch was most informal and one was made to feel at home. After lunch Queen and Princesses departed and I went back to King's study to discuss details of defence of Windsor. When liberated drove on to Ferney Close to snatch a few hours of paradise with you and the young.

On my drive out I turned to my chauffeur Parker (who had previously been employed by one of the Royal Princesses) and asked him whether he had been given his lunch all right. 'Oh yes,' he replied, 'I know my way around the castle well from former visits. What is more, I have come away with a spare chamois and sponge, they keep the best chamois and sponge that you can get anywhere.' I could only hope that the deficiency in chamois and sponge would not be connected with my visit.

Just back from motoring to Rag and calling at GHQ. Shelling and bombing appears to be rather less up to present tonight.

14 October

Started morning in the office and attended Chiefs of Staff meeting at 10.30 am where we discussed shortage of ammunition. Returned to office to interview Stewart, the Inspector of Royal Armoured Corps and Rusty Eastwood. After lunch attended Selection Board meeting in Dill's room, returning St Paul's about 5 pm. Left office at 8 pm in middle of heavy air raid with sky lit up by flares. Arrived outside club to find the whole street littered with glass and car unable to drive down Pall Mall. The Carlton Club had been hit by a bomb and set on fire! It is burning hard now and my room here is thick with smoke from it! There are several fire engines working and they seem to be getting it under control. The Germans have been very active in these parts tonight and have dropped many bombs in the vicinity. The moon is unfortunately far too bright!!

15 October

The Germans were very active last night in these parts. Besides burning out the Carlton Club, they hit the Monaco, Burton's and the church in Piccadilly, landed one in St James's Square, one at the bottom of the steps at the bottom end of Regent St, where they unfortunately killed Admiral Tower, who was my chief Naval Liaison Officer. Held a conference at St Paul's for Army Commanders lasting from 10 am to 1.30 pm. Started with Intelligence summary of invasion prospects. Followed by QMG and AG. After lunch Dill came and gave an excellent talk on the world situation. Tonight the Germans are hard at it again, but up to now not quite so near as last night!

16 October

The most noisy night we have had yet and I was kept awake till 3.00 am by continual bombing. Several pretty close including a parachute mine in St James's Park which blew in all the windows of Buckingham Palace and most houses surrounding the park. Spent the day with the 1st London Division going round Ramsgate salient, the bay immediately south of it, Deal, etc. The more I look at that Salient the more I dislike it, we are definitely too weak there, but I have nothing else to add to that part without depleting other fronts dangerously. I have now all moves prepared to get divisions back to train, but do not yet dare to do so. The most recent intercepts point to preparations for an invasion being on foot.* The force being assembled in the Scheldt on a programme lasting some 7 days. The information is fairly reliable, but it is difficult to believe that the Germans would attempt a serious invasion at this time of year. Luckily at present it is raining and an overcast sky so we may have a less disturbed night than the last two!

17 October

Evidence is amassing from wireless intercepts of impending invasion of some kind or other. Rotterdam is filling up with shipping, I have asked for it to be heavily bombed and for continuous reconnaissance of the Scheldt. Spent the morning in the office, then went to give Eves his last sitting for his picture. Found he had made excellent portraits of Gort and Auchinleck. He is leaving London as he can't sleep. Paget went off on leave, Lindsell is also away, so that if the Boche does attack they will be nice and fresh when they come back. Meanwhile I must bear the burden. Dined with Bertie this evening and found it most refreshing and helpful, I wish we could take him as a Corps Commander.

18 October

Very foggy morning and when I got to Hendon to fly to Bristol I was told I

---

*Bryant coyly substituted 'reports' for 'intercepts' in this entry, and omitted 'wireless intercepts' from the next one; and similarly on 24 Oct. *The Turn of the Tide* (London: Collins, 1957), pp. 224–25.

should have to wait for an hour or so for mist to lift off Bristol. Did not get off till after 10.30 am. Rose up through fog to find ourselves in beautiful sunshine looking down on a vast expanse of white cotton wool sea. Never saw the land all the way. On reaching Bristol wireless reported fog was down again so flew on to Bristol Channel where we dropped to sea level and flew along coast and landed at Weston-super-Mare, 25 miles from Whitchurch aerodrome where we should have been. Borrowed RAF motor and motored to Blaydon [Bleadon] where I met Auchinleck, Gammell, and Cmdr 8th Inf Bde and had lunch. Then watched infantry battalion exercise to retake aerodrome of Whitchurch from which I took off to fly back, reaching Hendon 4.30. Went to office till 8 pm.

19 October

Another day gone and thank God for it! Every day that passes must at least be one day less of this war. But there are times when the madness and the folly of war choke one! Why human beings must behave like children at this stage of the evolution of the human race is hard to understand. At any rate it proves that we have still got to go a long way on the road that leads to perfect human beings. And yet through all its destruction, uselessness and havoc I can see some progress. Progress that could never be achieved without the upheaval of war. Long standing institutions and social distinctions are shattered by war and make room for more modern methods of life. Those that would never release what they hold in peace, are forced to do so in war, to the benefit of the multitude. Ultimately I suppose that human beings from much suffering will become wiser and will appreciate that greater happiness can be found in this world by preferring their neighbours to themselves!

Meanwhile for all my philosophy I am very tired of this war and long for peace. A peace that will allow us to spend the remaining years of our life quietly together in a small cottage with a garden to work in, some trees to look after and perhaps a stream close by where I can watch the fish even if I don't catch them! And above all somewhere where I can bask in the sublime happiness of the sunshine of your company! But even if I can't be with you at present I still thank God for having allowed me to know you and for all the wonderful happiness of seeing you once a week. I am now counting the hours till tomorrow when I hope to start for my Sunday with you.

20 October

Sunday is gone, and as usual has flown like a dream of perfect happiness. You cannot realize what it means after a week of worries, responsibilities, doubts as to whether I am doing all I can, nights of bombing, and the continual desperate longing to be with you, to be able to step out of all that turmoil and at your side find perfect peace and happiness. To be able to mix with the interests of those two beloved wee souls and to enter their world where war does not exist but a thousand simple and healthy interests. To see them developing and to watch bits of your perfect self reflected in them, I cannot tell you darling what it all means to me, it is just heaven on earth. I do thank God and you for such a perfect blessing.

London was being lit up by flashes of fire as we approached. I was half drowsing as we slid along the Great West Road. Suddenly there was a terrific crash and the car after swaying badly lurched off to the side of the road! I thought for the first moment that it was a small bomb or AA dud shell, but we found that we had run into a stationary car standing in the middle of the road with no lamps on. Luckily there was no serious trouble beyond wings badly bent. So we went on and stopped at St Paul's School on way home. No special news. And yet we enter another week of tension and probability of invasion. These scares are trying and I shall be glad if we get through to next Sunday without an invasion.

21 October

After a fairly quiet night began day at office. Attended Chiefs of Staff meeting at 10.15 where we discussed small arms ammunition situation, defence of aerodromes, lack of intelligence, etc. Then had Rusty Eastwood for an hour to discuss reorganization of the Home Guard and findings of the Grigg Committee. Menzies came to lunch with me to give me most recent reports of secret service. He was followed at 3 pm by Sikorski, Polish PM and C-in-C, on an official visit owing to Polish troops being now under my orders. He was very interesting on the European situation and on the reports he had of the Russian situation. According to him Stalin is feeling very uneasy as to the future, the Germans having amassed strong force all along the Russian frontier. No further reports today of impending invasion.

22 October

Another foggy and relatively quiet night. Had breakfast at 7 am and left for Hendon at 7.30 am. On arrival there was told that visibility all the way to Newcastle was limited to 50 yards and unlikely to clear. I therefore gave up the idea of going north and went to office instead. As there was not much doing there went to club for lunch and put in some shopping. Piccadilly looked very sad and completely blocked where the 50/- fruit shop and the church have collapsed into the road! Paget returned off leave this evening. No more news of impending invasion, but still sufficient rumours to make it quite possible still.

23 October

Another quiet and peaceful night with little bombing owing to fog. Left club at 8.30 am and proceeded to Littlehampton where I met Bulgy Thorne, Brocas Burrows and Sandy Lawrence. The latter commanding the 201st Infantry Brigade, consisting of 4 new battalions who have just taken over beach defences between Littlehampton and West Wittering. Good battalions that promise very well, but require more officers. Returned London 6 pm and went to office till 7.45 pm.

24 October

Another quiet night with little bomber activity, and not much doing during the day. Is this the lull before the storm?! Tomorrow is supposed to be a dangerous date from the point of view of the moon and tide. We have had no further intercepts of any importance, and the weather is certainly unfavourable for the launching of any large scale attack. And yet it would be unwise to surmise that all was safe! It is just possible that under the cloak of Hitler's visit to Franco on the Franco-Spanish frontier, when all eyes are directed in that direction, that a sudden blow might be launched at England!

I have spent a day in the office with a series of interviews and preparations for my air-borne exercise at the Staff College.

25 October

Another fairly quiet night. Left here at 8.45 and motored to Frinton and Clacton to inspect the 233rd Bde. Massy and Money met me there also. Not quite as good a show as the 201st Bde. Got back to St Paul's School at 5.30 pm and put in 2 hours work in the office before returning to the club. Germans rather more active again tonight.

26 October

After spending the morning in the office and lunching at St Paul's proceeded home for 7 days' leave!

31 October

Had to proceed to London for a conference of Cs-in-C held by the PM in the Cabinet War Room. Meeting was attended by Chiefs of Staff, First Lord of Admiralty, S of S for Air, all Naval Cs-in-C, C-in-C Home Forces, C-in-C Ireland, and all Air Cs-in-C. We sat from 11 am to 1.15 and again from 3 pm to 5.15, but as far as I could see achieved little! The main subject of discussion was desirability of freeing more destroyers to hunt submarines in the Western Approaches. The Navy for the present seem to have the conviction that they are far better qualified to handle the Army than we are! Personally I wish they would concentrate their efforts on controlling the naval forces!

4 November

In the evening I went over from Ferney Close to the Staff College to watch a rehearsal for air-borne exercise I was to direct the next day.

5 November

Left home 9.30 am and motored to Staff College. At 10 am started exercise which I ran till 4 pm with an interval for lunch. On the whole I think we derived some benefit from it. Then motored back to GHQ with Dill and discussed plans generally with him. Finally put in 2½ hours in the office before going back to club. A quiet night so far except for a few distant bombs. But last night he hit the poor old Naval and Military Club, also the Ritz and the Green Park underground station.

6 November

Struggled the whole morning with files and various interruptions. At 12.30 Sir Findlater Stewart [PUS India, on special duty] came in to discuss Warren Fisher's plans for clearing demolished houses in London. We both came to the conclusion that Warren Fisher's present plans had little hope of achieving anything and that the baby would inevitably be handed back to the army to nurse! This is not a pleasant prospect as it is certain to spread to the provinces with further demands for help. Morrison (Minister for Home Affairs) came to lunch with me and was interesting, having only recently taken over the Home Office he does not quite know where he is yet. After lunch General Corap, Chief Liaison Officer with foreign contingents came to see me, and we discussed role of Polish and Czech contingents. Finally Williams came and discussed defensive arrangements. The usual heavy bombing started early and as we were driving through Green Park at 8.30 pm two bombs whistled in the near distance. I hear that the Naval and Military Chambers were blown in and two of the occupants wounded. It is lucky I had transferred myself from there to the Army and Navy Chambers!

7 November

A bad night with German planes hovering over, continuously overhead between 11 pm and 3 am, followed by a dull day in the office. Visits by Dorman-Smith and by Rusty Eastwood in the morning. In the evening dined with Bertie, a great Godsend to have these occasional dinners with him as a complete change and to be able to discuss with him fully all I am doing.

8 November

Left the Club at 8 am and proceeded to Hendon, which we found wrapped in fog. We had to wait till 10.45 for it to clear up sufficiently to admit of taking off. I found [illegible but probably Sir John Maffey], our government representative in Dublin, also waiting to start for Ireland and had an interesting talk with him on the situation in Ireland and the effect of Winston Churchill's last speech in the House concerning naval bases on the west coast of Ireland. I did not have my usual Flamingo, presumably owing to the fact that 2 of them have recently been crashed. They gave us instead a Lockheed machine which was slower. I flew to an aerodrome just NE of Norwich where I was met by Osborne and Beckie Smith. I visited 3 of the new Brigades which have replaced the 18th Div and flew back to Hendon by 4.30 pm. Went to St Paul's where I put in 3 hours work.

Up to now the Boche has been a little bit quieter presumably owing to mist and fog in France. However an odd machine keeps turning up and the thump of bombs can be heard periodically. It is a queer life knowing that bombs are being carted about the sky over one's head and may be released at any moment! The pictures of the demolished houses we have seen recently occasionally rise up vividly in one's mind and one can only thank God for the providence that guards over one, and leave the whole matter in His hands.

9 November
A morning in the office followed by lunch with the Lord Mayor at the Mansion House on the occasion of Lord Mayor's Day. I sat with Sinclair (S of S for Air) on my right and the Dean of St Paul's on my left. Winston Churchill made a very good and interesting speech with many references to the election of President Roosevelt and the present attitude of America. He was followed by the Archbishop of Canterbury proposing health of the last Lord Mayor. After lunch I returned to the office and worked till tea when I went home for the weekend!!

10 November
A *very* happy Sunday spent with you, including a visit to Mattingley Church in the morning.

11 November
Left Ferney Close at 8 am, worked from 9 to 1 in the office. Then lunched with Kirke at the Rag to discuss Home Guard in factories. After lunch back to the office where I had long discussion with Taylor who is at present running the bomb disposal squads and the working parties clearing bomb damage in London. All making great progress. In evening went to dine with Dill. Anthony Eden was there also but had to go off early as PM was having Chiefs of Staffs meeting to discuss Greek situation. Are we again going to have 'Salonika Supporters' like the last war. Why will politicians never learn the simple principle of concentration of force at the vital point, and the avoidance of dispersal of effort? Pouring rain and now a lovely quiet night with no bombers!!

12 November
After a lovely quiet night left here at 8.30 am for Ipswich where I attended a skeleton exercise of the 15th Division. A very useful exercise judging by the number of mistakes I saw! Got back to the office at 5.30 pm and put in 2½ hours work before coming back to the club, with some more work to do tonight. Nasty clear night with very bright moon and German planes fairly active.

13 November

A relatively quiet night considering the brightness of the moon! Motored down to the Thames Estuary to inspect the 221st Bde. Met Bulgy Thorne, Val Pollok [43rd Division] and Jumbo Goschen. The latter delighted at Geoffrey having been given an MC in Egypt. The Brigade was commanded by a queer specimen called Gotto, who had been commanding Dover defences up to now. Returned to the office by 5.30 and put two hours into the office. Dirty wet night and no bombing so far!

14 November

A quiet night again mainly due to weather. Spent morning in office with repeated interruptions saying goodbye to Gubbins and welcoming Maltby, the new commander of air force working with Home Forces. Also looked at invention of new mortar. Then lunched with Findlater Stewart who has asked Bevin (Minister for Labour) to meet us. I found him very interesting and most amusing. Apparently much enjoying pulling the leg of the other members of the Cabinet. Then returned to St Paul's where I saw Revell-Smith's mock up of his armoured Bofors. A very good model. Then back to WO to attend Army Council Meeting at 4 pm. Here we discussed the manpower situation and possibility of raising additional divisions to replace any withdrawn from this country. Remained in the meeting till 6.45 pm! Then a few words with Pope and back to St Paul's where I remained till 8 pm. A nasty clear night but so far Boche has not been excessively active.

15 November

Left club at 8.15 am to fly to Weymouth, but found Hendon wrapped in a pea soup fog. No hope of clearing before 12 noon. I therefore abandoned hope of going and proceeded to the office where I good full day's work. Finishing Appreciation of Defence of this country and plan for the defence next summer allowing for withdrawal of troops to other theatres. Heavy rain storms predicted for tonight, a good thing as the moon full! Coventry was badly hammered last night – 1000 casualties.

16 November

A real unpleasant night, and from midnight to close on 5 am there was almost incessant bombing of the vicinity of the Rag! The Orleans Club only about 150 yards away was hit, another dropped at bottom of St James's St, two in St James's Square, one in Duke St, 2 in Lloyds bank (Cox and Co), 1 in the Carlton and one in Hamptons besides several in St James's Park! Hamptons caught fire and burned merrily most of the night with noisy arrival of fire engines. I got up to look out of the window, it was a weird sight looking east to see the end of the street one blaze of flames and made it hard to realize this was London in 1940!

Got up feeling very sleepy, spent day in the office and at 5 pm started for Ditchley Park, Enstone (near Oxford) owned by Ronnie Tree, and where the PM was spending the weekend instead of Chequers owing to the full moon and the fear of night attacks by bombers. I dreaded the thought of being kept up till 2 am by the PM in my sleepy mood!! However I slept in the car on the way out and the evening went off better than I had hoped for and I was in bed by 2 am. House party included Brendan Bracken, the PM's Parliamentary Secretary.

17 November
Left Ditchley Park at 9 am and drove straight down to Ferney Close where I spent one of those heavenly Sundays with you and the children.

18 November
Left at 8 am and arrived at St Paul's shortly after 9 am. No Chiefs of Staff meeting. At 11.15 went to WO to see German war films. Then lunched at Savoy with Geoffrey Lloyd, head of Petroleum Ministry. After lunch went to see Petrol film showing Flammenwerfers etc. Then picked up my bag at the Club and moved into my room at St Paul's to see whether I can have a quieter life here! My bedroom is in the house of the Headmaster. With a little more furniture I shall be able to make it fairly comfortable.

19 November
My first night at St Paul's School was very comfortable and quiet with not even the sound of a bomb! After breakfast motored to Newbury to visit the 214th Bde which is eventually to move to the Isle of Wight. A good show. Finished up with tea in the Royal Box of the Newbury Race Course where one of the battalions is billeted! Came home and did a couple of hours work before going to dine with Bertie Brooke in his flat in Chesterfield House. We lamented that the Orleans Club was no more, but had a v.g. dinner!

20 November
Spent day in the office reading up appreciation we are preparing for the defence of the country next spring. Lunched at the Club and had my hair cut. Then selected birthday present for the Mr Ti. So far night is fairly quiet although unpleasantly clear, but the moon period is passing over.

21 November
In the morning had visit from 'Ugly' Barratt (who has just taken over the new Army Air Command) and Auchinleck who was on his way to Dill to be told that he was to be C-in-C India.

I then went out to Richmond Park to see demonstration of new methods of dealing with bombs that have not exploded. Most interesting methods of burning through casing with thermite, also of burning explosive without detonating it, and of breaking bomb open with plastic explosive without detonating it. Showman was Lord Suffolk, a queer specimen who has been buccaneering about the world mining in Australia and working before the mast. He introduced me to what he classified as the other members of the 'Holy Trinity' and who consisted of his so-called secretary lady [Miss Morden] and his mechanic [officially chauffeur, Mr Harts]!*

In afternoon motored to Staff College where I ran rehearsal of seaborne exercise and then went home to Ferney Close for the night.

22 November

Left home at 9.30 for the Staff College where I ran exercise from 10 am to 5 pm. It was very well attended and on the whole a success. Should form a good basis for further exercises in other Commands. Finally drove back in Dill's car. He confided to me that his wife is now very very ill having had a stroke and is paralysed on one side and unable to speak properly! It is pathetic, he is urgently in need of a rest, cannot I think face going home for a week's leave, and if he goes elsewhere he feels he must go visiting troops as he can't bear doing nothing and being left with his thoughts! He finds the P.M. very difficult to deal with and I feel that he is having a miserable life and do wish that I could think of somehow of providing a rest for him.

As far as Churchill was concerned, it would have been impossible for those two men to hit it off together. They were poles apart in all their outlooks on life. Dill's character was too fine and highly tempered to be able to put up with the 'gangster' transactions of politicians. It all jarred on him, and put him on edge. He had already had a part of his career ruined by Hore-Belisha, and now he foresaw that his final downfall from favour was imminent. Beaverbrook filled him with horror, and he found it hard to hide these feelings. There is no doubt that Beaverbrook did much to poison Winston's mind against Dill. In fact, whilst returning from the first Moscow mission, in the cruiser on the way home he told Pug Ismay that he considered that it was high time that Winston got rid of Dill, and that he would strongly recommend the appointment of Tim Pile in his stead.

Possibly if Dill had had a happy home life at that time he could have weathered the friction with the politicians better. As it was, every visit to his wife in Windsor was a desperate ordeal, she could not make herself understood, he kept guessing what she could mean, usually unsuccessfully, and finally with a disappointed look in her eyes she used to throw her head back on the pillow.

---

*There is a marvellous portrait of Suffolk and the Holy Trinity in Michael Ondaatje, *The English Patient* (London: Picador, 1993), pp. 184ff.

23 and 24 November

Finished work early so as to arrive home in time for Mr Ti's birthday party and to spend a weekend in perfect paradise with you. When I am with you 3 I can forget all about the war temporarily and it is such a rest and a relief.

25 November

An early start for Salisbury to join Monty at his Corps HQ and to take part in his preliminary Corps Conference of the big exercise he is about to carry out. A very interesting exercise embodying the use of an armoured div, a motorized div and an armoured bde, plus parachutists.

After lunch I said a few words to the meeting and then drove back here for another 2 hours office work. Had tea with Mrs Paget on the way home.

26 November

Spent morning in the office catching up work of weekend and of Monday. Lord Trenchard came to lunch and to discuss with me steps he was taking to rehabilitate the army in the eyes of the country. He is quite right: it has become far too much a habit to run down generals and the army in the press. After lunch attended a Selection Board meeting in Dill's office. Am now ready after dinner to start by night mail for Newcastle for a 2 days visit to Adam in Northern Command. The impossibility of continuing our regular flying at this time of the year makes it far harder to get about visiting the army as I ought to.

27 November

Left King's X at 11.50 and had a good run up to Newcastle where I arrived in time for breakfast. Met Adam and proceeded to North Shields visiting Home Guard observers post on the way. Spent day seeing coast defence gunners and new brigades, with visit to Northern Command Company Commanders School on way back to York. Tea in Adam's office and there discussed various points with him till dinner. Then home to his house to spend the night.

28 November

Early start for Spurn Head where I visited coast defences and then worked north, seeing new Brigade and X Corps school. From Bridlington returned to York where I visited MT School in York. I then caught 5.50 train back to London and only arrived at King's X at 3.15 am!! 5 hours late on a 4 hours run!! This was due to air raids in Liverpool which caused train to run dead slow.

29 November

Spent the day in the office. Anthony Eden came to lunch with us and was very interesting on his trips to the Middle East by air. Went to see Dill at 4 pm and spent 2 hours with him only getting back to St Paul's at 6.30. Several people to see me before I slipped off home for the night and to shoot with Bertie Fisher next day.

30 November
Went to Bertie Fisher's house at 8.10 am. Lovely frosty day. We had quite a good day, getting 33 pheasants and 2 woodcock.

1 December
At home with you.

2 December
Left Ferney Close at 8 am, put in an hour's work at GHQ and then went on to Chiefs of Staff meeting. Bertie Brooke then picked me up and took me out to Hendon aerodrome for lunch, where I subsequently inspected his anti-aircraft light automatic school. A very good show that wants establishing in all Commands. On returning Michael Barker came to see me. Finally left for Ferney Close to spend night there before going on to Monty's exercise. Paget motored down with me.

3 December
Paget picked me up at 7.30 am and we motored to Tilshead where we met Montgomery. We first of all saw the use of parachutists. 32 were dropped by 4 planes from a height of about 500ft, only one man was slightly hurt by twisting his knee. I was very much impressed and feel certain that we must develop an Airborne Brigade with the least possible delay, probably in Canada. I then went to see the Armoured Division advancing on Marlborough, on the whole moving fairly well. Then hunted for 4th Div, but without success as they were stuck in the mud on Larkhill ranges! Finally attended Monty's conference in Burbage and spent the night in the Forest Hotel, Savernake.

4 December
Made an early start to join Monty and looked up Swayne who had had a hard night of it sorting out the 4th Div. Then visited 10th Inf Brigade before closing down of exercise. Returned via Ferney Close where I had lunch. Spent rest of day in the office catching up on last few days.

5 December
Spent day in office. Gen Lee (American Military Attaché) came to see me in the

morning prior to his sailing back for the USA. Nosworthy then came to discuss his Officer Training week and to ask me to give them a talk about our retirement to the sea. Quiet evening so far and the all clear has just sounded at 10.15 pm. A record!!

6 December

Left GHQ at 8.30 am and proceeded to Pevensey Castle where I met Hughes commanding 219th (new) Inf Brigade. I went round his 4 battalions with him finishing up just west of Newhaven. Lunched with a Colonel Gwynne (late Mayor of Eastbourne) who gave us an excellent lunch! Got back about 5 pm and after 2 hours in office started for Ferney Close, where I arrived for dinner.

7 December

Went to Winchester where I attended Monty's V Corps conference on the big exercise he has just concluded. The conference was in the Odeon cinema and absolutely packed, at least 800 officers! Monty gave a first class discourse and I said a few words after him. Got back for lunch.

8 December

Spent Sunday at home with you. Mr Ti a little better from his flu. Lovely sunny day.

9 December

Left Ferney Close at 8 am and dropped Ronnie at [illegible] on the way back. A very busy morning in the office. In the afternoon conference by Anthony Eden on the new Army Cooperation Command of the Air Force. Archibald Sinclair attended and Freeman from Air Ministry. Deplorable situation as regards any cooperation generally. No machines, and not likely to materialise for some time. Proposals for training Bomber Command Squadrons also quite inadequate. On returning had long interview with Q. Martel who has just been appointed Commander of the Armoured Corps. His appointment should assist to get a move on.

10 December

Held an Army Commanders Conference which started at 10 am and went on till lunch. Adam, [Guy] Williams, Finlayson, Auchinleck (and Alexander who is taking over [Southern Command] from him), Bertie Brooke, Findlater Stewart, Ugly Barratt and Maltby attended. I discussed reorganization of home defences to cover impending withdrawals to the Middle East. For lunch Dill entertained us all including the whole Army Council. After lunch Dill gave us a talk on the world situation. I then caught the 7.30 pm [train] for Dundee.

11 December

Arrived at 6.45 am in Dundee, freezing hard and very cold! Bath and breakfast in the hotel and then reception of Kukiel [Commander of Polish Forces] and Sikorski, followed by Guard of Honour of Poles outside hotel and then continuous guards of honour, marches past, salutes, inspections and introductions from 9 am to 6 pm!! In between periods with Sikorski maintaining conversation in French with him: very interesting in parts but very exhausting! We were given a Polish lunch where I had to say a few words with a Polish interpreter. The day was unfortunately marred, as guard of honour which was to have been at Perth station met with an accident on the slippery road and killed one man and injured 2 more very seriously. Returned to Edinburgh and spent night with Carrington.

12 December

Started at night and visited one of the new infantry brigades. Also made full enquiries in the case of Lancaster, the CO of the 9th Foresters, who has been giving trouble. Then inspected Command Company Commanders School. Dined with Carrington and caught 10 pm train for London.

13 December

Train only arrived at 10.35 am, namely 3 hours late! Had no breakfast as I was due to attend conference of Anthony Eden's at 10.30 on armoured forces. After this conference had a busy day in the office. Fog and a quiet night. News of Egyptian success has had a cheering effect on all.

14 December

After a morning in the office went to the Staff College Camberley for the first rehearsal of our big Armoured Div Ex. There were several points to be put right. After tea went to Ferney Close.

15 December

Spent Sunday at home with you.

16 December

Left Ferney Close at 8 am, arrived office 9 am. Put in morning in the office and then went on to lunch given by the Army Council to the Canadian Defence Minister. Sat between Andy McNaughton and Sir Horace Wilson [Head of Civil Service]. Returned to the office where I worked till dinner time.

17 December

Left 8.30 am and motored to [illegible] where I spent the day with Crocker inspecting his 6th Armoured Division. It is beginning to take shape and should be good. Finished about 4 pm in Warminster and motored back. Arrived here 6.45 and put an hour into the office before dinner.

Rumours again fairly strong of German preparations for an invasion within the next few days.

18 December

Office in the morning. Then lunch at Dorchester to meet High Commissioner of Canada and the Defence Minister of Canada. Following were there: Beaverbrook, Alexander, Sinclair (S of S of Air), [illegible], Norman (Bank of England), Dill, Joubert de la Ferté, Dudley Pound, McNaughton, Crerar, etc. Sat between [illegible] and Duke of Devonshire. After lunch went to cinema to see Charlie Chaplin as a dictator, a wonderfully good propaganda film.

19 December

Proceeded to Aldershot to visit 38th Div with Snow, its commander. Division making very good progress. Had lunch at Div HQ in the 'White House' Upper Hall, the old 1st Guards Bde HQ. Returned to GHQ about 4 pm, worked till dinner time when I went to dine with Bertie at his flat.

20 December

Sholto Douglas (C-in-C Fighter Command) came over in the morning and discussed with me the co-operation of fighter aircraft in the event of invasion. Early lunch and motored over to Oxford to stop at New College for the final day of Nosworthy's Corps Exercise. Not a very good exercise, and one showing want of education in the use of armoured forces. Dined with dons in Hall and slept in one of the undergraduate rooms.

21 December

Gave a lecture on the part played by the II Corps in the operations in France prior to Dunkirk. This finished Nosworthy's Officers' Week. I then left for Ferney Close where I had a hurried lunch with you and then went on to shoot with Bertie. An amusing afternoon in which we got 13 pheasants.

22 December

Spent Sunday at home with you.

23 December

Left Ferney Close at 8 am. Arrived office 9 am and put in a good hour's work before going to Chiefs of Staff meeting. Returned here to see Lancaster commanding 9th Foresters whose battalion I have moved from Scotland to the 1st Armoured Division, owing to trouble he had in 46th Div. Then seeing King and Martel. Lunched at Savoy with Defence Minister of the Netherlands. Prince Bernhard was also there. Anthony Eden, Dill, and Haining from the WO. After lunch drove Anthony Eden back to WO to say goodbye as he leaves to take up appointment of S of S for Foreign Affairs. A great pity and a great loss to the WO. Attended Selection Board conference in CIGS room till 6.30 pm with one interruption of Army Council meeting to greet new S of S [Capt David Margesson, formerly Chief Whip] and say goodbye to old one. Finally returned here to work until 8 pm in the office. German bombers over London.

24 December

Finished off office work till lunch time. Then drove round past Hamley and Kodak [shops] on my way home for Xmas. Arrived in time for tea with you, and a lovely evening preparing stockings for children.

25 December

Xmas day with you.

26 December

Left Ferney Close at 9.30 am. Guy Williams came over in the morning to discuss training of Eastern Command. Dupuy, the Canadian Envoy to the Vichy Government, came to lunch with me and was very interesting about his interviews with Pétain and the attitude of France generally. He was with me for ½ hour in the office before lunch and explained to me French reaction to the treatment of their fleet. Ugly Barratt came at 3 pm to discuss equipping of army co-operation squadrons. At 5 pm went to see Dill where I remained till 7.45 pm!!

27 December

Proceeded to Camberley early in the morning and spent most of the day going over my Army Commanders' Course on Armoured Formations. I think it promises fairly well, and with luck ought to be of good value. Germans started bombing London again tonight after Xmas spell of peace.

28 December

Spent morning in the office polishing off remnants of work and after lunch started off for Ferney Close. These weekends are an absolute God send! You cannot imagine what it means being able to completely forget the war and all its worries for a few hours.

29 December

Spent Sunday with you and the children, namely occupied filling up the new coal cabinet!

30 December

Left Ferney Close at 8 am and motored up to St Paul's School. Spent morning in the office with various visits finishing up with one from Eastwood to discuss Home Guard and its terms of service which are not yet satisfactory. Crerar came to lunch and I then discussed future Canadian contingents with him. Apparently a 3rd Canadian Div and an Army Tank Brigade to be ready in the spring. Afterwards an Armoured Div to follow towards the end of the year. After lunch attended Selection Board meeting at the WO which lasted until 6.30 pm! Came back to finish off office work.

31 December

Left here at 9 am for Bedford to inspect the 37th Infantry Brigade. Delayed by fog and heavy traffic on the road and arrived about 20 minutes late. Met there by Osborne [44th Brigade] and Lovat who commands the brigade. Got back here about 6 pm and did office work until dinner time.

There are now only 45 minutes left to complete the year 1940! One of the years which will be handed down through history as the year Germany overran Europe, backed by Italy which stepped in at what she took to be the 11th hour, but which so far has not proved to be quite the end of the war. Dunkirk will take its place amongst the many examples of disasters due to political misappreciations of the requirements of war. It should also rank as one of the finest recoveries from disaster. I feel, however, that the air battle for England and the German defeat in its attempt at invasion will probably loom as one of the greatest successes of British arms, which will for ever remain famous in terms of the PM's incomparable sentence: 'Seldom in the field of human conflict have so many owed so much to so few'!

Personally I feel that it is the year of my life in which I have had to shoulder the heaviest burdens and face the greatest responsibilities. Looking back at the year in retrospect one fact looms large above all others, namely your influence on my life. You, and just what you represent in all that is most holy and divine on this earth. You, and your influence on my whole outlook on life and the hereafter. You, and your sublime exterior calm and confidence in God, which has every day increased my confidence and belief in Him. If I have succeeded in shouldering my burdens so far, 90% of the credit is due to you and what you mean for me. I thank God for one thing above all others in life, and that is for having allowed me to meet you and thus realize what perfection could be realized on this earth.

The year 1941 began with the fears of invasion abated. The winter was now setting in, and any form of sea borne attack was highly unlikely until the spring or early summer. It was however, impossible to estimate what form the war might have taken by then. My task as Commander-in-Chief of Home Forces was, however, quite clear. The Home Army must be welded into an effective force capable either to repel any invasion that might be launched against these islands during the year, or to form part of Expeditionary Forces in whatever theatre it might be decided to launch offensive operations.

This breathing space, with no immediate fear of invasion, was indeed a welcome one. There was an infinite amount of work required to fit our army for its future role. Units were only partly trained, equipment was still very short, especially in armoured forces, formations required a great deal of running in, army-air co-operation was practically non-existent, and most important of all, higher commanders required a great deal of training and weeding out before real efficiency could be achieved.

1 January 1941
Spent morning in the office. New Zealand Troop Commander came to say goodbye. Maude (Education) came to discuss education. New Secretary of State [Margesson] came to lunch. Keen and energetic and I should say ambitious, very interested in all we were doing. In the evening gave lecture to the GHQ staff on the operation of the II Corps in France. Weather turned bitterly cold and am suffering from heavy cold in the head which makes life less attractive for the present.

2 January
Left Hendon by air for Liverpool at 11 am. Weather bitterly cold and the country below covered in snow. Met by Copper [Finlayson] and visited one of the new Beach Inf Brigades with him. Then inspected his new battle headquarters [Western Command] and remained in his office with him till 8.30 pm. He then had Andy, Duncan and his GSO1 all to dinner to meet me. Lady F and Mary F also there. Streaming cold and feeling rotten.

3 January
Left at 9 am to visit Junior Leaders' School, Company Commanders' School and one battalion (KOSB) of the 5th Div. Weather still bitterly cold and my cold in the head streaming. Caught 3 pm train from Crewe, arrived Euston 3 hours later with nasty head produced by cold.

4 January
Moved into my new office near Cabinet War Room (under Office of Works). A very good office which should do well in the event of trouble. We are also to have one floor upstairs, but this is not ready yet.

The headquarters was deep down in the basement of the building and covered over with a thick apron of reinforced concrete. As part of it was under the large well in the centre of the building, this space was filled with several layers of anti-submarine nets to explode bombs on the way down. All offices were well fitted out with special ventilators, telephones, message conveyors, map rooms, etc. It was in every way an excellent battle headquarters, with only one fault, namely its proximity to Winston!

Said goodbye to Chevenix-Trench the signals officer and welcomed new one. Ralston the Canadian Defence Minister came to lunch and we had a useful talk. Came home in the evening.

5 January

Morning at Ferney Close and in evening went on to Staff College for the big exercise on armoured forces that I am running there. All C-in-Cs of Commands, 4 Corps Commanders, and all Armoured Div and Bde Commanders are attending. Gave opening address after dinner. Very large gathering: all 5 Army Commanders, 6 Corps Commanders and all Armoured Div Commanders and Armoured Bde Commanders. After opening address we had a lecture by MI [Military Intelligence] WO on German Armoured Divisions.

6 January

Lecture in the morning on armoured division organization, signal layout and administrative organization. After lunch demonstration of parachutists, gliders, bridging and various types of armoured vehicles. After dinner Dill came from WO and gave an excellent lecture. He was in better form than I had seen him for a long time.

7 January

A hard day! Started with Ritchie on air co-operation and spent rest of the day on running over Armoured Div exercise. I found it a heavy strain listening to successive answers and making up criticisms and serving up remarks as we went along. Snow and very cold.

8 January

Finished up final situations of armoured exercise and then had my final remarks. The latter gave me an opportunity of instilling a little more offensive spirit into the Army and also of expressing my views as regards the present stagnation of higher training. Lunched at Club, spent afternoon in office. Quiet night with no bombing due to weather.

9 January

Spent day in the office catching up on back work. Nasty clear moon lit night and Germans active again.

10 January

The PM held one of his quarterly conferences of Cs-in-C of the three Services. Attended by the 3 Secretaries of State, all Naval Cs-in-C, all the RAF Cs-in-C, Pownall [Northern Ireland], Pile [Anti-Aircraft] and self, besides of course the Chiefs of Staff and Pug Ismay. Only 3 points put up for discussion, two of which were mine, so I had a busy time. My points were connected with the increased danger of invasion owing to Axis reverses in the Mediterranean, and danger of withdrawal of too many forces from this country.

During the discussion I raised the lamentable lack of arms that still prevailed after 1½ years of war. Shortage of rifles, .303 ammunition, tracer ammunition, Boys rifles and their ammunition, anti-tank guns, tanks, armoured cars, etc etc. This did not please Winston at all, and after the meeting he complained to Dill that he considered it most ungrateful of me to complain of lack of equipment after all that had been done for me! Considering the period we had been at war, I consider that I had every right, and indeed it was my duty, to draw attention to the shortages that prevailed.

Conference lasted till lunch time. I then had heated argument with Tovey as regards employment of Home Fleet in event of invasion. Lunched at Club, did office work in the afternoon, and then dined with Bertie in the evening.

11 January

After morning in the office lunched with Jimmy Harrison and then headed for home where I arrived in time for tea.

12 January

Spent day at home with you.

13 January

Left 8 am, very foggy driving back. Lunched with Paget, Findlater Stewart, and the Editor of *The Times*. Quiet night so far with no bombing up to the present.

14 January

Bertie Brooke picked me up at 9.30 am and we spent the day going round the 24th Independent Brigade Group, commanded by Fraser. Mostly south of London in the Purley-Wimbledon area. Returned to the office in the evening and put in a couple of hours work before dinner.

15 January

Spent morning in the office and left in the afternoon for Ferney Close to attend Armoured Corps Conference at Minley Manor on next day. Snow had started to fall and road was bad.

16 January

Joined up at Minley Manor [Hants] at 9 am for start of armoured exercise. Run by 'Q' Martel. Large assembly of all commanders of Armoured Divisions and Army Tank Brigades. Returned home about 6 pm.

17 January

Another similar day at Minley Manor. The exercise is proving very good value and should do a great deal to help to bring on the Armoured Corps.

18 January

Armoured Corps exercise finished shortly after 1 pm and I returned to Ferney Close where I spent afternoon carpentering. More snow falling.

19 January

Spent most of the day carpentering. Snow stopped.

20 January

A dark and wet start at 8 am from Ferney Close. Attended a Chiefs of Staff meeting to discuss handling of refugees in event of invasion, probable use of gas by Germans, desire to restore signposts by Admiralty, and proposals for me to take over again the Orkney and Shetland Islands. Did office work during afternoon.

21 January

Started at 10 am to visit 55th Div. Found them busy doing a divisional TEWT [Tactical Exercise Without Troops] which finished after lunch. We then motored to Batsford Park (the home of Lord Dulverton), where 55th Div have their HQ. Dulverton came to dinner. After dinner I had to pay him a visit. Very cold and slushy snow all over the Cotswold Hills still.

22 January

Did a tour of inspection of the 55th Div till about 3 pm and then motored back to London to take part in our large scale Home Defence Exercise which began today. We have moved the whole advanced GHQ into our battle HQ and I am sleeping in my battle dug out next to my office for the next 3 nights. So far in the exercise the Germans have invaded the Canary Islands, Iceland and Ireland.

23 January
Home Defence exercise in full swing all day with invasions developing all over the coast from Scotland to Devon. Headquarters running smoothly.

24 January
Another day of hard fighting in the exercise! The S of S and the C-in-C [CIGS?] came round in the afternoon to see how the exercise was going.

25 January
Closed down the exercise at 1 pm and went home for the weekend. Glad to get out of the stuffiness of my underground office and bedroom.

26 January
Sunday at home mainly spent in carpentering and blowing my nose owing to a cold.

27 January
Office during the morning and then visit to XI Corps HQ for an exercise of 15th Div. Weather very wet and cold. Spent night with Massy at his HQ.

28 January
Up at 6.30 am to watch march of 15th Div in the dark. Very unpleasant day and cold in my head bad.

29 January
Cold better. Spent day in the office with conference at the War Office at 4.15 pm to settle details concerning split in Eastern Command and organization of my 7 new County Divisions. Lunched with Jimmy Harrison and Mrs Harrison.

For some time I had been worried by the fact that Eastern Command, which covered the main danger area, was far too large to be controlled efficiently by one Commander. It covered the whole of East Anglia from the Wash to the Thames, and the South Coast from the Thames to short of Portsmouth. The Thames and London itself split this area in two and made intercommunication difficult, and the lateral movement of reserves slow. Guy Williams had been commanding this large front since the beginning, but I was not entirely happy about his methods. Being an Engineer, his mind naturally turned to the construction of defensive lines. Such lines might have been all right if we had the troops to man them, but we had not. What little troops we had as reserves I did not want to lock up in defensive systems. I wanted to retain them for a mobile role of an offensive defensive, ready to strike rapidly at any enemy that gained a foothold on our beaches. I decided, therefore, to split Eastern Command in two on the line of the Thames, to retain Williams in command of the Northern Sector for the present, and to place Paget, my Chief of Staff, in command of the southern part. I selected Budget Loyd to succeed Paget. I was criticized by many for this decision owing to the fact that Budget had had a nervous breakdown during our retreat to Dunkirk. However, I knew all the circumstances of this breakdown and felt sure that Budget would not break down with me and that he would fill the job admirably.

30 January

Day in the office. Have now reached the stage where Paget is shortly to leave us and Budget Loyd take over from him the duties of CGS. Paget goes off to organize the new South Eastern Command. He will be a great loss at GHQ as he had been with it since its early days. Budget might however do very well, I am sure. Lunched with [illegible] at the Berkeley and discussed many things with him, mainly connected with the after war problems. In my mind these are going to be harder to solve than the actual war ones! Foggy weather and a few single machines over London during daylight.

31 January

Went to inspect the Eastern Command Company Commanders' School in Moor Park [Herts]. A good show doing very good work. After lunch Andy McNaughton came to see me about the misuse of the Canadian Corps during last week's exercise!! *(I had been forced, owing to the situation which occurred in the exercise, to split the Canadian Corps and employ one of its divisions in another Corps.)* Not according to the 'Convention'. However, with a little talk we settled the matter quite amicably and all is well now. However, the 'Constitution' does not make things easier and renders the use of Dominion troops even more difficult than that of allies!

I quote this as an example of McNaughton's warped attitude to this Charter. He had not sufficient strategic vision to realize that under conditions of extreme emergency no Charter could be allowed to impede the employment of troops from a purely strategic role.

1 February

Had rather a hectic morning in the office trying to finish off work rapidly in order to get off in time for lunch. Finally got off by 12.30 pm. Spent afternoon with you, going for short walk and doing some carpentering.

2 February

After a very long sleep got up to a lazy Sunday morning! Had to leave at 6 pm to go over to Chequers where I was due for the night. Arrived at 7.45 pm. Party consisted of PM, Mrs Churchill and daughter, Anthony Eden and wife, Attlee [Deputy PM], Professor Lindemann [PM's scientific advisor, 'the Prof'] and secretary. After dinner epidiascope [projector] was produced and I had to give a lecture on our recent Home Defence Exercise. They were all very interested in it and the PM very flattering about the defensive measures that had been taken. But he would not acknowledge that an invasion of this country on that scale was possible in the face of partial sea control and local air control.

He even implied that this had been done in order to influence him into considering the threat greater than it really was. I assured him that this was not the case, that no one connected with the exercise even knew that he would wish to be made familiar with it. I pressed on him the fact that from the umpires' point of view evidently it was essential to test out the defences with the fullest possible threat. Nothing that I said had much effect, his suspicious nature had been roused!

3 February
Left Chequers at 9 am and spent day in the office, finally dining with Bertie's ADC Ivan Cobbold at the Dorchester. Bertie was there, and the new First [Chief] Whip Stuart who has succeeded Margesson.

4 February
Left at 9 am to visit Home Guard commanders of Kent and Sussex. Met General Romer first of all who took me round. A grand lot of patriotic retired officers. Returned to War Office at 6 pm where I had an appointment with Dill. Remained with him till 8 pm discussing proposed cuts in Army Co-operation squadrons of RAF. I am not satisfied that the Air Ministry are transacting this business in an above board method. Also discussed promotions of Corps Commanders etc. And finally talked over the desirability of making the PM realize more clearly the impending threat of invasion. Apparently both Dill and Pound told him they considered invasion more than probable, but he preferred to believe Portal who considered it improbable.

5 February
A day in the office with visits in the morning and afternoon. First of all Findlater Stewart with draft of letter to Herbert Morrison to extract military labour which Warren Fisher is still employing for the clearing of London. Then Barker on the subject of the new police for guarding of vulnerable points. Then Lloyd (Minister for Fuel Oil) on the subject of means of lighting up the sea as part of the defence against invasion. In the evening had Basil [Brooke] (just arrived from Ireland) to dine with me at the Rag. Snowing again this morning.

6 February

Had to give up tour to Wales owing to bad weather. So visited Bomber Command instead to discuss role of bombers in the event of invasion. Had a useful discussion with him [C-in-C Bomber Command, AM Sir Richard Peirse] and had lunch with him. Remainder of the day in the office. Budget Loyd is taking over from Paget this week and promises to be very good.

7 February

Another day in the office and a busy one. Settling details for my next conference, my next Corps Commanders' exercise, examining all the details connected with our last exercises, interviewing Findlater Stewart as regards the evacuation of civilians in Kent and Essex sea coast towns. Received instructions to proceed to Windsor on Monday to run through last exercise with the King.

8 February

Office work in the morning followed by lunch at Rubens Hotel with General Sikorski. The lunch had been settled as a bargaining meeting in which the Poles were to try to extract equipment and especially tanks! I was given excellent caviar to soften my heart, but went away with the caviar and my tanks! I did however part with a few light automatics, MGs and Tommy guns. Then went to WO for interview with Dill as my new organization is temporarily stuck with finance!

9 February

Sunday at home with you. Your father there on a visit.

10 February

Went straight to Windsor Castle from Ferney Close for interview with the King, and to give him some details of our 'Victor' [home defence] exercise. He displayed great interest in all details, and was as usual quite charming. Then on up to London where I did office work till lunch when the Prime Minister and Pug Ismay came to lunch with us. He was in great form and did a complete tour of my headquarters after lunch. He finished up by inviting me to see his new flat in the building and we visited his study, sitting room, dining room, Mrs Churchill's bedroom, his room, kitchen, scullery etc!! (*He was just like a small boy showing his new toy and all it could do! He had certainly been very comfortably fitted out, and was just above the War Cabinet room, Map Rooms, Cabinet Staff, etc.*)

Finished up rest of afternoon in office, and am now waiting to catch the midnight train to Swansea, where I am going to inspect Belgians, 36th Bde, Beach Brigade and Linney Head Practice Camp for armoured forces.

11 February
Arrived Swansea at 8 am after a good train journey. Station badly damaged by bombing. Breakfast at the hotel and then proceeded along coast inspecting 224 Inf Bde, some beach defence gunners, and finally the Belgian contingent. They have made considerable progress but are not up to very much. Spent night at Imperial Hotel where Finlayson joined me with many notes in his book.

12 February
Motored on to inspect 36th Inf Bde and to meet Admiral, Coast Defence Commander, and Home Defence battalion Commander in Pembroke. Lunched with West Kents in Pembroke. Then on to visit battalion exercise in pouring rain through muddy fields. From there on to Area HQ where I met Arthur Main and Martin Graham. Finally reached Swansea 8.30 pm and after dinner at hotel caught 9.40 night mail back to London.

13 February
Arrived back 8 am. After breakfast to office for a hard day. First Chiefs of Staff meeting where I had heated arguments as regards control of Orkney and Shetland Islands. Also use of Special Companies in event of invasion. After lunch had to attend meeting of Secretary of State's to disentangle hopeless mess WO had made of my proposal to raise County Divisions for defence of beaches. Things looked bad for a bit as S of S had not got clear picture and had been influenced against scheme by PUS [Permanent Under Secretary] owing to bad handling of case by AG and QMG, and especially by Bob Haining who is quite useless as Vice Chief of [the General] Staff. He understands nothing about military matters and messes everything up. However I have now got the matter passed by S of S and all is well, except the time unnecessarily wasted. The plan was originally submitted to the WO on Dec 15th and it is now Feb 13th and not yet through.

14 February
Left here at 8.30 am and motored to vicinity of Eastbourne where I met Bulgy and proceeded with him in a Bren carrier over the Downs to watch a divisional advance by the 56th (London) Division. We then dropped in on Oswald Birley for lunch, where I saw his daughter for the first time. It was great fun seeing him again. After a very good lunch watched more of the exercise and then motored back and put in 2 hours in the office, returning here at 8.20 pm. A long day.

15 February
Had a long morning in the office and left for Ferney Close after lunch.

16 February
Spent day at home with you.

17 February
Returned early and spent most of the day in the office with a Selection Board in the afternoon. Unfortunately Dill is away, having left with Anthony Eden for the Middle East. He is likely to be away for 3 weeks and meanwhile Bob Haining officiates for him! A poor substitute and one who may well make some mistakes and will want watching. Luckily I do not think that an invasion is imminent. I think that the Germans are more likely to start with heavy attacks on Western Approaches by submarines and long range bombers combined with heavy bombing of Western Approach ports, namely to try to achieve a victory through strangulation as opposed to direct attack. Such a procedure even if unsuccessful would pave the way for invasion.

I have … always considered from the very start that our participation in the operations in Greece was a definite strategic blunder. Our hands were more than full at that time in the Middle East, and Greece could only result in the most dangerous dispersal of force.

18 February
A hard day. Started a conference of Commanders in Chief at 10 am and did not finish till 4.30 pm. Secretary of State came to lunch with us. At the end of conference had to comfort old Johnson for being retired from age, then attended lecture from 5 pm to 6.30 pm followed by day's work till 7.45. After dinner did 2 hours on our next exercise for Corps Commanders.

19 February
Did a final run over next big exercise I am running at the Staff College. Then an interview with Barratt, concerning his difficulties with Portal. Then at last finally left for my 3 days leave at home.

20 February
Spent most of the day carpentering.

21 February
Went to Hayling Island with Q Martel. There we met PM and S of S, also [Guy] Williams, Paget, Nosworthy etc. Had an interesting morning watching experiments of various methods of overcoming tube scaffolding erected in the sea or on land as an obstacle against invasion. Depth charges most successful against obstacle in sea. On land, tank succeeded in shooting its way through at close range. PM in good form. Got back shortly after 2 pm.

22 February
Busy carpentering, making combination for cine [camera] and Astro lens.

23 February
Church in the morning. In the afternoon experimented with my new Astro lens and the fitting I made to put cine Kodak onto it [for bird watching].

24 February
Left early and put a day in the office. Lunched with Lloyd, Minister for Oil Production. Hankey and Pug Ismay also there for lunch. After lunch proceeded to Shell Mex building to see films of petrol used as a weapon on beaches by lighting up the sea or the beaches.

This device sounded most promising, but in actual fact was never really successful as it was too dependent on the state of the sea. Even the smallest of waves precluded its use....It was very evident that Lloyd was anxious to 'sell' some of his ideas and to gain credit for his Ministry!

25 February
Left King's X at 10 am for York where I arrived at 1.40 pm and was met by Adam. We then proceeded in direction of Bridlington to watch exercise carried out by 2nd Division. Very cold and whole country covered with snow. Returned to York and put up with Adam.

26 February
Left 8.45 for far side of Leeds to visit 8th Armoured Division. Found the division going on well under Dick McCreery. We toured through Ripon and Catterick where I visited the AA wing of Northern Command Weapon Training School. On way back to York called in on Ronnie Stanyforth's home and met his mother. Another very cold day.

27 February
Left again at 8.45 am for Lincolnshire, to see exercise of 1st Division near Louth. A poisonous day! Bitterly cold rain and sleet driven by a north wind that was sweeping over a snow covered country. It was not an interesting day as Kenneth Anderson failed to find most of the units we were to see. Finally reached Doncaster in time to catch the 3.40 from Doncaster. However, train was 30 minutes late there and 1½ hours late by the time we reached London!

28 February

A very busy day in the office, with Lord Croft [Under Secretary WO] to lunch. Left about 5.30 pm for Camberley where I inspected preparations for 2 day armoured div exercise which I am to run. Then on to RMC [Royal Military College] for dinner and opening remarks. All Army and Corps Commanders were present.

1 March

First day of exercise lasting from 9 am to 7 pm.

2 March

Finished off exercise by 12 noon and went on to Ferney Close. Exercise seemed to have been a success and enjoyed by those who attended. I think that these exercises which I have run during the winter have done good in educating formation commanders as to how to handle their commands in the event of an invasion.

3 March

Returned to London early and put in day in the office. Chiefs of Staff's meeting in the morning. Dudley Pound is quite the slowest and most useless chairman one can imagine. How the PM abides him I can't imagine.

4 March

Left 9 am and motored with Otto Lund [MGRA] to visit gun defences of Dover, Deal, etc. Was met by Paget and Bulgy Thorne. We visited 9.2" and 12" railway guns and the new 5.5" coast defence guns. I went into the problem of the concentration of the fire of the super howitzers on the beaches in the event of a landing. Lunched with Bertie Ramsay in Dover Castle and met his wife for the first time. Then inspected 9.2" gun mountings. Also 'Winnie' and 'Pooh', the two guns that fire across the Channel into France. *(These guns were great pets of Winston, but to my mind the purpose they served did not warrant the personnel they absorbed.)*

Returned to Canterbury for the night, and arrived just in time to visit the cathedral before dark. In the half light it looked quite glorious. After dinner discussed with Bulgy various problems connected with the defence of his Corps.

5 March

Carried on with inspection of guns and amongst others saw 18" railway howitzer. It is mounted on the carriage I had with me in the last war with a 14" gun. The battery commander produced a photo of King George V on the mounting at an inspection in France in 1918 [at] which I had been present. When I returned I heard that Colonel ['Wild Bill'] Donovan (one of Roosevelt's envoys) wanted to have an interview with me. He was most interesting, had just returned from a tour round Bulgaria, Greece, Turkey, Yugoslavia and Spain. He gave me his appreciation which he was sending on to the President to read.* Dined with Bertie.

6 March

Spent in the office with Trenchard to lunch. Have now moved up in our new flat where we are very well established. Invitation to go to Chequers next weekend.

7 March

Spent day with Home Guard. Left 9 am with Rusty Eastwood and returned 6 pm, after visiting Home Guard units of Essex and Hertford. General Deedes took me round. A real good lot and most efficient from what I could see of them. Came back to office and had long interview with Portal and Freeman on the question of who should act at Home Forces as my link with the RAF. Unsatisfactory situation.

8 March

Spent a busy morning in the office including an attendance at the Chiefs of Staff meeting. As this matter concerned the garrison of Orkney and Shetland which I had previously settled, it did not take long in spite of Dudley Pound's inefficiency as Chairman! Came home in time for a late lunch. Spent afternoon fixing up my new Astro Tele Lens attachment for the Kodak Special Cine.

9 March

Spent day at home. In the evening departed for Chequers at 6.15 pm. Arrived there at 7.45 pm. Houseparty consisted of PM, Mr Menzies (PM of Australia), Sandys and his wife, PM's youngest daughter, Professor Lindemann, Sec etc. PM suffering from bronchitis came down to dinner in his 'siren suit', a one piece garment like a child's 'romper suit' of light blue! He was in great form, and after dinner sent for his rifle to give a demonstration of the 'long port', which he wanted to substitute for the 'slope'. He followed this up with some bayonet exercise! Had talk with Menzies after dinner and found him easy to get on with. Luckily PM decided to go to bed early and by midnight I was

---

*The legendary Donovan, soon to become head of the US Office of Strategic Services (forerunner of the CIA), had been on a semi-secret fact-finding mission, escorted by a senior member of the British War Cabinet secretariat, Brigadier Vivian Dykes, who reappears later in the diaries. Dykes kept a diary of his own, including a revealing account of 'The Donovan Trip'. See Alex Danchev (ed.), *Establishing the Anglo-American Alliance* (London: Brassey's, 1990), pp. 17–65.

comfortably tucked away in an Elizabethan four poster bed dated 1550! I could not help wondering, as I went to sleep, what wonderful stories the bed could tell of its various occupants during the last 400 years!

This evening remains very vivid in my mind as it was one of the first occasions on which I had seen Winston in one of his really lighthearted moods. I was convulsed watching him give this exhibition of bayonet exercises, dressed up in his romper suit and standing in the ancestral hall of Chequers. I remember wondering what Hitler would have made of this demonstration of skill at arms.

10 March

Left Chequers at 9 am all covered with a couple of inches of snow. Spent day in the office, with various visits from Gen Kirke, Air Marshal Barratt, Admiral Sir George D'Oyly Lyon, etc. Found Ronnie Stanyforth had had a narrow shave Saturday night by being in the Café de Paris when it was bombed and some 30 people killed! Brocas Burrows had also been with him.

11 March

Left Hendon Aerodrome at 9 am and flew to Barnstaple, picking up Alexander at Old Sarum on the way. Very foggy and forced to fly out to sea over Bristol Channel. Met there by Franklyn (Cmdr VIII Corps) and proceeded to inspect 48th Div. Not very impressed by what I saw, rather a sleepy and pudgy division without snap or drive in it. During my wandering came through Sheepwash and over bridge on Torridge where I succeeded in letting a salmon slip back into the river after landing it! Lunched in Okehampton with A/T regiment. Finished up at Exmouth where we spent the night in the hotel.

12 March

Left early and proceeded to inspect the 50th Division. Bitterly cold wind. Found a more live concern than the previous day. Finally flew back from Western [illegible] aerodrome, very foggy and pilot first of [all] disinclined to take it on and was preparing to drive back. Arrived back in London 5.30 pm and went to office.

13 March

A day in the office. I was to have attended a Chiefs of Staff meeting in the morning which was subsequently put off. Hugh Elles, Regional Commissioner for South West England, came to see me before lunch. After lunch I had to pose for a series of photographs for the National Portrait Gallery and for the *Illustrated*. The Rumour Season is beginning to accentuate itself. Where are the Germans going to push next? I would not be surprised to see a thrust into Russia. In many ways this is far the most promising line of action. However, wherever the next thrust may be on the continent it is certain that the process of attempted strangulation will continue full blast with attacks on trade routes, Western Approaches, Western Ports and industry. And if these attempts are sufficiently successful eventually invasion will be attempted. Meanwhile the preparation of our forces makes good progress.

14 March

Put in an hour in the office, and then left for Hendon to fly to Gatwick to inspect No. 239 and 26 Squadrons. Lunched with 239 Squadron and then flew on to Odiham to inspect No. 400 RC Squadron. At 4 pm flew back to Hendon and back to office where I put in another couple of hours work. A lovely day with the first real feeling of spring in it. Made plane fly over Ferney Close on way home, but although we did a circle round the house I could not see any signs of either you or the family.

15 March

Attended Chiefs of Staff Committee to discuss Vice Chief of Staff's paper on invasion. A poor paper. Left for Ferney Close after lunch.

16 March

Spent at home working on cine with astro lens.

17 March

Left Ferney Close 8 am, motored to London, did an hour's office work and then motored on to Kettering for an Armoured Corps exercise for support troops. Was met there by Prince Henry and was put up by him for the two nights of this exercise. Found him very charming but not easy to make conversation with. However he did most of the talking after dinner and we were lucky to get to bed by midnight. I was given the state bedroom which Ronnie tells me was specially prepared for Queen Mary when she came to stop there. It was certainly very comfortable.

18 March

Left at 8.30 am to see remainder of exercise. A useful exercise which served to assist in forming a doctrine for the employment of the armoured forces. Left about 3.20 pm to stay with Prince Henry. Was shown the grounds, stables etc. After tea read paper till near dinner time. After dinner Prince Henry began to recall his memories of his last few days in France, and I thought we should never get to bed!! And it was only Ronnie who saved us at 1 am by suggesting that it was time to go to bed. I was interested to find how bitter he was about his treatment by Gort at GHQ in France. Apparently there was a great deal of friction towards the end.

I had heard a certain amount of this from Gort's side and knew that Prince Henry had got on his nerves towards the end. So much so that he had asked me to take him to my Corps for a spell, and to attach him to one of the divisional headquarters for additional experience. I had put him in the 4th Division with Johnson, and as far as I can remember he was still there when the Germans attacked. What surprised me that evening was his astonishing memory for details. In his description of various events he always went into long explanations of the most trivial details. Where he had been standing or sitting, which way he faced, how the furniture was placed, how wide the door opened, where his drink was, whether he had half finished it, etc, etc. All these small facts, which most people forget, seemed to impress themselves deeply in his memory.

19 March
Left at 9 am and spent the day inspecting the 9th Armoured Division with Brocas Burrows. It is making great strides and should make a grand division eventually. Returned to office 7 pm and put in a final ½ hour's work. Found from Budget that Bob Haining is messing up matters worse than ever at the War Office. I do wish to God that Dill would return from Egypt and pull matters straight again.

20 March
Spent day in the office with many interruptions. First Lindsell, Budget, and Mockler-Ferryman. Then Rusty Eastwood with 2 Americans who had been visiting the Home Guard. Then an interview with Taylor on the work of his bomb disposal squadron. After lunch a visit to the film of myself in my office saying a few words for the news reel. Tea time Prince Henry came, after which Ugly Barratt to discuss army co-operation. Finally document from War Office on further reorganization of the army which has kept me up till 11.30 pm preparing notes for tomorrow's conference by S of S at 10.30 am.

21 March
Attended WO at 10.30 for S of S meeting to discuss WO reply to PM's directive on future role of the army. I had only received this document at 7 pm yesterday evening. The whole paper was hopeless[ly] adrift and based on quite a wrong conception of the problems of defence of this country. If only Dill had been here he would have discussed it with me in its initial stages and the whole matter would have been simple. As it was I had to crash the whole paper and got S of S to agree that the whole thing required redrafting. He kept me back after the meeting to discuss replacing of Williams and Carrington. And then asked me whether liaison with the WO was not as good as it should be and I had to confess that had Dill been there the whole matter would have been treated very differently.

22 March

Spent a busy morning in the office and at 4.30 pm attended WO to discuss redraft of document I had not agreed with on previous day. Found it much better in its new form. Finally arrived home just before dinner, and found Mr Ti still in bed and sorry for himself.

23 March

Went to Sandhurst to take the Church Parade March Past and then went round to [illegible] Welsh's house. A good parade but a little spoilt by rain.

24 March

Left Ferney Close at 8 am. At 11.15 am went to S of S for about an hour to discuss probable replacement of Guy Williams and Freddy Carrington. I think I have now got the best solution and am going to discuss it with Paget this week to see how it would suit him, as it would mean replacing Bulgy by Monty.

For some time I had been feeling that a few changes in the higher command had become necessary. Guy Williams had been with Eastern Command since the beginning; though gifted with great administrative and organizing ability, he had not got that strategic and tactical flair so necessary for one commanding one of the most threatened fronts in the island's defence. I had decided to replace him with Laurence Carr, in whom I had great faith, but who unfortunately did not turn out to have the right qualities. In Scotland it had become desirable to replace Freddy Carrington, and I decided on Bulgy Thorne for this command, and replaced him by Monty to command that dangerous South East corner of England.

Kirke asked me to lunch with him at the Rag, and had Lord Melchett with him – the latter just back from America where he had been taking a part in munition making. Then selection board meeting at WO.

25 March

Left here for Hendon at 9 am. On arriving there was told that the aerodrome at Langham, where I was supposed to go to was not yet finished so they would take me to one within 6 miles. We started off and I could not fathom our course on the map nor make out where we were going. When we landed I asked 'Where is this place near?' the reply was Nottingham! About 150 miles from the Norfolk coast where I hoped to be! The mistake had arisen owing to another aerodrome being in process of construction with name like Langham. Nothing for it but to re-embark and fly on again to Langham, where I arrived a little late. There met by Osborne and Ozanne (commanding Norfolk Div). Spent day touring front with him, finally finishing up in Norfolk at 5.30 where I was to pick up the plane. Unfortunately one of the motors refused to start and I was stuck in Norwich for the night and put up by Ozanne. Car sent from London arrived at 1 am.

26 March

Left Norwich at 8.45 am and motored to point south of Ipswich where I met John Priestman and spent day with him touring round his Division – the Essex County Division. Very wet day and country all under water. Dined with Bertie who had the American Editor of the USA *Daily News* to dinner.

27 March

Spent day in the office catching up the last two days' work.

28 March

Got Paget to come up in the morning to discuss possible move of Bulgy Thorne to Scotland to replace Freddy Carrington. The King then came to lunch. I met him at the door, took him up to my room by lift. Discussed my dispositions and then took him down to the battle headquarters and from there on to the mess for lunch. He was as usual perfectly charming and natural and gave one the impression that he enjoyed his visit. After he left I went down to the Canadian Corps Staff College, a well run show.

29 March

Put morning in the office and came home in time for late lunch.

30 March

Spent at home.

31 March

Left Ferney Close 8 am and put in hard day in office with Chiefs of Staff meeting in the morning. Interview with S of S in the afternoon. Also many interviews.

1 April

Left here at 8.30 am for Portsmouth. Foul weather, went through 2 snowstorms with 1 inch of snow on Hogs Back and hills near Petersfield. Visited units in Portsmouth. Was very much impressed by the results of bombing on Portsmouth, the place has been badly smashed up. Too rough to use speed boat to Isle of Wight, so went by ferry boat. Did complete tour of island returning by Yarmouth ferry. Now 5 bns on the island and dispositions for defence seem good. Saw two more bn HQs on mainland and finally went to V Corps HQ to spend night with Montgomery who made me very comfortable.

2 April

Left at 9 am. Proceeded to Sandbanks where I inspected bn of Suffolks and then proceeded along coast line to near Exeter. Foul weather again. Finally flew back from near Exeter. Bumpy and unpleasant with very poor visibility. Returned to office for a couple of hours' work.

3 April

Attended Chiefs of Staff meeting in the morning and spent most of the rest of the day busy with office work. Bertie came to tea and I took him round the battle HQ.

4 April

Heard on midnight news that we had lost Benghazi! Not at all a healthy sign and it looks as if we have reinforced Greece at the expense of Tripoli front to a dangerous degree.

Left Hendon and flew to Netheravon where I was met by car and motored to Tilshead to inspect RAF Army Cooperation Squadron. Lunched with them at Clinton St Mary which filled my mind with thoughts of old Ralph Harrison and the exercises we used to run in that area. Then motored back to Netheravon and flew on to West England to visit another squadron. Finally flew back to Hendon and did an hour in the office on the way back. Just heard that I am to lose another tank brigade.

5 April

Put in a morning in the office and came home for a late lunch, and assisted in the erection of the chicken house in the afternoon.

6 April

A cold, wintery day which I spent mainly making brass fittings for the camera stand.

7 April

Left 8 am for London. Lunched with Kirke at the Rag, who had chairman of ICI to lunch. After [lunch] worked hard. Basil to dinner at the Rag with me.

8 April

Motored over to see Williams's new Eastern Command HQ near Luton. Had long talk with him concerning his problems and troubles. Motored back and lunched with Ronnie in Cavalry Club. Then motored out to Wentworth [Cambs] to see our Rear HQ and to find out how our practice move to that HQ had gone today.

It consisted of deep dugouts with offices and sleeping accommodation and was linked to a general system of communication over England. Had I been bombed out of London during an invasion I could have moved to Wentworth and continued to control operations from there.

I hear Dill is due back on Thursday, am longing to have him back.

9 April
Spent morning in the office. Lunched in the club and then attended selection board meeting and after tea attended meeting of Sir John Anderson together with Minister of Propaganda, Health, Internal Security and Scotland to discuss evacuation problem of East Coast towns and also visits of holiday makers to East Coast towns. Dined with Bertie.

10 April
Left 9 am for Lewes to see 1st Canadian Div carry out an exercise with Canadian Corps Control. Andy McNaughton was in bed and Dempsey therefore took control. Rather depressed at the standard of efficiency of Canadian Divisional and Brigade Commanders. A great pity to see such excellent material as the Canadians being controlled by such indifferent commanders. Returned to office in the evening and put in two hours work.

11 April
After a day in the office I left at 5 pm for home and for 3 days' Easter leave.

12, 13 and 14 April
Spent at Ferney Close in a heavenly paradise of happiness and in oblivion of the war and its horrors and worries.

15 April
Left at 8 am. At 9.45 am I had a painful interview with Guy Williams who wanted to refuse the offer to proceed to New Zealand to look after the defences of that country. Dill came to lunch and I had a long talk with him. It is such a relief to feel that he is now back at the helm at the War Office.

16 April
Left here at 8.45 am. Took off from Hendon for Lincolnshire to visit Lincolnshire County Div. Met Carr (commanding I Corps), and Hay (commanding Lincoln Div). Spent day visiting units and defences, finishing up near

Grimsby from where I took off at 5.30 pm, landing Hendon 6.30 pm. Put in an hour in the office.

17 April

Held a conference of Cs-in-C beginning at 10 am and lasting till 1.30 pm. They lunched with us and after lunch Dill gave us a talk of 1½ hours on his recent trip with Anthony Eden to the Middle East. It was a wonderfully interesting talk. When I returned I was sent for by the S of S for a conference with him and QMG on the petrol situation which is deteriorating, and to discuss methods of effecting cuts. Not easy without affecting training.

18 April

Left 8.15 am for Dover where I met Bulgy Thorne and Charles Allfrey and went round with them defences of 43rd Div round from Dover through Walmer, Deal, Ramsgate, Margate, Herne Bay and Whitstable. Finally returned at 6.45 pm and put in an hour in the office.

19 April

Had a meeting with the Minister for Agriculture at 9.15 am to discuss with him the problem of neutralizing ground against hostile aircraft landings without interfering with agriculture. I found that he had an exaggerated idea of what we proposed to do. Then Jimmy Harrison came to lunch with me, and in the evening I went home for the weekend.

20 April

Another one of those perfect Sundays spent with you.

21 April

Left Ferney Close 8 am. Arrived office at 9.15. Spent an hour doing office work. Then attended meeting of Minister for Home Security (Herbert Morrison), attended by Minister for Health, Education, Food, Transport, Scotland etc. Not a very impressive gathering either to look at or to listen to! We were discussing desirability of allowing holiday makers to visit East Coast. From some of the arguments put forward one might well have imagined that no war was on! Monty came to lunch with me to be put in the picture of the new Corps he takes over from Bulgy. After lunch attended S of S conference till 5 pm. Followed by visits from Cory, concerning allied troops in this country, Maltby, concerning Army Cooperation squadrons, and Martel to discuss impending withdrawal of some 60 Cruiser tanks from this country for the Middle East! It is an appalling blow as far as the defence of this country is concerned. *(It was Dill's decision, and as it turned out, a right one, but a hard one for me to put up with at that time.)*

22 April

Left Hendon at 9.15 am for Plymouth. Had a grand fly, beautiful sunny morning with good visibility. Finished up by flying right over Dartmoor. Plymouth was still burning after last night's air raid! Landed at Rosborough aerodrome, having a look at Fort House while we were landing. Was met by Franklyn (VIII Corps), Morgan (Devon and Cornwall Div), Commander of Young Soldiers' Bn, Sailor commanding aerodrome, and Chief AT! Saw minor exercise near Rosborough. Then motored on to [illegible] Lodge to watch another company exercise. From there on to Slapton Sands, Dartmouth, Paignton, Torquay, Teignmouth and back to Exeter Airport, from which I took off at 5.30 pm for Hendon, where I arrived at 6.45. Then put in half hour in the office to pick up papers for tomorrow's Chiefs of Staff meeting.

23 April

Attended Chiefs of Staff meeting in the morning, followed by a lunch at the Rag to which the Wilkinsons came. It was a great joy seeing them both again. Then at 3.45 an interview with the Secretary of State trying to get him to adopt a firm attitude with the War Cabinet on the question of the probability of invasion. Finally motored down to Ferney Close for the night.

24 April

Attended an Administrative discussion run by Lindsell at the RMC Sandhurst. Very good value. Returned to Ferney Close about 7 pm.

25 April

Left Ferney Close 8 am for London. Morning in the office followed by Anzac Lunch at the Overseas Club. Sat next to de Lisle, was to have had Ian Hamilton on my left but he had a small stroke after the church ceremony. After lunch went to WO with Dill for long discussion. Lord Melchett and Kirke came to tea to discuss new explosive. Finally had dinner with Jimmy and Mrs Harrison at the Cadogan Hotel.

26 April

Put day in the office but left by car at 5 pm for Bury St Edmunds to see Eastern Command Ex with 6th Armoured Div, 42nd and 45th Divisions. After going through the scheme and having dinner motored over to XI Corps HQ to see Massy and to discuss his plans with him. Returned to Bury St Edmunds about 12.30 am.

27 April 1941

Got up early to attend 6th Armoured Division Conference. Good orders by

Crocker, but too slow in getting them out. Motored on to see 42nd and 45th Divs and after lunch saw bit of forward move of 6th Armoured Div. Had to leave early as I was due at Chequers for the night. Arrived back at 5.30 pm. When I had changed had tea and motored on to Chequers where I arrived 7 pm.

PM was broadcasting at 9 pm, so we had to wait for dinner till 9.50 pm. He was in great form after his broadcast and kept us up till 3.30 am!! Party consisted of Margesson (S of S), Kennedy (DMO), Pug Ismay, Professor Lindemann, Mrs Randolph Churchill, and Secretary. Kennedy tried to give PM a rather pompous discourse on strategy in which he contemplated a fairly free evacuation of Egypt! This infuriated the PM and we had some trouble calming him down! However I had good opportunity of discussing my troubles such as shortage of manpower, loss of tanks transferred to Egypt, danger of concentrating authority for destruction of petrol, danger of forming a multitude of detachments from main effort for such efforts as fire fighting, clearing of houses, agriculture, etc, which can equally well be done by civilians. Also pressed present very unsatisfactory air situation.

The Kennedy incident was a very typical one, poor old John had only intended to express that there might be worse things to lose than Egypt. It was, however, at once taken by Winston as being a defeatist attitude, and Kennedy was relegated amongst those 'many generals who are only too ready to surrender, and who should be made examples of like Admiral Byng!' The more Kennedy tried to explain what he meant, the more heated Winston got, and I was very thankful when we rose from the dinner table and went into the hall to discuss other matters.*

28 April
Left Chequers at 8.30 am. Spent day in office. Interviewed Bulgy prior to his taking over his new appointment as C-in-C Scottish Command.

29 April
Went to Bisley to see demonstration of new anti-tank weapons. Mainly based

---

*This was indeed a typical Churchillian soirée. Like most of those around the table, Kennedy too kept a diary. His account is graphic and chagrined. He noted at the time that AB did not intervene on his behalf, 'although I knew I had said nothing with which he did not agree'. His coda is equally pointed. 'Later, I realized the wisdom of the technique which Brooke acquired after many stormy passages with the Prime Minister. Brooke found it an invaluable rule never to tell Churchill more than was absolutely necessary. I remember him once scoring out nine-tenths of the draft of a minute to the Prime Minister, remarking as he did so, "The more you tell that man about the war, the more you hinder the winning of it."' Maj-Gen Sir John Kennedy, *The Business of War* (London: Hutchinson, 1957), pp. 104–8. See also Martin Gilbert, *Finest Hour: Winston S. Churchill 1939–41* (London: Heinemann, 1983), pp. 1070–71.

The unfortunate Admiral Byng was court-martialled for his irresolute conduct of an engagement with the French in 1756, acquitted of cowardice but found guilty of dereliction of duty, and executed by firing squad on his own quarterdeck. Voltaire interceded vainly on his behalf, and provided him with an immortal epitaph: 'In this country it is considered a good thing to kill an admiral from time to time to encourage the others.' *Candide*, trans. Roger Pearson (Oxford: OUP, 1990), p. 73.

on the new 'cutting explosive' and was very much impressed by the results. Am going to press hard for their rapid development, not only for protection of aerodromes and for the Home Guard, but also as an addition to Anti-Tank Regiments to replace paucity of 2 pdr A/T guns. Lord Melchett also came and I had interesting conversation with him concerning production of explosives. On way down caught up S of S who asked me to travel down with him.

30 April
After a day in the office moved to Headquarters South Eastern Command where I spent night with Paget.

1 May
Got up at 5.15 am to watch 1st Armoured Div exercise. Exercise was based on one I had carried out theoretically during the winter. Returned to office at 6 pm and after 1½ hours in the office dined with Bertie.

2 May
Spent the day visiting Area and Bn commanders of the Home Guard of Surrey and Hants. Starting Chichester and ending Southampton. The main meeting entailing a description of the present situation, role of Home Guard, questions as to their troubles etc. Returned 6.30 pm and put in an hour in the office.

3 May
Put morning in the office and then motored home for late lunch.

4 May
Lovely sunny day at home.

5 May
Left Ferney Close 8 am. Put in some time in office and then proceeded to 10 Downing Street for what the PM had called a 'Tank Parliament'. Consisted of PM, Beaverbrook, Duncan (Supply Minister) with 2 others, Crawford, Admiral Brown, Professor Lindemann, Margesson, Haining, Macready, Pope, Burrows, Norrie, Hobart, Crocker. Discussed production of tanks, possibility of acceleration, expansion problems, and organization. On the whole meeting was I think good value. Spent afternoon in the office.

It was a useful meeting, as it brought those responsible for the production of tanks in close contact with those responsible for commanding them in action. I was able to stress the importance of spare parts for tanks and spare tanks, but Winston always disliked the idea of the provision of spares, everything into the front window. Beaverbrook was even worse in his desire to establish high figures for production. This failure to provide adequate spare parts for tanks accounted for many of our failures and early difficulties in armoured fighting in North Africa.

6 May

Left here 9 am, motored to Wilton where I picked up Alexander, and we went to watch large scale exercise he was running which included 8th and 9th Armoured Div and 45th, 3rd and part of 4th Divisions. Went first to Fordingbridge area to watch 45th Division and was very disappointed at the performance of the new Div Commander (Morgan). I doubt very much whether he is good enough for the job. Returned to Wilton for tea, after which I fished in the Nadder till dinner. Spent night with Alexander.

7 May

Up early and off by 7.15 towards Marlborough to pick up 8th Armoured Div. Found Dick McCreery and obtained his plan from him. Back to [illegible] to watch first contacts, then back to Dick's HQ again. From there on to Lumsden's bn HQ at [illegible] Lodge, and Brocas Burrows's 9th Div HQ on Salisbury Race Course. After which lunch in Wilton and off to see 45th Div before coming home via Romsey and [illegible]. Half hour in office before meeting with Dill at 7 pm which lasted till 8.15 pm, settling successor for AG and for VCIGS which he wishes to change.

8 May

Morning in the office. Lunched with Jimmy Harrison at the Rag. On way back met Dill who took me off to War Office to discuss again the successor for Pownall as C-in-C Ireland. He is still hankering after Mason-MacFarlane, and I thought I had warned him off him for that appointment. He would be better retained with his Division a little longer as he has never yet commanded anything. Returned to office 5 pm for interview with Eastwood and Barratt and Martel. Finally leaving office close to 8 pm.

9 May

Very nasty feverish cold. Left Hendon 9 am and flew to Driffield aerodrome where I met Adam and Lawson and proceeded to inspect the Yorkshire County Division. Very cold wind but bright sun. Flew back landing Hendon 7 pm and proceeded for ½ hour to office. Did rapid change and then dined with Bertie.

10 May

Started day with S of S conference on manpower in response to memo I had sent in. Covered a lot of ground, but have not yet got at the source of the trouble ie that the quota of manpower at present allotted to the army is inadequate. Lunched with Martel and all Armoured Div Commanders at the Rag. Then went on with Martel to Luton to see the new heavy tank (some 35 tons), the A22, which is now nearing completion. Had a drive round and took over the steering from the dual control seat of the how[itzer] gunner. *(... found it very handy for its size, I even pursued a cock pheasant with it and chased it for some way through scrubby bushes.)*

Then visited factory to see tanks constructed on motor car principles. The tank promises extraordinarily well, I wish we had a hundred of them. Then motored on to Ferney Close.

11 May

A lovely peaceful day with you. Spent afternoon photographing blackbird with cine.

12 May

Left Ferney Close 8 am. Very busy morning in office. Lunched at Ritz with S of S to meet American Ambassador [John Gilbert Winant]. Was very favourably impressed by him. Evidently all out to do what he can to help. Even proposed to fly over to America and back to put production on a sounder basis. Then on to WO for conference with Dill and S of S on Air Co-operation. Barratt attended and I think we started matters in right direction. Followed up with Selection Board Meeting to select 3 new Divisional Commanders. Back to office for interviews with Martel, Lund and Loyd.

13 May

Spent morning in the office till 12 noon when I attended second Tank Parliament at 10 Downing St. Beaverbrook took the chair to start with when we discussed maintenance and spare parts. Next item was air co-operation and assembly was enlarged for this, consisting of PM, Beaverbrook, Lord Brabazon (Minister for Air Production), Duncan (Minister for Supply), S of S, Dill, Admiral Brown, Professor Lindemann, Martel and all AC [Armoured Corps] Divisional Commanders. Also CAS (Portal) and his awful satellite, Goddard. Before we had finished I became a bit heated and attacked the Air Ministry strongly, as regards recent attitude towards Army Co-operation. PM backed me strongly and meeting was a great success! Finished at 1.30 pm. I rushed up to Hendon, where I took off for the Orkneys at 2 pm. Had to drop a passenger in Glasgow so went by west route over Liverpool and close to Isle of Man. Only reached Glasgow at 6.30 pm including 4¼ hours flying. Told weather conditions were very bad so had to strike across to East Coast, hitting Dundee and working up the coast past Aberdeen and round via Lossiemouth and Nairn. Finally arrived at Inverness at 7.45 pm. Took off again in 5 minutes and after a very good fly landed at Kirkwall at 8.50 pm. Met by Kemp and Hancock. I then had to motor to Admiral's launch to proceed to Hoy to dine with Binney. There I found Tovey (C-in-C Home Fleet), and very good dinner and interesting evening with Tovey. Putting up with Binney in very comfortable Admiralty House on Hoy.

14 May

Discussed defence arrangements with Binney, then left with Kemp for main island and proceeded to visit two new aerodromes near Twatt and their defences. From there on to a cliff near Kitchener's Memorial, where we watched a peregrine falcon on her nest, also fulmars and guillemots. Back to Stromness for lunch, and then to Kirkwall aerodrome to emplane for Shetland. Very good fly over except for occasional snow squalls. After one hour fly landed south end of island and had tea with Black Watch. Then inspected defences of south end of island. From there to Cunningham's headquarters in Lerwick. After dinner at 9 pm started off for the bird sanctuary on the Isle of Noss. Blowing fairly hard and odd snow storm, but most interesting. Wonderful 600 ft cliff covered with gannets, guillemots, kittiwakes, and a few cormorants. Also fulmars in the air and an odd skua diving down onto the gannets. We took with us the Town Clerk who is a great bird authority and had worked with the Kearton brothers in the old days. Got back to Lerwick after 11 pm bitterly cold, but very interesting evening.

15 May

Left Cunningham's HQ at 9 am. The whole country white with snow! Inspected defences of Lerwick and the new road, finally reaching aerodrome at 11.30 am and took off in the de Havilland 'Rapide' for Lossiemouth. A good flight except for snow storms and landed just after 1 pm, having flown direct across the sea from Wick to Lossiemouth. Was met there by Neil Ritchie, and a real joy seeing him again. Bulgy Thorne also turned up. Spent rest of afternoon visiting units of the 51st Division. Unfortunately visit was somewhat spoilt by a snow blizzard which went on the whole afternoon. Finally finished up at 51st Div HQ for tea about 6 pm. Had intended to fish in the evening but weather far too cold to make it worth while. Met Mrs Ritchie in the Highland Hotel where I am stopping.

16 May

Left 51st Div HQ at 9 am, and proceeded to visit HQs of units of 51st Division. I found considerable improvement since my last visit, and Neil Ritchie making a first class show of the Division. Finally fetched up at Dyce aerodrome, near Aberdeen, about 4 pm. After tea took off at 4.20 pm and landed at Hendon at 6.25! Two hours and five minutes for the journey! There was a strong north wind blowing and we rose up to 11,000 ft and struck due south from Montrose to Berwick, and from there straight over the Cheviots. Very cold and ice formed on propeller when coming down through clouds, but plane was well warmed. Went straight to my office for half hour's work.

17 May

Spent the day in the office catching up back work. Ugly Barratt came to lunch with me and we discussed Army Co-operation expansion. In the evening came home for the weekend.

18 May

Spent at home with you, photographing starling from pantry and blackbird.

19 May

Left 8 am. Day in the office. Lunched with Budget and his wife, Lady Mountbatten also there who kindly invited me to fish Broadlands waters.

20 May

Left at 9 am and motored down to King's Castle, to HQ 47th Div, to spend day with Utterson-Kelso. I toured his front and saw one or two very good field firing exercises. Defence improving fast. Nosworthy came to dinner, and also Morrisson from Canadian Corps. I had a long talk to the latter concerning state of Canadian Corps.

21 May

Left at 8.15 am for the Romney Marshes to meet Monty Stopford (56th Div) and to tour part of his front. Spent a long time on the Dungeness front and not satisfied with Dungeness Point. Had lunch in Dymchurch redoubt. Then watched inter-company exercise. Finally tea with Monty before coming home for an hour's work in office before dinner.

22 May

Went to St Neots to see a bridging demonstration which was good value and introduced all the most recent productions. After lunch motored back and had interview with Ciriez and Liddell [Inspector General for Training] who is just back from Gibraltar.

23 May

Flew to aerodrome just far side of Ipswich (Martlesham). Was given the Duke of Windsor's 'Airspeed Envoy' a very comfortable machine. Met by Massy (Cmdr II Corps) and Oliver Leese (Cmdr 15th Div). Spent day working up coast towards Norwich visiting 15th Div units and defences. A very good show. Finally took off from Martlesham at 7 pm to fly back and landed Hendon shortly after 7.30 pm.

24 May

Spent morning in the office, with long visit by Barratt giving me the latest news about air support. Then lunched with Adam who was very full of what he was going to do as AG. Finally motored home.

25 May

Motored over to Bertie Fisher's house to see his keeper about a nightingale's nest and a hedge sparrow's nest with a cuckoo's egg in it. None of them yet hatched out, so waiting for next weekend. Then picnic lunch by river at Greywell, where I caught 4 trout weighing 5½ lbs. Finally took photos of [a] nuthatch.

*These occasional spells of bird watching did marvels as a means of 're-creation'. I was able for a short spell to forget the war [and] all the nightmare of responsibility. For a short spell I was able to step into that Sanctuary of Nature, which Sir Edward Grey describes so well in his Fallodon papers. A sanctuary unaffected by the horrors of war.**

26 May

Left 9.30 am to see motorcycle trials by GHQ Intercommunications Unit. Pouring with rain. Arrived office 12.30. After lunch conference with Bertie Brooke to settle details of composition of Guards Armoured Division. For the present various obstructions have been overcome and the show is sailing ahead.

27 May

A busy day. Morning spent in office and attending Martel's conference of his Armoured Division Cmdrs on the organization of our armoured cars and our Armoured Div. You came and had lunch and converted the day into one to be remembered amongst others. After lunch went to see S of S to discuss questions connected with air support of Home Forces. Finally attended one of the PM's Tank Parliaments where we discussed air co-operation, and also anti-tank weapons. PM in great form and on the whole a very successful meeting. It is

---

*See Viscount Grey, *Fallodon Papers* (London: Constable, 1928), p. 85. AB was introduced to this little volume by the American Ambassador, Winant, with whom he found himself in deep sympathy; the passage alluded to became one of his key points of reference. See 19 November 1943, and AB's Foreword to David Armitage Bannerman, *The Birds of the British Isles*, vol. I (Edinburgh: Oliver & Boyd, 1953), pp. xiii–xiv.

surprising how he maintains a light hearted exterior in spite of the vast burden he is bearing. He is quite the most wonderful man I have ever met, and is a source of never ending interest studying and getting to realize that occasionally such human beings make their appearance on this earth. Human beings who stand out head and shoulders above all others.

28 May

Left here 8.00 am, took off from Hendon in the Airspeed Envoy at 8.45 am. Very cloudy and flying at 3000 ft never saw the floor. Reached Newcastle at 10.20 am where I was met by Eastwood, who had just taken over from Adam (Northern Command), also Robin Money. We then toured Northumbrian coast up to just short of Bamburgh Castle. Finally took off from Acklington at 6.45 and did not reach Hendon till 8.45 pm. The defences of Northumberland are certainly alarmingly thin. But then the more I go round the coast the more I realize how desperately thin our defences are.

29 May

Morning in the office. First interview with Bertie Brooke concerning conversion of Guards Armoured Division. Then visits of Admiral Peters and his successor. Followed by Prince Henry who took both Budget and me round to Claridges Hotel where I gave lunch to General Sikorski and them. Sikorski was very interesting concerning his visit to Roosevelt and also as regards the situation in Europe, probability of German attack on Russia, Hess's visit, etc.

I always found Sikorski exceptionally well informed as to what was going on in Central Europe. His spy organization and contacts with Resistance groups in Warsaw was excellent. I remember on this occasion that he pulled out of his pocket a long strip of thin silk, about 5 yards long, on which was closely typed a long report from Warsaw. This had been brought out by one of his contacts, closely sewn in his jacket lining.

More office work and interviews. Finally dinner with Ronnie Stanyforth, his fiancée and his mother in law. The fiancée struck me as particularly charming, and should make Ronnie very happy.

30 May

Left Hendon at 8.45 am for Yorkshire to visit 11th Armoured Division. Very unpleasant day for flying with low clouds. Never saw the ground for the first hour and was flying in thick mist. Finally came in very low over aerodrome south of Catterick. Spent day with Hobo [Hobart], and found him in very good form and running a real good show. Motored from Leeds to Whitley and back to the aerodrome, where I took off at 6 pm, landing Hendon about 7.30 pm.

31 May

After morning in the office dashed home to wish you the very happiest of birthdays! My own darling. After tea went to see how cuckoo and nightingale were getting on. Put up hide for willow wren.

1 June

Church in the morning. Then took photo of willow wren. Nightingale not yet hatched out. Cuckoo hatched out but still a bit young.

2 June

Left Ferney Close at 8 am – busy morning in the office. Bertie came in to discuss the projected London exercise (ie attack by parachutists on London) which I want to try out. After lunch Philip Game, Gowers and Gale again to discuss the exercise. Afterwards went out to dine with Bertie.

3 June

Left Hendon at 10.15 for Birmingham where I was met by Lord Nuffield and went round the factory making the Mk VI Cruiser tank, and also inspected the mock up of the Mark VII Cruiser. A most interesting morning. Was given lunch in Queen's Hotel. Birmingham showing very appreciable signs of air raids! After lunch looked at factory producing carriers and a fuze. Landed back at Hendon at 4.20 pm. After tea had interview with Bridgeman concerning the Home Guard Bomb Disposal Squads. Then received call from S of S to come to him at 6.45 pm and for Dill to dine with him. So after finishing office work went to WO where Margesson discussed advisability of replacing Barratt by Stuffy Dowding! A doubtful advantage. Dined with Dill and then had good talk with him.

4 June

Spent the morning with Taylor in Richmond Park watching a demonstration of his Bomb Disposal methods and organization. He has made wonderful progress in the last 6 months in developing means and methods of overcoming delayed action bombs and of clearing away duds. After lunch went out to Stanmore to discuss with Sholto Douglas [Fighter Command] the question of protection of fighter aerodromes and also the question of fighter support for military forces in the event of invasion. I found him all out to help and full of assistance. It is a great help having worked with him for 2 years at the Imperial Defence College [1932–34].

5 June

Morning in the office with various interviews including one with Attlee which did not materialize. Then lunched with Astor at *The Times* Printing House. Delightful sort of private house dining room with oil paintings on the wall and very well served and cooked lunch. Sat between Astor and Dawson. Duncan (Minister of Supply) was also there. Then Selection Board followed by long interview with Barratt on reorganization of Army Cooperation Squadron.

6 June

Intended to fly to Nottingham and Liverpool but weather too bad so had to cancel. Spent day in the office. Had Adam to lunch and discussed with him the future of ADGB [Air Defence of Great Britain] and the possibility of it coming under Home Forces. After lunch Neil Ritchie came to say goodbye prior to leaving for the Middle East to act as vice Chief of Staff to Archie Wavell.

7 June

Escaped from office by about 1 pm and arrived home for late lunch. Before tea went to see grey wagtail's nest at Chadwick Healey House. After tea out to see nightingale and cuckoo with Bertie Fisher's keeper. Unfortunately cuckoo was dead! Keeper also had found sparrow hawk nest and spotted woodpecker.

8 June

Took photos of nightingale, grey wagtail, thrush and nuthatch.

9 June

Left Ferney Close at 8 am. Attended Chiefs of Staffs meeting at 11 am. In afternoon interview with Americans as to disposal of their first brigade if they come into the war! Also with the commander of parachutists to decide their use in event of invasion. Decided to go to Scotland by train instead of flying owing to weather being so bad. So leave by night mail.

10 June

Good journey up to Edinburgh where we arrived about ¾ hour late at 8 am. Breakfast with Bulgy and then out inspecting 52nd Division till 8 pm. Rosemary came to dinner.

11 June

Started early and finished inspecting 52nd Div by lunch time. Lunched with the Hamilton Dalrymples (Bulgy's sister) and owner of the Bass Rock. After lunch navy conveyed us to the Rock, preceeded by a minesweeper and followed by a relief ship! Glorious sunny afternoon and calm sea. Had a most interesting time on the Rock photographing gannets. Quite one of the most wonderful sights I have ever seen. Do hope photos will be good. Finally left aerodrome near North Berwick at 7 pm and flew back to Hendon in 1¾ hours!

12 June
Office all day. Interview with John Anderson in the morning to give him details of the proposed London air attack exercise. Lunched with Martel and commanders of armoured divisions. After lunch had interview with a Brigadier Inglis, recently returned from Crete fighting. He was useful in providing many details of the German methods of air attack.

13 June
Spent day in the office and left for home after tea. After changing went to meet Bertie Fisher and Musson, who had found a good spotted woodpecker's nest.

14 June
Nasty cloudy day with no sun and unfortunately bad for photography. Started by taking a colour spool of the grey wagtail in Chadwick Healey garden. After lunch got busy with the spotted woodpecker. As nest was some 30 ft up I had to use large Astro lens. Hope some results may be good in spite of bad light.

15 June
Left Ferney Close at 8.30 am. Picked up Barney in Guildford and went on to Horsham where I met Paget. Spent rest of day seeing large south eastern exercise in which Can Corps, 38th Div, 47th Div and 8th Armoured Div were employed. Gave special attention to Canadians and am not happy about some of their senior officers. Had a talk with Andy McNaughton on way home.

The more I saw of the Canadian Corps at that time the more convinced I became that Andy McNaughton had not got the required qualities to make a success of commanding the Corps. A man of exceptional ability where scientific matters were concerned, but lacking the required qualities of command. He did not know his subordinate commanders properly and was lacking in tactical outlook. It stood out clearly that he would have to be relieved of his command, not a very easy matter, as he had become somewhat of a hero in Canada.

16 June
Attended large meeting under chairmanship of John Anderson to study implications of my proposed large London exercise. Meeting attended by Herbert Morrison, Bevin (Labour), Llewellin (Transport), Morrison (Post Office), Margesson [WO], Woolton (Food), Philip Game (Police), Gowers (Regional Commissioner of London), James [P.J.] Grigg (PUS WO), etc. I opened by

explaining scope of airborne exercise on London, and explaining lessons to be derived from it. I was then questioned by each minister in succession, and in the end obtained unanimous agreement from all as to the necessity for such an exercise. Permanent Committee under Findlater Stewart is to be formed to deal with the minor difficulties to be overcome.

17 June

Office in the morning. At 12 noon one of the PM's meetings of his C-in-Cs, which in the long run turn out to be mainly a meeting of moth-eaten old admirals! The PM began with a survey of the world situation which was interesting. To my horror, he informed us that the present Libyan operations are intended to be a large scale operation! How can we undertake offensive operations on two fronts in the Middle East when we have not got sufficient for one? From the moment we decided to go into Syria we should have to put all our strength on that front to complete the operation with the least possible delay. If the operation is not pressed through quickly it may well lead to further complications. After the PM had finished he called on some of us to make statements and then the meeting closed.

Bertie Ramsay then came to lunch with me. In the evening I dined with Dill who had Stafford Cripps to dine. As he is just back from Moscow he is very interesting, but on the whole did not throw much light on the probability of military resistance on the part of Russia if pressed.

18 June

Left Hendon at 10 am and flew to Netheravon. From there motored to Larkhill to see demonstration of anti-tank weapons. I was disappointed with the standard raised and shall start a campaign to improve matters. Left Netheravon at 2.30 pm and flew back to London, changed, and then went to Savoy Chapel to attend Ronnie Stanyforth's wedding, and from there on to reception at the Savoy Hotel.

19 June

Started the day with Taylor and Findlater Stewart to discuss organization of Auxiliary Volunteer Home Guard Bomb Disposal organization. Made good progress. Then had interview with Oliver Leese as regards command of the Guards Armoured Div. You then came and we had a very happy little lunch together. After lunch I interviewed a Mr Glancy, an American businessman, on tank production in the USA and the desirability of instilling it with more drive. Finally attended the PM's Tank Parliament, at which I pressed for better spare parts organization and for the necessity of maintaining some 20% spare AFVs per formation. This was not appreciated by the PM, who likes to put the whole of his goods in the front window.

This was one of Winston's bad failings in which he persisted. Had he listened to me at this period we should have avoided a great deal of the spare part chaos which prevailed in Egypt at a later date, and which literally brought operations to a standstill. Unfortunately Beaverbrook aided and abetted in this false spare part outlook.

20 June

Left here at 8.10 am and took off from Hendon at 8.45 for Newcastle. Rather foggy fly up. Was met by Steele (commanding 59th Div) and Packenham-Walsh (who has just taken over IX Corps).

Spent day inspecting 59th Div, which has made great progress during the last year, since Steele took over. Finished up at Catterick and flew back from there at 6.30 pm. Whilst at Barnard Castle, saw some of Eves' last pictures, including the uncompleted ¾ length one of me which he was to have sent up to the [Royal] Academy this year if he had not suffered from paralysis.

21 June

Finished off office before lunch and motored off to Ferney Close. After tea went into hide to take sparrow hawk's photograph. Hen came and fed.

22 June

Julian [unidentified] came for the day. Had another go at the sparrow hawk.

Germany started march into Russia! And with it new phase of war opens up.

It certainly was a new phase of the war from my point of view. As long as the Germans were engaged in the invasion of Russia there was no possibility of an invasion of these islands. It would now depend on how long Russia could last and what resistance she would be able to put up. My own opinion at the time, and an opinion that was shared by most people, was that Russia would not last long, possibly 3 or 4 months, possibly slightly longer. Putting it at 4 months, and as we were then in June, it certainly looked as if Germany would be unable to launch an invasion of England until October, and by then the weather and winter would be against any such enterprise.

It therefore looked as if we should now be safe from invasion during 1941. This would put me in the position of devoting the whole of my energies towards converting the defence forces of this island into a thoroughly efficient army capable of undertaking overseas operations if and when such operations became possible.

We were now able to begin to think more offensively, and to begin to examine the problems of a re-entry into France, although such operations still lay in the dim future. We could, however, produce more formations for active operations in Africa.

23 June

Left Ferney Close at 8.30 am and drove to Odiham aerodrome where I took off for Norwich to see large Eastern Command Exercise. Spent whole day touring around XI Corps, II Corps, 45th Div, 1st Div, 46th Div and also attending conference to which both 6th and 9th Armoured Divs came. Finally flew back, making Hendon at 7.30 pm.

24 June

Left Hendon at 9.15 am for Cheltenham, where I was met by Bubbles [Michael] Barker and spent the day going round his division with him. On the whole was pleased with what I saw. Finally left Banbury at 6.45 pm and landed Hendon at 7.30 pm.

25 June

A day of continuous interviews! First Otto Lund, then Budget, followed by Liddell. Then Mountbatten who was most interesting about his experiences round Crete [commanding HMS *Kelly*] and concerning the fighting on Crete. Then a parade at the Horse Guards to inspect AA weapons for use with Armoured Forces. Lunch with you at the Club and took the Harrisons with us. Then after lunch Cericz [Liaison Officer] about Poles and Belgians, followed by Lewis about fire fighting organization, or rather lack of it. Then tea with Princess Mary [Princess Royal] who had been inspecting our Signals. After tea Budget again, also Young and Jack Gammon.

26 June

I ran a large conference of Commanders-in-Chief from 10 am to 1.30 pm. We then had lunch to which Dill, Grigg and Margesson came. Dill then gave us an excellent talk on the world situation which lasted 1½ hours. I then had interviews with Cave, Eastwood, Barratt and Alexander. And finally tried to finish off some of the work I had left undone yesterday.

27 June

Flew to Feltwell aerodrome, where I was met by Osborne (commanding II Corps) and Dempsey, who has just taken over 46th Div. Spent the day going round the 46th Div, a good show originally trained by Anderson, whose hallmark still exists in the division. In evening dined with Bertie.

28 June

Finished office by 1 pm and motored home. Tried to photograph sparrow hawk in evening but failed.

29 June

Spent day at home, photographing flycatchers, house martins and young sparrow hawks.

30 June

Left Hartley Wintney at 8 am. Spent day in the WO. Finally after dinner went to WO to meet Dill and Portal at 9.45 to discuss organization of air force to work with army. Did not get home till midnight. It is an uphill battle to try and get an adequate allotment of air force for the army!

1 July

Left at 8.45 am, but on arriving at Hendon found no plane, owing to an error of Ronnie's! However after ½ hour's delay they produced a Vega Gull usually flown by Balfour (USS for Air). Not so roomy as my usual Flamingo, but got us there all right, though late. Spent day with 42nd Div commanded by Miles. Massy also came round. Very hot and oppressive without a breath of air. A good division. Finally flew back from Bury St Edmunds. On arriving at aerodrome found my pilot had changed and that Herbert (the son of Air Commodore Herbert, agent of Duchy of Cornwall at Princetown), was to fly me back. He was lame and I asked him how he had done it, and he said as a result of a fall from a horse. It was not, however, till we landed at Hendon that I discovered that he had had to have his leg off due to the fall and was flying with a wooden leg!

2 July

I was to have visited 45th Division today, but was specifically requested by Dill to attend a Chiefs of Staff meeting connected with proposed raids on the continent. Unfortunately at the last moment the meeting was put off. However I put in useful day in the office, with meeting with Laurence Carr in the afternoon concerning scheme for having squadrons from Bomber Command. Afterwards visit from McNaughton about arrival of 3rd Canadian Division in the near future.

3 July

Spent day in the office, looking through lists of officers recommended for Divisions and sorting them out into some sort of order. Also making plans to employ 3" (20cwt) AA guns to engage 70 and 90 ton German tanks should any of these monsters be landed to overcome beach defences.

4 July

Left here at 8.30 am, proceeded to Canterbury where I met Horrocks, the new commander of the 44th Div. I discussed the dispositions of his division and then proceeded to inspect engineers bridging beach defences, Manston aerodrome, Ramsgate defences, the fort Julius Caesar used as his base when operating against Wales and Scotland!, field firing north of Sandwich, defences south of Deal, the new defences of Dover, and finally a ceremonial parade at Broome

Park, Kitchener's old home! Whilst watching the march past my thoughts wandered off to the accounts I used to hear of Kitchener and his plans for Broome Park. I could not help feeling how little Kitchener ever dreamt that Victor's brother would be inspecting a battalion on the sacred lawn of Broome Park. Finally returned here at 8.45 pm after a 12 hour day.

5 July

Short morning in the office and then home to Ferney Close. Discovered wryneck nesting in green woodpecker nesting box. Took photographs of him and of sparrow hawk.

6 July

Spent busily photographing wrynecks and sparrowhawks.

This was a great find and I proceeded to set up a hide and take coloured film. It may well be imagined that such an important event as a wryneck nesting in the garden put the war and all its troubles right out of my mind during those happy hours. I returned to my work a new man.

7 July

Left 8 am. Office work till lunch. Dill from 3 to 5. War film after tea followed by preparation of lecture for Staff College. Dined with Dill to meet Mr Fraser (PM of New Zealand). Then Defence Committee of the War Cabinet at 10 Downing Street to discuss aerodrome defence. Lasted till 1 am!! But did good work towards getting our man power quota somewhat increased.

8 July

The weather better than ever and a somewhat trying day. Started with an hour in the office. Then flew from Hendon to the 2nd Army Cooperation Squadron to inspect them (near Ware). After lunching with them, flew on to Newmarket to inspect another squadron. Heat oppressive. Flew from Newmarket to Farnborough through a thunderstorm and on to Staff College to give lecture on Home Defence. Poured with sweat during lecture! Then went on to Ferney Close for the night.

9 July

Left 8 am. Office work till 12 noon when I went to the PM's Room, House of Commons, to attend meeting of the War Cabinet. The subject to be discussed was my proposed London exercise to deal with a parachute attack. I had to make a statement as to the reason why I considered it advisable to hold the exercise and why we could not hold it as a theoretical exercise. I was supported by John Anderson, Herbert Morrison, Margesson, Sinclair and the Chiefs of Staff. All went well till Beaverbrook started pouring vitriol onto the idea. Purely owing to the fact that he has recently taken over the Ministry of Supply and cannot contemplate having his preliminary efforts interfered with! Attlee backed him owing to his fears of the effects of such an exercise on the public. The more I see of politicians the less I think of them! They are seldom influenced directly by the true aspects of a problem and are usually guided by some ulterior political reason! They are always terrified of public opinion as long as the enemy is sufficiently far, but when closely threatened by the enemy inclined to lose their heads, and then blame all their previous errors on the heads of the military whose advice they have failed to follow. The more I see of democracy the more I doubt our wisdom of attaching such importance to it! I cannot see how our present system of democracy can produce real qualified leaders of a nation.

I had perhaps had little experience of politicians at the time that I wrote those lines, and I was no doubt embittered by the results of the day. Our present system of democracy certainly did throw up one of the most wonderful national leaders of our history, Winston Churchill. One of his first acts, however, was virtually to convert that democracy into a dictatorship! Granted that he still was responsible to a Parliament, and granted that he still formed part of a Cabinet; yet his personality was such, and the power he acquired adequate, to place him in a position where both parliament and Cabinet were only minor inconveniences to be humoured occasionally, but which he held in the palm of his hand, able to swing both of them at his pleasure.

10 July

After an early breakfast I left for Hendon at 8 am. From there I flew to Netheravon to go to Larkhill to watch some anti-tank trials. Some improvement since I last saw them but much more improvement required. Took off from Netheravon again at 12.30 pm for London, where I arrived in time for late lunch. Office work and interviews till 6 pm and then I had to attend another Defence Committee meeting of the Cabinet. The subject for discussion was that of the defence of aerodromes. There is to be a secret debate in the House, and members of the Cabinet are expecting to be cross questioned on our dispositions. Hence considerable quibbling and attempts at defining the indefinable. Attlee made me nearly lose my temper, Margesson confused the issue in imagining he was clearing up matters. After 30 minutes of cross questioning and heating of the air, in the end I succeeded in pacifying them. But they did not rise in my estimation.

I remember always considering that Sir Henry Wilson's description of what he called the 'Frocks' must be exaggerated. Now I am surprised how true to life his descriptions are! It is impossible for soldiers and politicians ever to work satisfactorily together – they are, and always will be, poles apart. After the aerodrome defence we discussed assistance to Russia. Here Anthony Eden surprised me. As a late S of S for war he must know well what the army's situation is, and yet the proposals and suggestions he put forward might have been based on gross ignorance of the weakness of our defence of this country. If this is the best democracy can do it is high time we moved forward to some other form of government!*

11 July

Left here at 8.15 am and flew to St Ervan in Cornwall where I was met by Kenneth Anderson (commanding VIII Corps) and F. E. Morgan (commanding Devon and Cornwall Bde). Croft (commanding W. Cornwall Home Guard) also turned up. I then toured the defence with special attention to aerodromes. Touring round via Penzance. The defences of this end of England are getting too thin and I will not stand any further withdrawals. Finally took off from St Ervan shortly after 6 pm and was back in the flat by 8.15 pm, after another 12 hour day and 480 mile journey! Luckily the weather was cooler in Cornwall with a nice breeze blowing.

12 July

Put the morning in the office, and then motored to Fleet to see Mr Ti and to pick you up. Heavy thunderstorm in the afternoon, but succeeded in taking a few more photos of the wryneck.

13 July

Pouring rain. Visited Mr Ti in Fleet Hospital during the morning. In the evening rain cleared and I took more photos of the sparrow hawk. As usual she came to feed at 6.45 and remained for 30 minutes.

14 July

Left at 8 am and spent morning in the office. Raymond Lee, the American Military Attaché, and two of his assistants came to lunch. After lunch selection board at the War Office till tea. Finally more office work and interviews till dinner time.

15 July

Had intended to fly to Newcastle but weather was too bad, so caught 9.15 train to York instead. From there motored to Redcar and visited front of Durham County Division down to Scarborough. Finally motored back to York which we reached at 8.30 pm. Spent the night with Rusty Eastwood.

---

*The famous binary division was 'the frocks' (politicians, in frock coats) and 'the brass hats' (soldiers, in helmets). See Maj.-Gen. Sir C. E. Callwell (ed.), *Field Marshal Sir Henry Wilson* (London: Cassell, 1927).

16 July
Left at 9 am and motored to 1st Division where I spent the day seeing various exercises, finally finishing up at an aerodrome near Lincoln from which I flew back to London, arriving back here at 8.10 pm. At Hendon I met Lord and Lady Londonderry, who had just come over from Ireland and who were full of Basil's praise.

17 July
Left here at 8.30 am. Motored to Hendon where I joined up with Barratt and flew with him to West Raynham aerodrome. There we spent the morning watching a bomber squadron carrying out an exercise in close cooperation with the army. It was the climax of a week's training. Good progress had been made, but I was more convinced than ever that we cannot ever expect real close cooperation from bomber squadrons suddenly swinging from an independent role to that of close cooperation with the army. We lunched at the aerodrome and then flew on to Markham aerodrome to visit II Corps HQ and finally flew back to Hendon in time to put in an hour in the office before dinner.

18 July
Left here at 8.15 am and took off from Hendon for Cranage, near Crewe. Weather absolutely foul, had to fly at 2 to 3 hundred feet and even at that height lost our way. However finally landed and glad to find ourselves on firm land again. Met by Copper and Beckie Smith and proceeded round units of 18th Division. After lunch flew on to Speke aerodrome outside Liverpool. Finally flew back meeting foul weather outside London, and barely able to find Hendon aerodrome. Had received message that Dill wanted to see me so drove round to his flat to be told that more tanks were to be withdrawn from this country. Then proceeded to dine with Adam in Roehampton. After returning here had interview with Budget concerning withdrawal of Alexander from Southern Command for a special expedition.

19 July
In the morning Mr Thomas from Nuffield Works came with model of Bofors gun mounted on tank which I had asked him for. I had a meeting of experts to examine it, but as it cut across the cruiser tank production, I decided to mount it on wheeled vehicle for the present. Worked in office till 6.30 pm, then left for Chequers. As I arrived there at 7.45 pm Mr Maisky (Soviet Ambassador) was driving away. He had been there since 5 pm, and he had kept the PM from his evening rest, so I felt there was some chance of an earlier bed! But I was mistaken, and did not get off till 2 am!! However I did good work and succeeded in extracting 100,000 men out of the PM to make up my shortage. I only hope he keeps his promise after seeing Bevin! Mr Harry Hopkins, from USA, was also

there, I found him most interesting. The First Sea Lord (Dudley Pound) was also there, but not much more awake than usual. In addition Pug Ismay, another American, several others, Mrs Winston and Mrs Randolph [Churchill]. The PM in excellent form and very cheerful.

20 July
Left at 9 am and motored down to Ferney Close. Had another go at the sparrow hawk photography in the evening.

21 July
Left at 8 am. Had several interviews in the morning, including Paget and Alexander. The latter has just been pulled out of Southern Command to command 'Puma', the force intended for Atlantic operations. Sir William Spens (Regional Commissioner for East Anglia) and Sir Findlater Stewart came to lunch, after which I discussed with them points connected with evacuation of coast towns and undesirability of non-combatants joining in the shooting. Then visited Portal to settle details concerning RAF representation at my HQ which has been far from satisfactory owing to the Air Ministry up to now insisting on providing a representative in addition to Army Command RAF personnel. Then proceeded to see Beaverbrook concerning production of A/T ammunition for 3.7" and 3" AA guns to deal with large tanks should they be landed. After tea interview with Barratt to settle organization for handling squadrons from No 2 Group of Bomber Command in the event of invasion. Followed by Martel to settle details of PM's visit to 1st Armoured Division. Finally at 7.45 pm left for Ferney Close for 7 days' LEAVE!!

22 July
Have now been C-in-C Home Forces for 1 year and 2 days. Have flown just under 14,000 miles during that period and motored some 35,000 miles in my own car. As I have certainly done at least as much in other people's cars when touring round my total road mileage must be somewhere near 70,000 miles in the year.

Spent morning photographing bull finches.

22 to 29 July
Spent on leave at Ferney Close except for Tuesday 25th July when I motored to Tidworth with Martel to meet the PM. He was coming down to see the 1st Armoured Division to say a few words to them to let them know that he realized the losses they had sustained in having to send some 150 tanks to the Middle East. He then went to Beach's barn where the 3rd Division put up a very good field firing exercise for him. Finally motored back to Tidworth and had tea in Rifle Brigade Mess. Everywhere he had an astounding reception. He

drove in my car between troops lining both sides of the road. All of them cheering him as he went and shouting 'Good Old Winnie'. His popularity is quite astonishing.

29 July

Left Ferney Close this morning at 8 am and motored back to London with a distinct 'going back to school' feeling. Rather a sinking at heart at the thought of shouldering again the burden of responsibility and all the worries and doubts which endeavour to swamp one's mind and are not always easy to keep down. Those horrible question marks which seem to be everywhere at times! Have I really taken the proper dispositions for the defence of this country? Am I sufficiently insured in the South East? Can I reinforce this corner without taking undue risks in the North? Am I under appreciating the air threat? Ought I to further denude the beaches to cover the aerodromes? If I do am I opening the door to sea invasion? Will the air support be as efficient as the Air Ministry would like us to believe? How long will the Navy take to concentrate its forces in home waters? Shall we be able to hold the thrust of Armoured Divisions in Kent during this period?

These are all questions where a wrong answer may mean the end of life as we have known it in this country and the end of the British Empire! The PM last time I was at Chequers made a very wise statement. He said the human mind is like the 6 inch pipe running under a culvert, it is only constructed to take a certain volume of water, in a flood the water flows over the culvert. During the last two years I have frequently felt that my mind was unable to fully realize the volume and magnitude of events I was living through. It is a wonderful provision of nature, otherwise I do not know how one could shoulder heavy responsibility without cracking ere long.

Such periods of doubt and uncertainty must at times descend on all commanders bearing heavy responsibility. They are made all the more difficult to bear since it is essential that these inward doubts must never rise to the surface. Outwardly a commander must inspire confidence in all those serving under him, and equally to his superiors. How often have I seen Winston eyeing me carefully trying to read my innermost thoughts, searching for any doubts that might rest under the surface.

30 July

Left 9 am for Aldershot where I spent the whole day going round 55th Div. Returned London early to meet Dill at 6.30 pm. There I found Auchinleck, who had arrived last night from Egypt. I was there till 8.15 pm discussing High Command appointments. Then dashed off to dine with Ronnie in Putney.

31 July

Spent morning in the office. After lunch meeting in the WO with Dill and Staff on manpower situation. Then met Rollie Charrington, which was a real joy to see him home safely [from Greece]. Tea followed by interview with Ugly Barratt and Q Martel and some more office work took me up to 8 pm when I went to dine with Dill, Auchinleck (home from Egypt), was also there, and P.J. Grigg. Had an interesting evening.

1 August

Left at 8.30 am for Newhaven where I met commander of 2nd Canadian Division and toured front of Division, finishing off at Rye at 6 pm, and landed back here at 8 pm. Was agreeably surprised at the state of efficiency of this Division. They have come on a great deal lately and are I think better than the 1st Can Div now.

2 August

Spent the morning in the office and then came home for the weekend.

3 August

Spent day at house.

4 August

Left home at 8 am. I put the morning in the office, and in the afternoon went to see Anthony Eden at the Foreign Office as he wanted to discuss points connected with Home Forces prior to a speech of his in the House this week.

5 August

Left here at 9 am for Hendon. Very strong wind blowing and promised a bumpy trip to York, so it was! It took us 1 hour and 55 minutes to reach York instead of the usual hour. There I inspected the Army Cooperation Squadron and had lunch. Then flew on to Doncaster where I inspected another squadron and had tea. I then flew back and had another very bumpy trip, which proved too much for Malpy's [Maltby's] young RAF officer whom he had attached to me, and very nearly did old Barney in! Finally landed Hendon having spent some 3½ unpleasant hours in the air.

6 August

Spent the day with Monty going round one of his exercises and also having a look at the 25th Army Tank Bde. I am not very happy with what I saw of the latter. It is not up to standard and requires a change in its commander. In evening dined with Bertie, Hilda was there, and Rollie Charrington also came to dinner.

7 August
A dull day in the office with several visits and interruptions. Weather still cold and wintery.

8 August
Was to have flown to Boscombe Down but weather was too bad. Went by car and spent day there examining various new types of aircraft. All the large 4 engine bombers such as the Stirling, Halifax, Fortress etc, were there, which made it a most interesting day. Got back to office about 5.30 pm.

9 August
After a busy morning in the office left for Ferney Close after lunch. There I found you suffering from a bad cold and badly in want of a change and a rest. I hope you will soon get both.

10 August
Church in the morning. In the evening Bertie Fisher came over to discuss future CO of 17th Lancers, to replace one that had just been killed in an aeroplane accident.

11 August
Left at 8 am in deluge of rain. Interviews with Paget, American Engineer General, Bertie Brooke, and many others.

12 August
Left at 8.30 am for Hendon to fly to Weymouth. Had a lovely fly with wonderful visibility. Met at aerodrome by James Garnett and spent rest of the day with him visiting the 3rd Division, going through Dorchester, Blandford, Romsey, and finishing up to V Corps HQ in Lord Radnor's castle. In the evening went out fishing for an hour with Teddy Schreiber, but did no good.

13 August
Left at 9 pm and proceeded via Romsey, Christchurch, Winchester and Newbury, to inspect units of the 4th Div. Jack Swayne came along with me. Nasty cold day with a regular autumnal feel about it. Finally came back by Ferney Close to pack clothes for Scotland.

14 August
Spent a day in the office. In the evening dined with Lord Trenchard who had

kindly asked me to dine quickly with him to discuss the desirability of including a Civil Defence Member on the Chiefs of Staff Committee. He also wished to show me one of the last horrors committed by the Minister of Public Relations in the shape of a circular sent round on the question of Relations with the Press. I believe that it had Margesson's blessing, but must find out.

15 August

Had intended to fly around aerodromes to inspect young soldier battalions, but weather was again foul and quite impossible to fly in. I therefore only inspected our special photographic flight at Hendon, a good show commanded by a first class young airman. Rest of day spent in the office, studying our future organization.

16 August

Worked in the office till about 3 pm. Having interviews with Williams, who runs Soldiers' Welfare, and Marsh, who runs education, to try and settle ways and means of keeping the army occupied and happy during the coming winter. Went home to Ferney Close, which felt like an empty shell without life, owing to your being away.

17 August

Spent day at home and in the evening motored to London to get ready for tomorrow's early start.

18 August

Woke 6 am to find the country wrapped in deluges of rain. Thought that flying must be off, but got up on chance. Arrived Hendon 8 am, still in deluges of rain, but told it was only a 'minor depression'! and that weather up north was good. Started off at 8.10 am, barely able to see across aerodrome. However, weather soon improved and we had a lovely fly up over Durham, Newcastle, Berwick on Tweed, from where we struck right across over the sea to Aberdeen. From there to Lossiemouth and on to Wick, finally landing at Castletown at 11.15 am, having taken only 3 hours and 5 minutes for the journey. There I was met by Bulgy Thorne, Kemp, and Miller, commanding the 227th Bde defending Caithness. Spent the day touring the defences, and lunched at John o'Groats. Finally returned to Wick at 5.30 pm and flew back to Peterhead. There I was met by Wimberley, commanding 51st Div, who gave me details for the next day and also fixed up an evening's sea trout fishing to which I went after dinner, finally returned home to the Hotel at 10 pm, and whilst having a cup of tea listened to bombs falling on Peterhead jail! A pretty full day with much travelling.

19 August

Left Peterhead early and spent the day with Wimberley watching an exercise for the recapture of Dyce aerodrome. Thought the division was rather sticky and did not move as quickly as it ought.

At 5.00 pm flew from Aberdeen for Perth where I met Kukiel, the Polish Corps Commander, and was informed as to plans for next day. After dinner went with Bulgy to fish for salmon in the Tay in water belonging to a Glasgow millionaire called Colonel Hardy. A very pleasant evening in spite of catching no fish. Returned to hotel 10.30 pm, very tired!

20 August

Left at 9 am with Bulgy and Polish Commander to watch Polish forces carrying out attack with their new tanks. I thought they were very good and promise very well for the future. After the exercise drove on to Milden to shoot with Ivan Cobbold for 3 days. Arrived there about tea time, all guns still out shooting. They arrived back for a late tea, consisting of Cobbold, his wife, daughter and two boys, John Astor, Bertie Brooke, Humphrey de Trafford and Astor's boy.

21 August

A very pleasant day's shooting in which we shot 281 grouse, 18 hares and 6 rabbits.

22 August

A very hard climb up to the Black Moss beat which I found a bit trying on legs and wind. Birds were not as plentiful, but we shot 132 grouse and 4 hares.

23 August

Another lovely day in the mountains. Bag of 160 grouse, 2 snipe and 2 hares.

24 August

Left at 10.30 am and motored to Montrose to pick up my plane, which was a little late owing to weather. Left at 1 pm, landing Hendon at 4 pm. Put in a couple of hours in the office trying to pick up the threads again.

25 August

A bad day. First of all a Chiefs of Staff meeting at which nothing was decided, followed by a series of worries and hitches of various things going wrong. Freddy Carrington came to lunch, and very lost without work. Followed by Selection Board at which Dill forced Dickie Creagh on me to command an

Armoured Division in the making, namely conversion of 42nd Div from infantry to tanks. I am convinced he is not up to it. Finally dined with Adam.

26 August
Another hard day in the office with continual interruptions. Started with Budget and a long discussion to fix details for the C-in-Cs conference of next week. Then Prince Henry turned up with plans to go to Gibraltar and from there on to Egypt. Then an American general to lunch after which Dill came to discuss the prospects of carrying out raid across the Channel during the winter months. Then King came over from the WO to discuss RE matters. Followed by Barratt to report situation as regards army cooperation squadron. Finally Andy McCullough to discuss protection of Oil Board installations. By then it was 6 pm, and my tray had been filling all day.

27 August
Left at 8.30 am for South Wales, had a bumpy flight over Exmoor and then over Bristol Channel. Spent day with 31st Bde. Copper Finlayson turned up just before I took off for London at 6 pm. Arrived back home after having spent 3 hours in the air and only just in time for Bertie's dinner at 8.30 pm.

28 August
Started day with an hour in the office, followed by inspection of new barbed wire obstacle in St James's Park. Then inspection of new type stereoscopic photographs. Then at 12 noon an hour's interview with Walter Elliot, the Director of Public Relations at the WO, whose work is useless. As the only suggestion was that he should remove himself, it was hard to put this to him! Then lunch with Sikorski to discuss organization of Polish forces. After lunch an hour with Roger Keyes with whom I could make no headway to dispense with commandos and to carry out raids with my own formations. Finally dinner with Dill and Margesson to discuss manpower situation.

29 August
Left at 8.30 am to spend a day with the auxiliary units in Kent and Sussex. These units comprise two main elements – one an information one equipped with wireless, and another a sabotage one equipped with explosive and weapons. Both are intended to work behind the enemy in the event of an invasion. They are therefore organized into small patrols, and have prepared some 'hide outs' in the woods where they can live and hide their weapons. These are beautifully concealed and could be walked right over without ever detecting them. I was impressed with the type of man both regular and home guard employed in these units. The latter were the best type of yeoman farmers. After returning went to a sherry party given by General Sikorski and the Polish

forces at Claridges. There I met a very interesting Polish officer [probably General Anders] just back from Russia who was full of information as to the state of the Russian forces.

30 August

Proceeded to Biggin Hill to see a demonstration by South Eastern Command of vehicles suitable for defence of aerodromes. A rotten demonstration composed of vehicles which I had all seen before, and none of which were immediately available for aerodromes. I cannot imagine why Paget had such a demonstration except for some ill managed attempt at self advertisement! After lunch, proceeded home, where I arrived in time for tea to find you had a large party with Tom, Dawn and [illegible].

31 August

Church in the morning and a quiet afternoon at home. Lovely day.

1 September

Left 8 am, motored back to London. Interviews with Garrod about locating RAF training establishments on the South Coast, followed by Adam, about winter scheme of dissolution of units. After lunch Cory to discuss Allied troops in England.

2 September

Left Hendon 9 am and flew to Leeds to inspect the 31st Army Tank Brigade. Rather a dirty morning and took 1¾ hours for the trip. Very favourably impressed by the brigade, which is making good progress. Returned Hendon 6.30 pm and spent till 8 pm in the office, and now settling down to prepare notes for my C-in-C conference on Thursday.

3 September

Left Hendon 8.45 am, flew to Duxford where I inspected 70 Welsh Young Soldiers' Battalion. Dirty, but not a bad lot of boys. Then flew on to Debden to see A Coy of 70th KRRC [King's Royal Rifle Corps], quite good and should make a good battalion. By car to Castle Camp aerodrome to see B Coy 70th KRRC. Back to Debden aerodrome where I lunched with Churchill, the aerodrome commander. Left at 2.15 for Martlesham, to see A and B Coys of 70th Suffolks – a good battalion. On again by car to Southend, where I saw A and B Coys of 70th Essex, disappointing and half trained. Finally flew back to Hendon where I landed at 6 pm, just as Gort was taking off to fly back to Gibraltar. Remained in office till 8 pm and have now got heavy evening in front of me to prepare tomorrow's conference.

4 September

Held a long conference of Commanders-in-Chief lasting from 10 am to 1.30 pm. Main subject for discussion was winter organization, and reduction of our forces. Conference was, on the whole, useful. After lunch Dill gave us an excellent talk on the world situation. Grasett came to tea, having just returned from Hong Kong. It was a great joy to see him again. Budget departed on a few days' leave.

5 September

I was unable to fly owing to fog and therefore had to motor down to Tilshead to inspect the Canadian Army Tank Brigade. They have not been in the country long and are consequently in the early stages, but promise very well. Andy McNaughton and Worthington (the commander of the Brigade) met me in Tilshead and we then spent most of the day in carriers driving about Imber Downs. We lunched at Imber village and after lunch went to visit an Advanced Dressing Station located in a spot which is quite sacred to me and which you know well! It brought back such floods of memories that I found it very hard to concentrate on the bandaging of the stretcher case which I was intended to watch. I finally left after tea, arriving back here in time for dinner.

6 September

Spent morning in the office, and left for Ferney Close after lunch.

7 September

Went to church in the morning and spent afternoon in the garden.

8 September

Left Ferney Close 8 am, arrived in the office after studying briefs for COS meeting in the car to find that another important item had been added. This concerned a mad scheme put up by Joint Planning Committee for a feint attack on Cherbourg Salient to relieve pressure on the Russians.

COS meeting lasted from 10.30 to 12.30. It reminds me of the tea party in *Alice in Wonderland*, with Dill as Alice, Portal as the Hatter, and Dudley Pound as the Dormouse. I feel inclined to shout, 'put the dormouse in the teapot', to wake him up.

I then had a rush to Hendon to ferry to Newark. Early lunch on the plane. Then we saw the new digging machine which is to dig an approach trench for tanks at the rate of ¾ mile per hour! A wonderful piece of machinery. Flew back and landed at 6 pm. Rushed to office to see Bridgeman to discuss training of Home Guard. Dined with B Mess and showed bird films.

9 September

Left 8 am for Hendon. Weather very thick and only just able to take off for Netheravon. Motored on to Larkhill for anti-tank trials and conference on improvements. Anti-tank shooting beginning to make some progress. Had 2 pdr, 6 pdr, 25 pdr, 75 mm, Bofors and 3.7" AA gun all firing. Very glad to find that Bofors with Kerrison predictor came up to my expectations. Left from Netheravon at 12.45, had lunch in plane on way back, landing Hendon 2 pm. Put in ½ hour in office before going on to War Office for S of S Conference on plans for the winter. Conference lasted till 5 pm but we did fairly good work getting extra concessions for officers to use gov transport on payment on similar system to the men. Back to the office for interviews till 7.45 pm and a full hour of them after dinner, plus two hours work in my despatch case.

10 September

Called at 6.30 am and by 8 am I had left Hendon on a 2 hours flight to St Erwan in Cornwall. Cloudy weather so filled in time reading draft copy of our new pamphlet on 'The Division in the Advance', also appreciation of opposing sides for army manoeuvres. On arrival at St Erwan proceeded to VIII Corps advance report centre to watch 48th Div exercise. Then spent day with [Kenneth] Anderson going round seeing troops. Quite one of the worst divisional advances that I have seen in the last year! Settled on the spot with Anderson that Peters, the Div Commander, must be removed. Finally left at 5.30 pm and had another 2 hours in the air before landing back at Hendon. Again more interviews after dinner. Am feeling very sleepy!

11 September

A busy day in the office. In the first place Gen King the new Chief Engineer at the WO came to see me. Then Arthur Smith, Chief of Staff in Cairo, came for a talk. Then Montgomery who is acting as Chief Umpire for Manoeuvres came to lunch with me. After lunch I went to the WO as Margesson had asked me to have a talk with Halifax. I was with him for 1½ hours giving him the various problems connected with the defence of this country. Finally Walter Elliot came at 7 pm to discuss matters connected with Public Relations.

12 September

Called at 6.30 am and breakfast at 7 am. Then left for 6th Armoured Div parade for the King. Parade was held on far side of Newmarket and was a great success. First of all review of the whole division formed up. Then a march past followed by lunch for the King in 6th Armd Div Mess. I did not feel that the King really appreciated what he had seen and he disappointed me for the first time by being mainly concerned with how cold he had felt! Then motored back to office for a couple of hours work, after which I left for Chequers.

Arrived there about 8 pm, Davidson (DMI) and PM's brother only other guests. After dinner PM took me to his study where I remained with him till 1.30 am! Discussed proposal to reduce 77 bns which I am glad to say he objects to. Also plans for operations in Norway. He was in a very good mood and very pleasant to argue with.

13 September
Early start back after inspecting Chequers Guard. Spent morning in the office. After lunch at 3.15 went round to see Dill to tell him results of my visit to Chequers. Adam was also there. Warned them both of PM's attitude towards proposed infantry reductions. Finally went home for the weekend.

14 September
Peacefully at home with you and the two beloved young ones.

15 September
Left 8 am. Morning of interviews. Selection Board meeting from 3 pm to 5 pm, then interview with King-Hall. Finally dinner in Dill's flat with Archie Wavell who is home for few days from India, but as silent as usual!

16 September
My visit to Chequers of last Friday is bearing fruit. I had rubbed in the fact that the new 'manpower ceiling' which he had imposed was resulting in a reduction of 77 of my infantry battalions, namely a reduction of a ¼ of the infantry force of this country, and that the personnel thus provided were to be used for ADGB, Coast Defence, RASC [Royal Army Service Corps] and RAOC [Royal Army Ordnance Corps]. He has now taken this matter up with the object of preventing the reduction of these battalions. Nothing but good can come of this, we must stop putting such large proportion of our manpower into purely passive static organization. And again the 'tails' of our formations are far too large. Left 8.30 am for the far side of Newmarket to watch exercise by 6th Armoured Div. Most refreshing to see the progress they have made and the state of efficiency that has been reached. Returned 6.30 pm for an hour in the office before dinner.

17 September
Spent the day going round emplacements of 8", 9.2" and 15" guns which are being mounted round Dover. Also had a careful inspection of the new Radio Location organization which we are installing. Lunched with Bertie Ramsay, and Sholto Douglas also turned up, so we had our old IDC [Imperial Defence College] party together again. After lunch inspected the gun control organization. Beautiful clear day with French coast standing out well. With a telescope we were able to pick out one of the German gun emplacements.

18 September

Spent day in the office. First of all interview with Bridgeman in connection with the Home Guard and its future training to take over more of the roles of the Field Force army such as Coast Defence. Then Grasett came and lunched with me. After lunch Cory to discuss Allied Forces, followed by Pope to say goodbye before proceeding to the Middle East. Finally Bob Daubigny (Capitaine Ciriez, my old II Corps Liaison Officer) who is now 2nd in Command of a squadron in the 15th/19th Hussars.

19 September

Left Hendon at 8.45 am for Leamington to visit Czech forces. Had a murky flight up through mist in which pilot lost his way for a bit. Met on aerodrome by Mike Houston and Pollok who was in charge of Czechs. Then spent the day seeing the 2 battalions, 2 batteries, A/T battery, reconnaissance unit, etc. Found them a most efficient, though somewhat dirty, force. I am certain that they would give a very good account of themselves if required. The pity is that they are a waning force and are having great difficulties trying to raise recruits from America. When leaving 2nd Bn I was presented by the Bn Commander with a copy of *Benes* by Hitchcock, and a small medal depicting Czechoslovakia being crucified on a swastika. Returned back by air at 6 pm and put an hour in the office before dinner.

20 September

A fairly easy morning in the office during which I attended conference of COS of reconnaissance units. Came home for a late lunch.

21 September

Day spent at home with you, church, photographing Pooks with goat, and cutting tree down.

22 September

Left early. Attended Chiefs of Staff meeting at 11.30. In afternoon Monty came to give me details of his investigation of plans of opposing sides for our GHQ 'Bumper' Exercise.* Promises to make a very good battle. In evening dined with Basil and Cynthia.

---

*'Bumper' was one of the largest exercises ever held in Britain. It was designed to give senior commanders practice in handling mobile formations, to investigate the composition of an expeditionary force, and to test defences against invasion. See French, *Churchill's Army*, pp. 207–8.

23 September

Got up at 6.30 am to start for Scotland. Fog put off departure till 9.30 and then kept us at aerodrome till 10.45 before departure. Flew to Glasgow without ever seeing the floor except bit near Liverpool and Isle of Man. Lunched at aerodrome and motored to Inverary, about 70 miles, to visit Combined Operations training centre. Met there by Roger Keyes (Director of Combined Operations), Drew, his assistant, Grimslade, in charge of the school, also Admiral etc. Watched landing operations and visited transports. Impression that training is far too stereotyped to fit in with varying conditions of possible operations. Spent night in hotel in Inverary.

24 September

Spent morning with Grimslade visiting various beach base installations. Distinct progress but much more work required. Still thinking much too small in all our plans. Lunched on luxury liner converted to transport duties. Then drove to Troon with Roger Keyes. There we put up in the golf hotel. After dinner went out to watch commandos approach beach in open boats under cover of dark. Much too noisy and voices easily heard.

25 September

Spent morning going round commandos with Roger Keyes and Haydon. Saw very good cliff climbing demonstration.

The whole of my visit to Roger Keyes was on his part to try and convince me that our commando policy was right. He failed to do so, and I remained convinced till the end of the war that the commandos should never have been divorced from the army in the way they were. Each division should have been responsible for maintaining a divisional battle patrol capable of any commando work that might be asked of it.

Lunched at hotel and then drove to aerodrome where I took off at 2.30 pm for London. Arrived 5 pm. Went to office where I found Dill wanted to see me at 6.30, and Margesson at 7 pm. Was kept there till 8.30 and consequently only arrived at 8.45 to dine with Basil and Cynthia at the Coq d'Or. Just got back and have been sitting up till close to 1 am dealing with last few days correspondence. Am feeling very weary and sleepy!

26 September

Left here at 8.30 am and flew to Norwich where I was met by the Commander of the 15th Division and spent the rest of the day going round with him watching demonstrations of various battalions. The Division is a good one but still requires a few changes amongst senior officers. Finally flew back from Ipswich and put in an hour in the office before dinner. I now have a despatch case full of stuff to get rid of.

27 September

A busy morning. First of all a visit from [Pierre] Dupuy, after his return from Vichy [as Canadian Representative]. He was very interesting and cheering as regards state of affairs in France and better spirit prevailing there. Also less confidence in final victory amongst German officers.* At 11 am interview with the Press to prepare them for the large scale exercise (3rd Armd Div, 9th Inf Div, 2 Army Tank Bdes) which we are running next week. At 11.30 visit from Adam during which Dill arrived and at 12.30 when Venning was to come I had not yet started dealing with Adam. However Dill left soon and I then disposed of Venning and got Adam to come to lunch. After lunch both Martel and Budget to [illegible] with and left for Ferney Close about 4 pm.

28 September

Left home at 3.30 pm for Oxford to establish my control centre for the manoeuvres. Am living in the [illegible] Hotel with office just outside.

29 September

Left early to fly from Cowley (Oxford) to Norwich. But weather bad and did not get off till 9 am. Very dirty weather and forced to fly very low most of way. Went to see German HQ and had a talk with Carr. From there motored on to II Corps HQ and XI Corps HQ to find situation. Then flew from Honington to Reading where second car met me and took me round to Southern Command HQ, where I discussed Alexander's plans with him. Returned to Oxford where I ran conference at 8 pm on day's fighting. Then Admiral Ramsay came to dinner and I described situation to him afterwards.

30 September

Spent day touring front and visiting various headquarters by car and by air. Bertie Ramsay came with me. Dill turned up for final conference after dinner. Manoeuvres going very well and day most interesting.

1 October

Again rushing round by air from 8 am to 7 pm and conference till midnight after dinner. Grasett came round today with me. Sad mishandling of armoured forces by Higher Commanders.

---

*Dupuy was enlisted by Churchill to convey to the French Government 'his readiness to send divisions to North Africa in case the French Government should decide to abandon the metropolitan territory or considered it opportune to receive British support in North Africa'. See Gilbert, *Finest Hour*, pp. 957–59.

2 October

Another day of manoeuvres. Spent all day motoring and flying about. Have now ordered manoeuvres to close down at 6 am tomorrow. They have been a great success. I am delighted with the way armoured divisions have come on, but disappointed at the way Higher Commanders are handling them. They have all got a great deal to learn, and the sooner they learn the better.

3 October

At midnight received special messenger from the War Office with orders to carry out examination for attack on Trondheim (Norway) and preparation of plan of attack. The whole to be in by next Friday! Also that I was to dine tonight at Chequers and spend night there to discuss plans. I motored back to London in the morning and spent most of the afternoon studying details of the plan. At 6 pm picked up Dill at the WO and drove down to Chequers discussing details with him on the way. Dudley Pound, Portal and Attlee formed the party. We sat up till 2.15 am discussing the problem and I did my best to put the PM off attempting the plan. Air support cannot be adequately supplied and we shall fall into the same pitfall as we did before.

4 October

Resumed discussion at 11 am and went on till 1 pm, I think PM was beginning to weaken on the plan.

How little did I know him at that time, to imagine that he was weakening on this plan. From then onwards we were to be continually in trouble riding him off mad plans to go back to Norway. Why he wanted to go back and what he was going to do there, even if he did succeed in capturing Trondheim, we never found out. The only reason he ever gave was that Hitler had unrolled the map of Europe starting with Norway, and he would start rolling it up again from Norway. It should be remembered that the plan for the capture of Norway had already been examined by the Chiefs of Staff Committee, and had been turned down as impracticable owing to insufficient air support for the operation.

Now, at Chequers, I, in my capacity of C-in-C Home Forces, had just received orders from him to prepare a detailed plan for the capture of Trondheim, ready to the last button. A commander for the expedition was to be appointed by me and the plan was to be sufficiently ready only to require the order to start. I was given one week to prepare the plan. I said that if I was to do so I must have the C-in-C Home Fleet, AOC Fighter Command, AOC Bomber Command, Minister for Transportation and several others at my disposal for repeated conferences during the week. I was told that they were all to be made available. It was an unpleasant assignment, I had been told by Dill of the results of the Chiefs of Staff inspection of the problem, and I felt convinced that I should arrive at similar conclusions. It was going to entail a great deal of wasted work on the part of many busy people. Personally I was in the middle of the final work connected with 'Bumper' Exercise, and my time already fully booked up.

Returned to London and made arrangements for conference on Monday to start discussing plan.

Finally motored home in time for dinner. Very weary after hard week short of sleep.

5 October
Spent peacefully at home recuperating after last week, and building goat cart with Pooks and Ti.

6 October
Left home 8 am. Foggy. Conference at 11 am in Cabinet War Room at which I presided. Following were present: Cs-in-C Home Fleet, Fighter Command, Bomber Command, Coastal Command, Army Command, QMG, Minister of Transportation, my own staff, etc. The more we examine the problem of Trondheim the more certain I am that it would be folly to attempt it. Afternoon series of interviews, and after dinner 2 hours at my notes for next Friday's conference on the manoeuvres.

7 October
Had intended to fly to visit the Dutch forces, but the whole country was wrapped in fog the whole morning, so I had to postpone the visit. I therefore spent the day preparing notes for my final conference on my large exercise of last week which takes place at the Staff College next Friday morning.

8 October
Spent morning preparing notes for Friday's conference. Then went to Dill's wedding. I *do* hope he will be happy; if anybody deserves it, he does.* Lunched at Turf Club with Budget and then returned for conference on Trondheim attack. Finally conference with Monty on last week's exercise. It is lamentable how poor we are as regards Army and Corps Commanders. We ought to remove several, but heaven knows where we shall find anything very much better.

This shortage of real leaders was a constant source of anxiety to me during the war. I came to the conclusion that it was due to the cream of the manhood having been lost in the First World War. It was the real leaders, in the shape of platoon, company and battalion commanders, who were killed off. These were the men we were short of now. I found this shortage of leaders of quality applied to all three fighting services, and

---

*Dill's first wife died in December 1940, after a long series of paralytic strokes (cf. 22 November 1940). His second wife was the widowed Nancy Furlong, née Charrington. It was indeed a very happy marriage.

later I was able to observe that this same failing prevailed amongst politicians and diplomats.

9 October 1941

You and Mr Ti came up to lunch today and turned what might have been a dull dead day into a red letter day! We then chose carpets, after which I returned to my office.

The whole morning had been taken up with another of my meetings preparing the Trondheim operation. I had C-in-C Home Fleet, Fighter, Bomber and Coastal Commands, Minister of Transport, QMG etc. Our final survey of the operation convinced us more than ever of its impracticability. I have now been warned to attend Chequers next Sunday again! at 6 pm. I have to start for Newcastle the same night.

10 October

Left at 8 am for the final conference of our large 'Bumper' exercise. We held it at the Staff College. There were some 270 officers attending it. I began by turning to Monty to act as historian, and then I followed on with criticisms. A great relief to have it over. The last fortnight has been a hard one with the large exercise and the PM's task on top of it to examine the Trondheim operation.

11 October

Had a troublesome morning going through the final appreciation of Trondheim for the PM. After lunch Tovey (C-in-C Home Fleet) and Brind [his Chief of Staff] came round and we again went through the whole appreciation. I don't like its final shape and would have liked to recast the whole thing. But my conclusion would still remain the same – that the operation is impracticable. Arrived home for dinner.

12 October

After having made all the arrangements to go to Chequers and for special train to collect me at Wendover station at 1.45 am, I suddenly received message during afternoon that PM wanted us at 10 Downing St instead! Went there at 6.30 pm. All Chiefs of Staff, Tovey, Sholto [Douglas], Paget and I attended. PM very dissatisfied with our appreciation! Told me that he was expecting a detailed plan for the operation and instead of that I had submitted a masterly treatise on all the difficulties! He then proceeded to cross question me for nearly 2 hours on various items of the appreciation, trying to make out that I had unnecessarily increased the difficulties! However I was quite satisfied that there was only one conclusion to arrive at.

I repeatedly tried to bring him back to the main reason – the lack of air support. He avoided this issue and selected arguments such as: 'You state that you will be confronted by frosts and thaws which will render mobility difficult. How can you account for such a statement?' I replied that this was a relatively trivial matter and that the statement came from the 'Climate Book'. He at once sent for this book, from which it at once became evident that this extract had been copied straight out of the book. His next attack was: 'You state that it will take you some 24 hours to cover the ground between A and B. How can you account for so long being taken, explain to me exactly how every one of those 24 hours will be occupied'! As this time had been allowed for overcoming enemy resistance on the road, removal of road blocks and probable reparation to demolition of bridges and culverts, it was not an easy matter to paint a detailed picture of every hour of those 24. This led to a series of more questions, interspersed with sarcasm and criticism. A very unpleasant grilling to stand up to in a full room, but excellent training for what I had to stand up to on many occasions in later years!

Finally left at 8.30 pm, dined at Club, and embarked on train at 11 pm.

13 October
Arrived Newcastle at 9 am. Met by Rusty Eastwood. Proceeded after breakfast to Fenham Barracks report centre. Then toured front. Very disappointed with inefficiency of commanders. Both Pakenham-Walsh and Willcox quite incapable of handling the forces under their orders! Put up for the night by Lord Allendale who made me very comfortable.

14 October
Started again at 9 am to see rest of exercise. Again heartbreaking to see armoured forces wrongly handled. Caught 12.53 pm train back from Newcastle and landed London 7.30 pm – unable to fly owing to weather.

15 October
Drove down to [illegible] Island to [illegible] to watch training of raiding parties for French coast. Very good exercises, all in blue goggles to simulate darkness. Lunched with Chambers who is in charge of the course. After lunch watched demonstration of artillery support by means of No. 18 wireless sets in touch with infantry operating from carriers. Horrible accident had occurred a few days previously in which Monkey Morgan the commander of 55th Div had been seriously wounded in stomach by a burst bombard. Nosworthy was also hit in the face, his ADC lost his chin, and Oswald Birley the painter lost an eye! I put up for the night with Paget.

16 October
Started 8 am from Paget's HQ and spent day in the office with series of inter-

views. McNaughton in the morning, then Harry Crerar. Busy trying to fix up Crerar to command 2nd Can Div, which is now vacant. Am getting Canadian Defence Minister to lunch with me on Monday to try and square matters up. Lunched at Savoy with Norwegian Defence Minister. King Haakon and Crown Prince also there. Lunch rather spoilt for me by having to sit next to Sandys. Continuous afternoon till 8 pm.

McNaughton arrived one morning to inform me that he had been invited to Chequers for the following weekend and to discuss something about Norway! I told him all the back history and the fact that the operation had already been examined twice for Churchill and turned down each time as impracticable. I warned him that he might well now try to have the attack done by Canadian troops. He assured me that he would not dream of accepting such a task for his troops, and I asked him anyhow to come and see me on Monday after his visit to let me know the results of his talk.

On the following Monday a limp looking McNaughton walked into my room and literally poured himself into my armchair! I asked him how he had got on. He informed me that he had had a ghastly weekend, he had been kept up all hours of the morning until he did not know which way he was facing. Winston's control of the English language and his qualifications as a barrister had left him dumbfounded. When I pressed him as to what he had agreed to, he began to beat around the bush and would not be very precise. Finally, however, I extracted from him that [he] had agreed to examine the Trondheim operation. When he saw the effect on me he hurriedly added that he had since sent a telegram to [Prime Minister] Mackenzie King asking him on no account to agree to the employment of the Canadian forces in any operations in Norway! This was one way of shelving the responsibility of refusing, but as far as I was concerned, it made little difference. I knew that the Canadians would not now be used in this wild venture.

This ended Winston's third attempt to have his own way! It did not mean that he relinquished the idea – far from it – he was always hankering after it, and the sight of a Norwegian map alone was enough to start him off again.

17 October

Spent morning in the office examining my new organization for collecting information concerning the French coast for raiding purposes which I have been entrusted with. Early lunch and then proceeded with Bridgeman to visit Home Guard school near Dorking. Finally went to see Dill at 6.15 pm where I remained an hour discussing disposal of Osborne and Massy who should be replaced in command of corps.

18 October

Put through the morning's work as quickly as I could and left by 12.30. Had my sandwiches in the car, changed rapidly, and dashed out to Bertie Fisher's house to walk up outlying pheasants with him during the afternoon. Had a good walk and shot 13 pheasants between us.

19 October
Went to church in the morning and spent most of the afternoon working on the goat cart.

20 October 1941
Left Ferney Close at 8 am for a busy day. First of all Air Marshal Barratt came to discuss the organization of the Airborne force. Then I had Canadian Defence Minister to lunch with me at the Club where I discussed the future organization of the Canadian Corps and the next commander of the 2nd Canadian Division. From there straight to WO for a Selection Board which lasted till tea. At the conclusion, Pownall asked to see me and informed me that Beaverbrook was scheming for Tim Pile to be next CIGS after Dill!! There is no knowing what schemes are going on behind our backs!

I have known Tim Pile for a long time, and he has got certain valuable qualities, but he certainly had not got the necessary qualifications for a CIGS. In fact, I could not imagine a worse selection, but typical of Beaverbrook. I had heard that Pile was frequently spending weekends with Beaverbrook and there can be no doubt that on such occasions he would not waste his time; he is a 'climber' if he is nothing else.

Just at this time I also began to hear rumours that Beaverbrook was undermining Dill's position with Churchill. It did not take a great deal to do this, as Winston had never been fond of Dill. They were entirely different types of characters, and types that could never have worked harmoniously together. Dill was the essence of straight forwardness, blessed with the highest of principles and an unassailable integrity of character. I do not believe that any of these characteristics appealed to Winston, on the contrary, I think he disliked them as they accentuated his own shortcomings in this respect. At any rate, I know for certain that he could not abide the easy code of morals of some politicians and Winston's methods were frequently repulsive to him. I was filled with anxiety as to Dill's future, he was far and away the best man we had in the army for the post of CIGS, and any change could only be for the worse.*

Back to Home Forces where Sir George Shuster came to see me about the home guard. After finishing off some office work I went with Humfrey Gale to dine with Sir Ralph Glyn at the Senior, and am back again weary and ready for bed.

21 October
Put in an hour's work in the office followed by a motor down to Imber to watch a demonstration of fighter attacks on lorries, infantry and guns. Most impressive! There is no doubt that the single seater fighter is destined to play a serious part in ground attacks. Left to their own devices they could destroy

---

*On these turbulent relationships see Alex Danchev, 'Dilly-Dally, Or, Having the Last Word', *Journal of Contemporary History* 22 (1987), pp. 21–44, and 'Waltzing with Winston', *War in History* 2 (1995), pp. 202–30.

long columns even spaced out at 150 yards between vehicles. I must take steps to provide for their protection in future. The cannon aircraft may later on when equipped with a heavier gun become a formidable weapon against tanks. The small Jefferis bomb also promises well. Returned in time to change, put in an hour in the office, and on to the club to give Harry Crerar dinner. I had a long and useful discussion with him about the future of the Canadian Corps. I do hope that they give him the 2nd Canadian Division.

22 October

Picked up Bertie Brooke at his flat and took him down to 24th Guards Brigade Group to watch a demonstration by Browning of attacks on tanks. A first class show very well staged and full of useful lessons. I am arranging to have it made into an instructional film which ought to be useful. Also informed Browning that he had been selected for command of the Airborne Division, and what I wanted him to do about it. Motored back in time for afternoon in the WO. Finally gave dinner to Freda Forres [?] at the club for her to discuss some ATS friend of hers who had been badly treated, and the new club for Allied senior officers which she was proposing to run on Sunday evenings.

23 October

Spent a day in the office. Most of the morning was spent sorting out and adjusting senior officers to cover the various changes we must make. There are at least 3 Corps Commanders that must be changed, and possibly 4! Added to that, Alexander's removal for operations in the Mediterranean creates another vacancy in the Army Commanders. The dearth of suitable higher commanders is lamentable. I cannot quite make out to what it can be attributable. The only thing I feel can account for it is the fact that the flower of our manhood was wiped out some 20 years ago and it is just some of those that we lost then that we require now.

You and Mr Ti came up to lunch at Harrods, such a joy getting a glimpse of you in the middle of the week.

24 October

Left at 9 am for a long day at Aldershot with the 3rd Canadian Division. I was given what Price, the Divisional Commander, called many 'cross cuts'! These consisted in seeing mortars shooting, a battalion at rifle ranges, field guns doing anti-tank, RAS [Royal Army Signals] motorcycle display, battalion on polo ground doing various training, whole complete infantry brigade on cere-monial, RAMC [Royal Army Medical Corps] dressing stations, reconnaissance units in semi-ceremonial, two batteries occupying positions, RE bridging, and finally 'Retreat' by massed bands! The division has the makings of a first class division, if only its advance training can be carried out properly.

25 October
I had a fairly quiet morning in the office and escaped in time to have lunch at Ferney Close. Spent afternoon putting down new carpets.

26 October
Finished carpets in the morning and then got on with the goat cart.

At 6 pm left for Chequers, where I arrived about 7.45 pm. I found that the only other guest was Lindemann. Dinner lasted on till about 11 pm by the time we had finished having snuff etc! After dinner the PM sent for his dressing gown to put over his 'siren suit'. The dressing gown is a marvellous garment, rather like Joseph's many-coloured garment! We then proceeded upstairs where he has had a small cinema established. There we watched Russian and German films till about midnight. We then came down and spent from midnight to 1 am with an explanation of 'Bumper' which I had to give. The PM then dismissed Lindemann and told him he wanted to speak to me. He proceeded to discuss impending operations in North Africa and Mediterranean and all the hopes he attached to them. From that he went on to discuss defence of this country against invasion and the strength of the forces left for this purpose. I told him of the fears I had of being very short of tanks if we went on sending them to Russia as proposed. He assured me that I should have some 4,000 tanks in this country by the spring. Finally at 2.15 am he suggested we should proceed to the Hall to have some sandwiches, and I hoped that this might at last mean bed! But no!! We went on till 10 minutes to 3 am before he made a move for bed!! He had the gramophone turned on and in his many coloured dressing gown, with a sandwich in one hand and water cress in the other, he trotted round and round the hall giving occasional little skips to the time of the gramophone. On each lap near the fireplace he stopped to release some priceless quotation or thought. For instance he quoted a saying that a man's life is similar to a walk down a long passage with closed windows on either side. As you near each window an unknown hand opens it and the light it lets in only increases by contrast the darkness at the end of the passage.

27 October
Had breakfast at 9 am and at 10.30 am accompanied the PM to a demonstration of the 'Bombard'. This had been staged as Beaverbrook's Director of Research, Lucas (of Lucas Car Lighting System) had been crabbing the mortar and recommending that its production should be closed down. I think probably that the D of A's [Director of Artillery] department was at the back of the whole show! At any rate there was some kind of dirty work in the background which was frustrated by the PM.

I returned to town for lunch which I had with Martel and Dempsey who has just been given the 42nd Armoured Division. Later in the afternoon I saw Gairdner who has just returned from Middle East to command the 6th Armoured Division. Another extraction of armoured forces from this country this evening in the shape of a brigade from the 6th Armoured Div. When will WO learn not to break up formations which it has taken months to build up!

28 October

Left Euston at 8.40 am for Wolverhampton to see the Dutch forces. Was met at the station by Copper and Lt Gen Northoven van Goor. We then proceeded to lunch at the Headquarters Mess and from there on to see the bn of armoured cars and the skeleton bn. Finally left Wolverhampton at 4.15 and landed back at Euston at 8 pm. On the whole agreeably surprised at the type of soldier in the Dutch contingent: with a little more training should make quite a useful small contingent. Kennedy was there for dinner and informed me that the proposed Mediterranean expedition under Alexander to Sicily is off! This is good news.

29 October

Left at 9 am for New Alresford where I met Schreiber and Swayne and also [illegible]. I spent the morning round [illegible] on an exercise of the reconnaissance unit. It woke many memories of strolls with Freddy and Betty Pelly and made me long to be back in those peaceful days. On way back to London I picked you up to go on to Gorringe's Hotel and to see 'The 49th Parallel' that night.

30 October

A series of interviews starting with Liardet to discuss defence of aerodromes. Then Alexander who is coming back to Southern Command, followed by Martel. At 4.15 pm went to see CIGS to discuss future Corps Commanders, finally back to collect you to go on with Charlesworth to see Leslie Henson followed by supper at Claridge's.

31 October

Flew from Hendon with Barratt to Ringway near Manchester to see parachute units under Gale. Spent a very interesting day inspecting parachute training appliances, gliders etc. Finally saw very good demonstration by two gliders carrying ordinary aerodrome defence personnel. I left very impressed by the possibilities of airborne forces and flew back to London. In the evening we both went to see rather poor cinema.

1 November

A series of committees and visits filled this morning. First discussing composition of armoured forces. Then discussing with McNaughton the command of the Canadian Corps during the period he is to be laid up. Finally Pownall on training areas. At last succeeded in picking you up shortly after 1 pm to motor back to Ferney Close and a peaceful weekend.

2 November
Church in the morning, and construction of goat cart in the afternoon.

3 November
Spent the day with an Armoured Corps conference at Sandhurst, returning Ferney Close in the evening.

4 November
Spent morning again at Sandhurst with Armoured Corps conference. Motored back to office in the afternoon, where I remained till dinner.

5 November
A busy day. At 10 am I had a conference which Mountbatten attended. He has just been appointed to succeed Roger Keyes as advisor on Combined Operations. We discussed the future of commandos and the carrying out of raids on the South Coast. Arrived at a successful solution to the handling of commandos. Then Osborne came to say goodbye. I then lunched with Cud Thornhill at the Bath Church. Afternoon series of interviews. Came back to the Mess as I had Ralph Glyn dining with me.

After dinner had to return to the Cabinet War Room for a conference of the PM's on the withdrawal of tanks from Home Forces for the Middle East. It is intended to withdraw another 170 Valentines from Home Forces! This is mainly to make up deficiencies caused by gifts of tanks to Russia! PM in good form, but refusing to realize that there are different types of tanks, or rather that tactics call for certain types for distinct jobs. Beaverbrook attended meeting and was all smiles after having written most abusive memo in reply to CIGS memorandum. Wonderful bit of acting between Beaverbrook and his production representative by which they ran up the output of tanks for next 3 months from 2,400 to 3,000!!

6 November
Started my Cs-in-C conference at 10 am and continued till 1.30 pm. We then had lunch which was also attended by Dill, Adam and Mountbatten. After lunch Dill gave us a talk of 1¼ hours on the world situation. As usual absolutely first class.

I have known no man who could marshal strategic events and situations better than he could. He had that gift of realizing where all the essentials lay, and consequently never confused his landscape with unnecessary details when painting a strategic picture of the world situation.

I was also informed that Paget was to go off as C-in-C Far East to replace Brooke-Popham. We have also got Copper out of Western Command, and Osborne, Massy and Packenham-Walsh from their Corps. This is a pretty drastic clearing which ought to make place for the younger material. Finally went to dine with Dill where I remained till 11 pm discussing army air cooperation, filling of divisional vacancies, etc.

7 November
Spent the morning in the office with various interviews. After lunch went to see Kerrison's most recent inventions and the possibility of applying modern anti-aircraft methods for anti-tank purposes. I feel that there is still a great deal to be done to improve anti-tank shooting of all kinds.

8 November
Spent morning in the office and arrived home for late lunch.

9 November
Church in the morning for Armistice Service, and construction of goat cart in the afternoon.

10 November
Motored to Salisbury Plain in the morning to see further anti-tank demonstrations. I think that we have made some progress in the last 6 months. Lunched in the new Larkhill mess which brought back floods of memories of all Larkhill days and hours spent on the plans of the mess. Attended beginning of conference of CRAs and said few words to them. Motored back with Adam in car as far as Hartley Wintney, where I had tea. Dined with Bertie in the evening.

11 November
Spent morning in the office before meeting you and the Pooks at Harrods where we had lunch together and then did some shopping. After lunch proceeded to Curzon Theatre to see a film on bomb disposal – a good film. Then went on to the Army Photographic Department, where all photographs for the army are developed and printed. Then went on to Devonshire House to visit the Wireless Interception HQ. Most interesting, it is very encouraging to see what we are doing. But I feel that the whole organization still falls far short of what is required. We are not yet anywhere near the German organization, and are not tapping half the ether information.

12 November

I had my first journey today in my special train! the Prime Minister's Xmas present! I left Paddington at 8.15 am and had breakfast on the train, arriving Lavington at 10.30 am. Train very comfortably arranged with dining car divided into two compartments, making very comfortable sitting room and dining room. Well filled up with writing table, sofas and chairs. Also full sleeping compartment and truck for car when required. Spent day going round Guards Armoured Division, which is making good progress and shaping well. Should become first class division in time. Picked up my train at Wylie and was landed at Addison Road by 7 pm, after a very comfortable day's travelling.

13 November

Morning in the office with a series of interviews. First of all Nosworthy to say goodbye to me on vacating his Corps. Then Anderson and Irwin to interview before they took over their new Corps. Followed by Johnson to tick off following his disloyalty to Hobart, for which he had my full sympathy. I then had lunch with Kirke at the Club, who had Lord Galloway to lunch also. After lunch spent 1½ hours with Dill discussing various points such as the new quota of aeroplanes which the Air Ministry is now offering us in reply to our claims. It is better but still falls short. Also discussed with him the various rumours as to successor for him, such as Tim Pile, selected by Beaverbrook! He says Margesson would like to send Pile to the Far East! Again, Paget's appointment to the Far East is beginning to look fishy. They were insisting on sending him to Moscow first. Now Moscow trip is falling through and they still seem to be retaining him in this country. It looks as if they may wish to keep him as a substitute for Dill. It would be a tragedy, and a definite step towards losing the war!

There was also Archie Nye to be considered and Dill said that the PM had taken a great fancy to him. From many points of view he would have made an excellent CIGS. A first class brain, great character, courage in his own convictions, quick worker with great vision. As CIGS he would, however, have the serious handicap of being on the junior side, and would consequently have had some difficulty handling men such as Wavell, Auchinleck, Alexander, Monty and Paget, who were considerably senior to him. In our discussion, Dill made it clear to me that as far as he was concerned, if he had to go, the one person he wanted to hand over to was me.

Another invitation for Chequers next Sunday, I thought I had a few more weeks to go!

14 November

I had intended to fly to Exeter to visit Young Soldier Bns. But weather was very foggy and unsuitable. Therefore remained in the office, and in the evening motored to Ferney Close in anticipation of Bertie Fisher's shoot.

15 November

Lovely day, but unfortunately bad from a shooting point of view. Bertie had expected about 100 birds, but instead of that we only got 27! Birds were there but would not rise. The day was so lovely that it did not matter a bit.

16 November

Spent morning putting the goat cart together again after its painting, and at 5.30 pm left for Chequers. Found party consisted of Mountbatten, Prof (Cherwell), Pug Ismay and self. Mrs Churchill there for dinner. After dinner PM took me off to his study and told me that as Dill had had a very hard time and was a tired man he wanted to relieve him. That he would be made a Field Marshal and Governor of Bombay. He then went on to say that he wanted me to take over from Dill, and asked me whether I was prepared to do so.

It took me some time to reply as I was torn by many feelings. I hated the thought of old Dill going and our very close association coming to an end. I hated the thought of what this would mean for him. The thought of the magnitude of the job and the work entailed took the wind out of my sails. The fact that the extra work and ties would necessarily mean seeing far less of you tore at my heart strings. And finally a feeling of sadness at having to give up Home Forces after having worked them up to their present pitch.

The PM misunderstood my silence and said 'Do you not think you will be able to work with me? We have so far got on well together.' I had to assure him that those were not my thoughts, though I am well aware that my path will not be strewn with rose petals! But I have the greatest respect for him and real affection for him, so that I hope I may be able to stand the storms of abuse which I may well have to bear frequently. He then went on to explain the importance he attached to the appointment and the fact that the Chiefs of Staff Committee must be the body to direct military events over the whole world. He also stated that his relations with me must for now approximate those of a Prime Minister to one of his ministers. Nothing could have been kinder than he was, and finally when we went to bed at 2 am he came with me to my bedroom to get away from the others, took my hand and looking into my eyes with an exceptionally kind look said 'I wish you the very best of luck.'

I got into my bed with my brain in a whirl trying to fathom the magnitude of the task I am about to take on. I have no false conceptions as to the magnitude of the task and of the doubts whether I shall be able to compete with it. If it was in peace time I should love to try it, but in war the responsibility is almost overwhelming. The consequences of failures or mistakes are a nightmare to think about. I pray God from the very bottom of my heart that he may give me guidance and be at my side in the times I may have to go through. And then I have you, oh my darling, as my lighthouse in all stormy seas. Bless you for the help which you are to me. Many, many thoughts kept galloping through my head and by 4 am I was still tossing about without sleep.

There is no doubt that I was temporarily staggered by the magnitude of the task I was undertaking. Let it be remembered the situation we were in at that time, left alone and unsupported in the war against Germany. Let it be remembered the task we had in defeating Germany in the First World War, when we had the assistance of a strong France, Italy, Russia and finally the USA. Now we were faced with a possible invasion across the Channel, with increasing difficulties in the Middle East, a closed Mediterranean, dark clouds growing in the Far East and not an ally left to help us. The horizon was black from end to end with only one shaft of light, in the possible entry of America into the war. To pick up the strategic reins at the War Office at such a moment was surely sufficient to cause one the deepest of anxiety.

Added to that was the certain trial of working hand in hand with Winston in handling the direction of the war. I had seen enough of him to realize his impetuous nature, his gambler's spirit, and his determination to follow his own selected path at all costs, to realize fully what I was faced with. I can remember clearly that after he had taken me away to his study and had offered me this appointment, he left me alone temporarily to rejoin the others. I am not an exceptionally religious person, but I am not ashamed to confess that as soon as he was out of the room my first impulse was to kneel down and pray to God for guidance and support in the task I had undertaken.

17 November

Left Chequers at 8.45 am. Motored back to Basingstoke to inspect Young Soldiers' Bn. Saw 70th Hants and 70th Warwicks, going round by Stockbridge, Nether Wallop, Winchester and Southampton. Returned by [illegible] to pick up suitcases and have another tea. On returning had to go to War Office to see Margesson. He was very nice, full of congratulations and full of help. We had long discussion as to how to smooth over the blow for Macready [ACIGS], who is to be passed over by Archie Nye, the latter having been shot up to VCIGS by the PM over Macready's head. This will make matters more difficult. Returned for dinner at 9.30 pm.

18 November

Saw Dill this morning who was quite wonderful and is taking the blow just as one would expect. It is a frightful tragedy. He tells me the two other members of the Chiefs of Staff Committee went to see Winston about it to try and get him to reverse his decision. He also told me that the PM first of all wanted to put Archie Nye in to relieve Dill!! Dill had a job to rid him of this idea.

In the afternoon I attended Chiefs of Staff meeting and stopped on for my first meeting of the military members of the Army Council, to begin to get into the picture. Now I am just off by my special train at 9.30 pm.

19 November

Left last night at 9.30 pm by my special train. Had a very comfortable journey with quite a party consisting of QMG (Venning), DGAE [Director General

Army Equipment] (Weeks), DWS (Williams), Sir Alexander Roger, Budget and Humfrey Gale. After breakfast on train arrived with train right into the Central Ordnance Depot, Donnington. There I spent 2 very interesting hours inspecting the whole system of receipt, storage and issue of stores. At 11.15 entrained for Chilwell, where we arrived at 2 pm, having lunched on the train. There again we spent a most interesting visit till 4.15 pm, when we re-entrained for London. There we arrived at 7 pm, having had tea on the train. There is no doubt that this train is a great acquisition.

Today the papers published Dill's departure and my appointment as CIGS together with the other changes. I suppose I ought to be very grateful and happy at reaching the top of the ladder. I can't say that I do. I feel a heavy depression at Dill going after the close contacts I have had with him ever since the war started. I had never hoped or aspired at reaching these dizzy heights and now that I am stepping up onto the plateau land of my military career the landscape looks cold, black and lonely, with a ghastly responsibility hanging as a black thunder cloud over me. Perhaps I am feeling liverish for want of exercise today!

20 November
Spent day in the office beginning to sever my connections with Home Forces. Had interview with Browning in the morning to discuss progress he was making with the Airborne Division. I think that at last, after many uphill moments, it is beginning to make strides. Next saw Director of Security to discuss Boney Fuller and his Nazi activities with him. I cannot believe that he has any unpatriotic intentions. Finally saw Paget to discuss his taking over [Home Forces].

In the evening Archie Nye came to see me to explain to me that he had not been pulling any strings to obtain the post of VCIGS – I believe he is entirely honest.

21 November
Left at 8.45 am, taking Budget Loyd with me. We went to Honiton, Wattisham, and Martlesham aerodromes to see Young Soldier Bns, KRRC and Suffolks. The latter especially coming on fast and very good. Finished by going to Ivan Cobbold's house for Saturday's shoot.

22 November
Shot with Cobbold. Guns consisted of Bertie, Cobbold, uncle, Humphrey de Trafford, Budget Loyd and self. Glorious day and plenty of birds. It made a refreshing day during which I was able to cast off the shadow of the oncoming burden of CIGS duties! After tea drove back to town where I arrived at 9 pm. Found message that the S of S wanted to talk to me. Apparently PM somewhat upset at prospect that both Paget and I are to be on leave simultaneously next

week! As a result Paget to be recalled. In addition I am to hold myself in readiness to attend Defence Cabinet [Committee] meeting either Monday or Tuesday evening.

23 November

Finished off a few instructions for Barney and left for home shortly after 9 am. Happy to spend a quiet week before taking over CIGS. There seems, however, possibility that I may be called up during the week for Defence Committee meetings.

It was a very definite wrench leaving this Force which I had taken over in its early days, disorganized after Dunkirk, short of weapons, short of trained officers, and of somewhat doubtful morale. We had been through very anxious days together under the threat of imminent invasion. I had imposed endless work and exercises on the component formations, often under the most trying conditions of winter weather. Every man and officer had responded wholeheartedly and it had been a most encouraging and inspiring experience to watch this large force grow in efficiency and battleworthiness. Doctrines had been evolved for the employment of armoured forces, those doctrines had been imparted to higher commanders and had been absorbed. Anti-tank equipment and technique had been seriously taken in hand and made rapid progress. The foundation of airborne forces had been laid and was making marked progress in Browning's able hands. Battle schools had been started to train officers and men to live hard and to take a pride in their endurance. The Force had not been subjected to the high test of meeting an invasion; had this test been met I am confident that Home Forces would have given an account of itself well worthy of all the best traditions of the British Army.

24 to 30 November

Spent on leave.

1 December 1941 – 31 December 1942

Although Dill officially did not terminate his appointment of CIGS till December 25th, he had left for Scotland and Northern England on a tour to say goodbye and ceased to function as CIGS. I therefore virtually took over from him on December 1st and started to function from that day onwards.

I was taking over at a difficult moment as far as the Far East was concerned. Dark clouds had been gathering fast on this horizon and everything pointed towards an early entry of Japan into the war. On the other hand, it was essential that we should take no step that might precipitate hostile actions with Japan without the entry of the USA into the war. Had we known that the Pearl Harbor attack would eventually start hostilities, matters would have been greatly simplified, and we should have known for certain that the USA would be irrevocably dragged into the war. I had discussed the possibility of Japan entering the war with Dill. He had told me frankly that he had done practically nothing to meet this threat. He said that we were already so weak on all fronts that it was impossible to denude them any further to meet a possible threat. I think he was quite right in his dispositions and that he could not have done more to meet the probable Japanese entry into the war. It was undoubtedly correct not to create general weakness on all fronts in an attempt to meet all possible threats, but it left us in a lamentably dangerous position on the entry of Japan into the war.

1 December
Left Ferney Close at 8 am for my first day's work as CIGS. Arrived WO at 9.15, read telegrams, and was briefed by DMO and DMI for Chiefs of Staff meeting. 10.30 Chiefs of Staff meeting till 12.15 when we were sent for by PM to 10 Downing Street. There we discussed advisability of moving into Thailand Peninsula prior to any move by Japan. Decision being to wait till we are certain that USA comes in. Bruce [High Commissioner] and Page [Special Envoy] also turned up to represent Australian outlook. Not a pleasant one [illegible] with talk of withdrawal of Australian troops from Syria and cruisers from Mediterranean. Finished meeting 1.30 pm. Afternoon prepared my briefs for 6 pm Cabinet meeting when I had to give résumé of the week's fighting in Libya, Abyssinia and Russia. Meeting lasted till 7.30 pm. At 9.30 pm another COS meeting to complete what we had not done this morning. This lasted till 12.30 am. Dudley Pound the slowest chairman I have ever seen.

2 December
Chiefs of Staff meeting from 10.30 to 1.30 at which we discussed possibility of raid on Italian coast. Gave up project owing to threatening situation in Far East. At 5 pm another COS meeting which was attended by Anthony Eden to discuss his impending visit to Russia and the offers he could make to Stalin as

regards troops for Southern Russia. Owing to Libyan offensive having gone as badly as it has there will not be much available for Russia! We then examined latest telegram from Roosevelt, or rather from Halifax of conversations with Roosevelt. It was the most encouraging one received yet as to cooperation of USA with us in the event of war with Japan. Situation in the Far East looking far worse, submarines reported moving south from Saigon this evening. Dined at Club and returned to office for work till 11.30 pm.

3 December

COS meeting at 10.30 where Pug Ismay produced memo from PM to the effect that 18th and 50th Divs were to be offered to the Russians for their Southern front! Eden to make this offer to Stalin during his impending visit to Moscow! This would probably mean having to close down the Libyan offensive, whereas I am positive that our policy for the conduct of the war should be to direct both our military and political efforts towards the early conquest of North Africa. From there we shall be able to reopen the Mediterranean and to stage offensive operations against Italy.

It is interesting to note that already on December 3rd, my third day as CIGS, I had a clear cut idea as to what our policy should be. America was not even in the war at that time, and it was not yet possible to foresee our combined landings in Algeria and Morocco. Nevertheless it was already clear to me that we must clear North Africa to open the Mediterranean, and until we had done that we should never have enough shipping to stage major operations. It is some gratification to look back now, knowing that this policy was carried out, but only after many struggles and much opposition from many quarters.*

At 12 noon had to go to see King in Buckingham Palace. After that lunched at 10 Downing Street with PM and Mrs Churchill, she was as usual charming.

Back to WO to prepare brief for Cabinet Defence Committee meeting at 5.30. Here we discussed means of ensuring that the USA comes into Far East war in event of Japanese aggression. Also question of whether Eden was to offer 50th and 18th Divs to Stalin. Luckily we succeeded in riding PM off such a suggestion but only at expense of some 500 tanks to be sent to Russia, this according to Beaverbrook's suggestion. At any rate most of meeting, including Margesson, Amery [India and Burma], Eden, St Clair [Sinclair? Air], and Attlee all against giving the divisions to Russia. Tried to begin to make them realize that we must have one definite policy for the conduct of the war. I must get the PM to see the advantages of a real North African offensive policy.

*Whether it was quite as clear-cut as that – and how 'the Mediterranean strategy' may be construed – is dissected in Brian Bond, 'Alanbrooke and Britain's Mediterranean Strategy, 1942–1944', in Lawrence Freedman et al. (eds), *War, Strategy and International Politics* (Oxford: Clarendon, 1992), pp. 175–93; Alex Danchev, 'Britain: The Indirect Strategy' in David Reynolds et al. (eds), *Allies at War* (New York: St Martin's, 1994), pp. 1–26, and 'Biffing: The Saga of the Second Front', in Alex Danchev, *On Specialness* (London: Macmillan, 1998), pp. 29–45; and Michael Howard, *The Mediterranean Strategy in the Second World War* [1968] (London: Greenhill, 1993).

I remember well being appalled in those early days of my time as CIGS to find the
lack of a definite policy for the prosecution of the war. We worked from day to day, a
hand to mouth existence with a policy based on opportunism. Every wind that blew
swung us like a weathercock. As I was to find out, planned strategy was not
Winston's strong card. He preferred to work by intuition and impulse.

4 December

COS meeting at 10.30 am where we discussed 'Anklet' and 'Truncheon' operations. The former intended to seize a temporary base in Norway and the latter
an attack on Italian coast. Proceedings as usual painfully slow owing to old
Dudley Pound.

At 6 pm I attended War Cabinet at which Anthony Eden's visit to Moscow
was again discussed. I had to state results of my investigation as to whether any
tanks could be spared for Eden to offer to Stalin. I said best we could do was
300 Churchill tanks by 30th June, and that although this offer might be acceptable to Russia, I did not recommend such a gift as we should be seriously
denuding this country and prematurely disclosing a new pattern of tank.
Painted a picture of possible tank battles in this country such as were taking
place in Libya. These gave Kingsley Wood [Chancellor] the shivers and he
appealed to PM not to contemplate denuding this country. Debate became
interminable. Anthony Eden like a peevish child grumbling because he was
being sent off to see Uncle Stalin without suitable gifts, while Granny
Churchill was comforting him and explaining to him all the pretty speeches he
might make instead. Finally Eden succeeded in swinging Churchill round to a
gift of some 300 tanks and 300 aircraft. During most of the debate the conduct
of the war seemed to have been pushed into the background, self interests
seemed to predominate.

After dinner COS met at 10 pm with the Prime Minister presiding, and Attlee
and Anthony Eden present. During the dinner interval the PM had swung
right round again, tanks and aircraft had been put aside, the gift was now to
consist of 10 squadrons of aircraft to be made available immediately after the
Libyan offensive was finished. Portal agreed, but said offer was too definite.
This produced the most awful outburst of temper, we were told that we did
nothing but obstruct his intentions, we had no ideas of our own, and whenever he produced ideas we produced nothing but objections, etc. etc! Attlee paci-
fied him once, but he broke out again, then Anthony Eden soothed him
temporarily, but to no avail. Finally he looked at his papers for some 5
minutes, then slammed them together, closed the meeting and walked out of
the room! It was pathetic and entirely unnecessary. We were only trying to
save him from making definite promises which he might find hard to keep
later on. It is all the result of overworking himself and keeping too late hours.
Such a pity. God knows where we would be without him, but God knows
where we shall go with him!*

---

*Cf. Danchev, 'God Knows: Civil-Military Relations with Allies', in *Specialness*, pp. 46–73.

5 December

COS meeting at 10.30 am where we were greeted by a memorandum from the PM couched practically in identical terms with those we had asked him to accept last night! Also 'Anklet' alterations which last night raised much ire were now accepted. There was not much business at meeting so went to see Paget on way back to WO. After lunch had to see all the military attachés. The Japanese seemed gloomy and I wonder whether we should have them with us much longer! Then had a meeting with Margesson and Moore-Brabazon [Aircraft Production] on the question of the production of fighter aircraft with 40 mm gun. Finished up with a military members meeting of the Army Council and more office work.

6 December

A quiet morning in so far as there was no COS meeting, I therefore got through a good deal of office work and had intended to slip home for Sunday at about 4 or 5 pm. However, just as I was getting ready to leave a cablegram from Singapore came in with news of two convoys of Japanese transports, escorted by cruisers and destroyers, southwest of Saigon moving west. As a result First Sea Lord at once called a meeting of Chiefs of Staff. Cadogan [PUS] for Foreign Office came also.* We examined situation carefully, but from position of the transports it was not possible to tell whether they were going to Bangkok, to the Kra Peninsula, or whether they were just cruising round as a bluff. PM called up from Chequers to have results of our meeting phoned through to him. Second message came in while we were there, but it did not clear up situation in the least, and it only said that convoy had been lost and could not be picked up again.

Put off going home, dined at Club, returned to WO after dinner. Went home expecting to be called out again, but got off without it.

7 December

Went up to WO, still hoping that possibly I might get home for a bit. Soon disillusioned and told to attend COS meeting at 11.30 am. We remained there till 2.15 pm with a representative from the Foreign Office, discussing all the various alternatives that might lead to war and trying to ensure that in every case the USA would not be left out.

Had hurried lunch at the club followed by a fast lap around St James's Park. Then ½ hour with S of S to put him into the picture and discuss with him advisability of letting [General Alan] Cunningham down as easily as possible on his return from the Middle East, PM being inclined to hold up his dismissal as an example.

---

*Another diarist, chronically acidulous. 'Found report of reconnaissance of Japanese armada moving west, south of Cambodia point. Rang up A [Eden]. Broke into meeting of C[hiefs] of S[taff], who didn't seem to know quite where they were.' David Dilks (ed.), *The Diaries of Sir Alexander Cadogan* (London: Cassell, 1971), p. 416.

5 pm: another COS meeting again attended by Foreign Office representative. Finished about 7 pm, and after seeing DMO and DMI went home for dinner. After dinner listened to wireless to find that Japan had attacked America [at Pearl Harbor]!! All our work of last 48 hours wasted! The Japs themselves have now ensured that the USA are in the war.

Came back to Latimer Court for my last dinner there as I move out tomorrow. After dinner got through to DMO and DMI to find out situation and to discover whether another COS meeting would be required. Luckily not! So off to bed for some sleep before another hard day's work.

At one of our meetings shortly after the USA had come into the war, someone was still adopting the careful attitude that had been necessary before the entry of the USA to ensure that we did not let ourselves into a war with Japan without the USA being in it. Winston turned to him, and with a wicked leer in his eye, said: 'Oh! That is the way we talked to her while we were wooing her, now that she is in the harem we talk to her quite differently!'

8 December
Started with Chiefs of Staff meeting which was mainly preoccupied with examining new situation. At 12.30 went on to Cabinet Meeting. PM explained steps he had taken, conversation with Roosevelt, telegram to de Valera appealing for Ireland to join war, convening Parliament for 3 pm, etc. He also put before the Cabinet his plan to start this week for America to see Roosevelt to ensure that American help to this country does not dry up. Cabinet agreed to this decision. During afternoon was informed that First Sea Lord and CAS would accompany PM, but that one Chief of Staff had to remain behind and being hardly in the saddle this should fall to my lot! Sad, but only to be expected. However he has decided to take Dill, which I am delighted at as it will please Dill I am certain and no one could be better suited for the job.

9 December
Rather a dull COS meeting which lasted from 10.30 to lunch. During afternoon series of interviews starting with Prince Bernhard of the Netherlands, Stuart of the Armoured Corps to be relieved of his job, King, the Chief Engineer, concerning gas in the Far East, Paget with points about Home Forces, etc. Returned to hotel to be greeted by telephone saying that PM wanted Chiefs of Staff meeting under him in Cabinet War Room at 10 pm! I had Q Martel to dine with me to discuss his trip to the Far East. Then went to WO and after this to the meeting. PM mainly concerned with naval situation in the Pacific due to result of Japanese action on USA fleet in Honolulu in which 3 battleships were sunk and 3 badly damaged out of 8!! This has entirely upset the balance in Pacific and leaves Japs masters of the ocean until we can assemble some forces there. We therefore examined possibility of sending British battleship to restore situation. Finally left matter to be thought over and broke up at midnight.

10 December

Arrived at WO to be informed that both the *Prince of Wales* and *Repulse* had been sunk by the Japs! This on top of the tragedy of Honolulu puts us in a very serious position for the prosecution of the war. It means that for Africa east-wards to America through the Indian Ocean and the Pacific, we have lost command of the sea. This affects reinforcements to Middle East, India, Burma, Far East, Australia and New Zealand! Chiefs of Staff conference moved to 10 Downing Street at 12 noon, when we discussed naval situation with the PM. He had stood shock well. He had also heard from Roosevelt who did not like idea of his visit owing to secrecy reasons and suggested meeting should be held in Jan instead as he could not leave till Jan 5th – PM fretting a bit at this delay.

Spent afternoon in office with series of visits. Starting with Sir Keith Murdoch who controls group of Australian newspapers. Then de Gaulle to draw my attention to value of Madagascar base under new situation. Next Melchett again about bombards.

11 December

At COS this morning we were informed that PM's trip to USA had been put forward again and that he proposed to start tomorrow night. Also informed by Pug Ismay that the PM now wanted to send the 18th Div to Rangoon to attack Japs on Kra Isthmus, being now convinced that we had enough troops for this North African business!

In afternoon went to 10 Downing St to see PM about sending Dill to USA as our representative there – that is to say for him to go with PM and then remain there. PM agreed.

This agreement was not arrived at without a good deal of discussion. Winston's dislike for Dill was nearly upsetting my plan at one moment.... Thank heaven I suc-ceeded in convincing Winston as few men did more in furthering our cause of final victory than Dill. From the very start he built up a deep friendship with Marshall and proved to be an invaluable link beween British and American Chiefs of Staff. It is unfortunate that Winston never gave him the credit that was due to him. I look upon that half hour's discussion with Winston at 10 Downing Street on December 11th as one of my most important accomplishments during the war, or at any rate amongst those that bore most fruit.*

Dined with Bertie, but could not stop long as I had to go to COS meeting under PM at 10 pm. Meeting began badly and Portal nearly started another brain-storm on the subject of denuding Middle East for the Far East. With some diffi-culty we calmed him down and finally I got him to agree to transfer Burma back to C-in-C India and Iraq and Persia to Middle East. 18th Div to go to Bombay as reinforcement for India and Archie Wavell to decide how best to

---

*Dill's vital work in Washington is the subject of Alex Danchev, *Very Special Relationship* (London: Brassey's, 1986).

reinforce Burma and how to operate offensively against Jap L of C through Kra isthmus. This still leaves possibility of diverting 18th Div up Persian Gulf to Iraq for defence of oil should Germans look like attacking through Turkey. Finished meeting at 12.30 am.

12 December

COS meeting this morning to pass the message that PM had written as a result of our meeting of the previous evening. Not much to alter. Pug Ismay said PM was very tired last night and complaining of a pain inside. I hope to God that there is nothing wrong with him. This afternoon another COS meeting to decide on details of bombing large convoy in Mediterranean evidently intended to take supplies etc to Libya, hope we get some of them. Alan Cunningham, just back from Libya, came to see me very depresssed and hard to comfort.

Dill came in evening to say goodbye on eve of departure for USA – PM and his train load start tonight. I shall be left as Chairman of COS during their absence, with Deputy Chiefs for Navy and Air. Pug Ismay also remains behind. Attlee will officiate as PM. Shall be properly stretched as my VCIGS is in Moscow with Eden, my ACIGS is going with PM's party, and my DSD [Director of Staff Duties] is still in Middle East!!

13 December

PM and his party left last night. Dill called up this morning once more before sailing to settle final details. At 10.30 started my first Chiefs of Staff meeting as Chairman. Finished at 12 noon instead of 1.30 as we should have done with old Dudley Pound! Lunch with Adam and had a real good afternoon in the office and at last began to get level with some of my work. Two Italian cruisers sunk, Malaya still holding out well. Hong Kong garrison back into the island!

14 December

Went to the WO in morning and then home for rest of day – a great rest after last fortnight!

15 December

Left Ferney Close at 8 am, WO 9.15, read telegrams and briefed for COS at 10.30 am. Afternoon Cabinet Meeting at 5 pm and Defence Committee meeting at 6 pm which lasted till 8 pm. PM now away and meeting run by Attlee very efficiently and quickly. Far East situation far from rosy! I doubt whether Hong Kong will hold out a fortnight and Malaya a month!

16 December

Usual morning Chiefs of Staff meeting. PM decided to go to Bermuda and to fly on. Far East news no better. Lunched with de Gaulle a most unattractive specimen. We made a horrid mistake when we decided to make use of him! Gentilhomme was also there, but I had little chance of speaking to him. Old General Billotte's son sat on my right – his father was the general in command of Northern group of Armies before Dunkirk who was killed in a motor accident. At 5 pm second COS meeting to discuss evacuation of coast towns in the event of invasion, and also formation of aerodrome defence corps. Back to WO after dinner.

17 December

Long COS meeting to discuss reinforcements to Burma and Malaya. A very difficult problem trying to patch holes out there without interfering with Middle East offensive. Personally I do not feel that there is much hope of saving Singapore, but feel that we ought to try and make certain of Burma. Another COS meeting at 5 pm and dinner with Brendan Bracken at the Ministry of Information. A queer assembly to meet Sir Keith Murdoch including Citrine, J.J. Astor, Roger Keyes, Sholto Douglas and many other queer birds.

18 December

Long COS meeting this morning to consider the desirability of seizing North Madagascar to stop Japs getting it. Full of complications – means abandoning temporary scheme for taking Atlantic Islands in event of loss of Gibraltar unless we can get Americans to take on that job. Further complications due to de Gaulle wishing to cooperate with the Madagascar operations. His support is more likely to be an encumbrance. Lunched with [illegible] and had long talk with him about defence of Singapore. In evening discussed with Margesson the latest attacks by Duff Cooper on Percival's handling of Singapore defence, which he has submitted to PM in a wire and which I have had to produce covering remarks on.

19 December

A long COS meeting in the morning where we prepared a memorandum on our policy for the Far East. Not an easy document. After lunch went to see Arnold Lawson to have my eyes tested as they have been feeling the stress of all the reading I have been doing and I thought that stronger glasses might be necessary. However he advised sticking to present ones. At 3.30 a visit by the King of Greece. A definite personality. Not much opinion of the Foreign Off[ice], which he had been coming up against. Gave me rather a feeling that he was a bit German in his make up. Army Council Military Members meeting at 6 pm. At 9.30 pm Defence Committee meeting with Attlee in the chair to discuss the paper we had prepared this morning. Attlee ran the meeting very well, which was not easy as Sir Earle Page, the Australian representative, with the mentality of a greengrocer, wasted a lot of our time. In the end our paper was accepted. Finished at 12.30 am!

20 December

A fairly long COS meeting, mainly connected with various aspects of various measures required to counter the the increasing threats in the Far East. Reports came in that Hong Kong Island was half occupied by the Japs but still holding on. Sent wire to the GOC with congratulations on their defence. Had Adam with me to lunch at the Carlton Grill and a good talk with him. Rest of afternoon taken up with working off remnants left over from this week.

The more I look at the situation at present the more I dislike it! My hopes of carrying on with the conquest and reclamation of North Africa are beginning to look more and more impossible every day. From now on the Far East will make ever increasing inroads into our resources. The loss of the American battleships and the *Prince of Wales* and *Repulse* will take a long time to recover, and meanwhile we shall suffer many more losses in the Far East.

21 December

WO office just to read telegrams and then slipped home for the rest of the day.

22 December

Left home at 8 am. Hectic hour in WO priming up for COS meeting which lasted till 1.30 pm. Whilst at lunch I was collected by S of S to go round to Colonial Office to discuss with Lord Moyne wire for Hong Kong as regards degree of resistance to be put up by them. Moyne very flabby and required boosting up. Attlee came in and was good. 5 pm Cabinet meeting, nothing of much importance discussed. Hectic evening after it.

23 December

COS meeting mainly concerned with operation to capture Northern Madagascar to forestall any attempt on the part of the Japs, also discussion as to the advisability of USA force undertaking the capture of Atlantic Islands in the event of invasion of Spain and Portugal. After lunch Army Council meeting and selection board meeting. Then interview with General Gentilhomme who struck me as being a far better type than de Gaulle. Then Spanish Military Attaché and after that Brig for Middle East to interview. Then had to go round to India Office to see Amery with reference to appointment of new commander for Burma and for selection of new Chief of Staff for Archie Wavell to replace Hutton, who is to be C-in-C Burma. Dined with Jimmy Harrison and his wife.

24 December

Another hard day. COS meeting in the morning. The situation beginning to become difficult. Winston has arrived in Washington, far from the war, and is pushing for operations by USA and ourselves against North Africa and banking on further success of Middle East offensive towards Tripoli. On the other side Duff Cooper in Singapore by his demands is inspiring the Australians to ask for more and more for the Far East. In the middle Auchinleck struggling along with the forces at his disposal and sending optimistic personal and private messages to the PM little knowing that his activities must shortly be curtailed owing to transfer of air and sea reinforcements from the Middle East to the Far East. At 3 pm Defence Committee meeting to settle aerodrome defence and 'scorched earth' policy in Malay peninsula. Afterwards visits from Liddell [Inspector-General for Training] and DMT. Had hoped to get home for Xmas, but impossible now owing to urgent necessity for COS meeting tomorrow morning. So dined quietly with Barney and now off to an early bed.

25 December

Xmas day and my first official day as CIGS! Went to WO at 9.30 where I spent 2 hours studying paper prepared by the Joint Planning Committee on relative importance of our new Far East commitments, taken in relation with the Middle East. At 11.30 went to COS meeting to discuss same paper and to prepare wire to PM with reference to his desire to carry out 'Gymnast' operation (i.e. reinforcements to French North Africa in event of being called in). Problem complicated by the fact that it does not look as if we are likely to be called in, and secondly that PM is now toying with the idea of carrying out such a plan against resistance, and finally owing to the fact that shipping available does not admit of both occupying North Africa at request of French and reinforcing Far East sufficiently to secure Singapore, Burma, and Indian Ocean communications. We have laid down that first of all in importance come security of this country and its communications and after that Singapore and communications through Indian Ocean. This is correct as if the latter go the Middle East or possibly India may follow suit. Committee lasted till 6 pm! News received this evening that Hong Kong had fallen on Xmas Eve.

The situation was evidently fraught with many dangers and a false step at this stage might well lead to the worst of catastrophes. Operations in North Africa were evidently dependent on many factors, and we were not in a position at that moment to undertake further commitments until we could see more clearly how we stood. Winston was never good at looking at all the implications of any course of action which he favoured! In fact, he frequently refused to look at them. I was consequently at that time filled with fears lest some decision might be arrived at by him whilst away in USA which would launch us into a new commitment at this critical juncture.

26 December

Usual COS meeting where we discussed various points connected with reinforcing of Far East and Fiji Islands etc. In afternoon rung up by Attlee to find out whether we were ready for a Defence Committee meeting to keep Australians quiet as they were fretting about reinforcements to Singapore. Told him we had better wait until we had reply from PM. Later Mr Bruce [Commonwealth Governments] asked to see me and I had to explain to him what we were doing for the Far East. He went away satisfied. Just before dinner wire from PM for Auchinleck came in which necessitated holding impromptu COS meeting after dinner. Finally interview with S of S and bed at midnight. Very weary!

27 December

A long and wearying COS meeting with a series of difficult problems, mainly connected with the PM and his Chiefs of Staff committee in USA brewing up a series of discrepancies with what we are preparing here. In the afternoon a Cabinet Defence Committee meeting intended to satisfy Bruce and keep him quiet. Lasted till 7.30 pm. I then escaped home in the hope of being allowed to spend a quiet Sunday and recuperate from the effort of the last 3 weeks! A very peaceful evening at home.

28 December

A lovely peaceful day with you at Ferney Close, which was wonderfully restful and fitted me up to stand another week of this strain!

29 December

Left Ferney Close 8 am, dropped Ronnie on way up, arrived WO at 9.10 am. There I found new wires had been received from the PM at 5 am suggesting that new Combined Command should be formed in the Far East under Wavell!, with USA deputy C-in-C and American naval forces under Wavell. Special body in Washington to control operations under PM and USA president. The whole scheme wild and half baked and only catering for one area of action namely Western Pacific, one enemy Japan, and no central control.

Cabinet Conference at 10.30 am where I was asked for my views and asked for time for COS conference to consider. Attlee in the chair granted us time till 2.30 pm. We therefore gathered a COS meeting till 1.30 pm to thrash out our own views. [The] more we looked at our task the less we liked it. A very hurried lunch and at 2.30 pm another cabinet meeting where I had to describe military situation and then describe results of morning's work. Cabinet was forced to accept PM's new scheme owing to the fact that it was almost a fait accompli! Lasted till 4.30 pm and then another COS meeting at 5 pm to brief representatives whom we are sending to the Americans. Then a hurried hour in the War Office, followed by dinner with Bertie, where Chester Beattie, [illegible], and [illegible] were the guests.

I remember well that the two points that worried me about this telegram were that in the first place we were setting up a local organization to deal with one specific theatre and one enemy, whilst what was really required was a global organization providing for central control for all fronts and both enemies. Secondly, I could see no reason why at this stage, with American forces totally unprepared to play a major part, we should agree to a central control in Washington.

30 December

COS meeting from 10.30 till 12 noon with no items of great importance. But by afternoon the charter for the new Far East Supreme Commander (Archie Wavell) had come in for immediate criticism. We consequently had to convene meeting of the COS for 9.30 pm. The draft is far from satisfactory. In the first place Burma is included in the Far East command but *not* China. This is quite impossible since Burma must be base for China, leading in through Burma road through which reinforcements must flow to the Chinese so that they may bite Japan in the backside. Secondly Australia and New Zealand are not included in the command, whilst it is essential that they should act as bases of supply, reinforcements, etc. Finally the wording was such as to restrict the machinery to too slow a cadence for war purposes. In afternoon had interview with Ottley, just back from Malta.

31 December

Started day with COS meeting which I succeeded in completing by 12 noon. Then 1½ hours hard work in WO, followed by lunch with S of S at Turf Club, where we discussed successor to Archie Wavell as C-in-C India. Personally I feel Adam is only possible selection, but am afraid I may have Gort pushed on me! and I am convinced he is unsuitable. The other alternatives are Alexander, who has not got the brains, and Paget, who should be left with Home Forces. At 4 pm Cabinet Defence Committee in which I put up proposals for transfer of Iraq and Persia to Middle East Command from India Command. Amery of course defended retention with India, but remainder of meeting was with me. This evening we received a wire from Wavell who is in complete agreement with me as regards desirability of retaining Burma with India instead of placing it in Wavell's new command.

[1 January] 1942

Started new year wondering what it may have in store for us. One thing I fully realize is that it has got about as much work in store for me as I can possibly cope with. I pray God that He may give me sufficient strength to devote the energy and drive that it will require. Difficult times with the PM I see clearly ahead of me and there again I pray God to help me by giving me guidance as to how to handle the difficult situations which are certain to confront me.

Ran Chiefs of Staff conference till 12 noon, when we adjourned for a Cabinet meeting. There the time was mainly taken by Anthony Eden describing his visit to Moscow. His impressions of Stalin were very interesting and his accounts of the banquets most amusing. The dinner started at 10 pm and lasted till 5 am! Timoshenko arrived drunk and by continuous drinking restored himself to sobriety by 5 am. On the other hand, [Marshal] Voroshilov after at least arriving sober, had to be carried out before the evening was through!

I did not enter it in my diary, but I believe that as Voroshilov slumped under the table, Stalin turned to Anthony and said: 'Do your Generals also hold their drink so badly?' Anthony, the complete diplomat, replied: 'They may have a better capacity for drink, but they have not the same ability for winning battles!' I cannot vouch for this story!

The afternoon I spent in the office without many interruptions and by 5 pm had finished without necessity to return to WO after dinner. And now I hope for a real good night's sleep.

2 January

COS meeting – as usual I succeeded in finishing it by 12 noon, and am beginning to get things moving! Wonder what I shall do when Dudley Pound gets back from USA and takes the chair again? It will be awful putting up with the delays, I shall have to devise some way of overcoming them. Nothing much of importance, except discussion on Foreign Office difficulties in settling matters concerning Timor Island, and the Portuguese anger at their occupation by Australians. At 3 pm Cabinet Defence Committee where we discussed advisability of asking USA to occupy the Falkland Islands. Foreign Office nervous lest USA should hand them over to Argentina. Whilst we argue Japs likely to step in.

This evening moved into the new flat for first time. Barney has done wonders and it is most comfortable.

I moved in to No. 7 Westminster Gardens, where I remained till the end of the war. I took the flat over from Dill, who had occupied it since he had been bombed out of another flat in the same building. Barney Charlesworth, my ADC, did wonders to make us comfortable and brought down some of his own furniture for it. He ran a wonderful show and was a marvellous companion, as tight as a clam with any information, so that I could pour out my worries to him, which was a wonderful help.

3 January

Was sent for at 10.30 by Attlee to discuss with him, S of S and Amery the future C-in-C of India. All sorts of proposals – Dill, Platt, Alexander, Hartley, Adam, Paget. Amery and Viceroy were pressing for Auchinleck to be returned to India. Evidently impossible. Finally settled that Hartley should be suggested to Viceroy. Then went on to COS. In evening slipped home where I arrived for dinner.

4 January
Spent peacefully at home.

5 January
Left 8 am. COS meeting from 10.30 to 12 noon. Then at 12.30 another meeting with Attlee, Amery and S of S concerning future C-in-C of India. Amery and Viceroy still pressing for return of Auchinleck to India. PM wiring from USA that this was impossible. Auchinleck recommending Hartley with Ted Morris as his CGS. So for the present this has been settled. This evening old Copper Finlayson has been snooping round to see if he can't push himself as C-in-C India!! Busy day and back in WO till 11.30 pm.

6 January
COS as usual which included a long interview with Tennant who was captain of the *Repulse*, sunk off Singapore with the *Prince of Wales*. He was most interesting in the whole of his account of the action, which apparently lasted under 1½ hours! Spotted at 6 am by reconnaissance plane, first attack shortly after 11 am, and sunk before 1 pm! In afternoon interview with Browning concerning Airborne Division and also special General Staff Committee under my chairmanship concerning tank development. I think we made some progress.

Dined with Dr Dalton [responsible for Special Operations Executive (SOE)] and discussed with him his sabotage activities in Europe under Gubbins, and also the question of raising local forces in Europe to be armed and equipped at the last moment. There is a great deal to be done in this direction at present and I don't feel we are doing anything like enough. Finished up with one and a half hour's work in WO. Home at midnight very tired and sleepy!

7 January
Usual COS with multitude of small points, none of which were of much importance. Harry Crerar to lunch, and a good opportunity of discussing with him the future organization of the Canadian Corps now that it has expanded to such a size that it requires a Force HQ to control rear echelons, workshops, etc. Full afternoon, necessitating return to WO in the evening.

8 January
A COS meeting mainly concerned with organizing the special wireless intercept system so as to ensure that it will be able to deal with its new task in the Far East, and also to increase its efficiency in the existing task. The afternoon I spent in the WO getting level with the work there. After dinner back to WO and long talk with Nye on the organization of the Airborne Division, and instructed it to be pushed to the utmost and given preferential treatment.

9 January

COS meeting this morning where we had representatives from the Middle East to discuss with them the possibility of carrying out 'Acrobat' (ie attack on Tripoli) in spite of delays that had occurred in capture of Cyrenaica and new situation in Far East. In view of the fact that operation cannot be carried out for 6 weeks and that during this period reinforcements may well flow into Africa from Italy, I am beginning to wonder whether the operation is on. At any rate I feel that it ought if possible to be connected with the operation for occupying North Africa on the invitation of the French. But, first secure your invitation!

In afternoon Defence Committee meeting to examine implications of American occupation of Northern Ireland. Andrews, the Prime Minister of Northern Ireland, was there and I had to put before him all the implications of this relief. He was very nice about it. Meeting from 3.45 to 5.30 pm. Then Military Members meeting of Army Council.

10 January

Usual COS in the morning, after which I had Adam to lunch in the flat. Succeeded in escaping home about 6 pm.

11 January

Spent peacefully at home.

12 January

Left 8 am and dropped Ronnie on way up. Rather a dull COS meeting mainly concerned with small points. The area allotted to Wavell's Supreme Command (i.e. ABDA area, standing for America, British, Dutch, Australian area) is continually giving trouble owing to original mistake of including Burma and not including Australia and NZ. I expect that we shall gradually be forced to change these back again. Wavell very quick in getting his show going. Meanwhile situation in Malaya getting more and more critical daily. Only hope reinforcements are not intercepted.

13 January

COS meeting mainly concerned with discussion of possibility of carrying out Tripoli attack. After lunch visit by General Daufresne de la Chevalerie, C-in-C Belgian Forces. Interesting individual, used to ride at Olympia, escaped from Belgium through France to America and back here. Then Porter back from Egypt. Afterwards visit to Attlee to discuss appointment of Governor of Singapore, civilian or military, also organization of Intelligence and situation in Singapore. Finally interviews with ACIGS and DSD. Then Basil and Margesson came to dinner.

14 January

COS meeting at which we closed down investigations on plans to capture a port in Northern Sumatra to save it from a Jap attack! Also heard from America that enterprise called 'Gymnast', to occupy North Africa, had been put off. Had McNaughton to lunch to settle details of future of Canadian forces. Then interview with Gubbins concerning raising of armies in Northen France and North Africa. Also with Archie Nye and Weeks. Finally dined with Bertie, where Sholto Douglas and Basil were also dining.

15 January

COS as usual, which I finished earlier. Then I had Dupuy to lunch to discuss French situation. He is going back to Vichy again soon. After lunch visit from Paget to discuss various points, followed by General Chaney, the American general, with whom I discussed relief of troops in Ireland by Americans. Later, visit of QMG to discuss reduction of Australian rear service of troops by move from the Middle East to Far East to save shipping. Finally DMI on most recent intelligence and back to flat after 8 pm with more work after dinner.

16 January

A COS meeting with many items which I succeeded in killing off fairly quickly. Then a rush back to do a bit of office work, followed by lunch at Home Forces. Then gave talk to Cs-in-C conference on the situation in the world. Started with Russia and worked right round. Talk lasted about 1¼ hours and questions to follow.

Returned to WO to have interview with Franklyn and Air Force concerning new plan for Ulster Force to move into Eire in the event of invasion. 5.30 pm, Cabinet Defence Committee where I had to give details of recent military events, discuss proposed Far East Defence Council constructed to give Dominions and Dutch a voice in direction of events, and finally argue as to effect of withdrawal of force from Syria.

17 January

Usual COS meeting where we discovered that PM was flying through from Bermuda, and had landed Mount Batten [Plymouth] at 9 am. After lunch went to Paddington to meet his special [train], due at 3 pm. A queer crowd of Cabinet ministers in black slouch sombreros and astrakhan collars to meet him! He arrived about 3.15 and was given a great welcome. Went back to WO to find he was having a war cabinet meeting which Chiefs of Staff were to attend at 6 pm. This lasted till 7.30 pm, and was very interesting as it contained a full account of the trip to America and his impressions. Then returned home where I arrived after 9 pm.

18 January

After a nice sleep and breakfast, a telephone call from PM saying he wanted me to dine with him tonight! So left home 5.30, motored back on snow covered roads to WO, where I got into picture as to latest wires and then went on to the Annexe at Storey's Gate. Only Mrs Churchill and youngest daughter for dinner. A very pleasant, quiet, homely dinner. He could not have been nicer. After dinner went to his study where I remained till after midnight discussing the possibilities of Singapore Island holding out. Also drew his attention to the danger of Rangoon.

He has now changed his mind about Dill and no longer wants him as Deputy Defence Minister in USA but to replace Wemyss [Head of British Army Staff] instead.

As far as Dill's work was concerned, this was only a different title; instead of being Deputy Defence Minister he was to be Head of the British Military Mission in Washington. The former title would have been a more suitable title and one carrying more guns, but with a man like Dill it did not matter what you called him, he did what he considered was required of him. As matters turned out he did the work of a Deputy Ambassador and Deputy Defence Minister combined in one person.

19 January

COS meeting with Pound in chair again, as a result desperately slow! Went on till 1.15 pm although we had very little to get through. This evening Cabinet meeting at 6 pm which lasted till 9.30 pm!!!* Mainly taken up with long discourse by PM on the strategical situation in a series of interruptions of the Chiefs of Staff statements. We then discussed the proposed organization for centralizing equipment, shipping, supplies of materials etc., between the belligerents. Sir Earle Page, Australian representative, as usual wasted most of our time!

20 January

The COS meetings are very trying again with old Dudley Pound in the chair. He is deadly slow and inefficient! Lunched with Adam at Carlton Grill and then walked back through St James's Park in the snow, about 2 inches deep. This afternoon a fairly quiet time without many interruptions and succeeded in getting through a good deal of work between 3 pm and 8 pm and with 2 more hours after dinner. Very cold. News from the Far East is bad and I am beginning to be very doubtful whether Singapore will hold out much longer.

21 January

A hard day made unpleasant by a bad cold. First COS meeting till 1 pm, mainly

---

*The first of the triple exclamation marks!

taken up with discussing relative dangers of Singapore and Rangoon and arguing best destiny for further reinforcements. Then lunch with Sikorski, who was very interesting on his visit to Russia and interview with Stalin. We discussed many points: rearming of Polish division in Russia, sending of Polish officers from Scotland to Russia, move of Polish forces from Scotland, etc. Then back to WO with many interviews including S of S for ½ hour.

5 pm COS meeting concerning reinforcements to Singapore, followed at 6 pm by COS under PM, and finally Cabinet Defence Committee at 10 pm, which lasted till midnight. The latter finished with a climax caused by arrival of wire from Australia disagreeing with all the arrangements PM had with USA concerning higher direction of the war!!

22 January

COS this morning at which we examined most recent developments of situation caused by Australia insisting on being represented on a Defence Council in Washington instead of in London! PM had sent good telegram back. He had admitted the inclusion of one of their representatives in the War Cabinet, but told them to fix the Washington Council themselves!, knowing that they would fail to do so.

Lunched with S of S at Ritz, where he had been sick. Back to office and several interviews before the evening Cabinet meeting at 6 pm. PM in great form in spite of his cold. After failing to resist the temptation himself of continually wiring advice to Wavell, he said this evening: 'It is no good appointing a Supreme Commander if you have to spend your time teaching him to supreme command, I want to keep the flies away from the meat.' Another 2 hours after dinner.

23 January

COS meeting in morning, mainly concerned with situation in Burma and Singapore. We have now got all the reinforcements we can on the move and the difficulty now rests in deciding whether these reinforcements should go to Singapore or to Burma. Both are in a very dangerous position and each affects the other.

The problem was a difficult one, the retention of Singapore was certainly the most important for the future prosecution of the war, and for the protection of our communications through the Indian Ocean. On the other hand, reinforcements for Singapore might well be too late, as turned out to be the case with the 18ᵗʰ Division, whilst reinforcements to Burma might still save the situation there and secure Eastern approaches to India. Looking back on our decision to send 18ᵗʰ Division to Singapore, in the light of after events, I think we were wrong to send it to Singapore, and that it would have served a more useful purpose had it been sent to Rangoon.

Lucas and Weeks came to lunch and we discussed production of the Mark VII tank and use of cannon fighter aircraft against tanks. In afternoon long interview with Paget, and with General Odic, who had been Weygand's Chief of Staff in North Africa. He has no use for de Gaulle and was very frank about it.

24 January

Usual COS in the morning. After lunch visit by Melchett about new form of gun. Then long spell with DMI on German forces. Then just as I hoped to go home we had to have another COS meeting to draw up a reply for PM to an Australian SOS brought about by the threat to New Guinea. Finally left for home at 7 pm.

25 January

Spent quietly at home recovering from my cold and doing some glass blowing with the young!

26 January

Long COS in the morning. Then Martel to lunch to give me details of his trip to the Middle East.

Then briefing for Cabinet at 6 pm which lasted till 8.30 pm and necessitated my coming back to WO after dinner.

27 January

I was sent for on my way over to COS to see PM. Found him in bed with the red and golden dragon dressing gown on and a large cigar in his mouth. Busy working at his momentous speech. He wanted to discuss a sentence connected with move of Australian forces from Syria which I had asked him to withdraw, also one connected with continuance of supply of tanks to Russia.

This interview was typical of many future ones of this kind. The scene in his bedroom was always the same and I only wish some artist could have committed it to canvas. The red and gold dressing gown in itself was worth going miles to see, and only Winston could have thought of wearing it! He looked rather like some Chinese Mandarin! The few hairs were usually ruffled on his bald head. A large cigar stuck sideways out of his face. The bed was littered with papers and despatches. Sometimes the tray with his finished breakfast was still on the bed table. The bell was continually being rung for secretaries, typists, stenographers, or his faithful valet Sawyers.

Long COS mainly connected with trying to rectify errors of ABDA and ANZAC [Australia and New Zealand Army Corps] areas. The show will never run properly until these are amalgamated into one area. Grasett came to lunch. Great joy seeing him again. Selection Board in afternoon and two good hours work in the WO after dinner.

28 January

COS this morning at which we discussed at length the organization for the allocation of supplies in USA and this country. Nothing has been put down definitely yet and a lot wants clearing up.

Called up in the middle of the COS meeting by Lord Beaverbrook on the question of 2 pdr guns for the Middle East. I cannot make out what he is after but I do not trust him a yard.

Lunched at one of Lord Nathan of Churt's awful lunches. Afternoon in the office writing letters and finally dined with [FM] Lord Milne who was kindness itself. Full of advice, let me into many sidelights of political life. Reasons for Beaverbrook's hold on Winston, and beginning of the former's unpopularity. Party determined to see him out if they possibly can, but very disappointed at his return from America. Also informed me as to desire of House to get Margesson out. Wonderful what a clear and active mind old Milne has maintained in his old age.

I remain deeply grateful to this day for all the advice Milne gave me that evening. He had suggested to me that since he had been CIGS for many years [1926–33] he might perhaps be of help to me and asked me if I would dine with him. At the end of our talk he said that no doubt after I had held my appointment for a little longer I might care for another talk which he would be only too delighted to have. He visited the House of Lords fairly frequently and had his ear very close to the ground. He missed very little of what was going on and his deductions were as clear as a bell.

29 January

COS meeting at which I pressed hard for the amalgamation of the ABDA and ANZAC areas. Dudley Pound incapable of appreciating the real implications, but Portal did, however I doubt whether we convinced the PM! He had a great triumph in the House today with a vote of 464 to 1 [in a motion of no confidence]!

[Alan] Cunningham lunched with me and was most interesting about the desert fighting and Abyssinia. Then spent an hour with Ted Morris who is just off as CGS to C-in-C India. After that home with VCIGS and DMO and P followed by visit from PUS. Have just finished dinner and been reading Auchinleck's long letters on his proposed system of reorganization. Some of the ideas are good, but others I am not in agreement with.

I was at that time beginning to be upset by many messages that emanated from Auchinleck's office. I was beginning to be suspicious that 'Chink' Dorman-Smith, one of his staff officers, was beginning to exercise far too much influence on him. Dorman-Smith had a most fertile brain, continually producing new ideas, some of which (not many) were good and the rest useless. Archie Wavell had made use of him but was wise enough to discard all the bad and only retain the good. Auchinleck was incapable of doing so and allowed himself to fall far too deeply under Chink's influence. This became one, and possibly the major, cause of his downfall!

30 January

News bad on all sides. Benghazi has been lost again and Singapore is in a bad way. The defence is retiring onto the island tonight. I doubt whether the island holds out very long. The Benghazi business is bad and nothing less than bad generalship on the part of Auchinleck. He has been overconfident and has believed everything his overoptimistic [DMI] Shearer has told him. As a result he was not in a position to meet a counter blow.

I had been questioning him for some time as regards his intelligence reports which made out Rommel's strength as considerably lower than WO estimates. I finally discovered that Shearer had been basing his estimate of the enemy strength on far too heavy German and Italian casualties. I forget now the actual proportions, but to the best of my memory in each action the enemy casualties were based on a considerably heavier proportion than those we had suffered. As we had been attacking the whole time and the enemy had been on the defensive, it was unlikely that their casualties were even as heavy as ours.

The results of these underestimates lulled Auchinleck into a sense of false security which turned out to be most unfortunate. Auchinleck, to my mind, had most of the qualifications to make him one of the finest of commanders, but unfortunately he lacked the one most important of all – the ability to select the men to serve him. The selection of Corbett as his Chief of Staff, Dorman-Smith as his chief advisor, and Shearer as head of his intelligence service contributed most of all to his downfall.

This morning Defence Committee on provision of tanks for Far East. Although it is quite evident that we are incurring grave danger by going on supplying tanks to Russia it is Beaverbrook's firm intention that we should go on doing so, and he controls PM on such matters. At this morning's meeting PM did not attend but left Attlee to take the chair, having decided beforehand that he would not stop sending tanks to Russia!!

Ronnie Stanyforth and his wife came to lunch. Had a quiet afternoon in the office and got through a good deal of work.

31 January

An ordinary COS meeting followed by office work and a dash home. I have now finished two months' work as CIGS, and it feels as if it had been ten years!!

1 February

Woke to find whole country covered with snow! Snowed all day, so much so that I decided to return in the evening and not to trust myself to possibly frozen roads. Returned to WO by 6.30 pm and put in 2 hours work before dinner followed by 2 hours more before bed, so perhaps it is as well that I returned.

2 February

Usual COS meeting with no points of great importance. At 5 pm Cabinet meeting. As usual most unpleasant remarks by various ministers in connection with defeats of our forces! As we had retired into Singapore Island and lost [illegible], besides being pushed back in Libya, I had a good deal to account for! and found it hard to keep my temper with some of the criticisms that were raised. However we finally turned to discuss one para connected with Lend Lease Bill which was related to Empire Free Trade and various other tariff questions. The meeting then became a complete parrot house! We were to have had a COS meeting under the PM at 10 pm. However, luckily it was put off for 24 hours.

These were very difficult times for me in the Cabinet and Winston was the worst offender. He came out continually with remarks such as: 'Have you not got a single general in that army who can win battles, have none of them any ideas, must we continually lose battles in this way?' etc., etc. Such remarks lowered the confidence of other ministers in the efficiency of the army, and could be nothing but detrimental in the present crisis. He could have said anything he liked to me in private, but not in front of the whole Cabinet. This procedure usually also led to other ministers also making offensive remarks at the expense of the army. On one such occasion, when I was being hard pushed, and Winston had been particularly offensive, I was being bombarded with unpleasant remarks, when Bevin suddenly asked some question. I thought at the time that the remark was meant offensively, and my blood was up. I therefore turned on him and gave him a short and somewhat rude reply. He said nothing more at the time, but came up to me as we were going out and in a most charming manner explained that he had not been trying to get at me but was genuinely asking for information. A typical action on his part and nothing could have been nicer. I apologized for the rudeness of my reply, and asked him to dine quietly alone with me when he could ask me any questions he wished. This he did, and we had a most pleasant evening together. The more I saw of him in later years the more I liked him. A very great man.

3 February

Usual COS meeting, mainly connected with shortage of shipping, and attended by Mountbatten. During most of the discussion the First Sea Lord went sound to sleep, and looked like an old parrot asleep on his perch!

I find in my diary many unpleasant remarks about Dudley Pound's sleepiness and slowness over his work. Had I known that he was probably already suffering from the disease he died from I would certainly not have made these remarks. He was the most charming of colleagues to work with, had it not been for this failing of slowness and sleepiness.

Lunch at Claridges, where I had all the Cs-in-C of Allied Forces. Sikorski sat on my right and was in great form. The more I see of him the more I like him. On my left sat Chaney, the USA army commander just back from seeing the USA troops arrive in Ireland. De Gaulle looking if anything more sour than ever, a most unattractive specimen.

Busy afternoon, visited by Copper, whose main grouse was that he had not been awarded a GCB in the last Honours List! Was to have COS under PM at 10 pm, but luckily put off!

4 February

A short COS this morning and a good walk after lunch made me feel better. After lunch long talk with Bob Haining on situation in the Middle East. The more I find out from various quarters, the more disturbed I am at the situation out there. I do not like the combination of Shearer and the Auk. It is not a good combination! Then long talk on shipping with Archie Nye, DMO and Movements. The situation as regards shipping is most disturbing and one that the PM will not face, and yet it is the one situation which will affect our whole strategy during the coming year.

Until we could open up the Mediterranean we should remain one million tons short of shipping, and shipping must exercise a stranglehold on all our strategy. Yet for the present, with the entry of Japan into the war, and reverses in North Africa, the basic strategy at which I was aiming, of clearing North Africa, opening Mediterranean, and threatening Southern Europe, had shrunk into the background.

Finally dined with Bertie, and had long talk with Bulgy.

5 February

Rather a dull short COS. After lunch about an hour with S of S and rest of day trying to get level again with office work. Finished up with long letter to Auchinleck on the reorganization which he proposes to carry out, and on the very indifferent handling of his armoured forces.

6 February

COS as usual, with many points of minor importance, followed by lunch, a short walk, and an afternoon of office work. Small dinner party with Winant (American Ambassador) and Brendan Bracken (Minister of Propaganda), also Archie Nye. Winant is especially interesting character and what I saw of him I liked very much.

7 February

A short COS, some office work and then lunch with you and your father and Mary. A little more office work and then a drive home to the young. Such a happy change from the usual days!

8 February
A very happy day at home with you.

9 February
Left Ferney Close at 8 am. Roads very bad with soft rain freezing on the surface. A long Chiefs of Staff meeting mainly concerned with the Directive for the 'Combined Chiefs of Staff'. Ever since Portal and Pound came back from the USA I have told them that they 'sold the birthright for a plate of porridge' while in Washington. They have, up to now, denied it flatly. However this morning they were at last beginning to realize that the Americans are rapidly snatching more and more power with the ultimate intention of running the war in Washington! However, I now have them on my side.

An unpleasant Cabinet meeting. The news had just arrived that the Japs had got onto Singapore Island. As a result nothing but abuse for the army. The Auk's retreat in Cyrenaica is also making matters more sour! Finally this evening, at 10.45, I was sent for by PM to assist him in drafting a telegram to Wavell about the defence of Singapore, and the need for Staffs and Commanders to perish at their post.

10 February
COS as usual. Then after lunch interview with VCIGS and DSD to settle my paper on air requirements. A very difficult matter. Then DMO and P to discuss my paper on shipping for the CNS – I am getting more and more worried about the shipping situation and its effect on our strategy during the coming year. It may well be our undoing!! Finally an hour with S of S to assist him with his Estimate Speech in the House. At 6 pm first meeting of the new Pacific War Council. PM in chair, attended by Attlee, Anthony Eden, Dutch PM and Ambassador, Earle Page (Australia), Gordon (NZ), Amery (India and Burma). Meeting mainly concerned with statement by PM explaining organization. Finally this evening dinner for Dalton (Economic Warfare) and Findlater Stewart (Home Executive) also Ronald Weeks. Went well and good value.

11 February
The news of Singapore goes from bad to worse and now poor Archie Wavell has injured his back! PM sent for me this evening to discuss with him last wire from Wavell about Singapore from where he had just returned. It was a very gloomy wire and a depressing wire as regards the fighting efficiency of the troops on Singapore Island. It is hard to see why a better defence is not being put up, but I presume there must be some good reason. I can't see the place holding out more than a day or so now. The losses on the island will be vast, not only in men but in material.

I have during the last 10 years had an unpleasant feeling that the British Empire was decaying and that we were on a slippery decline!! I wonder if I was right? I certainly never expected that we should fall to pieces as fast as we are and to see Hong Kong and Singapore go in less than 3 months plus failure in the Western Desert is far from reassuring! We have had a wonderful power of recuperation in the past. I wonder whether we shall again bring off a comeback?

12 February
Went to the Staff College to give lecture to passing out batch. Then went on to have lunch with you and from there back to WO for an Army Council meeting at 4 pm. Then office work.

News of Singapore far worse, and that of Burma rapidly deteriorating. We are bound to lose the former before long and I am getting very nervous about the latter! We are paying very heavily now for failing to face the insurance premiums essential for security of an Empire! This has usually been the main cause for the loss of Empires in the past.

13 February
News of Singapore getting worse, and that of Burma beginning to deteriorate! Added to that the *Gneisenau*, *Scharnhorst* and *Prinz Eugen* succeeded in running the gauntlet of the Channel yesterday without being destroyed, whilst we lost some 40 aircraft to the 20 enemy planes brought down! These are black days! Even Russia is no longer doing as well as she was.

Adam came to lunch and walked back to the WO with me. A fairly peaceful day in the office today. Only one call from PM late in the evening.

14 February
Rather a dull COS in the morning, and a quiet afternoon till 4 pm, when I began to hope that I might be able to slip away. Of course just then wires began to pour in about Singapore, where the situation was getting far worse and the place unlikely to hold out long. PM called me up from Chequers to prepare a wire for Wavell stating that 'he alone could judge when further resistance would be useless'. I discussed matters with other Chiefs of Staff and then sent off wire. Finally went home, arriving in time for dinner.

15 February
Quiet day at home. [And fall of Singapore.]

16 February
Left Ferney Close 8 am, arrived WO 9.15. Read all wires and briefed for COS till 10.30. Then COS till 1.30 pm. Back from lunch by 2.30 pm. Busy afternoon studying repercussions of fall of Singapore on flow of reinforcements. By 5 pm Cabinet meeting from which I escaped at 7 pm. Considering that we have lost

Singapore, endangered Rangoon, allowed *Gneisenau* and *Scharnhorst* to sail up the Channel and lost 3 transports trying to reinforce Malta I was expecting that the Services would meet with some sarcastic remarks! However we got off far lighter than I expected.

7 pm to 8 pm working up for Defence Committee. 9 pm COS meeting till 10 pm when Defence Committee under PM started and lasted till after midnight, mainly concerned with decision as to whether attempts should be made to reinforce Java. Strategically this would definitely be unsound under present conditions. Politically it may be difficult not to do so. Provisionally decided to send Australian Division back to Australia and 70th Div to Burma and Ceylon. PM on the whole in a very good mood.

This was typical of Winston, in a real crisis he was always at his best, and stood all the heavy shocks without flinching.

17 February

Another hectic day. Started with COS at which we had visit from Dutch Admiral, and had to explain to him that we were recommending that Java should not be reinforced by Australians. Then had to proceed to 10 Downing St to see PM concerning Wavell's last wire. Found him in a dejected mood and he said that he was just back from dealing with a troublesome House. I am afraid that he is in for a lot more trouble. After lunch 1½ hours with Sinclair and Weeks to discuss results of their committee. Then ½ hour with S of S mainly to discuss political situation, and demand for a Defence Minister separate from the PM. An absolute impossibility with a personality such as his.

Frequently when the situation was bad there were suggestions that a separate Chairman for the COS should be found, or a deputy Defence Minister interposed between the PM and the COS. None of these alternatives was either possible or neces-sary. To my mind the PM in war must always deal directly with the COS, and the members of the COS must defend their actions personally in the Cabinet, using their Chairman as spokesman. The introduction of an outside chairman will never smooth over differences between members of the COS if these exist. Should there be such dif-ferences there is only one course, to change some or all of the members of the COS. It is essential that these three men should work together as a perfect trinity.

Then at 6 another ½ hour with the Dutch Admiral, followed by our second Pacific Council meeting which lasted till 8 pm. As I had expected it was a more difficult meeting than the previous one! But on the whole the Dutch took it wonderfully well that they could expect no Australian reinforcements. After dinner back to WO for another 3 hours work.

Am getting more and more worried by old Dudley Pound as First Sea Lord, with an old dodderer like him it is quite impossible for the COS to perform the function it should in the biggest Imperial war we are ever likely to be engaged in! He is asleep during 75% of the time he should be working.

18 February

A futile meandering COS meeting with practically no main points and with Dudley Pound half asleep!! Then went to see Paget taking part in his Victor [home defence] Exercise. Back to WO where I picked up sandwiches and went to Horse Guards to see controller of Victor Exercise and from there on to South Eastern Command to see Monty functioning. Back to WO by 5 pm, where I had interview with Martel to settle suitable AFV [Armoured Fighting Vehicle] commander for Middle East, having at last got the Auk to agree to have one! Then long sitting with ACIGS, and back to WO after dinner till about 11.45 pm.

Burma news now bad. Cannot work out why troops are not fighting better. If the army cannot fight better than it is doing at present we shall deserve to lose our Empire!

19 February

Received reply back from Wavell saying that he was prepared to accept Alexander to replace Hutton as C-in-C Burma, the latter having proved unsatisfactory as a commander. After lunch was sent for by PM, who said he agreed to Alexander being sent out. So made all arrangements and interviewed Alexander this evening and fixed up plan to fly him out direct to Cairo tomorrow. Shall try leaving Hutton as CGS, if this does not work shall have to carry out a change. Only hope Alexander arrives in time as situation in Burma is becoming very critical. Troops don't seem to be fighting well there either which is most depressing.

PM showed me his new Cabinet that he had reconstituted. A smaller one and much more efficient. Beaverbrook is out of it!! That is the greatest Godsend. He is off to America. Cranborne and Moyne both pushed out of War Cabinet. Stafford Cripps [Aircraft Production] and Oliver Lyttelton [Production] have been introduced. Kingsley Wood and Greenwood pass out. Apparently Secretaries for Services also out, but I am not yet certain. With a small War Cabinet like that we ought to be able to get on much faster. But the greatest blessing of all is to be rid of Beaverbrook!

20 February

Did not attend COS this morning, but instead went to Shoeburyness to see trials of rockets fired from fighters for attacks on tanks. May prove useful for attacks on shipping but am doubtful as to its value for attacking tanks. Lunched with Adam. Burma news getting worse. Very doubtful if we will succeed in holding Rangoon. Tanks due to arrive tomorrow may help to restore situation. Busy afternoon. Military Members meeting of Army Council, interview with Norwegian C-in-C, and series of interruptions. Stafford Cripps to dinner, also P.J. Grigg and Bertie. Then more home work to finish off. New Cabinet has been announced – general relief at riddance of Beaverbrook!!

21 February

A bad day! COS meeting from 10.30 am to 1.30 pm, and again from 4 pm to 7 pm, and finally Pacific Council from 9.30 to 11.30 pm. And all to do the work which could be done by one man in 1 hour!! And what's worse, when finished the work was not worth the paper it was written on!

All connected with the use of Dutch shipping in Java in the final stages of the evacuation, the use it was to be made of and the desirability or otherwise of risking it under Japanese bombing without adequate protection. I know well from personal experience that whatever we may say, the man on the spot is in the end the only one who can judge. As a result of all this work I was unable to slip home this evening.

22 February

The night continued to be as damnable as the day! Barely was I asleep when the First Sea Lord called me up at 1.45 am about destination of convoy with 7th Australian [Division] aboard. It is at present between Colombo and Rangoon marking time pending approval from Australians to use it in Burma. An approval which we are unlikely to obtain in spite of appeals from PM and President of the USA – as a result we shall probably lose Burma!

This division was on its way back from Middle East to Australia when the Burma situation deteriorated rapidly. We had therefore applied to Australian government for authority to employ this division in Burma as it was the nearest reinforcement available. Meanwhile in order to save time we had diverted this convoy from Ceylon towards Rangoon. The Australians were obdurate and insisted on the early return of the division. It must be remembered that this was the first time that Australia had been threatened and allowance must be made for the degree of nervousness created by this threat.

Looking back on the event, I still feel that the arrival of this division in Rangoon, at that time, might well have restored the situation and saved Burma. On the other hand, it was certainly never required for safety of Australia. The outlook prevailing in Australia at that time was definitely parochial and centred solely on its own direct personal security. Dr Evatt [Minister for External Affairs] was certainly the worst propagandist of this policy!

Barely was I asleep when the telephone rang again at 3.30 am to tell me car was coming down with message from Wavell. Nothing very special in it beyond statement of conditions in Java, which are rapidly getting worse. Finally as I was trying to take maybe ½ hour in bed on Sunday morning third telephone call, to inform me that we were to have a COS meeting at 10.30 to consider Wavell's telegram. It is now quite clear that we can at last dissolve the ABDA organization and run the war on a rational basis! So far there is very little that was settled at Washington which is surviving the test of time. Burma has gone back to India, ABDA and ANZAC become one, Pacific Council goes West, and for that matter so does the Combined Chiefs of Staffs – and thank God for it!!

We shall now run the war with two main spheres of interest: the Americans running the Pacific up to Asia, including Australia and New Zealand, and a British one running the opposite way round the globe, including Middle East, India, Burma and Indian Ocean. After COS dashed home for afternoon and evening.

23 February

Left Ferney Close 8 am, arrived WO 9.05. Read telegrams and briefed for COS. Then went to say goodbye to Margesson, who has been replaced [as S of S] by James Grigg [formerly PUS]. A good change which will make for efficiency, but I was sorry to see Margesson go as he seemed so very upset and took it so well. Long COS, well after lunch. 4.30, attended reception at Russian Embassy by Maisky to celebrate their Red Army Day. Finally, 6 pm, War Cabinet with all the new members.

24 February

COS as usual mainly concerned with the future safety of Malta. The serious situation that we are in is not yet fully realized! Unless we advance again in Cyrenaica, I do not think that Malta will be able to hold out as it will no longer be possible to run convoys in from the East or West. The former due to increased air threat and the latter due to deficiency of naval forces. Selection Board from 3.15 to 5.15. Very disturbed about Irwin practically refusing to serve under Carr. It means both will have to go eventually. Also faced with writing to Bertie to tell him he was now reaching age limit! Finally 6 to 7.30 Pacific Council. PM very tired and gave very gloomy statement. China attended for first time, represented by ambassador.

25 February

Discussed two more raids at the COS, also defence of the Andaman Islands. Then had to go to Cabinet meeting in the House of Commons to discuss possibility of diverting temporarily 72 Hurricanes to Russia. As usual failed to have any deduction made and informed that political aspect of keeping our promise to Russia overtook all strategical considerations! Personally I consider it absolute madness. We have never even asked Russia to inform us of the real degree of urgency of these reinforcements.

We had been put on the wrong foot from the very start by Beaverbrook in his mission to Moscow as regards the supply of equipment to Russia. His policy was to pour everything into their lap without even asking whether it was needed, and without ever asking anything in return. As a result we kept on supplying tanks and aeroplanes that could ill be spared and in doing so suffered the heaviest of losses in shipping conveying this equipment to Arctic Russia. We received nothing in return except abuse for handling the convoys inefficiently! We had absolutely no information as to what the

Russian situation was as regards equipment. Russia even refused to keep us informed as to the distribution of her forces, and the only way in which I knew Russian disposi-tions was through German messages which we intercepted. I do not pretend for one moment that Russia was not playing a vital part in the war and bearing the maximum brunt of the land warfare. I fully agree that it was essential to retain Russia in the war and to assist her to do so, but this would in no way [have] precluded getting fuller value for what we were doing.

In afternoon went to see film of *Wavell's 200,000*. A very good film. In evening Anthony Eden and his wife came to dine, and also Barney's wife.

26 February
A short COS this morning at which I raised the desirability of transferring Malta Command to Middle East, since continuance of supply and defence of Malta is closely connected with problems of further advance into Cyrenaica. Came back for interview with QMG about Macready's impending visit to America and possibility of relieving him by Weeks temporarily. This resulted in final visit to S of S. After lunch I had first of my interviews with new USA Military Attaché and then long talk with Spears. I got a good deal of valuable information from him about de Gaulle and about the Levant, but he is not a specimen I have got any particular admiration for! Finally dined with Bertie, to whom I had had to write a letter yesterday informing him that owing to his age he would have to retire soon. Seldom have I hated writing a letter more, and seldom have I received a nicer answer.

27 February
Short COS followed by several interviews before lunch. After lunch went to see the army film on security. Very good indeed and going to be liberated [dis-tributed]. When I came out I was sent for to 10 Downing St and had ½ hour with the PM, found him very tired but cheerful. He discussed situation in Burma with me, Ceylon, defence of India, dangers of denuding the Levant, Malta and Middle East etc. Came back and finished off the office work before dinner. Situation in Burma is a little better, but appears to be lull before the storm! I cannot see how we are to go on holding Rangoon much longer.

28 February
A short COS meeting after which I went to see Paget to discuss PM's visit to troops with him, also trouble between Carr and Irwin, which is going to necessitate both of them going. Left for Ferney Close after tea.

1 March
Comfortably and quietly spent at home. Crerar came to tea.

2 March

Another bad Monday. Left Ferney Close 8 am, WO at 9.05. Found PM had drafted a bad wire for Auchinleck in which he poured abuse on him for not attacking sooner, and for sending us an appreciation in which he did not propose to attack till June!! Long COS till 1.30, mainly deciding form of message from COS to go instead of PM's wire. Cabinet at 5.30 which was employed in discussing Rangoon and Java situations, both of which are very gloomy at present. Finished at 7 pm, put in 1 hour in WO, and hurried dinner to meet COS at 9.15 before Defence Committee at 10 pm, at which PM cross questioned Oliver Lyttelton [lately in Cairo] concerning Auk's situation in the Middle East. Much time wasted in hot air, but he finally accepted wire we had drafted to replace his. Back to flat at midnight and another hour's work to do.

Here we have another example of Winston's interference with a commander in the field. Without it being possible for him to be familiar with all aspects of the situation facing Auchinleck he is trying to force him to attack at an earlier date than is thought advisable, and what is more, tries to obtain his ends by an offensive wire. Thank heaven we were able to stop the wire and re-word it.

3 March

COS meeting mainly concerned with transfer of Malta to Middle East, and with appointment of Military Governor for Ceylon. Brooke-Popham and Pug Ismay came to lunch – the former was interesting about Singapore and the initial stages of the Japanese attack before his relief by Pownall. After lunch long interview with McCreery priming him up for his new appointment with Auchinleck.

I had been worried for some time by Auchinleck's handling of armoured formations, mainly due to his listening to the advice of Chink Dorman-Smith. I had therefore informed him that I was sending him out one of our best armoured divisional commanders to act as his advisor at headquarters on the use of armoured forces. I knew that Dick McCreery might have a difficult time with the Auk, and I warned him frankly that he might have a difficult furrow to plough. I must say that I had not expected that he would be practically ignored and never referred to by the Auk on the employment and use of armoured forces.

Then Pacific Council, rather a sad affair with most of the ABDA area gone and Java on its last legs. Had long talk after the meeting with Mr Wellington Koo (Chinese Ambassador) to discuss the Burma Road with him and the possible routes from Assam to join with it after loss of Rangoon.

4 March

A long and protracted COS taken up mainly with a heated argument as regards relative advantages between a single commander (or generalissimo), as opposed to the usual trinity of the three services. I was supporting the former and was being strongly opposed by CNS and CAS! The case in point being Ceylon, and our attempt at producing a military commander instead of the usual civil Governor. The argument itself and impossibility of arriving at any agreement convinced me more than anything else that I was right! But argument went on for close on 2 hours.

You came to lunch and it was a great joy showing you the flat. After lunch we went to Mme Tussaud's to see my wax figure! *(We were neither of us much impressed by this figure, but I remember one of the officials hoped I would give them a sitting to improve it!)*

Remainder of evening spent in office finishing up with interviews with Duncan Sandys [Financial Secretary WO] on question of Alan Cunningham his future employment and a question he had to answer in Parliament.

5 March

Short COS, but afternoon of continuous interviews. Finally dined with the Edens. PM and wife, and Oliver Lyttelton there. Early part of evening mainly taken up with crisis produced by new proposed India Bill. Situation is very strained, PM prepared to resign on Monday if necessary. If so Eden to raise new government. After dinner discussion of offensive in France to relieve pressure on Russians. Also Winston's proposed visit to Stalin to discuss post war boundaries. Eden apparently nervous lest Russia should make peace with Germans. Also rumours as to offensive through Turkey.

Informed by the PM that I am to take over the chairmanship of the COS from Dudley Pound, and that Mountbatten is to be additional member of the COS! Rather doubtful how that business will run! Only returned home at 2.30 am!

Mountbatten's inclusion in the COS was a snag. There was no justification for this move. His appointment as Chief of Combined Operations was excellent and he certainly played a remarkable role as the driving force and mainspring of this organization. Without his energy and drive it would never have reached the high standards it achieved. However, the holding of this appointment was no reason for his inclusion in the COS, where he frequently wasted both his own time and ours. We could easily have called him in to attend any meetings where matters connected with his organization were being discussed. I am not making this statement from personal reasons, on the contrary, I enjoyed Dicky's presence in the COS in spite of the fact that at times he was apt to concern himself with matters outside his sphere.... The title 'Chief of Combined Operations' was also badly chosen, since every operation we were engaged in was a 'combined' one. It was certainly not intended that he should direct combined strategy – his job was to evolve the technique, policy and equipment for the employment of the three Services in combined operations to effect landings against opposition.

6 March

COS mainly concerned with organization of defence of Ceylon and of organization of its supreme command. Then had talk with Paget concerning preparations for a very large scale raid into France in May or June. Adam and Hardy came to lunch. 5 pm discussed army air requirement paper with S of S. After that Military Members meeting of Army Council.

7 March

Arrived at COS to find letter from PM saying that I was to be chairman of the COS in future! Also that Mountbatten was to become a member of COS as Chief of Combined Operations! but only to attend 2 days a week when we are to discuss the large problems of the war. It will be rather awkward having to take the chair with old Dudley Pound still there, and with Portal whose turn it should have been next! But I do hope that I shall be able to speed up the business. It is quite hopelessly slow at present! Got off home all right about 5.30 pm after nervous last moment call by PM!!

8 March

Lovely peaceful quiet day at home, forgetting there is any war and playing with the beloved children.

9 March

Left 8 am, arrived WO 9.05. Bad rush with many important wires. First COS in which I took the chair went off all right and both Pound and Portal played up very well.

This is putting it mildly! Dudley Pound usually was late for our COS meetings and I rather dreaded taking his place in his absence, but to my surprise dear old Dudley on this morning made a point of arriving before the appointed time and I found him already seated in my chair with his chairman's seat empty. This was typical of the man, I feel certain that this gesture on his part was done on purpose to make matters easier for me, and to impress on me how ready he was to serve under my chairmanship. I was deeply grateful to him.

Loud discussion over latest suggestions of assistance from USA, as exemplified by wire from President to PM. Looks very hopeful on first examination with many prospects of increasing strength in Middle East.

    5.30 pm Cabinet meeting which lasted till 7.30 pm. Then rush to dine with Brendan Bracken at Claridges, to meet American editor of *Life* etc. Found him very interesting to talk to. Just back 11.30 pm, and a good 1½ hour's work in my despatch case.

10 March

Long COS with Mountbatten attending for the first time. We discussed the problem of assistance to Russia by operations in France, with large raid or lodgement. Decided only hope was to try to draw off air forces from Russia and that for this purpose raid must be carried out on Calais front. Now directed investigations to proceed further. Lunched with Hugh Elles. Then painful interview with Alan Cunningham, 2 Chinese attachés, Schreiber, Martel and S of S.

At 6 pm Pacific Council where PM read out new proposals by President for subdivision of areas of responsibility. USA to look after the Pacific, London after Burma, India and Middle East and Mediterranean, whilst Combined COS did Atlantic and land operations against Africa. Good in places but calculated to drive Australia, NZ and Canada into USA arms, and help to bust up Empire!

11 March

Long COS meeting at which we discussed the naval and army calls on the air force. It resulted in rather a heated debate which did not lead us on to much! I expect some pretty stormy passages within the next few weeks.

My expectations were certainly fulfilled! The Air Force was at this time engaged in an all-out air offensive on Germany and were putting every ounce of their strength into this effort. Many of them held the opinion that, given sufficient heavy bombers, Germany could be brought to her knees by air action alone. In these circumstances it is not surprising that the Air Ministry was anxious to develop its strength in those types of aircraft that were best suited for the attack on Germany. As a result the army was being starved of any types suitable for the direct support of land forces. We had gone to war with the obsolete Lysander machine, and since then nothing had materialized. Everything seemed to be devoted to the production of four-engine bombers which were unsuited for close cooperation with the army. All Air Force eyes were trained on Germany and consequently all the personnel trained for long distance raids, and little interest was displayed in close cooperation with land forces.

Many doubted that land forces would ever be again employed in large land operations on the Continent – why therefore provide for a contingency that would probably never arise? They could always produce the argument that the Air Force was at that time busy hitting the Germans hard – were they to reduce this effort for the problematical benefits to be derived by producing men and machines capable of cooperating with the Army in operations that were unlikely ever to take place! It was uphill work striving to obtain what I knew would be essential in the later stages of the war if we were ever to win!

The Navy were also fighting for greater air support in the anti-submarine war which they were engaged in, and on which our very existence depended. Then again the Naval operations seemed purely defensive, promised no decisive results of victory – were they therefore to be allowed to detract from the bomber offensive on Germany, which might hold decisive promises of success?

A busy afternoon of interviews and at 6.30 visit of COS to 10 Downing St where we did a gallop round the world which centred mainly on Madagascar and the possibility of capturing it shortly. Mountbatten was present. Decided to take up matter at COS tomorrow morning.

12 March

COS mainly concerned with discussion of Madagascar expedition. Mountbatten had produced a scheme for attack with 4 bns which was quite inadequate. So had to decide to go back to old scheme of 2 Brigades, with all incumbent drawbacks and delays. Mountbatten agreed that 4 bns were inadequate.

Pacific Council in evening, PM seemed very tired, we discussed again President's new proposal for subdivision of the world into spheres of influence, with main Pacific sphere under USA, Singapore, Burma, India, Middle East, Mediterranean sphere under UK, and Atlantic sphere under both. Australia and NZ not very happy at prospect of finding themselves in the USA sphere!

Dined with Trenchard. He was as usual quite charming in spite of heated discussion between us on the subject of Army air requirements.

13 March

Considered Auchinleck's refusal to come home [for consultations] at this morning's COS. Drafted letter to PM about it, however he called up from Chequers and I had to tell him about it. He was infuriated and at once again suggested relieving him of his command! Would not agree to Auchinleck's suggestion that I should go out with CAS.

At 12.30 I had to go to Buckingham Palace to see the King, mainly about Bertie's relief by Arthur Smith. Was kept there till 1.15 pm, when I dashed back for a lunch I was giving de Gaulle. As he had been getting deeper in disgrace during the last few days I thought situation would be strained! However it went off all right. In afternoon another telephone call from Chequers, PM saying that he would now send telegram to Auchinleck! I shudder at what he may put in it, and we shall have to vet it tomorrow morning! Another COS meeting at 6 pm to settle about expedition to Madagascar, decided to start it off. Nasty lot of work left over to finish after dinner!

14 March

Called up at lunch by PM and told that he wanted VCIGS to go to Middle East to meet Stafford Cripps there, and discuss with the Auk prospects of his offensive. Spent afternoon fixing details of this and then went home suffering from a foul cold.

15 March

Spent my morning in bed to air cold and walk in afternoon.

16 March

Left 8 am. COS all morning. Cabinet at 5.30 pm and another COS at 10.45 pm to vet the PM's wire to Roosevelt. A foul day!

17 March

A difficult COS this morning, discussing what we could do to help Russia in the event of this country [Russia] being invaded by Germany next spring. Not much that we can do to draw off land forces, but we might possibly assist in drawing off some of the land [actually air] forces by an attack on the Calais salient.

Rush back to WO after telephone call from PM on command in Burma, to see Prince Henry in anticipation of his visit to the Middle East. Lunch with Home Forces, and then 1¼ hour talk on world situation. Back to WO to do day's work. Finally dinner with Chaney, the American general, Ralph Glyn, and Paget; a great success and quite an amusing evening.

18 March

A long COS settling details of the Madagascar expedition, and interviewing commanders. Lunched at Club, after which interview with Irwin to inform him that I was sending him to India.

Basil came to dinner, after which I had to go to Defence Committee meeting which lasted till 1 am!

19 March

A very short COS meeting after which I had talk with Pug [Ismay] as to best method of tackling the air problem. With PM in his present mood, and with his desire to maintain air bombardment of Germany it will not be possible to get adequate support for either the Army or the Navy.

This evening dined with Lord Milne and had long talk with him, he was as usual most interesting and in great form. His advice on all matters is most valuable. He thinks Winston is drawing near unto his end and that he won't last much longer as PM. Predicts that Stafford Cripps will succeed him soon.

20 March

A useful COS to discuss Middle East situation. PM came in at the end of it and discussed Burma situation with us.

Lunched at Mansion House. Speeches by Kingsley Wood and [A.V.] Alexander, the latter very good. A very hard afternoon in the office with a series of interviews. Finally dinner with Copper at the Senior.

21 March
A dull COS at which I had to drive old Dudley Pound along. Lunched with Adam at the Carlton Grill. Left for home after tea.

22 March
Peacefully spent at home.

23 March
A short COS at which Dudley Pound acted as a continual drag and delayed action! Several interviews and a Cabinet meeting at 6 pm. A dull day on the whole, with spring sun shining, which made the war all the more unpleasant.

24 March
Called by PM before COS. Found him in bed with the dragon dressing gown on. Evidently still unhappy about delays in Auchinleck's attack. Even suggesting replacing Auchinleck with Archie Nye! I have already ridden him off trying to replace him by Gort! It is very exhausting, this continual protecting of Auchinleck, especially as I have not got the highest opinion of him! COS till lunch. Dudley Pound fast asleep most of the time. At lunch I had Ciriez, my old liaison officer, to pump him about de Gaulle. He has a very poor opinion of him. Then Selection Board from 3.15 to 5 pm, followed by Pacific Council from 6 to 7.30, and dinner with Jimmy Harrison, wife, and Lady Strathcona.

These impulsive ideas to change Auchinleck were typical of Winston. Gort had certainly not been a success in France and there was little reason to believe that he would be any more successful in North Africa. Archie Nye, although brilliant in most ways, had not yet been tried out as a commander in the field in any capacity. It would have been gambling with fate to place him in command of the main front. My faith in Auchinleck was getting more and more shaken, but I had not yet arrived at the stage where I thought it desirable to change him.

25 March
A short COS meeting with no points of great importance. After lunch ran CIGS Committee on organization of Inf and Armoured divisions from 3 to 5. Then interview with Johnson to tell him his job of Inspector of Infantry was being abolished. At 6.30 COS meeting under PM at which I argued strongly against sending aircraft to Russia from Middle East. CAS had been suggesting sending 6 fighter squadrons just at the time when we are at our wits' end as to how to build up an adequate air force for the Middle and Far East. PM finally agreed to postponement of offensive in Cyrenaica till mid-May.

26 March

A useful COS at which we discussed the Middle East situation at length. Afternoon spent with a series of interviews and conference on honours list. Finally this evening Defence Committee at 10 pm. Discussed sabotage of railways in Poland, attacks on German oil, spare parts for Hurricanes to Russia and finally agreement on postponement of date of offensive in Libya to May 15th. This entailed certain unpleasant remarks concerning Auchinleck and desire to relieve him. Finished meeting at 11.30 pm, which was mainly due to Lord Hankey having asked questions about late sittings!

27 March

A relief from COS at last!! I went to Aldershot to watch a demonstration of flame throwers. Interesting, but not very promising except the Churchill [tank] fit up. Returned about 2.30 pm to find that PM was seeing First Sea Lord and CAS at 4 pm. Decided to go round to 10 Downing St to attend meeting. Glad I did as I was able to influence withdrawal of aircraft from Middle East to India which PM was intending to carry out. As he had decided on Libyan offensive in May it was madness to withdraw fighters from Middle East for India now in spite of all risks Calcutta might run.

In the evening Oliver Lyttelton, P.J. Grigg, and Weeks came to dine, very good value and I picked up many threads concerning Middle East. Much of what was said corroborated opinion I had formed as to condition existing there as regards Arthur Smith, Auchinleck, Haining, Riddell-Webster [QMG], etc.

28 March

A difficult COS to handle. Paget and Sholto Douglas were both there, and Mountbatten. We were discussing ways and means of establishing new Western Front. I had propounded theory that a Western Front, to be of use, must force withdrawal of forces from Russia, that it was impossible with the land forces at our disposal to force the Germans to withdraw land forces from Russia; but that we might induce them to withdraw air forces. But to do this a landing must take place within our air umbrella, namely in vicinity of Calais or Boulogne. Mountbatten was still hankering after a landing near Cherbourg where proper air support is not possible. Finally I think we convinced him sufficiently to make his visit to Chequers this evening safe. After tea went home.

Dickie's visits were always dangerous moments and there was no knowing what discussions he might be led into and what he might let us in for! He was most loyal, and on those occasions frequently asked me what he was to say that night to the PM. As it was not easy to predict what he might be asked it was not possible to guard against all eventualities. On Monday morning he always gave us a full account of what had happened to him.

29 March
Very peacefully spent at home.

30 March
COS in morning to discuss proposed raid to Bayonne. Lunched with Margesson, who was now feeling happier, having been made a peer. Busy afternoon with many interviews culminating in Cabinet at 6 pm. After dinner had to go round to see PM at 10.30 pm.

(Later: was kept up till 1 am discussing possibilities of some kind of offensive in Northern France to assist Russia in the event of German attack being successful, as it probably will be. A difficult problem – this universal cry to start a western front is going to be hard to compete with, and yet what can we do with some 10 divisions against the German masses? Unfortunately the country fails to realize the situation we are in.)

This situation grew more and more difficult: the Beaverbrook press influencing public outlook in the direction of a western front, Albert Hall meetings, Trafalgar Square meetings, vast crowds shouting for immediate help for the Russians. Many seemed to imagine that Russia had only come into the war for our benefit! Certainly very few of them realized that a premature Western Front could only result in the most appalling shambles which must inevitably reduce the chances of ultimate victory to a minimum.

31 March
The last day of the first quarter of 1942, fateful year in which we have already lost a large proportion of the British Empire, and are on the high road to lose a great deal more of it!

During the last fortnight I have had for the first time since the war started a growing conviction that we are going to lose this war unless we control it very differently and fight it with more determination. But to begin with a democracy is at a great disadvantage against a dictatorship when it comes to war. Secondly a government with only one big man in it, and that one man a grave danger in many respects, is in a powerless way. Party politics, party interests, still override larger war issues. Petty jealousies colour discussions and influence destinies. Politicians still suffer from that little knowledge of military matters which gives them unwarranted confidence that they are born strategists! As a result they confuse issues, affect decisions, and convert simple problems and plans into confused tangles and hopeless muddles.

It is all desperately depressing. Furthermore it is made worse by the lack of good military commanders. Half our Corps and Divisional Commanders are totally unfit for their appointments, and yet if I were to sack them I could find no better! They lack character, imagination, drive and power of leadership. The reason for this state of affairs is to be found in the losses we sustained in the last war of all our best officers, who should now be our senior commanders. I wonder if we shall muddle through this time as we have done in the past? There are times when I wish to God I had not been placed at the helm of a ship that seems to be heading inevitably for the rocks. It is a great honour to find oneself entrusted with such a task, and the hope of saving the ship a most inspiring thought and one that does override all others. But may God help me in my task.

1 April

Looking back at what I wrote last night I wonder whether I was liverish! Life looks yellow at times, but as long as one can prevent one's thoughts and actions being tinged with yellow all is well! We have got to choose between pulling through and sinking, and it does not take long to make that choice! So why look at the black side of life more than is necessary to avoid falling into any unnecessary pitfalls.

A useful COS at which we examined the dangers to which India is exposed and prepared to relate these to those of the Middle East so as to be guided as to the best use of our resources. Lunched with Norwegians and sat next to King Haakon whom I found interesting and easy to talk to. After lunch had to tell Laurence Carr that he must give up Eastern Command, unpleasant interview, but on the whole he took it well. Followed up [General] Godwin-Austen to be told that he is unlikely to be employed again. Then Lord Portal to see me on necessity for economizing on rubber and consequently reducing issue of motor vehicles – easier said than done! Finally interview with Admiral Harwood who is about to take over Mediterranean fleet. Came home and had Harry Crerar to dinner. He was in very good form and good company.

2 April

A short COS but somewhat heated one at which I went near to losing my temper with old Dudley Pound. I find it almost impossible to stir him up into action, he is always lagging about 5 laps behind even when he is not sound asleep. This morning I could not get him to realize how essential it is for us to have a concerted plan with the Americans as regards the action of our Naval forces. Without such a plan we run grave risk of being defeated in detail.

A fairly quiet afternoon which I spent in catching up with some of my back work. Real spring at last.

3 April

Discovered at this morning's COS that First Sea Lord had agreed last night to the PM sending out instructions for the French battleship *Richelieu* to be attacked and destroyed if it attempted to enter the Mediterranean as it was expected to do! We did not like the possible implications and ordered Joint Planners to examine possible results. By 3 pm we had results of this work and decided to have second COS at which we formed recommendation to the PM to withdraw order to attack *Richelieu*. Dined out with Bertie.

4 April

After a shortish COS in the morning and a rush after lunch polishing off work I succeeded in getting off home about 4.30 pm. We found in the morning that the PM had refused to withdraw the order to sink the *Richelieu*! Luckily it had not come out.

5 April

Lovely Easter day at home with you.

6 April

Left 8 am and in WO by 9 am. On reaching COS I discovered that most of the Japanese fleet appeared to be in the Indian Ocean and our Eastern fleet retiring westwards. Up to present no signs of transports. I don't like the situation much as we are very weak in the Indian Ocean, I have been trying to get First Sea Lord to fix up with the Americans some counter move towards Japan to cover this very predicament that we are in, but he has failed to do so up to present. At any rate the air action over Ceylon was successful yesterday and we downed 27 Japs!

7 April

COS at which we looked into the unpleasant situation created by entrance of Japanese fleet into Indian Ocean. Just what I had been afraid of and had been trying to get First Sea Lord busy about during whole of last week. Also frantic calls for air support from Wavell, which according to Portal there is little chance of meeting. I suppose this Empire has never been in such a precarious position throughout its history! I do not like the look of things. And yet a miracle saved us at Dunkirk and we may pull through this time. But I wish I could see more daylight as to how we are to keep going through 1942!

A very gloomy Cabinet meeting! Both Bevin and Alexander reporting Labour disenchantment at course of war and difficulty of not being able to give them a full account.

8 April

Very difficult COS attended by Paget, Sholto Douglas and Mountbatten. Subject – attempt to assist Russia through action in France. Plan they had put up was a thoroughly bad one!!

Then went to Hendon to meet Marshall (USA CGS) and Harry Hopkins [FDR's emissary and 'best friend'] who had just flown from America. 3 to 4 interview with Giffard [C-in-C] just back from West Africa. 5 to 5.30 Amery at India Office to discuss Indian Airborne forces. 6 to 7 Arthur Smith [Chief of Staff, Cairo] back from Middle East to discuss with him all problems connected with that theatre. Then S of S from 7 to 7.30. Finally 8.30 pm dinner with PM at 10 Downing St to meet Marshall and Harry Hopkins. Attlee also there and Anthony Eden came after dinner. Neither Hopkins nor Marshall disclosed their proposed plans for which they have come over. However it was an interesting evening and a good chance to get to know Marshall. But did not get back until 1.30 am!!

9 April

Started COS at 9 am as Marshall was due at 10.30. He remained with us till 12.30 pm and gave us a long talk on his views concerning the desirability of starting western front next September and that the USA forces would take part. However, the total force which they could transport by then only consisted of 2½ divisions!! No very great contribution. Furthermore they had not begun to realize what all the implications of their proposed plan were! We then gave him and his party lunch at the Savoy. After lunch I saw Cadogan (Foreign Office) on the question of withdrawing Mason-MacFarlane from Russia.* Then Wemyss who is back from the USA Mission [in Washington]. After that another hour with Arthur Smith which was very good value.

Finally another COS meeting to do the work we had been unable to do in the morning. We spent some time examining relative importance of Middle East and Indian theatres and assessing best employment of very limited forces. Situation is most unpleasant! Large Japanese Naval forces are in the Indian Ocean operating with carriers, and have [been joined by] two cruisers and one aircraft carrier in the last two days.

I liked what I saw of Marshall, a pleasant and easy man to get on with, rather over-filled with his own importance. But I should not put him down as a great man.

These first impressions of mine about Marshall are interesting and of course incomplete. They were based on the day's discussions, which had made it quite clear that Marshall had up to date only touched the fringe of all the implications of a re-entry into France. In the light of the existing situation his plans for September of 1942 were just fantastic! Marshall had a long way to go at that time before realizing what we were faced with. It will be seen from my diary that during the next few days I was busy sizing up Marshall's character and military ability. It was very evident that we should have to work extremely closely together, and for this a close understanding of each other was essential.

10 April

A very busy day which started with usual COS meeting, mainly concerned in trying to save India from the Japs. A gloomy prospect with loss of command of

---

*'Went to see CIGS about various things. ... Found him rather impatient with our attitude of giving *everything* Russians ask and getting *nothing* in return. Of course the Russians are fighting – but for themselves and not for us – but I do sympathize with him rather.' Dilks (ed.), *Cadogan Diaries*, p. 446.

sea and air. Lunched with Adam and in evening had another COS meeting to discuss Joint Planning Staff report on Marshall's scheme for invasion of Europe. Then out to Chequers for dinner and the night. Harry Hopkins and Marshall there, also three Chiefs of Staff. We were kept up till 2 am doing a world survey, but little useful work.

I remember being amused at Marshall's reactions to Winston's late hours, he was evidently not used to being kept out of his bed till the small hours of the morning and not enjoying it much! He certainly had a much easier time of it working with Roosevelt, he informed me that he frequently did not see him for a month or six weeks. I was fortunate if I did not see Winston for 6 hours.

11 April
Back from Chequers and busy morning with COS and office work. Finally dashed off home at 5 pm.

12 April
Sunday at home pruning roses and playing with darling Pooks.

13 April
A bad COS with much loss of time and interruptions trying to frame a reply for Marshall. Then lunch with Portal and Freeman to settle 'off the record' the differences between Army and Air Force. Evidently little hope of arriving at any sort of settlement.

This was still connected with the fact that the Air Force would at that time still make no provision for Army cooperation and air support. Their energies and outlook were entirely absorbed with the air offensive against Germany, and they considered a re-entry by the Army into Europe as an unlikely contingency which should not be allowed to detract from the air offensive against Germany – through which alone success might be achieved. It was a difficult policy to counter in those days.

Cabinet at 5.30 pm, attended by Harry Hopkins, Marshall and Casey [Australian Minister to USA, then Minister Resident in ME]. Afterwards [COS] meeting to settle final details of reply to Marshall. Only got away after 8 pm and had Marshall to dine with me. The more I see of him the more I like him.

There was a great charm and dignity about Marshall which could not fail to appeal to one. A big man and a very great gentleman, who inspired trust, but did not impress me by the ability of his brain.

14 April

Another very busy day. Marshall attended our COS meeting at which I stated our reply to his memorandum and handed over the document to him. We then had a Cabinet meeting to settle a new programme of arms for Russia. I then dashed back to the flat to meet you and found you were unfortunately suffering from ear ache! Most distressing.

This earache had been caught from my son who only narrowly escaped mastoids, and at the time it looked as if my wife might also have to be operated on. This remained a source of deep anxiety for some time to come.

At 5 pm a meeting with Oliver Lyttelton to try and settle the co-ordination of strategy and production. From there back to WO for an interview with Archie Nye and a rush home to change for dinner at Savoy with Anthony Eden, de Gaulle, Peake [British Representative to French National Committee] and self. A difficult dinner in many ways as there was no knowing what de Gaulle might want to lead us to!

From there back to Downing Street for a Defence Committee attended by Hopkins and Marshall. A momentous meeting at which we acccepted their proposals for offensive action in Europe in 1942 perhaps and in 1943 for certain. They have not begun to realize all the implications of this plan and all the difficulties that lie ahead of us! The fear I have is that they should concentrate on this offensive at the expense of all else! We have therefore been pressing on them the importance of providing American assistance in the Indian Ocean and Middle East.

With the situation prevailing at that time it was not possible to take Marshall's 'castles in the air' too seriously! It must be remembered that we were at that time literally hanging on by our eye-lids! Australia and India were threatened by the Japanese, we had temporarily lost control of the Indian Ocean, the Germans were threatening Persia and our oil, Auchinleck was in precarious straits in the desert, and the submarine sinkings were heavy. Under such circumstances we were temporarily on the defensive, and when we returned to the offensive certain definite steps were necessary.

We were desperately short of shipping and could stage no large scale operations without additional shipping. This shipping could only be obtained by opening the Mediterranean and saving a million tons of shipping through the elimination of the Cape route. To clear the Mediterranean, North Africa must be cleared first. We might certainly start preparing plans for the European offensive, but such plans must not be allowed to interfere with the successive stages of operations essential to the ultimate execution of this plan.

15 April

Usual COS in morning. After lunch I had Marshall for nearly 2 hours in my office explaining to him our dispositions. He is, I should think, a good general at raising armies and providing the necessary links between the military and political worlds. But his strategical ability does not impress me at all!! In fact in many respects he is a very dangerous man whilst being a very charming one! He has found that King, the American Admiral, is proving more and more of a drain on his military resources, continually calling for land forces to capture and hold bases. On the other hand MacArthur [Commander South West Pacific Area from April 1942] in Australia constitutes another threat by asking for forces to develop an offensive from Australia. To counter these moves Marshall has started the European offensive plan and is going 100% all out on it! It is a clever move which fits in well with present political opinion and the desire to help Russia. It is also popular with all military men who are fretting for an offensive policy. But, and this is a very large 'but', his plan does not go beyond just landing on the far coast!! Whether we are to play baccarat or chemin de fer at Le Touquet, or possibly bathe at Paris Plage is not stipulated! I asked him this afternoon – do we go east, south or west after landing? He had not begun to think of it!!

Later in the afternoon attended an American sherry party at Claridges to meet Marshall. Finally dined 10 Downing Street [where the] King had been invited to meet Marshall and Harry Hopkins, also Pound, Portal, Mountbatten, Ismay and Hardinge [Private Secretary to the King] and self. After dinner heated discussion as to possible future of German plans. I propounded possible German move through Eastern Mediterranean with sea and air borne attacks against Cyprus and Syria. I suggested this might be an alternative if Germany did not feel strong enough to attack Russia. The King very interested and this resulted in good argument with Winston.

My conversation with Marshall that afternoon was an eye-opener! I discovered that he had not studied any of the strategic implications of a cross Channel operation. He argued that the main difficulty would be to achieve a landing. I granted that this would certainly present great difficulties, but that our real troubles would start after the landing. We should be operating with forces initially weaker than the enemy and in addition his rate of reinforcement would be at least twice as fast as ours. In addition his formations were fully trained and endured [inured?] to war whilst ours were raw and inexperienced.

I asked him to imagine that his landing had been safely carried out and asked him what his plans would then be. Would he move east towards Germany exposing his south flank? Would he move south to liberate France and expose his left flank? Would he move east to secure some lodgement? I found that he had not begun to consider any form of plan of action, and had not even begun to visualize the problems that would face an army after landing.

I saw a great deal of him throughout the rest of the war, and the more I saw of him the more clearly I appreciated that his strategic ability was of the poorest. A great man, a great gentleman and great organizer, but definitely not a strategist. I found that his stunted strategic outlook made it very difficult to discuss strategic plans with him, for the good reason that he did not understand them personally but backed the briefs prepared by his staff.

16 April

Important COS meeting at which we discussed plans for this year's invasion of the continent in collaboration with the Americans, and also plans for 1943. The plans are fraught with the gravest dangers. Public opinion is shouting for the formation of a new western front to assist the Russians. But they have no conception of the difficulties and dangers entailed! The prospects of success are small and dependent on a mass of unknowns, whilst the chances of disaster are great and dependent on a mass of well established military facts. Should Germany be getting the best of an attack on Russia, the pressure for invasion of France will be at its strongest, and yet this is just the most dangerous set of circumstances for us.

Took lunch in car and went to see the organization for breaking down ciphers [Bletchley Park] – a wonderful set of professors and genii! I marvel at the work they succeed in doing.

17 April

Short COS from which I went round to No. 10 Downing St to say goodbye to General Marshall before his departure for USA. He was very charming as usual and hoped I would be able to return his visit.

I then had Sikorski to lunch and found him most interesting as usual. We discussed his visit to America and the return of his Poles from Palestine. According to his secret sources of information the German concentration for their offensive is practically completed. I wonder if he can be right? We have no such information. At 3.30 attended Defence Committee which was unnecessarily protracted by an argument about oil between Eden and [Geoffrey] Lloyd! Their personal animosity seemed to influence the argument more than the point under discussion! Then a visit from Lindsell to say goodbye before departure for Middle East, followed by Military Members meeting of Army Council, a visit from S of S and finally a long visit from Casey. I was very much impressed by him and by his grasp of things – he should be excellent in the ME.

18 April

An annoying COS meeting at which much time was wasted. Pug Ismay arrived in great excitement with wire from President to PM suggesting that owing to new Laval government French North Africa might shake loose! Pug had even gone so far as to imagine that Pétain would fly over to assume command. As a result we were asked to examine necessary steps to be taken in various eventualities (which to my mind seemed impossibilities). Finally we instructed Joint Planners to carry out examination to be ready by 5.30 pm.

After lunch went with CAS to Northolt to see various types of tug aircraft, and also the new 25 seater glider. I was much impressed by the latter and its possibilities. We were to have gone up in it, but time did not admit. Returned to COS at 5.15 pm and finished it off by 6 pm. Then dashed off home to see how you were getting on with your bad ear ache.

19 April

Mainly spent trying to fix things up for you so that you could be kept a bit quieter and looked after properly.

20 April

Left usual time and WO by 9 am. COS mainly connected with naval and air situation in the Indian Ocean. After lunch revised air paper with Archie Nye and Watson. Finally Cabinet at 5.30 pm and another interview with Nye concerning reorganization of War Office General Staff.

21 April

COS meeting at which we discussed the possibility of staging a satisfactory air offensive over France with object of reducing German Air Force and forcing them to withdraw from the Russian Front. Then Cabinet meeting in PM's room at the House to discuss gas situation and advisability or otherwise of making a declaration that we should make use of gas if Germans made use of it against Russians. Evening at the WO and after dinner sent for to 10 Downing Street to discuss successor for Dobbie [Governor] in Malta, as apparently stress is beginning to tell. Also possibility of getting convoys into Malta.

22 April

We went on this morning with the problem of convoys to Malta and at 12 noon attended Defence Committee where we went on with the problem without much success. Recommendation had also come in that Dobbie should be changed. PM was not for it, but in view of the recommendation of all the three services I pressed for it and recommended that Gort should be sent to Malta as Commander-in-Chief. PM would not agree at first but called me up after lunch to say that he had come round and agreed.

After lunch Billotte (one of de Gaulle's staff), came to see me about organizing sabotage and forces in France to assist invasion. Then Cyril Falls for *The Times* came for a talk on the general situation. At 5.30 pm, another Defence Committee at which final decision was taken as regards supplies for Malta. PM had drawn up plan which was based on awaiting results of Cyrenaica offensive.

23 April

A very difficult COS connected with the proposed operation against Madagascar. The Admiralty who were the original supporters of the necessity for such an attack are now adopting a different attitude and doubting the necessity! I cannot see that the desirability of carrying out the operation (if it ever existed!) has in any way altered, but the change of government in France and the arrival of Laval puts a new complexion on the enterprise. The repercussions are more likely and may be more serious, we have to take into account the possibility of Bizerta being handed over to the Axis powers, or possibly the French fleet, or Gibraltar heavily bombed and the flow of aircraft interfered with, or Dakar falling into Axis hands. All the above would have a serious adverse effect on our power to prosecute the war.

After lunch attended reception given by Sikorski in honour of Anders, the Polish general from Moscow who has flown home in connection with the flow of Polish forces from Russia to the Middle East. There are two opposed camps in the Poles now. Sikorski and those in England wish to transfer a large contingent home to form force here, the others wish to form Polish forces in the Middle East. Personally I am in favour of the latter. Any forces in the Middle East this summer will be a Godsend to us.

24 April

A short COS which started at 10 am, to consider advisability of putting Madagascar operation on. We then had to go on to discuss the operation with the PM and Foreign Secretary at 11 am, and finally with Defence Committee at 12 noon. The main difficulty was to estimate what effect the operation might have on the new Laval government and consequently what the repercussions were likely to be. Personally I feel we have little to gain from carrying out the operation. The main object is to deny the use of Diego Suarez to the Japs, and I don't feel that they are likely to go there! The risks are Laval giving Germans a free run of Dakar, or Bizerta, or bombing Gibraltar, or handing over fleet. Personally I do not feel operation is worth it. However Winston decided for it at the present.

After lunch another interview with poor Alan Cunningham, who wishes his case judged definitely one way or another. Then a long talk with Anders, the Polish general from Russia. I found him most interesting. Luckily he is a strong supporter of leaving as many Poles as possible in the Middle East. Then an interview with Gubbins to discuss subversive operations in France, and the linking up of his work with Billotte. Then went for an interview with Sir Stafford Cripps, to discuss his journey to Middle East and on to India. He was most interesting as regards his time in India, but I am afraid that Wavell's silence did not impress him much. He has a far higher opinion of Auchinleck. He was evidently much more impressed by his qualities, and no doubt the Auk took far more pains to make himself pleasant than old Wavell would!

25 April

Attended ANZAC Day service at St Martin's in the Lane [Fields], where I met FM Birdwood. Ian Hamilton also attended, looking very old and doddery. Went on to COS meeting which I finished before lunch. After lunch made an early departure for Ferney Close as I was longing to find out how you were getting on.

26 April

Spent at home and delighted that you were a little better. Walked with children to Andrews' cottage to ask about kingfisher's nest.

27 April

Was very happy at being able to leave you suffering less than when I had arrived, and with less fever. Good run up and COS where First Sea Lord arrived having returned from America, where he had flown over and back again in last few days. Then interview with Tom Wintringham, who wishes to go to India to raise guerrilla fighters. Stafford Cripps had told me about him. Cabinet meeting at 5.20 which lasted till 7.30 pm.

28 April

An important COS meeting at which I assembled the QMG and his opposite numbers from Admiralty and Air Ministry with the object of forming an Administrative Chiefs of Staff Committee to work in close cooperation with us in connection with proposed large scale offensive in 1943. Afternoon with many interviews, Curtis back from Iceland, Andy McCulloch suggesting he might succeed Dobbie, Paget to tell me Schreiber's health was giving out. Also Selection Board meeting to decide honours and rewards.

After dinner asked by PM to come round at 10 pm and remained on till after midnight. He was in a good mood and we discussed many problems: the capture and future garrisoning of Madagascar, the Poles in Syria, Wavell and Ceylon, Alexander's transfer home to command Expeditionary Forces, the supplying of Malta, the bombing of the *Tirpitz*,* and our new divisional organization.

29 April

A busy day at COS. This morning we were again busy with details of the Madagascar expedition. After lunch Cassels [lately C-in-C India], just back from India, came to see me. At 6.15 I went to the Cabinet meeting, where we were intended to discuss the future operations on the Continent. But instead we got involved in a heavy discussion on army support from the air. I became involved in heated discussion with S of S for Air, I should have liked to have told him even more plainly that he was deliberately speaking untruths! However, PM backed me up, and rubbed into Sinclair the necessity for devoting more love and affection to those air forces destined for army requirements.

---

*The threat of the *Tirpitz* had caused the scattering and destruction of convoy PQ17 the previous month. She was based at Trondheim, Norway.

30 April
At this morning's COS we were busy discussing the possibility of establishing greater unity of command in West Africa. We had Giffard (C-in-C) and Gater from the Colonial Office, and moved a certain distance forward. Then a lunch at Claridges for Sikorski and General Anders from Russia. Quite interesting talk with both of them on the state of the Russian force and on their views concerning Hitler's speech. Then dashed back to see you and Mr Ti at the flat. Back to WO to meet Giffard at 4 pm, then long interview with Archie Nye. Finally back to flat where I had Bertie Ramsay to dine and had long talk with him.

1 May
A short COS fixing final details as regards announcing carrying out of Madagascar attack next Tuesday morning. Had a fairly quiet afternoon which gave me the chance of working off back work.

Sent for by PM in the evening to discuss Wavell's latest wire. He is protesting strongly at the fact that land, sea and air forces for defence of India are not being built up quicker. This is partly due to the Madagascar operation. Personally I wish we were not carrying it out. We do not stand to gain much by it, as it is very doubtful whether Japs would ever go there. On the other hand, with new Laval government we may suffer a great deal from the reaction. However I put the matter clearly to PM and Anthony Eden, and they said they did not apprehend any special reaction from Laval. On their heads may the responsibility for the decision rest!

2 May
Flew to Shrewton to watch demonstration on Larkhill ranges. Then lunched in Mess and flew back to Odiham where car met me and took me home. I found you up and basking in the porch.

3 May
Lovely warm day which you spent mostly on the porch sunning yourself, but I am afraid sun must have been too much for you, as it put temperature up again.

4 May
Left 8 am and had good run up to the WO. COS concerned with final arrangements for attack on Madagascar, which takes place tomorrow morning early. Also PM had received telegrams from Casey confirming necessity for relief of Dobbie in Malta by Gort. PM then invited all the Chiefs of Staff to lunch at 10 Downing Street, where he arrived a little later from Chequers. He was in good form and said he felt elated, I think probably mainly with excitement at

thought of attack on Madagascar! Attlee turned up after lunch and we did not get off till 3.45 pm. War Cabinet at 5.30 pm which lasted till 7.30 pm. Evatt, the new Australian representative, was there. Not very attractive at first sight!

5 May

A busy day with meetings till 5 pm, when I caught train up to Penrith to go to Lowther Castle to see the tank searchlight school and its application in attack and defence. We arrived about midnight and were there till about 4 am when we started back in the sleeper, arriving London about 10.45. A very interesting and promising demonstration.

6 May

Arrived just in time to go to COS meeting to turn down proposed attack on Alderney Island [Channel Islands] as a large raid by Guards Brigade. Afternoon series of interviews, including one with our new scientist (Darwin). At 6 pm meeting with PM to discuss [the] Airborne Division and made considerable progress. After meeting invited by the PM to sit in garden with him to discuss the Madagascar operation, which has been rather sticky during last 24 hours! Had Kenneth McLeod [GOC Burma 1938–41] to dinner and discussed Burma with him.

7 May

I was sent for on way to COS meeting to see PM in bed about wire which had come in from Auchinleck about the date of his attack which he is again putting right on ahead to July or August. PM as usual very upset about the whole business, wishing to bring Alexander back to take over half of Middle East! Luckily news fron Madagascar was better again and this took the edge off the trouble!

After COS went to Cabinet meeting in the House to discuss issue of gas masks (3 million!) to USSR, which they had asked for! Then left at 1 pm to motor to Canadian Corps demonstration of their pipe method of destruction of mine fields. A good show. Back to WO office where I arrived at 7.45 pm. On to flat where QMG, Weeks, Sinclair and Archie Nye came to dinner to discuss organization of General Staff in WO. I think we have made good progress.

8 May

An unpleasant day! Difficult COS meeting, first of all considering Auchinleck's wire in which he proposes to put off his attack from May 15th to June 15th. I do not like his message – it is a bad one based purely on number of tanks and not on the strategical situation. He never takes into account danger Malta is exposed to through his proposed delays. Next we had to examine the Sledgehammer operation, namely proposals for establishing a bridgehead across the Channel [in 1942]. After an examination, Home Forces and CCO

(Mountbatten) had come to the conclusion that the landing craft were insufficient for the operation.

Lunched with Adam and had a short walk to look at tulips in St James's Park.

Then Cabinet meeting at 3 pm to examine Auchinleck's wire. I had to open the ball and stated that I did not consider that we could order the Auk to attack about May 15th against his advice. That we should give him till June 15th and tell him to coordinate his attack with running of convoy to Malta, whilst being prepared to take advantage of any limited attack enemy might make as expected towards end of May. PM asked opinions of all attending meeting and finally drafted reply himself, in which he said that COS, Defence Committee and Cabinet were unanimously of opinion that attack should if possible be delivered before the end of May. From Cabinet went to see Cranborne [Colonies] about West Africa and appointment of supreme Commander-in-Chief for all colonies. He did not approve of Giffard being given the job.

9 May

Usual COS after which I lunched at flat and finished my work off in the office by 4.30 pm. I then picked Mary up, had tea with your father and came on to Fleet Hospital to collect you.

10 May

Called up after breakfast by DMO to be told that I was wanted for Cabinet meeting at 6 pm and COS meeting before that to discuss latest wire from Auchinleck. He had again stuck his toes in and was refusing to attack till a late date, and had sent in a very bad telegram in which he entirely failed to realize the importance of Malta and overestimated the danger to Egypt in the event of his being defeated. We framed a proposed policy at COS in which we laid down that we considered that the value of Malta was underestimated, whilst his arguments against attack were not very convincing. Finally we suggested that he should be allowed to wait to take advantage of possible limited German offensive for Tobruk to put in counter stroke, but that the June convoy to Malta should be the latest date as this afforded the last opportunity of assisting in the supply of Malta.

At Cabinet meeting I made statement of our decisions. PM then asked individual opinions of each Minister, who practically all agreed to our proposals. PM then withdrew to draft a proposed wire which he read out on his return. We did not quite like it so Chiefs of Staff were asked to withdraw to consider it and redraft it, which we did. Our proposal was accepted.

11 May

Two years ago I was up in Brussels at this time, preparing to hold Louvain! A great deal has happened since then! COS mainly concerned with various Combined Operations which CCO [Mountbatten] is planning. Also arranging for next steps in connection with Madagascar operation, namely taking of Majunga and Tamatave [Toamasina], and sending one of brigades to India. At 12 noon we had meeting with PM to discuss the giving up of the attack on Alderney, and raids planned as alternatives.

Then lunched at Savoy with Lord McGowan [Chairman ICI], the others being Lord Camrose, Vincent Massey, Lord Ashfield, Alexander, Adam and Kirke! Cabinet meeting at 5.30 which lasted till 7.30. After Cabinet Grigg and I tackled PM again about Cunningham and Godwin-Austen, but without any luck! I cannot make out his attitude about it – the moment their names are mentioned one might imagine they were criminals of the worst order.

12 May

A difficult COS this morning with a visit from Evatt of Australia. He produced 3 strong blackmail cards and then asked for greater allocation of aircraft from America to Australia. In fact, if we did not ensure that MacArthur's requests were met we should probably be forced to part with the 9th Aust Div from Middle East, or the Australian Squadron from England, or the diversion of 2nd Inf Div and 8th Armoured Div to Australia! He is a thoroughly unpleasant type of individual with no outlook beyond the shores of Australia.

I did my level best to make him listen to a short statement of the global situation, and where the main dangers existed. He refused to listen and gave me the impression that as far as he was concerned he did not mind what happened to anybody else as long as Australian shores could be made safe. It was quite impossible to make him realize that the security of Australia did not rest in Australia. He failed to see that defeat in the Middle East, India and Indian Ocean must inevitably lead to the invasion of Australia, no matter what reinforcements were sent them now.

Ronnie Stanyforth and his wife came to lunch. After that I went with PM to Horse Guards to see most recent type of American tank. Paget then came to see me. Dined with Bertie.

13 May

Main interest of morning's COS was examination of proposed large scale raid in the vicinity of Dieppe. Little did I ever think in the old days of my regular journeys of Newhaven-Dieppe that I should have been planning as I was this morning! Lunched at Savoy to meet Evatt again. He does not improve much on further meeting. Before lunch old Dobbie came to see me. I thought he looked very tired and worn out from his trying time in Malta. After lunch Admiral Stark, recently arrived from America, came to see me. A delightful old gentleman.

14 May

A short and rather uninteresting COS meeting. Lunched at GHQ Home Forces and then gave talk on world situation to Cs-in-C. Then interview with Gardiner, who is on his way out to the Middle East to run a High Command School for Auchinleck. Also interview with Hambro, who has now taken over the SOE activities, and came to beg for Gubbins, not long removed from here for Russia.

15 May
A short COS and a fairly quiet day disturbed by the fact that I had to inform Macready that he was to go to Washington instead of Wemyss, that the latter was to go as MS [Military Secretary] instead of [Floyer-]Acland, and that the latter was to remain unemployed until such date as we can find some work for him.

Madagascar producing difficulties. Eden was in a great hurry to declare that Free French would control the island, and the reaction out there has not been at all favourable to such a conception!

16 May
A short COS and finished off office work by 4.30 pm when I started off for home.

17 May
Spent at home photographing blackbirds and trying to get photos of fox cubs without much success.

18 May
Left home 8 am. Short COS concerned with Madagascar and failure of Americans to provide aircraft, also difficulty of next Russian convoy. Lunched with Sinclair, Grigg and Portal to discuss army air requirements. We made no headway at all, and are exactly where we were before. The situation is hopeless and I see no solution besides the provision of an army air arm. Cabinet at 5.30 pm where PM decided to send convoy to Russia against advice of Cabinet. He also refused to reconsider employment of either Cunningham or Godwin-Austen.

19 May
Difficult COS meeting at which we discussed Army and Navy air requirements. It led in the first place to heated arguments between me and Portal and subsequently between Pound and Portal! I had obtained agreement on a certain number of points, but had to carry forward several for Defence Committee to settle. It is a depressing situation and the Air Ministry outlook is now so divorced from the requirements of the army that I see no solution except an Army Air Arm.

During afternoon had interview with Scobie, who is back from the Middle East. I am not happy at all from all that I hear of the situation at Middle East Headquarters. Auchinleck's Chief of Staff (Corbett) is nothing like good enough for the job, and yet he insisted on selecting him. On the other hand I do not feel that Neil Ritchie is a big enough man to command the 8ᵗʰ Army, and I fear that the Auk is also losing confidence in him! It is all very depressing with an offensive impending.

20 May

Went to Hendon by 8.30 am to fly to Ireland but was delayed 1 hour before starting. Arrived Belfast after good fly. Met by Franklyn and proceeded to Majendie's HQ and the American Headquarters before lunching with Franklyn. After lunch visited 59ᵗʰ Div and Command Battle School, seeing Inf Exercise and Anti-Tank range. Finally returned to Belfast to put up with Basil and Cynthia at Storebrooke. Large sherry party with PM [Basil, AB's nephew, became PM of Northern Ireland], Naval and Air officers etc. Sheilah, Harry and Rosemary to dinner.

21 May

Motored to Lurgan to see III Corps HQ and from there to near Clogh, where 61ˢᵗ Div HQ was. Then right through Colebrooke [AB's childhood home]! I felt as if I were moving in a dream, driving on right through the place without stopping and finding huts with soldiers all round Ashbrooke. Could not help looking back and wondering how surprised if I had been able to peep into the future! Lunch at bn HQ near Enniskillen and then went on to Belun Mountain to see exercise. There I met Henry Richardson dressed as a Home Guardsman. After seeing one more exercise by bn, went to Ely Lodge to see American troops and had very interesting display of their weapons. Then by launch across Loch Erne to Killadeas to see American engineers. Finally back to Belfast by car as plane would not fly.

22 May

Left Belfast 9.30, good fly over, landing Hendon at 11.30. Found I had narrowly escaped being recalled last night for Defence Committee which went on till 2 am to prepare conference with Molotov [Soviet Foreign Minister]! Had to lunch 10 Downing St to meet Molotov. Maisky also there. Most of War Cabinet present: Eden, Bevin, Anderson, Cripps, Attlee, Alexander, Sinclair, Grigg, Chiefs of Staff and of course PM. Very busy evening to polish off work of last 2 days.

I was filled with interest to meet Molotov for the first time. Not very impressive to look at and with slight impediment in his speech, yet gave one a feeling of distinct ability and shrewdness.

23 May

Went round to 10 Downing St at 12.30 after COS where Mountbatten and I had long interview with PM discussing invasion possibilities. He was carried away with optimism at times and establishing lodgements all round the coast from Calais to Bordeaux, with little regard to strengths and landing facilities. We both lunched with him and did not get away till 3.30. Got off home about 4.30, to the great joy of finding you better.

24 May

At home with a much lighter heart owing to you being so much better.

25 May

Got back to WO by 9 am. Usual COS and fairly quiet day only disturbed by one telephone call of PM after dinner to discuss telegram based on Battle of Austerlitz, which he wanted to send to Auchinleck, and wanted my advice! I advised not to send but doubt whether he will take this advice as he wants to discuss further with me!

26 May

COS at which we had a Major Wilkinson who had been Staff Officer to MacArthur in the Philippines and was very interesting.

Then went out to lunch at Russian Embassy to meet Molotov again. A memorable lunch party held prior to signing new Anglo-Russian Treaty. Lunch attended by PM, Eden, Attlee, Stafford Cripps, Oliver Lyttelton, Evatt, Bevin, John Anderson, Chiefs of Staff etc. Many toasts and many speeches. Somehow the whole affair gave me the creeps and made me feel that humanity has still many centuries to live through before universal peace can be found. *(I had evidently not yet become hardened to the insincerity of statements contained in the speeches of politicians and statesmen on such occasions!!)*

PM asked me to drive back with him in his car and discussed his proposed wire to Auchinleck. I luckily succeeded in preventing him from sending it.

6.45 pm – War Cabinet which lasted till 8.30 pm. Then a rush to get to the Savoy to dine with Portal, who was giving a dinner to Arnold [Chief of US Army Air Force] and Towers who had just flown over from USA to try and break the deadlock which new proposals of President has caused in which he is trying to stop deliveries of aircraft to us in order to provide sufficient aircraft to USA pilots! Transactions are not going over well.

27 May

Had a long and difficult COS attended by Paget and Sholto Douglas and Bertie Ramsay on the organization of command for invasion of the Continent in 1943. The desirability or otherwise of a Generalissimo to control all Services, and the necessity of unified command over land, sea and air between USA and ourselves was thoroughly discussed. Only returned late for luncheon and missed some of you as you were lunching with me. We then went round to [Army & Navy] Stores to buy Mr Ti a bicycle.

Then back to WO, to see first Cunningham, to inform him of lack of success both Grigg and I had had with PM as regards his future employment. Then Galloway as regards his employment as DSD at the WO. Finally Paget concerning operations on the Continent.

At 5.30 went to 10 Downing St to discuss establishing of Western Front. PM in very good form and quite ready to appreciate that it is impossible to establish a front with landing craft only capable of lifting 4,000 men [in] first flight. He was very amenable to reason, but inclined to transfer the scene of action to Northern Norway! Which we are now to examine. Back to the flat where I had the American Admiral Stark, Bertie Ramsay, and Bertie Sergison-Brooke dining with me.

28 May

A pretty full COS. First of all we had the USA DMO [Eisenhower] and QMG who are over for a few days and discussed with them the higher organization for operations in Europe in '43. Then we had Dr Evatt again for ¾ [hour] pleading that Australia should be crammed full of forces at the expense of all other fronts. However he left with no more than he had come! I then took a sandwich lunch and motored to Tunbridge Wells to see Monty in a big exercise he is running between 12th and Canadian Corps in which he is trying out the new organization. Returned back here 7 pm and put in an hour before dinner.

Rommel has now started his expected attack and a large scale battle is raging in the Middle East.

A great deal depends on it. The Auk ought to be able to get the better of it, and has great chances in pushing a counter stroke home.

29 May

COS at which we again discussed Madagascar. Again Foreign Office with their mad desire to back de Gaulle are putting us into a position where we shall ultimately be forced to use more force to finally secure our position in the island. We then had interview with Morton in order to examine possibilities of further coordination between SIS [Secret Intelligence Service] and SOE activities. I still feel they should be under one Ministry and not two as at present.

You came to lunch, *such* a pleasure seeing you look better.

Then interview with Dykes, back from Washington, Eisenhower, the USA Director of Military Operations. Followed by Mason-MacFarlane just back from Russia. I had to take him in to see S of S. Then Selection Board meeting which lasted to 7.45. After which I had to rush off to the Dorchester to dine with Admiral Stark in large dinner party for Americans over here. Came back to find new telegram from Middle East had arrived which required calling up the PM to give him latest situation. Found that he is at Chequers looking at a film and not likely to be out till 1 am!! I am therefore waiting for him to call up before going to bed!

30 May
Usual COS then lunch followed by interview with Paget before finishing off work about 4.30 pm and coming round to tea with you and your father. Then drove home with you.

31 May
Your birthday, and day of many treats including the bees swarming and all our bee stings!!

This bee swarm was a memorable one. My wife had never taken a swarm before, but after reading about it in the book felt full of confidence. Certainly more than I did! No excuses availed, and I was roped in as assistant, provided with a veil and a pair of gardening gloves full of holes. My wife climbed up the step-ladder and detailed me to hold the skep [sic] upside down under the swarm ready to receive the bees when she shook the pear tree bough they were on. Things, however, did not go according to the book! Half the bees fell into the skep and the remainder flew all over us. They soon penetrated our defences and busily attacked my wife's neck and my wrists. Suddenly she shouted 'I can't stand it any longer', and fled into the house. I felt that honour was now satisfied and followed in her wake, shedding bees in all directions.

When we finally reached the safety of her bedroom I had to pull 22!! stings out of her neck and a dozen had to be removed from my wrists. I swelled up rapidly and had an uncomfortable week. She showed no discomfort till after tea when she complained of not feeling well and retired to bed. I found she had a temperature of 103° but by next morning was none the worse with no swelling of any kind!

1 June
COS meeting fixing up various operations this summer to help Russians. In afternoon Cabinet in which I gave details of Rommel's attack and consequent fighting in Cyrenaica.

2 June
COS meeting at which we examined paper by Joint Planning Staff for future war against Japan.

Lunched at Club, then finished final details of my reorganization of General Staff. Then interview with S of S. Finally at 6.30 had to go to 10 Downing St to meet PM and Eden to discuss future dispositions for Madagascar. Winston's support of Vichy French as opposed to Free French in conditions prevailing in

Madagascar was refreshing. Eden's support of de Gaulle will go near losing the war for us if we do not watch it.

3 June

A short COS which I finished by 11.30 am! Oswald Birley, his wife and Barney's wife came to lunch. I then went to Birley's studio to sit for my picture. He kept me there till 5.45 pm, and I think made a good start. It was the first time I had seen him since he lost his eye. He tells me that it does not now interfere with his painting and that he thinks his work is as good as usual.

4 June

A fairly dull COS meeting. I then had Cyril Falls to lunch and from there went on to give Oswald Birley another sitting of 2 hours. He certainly is a very hard worker and keeps at it the whole time without a check.

5 June

At this morning's COS we discussed again the various possibilities of helping Russia by proceeding to France, either as a lodgement or as a raid. Prospects not hopeful. We then turned to examine the PM's pet attack on Northern Norway which appears even more impossible, except possibly for limited operations to secure Petsamo in combination with the Russians. Monty came to lunch and I discussed with him his large exercise which he has just completed to try out the new divisional organization.

6 June

A short COS and lunch at the flat, after which I finished off office work by 4.30 pm and started off for home. Very hot!

7 June

Spent afternoon photographing mistle thrush.

8 June

A COS with many items from Madagascar to Spitzbergen. Then Cabinet at 5.30 where we again discussed Madagascar and the Yugoslav Forces in the Middle East. Finally long COS meeting with PM at 10.30 which lasted till 1 am and at which we discussed operations on Continent this year, recapture of Burma, Madagascar, alternatives of reinforcing India or Middle East, i.e. whether 8th Armoured Div and 44th Div were to go to ME or India; the operation for capturing North Norway and finally the sending of a force to Spitzbergen to deny it to the Germans.

9 June

At COS this morning we reviewed some of the good work we had done with PM last night, and had the Joint Planners in to give them further working orders concerning the preparation of plans for the attacks on Rangoon, Petsamo and Spitzbergen.

You came up and we had a quiet lunch together.

After lunch first of all interview with General Lee of USA who brought me over a carbine from General Somervell. Then Gale to discuss commander for Indian parachute Bde, followed by Nye, then Adam, and finally interview with S of S. Last thing before leaving an aide memoire came round from Pug for me to use tomorrow at our interview with Molotov concerning what we are doing to assist Russia.

10 June

COS meeting for which I had prepared a statement to be made at an interview we were to have had with Molotov who is on his way through from USA to Moscow. But apparently PM had covered all necessary points last night. After lunch Army Council meeting, a dull procedure at which we discussed little that was directly connected with the conduct of the war. Afterwards series of interviews and evening's work preparing for tomorrow's Cabinet meeting.

11 June

COS meeting at 10 am, followed by Cabinet meeting in the House to review the prospects of establishing Western Front, of retaking Rangoon, of capturing North Norway or of taking Spitzbergen! PM in good form and carried Cabinet with him in his proposed policy that we do not land in France in strength except to stop there, and we do not go there unless German morale is deteriorating. Dashed off to Hendon after Cabinet and flew to near Catterick to visit 42nd Div. Then flew on to Northumberland to spend night with Allendales. Went out after dinner and caught 3 trout.

12 June

[A] day I had been looking forward to for months, namely visit to Farne Islands. Unfortunately weather foul and heavy sea running. In trying to load up dinghy overturned as Rusty Eastwood stepped out, naval Captain, two sailors and *all* my camera gear fell into sea!! Luckily Captain rescued camera before it sank. However he was almost exhausted before he was pulled out, and another sailor fell in in the attempt. At last we replaced dinghy by larger ship from Seahouses and loaded up the ML [Motor Launch]. But camera, films, lenses and all were swimming in sea water! I had an awful job drying out the sea water. Impossible to use camera, opportunity missed, most depressing. Anyhow weather very poor and drizzling. Finally flew back from Acklington landing Hendon about 8.15 pm.

This day was a real tragedy! For 20 years I had been looking forward to the day when I should return to the Farne islands to take photographs there!

13 June 1942

COS prolonged by interview with Mason-MacFarlane concerning Russia and his new job as C-in-C Gibraltar. Mountbatten also turned up, having just returned from America, and full of news of Washington. PM also called me up on telephone and told me he was thinking of starting for Washington on Thursday next and would like me to come with him. He considered Roosevelt was getting a bit off the rails and some good talks as regards western front were required. Escaped home about 4.45 pm.

14 June

A Sunday disturbed by many calls from the PM who was much disturbed at bad turn taken by operations in the Middle East. Rommel certainly seems to be getting the better of Ritchie and to be out generalling him.

15 June

A real unpleasant Monday! Left Ferney Close at 8 am. Drove straight to Huntsman where I ordered thin clothes for Washington. Then to WO where PM called up during briefing for COS and delayed me badly. COS till 1 pm. Then lunch and ordered thin shirts and tried on thin suits with Huntsman.

3 pm goodbye to Acland.

3.30 pm to 4.30 pm conference with Weeks, Watson and Nye on organization of force for next year's offensive.

5.30 pm Cabinet meeting and very gloomy owing to bad news from Libya and from Malta convoys. Lasted till 7.30 pm.

After dinner 1 hour's hard work before 10.30 meeting with PM at 10 Downing St. Just back at 1.20 am!! And we did *nothing* except meander round from Burma to France and back. Also discussed upcoming meeting to [in] Washington, and nearly decided to start tomorrow morning at 11 am!! Now postponed to Wednesday at any rate!

16 June

A difficult and tiring COS this morning. First of all JIC [Joint Intelligence Committee], then Donovan from USA to explain organization of their secret service. Then discussion as to command of 'Round Up' operation and also as to part to be played by Mountbatten and his party. In afternoon another trying on of my clothes for Washington, then went to dine with Bertie and was called up whilst I was there to be told that PM contemplated starting tomorrow!! None of my thin clothes will be ready and all money and coupons will be wasted! But worst of all I shall miss my dinner with you tomorrow evening.

The uniform was a serious matter as the temperature in Washington in June is like a
Turkish bath and I had no thin uniform except what I had just ordered!

17 June

Decided early that by 10.30 am final decision was to be given as to whether we
started for America at 12.15 am. Bad rush to get some thin clothing finished.
Attended COS where we received verdict that we were off ! Went back to WO
and flat to pick up kit and Barney met me at Euston station with 2 half finished
thin suits! Travelled up to Stranraer [south-west Scotland] in PM's special
[train] – very comfortable. Had meals alone at table with him and thus able to
settle many points in anticipation of talk with Roosevelt. Arrived Stranraer
about 10.30 pm, where news was telephoned through to PM. Then went by
motor boat to the Boeing Clipper. Huge flying boat beautifully fitted up with
bunks to sleep in, dining saloon, stewards, lavatories etc.

   Party consists of PM, his doctor [Sir Charles Wilson, later Lord Moran], ADC,
secretary, clerk, butler, detective, Pug Ismay, myself and my staff officer,
Stewart. At 11.30 pm we took off. Just saw a bit of the Irish Coast and then at
5,000 ft found the machine above the clouds. At 12.30 wonderful red sky from
sun just below the horizon. Slept very comfortably, after paying visit to pilot in
his driving compartment on top bridge.

18 June

Had long morning in bed as the clock was going back and breakfast was not
available till 11 am (about 8 am real time). Still flying over blankets of cloud till
about 12.30 when we found the sea again and shortly afterwards flew over a
large convoy of some 35 ships. PM in tremendous form and enjoying himself
like a schoolboy! As we waited to embark he was singing a little song to himself
'We're here because we're here'. As I write we are over the Atlantic and within
about an hour's flying of Newfoundland.

Later – Now over Newfoundland which we reached after 14½ hours flying.
Beautiful clear sky and able to get a wonderful view of the country. We flew
direct to Gander, the new airport, and after circling over the airport to have a
good look at it flew on on more southerly course.

Later – Hit off Cape Breton Island, and on to Nova Scotia. Unfortunately
cloudy and unable to see ground. Flying about 5,000 ft up, but came over
Newfoundland at 1,500 ft so as to see country well.

Later – After leaving Cape Breton Island we ran into heavy fog and bumpy conditions till we reached Cape Cod. By then we found that adverse weather had
delayed us and that we should have no time to divert to look at New York. We
therefore flew straight on to Washington and landed on the [River] Potomac
after being 26½ hours continuously in the air. Met by Halifax [Ambassador],

Lee [British Army Staff], Dill etc. Dill very kindly putting me up. Halifax asked me to dine so had to rush to Dill's house, bathe and change and go on to the Embassy where PM is stopping. Have only just returned at 1.45 am, which is equivalent of 7.45 am by English time to which I have been working during rest of day!!

Our arrival in Washington is one of those episodes which remains almost as clear in my mind as if it had been only yesterday. The sight of this beautifully laid out town in the hazy light of the evening; the Potomac looked like a small silver ribbon running through the middle of it, so small at that height that it seemed quite impossible for the large Clipper to find sufficient space to accommodate it. And yet when the time came it slid down on the water like a great swan, and then we were in contact again with the more solid elements of this earth. I found it hard to realize that in one hop I had moved through space from Stranraer Loch to the Potomac.

19 June

Left here at 10 am and drove to the COS offices where I found Dill and had long talk with him. At 12.30 am attended Combined Chiefs of Staff meeting at which I gave statement of reasons for our visit which were connected with some of the doubts expressed by President to Mountbatten.* We then had a lunch given by Combined Chiefs of Staff. After lunch had another interview with Marshall and his staff at which we made further progress towards defining our policy for 1942 and 1943. Found that we were pretty well of the same accord as to our outlook. Came back to Dill's room and then did some shopping. Dined with Dill this evening in his house. On the whole made fine progress today, but am a little doubtful as to what PM and President may be brewing up together.

20 June

Stinking hot day!! Went up to the office in morning where I looked through the minutes of yesterday's meetings. Then attended another Chiefs of Staff meeting at 11 am. Here I met Admiral King [US Chief of Naval Operations] for the first time. Meeting was I think a success, at least as a military man he was in agreement as to policy we should adopt. But we fully appreciated that we might be up against many difficulties when confronted with the plans that the PM and the President had been brewing up together at 'Hyde Park' [FDR's residence]! We fear the worst and are certain that North Africa or North Norway

*'Doubts' about the lengthening absence of any large-scale engagement with the Germans by Anglo-American (especially American) land forces. Roosevelt and Churchill in particular were concerned to find a suitable theatre for such engagement and *soon*, i.e. in 1942. If that was too soon for a cross-Channel operation in continental Europe – the ultimate goal – then North Africa beckoned meanwhile. AB's presentation of the British position on the competing possibilities was not reassuring to the Americans. See Dykes's diary, 19 June 1942, in Danchev, *Anglo-American Alliance*, p. 158.

plans for 1942 will loom large in their proposals, whilst we are convinced that they are not possible!

After COS meeting had interview with Admiral Little [Head of British Admiralty Delegation in Washington] for about ½ hour to discuss possibility of Rangoon operations. Then Dill and I went round to Embassy to see Halifax. I think he was mainly concerned with obtaining an appreciation of the situation in Libya. From there we went on to lunch with General Marshall. A very pleasant quiet lunch in a delightful house amongst the trees. After lunch we went to see the Lee Memorial, his old house kept exactly as it was when he inhabited it. I was thrilled with it and could transfer myself back easily to the days when he was there. I could almost see him going through the crisis of his life, deciding on which side he would fight! The slave quarters were also very interesting.

Then back to office. And to sherry party given by Dill for us to meet all the Dominion and British officers employed in Washington. Finally dined with Undersecretary of War, where the Secretary [Henry L. Stimson] was dining. Disturbed there by wire telling me Willoughby Norrie was being sent home.

This dinner was my first opportunity of meeting Stimson, the Secretary for War. I found him an exceptionally charming man to meet, and certainly a fine administrative brain, but with a limited strategic outlook. He was one of the strong adherents of breaking our heads in too early operations across the Channel. Consequently strong supporter of Marshall.

21 June

Had planned a nice quiet morning with Dill, but it was not to be! As we dropped into office we were warned that I had to lunch at White House with President. Shortly afterwards Pug Ismay called up to say that PM wanted to see me and that he was very upset at the decisions we had come to with the Combined Chiefs of Staff meetings. Found him a bit peevish, but not too bad and after an hour's talk had him quiet again.

Then went with him to see President. I was much impressed by him – a *most* attractive personality. Harry Hopkins and Marshall also turned up and we had a general discussion of all the possible offensives in France, Africa and the Middle East.

This meeting with Roosevelt made a very vivid impression on my mind. I was dressed in a very old suit for my day out with Dill, and when I found I was to meet the President I implored Winston to let me slip home and change into uniform, but he would not let me and said he wanted me. When I walked into the President's room I felt very ill at ease being in such slovenly clothes. He was sitting at his desk and after Winston had introduced me I apologized for being so badly dressed and gave him the reasons. He replied 'What's wrong with you? Why not take your coat off like I have, you will feel far more comfortable!' It was so nicely said that it at once made me feel at ease and broke down all my discomfort.

At 1 pm we adjourned for lunch, where I met Mrs Roosevelt. During lunch he said 'When I was a boy a certain Sir Victor Brooke came to stop with us at Hyde Park, is he any relation?' I then discovered that father and Douglas [AB's brother] had stopped with them and he remembered them well. I could not help wondering what father would have thought if he had known then the circumstances in which Roosevelt and his youngest son would meet in the future!

After lunch we had another long conference lasting till 4.30 pm. In the middle the tragic news of the loss of Tobruk came in!

Churchill and I were standing beside the President's desk talking to him when Marshall walked in with a pink piece of paper containing a message of the fall of Tobruk! Neither Winston nor I had contemplated such an eventuality and it was a staggering blow. I cannot remember what the individual words were that the President used to convey his sympathy, but I remember vividly being impressed by the tact and real heartfelt sympathy that lay behind these words. There was not one word too much or too little.

Marshall at once got to work to see what he could do to furnish some tangible signs of their sympathy in the shape of active assistance. ... He proposed in the first place sending the First American Armoured Division to the ME. This division was only partially trained, and it would have entailed forming an American front in the ME. Consequently it was decided to send 300 Sherman tanks and 100 self-propelled guns at once to the ME. These tanks had already been issued to the Armoured Division and had to be withdrawn from them for this purpose. Anybody knowing what it entails withdrawing long-expected weapons from fighting troops just after they have received them will understand the depth of kindness that lay behind this gesture.

I always feel that the Tobruk episode in the President's study did a great deal towards laying the foundations of friendship and understanding built up during the war between the President and Marshall on the one hand and Churchill and myself on the other.

After the meeting I had ¾ hour with Harry Hopkins and then came back to Dill's house via the office.

As I was walking out of the President's room, Hopkins said: 'Would you care to come round to my room for a few moments' talk? I could give you some of the background which influenced the President in the statements he has just made and the opinions he has expressed.' I went with him expecting to be taken to his office. Instead we went to his bedroom where we sat on the edge of his bed looking at his shaving brush and tooth brush, whilst he let me into some of the President's inner thoughts!

I mention this meeting as it was so typical of this strange man with no official position, not even an office in the White House, and yet one of the most influential men with the President. A man who played a great and nebulous part in the war as the President's right hand man. A great part that did him all the more credit when his miserable health is taken into account.

We had an early dinner and went back to the White House by 9 pm when we had a meeting with President, PM, Dill, Marshall, King, Harry Hopkins, Little, Ismay and self. Discussed results of submarine warfare and necessity for greater action on the part of preventative measures. Then proposed operation in Pacific. Finally Middle East position, and accepted offer of American Armoured Div for ME. This may lead to a USA front in ME at expense of the European front. Did not finish till 1 am. A little cooler this evening, thank Heaven, as heat has been oppressive all day.

22 June

Held a conference in the morning to discuss the use of the USA aircraft carrier *Ranger* in connection with convoys to Russia, to Malta, and aircraft to Takoradi for ME. Also discussed implications of sending USA Armoured Div to ME on Bolero (ie Western front plan). Then did some shopping and lunched with Dill, after which we went to Mount Vernon to see Washington's home. *Most* interesting. It is kept very much as it was in his day and makes it possible to bring him to life before one's eyes. I now want to read all about him! After tea went back to office and finally dined at Embassy to meet Winston and various Naval, Army and Air officers of Mission here. Winston made me drive back with him to the White House in the President's car to discuss necessity to relieve Neil Ritchie. I felt this was bound to come and was prepared for it. I am devoted to Neil and hate to think of the disappointment this will mean to him.

23 June

Went to office in the morning and at 2.30 pm to the White House to attend meeting of President, PM, Harry Hopkins, Marshall, Arnold, Pug Ismay and self. We discussed what could be done to reinforce Middle East rapidly by diverting USA Air Force from India to ME and also details concerning sailing of an armoured division from this country. Afterwards visited museum with Dill. We finally went round to the White House at 7.40 in anticipation of entraining for tomorrow's army demonstration. However after waiting some time we were informed that the special train had met with a misadventure and would not be able to start for another 2 hours or so. We were therefore all invited to dine with the President who was in good form. After dinner we went to the train which was air conditioned and beautifully cool.

24 June

Slept well and had good breakfast on the train. Then short conference with Marshall under the PM. At 11 am we arrived at Camp Jackson in South Carolina. Met at the station by guard of honour, bands, and masses of cameras and correspondents.

As we got out of the train there was a fleet of cars to take us round for the day, and as there was a vacant seat in one of the rear cars, Marshall very kindly suggested that

Sawyers (the PM's butler) should accompany us. From then onwards Sawyers became one of the party, both as regards watching the displays and as regards absorbing refreshments. The latter he did fairly efficiently, and for the rest of the day was distinctly affected by what he had consumed. When we regained the train later on he was asked by an official if the luggage in front of him belonged to the PM, to which in a thick voice he replied: 'How the hell should I know!'

Then drove out to reviewing field where we were shown 3 combat teams from 8th, 30th, and 77th Divisions respectively. Fine hard looking men. We were next shown a parachuting display by over 600 parachutists. Only 3 casualties, one leg broken, one sprain, and one suspected skull fracture. We were then shown individual training by the 77th Division, after which we had lunch on the train. We then went to a field firing range and watched a disappointing exercise. Finally flew back some 350 miles from Owen Fields Columbia, reaching Washington a little after 7 pm.

Here Sawyers again distinguished himself. Winston had changed into his Zip suit on the plane and put on his Panama hat for his arrival. The brim of the Panama was turned up all the way round and he looked just like a small boy in a suit of rompers going down to the beach to dig in the sand! Sawyers took up a position in the middle of the plane and refused to let him pass. Winston asked him: 'What's wrong, Sawyers? Why are you getting in my way?' In a very thick voice Sawyers replied: 'The brim of your hat is turned up, does not look well, turn it down, turn it down!' This was accompanied by a waving gesture of his hand. Winston, rather red and looking angry, turned the brim down. Thereupon Sawyers stood to one side, muttering to himself 'That's much, much better, much better.'

A very interesting day. I drove round with Mr Stimson, the Sec of State for War, a very nice man of about 72! The American system of individual and elementary training seems excellent, but I am not so certain that their higher training is good enough, or that they have yet realized the standard of training required.

They certainly had not – and had a lot to learn! I next met them in Northern Ireland, and they still had a lot to learn, but seemed to prefer to learn in the hard school of war itself. As a result they learned a great deal more in North Africa! But in the art of war, as in polo, lawn tennis, golf etc, when they once got down to it they were determined to make a success of it.

25 June

Went round to the office by 8.45 am where we had a Joint Staff Meeting to discuss American reinforcements to Middle East. [Admiral] Cunningham had just arrived to replace Admiral Little. At 9.30 we went to a Combined Chiefs of Staff meeting where we examined the various alternatives of providing an American Armoured Div for Middle East. A project both PM and President were very keen on. Marshall put forward a new proposal to provide 300 Sherman tanks and 100 105 [mm] self propelled guns together with two train ferry ships to take the lot out to ME.

Marshall then lunched with Dill and I had a very satisfactory talk with him explaining to him that after examining his proposal I was all for accepting it, but that I might have great difficulty to get the PM to accept it as he would wish to conform to President's desire to produce fighting troops instead of equipment. He agreed situation might be delicate and hoped I would do my best.

At 2.45 went round to White House to put proposal before PM. Dill, Little, Evatt, Cunningham, and Pug Ismay were also present. Things went better than I expected and I was able to convince PM that military aspect of this problem and its advantages outweighed the political considerations. I then telephoned to Marshall who was delighted at result.

Then dashed off to see a demonstration of the new American rocket gun. I was very much impressed by it and consider that it should be rapidly developed in large numbers. I then returned to Dill's house to pack and dine. At 8.15 assembled at the Embassy under Secret Service arrangements and motored to Baltimore where we found our Clipper drawn up along the quay like a ship. By 11 pm we were off, having taken off in the dark, and were flying over the lights of Baltimore, heading for Newfoundland.

26 June

Had an excellent night's sleep and got up at 6.30 am as we were due to arrive at Botley about 8 am and were to breakfast first. Flew over very swampy and waterlogged part of Newfoundland, finally landed at Botley, small village of wood houses and wooden church. Very good landing and went ashore for a couple of hours whilst the Clipper took on petrol. Our party is much the same – PM, his doctor, Sir Charles Wilson, Martin, his secretary, Thompson, his flag lieutenant, his butler, clerk, detective and Pug Ismay. In addition my Staff Officer, Stewart, [Ian] Jacob, whom we are fetching back, and [Averell] Harriman [FDR's Special Envoy], who has joined the party. We are at present well above the clouds, sailing out into the Atlantic.

It has been a very interesting trip and real good value. I feel now in much closer touch with Marshall and his staff and know what he is working for and what his difficulties are. Also meeting King (the Admiral), makes it easier to realize the difficulties in obtaining close cooperation between the land and the sea forces of America. Especially when King looks out over the Pacific primarily, whilst Marshall has his eyes turned towards Europe. Then meeting the President was a matter of the greatest interest, a wonderful charm about him. But I do not think that his military sense is on a par with his political sense. His conceptions and plans are not based on a full grasp of all the implications. As a result he favours plans which are not possible owing to their administrative aspects. On that account Marshall has difficulties and is forced to disagree with the President. I found it difficult in the first few meetings to be able to appreciate the degree of importance to attach to the President's military suggestions, and I did not know how Marshall would react. With the PM and the President planning on their own in the White House it made it difficult at first to carry on business with Marshall. However, I finally got on sufficiently intimate terms with him to discuss freely with him the probable reactions of both President and PM to the plans we were discussing. There is no doubt that Dill is doing wonderful work and that we owe him a deep debt of gratitude!

The President had no military knowledge and was aware of this fact and consequently relied on Marshall and listened to Marshall's advice. Marshall never seemed to have any difficulty in countering any wildish plans which the President might put forward. My position was very different. Winston never had the slightest doubt that he had inherited all the military genius from his great ancestor Marlborough! His military plans and ideas varied from the most brilliant conceptions at one end to the wildest and most dangerous ideas at the other. To wean him away from these wilder plans required superhuman efforts and was never entirely successful in so far as he tended to return to these ideas again and again. I am convinced that on many occasions Marshall imagined that I was in agreement with some of Winston's wilder ideas; it was not easy for me to explain how matters stood without disloyalty to Winston. On several occasions I believe that Marshall thought that I was double crossing him. It was in this respect, amongst others, that Dill was such an invaluable help. Marshall had the highest respect for him and I was devoted to him, consequently he was in a unique position to reduce difficulties between us. Unfortunately Winston never liked Dill, and had been poisoned against him by Beaverbrook. He consequently never gave him credit for the magnificent part that he played in Washington.

Later – still above the clouds and approaching Ireland. It has now become dark and although only 10 pm by my watch, it is 4 am by English time. It is easy to realize how the pioneers of transatlantic flights must have felt at a moment like this!

Later – shortly after writing above I went up to sit in the second pilot's seat where I found the PM. Beautiful moon shining on a sea of clouds, as the moon was nearly full the scene was beyond words. Shortly afterwards the clouds began to break and the sea again became visible, with only patches of cloud lying about. Then out of the darkness dark patches loomed up out on the horizon, which turned out to be the north coast of Mayo! We soon struck the coast, only just visible in the moonlight. PM was as thrilled as I was! We skirted the north coast of Mayo and sailed in just south of the mouth of the Erne, and on right over the middle of Lough Erne, hitting the north coast at about Killadeas. On over Armagh, north corner of Lough Neagh, and just north of Belfast. Then across the Channel and back to Stranraer where we made a perfect landing at 11.10 pm by American time but 5.10 am by British time. Journey home had taken just 24 hours from Baltimore.

I remember as if it were yesterday the pilot coming to me and saying: 'We have just passed the point of no return.' My mind at once went back to those pioneers and what their feelings must have been on passing that land-mark of transatlantic journeys. I also remember clearly when up with the pilot and Winston staring into the darkness trying to make out if we could see land, the pilot saying that if our land fall was correct we should soon see a lighthouse. And then suddenly flicking out of the darkness was a small spark of light! We had crossed that vast expanse of water and struck the exact spot we hoped for. My feelings during that moonlight flight across Ireland can well be imagined. I was spell bound looking down on Lough Erne and remembering the days I had fished there for pike. Then passing over Colebrooke and all the memories it conjured up, whilst Belfast wrapped in all the morning mist, pierced by columns of smoke, raised a lump in my throat and a desperate longing for days of peace.

27 June
We then landed and got onto PM's train where I slept till 12 noon (British time) then got up and had lunch and went through a mass of papers that had been sent up to meet us. At 4.45 we arrived at Euston to be met by Mrs Churchill and daughter, also large assembly of Cabinet! I then drove back to flat where I left kit. From there on to Cabinet meeting at 5.30 pm where PM gave an account of his trip and I was made to give a statement also. After that I went to WO picked up more papers and drove home, and was given a wonderful reception by you and the two young. Such a joy to be back with you.

28 June
Put in a wonderful long sleep and a quiet day. The next week will be a difficult one, picking up threads and at the same time dealing with the Middle East situation which is about as unhealthy as it can be. And I do not very well see how it will end. As far as I can judge from here the trouble is due to our tanks being under armed as compared to the Germans. We have been too slow in getting the 6 pdr and the 3" AA gun into tanks that are fit to be used out of this country.

29 June
Left Ferney Close at 8 am. Usual COS at which I explained results of American visit. Cabinet meeting at which Bevin was full of uneducated peevish questions about Middle East operations. Continually asking questions on points I had just explained. A great deal of the day taken up in picking up lost threads. This evening very nice photo of Roosevelt arrived for me with specially nice inscription.

30 June
COS meeting at which we discussed operations on the Continent next year. Then lunched with Oswald Birley at the Turf Club, after which we drove round

to his studio for another sitting. However on arrival they had message for me to go to 10 Downing Street. Arrived there 3 pm for meeting with PM and Mountbatten to discuss the large raid which is to be carried out next Saturday morning on Dieppe. After this discussion he called me out into the garden and informed me that he proposed starting for Cairo by air on Sunday and that he wanted me to come with him! I told him that it would not be fair on Auk to descend on him unless situation had stabilized a little. I cannot imagine anything more trying than Winston descending on one in the middle of a serious battle!! However I think he is prepared to accept the fact that the situation must have settled a little before he goes out. Personally I am longing to go, but not in company of PM at the present juncture with the fate of the Delta and Cairo in the balance.

Rushed back to Birley to finish my sitting, he is very pleased with the picture. Dined with Adam in Roehampton. Very heavy thunderstorm during dinner, during which lightning struck house about 100 yards away! Hailstones like pigeon eggs.

1 July

At COS we had a difficult time concerned with possibility of establishing a western front. Russia, USA and the Press all clamouring for a 'Western Front' without thinking what it means, or what its implications are! One might think we were going across the Channel to play baccarat at Le Touquet, or to bathe at Paris Plage! Nobody stops to think what you can possibly do with some 6 divisions against a possible 20 to 30! PM is well aware of all the implications. And yet for all that we are likely to be forced to undergo all the handicaps of taking up the necessary shipping and sacrificing the required training in order to prepare for an operation which we are convinced is impracticable.

At 6 pm I was due to go to Buckingham Palace, but PM sent for me at 5.40 pm! However I escaped just in time and arrived at the Palace exactly at 6 pm! King kept me till 6.45, discussing trips to America, Libya, Home Forces, his trip to Ireland etc. As usual he was quite charming. Lewin came to dine, but before he left I was sent for by PM again to discuss his speech for tomorrow. I was afraid might be kept up late, but succeeded in escaping by 1 am.

2 July

Missed COS and went to Staff College to deliver final address to students. Gave them 1¼ hours. Then home to Ferney Close to lunch with you. Then back to London where I tried on shorts in anticipation of possible start for Middle East on Sunday. Then back to WO and on to COS meeting at 5.30 where we discussed worst possible conditions in event of Auchinleck failing to hold up the German attack. Back to WO and long talk with P.J. Grigg on today's debates, and results of the PM's speech in the House. Apparently a great success. Finally dined Dorchester to meet Eisenhower, the new American general who has come to replace Chaney.

It is strange that I did not write more about my probable visit. I had at that time reached the stage where I could no longer handle the situation in Cairo without going out to see for myself. This impending visit was so constantly in my thoughts that I may not ever have thought it necessary to refer to it in my diary. The next point of interest is my reference to Eisenhower. He certainly made no great impression on me at our first meeting [in fact second: see 28–29 May 1942], and if I had been told then of the future that lay in front of him I should have refused to believe it.

3 July

Usual COS followed by a Cabinet meeting at 12 noon. There the PM examined the implications of the worst possible case in the Middle East in the event of Rommel driving on to Alexandria and Cairo. Luckily we had been studying this yesterday at the COS and I was able to make a statement covering our first investigations. Also described question concerning demolitions that might have to be carried out.

Monty came to lunch. In afternoon [Sir Reginald] Dorman-Smith (late Governor of Burma) came and I had a long talk with him about the campaign in Burma. He was very interesting. Later on PM sent for me. In the lobby Brendan Bracken caught me and asked me to influence PM not to go to ME for the present, and told me [Leo] Amery's son was coming over to try and induce him to go. I then went in and shortly afterwards a most objectionable young pup turned up who was Amery's son [Julian], just back from Cairo. He calmly said that he had landed this morning, that two things were necessary to secure the Middle East, first more equipment and secondly better morale. The equipment was on its way but delays must occur before it arrived. He considered therefore that the necessity for raising morale was paramount and that this could only be done by the PM flying out to Egypt!! The cheek of the young brute was almost more than I could bear. I cross questioned him as to what he based his deductions on and gathered that it was based on conversations with a few officers in the bar of Shepheard's Hotel, Cairo!

After he left I had about ¾ hour with Winston, first of all trying to convince him that he should not try to fly out by Gib and the Mediterranean in a Liberator. And secondly that he should wait till the situation consolidates a little more in Egypt before flying out. As a result we definitely do not start on Sunday, and I hope that the trip is put off till Wednesday at the earliest. This should give more time to see how events are going.

I feel I was somewhat unkind about young Amery when I wrote my diary that evening! But I had been sorely tried by him that day, with his attempts to get Winston to go out to the Middle East just when we were trying to stop him from going. In addition his bumptious manner had annoyed me, sitting there and lecturing Winston and me on the morale of the Middle East force, when all he had to base his deductions on were conversations in Shepheard's Hotel in Cairo. He had absolutely no solid evidence of any kind to base his deductions on. And yet he impressed Winston because he had flattered him! After he had left the room Winston turned to me and said: 'That is a wonderful message that young man has brought back for me from the Middle East.' I replied: 'Yes, if you are prepared to listen to a bar lounger.' He then said: 'A what?', and I again said 'A BAR-LOUNGER.' He replied 'Ah, bar-lounger, perhaps.' I then had a hard time convincing Winston that he had better wait a little longer before going out, my task having been made all the more difficult by young Amery's chatter.

4 July

A short COS and finished off work by 4 pm, when I dashed off home.

5 July

Quiet Sunday at home with you, but left at 9 pm owing to early start for Ireland tomorrow morning.

6 July

Had an early breakfast and left Hendon aerodrome for Belfast shortly after 9 am. Flew in Lockheed Electra 4 seater, [Col.] Peter [Dunphie, his PA] came with me, and we gave a lift to Strathcona and one other. Very good 2 hours fly. Met by Franklyn and proceeded straight out to see his large scale exercise. Visited Majendie first, commanding Northern Force, and then on to see Ryder commanding 34th USA Div. After that lunch at Control HQ, where McKenna, the Free State C-in-C was introduced and sat next to me at lunch. A pretty rough diamond, evidently very interested in all military matters. After lunch went to 59th Div to see Pat Bradshaw and from there on to see Hartle, the USA general commanding the Southern Force. He was disappointing and had no grip whatever of the situation. Finally back by 61st Div, Fullbrook-Leggatt, and two of his Brigadiers. Then returned to Storebrooke to spend the night with Basil and Cynthia.

7 July

Another early rise and started off at 8.15 am to see attack by American Armoured Div just west of Belfast. Cold morning and troops very sticky. Waited on till after 10.30, and then left for aerodrome. It is evident that the USA troops have excellent material, but that they require a great deal more training. Good fly back to Hendon where I arrived at 1.30 pm.

Cabinet meeting at 5.30 pm. A dreadful exhibition of amateur strategy by Cabinet ministers! Bevin quite at his worst and posing as an authority! Eden and Cripps offering criticism as if they were leading authorities on strategy! PM unfortunately not in his usual form and unable to keep them in order. A most depressing and lamentable meeting.

8 July

Another difficult COS discussing results of yesterday's Cabinet meeting and trying to tidy up this year's policy concerning possible offensives. Also heated debate between First Sea Lord and CAS on air support of Navy. At 12.30 Cabinet meeting at 10 Downing Street at which PM ran down ME army in shocking way and criticized Auchinleck for not showing a more offensive spirit. I had an uphill task defending him and pointing out the difficulties of his present position. Also the fact that any rash move on his part at present would very quickly lose us Egypt. However PM was in one of his unpleasant moods going back over old ground and asking where the 750,000 men in the ME were, what they were doing, and why they were not fighting. After being thoroughly unpleasant during the Cabinet meeting, with that astounding charm of his he came up to me afterwards and said to me 'I am sorry Brookie if I had to be unpleasant about Auchinleck and the Middle East!' Had a good talk with Bevin after the Cabinet meeting. I think he means very well and tries to help but is rather clumsy about it!

Then you came to lunch, and I forgot about all my worries.

Afterwards I had visit from Eisenhower (USA general) to put him into the picture, and then finally went round with you to Oswald Birley to see my picture, and had tea there. Wainwright came to dinner.

9 July

At this morning's COS we had invited Andy McNaughton so as to give him the task of examining the possibility of capturing North Norway with the Canadian Corps! This was according to the PM's orders, it having been suggested by Attlee that with his more flexible and fertile brain he would find a way out where the Chiefs of Staff had failed! After lunch I sent for him to my office and informed him privately how matters stood as I did not want him afterwards to imagine that we were suggesting that the Canadians should undertake an operation which we considered impracticable.

Alexander turned up in the afternoon having landed home after his trip to Burma and the hard fighting he had there. He looks as if he requires some leave.

More worries as to interference by Foreign Office in Madagascar and insisting on sending Panchkov, the Free French representative, there, just when we are trying to complete negotiations with the local Vichy Government! The Foreign Office's love for de Gaulle will finish by losing us this war!

10 July

Alexander attended COS meeting and brought us back Wavell's ideas on the attack in Burma. Lunched at Claridges to entertain de Gaulle. He was in one of his better moods, but I fail to see how we are ever to make much use of him!

5 pm Meeting with PM which lasted till 7.30 pm. He was in a bad mood and meeting was not pleasant as we were discussing one of his pet schemes namely how it is that Middle East has 750,000 men on its ration strength and only produces 100,000 to fight Rommel!! Dill suffered from this in the past and he will

never be convinced by the arguments! We then discussed possibility of sending next convoy to Russia after losses of last one.

The ration strength versus fighting strength in ME was always an unpleasant subject. In the middle of a Cabinet meeting he would turn to me and say: 'Pray explain CIGS, how it is that in the ME 750,000 men always turn up for their pay and rations, but when it comes to fighting only 100,000 turn up!! Explain to us now exactly how the remaining 650,000 are occupied!' Not an easy answer to give in the middle of a Cabinet meeting. He could never understand, or at any rate refused to do so, that the ME was a vast base for operations in various theatres besides the Western Desert. It had catered for Somaliland, Abyssinia, Palestine, Lebanon, Greece, Crete, Iraq and Persia. The figures as put by him looked appalling, but when broken up into details were not over extravagant when modern mechanized requirements are taken into account.

Finally WO dinner at the Ritz for Eisenhower, Winant, Harriman and American generals.

11 July

Finished off the COS fairly early, but after lunch had difficulties with an unpleasant wire which the PM was insisting on sending to Auchinleck and which would have done no good. Pug Ismay had spent morning trying to stop him sending it without success! Finally arrived home just before dinner.

12 July

Conversation with PM after breakfast in which I found out that he had at least agreed to alter his wire, and to split it sending half to the Auk and half to Corbett!

13 July

A typical Monday! COS at which we discussed the possibility of sending next convoy to Russia after having suffered 75% casualties in the last one! Then Cabinet meeting at 5.30 at which PM abused WO owing to the fact that Middle East reported proportion of Valentines [tanks] arriving in bad state. Finally Defence Committee meeting at 10 pm to arrive at final decision about Russia Convoy. This decision took a long time to arrive at! However finally the meeting being unanimous, the PM gave the verdict against further continuance of convoys for the present. He then discussed alternative methods of helping Stalin and again returned to his attack on Norway. Pointing out how easy such an attack would be! Looked like working up to a storm at one time!!

Just as I was going was called back owing to wire just received from Smuts [South African PM, Minister of Defence and C-in-C South African Forces], very disturbed about Court of Enquiry on surrender of Tobruk, as rumours had been spread that SA [South African] Commander of troops was a fifth columnist!! Eden then suggested that I should wire to Wilson that he should cook his Court of Enquiry to ensure this SA commander should be exonerated! I suggested that Court of Enquiry must report true verdict, this could be kept secret and dealt with by Government as they thought best. This was agreed to.

14 July

Another difficult COS with First Sea Lord asleep most of the time! In afternoon Selection Board at which Tim Pile attended. As he gets older his face discloses more and more to the world his crookedness! He is a repulsive creature! Dined at White's Club with Ivan Cobbold.

15 July

COS at which most of my energy was spent in arriving at a suitable settlement between CNS and CAS. Oswald Birley and wife and Portal and wife came to lunch to introduce them to each other as Birley wanted to paint Portal. At 5 pm, Neil Ritchie came to see me. It was a sad meeting as I knew well how much he felt being pushed out of the 8th Army. However after a bit of a talk he warmed up and was most interesting about his experiences.

Neil Ritchie had done me so wonderfully well in France during the fighting leading to Dunkirk, and I had grown so fond of him, that I hated seeing him subjected to this serious reverse. I told him that I considered that he had been pushed on much too fast by Auchinleck, to be put in command of 8th Army in the field when he had never even commanded a division in action. I told him he must regain confidence in himself. To do this he must go back to what he had done so efficiently before, namely the command of a division at home. I told him that when he had regained confidence in himself I would give him a corps. This is just what happened.

At 7 pm had to go round to 10 Downing St to discuss with PM desirability of preparing division from India for ME should occasion arise for their use in the event of further penetration by Germans towards Caucasus. He was in a very pleasant mood and we sat out in the garden. I told him that if he found that he could not go to the Middle East I ought to go out on my own to visit Gibraltar, Malta and Middle East. He agreed.

We received news today that Marshall, King and Harry Hopkins are on their way to discuss future operations. It will be a queer party as Harry Hopkins is for operating in Africa, Marshall wants to operate in Europe, and King is determined to strike in the Pacific! We are I believe all to go down to Chequers next weekend to discuss these various alternatives.

I had by then learned that if you wanted to get Winston's agreement to something, you might have to wait several days for a propitious moment. To ask at the wrong moment was to court disaster! Once you had received a negative reply it was almost impossible to alter his verdict! I had been waiting for days, very precious days, to ask him to go to the ME on my own. I knew that the odds would be heavily against getting his sanction, that he would say he could not spare me, whilst in the back of his mind the real reason would be that he would hate me to go off on my own without him. Meanwhile the situation in the ME was not improving, the Auk was suggesting giving the 8th Army to Corbett. It was essential that I should go out to see for myself what was really wrong, and for that job I did not want Winston treading on my heels! Fortunately that lovely evening sitting in the garden of 10 Downing Street I found him in one of his amenable moods. I jumped in at once and to my joy got his approval. The only difficulty was that I could not start at once, as I should have to wait for the arrival of Harry Hopkins' party, and there was always the danger of Winston changing his mind or deciding to come with me.

16 July

A quiet day on the whole. Dull COS, not much work in the afternoon and finally Neil Ritchie to dinner. He remained till 1.15 am and it was great value seeing him again and hearing full details of all his fighting in the ME.

17 July

Spent most of COS meeting preparing for visit of Harry Hopkins, Marshall and King, who are on their way over now, arriving early tomorrow morning. They have come over as they are not satisfied that we are adhering sufficiently definitely to the plans for invading France in 1943, and if possible 1942. In my mind 1942 is dead off and without the slightest hope. 1943 must depend on what happens to Russia. If she breaks and is overrun there can be no invasion and we should then be prepared to go into North Africa instead. But Marshall seems to want some rigid form of plan that we are bound to adhere to in any case!*

I found Marshall's rigid form of strategy very difficult to cope with. He never fully appreciated what operations in France would mean – the different standard of training of German divisions as opposed to the raw American divisions and to most of our new divisions. He could not appreciate the fact that the Germans could reinforce the point of attack some 3 to 4 times faster than we could, nor would he understand that until the Mediterranean was open again we should always suffer from the crippling shortage of sea transport.

It was evident that if Russia cracked up the Germans could concentrate the bulk of their forces in France and make an invasion quite impossible. Under those circumstances our only hope would be to operate in Africa. But in any case from the moment I took over the job of CIGS I was convinced that the sequence of events should be:

a) liberate North Africa

b) open up Mediterranean and score a million tons of shipping

c) threaten Southern Europe by eliminating Italy

---

*Cf. Dykes diary, 17–19 July 1942, in Danchev, *Anglo-American Alliance*, pp. 175–77.

d) then, and only then, if Russia is still holding, liberate France and invade Germany.
Marshall hankered after direct action in France without appreciating that in the
early days such action could only result in the worst of disasters.

Lunch at Savoy with Lord Nuffield to see results of his research work in the
shape of floating lorries for amphibious landings. His engineers have made
great progress.

18 July

Went to Euston Station at 7.50 am to meet Harry Hopkins, Marshall, King and
a few more. Fairly long COS settling points for discussion with American
Chiefs of Staff. At 4 pm when I was getting near end of work and thinking of
soon going home was informed that all the Chiefs of Staff were wanted at
Chequers for the night!! Arrived there just in time for dinner. Pound, Portal,
Mountbatten, Ismay, Cherwell and self. After dinner we had long sitting
reviewing the whole war and relative advantages of various fronts. This lasted
till 2 am when we were taken to see a film! Finally to bed at 2.45 am.

19 July

Left Chequers at 9 am and drove straight to Ferney Close, where I had quiet
day with you.

20 July

Arrived WO 9 am. Found mass of messages. Troublesome COS with
Mountbatten again assuming wild powers unto himself! At 12.30 we went
round to 12 Downing Street to meet American Chiefs of Staff with PM! We had
originally intended to meet them at 10 am 'off the record' for a private talk,
but PM very suspicious and had informed me at Chequers that Marshall was
trying to assume powers of C-in-C of American troops which was [constitu-
tionally] President's prerogative!

After lunch at 3 pm we met Marshall and King and had long argument with
them. Found both of them still hankering after an attack across Channel this
year to take pressure off Russia. They failed to realize that such an action could
only lead to the loss of some 6 divisions without achieving any results! Next
argument was that we should take advantage of German preoccupation with
Russia to establish bridgehead for 1943 operation. Had to convince them that
there was no hope of such a bridgehead surviving the winter. Next discussed
alternative operations in North Africa which they are not much in favour of
preferring the Pacific [cf. 18 May 1943].*

---

*On the 'Pacific alternative' in American strategizing – which was not simply a bargaining tactic – see
Dykes diary, 14 July and 15 August 1942, in Danchev, *Anglo-American Alliance*, pp. 168 and 189; and
Mark A. Stoler, *Allies and Adversaries* (Chapel Hill: University of North Carolina Press, 2000).

Rushed back to WO to see S of S, VCIGS, DCIGS, DMO, DMI and MS. After dinner put in 2 hours hard [work] and was then sent for to 11 Downing Street. There I found Hopkins, Harriman and Beaverbrook with the PM. He kept me up alone with him after others had left till 1 am, giving the results of my talk with Marshall and King.

21 July

A short COS which started at 10 am, leading up to a meeting at 11 am with the American COS.

Disappointing start! Found ourselves much where we had started yesterday morning! Except that Marshall admitted that he saw no opportunity of staging an offensive in Europe to aid Russians by September. He missed the point that by September the Russians might be past requiring assistance and that the weather at any rate at that season was such as to make cross-Channel operations practically impossible! We went on arguing for 2 hours, during which time King remained with a face like a Sphinx, and only one idea, i.e. to transfer operations to the Pacific. Finally we parted at 1 pm, and I felt we had made a little headway. We are to meet again at 11 am tomorrow.

In the afternoon Norrie, back from ME came to see me and I had an hour with him. Also had long conference with DCIGS, VCIGS and DSD to settle the future policy of handling available manpower to the best advantage with the very limited resources available. Bevin and Adam came to dinner and we had a very useful talk. I like Bevin and feel that he is all out to help win the war. He gave us a very interesting account of his weekend at Chequers with Winston and Beaverbrook, when they tried to get him to remain as Minister of Labour under Beaverbrook in his proposed post of Minister of Production! Bevin refused flatly and said that he would serve in any other job but not under Beaverbrook!

At 11 pm I had to go back to 10 Downing St. Both Eden and Hopkins there, I was not allowed to join them for fear that Marshall and King should hear of it and feel that I had been briefed by Hopkins against them according to President's wishes!! PM therefore came up to Cabinet room to see me and find out results of our morning meeting! Got home by 12.30 am.

22 July

Started COS at 10 am and was sent for by PM at 10.45 to discuss proposed draft of telegram to hurry the Auk on to attack. I had telegram read to me by short-hand writer and asked to see it in type in order to save time and try and stop its despatch.

At 11 am met American Chiefs again. They handed in written memorandum adhering to an attack on Cherbourg salient as the preliminary move for an attack in 1943. The memorandum drew attention to all the advantages, but failed to recognize the main disadvantage that there was no hope of our still being in Cherbourg by next spring! I put all the disadvantages to them. They did not return to the attack but stated that they would now have to put the matter up to the President and wished to see the PM first. I therefore fixed up for 3 pm meeting with PM and went round to explain to him how matters stood and to discuss with him most profitable line of action.

You then came to lunch and it was such a joy and rest from my labours having a couple of hours with you.

At 3 pm we all went to Downing Street and remained there till 4 pm. PM informed American Chiefs that he was in agreement with opinion of his Chiefs of Staff and would put whole matter before War Cabinet at 5.30 pm. At the Cabinet meeting I had to open the ball by putting results of all our meetings before the Cabinet, and then marshalling the case against the Cherbourg attack in 1942. I had no trouble convincing Cabinet who were unanimously against it. American Chiefs are therefore wiring to America and we are waiting for the next phase of our meeting. I hope they will not be as exhausting as the last 7 hours of discussion! This evening Chiefs of Staff gave dinner for Americans at Claridges. On the whole went well.

23 July

My birthday! 59! I don't feel like it!

A difficult COS at which we discussed the necessary measures to guard against German attacks through Persia on Abadan oil field should Russian resistance break. Then lunched at Ritz with Turkish ambassador, he spent most of the meal explaining to me the various reasons why Turkey could not under any circumstances throw in her lot with the Germans! He did NOT entirely convince me! Whilst lunching received message that PM wanted Chiefs of Staff to meet him at 3 pm. Arrived there to be told latest developments in our negotiations with Americans. Roosevelt had wired back accepting fact that western front in 1942 was off. Also that he was in favour of attack in North Africa and was influencing his Chiefs in that direction. They were supposed to be working out various aspects with their staff and will probably meet us tomorrow. Winston anxious that I should not put Marshall off Africa by referring to Middle East dangers in 1943. Told him I must put whole strategic position in front of Americans. Foresee difficulties ahead of me!!

Auchinleck started new attack day before yesterday and not very happy with progress he is making. This evening had Marshall to dine with me, and got P.J.Grigg, Venning and Weeks to dine with me. Marshall in very pleasant and friendly mood.

24 July

During our COS meeting we received a note from Marshall saying that American Chiefs of Staff would be ready to see us at 12 noon. I was a bit nervous as to what they might have been brewing up since our last meeting! I wondered what new difficulties and troubles I might have to face! However, they produced a paper containing almost everything we had asked them to agree to at the start. We sat with them till 1.30 pm and only made minor alterations to their draft. We then parted till 3 pm, when we met again to examine the redraft. We then settled that the British COS should present paper to PM and to Cabinet for their approval, before final signatures by them and Americans as a 'Combined Chiefs of Staff Document'. They all agreed to giving up immediate attack on Continent, to prepare plans for attack on North Africa to be carried out if re-entry into Europe was impossible next year. In order to obtain this we were prepared to accept an American Armoured Division in Persia and to stand certain cuts in proposed air allotments.

At 4.30 pm we met PM and I put memorandum to him, he was delighted with it and passed it at once. At 5 pm Cabinet meeting first of all to discuss Stalin's reply to stopping Northern Convoy and intimation that western front was not possible. It was an unpleasant reply! Then PM got me to put up our memorandum to the Cabinet. From the start things went wrong! Anthony Eden and Cripps thought they saw a flaw in it, they began to argue about things they did not understand, others joined in, and very soon we had one of those situations I have now seen frequently in the Cabinet, where the real issue is completely lost in arguing out some detail which is misquoted and distorted in the discussion. I perspired heavily in my attempts to pull things straight and was engaged in heated arguments with Eden and Cripps with most of Cabinet taking sides. Bevin, John Anderson, Bruce and PM with me, Attlee, Oliver Lyttelton, Alexander against. In the end I triumphed and had the memorandum passed without a word being altered. Any changes would have been fatal, the Americans have gone a long way to meet us, and I should have to ask them for more.

A very trying week, but it is satisfactory to think that we have got just what we wanted out of the USA Chiefs. Just been told that I am for Chequers tomorrow night!

25 July

At the COS we examined advisability and possibility of completing the Madagascar expedition now that negotiations have failed, with the minimum disturbance to future operations in Burma and in North Africa. After lunch had interview with Paget to inform him as to results of last week's work. Then saw Andy McNaughton to find out how his planning of the North Norway expedition was getting on. Found out that he was asking for 5 divisions, 20 squadrons, and a large fleet!

Was then sent for by PM who wanted to hear results of our morning meeting with Marshall and King. I told him that we had fixed up question of North Africa. USA to find Supreme Commander with British deputy. Under him two Task Force Commanders, one USA for Casablanca front, and one British for Oran front. I wanted Alexander for Task Force Commander. He wanted him to do both Deputy Supreme Commander and Task Force Commander! Had an hour's argument with him from 6 to 7 pm about, finally had to stop as it was time to start for Chequers!!

Arrived there at 8 pm. Party consisted of PM, Mrs C, Marshall, King, Harry Hopkins, Harriman, 3 Chiefs of Staff, Pug, Martin and Tommy. After dinner American Chiefs were shown Cromwell's mask and Queen Elizabeth's ring. They then left by special [train] for Scotland to fly to America. After they left we were shown a good film, *The Younger Pitt*, and then 2 hours talk and bed at 2.45 am! Dog tired and grateful this week is over.

26 July
Called at 7.30 am and off by 9 am to Ferney Close where I spent a lovely peaceful Sunday only marred by one thought – namely that we were not to meet for 3 or 4 weeks owing to your journey to Cornwall and mine to Egypt, India, etc.

27 July
A COS where we decided next steps necessary to start active planning for North African venture and for the necessary deception plans. Afternoon started all necessary plans for my departure for Egypt next Thursday or Friday. Cabinet meeting at 5.30. Just before starting message from the Auk that he had launched new attack.

28 July
Considered necessity of abandoning Madagascar operation owing to difficulty of getting landing craft back in time for African enterprise. After lunch was inoculated against yellow fever in anticipation of my trip. Then series of interviews with [Alan] Cunningham, S of S, DCIGS, MS, VCIGS, and S of S again after his Cabinet meeting. He had returned infuriated as a Special Committee consisting of Attlee, Cripps and Eden were to examine possibility of reducing Army rear services!!

After dinner at 10 pm, meeting with PM at which we again discussed Madagascar and operations against Rangoon, also convoys to Russia. PM in very depressed mood as result of Auk's second attack being repulsed. Pouring out questions as to why Auk could not have done this or that and never giving him the least credit for doing the right thing. He is quite heart-breaking to work for. It is very trying having to fight battles to defend the Auk, when I am myself doubtful at times why on earth he does not act differently. Told PM I intended going on to India from Iraq. He was not in favour, suggesting I should get Wavell to come and meet me at Basra. May have difficulties in getting to India, but shall try to do so.

29 July
A short COS when we again reviewed the Middle East situation, relative importance of Egypt as opposed to Abadan oil fields, etc. A busy afternoon finishing off odd jobs before my departure for the ME. At 6.30 pm PM sent for me to 10

Downing Street where I spent an hour with him in the garden discussing the points he wishes me to look to whilst in the Middle East, Persia, Iraq, India etc. He is evidently very intent on following along close behind me if possible and wishes me to report what journey is like.

30 July

A short COS at which Portal broke the news that Winston had decided to follow me at once to the Middle East! I was sent for by him at 12 noon and told that after I left him yesterday he decided at dinner that he would fly out on Friday! He called War Cabinet meeting immediately after dinner and obtained their approval. Since then wire from Ambassador in Moscow had been received suggesting visit from Winston to Stalin was advisable! He was therefore contemplating going on to Russia and wanted me to go with him!! All my plans upset.

Early lunch and dashed off to Farnborough to see trials of the new Cromwell tank. A very promising model providing we get sufficient Meteor engines. Drove it round for a bit and liked it very much. Got back 6.30. Long interview with Paget. Then dinner at Savoy with Lucas, Rootes and Lord Weir, S of S, Green, Weeks, Nye, Bond, etc. Whilst there call from PM to go to 10 Downing St at 11.30. Kept there till 1 am discussing details of his journey. He now starts on Saturday and arrives Gib day after me, disguised in a grey beard! He then flies direct to Cairo, so that we arrive there same day. Proposal now is for us to meet Stalin at Astrakhan. I have now to take Cranborne out in my plane and leave him in Malta.

Shall start new book tomorrow as I dare not risk being caught with this should we be caught or crash.

31 July   Portreath, 300 miles, 1¾ hours

Attended a short COS then back to WO for lunch and my final packing up. At 5.30 pm left for Hendon with Adam and Peter [Dunphie]. There we found Cranborne [Dominions] and Aitken. The latter two were to come with us to Malta. We were given a Flamingo and had a very good flight down to Portreath in Cornwall where we arrived about 7.45 pm. We were given a good dinner and I am now off to bed for a few hours' sleep before taking off for Gib at 2 am tomorrow morning. It is a most lovely night, and I don't feel inclined to go to sleep!

1 August   Gibraltar, 1500 miles, 7 hours

After a doubtful 2 hours sleep, called and given breakfast at 1.30 am!! We then embarked and by 2 am were off into the darkness. I did not sleep over well because plane was very noisy. At a few minutes before 9 am we saw tops of mountains sliding out of the sea of clouds and shortly after clouds cleared and the Rock was visible before us. We flew round it once before landing, which was interesting. Mason-MacFarlane and his staff met us on landing.

Bath and breakfast after which I toured defences and tunnels with Mason-Mac. Large lunch with Admiral, Air Marshal, etc, after which another tour of defences till tea. We then went out in a motor launch and did a tour of the Rock by sea. All most interesting. Tremendous tunnelling work has been accomplished since beginning of war. Practically all stores, hospitals, distilleries, ammunition and accommodation for the garrison has been tunnelled out of the main rock. In addition a full sized lorry road connecting east and west sides of the Rock. After dinner we were given demonstration of barrage AA fire and searchlights. Finally emplaned at 11 pm and slid off into dark.

For the next hop it was essential to reach Malta before dawn, otherwise there were chances of being shot down by Italian fighters. Dill and Eden on their way to Greece had missed the island, overshot it, and had to turn back to find it, only reaching it just in time. I was especially anxious to visit Gort in Malta as I knew he was in a depressed state, feeling that he had been shoved away in a corner out of the real war, and in danger of his whole garrison being scuppered without much chance of giving an account of themselves. His depression had been increased by the fact that he insisted on living on the reduced standard of rations prevailing on the island, in spite of the fact that he was doing twice as much physical and mental work as any other member of the garrison. Owing to the shortage of petrol he was using a bicycle in that sweltering heat, and frequently had to carry his bicycle over demolished houses.

I wanted to tell him about the plans for a new Command in the Middle East with an advance westwards combined with American–British landings in West Africa moving eastwards, destined to meet eventually. I wanted him to feel that if all this came off he would find himself in an outpost of an advance instead of the backwater he considered himself in. I felt certain that to be able to look forward to something definite would do much to dispel his gloom.

2 August   Malta, 1250 miles, 6½ hours

A very comfortable smooth flight. I had borrowed ear plugs from Mason-Mac to drown noise of engines, which I found affected my ears during previous flight. I slept on and off and was snoozing properly when I woke to find the plane bumping badly and thought something had gone wrong till I realized that we were landing in Malta in the dark! It was just before dawn. Gort had sent Munster [his ADC] to meet us and Park the AOC was there also. We drove up to Gort's house where we had some tea and then went off to bed for a four hours' sleep till 10 am. Then discussed business with Gort till lunch, told him of future plans in Africa which interested him very much. For lunch Park and Leatham the Admiral came. Also Beckett [CRA]. After lunch went to the docks and to Valetta. The destruction is inconceivable and reminds one of Ypres, Arras, Lens at their worst during last war. We travelled about in Admiral's barge and examined wrecks of last convoy. Finally examined new dock workshops which have been mined into the rock. Had tea with Admiral in charge of docks. 5 air raid alarms during the day, but no serious bombing. Finally at 10.45 before we were to start a German plane came over, but did not remain.

It had been a very hot and tiring day, all the more so after a hard day in Gib, and two nights flying without much sleep, sitting up with a wooden box between my legs. The visit had been worthwhile and I think brought a new hope to Gort. The conditions prevailing in Malta at that time were distinctly depressing, to put it mildly! Shortage of rations, shortage of petrol, a hungry population that rubbed their tummies looking at Gort as he went by, destruction and ruin of docks, loss of convoys just as they approached the island, and the continual possibility of an attack on the island without much hope of help or reinforcements.

3 August   Cairo, 1250 miles, 7½ hours

We took off into the dark at 11 pm and had a very peaceful journey in spite of the fact that we ran right down 'Bombers' Alley' between Crete and Cyrenaica. We flew at between 8 and 10 thousand feet as on the previous days. Just as the day was breaking we struck the mouth of the Delta just east of Alexandria, and flew inland to look for an aerodrome on Alexandria-Cairo road. Unfortunately we struck a low blanket of clouds and could not get down for an hour, during which time we flew round in the morning sunshine over a sea of clouds. I had not slept much and my legs were rather cramped. Finally we descended at about 6.30 am and found a large gathering on the aerodrome awaiting PM, who was due shortly. [Ambassador] Miles Lampson, Casey, Tedder [AOC Mediterranean], Naval captain, CGS and Liddell. We did not wait for the PM but drove in the 25 miles to Cairo and the Embassy where I had a shave, bath and breakfast. PM then turned up delighted with his trip and looking remarkably fresh. He has got his Dr [Wilson] with him, who tells me he was a little worried about his pulse.

Went over to GHQ after breakfast and had long talk with Corbett the CGS. The more I saw of him the less I thought of him – he is a very small man.

One interview with him was enough to size him up. He was a very very small man unfit for his job of CGS and totally unsuited for command of the 8th Army, an appointment which the Auk had suggested. Consequently Corbett's selection reflected very unfavourably on the Auk's ability to select men and confirmed my fears in that respect.

Also had a long talk with Messervy, who was interesting on recent fighting. At lunchtime Smuts [PM South Africa] turned up having flown up from Pretoria. He was astounding good value and full of wit in answering PM's remarks.

After lunch snatched ¾ hour sleep before going to meet Auchinleck, who was coming back from the front. Had a short talk with him before we attended one of his C-in-C meetings. At 5.30 pm he came over to Embassy and we had long interview with PM, after which he called me in for further talks. He is fretting at the thought that there is to be no offensive till Sept 15th. I see already troublesome times ahead.

After dinner when I was dropping with sleepiness PM again called me in and kept me up till 1.30 am. Back to the same arguments that Auk must come back to the command of the ME and leave 8th Army. Exactly what I have always told him from the start! Then argued strongly for Gott to take over, whilst I know that Gott is very tired. Finally suggested that I should take it over!! I shall have a job to convince him that I am unsuited for the job, having never been trained in the desert.

It is interesting to note that Winston was already selecting Gott without having seen him. Personally I knew Gott very well indeed and had the highest opinion of him. He had been second in command to 'Bubbles' Barker in the bn of the 60th KRR attached to Aldershot Armoured Brigade when I commanded the 1st Mobile Division [in 1938]. He was a brilliant commander, but he had been in the desert since before the beginning of the war, and was beginning to feel the effects of it. He was no longer as fresh as he might be. I happened to know of a letter he had written to his wife in which he expressed feelings that pointed to the fact that he was tired. I did not feel therefore that Gott in his present state was the man to instil a new spirit of self confidence in the 8th Army. It would require someone like Montgomery, bounding with self confidence and capable of instilling this confidence in those under his command. At any rate I wanted to see Gott for myself to find out how tired he was before putting him down definitely as unfit for the 8th Army.

Winston's suggestion that I should take over the 8th Army personally gave rise to the most desperate longings in my heart! I had tasted the thrill of commanding a formation in war whilst commanding II Corps in France. For sheer thrill and excitement it stood in a category by itself, and not to be compared to a Staff appointment. Even that of CIGS, when working for a man like Winston, must mean constant frustration, friction, and untold difficulties in achieving the results one was after.

4 August

Met Auchinleck at 9 am and had a short talk with him before proceeding to attend a Joint Cs-in-C Conference with him, Tedder and the Admiral. We discussed the relative importance of Egypt as opposed to Abadan and all agreed that the latter's importance was paramount.

As all the motive power at sea, on land and in the air throughout the ME, Indian Ocean and India was entirely dependent on the oil from Abadan, if we lost this supply it could not be made good from American resources owing to shortage of tankers, and continuous losses of these ships through submarine action. Therefore if we lost the Persian oil we inevitably lost Egypt, command of the Indian Ocean, and endangered the whole Indian Burma situation.

Then returned to Embassy at 12 noon to have an hour with Smuts at which we discussed the relief of SA Bde from Madagascar at the earliest possible date, the transformation of SA Division to armour, and the situation here. He has a good opinion of the Auk but considers that he selects his subordinates badly and that several changes are desirable. Most of the changes he suggested coincided with my own views. He is the most delightful old man with a wonderfully clear brain.

I then lunched at the Mohammed Ali Club with the Auk, Tedder and the Admiral. After lunch returned to GHQ for long discussion with the Auk. A most useful one. I fortunately found that he was in agreement as to the necessary changes, i.e:

a) new commander for 8th Army Montgomery

b) new CGS to be selected vice Corbett

c) Jumbo Wilson [b. 1881] too old and to be replaced by Gott

d) Quinan unsuitable for 10th Army, to be replaced by Anderson.

These changes should lead to improvements but I must still pass them through the PM and there will be the difficulty.

I had been surprised that the Auk was prepared to accept Monty in command of 8th Army. I had expected some opposition, but I felt some very serious doubts as to whether an Auk-Monty combination would work. I felt that the Auk would interfere too much with Monty, would ride him on too tight a rein, and would consequently be liable to put him out of his stride. As I was very anxious to put Monty in command of the 8th Army, I felt this might necessitate moving the Auk to some other command.... Jumbo Wilson I knew intimately. We had sat at neighbouring desks at the Staff College in 1919. I was well aware of his exceptional ability, but had heard from all sides that he was showing signs of ageing and had lost his drive. I had been misinformed, and should not have attached so much importance to rumours. Luckily I discovered my mistake in time and made full use of him during the rest of the war.

Came back to Embassy at 5.45 pm for large conference under PM attended by Smuts, Auchinleck, Wavell, the Admiral, Tedder, Casey, Jacob and self. PM reviewed the whole situation and explained plans for offensive in North Africa with Americans, and its relation to western attack in ME. On whole he was fairly sound in most of his arguments. Finally cross questioned Auchinleck as to the probable date of his offensive. I could see that he did not approve of his replies! He is again pressing for an attack before Auchinleck can possibly get ready! I find him almost impossible to argue with on this point. Conference lasted 2¾ hours!! Just had time to rush off for a bath before 9 pm dinner!

After dinner I was dragged off into the garden by PM to report results of my day's work. As I expected my work was not approved of! Montgomery could not possibly arrive in time to hurry on the date of the attack! I told him no one else could. He then pressed for Gott, I told him I had discussed him with Auchinleck, who did not consider him up to it, and also that he was too tired. I then told him about the project to move Wilson as too old. He then said that I was failing to make use of the two best men: Gott and Wilson. He then said that he knew neither of them but that Eden had told him so!! I got level with him this time by suggesting that it was not astonishing that Eden should select old Green Jacket officers! This went home all right and he saw the logic of it and was very nice. However he kept me arguing till 1 am!! and we have got to get up at 4.45 am tomorrow!!! Moscow party is growing – Wavell is coming and probably Harriman.

5 August   250 miles, 1½ hours

Was called at 4.45 am and had early breakfast to admit of start at 5.45 am with PM and his doctor for Heliopolis aerodrome. There we emplaned for Burg el Arab aerodrome (situated about 20 miles west of Alexandria). PM in great form in spite of early start. We were met at aerodrome by Auchinleck, Tedder and [Air Marshal] Coningham [working with 8th Army, later forming 1st Tactical Air Force]. The Auk took the PM in his car and I travelled with Tedder and Coningham. We drove right up to El Alamein where we met the Australian and South African Divisional Commanders. We then motored back along the road, where Australians came to meet the PM. They all seemed delighted to meet him. We then motored on to 8th Army HQ where the Auk gave us a light breakfast and we also met Gott, Briggs, commanding 5th Ind Div, and Inglis, commanding the NZ Div as Freyberg is still injured. After breakfast PM started for home and I stopped on to continue my trip.

I started with a long talk with Ramsden who used to command 50th Div under Home Forces and now has a Corps. I then went on with Martin, the CCRA of the Corps, for a further tour. We started down the famous central ridge on which such heavy fighting has taken place recently. Lunched with Briggs at 5th Ind Div HQ. It was he who commanded the brigade that fought its way out of Benghazi. From there I motored south to Gott's HQ, and had a useful talk with him. There is no doubt that a rest home would do him a lot of good, and I do not feel that he would yet be ready to take over the 8th Army. He requires more experience. However I do not know what opinion the PM formed of him and how much he will press for him instead of Monty.

It was not till we were sitting at tea together that he began to open out his heart to me. He said, 'I think what is required out here is some new blood. I have tried most of my ideas on the Boche. We want someone with new ideas and plenty of confidence in them.' I knew Gott well enough to know that he would never talk about having 'tried most of his ideas' unless he was tired and had temporarily lost some of his drive. This confirmed my opinion that he was probably not the man to lead the 8th Army in an offensive to turn the tide of the war.

I then motored back to 8th Army HQ where I had tea with the Auk. It has been an interesting day. I was impressed by the dispersal which the air forces on the army, with all its evil consequences as regards maintenance and control. The lack of any real bold features also surprised me. I had expected that the various ridges would be more clearly marked. It is a strange life that this army leads in the desert, but the men look fit and hard. I was much impressed by the beauty of the turquoise blue of the Mediterranean along this coast. This colour is caused by specially white sand along this coast line. Left Auk about 5 pm and motored back to Burg el Arab where I emplaned again for Heliopolis. At the aerodrome I found Adam who had come down to settle plans for tomorrow. Again a late night with bed only after 1 am.

6 August

One of the most difficult days of my life, with momentous decisions to take as far as my own future and that of the war was concerned.

Whilst I was dressing and practically naked, the PM suddenly burst into my room. Very elated and informed me that his thoughts were taking shape and that he would soon commit himself to paper! I rather shuddered and wondered what he was up to! Ten minutes later he burst into my room again and invited me to breakfast with him. However, as I was in the middle of my breakfast by then he asked me to come as soon as I had finished my breakfast. When I went round he made me sit on the sofa whilst he walked up and down. First of all he said he had decided to split the ME Command in two. A Near East taking up to the canal, and a Middle East taking Syria, Palestine, Persia and Iraq. I argued with him that the Canal was an impossible boundary as both Palestine and Syria are based administratively on Egypt. He partially agreed, and then went on to say that he intended to remove the Auk to the Persia Iraq Command as he had lost confidence in him. And he wanted me to take over the Near East Command with Montgomery as my 8th Army Commander! This made my heart race very fast!! He said he did not require an answer at once, and that I could think it over if I wanted. However I told him without waiting that I was quite certain that it would be a wrong move. I knew nothing about desert warfare, and could never have time to grip hold of the show to my satisfaction before the necessity to attack became imperative.

Another point which I did not mention was that after working with the PM for close on 9 months I do feel at last that I can exercise a limited amount of control on some of his activities and that at last he is beginning to take my advice. I feel therefore that, tempting as the offer is by accepting it I should definitely be taking a course which would on the whole help the war the least. Finally I could not bear the thought that Auchinleck might think that I had come out here on purpose to work myself into his shoes! PM was not pleased with this reply but accepted it well.

At 10.30 we had a meeting with him, Lindsell, Adam and Corbett to examine details concerning tail of the army. It was not a happy meeting and he rather lost his temper with Corbett before it was over. Smuts attended. After the meeting I took Adam, Lindsell and Corbett onto the lawn to decide action to take to meet PM's requirements.

After lunch Smuts asked if he could see me for a bit, and we retired to a quiet room. He then started on the same story as the PM in the morning. Telling me what importance he attached to my taking it, and what a wonderful future it would have for me if I succeeded in defeating Rommel. I repeated exactly what I had said to PM. Thanked him for his kindness and told him that he did not really know me well enough to be so assured I should make a success of it. However, he replied that he knew I had taken a leading part in saving the BEF in France. At last I got him to agree that Alexander was a better selection than me. I have been giving it a great deal of thought all day and am *quite* convinced that my decision was a right one, and that I can do more by remaining as CIGS.

Then went round to GHQ where I had interview with Lumsden, Freyberg and Jumbo Wilson. Then on to an AG meeting to lay down policy for amalgamation of units owing to the shortage of reinforcements. Whilst there was sent for by the PM to meet him and Smuts and read their final decision. The telegram was to the War Cabinet recommending a splitting of the Middle East into Near East and Middle East. Auk to vacate the former and take over the latter. Alexander to take over Near East, Gott to take over the 8th Army. Ramsden to leave, Quinan [10th Army] to leave, Corbett and Dorman-Smith also to go. Considering everything this is perhaps the best solution. I accepted it. Alexander is to fly out at once to take over ME, and for us to see him before we leave. Went back to GHQ and gave talk on world situation. After that had ½ hour with Casey. Then back for bath and another interview with PM to see his last telegram.

... it had been one of the most difficult days of my life, and one with devastating heart burnings! I had been offered the finest command I could hope for, and I had turned it down!...I could not put the real reasons to Winston which were connected with the fact that, rightly or wrongly, I felt I could exercise some control over him. At any rate, whether I exercised any control or not, I knew by now the dangers to guard against. I had discovered the perils of his impetuous nature. I was now familiar with his method of suddenly arriving at some decision as it were by intuition without any kind of logical examination of the problem. I had, after many failures, discovered the best methods of approaching him. I knew that it would take at least six months for any successor taking over from me to become as familiar as I was with him and his ways. During those six months anything might happen. I would not suggest that I could exercise any real control over him; I never met anybody that could, but he had grown to have confidence in me, and I had found that he was listening more and more to any advice that I gave him. ...

It had been difficult to resist Winston's pressure, but it was doubly difficult to resist that of Smuts! I was a tremendous admirer of his, and any word he spoke carried immense weight with me....I must confess that whilst listening to him for a few moments my resolutions of the morning were shaken! For a few moments I hesitated and then, thank heaven, I remained firm. Looking back I am certain that my decision, hard as it was, was the right one and that by remaining CIGS I was able to render greater services to my country than if I had accepted the more attractive alternative. I had many heart-gnawing regrets, but at any rate the satisfaction of feeling that I had chosen the right course. ...

I had very serious misgivings about Gott's appointment in his tired state, but was not at that time sufficiently convinced of the degree of this disadvantage to oppose the appointment.

7 August

Spent most of the morning with Wavell discussing various problems connected with India, and getting his advice on the situations which we are faced with here. At 12 noon PM sent for me to see reply from Cabinet to his wire concerning changes. They are quibbling at the split in the Command. Their arguments are not very conclusive and he was able to deal with them fairly easily. Spent afternoon with Adam and Wavell, also interviews with Corbett and Dorman-Smith.

Just as I was starting for home for dinner I received the news that Gott had been killed this afternoon being shot down whilst flying back from Burg el Arab! A very hard blow coming on top of all the planning we had been doing. He was one of our linkpins! I do feel sorry for Mrs Gott. After dinner PM, Smuts and I had conference as to how the matter should be settled. Had some difficulty. PM rather in favour of Wilson. However Smuts assisted me and telegram has now been sent off to Cabinet ordering Montgomery out to take command of 8th Army. I hope we get Alexander and Montgomery out soon so that I may settle details of Corps Commanders and Chiefs of Staff with them.

Harriman arrived today, together with some Russians. They are to accompany us to Moscow. Also Maxwell the American General is to join us. De Gaulle turned up to lunch, as supercilious and self-satisfied as ever. I am longing to finish tidying up this front, and am having rather a job to keep the PM on the move.

Gott's death was a very serious blow, and the most unexpected one. He was flying back on the Burg el Arab-Heliopolis route, considered so safe that no escort had been found necessary for Winston when we flew out. It happened to be an individual German plane, driven out of high altitude in combat, and dashing home at lower altitude. It came across the slow transport plane on its way and shot it down in flames. It seemed almost like the hand of God suddenly appearing to set matters right where we had gone wrong. Looking back on those days with the knowledge of what occurred at Alamein and after it I am convinced that the whole course of the war might well have been altered if Gott had been in command of the 8th Army. In his tired condition I do not think that he would have had the energy and vitality to stage and fight this battle as Monty did. ... Let it not be imagined from these remarks of mine that I had not got a high opinion of Gott. On the contrary I held him in the highest esteem and capable of great things, but he was not at his best, had had too long a run in the desert, and wanted rest.

8 August

I was called early to go round to PM's bedroom as he had received reply from Cabinet. They had agreed rather reluctantly to splitting of Command, but disliked nomenclature!!! Middle East Command should remain ME Command and new one to be called Persia-Iraq Command. Perhaps they are right. However Montgomery was fixed and his replacement by K. Anderson [1st Army] was settled. Jacob was then sent off with PM's letter to Auchinleck and instructed to bring back reply. PM and I with Harriman then accompanied Dick McCreery in a visit to 8th, 9th and 24th Armoured Brigades. All of them awaiting issue of tanks. Fine lot of men looking very fit. Met many old friends including Charles Norman, Currie, [illegible] etc. Returned here at 2.30 pm, late for a large lunch attended by 3 of our Russian friends who are to accompany us on our journey to Moscow. I had a long talk to the General after lunch. Then back to office to tell Wavell latest developments, and on to the USA GHQ, where I met General Maxwell and was given a full account with film of their recent survey of the trans-African route.

Back to Embassy to see Jacob with PM. Result Auchinleck refuses new appointment and prefers retirement. He is I am sure wrong – the Iraq-Persian front is the one place where he might restore his reputation as active operations are more than probable.

I still think that he was wrong not to accept the Iraq-Persian Command, and although the Germans did not push through on this front, it was the vital strategic point at that time. It would also have been a more 'soldierly' act to accept what he was offered in war, instead of behaving like an offended film star.

However, I am not certain that we are not better off without him. This will now mean finding new Commander, and probably placing this front under India. Went back to GHQ to see Wavell about this, he agrees. Then went back to see Casey and had a long talk with him. Apparently he has been having a very difficult time of it with the Auk, and poured his heart out to me. Back to Embassy again to receive a long lecture from PM, with all his pet theories as to how essential it is for Alex to command both ME and 8th Army. I again had to give him a long lecture on the system of the chain of command in the Army! I fear that it did not sink much deeper than it has before!

9 August

Had settled to breakfast with the PM on his terrace at 8.30 am. At 7.15 am his valet woke me to inform me that the PM was awake and wanted to know when I should breakfast. I replied 8.30 am as settled. The valet was horrified and replied, 'But Sir Alan, the Prime Minister likes to breakfast when he wakes up!' I replied that if this was so then I regretted he would have to breakfast alone as I intended to breakfast at 8.30, and turned round for another snooze! At 8.30 I went round. He had finished but bore me no ill will. We were expecting Alexander, and I wanted to see him badly before the PM got hold of him and had instructed for him to be brought round to my room. Unfortunately he arrived whilst I was having breakfast on the veranda. The PM's flag lieutenant whispered in my ear that he had arrived, but PM overheard and had then to be told that Alex had gone to the lavatory! Finally I got an opportunity and dashed out to see him. I wanted to warn him as regards the PM's conception of the Command of the ME as opposed to that of the 8th Army, which he mixes together. I then brought Alex in to PM and we had a long talk after which I had a long go with Alex by himself.

At 12 noon I received a message from the Auk that he had arrived at GHQ and wanted to see me before we went to PM, for which he was already over 1 hour late! I slunk out and went round to GHQ where I found him in a highly stormy and rather unpleasant mood. He wanted to know what the decision had been based on, and I had to explain mainly lack of confidence in him. I then brought him round for the PM to see. He was with him till 1.30 pm and made lunch late. Especially as PM asked to see me as soon as Auk left to tell the results of his interview. Apparently Auk is still havering as to whether to accept Persia-Iraq Command, and PM has given him a few days to think it over. After lunch I had another interview with the Auk and again found him in an unpleasant mood. Later Alex turned up and I left the two together and went to have an interview with Wavell. Later he and I had ¾ hour with Tedder on the air aspect of the proposed new Command. Tedder was astonishingly pig-headed and has fallen in my estimation. He is, I am afraid, only a small brained man. Finally I had ½ hour with Maxwell the GHQ gunner on the artillery situation.

10 August

Breakfast with Alex on the terrace, PM keeping us company. Then call from Auk to GHQ. Had to bite him back as he was apt to snarl, that kept him quiet. Came back here to collect PM at 11 am to visit map room at GHQ. Interview with Wavell and back for lunch. Visit from Gatehouse at 3.30 pm. Then sent for Dick McCreery to congratulate him on being CGS and to give him a few words of advice. Next Corbett to tell him that he would be relieved of his job. He asked to finish soldiering as he is tired, and yet he is only 54! A poor speci-men of a man.

Back to Embassy to discuss transport with PM and Lindsell from 5 to 6 pm. Then Wavell to discuss with PM and me the new Iraq-Persia Command and its possible inclusion in India Command. Now I have just finished packing as we start off on the new venture to Moscow tonight, shortly after midnight.

11 August   Teheran, 1300 miles, 6½ hours

We left the Residency about midnight and drove out to the aerodrome where we emplaned in 3 Liberators. PM with his doctor and retinue [in one], I had with me in my plane Cadogan, Wavell, Tedder, Jacob and one other. We were kept waiting until after 2 am before taking off, why I do not know.

Our party was unnecessarily large, as Winston on these occasions loved to accumu-late a large number of Generals, Admirals and Air Marshals who were not much con-nected with the work on hand, but I think he felt it increased his dignity. On this trip there was little reason for Wavell's or Tedder's presence.

I had a fair sort of bed rigged up in the bomb racks and slept fairly well. Unfortunately I had no sort of window and was unable to look out when day-light came. I should have liked to see the Persian mountains. About 8.30 am we landed and drove to the Residency where we washed and had breakfast. We were to have gone on after an hour, but owing to our late start last night it became evident that we could only reach Kuibyshev tonight, and could not reach Moscow. It was therefore decided that we should spend the day here and leave early tomorrow morning for Moscow. PM consequently went off for lunch with the Shah whilst we lunched in Embassy. After lunch we came up to a delightful spot in the hills where the Legation staff live. Beautifully cool trees and a lovely clear stream running through the garden. In the centre of the garden a most beautiful old Persian tent, and almost in the tent a small blue tiled pond of clear water with goldfish in it! When compared with the surrounding arid country, a real paradise. The ground was originally given by one of the former Shahs to Queen Victoria, and the various houses on it make excellent dwellings for the various members of the Legation. The one we are stopping at is really the one for the Minister (Bullard), but he prefers the building in Teheran and has handed this one over to his second string, a man called Holman.

Went down again to Teheran this afternoon for meeting at 6 pm with the PM, attended by Harriman and several Americans, to discuss the advisability of handing over the development of rail and road communications in Persia to the Americans. On the whole this seems advisable, but we are to make a final decision on returning to Cairo. We were given a most excellent dinner by the Holmans in the most lovely Eastern setting, sitting under a very old Persian tent with a lovely blue tiled pool actually in the tent itself, with roses round it and goldfish swimming about. We started with caviar, and went on with excellent fresh brown trout. Early to bed for an early start.

12 August   Teheran, 2½ hours, 400 miles

Called at 4.45, breakfast at 5.15 and left the house at 5.30 to emplane by 6 am. As a matter of fact, owing to usual delays at the aerodrome, we did not take off till 6.45. After we had taken off I crawled to a rear part of the Liberator from which it is possible to see out, and had a good view of the country. After we had been up an hour we were told that one of the four engines had gone wrong, and that the adjustable propeller blades were stuck. We had to turn back, and spent a long time cruising round to reduce the overload of petrol before landing. The plane was examined and we were informed that we could not go on before tomorrow morning!! So back we went to the Embassy. We were on the whole fortunate as the trouble was a serious one, and might have set fire to the plane.

After lunch I had a first class sleep and a bath, and then tea followed by a walk through bits of Teheran with Cadogan and Archie Wavell. We have now dined and are making for an early bed as we are by way of taking off in a Russian plane at 5 am. The pilot to be the Russian who flew over the North Pole going from Russia to America!

It had been a disappointing day. I had seen Winston's plane disappearing into the distance as it headed for Moscow whilst we turned back to Teheran! I did not like seeing him go off out of my sight without knowing how we were going to follow him.

13 August   Moscow, 13 hours, 1800 miles

Called at 3.30 am, breakfast 4 am and off to aerodrome by 4.30 am. There we found a very fine Douglas aeroplane beautifully fitted up inside with 8 arm-chairs and two couches, also large table. A very nice Russian pilot interpreter and crew. At 5.30 we started off flying for Kazvin, very desolate sandy desert plain with high mountains to the north. At Kazvin we turned north to pass through the mountains and struck the Caspian Sea near Pahlevi. A wonderful change of scenery as we approached the Caspian. Instead of a bare treeless desert and hills one suddenly came in to wooded hills and green fields. A very attractive scenery which looked lovely from the plane. We then followed the coast of the Caspian Sea till we reached Baku at 8 am. Then we landed to have fill of petrol and took off again at 8.45. It is a bigger place than I had expected and very interesting seeing all the oil wells. (I am writing in the plane which is bumping about a bit, and hence bad writing!) We flew right up the west coast till we came to the swamps at the mouth of the Volga. Miles and miles of small lakes and marshes. We finally reached Astrakhan and crossed the Volga north of it. We then again came into miles of marshes followed by desert. It became unpleasantly bumpy about that time! At 3.15 pm we landed at Kuibyshev (the rear capital). We had been expected here for some time and were given a recep-tion on the aerodrome with masses of hors d'oeuvre, including caviar! and vodka! We then took off again at 4.15 pm, flew over the town, crossed the Volga again, and flew over the most lovely forest where I spotted an eagle hov-ering below. We are now over more open country, but the plane is bumping about a lot. Must stop.

We finally arrived in Moscow at 8.30 pm, having been some 13 hours in the air and 15 hours travelling. We were met at the airport by a large gathering including our Ambassador, Shaposhnikov, the Chief of Staff, also the General commanding Moscow and a mass of press correspondents. Anders was also there. We had to have groups [photos] taken, etc. Then drove to hotel for a quick change and on to dinner with the PM in his house just outside Moscow. Found him very well and on the whole pleased with his interview with Stalin yesterday.

At 11 pm we were due to go and meet Stalin in the Kremlin. It was very inter-esting meeting him, and I was much impressed by his astuteness, and his crafty cleverness. He is a realist, with little flattery about him, and not looking for much flattery either. Our meeting consisted of Stalin and Molotov and PM, Cadogan, Wavell, Tedder, Jacob, self and 2 interpreters. We remained there till about 1.45 am when I was dropping with sleepiness having been up since 3.30 am! The discussion ranged mainly round our inability to establish a Second Front, and the fact that they cannot understand why we cannot do so. Tomorrow at 3 pm I am to hold a military meeting with their Chiefs of Staff to go further into the matter with them. At 6 pm they are to give us a demonstra-tion of their new mortar. I do not feel that this evening's meeting was on the whole a success, and that it will do much towards drawing us much closer together. The two leaders, Churchill and Stalin, are poles apart as human beings, and I cannot see a friendship between them such as exists between

Roosevelt and Winston. Stalin is a realist if ever there was one, facts only count with him, plans, hypotheses, future possibilities mean little to him, but he is ready to face facts even when unpleasant. Winston, on the other hand, never seems anxious to face an unpleasantness until forced to do so. He appealed to sentiments in Stalin which do not I think exist there. Altogether I felt we were not gaining much ground, and were being accused of breaking our word, lack of courage to open a Second Front, incapable of realizing the importance of the Russian front, only giving them that equipment which we did not want, etc, etc.

Personally I feel our policy with the Russians has been wrong from the very start, and as begun by Beaverbrook. We have bowed and scraped to them, done all we could for them and never asked them for a single fact or figure concerning their production, strength, dispositions etc. As a result they despise us and have no use for us except for what they can get out of us.

Whilst in Baku our pilot was instructed to fly low under 200 ft and hug the line of the coast to avoid any German fighter that might be about, as their troops were now in the centre of the Caucasus. This suited me admirably, as we had a wonderful view of that strip of flat ground some 10 to 20 miles wide between the Caucasus and the Caspian which provides one of the main lines of advance from Russia into Persia. I was very anxious to see what defences were being erected by the Russians. I did not expect very much....I had, however, expected to find more than what I saw, which consisted of only one half completed anti-tank ditch, badly revetted and without any covering defences!...In fact the back door seemed to be wide open for the Germans to walk through for an attack on the Russian southern supply route, and more important still, the vital Middle East oil supplies of Persia and Iraq!

The marshes in the deltas of the Volga made me long to visit them for the purposes of photography! I could see white egrets, herons and duck flying about as we skimmed past flying low. On arriving at Kuibyshev I was very much impressed, as we circled round, to see all the work that was going on in the way of factory construction. Everywhere new works were springing out of the ground. When we landed we found a strange reception awaiting us! In one of the aerodrome buildings was a lunch evidently prepared for Winston, who had been expected the previous day. The meal had been left in the hope that at any rate we might turn up on the next day to eat it up! The corners of the sandwiches had begun to curl up, the open sardine tins had lost their lustre, and the whole meal had a somewhat faded appearance! However, the caviar was good and some of the vodka had to be consumed, a serious risk in view of the bumpiness of the trip!

14 August

Had a bit of a rest and breakfast at 9 am with caviar and every other description of food! After breakfast did a short tour of the town to see the Kremlin, Lenin's tomb, Red Square etc. Also did a little shopping. At 11 am Anders the Polish General came to see me and we discussed the evacuation of the Polish forces from Russia to Persia. It is now in full swing. Not very pleased at results of last night, and rather depressed at results of last convoy Malta which sustained heavy losses. Lunched with PM and sat next to American Ambassador. At 2.30 pm started off to see demonstration of new Rocket Mortars. Shaposhnikov and Voroshilov were both there. Quite a useful type [of] weapon which we might well make use of. Returned about 7 pm and was informed that Stalin's dinner at the Kremlin would not take place until 9 pm.

At 9 pm we proceeded to the Kremlin for the banquet, which was held in one of the state rooms. I kept wandering back into the past and wondering what very different scenes this room must have witnessed in the days of the Tsars. It was a big banquet attended by the whole of our party, Stalin, Molotov and most of the main civilian and military officials. From the beginning vodka flowed freely and one's glass kept being filled up. The tables groaned under every description of hors d'oeuvres and fish etc. Stalin sat at the centre of the table with PM on his right and Harriman on his left, then came an interpreter, then myself and Voroshilov on my left with a Foreign Office official beyond. Molotov was opposite Stalin, and started proposing toasts within 5 minutes of our having sat down. These toasts went on continuously. My turn came about 3rd or 4th and I replied proposing health of Red Army after which I was left in peace. Archie Wavell replied in Russian which met with great success.

The evening dragged slowly on, many members getting somewhat the worse for wear! I got so bored and so disgusted looking at food that I almost felt sick! There were 19 courses, and we only got up at 12.15 am, having been 3¼ hours at the table! Luckily the evening rapidly drew to a close as the PM said he was feeling too weary to attend a film which had been provided for him.

By the end of dinner Stalin was quite lively, walking around the table to click glasses with various people he was proposing the health of. He is an outstanding man, that there is no doubt about, but not an attractive one. He has got an unpleasantly cold, crafty, dead face, and whenever I look at him I can imagine his sending off people to their doom without ever turning a hair. On the other hand there is no doubt that he has a quick brain and a real grasp of the essentials of war. He strikes me as ageing and beginning to show distinct signs of wear. By 2.15 am I was in bed and very grateful to have got off as lightly, having expected to be kept up till 4 am!

Our life in Moscow was from one aspect somewhat that of prisoners. We each had a guard armed with revolvers perpetually in attendance. They stood outside one's room in the hotel and accompanied one everywhere, always shadowing one's footsteps.

Anders' visit was of course of some interest. I had last seen him at that sherry party of Sikorski's at Claridges. He had been sent back to Russia to extract the Polish prisoners captured by the Russians in their invasion of Poland when co-operating with the Germans. When he came into my hotel sitting room he beckoned to me to come and sit at a small table with him. He then pulled out his cigarette case and started tapping the table and speaking in a low voice. He said: 'As long as I keep tapping this table and talk like this we cannot be overheard by all the microphones in this room!' I must confess that till then I had not realized that my sitting room was full of microphones. I learned to realize that all rooms in Moscow had ears! Anders then proceeded to tell *me that hunt as he might he could not discover a large consignment of Polish prisoners which comprised most of the men of distinction in most walks of life. He had followed one clue half way across Siberia and then it fizzled out. He said he was certain that they were either being liquidated in one of the Siberian Convict Camps or that they had been murdered. It turned out that he was correct. This was the batch of prisoners that the Russians murdered and that the Germans found later on, Goebbels exploiting this find to the utmost.* Anders wanted me to fix up a meeting for him with Winston so that he might assist him in getting authority from Stalin to establish assembly areas for other collections of Polish prisoners, and for their despatch to Persia. He told me that their condition was deplorable, most of them being in a half starved condition. I had an opportunity of corroborating this fact later on in Teheran.*

The rocket mortar demonstration was quite interesting and the weapons very effective for area bombardments, such as the plastering of company localities. They consisted of slides mounted at an angle on lorries from which groups of rockets could be fired. The heavier rockets were actually fired out of the wooden crates in which they were packed. The crate was put in a rack at an angle of some 45 degrees and then the lid of the crate removed, the rocket being fired electronically. On returning from Moscow I got the War Office to apply for details and diagrams of these rockets through the Soviet Embassy, but we never received any reply to our enquiries.

I had heard a great deal about the Kremlin banquets from Anthony Eden who attended one during his visit and at which Voroshilov slumped under the table. Stalin had turned to Eden and asked him whether the British generals were any better at holding their liquor. Eden, the complete diplomat, I believe replied: 'They may perhaps hold their drinks better, but they are not so successful at winning battles!' Doubly insulting considering Voroshilov was not fit to win any battle, a flat catcher and an excellent example of a political general. He would not be President now if he had not been more politically than militarily minded throughout his life.

I was in dread of this banquet all day and shuddered at the idea of having to spend the evening dodging the effects of vodka. It turned out to be a complete orgy as I described in my diary. Continual toasts throughout the dinner, and a table groaning with food, mostly of a fishy and oily nature. During the first hour we must have got through at least a dozen toasts. Luckily, I had a jug of water in front of me, and when I was not being watched I filled up my glass with water instead of vodka. At this time Voroshilov said through his interpreter: 'This white vodka is no good. I am sending for yellow vodka.'!! I thought that he must have spotted me juggling with the water jug, but he had not, he genuinely preferred yellow vodka. The new drink arrived with a large red chilli, about the size of a large carrot, floating in the jug! Voroshilov filled my glass and said 'No heel taps', to which I replied 'Oh no, you know your yellow vodka, I have never tasted it and shall therefore sip this first glass.' This I proceeded to try to do, but after a couple of sips I found it impossible to swallow any more, it was just like drinking liquid cayenne pepper and completely choked up one's throat. I told

---

*A large number of Polish officers had been taken prisoner by the Russians in 1939. On the recommencement of diplomatic relations with the USSR in 1941, the Poles began to search for these men, who had disappeared. Most had, in fact, been massacred by the NKVD, and buried in mass graves at Katyn, Kharkov and near Kalinin. The Germans announced the discovery of some 4,400 corpses at Katyn in April 1943.

Voroshilov that I should stick to the white, but he said that he would now take to the yellow and proceeded to throw down two glasses in quick succession! The result did not take long to show itself. His forehead broke out in beads of perspiration which soon started to flow down his face. He became sullen and quiet sitting with a fixed stare straight to his front, and I wondered whether the moment had arrived for him to slip under the table. No – he retained his seat, but took little further interest in the proceedings.

The evening wore away slowly and I felt more and more despondent. In front of me amongst the many fish dishes was a small suckling pig covered with a blanket of white sauce. He had a black truffle eye and an orange peel mouth. He was never eaten and as the evening slipped by his black eye remained fixed on me, and the orange peel mouth developed a sardonic smile! I can still see that pig now if I shut my eyes. Towards the end of the banquet Stalin took up the running from Molotov and started a round of toasts. He filled his glass with vodka and must have had his eye on Voroshilov in his sad plight, for he descended straight on him. He came and stood alongside him holding his glass on high and started his toast with a broad grin on his face. Voroshilov had to stand whilst his toast was being proposed; this he was only just able to do. He held on tight to the table with both hands, swaying gently back-wards and forwards with a distant and vacant look in his eyes. The critical moment arrived – Stalin held up his glass for Voroshilov to click with. Voroshilov must have seen at least half a dozen glasses, a worried look came on his face, he tried to concen-trate his thoughts, finding that impossible he trusted to luck and lunged forward at one of the many glasses he was seeing. Fortune was with him and he clicked the right one! Stalin walked off to fill his glass another dozen times for further toasts, whilst Voroshilov with a deep sigh sank back on to his chair.

The end came at last and I rose from the table thanking heaven that I still had full control of my legs and my thoughts!

15 August

Took an easy morning in bed after our late night. Then went out for a short walk round Red Square with Archie. At 11 am we went to PM's house for final talk before our military interview which was timed for 12 noon. There we met Voroshilov and Shaposhnikov with one other general and interpreters. We consisted of Archie Wavell, Tedder, Maxwell (USA), US air man, Jacob and self. Our meeting lasted till 2.30 pm and for 2½ hours I argued against the possibili-ty of establishing a Western Front in 1942. It was very up hill work as they had no intention of being convinced and hoped to convince us that we were wrong. As they have not got the vaguest conception of the conditions prevail-ing in France and England nor any real ideas of the implications of amphibious operations, it was a hopeless task from the start. We remained quite friendly but entirely unconvinced.

They then gave us lunch during which I had a talk with Shaposhnikov who looks terribly ill and worn out. He has been chief of staff since the start and is a sick man suffering from his heart or something. But he is very charming to talk to, and I should think quite a good staff officer. Voroshilov is an attractive personality but the typical political general who owes his life now to his wits in the past.

After our meeting I went to report to the PM and then back to the hotel, hoping to be called for another meeting to discuss the Caucasus situation, as when I raised this point this afternoon I was told by Voroshilov that he had no authority to discuss it. He said he would endeavour to obtain authority for the Gov to meet us at 5pm to discuss this side of the problem. There is no doubt that they are anxious to get all they can out of us, but at the same time have no intention of giving us the smallest help of any kind. They are an astonishingly suspicious type of people and very difficult to arrive at that close cooperation in war which is essential. This visit may have done some good in forging some bonds of greater confidence between us, but on the whole it is highly unsatisfactory. We have never really got down to discuss the main problems of this war or how we can best circumvent our common difficulties. We agree easily enough that these difficulties exist and must be overcome, but since we approach them from diametrically opposed points of view solutions are hard to find!

At 6 pm I went over to visit the British Mission under Admiral Miles, and from there went on for a second meeting with Voroshilov to discuss the question of the defence of the Caucasus. He had now received permission from Stalin to discuss this point, but was still as sticky as could be. I then said that I had been frank with him as regards the strength of British forces and expected equal confidence on his part. He then agreed and said that there were 25 Russian divisions in the Caucasus with corresponding tank and air forces. This is the same figure as quoted by Stalin but I am certain it is not the truth. We then discussed possibility of sending air reinforcements to the Caucasus. This he took greater interest in, but was definitely looking 'the gift horse in the mouth' till I again got annoyed with him and got him into a better mood. In the end we got agreement concerning machinery to carry out the required preparations to receive the air forces if they can be spared for this front.

Rushed back after a touching parting with Voroshilov and Shaposhnikov and dined with Admiral Miles in his flat. Have now returned and am getting ready for an early bed in anticipation of an early start tomorrow morning. I am leaving Moscow with no regrets! If Moscow represents Bolshevism we must certainly look for something better. Even making allowance for war and its effect, the dejection, drabness and lack of any sort of joie de vivre is most marked.

I found the discussion with Voroshilov and Shaposhnikov was very heavy work. Voroshilov evidently understood nothing about it and his military knowledge was painfully limited, as exemplified by his questions, which were entirely childish. There was no difficulty in dealing with the questions, but the reply was never absorbed and the same question was reiterated unendingly. I gathered that Voroshilov's position alongside of Stalin was based more on personal friendship and early contacts. I believe that in the early days when Voroshilov commanded a battalion, Stalin was attached to his unit as a political Commissar. Doubtless the foundation of an understanding between them was set up in these days and cemented during the purge of generals, when doubtless Voroshilov played a considerable part in selecting those for liquidation! Whatever the relations they were certainly not based on his value as an advisor in military matters. I do not remember a single instance in which Stalin sought his advice in all our meetings. Shaposhnikov was a very different type. I believe he had been an officer in the Tsarist armies and had graduated at their Staff College. If so he had evidently turned Communist and turned in his lot with them. A pathetic figure evidently dying fast of some complaint since he only lasted a few months after our interview. He had a well trained military brain and his questions were far more to the point than those of Voroshilov.

Throughout our discussion Wavell was most useful to me; as he could understand Russian he wrote down a few notes and pushed them over to me even before the interpreter had time to get to work. I thus had a few additional seconds to frame my replies in. After 2½ hours of it I saw clearly that we could go on arguing till the cows came home without making any headway. I therefore said that it was useless continuing our talk on the Second Front, that I had given them all the strong reasons that made such an operation impossible in 1942, that the operation could not take place, and that I had nothing more to add to what I had already said. I continued saying that I now wanted to discuss their dispositions for the defence of the Caucasus against the German penetration. I drew their attention [to the fact] that their Southern route of supplies from the West was threatened and that our oil supply was endangered, consequently we both had an interest in the defence of this area. Evidently a discussion of those defences was desirable. Voroshilov replied that he had no authority from Stalin to discuss the Caucasus. I replied that this was very regrettable considering their importance and asked him to obtain the necessary authority.

As will have been seen from the diary he secured this authority after having given himself time to discuss with Stalin what he was to disclose. After having given me his reply of 25 divisions in the Caucasus, a number which I suspected as a gross exaggeration, I decided to test his veracity over the defences of the Caucasus. I knew that he would not realize that I had flown up the west coast of the Caspian instead of following the east coast as Winston had done. I therefore began by asking him questions concerning the central passes, but I could not check his answers. I then turned to the main approach route between the Caucasus and the Caspian. Here I drew him on and extracted out of him details of their strong lines of defence with anti-tank ditches and concrete pill boxes for anti tank guns and machine guns. A complete pack of lies from what I had been able to see for myself, as described in these notes!! I was thus able to estimate the small amount of faith one could attach to any of his statements.

Thank heaven, amongst his many mistakes, Hitler lost a golden opportunity by carrying on with the desperate attacks against Stalingrad instead of directing Von Paulus towards Persia and the Middle East oil. Instead of losing this army of 60,000 men captured by the Russians he would have found the road leading to one of the greatest strategic prizes practically open and devoid of defences.

Our visit to Moscow had now come to an end. It had been of intense interest and looking back on it I feel that it fulfilled a very useful purpose, that of creating the beginnings of a strange understanding between Winston and Stalin.

16 August   Teheran 9½ hours, 2000 miles

[in pencil]

My pen has run out and I dare not wait until tomorrow as events follow so fast on each other it is difficult to remember them. I was called at 3.15 pm and left Hotel at 4.15, raining heavily. However by the time we reached aerodrome it was only a drizzle, but rather a dull, drab gray dawn. A large crowd at the aerodrome – Guard of Honour, Press Cameras, press, officials etc.

PM was somewhat late and no wonder! He went to see Stalin for final visit at 7 pm and remained with him till 3 am!! He had no time for bed and after a bath came straight to the aerodrome. He arrived with Molotov. The band played the International, God save the King, and the Star Spangled Banner; during which period we all stood to attention and saluted! Then a series of goodbyes to Molotov, Shaposhnikov, Anders, etc, etc. Finally 5.30 am we took off in 4 Liberators and flew off in formation.

The Liberator was not as comfortable as the Douglas Russian plane we had flown up [in], but faster, being capable of 200 miles per hour. We flew over Kuibyshev, then on to the Ural River where I moved up into second pilot's seat and had a grand view. We flew right down the Ural River through deserts and swamps to the Caspian, then we came down the east coast for a change which was interesting. Finally we cut across the southern Caspian to Pahlevi, over the mountains to Kazvin and back to Teheran where we landed after an excellent non-stop 9½ hours flight. We all went up to the hill Legation where we had an excellent dinner under the lovely Persian tent with the blue pool with gold fish. Now off to bed for another early start tomorrow morning.

Winston's final visit to Stalin had been a useful one judging by the interpreter's notes of the interview. During the course of the evening they became on very friendly terms and began to ask each other why they had done various things in the past. Winston asked Stalin how it was that he had double crossed us at the beginning of the war when our mission was in Moscow apparently making good progress and suddenly he swung right over to sign an agreement with Ribbentrop? Stalin replied that he thought England must be bluffing, he knew we had only 2 divisions we could mobilize at once and he thought we must know how bad the French Army was and how little reliance could be placed on it. He could not imagine we should enter the war with such weakness. On the other hand he said he knew Germany was certain ultimately to attack Russia. He was not ready to withstand that attack; by attacking Poland with Germany he could make more ground, ground was equal to time, and he would consequently have a longer period of time to get ready. I should think that this was probably a fairly true statement of the reasons that led to his decision.

Stalin then asked Winston why he bombed his Molotov when he sent him to Berlin. Winston replied that in war no advantages can ever be neglected. Stalin then said that Molotov was engaged in conversation with Ribbentrop who was saying that the British Empire was now finished and that the time had come to work out the partition of those lands between Germany and Russia. At this moment the bombers arrived and Ribbentrop decided to continue the discussion in the dug out. When safely established underground Ribbentrop continued saying that as he had already mentioned the British Empire need no longer be taken account of. Molotov interrupted at this point with the awkward question: 'Then why are we down here now?' This had pleased Stalin very much and he told Winston that his Molotov had a good sense of humour. Personally I had never credited him as possessing any sense of humour!

The only tragedy concerning this last visit of Winston to Stalin was connected with poor Anders. I had succeeded in getting him his interview which was to have taken place at 8.30 pm that evening on Winston's return from Stalin. Anders waited until 3 am for him and when he returned he said 'Ah, my poor Anders. I have been detained by M. Stalin and now I must fly off, but you come along to Cairo and we shall have a talk then!!' Anders had already flown from Tashkent to Moscow to see him and now he was asked to come to Cairo as if it was in the next street. To give Anders credit he got into his plane and followed laboriously in our wake, reaching Cairo before we had left there and had his long sought interview!

While we were flying away from Moscow I had established myself with Archie Wavell in the small cabin in the rear of the Liberator. We were lying on the floor as there were no seats. I was reading but Archie was busy writing notes in his corner. I wondered what he was writing about and wondered whether he was busy writing notes on our meetings in Moscow and wondered whether I was neglecting my duties not following his example. Suddenly he stopped and threw across to me the results of his labours. The paper was headed 'Ballad of the Second Front'. It ran as follows:

MOST PERSONAL AND VERY SECRET
BALLADE OF THE SECOND FRONT
P.M. Loquitur
1. *I do not like the job I have to do. I cannot think my views will go down well.*
   Can I convince them of our settled view; will Stalin use Caucasian oaths and yell?
   Or can I bind him with my midnight spell; I'm really feeling rather in a stew.
   It's not so hot a thing to have to sell; No Second Front in 1942.
2. *I thought so, things are stickier than glue; they simply hate the tale I have to tell.*
   Stalin and Molotov are looking blue; if they give in an inch they'll take an ell.
   I wonder if they'll put me in a cell, and deal with me like Hitler with a Jew.
   It's not so hot a thing to have to sell; No Second Front in 1942.
3. *Come, things are taking on a rosier hue; the whole affair has got a better smell.*
   I think that after all we'll put it thru; though not as merry as a wedding bell.
   The sound is now less like a funeral knell; another vodka for? Here's Fortune – Phew!
   I've got away with what I came to sell; No Second Front in 1942.

ENVOI
4. *Prince of the Kremlin, here's a fond farewell;*
   I've had to deal with many worse than you.
   You took it though you hated it like hell;
   No Second Front in 1942.

17 August   Cairo 5½ hours, 1300 miles
Another 4.30 am rise and off by 6 am. We had a wonderful fly back to Cairo averaging well over 200 miles per hour. I went up into the second pilot's seat

after we had taken off and remained there till just before landing. We rose steadily to 15,000 ft (height of Mont Blanc) to clear the hills in our path and then remained between 14 and 15 thousand feet up to avoid the bumps owing to heat off desert and hills. Glorious wild mountain ranges which I was very interested in in connection with the defence of Persian oil against invasion from the Caucasus. After the mountains we passed over the valley of the Tigris and the Euphrates. We were some way south of Baghdad. We then had a very bleak stretch of desert before reaching Amman, the only interesting part in this section being the oil pipes which we flew along for some time. We struck the Dead Sea near its northern end flying at 14,000 ft with beautiful visibility. I was able to see the whole Dead Sea from end to end, Jerusalem, Bethlehem and Hebron all at the same time. It was a thrilling sight. As I looked down on the Dead Sea from above I thought of our Lord walking on the water and from the height we were at it seemed quite a natural thing to do, the water looked like a solid. We then flew over Beersheba and I could see Gaza and the sea in the distance. Finally we crossed the top of the Sinai Peninsula and struck the canal at Ismailia, from which we glided down to Heliopolis Aerodrome in Cairo. We were met there by Miles Lampson [Ambassador] and Casey [Minister]. Adam and Alexander also turned up.

After lunch PM, Alexander and I had a long conference on his plans and on the reorganization of his army. Casey also had a talk with me to tell me that Auchinleck refused the Iraq-Persia Command. I hear from Alexander that he has been very difficult and most unpleasant of late, looked for an offence in everything. Monty I hear is settling down well and going great guns. I pray to God that the new Alexander-Monty combination will be a success, I can think of nothing better. The more I look back at our decision to get rid of Auchinleck the more convinced I am that we are correct.

18 August   Cairo

Determined at last to have a good night's sleep. I slept solidly from midnight to 8.30 am. Whilst dressing the PM breezed in in his dressing gown and told me he had been thinking over the urgency of the attack against Rommel. He then started producing all the arguments that I have so frequently battled against for speeding up the date. I had to point out that it was exactly 2 days!! ago that Alex had taken over and Monty arrived, and that there was a mess to be put right, etc etc. I know that from now on I shall have a difficult time curbing his impatience. I then went round to GHQ to meet Archie [Wavell] and explain to him my latest plan. Namely: Iraq and Persia to be handed over at once to India from Middle East so as to free Alex of this responsibility. Archie Wavell to act as a foster parent and to prepare this Command for an independent existence at the earliest possible date. I feel convinced that we cannot leave the all vital Abadan Oil centre in a sector where it represents the poor sister of either Middle East or India. It must have a life and entity of its own and be prepared by an energetic commander for the vital conflict which may take place in this area if the Caucasus breaks. Archie Wavell agreed with me. Then held an interview with Peirse (Archie's AOC) who pleaded for the Auk's future.

Back to the Embassy to see Auchinleck after he had said goodbye to PM at 12 noon. Did not look forward to this interview, but he was in a much more pleasant mood and the interview went off well. We parted on friendly terms.

At lunch Alex and Pinard (the SA Div Commander) were present. After lunch Pinard gave us an interesting account of recent fighting.

At 5 pm, a big conference attended by PM, Miles Lampson, Iraqi Ambassaor, Wavell, Alexander, Tedder, Peirse, Admiral, Lindsell and Jacob to decide on future of Iraq-Persia Command. PM is taken with my scheme, and meeting took to it too. Very satisfactory. Committee appointed to go into details and report day after tomorrow. After meeting I found that PM was evidently again toying with the idea of stopping on here till the 30th!! This is because there is an indication of a possible attack on the 26th and he would like to be here for it!! I had to be as firm as I could with him and told him that he would put himself in an impossible position if he stopped on and would be accused of taking control. (It would be far worse than his Antwerp visit in the last war, but I did not say so and only implied it!) I told him we must arrange to start next Saturday or Sunday at latest. I think I have brought him round, and hope he will not slip back!

In my diary I state that we had an 'indication' that Rommel would attack. No doubt I used this term for security reason[s] for we had far more than an indication. We had the most reliable of wireless intercepts giving details as to this intention and the probable date. In fact everything except details as to the front of attack.

Dined out with Shone (1st Secretary), where Alexander, Archie and Adam were also dining. Pamela Wavell [daughter] was also there – I had not seen her since she showed us round Gov House in Salisbury when we were moving in before the war.

19 August Desert
Started with breakfast on terrace with PM. Then over to GHQ for final talk with Adam before his departure for home. From there on to see Wavell and had a long argument with him and Peirse as regards future of Iraq Persia Command and the difficult problem of allotting the Air to this theatre. Did not get much further with the problem.

Back to the Embassy to read recent telegrams about Dieppe Raid and to pack for our departure for desert after lunch. Alex came along with us. We left Embassy at 3.15 pm and motored the whole way out, only reaching 8th Army HQ at about 7.30 pm. There Monty gave us an excellent appreciation of the situation and what he proposed to do if Rommel attacked before he was ready and also his plans in the event of his starting the offensive. He is in tremendous form, delighted at being sent out here, and gave me a wonderful feeling of relief at having got him out here. We dined at their Mess and I slept in an ambulance converted into a caravan for Alex. Very comfortable, lovely night with the sound of the waves only a few yards away. On way to bed PM took me down to the beach, where he was transformed into a small boy wishing to dip his fingers into the sea! In the process he became very wet indeed!!

20 August   Cairo, 40 minutes, 100 miles

Called at 6 am. PM had a sea bathe before breakfast. We then proceeded to the front where we visited 44th Division, 22nd Armoured Brigade, 4th Light Brigade, 7th Motor Brigade, and New Zealanders, finally lunching at 13th Corps HQ with Horrocks. After lunch PM visited squadron of the 4th Hussars, his old regiment. We then motored back to 8th Army HQ where we had a sea bathe and tea. Then on to Alexandria, from where we flew back to Cairo, arriving there about 6.15 pm.

At 7 pm conference on Iraq-Persia. Committee had sat and produced report on transfer to India. Still impossible to obtain decision from PM!! Usual Air Force difficulties and he will not face up to them. I pointed out that while we are talking the Germans are walking through the Caucasus. He nevertheless decided he would write a paper which we should discuss tomorrow! After dinner he suddenly said that he did not think we could get off before Monday! I had another long argument and have brought him back to Sunday, but shall probably again have difficulties tomorrow!

21 August   Cairo

Breakfast on the terrace with PM and Gort. During the night PM had produced a new paper on the organization of the Persia-Iraq front which is nothing more than the original plan of making it an independent Command from the very start. He has not yet solved the main difficulty namely the control of air forces. However it is a possible start and one which can be built on provided we make use of Jumbo Wilson for this purpose. He is not ideal being too old but might get the show started. Then went round to GHQ to discuss with Wavell and McCreery the allocation of forces to the new command. After this I went to see the Admiral, and had a long interview with Anders, who has returned from Moscow via Tashkent and who is very upset about the organization of his forces in Palestine. Apparently he and Sikorski are not seeing eye to eye.

At lunch Vice President of Greek government was there. Not very inspiring specimen. After lunch had long talk with Gort to put him into the picture of recent events. At 5 pm went out with the Ambassador and his wife to be taken round the shops to purchase presents. It was rather an interesting part of Cairo I had not been in before.

Had to return to Embassy at 7 pm as PM was having conference there to settle question of handing over the running of the Persian Railway to the Americans to develop. Decided that the PM should on Harriman's recommendation wire to the President asking if he would be kind enough to take it over. I then remained on with PM to settle final details concerning formation of

Iraq-Persia Command. Decided to hand it over to Jumbo Wilson to start it. I had sent for Jumbo and went out to probe him to find out whether he was prepared to take it on. He said he was delighted to do so. He is too old really for the job, but I see no alternative to letting him start the show. It is imperative that something should be done quickly as the Germans are pushing on into the Caucasus rapidly. Our defences in Iraq-Persia are lamentably weak. Jumbo Wilson will have an uphill task! He and Dick McCreery came to dine. Dick has settled down to the CGS job well and should I think make a success of it. We have carried out some drastic changes while we have been out here, I feel convinced they are for the better, and do hope events will prove this the case.

Looking back at my remarks about Jumbo Wilson it is interesting to notice how I misjudged at that time the effect that age had had on him. He had become very large and fat and I thought that age was telling fast on him, slowing him up and reducing his value as a commander. I was totally wrong as I soon discovered, and he was still capable of giving the most valuable service. An exceptionally clear brain, a strong personality, and an imperturbable character.

22 August   35 minutes, 100 miles

I had breakfast at 6.15 and left at 6.45 with the PM to visit the caves of Tura. They are caves that were created by the quarrying of the pyramid stones, and are now being used as vast workshops by the RAF for repair of aircraft engines and for overhauls. From there we drove to Heliopolis aerodrome, where we emplaned for Abu Suweir where bomber squadrons are located. We had breakfast there and then motored on to inspect the 51st Division at Quassassin. They have only just arrived out here and were recently in the Aldershot, Camberley, Hartley Wintney area! Men looking very fit after their sea journey but not yet tanned by the sun. We spent about 1½ hours with them and then motored back arriving in time for a late lunch.

After lunch PM called Alex and me into his study for an hour's discussion on prospects of Rommel's possible attack on 25th. I suggested that petrol reserves at pumps should be reduced in case of temporary breakthrough with thrust on Cairo. Miles Lampson called in and put in contact with Alex to attend to this danger. I am surprised that it was not looked into sooner. Then had my hair cut and shampooed, both badly required. Then 5 to 6.15 long interview with Jumbo Wilson to discuss future details concerning his new command. He has been getting busy and made good progress in the preliminary measures. I then went off to look up Casey, who has been ill, and to tell him of all the recent developments. I do not feel that he is of big enough calibre for the job, and in any case doubt whether his health will stand up to it. Platt (C-in-C East Africa), turned up this evening. Alex also came to dinner.

This should be my last evening here, and I feel that during the last 3 weeks I have lived through a very full quota! First the necessary changes here, removal of Auchinleck, Corbett, Dorman-Smith and their replacement. Then the reorganization of the Middle East Command into two with all the discussions and work it entailed. The loss of Gott at the critical moment when we had selected him for 8th Army. The handing over of the Persia Railway to the Americans. The Western Front discussions with the Russians. Meetings with outstanding men such as Smuts, Stalin, Molotov, Voroshilov, Shaposhnikov, etc. It has all been intensely interesting, but very hard work when the background of constant contact with Winston is taken in to account! And yet nothing could have been kinder and more charming than he has been throughout this trip.

23 August

Breakfast on the terrace with PM and Gort. Then long interview with Platt (C-in-C East Africa) concerning operations in Madagascar and raising of East African forces. We both then went to see the PM and had long discussion with him. Jumbo Wilson then came round to discuss further the issue of the organization of Command in Iraq-Persia and to decide what we were to do with Quinan. After him Alex and Dick McCreery came round to discuss their proposed organization of the Armoured and ordinary divisions. This conforms to home except for some minor differences, and is much sounder than the Auk's wild schemes. Casey and his wife, Spears and Stone came to lunch. PM worried about Stone as commander of Cairo defences and decided that Jumbo Wilson should be prepared to take job on should Rommel attack during next few days. Spears full of the de Gaulle difficulties.

All preparations now made for our secret departure. PM goes off as if visiting Casey and then slips off to aerodrome. Cadogan and I leave here at 5.15 pm. I think plane is timed to take off about 7 pm. I am glad to be off as I want to pick up threads at home, where there is a great deal to be done. However I am delighted that we came out as I could never have put matters right here from a distance. It has also been very interesting to meet men such as Smuts and Stalin. Such a contrast! Smuts I look upon as one of the biggest of nature's gentlemen I have ever seen. A wonderful clear grasp of all things, coupled with the most exceptional charm. Interested in all matters and gifted with marvellous judgement. Stalin, on the other hand, a crafty, brilliant, realistic mind, devoid of any sense of human pity or kindness. Gives one almost an uncanny feeling to be in his presence. But undoubtedly a big and shrewd brain with clear cut views as to what he wants and expects to get.

At 5.15 Cadogan and I left Embassy for the aerodrome. PM had gone ahead, dropping in on Casey to simulate a proposed visit there. The aerodrome was in an unpleasant condition, with continuous minor sandstorms. Finally by 7.30 we took off, PM being 15 minutes ahead in his plane, 12 fighters overhead to cover us. We climbed steadily and headed SW.

24 August   Gibraltar, 13¾ hours, 2500 miles

Our party consisted of Cadogan, Jacob, Peter Dunphie, Mr Kinna [Churchill's clerk] and our airmen. We headed SW and then turned west, passing only 200 to 250 miles south of Benghazi! from there straight on over south Tripoli,

Algeria, and finally came out over Spanish Morocco into the western part of the Gibraltar Channel. Here we bore north for a bit and then turned east to approach the Rock as if we were coming from home, for security purposes. Low lying clouds through which the jagged top of the Rock stuck out. Not much of the runway to be seen through the clouds. However, pilot did a wonderful landing and put us down at 9.15 am. I was not feeling very fresh having tried to sleep on a hard floor with a thin mattress (1 in thick) on top of it. I felt rather as if a steam roller had been over me. We had also done a good deal of the journey at 15,000 feet, and lying down at that height makes one very short of breath. After a bit the oxygen supply was turned on and we put on masks like the dentist produces to give one gas, not comfortable for sleeping in.

We came straight up to Government House for a shave, bath and breakfast. PM had arrived in his plane with Harriman and Sir Charles Wilson just 15 minutes before us. Weather reports over England are unfavourable, apparently foggy mornings likely to prevail for a bit. The possibility of going on again in a few hours and doing the journey by day instead of by night is being examined at present. Mason-MacFarlane is away at present, discussing plans at home, so Colin Jardine is doing the honours. PM is in any case to be confined to house for security reasons. He discussed disguising himself as an Egyptian demi-mondaine, or an Armenian suffering from toothache so as to be allowed out! I do not think that he will be allowed either of these alternatives. I feel that it is a great triumph having got him to start from Egypt last night. He had every intention of wriggling out of it if he could! He felt that the Cabinet had given him leave till the 30th and that he should be allowed to stop on till then. On the other hand I know that he would have given anything to stop on this week so as to be there if Rommel attacks on the 25th Aug!

Later – At 1 pm just as we were going for lunch we were suddenly informed that London had approved doing journey by day and that we were to start at 1.30 pm!! This entailed desperate rush as we had to change, pack, lunch and get down to aerodrome in 30 minutes.

London, 8 hours, 1600 miles
By 1.45 pm we were off, skirting along the Spanish coast as far as Trafalgar Point, from there we lost sight of land and sailed out to sea. While we were in the Bay of Biscay I went up to the second pilot's seat and remained most of the journey there. There were nice cloud banks that we kept close to in case of attention by German planes operating from Brest. We saw none, and had a peaceful journey until we approached England. Here we ran into dirty weather, heavy cloud and electric storms. Wireless failed to function and we were there-fore deprived of directions of locations, and after flying some 7 hours over the sea I think there were some doubts as to where we had got. However finally as light was beginning to fail we struck the coast of Wales north of Pembroke. Most of us thought we were over Cornwall, and mistook the Welsh mountains for Dartmoor! Finally, with the light almost gone, the pilot made an excellent landing at Lyneham (near Swindon). There we found the PM had landed 10

minutes before. He had been met by Mrs Churchill, Randolph and CAS and Harriman's daughter. We motored to special train where we dined on the way to London. Arrived at 11.15 pm to find large crowd, and a great joy to see you were amongst them.

I had been away just over three weeks and had covered a great deal of ground in that time. I had visited Gibraltar, Malta and Cairo Commands, including detailed visit to 8th Army. I had met C-in-C India (Wavell) and East Africa (Platt). I had also met Smuts and had opportunities of discussing South African forces with him. In addition I had seen Persia and a good deal of its mountainous country from the air, also a glimpse of Iraq. Beyond that the visit to Moscow had been of intense interest and placed me in a far better position to appreciate the Russian situation. But above all the most important part of all lay in organizing the command of the Middle East, and restoring confidence of the fighting troops in their leaders. The separation of Iraq-Persia Command from Middle East I also look upon as a step of great importance.

> I pray God that the decisions we arrived at may be correct,
> and that they may bear fruit.

When looking back at those days in the light of after events one may be apt to over-look those ghastly moments of doubt which at times crowded in on me. Moments when one wondered whether one had weighed up situations correctly, arrived at the right conclusion, and taken suitable action. This little short prayer of 2 lines was not just a figure of speech, it was a very real, deep felt and agonized prayer written at a moment of considerable mental and physical exhaustion at the end of 3 most memorable weeks!

As regards distance covered in the 3 weeks I have flown 15,650 miles, and have been in the air some 84 hours, the equivalent of 3½ days spent flying.

25 August

I had a late breakfast which you came and shared with me to my great joy. After breakfast we had a talk and I then took you back to your hotel and went on to the WO. I have spent most of the day gradually picking up threads again and finding out what had been happening whilst I was away. Finished up with Cabinet meeting where PM explained results of trip. Dill putting up here and I had dinner with him. Rather hard settling down to the routine work again. Just heard that the Duke of Kent has been killed in an air crash!

26 August

A difficult COS meeting trying to find out where we are with Torch operation, things have been going wrong lately and I am not at all happy at the time events have taken! For some reason landings at Casablanca have been abandoned, others of a doubtful nature at Philippeville and Bône have been inserted, etc. Now the PM steps in and sends a wire to the President settling Oct 14ᵗʰ as a definite date without reference to the COS. We had to have a second COS meeting at 6.30 at which I am afraid I was rather rude to all members of the COS including poor old Dudley Pound – but he is quite maddening and long past retirement.

27 August

COS met at 10 am to prepare answer to American proposal to cut down North African enterprise to Casablanca and Oran only, instead of Oran, Algiers and Bône as settled at present. Met PM at 11 am to discuss matter with him, and again at 12.30 to discuss formal drafts of telegram from PM and from COS on same matter.

Afternoon had visit from the Duke of Gloucester and from Paget. The former is suggesting that I should give him some employment connected with me!! Bertie and Weeks came to dine, Dill still here.

The Duke of Gloucester suggesting that he might serve on my staff put me in a diffi-cult position, and I had to prevaricate. From what I had seen of him in France I knew that he would not have stood the pace, and that used as a personal assistant he would have acted as a permanent drag, which could not be countenanced. Fortunately he did not press the matter!

28 August

A short COS. At 12.30 went to pay visit to King, who discussed our trip to Moscow etc. We also talked about the death of the Duke of Kent, and the fact that he wanted me to find some form of employment for the Duke of Gloucester! This will not be very easy, however he no longer suggests a command. He was as usual perfectly charming. In the evening motored over to Chequers. Eisenhower, [US General Mark] Clark, Mountbatten, Pug Ismay, Anthony Eden and self made up party. After dinner we saw films, including a Walt Disney one! However did not get to bed till after 2 am.

29 August

At 11 am PM held conference to discuss North African enterprise in the light of latest USA message. Finally agreed that we should examine possibility of doing Casablanca, Oran and Algiers instead of Oran, Algiers and Bône. This is I think a much wiser plan and conforms much more to the USA outlook. The difficulty is that we shall require additional forces for it which can only be found by drawing on Pacific. This will not suit Admiral King. We shall have again to remind the Americans that Germany must remain our primary concern and that the defeat of Japan must take second place. Lunched at Chequers and returned to WO by 4 pm, where I worked till 8 pm, trying to work off some of the accumulation of work which has been collecting itself while I have been away.

30 August

Spent whole morning polishing off back work in the War Office. In afternoon took a walk and then went back to polish off last remnants at the WO. I can now start next week square again. PM called me up this evening convinced Rommel will attack tonight as he was keeping area clear with his fighters today.

31 August

A bad day!

Unsatisfactory COS at which I bit First Sea Lord, and felt depressed rest of day at having bitten a corpse!

The first 3 lines of this day's diary must never be published. Had I known how ill Dudley Pound was at that time I should of course never write like that. In any case the only excuse I can offer … is the fact that they were written at the end of a very long tiring day.

Called up at lunch and asked to have coffee at 2.30 pm with PM to discuss reply from Roosevelt. Said I could not as I was due at Millbank at 2.30 to treat elbow for arthritis. Went 12 Downing St at 3.30 to discuss President's telegram, which was almost unintelligible. At least two points stood out in it. First that Casablanca should be one port of entry. Secondly that Americans should act as vanguard and that British should only follow a month later! We argued with PM till about 5 pm, then went off for COS meeting with Eisenhower and Clark attending. Meeting lasted till 7.30 pm. We decided that Americans must do Casablanca, Oran and Algiers. British to follow up. That is if we are to adopt President's proposals. Lewin dined. After dinner another meeting under PM, attended by Attlee, Eden and Lyttelton. PM inclined to accept our proposals, Eden also, Lyttelton against it, Attlee no special opinion. In end PM decided draft wire in accordance with our proposals. Meanwhile plane to be held ready for possible departure for Washington! And as a background to it all news from the Middle East that Rommel has started his attack!! Not much news of it yet.

1 September

A short Chiefs of Staff till 11 am when we went to meet PM to discuss his proposed wire to President. Before going there Sir Charles Wilson (the PM's doctor) asked to see me. He told me that he had heard that the PM was thinking of going over to America to try and straighten out the North African attack. He said that the last time PM was in Washington he had had trouble with his heart and that he thought it very unwise for him to go. He asked whether I could not offer to go instead of him. I should be only too delighted to do so but as the problem is mainly a political one it is essential that some Cabinet Minister should come with me.

We discussed PM's reply from 11 am to 12.45 pm and made several minor alterations. Attlee, Oliver Lyttelton and Eden were there. PM's reply conceded to the President the fact that they were at liberty to take full responsibility for the expedition and to base their hopes on a political re-entry without the necessity of force. He pointed out however all the dangers and pressed for the inclusion of Algiers at any rate. PM seemed dejected, tired and depressed.

Lunched with Admiral Stark. Dill, Dudley Pound and Mountbatten also there. Then Selection Board meeting followed by interview with Paget concerning the removal of Marshall-Cornwall [Western Command]. Then visit from Sir Samuel Hoare on Spain and probable reactions to our reentry into North Africa. He painted a gloomy picture. It is very hard to maintain one's determination to carry out an operation when everybody keeps pouring into one's ear all the awful dangers one is likely to meet. It takes far more moral courage than anyone would believe to stick to one's plan and to refuse to be diverted.

Crerar came to dinner and gave me a very good account of the Dieppe raid and of its difficulties. The casualties were undoubtedly far too heavy – to lose 2,700 men out of 5,000 on such an enterprise is too heavy a cost.

2 September

Dill turned up at the COS to discuss the question of use of American aircraft in India. You and the young came to lunch and tea which was a great joy. In afternoon I had to go and see Amery with reference to Auchinleck, as he wanted to know what his future might be. Lord Milne, Adam and Portal came to dinner.

3 September

Arrived at COS to find that PM had just received President's reply to his wire! He had ordered
us to meet him 10 Downing St at 11 am. This was quite useless as the President's wire required examining with experts to arrive at implications. He kept us waiting till 11.15 then talked round the subject till 11.45 when Attlee, Eden and Oliver Lyttelton turned up. We then talked more hot air and at last I obtained leave to withdraw COS to consider the matter and report at 5 pm. We sent at once for Eisenhower and Clark and also for Ramsay. The new plan contemplated an assault force of some 34,000 at Casablanca, where the surf will probably render a landing impossible, and only 10,000 at Algiers, which is the key to the whole front. We concluded that the Casablanca landing must be cut by some 10 to 12 thousand to make Algiers possible. PM and ministers agreed, he then took me and Eisenhower to draft reply to President suggesting this change. He is sending Eisenhower, Ramsay and Mountbatten to Washington and asked me whether I thought I ought to go over. I said I felt that main difference rested on matter of shipping, assault craft and naval cover, that I did not feel I could assist much, especially so in view of the fact that Dill is also going back and can deal with the major points.

This day is a good example of the way Winston's impetuosity was apt to delay matters and waste one's time. If only he had given us time to consider this wire before meeting him we should not have wasted half the morning, nor would his time and that of Eden, Attlee and Lyttelton also [have] been wasted. We could easily have stated the time by which we should have been ready, much confusion would have been avoided and time saved. Unfortunately he always wished to stick his fingers into a pie before it was cooked!

4 September

We received rumours in the morning that the President would probably agree to our proposal except that he would only reduce the Casablanca attack by 5,000 men instead of 10 to 12 thousand. By the evening it looked as if I should be caught and fail to get off for my Saturday off! President's wire was reported to be coming in late that evening. Finally I escaped and went home feeling very weary!

5 September

Spent resting at home. Call from Nye and Special DR with copies of telegram from President brought me up to date. 'Torch' is now again in full swing and most difficulties have been overcome for the present. Meanwhile news from Alexander continues to be good. Rommel continues to retire.

6 September

Went to church in morning. Otherwise lazy day.

7 September

COS in morning of no great importance. Cabinet at 5.30 pm after which Grigg came to tell me of his troubles with Duncan Sandys [Financial Secretary] and Henderson [Under Secretary]. The two, apparently working together, consider they have not enough control of things. Meanwhile Sandys spends his time snooping about and reporting to PM! Grigg very upset. Dill back and dined in. After dinner had to go round to 10 Downing St to discuss PM's speech for tomorrow with him. Just back near 1 am!

Poor Grigg at that time was in a very unhappy state, and I do not wonder at it! It must be remembered that Duncan Sandys was Winston's son-in-law and is exceptionally ambitious. Rightly or wrongly, he was giving Grigg the impression that he was playing the role of a cuckoo bird, working to push Grigg out of the nest so as to replace him! I cannot say that I had formed any personal affection for Sandys. I would not have trusted him very far!

8 September

A fairly quiet day. We considered possibility of sending arms to Turkey at the COS. Not an easy matter considering how short we already are in Persia! You came to lunch which was a great treat. After lunch did Millbank and took you to Waterloo. Then returned to WO to interview Liddell to discuss with him advisability of closing down his job as Inspector General of Training. He agreed that it should lapse on October 21st.

Not much more news from Middle East. Rommel is now practically back to where he started from. My next trouble will now be to stop Winston from fussing Alex and Monty and egging them on to attack before they are ready. It is a regular disease that he suffers from, this frightful impatience to get an attack launched!

9 September

Started with COS at which we discussed possibility of getting more fuel into Malta, to assist in playing its part in future offensives. Fast minelayer *Welshman* seems only solution. At 12 noon went off to Abbey for memorial service for Duke of Kent. From there on to Dorchester for solitary *tête-à-tête* with Sikorski. He was charming as usual and very interesting about probable future intentions of Germans. According to him they will be satisfied with capture of Stalingrad and Grozny for 1942, and will not go on to Baku. They are organizing a large labour army to develop the Ukraine, and have every intention of rendering themselves self-supporting as regards grain and oil. They will withdraw large air forces for air attacks on this country during winter nights. Furthermore one of his agents from France is returning shortly with messages from Giraud [French General, prospective commander of Allied French forces after North African invasion], and he will invite me to meet him.

This evening Dill and I dined out with Admiral Stark in his flat. He was quite charming and evidently delighted with his flat, which he has just moved into. Dill is off back to America tomorrow. I shall miss him badly.

At 6 pm PM sent for me to 10 Downing Street. He was in a very good mood. Began by discussing prospects of North African venture being up to date, and if not of putting an extra PQ convoy to North Russia. Then went on to discuss the WO and the Political Under Secretaries, Croft, Sandys and Henderson. He considers Grigg does not give them enough scope. This is all produced, I think, by Sandys' underhand working and his reporting to father-in-law. It is all a very unhappy situation, and one under which P.J. Grigg may well be pushed out in the end. I should be very sorry, and sorrier still if Sandys were to replace him!!! It would be a desperate situation.

Of the two there was no comparison. P.J. had ten times the ability, but what was infinitely more important he was just as straight as they make them. Had Sandys succeeded in replacing P.J. I should have had no alternative but to resign.

We then went on to discuss the PM's desire to send out Hobart, in command of 11th Div, to North Africa, in spite of his being 57 years old and reported on by doctors and board as being a very doubtful medical case.

10 September

Madagascar attack of Majunga started this morning and appears to have been successful. Long argument in COS on question of command of air force in Iraq-Persia Command. Birley and wife came to lunch and I then went on for a final sitting. I think he improved picture a great deal. Ciriez came to dinner and I had long discussion with him about de Gaulle, Free French and those Frenchmen who do not wish to associate with him and yet want to go on fighting for France.

11 September

I had a busy day which finished off with a visit to Chequers. Eisenhower, Clark, Mountbatten, Leathers, Hollis, Rowan [secretary] and self. After dinner we had a film from 11 pm to 1 am and then sat from 1 am to 3 am!! arguing on the prospects of the North African attack and the reception which the Americans are likely to receive.

12 September

At 10 am we had a conference. Dudley Pound turned up back from Scotland, and Holmes (Transportation) also came. We discussed the likelihood of being able to carry out the North Africa attack before November 15th, and in that case the desirability of trying to put in an extra convoy to Russia before it. Many various facts to consider, danger to naval forces employed, thus rendering them possibly non-available to support North African venture. Secondly, result of locking up some 80 ships in Archangel during whole winter etc etc. PM as usual trying to get the last ounce out of the Naval forces and consequently wanting to run the convoy if possible. Left in time to get back for lunch and Adam lunched with me and we discussed difficulties which exist between that objectionable specimen Duncan Sandys and P.J. Grigg. It is gradually working to a climax. Sandys reports to PM that S of S is not giving him enough responsibility. PM then tackles Grigg who has no intention of pandering to Sandys, and rightly so too.

After lunch long interview with Paget on organization of Army Air Force. Paget has been got at by Sholto [Douglas] and is prepared to sacrifice all the work we have done of late to secure suitable air forces for the army! Next Bovenschen [Deputy Under Secretary at WO] came to discuss the Sandys-Grigg trouble! Wanted me to discuss with Army Councillors the suggested allocation of duties for Sandys and then put up proposal to S of S. I declined as I consider that this can only be done by S of S himself. Came home in evening.

13 September

Quiet day at home. Rollie, Stella and young [Charringtons] came to tea. Rosemary home [AB's elder daughter, then a subaltern in the ATS].

14 September

Dropped Rosemary on way up. Dull COS and equally dull Cabinet meeting. Had heated argument with S of S on air situation. He has evidently been got at by Paget!

15 September

A busy day! First a COS meeting at which I had a difference of opinion with CAS on subject of airborne forces. Then at 12.30 we went to meet the PM to discuss the possibility of capturing North Norway in January! He had promised something of this kind to Stalin in his last interview with him! Now he is trying to drive us into it. In my mind it is quite impossible at the same time as the North African expedition. Shipping alone will make it impossible. He would not agree and we had a difficult hour of it till 1.30 pm.

After lunch went to Millbank for my arm. At 3.30 pm Duke of Gloucester came to see me about job he is to be found at the WO! Not an easy job!! Then Mr [Walter] Lippmann an American Newspaper magnate [more a corre-spondent]. I gave him ½ hour. I then went on to see Anthony Eden to discuss with him the difficulties S of S is having with PM's son-in-law (Duncan Sandys). I told him that I feared Sandys was trying to replace S of S and that it would lead to chaos. Also told him that present situation would lead to S of S resigning if we did not watch it, and that we had already had 5!! Ss of S since the war started and could not go on changing. He was very nice and promised to help.

Finally dined out with Lucas (of Lucas Lights), and his wife, Mr and Mrs Nelson also there, Duncan, Minister of Supply and Admiral Stark all there.

The Grigg-Sandys situation had become so critical that I felt I must do something about it. I did not like to tackle PM directly owing to the close relationship with Sandys, so decided to consult Eden. He was most understanding and sympathetic and entirely appreciated our trouble. He said with a twinkle in his eye that he would do what he could with Winston short of accepting Sandys in the Foreign Office! I do not know what he did but the situation eased shortly after this interview, and it was not long before Sandys was moved away from the WO to the infinite relief of all of us.

16 September

A very difficult COS meeting deciding how to deal with the PM's present desire for a North Norway enterprise at the same time as the North African one! We have put it to the Joint Planners to prepare a case. I then lunched at Claridges – a gov[ernment] lunch for the Maharajah Jam Saheb of Nawanagar and Sir

Ramaswami Mudaliar. A dull lunch. I sat next to Duke of Devonshire and he was not very entertaining. At 7 pm PM sent for me to 10 Downing St where I found Eden, Cranborne [Dominions], First Lord and First Sea Lord. We discussed peace proposals from Cruet in Madagascar, or rather his wish to send plenipotentiaries. This took a long time and I did not escape until 8.30 pm! Bad as I had John Anderson and P.J. Grigg and their wives coming to dinner! They have just left and I must now prepare my speech for the opening of the photographic exhibition at Selfridges!!

17 September

A COS meeting mainly devoted to defeating Winston in his latest venture in North Norway! Then a visit to Mountbatten's Dieppe room. Hurried back to lunch at the flat where I had Sikorski and Kleber lunching. The latter just back from France, having had contacts with Giraud, Pétain, Laval etc. He was very interesting and may prove useful. Rushed off at 2.30 to Selfridges to open a photographic exhibition where I had to make a speech. Afterwards had interesting lunch with the Mayoress of Marylebone! Then back to WO to do some work and then on to 18 Kensington Gardens to a reception by the President of Poland. Back to WO again and finally to flat where I had Clark (USA General), Cranborne and Speed (Financial PUS) dining with me. I like Clark. He is a most charming personality. Speed always refreshing and Cranborne a delightful person to meet. Just been packing for my few days leave.

18 September

After the COS I drove round to Hendon with Barney and we flew to Catterick aerodrome. From there we went to Barnard's Castle to see the Infantry School and had tea there. Left there 6.30 and motored to Barney Charlesworth's grouse lodge.

19 September

Shot the far beat. Ronnie Stanyforth there. 60 brace. On returning to the house found message from PM that I was to go to nearest scrambler for telephone conversation! This turned out to be at Catterick aerodrome, about 15 miles away. When I got there found bad line and I could only just hear the PM. All he wanted was to know what my reactions had been to a wire he had received from Alexander putting off date of attack. As I had not seen the wire I had to have a copy sent up by the Contact Officer.

The above statement requires expounding slightly. As I returned rather weary from the day's shoot there was a note awaiting me asking me to call him up after 8 pm on the nearest scrambler. As this meant a 30 mile journey I called him up to find out if I might come at once instead of travelling through the night, which he agreed to. When I finally got through to him on the telephone and he asked me what I thought of

Alex's last message I replied, 'I have not seen it.' This met with grave disapproval, and he replied, 'You have not seen it? Do you mean to say you are out of touch with the strategic situation?' I replied, 'I told you I was going grouse shooting today, and I have not yet solved how I am to remain in touch with the strategic situation whilst in a grouse butt.' 'Well, what are you going to do about it now?' was his next answer, to which I replied, 'If you want to know what I think of Alex's wire, I shall have to have it sent up here tonight and shall let you know tomorrow.' Back came, 'How? Will you send a telegram? Have you got a cipher officer with you?' My temper was now beginning to get worn and I replied, 'No, I do not take a cipher officer to load for me when I go grouse shooting! I shall come back here tomorrow evening and continue this conversation with you on the scrambler when I have read Alex's wire.' This finished the conversation and I then had to get through to the WO to arrange for an unfortunate contact officer to be sent up to Darlington with a copy of the wire on his motorcycle.

The annoying part of the whole thing was that there was nothing in Alex's wire which could not easily have waited till I returned. It was very typical of him, he hated letting me go off without continually calling up for one reason or another to find out whether one still remained accessible. My Sundays at home were always subjected to a series of calls throughout the day, When shooting with Ivan Cobbold at Glenham he called me up at 1 am on some trivial matter. As the night telephone was beside Ivan's bed his wife had to turn out at this early hour so that I might, in a half-awake condition, have a talk with Winston as I sat shivering on the edge of Ivan's bed!

20 September
Sunday. Low mist and rain. Drove to Catterick aerodrome for another talk with PM. I had by then received a copy of the telegram and Alexander's reasons, which I thought were excellent. I told him so on telephone and thought he said that he agreed with me. As a matter of fact he sent a wire to Alex, I discovered afterwards, trying to make him hurry up! We lunched with people in Richmond and went for a walk in evening.

21 September
Blowing hard but no mist, very good day with bag of 150 brace.

22 September
Weather held up again but very windy. Two drives badly upset by wind. Total bag 66 brace. Left after dinner for Darlington and returned by night mail.

23 September
Started COS work with much reluctance. Found many troublesome things afoot! PM more set than ever on North Norway campaign, and now settled to send Andy McNaughton to Moscow! to start staff discussions with Stalin!

After lunch PM sent for me to discuss a reply wire he wanted to send to

Alexander. I tried to stop him and told him that he was only letting Alex see that he was losing confidence in him which was a most disconcerting thing before a battle. He then started all his worst arguments about generals only thinking of themselves and their reputations, and never attacking unless matters were a certainty, and never prepared to take risks, etc, etc. He said this delay would result in Rommel fortifying a belt 20 miles deep by 40 miles broad that we should never break through owing to a series of Maginot defences etc etc! I had a very unpleasant ¾ hour! However, I succeeded in getting a very definite tempering of the message. After dinner at 10 pm I was sent for again, this time about tanks for Turkey. We had a hammer and tongs argument which ended on friendly terms.

24 September

Another COS connected with the mission to Moscow to discuss North Norway attack! McNaughton now not for it! Apparently sent his staff officer by air to Canada to explain details of the attack! We had also further details from Joint Planners as to impossibility of carrying out operations in Feb. We therefore prepared minute for PM on the subject to be sent to him with McNaughton's letter. After lunch I ran Selection Board committee and was then sent for by PM. He had just received telegram from Canadian PM who stated that he did not think it advisable to send McNaughton to Moscow, and giving all the reasons for it! I asked him if he had yet seen McNaughton's letter. He said he had not, and I told him the contents of it. He then became very worked up about the whole show and in the end was very pathetic. He said this machine of war with Russia at one end and America at the other was too cumbersome to run any war with. It was so much easier to do nothing! He could so easily sit around and wait for work to come to him. Nothing was harder than doing things, and everybody did nothing but produce difficulties. He is a wonderful mixture, one never knows what mood he will be in next!

We then find him adopting the attitude that he was the only one trying to win the war, that he was the only one who produced any ideas, that he was quite alone in all his attempts, no one supported him. Indeed, instead of supporting him all we did was provide and plan difficulties etc etc. Frequently in this oration he worked himself up into such a state from the woeful picture he had painted, that tears streamed down his face! It was very difficult on those occasions not to be filled with sympathy for him when one realized the colossal burden he was bearing and the weight of responsibility he shouldered. On the other hand if we had not checked some of his wild ideas, heaven knows where we should be now!

Basil and Cynthia came to dine.

25 September

Expected to be sent for during the morning by the PM, but it was not till after

4 pm that the call came. Anthony Eden also sent for. He [Churchill] discussed alternatives as regards the Russians, and I think is giving up the idea of the North Norway attack! At any rate we hope so, but he may well return to the attack. Lunched with Adam at the Carlton Grill and went for a walk with him in St James's Park.

26 September

A short COS and an early start for home where I unfortunately found you all three the worse for wear for something you had eaten the previous evening.

27 September

Also followed suit and apparently ate the remainder of that self same something with sad results!

28 September

First fog of the winter. Long COS attended by Cater of Colonial Office and by Mr Rowntree, catering advisor to the Governor of Malta. He had sad tales about food situation in Malta! Somewhat of an alarmist. I do not think that he was examining the problem from a war point of view. Slaughtering cattle and horses had certainly not been taken fully into account in his calculations. In any case we must have a definite estimate of the situation from the Governor himself.

Cabinet at 5.30, with PM in quite good form. He is at last taking a firmer attitude towards Maisky's unpleasant remarks and criticism as to the handling of our naval forces.

29 September

COS at which we had interview with Admiral Miles back from Moscow. Also discussed difficult problem of providing adequate protection for Persia whilst at same time maintaining supplies to Russia. Also alarming information of loss of a Catalina [flying boat] between Lisbon and Gibraltar, and bodies washed up at Cadiz with letters in their pockets containing details of North African attack plans! Madagascar operation almost completed. Spent afternoon in the office battling with Portal's latest ideas for the policy of conduct of this war. Needless to say it is based on bombing Germany at the expense of everything else.

30 September

Main point of interest at today's COS was deciding whether we should approve of Wavell's plan to attack Akyab [Burma] this year. I don't like the idea of Akyab as an isolated operation without the full scale operation for Rangoon, Moulmein, etc, for which we are not yet strong enough.

During afternoon Hawkes and Lennox from MI5 came to see me with reference to a conversation between Kenneth de Courcy [founder of Imperial Policy Group] and Raikes which they had intercepted on a concealed microphone in their room. It went very near having discovered all about the North African attack, and evidently had been obtained from someone in possession of plans. They did not dare show it to Duff Cooper [Information], their legitimate boss, as they were uncertain how much he knew about this plan of attack. I discussed it with Pug Ismay and decided it was safe for Duff Cooper to see, but that he should let PM see the conversation.

At 7 pm had to go to 10 Downing St. Arrived there as de Gaulle was coming out, having just attended a memorable meeting with PM and Foreign Sec where he had adopted a very high handed attitude and the meeting had almost broken up in disorder!! We then discovered that he was due to broadcast at 8.15 pm!! BBC had to be called up by the PM and instructed to cut off broadcast at once if he departed from script! Then discussed desirability of even gaining one or two days in advance of Alexander's attack so that effect of this operation would have time to exercise its effects on Spanish opinion and make it easier to accept preparations for North Africa. PM very reasonable and handed over his draft telegram for us to adjust.

1 October

Whilst I was sitting with the COS I was sent for by PM. Found him in bed with Duff Cooper *(not both in bed!!)* who had just given him the intercepted conversation between Kenneth de Courcy and Raikes. To my horror Duff Cooper said that he suspected Kennedy (my DMO) had provided the information on secret operation which de Courcy referred to as having obtained from a 'Director of Plans'. PM asked me to look into the matter as soon as possible. I was lunching with Nelson and the Board of Directors of GEC so went on to look up Kennedy who is at present ill, in his flat. To my relief he said that he had only met de Courcy once, and that was whilst he was dining with Mackessie on June 23rd, and that so far as he could remember he had said nothing to him at that time. However, as June 23rd was before the operation discussed had even been planned, all was quite safe and Kennedy completely absolved. However we have still got to find the culprit – but that is Duff Cooper's job with his agents.

Long talk this evening with Paget about reduction of forces in this country and necessity to assess whether we are sufficiently insured against possible invasion next spring, unlikely as such an event may appear for the present.

2 October

Our COS meeting was again mainly taken up with discussing plans for the future feeding of Malta. The present supplies finish about the middle of October. Future supplies will depend on success of Middle East offensive and North African venture. If neither succeeds God knows how we shall keep Malta alive, and even so the timing of both these alternatives will inevitably run Malta very low before relief can come. Spent afternoon in WO working steadily from 3 pm to 8 pm without stopping. Then collected Cynthia and Henry [her son] to come and dine at the flat.

3 October

A short COS and a rapid afternoon's work followed by a dash home.

4 October

A lovely day, spent in collecting apples.

5 October

Mason-MacFarlane came again to the COS meeting where we discussed again placing of Gibraltar under command of Eisenhower during North Africa operation. Also discussed long paper prepared by Joint Planners on operations in 1943 in which they had badly missed the salient points of next year's strategy.

Cabinet meeting at 5.30 pm and a meeting at 10 pm under the PM for Portal, Sinclair, P.J. Grigg and self to discuss our Army Air support differences. Air Ministry have again gone back on their word. Having at last agreed to provide an Army Support Group they now propose to take it back again!! The meeting was a hopeless one at which Winston never began to understand what we were arguing about.

6 October

Another hard day. Started with a difficult COS meeting with a series of problems connected to the North African attack. Then lunched with Vincent Massey to meet Canadian Defence Minister [Ralston]. From there went on to Claridges to meet the King of Greece who had said he wanted an interview with me. I found all he wanted was that the liaison officer with the Greek Forces in the Middle East should be raised from a Lt Col to a Brigadier to raise the status of the Greek forces!!! Returned to WO for interview with Harker of MI5 about Kenneth de Courcy. He has now found that the culprit is one Hannon of the SOE who has been talking too freely. Then an interview with Stewart, Canadian Chief of Staff, who is anxious for Canadian forces to be given a more active role. At 6 pm Cabinet meeting to prepare reply telegram for Roosevelt with reference to supplies to Russia. A meandering meeting with little accomplished. Bed by 1 am.

7 October

COS again mainly occupied with North African attack and cooperation of Malta. Also defence of Iraq-Persia for next spring.

12.30 Cabinet meeting in the House, Winston away owing to a cold and Attlee in the chair. Discussions on draft telegram to Stalin, telling him that

North African operation may interfere with Northern Convoys and suggesting support by air in the Caucasus. Took lunch in car and went with DMI to see the institution engaged in assisting escapes of our prisoners and of codes to them [SOE training school, Beaulieu, New Forest?]. Also interrogation of German prisoners under special means with microphones and 'stool pigeons'. A very well run and interesting organization, under a live wire.

8 October
COS meeting at which we again considered final draft of telegram to Stalin. We also spent some time with the new German threat to put Dieppe prisoners in irons, owing to the tying together of prisoners' hands in the last raid. In the afternoon had interview with Ramsden just back from the ME and also with Hardinge who was arranging King's visits to formations about to proceed abroad. Informed that I had been appointed General ADC to King.

9 October
Finished off the COS meeting by 11.30!! Almost a record. Lunched out with the Mountbattens. Bullitt, the American Ambassador to France at the beginning of the war was there. I would not trust him very far! This evening Eisenhower, Riddell-Webster [?] and Kennedy came to dinner.

10 October
A fairly busy COS meeting. After lunch and some office work went to Staff College to give a talk on the world situation to all Army Commanders, Corps and Div Commanders of Home Forces. Talked for 1½ hours but for all that most of them were still listening at the end! Then had interview with Hobo [Hobart] about his not accompanying his div to North Africa owing to age.

11 October
Quiet day at home with you.

12 October
Early start as usual and for once a quiet Monday with short COS meeting and short Cabinet meeting in afternoon, perhaps mainly owing to the PM being away!

13 October
The PM turned up at 11 am in the middle of our COS meeting and wasted nearly an hour as he had nothing special to discuss and only wanted a general talk! We then had a visit from Cunningham the Admiral back from

Washington in anticipation of commanding naval forces in North African expedition. He gave us latest gossip about America and its varying moods.

In afternoon had interview with our Military Attaché, just back from Tokyo. He was very interesting on Japan and on the period leading up to the war. Dined with the PM in the Annexe. Eisenhower, Clark, [Bedell] Smith and Cunningham were there. Smuts who had just arrived from Cairo came in after dinner. He gave us the latest news from Egypt. We then discussed the North African operation in all its various aspects and its possibilities and limitations. Just back now in the flat after midnight, and must prepare brief on Airborne Division for tomorrow's Chiefs of Staff meeting.

14 October

Oliver Lyttelton attended our COS meeting and we discussed the date of his impending visit to USA and the points he was to discuss. The whole problem depends on our being able to complete the necessary information for him to proceed over there before some of their plans become crystallized out. At 12 noon Smuts came to WO to see me to discuss plans for the North African venture. In afternoon visits from Cory about Allied troops, followed by Porter, giving me Montgomery's plan for his attack against Rommel. At 5.30 Cabinet meeting to welcome Smuts. In evening Sholto Douglas, Ramsay and Bertie came to dinner.

This had been an important day as I had now received a detailed plan of Monty's attack and also probable date. He asked me to take every possible care that no details of this plan leaked out. As I had no confidence in Winston's ability to keep anything secret I decided not to tell him about this plan. I knew, however, that I should have difficulties as Winston was continually fretting to advance the date and asking me why we were not being informed of the proposed date of attack. I had to judge between the relative importance of maintaining complete secrecy and on the other hand of stopping Winston from wiring to Alex and Monty and upsetting their plans with his impatience.

15 October

At this morning's COS meeting we had Cunningham, [Kenneth] Anderson and Welsh in, the three service commandrs taking part in the North African expedition. We discussed with them various details connected with the expedition. After lunch Ralston (Defence Minister of Canada) with Vincent Massey and Stewart came to see me as regards the possible role of Canadian forces in 1943! Not an easy matter to lock them into any of our proposed offensives. Then Eisenhower came round to see me. I had asked him to come to discuss the directive to Anderson which had upset him, and also to find out what the arrangements were for the command of American troops in England after the departure of Eisenhower to Gib. He tells me that Hartle will be in command which does not fill me with joy as I am certain that he is useless!

The directive which had upset Ike was a copy of the usual directive given to any British Commander working under the order of an Allied C-in-C. It was the same as Douglas Haig had had during the 1914–18 war, the same Gort had had, and the same I had had. It was therefore quite easy to explain the wording he objected to and which I think we adjusted slightly to suit him.

This evening Strathcona, Cobbold, Peter Fleming and Mockler-Ferryman came to dine. I found Peter Fleming [author of *News from Tartary* etc, brother of Ian] most interesting about both Russians and Japanese and had a very long talk with him.

16 October
We again discussed various alternatives open to us in the event of Spain turning sour during the North African operation and decided to prepare special forces to deal with the various eventualities. Then discussed with Secret Service the raising of Special Forces in France to meet future eventualities. Then lunched 10 Downing St. PM in the very best of form. After lunch I gave him the details of dates and plans for Middle East attack which had been brought back by Porter. He seemed very pleased at date of attack having been put forward.

I had come to the conclusion that I should not be able to hold Winston and that in his impatience he would wire out to the Middle East and upset Alex and Monty at this critical juncture. He was in a good mood that day so I thought that if I told him I could impress on him the absolute importance of secrecy.

17 October
When I arrived at the Chiefs of Staff meeting I found Pug Ismay in one of his excited moods! He had received a telephone message from Eisenhower that the latter had received 3 telegrams from Marshall which affected the whole North African operation drastically. He was drafting a reply but considered that he would probably have to dicuss this reply with PM and COS. We did the ordinary work and at 12 noon I had to go back to meet Paget and McNaughton to discuss with them the provision of additional forces to attack the Canaries and Spanish Morocco should this become necessary. Return to COS at 12.30 to read Eisenhower telegrams. They were connected with Murphy's most recent activities in North Africa where he had begun to establish contacts with Giraud and with Darlan!! Murphy had suggested we should send representatives to discuss matters.* Proposal was to send Clark to state we were prepared to make Giraud

---

*Robert Murphy was US representative in North Africa with the rank of minister from 1941. He helped to establish contacts with the French forces in the area in an effort to aid the landings, and then became political advisor to Eisenhower during the campaign. Admiral François Darlan was a highly placed minister in the Vichy government, and an ardent collaborator with the Germans. They

Governor of North Africa with Darlan as Deputy Commander under Eisenhower. It is difficult to decide degree of authenticity of these reports. We must not give away plans prematurely, hence difficult situation. PM, Smuts and Eden returned from Chequers for meeting with COS at 4.30 pm to approve Eisenhower's telegram and to decide on plan of action for Clark. Left for home about 6 pm.

18 October

Quiet day at home.

19 October

Left 8 am, in WO shortly after 9 am. At COS arguments with Portal as regards expansion of Bomber Command at the expense of air forces operating with other services. Heated argument as usual, for once CNS sufficiently awake to support me!

Cabinet at 5.30 pm when I again approached Smuts and asked him to assist me with reference to [General] Cunningham and Godwin-Austen. I think that at last we may overcome Winston's objections to employing them again.

According to him these officers had failed in action, had proved themselves deficient of offensive spirit, should never be employed again and could indeed consider themselves lucky they were not being made a public example of as in the case of Admiral Byng!

20 October

A long COS meeting when I again had heated arguments with Portal concerning Airborne forces.

In afternoon had meetings with Paget and with Ralph Glyn. Dined with Oliver Lyttelton, who is stopping at the King's dug-out flat next to the Lansdowne Club with Portal. Quite an amusing dinner at which we discussed the future of Europe after the war!

21 October

During this morning's COS we had Eisenhower and Smith in to discuss final arrangements for North African campaign. All preparations seem to be going well. Clark arrived safely in Gib yesterday and proceeded on by submarine to establish contact with Murphy in North Africa. This evening dissipated myself,

---

replaced him with Laval in 1942. He was in Algiers when the Allies landed, and assumed command of the Vichy French forces opposing them. After arranging a ceasefire on 10 November, he agreed to work for the Allies, and was appointed High Commissioner for French North Africa. He was killed on Christmas Eve 1942 by a young French royalist, trained by, but not under the control of, SOE. He was replaced by General Henri-Honoré Giraud, who was already C-in-C of local Free French forces.

and took an evening off with Barney to go and see a play! It was *A Quiet Weekend* and most amusing.

22 October

I had been expecting that Monty's attack might start last night. Probably will be tonight instead.

A heated COS at which I had a hammer and tongs argument with Portal on the policy for the conduct of the war. He wants to devote all efforts to an intensive air bombardment of Germany on the basis that a decisive result can be obtained in this way. I am only prepared to look on the bombing of Germany as one of the many ways by which we shall bring Germany to her knees.

At 12 noon we went round to see PM to discuss the raising of 50 bomber squadrons before the end of the year at the expense of all the other squadrons. Then I discovered that Winston, after giving me a solemn undertaking that he would not tell anybody what I had told him about details of impending ME attack had calmly gone and told Eisenhower and [Bedell] Smith!! I rubbed his iniquity into him and he was very nice and repentant and said he would send for Eisenhower at once to impress necessity for secrecy on him. I then came back to WO to find that P.J. Grigg, the only other person I had told about it, had also gone and told DDMI [Deputy Director of Military Intelligence] and the Director of Public Relations!! It is absolutely fatal to tell any politician any secret, they are incapable of keeping it to themselves.

Lunched with St Clair and his wife at the Senior. They have got one son a prisoner in Germany.

Shall be lucky if I get through tonight without being called up by PM to ask how it is the ME attack has not started yet!

I had had great doubts as to whether Winston would keep his secret, and my doubts were not misplaced! The newspaper reporter in him was coming to the fore. News was not something to sit on, it must be cashed in on at once, even if that cash only meant importance. He had no reason whatever to tell Eisenhower, this attack did not concern him in the least at that moment, and what is more important, Ike's HQ was conspicuously leaky as regards information and secrets at that time.

23 October

Another long and difficult COS trying to arrive at agreement concerning future policy for the conduct of the war. We are getting a little nearer, but the divergence between Portal's outlook and mine is still very great. He is convinced that Germany can be defeated by bombing alone, while I consider that bombing can only be one of the contributory causes towards achieving that end. Mountbatten's half-baked thoughts thrown into the discussion certainly don't assist.

At 3.30 pm went to see Bruce who has received telegrams from Australia shouting for the 9th Australian Division from the Middle East. A bad moment just as the attack is starting!! This evening after dinner received call from War Office to say that Middle East attack had started! We are bound to have some desperately anxious moments as to what success is to be achieved. There are great possibilities and great dangers! It may be the turning point of the war, leading to further success combined with the North African attack, or it may mean nothing. If it fails I don't quite know how I shall bear it, I have pinned such hopes on these two offensives.

It may be remembered that just after taking on CIGS I had planned my policy for running the war. I wanted to clear North Africa, open the Mediterranean, threaten Southern Europe and at some later date liberate France. Since then we had had one blow after another. Japan had come in, we had lost HMS Prince of Wales *and* Repulse, *Hong Kong, Singapore, Rangoon, Burma, most of our Middle East gains, Cairo was threatened, our oil was threatened, India and Australia were also threatened. And at last we had been able to return to my original plans which were now greatly helped by the entry of America and their participation in the North African operation. The stage was now set, after much trouble, for a possible change in the tide of the war.*

Since our return from Cairo I had been inwardly eaten up with anxiety as to the results of this attack. The very fact that these feelings had to be kept entirely to myself had made them all the harder to bear. The waiting period was now over and we should now soon know the results. So much depended on it all, and I had such deep hopes of success, that I wondered how I should face failure should this be necessary. I knew well that the next few days would mean acute agony of expectation. The anxiety of watching a battle from a distance is far worse than being mixed up in the middle of it and absorbed by running it.

24 October
Left Hendon at 9.15 am and flew to Shrewton landing ground to watch demonstrations of A/T and A/A guns. Lovely day and good demonstrations. Lunched at RA Mess Larkhill after which I flew back to Odiham and arrived home for tea. Not much information of the attack come in.

25 October
A quiet day at home with 3 calls by PM to find out how the Middle East battle was getting on.

26 October
An early start for London, a hectic hour and a half briefing, and a long COS till 1.15 trying to knock our paper on future strategy into some shape. It is beginning at last to look a little better.

Then lunch with PM to listen to Clark's adventures in North Africa.

Eisenhower, Smith and Pound also there. Apparently Clark flew to Gib; as no rendezvous had yet arrived he went on by submarine and had the rendezvous wirelessed to him. Meeting point was signalled by lamp with white blanket behind it shining through window. Went ashore in canvas boat and upset by surf on landing. Met by Murphy, French Staff Officers and later by command- ing French General. All contacts most favourable and every chance of Giraud coming over! Meeting interrupted by police. Clark and his companions hid in wine cellar when one of them, a British captain, started coughing fit! Clark asked him if chewing gum would help him and gave him bit out of his own mouth!! After a bit the captain asked for more. Clark said he hoped he hadn't swallowed it. The captain said, 'No, but the bit you gave me has not got much taste!' Clark replied, 'That is not surprising, as I have been chewing it for two hours'!!! The party then had a desperate time getting back again and were nearly drowned, the boats being swamped repeatedly. However, trip was a great success.

Cabinet at 5.30 pm and after that dined in Naval mess Greenwich at dinner for Smuts, where he made a very good speech.

27 October

Another long COS meeting with many items. First Sea Lord more sound asleep than ever! Lunched with Hugh Elles and listened to his work in the bombing of Exeter and Bath during the last 6 months. In afternoon Morgenthau [US Treasury Secretary] came to see me before returning to USA. I found him an attractive personality. He seemed to be impressed with the fact that war was going better than he had imagined before he came over here. Long interview with MS discussing various appointments for Selection Board tomorrow.

Dined with Churchills, Mrs Roosevelt, her secretary, Lady Limerick, Dame [Rachel] Thornhill, one other lady, Brendan Bracken and self. After dinner PM kept me on to discuss Middle East operations and a telegram he was sending to Gort to tell him he was putting him up for Field Marshal from January. He also showed me answer he had written to P.J. Grigg and told me he was prepared to accept his resignation if he sent it in. This was in answer to last letter P.J. had sent in. The whole trouble emanated from Duncan Sandys. I fear the worst as P.J. is not gifted with overmuch tact in these matters. It will be a great mistake to have him out. He is, I think, the best S of S we have had for some time.

28 October

An unpleasant day. Started with a long COS at which we examined future policy in Mediterranean. Then had interview with Craigie, late Ambassador in Tokyo. He was very interesting in his views about the Japanese, their powers of resistance, etc. Finished at 1.15 pm.

At 3 pm a most futile Army Council meeting at which we discussed points such as saluting, polishing brass, provision of officers, etc. Finished at 5 pm and went straight on with Selection Board meeting till 6.30 pm. I had to go to

10 Downing Street for a meeting under PM at which we discussed Oliver Lyttelton's paper on the proposed discussion with Americans next week. Finally finished at 8 pm and collected all the day's work to do after dinner.

29 October

Before I got up this morning I was presented with a telegram which PM wanted to send to Alexander! Not a pleasant one and brought about purely by the fact that Anthony Eden had come round late last night to have a drink with him and had shaken his confidence in Montgomery and Alexander, and had given him the impression that the Middle East offensive was petering out!!

During COS, just while we were having the final interview with Eisenhower, I was sent for by the PM and had to tell him fairly plainly what I thought of Anthony Eden's ability to judge a tactical situation at this distance!

Then at 12.30 we had a COS meeting under PM attended by Smuts, Attlee, Eden and Oliver Lyttelton. Here again the whole question of the Middle East situation was raised. Eden made a statement as to his worst fears. I refuted this statement and the PM then turned to Smuts who (thank God) said, 'You are aware, Prime Minister, that I have had no opportunity of discussing this matter with the CIGS, but I am in entire agreement with all the opinions he has expressed!!' This settled the situation, and I was very grateful to him.

During afternoon I had interviews with Dobbie [Governor Malta], the Greek Deputy Prime Minister and Anderson prior to his departure on his new venture. At 5.30 pm Cabinet meeting to discuss Oliver Lyttelton's expedition to America. Dined with Bertie, Ivan Cobbold there. Afterwards had to go to PM at 11.30 pm. He had specially good intercept he wanted me to see and was specially nice. Referring to Middle East he said, 'Would you not like to have accepted the offer of Command I made to you, and be out there now?' I said , 'Yes', and meant it. And he said, 'Smuts told me your reasons, and that you thought you could serve your country best by remaining with me, and I am very grateful for this decision.'! This forged one more link between him and me! He is the most difficult man I have ever served with, but thank God for having given me the opportunity of trying to serve such a man in a crisis such as the one this country is going through at present.

When I went to see Winston, having been sent for from the COS meeting, I was met by a flow of abuse of Monty. What was <u>my</u> Monty doing now, allowing the battle to peter out (Monty was always <u>my</u> Monty when he was out of favour!). He had done nothing now for the last three days, and now he was withdrawing troops from the front. Why had he told us he would be through in seven days if all he intended to do was to fight a half hearted battle? Had we not got a single general who could even win one single battle? etc, etc. When he stopped to regain his breath I asked him what had suddenly influenced him to arrive at these conclusions. He said that Anthony Eden had been with him last night and that he was very worried with the course the battle was taking, and that neither Monty nor Alex was gripping the situation and showing a true offensive spirit. The strain of the battle had had its effect on me, the anxiety was growing more and more intense each day and my temper was on edge. I felt very angry with Eden and asked Winston why he consulted his Foreign Secretary when he wanted advice on strategic and tactical matters. He flared up and asked whether he was not entitled to consult whoever he wished! To which I replied he certainly could, provided he did not let those who knew little about military matters upset his equilibrium. He continued by stating that he was dissatisfied with the course of the battle and would hold a COS meeting under his Chairmanship at 12.30 to be attended by some of his colleagues.

At 12.30 we met and he turned to Eden and asked him to express his views. To which Anthony said that he considered that Monty was allowing the battle to peter out, that he had done nothing for the last three days and that now he was withdrawing formations to the rear. I was then asked by Winston what my views were. I replied that the Foreign Secretary's view of the battle must have been very superficial if he had come to the conclusions he had just expressed. He had said that during 3 days Monty had done nothing; he had therefore evidently failed to observe that during that period Monty had withstood a series of determined counterattacks delivered by Rommel, none of which had made any head way. During that period Rommel had therefore suffered very heavy casualties, all of which played an important part in securing ultimate success in this battle. And again, I said since the Foreign Secretary had been a Staff Captain in the last war he must be familiar with administrative matters. (Winston was always drawing my attention to the fact that Eden had been a Staff Captain and therefore familiar with military matters!) Had he not observed that Monty's attack had advanced the front several thousand yards, did he not remember this entailed a forward move of artillery and the establishment of new stocks of ammunition before another attack could be staged? Finally the Foreign Secretary accused Monty of withdrawing formations. Had he forgotten that the fundamental principle of all strategy and tactics lay in immediately forming new reserves for the next blow? I then went on to say that I was satisfied with the course of the battle up to the present and that everything I saw convinced me that Monty was preparing for his next blow.

We have seen in the diary how fortunate I was to have Smuts' full support. The flow of words from the mouth of that wonderful statesman was as if oil had been poured on the troubled waters! The temperamental film-stars returned to their tasks – peace reigned in the dove cot!

Personally however I was far from being at peace. I had my own doubts and my own anxieties as to the course of events, but these had to be kept entirely to myself. On returning to my office I paced up and down, suffering from a desperate feeling of loneliness. I had, during that morning's discussion, tried to maintain an exterior of complete confidence. It had worked, confidence had been restored. I had then told them what I thought Monty must be doing, and I knew Monty well, but there was still just the possibility that I was wrong and that Monty was beat. The loneliness of those moments of anxiety, when there is no one one can turn to, have to be lived through to realize their intense bitterness.

30 October

We finally finished off our policy for the conduct of the war in 1943 at this morning's COS. You and the children came to lunch and we went to the [Royal] Academy to see my portrait by Birley. I am afraid it was a boring afternoon for Miss Pooks and Mr Ti, but I had two very deliciously clammy little hands grasping my hands tightly as we walked through the rooms, and I could feel tiny electric impulses registered through those dear hands that they felt they were not in an altogether friendly atmosphere!

During afternoon I had interviews with Arnold, Military Attaché in Turkey, Alan Cunningham to arrange for his future appointment, and the DGAMS [Director General Army Medical Services] to discuss malaria in various theatres, and its cure now that quinine is running short. Finished up with dinner party run by Barney which was good value.

31 October

Adam came to lunch and brought Harding [possibly future FM Sir John Harding] along with him. It was some time since we had had a lunch together and we had a good deal to discuss. I finished off early and was home for tea, bringing rabbits with me for P and T!

1 November

Poured with rain all day, most of which we spent indoors.

2 November

Made an early start on a very cold day. At COS meeting we were informed that Murphy had been suggesting that date for North African operation might be put forward 14 days. This may have been to meet Giraud's request, we know not, but whatever it may be it is quite impossible. Most of the first flight convoys have now all started and there is no going back. We had a memorable lunch at 10 Downing St, PM, Smuts, Eisenhower, Clark, Smith, Pound, Portal, Mountbatten and self. It was to bid Eisenhower and Clark farewell, for they are off tonight.

During afternoon wire arrived stating Monty had attacked again with New Zealanders and 151st and 152nd Inf Bdes. Usual Cabinet meeting at 5.30 pm.

3 November

Made an early start and motored down to Andover to visit Airborne Division. Started with inspection of Border Regiment, a first class show and a real workmanlike organization for an airborne battalion. Then proceeded to lunch in Syrencot House, the HQ of the division. This brought back many memories of 3 of the happiest years of my life. After lunch inspected Parachute Bn, grand lot of men, and then representative groups from all the units. Was also shown method of loading gliders, ambulance and RE organization, etc. After tea was shown glider using parachute to allow of steeper descent. Also had a trip in a Wellesley aircraft fitted with 'Rebecca', a new homing system for finding objectives. I was then taken in a Horsa glider pulled by an Albermarle from Netheravon to Shrewton. A delightful and most inspiring trip. Finally watched a night landing by Hotspurs. Came away more convinced than ever that there is a great future for airborne forces.

Whilst at lunch I was called up by DMI and informed of two recent intercepts of Rommel's messages to GHQ and Hitler in which he practically stated that his army was faced with a desperate defeat from which he could extract only remnants! Motored back to Ferney Close after midnight.

4 November

Very foggy drive up to London. Took 1¾ hours! Sent for by PM at 10.20 am to show me an intercept of Hitler saying to Rommel that he was to hold on and that his men should select between 'death and victory'. PM delighted. At 3.30 pm he sent for me again to discuss prospect of ringing church bells. I implored him to wait a little longer till we were quite certain that we should have no cause for regretting ringing them. More good reports from Alex during afternoon. At 11 pm sent for again by PM who was busy dictating messages to Roosevelt, Stalin, Dominions, Commanders, etc. He was in great state of excitement. Anthony Eden came in later, also Brendan Bracken who was mainly interested in results of American election which has gone badly for Roosevelt. But PM refused to be depressed by this!

The Middle East news has the making of the vast victory I have been praying and hoping for! A great deal depends on it as one of the main moves in this winter's campaign in North Africa. Success in Libya should put Spaniards and French in better frame of mind to make Torch a success. And if Torch succeeds we are beginning to stop losing this war and working towards winning it! However, after my visit to Cairo and the work I had done to put things straight, if we had failed again I should have had little else to suggest beyond my relief by someone with fresh and new ideas! It is very encouraging at last to begin to see results from a year's hard labour.

5 November

News continues to be good and Monty has now got the whole of Rommel's army on the move: as they are very short of both transport and petrol he has chances of a tremendous haul. If only luck will be really kind to us!

The North African preparations are going well, and so far have not created too much excitement amongst Spaniards, French and Germans! I had never hoped we should get off with it so quietly.

Eisenhower left this morning, and tonight the submarine should pick up Giraud to convey him to Gibraltar. A great deal of history will be written one way or another during the next week!

6 November

Our Chiefs of Staff meeting was mainly concerned with the final arrangements for the North African landings. We were again mainly concerned with the probable Spanish reaction. At 12.30 we were called to a meeting under the PM to discuss most recent telegram from Sam Hoare in which he stated a certain uneasiness prevailed in Madrid as to our probable future action. They knew a hammer was about to fall, but where? If it fell in French Morocco this might well cause native uprisings which would spread to Spanish Morocco. They therefore hoped no such action was contemplated. We were not certain that these manoeuvres were paving the way for a move into French Morocco to the Sebou River!

Middle East news continues to be excellent, and chances of driving Rommel out of Africa are excellent. Lunched with old General Laurence, picking up Bertie on the way. In evening motored to Glenham, taking Bertie out in order to shoot with Ivan Cobbold on Saturday.

7 November

Pouring with rain in morning, which rather spoiled our shoot, but fine evening. Very jolly shoot with just Bertie, Ivan, Barney and self. Motored back here in evening arriving 9 pm, and have been dealing with the day's papers since dinner. All preparations for North Africa proceeding according to plan and with very little interference. It is quite unbelievable that things should have gone so well up to date. It is a great gamble for a great stake, and I pray God that it may come off!!

The Middle East victory should be of great assistance in influencing public opinion in our favour. Giraud was reported this evening as having landed at Gibraltar in his submarine. He should be a great contribution to this venture, and may ultimately assist us in solving the de Gaulle 'impasse'.

8 November

This morning the landings at Casablanca, Oran and Algiers, or rather in the vicinity of these places, were carried out almost like clockwork. They met, however, with considerable opposition in places and this opposition has not yet been overcome by any means. Giraud also turned sour and apparently refuses to play unless he is given supreme command of all forces, and liberty to use them as he wishes. As one of his intentions appears to be to re-enter France with them, it is pretty clear that such a plan is for the present quite impossible. However I am afraid that his personal vanity may well upset some of our schemes!!

Meanwhile Monty goes on gaining ground and has I think by now driven Rommel back across the frontier. I remained up here [in London] today and did not go home for my usual Sunday at home. The coming week will be a busy one.

9 November

News of Middle East continues to be very good. That of North Africa on the whole good, but there are still some dangerous moments in the operation. A lot depends on the extent to which Giraud will succeed in swinging over the military opinion in North Africa. At any rate Spain is keeping wonderfully quiet. Long Cabinet this evening which lasted till 8.30 pm, at which Winston revelled over our success! But did not give the Army quite the credit it deserved. However he did finish up by suggesting that the Cabinet might congratulate the CIGS and the S of S for the fine performance put up by the Army.

I think this is the only occasion on which he expressed publicly any appreciation or thanks for work I had done during the whole of the period I worked for him.

10 November

North African news continues to be puzzling! Giraud, Clark and Anderson are now all in North Africa in Algiers. Yesterday Giraud looked like giving trouble and of being unable to see the larger picture through his own personal pride. The fighting at Oran continued throughout the morning. This evening we received news that Darlan had signed a separate peace with Clark, and that he was issuing orders for fighting to stop throughout Africa! Meanwhile the Germans have started to land forces in Tunisia by air. There seem great hopes of possibly achieving our objectives of ultimately clearing North Africa of Germans. PM sent for me this evening while he was dressing for dinner to make certain we were taking all necessary steps to take advantage of this situation.

Lunched at Mansion House. PM made very good speech and in referring to good war news he said: 'This must not be considered as the end, it may possibly be the beginning of the end, but it is certainly the end of the beginning.'!!

11 November

Nasty foggy morning. At 9.50 I deposited wreath of the Army Council at the Cenotaph. PM then sent for me. I could not quite make out why as he did not want anything special, but only wanted to be assured that we were pushing on as fast as possible in the Middle East and remembering the urgency of Malta. Lunched with Adam at the Carlton Grill. Desperate heavy fog came on in the evening, making it impossible for any traffic to move! Consequently had to walk home.

Events moving fast. Germany now invading unoccupied France, Fleet moved out from Toulon, Oran and Casablanca now captured. But Germans landing airborne forces in Tunisia. We have moved to Bougie and making all preparations for early push eastward by land, sea and air. Meanwhile political side in the balance. Giraud has not moved and Darlan remains an unknown factor.

12 November

The situation has not unfolded itself much during the day. Rommel is no doubt in a very bad way and retiring about as fast as he can. Meanwhile Mussolini abuses him for abandoning Italian troops! On the other side the Germans are occupying France and Corsica fast, and endeavouring to build up a bridgehead in Tunisia. We are rushing troops over as fast as is possible to evict them out of it.

Lunched with Sir John and Lady Anderson. I like him and always feel he is quite one of the best in the Cabinet.

13 November

We had General [Bedell] Smith (Chief of Staff to Eisenhower) in to the COS to discuss the problem of organizing future offensive against Sardinia, and to estimate the repercussions on our very limited shipping. Lunched with Lord Kemsley (Editor of the *Sunday Times*). Attended Army Council meeting in the evening.

14 November

Left early (7.45 am) with Barney. Picked you up on the way and went on to Preshaw to shoot. Lovely day, and unbelievable joy to be away from the WO and work! Motored back to Ferney Close in evening.

15 November

Left Ferney Close at 9 am and motored over to Chequers where I attended conference at 11 am on future strategy in the Mediterranean. PM presided, and attended by Smuts, Eden, Leathers, CNS, CAS, CCO, Pug and me. We lunched there and then had a second meeting with Smith and Humfrey Gale there. Most of the discussion centred on the advisability of letting Darlan take charge of the French in North Africa. Eden opposed. PM for it. In any case, no alternative for the present. After the meeting motored back to Ferney Close where I arrived at 5.30 pm after a puncture.

16 November

Left usual early hour, in WO by 9.10 am. Lots to read before COS. Then difficult COS till 1 pm, correcting PM's directive on strategy. Lunched Dorchester, alone with Sikorski, as usual quite charming and full of congratulations on our recent success. Walked back to WO to put in crammed work from 3 to 6 pm. Then Cabinet meeting 6 to 8 pm at which I had to do much of talking explaining military situation. After dinner COS meeting again at 9.30 to 10 pm, followed by Defence Committee meeting from 10 pm to 12.15 am, still discussing Mediterranean strategy, which is now fairly clear.

17 November

A fairly short COS meeting and a Selection Board meeting in the afternoon were the main items today. Was told on the 7 am News that I had been promoted to Knight Grand Cross of Order of Bath [GCB] for work done in connection with North African campaigns. Not much more news from either front.

18 November

COS at which we discussed Portal's plan for the air attack of Germany. Then collected the Wilkinsons for lunch, and met you on door step. Dined with Copper at the Senior. Not much news from either front. Tunis advance progressing rather slowly and Monty delayed by administrative problems. On the other hand from secret sources it is plain that Rommel is at present in a very bad state, lacking reinforcements, tanks, ammunition, transport and petrol. Unfortunately we are not in a position to take full advantage of his condition. By the time Monty has overcome his administrative difficulties the situation will no longer be so rosy.

19 November

COS mainly concerned with support Malta could be expected to give operations directed against Tunis. All dependent on convoy to Malta arriving safely and being unloaded. After lunch had to go round to see Field Marshal Smuts at Hyde Park Hotel with reference to mechanization of SA force in the Middle East. Afterwards McNaughton came round to discuss organization of Canadian forces to fit in with their probable role in 1943. News from Tunisia rather sticky, only hope Anderson is pushing on sufficiently fast. Benghazi looks like being captured within next 24 hours.

20 November

Malta convoy of 4 ships arrived safely, thank God. This puts the island safe again for a bit. Benghazi was also evacuated by Rommel. Attacks against Tunis and Bizerta not going quite as fast as I should like, and reinforcements of Germans and Italians arriving fairly freely. Discussed with the Chief Administrative Officers the gradual build up of American forces in this country and the tendency to stop the build up after completing the first 5 divisions! Adam came to lunch with me. Quiet evening with few interruptions.

21 November

Usual COS followed by a Cabinet meeting at 12 noon to discuss the proposed agreement between Eisenhower and Darlan. As far as I could see there is at present nothing to do but to accept the Darlan situation and get on with pushing the Germans out of Tunisia. And yet Anthony Eden was for further delays and wasted a long time before Winston finally got some form of general agreement. Went home in the evening.

22 November
Very happy restful Sunday at home with you three.

23 November
Arrived back in WO just after eight following a very cold drive up. Masses of situation wires, maps and briefs to look through before 10.30. Then COS till lunch. After lunch series of interviews to stop me preparing statement for Cabinet on week's fighting. 5.30 to 7.30 Cabinet at which I had to make long statement. Then ½ hour before dinner and 1 hour after dinner all out trying to do day's files. Finally 10 pm to 12.45 am meeting with PM to discuss telegram about return of 9th Aust Div and NZ Division, convoys to Russia, sending of aircraft carriers to Pacific, etc. Operations in Tunisia not going as fast as they should and on the other hand Monty's pursuit of Rommel badly delayed by weather. As a result Rommel given more time than I like to re-establish himself.

24 November
Finished my COS fairly early. After lunch hair cut and then went to see map producing department. Pound, Croft and Kennedy came to dinner. Am still very worried with slow rate of progress in Tunisia, in spite of long report from Eisenhower.

It must be remembered that Eisenhower had never even commanded a battalion in action when he found himself commanding a group of armies in North Africa! No wonder he was at a loss as to what to do, and allowed himself to be absorbed in the political situation at the expense of the tactical. I had little confidence in his having the ability to handle the military situation confronting him, and he caused me great anxiety.

25 November
A very difficult and long COS at which we tried to clear up future operations in the Mediterranean. The first thing that requires deciding is the organization of control of operations, namely the High Command. It is quite one of the most tricky problems I have met. You then came up for lunch. After that I had an interview with General Gentilhomme, who annoyed me with a very narrow outlook on the war. I then had Lord Rennell [Civil Affairs Administration] on the political situation in Madagascar, where he had just returned from. He backed up all my views as to the unpopularity of the de Gaullists. At 5.30 I had to go to 10 Downing Street to discuss Alexander's operations with him. Then

dinner party with Mountbattens, Strathcona, and Diana Charlesworth. Finally meeting with PM attended by [Bedell] Smith just back from Tunisia to discuss future clearance of North Africa and operations for it.

26 November
Escaped COS this morning and went to Staff College to deliver lecture instead. Then lunched with you and from there to Buckingham Palace to attend reception for American officers. No official news from Tunisia, but the intercepts point to operations proceeding successfully. Kesselring [German commander, North Africa] states that he has insufficient forces to hold both Tunis and Bizerta and wonders which he should hold, since neither of them individually can achieve much. If this is correct there should be a chance of pushing him into the sea before long.

27 November
Again long discussions at the COS concerning problems of command in the Mediterranean. There is I feel no solution except an Allied Command in North Africa under a Supreme Commander (Eisenhower) and the present arrangements of a trinity in the Eastern Mediterranean with a dividing line through Tripoli-Tunis frontier prolonged to Corfu so as to include Malta. Unfortunately Portal wishes to have unified air command from Gibraltar to the Indian frontier!! Quite impossible. Afternoon interview with de Gaulle at 3.30, which went off quite well and he was quite pleasant and did not allude to Darlan! He was only preoccupied with cooperation with Leclerc [Free French Commander] who is coming up from Lake Chad area into Southern Tripoli. Army Council meeting in the evening.

28 November
A short COS which allowed me to fit in a good deal of work before lunch. Lunched with Adam at the Carlton Grill, walked back through park, and then finished off work quickly so as to come home for a late tea.

29 November
A very happy peaceful Sunday with you.

30 November
Good run up followed by hectic period of briefing and of examination of most recent telegrams.

COS at which we examined most recent ideas of PM for a re-entry into the Continent in 1943, and where he is again trying to commit us to a definite plan of action. After lunch interview with S of S on new proposed manpower cuts of PM. He never faces realities, at one moment we are reducing our forces, and the next we are invading the Continent with vast armies for which there is no hope of finding the shipping. He is quite incorrigible and I am quite exhausted!

Cabinet from 5.30 pm to 8 pm and now we are off for another meeting with him from 10.30 to God knows when, to discuss more ambitious and impossible plans for the reconquest of Burma!

It is now 1 am and I am just back from our meeting. With today I complete my first year as CIGS, not that I think I shall complete a second one! Age or exhaustion will force me to relinquish the job before another year is finished. It has been quite the hardest year of my life, but a wonderful one in some ways to have lived through! I had only been in the saddle one week when Japan came into the war, and by the end of the third week I thought I was finished and that I could never compete with the job! Then disaster followed disaster and politicians under those circumstances are never easy people to handle. At times life was most unpleasant. The PM was desperately trying at times but with his wonderful qualities it is easy to forgive him all. A hard taskmaster, and the most difficult man to serve that I have ever met, but it is worth all these difficulties to have the privilege to work with such a man. And now, at last the tide has begun to turn a little, probably only a temporary lull and many more troubles may be in store. But the recent successes have had a most heartening effect and I start a new year with great hopes for the future.

1 December

First day of a new year! Long COS where I had a difference of opinion with the CAS as to command of air forces in the Mediterranean. Then interview with Russian Military Attaché after lunch, followed by Honours Selection Board. Finally another Cabinet of 2 hours on manpower and necessary cuts. Then an anniversary dinner party to commemorate end of first year as CIGS.

2 December

After COS went to Palace at 12.15 for investiture of GCB. King was as usual perfectly charming and most interested in the war. I was there for about ¾ hour giving him details of the war.

After lunch had visit from General Catroux [C-in-C Free French in Levant], found him very helpful and full of the better sentiments of cooperation between various French factions. I feel now that there is some hope of French amalgamation to defeat Germany and free France. This evening dined with Kennedy and his new wife, a delightful couple.

3 December

COS meeting at which we were faced with a new paper written by the PM, again swinging back   towards a western front during 1943!! After having repeatedly said that North Africa must act as a 'springboard' and not as a 'sofa' to future action! After urging attacks on Sardinia and Sicily he is now swinging away from these for a possible invasion of France in 1943! Lunched with de Gaulle, he was on the whole in a good mood but very bitter against Darlan. Catroux, Gentilhomme, etc were also lunching there.

In the evening, 5.30 pm meeting of COS with PM, Attlee, Eden, Leathers. Long harangue by the PM that army must in 1943 fight German army! However, after proving to him small forces that might be made available, inclined to agree that we might perhaps do more in the Mediterranean, unless there are signs of great weakness in Germany. This evening Bertie, Basil and Ivan Cobbold came to dinner.

At that afternoon meeting after saying that the Army would have to fight the German Army in 1943, he said, 'You must not think that you can get off with your "sardines" (referring to Sicily and Sardinia) in 1943, no – we must establish a western front, and what is more we promised Stalin we should do so when in Moscow.' To which I replied, 'No, we did not promise!' He then stopped and stared at me for a few seconds, during which I think he remembered that if any promise was made it was during that last evening when he went to say goodbye to Stalin, and when I was not there! He said no more . ...

4 December

COS meeting at which we once again examined PM's recent swing round to invasion of France instead of Mediterranean operations. After lunch had to go round to see Amery, who had letter from Viceroy about Auchinleck and his future. He is apparently becoming somewhat restless. Military Members meeting of Army Council in evening. News from Tunisia not too good today, and I don't like much the way things are going there.

5 December

A fairly short COS at which we laboured with the difficulties of arriving at a settlement over Dakar with Boisson [Governor General West Africa] without de Gaulle handing over Vichy prisoners in exchange for our prisoners held by Dakar. In evening came home.

6 December

Quiet and very happy Sunday at home.

7 December

A quieter Monday than usual. Situation in North Africa none too good. Eisenhower far too busy with political matters connected with Dakar and Boisson. Not paying enough attention to the Germans, who are making far too much progress and will now take a great deal of dislodging out of Tunis and Bizerta! Cabinet at 5.30.

8 December

Finished off COS fairly early. We were busy deciding line of action to adopt in order to influence the PM to abandon ideas of invasion of France in 1943 for more attractive prospects in the Mediterranean.

You came to lunch and we also went to a play followed by supper at the flat. A *very* happy day.

9 December

Clark Kerr, Ambassador in Moscow, came to see me this evening and I had a long talk with him.

He corroborates all my worst fears, namely that we are going to have great difficulties in getting out of Winston's promise to Stalin, namely the establishment of a western front in 1943! Stalin seems to be banking on it, and Clark Kerr fears a possible peace between Hitler and Stalin if we disappoint the latter. Personally I cannot see such a settlement. Stalin is just beginning to get the better of the Boche and would only accept a settlement entailing restoration of old frontiers plus Baltic States, plus share of Balkans, plus many guarantees for the future which Germany cannot give. On the German side, Germany cannot carry on without grain from Ukraine and oil from Caucasus plus oil from Rumania. I therefore feel that the danger of a peace between Russia and Germany is mainly useful propaganda from either side to secure their own ends!

10 December

Short COS at which we discussed Winston's new project of making battleships and aircraft carriers out of ice!! After lunch Paget came for a long interview connected with a change of role of Home Forces from a defensive role to an offensive one. Also use of tank searchlights in landings. Then Admiral Stark came round to discuss world situation before returning to America to see the President. Little news from North Africa during the last two days.

11 December

A very short COS followed by a Cabinet meeting at 11.30 on manpower cuts. It was more peaceful than I had expected. The possible future reduction of 4 divisions was accepted more easily than I had expected. After the meeting he called me up to discuss the rescinding of one of our ACIs [Army Council Instructions] connected with shoulder badges. He has been behaving like a child in this connection and has been wasting a lot of our time.

This evening received wire from Dill, giving insight into Marshall's brain:

apparently he considers we should close down operations in the Mediterranean once we have pushed Germans out, and then concentrate for preparing for re-entry into France, combined with a move through Turkey. I think he is wrong and that the Mediterranean gives us far better facilities for wearing out German forces, both land and air, and of withdrawing strength from Russia.

12 December
Left London early. Picked you up and we went to shoot with Ronnie. A lovely day.

13 December
A quiet day at home.

14 December
Gave Rollie a lift up to London. Then COS meeting to settle future policy paper which we propose to send to PM in which we disagree with his paper. Tomorrow evening we have to discuss it with him.

Lunched with John Anderson, Duke of Alba (Spanish Ambassador), the Jam Saheb, Lord Portal and two others. Cabinet at 5.30 at which Winston was troublesome about the strength of rear troops in Tunisia. Then dined with Cranborne, who had two Americans, Sir John Simon, Brendan Bracken and one other dining there.

15 December
We finished off our paper refuting PM's argument for a western front in France and pressing for a Mediterranean policy aiming at pushing Italy out of the war and Turkey into it. By these means we aim at relieving the maximum possible pressure off Russia. Clark Kerr, the Ambassador in Moscow, gave us an hour on his views of Stalin's reactions if we do not start a western front in France. He argued that such a course might well lead to Stalin making a separate peace with Hitler. I refuse to believe such a thing is possible, and fail to see how any common agreement could ever be arrived at between them which would not irreparably lower the prestige of one or the other in the eyes of their own people.

Bertie Brooke came to lunch before his departure for Cairo [as Red Cross Commissioner]. I am very sorry at seeing him go. After lunch Casey came and I had a long talk with him about the situation in the Middle East. Probed him as to the rumours of Monty being sticky in his pursuit. Stirling [Cabinet Secretariat] also came in the evening, just back from Algeria with all the latest news from Eisenhower and Anderson.

My enquiries from Casey concerning Monty were due to the fact that at that time there were many rumours afloat that Monty was far too sticky, that he only thought of his own reputation, would never take risks, played for certainties, etc, etc. I discovered that these rumours emanated from the two airmen, Coningham and Tedder, who were responsible for the air support. I felt convinced that they were unjustified and wanted Casey's opinion. I found on several occasions in the war that airmen, entirely disconnected with the administrative problems of supply, which were mainly done for them, and with the very vaguest of conceptions as to requirements of land tactics, were only too free in offering criticisms and accusing the Army of moving too slowly.

16 December
COS as usual. Then lunch with Oswald Birley to meet [? Gen. Sir John] Brind [Deputy Regional Commissioner, North East]. Lunched in studio. She [his wife] was also there. After lunch went round with him to see a bust of Winston which some woman was making.

At 6 pm we had a COS meeting with PM. Anthony Eden also there. All about policy for 1943. As the paper we put in went straight against Winston, who was pressing for a western front in France, whilst we pressed for amphibious operations in the Mediterranean, I feared the worst!! However, meeting went well from the start and I succeeded in swinging him round. I think he is now fairly safe, but I have still the Americans to convince first, and then Stalin next!!

17 December
A difficult COS in which I could not get agreement between CAS and CNS on the employment of new radio-location devices. CAS quite clear as to what he wanted, but CNS waffling about and leaving me to do all the work. In the evening Cabinet at 6 pm at which cannibalization of 2 divisions in ME was to be discussed. Spent an hour preparing myself to fight Winston, and then found there was no fight at all!!! Not the first time.

18 December
A very short COS followed by office work and Adam to lunch with me. Then interview with old [illegible] to tell him he was getting too old for the job, he took it very well, but the sort of interview that makes me almost sick before starting them! At 5 pm left for Cobbold's house, pouring rain and misty, did not arrive till close on 9 pm. At 1 am, PM called up and wanted to talk to me about brigade of 46th Div which we had advanced for the 1st Army and had been told by Eisenhower's HQ that they could not take it in. I had dealt with the matter in the morning and there was nothing more to be done so I don't know why the hell he wanted to disturb everybody, except for the fun of it!!

19 December
Shot with Ivan Cobbold. Very pleasant day. Returned to flat in evening and went through day's telegrams.

20 December

After spending about 2 hours in the WO I slipped home for the rest of the day.

21 December

Left home at 8 am as usual. During COS discussed Cunningham's report on Anderson, which accused him of lack of cooperation with Commander of the Air. As a result wrote letter to Anderson. Cabinet at 5.30 pm and about 1½ hours work after dinner. Russian news excellent.

22 December

I had a very heated discussion in the COS lasting about an hour, concerning the role and charter of Mountbatten [as Chief of Combined Operations]. The suggestion being that he should command the naval forces for an invasion of France. Portal and Pug Ismay were supporting him, and Dudley Pound and I were dead against it on the basis that his job is one of an advisor and not of a commander. We finally shook the other two and went a long way towards making the point.

After lunch a long Selection Board which took us till 5 pm. Then an interview with Paget on question of command of air forces in event of an invasion of France. Roosevelt has sent message to Winston suggesting a meeting in North Africa, somewhere near Casablanca, about January 15th. We shall consequently soon be travelling again.

23 December

Had to turn down a very bad plan for the capture of Sardinia worked out by Eisenhower. It never went beyond the landing on the beaches and failed to examine the operations required after the landing is completed. A typical bit of work of the Combined Operations department of Mountbatten's. Instructed Joint Planners to work out complete plan.

Further discussion as to where this oasis is to be found where President and PM are to meet [ultimately Casablanca]. Looks as if we start early in January. Norwegian General came after lunch to try and get more plans with which to extract Norwegians out of Sweden. Cabinet at 5.30 pm at which Duncan Sandys gave an account of his travels in ME and North Africa.

24 December

Had hoped to get off early to go home, but found note from Winston that he wanted to see S of S and myself at 3 pm to discuss increased number of 6 pdr gun tanks to the 11th Armoured Div for North Africa. Succeeded in shifting meeting to 12.30. He was peevish and troublesome, but more or less satisfied by increasing troops by an additional 6 pdr tank. Then went home.

25 December
Happily and peacefully spent at home.

26 December
Spent at Preshaw.

27 December
Another peaceful day at home.

28 December
An unpleasant day to start work again! Left 8 am, arrived WO 9.10, then continual rush till 10.30 studying situation on various fronts, reading all telegrams, and looking through briefs for COS meeting. From 10.30 to 1.30 pm long and difficult COS, all on future strategy and preparing paper to bring the Americans to our way of thinking. From 2.45 to 5.30 continuous interviews, then Cabinet till 7 pm, followed by ¾ hour with PM, who now wants to pull Alexander out of Middle East to replace Anderson! at the same time giving Jumbo Wilson the Middle East Command! Rushed back to WO to pick up papers, home for dinner followed by 1 hour's hard work before going round to Defence Committee Meeting at 10 pm. This lasted till midnight and was mainly filled up with an examination of Eisenhower's situation and his intention to put off attacks for 2 months! I am afraid that Eisenhower as a general is hopeless! He submerges himself in politics and neglects his military duties, partly, I am afraid, because he knows little if anything about military matters. I don't like the situation in Tunisia at all!

These remarks about Eisenhower are pretty drastic! My opinion, however, never changed much as regards his tactical ability or his powers of command. In these early days he literally knew nothing of the requirements of a commander in action.... Where he shone was in his ability to handle allied forces, to treat them all with strict impartiality, and to get the very best out of an inter-allied force.... As Supreme Commander, what he may have lacked in military ability he greatly made up for by the charm of his personality.

29 December
Another long COS at which we considered a telegram to Eisenhower and to Washington concerning Tunisia. Also our future strategy paper which we had had approved by Defence Committee last night and wish to send on to Washington in anticipation of our proposed meetings.

After lunch interview with Crocker concerning the departure of his Corps HQ for Tunisia. Then Giffard who is just back from West Africa, followed by MS, interview with S of S, talk with VCIGS and Director of Air, with final visit by DMI. Have now been struggling with files after dinner and am just off to Defence Committee Meeting at 10.30 pm tonight.

30 December

A more peaceful day. Relatively short COS. Lunched with Adam and walked round St James's Park to look at ducks. Then interview with Grasett to ask him to take on the Allied Forces. I could see he was disappointed, and being one of my best friends it was naturally a painful interview. Then had a talk with Gatehouse, just back from ME. Finally dined with Duncan Sandys to discuss his tour abroad. Now off for an early bed.

31 December

A very unpleasant day with continuous annoyances and troubles. First a ridiculous plan put up by Eisenhower for prosecution of war in Tunisia. Then difficulties at COS meeting with reference to dropping of Italian prisoners' mail by air. In the afternoon first interview with Nosworthy who wanted to know why he was not being employed any further. A false idea of his value, consequently some difficulty in making him realize that he had reached his ceiling. Then Beckett back from Malta with long talk why Gort had better be relieved. Then Andy McNaughton to discuss employment of Canadians. Then QMG and DCIGS to discuss rate of arrival which could be contemplated as maximum for American divisions and date of departures of Tank Brigade for Tunisia. From there to S of S and finally with PM for 6.30 to 8.15 pm. Back to flat with lots of work after dinner. This is a dog's life!!

1 January – 31 December 1943

1 January 1943

New year started. I cannot help glancing back at Jan 1st last year when I could see nothing but calamities ahead; Hong Kong gone, Singapore going, Java etc very doubtful, even Burma unsafe, would we be able to save India and Australia? Horrible doubts, horrible nightmares, which grew larger and larger as the days went on till it felt as if the whole Empire was collapsing round my head. Wherever I looked I could see nothing but trouble. Middle East began to crumble, Egypt was threatened. I felt Russia could never hold, Caucasus was bound to be penetrated, and Abadan (our Achilles Heel) would be captured with the consequent collapse of Middle East, India, etc.

After Russia's defeat how were we to handle the German land and air forces liberated? England would be again bombarded, threat of invasion revived. Throughout it all Cabinet Ministers' nerves would be more and more on edge and clear thinking would become more and more difficult.

And now! We start 1943 under conditions I would never have dared to hope. Russia has held, Egypt for the present is safe. There is a hope of clearing North Africa of Germans in the near future. The Mediterranean may be partially opened. Malta is safe for the present. We can now work freely against Italy, and Russia is scoring wonderful successes in Southern Russia. We are certain to have many setbacks to face, many troubles, and many shattered hopes, but for all that the horizon is infinitely brighter.

From a personal point of view life is also now a bit easier. With 13 months of this job behind me I feel just a little more confident than I did in those awful early days when I felt completely lost and out of place. I pray God that He may go on giving me the help he has given me during the last year.

Started the year with a slightly easier day. A long COS. In afternoon visit from Baxter the Military Attaché in Portugal, and Browning Commander of the Airborne Div who is just back from North Africa. Finally Army Council Meeting at 5 pm.

2 January

A fairly peaceful Saturday morning. COS mainly filled with preparations for our trip next week to Casablanca. Got home for tea.

3 January

Peaceful day at home.

4 January

Jacob just back from North Africa came to COS with most recent news.

Apparently Clark has been creating trouble. Very ambitious and unscrupulous, has been egging on Giraud to state that French troops could not fight under British! so as to ensure that he should be given the Tunisian Front! Account of Eisenhower's HQ and staff work are pretty shattering. High time I got out there and had a chance of looking round.

The news about Clark was a bit of an eye opener and quite unexpected. However, from everything I gathered, there was no doubt that he was trying to discredit the British in the eyes of the French in order to obtain for himself the command of the Tunisian Front. Eisenhower evidently became aware of this manoeuvre and with his high quality of impartiality rid himself of Clark as his Deputy Commander and sent him back to command the reserve forces in Morocco. Through this action Ike greatly rose in my estimation.

Gort turned up after lunch looking very run down and tired, and only just recovered from his bad burns. Cabinet at 6 pm.

5 January
Fairly short COS concerned mainly with situation in North Africa and our impending departure. A quiet afternoon with a call from Winston at 7.15 pm to vet our telegram to the JSM [Joint Staff Mission] Washington in which we criticize Eisenhower's strategy. However we settled the matter by sending the wire and stating that we would await discussions in Casablanca before sending a message to Eisenhower.

6 January
A very trying COS, arguing about landing craft figures produced by Mountbatten and Dudley Pound. The former was, as usual, confused in his figures and facts and the latter was as usual asleep! Chairmanship of the meeting was consequently difficult!!

You came up for lunch, which produced a very beautiful ray of sunshine in an otherwise very cloudy sky.

In afternoon visit from new Norwegian Military Attaché. All plans for the departure next Monday are progressing well. I foresee that I shall have a difficult time.

7 January
Great discussion at the COS as to how we are to get to Africa! Weather reports bad and odds against our being able to start on Monday [11 January]. PM suggests cruiser, Dudley Pound against this owing to submarine threat. Finally PM decides we must be ready to start Sunday. Later this is cancelled – for the present we are to be ready by Monday. Lunched at Latimer Court with Home Forces and then talked for 1½ hours on world situation. Then back to WO to finish off ordinary work.

8 January

One of those awful COS meetings where Mountbatten and Dudley Pound drive me completely to desperation. The former is quite irresponsible, suffers from the most desperate illogical brain, always producing red herrings, the latter is asleep 90% of the time and the remaining 10% is none too sure what he is arguing about. Never finished till after 1 pm. After lunch interview with Giffard followed by [Kingsley] Wood, just back from North Africa. Then Military Members meeting of Army Council. And finally the very *very* bright spot of fetching you to come and dine with me.

9 January

Finished off COS meeting relatively early and then completed office work by lunch. You then lunched with me and we had a lovely drive down to Ferney Close together.

10 January

Spent quietly at home, mainly occupied in polishing off my new Dresser's Book of Birds of Europe.

11 January

Left early as usual. Arrived WO just after 9 am and spent hectic 1½ hours reading telegrams and absorbing situation. 10.30 to 12 noon COS meeting. Then War Cabinet till 1.30. After lunch packed up and made all preparations to leave for Casablanca at 5.30 pm by air. But at 4.45 pm informed that weather was unsuitable and journey put off. All the Chiefs of Staff, Joint Planners, PM, Lord Leathers, and Harriman are proceeding there to meet American COS, Roosevelt and Dill. We are to discuss strategy for 1943 and I feel that we shall have a difficult time.

12 January

At 7.30 pm I left London by car for Casablanca, embarking at Lyne [Lyneham] at 2 am. The account of my journey is contained in a separate diary, covering the period from Jan 12th to Feb 7th.

12 January   1,400 miles

After our very happy lunch and shopping and leaving you at Waterloo I returned to the WO. I was then told that all plans were changed. We were not going by Clipper as the sea was too rough at Gibraltar, but should go by Liberator instead. We were to go by car, leaving London at 7.30 pm and motor some ninety miles in the dark to an aerodrome near Swindon. We took off at 2 am and had a very good journey. We had to wear flying kit to counteract the cold, but with fur lined clothes kept very nice and warm.

Our departure had been kept remarkably secret in London and we did not even know what aerodrome we were going to. We were given a rendezvous when the cars met and were led to the aerodrome, which I think must have been Lyne. There we had a long wait, being issued with flying kit and lectured as to what we did if we landed in the sea. Finally we embarked in one of the uncomfortable converted Liberators. I slept on the floor of the little cabin in the rear of the plane and had Dickie Mountbatten sleeping next to me. I did not find him a pleasant bed companion, as every time he turned round he overlay me, and I had to use my knees and elbows to establish my rights to my allotted floor space! I cannot quite remember but believe we landed in Rabat before proceeding onto Casablanca.

13 January   Casablanca

Arrived at Casablanca at 11 am after quite an interesting flight down the coast. Here we are stopping in a very comfortable modern hotel just outside the town, with two modern villas close by, one for Winston and one for Roosevelt. The former arrived at the same time as we did and the latter should arrive here to-morrow. We are quite a large party – PM, Lord Leathers, 3 Chiefs of Staff, Pug Ismay, Mountbatten, Jacob, Kennedy, Slessor, 3 Joint Planners and many others. On American side President, Marshall, King, Arnold, Cooke, Somervell, Clark, Eisenhower, Leahy, Dill, Harriman etc. In addition Alexander and Tedder arrive to-morrow. At 4.30 pm we had Chiefs of Staff meeting for Dill to give us the American outlook. At 6 pm a meeting with PM to discuss with him the most recent conclusions as regards relative advantages of Sardinia versus Sicily. Then dined with Marshall and had long talk with him after dinner. Am now tired and very sleepy, but must prepare my address to the Combined Chiefs of Staff meeting on the world situation and proposed policy.

In settling our future Mediterranean policy we had had long discussions as to whether we should invade Sicily or Sardinia once we had cleared North Africa. I could see very few advantages in selecting Sardinia, and had been a strong supporter of Sicily; distances were shorter, landings easier to support, and it was on the direct route to Italy. I had had some problems with the Joint Planners, who were inclined to favour Sardinia, their argument being, as far as I can remember, that the opposition on the beaches would be less and that aerodromes in Sardinia would be better placed for air action against Italy. I had finally got agreement to settle on Sicily, and it was the Sicily landing that I was to put forward to the Americans as our next objective. I was, however, destined to still have some trouble with the Planning Committee in this respect.

14 January (2 am)

A very long and laborious day. Breakfast at 8.30 am followed by 1½ hour's hard work preparing my opening statement for our first meeting with the American Chiefs of Staff. At 10.30 we met. I started off with a statement of about 1 hour giving our outlook on the present war situation and our opinion as to the future policy we should adopt. Marshall then followed on with a statement showing where they disagreed with our policy. We stopped for lunch and met again at 2.30 pm. I then asked them to explain their views as to the running of the Pacific War. Admiral King then did so, and it became clear at once that his idea was an 'all-out' war against Japan instead of holding operations. He then proposed that 30 per cent of the war effort should be directed to the Pacific and 70 per cent to the rest. We pointed out that this was hardly a scientific way of approaching war strategy! After considerable argument we got them to agree to our detailing the Combined Planners to examine and report on the minimum holding operations required in the Pacific and forces necessary for that action. We broke up the meeting at about 5 pm, had tea, and then had a meeting with our Joint Planners to instruct them on the line of action to take.

I then went for a walk with John Kennedy to the beach to look for birds.

Returned to find invitation to dine with the President who had arrived that afternoon. Party consisted of PM, President, Harry Hopkins, Harriman, Elliot Roosevelt, Marshall, King, Arnold, Dudley Pound, Portal, Mountbatten and self. King became nicely lit up towards the end of the evening. As a result he got more and more pompous, and with a thick voice and many gesticulations explained to the President the best way to organize the Political French organization for control of North Africa! This led to many arguments with PM who failed to appreciate fully the condition King was in! Most amusing to watch. At about 1.30 am an alarm was received, lights were put out, and we sat around the table with faces lit by 6 candles. The PM and President in that light and surroundings would have made a wonderful picture.

15 January (1.15 am!)

Another hard day. Got up fairly early and by 8.45 am started off for a walk with Kennedy to look for birds. Delightful 1½ hours, during which we saw goldfinch, stonechat, warblers of all sorts, white wagtail and several kinds of waders on the sea-shore, such as sanderlings, ring plover, grey plover and turnstones!

Then COS conference till 12 noon, when PM came and I told him what we had done the previous day. After lunch Combined Chiefs of Staff meeting, first discussing security of communications, and secondly, relative advantages between Western Front in France and Mediterranean amphibious operations. I made long statement in favour of the latter which went down fairly well and remains to be argued further to-morrow. Eisenhower also came to give statement of operations in Tunisia. I had to criticize his operation against Sfax, which is in no way co-ordinated with either 1st Army or 8th Army operations. At 5.30 pm Combined Staffs, Eisenhower, Alexander and Tedder met President and PM, at which we did little except that President expressed views favouring operations in the Mediterranean. Both Eisenhower and Alexander made statements of their operations. Finally dined with PM. Alexander, Tedder, Portal and I. After dinner Hopkins and Harriman came in, the former in rather a bitter mood which I had not yet seen him in.

There is no doubt that we are too closely related to the Americans to make co-operation between us anything but easy.*

16 January

Got up with somewhat of an effort after two late nights. After breakfast at 9.30 conference till 10.30 with Eisenhower and Alexander to coordinate the attacks on Tunisia. Eisenhower's previous plan was a real bad one which could only result in the various attacks being defeated in detail. As a result of our talk a better plan was drawn up.

From 10.30 to 1 pm Combined Chiefs of Staff meeting at which I had again to put forward all the advantages of our proposed Mediterranean [strategy] and counter arguments in favour of a French front plan. It is a slow and tiring business which requires a lot of patience. They can't be pushed and hurried, and must be made gradually to assimilate our proposed policy. After lunch went for a walk with Alexander when I had a long discussion with him about the Middle East, commanders, his hopes and proposed operations, etc. From 3.30 to 5.15 pm another Combined Chiefs of Staff meeting. I think we are beginning to make some progress and that they are getting interested in our proposals. At 5.30 pm we had to go to the PM for me to report progress of our work. He was in a very good mood, and had spent most of the day planning a conciliation between de Gaulle and Giraud [now High Commissioner of French North and West Africa]. Back here and off to dine with General Patton, the American general who carried out the landing on the Morocco Front. A real fire-eater and a definite character. He is living in the house that had been occupied by the German Armistice Commission, owned by a Jew newspaper proprietor. A small marble palace with all possible modern comforts.

Now I am off to bed early for once and feeling dog-tired as a result of the last few days' work! It is a slow tedious process, as all matters have to be carefully explained and reexplained before they can be absorbed. And finally the counter-arguments put forward often show that even then the true conception has not been grasped and the process has to be started again.

The whole process was made all the more difficult by the fact that amongst Marshall's very high qualities he did not possess those of a strategist. It was almost impossible to make him grasp the true concepts of a strategic situation. He was unable to argue out a strategic situation and preferred to hedge and defer decisions until such time as he had to consult his assistants. Unfortunately his assistants were not of the required calibre, and Cooke [Naval Planner] was of a very low category.

My meeting with Patton had been of great interest. I had already heard of him, but must confess that his swash-buckling personality exceeded my expectation. I did not

---

*Misread by Bryant as 'there is no doubt that we are too closely related to the Americans to make co-operation easy', provoking a puzzled comment from AB. *Turn*, p. 547.

form any high opinion of him, nor had I any reason to alter this view at a later date. A dashing, courageous, wild and unbalanced leader, good for operations requiring thrust and push but at a loss in any operation requiring skill and judgment.

17 January

A desperate day! We are further from obtaining agreement than we ever were! Started Combined Chiefs of Staff meeting to be told by Marshall that there was disagreement between the Joint Planners on the question of Burma. Then a long harangue again on the question of the Pacific from Marshall, and finally questions about Iceland!! Decided that it was useless going on conferring until the Joint Planners had made more headway. Had a meeting between Chiefs of Staff and our Joint Planners when we found that the main difficulty rested with the fact that the USA Joint Planners did not agree with Germany being the primary enemy and were wishing to defeat Japan first!!! We have therefore prepared a new paper for discussion to-morrow at which we must get this basic principle settled.

Went for another good walk, during which I found a new white heron, quite distinct from the egret, and a new small owl which we could not place. After dinner another meeting with Joint Planning Staff which took us up to 11 pm.

18 January

Went out early with John Kennedy for a bird walk. We saw all our wader friends on the beach and then found a black stone-chat on the way home.

From 10.30 to 1 pm a very heated Combined Chiefs of Staff meeting at which we seemed to be making no headway. King still evidently wrapped up in the war of the Pacific at the expense of everything else! However immediately after lunch I sat down with Dill, I must confess without much hope, trying to define the line of our general agreement. In the middle Portal came in with a better paper. I therefore decided on the spur of the moment, and without a chance of seeing the First Sea Lord, to try to use this proposed policy as a bridge for our difficulties.

We met again at 3 pm and I produced our paper which was accepted with few alterations!!! I could hardly believe our luck. Shortly afterwards we were informed that the President would hold a full meeting with the PM and all Combined Chiefs of Staff to hear results we had reached. We met at his villa at 5.30 pm. I was asked to sit next to him, and he asked me who had been acting as our Chairman and I told him that Marshall had been invited by us to perform that function. He then called on Marshall, who at once asked me to expound the results of our meetings. It was a difficult moment, we had only just succeeded in getting the American Chiefs of Staff to agree with us. However the statement went all right, was approved by the Americans and by the President and PM, receiving a full blessing. So we have reached some results after all.

We were then all photographed together!

Finished up the day by dining with Giraud. He asked me to come at 7.15 pm and I had ¾ hour alone with him. He could not have been more charming. We talked of old times in France, his lunch with the King, his advance to Breda, his escape from Germany, his interviews with Laval etc. Finally at 8 pm we went in to dine, where we found Harriman, Murphy and Macmillan [Minister Resident in Mediterranean; another inveterate diarist], also 2 French officers. A very pleasant informal dinner, with no pomp and a great deal of genuine friendliness. He is no politician, a very indifferent general, but a high principled gentleman with a whole-hearted desire to defeat the Germans.

The fact that we had finally secured an agreement with the Americans on this memorable day was for the greater part due to Dill. I cannot think why I did not give him credit for this in my diary, but am glad that the details remain fresh in my memory so that I may remedy my omission and do him justice now. That morning as we had left the Combined COS meeting I was in despair and in the depths of gloom. Whilst walking upstairs I said to Dill: 'It is no use, we shall never get agreement with them!' To which he replied: 'On the contrary, you have already got agreement to most of the points, and it only remains to settle the rest. Let's come to your room after lunch and discuss it.' We sat on my bed after lunch and he went through all the points on which we had agreement and then passed on to those where we were stuck, asking me how far I would go to get agreement. When I replied that I would not move an inch, he said, 'Oh yes, you will. You know that you must come to some agreement with the Americans and that you cannot bring the unsolved problem up to the Prime Minister and the President. You know as well as I do what a mess they would make of it!' He then put up a few suggestions for agreement and asked me if I would agree to his discussing these with Marshall. I had such implicit trust in his ability and integrity that I agreed.

At this juncture Portal arrived with his proposed plan for seeking agreement, which was somewhat similar to some of Dill's suggestions, and we decided to adopt it. Thereupon Dill proceeded to see Marshall before the meeting to discuss these suggestions. I am certain that the final agreement being reached was due more to Dill than to anyone else, acting as the best possible intermediary between Marshall and myself. I owe him an unbounded debt of gratitude for his help on that occasion and in many other similar ones.

Giraud's story of his escape was most interesting. First a code was established with his wife through the medium of a repatriated officer. Then she sent him a wire cable in lengths of 1 metre hidden in butter tins. She sent him chocolate which he sold to his guard and with the money bought other articles. He collected goggles, a Homburg hat, a cape, trousers etc. On the given day he scaled down the wall with his cable, hid in a small copse, shaved and changed He then met the contact his wife had arranged for him outside the Railway Station, the code word being 'Güten Abend Heinrich'. Then walked into the waiting room where the contact man handed him a suit case with clothes and identity card as a business man of some kind, also a ticket. The journey to the Swiss frontier took several days, and he finally made a rush over the frontier. Then he was arrested, put in prison, but luckily remembered a Swiss schoolfriend in Berne whom he asked to come and identify him! He was returned to France and very nearly handed back to the Germans by Laval! He also gave me details of his trip by submarine and flying boat from the vicinity of Toulon to Gibraltar. Also a cloak and dagger trip.

Poor Giraud. He was an attractive personality with great charm, but the very wildest ideas as to what was possible, militarily. Politically he was no match for de Gaulle, whom I think he inwardly despised. He was one of those queer personalities that fortune occasionally throws forward into positions of responsibility which they are totally unfitted for.

We had at that time a strange set up in North Africa. A C-in-C deficient of experience and of limited ability in the shape of Eisenhower, and three possible French leaders, Darlan who had ability but no integrity, Giraud who had charm but no ability, and de Gaulle who had the mentality of a dictator combined with a most objectionable personality!*

19 January

Started off early with John [Kennedy] to look for birds, and I think located a pair of spur-winged plover.

From 10 to 12 a Combined meeting settling details required by our main policy. From 2 to 3 pm a COS meeting in anticipation of a Combined meeting from 3 to 5. At 5 General Giraud came round to see the Combined Chiefs of Staff and made a series of statements concerning French forces he considered could be raised in North Africa provided equipment was found for them. The force amounted to 3 Armoured and 10 Motorised divisions!

I then went for another walk with John Kennedy but found no birds.

Just before dinner PM came round to the hotel and told me he proposed to go to Marrakesh on Saturday. That I was to accompany him there, and that from there we should go on to Cairo. Whilst there he hoped to go on to Cyprus to meet Turks and prepare for their entry into the war. We should then go on to Tripoli, which he hoped would be captured by then and from there home. A very interesting trip and I hope it comes off all right.

In discussing this trip he told me that he proposed to see the President fly off from the Marrakesh aerodrome and that he would subsequently spend two days in Marrakesh to rest and to paint. He told me that it was seven years since he had painted in Marrakesh, and that he had brought his paints on purpose, and was very much looking forward to the opportunity – I thought the plan was excellent. I was feeling a bit tired after all the recent work, and at once made plans for one day's tour in the Atlas mountains and one day's partridge shooting with a local sheik. We shall see however that those lovely plans were to be interfered with! L'homme propose et Dieu dispose! [Man proposes and God disposes!]

---

*In fact, as already noted, Darlan was assassinated on Christmas Eve 1942. AB seems to have forgotten this when he wrote his Notes.

20 January

Got up a little earlier and went for a walk with John Kennedy. Very little luck with the birds and we found nothing except 2 little owls and some larks we had already seen. At 10 am we had a Combined Chiefs of Staff meeting at which we started with a shipping discussion for which we brought Lord Leathers in. We then thrashed out the system of command in Tunisia after arrival of the Eighth Army, deciding that it must then be transferred to Eisenhower's command. In order to assist in the control and co-ordination of the First and Eighth Armies and the French and Americans in Tunisia, Alexander to become Eisenhower's Deputy. The Air Command, with Tedder as Supreme Commander of Mediterranean, was also settled at the same time.

American Chiefs then withdrew to see the President and we carried on with a Chiefs of Staff meeting which lasted till 12.45 and at which we discussed the Sicilian operation. At 12.45 we went round to the PM's villa to be photographed with him. At 2 pm we again met as Combined Chiefs and thrashed out plans for the capture of Sicily. The meeting went far better than I had hoped for and finished about 4 pm, when I went round to the PM's house to discuss details of my journey with him to Cairo.

Finally another walk with Kennedy, during which we added three new specimens to our finds in the shape of a wimbrel, sandpiper and yellow wagtail.

The back of the work here is broken and thank God for it! It has been one of the most difficult tasks I have had to do, and at one time I began to despair of our arriving at any sort of agreement. Now we have got practically all we hoped to get when we came here! They are difficult though charming people to work with. Marshall has got practically no strategic vision, his thoughts revolve round the creation of forces and not on their employment. He arrived here without a single real strategic concept, he has initiated nothing in the policy for the future conduct of the war. His part has been that of somewhat clumsy criticism of the plans we put forward. King on the other hand is a shrewd and somewhat swollen headed individual. His vision is mainly limited to the Pacific, and any operation calculated to distract from the force available in the Pacific does not meet with his support or approval. He does not approach the problems with a worldwide war point of view, but instead with one biased entirely in favour of the Pacific. Although he pays lip service to the fundamental policy that we must first defeat Germany and then turn on Japan, he fails to apply it in any problems connected with the war. Arnold limits his outlook to the air and seldom mixes himself up with other matters. But as a team to have to discuss with they are friendliness itself, and although our discussions have become somewhat heated at times, yet our relations have never been strained. I hope we shall leave here with a more closely united outlook on the war.

When I returned from my walk this evening I went to have a drink and was just leaving for my bath when Mack (Foreign Office Representative with Eisenhower) dumped Giraud down on top of me. I got involved in a long conversation from which I could not escape for half an hour and had to listen to all sorts of short cuts towards winning this war which failed entirely to take administrative considerations into account.

AB's wife, Benita, in the late 1930s.

Benita Brooke with the children, Victor (Mr Ti) on pony, and Kathleen (Pooks) on foot.

AB at the centre of a group photo aboard the trawler *Cambridgeshire*, en route from northern France to Plymouth, probably 19 June 1940.

AB walking from plane during 'Bumper' exercise, 28 September to 3 October 1941. Barney Charlesworth is on the left.

AB dining from back of car during 'Bumper'.

AB with Nye in CIGS's office, War Office, early June 1942.

AB at embassy in Teheran, 11 August 1942. Photo by Archie Wavell.

Left: Going up: the
Combined Chiefs of
Staff in a lift, Casablanca
conference, January 1943.
From the left: Arnold,
Dill, Marshall, AB, Pound,
Portal.

Below: AB chairing
combined chiefs of staff
meeting at Casablanca.
From the right: Portal,
AB, Pound, Mountbatten,
Ismay, Wedemeyer, Dykes,
Somervell, Arnold,
Marshall, King.

The British delegation at Casablanca. Front row, from the left: Portal, Pound, Churchill, Dill,
AB. Back row, from the left: Commander C.R. Thompson, Dykes, Alexander, John Martin,
Mountbatten, Ismay, Lord Leathers, Macmillan, Leslie Rowan, Jacob.

AB, Grigg and Paget, in Secretary of State's room at War Office, sometime in 1943.

Top: Triumph in his vest: Oriskany Fishing Club, Quebec, 16–20 September 1944. From the right: Cunningham, Portal, AB, Leckie (Canadian CAS).

Above: Is it a bird? Is it a plane? Probably a bird. AB indicates points of interest to Marshall and King, on Malta, 2 February 1945. Brooke had probably just heard news of the death of Barney Charlesworth.

Right: AB and Bradley
at 9th US Army HQ,
Rheinberg,
25 March 1945.

Below: The Watch on the
Rhine: Churchill,
Montgomery and AB near
Wesel, 25 March 1945.

AB leaving the Yalta conference, 9 February 1945.

On this date we had achieved another marked success. We had got agreement on the organization of Higher Command in North Africa. We had had many troublesome discussions on this matter in our own Chiefs of Staff Meetings which had gone a long way to clear the air. It was clear that centralized command was essential to co-ordinate the actions of the First and Eighth Armies and the American and French forces; but who was to be placed in this responsible position? From many points of view it was desirable to hand this Command over to the Americans, but unfortunately up to now Eisenhower certainly did not seem to possess the basic qualities required from such a Commander. He had neither the experience nor the tactical and strategical experience required for such a task. By bringing Alexander over from the Middle East and appointing him as Deputy to Eisenhower, we were carrying out a move which could not help flattering and pleasing the Americans in so far as we were placing our senior and experienced commander to function under their commander who had no war experience. Such a plan was consequently quite acceptable to them, and they did not at the time fully appreciate the underlying intentions. We were pushing Eisenhower up into the stratosphere and rarified atmosphere of a Supreme Commander, where he would be free to devote his time to the political and inter-allied problems, whilst we inserted under him one of our own commanders to deal with the military situations and to restore the necessary drive and co-ordination which had been so seriously lacking of late! I must confess that I had some doubts as to whether Alexander would have the ability to handle this difficult task. I had however great faith in his Chief of Staff, Dick McCreery, and I hoped that between them all would be well. The battle of Tunis proved the accuracy of this forecast, but I have never felt that McCreery received all the credit due to him for the part he played in these operations.

My estimates of the American Chiefs of Staff as written on our first Combined Meetings were remarkably accurate, and I have never had much cause to depart from these first impressions throughout the many subsequent meetings that we had.

21 January

Started the day with a COS meeting from 9.30 am to 10 am. We then carried on with Combined COS meeting till 12 noon, during which we discussed the building up of American Forces in England during 1943 and their employment. At 12 noon we met the PM and remained with him till 1.15 discussing the possibilities of expediting operations in the Mediterranean. At 2 pm we again met the Combined Staffs and carried on until 4 pm when we went down to Casablanca to inspect a Headquarters ship which Mountbatten had got ready for us. Whilst there we also saw the French battleship the *Jean Bart* which had been hit by 3 1000 lb bombs during the American bombardment of the harbour. The bow and stern were almost completely blown off. Came back and spent rest of evening preparing for a [British] Chiefs of Staff meeting after dinner, which lasted from 9 pm to 12 midnight.

There we had long and protracted arguments as to the relative advantages of Sardinia as opposed to Sicily as an objective. There are a thousand different factors connected with this problem. In my own mind there is not the least doubt that Sicily should be selected, but on the whole the majority of opinion is hardening against me. When an operation has finally been completed it all looks so easy, but so few people ever realize the infinite difficulties of maintaining an object or a plan and refusing to be driven off it by other people for a thousand good reasons! A good plan pressed through is better than many ideal ones which are continually changing. Advice without responsibility is easy to give.

This is the most exhausting job, trying to keep the ship of war on a straight course despite all the contrary winds that blow is a superhuman job!

I have the most vivid recollection of that exhausting evening! I had already had a long day when we started, and had a very heavy encounter with the bulk of the COS against me! We had had many debates on the relative advantages of Sardinia and Sicily before leaving England, and it was only at the end of much hard work that I had obtained general agreement on Sicily. All my arguments with Marshall had been based on the invasion of Sicily and I had obtained his agreement. And now suddenly the Joint Planning Staff reappeared on the scene with a strong preference for Sardinia and expressing most serious doubts about our ability to take on the Sicilian operation! They had carried with them Mountbatten who never had any very decided opinions of his own. Peter Portal and Pug Ismay were beginning to waver, and dear old Dudley Pound was, as usual, asleep and with no views either way!

I had a three hours hammer and tongs battle to keep the team together and to stop it from wavering. I told them that I flatly refused to go back to the American Chiefs of Staff and tell them that we did not know our own minds and that, instead of Sicily, we now wanted to invade Sardinia. I told them that such a step would irrevocably shake their confidence in our judgement. What is more, I told them frankly that I disagreed with them entirely and adhered to our original decision to invade Sicily and would not go back on it.

As I wrote in my diary it was an example of one of those occasions, which occurred frequently, when it was a matter of utmost difficulty to adhere to one's plans and not to be shaken in one's decisions. So easy to look back at, in the light of after knowledge, but so difficult and trying at the time!

22 January

I went in to our Combined Chiefs of Staff meeting at 10 am with some misgivings! We had had an evening with definite signs that our Joint Planners were trying to swing us away from the Sicily operation to a Sardinian one! Such a change at the last moment was not to be contemplated. The Americans I knew would not look at Sardinia and might well accuse us of not knowing our own minds, and wish to close down operations in the Mediterranean. It was with some difficulty, and against their inclination that we had succeeded in drawing them away from a re-entry into France for a continuance in the Mediterranean. The meeting however went off far better than I had hoped, and the determination to proceed with our plans for Sicily were confirmed subject to a revision at a later date as regards resources and training. This was really the culmination of all my efforts. I wanted first to ensure that Germany should continue to be regarded as our primary enemy and that the defeat of Japan must come after that of Germany. Secondly that for the present Germany can best be attacked through the medium of Italy in the Mediterranean, and thirdly that this can best be achieved with a policy directed against Sicily. All these points have been secured, and in addition many minor ones connected with Turkey, command of operations in Tunisia and at home, etc. It has been quite the hardest 10 days I have had from the point of view of difficulty of handling the work.

At 12 noon we all went round to the President's villa for photographs to be taken of the President, PM and Combined Staffs. After lunch, which I had with the PM, Randolph and Ismay there, we met again at 2.30 in a Combined meeting which lasted till about 4.30.

After tea I went for a walk with John Kennedy. We found five of the small owls and a marsh harrier.

It is an untold relief that this meeting is drawing to a close. It has done a great deal, I feel certain that we now understand each other and our respective difficulties far better.

Am just back from seeing the PM, who wanted to get Alexander back to Marrakesh on Sunday to see him! As he has already been away from his Command for a week at this critical moment I did not think it desirable and told him so. He had been seeing de Gaulle after his historic meeting with Giraud. Apparently this interview did not go too smoothly, and I doubt whether such opposed characters can possibly pull together.

23 January

We met again at 10 am to thrash out the final points and to discuss our report to the President and Prime Minister on the work of the meeting. After lunch we motored out to Fédala, the site of one of the American landings. We collected an American Colonel Ratlye to come with us who had actually taken part in this landing. It was most interesting, and quite evident that, if the French had put up any real resistance the landing could not have been carried out. On the way back I saw 3 storks close to the road, the ordinary type as far as I could see. On the way back we did some shopping at the Galeries Lafayette.

At 5.30 pm we attended meeting with President and PM in the chair. Lasted till 7.30 pm. We were congratulated by both of them on the results of our work and informed that we had produced the most complete strategic plan for a world-wide war that had ever been conceived, and far exceeding the accomplishments of the last war. They then discussed details, tried to push forward the Sicilian date, insisted on more stress as to the assistance to China, and a few other minor points. Finally we had our last meeting at 9.30 pm to bring this final document into line with the remarks of the President and PM. This meeting ended up with a series of small speeches of appreciation for the spirit in which we had met each other's difficulties.

I am convinced that this meeting has achieved a great deal. It has brought us all much closer together and helped us to understand each other's difficulties in a way which we could never have done at a distance. It has been a very tiring 10 days and I am glad that it is over, and delighted that the results are so satisfactory.

I was quite correct in what I wrote that evening. The meeting had drawn us far closer together, but we were soon to discover that as soon as we parted we began to drift away from each other, and misunderstandings grew up between us. We found that it was essential to have frequent Combined Chiefs of Staff meetings to regain our common understanding.

24 January   Marrakesh (150 miles)

Finished packing up, everybody dispersing in different directions. Marshall for Algiers and back to America, Dill for Algiers and on to Delhi, Arnold also for Delhi and on to Chungking from there. Portal Algiers, Malta and home. Dudley Pound Algiers and home. I came on here with Jacob, Stirling [Cabinet Secretariat] and Boyle [Military Assistant] by Liberator and had a lovely fly with excellent view of the country. It is an amazing sight as one approaches the Atlas mountains to see mile upon mile of snow peaks in front of one. President and PM were to come on by road.

We arrived in time for lunch and were taken by Pendar the American Consul in Morocco to a house owned by a Mrs Taylor for lunch. It is the house the President and PM are to stop in. Built in complete Moroccan architecture in the middle of what used to be an olive plantation. Very ornate and Moroccan with a wonderful garden round it. After lunch we climbed up into the tower to see the view. An astonishing mixture with palm trees and Arab Moroccan town in the foreground and lovely snow coloured peaks in the background! From my hotel window I have a wonderful view right over an orange plantation, covered with oranges, and through a fringe of palm trees the glistening snow peaks in rear. Absolutely lovely.

I spent a real peaceful afternoon looking for birds in the lovely garden of the hotel and found several very interesting specimens. It is great fun identifying the European specimens in the form of some sub-species with minor variations. For instance I found the ordinary chaffinch, but the cock with a blue grey head instead of the red-brown of the home specimen. It is also very interesting seeing what a great difference there is between the bird life at Casablanca and that of Marrakesh, although the distance between them is only some 130 miles.

25 January

We had made lovely plans for two quiet days here with a day's partridge shooting! But it was not to be! PM sent for me this morning and said he wanted to start tonight for Cairo.

I had frequently seen him in bed, but never anything to touch the present setting! It was all I could do to remain serious. The room must have been Mrs Taylor's bedroom and was done up in Moorish style, the ceiling was a marvellous fresco of green, blue and gold. The head of the bed rested in an alcove of Moroccan design with a religious light shining on either side, the bed was covered in a light blue silk covering with a 6 in wide lace 'entre deux' and the rest of the room in harmony with the Arabic ceiling. And there in the bed was Winston in his green, red and gold dragon dressing gown, his hair, or what there was of it, standing on end, the religious lights shining on his cheeks, and a large cigar in his face!! I would have given anything to have been able to take a coloured photograph of him.

He greeted me by telling me that we were off at 6 pm! I replied that I was under the impression that we had come here to paint the scenery he had been longing to get at for the past 6 years. He said he would paint 2 hours in the afternoon and that we should start at 6 pm. I drew his attention to the fact that even he could not hope to do justice to the wonderful effects of palm trees and snow peaks in 2 hours! He replied again 'I am off at 6 pm', by way of clinching the argument. I then said 'All right, if we are off at 6 pm, where are we going?' His reply was typical, 'I have not decided yet!' On being asked as to what the alternatives might be, he replied, 'I am either going to answer questions in the House tomorrow, or I am going to Cairo.' On being further questioned as to what would decide him I was informed that he was awaiting a telegram from Anthony Eden about his proposed visit to the Turks. If the Cabinet agreed, we should go to Cairo.

We sent for pilot, who said weather conditions were excellent. Telegrams were therefore sent to Miles Lampson that we were coming and to Jumbo Wilson [C-in-C ME] to come to Cairo. Our plan now is to arrive at Cairo tomorrow early, and go to Cyprus if Cabinet removes objections to PM meeting Turks, which they don't seem to like. Then to Tripoli to meet Montgomery and Anderson and from there home.

After lunch drove off into the Atlas Mountains and had a lovely drive. We went well up into the hills and stopped to hunt for birds. Saw an eagle in the distance but too far away to make out what it was. Meanwhile Winston had climbed up the tower of Mrs Taylor's house with his easel and oil paints and was busy painting. He had been in Marrakesh about 6 years ago and did some painting then. So on this trip he brought his paints with the determination to go back there to paint again. I had hoped that this desire would lead him to spend a day or two at Marrakesh, but it was not to be! At 5.30 pm, after having tea with the Danish Consul and his wife, we left the Hotel Mamounia for the aerodrome. We had two Liberators, one for PM, Randolph, Doctor, Sec, Flag officer, detective and valet. The other for me, Jacob, Rowan the other sec, the chief clerk, another detective, and Boyle. We took off at 6.30 pm and after climbing round in rings gradually struck out to cross the snowy peaks of the Atlas Mountains. We climbed to 14,500 ft before crossing, it became bitterly cold, but the view was glorious. The sun was setting, there was not a cloud in the sky, and the horizon all round was lit with a pink glow which was reflected on the snowy peaks. As we passed over the mountains the sun set, and the whole scenery gradually disappeared into darkness, till we were left alone in the dark, driving into the unknown with 2300 miles of desert in front of us. We then had dinner of boiled eggs and sandwiches. After that rolled up for the night and packed stacks of blankets on top to keep warm. We had dropped down again to 9000 ft, which was more comfortable but still very cold.

26 January   Cairo (2300 miles)

After a somewhat uncomfortable night, looked out to see dawn breaking over the desert. We had been flying for about 11 hours. Shortly afterwards we landed, having arrived a few minutes before the PM. Casey, Moyne [Deputy Minister of State, Cairo], Alexander and Sholto Douglas were all on the aerodrome to meet us. We drove straight to the Embassy where we were met by Miles Lampson and Jacqueline. We were given a good breakfast after which I had a bath and shave.

Just after arriving in the Embassy, and being greeted by the Miles Lampsons, Winston turned to me and said, 'Shall we have breakfast now?' I felt that he should have addressed this question to Jacqueline, so replied, 'I think we had better first of all get washed and have a shave.' This did not suit him, and he went on with 'No! we shall have breakfast now', and then turned to Jacqueline and asked her if breakfast was ready. She assured him that it was and led him to the dining room where she offered him a cup of tea. This offer was not at all acceptable and he asked for a glass of white wine! A tumbler was brought which he drained in one go, and then licked his lips, turned to Jacqueline and said, 'Ah! that is good, but you know, I have already had two whiskies and soda and 2 cigars this morning.'!! It was then only shortly after 7.30 am. We had travelled all night in poor comfort, covering some 2300 miles in a flight of over 11 hours, a proportion of which at over 14,000 ft, and there he was, as fresh as paint, drinking white wine on top of two previous whiskies and 2 cigars!!

I got Alexander to come round at 10.30 and had a long talk with him on the clearing of Tunisia and on the Sicilian operation.

It is very strange being back here after little more than 5 months, and so much has happened in that time! When I was last here I kept wondering whether the day would come when Germans would be firing across the Nile into the Embassy Gardens, and now they are on the point of being driven out of Tripoli! After lunch I went round with Alexander to his map room to examine the situation in Tripoli and the prospects of opening the port. Whilst there the PM turned up and became involved in a long discussion on the situation of the French naval forces under Godfroy in Alexandria with Admiral Harwood [C-in-C Levant and Eastern Mediterranean]. PM all for a firmer attitude with these forces to induce them to join the French movement to free France. Either under Giraud or under de Gaulle. Did not succeed in getting off to bed till near 1 am. Very sleepy after poor previous night in the plane.

27 January

Had a grand sleep to make up for previous night. At 10.30 am attended Alexander's Staff Conference at which all intelligence was reviewed. After conference had an interview with Morshead (Commander 9th Aust Div) to say goodbye to him before his departure with his division for Australia. Then Jumbo Wilson turned up from Baghdad and I put him into the picture and settled details as to his taking over from Alexander, what his tasks would be in the administration of 8th Army, training formations for the Sicilian operation, and preparing troops for Turkey.

Reply had come from Turkey stating that they were delighted with proposed visit, but suggesting we should come to Angora [? Ankara]. However for security decided that meeting had better take place near frontier. Plans being worked out on that basis. To lunch today, Casey and his wife, Jumbo Wilson, Dill (on his way to India with Arnold), Alexander, and usual party. After lunch photographs were taken, and the PM held conference with Casey, Wilson and me to discuss future of Iraq-Persia Command. He wanted to amalgamate it with Middle East, but I succeeded in his agreeing to maintaining it as a separate Command, probably with Giffard as a commander. Being back here reminds me the whole time of that nightmare of a first week last August with all the unpleasantness of pushing Auchinleck out and reconstituting the command and staff of the Middle East. Thank heaven that is all over now and this visit is consequently much more pleasant.

Slipped out before dinner to collect some Turkish Delight for the young. Bertie Brooke came to dine – it was a great joy seeing him again. Just before dinner I received a letter from Montgomery reporting that the clearing of Tripoli harbour was not proceeding quickly enough. After dinner I told PM we ought to do something about it. He telephoned for Admiral Harwood to come at once. We have just had an interview with him and his staff officer. As a result we are now convinced that bad organization and lack of drive has resulted in this delay. I think they may now get more move on. 1.30 am, and I am very sleepy!

28 January   800 miles

Left Embassy at 9.30, and took off from Heliopolis aerodrome for Siwa Oasis at 10 am. Strong head wind and the 400 miles took us 2¾ hours. A most interesting spot, surrounded by sandy crags and small sandy hills of queer terraced shapes due to erosion of wind and rain. Most of the water of the oasis is salty in various degrees, but 2 or 3 springs are of the most lovely clear water welling straight up from the bottom of a deep hole. We had lunch alongside the biggest of these holes and two of the main sheikhs came with offerings of dates and sweet lemons in the most attractive baskets made of palm leaves. After lunch we examined one of the two main villages which had to be evacuated in recent times owing to a cloud burst which washed most of the structure of the houses away. However in washing the houses away the remnants of a well built stone temple appeared which is considered to be that of the famous

Oracle of Siwa, which even Alexander the Great went to consult. The total population of the oasis is about 4,000 and they exist through the cultivation of dates and olives, plus a limited amount of grain they grow.

We then went on to the next village where we were given an official reception by the Sheikhs all in their best clothes and with their swords of office on. The local band also turned out for us, and a small choir of women who produced their welcome song. It was something between a Red Indian call and an owl hooting. We sat under a covering of palm tree trunks covered with palm leaf mats, and ate dates and drank small glasses of very highly flavoured tea. We were also presented with the top of a palm tree to take away and eat! They seemed a thoroughly cheerful and happy little community in spite of the alternative occupation of Italian, British and German forces according to the various swaying backwards and forwards of the fighting in Libya. Their opinion of the Italians was not very high as owing to shortage of rations the Italians had stolen and eaten some of their donkeys. However there are still some supporters of the Italians amongst the population. And even in some families there is a division between 'British' and 'Italian' members of the family. We left at 3.20 pm, and with a strong following wind made the journey in 2 hours.

Both going and coming we had an opportunity of seeing the famous Qattara Depression from the air. It was a most interesting day that I would not have missed for a great deal. I had hoped to see some bird life of interest, but the resident types are few, and it is only during the migration that bird life is plentiful. I did see a white rumped chat, which I had not seen before, and otherwise only 2 ravens and 1 hooded crow. For dinner this evening the American Ambassador, General Arnold (USA), General Andrews (USA), General Spaatz (USA). Kept up till 1 am by the PM who was busy arguing how he could best deal with the French Admiral Godfroy.

29 January

Attended Intelligence meeting at GHQ at 9.15. I then gave the Commanders in Chief ½ hour on proposed plans in the Mediterranean. Then discussed with Alexander the organization of his planning staff for Sicily. Back to the embassy to try and raise some clothes (plain) to proceed to Turkey in as we are not supposed to wear uniform while we are there. Bertie is trying to assist. It is settled now that we start tomorrow.

Later – I have now succeeded in raising the different outfits. Some are too tight in the waist, some too long in the legs, some too thin in the material, but I hope out of the lot to produce something in which I can appear without shame in front of the President of Turkey.

I have often wondered what the Turks must have thought of us when they saw us arrive in our strange clothes. Jumbo Wilson had borrowed a suit from Miles Lampson that even he could not fill adequately, and the jacket on him had the appearance of a maternity garment! I had borrowed Lampson's ADC's clothes, and as he was quite 8 inches taller and very long in the leg, I had serious trouble with the trousers. I braced them up till they caught in my armpits and would go no further, and then found that the top fly button appeared above the waistcoat opening and half concealed my tie! We looked more like a third rate travelling theatre company than anything else!

For lunch today Morshead, who commanded 9th Australian Div and is just off back to Australia, Alex Cadogan who has just arrived from England, Sholto Douglas and Tedder. At 3 pm held conference at GHQ to decide final details of our conference with the Turks tomorrow. Then this evening another hour with PM to discuss the notes he had prepared and the results of our conference. Dined with Sholto Douglas, mostly Americans for dinner, including Generals Andrews, [illegible], Spaatz, etc. Am now going to pack up for our early start tomorrow.

30 January   Adana, 700 miles

We left the embassy at 9 am for the aerodrome, from which we departed at 10 am for Adana in Turkey. We skirted up the coast of Palestine and Syria, and saw Haifa, Beirut, Gaza, Tripoli etc on the way up. Weather bad and trip very bumpy. We saw two water spouts from the air, which was interesting. Finally arrived Adana at 1 pm, after 3 hours flying. There we were met by the Prime Minister, Sükrü Saracoglu and the Foreign Minister Numan Menemencoglu. Country all round soaking wet and under water from recent rains. A certain delay then occurred as our train had not yet arrived. Finally we boarded the train and lunched as we pushed out some 20 miles west where we joined the President's train. There we met the President, General Ismet Inönü (late Ismet Pasha of old) and Field Marshal Fevzi Çakmak. We had first of all a very awkward phase of meetings and polite speeches which were very protracted. However finally we started our conference with opening speech in French by PM.

The political heads then withdrew and the military heads got busy. Çakmak presiding on one side and I on the other. I soon found that Çakmak had no conception of the administrative aspect of handling armies, he had not prepared his case, consequently was continually involved in discussions with his advisors and made it hard to keep one's temper. We went on till about 6 pm and covered a great deal of ground, and have I think got them definitely working towards fulfilling my hopes of ultimately coming to our assistance. But they have got a long way to go before they can be considered as [a] real efficient force, and how we are to provide them with the necessary equipment in spite of their poor communications is a mystery!

Finally we finished up with a dinner with the President at which the PM was a great success, and the day ended on the whole most successfully. Our party consists of PM, Cadogan, Lord Wilson [Moran] (doctor), Alexander, [Jumbo] Wilson, Jacob, Drummond, Martin, Thompson, two detectives and the valet. We are living and feeding and sleeping in the train in a siding in a wilderness of cotton cultivation, a sea of mud at present.

On our arrival in Adana the Turkish Foreign Minister after greeting me told me how delighted the whole of Turkey was at the visit by the PM. I asked him how this could be, since the visit was being kept as a matter of first class secrecy nobody could know that he had arrived. To this he replied, 'How could you keep an event of that kind secret? Of course everybody knows about it!' This was disconcerting as the necessity for secrecy had been strongly impressed on him. The situation was far from safe; there was a German company working in the vicinity of Adana reclaiming marshland. They were certain to become aware of the visit and the Turkish security arrangements were not likely to be of a very efficient nature.

Our two trains were drawn up tail to tail in the middle of an open plain, and were supposed to be surrounded by Turkish sentries. I thought it advisable to have a look round these sentries and found just what I expected. As it was raining each sentry had sat down on his hunkers and put his blanket over his head. Their primary concern was to keep dry and the security of the PM ranked as a very bad second. When I returned to the train from this investigation I looked for the PM's detective, whom I found in the dining car feeding, also more concerned with his personal comforts than with the PM's safety. I told him that the security arrangements were very poor and that he and his assistant must make a point of occasionally patrolling round Winston's sleeper through the night. He replied in an insolent manner, 'Am I expected to work all night as well as all day?' I then told him that he had travelled in identical comfort with the rest of the party, and that I was certainly not aware that he had even started working that day, and I most certainly would ensure that he did not leave a stone unturned to ensure the safety of the PM throughout the night. ...

During our discussion with Çakmak I was facing him seated at a long central table running down the centre of the railway carriage. Whilst talking to him I could see out of the window behind him, and suddenly spotted what I thought was a pallid harrier busy quartering over the plain. I had never seen a pallid harrier, and was not certain whether what I was looking at was one, or a hen harrier. I was consequently very intent on looking out of that window, much to Çakmak's discomforture, who kept looking round and possibly thought that I had spotted someone getting ready to have a shot at him! It was not possible for me to explain through the interpreter that I was only 'bird-watching'!!

The dinner party was a screaming success, Winston was quite at his best and had the whole party convulsed with laughter. In his astounding French, consisting of a combination of the most high flown French words mixed with English words pronounced in French, he embarked on the most complicated stories, which would have been difficult to put across adequately in English. On leaving the dinner table for his cabin he asked me to come along with him. He then informed me that he proposed to stop on for an additional day, that he had a great deal more to discuss with Inönü and would require at least another day. He also said that he felt certain I required much more time. I told him that it was highly undesirable that he should stop on and that all arrangements had been made for our departure for Cyprus by 12 noon the next day. I told him how inadequate the security arrangements were, and pointing to his berth told him it would be quite easy for anybody to blow him sky high in his bed! He gave the berth one perturbed look and said, 'Oh! do you think so?' I assured him that I had instructed his detectives to take every precaution against such a regrettable *contingency, so considered he would probably have a good night. Once more I impressed on him the fact that we must stick to our plan and be ready to depart on the morrow. Once more he repeated all the arguments that made it necessary to stop on. I bade him goodnight and left him, hoping for the best.*

31 January   Cyprus, 150 miles

Moderately comfortable night in a very dirty sleeping car, with continual hammering of hot water system. At 11 am we were by way of having another military conference with Çakmak. However owing to some hitch Çakmak had not been warned, and they were not ready. However we met again at 11.45 am and went over a draft of the conclusions arrived at during previous meeting. All went very well, but I found both these meetings very hard work, having to take the chair for our side and carry out all the negotiations in French. Added to the language trouble Çakmak's ideas of modern war are somewhat elementary, and it was very difficult to make him realize what the requirements of mechanization mean in terms of training, maintenance, repair, etc. Another grave difficulty arises out of the poor communications, both road and rail, in that country. Supply of equipment is consequently limited by what can be carried, and that is dependent on many of the civil wants such as corn, coal, petrol, etc.

On the whole the visit was a tremendous success. PM is delighted. Turkey's neutrality will from now on assume a far more biased nature in favour of the Allies, I hope somewhat similar to that of the Americans prior to their entry into the war.

Finally we all had lunch again with the President as the train moved off for Adana again. On arrival we had a great rush for the plane as at that moment plans were to return direct to Cairo. Plans on the previous evening were changed by PM who had decided that we were to stop one more night with the Turks! I had implored him not to as security arrangements were very poor and most of Turkey was aware of his presence. This morning I succeeded, with the help of Cadogan, to get him to decide not to stop in Turkey. However he then decided to return straight to Cairo instead of going to Cyprus. We had already got into the plane to go to Cairo when he discovered that the pilot was still under the impression that he was going to Cyprus! This was enough for a change of plans! The PM now decided that we should adhere to our original plan and go to Cyprus! Off we started down the runway but in turning one of the corners a wheel got off the runway and sank up to the axle. So we all got out again and for nearly an hour a crowd of jabbering Turks endeavoured to pull the wheel out of the mud. As they were making no progress we decided to change to the second Liberator, so out came all the luggage out of both machines and ours was transhipped. We then all packed in, warmed up the engines and were moving down the runway when we were told that our own plane had now been pulled out of the mud! However we decided to stick where we were and took off for Cyprus.

As we rose up and left Adana we had a wonderful view of the whole of the

Taurus range of mountains from one end to the other, all covered with snow glittering in the wintery sun. After about ½ an hour's flying we struck the east end of the island and had a very jolly fly over it with good visibility and lovely evening lights. The Governor met us and we are now very comfortably installed in Government House. A very good house which was built over the remains of the old house, burned down during the rising in Story's governorship. Our party has been reduced to the PM, Cadogan, Randolph, Martin, Thompson, Secretary, Detective and valet. Finished the day with large dinner party at Government House. Sat next to Lady Woolley, Governor's wife, and Hughes, commander of troops in Cyprus. After dinner had long talk to government official who is an expert on birds. Finally after PM had gone off to bed Lady Woolley played two bits on the piano which were quite lovely. Now to bed for a good sleep as I feel very tired. This is a very attractive house with two marvellous walls in the drawing room which slide bodily upwards turning 3 drawing rooms into one large room.

[Churchill] loved these sudden changes of plans. Unfortunately he often wished to carry out similar sudden changes in strategy! I had the greatest difficulty in making him realize that strategy was a long term process in which you could not frequently change your mind. He did not like being reminded of this fact and frequently shook his fist in my face and said, 'I do not want any of your long term projects, all they do is cripple initiative.' I agreed that it might possibly cripple initiative but all I wanted was to know when he would put his left foot down after having put down his right, and that I refused to look upon that as a 'long term project'.

1 February   Cairo, 600 miles

Had a grand sleep and comfortable morning with breakfast at 9 am. After breakfast talked to large gathering of representative magnates of Cyprus who had come to see the PM. Finally he appeared on the scene and made a very nice little speech to them. I then went off with Hughes (late commander 44th Div) who now commands the troops in Cyprus. We went to his HQ and climbed onto the roof from which we had an excellent view of the whole island. He explained to me the defensive organization and plans to meet attacks. We then drove up to the passes on the road from Nicosia (the capital) to Kyrenia on the north coast and a possible point of landing and attack on the capital. We then drove back to lunch with Hughes at his mess, and from there down to the aerodrome. Meanwhile PM had been inspecting the 4th Hussars. We all met and took off about 2 pm. Lovely clear weather and we had a beautiful fly back to Cairo. I climbed in to 2nd pilot's seat and had a lovely view. From Cyprus we went straight to Haifa, and then down along the coast to the boundary between Egypt and Palestine. From there we struck for Ismailia, where we crossed the Canal and on to pass just north of Cairo and came down at our usual landing ground.

It has been a most satisfactory trip and I never thought that we should make such headway with the Turks. Some of my wild dreams of bringing Turkey along with us no longer look quite so wild!

After tea Alexander and Dick McCreery came to see me to discuss the organization of the planning staff for the Sicilian operation. I then went out to dine with Bertie at the Mohammed Ali Club and had a grand long talk with him.

My 'wild dreams' about Turkey unfortunately remained wild dreams! Von Papen fooled the Turks about fictitious concentrations of German troops in Bulgaria which never existed. This was enough to keep them sitting on the fence. It is a pity as the entry of Turkey would have made a considerable difference, not that the Turkish forces could ever have been trained up and equipped to be much use. The real value would have been the use of Turkey for aerodromes and as a jumping off place for future action.

2 February

Started the day by attending GHQ 9.15 am conference to hear the latest about the general situation. Then spent an hour with Jumbo Wilson running through his task with him, and settling details as to how he is to look after administration of 8th Army, attend to equipping of Turks, and at the same time ensure that formations required for amphibious operations receive their full training. Came back to Embassy and was given telegram from PM to Roosevelt to check over. It was rather too optimistic as to what we are likely to be able to do during 1943, and I had to go to him to tone it down. Then lunched with Casey, a large party with PM, Moyne, Lampson, Spears, Cadogan, Sholto Douglas, etc. After lunch did some shopping and attended a film at the American Embassy of our trip to Turkey and also of the re-entry into Tripoli. All plans are now made for our departure to Tripoli tomorrow morning early, weather permitting. I only hope he will not suggest any more changes of plans at the last moment! It is high time we started turning homewards, and I shudder at the work to catch up again with events when I get home.

3 February   Tripoli, 1200 miles

We said goodbye to the Embassy at 8.30 and left for the aerodrome where we took off at 9.45 am. We had a lovely calm fly and most interesting. After lunch I went forwards to the 2nd Pilot's seat. We were just over El Alamein at that time and from there on I was able to look down on the various battle scenes, Buerat and then Misurata where we picked up an escort of fighters to accompany us forward. Up to then we had flown continuously over never ending desert. Now we came into the beginning of some form of elementary farming. Mussolini colonizing settlements consisting of little white cottages, a well and a few palm trees. Finally at 4.30 pm we landed at Castel Benito aerodrome outside Tripoli and were met by Monty and Alex. We drove off to Monty's camp, where Monty gave the PM and me a long talk on his situation. He then paraded the whole of his HQ which was addressed by the PM on a loudspeaker. Then we had further talks with Monty and dined in his Mess, the same tent we had dined with him in before the battle of El Alamein!!

Now I have retired to my caravan. It is infernally cold, so shall get into bed quick so as to get warm. It is a wonderful feeling finding myself back with 8th Army HQ and Monty after the last few months and to feel that during that short space the whole aspect of the war in North Africa has been changed.

4 February Tripoli

PM and I have been stopping in Montgomery's camp whilst rest of party were with Alexander.

At 9.30 am we all assembled and started off by car for Tripoli. It was most interesting seeing the place for the first time. The streets and housetops were lined with sentries, who held back the local inhabitants. When we arrived on the main square and sea front we found there the bulk of the 51st Division formed up on the sea front and main square. The last time we had seen them was near Ismailia just after their arrival in the Middle East. Then they were still pink and white, now they were bronzed warriors of many battles and of a victorious advance. I have seldom seen a finer body of men or one that looked prouder of being soldiers. We drove slowly round the line and then came back with the men cheering him all the way. We then took up our position on a prepared stand and the whole Division marched past with a bagpipe band playing. It was quite one of the most impressive sights I have ever seen. The whole Division was most beautifully turned out, and might have been in barracks for the last 3 months instead of having marched some 1200 miles and fought many battles during the same period. After the review we drove out into the country to see some of the Corps troops, Medium Artillery, Field Artillery, Anti Tank, Engineers, etc. In many places the native population cheered and clapped their hands as we went by. Oliver Leese, the Corps Commander, gave us a most excellent open air lunch after which we examined the various types of mines used by the enemy and the ways of defeating them.

From there we went to the New Zealand Div which was formed up complete on parade, with Bernard Freyberg at its head! He gave a General Salute by microphone and loud speaker which was admirably carried out. We then drove round the parade and finally the whole Division marched past. We then had some tea and drove to Castel Benito aerodrome for the PM to visit the Air Force. From there down to the harbour where we did a complete tour of the harbour in a launch and visited the blockships which they are busy clearing. They had just succeeded in bringing in a 2,900 ton ship, the first to get through. We finished up the harbour by seeing the destruction of the wharfs and quays carried out by Germans and the work we are doing to put it right. The Germans did a very thorough job of it and a great deal of work is required.

Returned to camp to find telegram from home trying to stop PM from going to Algiers owing to a message which had been intercepted pointing towards attempts on his life in Algiers. He decided to carry on with his original plan. We therefore start at 5 am tomorrow for Algiers and there are not many hours left for sleep. While I write a heavy air raid on Tripoli is going on and we have been watching the shells bursting.

As I stood alongside of Winston watching the Division march past, with the wild music of the pipes in my ears, I felt a large lump rise in my throat and a tear run down my face. I looked round at Winston and saw several tears on his face, from which I knew that he was being stirred inwardly by the self same feelings that were causing such upheaval in me. It was partly due to the fact that the transformation of these men from their raw pink and white appearance in Ismailia to their bronzed war-hewn countenances provided a tangible and visible sign of the turn of the tide of war. The meaning of this momentous change was brought home to me more forcibly than it had been up to the present. For the first time I was beginning to live through the thrill of those first successes that were now rendering ultimate victory possible. The depth of these feelings can only be gauged when considered in relation to the utter darkness of those early days of calamities when no single ray of hope could pierce the depth of gloom. It was only after having stared utter perdition in the face that one could sense the fathomless depth of relief caused by a realization that victory had now become a practical proposition. I felt no shame that tears should have betrayed my feelings, only a deep relief.

5 February Algiers, 900 miles

I was called at 3 am, had a little breakfast 3.30 and by 4 am started off for Castel Benito aerodrome. We arrived there about 5 am and by 5.30 am sailed off into the dark. We had to head south west first to avoid Tunisia and finally north for Algiers. The journey resulted in some 900 miles. I slept for the first 3 hours of it and then spent the last hour looking out on southern Algeria. We finally arrived at 10 am on Maison Blanche aerodrome. There I found Eisenhower to meet me. He told me that PM had landed some 10 minutes pre-viously and that he had sent him on in his half-armoured car with windows smeared with oil and mud. He was to go by a circuitous route. I could see Eisenhower was somewhat worried with the responsibility of having him on his hands. I then got into Eisenhower's car and we drove back by the direct route with a man armed with a Tommy gun beside the driver and Eisenhower with a revolver. We saw no suspicious characters. On arriving here I had break-fast, bath and shave in Eisenhower's house. Anderson then turned up from 1st Army and I had long talk with him on questions affecting his front. It was a useful meeting as it became clear to me at once that he required more infantry. On this strength I got Eisenhower to send a telegram on my behalf to the WO to order an additional infantry division. Anderson and I then had to go to the PM. We found him in bed. He started by saying he proposed to stop another day! I told him that if the weather was good he should decide to go tonight. After some difficulty got him to agree.

I then attended large lunch given by Eisenhower, and attended by PM, Giraud, Noguès, Boisson, Peyrouton [Governor-General Algeria], Alex Cadogan and Cunningham. I was interested at meeting Noguès [Resident-General and C-in-C Morocco] and Boisson [Governor-General of West Africa]. Did not think much of the former, but the latter impressed me much more favourably. After lunch I had a long talk with Cunningham, and then had a walk round looking for birds in the garden. Discovered the same African bluetit that I saw at Marrakesh.

Had tea with Eisenhower and a long talk with him before dinner, which we had in Admiral Cunningham's villa. PM, Cunningham, Randolph, Doctor, Bedell Smith etc were there. After dinner we formed a convoy and departed for the aerodrome. I got into the aeroplane, put on pyjamas and flying suit on top with fur lined boots and prepared to take off. Engines warmed up and went on turning round, and yet we never took off! At last pilot sent word to get out again one by one and to watch the propellers not to be hit by them. We discovered that one of the two magnetos of engine no 1 of the PM's plane had refused to function and would have to be changed! We soon found that the delay would make it impossible for us to start, so there was nothing for it but to dress again and return to Eisenhower's house again for the night. Finally rolled into bed at 2 am dog tired.

I did not mention in my diary that the bed I rolled into was that of Butcher, Ike's ADC, and that the bed was still warm as the unfortunate Butcher was turned out of it to make room for me!

6 February   Gibraltar, 500 miles

I had a grand sleep till 9 am, a good breakfast, and then went round to see the PM about the journey on. I had discovered from my pilot that he did not at all like the idea of going direct from Algiers to England as he was not so well fitted out with radio directional gear as Van de Gould, the PM's pilot. We therefore decided that I should go direct to Gibraltar and on whilst the PM went direct and that we should time to arrive about the same time. I consequently had an early lunch with Eisenhower and was at the Maison Blanche aerodrome by 2 pm. Just as we were moving off to get into position to take off, two fighter planes came in simultaneously apparently not seeing each other. They both crashed on the runway, one of them turning over onto the pilot and bursting into flames at once! The other pilot luckily did not catch fire and I do not know whether he was damaged or not. We had to move right up to within about 30 yards of the crash in order to get sufficient of the runway to take off.

We had an excellent journey leaving at 2.30 and reaching Gibraltar at 5 pm. We skirted along the African coast, passing Oran and Melilla. Arrived here with lovely lights over the Rock. Mason-MacFarlane met us on the aerodrome and took us up to Government House where we had tea. After tea I had a walk in the garden looking for birds, saw a peregrine falcon high up in the sky. Mason-MacFarlane staged a defensive fire demonstration for us after dinner. We were motored up to the top of the Rock at about 11 pm and from there had a wonderful view of the tracer bullets of machine guns firing out to sea in a zone illuminated by searchlights. At the same time searchlights and all AA guns engaged imaginary targets in the air. It was a most impressive sight.

At 1.15 am we went down to the aerodrome and at 2.15 am sailed into the darkness on the last stage of the journey.

7 February   Ferney Close, 1500 miles

A cold and uncomfortable night. At 9 am we were over the Scilly Isles and 10 minutes later came to Land's End. Clouds were low and the going very bumpy. However by 10 am we reached Lyneham aerodrome and made a safe landing. We found that we were about 30 minutes ahead of the Prime Minister's plane which had flown straight from Algiers. Cadogan and I went on direct to the train where we had breakfast and a wash and greeted the PM a few minutes later. By 1 pm we arrived in London where to my great joy you met me.

I had finished a journey of some 10,200 miles, which had been full of interest and had resulted in agreements with Americans and Turks far above anything I had hoped for. In the last two years I have flown just under 55,000 miles!!

I now foresee some hard work ahead to convert some of the paper work of the last 3 weeks into facts and actions.

8 February

After a peaceful Sunday evening and Monday morning I left Ferney Close for London. Arrived at the flat at 1 pm and after lunch walked to the WO to start work there again. At 5.30 pm we had the usual Monday Cabinet which was taken by Attlee. Since dinner I have been digging into old files and trying to get level with the work again. It is funny how quickly one settles back into the old groove. I hardly feel as if I had been away and can hardly realize that in the last 3 weeks I have covered over 10,000 miles and visited Casablanca, Marrakesh, Cairo, Adana, Cyprus, Cairo, Tripoli, Algiers and Gibraltar.

9 February

Back into the ordinary routine again!! COS all morning, then McNaughton and Stewart from 3.30 to 4.30 and Paget from 4.30 to 5.30 pm. The S of S from 5.30 to 7.30 pm! Not much time left and DMO to see. Finally Basil to dine and at 11 pm sat down to try and work off some of the files that had accumulated all day.

10 February

At this morning's COS we struggled with attempts to put date of attack on Sicily further into June [i.e. mount it sooner]. Both President and PM are hankering after this, personally I feel we are running grave risks of wrecking the whole show by trying to rush it. After lunch I had interview with Godwin-Austen to ensure that he devoted sufficient attention to the difficulties of fighting mines when attending Montgomery's conference in Tripoli. Then a mass of files, including checking up the PM's speech for tomorrow. Finally Harry Crerar to dinner and a long harangue from him as to the necessity of getting some Canadians fighting soon for Imperial and political reasons. I fully see his point and his difficulties – I wish he could see mine and all their complexity!!!

11 February
Started the day by being sent for by the PM to discuss one or two of the bits out of his speech for the House. Then a fairly short COS. Neil Ritchie came to lunch with me, and in the afternoon I had interviews with the S of S and Ronnie Weeks.

12 February
Finished off our COS meeting fairly quickly. Then interview with S of S, followed by visit from new Spanish Military Attaché. Then lunched with [Benita's sister] Madeline and Jack [Lees] at Brown's Hotel and went round to the Annexe at 3 pm to see PM concerning desirability or not of offering Iraq-Persia Command to Auchinleck. PM in bed with fever, I hope it won't be bad. Got him to agree that Auchinleck should not be offered this command. I had intended to discuss other questions of command, but did not like to worry him when he had this fever.

   Army Council meeting at 5.30 pm with no important items. Then dined with Cobbold at Dorchester at dinner he gave to Andrews, the new American General over here.

13 February
A very short COS which allowed me to finish most of the office work before lunch. Adam came to lunch and we had a long talk together. After lunch I had a long go with Ronnie Weeks and Sandy Galloway and then started off for home.

14 February
A peaceful Sunday at home with you.

15 February
Spent most of the COS meeting in examining the possibility of shifting forward date of Sicily attack to June instead of July, all on the assumption that Tunis can be cleared by May 1st. As both American and the British considerations have to be taken into account it is not easy to arrive at a conclusion. Gort came to lunch, his lip is not yet right but he looks much better than he did. Cabinet at 6 pm. Winston there but with very bad sore throat and cold. Dined with Harriman to meet Andrews. Big party with Grigg, Sinclair, Alexander, Cripps, Leathers, Pound, Mountbatten, Stark, Pug Ismay and several Americans.

16 February
Finished COS fairly early and had quiet afternoon except for a Selection Board.

17 February

At this morning's COS we had Andrews, the new American General, and also the Principal Administrative Officers to discuss the flow of American reinforcements into this country to build up an American force. Something has gone wrong with our Casablanca agreement and the flow has not started at all.

After lunch I had several interviews. First a Mr Wagg, American war correspondent, sent to me by Evelyn Wrench. He was very upset with [illegible, even to the diarist] and his lack of appreciation of American outlook, and consequently the way in which he was widening the rift between us and the Americans in India. Then General d'Astier de la Vigerie, de Gaulle's second string. He wanted more planes to drop arms in France. I told him what I thought of the French lack of realization of the true situation, and of their failure to get together to fight Germany instead of squabbling amongst themselves. After him came Percy Hambro saying that he had heard that Bulgy Thorne was leaving Scotland and would love to have him working with him in Subversive Activities. I told him that this was the first I had heard about it. Then Exham just back from Moscow whom I had to pump on the most recent developments. He corroborated all I knew as to the Russian attitude and their desire to get as much as they could and give as little back as possible.

18 February

Bertie Ramsay just back from North Africa came to our COS meeting and gave us the most recent information about the planning side of the Sicilian operations. Evidently Eisenhower does not think he can possibly undertake the operation before July moon in spite of the pressure that is being applied to him to do it in June. In any case after the recent defeat he has suffered in Tunisia I doubt very much whether he can clear Tunisia of Germans before May at the very earliest if even then!

Attended dull Cabinet at 6 pm to decide about Tizard's mission to Moscow, and the desirability that he should collect some information. This evening heated argument with S of S trying to prevent a most awful broadcast by Commanders-in-Chief during a BBC Army Week. He is adopting a peevish child attitude about it which makes him impossible to deal with.

This last paragraph surprises me! It cannot have been a very heated argument as I remember nothing about it! It must have been a very exceptional occasion for P.J. to adopt a 'peevish or childish attitude' as I cannot remember his ever being in that frame of mind. It seems more probable that I was in a peevish and childish mood myself!

19 February

A long COS meeting at which Dickie Mountbatten gave me a heap of trouble with a proposed attack on the Channel Islands which was not in its proper strategical setting and tactically quite adrift. Lunched with Adam and had a walk in [St James's] Park where crocuses are coming out fast. Visits from Grasett [Allied Forces] and Crocker [IX Corps Tunisia] in the afternoon. Discussed future of Polish forces with the former.

20 February
Succeeded in finishing COS fairly early. Then went to Embankment to see a specimen of [illegible] Landing Craft. Lunched with myself at the flat and finished work quickly at WO. Then drove Barney to Camberley and went on to Ferney Close.

21 February
Quietly at home, but spoilt by bad news from Tunisia. I am afraid the American troops will take a great deal more training before they will be any use, and that Anderson [1st Army] is not much good! Sent wire to Alex telling him to get rid of him if he thinks he is no good.

I remember being very disturbed at the reports and rumours I heard about Anderson at this period. I had formed a high opinion of his fighting ability in France before Dunkirk, but felt that he was not living up to that opinion. From a distance it was hard to judge, and I had some doubts as to whether Alexander would have enough grit to get rid of him if it became necessary. Luckily such a course never became necessary.

22 February
COS meeting mainly concerned with meeting with Mason-Mac and deciding details about Gib. You and Pooks came to lunch.

When I returned to WO found urgent message from PM to come round at once. He wanted to see me before he went to sleep as he had had letter from [the] King saying he was most disturbed by situation in North Africa, both political and military. Rushed round and read King's message, thought it very regrettable that he should disturb the PM when he was ill. Advised PM to alter two paras of his letter. Thought he was still looking very ill, although he said that he was much better with a temperature of only 100 and was quite ready to joke.

Cabinet at 6 pm, peevish and full of questions about Tunisia. Lewin came to dinner. I am not at all happy about Tunisia and very doubtful if Alexander is man enough to pull it straight!

It had been made quite clear by what had happened up to date that Eisenhower had not got the required ability to ensure success in this theatre. Alexander, his deputy, had many very fine qualities but no very great strategic vision. He had been carried by Montgomery through North Africa as regards the strategic and tactical handling of the situation. Monty was now far from him, and Anderson certainly had not got the required qualities to inspire Alex. It was very doubtful whether he was fit to command his Army. The only comfort rested in the fact that Dick McCreery was still Alex's Chief of Staff and I had the very greatest confidence in his ability.

23 February

Started with a COS which lasted till close on 12 noon. Then had to go to Cabinet meeting in the House where we discussed desirability of introducing restrictions on visitors to the South Coast.

After lunch, long talk with James Drew [Training Combined Operations]. Followed by Wilson who is just back from accompanying Dill to Chungking and Delhi. At 5 pm went to Soviet Embassy for their entertainment and after dinner am now just off for a Defence Committee at 10 pm. Hope we may not be kept up too late.

24 February

Very short and uninteresting COS. Lady Margaret Alexander came to lunch to hear latest news of Alex. After lunch, visit by Chinese General over from Washington. Followed by Franklyn [Home Forces] to explain his proposed lay out for the Home Forces and ADG[B] organization. Then conference with S of S on Airborne Forces and Army Air Support. Then Martel wishing to find out what his future fate was to be and what the reasons were why we were not giving him a command at once. Then Paget with news of his trip to Tripoli and to discuss his exercise which starts next week, and during which McNaughton is to command one side.

Whilst taking my midday exercise in the Park I ran into Hore-Belisha! Looking more greasy and objectionable than ever, he insisted on walking with me which annoyed me as I did not want to talk to him and wanted to look for the scaup duck on the lake which I have been unfortunate enough not to find yet.

25 February

A fairly short COS, then lunched with Ronnie Weeks at his flat. Walked back to WO and again met Hore-Belisha in the Park, who again began to pump me on Tunisia. At 3.30 did short broadcast for winding up of the introduction to the Army Week on the BBC. At 4.30 to Buckingham Palace where I had an hour's interview with the King. He asked me all about the military situation and took the greatest interest in all details. Came back to WO and attended a film in the WO of our going to North Africa which was quite good. Am very worried by way in which Americans are failing to live up to our Casablanca agreements. They are entirely breaking down over promises of American divisions to arrive in this country.

26 February

I had to attack Portal this morning on the paucity of bomber squadrons with the 1st Army in Tunisia. But unfortunately with the usual results! Sikorski came to lunch with me. I found him in rather a depressed mood. I think the burdens of his job were weighing specially heavily on him, as they do on all of us at times! He was having trouble with the commanders of both Scottish and Iraq Polish forces, and in addition Russia and also the Foreign Office were troubling him. Nonetheless he was quite as charming as ever and we settled a good deal together. After lunch had interview with Browning [1st Airborne Division], found he had badly smashed himself up in a bad glider landing! Looked ill, wanted rest. Told him he must take full fortnight's leave at least. Then told him off for causing trouble by writing letters to politicians, he took it very well. Attended Army Council Meeting and then dined with Stark at dinner to meet Andrews who had been ill with flu and looked none too well.

27 February
A nice peaceful Saturday on which I finished work early and slipped off home a few minutes after 4 pm!

28 February
Lovely quiet Sunday at home with you.

1 March
Left home 8 am. War Office by 9.10 am. Masses of telegrams in over the weekend, and S of S also wanting to see me before COS meeting. COS mainly concerned with shipping situation and fact that American COS are not living up to our Casablanca agreements. Marshall is quite hopeless and has no strategic concepts of any kind. He now proposes to waste shipping equipping French forces which can play no part in the strategy of 1943.

At 3.30 pm another conference with DCIGS Movements, Q [QMG], and DMO on shipping. Then Cabinet at 5.30 pm fairly quickly finished as Winston is still absent. Dined Nuffield Club with Americans and sat between Andrews and Hartle. At 10 pm had to go to PM where I spent an hour settling various appointments. Pownall to Iraq-Persia, Martel to Moscow, Auchinleck to a Governorship and Giffard or Platt to Burma Command. PM very much better. Anthony Eden came in while I was there. Winston produced a beauty in referring to the manner in which we treated the Turks. He said: 'We must start by treating them purry-purry puss-puss, then later we shall harden!'

2 March
A long and difficult COS on shipping attended by Lord Leathers and Lord Cherwell. The Americans are letting us down, and we cannot find the shipping for all our enterprises. Some centralized Shipping Control Board handling the globular shipping is essential. I then lunched with Colonel Kalla to meet

President Benes. He was very interesting on the future of Czechoslovakia, Russia, the collapse of Germany, the future of the League of Nations, etc. Came back to WO to meet a French General over from France who is organizing secret forces in France. Then interview with Gort prior to his return to Malta and to discuss his probable visit to present sword to Stalingrad. Finally Defence Committee at 6 pm.

3 March

Gort came to the COS this morning and we had a long discussion concerning his directive which is not very easy to prepare owing to the very complicated system of command in the Mediterranean. We also had a long discussion about the organization of the wireless interception service. I had d'Astier de la Vigerie, Billotte and Archdale to lunch. Conversation mainly centred round the provision of arms and explosives for the secret forces in France. Back to WO where I picked you up for tea about 4 pm, and saw you off at Waterloo. In the evening the Strathconas and Lady Jean Rankin came to dinner and we had a film show after dinner. Heavy air raid in the distance as retaliation for attack on Berlin, but it failed to penetrate to the centre of London as far as we could tell.

4 March

I was expecting an attack by Rommel on Montgomery today. But so far no news about it. COS mostly concerned with subversive activities. After lunch went to see Amery in India Office about Auchinleck and Air Transport as usual. Then had to inform Martel that he was for Moscow [Head of Military Mission] which he did not appreciate very much!

5 March

A long and tiring COS first fighting CAS who wished to give American airmen priority over Canadian troops in the limited shipping. Then more differences with him as regards provision of Airborne Forces. Finally telegram from PM to Stalin concerning stopping of convoys to Russia had to be redrafted and took us to 1.30 pm. We all three of us had to give up any idea of going to the Guildhall lunch of 'Wings for Victory'. During afternoon Martel came back to see me again, evidently not happy about his trip to Russia. At 6.30 went to see Tripoli film, and after that dinner at Dorchester by Army Council for Andrews.

6 March

Fairly short COS. Then had Rollie Charrington to lunch and motored him home after lunch. Great excitement [at Ferney Close] as two small white goats were born during the afternoon.

7 March

Left at 9 am with Adam to see 'Spartan', a Home Forces Exercise. Started by motoring to Godalming to see Andy McNaughton commanding Canadian Army, and proving my worst fears that he is quite incompetent to command an army! He does not know how to begin the job and was tying up his forces into the most awful muddle. Then went to Newbury to see Crerar and his Corps HQ, a real good show. He has improved that Corps out of all recognition. From there on to Oxford to see the Control Centre. Met S of S, Paget and Budget Loyd there. Quite clear that Paget was quite incapable of realizing how bad Andy McNaughton is! Went on through Bicester to see Herbert Lumsden and his Corps. Then I missed Gammell. Got home at 8 pm.

8 March

Drove Rollie Charrington up. Lunched with Gort at Turf Club. Dull Cabinet without PM at 5.30 pm. Quiet evening.

9 March

Another difficult COS meeting at which we again discusssed shipping with Lord Leathers and Cherwell. You came up to lunch and we went to Harrods to select a book case (*for bird books*). Fairly peaceful afternoon.

10 March

Very heated argument at COS with Mountbatten who was again putting up wild proposals disconnected with his direct duties. He will insist on doing work of Force Commanders and does it infernally badly! Both Portal and I were driven to distraction by him. After lunch visited [illegible] Secret Service organization. Very interesting, but did not satisfy me as to secret agent organization in Italy, Sicily and Sardinia, which to all intents and purposes is non-existent.

11 March

During our COS meeting this morning we were visited by Andrews and discussed defence of Scotland with him. In afternoon had long interview with Hobart to explain to him new job I wish him to take on connected with flotation tanks, searchlight tanks, anti-mine tanks and self-propelled guns. This evening dined at Claridges with Chinese Chargé d'Affaires to meet General H. Soong who is at present over here from America.

12 March

Fairly short COS meeting followed by office work and a good walk in the Park where I had an excellent look at the scaup duck. Then more office work before

Army Council meeting. Then dinner party with Archie Nye and his wife and Mrs Knox the head of the ATS an awful woman!! and I should say totally unsuited for her present appointment. Shallow, self-opinionated, conceited, perhaps efficient, but with so little knowledge of the world as to make her quite unsuitable for her present appointment!

13 March
Finished off early and went home after lunch.

14 March
Started flu after tea and went to bed where I remained whole of the week, nursed by you till you also caught it.

[No entries for 15–23 March 1943.]

24 March
Returned to work midday. Found a lot of worries to meet me. Montgomery's attack not going well and driven back on the sea. The plans for Sicily all altered. More difficulties as regards organization of Supreme Command for overseas operations etc. PM sent for me on way back to flat and was very nice, saying that I was not to overwork and that I should take it easy for the next few days.

25 March
Had fairly long COS meeting at which we discussed organization for planning re-entry into Europe, and the appointment of a Chief of Staff until such time as we are able to appoint a Supreme Commander. After lunch Alexander Hardinge came to see me to discuss [the] King's proposed visit to North Africa as soon as Tunisia has been cleared. King apparently keen to go out and it seems a very good moment for him. Then at 5.15 pm meeting under PM to discuss Eisenhower's new alterations to plans for attack on Sicily and preparation of telegram in which we expressed our disapproval of his proposed plans. Finished office before dinner and had a quiet evening with bird books.

26 March
Andrews (USA General) attended COS meeting at which we discussed organization of the staff to plan the future re-entry into France. During the meeting the PM sent for me. By the time I was rid of Andrews and had reached him in the Annexe he was in his bath! However he received me as soon as he came out, looking like a Roman Centurion with nothing on except a large bath towel draped around him! He shook me warmly by the hand in this get up and told me to sit down while he dressed. A most interesting procedure, first he stepped into a white silk vest, then white silk drawers, and walked up and down the

room in this kit, looking rather like 'Humpty Dumpty', with a large body and small thin legs! Then a white shirt which refused to join comfortably round the neck and so was left open with a bow tie to keep it together. Then the hair (what there is of it!) took much attention, a handkerchief was sprayed with scent and then rubbed over his head. The few hairs were then brushed, and finally sprayed direct! Finally trousers, waistcoat and coat, and meanwhile he rippled on the whole time about Monty's battle and our proposed visit to North Africa. However, the main thing he wanted to say was that he thought I looked tired last night at the meeting we had and that I was to take a long weekend!

This evening Army Council meeting. After dinner, Bertie suddenly turned up having returned suddenly from Cairo.

27 March
Finished off work before lunch. Bertie Brooke came to lunch, having just arrived back from Cairo. Received news of Julian Brooke's death [Basil's son] near Mareth Line. Went home after lunch.

28 March
Peaceful day at home, but unfortunately with you in bed [flu].

29 March
Made usual early start. Arrived office 9.15 am to find my table littered with telegrams and letters, and a message from PM that he wished to speak to me. I found that he was upset that Alexander was not sending him messages and that he was receiving them direct from Monty. He was suspecting that Eisenhower was interfering with Alexander's free channel of communication to him! This I discovered later was due to a message that he had received from Macmillan to the effect that Eisenhower had expressed dissatisfaction with [the] King's message being sent direct to Monty!

Lunched with Sikorski who was as usual quite charming. Then Cabinet at 5.30 pm after which I had to go and dine with Winston, a *tête-à-tête* dinner sitting in arm chairs in the drawing room. Dinner consisted of plover's eggs, chicken broth, chicken pie, chocolate soufflé and with it a bottle of champagne between us, port and brandy! We discussed the organization of Europe after the war, his disapproval of Roosevelt's plan to build up China whilst neglecting France etc. But the main subject was his disappointment about Eisenhower, and plans for our next trip to North Africa. At 10.30 pm we went to a meeting with the Joint Planners to listen to an account of the proposed plan for the capture of Sicily. He took it fairly well but as usual considered we were using far too much strength and that we ought to be capturing both Southern Italy and Greece at the same time. Now rolling to bed about 1 am, dog tired!!

30 March
A fairly short COS meeting. At 3 pm a Selection Board followed by a Military Members meeting to discuss PM's unsound plan for bringing in a war medal. Then Martel came to say goodbye before his departure for Moscow and then General Lee (USA Commander of Airborne Forces) came to discuss results of his visit over here.

31 March
I was sent for by PM at 10.15 am to examine telegram he proposed to send to Alexander concerning lack of information received from him. The telegram was all right luckily so the interview remained a peaceful one. Then short COS followed by lunch at Mansion House to meet Queen Wilhelmina [Netherlands], who came with Prince Bernhard. I sat opposite to her with Nuffield on my right and Rothschild on my left. In afternoon Percy Hambro came to discuss degree to which the Foreign Office was interfering in his SOE activities. Then interview with S of S, followed by conference on reorganization of the infantry battalion. Finally Crerar came to dinner and I had a long discussion with him as to which was the best method of having McNaughton recalled back to Canada to avoid his commanding a Canadian Army which he is totally incapable of doing!

1 April
A fairly short COS occupied in organizing the staff of the Chief of Staff for future Supreme Commander in this island. (*For liberation of France.*) Then after lunch interview with Ludlow Hewitt on organization of Air Force destined to cooperate with Army. Then Hobart on questions of organization of his division to handle various specialized forms of armoured vehicles such as amphibious tanks, search light tanks, mine destroying tanks, flame throwers etc. Then Butler back from Abyssinia. Finally dinner party with Mrs Eden, Barney's sister, John Kennedy and Lady Jean Rankin and her husband, at which we showed film of birds.

2 April
In the afternoon had visit from Sir Arthur [Archibald] Sinclair just back from Washington, then Wilkinson who is sort of liaison officer with MacArthur and quite interesting in his accounts of the prima donna!

At 5 pm an Army Council meeting to discuss PM's proposals for a medal.

3 April
Adam came to lunch prior to departing on a trip to India and back. And then went home where I found you up but very flat and tired after your flu.

4 April
A quiet day at home with rose pruning.

5 April
An early start back and protracted COS. In evening Cabinet meeting. Mountbatten gone sick.

6 April
In the evening whilst in a conference with Secretary of State on subject of reorganization of Home Forces on an Expeditionary Force basis, I was sent for by PM. This was to hear Monty's account of his successful Gabes Gap attack [in Tunisia]. PM wanted to issue information at once and I had difficulty in checking him considering that he had only received Monty's illicit short cut report, and no official report from Eisenhower or Alex. Luckily got him to agree. Dined with Cobbold to meet Bertie, also many American officers. In afternoon sent for by Amery to discuss question of divorcing commander of Burma operations from C-in-C India. There is a great deal in what he says and many aspects of the problem.

7 April
After COS lunched with Spanish Ambassador (Alba). PM also there and Minister of Agriculture, Croft, Portuguese Ambassador, Cadogan, etc. Dined with Birley and his wife. Victor Warrender [Parliamentary Secretary, Admiralty] also there.

8 April
A difficult COS meeting. We had the Joint Planners in and discussed future Mediterranean policy after capture of Sicily. I had difficulty with both Portal and Pound, who wandered about in their fluid elements and seldom touched the ground with their feet! After lunch had long interview with Paget on future employment of Canadians. Finally quiet evening with bird books.

9 April
First of all a COS which lasted till 12 noon. Then a Cabinet meeting on supplies and arms for Russia at 12 noon. From 3 pm to 5 pm a difficult Staff meeting under PM on shipping, concerning the minimum supplies required to maintain the British Isles, shipping required for India, and possibilities of running early supplies through the Mediterranean. Then 5 pm to 6 pm with Gardiner on plans for [Operation] Husky [Sicily] and the difficulties of arriving at coordinated action owing to Montgomery's egotistical outlook.

Then S of S to 6.30 pm on command of West Africa, probable arrival of

Marshall and Hopkins in the near future, recall of Wavell, Peirse and Somerville to discuss future attacks on Burma. At last finally dinner with Bertie, S of S, Lord Leathers and Harriman which went off quite successfully.

10 April

Short COS and an early departure for home.

11 April

Spent arranging cases for Gould's books, ironing tissue paper in Meyer's book with you, and arranging black cupboard for you here.

12 April

Early departure from home, with puncture on way to WO. Then a busy day culminating with Cabinet at 6 pm where I had long statement to make connected with fighting in Tunisia, where Monty is securing Sousse.

13 April

Tunisian news continues to be excellent. COS meeting at which we discussed future moves after capture of Sicily. This evening meeting with PM which started being stormy and then improved. Discussing advisability of removing all landing craft from this country to the Mediterranean for 1943 and devoting the whole of our energies to the Mediterranean. Luckily PM finally agreed but we are to put paper up to Defence Committee to prove our case. Basil came to dine.

14 April

We were busy again with future operations in the Mediterranean and elaborate deception plans.

You came up to lunch at 10 Downing Street where we found Portuguese Ambassador and his wife, Lady Harlech, Oliver Lyttelton, Mrs Randolph Churchill and one other. After lunch we shopped together.

15 April

A depressing COS as recent telegrams from America show that we are just about back where we were before Casablanca! Their hearts are really in the Pacific, we are trying to run two wars at once which is quite impossible with limited resources of shipping. All we can hope for is to go all out to defeat Italy and thus produce the greatest dispersal of German forces and make the going easier for the Russians. If we even knew what the Russians hope to do!! But we have no inkling.

Lunched at Claridges to meet Jones, the New Zealand Defence Minister. Not very impressive to meet. After lunch Strang came round from Australia House having been sent by Bruce to discuss ways and means of sharing information on jungle fighting between India and Australia.

16 April
A fairly short COS. After lunch interview with American Director of Military Operations, General Handy. Then a Military Members meeting of the Army Council. And in the evening a dinner for Generals Andrews, Paget and McNaughton. After lunch I was sent for by PM to 10 Downing St where he had Jones to lunch to discuss question of retention of NZ forces for employment in Sicily operation and also regarding possibility of promoting Freyberg to command a Corps.

17 April
Whilst at COS received instructions from PM to go round to see Attlee to discuss possibility of using NZ Div for Sicily operation. Fraser had wired back that he could not give decision till House met on April [May] 19th! and disinclined to assemble House on purpose. Settled with Attlee for him to discuss it with NZ Defence Minister, at present over here, and state that if Fraser was certain enough of carrying House delay would not matter.

Went home. After tea PM called up concerning ridiculous wire he had received from Marshall concerning advisability of starting attack on Sicily before Tunisia was clear!! Quite mad and quite impossible, but PM delighted with this idea which showed according to him 'a high strategic conception'. I had half hour row with him on the telephone.

18 April
Quiet day at home.

19 April
Went straight to Hatfield aerodrome where we saw a demonstration of all the most recent types of aircraft, specially arranged for PM. We were also shown latest aircraft without propellers, driven by air sucked in in front and squirted out behind! Apparently likely to be the fighter of the future. Drove back to London with PM who had forgiven my frankness of Saturday [17 April]. Busy afternoon in office, then Cabinet from 5.30 to 8.15 pm. After dinner hard work till 10 pm. Then visit to PM to explain plan of attack in Tunis, which starts tonight! After that meeting with PM to examine plan for recapture of Burma which lasted till close on 1 am. Very tired off to bed!

Winston did not like the plan for the capture of Burma, and produced one of his priceless sentences by saying, 'You might as well eat a porcupine one quill at a time'!

20 April

No news yet of the start of the Tunis attack. Long discussion at the Chiefs of Staff meeting concerning future moves after capture of Sicily. Very difficult to appreciate what form the collapse of Italy may take and what its implications may mean for us. You and Ti came up to lunch to my great joy, and we went on to Harrods. At 3.15 meeting with MS and Selection Board to settle honours and awards for King's birthday.

21 April

Remarkably quiet day! A short COS, no interviews and not much office work. Spent most of the afternoon appreciating probable course of action by the Germans during 1943. Not a very easy problem. I think however that their policy will aim at maximum offensive against our shipping at sea and defensive on land and in the air on all other fronts. Should have departed for week's salmon fishing on the Dee today with Ivan Cobbold if it had not been for Wavell's impending arrival!!!

22 April

While I was sipping my tea in bed at 8.15 am I was suddenly told that Archie Wavell was arriving at Hendon at 8.45 am!! I had a rush to dress and have breakfast. Arrived Hendon 9.15 and was told that he had landed at Elstree aerodrome instead. Had a hunt for this aerodrome and found Handley Page aerodrome instead! Finally discovered Archie and Peirse having a cup of tea! Dropped Archie at flat and dashed off to COS meeting which lasted till lunch. Then back to flat to lunch with Archie and take him for a meeting at 10 Downing St to discuss plans for attack on Burma. Peirse and Somerville were also there. PM gave his views why he considered the operation like 'munching a porcupine quill by quill'! He considered we should wait till we got Russia in against Japan. We should then establish air bases near Vladivostok from which Japan could be bombed, and according to him we should then sing the Ladybird Song to the Japs, namely, 'Ladybird, ladybird, fly away home, your house is on fire and your children at home!'

Then back to WO to work at routine and interview with Amery at 6 pm. He was again propounding the Viceroy's theory about the necessity of constituting a new front for Burma independent of India.

23 April

A tiring morning. Started COS meeting with USA General to discuss the organization of large scale feints this year to simulate impending attacks. American made some difficulty about Morgan running the show as it might detract from his energies in preparing plans for 1944!!* Andrews remained for an hour to

---

*F.E. Morgan was newly appointed COSSAC (Chief of Staff, Supreme Allied Commander), with responsibility for planning the invasion of Europe. Outlining his job to him, Brooke said, 'Well, there it is. It won't work, but you must bloody well make it.'

settle what should have been done in 15 minutes and I grew peevish towards the end. Then at 11.30 Archie Wavell, Peirse and Somerville came to discuss the prospects of Burma Campaign, and we were there till 1.15 pm. Archie propounded all the difficulties and a very fair estimate of the poor means of solving these problems. Peirse and Somerville apparently have no ideas and take little interest in the solution of the problem! A typical example of the Navy and Air Force dislike for taking any responsibility or producing any ideas and in fact handing over control to Army and yet always up in arms when any idea is put forward for unity of control!

After lunch saw Paget and McNaughton and arranged for replacing of 3rd Div by a Canadian Division in the plans for attack on Sicily. Although Canadians have continually been asking for this I received no sign of gratitude from McNaughton! Archie Wavell still stopping here.

24 April

A very hurried morning. I sent Wavell off to his sister, and then home for Easter!

25 and 26 April

Quietly at home for Easter and Bank Holiday.

27 April

Left early as usual. Attended ANZAC Service at St Martin's in the Field[s]. Then lunch with Archie. COS at 3.15. Mountbatten back from his bed of sickness. At 6.15 Cabinet till 8.15. Then Grigg and Amery to dine to discuss organization of Burma Command. Wavell very disappointing, just as silent as usual and refusing to express his views!!

28 April

A long and very tiring COS at which we had the attendance of the Indian Cs-in-C and all the planners. We discussed lengthily the various alternatives open to offensive from India directed against Burma or Sumatra etc. Came to the conclusion that the offensive for 43/44 must be reduced to a very minor one. To consist mainly in the development of the air route to China from Assam. Lunched with Home Forces and then gave talk on world situation. Back to the office for interviews with S of S, Nosworthy before his start for West Africa, Weeks before his journey to North Africa, MS, VCIGS, etc. Back to flat for dinner. Archie Wavell dining with PM.

29 April

A troublesome day! Whilst at COS Portal first of all informed me that PM last night had decided to start with Chiefs of Staff for Washington on Wednesday next! Then Dudley Pound said that he had just been with him and we were to start on Sunday!! (*It was then already Thursday.*) At noon a Cabinet meeting at which Wavell, Peirse and Somerville disclosed their views on the Burma Campaign. This lasted till 1.30 pm and at 1.15 I was due at the Dorchester to lunch with Stark, who had King [Crown Prince] Olaf lunching with him! Arrived there at 1.45 pm!! Sat between Turkish Ambassador and Stark's Staff Officer. Besides the King, Winant, Andrews etc lunching, also Bullin [?Bullitt]. At 5 pm meeting with PM to try and postpone date of departure. I told him we were not yet ready to discuss the plans on far side yet. He said we should have time on the *Queen Mary*! Luckily Transportation said *Queen Mary* was full of vermin!! Vermin became our allies and our departure is now postponed till next Wednesday. Dined with Home Forces, Wavell with me.

30 April

More preparations for our departure. But no reply yet from USA. A meeting convened at 4 pm by PM to discuss security of the trip. Apparently impossible to conceal nature of preparation on the *Queen Mary*, and quite possible news might get over to Dublin. German Ambassador there might cable or wireless the news to Germany. We were assured that in either case messages would be intercepted although wireless ones could not be stopped. We should know however and could then change to go by air. Pound also explained that a carrier had been detailed to act as escort in area where Focke-Wulf aircraft might operate. Also cruisers detailed to provide protection on sections of the journey. As a result of conference decided to carry on with the original plan and to prepare departure for Wednesday. Quite possible however that we may not be welcomed on far side.

News in paper tonight that Basil has been appointed PM of Northern Ireland. Real good news.

1 May

Still no decision as to whether we are to start for America on Wednesday or not! Anyhow, all prepartions continue. Lewin came to lunch, after which I motored home.

2 May

Quiet Sunday at home.

3 May

A long day! An early start from Ferney Close. Arrived WO 9.15, found my table full of messages, situation reports and maps. Then briefing for COS, followed by interview with the S of S and then COS till 12.30. Half hour crammed with files. Lunch. Then interview with General Bouscat who has been sent over by General Giraud for contacts with de Gaulle. Seems one of the better sort.

Another interview with S of S and Cabinet at 5.30. More work and briefing for night's meeting.

At 10.30 Defence Committee till 12.30 am to discuss tank production and tank armament. A complete Alice in Wonderland meeting. Clark D of A [Armour] expressing the usual technician opinion entirely detached from tactical and operational requirements. Duncan Sandys expressing a self-opinionated amateur's view devoid of all sound basis. Lord Cherwell wandering off into impossibilities etc etc.

We heard definitely this morning that we are to go to Washington and that we start tomorrow evening by train.

4 May

A very artificial day during which I have lived an ordinary day feeling anything but 'ordinary' owing to the impending departure. We had our usual COS at which we made final preparations for all the work on the journey. I then lunched with Alexander Cadogan and his wife at the Savoy. John Anderson and his wife, Olliphant (Brussels Ambassador) and his wife and several more I did not know were all present. Then back to WO for a Selection Board and a series of interviews. Finally back to flat at 8 pm for dinner and packing. I am now just off to the station to start on my journey to Washington. A busy time ahead, and am feeling uncommonly tired and weary before starting, but sea journey should freshen me up before the hard work of the conference starts. I don't feel very hopeful as to results. Casablanca has taught me too much. Agreement after agreement may be secured on paper but if their hearts are not in it they soon drift away again!

5 May

Last night after dinner at 11.15 pm I started for the station outside Olympia (Addison Road) where our special train was waiting for us. Barney came to station with me although he was only embarking the next morning early at 5.30 am. I had a good sleep and comfortable breakfast and lunch on the train. Our party consists of PM, Averell Harriman, Beaverbrook, Leathers, Charles Wilson, Cherwell, Wavell, Peirse, Somerville, 3 Chiefs of Staff, all Joint Planners and in addition shipping, movement, administrative, intelligence etc, staff officers from the Admiralty, WO and Air Ministry, and finally many clerks, detectives, etc. We arrived at Greenock at 3.40 pm, and then transferred to a launch which took us to the *Queen Mary*. The height of her was most impressive as we drew up along side of her, and when we got on board it was a job to find one's way about. She had been completely stripped and turned into a troop carrier, and it has entailed considerable work restoring her into a suitable condition to take PM and us. They have done marvels in the short time, and the cabin I am in must be almost up to pre war standard. A very large double room very well fitted with sitting room, 2 bath rooms, box room and masses of cupboards, arm chairs, sofas, etc, etc. There are about 3,000 troops on board with us, but she can carry 15,000. This leaves her almost empty. We started at 5.30 and Dudley Pound took me and Portal up to the bridge, where he introduced us to the captain. We remained there for a couple of hours, till we had sailed down the coast past Ayr, which brought back many memories of our visits there with you bathing and Mr Rex [the dog] going in with you.

I have just had dinner and a talk with Wavell and am now preparing to go off to bed. Just before dark we saw the northern coast of Ireland and the Giant's Causeway. Tomorrow we have an escort of an aircraft carrier and a cruiser to look after us.

6 May

We started the day with a boat drill parade, during which we were taken and shown the lifeboat we should use in the event of being sunk by submarine. At 10.30 we had COS meeting attended by Indian Cs-in-C [Wavell, Peirse, Somerville]. We also had Leathers [Minister of Transport] and Holmes [Director of Movements] in and discussed the shipping situation at some length. There is no doubt that unless Americans are prepared to withdraw more shipping from the Pacific our strategy in Europe will be drastically affected. Up to the present the bulk of the American navy is in the Pacific and larger land and air forces have gone to this theatre than to Europe in spite of all we have said about the necessity of defeating Germany first!

Before lunch I went up onto the bridge with Pound and Portal and watched our accompanying cruiser ploughing through the fairly heavy seas. In the sky we were being accompanied by a Sunderland Flying Boat whilst ahead we had an aircraft carrier. Fairly rough seas and we were rolling a bit, but not enough to upset one. After lunch I went for good walk on the deck where I met Cherwell and listened to him for about an hour. After tea I got down to work again preparing for our coming meetings. In the evening dined with PM. He had Beaverbrook, Leathers, Harriman, Wavell, Pug Ismay and self. He was in great form and thoroughly enjoying the trip. Tonight we go through the worst part of the run and there are several submarines spread out on our course, but they are mainly on their way to and from the Ports of Biscay and Northern Convoy Routes. Escaped reasonably early, and in bed by midnight.

7 May

We got through the submarine belt safely and by the morning we were about 500 miles west of Cape Finisterre and altered course about 12 noon for our bearing fairly direct on New York. We received news of 13 ships having been sunk out of one of our convoys between Newfoundland and Greenland, but at the cost of 5 German submarines! At 10.30 we had a COS meeting at which we discussed lines of action to take at our impending meeting with Dr Evatt of Australia who will be in Washington when we get there endeavouring to extract additional forces for the security of Australia.

After lunch I had more papers to go through followed by a walk on deck and after tea another COS meeting to discuss lines on which we are to approach our American friends to tell them that the reconquest of Burma in 1943/44 is not possible. Just before dinner good news came in of operations in Tunisia where Alexander's last offensive is making good progress. We have again altered course a little further south and temperature is much milder. We are being very well looked after and cooking is very good. There are only 3,000 troops on board instead of full 15,000, so that we are not crowded at all. Sea calm and practically no motion.

8 May

Another day mainly devoted to conferences. We started the day with a discussion over my opening statement at the conference in Washington. We then had another discussion on shipping attended by Lord Leathers and Cherwell, a good conference which has gone a long way towards clearing the air. The afternoon I spent reading up a paper on our action in the event of a collapse of Italian nation, which we then discussed at 5.30 pm.

Meanwhile the PM had been writing a long paper on our future action against Japan in which he forgot to take into account the basic limitation of our strategy, namely shipping. He also offended Archie Wavell by adversely criticizing the operations in Burma which have just been completed. So much so that Archie was indignant and I had to pacify him. Running a war seems to consist in making plans and then ensuring that all those destined to carry it out don't quarrel with each other instead of the enemy. Capture of Tunis and Bizerta seems to be confirmed. We altered course even further to the south today and as a result temperature much milder.

9 May

More troubles! Archie Wavell's Permanent Assistant [sic] arrived while I was shaving with a note from Archie in which he said that he had been unable to sleep and was so upset by Winston's references to the Burma operations that he proposed to send him a letter which he enclosed. In that letter he said that since Winston had lost confidence in him it was better for him to send in his resignation!! I went round and saw him and advised him not to send the letter. Later he saw Winston, had a talk with him and now all is quiet and I may shave in peace tomorrow!!

I remember that when I was discussing the matter with Wavell and trying to stop him from sending in his resignation, I told him that if I were to take offence when abused by Winston and given to understand that he had no confidence in me, I should have to resign at least once every day! But that I never felt that any such resignations were likely to have the least effect in reforming Winston's wicked ways! I think this argument fortunately convinced him that it was a bad step to take.

Our British escort left us today and we picked up two American cruisers and four of their destroyers. COS again from 10.30 to lunch and from 5 pm to dinner with much reading in between. I am very *very* weary with work and at times feel that I just can't face another day of it!

10 May

This should be our last day at sea as we are due to arrive tomorrow morning if we go on defeating submarines as we have done up to the present. There are about 100 of them operating in the North Atlantic at present, but most of them are concentrated further north. There are only two reported in front of us on the approaches to New York. But as we have now also picked up a Catalina flying boat in addition to our two cruisers and four destroyers we should be well protected. News from Tunisia continues to be excellent.

This morning from 10.30 to 11.30 we had our final COS meeting on our proposed Mediterranean strategy. We then went on to the PM at 11.30 and discussed the Far East strategy till 1.30 pm. A thoroughly unsatisfactory meeting at which he again showed that he cannot grasp the relation of various theatres of war to each other. He always gets carried away by the one he is examining and in prosecuting it is prepared to sacrifice most of the others. I have never in the 1½ years that I have worked with him succeeded in making him review the war as a whole and to relate the importance of the various fronts to each other. At 5.30 pm we had another meeting with the PM that lasted till close on 7 pm. We were intended to discuss the Mediterranean strategy, but it was not long before we were drawn off again to his pet of the moment in the shape of an attack on Northern Sumatra or Penang!! A different theatre, but not only that – a theatre entirely secondary to the European one which must remain our primary one!

After the meeting Pound ran a small sherry party for the naval officers in charge of the ship which we were invited to attend. Now I am off to bed, and if we do not meet a submarine we should be in New York fairly early tomorrow morning. It has been a very comfortable trip, with plenty of work to fill in the time, and we should by now be ready for our conferences with the American Chiefs of Staff. I do NOT look forward to these meetings in fact I hate the thought of them. They will entail hours of argument and hard work trying to convince them that Germany must be defeated first. After much argument, they will pretend to understand, will sign many agreements and…will continue as at present to devote the bulk of their strength to try and defeat Japan!! In fact Casablanca will be repeated. It is all so maddening as it is not difficult in this case to see that unless our united effort is directed to defeat Germany and hold Japan the war may go on indefinitely. However it is not sufficient to see something clearly. You have got to try and convince countless people as to where the truth lies when they don't want to be acquainted with that fact. It is an exhausting process and I am very *very* tired, and shudder at the useless struggles that lie ahead.

On reading over these pages of my diary I think that I must have been still suffering from the after effects of that go of flu which I had only recently recovered from.... It was easy enough to lay down, and to accept, the concept that Germany must be defeated first. Where the difficulty rested however was to decide how much effort should be devoted to hold Japan. The holding of Japan provided all the excuse necessary for a continual diversion of effort not truly required for a holding role. I still feel that if at that stage of the war our basic strategy had been more strictly adhered to we should have finished the war a few months sooner.

11 May

I rose earlier so as not to miss any of the sights on the way to New York. But fate was unkind and I was again destined to see nothing of New York!! There was a heavy mist and then rain which made it difficult even to see the shore or the approaches. We stopped a long way short for security reasons, and were taken ashore in a small craft to a station in some docks. We had lunch on the train and saw nothing of New York on our way out. Reached Washington at 6.30 pm where we were met by Roosevelt, Marshall, King, Dill, etc. We had to go straight to a cocktail party given in our honour in a large hotel. From there we did not escape till 8.15 pm. We then returned to Dill's house where Archie Wavell and I are being very kindly put up. Dill is only just recovering from his operation for hernia and not looking at all well.

Rather hot and sticky night. I must now prepare my opening remarks for tomorrow's Combined Chiefs of Staff conference and muster up all our arguments. We have a very heavy week's work in front of us!

12 May

Started the day with a conference at 9.30 with the Joint Staff Mission and Dill to find out what the probable reaction would be to our proposals. We then lunched with Leahy, Marshall, King etc. At 2.30 pm we went on to the White House to attend meeting with the President at which they laid down their conception of the future strategy. I could not help wandering back to eleven months ago when PM and I were alone with President in that room and Marshall came in with news of the surrender of Tobruk!! I could see us standing there and the effect it had on us. And then I wandered through the last 11 months with all their anxieties, hopes, disappointments and worries. And now! At last the first stage of my proposed strategy accomplished in spite of all the various factors that have been trying to prevent it. I felt rather as if in a dream, to be there planning two stages ahead, with the first stage finished and accomplished.

PM gave very good opening address, followed by President, who showed less grasp of strategy.

At 5 pm another meeting with JSM officers to put them into the picture as far as is possible.

13 May

We started our first Combined Meeting this morning at 10.30. Leahy began by restating the American conception of the global strategy, which differs considerably from ours in two respects:

First in allowing too much latitude for the diversion of force to the Pacific. Secondly by imagining that the war could be more quickly finished by starting a Western front in France. It is quite clear from our discussion that they do not even begin to realize the requirements of European strategy and the part that Russia must play. I am afraid that we shall have a very difficult time and that we shall leave here having accomplished little towards altering the conception which is deeply rooted in their hearts. I am thoroughly depressed with the prospects of our visit!

We lunched with the Chiefs of Staff, after which Marshall took me round the new War Department building, the American War Office. A vast building which has only just been completed. At 5.30 we had a British COS meeting attended by Dill to discuss line of action to take tomorrow. Dined quietly with Dill.

14 May

Started our Combined Chiefs of Staff Meeting at 10.30 when we stated that we did not agree with their paper on global strategy. I then had to make a statement on the Anakim operation (ie Burma) and various alternatives. Stilwell followed and disagreed with most of what Wavell had said and we left the problem more confused than when we had started.

We then lunched with American COS and went on to the White House at 2 pm where we met President and PM and again discussed the whole of Burma. First President, then PM made statements. Then Wavell was called upon followed by Somervell who contradicted him! Then Stilwell who disagreed with both and with himself as far as I could see! He is a small man with no conception of strategy. The whole problem seemed to hinge on the necessity of keeping Chiang Kai-shek in the war. Chennault was then called upon followed by more Stilwell and more confusion! President and PM had some more to say about it in the end, and by the time we left what is not a very simple problem had become a tangled mass of confusion.

At 5.30 one of our COS meetings to discuss the trend of the conference, which is most unfavourable and unpromising at present! Dill gave dinner party in the evening.

The President's writing table always interests me owing to the congestion on it. I tried to memorize the queer collection. Blue vase lamp, two frames, bronze bust of Mrs R, bronze ship's steering wheel clock, 4 cloth toy donkeys, one tin toy motor car, one small donkey made of two hazel nuts, jug of iced water, medicine bottle, pile of books, large circular match stand and inkpot plus many other articles that I cannot remember. Most of the donkeys have been there since I was in Washington last July!

It may well be argued that I would have been better employed trying to reduce the confusion that the conference had got into than to memorize the articles on the President's table! I remember feeling the absolute hopelessness. The Americans were trying to make us undertake an advance from Assam into Burma without adequate resources. In fact an advance which was only ultimately made possible by the provision of air transport for supply purposes. Except for Wavell, those arguing certainly did nothing to clarify the situation. Somervell had never seen the country and had no conception of the administrative problems. Stilwell was a strange character known as Vinegar Joe, a name that suited him admirably. One of Marshall's selections, and he had a high opinion of him. Except for the fact that he was a stout hearted fighter, suitable to lead a brigade of Chinese scallywags, I could see no qualities in him. He was a Chinese linguist, but had little military knowledge and no strategic ability of any kind. His worst failing, however, was his deep rooted hatred of anybody or anything British! It was practically impossible to establish friendly relations with either him or the troops under his command. He did a vast amount of harm by vitiating the relations between Americans and British both in India and Burma. Chennault, a very gallant airman, had originally commanded a volunteer American Air Force supporting the Chinese. A fine fighting man, but of limited ability, who added little of use to our discussions that day.

15 May Williamsburg

Started the day with a Combined Chiefs of Staff meeting which on the whole was most unsatisfactory. We are a long way apart in our strategy for the European theatre, and I feel great doubts whether the end of next week will see us much closer!

After lunch drove down to aerodrome and flew down to an aerodrome some 20 miles from Williamsburg to which we went by car. On arrival there we visited the Capitol first, and then went into the main inn all restored exactly as it was in its original days. Apparently Rockefeller spent a fortune in restoring the whole village to its original condition as the heart of Virginia. It has been marvellously done. We dined in a hotel nearby, and after dinner visited the Governor's House, lit up by candlelight. It was a most impressive sight. I kept on feeling that I had been transported back to old days, and expected the Governor to appear at any moment. The flowers in the various rooms were one of the most impressive sights, and had been done by one of the ladies of the university who has made a study of flower decorations of that period. They were quite lovely and gave the final touch to the whole scene. In addition odd bits of garments, etc, were lying about as if the house was inhabited. In the sitting room the chessmen were out on a board, in the Governor's wife's room her dress was thrown across the sofa, and a collar across the back of a chair. Gloves were lying on a table and books pulled out from a bookcase for reference etc.

16 May

Got up leisurely and breakfasted on the terrace outside the hotel. We then went on to the old Colonial church for morning service. The church was crammed, the singing very good, and the [illegible] service and sermon very good. The congregation impressed me with their high standard. All women beautifully turned out, no poverty and all well educated. Dudley Pound read the second lesson. We were then given a long lunch attended by the Mayor of Williamsburg. After that we flew back (160 m) to Washington, and at 5.30 had a COS meeting to prepare for tomorrow's work.

Then on to Embassy to dine. Wavell came with me. The American Under Secretary for War and his wife, Law [Minister FO] and Mrs Gibbs constituted the guests. Felt very sorry for Lady Halifax who showed distinct signs of the sad time she has been through during the last year [one son killed in action in 1942, another seriously wounded in 1943]. Temperature much warmer and have now changed into thin clothes. I wish the next week was over, don't look forward to it!! We have some heavy work ahead of us.

17 May

Another very disappointing day. We had long meeting with Combined COS from 10.30 am onwards, again discussing 'Global Strategy', which led us nowhere. The trouble is that the American mind likes proceeding from the general to the particular, whilst in the problem we have to solve we cannot evolve any form of general doctrine until we have carefully examined the particular details of each problem. The background really arises out of King's desire to find every loophole he possibly can to divert troops to the Pacific!

Lunch with the American Chiefs, and then at 2.30 pm went to see Winston about command of formations at home. He was in a bad mood, mainly owing to his dislike for Paget and we got no further ahead. At 5.30 a long COS meeting till 7.30 pm preparing for tomorrow's meeting on the future war against Germany. Then dinner with Macready [British Army Staff], where we found Rex Benson [British Military Attaché] and his wife, Mrs Gibbs, etc.

18 May

Met American Chiefs at 10.30 am, but their paper on the European Theatre was not yet ready! and what's more they had not yet properly digested ours. We therefore accomplished nothing!!!

It is quite apparent now that we are a long way apart. What is more the Americans are now taking up the attitude that we led them down the garden path taking them to North Africa! That at Casablanca we again misled them by inducing them to attack Sicily!! And now they are not going to be led astray again. Added to that the swing towards the Pacific is stronger than ever and before long they will be urging that we should defeat Japan first!

We have now at last received their paper and are to discuss it tomorrow. I shudder at the results.

Had a talk to Bedell Smith off the record this evening. He thinks a solution may be put forward which will limit the European Theatre, both cross Channel and Mediterranean, for the benefit of the Pacific! Dined with Admiral King who received us on his ship and produced films after dinner.

It is evident from the diary that at this period I went through a phase of deep depression. I think this was due to the fact that in spite of all my hard work at Casablanca and in spite of the rich fruits which we had gathered up to date as a result of our strategy, the Americans still failed to grasp how we were preparing for a re-entry into France through our actions in the Mediterranean. We had now opened the Mediterranean, and in doing so had regained the equivalent of about a million tons of shipping, thus regaining a great deal of the strategic mobility which we had lost. We had taken a quarter of a million prisoners and inflicted very heavy losses on the enemy both at sea and in the air. We had now opened the way for an attack on Sicily and Italy and we were forcing the enemy to expend forces for the defence of Southern Europe, a region of bad intercommunication and likely to absorb more than its share. We were in fact taking the best road for the liberation of France and final defeat of Germany, which was being subjected to ceaseless bombardment.

And yet in spite of all these advantages it was I think about this time that as I was walking with Marshall and Dill to one of our meetings Marshall said to me, 'I find it very hard even now not to look on your North African strategy with a jaundiced eye!!' I replied, 'What strategy would you have preferred?' To which he answered, 'Cross Channel operations for the liberation of France and advance on Germany, we should finish the war quicker.' I remember replying, 'Yes, probably, but not the way we hope to finish it!'

It was quite evident that Marshall was quite incapable of grasping the objects of our strategy nor the magnitude of operations connected with cross Channel strategy. On top of it all King had been gaining ground recently and was diverting more and more strength to the Pacific. Any attempts to unduly push our strategy on Marshall had a distinct tendency to drive him into King's Pacific Camp. He even stated once or twice that if our strategy was to be one of wasting our time in the Mediterranean, the American forces might well be better employed in the Pacific!

To me the strategy which I had advocated from the very start, and which was at last shaping so successfully, stood out clearer and clearer every day. It was therefore not surprising that at this period my temporary inability to bring the Americans along with us filled me with depression, and at times almost with despair!

19 May

Started the most difficult day of the conference. Up in the office by 8.30 am to study again the American paper. Then COS conference at 9 am where we decided the line of action I was to take up. At 10.30 am we met American COS and started by criticizing each other's papers on the proposed European strategy. Then Marshall suggested the meeting should be cleared for an 'off the record' meeting between Chiefs of Staff alone. We then had heart to heart talk and as a result of it at last found a bridge across which we could meet! Not altogether a satisfactory one, but far better than a break up of the conference! We met again at 4 pm in a COS meeting to consider draft of conclusions. At 4.30 pm we returned to a Combined Chiefs of Staff meeting to pass our resolutions, and at 6 pm we went round to the White House to report to the President and PM the results of our work.

Our conclusions are that we are to prepare some 29 divisions for entry into France early in 1944, and at the same time a continuance of pressure against Italy in the Med. The latter is a triumph as Americans wanted to close down all operations in Med after capture of Sicily.

I think that this must have been the first of our 'off the record' meetings, a procedure we had to adopt on several occasions when we had arrived at loggerheads. It always helped to clear the air. The trouble was often due to the fact that the number of attendants during our conferences had grown far too large. The Americans had gone on adding more and more staff officers and we had followed suit. This had resulted in some 20–30 odd people coming in besides the Chiefs of Staff. We sat facing each other, and behind us, on each side, seated on chairs, was a row of some 15 staff officers. I felt that frequently Marshall did not like shifting from some policy he had been briefed on by his Staff lest they should think he was lacking in determination. The off the record meetings consisted only of the Chiefs of Staff and a secretary. Leahy remained of course, as Chairman of the American COS and Dill also remained with us, head of the British [Joint] Staff [Mission] in Washington.

Dined with Admiral Noble [British Admiralty Delegation], Archie Wavell coming with me. Heavy thunderstorms at present cooling the air, and thank heaven for it as evening was very oppressive.

20 May

A very full day:

8.30 to 9 am Office, trying to read through masses of papers produced during the night for today's conference.

9.00 to 11.30 COS meeting during which we had to decide the attitude we would take to resist American pressure to do impossible operations in Burma in order to satisfy Chinese and public opinion.

11.30 to 1.30 Combined COS at which we reached a complete impasse with a suggestion by Leahy that we should send in separate reports. They were still pressing for a full scale advance from Assam into Burma contrary to all administrative possibilities. However we finally decided to have an 'off the record' meeting in the afternoon to try and reconcile our differences.

1.30 to 2.30 Lunch.

2.30 to 3.30 Another COS meeting at which we decided line of action to adopt and drew up proposed agreement.

3.30 to 5.00 'Off the record' Combined COS meeting at which we finally reached agreement and obtained practically exactly what we had originally put forward as a result of work on board ship!

5 to 5.45 Garden party at the White House with Marine Band.

5.45 to 7.30 Meeting of Dominion Representatives under PM, including Mackenzie King (Canadian PM) and Dr Evatt (Australian nuisance!). PM reviewed world situation.

7.30 to 8.00 Dashed back through office to meet Secretary Stimson (S of S for War).

8 to 11.30 Dinner at the hotel, which we gave for American Chiefs of Staff! And now at last bed and rest!

21 May

Rather an easier day which started again with a COS meeting at 9 am and followed up with a Combined meeting at 10.30. The work was easier and there was less controversy. We dealt with the Pacific and accepted what was put forward.

In the evening at 5 pm we had another White House Conference with PM and President, when we put up the results of our work. It was all accepted and we received congratulations on our work, but I do not think they realized how near we were to a failure to reach agreement! We spent about 1½ hours listening to PM and President holding forth on strategy and shivering lest either of them should suddenly put their fat foot right into it and reopen some of the differences which we had reconciled with such difficulty! It would not have taken much to start some of our troubles again. Thank heaven we got through it safely!

After the meeting PM called us all in and started discussing whether Archie Wavell still had enough drive and energy to carry on with his job, and to discuss his proposed plans for changes. He wishes to restrict the C-in-C in India to pure command of India alone, and divorce him from all operations outside, also to replace Hartley by Auchinleck, and then to appoint a young Corps Commander to control operations outside India. The problem is complicated by the desirability of appointing a Supreme Commander to coordinate the actions of Americans and British in this theatre. The whole problem bristles with difficulties.

Came down to meet Mrs Stark before dinner and then went out to dine with Colonel Donovan, who runs American Secret Service, Subversive Activities and Political Warfare. After dinner he produced a film for us which was ghastly!

22 May

A very much easier day. We cut out the early morning COS and went straight to the Combined meeting at 10.30 am. There we discussed the submarine warfare, which led to a small altercation between King and Pound. Otherwise we did not do much business beyond being photographed in session. Closed at 12 noon and I went to get my hair cut before lunch, and after lunch fell down 14 stone stairs with serious bruising all over my body but no real harm. In the evening we went to the Mellon Picture Gallery and I was dumbstruck by the pictures and their wonderful setting. Mr Finlay, the curator, took us round and was quite charming. For dinner Mrs Marshall came and also Mrs Marriott (daughter of Otto Kahn). Weather very much cooler.

23 May

Sunday. We started with a COS meeting at which we invited Lord Leathers and Cherwell, and discussed the whole of the shipping situation in relation to the plans we had been making. Luckily the shipping worked out all right and covered all our plans. At 2 pm we had a Combined COS meeting and did not meet with very much difficulty in making the American Chiefs agree to the arguments put up. It was a very satisfactory ending to a difficult period. I then went for a short walk with Dill and in the evening dined out with the Rex Bensons.

Any agreement and progress we may have made at this conference was again very greatly due to Dill and his help. He was a sick man, suffering from an infection which had followed his operation for hernia. He ran low temperatures, suffered from heavy perspiration at night, and looked very run down. Yet in spite of it all he was always ready to act as an intermediary between Marshall and me.

24 May

Today we reached the final stages of the conference, the 'Global Statement of our Strategy'. We started with a COS at 9 am to look over proposals and followed up with a long Combined meeting at which we still had many different opinions which were only resolved with difficulty!

Our difficulties still depended on our different outlook as regards the Pacific. I still feel that we may write a lot on paper but that it all has only little influence on our basic outlooks which might be classified as under:

a) King thinks the war can only be won by action in the Pacific at the expense of all other fronts.

b) Marshall considers that our solution lies in a cross Channel operation with some 20 to 30 divisions, irrespective of the situation on the Russian front, with which he proposes to clear Europe and win the war.

c) Portal considers that success lies in accumulating the largest air force possible in England and that then, and then only, success lies assured through the bombing of Europe.

d) Dudley Pound on the other hand is obsessed with the anti-U-boat warfare and considers that success can only be secured by the defeat of this menace.

e) AFB [Alanbrooke] considers that success can only be secured by pressing operations in the Mediterranean to force a dispersal of German forces, help Russia, and thus eventually produce a situation where cross Channel operations are possible.

f) And Winston??? Thinks one thing at one moment and another at another moment. At times the war may be won by bombing and all must be sacrificed to it. At others it becomes essential for us to bleed ourselves dry on the Continent because Russia is doing the same. At others our main effort must be in the Mediterranean, directed against Italy or Balkans alternatively, with sporadic desires to invade Norway and 'roll up the map in the opposite direction to Hitler'! But more often than all he wants to carry out ALL operations simultaneously irrespective of shortages of shipping!

After lunch I had meeting with Mary Venning, Pratt, St Clair on tank production.

At 4.45 pm we went to the White House, first to be photographed, and then to attend conference with President and PM. There the PM entirely repudiated the paper we had passed, agreed to, and been congratulated on at our last meeting!! He wished to alter all the Mediterranean decisions! He had no idea of the difficulties we had been through and just crashed in 'where angels fear to tread'. As a result he created situation of suspicion in the American Chiefs that we had been behind their backs, and has made matters far more difficult for us in the future!! There are times when he drives me to desperation! Now we are threatened by a redraft by him and more difficulties tomorrow!

On leaving White House I went round to Butler, Director of Public Relations, who was having a cocktail party for Chiefs of Staff to meet Press Representatives. I was there from 7.30 to 8.30 pm and missed a baseball match I was to have seen. Thank God our visit here is almost over!

Winston's attitude at the White House Conference was tragic. He had originally agreed entirely to the paper we were discussing and with Roosevelt had congratulated us on it. Now at the eleventh hour he wished to repudiate half of it. Some of the alterations he wished to make were on points we had been forced to concede to the Americans in order to secure more important ones. From the attitude he took up the American Chiefs might well have believed that we had gone behind their backs in an attempt to obtain those points through Winston. On their side they knew that Roosevelt would not take such action unless briefed to do so by his Chiefs of Staff, and it was not possible to explain to them how independent Winston was in his actions.

... in later conferences he always feared that we should 'frame up' (he actually accused me in those terms one day) with the American Chiefs of Staff against him! He knew the Americans could carry the President with them, and he feared being opposed by a combined Anglo-American block of Chiefs of Staff plus President. As a matter of fact on those occasions I was far from 'framing up' with Marshall and on the contrary was more liable to be at loggerheads with him over Pacific and cross Channel strategy. Under such circumstances it may be imagined how complicated matters became!

25 May

I went over to office early to find out results of PM's attempts to alter wording of our agreement. I discovered from Ismay that the PM had produced an impossible addition to our agreement which would have crashed the whole discussion, as we could never have got the American COS to agree. However luckily Harry Hopkins succeeded in getting him to withdraw it at the last moment and he finally only put up a matter of wording which only altered details and none of the principles. We were therefore exactly as we had started so far as the paper we had submitted to the President and PM was concerned, but the PM had done untold harm by rousing all the suspicions as regards ventures in the Balkans which I had been endeavouring to suppress. He had however succeeded in getting the President to agree to Marshall coming with us to North Africa on our coming visit. This has now become essential as otherwise, after the PM's statements, I feel certain that a visit by the PM and myself to North Africa would be looked upon with grave suspicion as an attempt to swing Eisenhower in our direction at the expense of decisions arrived at in Washington.

We met as a COS at 8.45 am to consider PM's amendments. At 10.30 we met for the last time as a Combined COS meeting of TRIDENT (name given to present meeting). The meeting was short and we went on to the White House where we again reported to President and PM at 11.30 am. Meeting lasted till 1 pm without any startling developments and finished up with cocktails.

Before lunch I had opportunity to thank Harry Hopkins for all his help. We then assembled for a vast lunch in the White House, given to Chiefs of Staff, Planners, Shipping experts, etc, etc. I sat between Secretary Stimson, for War, and one of the USA admirals. Cordell Hull [Secretary of State], [illegible], etc, were there. President and PM made speeches at the end.

I then went to do final shopping before starting back, feeling very flat after all the exertions of the last 2 weeks! Came home and dined quietly with Dill and finished arrangements for early departure tomorrow. Another Combined Conference over. I have now attended four, two small ones in London with Marshall and King, and two large ones at Casablanca and here. They are the most exhausting entertainments imaginable. I am convinced they do a lot of good in securing greater understanding between us, and yet – they fall short in so far as our basic convictions remain unaltered. King still remains determined to press Pacific at the expense of all other fronts. Marshall wishes to ensure cross Channel operation at expense of Mediterranean. Brooke still feels that Mediterranean offers far more hope of adding to final success. Portal in his heart feels that if we left him a free hand bombing alone might well win the war. And dear old Dudley Pound when he wakes up wishes we would place submarine warfare above all other requirements. Out of the above compromise emerges and the war is prolonged, whilst we age and get more and more weary!!

Looking back on the conference in the light of the results that ensued, the compromise that emerged was almost exactly what I wanted! We continued with the war in Italy with the aim of eliminating Italy. We forced dispersement of German forces under strategically bad conditions in Southern Europe.

26 May   Botwood [Newfoundland], 2300 miles

At 7.30 am a security car came to pick me up at Dill's house, and took me to the moorings of the clipper 'Bristol' on the Potomac just below Washington. The President came down himself with the PM who told me to go and sit with him for a few minutes in his car. He was as usual most charming and said that next time I came over I must come to Hyde Park to see where my father and Douglas had looked for birds. The Halifaxes also came down to see us off, and Dill had come with me. Harriman and Harry Hopkins were there. At 8.30 am we took off in fairly heavy rain and were soon in the mist. We saw a little bit of Nova Scotia, but the weather cleared well as we struck the south coast of Newfoundland. I was surprised to see a lot of snow still lying, especially along the southern coast. The southern part of the island is practically uninhabited, at any rate along the route we took. At about 5 pm Washington time, we made a very good landing and went up to the Air Force Mess for dinner, as by their time it was about 7.30 pm. The PM was kept very busy signing up 'short snorters'! At 9 pm we started off again, and only just in time as the weather was clouding up fast and clouds lowering. PM sat talking for some time, but luckily we succeeded in getting him off to bed at a reasonable time.

The 'short snorters' referred to were at that time very popular. Originally you could only become one if you had flown the Atlantic. It cost you 5/- and you were initiated by someone who already belonged to this sect. Your name was entered on a bank note, and you then collected signatures of all other 'short snorters' till you had to gum several banknotes together. Mine consisted of a Russian note, a Turkish note and an American one, and was covered with signatures including President, PM, Hopkins, Harriman, Anthony Eden, Attlee, Inönü, etc, etc.

27 May   mid-Atlantic 3260 miles

I had quite a fair night and got up at 8 am, which according to Washington time was about 3 or 4 am! We are now somewhere north of the Azores heading for Gibraltar, and according to the estimates should reach there about 4 pm. We have now got a tail wind which has put our speed up a bit. The total distance from Washington to Gibraltar should be about 3260 miles. It is rather difficult to compete with the changes of temperature. Washington very hot and stuffy, Botwood [base of North Atlantic air patrols] bitterly cold, and the outside temperature zero at 7000 ft, the height we are flying at. I had rather a job to keep warm enough at night. Beautiful calm sea below now and patches of fleecy clouds.

Later – Gibraltar

During last night I heard two bangs followed by a flash as if something had hit the hull of the flying ship. I was informed in the morning that this was the result of two electric discharges, like lightning flashes, that had hit the bows of the machine.

At 3.30 pm we made a perfect landfall just off Cape St Vincent and then skirted the Southern Portuguese coast, and cutting across the bay of Cadiz struck Cape Trafalgar, round the point and saw the top of the Rock emerging from a blanket of clouds. It looked at first as if the bay was covered in mist, but this turned out to be only a strip outside the harbour. The boat made a perfect landing and we were towed in to a buoy where Mason-MacFarlane with his launch picked us up. We had been 17 hours flying, unfortunately it was now too late to go on to Algiers, and we were forced to spend the night in Gib. After dinner Mason-MacFarlane produced a display of defensive fire for the PM which we watched from the top of the Rock.

28 May   Algiers 450 miles

Had a very comfortable and good night's sleep. At breakfast General Catroux and Macmillan turned up from England on their way to Algiers where they are preparing for de Gaulle's arrival tomorrow. I had a talk with Catroux at breakfast. He seemed very relieved that his negotiations between Giraud and de Gaulle were at last coming to a conclusion of some kind. Personally I have serious doubts whether there can ever be any form of permanency in any Giraud-de Gaulle agreement, their characters are not calculated to blend into any form of strongly united combination. Weather in Gib cooler than I had expected.

At 11.30 am PM, Marshall and I went with Mason-Mac for a tour of the Rock. We did not have time to do much as we were due to emplane at 1.30 pm. It was our first trip in the PM's new plane, a Lancaster converted for him and called a York. Very comfortable, with special cabin for PM, drawing room, berths for 4 besides PM and lavatory. We took off at 1.40 and had a lovely trip. We crossed African coastline east of Melilla and travelled some 10 to 15 miles south of the coastline. Lovely clear day and very good view of all the country. We arrived Algiers at 4.30 pm. Eisenhower, [Andrew] Cunningham, Alexander and Coningham were all on Maison Blanche aerodrome. Drove up to Eisenhower's house, where I am in same room as I had last time. Tonight Marshall and I dined with Cunningham, where the PM is stopping, the dinner consisted of PM, Cunningham, Marshall, Eisenhower, Tedder, Bedell Smith, Ismay, Alexander and some of Cunningham's staff. After dinner we had a long discussion as to what our future action in the Mediterranean should be. PM and I were busy trying to impress on Eisenhower what is to be obtained by knocking Italy out of the war. I still do not think that Marshall realizes this, and I am quite certain that Eisenhower does not begin to realize the possibilities that lie ahead of us in this theatre. Alexander too is somewhat disappointing and only realizes half the situation.

29 May

Had a good night's sleep and woke up to a very warm day. After breakfast Eisenhower came into my bedroom, hung round with the ribbon of a Grand Commander of the Legion of Honour which Giraud had hung round his neck at a ceremony this morning. He had said that no one could say that he was not entitled to it as it was his own one, which had been put round his neck on the field of battle! Eisenhower said he accepted it as a token of the strength of Allied friendship, but that he would on his part refrain from wearing it until they met in Metz!

Later – I now hear that de Gaulle is indignant that Giraud should have done this without consulting him!

Alexander came to see me in the morning and I had a long talk with him until sent for by the PM.

I lunched in Cunningham's villa to meet Giraud and Georges, who were lunching there to meet the PM. Georges has just been extracted out of France by us. I had not seen him since that memorable meeting with him and Weygand, when I was instructed to 'hold Brittany', after returning to France for the final days subsequent to Dunkirk. He has aged a great deal, but was very interesting on the question of conditions in France, German morale and Italian morale.

After lunch Humfrey Gale came to see me. He is the British Chief Administrative Officer with Eisenhower. I discussed all his difficulties with him from 3 to 4, when Alexander came back for another talk, which lasted till 5 pm. We then had a conference with the PM to discuss conclusions of Washington Conference and to find out what Eisenhower's reactions were. The meeting was of good value, and I think went a long way towards securing the action after Sicily that we look for. I then had another talk with PM at which I recommended that Wavell should be made Governor of Australia. PM liked the idea and wired home about it. Dined with Eisenhower and Marshall.

30 May

At 10.30 am Humfrey Gale sent a car up to pick me up and bring me down to the Headquarters Office, where I spent about an hour going round the offices and being introduced to the various officers. Most of the rooms are occupied by Combined Staffs of American and British, and it is a wonderful example of what can be done in the way of close cooperation between Allies. At 11.30 a car from Alexander collected me and brought me out through his HQ to his camp in the woods, some 10 miles west of Algiers. A most delightful spot right in the middle of pine trees and looking down onto the sea. We had lunch there and then went to look at the beaches west of Algiers, where the Americans landed originally. Then we had a walk along the beach and a very pleasant bathe. We came back to have tea and then drove back home, where I spent an hour in the garden looking for birds before going to dine in the Senior Staff Mess with Humfrey Gale. Returned back here to find a very sleepy Eisenhower waiting for the PM who had telephoned through saying he wanted to see him on return from dining with Alex!! I smiled at his distress, having suffered from this type of treatment repeatedly.

31 May **400 miles**

Alex came to pick me up at about 9.30 and we drove to Maison Blanche aerodrome to pick up his aeroplane to go on to inspect the 51st Div. We flew first to Sétif, but landed on a wrong aerodrome and had to take off again to find the right one. When we did find it, it was so late that it was not possible to motor from there to Jijelli, which we had intended to do to see the lovely country. We therefore emplaned again and flew to Jijelli and from there on to see 51st Div. We found them in a lovely bit of country just east of Bougie. I had no conception that North Africa could be so beautiful. Lovely cork tree forests with carpets of spring flowers, golden fields of calendulas, hedges covered with convolvulus, and lovely green fields leading to tree covered hills on one side and to a lovely blue Mediterranean on the other. A lovely place to rest a war-weary division.

At 3.15 we flew back and arrived back at 5.30 pm, half an hour late for a conference of the PM on the same subject as we discussed the other day. Anthony Eden turned up having been wired for by the PM so that he might become familiar with the de Gaulle aspect in this country. We did not get very much further at the meeting and the situation is on the whole much as we settled it in Washington which is as it should be. After the conference Cunningham suddenly informed me that the PM's latest idea is to go to Moscow from here!!

Later Eisenhower gave a large dinner to which the following came, PM, Anthony Eden, Macmillan, Murphy, the USA Under Sec for Air, Marshall, Cunningham, Tedder, USA Admiral, Ismay, etc. Before dinner Anthony Eden drew me aside to ask me about the Moscow plan. I told him I considered we should stop the PM at all costs owing to the strain on his health. I said that it was very necessary that I should get home soon, but that if going with Eden might stop the PM from going then I should be only too ready to do so! I just *hate* the thought and am longing to get home where there is masses for me to do. Eden was very nice in congratulating me on the results of Washington, he said he had read the minutes and considered I could not have handled the affairs better. Which is satisfactory.

1 June

We left at 8.30 am for Maison Blanche aerodrome where we emplaned in the PM's York and flew to Chateau d'Un aerodrome. There we attended the briefing parade of an American squadron starting off to bomb Pantelleria defences. We then watched the bombers take off on their mission. At 11.30 am we left for El Anerin aerodrome just outside Tunis. From there we motored to Carthage where a large party of men had been collected in the old Roman amphitheatre. It was a most wonderful setting for the PM's address to the men and the acoustics were so perfect that no loud speakers were necessary. It was hard to realize that in the same spot years ago Christian girls had been thrown to the lions to tear!

We then lunched at 1st Army HQ in a very comfortable house close by. There I met Charles Allfrey [V Corps], Evelegh [78th Division], Anderson and many others. After lunch we motored through Tunis and on towards Tébourba examining the main line of the attack on Tunis. We also saw elements of Corps HQ and of the 46th Div and 34th USA Div (which I had not seen since Ireland). It was a most interesting trip and I was much impressed by the wonderful tank country over which the attack was made. Finished up by going to Eisenhower's 'Fairfield Camp' where we were made very comfortable for the night. We had a very amusing dinner party consisting of PM, Anthony Eden, Pug Ismay, Randolph, Tommy [Flag officer] and self. We had tremendous arguments as to how the de Gaulle-Giraud difficulties should be settled. PM was in remarkable form, delighted at having had a chance of speaking from the Carthage amphitheatre. 'Yes, I was speaking where the cries of Christian virgins rent the air whilst roaring lions devoured them, and yet I am no lion and am certainly not a virgin!!' We slept in very comfortable tents with a lovely cool breeze blowing through.

2 June   900 miles

Left camp at 9 am and proceeded to see 34th USA Div gunners. From there to Tunis where we examined a Mark VI (Tiger) German tank. Most interesting. From there we went on to see more of 46th Div, then 4th Div and finally 6th Armoured, and 201st Guards Bde. Keightley gave us an explanation on the ground of the action of his Division (6th Armoured) at Hammam-Lif, most interesting with actual details of the positions held by the enemy and method by which they were defeated. We then went on to lunch with Coningham (RAF) in a wonderful villa owned by a Mr Germain, a Spaniard. Rumour says that Mrs Simpson used to go there with Mr Simpson! A most unattractive house in many ways, with black marble baths etc. Here we had an excellent lunch and then went on to Grombalia aerodrome where we took off for Algiers. PM took the controls and gave us somewhat of a swaying passage for a bit! Returned here by 8 pm and dined with Eisenhower followed by an early bed.

The last two days have been intensely interesting. It is a great joy at last to see the real ground after looking at the maps for weeks and weeks trying to imagine what it is like. After seeing the ground, and discussing the recent fighting with most of the commanders, I feel fairly certain that our future plans are on the right lines. We have got the Germans in a definitely difficult position. They must do something in Russia, and yet have not got the resources to do anything on a large scale. At the same time the Italian situation cannot fail to cause them the gravest anxiety. We can at present help Russia by hitting Italy.

I have since the start and in spite of many tribulations aimed at 3 main points:

a) Secure the whole of North Africa (which we have now done).

b) Eliminate Italy (which we may hope to do before too long).

c) Bring Turkey in (which must remain dependent on situation in Russia).

If once we succeed in attaining these three points a re-entry into France and a conclusion of the war should not be long delayed, all dependent on the situation in Russia. In any case the horizon is far brighter than it has been for some time.

3 June

PM sent for me during breakfast and told me he was now considering starting tomorrow! It is only yesterday that we had settled that Alexander and I should start back with Anthony Eden on Friday (4th) whilst the PM stopped on to greet the next visitor here [the King]. However, whilst we were discussing the question he began to swing towards leaving on Saturday instead! He also discussed various questions of command and showed me a wire to Curtin [Australian PM] suggesting Wavell as future Gov General of Australia. I failed however to get any definite decisions as regards commanders in any theatre.

Montgomery arrived last night and I had a long talk with him until PM sent for him. He requires a lot of educating to make him see the whole situation, and the war as a whole outside 8th Army orbit. A difficult mixture to handle, brilliant commander in action and trainer of men, but liable to commit untold errors in lack of tact, lack of appreciation of other people's outlook. It is most distressing that the Americans do not like him and it will always be a difficult matter to have him fighting in close proximity to them. He wants guiding and watching continually and I do not think that Alex is sufficiently strong and rough with him. After the PM finished he came back and we had another long talk till 12.30 pm.

I then drove out to Alex's HQ and had lunch with him in his camp, after which I went for a short walk in the pine woods round his camp to look for birds. I found a cross-bill, several green finches and some doves, but not much else. Then picked up Alex and drove back here where I had told Monty to meet me at 4 pm. We had tea in my bedroom and discussed commanders. Then at 5 pm we had another conference with PM, which did not get us much further, but we reviewed all the agreements we had arrived at during the last few days. On the whole I think the visit has been a success in ensuring that the decisions arrived at in Washington were correctly interpreted here.

In the evening I dined at the Admiral's villa at request of the PM. The party consisted of PM, Cunningham, Marshall, Eisenhower, Tedder and Montgomery. After dinner Anthony Eden and Macmillan dropped in with latest information concerning Giraud-de Gaulle negotiations which have made great strides during the last 24 hours. As a result there is going to be a great lunch party tomorrow to celebrate the fusion of the parties, just prior to our departure.

My morning interview with Monty was another of those instances where I had to haul him over the coals for the trouble he was creating through his usual lack of tact and egotistical outlook which seemed to prevent him appreciating other people's feelings. When we arrived in Algiers he was in England having a very well earned period of rest after the fighting from El Alamein to Tunis. I was reluctant to call him back, but found it was essential that I should see him before leaving North Africa and this only entailed curtailing his leave by a few days.

In my first interview with Eisenhower I discovered that he was boiling over internally with anger over Monty's insistence on extracting a Fortress aircraft out of him for Monty's personal services. The matter had originated from a remark which Bedell Smith had made jokingly whilst visiting Monty. He said to him that if he cleared Sousse of the enemy by a certain date he would earn a Fortress aircraft. This statement had been lightheartedly made and far more as a joke than a real promise. However, Monty reached Sousse by the date mentioned and promptly wired to Bedell Smith for his Fortress aircraft! Bedell Smith still looked upon the matter as a joke and tried to laugh it off in his reply. This apparently did not satisfy Monty, who wired back stating that he was still expecting delivery of his aircraft. Bedell Smith was then forced to take the matter to Eisenhower, who was infuriated that he should be bounced in this way by Monty! However, being the past master at cementing inter-Allied relations, Eisenhower ordered that Monty should be given the Fortress aircraft, together with the American crew to fly it. Monty had thus gained his aircraft, but in doing so he had annoyed Eisenhower intensely, and laid the foundations of distrust and dislike which remained with Eisenhower during the rest of the war.

The above details are based on the story given to me by Ike and Bedell Smith. I did my best to smooth over the harm that had been done, but realized that my efforts were falling short of what I hoped to achieve. When I accused Monty of crass stupidity for impairing his relations with Eisenhower for the sake of an aircraft which might have been provided from our resources, he told me that he had been under the impression that Eisenhower had considered the whole transaction as an excellent joke! I told him that if he had heard Ike express his views to me he would certainly have had no such illusions. He was as usual most grateful for having his failings pointed out to him. This gratitude was genuine and not assumed, of that I am certain. I am also convinced that with his inability of assessing other people's feelings, through excessive concentration on his own, he was genuinely under the impression that his insistence on obtaining his aircraft was looked on as a joke by Ike!

4 June 500 miles

In the air between Oran and Gib. Packed up my kit in the morning and had long talk with Eisenhower. Later Monty came and we had a final talk about impending operations. At 12.45 I went to Admiral's house for lunch party to celebrate the drawing together of Giraud and de Gaulle. Lunch party consisted of: PM, Anthony Eden, Admiral Cunningham, Giraud, de Gaulle, Catroux, Georges, Phillip [Commissioner of the Interior], Monnet [economic advisor to Giraud], Margerie [former Chef de Cabinet] and Macmillan. I sat between de Gaulle and Margerie. De Gaulle very sticky and stiff. Giraud very pleasant, old Georges quite delightful. I had several interesting talks with Georges, who described to me what his feelings were at the beginning of the war, and how well he realized the deficiencies of the French Army. At the end of lunch PM made an excellent speech in French followed by Giraud and then de Gaulle. Anthony Eden then spoke and finally old Georges said a few words. Photos were taken and they departed.

We then left for Maison Blanche aerodrome at once, and shortly after 3.30

took off for Gibraltar in the PM's York. Party on board comprising PM, Anthony Eden, Alexander, Rowan, Tommy and self. 6 pm we are fast approaching Gib.

Later: Arrived in Gib to be told that we could not go on owing to weather!! PM depth of gloom.

However, at end of dinner we were suddenly informed that we might go, starting at 10 pm. This meant a bad rush, but by 10.30 we were off, in the York, not the Boeing Clipper as we had intended.

5 June   London, 1400 miles
Arrived at Northolt at 6 am after an excellent trip back. Bath and shave and then collected you at Goring Hotel and went home to Ferney Close for a quiet weekend.

6 June
Long sleep and lovely peaceful day.

7 June
Usual early start and busy day in WO. Spent morning seeing S of S, DMO and DMI. After lunch long go with VCIGS. Cabinet at 5.30 pm and finally a desperate meeting with PM at 10 pm about the Azores. We sat for 2 hours and did absolutely nothing!! PM in bad mood, arguing against Foreign Secretary and refusing to make up his mind in any direction.

8 June
Started in again with the COS meeting. You and your father came up to lunch. At 5 pm went to see Amery who had asked for me. We had a long discussion on the future set up for Army operations from India against Japan. Dined with Brendan Bracken who was entertaining some 3 Australian newspaper magnates. Attlee, Bruce, Selborne, Walter Layton, Dudley Pound and many others were there.

9 June
Started with the shortest COS we have ever had. Then visit to [the] King at 12 noon which lasted till 1 pm, mainly connected with his impending visit to North Africa. Lunched with Adam at Carlton Grill and heard all about his trip to India. Then DCIGS at 3.30 till 4.30 pm to discuss recent developments and his visit to North Africa. From there to S of S to settle final points before his departure with King. Finally finished by dining with Ivan Cobbold to meet some American officers.

10 June

As soon as the COS was over I returned to flat, changed, and motored to Hendon with Barney. We took off at 1.30 pm and flew to Acklington in Northumberland where we arrived at 3.30. On the way we had a very good lunch of gulls' eggs and crab sandwiches. Luckily the air was not rough! Spent most of the afternoon inspecting searchlight tanks. Finally fetched up for the night with the Allendales. Dined with the Strachans and fished for trout after dinner, without success owing to thunderstorm.

11 June

Left 9 am for Seahouses, where Admiral met us with a ship to proceed to Farne Islands. Practically the same naval party as last year with bird watchers. Ronnie Stanyforth also turned up. We had a delightful day and I took many photographs of eider duck, fulmar petrel, kittiwakes, guillemots, razor bills, puffins and shags. Weather held up well. Finally returned to Blythe with 2 hours sea trip through heavy storms.

12 June

Flew back to Odiham and was home by 12 noon.

13 and 14 June

Quiet Whitsun weekend at home with a heavy cold. Photographed fly catcher.

15 June

Motored back to London, still streaming with cold. COS lasted till 12 noon. After lunch series of interviews till Cabinet at 5 pm. PM called me in just before the meeting to tell me that he had been wanting to tell me during the last few days that he wanted me to take the Supreme Command of Operations from this country across the Channel when the time was suitable. He said many nice things about having full confidence in me, etc. Am now off for one of his evening meetings at 10 pm on tank armament.

This was the first time that the PM definitely told me that he wanted me to have the Supreme Command of the Liberation Armies when the re-entry into France became possible [for the second see 7 July 1943]. He had hinted at the possibility but had not yet made a definite statement. This news gave me one of my greatest thrills during the war. I felt that it would be the perfect climax to all my struggles to guide the strategy of the war into channels which would ultimately make a reentry into France possible, to find myself ultimately in command of the Allied forces destined for this liberation! I was sworn to secrecy by Winston and consequently did not even tell my wife. At a later date when he met her he at once asked her how she liked the idea of my assuming Supreme Command of the Liberation Armies. He was very surprised when he found out I had not even told her.

Later: we had a desperate meeting with PM, up till 1.30 am and never arrived [at] a single decision! The following were present: Oliver Lyttelton, Duncan Sandys, Cherwell, Micklem (Tank Board), Geoffrey Lloyd, Donald Banks, Ronnie Weeks, Bond and AB. Discussions according to agenda should have been connected with armament of tanks, but as a matter of fact centred round the fact that the PM, as a result of conversation with Harriman, is very anxious to accept another 2000 tanks from USA at the expense of home production, which would have to be reduced.

16 June

Just before starting for last night's meeting PM sent me a copy of proposed telegram for Viceroy offering C-in-C India to Auchinleck as a result of offer of Viceroyalty to Wavell. Short COS in morning. Cabinet at 5 pm at which proposed armistice terms for Germany were discussed. Now at 10.30 the PM is holding another meeting to go through the plans for attack of Sicily.

The Indian problem was at last settling itself after much shuffling. Australia having fallen through, the Viceroyalty of India was offered to Wavell, who accepted. This left the post of C-in-C India vacant. Up to now, during the defensive period and the minor offensives, the operations in Burma had been conducted by the C-in-C India. It was now decided to divorce the questions in Burma from the Command of India. A separate Commander was to be appointed for the offensive operations, whilst India would remain the base from which the operations would be run. Auchinleck was still unemployed, and with his intimate knowledge of the Indian Army, he was evidently the most suitable C-in-C under the new organization.

17 June

After COS meeting Portal informed me that PM had just told him that he had selected Sholto Douglas as Supreme Commander for Eastern Asia Command. I am delighted. He should do it well.

We had had several discussions with PM concerning selection of a Supreme Commander for South East Asia and had recommended Sholto Douglas to him. Unfortunately we shall see that the Americans objected to him for some reason I have never known. Ultimately the cloak fell on Dickie Mountbatten's shoulders, but I am convinced that Sholto Douglas would have filled the bill better, provided he remained active and did not grow too fat!

During afternoon had interviews with Crocker and Hobart, the latter very pleased with his new job of working up procedures for amphibious tanks, searchlight tanks, and flamethrowers. Morgan (Chief Staff Officer for Cross Channel Operations) also came to see me to discuss various minor difficulties he has come up against.

18 June

Our morning COS was greatly taken up with an interview with the deputy of the Minister of Information [Bracken] in order to try and regulate the press which as usual is discussing the fact that it is inevitable that we should carry out exactly what we propose to do! So far it has worked quite well as a 'double cross', as the Germans cannot imagine that we should be such fools as to give the press such liberty! But we cannot hope to go on fooling them in this way.

After lunch I had a visit from the Duke of Gloucester and after that Arthur Smith and Gascoyne came round for a long discussion on reinforcement situation in the Guards, and desirability of abolishing the 201st Guards Brigade. However I am refusing to do away with troops in North Africa at present and am prepared to run short at home. Crerar came to dine in the evening and poured his heart out to me as regards his worries connected with the Canadian forces. He is very unhappy about Andy McNaughton who is in a restless mood and undoubtedly quite unsuitable to command an army. I only wish I could find some job we could remove him to, but that is not easy.

19 June

Adam came to lunch with me, and we had another long talk about all his visits during his tour to Algeria, Middle East and India. He surprised me by telling me that Eisenhower had said that although he was very fond of Alexander and admired him, he did not think that he was a big man, and that he did not consider him fit to take on a Supreme Commander's job. I did not realize that he had appreciated this fact. He went on to tell Adam that he considered that there were only two men to take on the Supreme Command in this country and that one was Marshall and the other myself. That also astonished me, as I did not believe that he had much of an opinion of me.

20 June

Spent peacefully at home, except for being chased by your bees!

21 June

Usual COS, then lunch at Claridges with Lord McGowan (of ICI). Following also were there: Winant, Devers (new American General replacing Andrews), Portal, Leathers, Bevin, and many others. After lunch interview with K. Anderson just back from Tunis. Then at 5.30 pm Cabinet, mainly preoccupied with de Gaulle's future. Personally I am convinced that there is only one course to follow, and that is to get rid of him at the earliest possible date. Now I have to go off for a PM's meeting of Chiefs of Staff at 10.30 pm to discuss implications of protection for Portugal in the event of occupying the Azores. I feel that we are not in a position to guarantee security of Portugal.

22 June

A fairly quiet COS after which I had a hair cut, bank, lunch, and then went and invested capital in a set of *Gould's Birds*. It remains to be seen whether my forecast of the set going up in value come[s] true!

My purchase of Gould's Birds *was a big venture! There were 45 volumes for which I gave just over £1500, but my forecast was correct and at the end of the war I sold these books for twice their original cost. Meanwhile I had had wonderful value from them as an antidote to the war and to Winston! Whilst looking at Gould's wonderful pictures I was able to forget every thing connected with the war.*

Then had visits from Dick McCreery, Devers, and finally Arthur Smith and Gascoyne. With the latter I fixed final details for retaining the 201st Guards Bde and providing the necessary reinforcements to keep it going. [The] King reported safely back from Malta.

23 June

At our COS meeting we had a visit from Scobie, back from Middle East, and discussed with him the allocation of forces from the Middle East to assist Eisenhower in his operations against Italy. At 12.30 I started off with Barney for Kodak Works at Harrow on an invitation to visit the works. Lunched with them and had a very interesting afternoon, finishing with a gift of 200 ft of Kodachrome [film].

Back to WO in time for PM's conference at 5.30 on the use of special means to counter German air defences in bomber raids. A debatable point as the weapon is two edged and can be turned onto us. However, in view of heavy losses suffered by Bomber Command decided to make use of it. I hope that we may have been right.

The code name 'Window[s]' was given to this new weapon; it consisted of strips of metal ribbon dropped from the air to confuse radar readings. The Germans certainly also soon made use of this device to confuse our radar.

24 June

A fairly quiet day finishing up with a dinner party with you, Basil and Cynthia, and Devers.

25 June

Lunched Savoy with Alec Cadogan; lunch mainly for King Haakon of Norway, Duke of Alba also there and several others. In the evening went to see *Arsenic and Old Lace* with you, Grass [Grasett?] came also. A most amusing play.

26 June
After lunch drove down with you through Reading to look up Mr Ti at his school and from there on home.

27 June
A quiet day at home.

28 June
Usual early start followed by War Office rush and COS meeting. Then in evening Cabinet mainly filled with long talk by PM to the effect that he would not let his relations with the President be affected by de Gaulle, that he would be quite prepared to dispense with his services if he gave trouble. Attlee and Amery were still supporting de Gaulle. Eden on the other hand has at last learned wisdom, and I think sees through de Gaulle now. At any rate he has different views from this time last year.

29 June
A fairly short COS, a hunt in Harrods for a bookcase after lunch, followed by an hour with Franklyn prior to his taking over the new Home Forces. Then I went to see a Russian play at Mr Maisky's invitation with you. Well acted and a good picture of what Russian life is like at present. Then dinner at the flat with you followed by a meeting with PM, attended by Eden, Lyttelton, Morrison, Cripps, COS, Sandys, Crow [rocket expert], Professor [Lindemann], etc, etc. We met to discuss the new rocket weapon which the Germans are supposed to be developing and which Sandys has been enquiring into. Arrived at conclusion that definite threat exists, and that we should bomb Peenemünde (experimental station) [on the Baltic coast of Germany] at earliest possible date.

This was one of the first conferences connected with the V2 threat. In photographs taken of Peenemünde large cigar shaped objects could be clearly seen, but information was lacking as to how these projectiles could be launched and considerable divergence of opinion existed amongst the scientists. None of them was ever near the real solution. It is very fortunate that this weapon did not materialize at that time and never appeared till the final stages of the war.

30 June
We had to rush the COS this morning in order to get away in time for the Guildhall ceremony of the presentation of the Freedom of the City to Winston. I was very impressed by this ceremony, having never seen it before. I had an excellent seat on the dais next to Lord Cherwell and not far from Winston's back and the Lord Mayor. Winston made a first class speech which received a great reception. After the ceremony we went to lunch at the

Mansion House. I sat with Lord Samuel on my left and Lord Bennett on my right, Wavell one further off on the left and Bishop of London one further off on right. In front Archbishop of Canterbury, his wife, Duke of Marlborough, his wife, Anthony Eden and his wife. Lord Mayor made good short speech followed by an excellent short speech by Winston.

In evening Casey came for 1½ hour's talk on the Middle East situation, Syria and the rogue [illegible], Palestine and the Jews, Persia and the Poles etc. Finally home to a quiet dinner with you in the flat and looking at Gould's bird books.

1 July
We were worried this morning with the repercussions on Portugal by proposed operations in the Azores, and our attempts to get Portugal to hand over these islands to help us overcome submarines. After lunch I had an interview with two of the officers of Wingate's brigade [Chindits] which has been operating far into Burma. They were very interesting. Then a long discussion with Archie Nye on various aspects of the WO. Finally a small dinner party with the Adams which you attended, followed by a few bird films. This evening we received troublesome telegrams from the President to PM about South East Asia Command and Portugal.

2 July
A hard day. First a long COS to consider two telegrams from the President. The first suggested sending a whole division plus 400 AA guns and some 14 squadrons of fighters to support Portugal in the event of Salazar [Portuguese Prime Minister] granting us facilities on the Azores for submarine hunting aircraft. Such action in my mind would inevitably endanger our relations with Spain and bring Germany into Spain to counter what she would consider the first steps towards starting a Peninsular offensive. The whole situation is very dangerous and we may well find ourselves driven into Peninsular war against our wishes! The next telegram for PM was connected with the organization of the new South East Asia Command. There again the proposals cannot meet our requirements.

Lewin lunched with me and at 3 pm I went to 10 Downing St for a two hours meeting with the PM. We warded off all the immediate dangers, but I am not certain that he realizes all the dangers that lie ahead of us in connection with our Azores policy. Came back to WO just in time for an Army Council meeting which lasted till 6.30 pm when I got on with ordinary office work. Archie Nye and his wife came to dinner.

3 July
I finished off the COS early and then went round to Sullivan's for half an hour to discuss Gould's books. Lunched with Adam at the Carlton and afterwards drove home.

4 July

Peacefully at home.

5 July

Left home early as usual and had COS discussion on future Supreme Commander for South East Asia Command. PM wanted Oliver Leese who is quite raw and should command an Army before going to a Supreme Command. Sholto [Douglas], whom we want, is not being accepted by the President and we feel we must induce PM to approach President again. After lunch Stewart, Canadian Chief of Staff, came to see me. Apparently he realizes that McNaughton is unsuitable to command the Canadian Army! We discussed possible ways of eliminating him, not an easy job! Best solution is to split Canadian forces between the Mediterranean and European theatres, but this is easier said than done! USA look at present like trying to close Mediterranean theatre, if they can, after Sicily. We must wait and see how Sicily operations go and what I can do at next Combined Chiefs of Staff [meeting]. Cabinet at 6 pm and at 10.30 pm Staff meeting with PM at which we convinced him of desirability to have one more shot to get Sholto Douglas accepted. Heard today of tragedy of Sikorski's death in an aeroplane accident at Gibraltar. He is a terrible loss, and I feel I have lost a great friend.

6 July

Finished off COS quickly. Lunched with Anthony Eden in Foreign Office. Ambassadors of Portugal, America, Norway, China and Poland, Cranborne and Morrison (Post Office) were there.

After lunch a Selection Board meeting followed by interviews with old and new Indian Army Generals with India Office. Macready just off for America, Dewing just back from Australia, and S of S back from Algeria. Then dinner with Arthur Smith with the King's Guard in St James's Palace. Wavell also dining there.

7 July

We had a short COS at which we had to review some of the final arrangements for the capture of Sicily. After lunch I had another interview with Dewing about Australia, MacArthur's strategy, Blamey [Australian C-in-C], Curtin etc, etc. Very interesting, and very instructive, but mainly refreshing in so far as the Australians are still above all desirous of remaining in the Commonwealth. At 6 pm we saw a film of the PM's last tour and of the King's trip to North Africa. Finally dined with PM to meet King, dinner consisted of Grigg, Alexander, Sinclair, Pound, Portal, Pug Ismay and self. The King as usual quite charming. He noticed that Ismay and I had put Sam Browne belts on, and very kindly suggested that we might remove them for dinner. PM made him into a 'short snorter' and he kindly signed all our notes for us [see 26 May 1943]. He remained on till midnight. Pound in great form and full of stories. After King had left PM kept us on till 1.30 am. Finally when we were saying goodbye he took me off into the garden at 10 Downing St in the dark, and again told me that he wanted me to take over the Supreme Command of operations out of this country, but that I was to stop on as CIGS till January or February and that I should only take over if it looked pretty certain that the operation was possible. He could not have been nicer and said that I was the only man he had sufficient confidence in to take over the job.

This was the second time that Winston was promising me the Supreme Command of the European Liberating Force [cf. 15 June 1943]! This time he was actually mention-ing a date for my take over, a date only just over half a year ahead! I was too excited to go to sleep when I returned home, and kept on turning the thought over and over in my mind. Was fate going to allow me to command the force destined to play the final part in the strategy I had been struggling for? It seemed too much to hope for that the strategy should pan out as I had wanted and that in addition I should command the forces destined for the final blow. Fortunately I realized well all the factors that might yet influence the final decision and did not let my optimism carry me off my feet.

8 July

Left COS at 10.45 in order to lecture at Camberley to passing out batch. Then lunched with you.

Back to London by 4 pm to see Spears, back from Syria, who wished to inform me that our present plans for re-entry into France were all wrong as regards use of French troops. However I could not see that his suggested solu-tion was any better. After dinner at 10.30 meeting with PM, Eden and Cadogan to discuss latest news from Lisbon as regards use of Azores. However from 10.30 to 11.20 we listened to a heated argument between PM and Eden as regards recognition of French National Committee in Algiers and a long tirade of abuse of de Gaulle from Winston which I heartily agreed with. Unfortunately his dislike for de Gaulle has come rather late, he should have been cast overboard a year ago and gave plenty of opportunities for such action! But on every occasion Anthony pleaded with him and Winston forgave. We then discussed Lisbon for ten minutes, and then answered series of questions on impending Sicily operation. Finally we were liberated at midnight, having wasted an evening to do only 10 minutes work!

9 July

Speeded up COS as at 10.45 we had to attend Cabinet Meeting on manpower. We have now reached a stage where all three services and industry supplying them are living above their means in manpower. Cuts must be made. Unfortunately, whilst recognizing that cuts must be made, Winston won't face up to reducing formations. It is useless retaining emaciated formations which we cannot maintain and I refuse to do so, and that leads to differences of opinion of the severest nature with Winston! However, this morning matters went off more quietly.

Winston's desire was to retain formations long after it had been made clear that the manpower conditions no longer admitted of their retention. It was almost a childish dislike to have his battalions and divisions reduced. This failing increased as the USA formations outnumbered ours. I could not make him realize that it was a matter of living in a fool's paradise to maintain emaciated divisions. I tried repeatedly to explain that the efficiency of formations rapidly deteriorated when unable to maintain their numbers. It was all of no use. He became more and more obstinate, and it was only with the greatest difficulty that I obtained my way in this matter.

After lunch Irwin who had been sent home from his command on the Burma front came to see me. An unpleasant kind of interview which I dislike intensely. However we did not discuss the future as all reports were not in, and confined ourselves to discussing the Burma campaign and all its lessons. I was appalled at listening to what he had to say as regards the morale of the troops and their inferiority complex in relation to the Japs. We shall have to do something very drastic to get matters right.

Tonight the attack on Sicily starts, and thank heaven the suspense will be over! It has been getting more and more trying waiting for operations to start. The reports of the weather were perfect.

10 July
A thrilling day with reports of Sicily coming in. Few people, if any, realize what the weight of responsibility of this attack is like! I feel specially responsible. First I had to convince the Chiefs of Staff and had difficulty – they favoured Sardinia. Then I had battles with the PM to induce him to remain in the Mediterranean and not return to the English Channel. Then finally whilst busy battling with the American Chiefs of Staff the Joint Planning Staff went against me and tried to swing back to Sardinia!! It took a lot of will power to keep on with the Sicily objective. And now it remains to prove that I was right, or wrong!?! Anyhow the start has been good.

11 July
Peacefully spent at home moving book cases and working hard at repairing the Pook's goat cart to keep my mind occupied and my thoughts away from Sicily. Reports all good thank heaven.

12 July
Back to work as usual. Reports from Sicily continue to be good. Cabinet at 6 pm, when I had to give full account of operations. This evening dined with Cobbold at the Nuffield Club for American officers. Dinner in honour of Wavell.

13 July

A very difficult COS. We were discussing the Commander for South East Asia Supreme Command. The Americans are turning down Sholto Douglas and we do not feel that they have any reason or right to do so. Matter is rendered more difficult by PM wishing to appoint a 'dashing young Corps Commander from North Africa'. Probably Oliver Leese who will make a first class Army Commander, but has not yet got the experience to become a Supreme Commander.

The Finlaysons came to lunch with us and then you and I went round to Harrods. In afternoon I interviewed General Mathinet who has been sent by Giraud to act as Liaison Officer between him and me. Quite a delicate business as I do not know how de Gaulle fits into this business. Dined with Rollie Charrington at Boodles and had a delightful time with him.

14 July

Still very worried about a possible Supreme Commander for South East Asia Command! Winston will not press President to accept Sholto Douglas against their wishes. I am now turning over Jumbo Wilson, Giffard, Platt and Pownall as possibilities. Probably the former. Lunched with the 30 Club who were entertaining Basil. He made an excellent speech, followed by Herbert Morrison. Back to WO to see Jamie Drew and then on to meet you and the Pooks here for tea. From tea to station to see Pooks and Crow [governess] off and then to 10 Downing Street for sherry party. PM then asked you how you liked the idea of my becoming Supreme Commander of the Invasion of France! And I had not yet told you anything about it as it was still all so distant and indecisive. We met many people including Wavell and Queenie [his wife], Cranborne, Marlborough, Bevins, Ismay, Griggs, Bracken etc, etc.

Here we have the third case of Winston referring to my assuming the Supreme Command for the liberation of France [cf. 15 June and 7 July 1943]. He now asked my wife what her reactions were to this appointment which must therefore have been fairly definite in his mind. I had not mentioned it to her as he had told me to keep the matter secret, and as the appointment was still some way off and uncertain.

15 July

A very long day. Commenced earlier as COS was at 10 am. From 9 to 10 am dealt with a mass of wires on general situation and briefing for COS. Then meeting of COS with Joint Planners at which we discussed future of Mediterranean campaign.

At 11.10 we all left for poor Sikorski's funeral at Westminster Cathedral. The service was too theatrical and fussy to stir up my feelings till the very end. But when I saw the empty stand where the coffin had been with 6 'sierges' [candles] burning round it, and on either flank representative 'colours' of regiments borne by officer parties it struck me as a sad picture of Poland's plight:

both its state and its army left without a leader when a change of the tide seems in sight. I was very fond of Sikorski personally and shall miss him badly.

Went straight from Cathedral to Hendon to fly to Norfolk. Attending funerals in war of victims of air accidents is not a sustaining process to one's flying nerves, and should be avoided! Had a bumpy fly. Met by Hobart and taken to see his amphibious tanks. Most interesting and inspiring. I finished with a sail in one of them. Delighted to see old Hobo so happy and so well employed.

Flew back to Hendon and put very busy hour in at WO, before dinner party at flat with Basil, Cadogans and Birleys.

Then at 10.30 had to go to 10 Downing Street for meeting of COS with PM, Herbert Morrison and Lord Cherwell to discuss the probable German reactions to the use of aluminium leaves dropped by bombers as a counter to German Radio Location. Also to discuss Morrison's claims for additional shelters to meet threat of German rocket. We then discussed next meeting with Americans, in Quebec in early August, and finally again attacked South East Asia Command. Decided to get Sholto Douglas home to answer some of the charges raised against him by the Americans. As I walked out, feeling very weary, PM said 'You look tired CIGS, are you doing too much? Don't go flying about too much.' Coming from him a remark like that means a lot and more than compensates for any extra strain. At last at 1.30 am I am off to bed!

16 July

We had a short COS as we were due at House of Commons for a Cabinet meeting at 11.15 am.

The whole period till 1.30 pm was occupied with the question of manpower. It is quite evident that we have reached a stage where cuts have to be made, but nobody wants to accept a cut!! The PM is dealing with the matter by services or industries in succession, whereas the problem can only be approached as a whole. We must relate manpower to our strategy and it must be allotted according to the strategic requirements of the services.

I had a busy time with office work in the afternoon and finished up with an Army Council meeting. News from Sicily continues to be good and thank heaven for it! I don't know what I should have done if things had gone badly as I had supported the operation against continual opposition from its inception! I shall never forget the battle I had with the Joint Planners and COS at Casablanca when they tried to run out at the very last moment!

17 July

A short COS followed by Adam to lunch and a rush home to just arrive in time to help making hay.

18 July

Quiet day at home, busy photographing greenfinch.

19 July

A long COS trying to decide what our next best plan should be after Sicily. We were examining a tempting attack direct on Naples. Air cover bad and dependent on carriers, also plan put forward with only 3 divisions – quite inadequate. Rate of build up also slower than that of the Germans. Unfortunately Intelligence Branch are not good at deciding probable enemy moves! Busy afternoon in office followed by Cabinet at 6 pm, when luckily news of Sicily was good and cheerful. At 8.30 pm received new appreciation of attack on Naples which I studied till 9.30 pm. A bad paper again! We then met as Chiefs of Staff till 10.30, when PM, Eden, Attlee and Oliver Lyttelton came along to discuss prospects. A real amateur strategists' meeting as far as the last 3 were concerned! Winston on the whole very open to reason and on the right lines. We shall have a busy job to knock it into some shape to wire out to Eisenhower, and to bring Marshall along with us without frightening him out of the Mediterranean!!

20 July

Our COS meeting was mainly concerned with adjusting future planning in accordance with last night's meeting with the PM. We drafted a telegram for Washington supporting Marshall's aspirations for Naples but pointing out that this must entail certain changes and retentions in the Mediterranean at the expense of operations in Burma and across the Channel. This will not be greeted with great joy!!

During afternoon I had interviews first with Morgan to discuss cross Channel planning, then with Mallaby back from India [DMO] to discuss South East Asia Command and war against Japan. Then interview with S of S about future appointments and on to sherry party with the Birleys. Finally dinner party for Giraud at Claridges where I sat next to him and found him in great form after his visit to America. Drove Grasett back who came in and had a talk, so very refreshing having a chance of a talk with him.

21 July

At our COS meeting this morning General Giraud turned up at 11 am and remained for close on 1½ hours. He was in an excellent mood, convinced that the right theatre of operations is the Italian one, and except for small attention to any administrative difficulties talked very good common sense! After lunch at 4 pm I went to see Mr Amery, had tea with him in the India Office and discussed with him ways and means of providing adequate mountain warfare troops for fighting in mountainous Italy. He was very kind and helpful.

Came back to WO to meet an infuriated General McNaughton who had gone all the way to Malta to see Canadian troops in Sicily and had not been allowed by Alex (apparently owing to Monty's wishes) to visit Canadians in Sicily!! He has reported matter to his government and was livid with rage! I spent 1¼ hours pacifying him! although I felt inclined to tell him that he and his government had already made more fuss than the whole of the rest of the Commonwealth concerning the employment of Dominion forces!

The McNaughton incident was an excellent example of unnecessary clashes caused by failings in various personalities. In the first place it was typical of Monty to try and stop McNaughton for no valid reason, and to fail to realize, from the Commonwealth point of view, need for McNaughton to visit the Canadians under his orders the first time they had been committed to action. Secondly it was typical of Alex not to have the strength of character to sit on Monty and stop him being foolish. Thirdly it was typical of McNaughton's ultra political outlook always to look for some slight to his position as a servant of the Canadian government. The troubles we had did not, I am sure, emanate from Canada, but were born in McNaughton's brain. He was devoid of any kind of strategic outlook, and would sooner have risked losing the war than agreed to splitting the Dominion forces. The move of one of his divisions to the Mediterranean had not been achieved without applying considerable pressure from Canada on him, it was therefore doubly unfortunate that through Monty's foolishness he had been prevented from visiting the Canadian division!

Finally dined with John Kennedy, who had Devonshires and Bannerman to dine. The latter is busy preparing a new book of birds to be illustrated by Lodge and brought with him some lovely pictures which Lodge has been painting for this book.

22 July

A strenuous day. Started with a usual meeting with Joint Planners at the COS, at which we discussed the Naples attack and its prospects of success. Came to the conclusion that it was a gamble but probably one worth taking. Then Devers and Morgan came to discuss re-entry into France in the event of a collapse. From there to a Cabinet meeting in the House to discuss manpower which lasted till 1.15 pm and made us late for lunch Giraud was giving at the Ritz. There I sat between Giraud and Vanier [Canadian Representative]. Giraud in great form. Rushed back to WO to meet the new Polish C-in-C who has succeeded Sikorski [Sosnkowski]. He is definitely not up to the standard of his predecessor but quite a pleasant individual to meet. After him an hour with Mallaby [DMO India] on the future set up of the new South East Asia Command and all its difficulties and snags. Then an hour with DMI and office work. Followed at 7.15 by a rush to Pug Ismay's sherry party so as to return by 8 pm for dinner party for P.J. and Lady Grigg, Weeks and his wife. After dinner Dill arrived from America at about 10.30 pm, looking very thin, but he says he is now quite fit again.

It may seem that I was attending very many dinner parties, lunches and sherry parties, considering we were heavily engaged in war! It must, however, be remembered that a great deal of work was done at these off the record meetings. Opportunities occurred for quiet talks, and for the gathering of important details which one might otherwise miss.

23 July

My 60th birthday, when I pass out of the active list of the Army!

A longish COS, where we discussed Auchinleck's plan for the Burma campaign and had Mallaby in to discuss it with. Then lunch with Admiral Stark. Dill came along with me and Devers was also there. Stark apparently knew it was my birthday and presented me with a lovely birthday cake with candles which he suggested I should take home! From the Dorchester we went straight to Lady Pound's funeral at St Michael's Chester Square. From there back to WO to meet Alan Cunningham and tell him I was sending him to command Northern Ireland.

24 July

A very disappointing wire from American COS – Marshall absolutely fails to realize what strategic treasures lie at our feet in the Mediterranean, and always hankers after cross Channel operations. He admits that our object must be to eliminate Italy and yet is always afraid of facing the consequences of doing so. He cannot see beyond the tip of his nose and is maddening.

Lunched with Adam. Dill was there also. After lunch proceeded home where I arrived for a wonderful birthday tea!

25 July

A quiet morning at home and at 4 pm you and I started off for Chequers. We found Winston, Clemmie, Mary, RAF daughter [Sarah], Cherwell, Martin etc there for the night. Before dinner Winston took me off to seat in the orchard where he again propounded desire for Oliver Leese as Supreme Commander South East Asia. I again rode him off it. He then wanted Wingate as an Army Commander of South East Asia and I again had trouble. We then discussed future Mediterranean strategy. We are both in complete agreement but fully realize the trouble we shall have with the Americans. After dinner we had a film, *Sous les Toits de Paris*. In the middle came news of Mussolini's abdication!!! Winston dashed off to talk with Eden. A memorable moment and at least a change over from 'the end of the beginning' to 'the beginning of the end'! Escaped to bed by 1.30 am.

26 July

Busy day. Long COS, then at 4.30 another COS on the Italian situation, armistice terms, etc. 5.30 War Cabinet, 6.30 ordinary Cabinet till 7.45 pm and finally a dinner party for Allendales and Katie Seymour to see bird films.

27 July

A difficult COS meeting dealing with shortage of manpower and trying to arrive at a decision as to which service should be cut. After lunch Stewart, the Canadian CGS, came to see me. He suggested splitting the Canadian force between Home and Mediterranean so as to dispose of McNaughton as an Army Commander! He is right. It is the only way to save the outfit. Then Paget came for a talk, and Weeks and Kennedy. Finally interview with S of S and then home.

28 July

A long COS discussing armistice terms which Eisenhower proposed to broadcast to Italians before any overtures from Italians. All agreed this was wrong. Charrington came to lunch and Nancy and Jack Dill also there. After lunch interview with Turkish MA, also with Wedemeyer on his way back to America. For dinner Dills, Adam, Strang and Stark. Wavell dropped in after dinner. Finally meeting with PM to discuss armistice terms and also future operations in South East Asia. PM now prepared to take Alan Cunningham in spite of turning him down every time I put him forward!

29 July

Our COS was again occupied with armistice terms, telegram to Eisenhower for broadcast to Italians etc, etc. During the afternoon had interview with a QMS [Quartermaster Sergeant] Cook of the Airborne Division, who put up a very fine fight against Boche in Tunisia, was captured, taken to Italy, dug tunnel to escape, was caught, put into solitary confinement, beaten up, transferred to hospital, escaped, got into Vatican and was eventually repatriated home! Finally spent some time with Weeks setting up organization of Army part of South East Asia Command. Dill also dropped in to discuss what he should say to Soong [Chinese Foreign Minister] about future operations in Burma.

30 July

We were fortunate last night! A wire arrived at 1.30 am from Eisenhower about armistice terms for Italians. PM considered it sufficiently urgent to turn whole War Cabinet out of bed and kept up till 4 am!! Thank heaven we escaped and were not sent for.

During COS we had Devers and Eaker in to discuss desirability of transferring American bomber squadrons to Mediterranean to help Eisenhower. Decided against it owing to air battle on at present between American Fortresses and German fighter strength. This evening Army Council meeting.

31 July

A very hot day. Luckily short COS. Lunch and then drove down with Barney, whom I dropped at Sandhurst. Jones brought Gould books down for me.

1 August
Quiet Sunday at home.

2 August
Early rise. Found table crammed with messages about Italians prepared to surrender in Dodecanese, Crete, Balkans etc. Very long COS trying to decide how to deal with the Azores. We are again coming very near committing ourselves to the Portuguese to come to their assistance. COS lasted till 1.30 pm. Bad afternoon with long interview with DMO, DCIGS and QMG discussing what we could do in Italy. At 6 pm Cabinet that lasted till 8.20 pm and I then had to rush to the Dorchester to dine with Devers and Congressmen. From there I just escaped in time for a Defence Committee meeting at 10.30 pm which lasted till 1.30 am. PM in bad and peevish mood. Selborne [responsible for SOE] there pleading for more aircraft for his activities. He asked PM to approach President with a view to securing more Liberators. PM replied, 'What you are after is for me to pull the teat off the cow'!!! Then discussed Portugal again with the Azores, which resulted in friction between Eden and Winston. Finally telegram from America stating that President was considering agreeing to Rome being an 'open town' [to preserve it from destruction], this was the climax of an unpleasant evening!

3 August
Another hard day. Long COS with difficult manpower problem, trying to arrive at proportional cut between Land and Air forces! As usual in such cases impossible to arrive at a decision! Then Dr Soong came to see us to enquire on behalf of Chiang Kai-shek as to how we were getting on with preparations for operations against Burma. A delicate problem as Dr Soong was very inquisitive and there was a good deal to conceal from him. He remained for over an hour with us till close on 1.45 pm. At 3 pm Ralston, Canadian Defence Minister, came to see me and remained nearly two hours discussing how we are to get rid of Andy McNaughton as an Army Commander! No easy problem. Then Browning just back from Sicily and full of details of Airborne forces and their landings and work in the attack. After much uphill work they promise well for the future. Then MS for ½ hour. Finally Weeks and Nye for discussion on many points. By then 8 pm and none of my trays empty! Consequently a long evening's work in front of me now.

Preparations for departure to Quebec are moving on. I hate going, and dread the Conferences in front of us, the work will be never ending and very trying!

4 August
Another hard day continually on the rush. [Monkey] Morgan came to COS to discuss his plans for cross Channel invasion – very over optimistic in places. Had another heated argument with CAS on question of finding the deficient manpower from either Army or Air Force. We got no further.

At 1 pm Cabinet meeting to discuss President's wires insisting on declaring Rome an 'open town'. COS and Cabinet all strongly opposed.

Afternoon: long and interesting talk with Ramsay who gave me many side-lights on various personalities connected with Sicily operations. Then a visit from Wingate, back from Burma, to discuss his mobile column tactics. Long talk with S of S on manpower and on many appointments. Finally series of talks with DMI, DCIGS and VCIGS on all sorts of pending matters. Then dined at 7 pm and proceeded at 8.20 to catch train for the North to board *Queen Mary* for Canada. Difficult times lie ahead and I do *not* look forward to our meeting with American COS!!

I was very interested in meeting Wingate whom I had heard a lot about. He had orig-inally been operating in Abyssinia, after which he had a nervous breakdown and tried to commit suicide by cutting his throat. He was saved and after some nursing fit for work again. Amery had then asked me whether I would consider sending him out to Burma where he might prove useful. I wired to Wavell asking him whether he wanted him and he replied he could make use of him. He turned out a great success and orig-inated the long range penetration forces which worked right in Japanese territory. In the discussion I had with him he explained that he considered that what he had done on a small scale could be run with much larger forces. He required, however, for these forces the cream of everything: the best men, the best NCOs, the best officers, the best equipment and a large airlift. I considered that the results of his form of attacks were certainly worth backing within reason. I provided him with all the contacts in England to obtain what he wanted, and told him that on my return from Canada I would go into the whole matter with him to see that he had obtained what he wanted.

On arrival at Addison Road station, to my astonishment I was informed that Winston was taking Wingate and his wife with him to Canada! It could only be to bring him over as a museum piece to impress the Americans! There was no other reason to justify this move. It was sheer loss of time for Wingate and the work he had to do in England.

5 August

Left London last night after dinner from Addison Road station shortly after 9 pm. In the morning found ourselves on the banks of the Clyde. After breakfast we embarked on one of the old Calais-Dover steamers and were taken to the *Queen Mary*. She has been painted lately and looked much smarter than last time. We arrived on board before lunch and PM's train arrived shortly after lunch. Party consists of PM, Mrs Churchill, Mary, Averell Harriman and his daughter, living with PM, the whole of COS, Lord Leathers, Lord Moran, Riddell-Webster [QMG], Wingate (whom PM has brought along with his wife!!!) and all the various planners, intelligence, transportation etc, etc staff. We had a COS meeting after tea, and Winston asked me to dine. Dinner con-sisted of Winston, Clemmie, Mary, Harriman, his daughter, Leathers, [illegi-ble], and self. After dinner Winston started a game of rubicon bezique with

Harriman and Leathers and I slipped off.* Dirty windy weather, very overcast and forecast of weather bad for 36 hours! Fortunately so far *Queen Mary* is not wobbling about much!

The nearer I get to this next conference the less I like it, I know we shall have hard fighting with our American friends!! I now know too well what these conferences are like and how much they take out of one.

At dinner this evening the steward was filling tumblers with water before going round with the champagne. Winston stopped him by saying, 'Stop pouring all that water out, it is too depressing a sight'!

6 August

Blowing a bit last night, but only just affected the *Queen Mary* sufficiently to make her roll slightly. Started with a COS meeting at 10.30 at which we discussed how best to tackle the Mediterranean situation [with the Americans]. Decided to relate the action in this theatre to the requirements of Northern France suitable to admit of an invasion. In my mind it is all so clear and palpable that the policy we must pursue is to complete the elimination of Italy, profit from the situation by occupying as much of Italy as we require to improve bombing facilities of Southern Germany, and to force a withdrawal of German forces from Russia, Balkans and France. If we pin Germany in Italy she cannot find enough forces to meet all her commitments. Spent rest of day reading Morgan's plans for cross Channel operation. A good plan but too optimistic as to rate of advance to be expected.

After tea sent for by PM to discuss manpower cuts in the Army, and also South East Asia Command. Got him to agree to Giffard commanding the Land Forces, and Wingate to have the long range jungle groups. He also informed me that he now contemplated giving Dickie Mountbatten the Supreme Command of South East Asia!! He will require a very efficient Chief of Staff to pull him through!

We have been well looked after today by an aircraft carrier, a cruiser and three destroyers, plus flying boats from Northern Ireland.

7 August

Spent whole morning with COS discussing the cross Channel operation and examining the possibility of such an operation and the reduction of German forces in France necessary to render such an operation possible. After lunch had interview with Wingate to discuss what he could do in Burma. Then a talk with Mallaby on question of command in South East Asia. At 6.30 pm a meeting with Winston when I had a hammer and tongs argument with him on the set up of command in South East Asia. He was upholding the theory that

---

*Bezique is a card game for two, three or four people, played with two packs, from which all cards below the seven have been removed; the winning combination in one hand (the bezique) being the knave of diamonds and the queen of spades. To rubicon is to win the game before one's opponent scores 100.

no Army Commander was necessary in Assam, that the commander of land forces of South East Asia working with Supreme Commander, and also responsible for any operations in Malaya, should be capable of doing both jobs from Delhi! After an hour's bitter arguing I partially convinced him, but may well have to start it all over again tomorrow! Dirty weather again today.

8 August

News from Sicily good. The Etna position is being rapidly turned on the North. A difficult COS at which we discussed the line to take concerning Burma campaign. We got Wingate to come in and discussed what could be done with the Long Range Penetration Group organization and finally arrived at a line of action with which to take on the American Chiefs of Staff and to prove to them that we are in no way neglecting the operations in Burma.

After lunch PM sent for me and I had about an hour with him. In the first place he argued with me as regards organization of command in South East Asia, and agreed to all he had argued so hard against yesterday. Then he informed me as to his views concerning Sumatra and his wish to localize an offensive on this island to the North of the island, and not to carry it across on to the mainland at Penang. I also informed him of rumours I had gathered from Leathers that a movement was on foot in America to replace Marshall by Somervell. That the latter was scheming with this end in view, and had King as an ally!

Attended sherry party of Dudley Pound for ship's officers. After dinner went to see second part of American film of events leading to the war. Two American cruisers and four destroyers have now taken up escort work. Received message from Washington that we are to have a very difficult time of it at this conference. Americans determined to carry on with preparations for re-entry into France and for Burma campaign at expense of Italy. They do not seem to realize the truth of the motto that 'A bird in the hand is worth two in the bush'!

I do not know when Leathers had raised the rumour about Somervell. I certainly would not have put it beyond him and King, but do not think that there was a word of truth in it.

This was, I think, the first day on which Winston began to develop his affection for the Northern tip of Sumatra. As we shall see it became an obsession with him, somewhat similar to Trondheim (Norway) in the early days, and we were destined to have many discussions and heated words in connection with this idea of his!

9 August

We had our usual COS at 10.30 to deal with various small points including the scheme for making aircraft carriers out of ice! One of Dickie Mountbatten's bright ideas!

During afternoon land loomed up in sight and we gradually approached

Halifax. From the bridge, where I joined PM, Mrs Churchill, Mary, Pound, Portal and Mountbatten, we had a wonderful view of the harbour and of the pilot carrying out the difficult task of bringing the vast *Queen Mary* into port. When we arrived alongside I found one named Donnie White on the wharf. He was Brigade Major of the Canadian Divisional Artilleries during the last war and a great friend of mine while I was in the Canadian Corps. I had not seen him since 1919! We were given a very comfortable train with the most wonderful compartments. My sleeping berth had a double bed in it. The attendant informed me that the last 'important personage' to sleep in that berth was Wendell Wilkie [Republican opponent of FDR in 1940 Presidential election; author of *One World*]!

10 August

After a very comfortable night I woke to look out on a country that reminded me most of Scotland. Very attractive rivers and lakes that I should have loved to fish in! We had an interesting journey which I thoroughly enjoyed, with opportunities of looking at a new country. Just before crossing the St Lawrence River the train stopped and the PM and family were collected by Mackenzie King [Canadian PM] and taken on by road. We went on by train arriving at Quebec station about 5.30. There we were met by the Washington Joint Staff Mission and taken up to the Chateau Frontenac Hotel, where I have been given a most comfortable bedroom and sitting room looking right up the St Lawrence. We have taken the whole Hotel for our conference. The Americans do not arrive till Friday, which is a pity and means wasting a few days.

11 August

We started the day at 10.30 with a meeting with Joint Staff Mission to discuss the background to our coming meeting, and to gather from them what lies at the back of all the opposition which we have been meeting lately. As far as I can gather King is at the back of most of the trouble and with his Pacific outlook is always opposed to most operations in Europe. In addition Marshall still feels injured that we turned down his plans for cross Channel operations last year. I am not looking forward to this coming meeting, and feel we shall have a very difficult time.

After lunch we had a meeting with the Canadian Chiefs of Staff to explain to them the general trend of operations. After that I was kept at it till 8 pm reading appreciations of the situation carried out by the Americans, and also examining Wingate's proposals for the Burma campaign.

Pouring rain and strong wind most of the day. Winston left for Hyde Park to spend a few days with Roosevelt.

12 August

We all took a day off! Pound, Portal, Riddell-Webster, Mountbatten and self all started at 9 am, motored 40 miles due north, then on foot for ¾ hour on a bush trail till we came to a lake. There we took to a motor launch and crossed the lake to a small fishing lodge owned by a French Canadian. The country was lovely. Pine tree covered hills leading down to the lake, and wild enough for moose to come down to the lake, whilst bears live in the woods, and beavers had one of their dwellings on the upper of the two lakes that we fished. The fishing was poor, only small trout and not many of them, but that did not matter or detract from our enjoyment. Everything was provided: rods, lines, flies and a vast lunch. (*The lakes we went to are, I believe called St Vincent and St Guillaume.*) On the way home I passed a chipmunk within a couple of yards, and was fascinated by it, a most delicious creature. Finally on our way home a skunk crossed the road in the beam of the headlights. We got out to look for it, but it was gone.

By the time we returned to the hotel it was close on 10 pm and we had had a good full 12 hour day away from work! I only wish to heaven I could go on escaping into the country instead of having to face up to a conference with our American friends, who have no strategic outlook, cannot see beyond the ends of their noses, and imagine that the war can be run by a series of legal contracts based on false concepts as to what may prevail six months ahead! I am tired of arguing with them!

This was the first day on which we noticed signs of failing on the part of Dudley Pound. On the way out he had lost his balance and nearly fallen into a small ravine, only just caught in time by Dickie Mountbatten. On the way back we had great difficulty in getting him back to the car. He seemed completely exhausted.

13 August

A long and tiring day. Met Dill just after breakfast and had to tell him how we stood. Then a rush trying to read correspondence of 2 days in 30 minutes! Then COS from 10.30 to 1 pm with the Joint Staff Mission from Washington with us. Followed by photograph with Canadian Chiefs of Staff before lunch. After lunch 3 hours hard reading till 5.30 pm when we had a second COS meeting which lasted till 7.30. Dinner with Marshall, Arnold and Somervell, followed by reception by Mackenzie King and the PM of Quebec, which lasted till midnight.

Now I must get down to prepare my remarks on the American papers on European strategy which we received today. I am delighted with the papers and feel that at last they are beginning to see some daylight in the problems confronting us. But we still have several difficult points to settle and shall not have a rose petalled path to tread!

As our Combined COS conference was being held on British soil, according to our rule I should have to take the Chair for the meeting. This entailed a good deal more work, for not only had one to prepare to deal with all the aspects of the strategic problems, and to marshal the arguments in support of our policy, but in addition one had to clear one's mind as regards the best lines on which to steer the conference. These meetings in any case meant working at hard pressure, first rendering oneself thoroughly familiar with the matter to be discussed, which entailed a great deal of reading, secondly running our own COS meeting to ensure we were speaking with one voice, then meetings with our American colleagues, and finally meetings with Winston to keep him acquainted with what we were settling, or failing to get agreement on.

14 August

At 10.30 we started our first Combined meeting. Not a difficult one. Our first task being to settle the agenda for the conference, and secondly to run through a general outline of the war as we saw it. Before lunch we finished the European Theatre in complete accord. After lunch we went on with the Pacific Theatre till 4 pm, but meanwhile we had received a telegram from Auchinleck giving full details of the floods west of Calcutta. These floods look like affecting the Burma Campaign drastically and put us in a difficult position in view of the pressure put on us by our American friends to carry out a Burma Campaign.

Lunched with Mrs Churchill in the Citadel. Leahy and Ismay came to lunch. This evening after dinner went with Stewart (Canadian CGS) to see a Canadian show run entirely by Canadian army personnel. Sat in a box with Mackenzie King, Mrs Churchill, Dill, Marshall and King. A first class show.

15 August

The end of a gloomy and unpleasant day. Started with a tiring COS which was made rather heavier by the attendance of the Washington Joint Staff Mission, Dill and the QMG. Then Winston sent for me asking to see me ¼ hour before lunch. He had just returned from being with the President and Harry Hopkins. Apparently the latter pressed hard for the appointment of Marshall as Supreme Commander for the cross Channel operations and as far as I can gather Winston gave in, in spite of having previously promised me the job!! He asked me how I felt about it and I told him that I could not feel otherwise than disappointed. He then said that Eisenhower would replace Marshall and that Alexander was to replace Eisenhower, whilst Monty would be required home to take Paget's command. In addition Dickie Mountbatten had been offered to the President for the Supreme Command of SE Asia and was acceptable to President. He asked me whether I had thought any further about this appointment and I told him that I still considered that he lacked balance for such a job.

I remember it as if it was yesterday as we walked up and down on the terrace outside the drawing room of the Citadel. Looking down on to that wonderful view of the St Lawrence River, and the fateful scene of Wolfe's battle for the heights of Quebec. As Winston spoke all that scenery was swamped by a dark cloud of despair. I had voluntarily given up the opportunity of taking over the North African Command before El

Alamein [in 1942] and recommended that Alexander should be appointed instead. I had done so, as I have previously stated, because I felt at that time I could probably serve a more useful purpose by remaining with Winston. But now the strategy of the war had been guided to the final stage, the stage when the real triumph of victory was to be gathered, I felt no longer necessarily tied to Winston, and free to assume this Supreme Command which he had already promised me on three separate occasions. It was a crashing blow to hear from him that he was now handing over this appoint-ment to the Americans, and had in exchange received the agreement of the President to Mountbatten's appointment as Supreme Commander for South East Asia!

Not for one moment did he realize what this meant to me. He offered no sympathy, no regrets at having had to change his mind, and dealt with the matter as if it were one of minor importance! The only reference to my feelings in his official history [war memoirs] (V, p.76) is that I 'bore the great disappointment with soldierly dignity'. On this same page he describes the reasons that lay behind this change, namely the fact that it was now evident that in the cross-Channel operations the proportion of American forces would be considerably in excess of ours. It was better therefore that the Supreme Commander should be an American. At the time this fact did not soften the blow, which took me several months to recover from.

The whole COS lunched with PM and then went hurriedly back for our 2.30 conference with the American Chiefs of Staff. It was a most painful meeting and we settled nothing. I entirely failed to get Marshall to realize the relation between cross Channel and Italian operations, and the repercussions which the one exercises on the other. It is quite impossible to argue with him as he does not even begin to understand a strategic problem! He had not even read the plans worked out by Morgan for the cross Channel operation and conse-quently was not even in a position to begin to appreciate its difficulties and requirements. The only real argument he produced was a threat to the effect that if we pressed our point the build up in England would be reduced to that of a small Corps and the whole war reoriented towards Japan. We parted at 5.30, having sat for 3 very unpleasant hours.

I did more office work and then went for a short walk for a breath of fresh air. Dined by myself as I wanted to be with myself! After dinner discussed with Dill till midnight what our best plan of action was. Dill had been for a private talk with Marshall and had found him most unmanageable and irreconcilable, even threatening to resign if we pressed our point.

My troubles with Marshall that day had arisen from the fact that he wanted to give from now on absolute priority to the cross Channel operation, if necessary at the expense of the Italian theatre. My contention was that the Italian theatre was essen-tial to render the cross Channel operation possible and consequently the two opera-tions were inter-dependent. By giving full priority to the cross Channel preparations you might well cripple the Italian theatre and thus render it unable to contain the German forces necessary to render the cross Channel operation possible.

16 August

Just as we had settled down at our morning COS to decide our plan of action for our Combined meeting Winston sent for us! He wanted to discuss a telegram from Anthony Eden forwarded from Sam Hoare. In it he gave an account of an interview with a General sent by Badoglio [Italian Prime Minister] to settle peace terms with us on the basis of proposed cooperation of Italian troops with us in clearing German troops out of Italy. The whole matter wants going into carefully to decide how best to make use of this offer. We had our conference with Winston in his bed and he read to us the telegram he was sending to Roosevelt on this matter.

We then came back and had the difficult task of finding a bridge to span over our differences with the Americans. This took us till 1.30 pm. At 2.30 pm we met them in a small session with all secretaries and planners removed. Our talk was pretty frank, I opened by telling them that the root of the matter was that we were not trusting each other. They doubted our real intention to put our full hearts into the cross Channel operation next spring, and we had not full confidence that they would not in future insist on our carrying out previous agreements irrespective of changed strategic conditions. I then had to go over our whole Mediterranean strategy to prove its objects which they have never fully realized, and finally I had to produce countless arguments to prove the close relation that exists between cross Channel and Italian operations. In the end I think our arguments did have some effect on Marshall. Unfortunately Marshall has no strategic outlook of any kind, and King has only one thought and that is based on the Pacific. We finished the conference at 5.30 pm, having been 3 hours at it!

A walk in the fresh air before dinner did me some good, but it is not a cheerful thought to feel that I have a continuous week of such days in front of me! This is the sixth of these meetings with the American Chiefs that I have run, and I do not feel that I can possibly stand any more!

17 August

Most of morning COS was taken up with preparations to meet the situation created by the most recent peace offers from Badoglio. We prepared a message to Eisenhower instructing him to send a staff officer to Lisbon to meet the Italian General. The matter is a difficult one to handle since if Badoglio does too much to help us before our arrival in strength he will be replaced by some Quisling by the Germans.

At 2.30 we had our meeting with the Americans and started with a closed session with only Chiefs of Staff attending. To my great relief they accepted the proposals for the European theatre so that all our arguing has borne fruit and we have obtained quite fair results. We then went on to discuss the Pacific and the Burma campaigns. Quite a good meeting at which I produced Wingate who gave a first class talk of his ideas and of his views on the running of the Burma campaign. Unfortunately the heavy floods west of Calcutta have seriously affected all our plans and schemes.

At 6 pm I went with Dill and Somervell to the Citadel to attend a cocktail party given by the Governor General (Lord Athlone) to celebrate the President's arrival. As soon as I arrived I was roped in by the PM to discuss with him, the President and Admiral Leahy the wire to be sent to Eisenhower connected with Badoglio's proposals. The President altered one sentence concerning bombing, otherwise was in full agreement and we sent it off.

Dill was as usual of the greatest help throughout this conference. I do not know what I should have done without him. He knew Marshall so well that he was able to explain to me the working of his brain. And as both Marshall and I trusted him implicitly he was the most excellent intermediary, and repeatedly brought us together again when we were at loggerheads.

18 August

A fairly easy COS meeting at which our main difficulty was connected with landing craft. We then proceeded to the Citadel for lunch with the Athlones, a large lunch to meet the President. After lunch a series of photographs were taken of groups. We had to rush back to get on with our afternoon Combined meeting. There we had a considerable discussion on the question of Stilwell and how he was to perform the multitude of duties assigned to him! The meeting however remained on friendly terms and went fairly fast.

We then went to the Heights of Abraham to study Wolfe's attack on the French during the battle of Quebec. In the evening we all went to a large dinner given by Mackenzie King. We finished up with a short speech by him answered by the President and the PM. The evening finished with some dull films.

19 August

Another poisonous day! I had rushed time going through papers from 9 to 10.30. Then a difficult COS till 12 noon when we went to Citadel to see the PM to discuss South East Asia operations. I had another row with him. He is insisting on capturing the top of Sumatra Island irrespective of what our general plan for the war against Japan may be! He refused to accept that any general plan was necessary, recommended a purely opportunistic policy and behaved like a spoilt child that wants a toy in a shop irrespective of the fact that its parents tell it that it is no good! Got nowhere with him, and settled nothing! This makes my arguments with the Americans practically impossible!

Back to the hotel for a rushed lunch followed by a meeting with the Americans at 2.30 pm, followed by one with President and PM at 5.30. We gave them results of our work up to date and got our agreements accepted fairly easily.

Back to Hotel in time for dinner with QMG to discuss the Burma administrative aspect. From dinner straight to Marshall's room for an hour's talk on the Burma and Japan war. Then to my room where Mallaby (DMO for India) was awaiting me to go on discussing India and its power to conduct operations in Burma and Sumatra simultaneously. Dill joined us and they remained till midnight. I then had to settle down to it and read for an hour to get ready for tomorrow.

I feel cooked and unable to face another day of conferences. It is quite impossible to run a conference such as present one with PM chasing hares in the background!

Winston was by now revolving round the northern end of Sumatra as he had done over Trondheim in the past! He had discovered with a pair of dividers that we could bomb Singapore from this point and he had set his heart on going there. It was not a suitable base for further operations against Malaya, but I could not get any definite reply from him as to what he hoped to accomplish from there. When I drew his attention to the fact that when he put his left foot down he should know where the right foot was going to, he shook his fist in my face, saying, 'I do not want any of your long term projects, they cripple initiative!' I agreed that they did hamper initiative, but told him that I could not look upon knowing where our next step was going as constituting a long term project! I told him he must know where he was going, to which he replied that he did not want to know! All this made arguing impossible, and made it difficult to stop him chasing this hare at this critical moment. We were having difficulties enough with the Americans to arrive at an agreement on our Burma operation without bringing in extra complications such as Sumatra.

Dickie had come up to me just before our Combined COS meeting, at which I knew I was going to have difficulties with Marshall, and asked me if he might explain to the Americans the progress that had been made with 'Habbakuk'. I am afraid that I replied 'To hell with Habbakuk, we are about to have the most difficult time with our American friends and shall not have time for your ice carriers.' However, he went on begging that I should remember if there was time.

The meeting was, as I expected, a heated one, and half way through I suggested to Marshall that we should clear the room of the sixty odd officers that had attended these meetings, and that we should have an 'off the record' meeting to try and solve our differences. He agreed, and after further heated arguments in our closed session we ultimately arrived at an agreement and were just breaking up the meeting when Dickie rushed up to remind me of 'Habbakuk'! I therefore asked Marshall if he and the American Chiefs would allow Dickie to give an account of recent developments in 'Habbakuk'. He kindly agreed and we all sat down again.

Dickie now having been let loose gave a signal, whereupon a string of attendants brought in large cubes of ice which were established at the end of the room. Dickie then proceeded to explain that the cube on the left was ordinary pure ice, whereas that on the right contained many ingredients which made it far more resilient, less liable to splinter, and consequently a far more suitable material for the construction of aircraft carriers. He then informed us that in order to prove his statements he had brought a revolver with him and intended to fire shots at the cubes to prove their properties! As he now pulled a revolver out of his pocket we all rose and discreetly moved behind him. He then warned us that he would fire at the ordinary block of ice to show how it splintered and warned us to watch the splinters. He proceeded to fire and we were subjected to a hail of ice splinters! 'There,' said Dickie, 'that is just what I told you; now I shall fire at the block on the right to show you the difference.' He fired, and there certainly was a difference; the bullet rebounded out of the block and buzzed round our legs like an angry bee!

That was the end of the display of shooting in the Frontenac Hotel drawing rooms, but it was not the end of the story.

It will be remembered that when our original meeting had become too heated, we had cleared the room of all the attending staff. They were waiting in an adjoining room, and when the revolver shots were heard, the wag of the party shouted: 'Good heavens, they've started shooting now!!'

20 August

We struggled with the war with Japan till after 1 pm in our morning COS meeting without arriving at any very definite conclusions. The problem is a very difficult one and made all the more difficult by the PM's childish attitude of selecting one operation and wishing to close his eyes to all the rest! At 2.30 we met the American Chiefs and had a difficult time keeping the conference away from any definite conclusions until such time as we had held a final discussion with the PM.

I then went for a walk which was badly needed as I was in a foul temper from continuous work and no exercise.

After dinner Planners came to my room and were joined later by Dill and Portal. With their aid we finally arrived at a suitable document to continue with tomorrow. I propose first of all to get it through the COS then to take it to Winston and finally get it approved by our American friends.

21 August

Another difficult day! We started our COS by considering the paper Portal, Dill and I, aided by Planners, had produced yesterday evening. We altered it slightly and accepted it. We then had to meet Winston at 12 noon to discuss it with him. He was more reasonable, and did accept the fact that an overall plan for the defeat of Japan was required, but still shouted for the Sumatra operation like a spoilt child! However, he accepted our paper. At 2.30 pm we met the Americans and presented the paper to them, suggesting that we should withdraw to let them discuss it between themselves. For this they took a full hour and when we returned we found that they wished to amend those points which would have made the paper entirely unacceptable to Winston! More discussions ensued in getting them to agree to a form which should be acceptable to Winston and to ourselves. This was a relief as it broke the final difficulties of this conference and practically finished our work.

We then embarked on a ship provided by the Canadian Government for a trip up the Saguenay River.

22 August

Our party consisted of some 300 Americans, Canadians and British who had been taking part in the conference. We spent the whole night sailing down the St Lawrence River and then up the Saguenay River. At dawn we turned round and sailed back. The scenery was quite beautiful and the ship very comfortable. A great rest after the strenuous week we had just finished. We arrived back in the hotel about 8.30.

I found a letter from you with an account of Mr Ti's accident. Thank God it was not worse!

He had been knocked down by a car near the Houses of Parliament and taken off unconscious to the hospital in an ambulance. A terrible experience for my wife and very fortunate it did not turn out to be more serious.

23 August

Last day but one of our conference – and thank God for it! I do not think that I could possibly stand another day of these meetings. The strain of arguing diffi- cult problems with the Americans who try to run the war on a series of lawyer's agreements which, when once signed, can never be departed from, is trying enough. But when you add to it all the background of a peevish temperamental prima donna of a Prime Minister, suspicious to the very limits of imagination, always fearing a military combination of effort against political dominance, the whole matter becomes quite unbearable! He has been more unreasonable and trying than ever this time. He has during the sea voyage in a few idle moments become married to the idea that success against Japan can only be secured through the capture of the north tip of Sumatra! He has become like a peevish child asking for a forbiddden toy. We have had no real opportunity of even studying the operation for its merits and possibilities and yet he wants us to press the Americans for its execution! We have struggled all day with a series of COS, Combined COS, and Plenipotentiary meetings with PM and President. As a result we have practically broken the back of all the work and have had our proposals accepted and approved by the Almighty! I am not really satisfied with the results, we have not really arrived at the best strategy, but I suppose that when working with allies, compromises, with all their evils, become inevitable.

24 August

The conference is finished and I am feeling the inevitable flatness and depres- sion which swamps me after a spell of continuous work, and of battling against difficulties, differences of opinion, stubbornness, stupidity, pettiness, and pig- headedness. When suddenly the whole struggle stops abruptly and all the par- ticipants of the conference disperse in all directions, a feeling of emptiness, depression, loneliness and dissatisfaction over results attacks one and swamps one! After Casablanca, wandering alone in the garden of the Mamounia Hotel in Marrakesh, if it had not been for the birds and the company they provided,

I could almost have sobbed with the loneliness. Tonight the same feelings overwhelm me, and there are no birds!

We had an early COS at 9.45, followed by CCS at 10.30 to clear up the few remaining points requiring discussion. During this meeting Dr Soong came to visit us and asked indiscreet questions which could not be answered, mainly owing to the fact that the Japanese have broken into Dr Soong's cipher and intercept all his messages!

At 1 pm we joined with the American Chiefs to lunch the Canadian Chiefs of Staff. After lunch we broke up, and all went their respective ways. The Americans started back for Washington, Dill accompanied Marshall and the Hotel rapidly emptied. Portal and I are stopping on till Saturday when we fly back. Meanwhile we propose to go fishing for two days. We therefore proceeded to purchase casts, flies, trousers and socks to go fishing with. I also had a final interview with Mallaby and Wingate to settle details of the Long Range Penetration Groups to be raised to fight the Japs.

Just before dinner Winston requested to talk to me on the scrambler. He was in a bad 'prima donna' highly strung condition. Notes for a lecture given to CCS had set him off. In it one of Alexander's staff officers had stated that six divisions would not be installed in Naples until about 1st December. The lateness of this forecast sent him quite mad and during a 20 minutes talk I failed to calm him. I must now go to see him at 10 am to discuss this situation further!

25 August

Reading over what I wrote last night I feel that I must have been very liverish! And I should like to remove these pages and should if it did not mean having to write them again in a less despondent strain.

The morning started with a conference with Winston postponed from 10 am to 11 am. He was still in a very peevish and difficult mood about rate of build up of our divisions in Italy and had already prepared a wire for Alex.

After the conference I rushed back, lunched early, changed into plain clothes and started off with Portal and a Mr Campbell for Lac des Neiges to fish for 2 days!! Campbell was there to look after us and we were to go to a camp owned by a Colonel Clarke who was also coming with PM and family. They were to stop at a lower camp and join us on the lake. After 60 odd miles of road mostly through the bush we arrived at the lake and embarked in motor boats for the camp some two miles up the lake. There we found a delightful camp with sitting room, dining room and dormitory, guides, canoes etc. Portal and I started fishing at once. I was getting on very well in an excellent spot, when to my horror up turned Winston with Clarke and I had to turn out. I could have shot them both I felt so angry. However before dinner I had caught 10 lovely trout averaging about 1½ lbs.

26 August

Portal and I got up at 6 am. Pouring rain and damned cold! We fished practically all day, and I finished up with 40 trout again averaging about 1½ lbs and best about 3 lbs. Also saw an osprey at close quarters as he sat about 50 yards from me. Also a great northern diver, a spruce partridge and a black duck. I also saw a falcon which I thought was a 'duck hawk', but am not certain. The lake is a grand wild spot with virgin woods down to it on all sides which they are cutting for pulp wood. Bears frequent and one frightened Louise the cook when she walked out to empty slops behind the camp some time ago!

27 August

Another 6 am rise to find a glorious morning but the lake shrouded in mist. It did not last long however. Portal and I had tossed on previous evening as to who should go up and who should go down [the lake]. He won the toss and had a wonderful morning with 50 trout, whilst I caught 9!! However, we changed over at lunch and I followed him in the spots where he had been and caught 45! So I finished the day with 54 trout over 1¼ lb average and including several of about 2½ to 3 lbs! The total bag for me was 94 trout in about 2 days fishing! I have never had such lake fishing! We left lake at 7 pm and motored to PM's camp which we reached at 8.30 pm, and dined with Clemmie, Mary, Anthony Eden, Cadogan, Moran, Martin and Thompson, plus our hosts Clarke and Campbell. After dinner we motored on here where we arrived at midnight and I am feeling dog tired but very much the better for my 2 days. Tomorrow we are by way of leaving.

28 August

The morning was spent in packing, visiting old Dudley Pound, and running round to a bookshop to collect a book I had ordered on Canadian birds. At 11 am we left the hotel and dropped down to the landing stage where we embarked on a launch to take us to the Clipper which was lying out in the St Lawrence just below Quebec Citadel. Our party consisted of Anthony Eden, Portal, Mountbatten, Jacob, Boyle, Barney and 3 others. At 11.45 am we made a perfect take off up the river and then swung round over Quebec and on down the St Lawrence. Lovely scenery most of the way. We lunched shortly after leaving and arrived at Botwood [Newfoundland] for dinner having to put clock on a couple of hours.

After dinner we made a lovely take off just as the sun was setting and sailed off into the darkness. We are now over the eastern edges of Newfoundland and shall soon be heading off into the Atlantic. It is now my third trip in this direction but it still has the same thrill as the first crossing, a thrill which present generations will never have as the background of the difficulties of early flights across Atlantic can never mean the same to them, not having lived through those days.

Little did I realize on saying goodbye to old Dudley Pound that I should never see him again! He was sitting in an armchair with his feet up and looked far from well. It was

very shortly after this that he had his first stroke on arrival in Washington. He trav-
elled back a sick man, was met by an ambulance on arrival in London, and died
shortly afterwards [on 21 October]. A very gallant man who literally went on working
till he dropped. I am certain that he had been suffering from his complaint for some
time. He fell asleep oftener and deeper than he had done before during meetings, and
I always felt nervous lest the naval aspect of our problems should be not be adequate-
ly represented owing to his being so often asleep. He was a grand colleague to work
with, and now that I realize how sick a man he was lately I withdraw any unkind
remarks I may have made in my diary concerning his slowness and lack of drive.

29 August

A very calm but cold night. I got up at 9 am (British time), about equivalent to
4 am (Canadian time) and after a good breakfast hoped to see our landfall off
the coast of Ireland. Unfortunately the whole of Ireland and England were
covered by clouds. We flew right over Lough Erne and Belfast, but never saw a
thing. We had one glimpse of the Irish Channel, a bit of Wales near
Shrewsbury, some of Salisbury Plain, what I think may have been Salisbury
Cathedral through a hole in the clouds, and finally reached Poole harbour
where we descended through the clouds and made a perfect landing at 2 pm
after an 18 to 19 hours journey from Quebec. There we were met by a coach
and taken to a special train which reached London about 5 pm. I came straight
on home to you by car, and a great joy and relief to be peacefully home.

30 August

Went up to WO at usual time and spent a busy time with a series of interviews,
S of S, DMI, DMO, Mallaby, VCIGS, DCIGS and MS. All of them had to be
informed of latest decisions from Quebec and then I had to hear from them
the latest news from the WO.

At 5.30 pm you picked me up and we went off to the Hippodrome to meet
Admiral Stark and Nancy Dill. The play *A Lisbon Story* was excellent. We afterwards dined with Stark at the Dorchester and then drove home to Ferney Close
with the comfortable feeling of a few days in front of me.

Soon I shall be back at the usual grinding work, but feel badly in want of a let
up at present. The Quebec conference has left me absolutely cooked. Winston
made matters almost impossible, temperamental like a film star, and peevish
like a spoilt child. He has an unfortunate trick of picking up some isolated
operation and without ever really having looked into it, setting his heart on it.
When he once gets in one of those moods he feels everybody is trying to
thwart him and to produce difficulties. He becomes then more and more set on
the operation brushing everything aside, and when planners prove the operation to be impossible he then appoints new planners in the hope that they will
prove that the operation is possible. It is an untold relief to be away from him
for a bit.

I wonder whether any historian of the future will ever be able to paint

Winston in his true colours. It is a wonderful character – the most marvellous qualities and superhuman genius mixed with an astonishing lack of vision at times, and an impetuosity which if not guided must inevitably bring him into trouble again and again. Perhaps the most remarkable failing of his is that he can never see a whole strategical problem at once. His gaze always settles on some definite part of the canvas and the rest of the picture is lost. It is difficult to make him realize the influence of one theatre on another. The general handling of the German reserves in Europe can never be fully grasped by him. This failing is accentuated by the fact that often he does not want to see the whole picture, especially if this wider vision should in any way interfere with the operation he may have temporarily set his heart on. He is quite the most difficult man to work with that I have ever struck, but I should not have missed the chance of working with him for anything on earth!*

3 September
Flew up to Catterick Bridge and from there went on to stop with Barney till Tuesday 7th, when I flew down to Odiham again. [No entries 4–7 September.]

8 September
Went up to War Office in the morning where I discovered that all plans were made to announce the armistice with Italy that evening and to invade Naples the next morning, combined with an airborne landing near Rome. However in the middle of the day wire arrived from Eisenhower to the effect that Badoglio was ratting and that he did not consider that he could hold the Germans in check. However decided to continue with operations except for the airborne landing outside Rome. I attended lunch given by Anthony Eden to Maisky and his wife at the Dorchester in anticipation of their departure for Russia. Halifax, Lloyd George, Bevin, Cripps, Kingsley Wood, John Anderson, Grigg and many others were present. I sat next to Mrs Jordan [wife of NZ High Commissioner] and a Russian. In evening attended Army Council dinner for Wavell. Pownall also there, and I informed him of the proposal for him to be Chief of Staff to Dickie Mountbatten.

I had selected Henry Pownall as the most suitable staff officer for Mountbatten. I had full confidence in his ability and considered he might counter some of Dickie's lack of balance and general ignorance in the handling of land forces. Whilst we were in Quebec, and just after he had been informed of his selection as Supreme Commander for South East Asia Command, Dickie had come up to me and asked me if I would give him one of my tunic buttons! He told me that he intended to put a similar request to Portal, and that the reason [was] that he wanted to have them sewn on his tunic. He would then have on him buttons of the three services on his jacket and felt that

---

*In the original diary the last clause ('but ...') is in different ink; it may have been added on rereading the entry the following day (cf. 25 August).

such an arrangement was a suitable one for a Supreme Commander. I only quote this story as an example of the trivial matters of outer importance that were apt to occupy Dickie's thoughts at times when the heart of the problem facing him should have absorbed him entirely.

The next few days should be momentous ones in the Italian Campaign. We are gambling and taking risks, but I feel we are justified in doing so.

[No entries 9–12 September.]

13 September

This date brought to an end the first real spell of leave that I had had since taking on the job of CIGS. I returned to work with a very flat feeling and a desperate disinclination to work! I feel that nothing less than 6 months leave could really restore the necessary drive and vitality to pick up this burden again! I hope I shall feel better tomorrow. Archie Nye took the COS meeting whilst I read hard to bring myself up to date again. A great deal had been going on and a good deal of what I saw I did not like. The Salerno landing in my view seems doomed to failure. The build up of forces has not been fast enough, whilst the Taranto-Brindisi landings are not being made sufficient use of. I am afraid that neither Eisenhower nor Alexander will ever have sufficient vision to be big soldiers. Meanwhile it is hell to have to face (*the chance of*) being driven out of Salerno at this juncture! Such a set back will (*would*) do us no good.*

We had a family lunch party after which I took you all off to Ti's doctor and then returned to work and a Cabinet at 5.30 pm. A Cabinet under Attlee, how different from those under Winston! In many ways more efficient and more to the point, but in others a Cabinet without a head.

14 September

News about Salerno landings is going from bad to worse and I feel we are bound to be pushed back into the sea! It is maddening not to be able to get the Americans to realize that they are going to burn their fingers *before* they do so. Started again with the morning COS which gave me a feeling of repulsion at the very thought of it. Then in afternoon a Defence Committee under Attlee which lasted for 2 hours when 30 minutes should have been sufficient. Finally Wavell came to dinner and we had a long talk till 11.30 during which I gave him full details of the Quebec meeting and the most recent developments of the new South East Asia Command. He was as delightful and charming as usual, but I do not think he spoke more than 100 words in the whole evening.

---

*The variants in italics were amendments made by AB on rereading the diary after the war – presumably because, as it turned out, the pessimism of the diarist was premature and the Allies were not driven out of Salerno after all.

15 September

The Salerno news is thank God a little better, and the chances of remaining there now seem more hopeful. A day of COS and interviews. During the afternoon I had a visit from Paget, who is not improving and is I fear on the decline slope. Then saw Platt, back from East Africa. He has aged a lot and made me feel very old! In the evening I had Harry Crerar to dine and we had a long talk, in fact he remained till 12.30 am! All in a very despondent mood about the Canadians not being sufficiently in the limelight, and the fact that the Americans, although later to enter the war, were playing a greater and more conspicuous part. He made me quite angry with some of his petty criticisms and remarks, however we parted the best of friends.

16 September

News of Salerno improving. Very long COS which lasted till lunch all connected with next year's plans for invasion of the Continent. After lunch Arthur Smith came to discuss desirability of forming Guards Armoured Division. Then Pownall to discuss the South East Asia Command after which I went to the India Office for a talk with Amery on the raising of mountain warfare forces.

17 September

News from Salerno goes on improving. COS this morning was mainly filled up with visits from Devers and from Platt back from East Africa. After lunch I had a long interview with Carton de Wiart who had been sent back by Badoglio in his attempts to establish contacts and bona fides. He was very interesting about his attempt at escape from prison and general Italian attitude. Then Army Council meeting followed by interview with QMG back from Middle East and finally dinner by Winant for Knox (Sec American Navy). Finished up with two excellent speeches by Knox and Alexander. Sat next to Attlee who was very pleasant.

18 September

Salerno landing now seems safe. A short COS, then lunch with Adam and off home for the weekend.

19 September

Rusty Eastwood and his wife came to tea and to see bird books.

Had to leave early to meet Winston at 9 pm at Euston [on his return from US]. Large crowd to meet the train. Afterwards Weeks came to my flat and discussed results of his trip to North Africa for an hour. Then had mass of telegrams to go through, mainly connected with future policy regarding Badoglio's government and degree of recognition it is to receive. This presents some difficult problems! Sardinia has been evacuated and it looks as if Corsica will also be free of Germans before long.

20 September

I succeeded in finishing off the COS fairly early. Then lunched with General Sosnkowski (Sikorski's successor) at the Ritz. He is very pleasant, but not in the same category as Sikorski was. After lunch prepared for Cabinet which started at 5.30 pm and lasted till 8.30 pm!! After Cabinet Winston called me up to find out if I had read his speech which I had not done! He said he hoped I would do so as he would probably want to discuss it with me after dinner. As I had Ivan Cobbold dining with me there was not much chance to read through it! Shortly after dinner I was called up and had to go round to 10 Downing St, where I was kept till 2 am discussing and checking the speech. He spent an infinity of work over it and was attending to meticulous details.

On several occasions I had to participate in the final stages of Winston's preparations for a speech. The whole Cabinet table had usually been littered with segments of the speech which had been returned by various people with remarks or criticisms. He worked at tremendous pressure on these occasions and by the small hours of the morning order began to replace the original chaos.

21 September

Short COS again. After lunch interview with Sir Percy Hambro who had given up his job with SOE. Then General d'Astier de la Vigerie who is returning to North Africa. Followed by Pug Ismay who wishes to substitute Archie Nye [for himself] in his trip with Anthony Eden to Moscow. Finally had a talk with P.J. Grigg who is very upset at the thought of having to remove Paget from the Exp[editionary] Force to make way for Montgomery. Home to the flat where Bertie Ramsay and Lewin came to dine with me. Ramsay very upset about delays in appointing new First Sea Lord.

The replacement of Paget with Montgomery for the liberation of France was a matter which was causing me much anxiety. Since the threat of invasion had lapsed Paget had been placed in command of the forces in this country destined ultimately for the cross Channel operations. He had done a marvellous job in training up these forces and in raising their general efficiency and I wish it had been possible to leave him in command for D Day. I had a great personal admiration and affection for him which made it all the more difficult to have to replace him at the last moment. He had, however, had no experience in this war of commanding a large formation in action, his abilities in my mind suited him better for the duties of a Chief of Staff than for a Commander. Finally, I felt that it was essential to select some general who had already proved his worth and in whom all had confidence. I had selected Monty for this job in my own mind, but thought that I might well have trouble with Winston and Ike (or Marshall) who might prefer Alexander. Meanwhile P.J. Grigg, who had a great admiration for Paget, was pressing for his retention, and although I was in complete sympathy with most of his feelings, I knew I must press for the appointment of Monty.

22 September

Busy fixing up details for South East Asia Command this morning at the COS. Then lunched with the Mountbattens, where Winston and Clemmie were lunching, also Portal and his wife. PM pretty well decided to appoint Fraser as First Sea Lord. Spent evening preparing my talk for tomorrow to the Staff College and Commanders-in-Chief on the world situation.

It was indeed fortunate that Winston did not decide to appoint Fraser as First Sea Lord, he had not got a quarter of the ability of Andrew Cunningham.*

23 September

Left early for Camberley where I gave a final talk to the Camberley students. Then drove to Teddington where I lunched with Franklyn and Home Forces HQ and gave another talk to Commanders-in-Chief returning to WO about 5 pm.

24 September

I had a busy day. Started with usual COS which left me about ¾ hour office work before lunch. Then after lunch Cabinet at 3 pm to discuss Indian food situation, followed by visit to [the] King at 4 pm when he kept me for an hour discussing world situation. On to Nepalese Legation for cocktail party to meet Gurkhas and men of 4ᵗʰ Indian Div. Back to WO to finish office work and to see DCIGS, MS and DMI. Rushed home and changed to dine at Claridges at 8 pm to meet Nelson [War Production] from America. He read a speech for 30 minutes!! Home to flat to finish office work.

25 September

Short COS and home after lunch.

26 September

Quiet Sunday at home.

27 September

A long COS. After lunch first of all a visit from Morgan and Barker to explain Marshall's wishes as regards the organization of the HQ of the Supreme Command in accordance with his wishes. Then a visit from Harker [MI5], to give me details of Martel's latest indiscretions through the post, in the shape of

---

*In fact, Churchill offered Fraser the job, but he declined it in favour of Cunningham, who became First Sea Lord in October 1943. As C-in-C Home Fleet, Fraser was responsible for sinking the German battle cruiser *Scharnhorst* off the North Cape in December 1943.

a letter to that drunkard Mackessie who used to be Military Correspondent to the *Daily Telegraph*. Then a long visit by Mathinet to discuss his relations here as liaison officer with me from Giraud and de Gaulle. Finally Mountbatten sherry party at the Dorchester as goodbye party prior to his departure for India. In the evening Alexander's ADC arrived with plans for future moves in Italy.

Martel was at that time in Moscow and had written a letter to Mackessie in which he had been very critical of his appointment to Moscow, and implying that I was unable to judge merit where it lay. That he, Martel, as the greatest authority on the handling of armoured forces, ought to be selected for an important command in the cross Channel operations, instead of being relegated to Russia etc. As Mackessie was a close friend of Kenneth de Courcy, whom we had already had trouble with just before the North African landings, all Mackessie's correspondence was being watched. It was known that he was very partial to brandy and might be made to speak when he had had a little too much. I see that in my diary I classed Mackessie as a drunkard, and I think that this is too severe a word to apply to him; his failing did not extend beyond fairly frequently taking more than was good for him. MI5 had come to me to warn Martel to be careful in what he wrote to Mackessie, which was not an easy matter without informing him that his correspondence had been intercepted.

28 September

COS at which we discussed PM's wild minute about proposed operations in the Indian Ocean. Now in addition to the impossible Sumatra operation he hopes to do Akyab, Ramree and the Rangoon operation all in 1944!! If Germany is defeated by the end of this year, there may be some hope of doing something out there, but Germany is not yet defeated and his wild schemes can have only one result, to detract forces from the main front. Cabinet at 5.30 which lasted till 7.45. We then had a COS meeting from 9 to 10.30 to prepare for a PM's meeting which lasted from 10.30 to 1 am. We did practically nothing, or at any rate nothing that could not have been finished in an hour. He was in a foul mood and convinced that we are finding every excuse we can to avoid doing the Sumatra operation.

29 September

I was sent for by the PM after the morning's COS meeting, and found him in a much more pleasant and cooperative mood. He started by saying that he was just as anxious as I was about our Mediterranean strategy and for not doing anything that might draw forces away from the Mediterranean. I think he felt that he had been in a very unpleasant mood the previous evening and wanted to make some amends for it. He told me that at the end of October, on his way to Teheran to meet Stalin, he proposed to go via Algiers and then on to Italy to see Alex. He hoped we might be in Rome by then. He also said that he wanted me to come with him for the first part of the journey, but probably not for Teheran, which was probably only to be political and not military.

This evening dined with Mathinet at the Ritz. He is very anxious that in future there should be no division between the de Gaullists and other Frenchmen.

30 September

We again struggled with the north Sumatra tip operation to see whether it could possibly be done without affecting the Mediterranean operations. Intelligence is inadequate, and it is therefore hard to form a true picture. Gave official lunch for Turkish Ambassador at the Ritz. He is still off colour, having suffered from pneumonia lately. In evening attended sherry party given by Mr Anthony Eden and Mr Littlejohn Cook at a club for Allied officers. Said goodbye to Platt prior to his departure for East Africa.

1 October

A rushed morning with COS till 12 noon, then meeting with PM, COS, Dickie Mountbatten and Pownall. This resulted in an hour's pitched battle between me and the PM on the question of withdrawing troops from the Mediterranean for the Indian Ocean offensive. I was refusing to impair our amphibious potential power in the Mediterranean in order to equip Mountbatten for adventures in Sumatra. He on the other hand was prepared to scrap our basic policy and put Japan before Germany. However I defeated most of his evil intentions in the end! Rushed work during afternoon and left for Cobbold House, Glenham Hall, at 5.10 pm, arrived in time for dinner.

2 October

Glorious day and had an excellent shoot with some 80 brace of partridge and about 30 pheasants.

3 October

Shot again during morning, about 35 brace partridges and some 25 pheasants. Then motored back to London in the evening.

4 October

Found PM in a great flutter owing to the attack on Kos island [in the Aegean]. Cabinet in the evening at which Kos situation was lengthily discussed.

5 October

Had to rush COS as I was due at Stanmore at 1 pm to lunch with President of the Polish Republic in order to have the order of 'Restored Poland' conferred on me. Nye, Grasett, Pug Ismay, Tim Pile and Carton de Wiart were also invited whilst on the Polish side Sosnkowski, Kukiel and some 5 others were also present. The President made a small speech before presenting the order which I had to reply to, and then I had to shake hands with all the Polish officers present. We then finished up with an excellent lunch followed by photograph.

I had to rush back for a Selection Board and a Cabinet at 5.30 which lasted till 7.30 pm. We were by way of discussing Foreign Secretary's paper on line he was to take up during his coming visit to Moscow, all concerning post war handling of Germany. Unfortunately PM was in one of his peevish moods and we did nothing and settled less, much to Anthony Eden's annoyance. Smuts appeared having arrived in the morning, he raised the interesting point as to whether we really wanted to dismember Germany now, or whether a strong Germany in the future might not assist in balancing power in Europe against Russia. He said he had no doubts last year about dismembering Germany, but now was doubtful about it.

6 October

Our COS was employed in examining the situation created by the German attack on Kos Island, and its capture by them; the PM's anxiety to recapture this wonderful trophy and the effect of its loss on the proposed operations to capture Rhodes. It is pretty clear in my mind that with the commitments we have in Italy we should not undertake serious operations in the Aegean. At 3.15 pm we were summoned to a Staff conference under the PM. Andrew Cunningham and Sholto Douglas were both there. PM by now determined to go for Rhodes without looking at the effects on Italy or at any rate refusing to look the implications square in the face. I had a heated argument with him, and no support from Portal, in fact the very reverse!

7 October

Another day of Rhodes madness. Another 3 pm conference, another 1½ hours battle with PM to hold on to what I think is right. The same arguments brought up again and again! And then finally sent for at 10.30 pm to try and swing me and get me to agree in a *tête-à-tête* interview. However I arrived in the middle of an air raid. As I walked in Winston was dashing out with Mary, who was on leave, to take her back to her AA battery in Hyde Park. I was whisked off with them! By the time we arrived the raid was over, we therefore walked round the battery position for half an hour. Winston started reminiscing and told me this was the very spot Mrs Everest (his nurse) used to take him out when he was a small boy whilst he was longing the whole time to get back to his soldiers! And now it was a battery position in which his daughter was serving! He next broke the news to me that on Saturday (today being Thursday evening 11 pm) I was to start with him for a conference in Tunis!! and that we should come back on Tuesday!! This is all to decide whether we should try and take Rhodes which he has set his heart on! He is in a very dangerous condition, most unbalanced, and God knows how we shall finish this war if this goes on.

8 October

I am slowly becoming convinced that in his old age Winston is becoming less and less well balanced! I can control him no more. He has worked himself into a frenzy of excitement about the Rhodes attack, has magnified its importance so that he can no longer see anything else and has set his heart on capturing this one island even at the expense of endangering his relations with the President and with the Americans, and also the whole future of the Italian campaign. He refuses to listen to any arguments or to see any dangers! He wired to the President asking for Marshall to come out to the Mediterranean for a conference in Tunis to settle the matter, hoping in his heart to be able to swing the meeting by his personality. However, the President sent him back a very cold reply asking him not to influence operations in the Mediterranean. This did not satisfy him and he wired back again asking President to reconsider the matter. The whole thing is sheer madness, and he is placing himself quite unnecessarily in a very false position! The Americans are already desperately suspicious of him, and this will make matters far worse.

Meanwhile it is nearly midnight Friday and we none of us yet know whether we are to start for Tunis tomorrow or not! It is quite maddening and all most futile, but the worst of the whole matter is that I am afraid matters will go on deteriorating rather than improving. If they do I shall not be able to stick it much longer!

It should be remembered that the Americans always suspected Winston of having concealed desires to spread into the Balkans. These fears were not entirely ungrounded! They were determined that whatever happened they would not be led into the Balkans. At times I think that they imagined I supported Winston's Balkan ambitions, which was far from being the case. Anyhow the Balkan ghost in the cupboard made my road none the easier in leading the Americans by the hand through Italy!

9 October

A short COS. Then Adam to dine and went home to meet you.

10 October

A quiet day at home!!! with continuous telephone calls connected with Roosevelt's last reply to PM's wire. I spent ½ an hour with him on telephone, during which he stated everyone was against him, but that the situation was so changed in Italy that we must readjust our thoughts!! Any changes there are only due to everything I have been trying to drill into him during the last week! I can't stick much more of these eel-like tactics!!

11 October

Motored up with you and spent usual Monday with Cabinet conference that was to have been followed by a Defence Committee meeting that did not materialize. Dined out with Medlicott [21ˢᵗ Army Group] and consequently missed the joy of dining with you.

12 October

Finished COS fairly quickly without any very important matters. Our worst troubles arose out of the Foreign Office attempting to support the King of Greece at the expense of the EMA, the secret organization which at present provides us with the maximum support against the Germans. Had a quiet afternoon during which I accomplished a lot of work.

13 October

Bert Harris of Bomber Command came to see us this morning during the COS meeting. According to him the only reason why the Russian army has succeeded in advancing is due to the results of bomber offensive!! According to him I am certain that we are all preventing him from winning the war. If Bomber Command was left to itself it would make much shorter work of it all!

Madeline [Lees] came with you to lunch and I left you at Eaton Square after lunch. After lunch I was photographed by a Canadian photographer,* then had long interview with Tommy Lindsell who is going out to Delhi shortly [as Principal Administrative Officer]. Finally saw Canadian AG.

14 October

Our COS did not last very long, and was mainly taken up with trying to find some solution to centralizing the command in the Mediterranean. In the afternoon I had a visit from Van Reinweld, the South African Chief of their Staff. He remained about an hour, whilst we discussed the employment of the South African Forces. Before dinner I attended Sosnkowski's (Polish C-in-C) sherry party at the Savoy. In the evening Harry Crerar came to dine with me to discuss details of the moves of Canadian Corps to North Africa.

15 October

At this morning's COS we had Van Reinweld, the SA CGS, for an interview. His heart seemed to us to be as much in this war as anybody else's heart. In the afternoon I had interviews with the Egyptian MA and with Paget. Bertie and Hilda came to dinner in the evening. It was a great joy having them back.

---

*The celebrated Karsh of Ottawa. This portrait appears on the jacket of the present volume.

16 October

After a rushed morning I dashed off to St James's Church, Spanish Place, to meet you at Ross's wedding. After the ceremony we both attended Ross's reception and the Finlaysons' reception. Finally we drove home, taking you, Patricia and the Pooks back in the car.

17 October

Quiet Sunday at home, but had to come up to town before dinner.

18 October

An uninteresting COS which I found it hard to pay attention to. A series of interviews, a Cabinet meeting, more work, and another Monday gone.

19 October

COS at which we received note from PM wishing to swing round the strategy back to the Mediterranean at the expense of the cross Channel operation. I am in many ways entirely with him, but God knows where that may lead us to as regards clashes with Americans.

This evening another meeting with PM at 10.30 pm attended by Smuts, Attlee, Cadogan, Lyttelton, Leathers etc. Here again PM worked on same scheme and advocated another Combined Chiefs of Staff meeting next month, and early at that. He suggested first week in November which is quite impossible. I shudder at the thought of another meeting with the American Chiefs of Staff, and wonder whether I can face up to the strain of it.

20 October

One of those days when even sunshine fails to dispel the gloom that lies on one. All life, and all its enterprises looked black. In every problem the molehills became mountains, and failure seemed to be the inevitable result of all enterprise. A desperate feeling of failure, incompetency and incapacity to carry this burden any longer!

Dined with Ralph Glyn and 3 other members of Parliament all engaged on a committee to reduce war expenditure. We dined at the Euston Station Hotel, and I was bombarded with questions for some two hours on end. I felt in no mood for it.

21 October

Heard news of poor old Dudley Pound's death, it must be a blessing from his point of view as he was deriving little benefit from life in his paralysed state. Cunningham, the new First Sea Lord, now attends the COS. It is too early yet to say what assistance he will be.

Andrew Cunningham's arrival in the COS was indeed a happy event for me. I found him first and foremost one of the most attractive of friends, secondly a charming associate to work with, and finally the staunchest of campaigners when it came to supporting a policy agreed to amongst ourselves, no matter what inclement winds might be brought to bear on it. I carry away ... nothing but the very happiest recollections of all my dealings with him. His personality, his charming smile, and heart-warming laugh were enough to disperse at once those miasmas of gloom and despondency which occasionally endeavoured to swamp the COS.

Duke of Gloucester came during the afternoon for one of his visits and as usual was very nice and luckily did not stop too long.

I am still suffering from a dislike for life and even greater dislike for work!

22 October

We received a wire from Moscow giving the latest results of Eden's talks and asking for replies as to lines he was to take regarding Russia's desire to get Turkey and Sweden in to the war. I then picked you up at the flat to take you to lunch at the Spanish Embassy. There we found the PM and Clemmie, Cadogan and his wife, John Anderson and Ava, Duke d'Alba's daughter, her cousin, and various naval and military attachés. The food as usual was beyond description in its perfection! After lunch a meeting with PM at 4.15 pm which took us up to 5.10 pm. I then left with Barney for Cobbold's shoot where I found Bertie and Hilda.

23 October

A very pleasant shoot with 132 partridges and 64 pheasants. Inclined to be wet in morning but lovely afternoon.

24 October

Shot again in the morning with 41 partridges and 2 pheasants. Glorious sunny morning. After lunch motored back to London where we arrived about 5.30 pm. As cook was busy getting married I went out to dine with Barney at the Turf Club.

25 October

It is becoming more and more evident that our operations in Italy are coming to a standstill and that owing to lack of resources we shall not only come to a standstill, but also find ourselves in a very dangerous position unless the Russians go on from one success to another. Our build up in Italy is much slower than the German, and far slower than I had expected. We shall have an almighty row with the Americans who have put us in this position with their insistence to abandon the Mediterranean operations for the very problematical cross Channel operations. We are now beginning to see the full beauty of the

Marshall strategy!! It is quite heartbreaking when we see what we might have done this year if our strategy had not been distorted by the Americans.

26 October

I was sent for by Winston at 10 am to discuss Alexander's last wire stating that operations in Italy were coming to a standstill. Discussed with him the best methods of getting the Americans to realize that we must for the present concentrate on the Mediterranean. Then met COS and prepared a wire for Washington which we discussed with Winston at 12.15.

After lunch attended poor dear old Dudley Pound's funeral, and felt as I sat next to his coffin in the Abbey, that amongst the 3 of the Chiefs of the Staff he had certainly chosen the one road that led at last to peace and an end to these worldly struggles, and in some ways I envied him.

Bertie and Hilda came to dinner before his departure back to the ME and North Africa.

27 October

I was to have attended an Anniversary Parade of the Czechoslovak forces. Unfortunately weather was so foggy that it was impossible to attempt it. This afternoon had long interview with Lord Rennell who is just back from Alex's HQ. He was rather depressing about conditions prevailing at Eisenhower's HQ and compared it to Cairo at its worst!!

At 6 pm Cabinet meeting at which PM and Smuts gave a long discourse on relative merits of Mediterranean theatre as opposed to cross Channel operation. I believe the whole of it was intended for Beaverbrook with an idea of educating him! Finally PM turned to him and asked him what he thought about it. He replied that he had always been an ardent supporter of the cross Channel operation, but that now that we were committed to the Mediterranean, we should make a job of it.

The stagnation of our operations at that time was very disturbing. The winter weather settling in no doubt added to our difficulties, but the main trouble was the American desire to now swing priorities round to the Channel and in doing so render it impossible to gather the full fruits of our present strategic position. We were now firmly established in the lower part of the leg of Italy. We had command of the air and command of the sea. The enemy flanks therefore remained open to combined operations on both sides throughout the length of Italy. The main artery of rail communication consisted of one double line of railway open to air attack throughout its length. The Italian forces had only one desire, and that was to finish with the war. Conditions were therefore ideal for hitting the enemy hard, and for enforcing on him the use of reserves in the defence of Italy.

The attitude of Ike's HQ was not encouraging. I knew that he never really appreciated the strategic advantages of Italy, and that the American blindfolded cross Channel policy must appeal to him as being easier to understand.

We had certainly arrived at the time when the most active planning and prepara-
tion was necessary for next year's cross Channel operation, but these plans and prepa-
rations must NOT be allowed to slow down operations in Italy, which were
themselves one of the most important of the preparations. The American outlook was
unfortunately one of, 'We have already wasted far too much time in the
Mediterranean doing nothing, let us now lose no more time in this secondary theatre.
Let us transfer and allot all available resources to the main theatre and finish the war
quickly in Germany.'

28 October

A difficult COS at which we discussed the desirability or otherwise of vacating
Leros. A very nasty problem, Middle East [Command] have not been either
wise or cunning and have now got themselves into the difficult situation that
they can neither hold nor evacuate Leros. Our only hope would be assistance
from Turkey, the provision of airfields from which the required air cover could
be provided.

Lunched at the Mansion House at a meal given in honour of new Soviet
Ambassador [F.T. 'Frogface' Gousev, a former butcher]. He is certainly not as
impressive as that ruffian Maisky was! In afternoon had long interview with
Boy Browning to discuss his visit to India and plans for airborne division in
that country. News from Russia continues to be excellent.

It is rather strange that I did not refer more frequently to the news from Russia. It con-
tinued to be the vital point on which the whole of our strategy hinged. If Russia had
collapsed all our strategic plans would have gone west. German forces liberated from
Russia would have made a cross Channel operation impossible and would have
endangered our position in Italy and Middle East. Further afield the Indian and
Australian dangers would again have come to the fore. Russia therefore remained of
vital importance throughout these anxious days, but luckily the signs of a turn in the
tide were becoming more and more apparent.

29 October

A rather long and busy day and especially trying owing to a heavy cold! Started
with long COS which lasted till 12.30. Then at 3 pm met PM to discuss South
East Asia operations and thank God succeeded in getting decisions out of him.
Then discussed control of Mediterranean and found that as usual PM could not
realize real facts and failed to get a clear picture of what command really
means.

After our meeting I asked him whether he would agree to put Dill up for a
peerage in the New Year's Honours List. I felt very doubtful how he would
react and was surprised to find that he jumped at it. He only asked whether he
might perhaps prefer an OM [Order of Merit]! I must now see that he sticks to
it.

This was my first attempt to obtain Dill a peerage. For my next attempt I brought P.J. Grigg with me. The results were the same; agreement and promises. Then nothing! I do not believe he had any intention of ever ensuring that Dill received a peerage [cf. 5 November 1944]! And yet there are very few people to whom he owed more than he did to Dill for the exceptional relations he had established with Marshall.

Rushed back to WO for Army Council Meeting from 5 to 6.15 pm with long discussion concerning Home Guard morale. Then dashed off with you to Turkish Embassy cocktail party. Finally finished up day by entertaining General and Madame Sosnkowski to dinner.

30 October

For a marvel there was no COS meeting this morning!! As I had a heavy cold arranged to start off at 11.30 am with you to get back to Ferney Close by lunch time. Spent rest of afternoon with my bird books nursing my cold.

31 October

Late morning in bed and quiet day indoors mostly spent looking after my cold.

1 November

Early start back. Found my table groaning with telegrams! A rushed briefing period followed by fairly long COS. In afternoon had interview with Andy McNaughton and a Cabinet meeting at 5.30 pm. Now I am off for another 10.30 pm meeting, and I am 'sick unto death' of these night meetings! We are to discuss plans for another Combined Chiefs of Staff meeting, and the stink of the last one is not yet out of my nostrils! My God! how I hate those meetings and how weary I am of them! I now unfortunately know the limitations of Marshall's brain and the impossibility of ever making him realize any strategical situation or its requirements. In strategy I doubt if he can ever, ever see the end of his nose.

When I look at the Mediterranean I realize only too well how far I have failed in my task during the last 2 years! If only I had had sufficient force of character to swing those American Chiefs of Staff and make them see daylight, how different the war might be. We should have been in a position to force the Dardanelles by the capture of Crete and Rhodes, we should have the whole Balkans ablaze by now, and the war might have been finished in 1943!! Instead, to satisfy American shortsightedness we have been led into agreeing to the withdrawal of forces from the Mediterranean for a nebulous 2nd Front, and have emasculated our offensive strategy!! It is heartbreaking. I blame myself and yet at the same time doubt whether it was humanly possible to alter the American point of view more than I succeeded in doing?

At the time I wrote the above remarks I was evidently suffering from a heavy cold and had also not yet fully recovered from the strain of the Quebec Conference. Reading between some of the lines I wrote I am inclined to think that I cannot have been very far off from nervous breakdown at that time. Nevertheless there is a great deal in what I wrote on the evening of November 1ˢᵗ. If the Americans had cooperated whole heartedly in the Mediterranean and had been able to appreciate the advantages to be gained events might well have turned out to our advantage. Unfortunately just at a moment when there were some fruits to be gained from the efforts we had made, the Americans selected this as a moment to damp down our efforts; troops, landing craft and transport were removed and reallocated. At very little cost Crete and Rhodes could have been rendered possible operations without affecting operations in Italy, whereas as matters stood these operations were only possible at the expense of Italian opera-tions and consequently ruled out. Success in Crete and Rhodes might have had the happiest repercussions in Turkey and the Balkans without ever committing a single man in the Balkans; we could have benefited better than before by the actions of the Resistance movements in these countries.

2 November

A long COS which started with our weekly interview with Joint Intelligence Committee. I had to disagree with a report they had submitted as to number of divisions that could concentrate in Northern Italy. They did not like this and consequently I am very unpopular with them now. I then met you, Pooks and Pat at Waterloo and brought you home to lunch and then on to the cinema. Then interview with Barington back from Moscow, and with the Adjutant General who is just off on a journey to North Africa and India. Was also sent for by PM to discuss with me the appointment of Monty Stopford to Commander of South East Asia Overseas Expeditions. Did not have much trouble with him as he was in a good mood. Also discussed McNaughton and ways and means of finding a new appointment for him. P.J. Grigg and Lady G came to dine with us and we then went on to see a film which has been pre-pared as a sequel to *Desert Victory*. From there I had to attend Defence Committee meeting with PM who kept us up till midnight. Mainly discussing impending journey to Mediterranean.

3 November

This morning's COS took a nasty turn in the shape of a long discussion between CAS and the new First Sea Lord [Cunningham]!!! Neither would give in and I had a difficult time, I wonder if this is the first of many more of this kind! After lunch I had interview with Bob Laycock, who replaced Dickie Mountbatten as CCO. Finally dined with PM at 10 Downing St for dinner for the King. Portal, Cunningham, Hollis and I were the guests. PM in very good form and produced some nuggets which although I intended to write down tonight I find are all forgotten except the following: He had wanted to send a wire to Eden on his way back from Moscow and who has been instructed to coerce the Turks into the war, that it was necessary to 'remind the Turkey that Xmas was coming'! The King was as usual perfectly charming and remained there till 12.30 am. We were then kept up for another hour by the PM and only returned home shortly before 2 am.

4 November

A long discussion with the Planners to decide best method of presenting the problem of the Mediterranean dilemma to the Combined Chiefs of Staff. Then lunch at the Butlers followed by a call from PM for 3 pm meeting to discuss Eisenhower's last telegram, and to frame new wire to Washington to try to straighten out the situation. Finally Cabinet at 6 pm to discuss this development and Winston's wire to the President backing up our wire. In evening dinner party for Reinweld and Mathinet.

5 November

It was a 'manpower' morning! First with a discussion at the COS and then a Cabinet meeting from 11.30 to 1.30 pm. We discussed the policy of banking on the defeat of Germany in 1944 and of retaining intensity of war at maximum whilst allowing for a cessation of hostilities in 1945 except for Japan and armies of occupation. At lunch the Vivians and Wainwrights. After lunch interview with Bertie Ramsay and finally theatre with Grasett and dinner at the Ritz. Cannot shake off remnants of my cold and feeling rotten all last week. No energy, no drive and a desperate dislike for work!

6 November

After lunch I drove to Ti's school where I found you and Mr Ti. We had tea with the Pursers and then after returning Mr Ti drove back to Hartley Wintney.

7 November

A quiet Sunday at home nursing the remnants of my cold. Lovely sunny day.

8 November

Usual early start, arrived at WO to find table littered with telegrams from Moscow and from Washington. One from Washington with a ridiculous suggestion by Leahy that Marshall should be made Supreme Commander of European Theatre, to combine North Africa with cross Channel! Luckily PM was entirely with us and sent back strong telegram to Dill with his views as to the absurdity of the proposal! The trouble is that meanwhile our proposal to combine the control and command of the Mediterranean is being sidetracked.

Lunched at Hyde Park Hotel with Smuts, who had PM and 3 Chiefs of Staff lunching, also John Anderson and Cranborne. I sat next to High

Commissioner and SA representative in Sweden. Then back to WO for a rush of work including interview with Ralston and Stewart from Canada connected with desirability of relieving Andy McNaughton of his command of the Canadian Army. At 5.15 rushed off to Soviet Embassy to attend reception in honour of the foundation of the Soviet regime. Rooms packed and had too much vodka pressed on me. Back to Cabinet at 6 pm which lasted till 8.15 pm. PM in very good form and produced several gems. Referring to plans for dismissing King of Italy he said, 'Why break off the handle of the jug before we get to Rome and have a chance of securing a new handle for it!'

Dined out with Bannerman and had a glorious evening of bird talk which I thoroughly enjoyed.

9 November

Long discussion at our COS meeting on future Mediterranean strategy. I was not in full accord with plans put forward by Planners. Essential that we should clear our minds as to our recommendations before meeting the American Chiefs. A few things stand out clearly. First, we must go in Italy till we reach the Pisa-Rimini Line. This will entail postponing cross Channel operations some 2 months. Secondly we must centralize command of Mediterranean. Thirdly the partisans in Balkans must be rearmed at far greater rate than at present. Fourthly, Turkey must be brought into the war and the Dardanelles opened again. Fifthly, Balkan states must be made to sue for peace. The above seems rough outline to go for.

Lunch at Mansion House for Lord Mayor's day. PM's speech not quite up to his usual standard.

In the evening fetched you from Goring Hotel to dine at the flat.

10 November

We had a long COS again. We were busy formulating our Mediterranean policy for the forthcoming meeting with the American Chiefs of Staff at which we are bound to have a pretty stiff contest!

I then fetched you for lunch, after which I left you with Mr Squirrell and back to the WO for a series of interviews. First with DCIGS concerning the build up of vehicles in the Italian Theatre. Then Paget concerning McNaughton and his interviews with him about his report from Ralston as regards being unsuitable for command of the 1st Canadian Army. Finally Mathinet came to see me with many minor points and a very definite doubt in his mind as to his future now that the French National Assembly have got rid of Giraud and Georges!!

Finally picked you up for our dinner at Buckingham Palace where the party consisted of King and Queen, Duke of Gloucester and Duchess, Duchess of Kent, Philip Chetwode, PM and Mrs Churchill, Law etc. A very good dinner! Sat between Lascelles and Lady Chetwode. After ladies left was called up to sit between the King and Duke of Gloucester. Had long talk with the former about the Brigade of Guards and the required changes. He seemed to agree that Arthur Smith [Commander] might well be relieved by Budget Loyd. Then moved into drawing room where I had a talk with the Queen and with the Duchess of Kent, whom I found much easier to talk to than the Duchess of Gloucester.

11 November

Rather a rushed morning! First of all sorting out of kit for our journey to Cairo. Then a rush in the WO as I had to lay a wreath on the Cenotaph at 9.55 am. Then S of S sent for me before COS meeting and said he had been helping to get Bertie the London Police job as Philip Game was going. I told him how grateful I was to him. [Nothing came of this.] Then long COS with the Joint Intelligence Committee and Duncan Sandys to reorganize the research organization and necessary action required by the German rocket[s]. Then interview with St Clair concerning production during 1944, 45 and 46. Not easy matters to predict for. Then fetched you for lunch and we had a walk in St James's Park, wrote our names in the book at Buckingham Palace and then I left you at the Hotel before going on for my hair cut. Franklyn came to see me in the afternoon and finally I collected you and the Kennedys for dinner and for some bird films.

We are now getting near our departure for Cairo. I feel that we shall have a pretty serious set to, which may strain our relations with the Americans, but I am tired of seeing our strategy warped by their shortsightedness and their incompetency!

12 November

A busy day. We started with a long COS, which was mainly spent in listening to the junior planners just back from Washington on the problem of the war in the Pacific. Having been ordered by the Americans to produce a plan to defeat Japan in 2 years they had done their best and in my opinion produced a rotten plan with little hope of success!

Dashed back to WO and from there to pick you up for lunch at the flat before taking you on to the station to catch the 1.54 to Winchfield. Then on to the Birleys who had specially asked me to come. There I found them both very distressed because Maxine their daughter had volunteered her services for special duties in France with the Saboteurs! Rhoda had discovered it in confidence from Maxine, had tried to dissuade her and failed. Oswald had also tried but with no more success. I was asked could I do anything to save her without disclosing to her that they had approached me! Dashed back to WO and put DMI on job to tackle SOE department. Then attended Cabinet at 3.30 pm to discuss crisis that has occurred in the Lebanon owing to de Gaulle's dictatorial action.

Back to WO for Army Council meeting at 5 pm followed by interview with Ralston (Canadian Defence Minister) and Stewart (Canadian Chief of Staff).

Apparently former had informed McNaughton that neither I nor Paget had confidence in him as an Army Commander in action.

McNaughton had been to see Paget and on the strength of his interview with him had wired to Mackenzie King that Ralston and Stewart had fitted up a case against him which was in no way supported by Paget, and had given a completely erroneous interpretation of his interview with Paget. It rather looks to me as if McNaughton is going off his head! At any rate I was stuck with Ralston for over an hour.

Then final interviews with P. J. Grigg, VCIGS, PUS, DMI, DCIGS etc before my departure. It now only remains to go shooting with Alwyne tomorrow, spend the next day with you quietly at home, and then to start on one more of those long journeys and difficult meetings with our American friends. I feel very weary and disinclined to go.

13 November
Barney and I after an early start left here at 7.45 am. By 8.45 am we were at Ferney Close to pick you up, together with Pooks and Sneezer [Patricia Pelly], and the lunch. By 9.45 we were at Preshaw for [Benita's brother] Alwyne's shoot. Very wet but it cleared up in the afternoon and was not bad at all from the weather point of view. Lots of birds and we had great fun. Motored back to Ferney Close in the evening.

14 November
Quiet day at home and pouring rain all day. Was to have started for Gibraltar in the evening, but at 4.30 pm message came through postponing departure for 48 hours owing to icing conditions.

15 November
Left early attended COS in the morning and then picked you up at Waterloo for lunch and then on to your meeting. Cabinet in the evening run by Attlee as Winston is in [HMS] *Renown* on his way to Gib or Malta. Our journey again put off for 24 hours, this is bad as Winston will be off to Italy without me and I want to be there when he sees Alexander and Monty!

16 November
Another COS with a meeting of the Joint Intelligence Committee. In afternoon Cabinet at 5.30 at which we discussed the question of supporting partisans in Greece. I had considerable difference of opinion with Anthony Eden who is for cutting support to those partisans who have been doing most of the work, as their views are communistic and against the future government of Greece as backed by the Foreign Office. Succeeded in getting Cabinet to agree with me.

Weather now reported good enough and we are to take off from Northolt at

1 am for Gib. I am not looking forward to the trip as it is beastly cold and we shall probably have to fly very high! Unfortunately we are already two days late and the PM will be getting over to Italy without me!

Here we were off again on one of our Combined conferences. This one, however, was badly prepared for, and what was far more serious, badly staged. We had stated that we wanted to meet the Americans first to clear our minds with them and establish a common policy. Then to meet the Russians to complete matter with the defeat of Germany and finally to meet Chiang Kai-shek to discuss operations against Japan. Owing to American pressure we let the tail wag the dog and started with Chiang Kai-shek!

17 November   Gibraltar and Malta

I am writing this flying over the Western Mediterranean having left Gib about an hour ago. Left my flat at 11.30 pm for Northolt. Had not been gone long when I remembered my pyjamas had not been packed! Went back to get them. Arrived aerodrome at 12.30 am and found Portal, Bowhill, Van Reinweld and CCO [Laycock] all there. Bowhill was only there to see us off. At 1 am the engines roared and we dashed off into the darkness and the unknown. We are travelling in the PM's York and I am in his state cabin and therefore very comfortable. Bed with sheets, small table, chair and lavatory complete!! At 7 am, steward woke me up with a cup of tea. After a wash, shave and dress I looked out, the sun was just rising in a cloudless sky, both Spanish and African coastlines were being lit up with a red glow. Lovely soft lights.

By 8 am (only 7 hours from London!) we were hovering over the Rock prior to landing. The Rock looked quite its best shining in the sun. We did a beautiful landing and were met by Mason-MacFarlane who took us up to Government House for breakfast. He was very interesting on all his recent mission work with Badoglio and the King of Italy. The Ambassador from Chungking was also at breakfast on his way home and delayed several nights by weather. At 10 am we took off again, after 1½ hours filling tanks, and are now on our way to Malta, hoping to make it before dark. Lovely calm sea and bright blue sky with a few fleecy clouds.

Later:

We had a lovely fly along the North African coast and saw Oran, Algiers, Bougie, Philippeville and Bône. Passed just south of Tunis and saw Pantelleria Island in the distance. We were given an excellent hot lunch, with soup, steak and fruit flan! Finally arrived at Malta at 3 pm, having only left Northolt at 1 am the same day! 12 hours flying to cover 2500 miles!! I was met on the aerodrome by a Guard of Honour and Park, the AOC, Tedder and Oxley, the OC troops. Drove up to the Palace where I found Gort and Alexander and also Eisenhower. PM had not yet arrived and was coming by sea, we had passed his battleship and cruiser escorted by their destroyers some way out to sea and supposed he must be in it. I can't help feeling what a very different visit from my last one to Malta, August a year ago, when I crept in at night, had 18 air raid alarms during the day, and crept out again in the dark! The whole island on short rations and Gort in a very depressed mood, whilst I tried to cheer him up with the prospects of North African operations!

Thank God those days are over!

PM arrived about 7.30 pm, bringing with him Winant, Mrs Vic Oliver [Sarah Churchill], Pug, Martin, Cunningham. Dined 8.30 pm and afterwards much talking which kept us away from bed till after midnight. Dead tired I am dropping off to bed, the last 23 hours have been pretty full and have covered many miles!

18 November   Malta

It had been decided last night with the PM that we should have a meeting with him at 11 am and that at 2 pm he should start off with Alex and me for Italy. This morning all plans were changed! First of all the PM had a cold and therefore could not go to Italy, secondly he wanted to have a talk with Alexander in the afternoon therefore Alex and I could not start for Italy, and thirdly the President had wired that in view of the fact that security had been violated and the Germans had already published the fact that we were all meeting in Cairo, we should have to find another place. He suggested Khartoum! PM suggested Malta, Gort was horrified at the thought of it, wires flew in all directions, and I think that in the end we shall go on going to Cairo! Had a talk of about 1 hour with Alex in the garden which was good value.

We then had our conference with PM in bed, Chiefs of Staff, John Cunningham [C-in-C Mediterranean] and Tedder [AOC Mediterranean]. PM gave long tirade on evils of Americans and of our losses in the Aegean and Dalmatian coast. He was not at his best, and I feel nervous as to the line he may adopt at this conference. He is inclined to say to the Americans, all right if you won't play with us in the Mediterranean we won't play with you in the English Channel. And if they say all right well then we shall direct our main effort in the Pacific, to reply you are welcome to do so if you wish! I do not think that such tactics will pay. After lunch Alex, Moran and I went for a drive round Malta and went to northern point from which we could see the islands of Gozo and Comino. PM in bed all day, but by way of getting up for dinner.

Later:

PM got up for dinner, saying he was feeling better. He kept us up only to close on midnight. Alex and I have planned to start for Bari in his plane at 9 am tomorrow, PM says he may follow on in the evening. Long military discussions at dinner and after dinner, which filled me with gloom! There are times when I feel that it is all a horrid nightmare which I must wake up out of soon. All this floundering about, this lack of clear vision, and lack of vision! PM examining war by theatres and without perspective, no clear appreciation of the influence of one theatre on another! Then he discusses Command and Commanders and has never yet gained a true grasp of Higher Command organization and what it means.

On the other hand Alexander charming as he is fills me with gloom, he is a very, very, small man and cannot see big. Unfortunately he does not recognize this fact and is oblivious to his shortcomings! Perhaps it is as well or he might get an inferiority complex. But I shudder at the thought of him as a Supreme Commander! He will never have the personality or vision to command three services! It is hard to advise him as he fails really to grasp the significance of things.

First of all the new feelings of spitefulness which had been apparent lately with Winston since the strength of the American forces were now building up fast and exceeding ours. He hated having to give up the position of the dominant partner which we had held at the start. As a result he became inclined at times to put up strategic proposals which he knew were unsound purely to spite the Americans. He was in fact aiming at 'cutting off his nose to spite his face'. It was usually fairly easy to swing him back on the right line and to get rid of these whims. There lay, however, in the back of his mind the desire to form a purely British theatre when the laurels would be all ours. . . . Austria or the Balkans seemed to attract him for such a front.

Winston's views on command always remained confused throughout the war. He could not or would not follow how a chain of command was applied. He was always wanting a Commander-in-Chief to suddenly vacate his post and concentrate on commanding one individual element of his command at the expense of all the rest. It was therefore a matter of considerable difficulty when the system of command in the various theatres had to be readjusted to meet new developments.

In the last paragraph of this day's diary I may perhaps have been unnecessarily hard on Alex, and yet when I read it through again there is nothing that I want to alter! There is no doubt that he held some of the highest qualities of a Commander: unbounded courage, never ruffled or upset, great charm and a composure that inspired confidence in those around him. But when it came to working on a higher plain, and deciding matters of higher tactics and of strategy he was at once out of his depth, had no ideas of his own, and always sought someone to lean on. Up to now he had fitted admirably into the various jobs I had asked him to do, but looking ahead I foresaw some stormy seas with rocks, crags and sandbanks and had the gravest doubts as to Alex's ability to navigate such waters. Fortune favoured me and I was able to retain him in Italy.

19 November   Malta

Woke up to find it pouring with rain. Reports from aerodrome were uncertain and undecided. We started for the aerodrome and got half way there when we were met and informed that there would be no flying today and probably none tomorrow! This knocks my trip to Italy on the head. Meanwhile no further news from President as to whether he is prepared to stick to Cairo for our meeting.

During morning Alex and I went off to visit the Palace and also the Church of St John, the old Knight Templars' church, most interesting. In the afternoon I went with Winant (American Ambassador), Portal and Alex to see the collection of old books and documents in the library. A most wonderful collection with letters from Henry VIII, Queen Anne, various Georges, Marie Antoinette etc. Also a wonderful collection of old bibles and books marvellously painted and illustrated. PM has now decided to go on by sea to Alexandria. I hope therefore to fly on to Cairo in his York leaving here about 9 am weather permitting.

Later:

When I came down for dinner I was informed that PM had decided that if no reply from Roosevelt came in before 10 pm (and he considered chances 1000 to 1 against!) he would stop on another night and would require his York aircraft to remain in Malta in case he required it! We had therefore arranged for a Dakota to take me on instead. However, during dinner a wire arrived stating that President was prepared to come to Cairo, so PM decided to sail at 11.30 pm in *Renown*, and the York again became available for me. He was in very good form at dinner and finished up with a long dissertation on his post war reconstruction ideas, and his slogan of 'food, house and work for everyone'. Also his instruction to Woolton working with Oliver Lyttelton to produce these requirements. After dinner he left to embark and Gort accompanied him.

The events of this day have always remained very deeply rooted in my mind as it was the first day that I really got to know and understand Winant. First I had been with him in the library where I had invited him to come with us, and afterwards we went for a drive around the island together. I had always been taken by him, but had never up till then been able to break through the 'iron curtain' of reserve that kept out the outer world. What I found behind this curtain was quite enchanting. A man who had made a deep study of life and had not arrived at his convictions easily. What he had arrived at was well worth hearing from his own lips. We were both discussing the wonderful rehabilitation to be acquired through close contacts with nature, and especially so in time of war. He said that no doubt I must have read Earl Grey's views on these matters as contained in the Fallodon Papers? *I had to confess that I had not! Whereupon he at once said he must rectify this defect and that he would send me a copy immediately on his return. He kept his promise and this book has remained one of my most treasured possessions. Later he gave me a wonderful folio copy of some 12 volumes of Audubon's* Birds of America. *His friendship I always look upon as one of those great blessings which the war occasionally provided as an antidote to all its horrors.*

20 November   Cairo

At 9 am we had a general exodus and farewell to Gort. Alexander was off to Bari, Portal off to Tunis, and I, accompanied by Bob Laycock (CCO), started for Cairo. I am at present writing in the air flying along the edge of the African coast east of Tripoli. We struck due south on leaving Malta so as to avoid Crete and any possible contacts with Germans from that island. Start of journey was a bit bumpy but has now smoothed down. We are flying over the edge of that sea of yellow and brown sand looking out over the deep blue of the Mediterranean which gradually shades off into the light blue of the horizon and leaves the horizon ill defined. Below us is the black bootlace of the tarmacked desert road. Last time I was over it on my way to Tripoli it was alive with lice-like lorries spaced out every hundred yards, busy building up our forces for the invasion of Tunisia. Now it is desolate and deserted without a vestige of life to be seen on it!

I wish our conference was over. It will be an unpleasant one, the most unpleasant one we have had yet, and that is saying a good deal. I despair of ever getting our American friends to have any sort of strategic vision. Their drag on us has seriously affected our Mediterranean strategy and the whole conduct of the war. If they had come wholeheartedly into the Mediterranean with us we should by now have Rome securely, the Balkans would be ablaze, the Dardanelles would be open, and we should be over the high way towards getting Rumania and Bulgaria out of the war. I blame myself for having had the vision to foresee these possibilities and yet to have failed to overcome the American shortsightedness and allowed my better judgement to have been affected by them. It would have been better to have resigned my appointment than to allow any form of compromise. And yet I wonder whether any such action would have borne any fruits. I rather doubt it. However I approach this conference full of misgivings as to the possibilities of our sacrificing further prospects through this process of compromise.

Later:

At 3.30 we arrived on the aerodrome beyond Mena. Jumbo Wilson [C-in-C ME] and Adam were on the aerodrome to meet me and took me to the villa which I am to live in with Dill, Portal and Cunningham, with Boyle and Barney also there. It is a villa outside Cairo on the way to Mena and belongs to some Egyptian princess. It is quite comfortable except for the plumbing which is none too good and water seldom hot. Dill turned up shortly after I had arrived, and we both went to dine with Jumbo Wilson.

We had left far behind the period of stopping Marshall from going across the Channel under entirely unsuitable conditions. We were beyond the days of coaxing them into North Africa and from there on into Sicily. We had made one million tons of shipping by opening up the Mediterranean, we had achieved a partial agreement to the elimination of Italy and an advance into that country. During this period Russia had held and was now beginning to show some offensive power. The bombing of Germany was gradually ripening up Germany for the final stages whilst at sea the German submarines were being checked. In fact all had gone admirably in our preliminary stages of preparation for the liberation of France.

We had now arrived in the orchard and our next step should be to shake the fruit trees and gather the apples. Southern Europe was now threatened on all sides; Italy was tottering and seeking for a way out of the war; all partisans in the Balkan states had been inspired by our successes and stirred to new activities; Turkey, which had for some time been sitting on the fence, was showing signs of leaning towards our side. Success breeds success in these cases, and the ball was at our feet. A quick elimination of Italy, coupled with a show of forces in the approach to the Dardanelles, including the capture of Crete and Rhodes, might well have borne valuable fruits. No liberation of the Balkans should be undertaken. This was unnecessary and would commit too much force. What was wanted was to knock all the props from under the Germans in the defence of the Mediterranean, let them alone to bear this full burden. We had been forced to miss some opportunities through lack of forces in the Mediterranean.

Europe was just one large strategic front with German forces distributed round the perimeter in accordance with the existing threats in each respective theatre. Forces in France watched the Channel approaches, those in Norway and Denmark held down those countries, from there westwards and southwards vast armies contained the Russians, in the south further detachments threatened Turkey and kept peace in the Balkans, whilst finally considerable force was employed in holding onto Italy and guarding Southern France. All these forces were handled centrally, and served by the most perfect East and West railway system in existence. A system which had been built up in the First World War and reinforced by the autobahn system of roads. It was easier for the Germans to convey divisions from the Russian front to the French front than it was for us to convey similar formations from the Italian front by sea to the French front. The North and South communications were, however, nothing like as efficient, comprising only one double line of railway through the leg of Italy and one through the Balkans to Greece.

Our strategy had now become a delicate matter of balancing. Our aim must be to draw as many divisions as possible from the French Channel and to retain them in Southern Europe as long as possible. Any failure to draw full advantage from our present position must also fail in drawing reserves away from the Channel. On the other hand any tendency to weaken our forces in the Mediterranean would at once lead to the move of German forces to the Channel.

When arguing with Marshall I could never get him to appreciate the very close connection that existed between the various German fronts. For him they might have been separate wars, a Russian war on the one side, a Mediterranean war on another and a cross Channel one to be started as soon as possible. I have often wondered since the war how different matters might have been if I had had MacArthur instead of Marshall to deal with. From everything I saw of him I put him down as the greatest general of the last war. He certainly showed a far greater strategic grasp than Marshall. I must however confess that Winston was no great help in the handling of Marshall, in fact the reverse. Marshall had a holy fear of Winston's Balkans and Dardanelles ventures, and was always guarding against these dangers even when they did not exist.

21 November

Went to GHQ to attend the intelligence conference. Then had long talk with Jumbo Wilson on a multitude of points. He came to lunch with me and at 2.30 pm we went to meet the PM on his arrival by plane from Alexandria. I then went to the Mena Hotel which has been taken over for our offices and conference rooms. Then I went through a series of documents which the American Chiefs of Staff had produced. Finally dined with PM, together with Dill, Portal, Wilson, Sholto Douglas, Mountbatten and Casey. PM kept us up till after 1 am. He was in a very excitable mood. I am not happy at the line he proposes to take in approaching the conference. We decided on the programme and are to start by dealing with Chiang Kai-shek who has arrived with Madame. And then we shall start on our Mediterranean discussion. The whole programme is affected by Stalin's visit to Teheran and the necessity of meeting him there by a given date after concluding our talks here.

The whole conference had been thrown out of gear by Chiang Kai-shek arriving here too soon. We should never have started our conference with Chiang; by doing so we were putting the cart before the horse. He had nothing to contribute towards the defeat of the Germans, and for the matter of that uncommonly little towards the defeat of the Japanese. Why the Americans attached such importance to Chiang I have never discovered. All he did was lead them down a garden path to a communist China! We should have started this conference by thrashing out thoroughly with the Americans the policy and strategy for the defeat of Germany. We could then have shown a united front to Stalin and finally, if time admitted, seen Chiang and Madame.

22 November

Started the day with a COS at 10 am at which we discussed our procedure for the rest of the meeting. After lunch had our first Combined meeting when we again decided on procedure. Martel then came to see me. Dill and I then called on Miles Lampson and Caseys. After dinner meeting with President, PM, all Chiefs of Staff, Mountbatten, Stilwell, Chennault, Harry Hopkins, to discuss Dickie Mountbatten's plans [for SE Asia] and to prepare for meetings with Chiang Kai-shek. After that PM took Dill, Portal and I to his villa. He was very pleased with results of his talks with the President, and thinks we shall not have so very much difficulty. Personally I doubt this. Got home after midnight.

23 November

We started the day with a rather rushed COS meeting as at 11 am we were due to go to the President's villa for a meeting with Chiang Kai-shek. It was a historical meeting with the President, Prime Minister, Harry Hopkins, Chiang Kai-shek, Madame CKS, all the Chiefs of Staff, Dickie Mountbatten, Stilwell, Chennault, Carton de Wiart and a full house of Chinese Generals!

I was very interested in the Chinese pair. The Generalissimo reminded me more of a cross between a pine marten and a ferret than anything else. A shrewd, foxy sort of face. Evidently with no grasp of war in its larger aspects but determined to get the best of the bargains. Madame was a study in herself, a queer character in which sex and politics seemed to predominate, both being used indiscriminately individually or unitedly to achieve her ends. Not good looking, with a flat Mongolian face with high cheek bones and a flat, turned up nose with two long circular nostrils looking like two dark holes leading into her head. Jet black hair and sallow complexion. If not good looking she had certainly made the best of herself and was well turned out. A black satin dress with a yellow chrysanthemum pattern on it, a neat black jacket, big black tulle bows at the back of her head and a black veil over her face, light coloured stockings and black shoes with large brass nails covering small feet. Tapered fingers playing with a long cigarette holder in which she smoked continuous cigarettes. The meeting was a slow performance with everything interpreted by a Chinese General reinforced by Madame! Dickie Mountbatten explained his whole plan, then a few questions were asked by Chiang. Finally a long discussion in which Chiang seemed to make whole operations dependent on presence of naval forces in the Indian Ocean.

After lunch meeting with CCS which became somewhat heated with King on the subject of the Andaman Islands and the possibility of landing craft being diverted from this operation to the Aegean. At 3.30 the Chinese came in and I had a desperate time with them to try and get them to speak. All they wanted to do was to listen and as we had nothing more to say except to argue with them and answer their questions, the meeting came to a standstill!! We had to suggest that they should examine the plan a little deeper and return tomorrow. Thus wasting more of our precious time! After the meeting I had an hour with Dickie Mountbatten. Then finished off office work and returned here by 7 pm.

We then had Leahy, King and Arnold to dine. Unfortunately Marshall was unable to come. The cook gave us an excellent dinner and things went well. King was as nice as could be and quite transformed from his afternoon attitude.

This very Chinese day has remained rooted in my memory. I have never known whether Madame Chiang gatecrashed into the morning's meeting or whether she was actually invited. It makes little difference, for I feel certain she would have turned up whether she was invited or not. She was the only woman amongst a very large gathering of men, and was determined to bring into action all the charms nature had blessed her with. Although not good looking she certainly had a good figure which she knew how to display at its best. Also gifted with great charm and gracefulness, every small movement of hers arrested and pleased the eye. For instance at one critical moment her closely clinging black dress of black satin with yellow chrysanthemums displayed a slit which extended to her hip bone and exposed one of the most shapely of legs. This caused a rustle amongst those attending the conference and I even thought I heard a suppressed neigh come from a group of some of the younger members!

The trouble that lay behind all this was that we were left wondering whether we were dealing with Chiang or with Madame. Whenever he was addressed his Chinese General sitting on his right interpreted for him, but as soon as he had finished Madame said 'Excuse me gentlemen, I do not think that the interpreter has conveyed the full meaning to the Generalissimo!' Similarly, whenever Chiang spoke his General duly interpreted the statement, but Madame rose to say in the most perfect English, 'Excuse me Gentlemen, but the General has failed to convey to you the full meaning of the thoughts that the Generalissimo wishes to express. If you will allow me I shall put before you his real thoughts.' You were left wondering as to whom you were dealing with. I certainly felt that she was the leading spirit of the two and that I would not trust her very far.

As for Chiang, I think the description I gave of him fits him very well: a shrewd but small man. He was certainly very successful in leading the Americans down the garden path. He and his Chinese forces never did much against the Japs during the war, and did not even succeed in keeping his country from becoming communist after the war. And yet the Americans never saw through all his shortcomings, pinned their hopes to him and induced us to do the same. I often wonder how Marshall failed to realize what a broken reed Chiang was when he went out to China just after the defeat of Japan. Marshall's advisors were bad. Stilwell was nothing more than a hopeless crank with no vision and Chennault a very gallant airman with a limited brain.

Anyhow, here we were on 23rd Nov 1943, sitting in a plenary conference with President, PM, Chiang and Madame to decide how we could meet his wishes for operations in the Indian Ocean intended to support the armies near Chungking. What is more we were prepared to pander sufficiently to Chiang to affect possible operations in the Aegean against our primary enemy!

The second Chinese farce on this day took place in the afternoon when three Chinese Chiefs of Staff attended our meeting to discuss operations in Burma. We had previously provided them with our proposed plans and intentions in Burma and asked them to read these so as to discuss them with us at our Combined Chiefs of Staff meeting. As the Conference was on British soil I was in the Chair and welcomed them as they arrived. I told them how much we had looked forward to this opportunity of discussing our plans in the war against Japan with them. We felt that with their long contacts with the Japanese both as neighbours and as enemies they must be in a special position to know how to bring about their ultimate defeat. I told them we had spent many hours in preparing the plans we had given them to examine and that we hoped now to receive their help and assistance in perfecting those plans. And I finally asked them for their views and their criticisms. There ensued the most ghastly silence!

The room was packed with some 60 to 70 British and American Staff Officers and at the end of the table a dozen or so Chinese staff all whispering together in a state of excitement. At last a Chinese spokesman arose and said, 'We wish to listen to your deliberations'! This was followed by a silence in which you could have heard a pin drop, whilst I wracked my brain as to what to do next! I then explained to them carefully that we had already spent hours of deliberation to arrive at the plans we had submitted. That our deliberations on these plans were now finished, and that the plans rested with them to express their views in relation to them. Finally I asked them once more to express their own views and criticisms. This was followed by another of those deadly silences broken only by Chinese whisperings. Just when I could no longer bear the silence up got the same Chinese spokesman and repeated the very same words: 'We wish to listen to your deliberations'!

I felt all eyes turn on me with a suppressed sound of amusement wondering what I *should do next. And for a few seconds I had no idea what I should do next. Then I rose and told them that possibly they had not had time enough to study the plans, or perhaps had not been able entirely to understand them. I suggested we should give them a further 24 hours to study the plans and that we should attach to them special staff officers to explain these plans. As soon as this suggestion had been interpreted there was a real 'flutter in the dovecot' and before we had time to realize it they had all slipped out through the door and disappeared! Mopping my brow I turned to Marshall and said, 'That was a ghastly waste of time!' To which he replied, 'You're telling me!' Considering that it was thanks to him and the American outlook that we had had to suffer this distressing interlude I felt that he might have expressed his regret otherwise.*

These two episodes on one day went a long way to convince me that there was little to be hoped for from Chiang's China.

24 November

We started with our usual COS meeting which lasted till 11 am when we all went over to the President's villa for a meeting with him and the Prime Minister. The President started with a general statement expressing his views as to the conduct of the war. This did not last very long and then the PM gave a masterly statement on his views concerning the European strategy and the best ways of maintaining the pressure on Germany during the winter months, and the dangers of spelling Overlord (codename for cross Channel operations) T-Y-R-A-N-T. It was a good address and should help us in our deliberations.

After lunch we met the American Chiefs at 2.30. Marshall was late as he had been lunching with Chiang Kai-shek who had suddenly decided that unless several impossible conditions could be fulfilled he refused to play his part in the operations! Shortly afterwards the Chinese Chiefs arrived and spent an hour asking the most futile questions. Finally Stilwell, as spokesman for Chiang, repeated what Marshall had said. We decided to send Mountbatten round to discuss matters with him and to aim at obtaining an agreement.

Finished up with dinner with Bertie Brooke, Clark Kerr – Ambassador in Moscow – and the American Undersecretary for War. We are making slow progress, and after several days' deliberations we have made no progress whatever!

The return of the Chinese Chiefs to the Combined Meeting was again a lamentable fiasco! When I had them assembled I now again asked them if they had any questions or criticisms they wished to put forward. After another one of those devastating silences only filled by Chinese whispers, the spokesman got up and asked: 'What is the proportion of Indian troops as opposed to British troops which will take part in this proposed operation?' I then reminded him that we had provided them with staff officers to answer just such questions and then gave them the figures they had asked for. With the greatest difficulty I extracted a few more such futile questions and then gave up the conflict in despair. It was evident that they understood nothing about strategy or higher tactics and were quite unfit to discuss these questions.

Chiang's latest haggling manoeuvres were typical of the man.

25 November

We started this morning with our usual COS at which we decided best line of action for the afternoon Combined meeting. At 12 noon we went round to President's villa when a series of photos, both still and movie, were taken. First of all the high and mighty: President, PM and Generalissimo. Then the above with Chiefs of Staff and Chinese Generals. Finally the above with politicians and diplomats etc. Not a very attractive lot to look at! I have no doubt that we were not much more beautiful in the military groups, but I pray to heaven that we may have been both individually and collectively less crooked!

At 2.30 pm we had an off the record Combined meeting and made considerable progress. I put forward our counter proposals for continuing active operations in the Mediterranean at the expense of a postponement of Overlord date. We did not meet with half the reaction we were expecting. On the other hand the Chinese negotiations are not going well and Chiang Kai-shek is busy bargaining to obtain the maximum possible out of us.

At 6 pm we had a service in the Cathedral for the Americans in honour of Thanksgiving Day. It was a sad fiasco and abominably badly run from the pre-reservations [of seats] to the Bishop's sermon included. I was in a cold sweat of agony throughout.

26 November

A long COS meeting to decide line to work on during afternoon. We had Commanders-in-Chief Middle East to hear their views about the Aegean operations. Admiral John Cunningham and Wilson came to lunch.

At 2.30 met Americans. It was not long before Marshall and I had the father and mother of a row! We had to come down to an off the record meeting and we again made more progress. In the end we secured most of the points we were after.

At 5 pm attended a tea party given by Chiang Kai-shek and Madame – a dismal show. Very hot and stuffy room. Had some 15 minutes talk with him through an interpreter. He did not impress me much, but hard to tell meeting him like that. Meanwhile Madame holding a court of admirers. The more I see of her the less I like her!

Dined with Bertie at the Mohammed Ali Club. Found Eisenhower and Donovan there, also the King of Greece with his lady friend, very attractive looking.

27 November   Teheran, 1300 miles

We had an unpleasantly early rise, being called at 4.30 am! By 5.45 am we were leaving our villa in the dark and light mist for the aerodrome. When we arrived there we were told that the mist would delay our departure. However, by 7 am we were moving down the 'runway' for our take off for Teheran. Our party consisted of Dill, Cunningham, Portal, Pug Ismay and Boyle and other secretaries. We were travelling in the new York designed for the Chiefs of Staff. Very comfortable. We crossed the canal near Suez and could see Italian battle-ships in the Bitter Lakes. Then across the Sinai Peninsula until we struck Beersheba. From there on across the top of Dead Sea and as visibility was good we could see Jerusalem, Bethlehem, Hebron and Jericho. We then headed for Habbaniya aerodrome near Baghdad where we came down and spent an hour looking round the aerodrome and being told story of the attack on the aero-drome in the early days of the war. After taking off again we were served with a most excellent lunch and with oxygen for those who wanted it. We had to travel at 14,000 feet for a long bit of the way, but I found it did not bother me and that I did not require any oxygen.

We arrived at Teheran a few minutes behind the PM who had started an hour later but flown direct. We were met by Selby commanding troops here temporarily and taken up to the British Legation. They have had an awful job to fit us all in but have made a good business of it. We are not yet certain whether Stalin has arrived or not. According to rumours he is here. I am not looking forward to the next few days. The conferences will be difficult and there is no saying where they may lead us to! Great change in temperature between Cairo and this place!

One amusing rumour, which apparently I failed to enter in my diary, was the local Teheran explanation for this sudden gathering of important people in their capital. Our visit happened to almost coincide with some local election that was being held. It was therefore decided that all these 'Very Important Personages' had gathered together here to ensure that the Persian elections were run on impartial lines!!

The security arrangements were not of the best, and as the American Embassy lay some way out of the centre of the town, it was decided to house the President in the Soviet Embassy, where they had room, and to hold our conferences in this Embassy also. As the British Legation buildings were just alongside of the Soviet ones, we had only one road to cross to attend meetings and the PM's security was also made easier.

28 November   Teheran

Had a quiet morning to make up for previous night's lack of sleep. Then spent an hour in office prior to running a COS meeting till lunch. We were very worried with the whole situation. We have not got agreement with the Americans on the main points for discussion, and it was evident that we are heading towards chaos. PM has bad throat and has practically lost his voice. He is not fit and consequently not in the best of moods. We tried to get him to agree to going on with the Andaman operation so as to get American agreement in the Mediterranean. He would not do so.

At 4 pm we went over to the Russian embassy for our first plenary meeting. The following were present: Stalin, Roosevelt, Winston, Anthony Eden, Harry Hopkins, Molotov, Voroshilov, Dill, Portal, Cunningham, Leahy and King, plus Ismay, Royal [Adm Sir G.C.C. Royle], Deane and 3 interpreters. Stalin turned up in his uniform of Field Marshal, but to my mind [looked] no more attractive than I thought him last time I saw him. Molotov looked almost saturnine! We all sat around a large round table. The President started off with an introductory statement which he followed up by a brief review of the war in the Pacific. To this Stalin replied that he much appreciated what we were doing in that theatre, and that it was only the fact that the Germans fully engaged him that prevented him cooperating with us! This was cheering news and implied Russian help as soon as Germany was defeated. The President then alluded to the Western Front and read a poor and not very helpful speech. From then onwards the conference went from bad to worse!

Stalin replied advocating cross Channel operations at the expense of all else. Winston replied and was not at his best. President chipped in and made matters worse. We finished up with a suggestion partly sponsored by the President that we should close operations in Italy before taking Rome. That we should land some 6 divs in southern France at the beginning of April and carry out Overlord on May 1ˢᵗ [1944]. Turkey according to Stalin was beyond hope and nothing could induce her to come into the war on any account. Dardanelles were apparently not worth opening.

In fact after complaining that we were not holding sufficient divisions away from Russia Stalin's suggestion was that practically no action should take place during the winter months! We sat for 3½ hours and finished up this conference by confusing plans more than they ever have been before!

The meeting had, however, been of intense interest and a great deal had been made clear which I had not yet realized. This was the first occasion during the war when Stalin, Roosevelt and Winston sat round a table to discuss the war we were waging together. I found it quite enthralling looking at their faces and trying to estimate what lay behind. With Churchill of course I knew fairly well, and I was beginning to understand the workings of Roosevelt's brain, as we had had several meetings with him, but Stalin was still very much of an enigma. I had already formed a very high idea of his ability, force of character and shrewdness, but did not know yet whether he was also a strategist. I knew that Voroshilov would provide him with nothing in the shape of strategic vision. My last visit to Moscow had made that quite clear to me, when I had spent several hours with Voroshilov discussing the problem of a Second Front with him.

During this meeting and all the subsequent ones which we had with Stalin, I rapidly grew to appreciate the fact that he had a military brain of the very highest calibre. Never once in any of his statements did he make any strategic error, nor did he ever fail to appreciate all the implications of a situation with a quick and unerring eye.

In this respect he stood out when compared with his two colleagues. Roosevelt never made any great pretence at being a strategist and left Marshall or Leahy to talk for him. Winston, on the other hand, was far more erratic, brilliant at times but far too impulsive and inclined to favour quite unsuitable plans without giving them the preliminary deep thought they required. ...

... Stalin was now evidently far better satisfied with his defensive position [on the

Eastern Front]. He was beginning to feel that the Germans had shot their bolt; immediate pressure on the West was no longer so urgently required. What is more, from his
point of view the entry of Turkey was no longer so desirable. He no longer had (if he
had ever had) any great desire for the opening of the Dardanelles. This would bring in
the British and the Americans on his left flank in an advance westward through the
Balkans. He had by then pretty definite ideas about how he wanted the Balkans run
after the war and this would entail, if possible, their total inclusion in the future
Union of Soviet Republics. British and American assistance was therefore no longer
desirable in the Eastern Mediterranean.

His new outlook on Italy was also interesting. There was now no pressure on our
forces to push up the leg of Italy. Such an advance led too directly towards Yugoslavia
and Austria, on which no doubt he had by now cast covetous eyes. He approved of
Roosevelt's futile proposals to close down operations in Italy and to transfer six divisions to invade Southern France on April 1st, whilst the main Channel operation
would take place on 1st May. I am certain he did not approve such operations for their
strategic value, but because they fitted in with his future political plans. He was too
good a strategist not to see the weakness of the American plan. To cease operations in
Italy before Rome would at once free the required reinforcements to meet six of our
divisions under the precarious conditions of a landing and all the subsequent administrative problems connected with their maintenance on this new front. The potential
war effort of our divisions on transfer from Italy to Southern France would in the early
stages have been reduced by half. Furthermore this plan allowed for the whole of the
month of April for the annihilation of these six divisions whilst fighting in Italy was
at a standstill and OVERLORD had not yet started. I feel certain that Stalin saw
through these strategical misconceptions, but to him they mattered little; his political
and military requirements could now be best met by the greatest squandering of
British and American lives in the French theatre.

We were reaching a very dangerous point where Stalin's shrewdness, assisted by
American shortsightedness, might lead us anywhere.

29 November

7 hours spent in conferences and 6 of them through interpreters!! We started
the morning with a staff meeting at 10.30, consisting of Leahy, Marshall,
Voroshilov, Portal and myself. We spent 3 hours at it, and at the end were no
further advanced. Voroshilov's main theme was that the cross Channel operation must have preference over all others and that the date must remain May
1st. In vain I argued that by closing operations in the Mediterranean German
forces would be free to proceed to other theatres! Our friend Voroshilov refused
to see any of these arguments having been evidently briefed by Stalin who no
doubt had also been prompted by Averell Harriman. Anyway Leahy said
nothing and Marshall only stressed the importance that the Americans had
always attached to cross Channel operations. By 1.30 I adjourned the meeting.

At that hour Trott whom we are putting up with was having a lunch party
for Cadogan and Clark Kerr. It turned out to be a Persian lunch, not very
attractive. At 2.45 we held a short COS to compare notes and frame future

action. At 3.30 pm we went over to the Russian Embassy to see Winston present the Stalingrad Sword to Stalin. Bands, Guards of Honour, national anthems etc. Speech by Winston after which he handed sword over in name of King to Stalin. Stalin kissed sword and handed it over to Voroshilov, who promptly dropped sword out of its scabbard! However finally it was handed over to commander of Russian Guard of Honour and marched off securely. Then photographs of usual groups.*

We then sat down at 4 pm to another long 3 hour conference! Bad from beginning to end. Winston was not good and Roosevelt even worse. Stalin meticulous with only two arguments. Cross Channel operation on May 1st, and also offensive in Southern France! Americans supported this view quite unaware of the fact that it is already an impossibility. Finally decided that Americans and ourselves should have another meeting tomorrow with a view to arriving at some form of solution for our final plenary meeting at 4 pm.

I have little hope of any form of agreement in discussions. After listening to the arguments put forward during the last 2 days I feel more like entering a lunatic asylum or a nursing home than continuing with my present job. I am *absolutely* disgusted with the politicians' methods of waging a war!! Why will they imagine that they are experts at a job they know nothing about! It is lamentable to listen to them! May God help us in the future prosecution of this war, we have every hope of making an unholy mess of it and of being defeated yet!

As I stated before, the Americans had forced us to put the cart before the horse in the early stages by meeting Chiang Kai-shek before having our meetings with them. Now the same was occurring with the Russians. We had reached the stage where we had put the horse in the cart and were pulling it around without knowing where we were heading for.

*I notice that in this day's diary I level an accusation against Averell Harriman that may well be entirely unfounded. But I had a distinct feeling throughout the meeting that Harriman had been endeavouring to improve the American situation with Stalin at our expense. That he had been pointing out how anxious the Americans had been to establish a Second Front from the start and that they had been prevented from doing so by the British. I would not have been surprised if he had also mentioned me personally by name as being one of the strongest opponents to the Western Front policy.***

---

*Inscribed on the blade of the sword, in English and in Russian, were the words: 'To the steel-hearted citizens of Stalingrad, the gift of King George VI, in token of the homage of the British people.' The Sword of Stalingrad is one of the motifs or inspirations of perhaps the greatest novel of this war, the *Sword of Honour* trilogy (1964) by Evelyn Waugh. See Alex Danchev, 'The Real Waugh', *Diplomatic History* 25 (2001), forthcoming; and David Wykes, 'Evelyn Waugh's Sword of Volgograd', *Dutch Review of Anglo-American Letters* 7 (1977), pp. 82–99. The sword itself is on permanent display in the Museum of the Defence of Stalingrad.

**AB does not figure prominently in Harriman's own memoir. As a kind of countervailing implication, there is some suggestion of AB's reluctance to cede control to the Americans, but no obvious antipathy. W. Averell Harriman and Elie Abel, *Special Envoy to Churchill and Stalin* (London: Hutchinson, 1976), e.g. p. 166.

30 November

The PM's 69th Birthday. Got up with the feeling that we had an unpleasant day in front of us, but it did not turn out to be so bad after all! We began with an ordinary COS meeting at 8.45 am. This was followed by a CCS with Americans at 9.30. Here we had a difficult time trying to arrive at some agreement which we could put before our Russian friends in the afternoon. After much argument we decided that the cross Channel operation could be put off to June 1st. This did not meet all our requirements, but was arranged to fit in with proposed Russian spring offensive. We also decided to stage what we could in the way of operations in Southern France. I pressed hard again to obtain the abandonment of the Andaman Island attack so as to render more landing craft available for the Mediterranean. Still same political difficulties with President.

At 12.30 we adjourned to see PM and inform him of results. Then lunch with Bullard [British Ambassador] in Legation building. After that out for ¾ hours shopping in the curio shop near gate of Legation. Then another talk with Winston before attending another Plenary meeting to report results of our morning meeting. This was quite a short meeting at which I gave out the results of our decisions and President, PM and Stalin made pretty speeches. Finished up meeting by drafting military part of the communiqué.

This finishes up the first of our tripartite meetings with the Russians. One thing is quite clear, the more politicians you put together to settle the prosecution of the war the longer you postpone its conclusion!

We finished the day with a banquet in the Legation building to celebrate Winston's 69th birthday!

The guests consisted of President, Stalin, Molotov, Anthony Eden, Harry Hopkins, Harriman, Clark Kerr, Bullard, Holman, Voroshilov, American Chiefs of Staff, British Chiefs of Staff, Winant, Somervell, Randolph and Sarah Churchill, Roosevelt's son and son in law. On our side Winston sat with President on his right and on the other Anthony with Molotov on his right and Harry Hopkins on his left. On the centre of the table was a large cake with 69 candles burning!!

We had not been seated long when the PM said that we should dine in the Russian manner, and that anybody that liked could propose a toast at any time during the meal. He therefore started pretty soon by proposing health of King, President USA and President Soviet Republic. Then speeches came fast and furious without a stop. We had not been going long when the President made a nice speech alluding to our fathers having known each other when he and I were boys and proposing my health. Stalin then chipped in and said that as a result of this meeting and of having come to such unanimous agreement he hoped that I would no longer look upon Russians with such suspicion and that if I really got to know them I should find that they were quite good chaps!! This was a most unexpected and uncalled for attack and I am certain that Averell Harriman, the new USA Ambassador, must have been making mischief as he is very busy at the moment trying to improve his USA position at our expense.

I could not let this accusation pass, so waited for a propitious moment to get up. It was rather nervous work, considering what the audience was! I thanked the President for his very kind words which I assured him I had deeply appreciated. I then turned to Stalin and reminded him that in the afternoon's conference the PM had said that 'in war the truth must be accompanied by an escort of lies to ensure its security'. I reminded him that he himself had described how in all big offensives he produced masses of dummy tanks and aeroplanes on the fronts he was not going to attack, whilst he moved up forces quietly and under cover of darkness on the front of attack. After four years of war and the continual cultivation of false appearances for the enemy was it not possible that one's outward appearance might even deceive one's friends? I felt convinced that he must have been looking at the dummy aeroplanes and guns and had failed to observe the real and true offensive in the shape of real friendship and comradeship which I felt towards him and all the Soviet forces! This went very well and met with some success. After dinner I returned to the attack and we finished the best of friends with long hand shakes and almost with our arms round each other's necks! He said that he liked the bold and soldierlike way in which I had spoken and the military strength of my voice! These were true military qualities that he liked and admired, and that we were now on the best of terms; furthermore that it must be remembered that some of the best friendships of this world were founded on original misunderstandings!

It was a wonderful evening full of the most witty speeches on the part of Winston, President and Stalin. On one occasion, when Winston was referring to political tendencies in England he said the whole political world was now a matter of tints and that England could be said to have now quite a pink look. Without a moment's hesitation Stalin snapped back 'a sign of good health'! The President finished up by returning to the tint theme and said that the effect of this war would be to blend all those multitudinous tints, shades and colours into one rainbow where their individuality would be lost in the whole, and that this whole represented the emblem of hope! It was a fine idea and far better put than I have. Finally by 1.30 am I was able to escape to bed.

November 30th had been an important day from many points of view. The constant drip of water can eventually erode stone. In the same way the constant repetition of an argument eventually made some impression on the American Chiefs of Staff! We had at least moved the date of OVERLORD from May 1st to June 1st. The operations in the South of France had now taken on the shape of to 'stage what we could in the way of operations in the South of France'. The present operations in Italy were therefore now on a firmer footing. It must be remembered that to remove a division from the Italian front, to embark it, to transfer it by sea in convoy through the Mediterranean and Bay of Biscay, to unload it in England, locate it in new formations and new training areas, and finally to train it for the most difficult of operations – a combined landing against strong opposition – required a period which could only be measured in terms of months. It will therefore be seen that every division withdrawn from Italy to England for operation OVERLORD was a division washed off the slate for a period of months.

I found these conferences very trying, and I became more and more peevish as they went on, which accounts a great deal for the over critical attitude assumed at times in my diaries. In my mind the course to be adopted seemed so clear and obvious that I found it maddening not to be able to make them see as clearly as I saw. Not being gifted with an over patient nature it reacted on me by making me take an over gloomy view of the progress we were making. ...

I found it a very trying nervous test getting up to reply to Stalin's toast in front of that audience! I had a very trying quarter of an hour preparing my reply during which I would have given almost anything to remain seated. I had, however, by then seen enough of Stalin during our Moscow visits to know that if I remained seated and sat under his insults I was finished in his eyes for good and all and written off as spineless. Luckily by the time I made my speech he had consumed a fair share of champagne which he was not so well used to as vodka! ...

The whole episode still lives clearly in my mind and I might at this moment still be sitting in the Legation dining room. A dining room which I believe had originally been built by the Royal Engineers in Persian style. One might almost have been inside a Persian temple. The whole of the walls were covered in a mosaic of small pieces of looking glass set at every conceivable angle. The windows were covered with heavy deep red curtains, and the walls had on them the pictures of the Royal Family which one expects in an Embassy or Legation. The Persian waiters were in blue and red liveries with white cotton gloves, the tips of the fingers of which hung limply and flapped about as they handed plates around.

When we came to the sweet course, the Chief of the Legation Cuisine produced his trump card. It consisted of a base of ice 1 foot square and some 4 inches deep. In the centre a round hole of some 3 inches diameter had been bored, and in this hole a religious nightlight had been inserted. Over the lamp and hole a perforated iron tube stood erect some 10 inches over the ice. On the top of this tube a large plate had been secured with icing sugar. On the plate rested a vast cream ice, whilst a small frieze of icing sugar decorated the edge of the plate! When lit up and carried in by white gloved hands with long white fingertips the total effect was beyond description. Two such edifices entered and proceeded solemnly round the table whilst each guest dug into the ice. I watched the tower approaching us carefully and noticed that the heat of the lamp had affected the block of ice that it rested in. The perforated iron tower had been affected by the melting away of its base. It was no longer perpendicular and now looked more like the Tower of Pisa! The plate on top, conforming to the general subsidence of its support, had now assumed a rakish tilt! An accident was now inevitable, and safety measures must be taken at once. The ice was by now practically over Martin's head, but sloping rapidly towards mine. I seized Somervell, my right hand neighbour, and shouted to him to duck. We both buried our faces in our empty plates, and only just in time. With the noise of an avalanche the whole wonderful construction slid over our heads and exploded in a clatter of plates between me and Berejkov. The unfortunate Berejkov was at that moment standing up translating a speech for Stalin and he came in for the full blast! He was splashed from his head to his feet, but I suppose it was more than his life was worth to stop interpreting! In any case he carried on manfully whilst I sent for towels and with the help of the Persian waiters proceeded to mop him down. To this day I can still see large lumps of white ice cream sitting on his shoes, and melting over the edges and through the lace holes!

1 December   Jerusalem

We had an early rise, said goodbye to Mr Trott, who had been putting us up in his house. He is the Oriental Secretary and very interested in birds so I made the most of him and got him to show me all the bird skins he had been collecting. We left the Legation at 7.30 am and by 8 am were roaring down the runway taking off for Jerusalem. We had a very good journey and landed on an aerodrome some 35 miles from Jerusalem [Lydda]. There we were joined by Marshall, King, Somervell and Arnold. We then drove to the King David Hotel, where we are being done quite exceptionally well. This was intended as returning the Williamsburg hospitality [15–16 May 1943].

After lunch we did a tour of Jerusalem with a monk guide and were shown all the usual sights. I was very interested in it all, but cannot help feeling that it is all so far detached from real events that I would sooner retain my own conceptions of all those episodes. However, from the historical point of view of all the various events that have occurred since the Crucifixion and their vast influence on the whole destiny of Europe it is quite enthralling. We returned to tea, and afterwards went to call on the Governor, or whatever he calls himself [High Commissioner]. We finished up the day with a banquet for the American Chiefs, a band and a dance in the hall. On the whole the show so far has been a success. We presented all Chiefs of Staff with a small olive wood cigarette box with silver plate on it with their names inscribed.

2 December   Cairo

We left hotel at 8.30 and returned to Jerusalem city to visit the Dome of the Rock or Dome of Omar. I was fascinated by it and thought it quite one of the most attractive sights we had seen. Then we went on to the Garden of Gethsemane which finished our tour. We returned to the hotel, said goodbye to the St Franciscan monk who had acted as our guide, and then motored back to Lydda aerodrome. Then we took off for Cairo where we arrived in time for a late lunch. On arriving on the aerodrome we were informed that the PM and President were expected in a few minutes having changed their plans. They are now all safely back here, including PM and President. Afternoon getting hair cut and going through papers. In the evening we had Jumbo Wilson, Sholto Douglas and Wedemeyer to dine.

3 December   Cairo

Started with a COS to try and sort matters out. Then at 12.30 went round for a meeting with PM. Found him in a poor temper having just completed inspection of 4th Hussars. Also discovered that he had been queering our pitch by suggesting to Leahy that if we did not attack Rhodes we might at any rate starve the place out. We then lunched with the PM and at 2.30 went back for our meeting with the Combined Chiefs of Staff. We were dumbfounded by being informed that the meeting must finish on Sunday at the latest (in 48 hours) as the President was off! No apologies, nothing. They have completely upset the whole meeting by wasting our time with Chiang Kai-shek and Stalin before we had settled any points with them. And now with nothing settled they propose to disappear into the blue and leave all the main points connected with the Mediterranean unsettled! It all looks like some of the worst sharp practice that I have seen for some time. The rest of the meeting was quite hopeless and we settled little else. Attended Jumbo Wilson's cocktail party for Scobie prior to his departure for III Corps.

I am afraid I was unnecessarily bitter with the American Chiefs of Staff then, and evidently at the end of my tether! I withdraw every word connected with 'sharp practice' and am quite certain that the one thing that Marshall would never have tolerated was anything connected with 'sharp practice'. I have seldom met a straighter or more reliable man in my life and thank heaven for these qualities of his. It was only in his lack of strategic vision that my patience with him used to become frayed.

4 December

A difficult day! First a COS meeting to try and decide how best to tackle our American friends, this lasted from 9.45 to 10.15 when we went to the PM. He was not in a good temper, and upset by Dickie Mountbatten's latest telegram asking for more forces for capture of Andaman Isles! Poor Monty Stopford [XXXIII Corps, Burma] came in for a bad passage.

Then at 11 am round for interview with President and Americans. PM gave long discourse and then called on me to express my views. I said that this conference had been most unsatisfactory. Usually at these meetings we discussed matters till we arrived at a policy which we put before the PM and President for approval and amendment, and that we subsequently examined whether ways and means admitted of this policy being carried out. Finally putting up a paper for approval which formed our policy for future conduct of the war. This time such a procedure had been impossible. We had straight away been thrown into high level conference with the Chinese. These had hardly been finished when we were rushed off to Teheran for similar conferences with Stalin, and now that we were back we were only given two days to arrive at any concerted policy. We then proceeded with the desirability to give up the Andaman Islands in order to concentrate on the European front. Here at once we came up against political difficulties. The President had made promises to Generalissimo [Chiang Kai-shek] of an amphibious operation and did not like to go back on him. We made no progress!! Dashed back to house where I had Sosnkowski and Anders lunching with me. Then back for 2.30 pm conference with Americans where we did not get much further.

Finally asked to dine alone with Winston to discuss questions of command. President had today decided that Eisenhower was to command Overlord whilst Marshall remained as Chief of Staff [of US Army as a whole]. I argued with PM that Alexander was not of sufficiently high calibre to take on the new centralized Mediterranean Command. I suggested Jumbo Wilson as Supreme Commander for Mediterranean, Alexander as Commander in Chief Italian Land Forces, Paget for Middle East, Montgomery *vice* Paget, and Oliver Leese *vice* Montgomery. He was inclined to agree. He said that he had at one time thought of me for Supreme Commander of Mediterranean, and Wilson as Chief of [Imperial General] Staff, but that it would be better if I remained where I was. I agreed that it would be best. Jumbo Wilson would have a great deal to pick up to become CIGS, whereas he knew ½ Mediterranean intimately. I hope he does not change his mind again!

I found him very tired that evening, and it was with difficulty that I could get him to absorb all the intricate points connected with it. I had devoted a great deal of thought to this problem, had found it hard to solve, but was now perfectly clear in my own mind. First of all the selection of Eisenhower rather than Marshall was a good one. Eisenhower had now a certain amount of experience as a Commander and was beginning to find his feet. The combination of Eisenhower and Bedell Smith [as his Chief of Staff] had much to be said for it. On the other hand Marshall had never commanded anything in war except, I believe, a company in the First World War.

The removal of Ike from the Mediterranean left a difficult gap to fill. I did not want to touch either Alex or Monty for this job as I required them for the Italian campaign and for the British contingent of Overlord. Had I had my own way I would select Monty for Overlord and Alex for Italy, but I knew that I might well have difficulties with this preference of mine, first with Winston and secondly with Eisenhower. I therefore introduced Jumbo Wilson for the Supreme Command Mediterranean, and to take over from Ike. For the rest I banked on Alex for Italy, Monty for Overlord and to relieve Paget, who could then take over Middle East, whilst Oliver Leese relieved Monty in the 8ᵗʰ Army.

5 December

A very difficult day filled with a series of meetings from COS to Plenary Meetings, but negotiations remained at a deadlock as we were holding out for cancelling the Andaman Island attack, whilst the President having made promises to Chiang Kai-shek would not cancel. It all proved too clearly that we had been quite right in insisting that Chiang Kai-shek should only come at the end instead of the start of the meeting.

We lunched at the Embassy, large lunch with Mohammed Ali, Egyptian Prime Minister, Winston, Eden, American Chiefs etc. In afternoon another CCS meeting at which we called in Stopford and Troubridge [Force Commanders for Andaman operation] to discuss the Andaman Islands and whether any alternative small operation could not be found to 'save face' with Chiang. Finally dined with American Chiefs of Staff.

6 December

To our joy this morning we discovered that the President had at last agreed to cancel Andaman Islands attack! He had sent a wire to that effect to Generalissimo, this may lead to his [Chiang's] refusing to carry out his part of the Burma campaign. If he does so it is no very great loss! At any rate we can now concentrate all our resources in the European theatre. Again a series of meetings ending up with a Plenary meeting at 6 pm at which we handed in our final report to the President and the Prime Minister who expressed their full satisfaction. Old Smuts had turned up for the final meeting. Bertie came to dine with me. I shall rest very well tonight and feel very satisfied at the final results of this meeting.

7 December

We started the day with another COS meeting followed by a Combined Chiefs of Staff meeting to settle a few additional points. The President had left early in the morning, and later on Inönü (President of Turkey) also left. After lunch we went round to the PM's villa to listen to MacArthur's Chief of Staff, Sutherland, explain the future plans and views of General MacArthur.

I then went shopping with Barney. At 7.30 pm we met at our house for a brief Chiefs of Staff meeting to consider a minute written by the PM concerning operation in Turkey in anticipation of their entry into the war. Finally dined with the PM, Smuts, Dill, Portal, Cunningham, Marshall, King, Arnold, Leathers and Hollis. Eden came in just as dinner was finishing. King consumed more than a bottle of champagne to his own head and was showing signs of wear. Sat next to Arnold and Anthony Eden when he came in. PM in tremendous form and Smuts as charming as ever. During the dinner the PM asked us all to express our views as to when Germany would be defeated. Marshall predicted March and if not then November [1944]. Dill gave even money on March. I gave 6 to 4 on March, remainder favoured March or November.*

8 December

Portal and Cunningham left early in the morning and Dill went off immediately after breakfast. I had long talk with Jumbo Wilson in his HQ explaining to him possibilities of the future. Then he and I went off with Smuts to inspect march past of South African Division, a very impressive show. After lunching out there we motored home and I went to the Mena offices for an hour's work. Then visited Pug Ismay who is unwell. Back to my house for an interview with Sosnkowski. From there on to the Embassy to dine. PM, Smuts, Eden, Cadogan,

---

*'At the end of the first week of that December, History records, Mr Winston Churchill introduced Mr Roosevelt to the Sphinx. Fortified by the assurances of their military advisers that the Germans would surrender that winter, the two puissant old gentlemen circumambulated the colossus and silently watched the shadows of the evening obliterate its famous features.' Evelyn Waugh, the *Sword of Honour* trilogy (London: Everyman, 1994), p. 600.

Casey and his wife, young Jellicoe, Maclean [Brigadier Commanding British Military Mission] back from Yugoslavia, Randolph, Sarah, Jumbo Wilson.

Kept up late and finally had to drive back here with the PM. All my good work of the dinner [with him] is gone! He is now back again wanting Alexander as Supreme Commander for the Mediterranean, and has pushed old Jumbo Wilson aside! I shall have heavy work ahead. All the trouble has been caused by Macmillan who has had a long talk with the PM suggesting that Alex is the man for the job and that he, Macmillan, can take the political load off him. He [Macmillan] came round to see me for an hour this evening and evidently does not even begin to understand what the functions of a Supreme Commander should be. Why must the PM consult everybody except those who can give him real advice!!

This interference on the part of Macmilllan made me very angry. I had been informed by the PM that Macmillan had an excellent solution to the problem of supreme command in the Mediterranean, and asking me to discuss it with Macmillan. I at once smelled a rat there, and wondered what he was poking his nose into. I sent for him, and as I state in my diary, very soon discovered that he had only the haziest of ideas as to what the duties of a Supreme Commander were. Consequently his plan was quite unworkable. I also asked him, when he had these bright ideas on military organization, to discuss these matters with me first before seeing the PM. What I did realize very quickly whilst discussing this problem of command with Macmillan was that he knew he could handle Alex, and that he would be as a piece of putty in his hand; but on the other hand Jumbo Wilson was made of much rougher material which would not be so pliable and easy to handle. If Macmillan were at any time to have to act as Minister for the Mediterranean it is evident that Alex would be far easier to control and influence.

9 December

Started this day by picking up Bertie to take him with me to see old Smuts off, as the latter had said that he wanted to see Bertie. There was quite a gathering on the aerodrome including Ambassador and Jacqueline [Lampson], Jumbo Wilson, King of Greece's brother seeing his wife off etc. Smuts was as charming as ever. Last night at the Embassy dinner he pulled me aside to tell me he was not at all happy about the condition of the PM. He considered he worked far too hard, exhausted himself, and then had to rely on drink to stimulate him again. He said he was beginning to doubt whether he would stay the course, that he was noticing changes in him. He then said that he fully realized my task was getting more and more difficult with the PM, but that I must stick to it

---

*In its own feline way, Macmillan's account of this interview corresponds closely to AB's. 'Of course, I have to tread very carefully in all this, for if the Wilson appointment is made – as I believe it will be – I do not want to start on the wrong foot with him. And I am sure I *can* work with him – only, Alex is a younger man and I know him now so well, that I should prefer General Alexander. But Wilson is a good man too, and I naturally do not want him to think that I am working against this choice. But since Winston asked me, I felt I must give him my views. ...' *War Diaries* (Macmillan, 1984), p. 322.

and do my best to keep him on the right track. He said that he had been saying things to the PM to try and assist me in my task. He fully realized that I had been correct in sticking to my job when he and the PM had tried to get me to replace Auchinleck, he also fully appreciated what a heavy responsibility it entailed and what a heavy task it was. I was very sorry to see him disappear in his silver aeroplane over the horizon. Then drove Bertie back and went on to discuss Yugoslavia and Greece with Jumbo.

From there I was ordered for a *tête-à-tête* with PM. We lunched in the garden, he was looking very tired and said he felt very flat, tired and had pains across his loins. However he swatted flies with his flap throughout lunch and counted their corpses. We discussed command in the Mediterranean. He kept on harping back and repeating details which were of no consequence and I saw that it was useless in his tired state to discuss the larger issues. Halfway through lunch he asked me whether I did not think I had better be made a Field Marshal in view of all the responsibility I was carrying! I told him there was nothing I would appreciate more when he considered I had deserved it. He then said that Portal was to be made an Air Chief Marshal and he considered I should be a Field Marshal. He said he would speak to the King about it.

After lunch I went off sight seeing, and secured the assistance of one of the scientific research department of the Gov of Egypt called Emery. He was quite excellent and most interesting. We went to the old capital of Egypt, inspected one sample tomb, and were shown all the recent excavations round the old step pyramid. In evening dined with Bertie at the Mohammed Ali Club.

My talk with Smuts on the previous day had again opened my eyes as to that man's wonderful grasp of things. He was realizing far better than anyone, even Moran, the PM's doctor, how near Winston was getting to a breakdown! He was at that moment on the verge of his go of pneumonia which he was to develop in Tunisia, and had within the last few days been sitting in on a series of high level conferences with Roosevelt, Stalin, Chiang Kai-shek and Inönü, and he was worn out. The degree of his fatigue was easily measured by his complete inability to discuss anything that day at lunch. I shall always remember that lunch as a bad nightmare. He was dressed in his grey zip suit, with zip shoes and his vast Mexican hat on. We sat amongst the flower beds at a small card table and were served with an excellent lunch by two Egyptian liveried waiters. He held a fly whisk in his hand. After two spoonfuls of soup he started discussing the question of the command of the Mediterranean, and said, 'It is all quite simple, there are ...', then down came the fly whisk with a crash, and a fly corpse was collected and placed in a fly mortuary near the corner of the table. He then had two more spoonfuls of soup and said: 'This is the most deelicious soup' followed by another spoonful. He then started again, 'As I was saying, it is all quite simple, there are just three areas ...' Crash, down came the fly whisk and another fly was conveyed to the mortuary! This procedure went on through most of the lunch, but we never got beyond the 'three areas' before having to convey another fly to the mortuary!

The interesting part was that there were not 'three areas' in this problem of command, and yet I knew well that in his present worn out condition it was quite impossible to make him grasp this fact! I let him go on killing flies and talking about the 'deelicious' food, knowing well that there was no possibility of doing any work. I felt desperately anxious about him at that lunch. I had just been listening on the previous evening to Smuts's fears about him, and I began to wonder how near he was to a crash and how serious that crash would be. I am quite certain that he never remembered much about this lunch, and that my recommendation for a baton had probably been started by Smuts in his talk with him on previous days.

10 December   650 miles

Got up at 5.15 am and by 6.15 was off for Luxor. I had borrowed Sholto Douglas's plane, and fixed up for Emery to come with me. We picked him up on the way to Heliopolis aerodrome and at 7 am we took off. We had an excellent journey and arrived at the small aerodrome near Luxor at 9 am. Here we were met by a shaky old car which took us to the office where we secured the necessary tickets and then went to the river bank to cross over to the west bank. Here an old Ford in the last stages of decay met us and we started a precarious journey to the Valley of the Kings.

The car repeatedly stopped in spite of one attendant spending his whole time inside the bonnet whilst the car was running! Emery was quite invaluable as he knew just what to take us to in the very limited time. We began with Tutankhamen's tomb which thrilled me. We then did two more of the Kings' tombs, after which Emery took us to see a tomb which he had discovered himself. It was the tomb of the Prime Minister of one of the Kings, and of special interest as being a good example showing how the finished work existed alongside of started work, and the whole procedure.

We then went to visit the large temple and palace on the west bank, finally motoring back past the two colossus figures. Here the inevitable happened and one of the front tyres burst! No spare wheel, a jack that did not work, but nothing stopped our mechanics! The car was lifted by hand, the tyre removed, and we rumbled on on the rim! We re-crossed the Nile and went to the Desert Palace Hotel for lunch. After lunch we visited the Luxor temple and the old large temple further north on the way back to the aerodrome. We took off at 4.30 pm and flew back in the moonlight. A full moon shining on the desert and reflected in the Nile. A glorious sight.

Jumbo Wilson and Sholto Douglas came to dine after which we discussed the prospects and timing of the Rhodes attack. At 11 pm we drove round to the Embassy where PM was dining. At midnight after saying goodbye to Ambassador, Jacqueline, Caseys, Jumbo, Sholto etc we started off. I drove with PM to aerodrome and he went on discussing the organization of command all the way. Finally, at 1 am we took off in the York. Party consisting of PM, Lord Moran, Sarah, Randolph, Martin, Tommy and self.

11 December   Tunis, 1550 miles

At 9.30 am we arrived over Tunis after a very good journey, but not much sleep as plane was over heated inside. Owing to a mistake we landed at wrong aerodrome first and had to take off again. Finally we arrived at the right place, and there we found Eisenhower and Tedder waiting for us. PM very tired and flat, he seems to be in a bad way. The conference has tired him out and he will not rest properly and insists on working. I cannot think that it is wise for him to go to Italy in this condition. After breakfast he went and rested till lunch.

Meanwhile I had a very useful conference with Eisenhower and Tedder on various points connected with operations in the Mediterranean, but mainly on the question of the selection of his successor and of the organization of the Command. I warned him of the attitude the PM was taking and asked him to assist me in making it quite clear to the PM what the organization should be. I told him that I had been at the PM for some time now trying to get him to understand, but that he always returned to his own faulty conceptions. Ike's suggested solution was to put Wilson in Supreme Command, replace Alex by Monty, and take Alex home to command the land forces for Overlord. This almost fits in with my idea except I would invert Alex and Monty, but I don't mind much. Ike and Tedder remained to lunch and did excellent work with the PM but I fear he may swing back.

Then went out to look at the ruins of Carthage. We are in the same house that we lunched in with Anderson last time we were here. It was recently refurbished for the President and then kept on for the PM. PM rather more rested at lunch. I tried to induce him not to go to Italy, but so far have failed. He has spent most of the afternoon resting.

It was very useful being able to have this talk with Ike in which I discovered, as I had expected, that he would sooner have Alex with him for Overlord than Monty. He also knew that he could handle Alex, but was not fond of Monty and certainly did not know how to handle him. I am surprised that in my diary I wrote that between the selection of Alex or Monty for Overlord 'I don't mind much'! I certainly minded a great deal and would have had little confidence in Alex running that show.

I was getting very worried about Winston's health. He seemed to be going from bad to worse. It was most unfortunate that we had come down on the wrong aerodrome as they took him out of the plane and he sat on his suitcase in a very cold morning wind, looking like nothing on earth. We were then there about an hour before we moved on and he was chilled through by then.

I felt that a trip to Italy in December with snow and seas of mud, living in cold caravans, would finish him off. I discussed the matter with Moran who entirely agreed. I therefore tackled Winston in the evening and told him that he was wrong in wanting to go to Italy. I granted that the troops would be delighted to see him and that he would enjoy the trip, but said that I did not think that he had any right to risk his health in this way when he had far more important matters in front of him connected with the war. I was beginning to make a little progress, and then I foolishly said, 'And what is more, Moran entirely agrees with me.' He rose up on his elbow in his bed, shook his fist in my face and said: 'Don't you get in league with that bloody old man!!!'

After that there was no alternative but to leave the matter alone for a bit.... Thank heaven, God took a hand in the matter and the next day he was running a temperature!

12 December

I was dog tired last night and sleeping like a log at 4 am when I was woken by a raucous voice re-echoing through the room with a series of mournful, 'Hullo, Hullo, Hullo!' When I had woken sufficiently I said, 'Who the hell is that?' and switched on my torch. To my dismay I found the PM in his dragon dressing gown with a brown bandage wrapped round his head, wandering about my room! He said he was looking for Lord Moran, that he had a bad headache. I led him to Moran's room and retired back to bed. But for the next hour the whole house resounded with the noise of people waking up and running around. This morning, on getting up, I discovered that the PM has got a temperature of about 102 and is not in too good a way at all. Moran is uncertain as to what the trouble is, but is anxious to get him home as quickly as possible. The visit to Italy must be definitely off as far as he is concerned, and I am rather doubtful whether I shall be able to make it, or shall have to accompany him back.

Later:

Alexander turned up during the morning and we had a long talk after which he went for a talk with the PM. As might be expected Alex is ready to do just what he is told and does not show any great signs of disappointment at not being appointed Supreme Commander. PM's temperature went down considerably during the day but Moran did not think he was so well again in the evening. Eisenhower came round in the afternoon and we had a long talk with him and Alex. Tedder came to dine. Settled that Alex should go back to Italy tomorrow and that I should accompany him.

After this bad night of Winston's, and in view of the temperature he was running, I asked Moran what he diagnosed the trouble was. He said that as far as he could judge at present it might be another go of pneumonia, or it might just be a case of flu. I asked him what he would require if it was a case of pneumonia and he replied that in that case he would have to have a pathologist, 2 nurses and a portable X-ray set. I asked him where these would have to come from, and he said the two former from Cairo and the latter probably from Algiers. I told him these would take some time to get and that we should wire at once for them. To my surprise he begged me not to wire as this might be a false diagnosis. I told him that I could not see that it could matter if it was a false diagnosis. In that case, thank heaven, they would not be required and could be flown back. On the other hand if it was pneumonia we should never forgive ourselves for having wasted 24 hours. It is fortunate those wires were sent to Cairo. I think that by then Clemmie had also been wired for.

In my talk with Alexander about command, I found him, as always, quite charm-ing to deal with, always ready to do what was requested of him, never scheming or pulling strings. A soldier of the very highest principles.

13 December   Bari, 600 miles

PM not too well during early part of night and Moran was up with him for a long time. We wired for pathologist and 2 nurses yesterday who are due at 2.30 pm. I am by way of starting at 11.30 with Alex for Italy but am still rather doubtful about leaving the PM in his present state. However, I do not feel that there is much that I can do here by my presence. Have just sent a wire to Algiers for a portable X ray set, as Moran wants to take a photograph of his lungs to make certain they are not affected.

Later:

I went to see PM. Found him looking much more cheerful and he was all for my going off. I therefore put Tedder in touch with Moran so that he should have someone to appeal to for help if necessary. At 11.30 left with Alex for the aerodrome where we took off in his plane at 12 noon for Bari. We had a lovely fly, first over the Bône peninsula, then close to Pantelleria, and struck Sicily on the southern coast about the centre. I had an excellent view of the landing places of American, Canadian and British forces. We then crossed over the south eastern corner of the island to the Catania plain which we did a good circle around to look at it properly. Mount Etna looked glorious with its lovely white snow covered top looking through a blanket of low clouds which ringed the mountain half way up. We then worked along the east coast of the island towards Messina. I had no idea that coast was as lovely as it is. The sun was shining on it and bits of it were lovely. We then crossed over to the Italian coast and skirted along the sole and ball of the foot, crossing the bay under the instep and striking Taranto harbour. From there we crossed the heel and landed at Bari after a four hours most interesting flight.

It gave me a great thrill setting foot on European soil again; a full four years after I had stepped off at St Nazaire. Little did I know at St Nazaire that after four years I should step back at Bari!

Went with Alex to his office and listened to the latest news. Then came back to my room to sort out my kit for tomorrow's move on to Montgomery's HQ. While I was doing so the Germans arrived over Bari port for a raid, and I spent half an hour in watching the most beautiful fireworks as all the AA let loose on them. I was quite safe being some 5 miles out of Bari, so was able to watch and enjoy at my leisure! This is the second heavy raid on this place. In the last one they destroyed some 17 ships by fire owing to an ammunition ship blowing up.

The question of the Supreme Commander for the Mediterranean is I think settling as I wanted after many ups and downs and many tribulations. The PM has I think now pretty well settled on Wilson for Supreme Commander, Alex to command forces in Italy, and Monty to come home to command the land forces in Overlord. I pray and hope he does not again change his mind!

14 December   Monty's battle HQ on Sangro River, 150 and 50 miles

I started the day by attending Alex's intelligence conference at his HQ. We then had an early lunch shortly after 12 noon and by 1.30 pm left Bari aerodrome in Alex's plane to fly to Termoli, about 130 miles up the east coast. On the way we flew over the battleground of Cannae and flew rings round it low so as to have a good look at it. On the aerodrome we were met by the 8th Army AOC, who took us up in a Stork, a German one which had been flown over from Yugoslavia. A most wonderful machine in which we flipped amongst tree tops and chimney stacks obtaining a wonderful view of all the country as we went. We have been making extensive use of the American Stimson machine for this hedgehopping job, but the Stork has the best visibility and a wonderfully restricted take off and landing. These machines are known as 'puddlehoppers' or 'whizzers'. We had an excellent view of all the battleground on the way up and finished with a reconnaissance of the Sangro river and all its difficult crossings. We landed on a small strip near the mouth of the river and were met there by Montgomery. He took us in his open car along the Sangro river explaining all his plans and difficulties connected with the crossings of the river. We then returned to his camp in a field on the high ground just south of the river and I was shown my caravan for the night. We had tea followed by a long talk with Monty. For dinner both Dempsey and Charles Allfrey came.

Off to bed early. Weather not as cold as I had expected. Monty strikes me as looking tired, and definitely wants a rest or a change. I can see that he does not feel that Clark is running the 5th [US] Army right, nor that Alex is gripping the show sufficiently. He called me into his caravan just before dinner and asked me how much importance we attached to an early capture of Rome, as he saw little hope of capturing it before March!! To my mind it is quite clear that Alex is not gripping this show. There is no real plan for the capture of Rome beyond a thrust up the coast by Monty and no longer any talk of a turn to the left by his forces towards Rome. The mountain roads are considered too difficult for any real chance of success based on such a swinging movement. I must now see during next few days what hopes rest in the plans of 5th Army. Frankly I am rather depressed from what I have seen and heard today. Monty is tired out, and Alex fails to grip the show!!

15 December   Alex's forward camp near Vasto, 50 miles

Left Monty's camp at 9 am and dropped down into the valley of the Sangro which we followed till we crossed it and its tributary and arrived at Freyberg's Div HQ. He was on the road to meet us, and had formed up for our inspection a batch of some 30 prisoners caught that night. They were a very poor lot of humanity of all ages, sizes and shapes. I had a long talk with him and we then drove on to the 8th Indian Div HQ to see Russell the commander. On the way we passed the badly bombed and shelled villages which the Germans had held whilst defending the north bank of the Sangro. After speaking to Russell for some time we went on to the Canadian Div HQ, and talked to [illegible]. Then back to the mouth of the Sangro where we had lunch, after which we were picked up in a Whizzer by Broadhurst the 8ᵗʰ Army AOC and flew back here, where Alex has an advanced HQ alongside of 8ᵗʰ Army Main HQ. We had tea with 8ᵗʰ Army officers and then came back here for dinner.

My impression of the day is that we are stuck in our offensive here and shall make no real progress till the ground dries, unless we make greater use of our amphibious power. I have an impression that Monty is tired and that Alex has not fully recovered from his jaundice. The offensive is stagnating badly and something must be done about it as soon as I get back.

16 December   Alex's camp at 5th Army HQ, Caserta, 150 miles

Left camp at 8 am and motored to a brand new landing strip just south of Vasto near the beach. There we took off at 9 am, with an escort of fighters, to fly to Naples. It was a lovely morning and turned out to be a lovely flight. We headed for Foggia first and then turned west over the hills. The scenery was quite lovely. After ¾ hour we began to drop again and Mt Vesuvius came into sight with quite a large feather of smoke coming out of its summit. We landed at 10 am on the Naples landing ground and proceeded to the American HQ commanding the town. Robertson (son of the old Field Marshal) was with us also. We then did a detailed tour of the port to see the marvels that had been accomplished in the way of clearing up all the debris from the German destruction. Ships had been raised from the bottom, others left on their side were being used as new quays, whilst the sunken ones had superstructures built on them to allow of their use as landing stages. A real fine performance. We then lunched with Robertson in a marvellous villa just north of Naples.

After lunch we went off to visit Pompeii and had a most interesting afternoon, spending about 2 hours amongst the ruins. I wish we had had longer. We then motored out to the American 5ᵗʰ Army HQ camp where Alexander has a small camp also. We dined with Clark and his mess. I had a long talk with him about the offensive on his front and do not feel very cheered up as to the prospects for the future from what I heard from him. He seems to be planning nothing but penny packet attacks and nothing sufficiently substantial.

17 December   Caserta

Got up early and left camp by 8 am in a jeep. A very cold morning, and a jeep is not a warm vehicle for driving in! I had not been able to see the camp last night as we arrived after dark. I found that it was in the gardens of Caserta Castle which was built as a copy of Versailles. We motored up through Capua to visit Dick McCreery's X Corps HQ. There I had a talk to various members of his HQ and then went on in his jeep to the front. On the way we met Harry Arkwright and Colvin, commanding 201ˢᵗ Guards Brigade. We finally met

Hawkesworth, commanding 46th Div, who gave us a description of his front. We then motored in our jeeps to within 2500 yards of the Boche and in full view of him without being fired on. Hawkesworth then gave us a description of the attack on Mount Camino from our old front line. We then motored up the slope as far as the jeeps would go, and then took to horses to go up a perpendicular mule track to a small plateau below Monastery Hill. Here Brig Lyne gave us an excellent description of how his brigade of Queen's bns stormed this frightful height. It was all most interesting and very vivid as the old Boche trenches and equipment were still lying about, and they were even burying Boche still while we were there. We then rode down at the risk of breaking our necks, and had lunch at the bottom. We then visited the rest of the front in a jeep, and after having tea with McCreery got back to camp at 8 pm. Very weary after 12 hours hard work. Before coming home we looked up Templer (Div Commander of 56th Div) who was in hospital. We also went to say goodbye to Clark.

This had been a tiring but very useful day. I had found more life on Dick McCreery's Corps' Front than I had found on the rest of the Italian front, and I was impressed with the way he was running his Corps. I had been provided with a grey pony with a very straight shoulder, and found it unpleasantly straight when going down steep slopes! The great value that day was to have been given such excellent accounts of the fighting that had been taking place. I was able to make a very good mental picture of the types of operation that were required, and was frequently far better able to visualize the fighting when back in London. From the top of Mount Camino I had been able to see quite clearly Mount Cassino and the country round, and had discussed with Alex the very nasty nut we should have to crack there. All this experience proved invaluable at a later date when I had difficult times with Winston concerning Alex's attacks on Mount Cassino.

I remember finding a very disgruntled Templer at having to be confined to his bed. I have vague recollections that a piano had been dropped on his car in a collision with a lorry, but I may be wrong.*

18 December   Tunis, 650 miles

Left Caserta at 8 am and motored to Naples airport. There we emplaned for Bari. On the way we visited Mt Vesuvius and flew within about 100 yards of the open crater, which was belching out smoke, fire and hot ashes! A most impressive sight. We then flew over Salerno bay and had a good look at operations connected with the landings. We reached Bari at 10.30 am where I said goodbye to Alex and at 10.45 started off again in his plane for Tunis. We flew back across Italy coming out at southern end of Salerno bay and then cut

---

*In fact Templer was struck low by illness at this point. But the story of his encounter with the piano was much told, and thoroughly investigated by his biographer. It took place on 5 August 1944. Templer was hit in the back by the rear wheel of a Guards Brigade HQ 'camp truck' when it was blown up by a mine. For the conspiratorially or musically minded, however, it seems the truck was carrying a piano, or pieces of a piano…John Cloake, *Templer* (London: Harrap, 1985), pp. 139–40, 469–70.

straight across the sea to the corner of Sicily just west of Palermo. Very bumpy for a bit. By 1.45 pm we were landing in Tunis. I went to see the PM after having long talk with Moran about his health.

Winston started by telling me that the King was very pleased to make me a Field Marshal, and that it would be announced on 1st Jan. He then told me that his temperature was now normal, but that his heart was the trouble. I told him all about my trip to Italy and he wanted to hear all details. We settled up final details about Command. He has now settled definitely about Jumbo Wilson for Supreme Command of the Mediterranean. He instructed me to get Martin to draft the wire to President Roosevelt to that effect. He was rather upset when I told him I was off tomorrow morning, and I had to be firm as he was suggesting my stopping on for several days!

Later:

After his afternoon rest I went back again to see him and to discuss draft Mr Martin had prepared of a telegram for the President about the Command. It is now decided that Wilson becomes Supreme Commander Mediterranean, that Alexander stays in Italy, and that Monty comes home to command land forces for Overlord, whilst Oliver Leese takes over 8th Army, and Paget relieves Jumbo in the Middle East. It is a great relief having those various points settled. After dinner I had to go back again to say goodbye to the PM. Clemmie was sitting on the bed with him and Randolph was also there. He was in very good form, but objecting to have to spend a week in bed before going on to Marrakesh for his fortnight's recuperation.

In my talk with Winston I of course said nothing to him about the depressing impressions I had gained whilst in Italy. I knew from experience that it would be fatal to draw his attention to such defects. He would only want to rush into some solution which would probably make matters worse. No, I had to keep all these misgivings to myself and look for a cure.

I did not mention in my diary that on that day my PA (Brian Boyle) had acquired a turkey, alive and on the hoof, for his Christmas at home. From now onwards this turkey became one of the passengers and was allowed to walk about the plane, and occasionally held up to look out of the window.

19 December   Gibraltar, 1000 miles

I slept in Eisenhower's villa and went to the PM's house for breakfast. There I met Lord Moran who said PM had had a good night and that he was still normal, that he could now be considered as safe from the pneumonia, but that his heart was the only danger. He had had during last few days two goes of heart flutter with pulse of 130, and that as a result of such a flutter a clot might form that would affect his brain. He must therefore be kept quiet, but was proving troublesome!

Went to aerodrome at 9 am to get into the Liberator Mrs Churchill had flown out in. At 10 am we took off. A very wild blustery day, but as soon as we were up it was quite smooth. We flew round Bizerta and then along the African coast. We had a strong head wind and it took us 5½ hours flying, only arriving here at 3.30 pm. We came up to Government House where we are to have dinner, waiting for the verdict as to whether the weather conditions will be good enough for us to fly on to England tonight. The chances are not too good as the weather has been very bad over England lately. Mason-MacFarlane is in England at present and Heyland is commanding here in his absence.

It is very hard to believe that I have not been away quite 5 weeks, it feels more like 5 years! So much has been done during that period, so much ground covered, so many conferences, so many decisions, so many visits, and so many impressions. My brain is feeling tired and confused, and a desperate longing for a long rest. I suppose I might as well long for the moon!

Later:
After dinner we were told that the weather was good enough for us to fly, and that we were to embark between midnight and 1 am, ready to fly by 1 am. We came down to the aerodrome shortly after midnight and made ourselves as comfortable as we could in the plane. Poor Boyle had started a go of jaundice so we gave him the only bed available. By 1.30 am we were off.

20 December   London, 1500 miles

We had a very good journey, made an excellent landfall, and 9.30 am were running down the runway at Northolt. By 10.30 am we were back again in:

LONDON

having been away just under 5 weeks and having covered some 13,000 miles by air during that period! It has been a useful and interesting trip and I feel that we have accomplished some useful work. After a bath and breakfast I went up to the WO where I had an hour's interview with the Secretary of State. I then met you and the Pooks at Waterloo and you both had lunch with me. The afternoon was spent in getting myself up to date again and in going through recent papers, together with interviews with VCIGS, QMG, Humfrey Gale, DMI and MS. Am feeling very sleepy and dog tired as I did not get much sleep in the plane last night.

I had some reason for satisfaction as to results of the trip as I had secured the main points I was after. In the first place I had got the date of Overlord pushed on to June 1ˢᵗ so that it would not cripple the Italian campaign, then I had turned the South France offensive into something more plastic, which could be adjusted without affecting Italy seriously. Then the Andaman attack had been put off, thus allowing landing equipment to be assembled in the Mediterranean, and not diverted to war against Japan before Germany was defeated. Finally I had fixed up the intricate problem of command in the Mediterranean in spite of many difficulties. In addition my visit to Italy had brought home to me the importance of making use of our amphibious power in this theatre by opening up a bridgehead near Rome.

My poor Boyle went down with jaundice and was taken off to hospital. I found myself landed with his turkey, which we had named 'Macaroni'. In the morning I had left the turkey in a basket at the flat. Suddenly in the evening on returning to the flat I remembered the poor bird. I asked the batman what he had done with it. He was rather a pompous young man and replied, 'There was no bird sir, only some fish!' I went round to see the fish and was greeted by a chirrup from my old friend, still in the bag! It was quickly liberated, given food and drink, and remained at large in the flat till I went down to Ferney Close and took it with me. There it lived for many happy days and even contributed 11 lovely eggs to our meagre rations.

21 December
Attended Chiefs of Staff meeting in the morning to listen to discussions on probability of pilotless aeroplane attacks on London. Then made a statement concerning my visit to Italy and necessity for amphibious operations on this front. At 3.15 pm went to see the King, who kept me for 1¼ hours. He was in excellent form and most interested in all details of conferences and of my visit to Italy. He has a wonderful knowledge of what is going on. Then an interview with Ralston, Canadian Defence Minister, concerning replacement of McNaughton who is now very ill. Also visit from Mason-MacFarlane, who is home from Gib.

22 to 29 December
Proceeded home for my Xmas leave with you and the children.

30 December
Left at 8.30 am and was in WO by 9.30. Spent morning going through papers and getting up to date. My recommendations for strong amphibious operations in Rome area are being acted on which is good. In afternoon had interviews with Philip Neame just back after escaping from Italian Prisoners' Camp. He was very interesting and praised the Italians for the assistance they had given him. Then Jumbo Wilson for a long interview to discuss his new job of Supreme Commander Mediterranean. After that with Harding who is just going out to act as Chief of Staff to Alexander. Then VCIGS followed by QMG and DCIGS.

31 December
Attended my first COS meeting for many weeks! It was not a very arduous one. Mainly concerned with pulling straight telegrams from PM who is now becoming very active again! In the afternoon had interviews with Duff Cooper, Laycock and with Capt Power RN concerning Rome amphibious operation. Then Army Council meeting and an interview with Bedell Smith concerning setting up of HQ for cross Channel operations. He and Eisenhower are anxious

to take all the heads of Staff departments out of the Mediterranean!! This will want watching! Considered that Bedell Smith had gone off a lot and was suffering from a swollen head. Army Council meeting in the evening.

Bedell Smith had been sent home with Ike to begin to organize his HQ for Overlord. He was decidedly bumptious and imagined that the Mediterranean HQ could now be robbed of all its best officers to form the new HQ. I had to put Bedell Smith in his place and inform him that I was responsible for the distribution of the Staff on all fronts, and could be relied on to take their various requirements into account. I told him I would have no string pulling.

1 January – 31 December 1944

1 January 1944

Heard on the 8 am wireless that I had been promoted to Field Marshal! It gave me a curious peaceful feeling that I had at last, and unexpectedly, succeeded in reaching the top rung of the ladder!! I certainly never set out to reach this position, nor did I ever hope to do so, even in my wildest moments. When I look back over my life no one could be more surprised than I am to find where I have got to!!

Left the WO early, changed into shooting clothes, and motored down to Fisher's home for an afternoon's shooting. From there on home.

2 January

Spent very very happily at home with you, Pooks and Mr Ti.

3 January

Early start. Picked up my jacket, converted to FM badges, and then went on to WO and to COS. After lunch meeting with Monty to discuss his ideas on plans for invasion. Then Cabinet meeting where Portal and I were congratulated on our promotion. Finally dined with Cobbold to say goodbye to Devers who is returning to North Africa as second in command to Wilson. Saw that the scaup [duck] had returned on the St James's Park lake.

The return of the scaup amongst the St James's Park duck was a great event! It had been there the whole previous winter, but left during breeding season, only to return again this winter.

4 January

A long COS meeting at which we did our weekly review of the threat of the rocket or pilotless plane. Evidence goes on accumulating. Also had a talk with Jumbo Wilson and discussed attack on Rome. In afternoon O'Connor, just back from Italian prison, came to see me. He is in good shape and will be given a Corps at once. Then Paget came to say goodbye. He is evidently upset and sad at being superseded by Monty, but is taking it all very well. Now I have to work out all the other incumbent changes.

5 January

A COS at which we were employed trying to sort out a tangle existing in the

Mediterranean. Most of the difficulties are caused by the PM, at Marrakesh convalescing and trying to run the war from there!! The latest suggestion arrived tonight is that I should fly out to Marrakesh for a conference this weekend with Alexander, Bedell Smith etc, on operations in the Mediterranean!! The prospects are not very attractive to say the least! Lunched with Franklyn at Home Forces HQ and gave talk on the world situation. Tonight Bannerman, Kennedy and Bevan came to dine, and we had a bird evening!

It must be remembered that Ike as Supreme Commander came directly under the orders of the Combined Chiefs of Staff, and that orders for him always required the agreement of both President and PM. It will be realized therefore that direct interference by PM with Alex and Bedell Smith could only annoy the Americans and raise their suspicions.

6 January
Discussed the desirability of flying out to Marrakesh with COS. Both Portal and Cunningham not in favour owing to the fact that unless Marshall is also present Americans may well accuse us of exercising unilateral control of operations in Mediterranean. Lord Milne came to lunch with me to talk about uneasiness in the Royal Regiment [of Artillery] that their interests were not sufficiently attended to in WO. He was most useful in providing outside opinions which I would otherwise not receive. I think I can do a good deal to put these matters right. In the afternoon interviews with Nosworthy, back from West Africa, Noel Irwin, still unhappy about his fate, and Jumbo Wilson for a final word before departure for Supreme Commander Mediterranean. Finished up by dining with Oswald Birley.

7 January
A difficult COS, as Winston, sitting in Marrakesh is now full of beans and trying to win the war from there! As a result a 3 cornered flow of telegrams in all directions is gradually resulting in utter confusion! I wish to God that he would come home and get under control.

After lunch went to see Amery who, having just been appointed President of the Alpine Club, has become more mountain warfare minded than ever! He would almost convert the whole army in Italy into mountaineers! However, there is a great deal in what he says, and I don't think that Alexander realizes half enough the necessity of training mountaineers on his front. I then attended an Army Council meeting and finished up with Lewin coming to dine.

8 January
A short COS, a rush through files, a hurried lunch and a drive home reading more files, and a peaceful evening to follow!

9 January
Peaceful Sunday at home.

10 January
Usual early start. Found a mass of telegrams in as a result of the PM's conference at Marrakesh.

The operation for the attack just south of Rome is now all settled for the 22nd of this month. Pray God that the weather may be fine for it, otherwise it might well end in a bad disaster. Unfortunately weather is none too certain at this time of year. Also telegrams from PM about handing over Italian ships to Russia. There are no military advantages to this that I can see, nothing but a political gesture which may well have serious military repercussions. Then very small War Cabinet at 5 pm at which I had to explain the outline of the Italian Rome amphibious operation. At 5.30 pm we went on with the usual Cabinet. Plans now being made for return of PM.

11 January
We had our weekly examination at the COS of the prospects of the pilotless plane and of the counter measures. The bombing of the launching emplacements in North France is not going well, and the bombing has been very inaccurate. We next considered handing over of Italian naval ships to Russians. Militarily there are nothing but disadvantages in such a procedure. Unfortunately during moments of special friendship fomented by wine promises were made by the powerful ones to Stalin in Teheran. After lunch we had a long Selection Board, the first one attended by Monty. We have now, I think, settled all the various appointments incumbent on the major changes and on the preparations for the over-Channel operation.

12 January
A dull COS. After lunch Layton, who had been out to Australia seeing Curtin [Australian PM], MacArthur, Blamey etc, came to see me and was most interesting. Apparently Curtin is no longer quite so much in MacArthur's pocket! In the morning Casey came to say goodbye before leaving for India to take over Governorship of Bengal, not a very pleasant job just at present!!

13 January
Ran the usual COS meeting during the morning, and after lunch left the WO at 3 pm for Sandringham. I took Lockwood [batman] and Parker [driver] with me, both delighted at the opportunity of re-establishing contacts with the former Royal entourage they worked with. We had a very good run and in spite of the dark reached Sandringham just about 6 pm. We however found Sandringham empty, as the King is using a smaller house close by which the late King had

given the Queen of Norway. At the gate we were stopped by a policeman who after examining our identities turned on a series of little magic blue lights on either side of the avenue up to the house. On arrival there I was met by Piers Legh [Equerry to the King], who took me round to the drawing room. There I found the Queen alone with the two princesses. She said she had some tea for me, which she rang for and then poured out for me. The older of the two princesses also came along to assist in entertaining me, whilst the younger one remained on the sofa reading *Punches* and emitting ripples of giggles and laughter at the jokes.

The King came in a little later and also sat at the small table whilst I drank my tea. After tea the King asked me to come to his study and I had about an hour with him, discussing the war, various appointments, the Prime Minister, the new medals etc. In every subject he displays the greatest interest and is evidently taking the greatest trouble to keep himself abreast of everything. I then went up to dress for dinner which was not till 8.45. We assembled in the drawing room, consisting of Lady Delia Peel (lady in waiting), Lascelles (Secretary), Piers Legh (Controller) and Arthur Penn [Private Secretary to the Queen] who had arrived just before dinner. After a bit the King, Queen and eldest princess came in and we all did the necessary bowing and curtsying. We went in to dinner where I sat on the Queen's right. I found her throughout the whole of my visit quite charming and very easy to get on with. An exceptional charm and naturalness, backed by a good sense of humour and complete lack of pomposity, made her exceptionally attractive. After the Queen had left, the King got me to sit next to him and we sat on for another ½ hour. When we came to the drawing room the Queen offered us tea which she poured out and we talked till 11.30 pm when we all went off to bed.

14 January

Breakfast was at nine and was not attended by any of the royal family. After breakfast Harry Cator (brother in law of Queen) and Oliver Birbeck (Master of local hounds) came as the two additional guns, which made us 6 in all as Lascelles did not shoot. We started at 10 am, and walked to the first beat. The King throughout the day took complete charge and posted all guns himself. It was all very informal and pleasant. The Queen and family turned up during the morning and kept with the King most of the time. A very happy little family group, full of jokes and laughter. We had a very good day and shot 348 pheasants (all wild birds), 65 partridges etc. The day was quite glorious, a lovely sunny day with no wind and ideal temperature. We returned about 4.30 pm, and after changing assembled in the drawing room for an excellent 'sit down' tea at a long table with the Queen pouring out at one end. After tea I attended to an envelope of papers sent up from the War Office and shortly afterwards the King came to fetch me for another talk with him in his study. This was followed by dinner on the same lines as the former evening except that I sat on the Queen's left this time.

The day had started with Lockwood calling me…Lockwood had been the Duke of Kent's valet for 17 years and for a matter of fact had only left him some months before his death. Had he remained on he would have been killed in the aeroplane with the Duke of Kent. Well, Lockwood was quite familiar with all the Sandringham habits. He also knew that I was interested in the 'Buck Ryan' serial in the Daily Mirror. *He therefore brought in my tea with a copy of the* Mirror *and said, 'I must draw your attention, Sir, to the fact that this paper is somewhat frowned on in this establishment, so I should not walk about with it. Yet as there is only one copy of it there is quite a queue forming up for it as soon as you have finished with it!' He was loading for me, which he did admirably, and at one stand he suddenly asked me, 'Do you like Cox's Orange Pippin Apples, because they grow a very good brand here. If you like them we could bring some home with us!' When I told him he must certainly not take any he said 'Oh! I would not dream of doing that! They send them to market from here and I can pay the gardener.' I agreed that as long as they were legitimately paid for that there would be no harm in taking a few.*

15 January

The two outside guns today were Lord Coke and a local farmer, A. Keith. The weather was not quite so good during the morning owing to mist, but this cleared up and the latter part of the day was again glorious. The Queen and family again came out during the morning. This time we lunched out in sort of tin School House. We had another very good day with 312 pheasants and 23 partridges etc. During the afternoon we saw some woodcock and shot 9 of them. The evening was again filled up with the same routine as on the previous days. Before going to bed the Queen said goodbye, but the King said he would be down before I left.

16 January

This morning at 10 am the car was all loaded up and ready. The King had been down talking to me for about a quarter of an hour. He then very kindly asked whether he could talk to Parker as he had driven him when he visited Gort in France. Parker beamed all over. The King had also had a little talk with Lockwood whilst we were shooting, which delighted him. In fact both Lockwood and Parker were in seventh heaven. Finally I said goodbye to the King, thanked him profusely and drove off.

… I had one ghastly moment that he would find the whole of the back of the car packed with his best Cox's Orange Pippins. But Lockwood was too clever to be caught out like that: there were lots of them, all carefully hidden and all had been paid for.

It has been a most interesting experience, and one which has greatly impressed me. The one main impression that I have carried away with me is that the King, Queen and their two daughters provide one of the very best examples of English family life. A thoroughly closely knit and happy family all wrapped up in each other. Secondly I was greatly impressed by the wonderful atmosphere entirely devoid of all pomposity, stiffness or awkwardness. They both have a wonderful gift of making one feel entirely at home. The Queen, I think, grows on one the more one sees her and realizes the wonderful qualities she possesses.

I had a bad journey back owing to fog, which got thicker as we approached London. I had hoped to come on to Ferney Close but found it quite impossible owing to the fog. In any case I had a lot of work to do and a large bag to go through which kept me busy the whole afternoon. In addition I had a lot of letters to answer and business to look to.

I forgot to mention that one of the Sandringham rules is that no tips are given to anybody. In addition I was provided with most of my cartridges!!

17 January

This morning's COS consisted of nothing but dealing with a mass of various telegrams on a mass of subjects such as: parachutists for South East Asia, arguments concerning landing craft to be withdrawn from South East Asia to Med, Chiang Kai-shek's refusal to use his Yunnan forces, latest reports on German pilotless aeroplanes, desirability of infiltrating Spitfires into Turkey, difficulties with Portuguese concerning American attempts to share use of Azores with us, etc, etc.

After lunch Eisenhower came round to see me, in very good form. He is apparently quite prepared to face the question of curtailing south of France operation on its merits. Finally Cabinet, the last to be run without Winston who returns tomorrow.

I foresee troublesome times the moment he returns. For one thing he wants again to get Adam out of AG job, and wishes to send him to Gibraltar!* Luckily S of S is prepared to fight this alongside of me. He also has some idea of kicking Giffard [11ᵗʰ Army Group] out without any reasonable grounds for it.

18 January

This morning was somewhat upset by the return of the PM who arrived at Paddington at 10 am, where we all proceeded to meet him. Then COS with Cherwell attending to the latest reports of progress made by the German pilotless aeroplane, and our bombing of the launching points in France. At 12.15 a Cabinet to listen to PM, who rambled on till 1.30 pm. He was looking very well, but I did not like the functioning of his brain much! Too much unconnected rambling from one subject to another. After lunch I had an hour with Alex [Alan] Hartley, just back from India, to hear all the latest news. Then a sad interview with Kenneth Anderson to tell him he would not be commanding

---

*Following a pattern of expulsion or attempted expulsion from the Churchillian inner circle of those who did not find favour there: for Dill, 'a position of great honour, followed by a bodyguard with lances' (Governor-General of Bombay); for Halifax, 'a glorious opportunity in America' (Ambassador in Washington); for Wavell, 'a seat under the pagoda tree' (C-in-C India).

the 2nd Army in the forthcoming offensive, as Dempsey is to replace him. He took it very well.

19 January

The PM is starting off in his usual style!! We had a Staff meeting with him at 5.30 pm for 2 hours, and a Defence Committee from 10.30 pm for another two hours. And we accomplished nothing!! I don't think I can stand much more of it. We waffled about with all the usual criticisms, all the usual optimist's plans, no long term vision, and we settled nothing. In all his plans he lives from hand to mouth. He can never grasp a whole plan, either in its width (ie all fronts) or its depth (long term projects). His method is entirely opportunist, gathering one flower here another there! My God how tired I am of working for him! I had not fully realized how awful it is until I suddenly found myself thrown into it again after a rest! Lunched with Sosnkowski at Claridges, he was in good form and very nice.

20 January

Operations in Italy going better. Oh! How I hope that the Rome amphibious operation [at Anzio] will be a success! I feel a special responsibility for it [as I] have resuscitated it after my visit to Italy and found things stagnating there. It may fail, but I know it was the right thing to do, to double the amphibious operation and carry on with the outflanking plan. You came up to lunch. In the afternoon Cranborne came to see me to tell me that McNaughton was preparing to do a lot of harm on his return to Canada. He is evidently very embittered about his removal from command of the Canadian Army. Dined with Bas and Olave.

21 January

Started with a COS from which I went on to a Cabinet starting at 12.15. This lasted till 1.30 pm. Then dashed off to lunch with Adam followed by an hour in the WO and then a motor drive to Glenham to shoot with Ivan Cobbold.

22 January

Very good shoot, only 4 guns: Cobbold, uncle Philip, Barney and I. Howling wind, almost gale force. Shot 172 pheasants. At lunch was called up by WO and told that landing south of Rome had been a complete surprise. This was a wonderful relief!

23 January

Left Glenham 10 am and reached flat by 12 noon. Repacked and off again at 12.15 with my brown bag of papers from WO. Worked all the way home where I arrived at 1.15 pm.

24 January

Left home 8 am. Had a long COS at which Eisenhower turned up to discuss his paper proposing increase of cross Channel operation at expense of Southern France operation. I entirely agree with the proposal but it is certainly not his idea, and is one of Monty's. Eisenhower has got absolutely no strategical outlook and is really totally unfit for the post he holds from an operational point of view. He makes up, however, by the way he works for good cooperation between allies. After lunch Monty came to see me and I had to tell him off for falling foul of both the King and the S of S in a very short time. He took it well, as usual.

Long Cabinet from 6 to 8.15 pm with Winston in great form. He was discussing Stalin's latest iniquities in allowing *Pravda* to publish the bogus information that England was negotiating with Germany about a peace. He said: 'Trying to maintain good relations with a communist is like wooing a crocodile, you do not know whether to tickle it under the chin or to beat it on the head. When it opens its mouth you cannot tell whether it is trying to smile, or preparing to eat you up.' After dinner another meeting from 10 to 12 midnight, to discuss artificial harbours for the invasion. Here again he was in very good form.

25 January

We had a long and tedious meeting this morning. First of all Cherwell and Duncan Sandys were with us whilst we discussed the situation concerning the pilotless planes and the rocket. Then representatives from Foreign Office and SOE to discuss various aspects of SOE activities in Greece, Yugoslavia, Poland and Czechoslovakia. After lunch Gibbon came to see me about Tom, and the fact that he had better now go to a Service unit. News of Rome landings continues to be good, but I am not happy about our relative strength in Italy. We have not got a sufficient margin to be able to guarantee making a success of our attacks, and the ground unfortunately favours the defence.

26 January

I finished up COS fairly early and put in close on an hour in the office before lunch. You came up and we lunched with the Hutton Crofts. Duke of Gloucester came to call after lunch and was very nice, and did not stop too long. Have just dined and am now off by train for a day with 'Hobo' and his swimming tanks and mine destroyers.

27 January

Eisenhower met me at the station last night and we travelled up by special train through the night. Hobart collected us at 9 am and took us first to his HQ, where he showed us his models, and his proposed assault organization. We then went on to see various exhibits such as the Sherman tank for destroying tank mines, with chains on a drum driven by the engine, various methods of climbing walls with tanks, blowing up of minefields and walls, flame throwing Churchill tanks, wall destroying engineer parties, floating tanks, teaching men how to escape from sunken tanks, etc, etc. A most interesting day, and one which Eisenhower seemed to enjoy thoroughly. Hobart has been doing wonders in his present job and I am delighted that we put him into it.

28 January

There was little for the COS to do this morning, and I finished it off in just under the hour. I had to lunch with the Military Attachés Association, a large lunch of about 50, comprising 18 different nationalities. Colonel Kalia, the Czechoslovakian Attaché, acted as the doyen and made a very nice speech, at the end congratulating me on my promotion and presenting me with a book from them all with their signatures in it. I had to reply, thanking them, and after lunch had talks to as many of them as we could fit in.

At 4.30 pm Winston suddenly convened a meeting as he had misread some of the intercepted secret information and thought that an additional division was being sent to oppose the Rome landing. He was also full of doubts as to whether Lucas was handling this landing efficiently. I had some job quieting him down again! Unfortunately this time I feel there are reasons for uneasiness!

29 January

We had no COS this morning so I succeeded in escaping early and arrived home for lunch. Called up by Winston [on the 'scrambler'] after midnight.

30 January

A quiet Sunday at home except for long talk on telephone with PM.

31 January

Usual early start and rush of Monday. First a COS during morning. Then a Cabinet in the afternoon, and finally Staff meeting after dinner with the PM to discuss preparation of improvised ports for cross Channel operations. PM in great form and full of chaff and leg pulling. I had a nice quiet evening as I was not involved in the discussion. News from Italy bad and the landing south of Rome [Anzio] is making little progress, mainly due to the lack of initiative in the early stages. I am at present rather doubtful as to how we are to disentangle the situation. Hitler has reacted very strongly and is sending reinforcements fast.

1 February

News continues to be poor from Italy. COS concerned with German rockets and pilotless planes for attack on London, and measures to deal with them. At 3.15 long Selection Board. Finally dined at Mansion House dinner given for Americans.

2 February

A busy day. First the usual COS, with some difficult problems. Then office work, followed by a lunch for the Chinese. Then interview with Budget Loyd telling him he was for London District, and Arthur Smith that he was for Iraq-Persia Command. Finally dinner at 10 Downing Street, where the guests were [the] King, Eisenhower, Bedell Smith, Monty, Lascelles and 3 Chiefs of Staff. PM in good form and brought out many gems. I only wish I could remember them. Amongst others:

'Politics are very much like war, we may even have to use poison gas at times.'

'In politics if you have something good to give, give a little at a time, but if you have something bad to get rid of, give it all together and brace the recipients to receive it.'

King remained till 1 am!! Ike stopped on a little longer, and it was 1.30 when I reached home, worn out! Winston's last statement referring to American desire to sack King of Italy and Bagoglio was: 'Why break the handle of the coffee pot at this stage and burn your fingers trying to hold it, why not wait till we get to Rome, and let it cool off.'

3 February

We had a long COS discussing the wire to send back to American Chiefs of Staff to convince them that with the turn operations have taken in the Mediterranean, the only thing to do is to go on fighting the war in Italy and give up any idea of a weak landing in Southern France. The American correspondent Wagg came to dinner with me and was interesting. Dined at Chinese Embassy and then went to attend PM's meeting from 10 to midnight on the question of measures taken to deal with pilotless planes and subversive activities in Poland and Czechoslovakia.

4 February

Pug wasted a great deal of our time at the COS. He has been having a row with the PM in defending a document we had produced yesterday. Winston had asked us to consider the advisability of pressing de Valera to sack the German Ambassador in Dublin for security's sake. We had discovered that as we had broken the German cipher we could control all cable messages, and as wireless sets had been removed, it was perhaps better to remain with the devil we knew, as opposed to the devil we did not know. Winston apparently wished for another answer and was very angry because he did not get it.

Lunched with the Sosnkowskis with you there also. At end of lunch was called off for a meeting with PM at 3 pm to discuss our cable to the Americans, which he approved. This is a wire connected with our intention to concentrate on the Italian campaign and to give up the idea of a subsidiary landing in the South of France. Army Council at 5 pm and after that went to a play with you, the Adams and Admiral Stark coming back to the flat for dinner.

5 February
After the COS and lunch we motored back together to Ferney Close.

6 February
Quiet Sunday at home.

7 February
Usual early start, and found my table full of telegrams, including some of American Chiefs of Staff disagreeing with us as regards cancelling the South of France operation. Nothing left but to wire and ask them to come over and discuss. Time now too short for any other course.

After lunch Jack Collins [Staff College] came as I had asked him to call and discuss a letter of his opened by the censor on its way to Ireland addressed to MacNamara. He had criticized the selection of Montgomery versus Paget and I had to tell him how we stood. While he was there, PM sent for me and kept me for ¾ hour discussing with him the situation in Italy. He was in the depths of gloom and I had a hard time cheering him up. At 5.30 pm Cabinet, by which time he was more cheerful.

8 February
A day spent almost continuously with the PM! Started with a call to go and see him at 9.15 am! That was put off to 12 instead, when he kept me till 1.15 pm. At 6 pm we met again till 7.45 and finally from 10 to 12 midnight! A great deal of this was concerned with a proposed wild venture of his to land 2 Armoured Divisions in Bordeaux 20 days after the cross Channel operations. I think we have ridden him off this for the present. Next a wild scheme for raising additional transport planes for the airborne lift.

This afternoon Stewart (Canadian) came to see me. I think that for the present the Canadian problems are settled. Next Donovan (USA) came. He was interesting: having been on the Rome landing he was able to paint a clear picture of the failure to exercise sufficient drive. I am afraid that Winston is beginning to see some of Alex's shortcomings! It was bound to come some time or other, but means difficult times ahead. I wonder how I have succeeded in keeping him covered up to now!

9 February

Another hard day. Started with a short COS and then WO work, followed by lunch 10 Downing St to which you came. Then Dutch Ambassador came to see me.

At 5.15 pm I was handed a 5 page telegram which PM had drafted for President covering the whole strategy of the war, and most of it wrong! He asked for it to be discussed with him at 10.30 pm. Unfortunately there was a Cabinet at 5.30 pm. There I had a royal battle with him concerning the imposition of a ban on visitors to the South Coast in anticipation of our proposed operation. For some unaccountable reason he was against the ban and supported Morrison. I had most of the rest of the Cabinet with me, including Stafford Cripps, Bevin, Oliver Lyttelton and P.J. We had a royal scrap and I think I had the best of it. At 7.30 pm we came out and had a hurried COS meeting to examine PM's wire which required drastic amending. At 8.15 I had Eisenhower, Grigg and Andrew Cunningham to dine. At 10.30 back again for meeting with PM to get him to alter his wire. We expected a holy row! Luckily another wire from Roosevelt came in which cut right across the one we were considering and saved most of the trouble. Now midnight and I am dog tired.

10 February

We had a long COS which Eisenhower and Bedell Smith attended at 12 noon. They had prepared a paper showing the requirements for the cross Channel operation which coincided with our views. Marshall had also wired that he left it to Eisenhower to take final decision. Therefore all seems to be going well at present. We only await decision of experts on technical matters who are flying out. PM insisted on seeing us after our meeting with Ike. He was in bed looking ill and old. He still wanted to express tactical aspects of case and we had to ride him off them.

Then lunch with Lord Camrose of *Daily Telegraph* at the *DT* office. Back to WO to finish off work and at 4.30 pm started for Larkhill. There I dined in the Mess, big dinner with Master Gunner and Colonel Commandant, the evening being given up to a reception of American gunners. I had to propose the toast to the guests. We had the RHA trumpeters, bands, Woolwich plate, powdered waiters etc. I think the evening was a success. After dinner motored back to Hartley Wintney.

11 February

Left Ferney Close at 11 am for the Staff College where I gave 1 hour lecture on world situation. Then on to London to deal with the usual work. Dined with Bannerman when Lodge came to dine, who is drawing all the plates for Bannerman's future book of the birds of GB. Lodge 82 years old, most attractive old man, found he knew Wolf well and had painted with him. His plates are quite wonderful and should make a historical book.

12 February

For once, thank heaven, there was not sufficient material for a COS. I therefore finished off work before lunch and came home.

13 February

Quiet Sunday at home.

14 February

A long COS, attended by Leathers, with a long discussion on shipping. News of Italy still none too good, but I feel the bridgehead south of Rome should hold all right, and that ultimately we may score by not having an early easy success. Hitler has been determined to fight for Rome and may give us a better chance of inflicting heavy blows under the new conditions.

In the afternoon Lumsden [British LO with MacArthur] came to see me and was most interesting concerning conditions in the Pacific. Apparently Nimitz and MacArthur have never yet even met although working side by side! King and MacArthur are totally opposed in their plans. Marshall and King are frightened of MacArthur standing for presidency, Marshall hopes for vice-presidency and consequently won't fall foul of King. General opinion is that King has finished serving his useful period [as Chief of US Naval Staff], etc etc. All military plans shadowed by political backgrounds. God knows how this will straighten itself out!

At 5.45 usual Cabinet meeting which lasted till 7.50. Then 10 pm meeting with PM to listen to Wedemeyer's plan which he had brought back from Dickie Mountbatten [in South East Asia]. I had long and difficult arguments with the PM. He was again set on carrying out an attack of north tip of Sumatra and refusing to look at any long term projects or concrete plans for the defeat of Japan. Again showing his terrible failing of lack of width or depth in his strategic vision. He lives for the impulse and for the present, and refuses to look at lateral implications or future commitments. Now that I know him well episodes such as Antwerp and the Dardanelles no longer puzzle me! But meanwhile I often doubt whether I am going mad or whether he is really sane. The arguments were difficult as Wedemeyer and his party were of course trying to sell their goods, namely operations through the Malacca Straits and these operations entailed the capture of Sumatra which the PM wanted. But he refused to argue the relative merits of opening the Malacca Straits as opposed to working via Australia. After much hard work I began to make him see that we must have an overall plan for the defeat of Japan and then fit in the details.

15 February

Our COS finished about 12 noon and I then went round to listen to Admiral Cooke (USA) give an hour's lecture on the fighting for the Marshall Islands. The subject was interesting, but Cooke nearly sent me to sleep! After lunch

Harrison, one of Mountbatten's staff officers, came to see me. We discussed Dickie's plans and his requirements for his offensive. Then Charles Allfrey back from Italy came to see me, he is back from Italy having his eyes looked at and goes back next week. Finally Arthur Smith coming to say goodbye before departure for Iraq Persia Command. There is no doubt that he is a very fine man, entirely selfless and with only one thought, that of serving his country. After finishing the above received telegram from Alex that he was not satisfied with Lucas as Commander of Corps in bridgehead south of Rome and asking me to consult Eisenhower. This resulted in a long series of telephone calls to Eisenhower and to PM and I only got to bed by 1 am.

16 February

I had hardly arrived in the office when I was sent for by PM who wanted to send Alexander to command the troops in the bridgehead and Wilson to command the main front! I am afraid I rather lost my temper with him over this and asked him if he could not for once trust his commanders to organize the command for themselves without interfering and upsetting all the chain and sequence of command. He gave up his idea for the present, but may well return to the attack!!

A fairly long COS with shipping and SOE problems. For lunch the St Clairs and Stanyforths came. Had intended to visit display of new jet aircraft, but weather was too bad. Visit from Budget, who has just taken over London District, to settle reduction of Guards Brigades.

17 February

Bitterly cold and feels like snow. A long COS and being mostly concerned with post-hostilities matters, and it is not yet easy to concentrate one's thoughts on after war matters! We were at it hard from 10.30 to 1.15 pm, and even then only skimmed the surface. After lunch I had an interview with Brocas Burrows, who is off to Moscow (to replace Martel) and found that the Foreign Office had been briefing him on such a completely conciliatory basis that he did not imagine that he was to get anything back out of the Russians! Typical of the Foreign Office – the more I see of them the more appalled I am at their inefficiency.

18 February

Our COS was mainly concerned with the situation in Greece, where Mr Leeper, the Ambassador and the Foreign Office have succeeded in stopping all guerilla activities by trying to look for some ultimate settlement which will admit of a political situation suitable for the reentry of the King at the end of hostilities. In fact, in searching for some ultimate political ideal we are losing sight of the current military necessities! In the afternoon an Army Council Meeting and finally Monty to dinner quietly with me which was good value and most helpful.

19 February

We had a very long COS. First of all Eisenhower, Bedell Smith, Tedder and Cooke etc all came in representing American Chiefs of Staff to discuss desirability of having an amphibious attack against South of France to coincide with cross Channel operations. Luckily I had discovered last night from Monty that he and Bertie Ramsay had foolishly agreed to curtail the cross Channel operation to allow for a South of France operation. If they had had any sense they would have realized that the situation in Italy now makes such an operation impossible. They had agreed to please Eisenhower, who was pressing for it to please Marshall!!! What a way to run a war! I had a little difficulty with Eisenhower, but not much to make him see sense, as all he required was a little pressure to go back to the plan that he really liked best now that he had shown some attempt to support Marshall's foolish idea! I think the matter is now all right.

We then had Nash from New Zealand to discuss whether cuts could be made in the employment of New Zealand forces, as more men are required at home for agriculture. I started for home after lunch.

20 February

Quiet Sunday at home.

21 February

Returned to London to find considerable damage done by bombs during previous night. One bomb [in] middle of Whitehall opposite Treasury had done much harm and blown in all windows of War Office except mine! Two bombs in middle of Horse Guards had blown in all 10 Downing St, Admiralty, Horse Guards windows etc. One bomb end of St James's. Guards Memorial badly chipped by bomb.

Long COS with Planners, discussing Pacific strategy and deciding on plan of action to tackle the PM with, to convince him that we cannot take the tip of Sumatra for him. We shall have very serious trouble with him over this. But we have definitely decided that our strategy should be to operate from Australia with the Americans and not from India through Malacca Straits. Cabinet at 6 pm.

22 February

A very long and difficult COS. Eisenhower came again to represent the American Chiefs of Staff and to argue their point concerning the Mediterranean. It is quite clear to me from Marshall's wire that he does not begin to understand the Italian campaign! He cannot realize that to maintain an offensive a proportion of reserve divisions are required. He considers that this reserve can be withdrawn for a new offensive in the South of France and that the momentum in Italy can still be maintained. Eisenhower sees the situation a little more clearly, but he is too frightened of disagreeing with Marshall to be able to express his views clearly. After Eisenhower, Wedemeyer came next to argue out and explain the Burma campaigns. I am not a bit happy about the final plans, there is no definite objective and large forces of Long Range Penetration groups are being launched for no definite purpose. If ever there was a campaign that has been mishandled it is the Burma one, and mainly due to the influence exerted by Chiang Kai-shek through the President on the American Chiefs of Staff. During afternoon visits by Macleod and by Stewart to fix up details of withdrawal of Crerar from Italy. I am feeling very weary and old and wish to God the war would finish!

23 February

Another long COS. First interview with Joint Intelligence Committee, then visit by Duncan Sandys whilst we discussed German progress with rocket and pilotless planes, and results of our attacks on them. Then checking off telegram to American COS as a result of our meeting with Eisenhower yesterday. We have got all we want but must word the wire to let the Americans 'save face' as much as possible! Finally Sir Orme Sargent from the Foreign Office to discuss the Greek situation and to try and make some sense out of the present Foreign Office policy in Greece! As this policy is mainly based on the future post war political regime in Greece it pays little attention to the requirements of guerilla warfare! It is a typical Foreign Office concern.

You came to lunch, also Pongo and Lillian Pelly. In the evening Soviet sherry party to commemorate Red Army Day. Returned to WO to find that Russians had awarded me the Order of Suvorov, First Degree!

24 February

A short COS for a change with no difficult problems, but tomorrow promises badly as we then discuss the Pacific strategy with the PM and he will wish to fasten onto the tip of Sumatra like a limpet. During the afternoon went for a walk to look at last night's air raid damage. Corner of St James's and Pall Mall badly smashed up by a stick of bombs. All windows of St James's Palace and the clock are gone, Hardy [fishing shop] and all adjoining shops, Conservative Club windows all blown in, Spinks completely gone and also picture shop alongside of poor old Orleans Club! German bombs seem to be much more powerful than they were. In the evening went to study plans for artificial ports. After dinner, another German air raid, lasting 1½ hours and very noisy!

25 February

I am quite exhausted after spending 7½ hours today with Winston, and most of that time engaged in heavy argument. First of all we discovered at the COS that the PM had never been informed by the Secret Service that the Japanese main fleet had moved to Singapore although we had known this fact for the last few days! This had to be rectified at once and entailed Menzies getting ticked off. At 12 noon the Chiefs of Staff met the PM and were kept till 1.45 pm. He was still insisting on doing the North Sumatra operation, would not discuss any other operation and was in a thoroughly disgruntled and bad temper. I had a series of heated discussions with him.

Then a hurried lunch and at 3 pm we met again. This time he had packed the house against us, and was accompanied by Anthony Eden, Oliver Lyttelton, and Attlee, in addition the whole of Dickie Mountbatten's party consisting of Wedemeyer, Binney, Macleod, Dewing, Naval and Air Officers. The whole party were against the Chiefs of Staff! Thank God I have got Andrew Cunningham to support me! It just makes all the difference from the days of poor old Dudley Pound. We argued from 3 pm to 5.30 pm. I got very heated at times, especially when Anthony Eden chipped in knowing nothing about Pacific strategy! Winston pretended that this was all a frame up against his pet Sumatra operation and almost took it up as a personal matter. Furthermore his dislike for Curtin and the Australians at once affected any discussion for co-operation with Australian forces through New Guinea towards the Philippines. Dewing chipped in and talked unadulterated nonsense, and I almost lost my temper with him. It was a desperate meeting, with no opportunity of discussing strategy on its merits.

I then rushed to WO for a talk with Wedemeyer before his return to America. Then an interview with Swayne to break the news to him that he is to go to India as Chief of Staff. Then Strang, just back from Australia, followed by MS, DMO and DMI.

Meanwhile PM called up and asked me to dine. I thought it was to tell me that he couldn't stick my disagreements any longer and proposed to sack me! On the contrary we had a *tête-à-tête* dinner at which he was quite charming, as if he meant to make up for some of the rough passages of the day. He has astonishing sides to his character. We discussed Randolph and his difficulties of controlling him and my difficulties with Tom. His daughters, my daughters. The President's unpleasant attitude lately. The fact that we may have to go to America soon, the Italian front, the air raids etc, etc.

At 10 pm another COS meeting which lasted till 12 midnight. PM in much more reasonable mood, and I think that a great deal of what we have been doing has soaked in. I hope so at least, as I don't want another day like today!

It was as well that I did not know all that lay ahead of me connected with the tip of Sumatra! It was indeed a pious hope to think that anything we had done up to date had 'soaked in'! We were just at the very beginning of the most difficult period I had with Winston during the whole of the war. It was all connected with our future policy for the defeat of Japan, and need never have arisen had fate allowed us to look into the future and to realize that Japan would collapse as early as it did. Not being able to crystal gaze we had to plan a strategy for the British part in the final operation against Japan as soon as the defeat of Germany made it possible to deploy forces in this theatre. Two major alternative strategies were open to us:

The first consisted of operations based on India, carried out in Indian Ocean by

South East Asia Command, with the object of liberating Burma, Singapore and possibly Java, Sumatra or Borneo. The second alternative consisted of operations based on Australia, carried out by Naval, Land and Air forces cooperating closely with American and Australian forces in the Pacific. The first of these alternatives was the easiest to stage, but limited itself to the recapture of British possessions without any direct participation with American and Australian forces in the defeat of Japan. I felt that at this stage of the war it was vital that British forces should participate in direct action against Japan in the Pacific. First of all, from a Commonwealth point of view, to prove to Australia our willingness and desire to fight with them for the defence of Australia as soon as the defeat of Germany rendered such action possible. Secondly I felt that it was important that we should cooperate with all three services alongside of the Americans in the Pacific against Japan in the final stages of this war. I therefore considered that our strategy should aim at the liberation of Burma by South East Asia Command based on India, and the deployment of new sea, land and air forces to operate with bases in Australia alongside of forces in the Pacific.

There was a great deal to be said for all the various alternatives and combinations, but they must be discussed from the broadest aspect so as to arrive at a general strategic policy. The trouble was that Winston had now got all his desires centred onto the north tip of Sumatra, just in the same way as he had been set on Trondheim in the early days. He refused to look at any strategy or operation that did not contemplate the capture of the tip of Sumatra as its first stage, or indeed as its only stage, as I never got out of him what his subsequent stage would be. Such enquiries were classified as 'long term projects that crippled initiative'. The situation was complicated by the fact that South East Asia Command was ready at all times to foster attacks on Sumatra, since this would at least lead to the allotment of forces to that command. The Americans, on the other hand, were not over anxious for our arrival in the Pacific to share their victories in the final stages and at a period [when] they were beginning to feel that they could probably defeat Japan on their own. They were more anxious for our cooperation with Chiang Kai-shek by the freeing of Burma.

26 February
A feeling of the lull after a storm, and yet we had a fairly long COS, after which I lunched with Adam and then went home for the weekend.

27 February
Quiet Sunday at home.

28 February
Usual bad Monday! Long COS. Visit from Franklyn, usual briefing for the Cabinet at 6 pm, when Winston was in an impossible mood, with nothing but abuse about everything the Army was doing! Every commander from Jumbo Wilson to last company commander was useless, the organization was useless, the Americans hopeless etc. It was all I could do to contain my temper.

Ramsay then came to dine and gave me some side lights as to how Monty was functioning. He is wandering around visiting troops and failing to get down to basic facts. Shall have to have him up again and kick his backside again!

Have been awarded the Order of Suvorov (first class) by Soviet Government. As far as I can gather this was done by specific order of Marshal Stalin!! My speech in Teheran must have gone deeper than I had thought.

Just before going to bed I received a disturbing wire from Alexander. He evidently is not very happy about bridgehead, proposes to relieve 56th Div by 5th Div and to add extra Div. This at once reacts on number of landing craft available for the cross-Channel operation as if we begin returning those that should go home the bridgehead will be affected! He also proposes to reorganize defence by bringing 8th Army over to Cassino front, in this I think he is right.

29 February

Sent Alex's cable onto the PM, knowing it would cause trouble during day. Then went to COS, from there on to see models of artificial ports. After lunch PM called up and after discussion with him suggested we should meet at 4 pm. We remained till 5.30 pm. I then dined with Ivan Cobbold and at 10 pm had another meeting with PM. This time Ike and Bedell Smith attended. We worded a wire to send to American Chiefs of Staff. Referring to the Anzio beach head, Winston said: 'We hoped to land a wildcat that would tear out the bowels of the Boche. Instead we have stranded a vast whale with its tail flopping about in the water!'

1 March

A fairly short COS. You came up at lunch time, after which I went to receive my baton from the King, after which we attended the King's party. Then back to the WO for a rush, followed by a Cabinet at 6 pm lasting till 8 pm. We again discussed the security measures under which we wish to impose a ban on visitors to the coast. Winston waffling badly! I can't make out what is at the back of it all. I feel it must be Beaverbrook again! I cannot think what else would induce him to take such a line.

Whilst receiving my baton: the King said that he understood that there was some idea about continuing our Pacific operations from Australia instead of India. Had I any appreciations or maps that would explain what was intended. I told him we had just prepared an appreciation. He then said that he would like to see it. I then found myself in a difficult position, if I went further I might be considered as trying to rope in the King's support against the PM!! As I was going out the King again asked for a copy of this appreciation!

2 March

A short COS, after which I asked to see the PM and went round at 12.45. I wanted to discuss the King's request. I told him I wanted his advice and he started talking about quite a different subject! I then returned to my point and told him my trouble about the King's request and that I did not want to go behind his back about it. He then said that he had written a new paper about it, rang the bell to get it and started reading it!! I returned to my point and reminded him that I had come to ask his advice! He replied that he must just read this bit of his new paper to me!! And so we went on fencing! Finally I said to him that his paper would certainly be considered later by the COS but what I wanted was a definite decision as to what action I was to take. I said I proposed to inform the King that the PM had not yet had time to see our paper, and that I thought, owing to our differences of opinion, he should be given some time to consider it and prepare his remarks. He agreed to this procedure.

By then 1.30 pm and I was 15 minutes late for my lunch party which I dashed back to, with General Mathinet, General Ragowski and Bas, Lady Margaret Alexander and Barney. After lunch work and interview with Harry, finishing off with a dinner party for Bas, Pug Ismay and wife and Lady Strathcona and Barney with you of course. Now bed and I am tired.

3 March

A very long COS, for as soon as we had finished our ordinary discussions, Portal asked for the meeting to be cleared of secretaries and explained his difficulties of command of the air force under Eisenhower. PM had been stepping in and muddling things badly as he has been 'crashing in where angels fear to tread'! Apparently Tedder, who was Deputy Chief, is now to assume more direct command, as far as I can see it this can only be done by chucking out Leigh-Mallory [C-in-C, Allied Expeditionary Air Force]. I do not know what the final result will be.

Then I had to discuss the very difficult problem which is brewing up, and in which the PM is trying at present to frame up the War Cabinet against the Chiefs of Staff Committee. It is all about the future Pacific strategy, it looks very serious and may well lead to the resignation of the Chiefs of Staff Committee. I am shattered by the present condition of the PM. He has lost all balance and is in a very dangerous mood. Army Council meeting. In evening the Weeks and Bannermans came to dine.

4 March

After the COS I came back for lunch with you in the flat and then we motored home together.

5 March

A quiet Sunday at home together.

6 March

An early start. During the COS we discussed how to handle the PM in the bad mood he has got into concerning the future plans for the war against Japan. We are preparing a reply to the desperate paper he has produced, and on Wednesday after dinner we are to have a meeting with him. He is to bring his chorus of 'Yes' men (Eden, Attlee, Oliver Lyttelton and Leathers) with him. It will be a gloomy evening and one during which it will be hard to keep one's temper. Cabinet at 7 pm which was luckily a short one.

In classifying these four statesmen as 'Yes' men I was considering them from the point of view of Pacific strategy. None of them had given any deep thought to the matter, had, in fact, only scratched the surface of the problem, as was palpable from their remarks, and as for Leathers; from what I had seen of him no matter what he might have found in scratching the surface he would have continued to trim his sails to whatever wind Winston blew. Somehow the presence of these four 'colleagues' of Winston's at those discussions always infuriated me and put me into a bad temper from the start. It was so palpable that they were brought along by him to support him, which they proceeded to do irrespective of the degree of lunacy connected with some of Winston's proposals. It must be remembered that the war had been going on for several years and tempers were becoming distinctly frayed.

7 March

Most of our COS meeting was devoted to preparing notes for tomorrow evening's meeting with the PM concerning the South East Asia strategy. He has produced the worst paper I have seen him write yet. Trying to make a case for an attack on the top of the island of Sumatra! He compared this plan to our outline plan for the defeat of Japan operating with Americans and Australians from Australia through New Guinea towards Philippines, Formosa etc. He has now taken Eden, Attlee and Oliver Lyttelton in tow, none of whom understand anything about it all, but who are useful as they are prepared to agree with him! We shall, I feel, have a royal row about this matter.

In the afternoon I ran the usual monthly Selection Board. After that Macmillan came to see me and we concerted as to how we could best save Jumbo Wilson from the PM's wrath! He is angry with him as he does not feel he is having sufficient control over him and will not recognize his inter-allied position. I foresee untold trouble over this.

The whole trouble was due to the fact that old Jumbo Wilson was not as pliable in Winston's hands as Alex would have been. Wilson was a tough old specimen and he just let Winston's abuse run over him like water rolls off a duck's back! The only thing that worried me was that I was not quite certain how far Macmillan would cooperate with me in saving Wilson. I felt that he might well be more inclined to cooperate with Winston in getting him out.

8 March

An unpleasantly heavy day! First a COS meeting where we discussed papers prepared to counter the PM's wild statements about the Pacific strategy. Then a long meeting with MS, followed by one with S of S on the question of appointing Loch as MGO in India. Back to lunch to meet Swayne for a final talk with him before he starts for India as Chief of Staff. At 3.30 pm interview with Lord Moran who is worried about Winston's latest attempts to start off wandering again whilst he does not think his health is up to it, wanted my assistance to stop him. At 4 pm interview with King of Greece, who wishes Greek brigade to be moved to Italy as soon as possible, and who is worried by various guerilla factions in Greece. Back for meeting with QMG and DMO to discuss relative merits of India as opposed to Australia from an administrative point of view, as a base for operations in South Pacific.

At 6 pm Cabinet meeting to discuss security arrangements for Overlord (cross Channel operation). Winston in a hopeless mood, incapable of taking any real decision. We finished by leaving the two main difficulties, the diplomatic channels and the coastal belt ban, undecided. Back to dinner for more work immediately after it, and finally at 10 pm off for our meeting with the PM on the Pacific strategy.

The meeting consisted of the PM, who had brought with him to support him Attlee, Eden, Oliver Lyttelton and Leathers! Our party consisted of Chiefs of Staff. Portal as usual not too anxious to argue against PM, and dear old Cunningham so wild with rage that he hardly dared let himself speak!! I therefore had to do most of the arguing and for 2½ hours, from 10 pm to 12.30 am I went at it hard arguing with the PM and 4 Cabinet Ministers. The arguments of the latter were so puerile that it made me ashamed to think they were Cabinet Ministers!* It was only too evident that they did not know their subject, had not read the various papers connected with it, and had purely been brought along to support Winston! And damned badly they did it too! I had little difficulty in dealing with any of the arguments they put forward. Finally we had succeeded in getting the PM to agree to reconnaissances of Australia being carried out as a possible base for future action and we had got him to realize that his plans for the defeat of Japan must go beyond the mere capture of the tip of Sumatra.

9 March

A fairly short COS followed by an interview with S of S to give him results of previous day's work and of visit of King of Greece. After lunch, which I had with the Boiler Makers' Club [the Worshipful Order of Boiler Makers], I saw Lumsden, before his departure for Australia and Burrows before leaving for Moscow. I then attended sherry party at Nepalese Embassy.

10 March

I was sent for before COS by PM who wanted to discuss most recent intercept

---

*This sentence censored by Bryant. Cf. *Triumph in the West* (London: Collins, 1959), p. 163.

of Kesselring's latest appreciation of the situation! A most useful document giving his outlook on the whole of the fighting in Italy. PM then told me that he had decided after all to allow the 'visitors ban' to be imposed!! A triumph after the long battle I had with him. After lunch cine films taken of me with 'Salute the Soldier' campaign message [about savings]. In evening a very useful visit by Monty to tell me how he was getting on with his preparations for the attack. He is making good headway in making plans, and equally successful in making enemies as far as I can see! I have to spend a great deal of my time soothing off some of these troubles.

11 March

Adam came to lunch after the COS committee and we had a long talk together. I then drove home for the weekend.

12 March

A quiet Sunday at home.

13 March

Faced again with the PM's restlessness! He now wants to go to Bermuda to meet the President on the 25th of this month! There is nothing special that we want to discuss as Chiefs of Staff. In fact, we do not want to meet American Chiefs until we have arrived at some form of agreement with the PM about the Pacific Strategy. Medically it is all wrong that he should go, but Moran has not got the guts to stop him! Cabinet at 6.30 pm. PM has now got the Joint Planners with him to discuss the Pacific strategy, heaven knows what he is up to, and what trouble he is brewing for us tomorrow!!

14 March

Apparently PM is now prepared to put off the date of departure to 31st March, but still hopes to go to Bermuda. I had another interview with Moran yesterday, to try and stop the PM on medical grounds. He tells me that he is writing to the PM to tell him that there are 3 good reasons why he should not go:

a) he may become a permanent invalid if he does,

b) owing to his very recent go of pneumonia he is quite likely to get another if he exposes himself to the hardships and fatigues of a journey and

c) he is liable to bring on a heart attack.

However, as he is intent on escaping from the minor worries of parliamentary life, etc, he may well risk all for some peace.

Russian operations continue to go well. Just heard from Alexander that Freyberg's attack is to be launched tonight. Sirens have just been blown for another air raid, but so far no gunfire.

15 March

The Germans are in a bad way in South Russia. I have said all along that there could be no military reasons to justify their strategy in south Russia, and that I could only account for their actions by attributing them to Hitler's orders or to political reasons connected with Rumania. Well, it looks now as if the Germans are about to pay the penalty for their faulty strategy!

Jumbo Goschen [Col. Commandant RHA] came to lunch, a great joy to see him again, he has a wonderful outlook on life which always does me good to come into contact with. Spent the afternoon putting finishing touches to my Trafalgar Square speech for the opening ceremony of the 'Salute the Soldier' campaign.

16 March

We had the Planners in our meeting this morning and discussed with them the instructions the PM gave them on Monday night concerning planning for the capture of Sumatra. I believe that Winston is softening fast. He sent me and the DMI separate minutes drawing our attention to the fact that Freyberg's name had been spelt Freyburg in this morning's intelligence reports! This evening went to see the new Anglo-American Tunis film, it is on the whole disappointing, and could have been made much better.

17 March

On conclusion of our COS meeting we were sent for by the PM to discuss latest American moves of their forces through the Pacific, which have been speeded up by several months in view of their recent successes with Marshall and Admiralty islands. He then informed us that he had discovered a new island just west of Sumatra, I think it is called something like Simmular [Simeuluë]. He had worked out that the capture of this island, when once developed, would answer as well as the top of Sumatra and would require far less strength!! However, by the time he had asked Portal his view he had discovered that from the point of view of the air he had little hope of building up his aerodromes and strength before being bumped off. From Cunningham he found out that from a naval point of view, with the Jap fleet at Singapore he was courting disaster!!! Both Portal and Cunningham were *entirely* correct, and I began to wonder whether I was Alice in Wonderland, or whether I was really fit for a lunatic asylum! I am honestly getting very doubtful about his balance of mind and it just gives me the cold shivers. I don't know where we are or where we are going as regards our strategy, and I just cannot get him to face the true facts! It is a ghastly situation.

In afternoon tried to comfort Neame as to the lack of jobs for him. Then Army Council meeting followed by Lewin to dinner.

18 March

Just as we were finishing our COS, we were told that the PM wanted to see us.

This was to inform us that he proposed to wire to the President that we should go to Bermuda for Easter, and that we were to have a Combined Chiefs of Staff meeting there! As there is nothing for us to meet about, and [on] the Pacific strategy we have up to now failed to arrive at an agreement with the Prime Minister, I do not see what we can do! He insists on going however, and proposes to fly from there to Gibraltar and then on to Italy, which will probably be the end of him! Lunched with Adam and then went home for the weekend.

19 March
Quiet Sunday at home.

20 March
One of the worst of Cabinet meetings with Winston in one of his worst moods! Nothing that the Army does can be right and he did nothing but belittle its efforts in the eyes of the whole Cabinet. I cannot stick any more meetings like it! He has now produced an impossible document on the Pacific strategy in which he is overriding our opinions and our advice!

21 March
We discussed at the COS how best to deal with Winston's last impossible document. It is full of false statements, false deductions and defective strategy. We cannot accept it as it stands, and it would be better if we all three resigned rather than accept his solution. We are telling him that it will be essential for us to put in a written reply, but that we can if he likes discuss with him his paper before we put in our reply. I don't know how tiresome he will insist in being. He may perhaps see some reason, otherwise we may well be faced with a most serious situation.

In the afternoon went to Farnborough to see experimental models of aeroplanes, including some of the new jet propelled planes.

22 March
A very tiring day. First of all COS from 10.30 to 1.15 with a long discussion with Planners concerning the latest appreciation by Wilson for the abolition of Anvil [operation in Southern France]. Then Eisenhower and Bedell Smith came up to discuss their report, which agreed with what we wanted. I now hope that at last all may be well and that the American Chiefs of Staff will at last see some wisdom!

After lunch I had a series of interviews, and finally we had a meeting with the PM to tell him what we had settled. He was in a good mood, and all went well, beyond wasting an hour with interruptions of every description. Had we seen the latest wire to Stalin? What was happening in Hungary ? Why would we use the word 'intensive' when the correct word was 'intense'? He had had a lovely view of last night's raid from the roof. He was going to broadcast on Sunday night. What a strain we had been having for the last 3 years. Why could not Wilson be more intelligent? etc, etc, etc. All these sandwiched between each paragraph of the minutes he was looking through! Thank heaven Roosevelt cannot meet him in Bermuda so our trip next week is off!

23 March

The situation gets more hopeless than ever, Wingate is now wiring direct to the PM through Mountbatten who expresses no definite opinion on the proposals put forward by Wingate. It looks as if the strain of operations had sent Wingate off his head. Meanwhile American wire stating that we should push on in Burma and give up all thoughts of Sumatra. PM's reaction was to wire direct to Mountbatten saying if you will conform to American requirements in Burma I shall back you in Sumatra and see that you are allowed to carry out the operation!!! We stopped that wire, but heaven knows where we are going. I feel like a man chained to the chariot of a lunatic!! It is getting beyond my powers to control him.

This afternoon Martel came to see me about the necessity of appointing a senior general in charge of the Armoured Corps, it was only too clear that in his mind he was the one man for the job! This evening both Kennedy and Bevan came to dine.

24 March

Attended Mansion House lunch to open 'Salute the Soldier Week'. P.J. Grigg and Monty made excellent speeches. After lunch I had to go round to St John's Wood to do another recording with Lord Kindersley of my statement for the 'Salute the Soldier' campaign. I then finally went out to dine with Riddell-Webster beyond Richmond. Tomorrow I have my Trafalgar Square speech to make, and I am not looking forward to it at all!

25 March

A trying day! I started with the usual COS, then rushed back to the WO, and at 11.45 left with 60 Despatch Rider escort (!) for Trafalgar Square. There I was met by the Mayor of Westminster who introduced me to the Lord Mayor. We then started the ceremony and the Mayor of Westminster introduced the Lord Mayor who then introduced me. I then made my 'Salute the Soldier' speech. I then had to lunch at the Savoy with both Mayors, and again more speeches. Finally escaped at 3 pm, and collected you and the Pooks for a short trip to the zoo. From there on home.

Trafalgar Square is certainly not an attractive place to speak in! We had a large plat-form from which we looked down on some 3 or 4 hundred people below us, but the life of London went on all around. Buses rumbling round, taxis and cars hooting, children playing, women gossiping etc, etc. Not a very inspiring audience to talk to. I cannot believe that either my speech or my 60 despatch riders did much towards promoting national economy!

26 March
Quiet Sunday at home.

27 March
Early start. Table crammed with telegrams. News not too good. Wingate report-ed killed. Marripan [Manipur] threatened by the Japs. Alexander stuck at Cassino. Marshall insisting on doing Anvil operation, etc, etc! Left at 12 noon to lunch with Eisenhower at Bushey Park [Herts] where he was lunching the War Cabinet. After lunch conference with Ike concerning Marshall's last wire. Back to London to rush for Cabinet which lasted till 8.30 pm. Then Monty to dine. He was in very good form, and brought all his proposed plans for the offensive – I liked his plans.

28 March
After the morning's COS we were sent for by the PM to discuss the latest American wire about Mediterranean operations and our proposed reply. We found him in a desperately tired mood. I am afraid that he is losing ground rapidly. He seems quite incapable of concentrating for a few minutes on end, and keeps wandering dangerously. He kept yawning and saying he felt desperately tired.

If I had been told at that time that Winston would be still Prime Minister of this country in 1955, I would have refused to believe it! I had been working closely with him practically since the start of the war, and had been watching him closely. I had seen a very definite deterioration during the last 6 months, and even a rapid decline since the last pneumonia attack. I began to feel at that time that the stupendous burden he had been carrying so valiantly throughout the war was gradually crushing him. With his marvellous vitality he carried on in a marvellous way, but it had become more difficult than ever to work with him. When we take into account that I was also getting a little stale, it is to be marvelled that we did not finish with an almighty row before the end of the war!

29 March
A very difficult COS when we discussed the production of landing craft for the Pacific in 1945. Third Sea Lord, Hurcomb [Transportation], and Sinclair all attended. It is one of those awful jigsaw problems when it becomes very difficult to fit in all the right pieces.

I then had Jack Collins and Crerar back to lunch. He [Crerar] is just back from Italy and is taking over the Canadian Army. It has been a difficult move to accomplish!! I have had to get rid of Andy McNaughton, give Crerar sufficient war experience in Italy, and get Monty to accept him with very limited active experience. All has now been accomplished with much anguish and many difficulties, but I have full confidence that Crerar will not let me down. I have, however, I am afraid, lost a very good friend in the shape of Andy McNaughton. I only hope that he may be able to realize the true situation to rise high enough for me not to lose his friendship.

30 March

Telegram from Dill showing that the American Chiefs of Staff are again going to fail to realize what the real strategic situation is in Italy. An easy afternoon and evening.

31 March

Telegram from American COS came in, quite impossible to accept. Again arguing that after uniting Anzio bridgehead and main front we should go on the defensive in Italy, and start a new front in Southern France. They fail to realize that the forces available do not admit of two fronts in the Mediterranean! I am afraid that our Joint Staff Mission in Washington are now only acting as a PO [Post Office] and not expressing views and opinions of their own.

In the afternoon I received an interesting letter from Wilson and Alexander. Evidently, just as I suspected, Freyberg has been fighting with a casualty conscious mind. He has been sparing the NZ infantry and hoping to accomplish results by use of heavy bombers and infantry, without risking too much infantry. As a result he has failed. In the evening saw Kenneth Anderson just back from Italy, who was very interesting and confirmed all my impressions as to Freyberg's weakness and Clark's unsuitability for an Army Command, etc. This evening Kennedys, Burrows and Diana Charlesworth to dinner.

In reading the above remarks about Freyberg it must be made clear that they in no way reflect on his own dash and ability to command. He had already more than proved these qualities in North Africa. The situation was now somewhat changed. The New Zealanders had suffered their full share of casualties for such a small country. It had recently been frequently impressed on Freyberg by the NZ Government that it was most desirable to avoid unnecessary heavy casualties in future. The war was evidently drawing near its close, and there was a reluctance to go on risking the lives of gallant men who had already risked them so frequently. All these considerations were weighing heavily on Freyberg and making him loath to risk heavy losses. Unfortunately it is hard in war to make omelettes without breaking eggs, and it is often in trying to do so that we break most eggs!

1 April

Had hoped to get off without a COS meeting, but found it necessary to meet in order to form our new reply to the last American note about the South of France invasion. Marshall is quite hopeless. I have seldom seen a poorer strategist! He cannot see beyond the end of his nose. The strategy he advocates can only result in two months without any operations in the Mediterranean, just at the very moment when we require them most owing to the date of the cross Channel operation. Drove Diana and Barney back to their house on my way home where I arrived in time for a late lunch.

2 April

Quiet Sunday spent at home.

3 April

Nasty rush of telegrams to deal with on my arrival at WO. Then busy COS finishing off our wire back to Americans. Cabinet from 5.30 to 8 pm at which Winston meandered about, talking continuously to say very little, and evidently loving to hear his voice! After dinner another meeting at 10.30 pm! We discussed the construction of 'Landing Ships Tank', and the provision of a Fleet train for the navy in the war against Japan. Meeting comprised PM, Lyttelton, Cherwell, Leathers, Sinclair, Alexander, 3 Chiefs of Staff, Pug and Jacob. We again beat round and round the bush. Cherwell with one thought only namely shipping for home imports! Leathers as slippery as ever and trimming his sails to the wind all the time. Lyttelton with apparently few ideas in his head, but many smiles. PM aged, tired, and failing to really grasp matters. It is a depressing sight to see him gradually deteriorating. I wonder how long he will last, not long enough to see the war through I fear.

4 April

I had intended to fly to Netheravon to watch a trial between a 4.2" mortar and 95 mm gun, but the weather was too bad. Consequently attended COS instead, and examined Air Force progress in bombing of launching sites for pilotless planes. In the afternoon Stewart (Canadian) came to see me, and then Budget Loyd, back from Italy where he has been touring round visiting Guards units. He is worried about reinforcements for Guards units, and the necessity to cannibalize.

5 April

Difficulties again with our American friends who still persist in wanting to close down operations in Italy [and] open new ones in South of France, just at the most critical moment. I don't believe they have any tactical or strategical perspective of any kind. Bertie Ramsay came to dine and was interesting concerning the naval preparations for cross Channel operations. At 10.30 had to attend one of those awful evening meetings of the PM. We were kept up till 12.45 am discussing use of heavy bombers in support of invasion of France. He is opposed to Tedder's plan to use them on the railways because he does not think that the results to be achieved will be much and secondly owing to casualties amongst French civilians which must result from it.

6 April

A quiet day on the whole. Went to see Amery in the afternoon again to discuss the value of mountain warfare in Italy. Then had interview with Lyon who is back from a very bold penetration to Singapore where he blew up 7 Japanese ships. He is now just off on a new mission on a larger scale.

7 April

A long day with Monty! At 9 am I paraded at St Paul's School to attend a wonderful day Monty ran to run over all the plans for the coming offensive. He started with some very good opening remarks, then we had Ramsay to explain naval plans and Leigh-Mallory to explain air plans. Lunch followed and after that Bradley and his two Corps Commanders, followed by Dempsey [2nd Army], Bucknall [XXX Corps] and Crocker [I Corps]. Bucknall was very weak, and I am certain quite unfit to command a Corps. After that Monty produced a summing up and the PM turned up and addressed a few remarks to the meeting. He was in a very weepy condition, looking old and lacking a great deal of his usual vitality.

After the meeting P.J. Grigg, Monty and I had an interview with the PM, to get him to face the reduction of formations in the Guards Division, as they can no longer find reinforcements. We had the usual difficulties, as it entailed abolishing the Guards Brigade (Army Tanks). He has been got at by MPs and produced every sort of futile argument against what is an inevitable necessity.

The King of Greece came for a *tête-à-tête* dinner with me. I am sorry for him. His Greek forces are mutinying and the whole of the Greeks are rent by political dissension. He has no Greek he can turn to for advice and help. He was very nice and left early.

8 April

Another difficult COS dealing with last reply from American COS on Mediterranean strategy. They have at last agreed to our policy, but withdrawn their offer of landing craft from Pacific!! This is typical of their methods of running strategy. Although we have agreed that the European theatre must take precedence over the Pacific, yet they use some of their available landing forces as bargaining counters in trying to get their false strategy followed. Left for home after lunch.

9 and 10 April
Spent peaceful Easter and Bank Holiday at home.

11 April
Back to work. Series of telegrams from PM to go through. He wishes to wire to Marshall to make one further attempt to obtain landing craft from the Pacific! In the afternoon Alexander turned up to see me, back from Italy. Whenever I meet him again my first impression is one of marvelling at what a small calibre man he is! He just shatters me, he is floating in the ether with very little realization of what he is doing. And yet the PM has never realized what a small calibre man he is. I discussed Alexander's plan of attack with him. It is not ideal. But he is handicapped by all the nationalities he has to deal with. At 10 pm we had a meeting with the PM attended by Alex. It lasted till 1 am. Our time was spent in going through his telegram to Marshall. Waste of time as I feel certain the reply will be in the negative.

Perhaps I was a little unkind that evening in my remarks on Alex, but he had annoyed me again by being so palpably devoid of any real ideas of his own. Up to now, throughout North Africa, he had been carried on Monty's back and McCreery's efficiency. Now that he had lost both of these he was climbing onto Oliver Leese's back and relying on John Harding's help [Chief of Staff 15th Army Group]. Neither of these were as high class ponies, or as used to first class polo, as the former two had been. I still marvel at Alex: there were so many sterling qualities in him and yet such a ghastly void behind it all.

12 April
A short COS. In afternoon a series of interviews. Wedemeyer to report on results of his visit to Washington and before returning to Mountbatten. Then the WO Scientific advisor to discuss the action of rockets controlled by radar against jet aeroplanes operating in the stratosphere. Followed by Joubert de la Ferté [Deputy Chief of Staff SEAC] to discuss India and Dickie Mountbatten's problems. Finally Willoughby Norrie on the eve of his departure for Algiers to take up his duties as head of Military Mission with Duff Cooper operating with de Gaulle.

13 April
A tiring day. First a long COS at which the Lethbridge Committee attended. They have just been touring the world: Washington, Canada, Honolulu, Fiji, New Zealand, Australia, New Guinea, India, Burma etc, studying the requirements for war against Japan. Their report is very good and provides much food for thought and progress.

After lunch series of interviews. First Symes, back from Burma having been second in command to Wingate, discussed Burma fully with him. Then Sir A.

Rowlands, Indian Civil Department, sent back by Viceroy. Had long discussion with him on Indian internal situation, grain situation, transportation etc, very useful hour spent with him. He was followed by McNarney (Marshall's deputy) and McCloy (Under Sec of State for USA War). Spent an hour with them discussing all fronts and mostly the existing differences of outlook between the British and USA Chiefs of Staff concerning our strategy in the Mediterranean. At 6.30 pm Cabinet to discuss distribution of manpower after defeat of Germany between industry and home development, occupation of Germany, and Japanese war. This lasted till 8.15 pm. Dined with Rollie Charrington at Boodles and at 10.30 pm went on to Defence Committee to discuss air strategy of bombing railway communications in France prior to attack. Am far from convinced that we should not be better employed spending that effort on German aircraft industry. PM scared of casualties to the French entailed by this policy. Meeting lasted till midnight and PM then called me for a private talk till 12.30. Luckily I got him to agree to my having a week's leave!! I feel that I want it badly and for the first time since I have held this job I feel thoroughly stale and almost whacked by the work!

14 April

We had a long COS meeting attended by the Planners at which we discussed the future Pacific strategy and examined the possibility and advantages of a line of advance on an axis from Darwin towards North Borneo. This might give us a chance of running an entirely British Imperial campaign, instead of just furnishing reinforcements for American operations. However, our whole trouble and difficulty in arriving at a conclusion is due to the extremely optimistic American forecast as to their probable rate of advance.

After lunch Davidson [DMI] came for an interview prior to his departure, and a Major Wilkinson just back from Yugoslavia who was very interesting. Unfortunately, whilst he was with me we were sent for by the PM. He had been drafting a reply to the wire he had received from Marshall about the Mediterranean strategy. It was an awful wire! Giving away all we had been fighting for during the past 6 weeks. I had a hard set to with him, and I hope convinced him that it would be a fatal error. He agreed to redraft the wire on our advised line. I only hope that he does so! I am finding these battles with him quite exhausting. I came out of this one quite cooked and feeling dog tired.

15 April

I finished off the COS early and arrived for a late lunch. Seldom have I felt more tired of work and more in need of a rest.

16 April

Sunday spent peacefully at home.

17 April

Arrived back early in office to find myself swamped with telegrams. After COS lunched with PM at 10 Downing St. Eisenhower, Bedell Smith and Alexander were there. The conversation at once again turned to the Mediterranean strategy and to the American Chiefs of Staff's failure to agree with us as to the necessity to press on with operations in Italy without impairing the prospects by preparations for an offensive against Southern France. Eisenhower produced all the arguments we heard the other day, Alexander succeeded in saying the wrong thing most of the time, and I had an unpleasant lunch! After lunch took Alex to the WO to have a talk. I am more and more appalled to see what a small man he is, and how far short he falls of requirements!

Cabinet at 6.30 which lasted till 8.30 pm. Received news that Tom is to go to North Africa on the 26ᵗʰ of this month.

18 April

A long COS at which we had first the Joint Intelligence Committee to discuss German Forces in Europe and their resources available to meet our offensive. Secondly Lord Cherwell and Duncan Sandys to discuss the threat of rockets and pilotless planes on this country. Then, at 12.15 a meeting with PM on ammunition, attended by Alex, Oliver Lyttelton, Duncan Sandys, P.J. Grigg, and Weeks. After lunch Selection Board. Then meeting with Billet, the American Director of Military Intelligence. I found him well on the spot and a good man at his job. Finally dinner for Birleys and Cranbornes.

19 April

At last all our troubles about Anvil (the South France invasion) are over. We have got the Americans to agree, but have lost the additional landing craft they were prepared to provide. History will never forgive them for bargaining equipment against strategy and for trying to blackmail us into agreeing with them by holding the pistol of withdrawing craft at our heads!

This afternoon had an interview with Wilkinson just back from Tito's forces in Yugoslavia and then Downe commanding the Indian Airborne Division, with plans for attack of Burma from the air. Am now off for one of those awful night meetings with the PM. We are to discuss the recent Egyptian crisis and the bombing of French railways in preparation for invasion. PM is afraid we are killing too many Frenchmen.

Later: A terrible meeting from 10.30 to just on 1 am!! First, as regards bombing of railways, the matter put back for another week's consideration, at a time when we are within 5 weeks of the attack and definite decisions are required. Secondly, Egypt. There gain a week by delay so as to clear the Greek situation. But the PM's best remark of the evening was that 'King Farouk was wallowing like a sow in the trough of luxury!' This was the only nugget of the evening – otherwise PM tired, lifeless and lacking decision.

20 April

A long COS with meeting of the Planners. We discussed again the Egyptian crisis and a very poor report we had from the Middle East. Tom came to lunch, being up in town to collect kit before starting for North Africa. Another evening Cabinet at 6.30 pm to 8.30 pm, mainly taken up with the Egyptian situation again!

21 April

Our COS was mainly concerned with arranging for subversive operations in Hungary and pressing on with the building of all the harbour equipment for the landings in France. Adam came to lunch and we had a long talk together. An Army Council meeting in the afternoon and the settling of all final details before my departure for Scotland to stop with Ivan Cobbold at Cairnton.

30 April

On the 22ⁿᵈ I flew up to Dundee in the morning, early, taking Ronnie Weeks with me. We spent the day visiting the 52ⁿᵈ Division [mountain warfare] and finally finished up at Cairnton where I found Ivan Cobbold. I had a heavenly week there fishing all day, leaving the house at 9.30 in the morning and not returning till after 11 pm except for about an hour at lunch and at dinner. I caught 12 salmon, but lost 9 and was fishing badly. I feel infinitely better.

This morning took off from Dyce aerodrome (Aberdeen) at 10 am and landed at Hendon 12.15 pm. Fast flight with wind behind us. Lunched at White's with Ivan and then came back to the flat for work so as to start square tomorrow.

1 May

Very reluctantly, I started work again! First a COS meeting at 10.30. Then at 12 noon the opening meeting of the conference of Empire PMs. Met Fraser (PM of NZ) at the door, who was very friendly and nice. Was then introduced to Curtin (PM of Australia) and could not make out which of his eyes was looking at me! Not an impressive head to look at sideways – there is no back to it! Mackenzie King (Canada) also very friendly. But by far the most attractive of the lot was dear old Smuts, just the same as ever and with the same dear refreshing outlook on life. A meeting with various polite speeches, and then photographs in the garden of 10 Downing Street, followed by a glass of sherry.

After lunch I had an hour with Wilson, who had just flown home for discussions on future strategy in the Mediterranean. At 5.30 pm another Dominion PMs' conference. Winston spoke for 1½ hours on the strategic situation in Europe. He was far from being at his best, and gave a pathetically bad survey. Dull, lifeless and missing the main points. He looked very old and tired, and in my opinion is failing fast. I wonder if he lasts another 3 months?

2 May

A desperate day! COS at 10.30 which we had to rush to finish before 11.30 when we again met the Dominion PMs. I had to give them a survey of the European Theatre. It took me about an hour, but seemed to keep them quiet and dealt with their questions. We did not finish the meeting till 1.30 pm. Had a rushed lunch, and then walked back to the office where I had half an hour with AG. Then went through briefs for Cabinet and at 4 pm Jumbo Wilson came to propound his various plans. He remained till 5.30 when I dashed off to the Cabinet. This was attended by Dominion PMs. My usual statement on the military situation was drawn out to an hour by continuous interruptions! The Cabinet finished with another long discussion on the bombing strategy of attack on French railways and killing of Frenchmen. More waffling about and vacillating politicians unable to accept the consequences of war, etc. Cabinet lasted till 8.30 pm. Then dashed home to dine with Jumbo Wilson and take him off to a meeting with the PM to explain all his various alternative plans. We finished up by again getting onto the bombing of the French railways, and were kept up till 1.30 am. Shall not get to bed before 2 am!

3 May

Another unpleasant day! Started with a COS at 10.30 at which Jumbo Wilson attended to discuss future plans for Mediterranean. Then Imperial meeting with Dominion PMs. Smuts opened with long statement expressing his doubts as to advisability of departing from Mediterranean strategy for cross Channel operation. After that Fraser (NZ) made somewhat of an ass of himself and got ticked off by Winston. Meeting broke up at 1.15. I then had lunch and dashed off to Franklyn's Home Forces HQ to give a talk on the world situation. Back to WO for a rush of work followed by another Imperial Conference from 5.30 to 7.30 pm. Then Basil, Cynthia, Adam, Dorothy, Boyle and Barney dining with us, you having turned up just before dinner. At 10.30 pm another meeting with PM on bombing of railways which lasted till 1.15 am!! Winston gradually coming round to the policy.

4 May

A long COS with a series of items and interviews with the Planners. Then lunch at Claridges with Bruce (High Commissioner for Australia) in honour of Curtin. I sat between Lord Camrose and Sir Edward Peacock. In the afternoon I collected you at the flat and we went to the Downing Street sherry party. Unfortunately raining so that we were unable to be in the garden.

After dinner another of Winston's awful meetings. This time on the provision of the synthetic ports and preparations for them and on methods of dealing with underwater obstacles. PM quite exhausted, the meeting meandered on, lasting till after midnight, when it might easily have been finished in ½ an hour. Hopeless waste of time!

5 May

Blamey (Australian C-in-C) attended COS and we discussed possible future operations from Australia and size of effort which Australia could support. Blamey is not an impressive specimen. He looks entirely drink sodden and somewhat repulsive. Lunched with you at 10 Downing Street to meet Mr Fraser (PM of NZ). In afternoon attended Australian sherry party. I finished off by going to see a play with you.

6 May

The day was spent in trying to get level with some of the work I had been unable to get through during the week. In the evening motored to Chequers with you for the weekend. The party consisted of Mackenzie King (PM of Canada), the PM of South Rhodesia [Godfrey Huggins], Lord Cherwell, Winston's brother, Mary and Sarah. We had a walk with Clemmie before dinner, and a film after dinner. Got to bed by midnight.

7 May

In the morning we went to church with Clemmie and Mary. After lunch did some work and after tea we went for a walk. Dinner was followed by the usual film after which Winston took me down to the little study where the secretaries work. There he sat by the fire and drank his soup. He looked very old and very tired. He said Roosevelt was not well and that he was no longer the man that he had been, this he said also applied to himself (Winston). He said he could still always sleep well, eat well and especially drink well! but that he no longer jumped out of bed the way he used to, and felt as if he would be quite content to spend the whole day in bed. I have never yet heard him admit that he was beginning to fail. He then said some very nice things about the excellent opinion that the whole Defence Committee and War Cabinet had of me and that they had said that we could not have a better CIGS. Got to bed by 1am.

Considering the difficult times I had had recently with Winston, I appreciated tremendously his kindness in passing on these remarks to me at the end of our talk. I did not often get any form of appreciation of my work from him, and therefore treasured it all the more on the rare occasions. He was an astounding mixture, could drive you to complete desperation and to the brink of despair for weeks on end, and then would ask you to spend a couple of hours or so alone with him and would produce the most homely and attractive personality. All that unrelenting tension was temporarily relaxed, he ceased to work himself into one fury or another, and you left him with the feeling that you would do anything within your power to help him carry the stupendous burden he had shouldered.

8 May

Made an early start, and back in WO by 9.30. Portal and Cunningham away on leave and absent from COS. Very busy afternon followed by dinner at Greenwich attended by Curtin, Fraser, Smuts, Attlee, Amery, Bruce, Leathers, Grigg etc. Cunningham and I had to rush back to attend meeting with PM at 11 pm to discuss our directive for Mountbatten. Winston terribly tired and very peevish, required great patience to handle him, but got what we wanted through. Now 1.30 am, sleepy and off to bed.

9 May

Our COS was mainly concerned with working out strength of force that could be deployed from Australia after Germany had been defeated. In the evening attended dinner at 10 Downing St for Dominion PMs. A series of speeches again from PM, Mackenzie King, Curtin, Fraser, Smuts, Sir Firoz Khan Noon [Indian Representative, British Cabinet] and Huggins [Southern Rhodesia]. Smuts as usual made a first class speech. Judging by the general atmosphere the Imperial bonds seem at present to be strong.

10 May

A day of continuous rush and little to show for it. At 10.45 COS meeting till 11.30, and then a rush to the Guildhall to arrive in time for Freedom of the City ceremony for Curtin and Fraser. Then lunch at the Mansion House with two more speeches by Fraser and Curtin. The latter made two excellent speeches but Fraser was inclined to be too long winded. Back to WO to interview Sosnkowski, who wanted to know why Polish evacuees were being held up in Gibraltar, why we would not enlist in British Forces Polish Jews who left Polish Forces, why casualties from Italy could not be reported home quicker, why he could not be allowed out of the country to visit Italy in spite of the special rule barring all movement till after invasion of France, etc etc. He was followed by Blamey (Australia), who remained a full 1½ hours! We discussed many of the Pacific problems. I found him easy to get on with, but not inspiring!

After that dinner at the Ritz to entertain Dominion Military, Naval and Air representatives. I suppose this all serves some purpose in welding Imperial bonds, but I doubt it at times. All these speeches strike me as being so much hot air, or perhaps better, so much alcoholic vapour, which goes to everyone's head, producing a beatific and complacent attitude of wonderful imperial understanding. But how much of all this remains there in the bleak reality of the morning after?

11 May

Nothing of importance at COS. Lunched with Sir John and Lady Anderson. Guests were Smuts, Duchess of Northumberland, Lord and Lady Camrose. During afternoon had interviews with Puttick (NZ Chief of Staff), spent an hour with him discussing the future of New Zealand forces, garrisoning of Pacific isles near NZ and Australia, supply of NZ officers to British forces etc.

After him Brig Salisbury Jones, our Liaison officer in South Africa. Rollie Charrington came to dine, seems to have entirely recovered and was in great form.

Tonight at 11 pm the Italian attack [Alexander's spring offensive, DIADEM, involving attack on Gustav Line and Monte Cassino] starts. I pray to God that it may be successful. A great deal depends on it.

12 May

Attack started up to time, but no news all day! I am now (11.30 pm) awaiting a message which is being deciphered. It is very trying having to wait for this information.

At morning COS Blamey (Aust C-in-C) and Puttick (NZ Chief of Staff) came to discuss future operations from Australia. Blamey looked as if he had the most frightful 'hangover' from a debauched night! His eyes were swimming in alcohol! However we made considerable progress and have now got a forecast of the total British, Australian and New Zealand forces which could be made available. I then went to lunch with Rollie Charrington at his brewery and went round the whole brewery with him. Came back to WO for interview with Koenig, de Gaulle's emissary here. He was the defender of Bir El Hachim, seemed quite pleasant and ready to cooperate. Preparation for cross Channel operation going on full blast, and date drawing very near!

13 May

A very short COS after which I escaped and returned home for lunch.

14 May

Spent Sunday quietly at home and photographed marsh tit.

Those 2 hours in a hide close to a marsh tit at its nest made Winston and the war disappear in a cloud of smoke. It was like rubbing Aladdin's lamp, I was transplanted to a fairyland and returned infinitely refreshed and recreated.

15 May

Went straight from home to St Paul's School to attend Eisenhower's final run over plans for cross-Channel offensive. The King, PM, Smuts, and all Chiefs of Staff were present. The main impression I gathered was that Eisenhower was a swinger and no real director of thought, plans, energy or direction! Just a coordinator – a good mixer, a champion of inter-allied cooperation, and in those respects few can hold a candle to him. But is that enough? Or can we not find all qualities of a commander in one man? Maybe I am getting too hard to please, but I doubt it. Monty made excellent speech. Bertie Ramsay indifferent, and overwhelmed by all his own difficulties. Spaatz [US VIIIth Army Air Force] read every word of a poor statement. Bert Harris [Bomber Command] told us how well he might have won this war if it had not been for the handicap imposed by the existence of the two other services!! Sholto Douglas [Fighter Command] seemed disappointed at the smallness of his task, and so was I. Then Humfrey Gale and Graham on Administration, followed by Grasett on civil control of France.

A useful run through. [The] King made a few well chosen remarks. After lunch he presented the CB to Bradley and two other decorations. Back to WO and finished up with Monty dining quietly with me. He was in very good form and bearing his responsibilities well.

16 May

A busy day which started with a fairly full COS at which we considered most recent evidence of German rocket bombs and pilotless planes together with the results of our counter measures. At 12.45 a final meeting of the Imperial Conference to hear speeches of all the various PMs and to see the final document signed. You turned up to lunch, and after a quick visit to my dentist we started off for the Russian embassy to receive the Order of Suvorov. Admiral Tovey and Air Vice Marshal Harris also recipients. Ambassador Gousev made a small speech, and Tovey answered for all of us. After presentation some vodka and caviar.

Then back to WO to be briefed for Cabinet at 5.30 which was attended by Dominion PMs. Luckily the Italian news continues to be good. Finally Crerar came to dine and we talked shop the whole evening.

17 May

Started with usual COS, then PM sent for me. He was in bed, obviously very tired having been up till 3 am at a dinner with Anthony Eden! He was very disturbed at statements made by Humfrey Gale and Graham at the Monday meeting connected with the 1000 clerks of the 3rd echelon and the fact that the invasion catered for one lorry for every 5 men. It took me ¾ hour to pacify him and I cursed Humfrey Gale and Graham and all their ancestors before I had finished! Pongo came to lunch. I then had interviews with Keith Murdoch of the Australian press, and with Hobo [Hobart] concerning all his accessory armoured vehicles. Finally a dinner party for Bedell Smith, Duke de Luna of Spanish Embassy, and Ivan Cobbold, most of the time was spent discussing fishing.

18 May

Another day of continuous work. First a long COS when we had a meeting of the Planners in order to try and settle a final Pacific strategy to put up to the PM. The problem is full of difficulties, although the strategy is quite clear. Unfortunately the right course to follow is troubled by personalities, questions of command, vested interests, inter-allied jealousies, etc etc. Curtin and MacArthur are determined to stand together, support each other and allow no outside interference. Winston is determined Mountbatten must be given some operation to carry out, Andrew Cunningham is equally determined that Mountbatten should not control the Eastern Fleet. Americans wish to gather all laurels connected with Pacific fighting, Winston is equally determined that we should not be tied to the apron strings of the Americans!! How on earth are we to steer a straight course between all these snags and difficulties?

Lunched at Dorchester with Australian Club, speeches by Duke of Gloucester, Winston, Curtin and Bruce, none of them very good. From 3 to 4 pm, meeting with PM, Eden, Bedell Smith and the Chiefs of Staff to decide how to handle de Gaulle before the invasion whilst still retaining secrecy. Eden as usual intended to soften and allow de Gaulle's new Republican Committee to be recognized. Back to the office for interview with American correspondent and Yugoslav General together with Maclean. Then another Cabinet meeting from 7 pm to 8.30 pm!! Finally John Kennedy and his wife to dine and to look at bird books.

19 May

Thank heaven the Italian attack is going well [the Gustav Line had been broken, and Monte Cassino finally taken], and it should play its part in holding formations in Italy and keeping them away from the Channel. At any rate we have proved that Marshall and the American Chiefs of Staff were all wrong arguing that the Italians would retire before we could attack them and leave only some 6 divs to cover their rear, leaving us with large forces stranded in Italy which we could not engage! Such a withdrawal may be forced on them later but not I hope until we have knocked the stuffing out of them.

This morning the Canadian Chiefs of Staff attended our meeting and we discussed the probable Canadian effort in this war after the defeat of Germany. I then lunched with Meinertzhagen who very kindly gave me some of the bird books which he no longer wanted. I found him a very interesting specimen. In the afternoon an Army Council meeting followed by a quiet evening which I felt I wanted badly!

I referred that evening in my diary to an attitude of Marshall which I had not previously mentioned. One of his arguments for withdrawing troops from this [Mediterranean] theatre was that the enemy would now start withdrawing forces from this front and leave rear guard forces covering this movement. Had this happened we should have been left with some redundant forces in Italy. This was quite a sound argument strategically, but it failed entirely to take Hitler's mentality into account. Nowhere yet had he retired voluntarily on any front and in not doing so had committed grave strategic blunders which led to his ultimate defeat. First Stalingrad, which resulted in the loss of Von Paulus's army of 90,000 men and countless casualties, secondly Tunisia with the loss of 250,000 men and much equipment, shipping and material, thirdly the Dnieper River Bend where he might have materially increased his reserves by shortening his front. It was not in Hitler's character to retire, he certainly would not give up Italy unless he was driven out of it, and he would fight against such a contingency. I therefore felt quite safe in arguing to Marshall that Hitler would not withdraw forces out of Italy unless we went on the defensive and started removing formations, in which case he could bring [them] on interior lines to counter these moves to meet the new threats. It was satisfactory to find that the reactions to Alex's offensive proved that my argument had been right.

20 May

Alexander's news of Italian fighting continues to be excellent. Thank heaven for it! I have staked a great deal on the Italian campaign in all our arguments with the Americans. I felt throughout that we had wonderful opportunities of inflicting a real telling defeat on the Germans which would be worth anything in connection with the cross Channel operation. The only danger was that the Americans should have their way and plan to withdraw forces from Italy at the critical moment. They nearly succeeded in ruining our strategy, and now I pray God we may be allowed to reap the full benefits of our strategy! Slipped home for lunch.

21 May

A quiet Sunday at home.

22 May

Back to work, and a long COS where we met the Australians (Blamey and his sailor and airman) to discuss sending a reconnaissance party to Australia. Blamey in complete agreement, so much so that we shall now be accused by Winston of settling things without his agreement and behind his back! Finished day with a long Cabinet lasting from 6 pm to 8 pm. Then dined with Rollie Charrington.

23 May

Meeting with Joint Intelligence Committee and long discussion with them as to situation in France as regards accumulation of German divisions to meet invasion. Close on 60 divisions accumulated!

Alex's offensive from Anzio bridgehead started this morning together with offensive in Liri Valley. I am rather afraid that he has launched bridgehead offensive too soon, and that he may not reap full benefits of favourable situation confronting him. However he alone can judge being on the spot. At 1.30 pm flew from Hendon, eating lunch on the way, to Oxford to inspect the Glider Pilot Regiment of which I am Colonel. They are a wonderful lot of men. They gave a demonstration of 20 Hansa Gliders taking off in 14 minutes, and subsequently the gliders landing in 8 minutes! Then flew back to London and finished office work.

24 May

A very full day. The COS was a long one and lasted till near lunchtime. Then Jack Collins [Staff College] and Jumbo Goschen [Chatham District] came to lunch, after which I rushed off to the dentist. Came back to WO to see a film of Lethbridge's tour in the Pacific. A good film giving good idea of fighting conditions. Then Sam Hoare came and gave me a general picture of conditions in Spain. Then rushed off to Cabinet meeting on transfer of RAF Regiment personnel to the Army. PM gave Archie Sinclair [Air] good ticking off and appointed a committee under John Anderson to go into the matter.

Then solitary dinner with Winston. He was very upset with the President's proposed broadcast to Germany to coincide with invasion. We also discussed Pacific strategy, and I found him in a very good mood. At 10 pm we had Chiefs of Staff meeting with him to discuss progress made in pumping out of Phoenixes [see 25 May 1944] and Pacific strategy. I think we have at last got him swung to an Australian based strategy as opposed to his old love of the 'Sumatra tip'!

25 May

Long COS, with meetings with Planners, Lord Leathers and Henry Pownall. Then hurried lunch and dash to Portsmouth where motor launch took me to vicinity of Isle of Wight to see the 'Whales', new piers for the invasion. A wonderful sight. From there to Selsey Bill to see the Phoenixes, the large concrete caissons for the breakwaters for the artificial harbours. A wonderful piece of engineering. From there to Monty's HQ to dine with him. I had to tell him off and ask him to concentrate more on his own job and not meddle himself in everybody else's affairs. Such as wanting to advise Alex on his battle, New Zealand PM on what to do with Freyberg, or WO how to obtain reinforcements! As usual he took it well. He then motored back to London with me.

Just heard Anzio bridgehead and main front are joined up together. Thank heaven for it!!

26 May

The Italian offensive is going on well, [enemy] reserves are being drawn in, and it is performing just the function we wanted with reference to the cross Channel operation.

Another very full day which started with a COS from 10.30 to 11.30. Then a meeting with PM, Eden, Attlee, Oliver Lyttelton, Leathers, Curtin, Blamey and Chiefs of Staff to consider our future strategy. The meeting started badly as Curtin who is entirely in MacArthur's pocket was afraid we were trying to oust MacArthur! He consequently showed very little desire for British forces to operate from Australia. On the other hand I know this outlook was not shared by the rest of Australia. However as the meeting went on it took a far better turn and in the end we obtained all we wanted for the present. Namely Darwin and Fremantle to be developed for future operations by us and representatives of our staff to be accepted to work with the Australian General Staff. Meeting lasted till 1.30 pm.

Then a rush home for lunch with Martin of the *Daily Telegraph*. After lunch interview with Blamey, with whom I made good progress. After Blamey, Ted Morris back from being Chief of Staff in Delhi and from whom I had a lot to gather. He was followed by Admiral Noble from Washington who tells me Dill is showing signs of age and is tired. Then a long talk with Pownall, just back from Mountbatten's HQ in Ceylon with the news that Dickie wants to get rid of George Giffard [11th Army Group]. I am very sorry for it. Finally visit from Weeks with answers to a series of minutes from the PM.

The news of Dill had been bad of late. He had never really recovered from the infection he suffered from after his operation for the hernia he had contracted whilst riding Archie Wavell's horses on a visit to Delhi. He had contracted this sort of anaemia which he could not shake off. I was more and more distressed every time I saw him. For all that he continued to do the most invaluable work in Washington.

Dickie Mountbatten made a fatal mistake in getting rid of Giffard, who would have done him admirably, and better than Oliver Leese who replaced him.

Winston had a habit of addressing minutes to various members of the General Staff of the War Office. I had instructed them that when they received such minutes they were to prepare answers back for my signature. All replies, having been checked by me, were signed by me. He tackled me one day and said, 'How is it that whenever I write to any officer of the General Staff at the War Office I get a reply from you?' I informed him that as I was responsible for the General Staff I considered it my duty to answer minutes of his, that I should prefer him to address such minutes direct to me, but that even if he chose to ignore the chain of responsibility he would still get replies from me!

27 May

A very full COS which I got through all right by going fast and keeping the ball rolling. By 12 noon I was off for Whit Monday weekend, and just longing for a rest of a few hours from continual war responsibility. The hardest part of bearing such responsibility is pretending that you are absolutely confident of success when you are really torn to shreds with doubts and misgivings! But when once decisions are taken the time for doubts is gone, and what is required is to breathe the confidence of success into all those around. This is made doubly hard when subjected to the ravings of prima donnas in the shape of politicians, who seem to be incapable of having real faith in their own decisions!

I never want again to go through a time like the present one. The cross Channel operation [D-Day] is just eating into my heart. I wish to God we could start and have done with it!!

Went home for the weekend.

28 May
Quiet Sunday at home.

29 May
Quiet Whit Monday at home.

30 May
A long COS. Then lunch at the Amerys with you there. After lunch visit by Cooke and Handy from Washington to discuss American Chiefs visit. Then Cabinet. Winston at his worst. Although Alex had brought off a master stroke, not a single word of praise for him, only threats as to what he would think of him if he did not bring off a scoop! I got so angry that I lost my temper. Cabinet lasted till 8.30 pm. Then dashed off to dine with [Duke of] Alba at Spanish Embassy. Amery, Woolton, Hudson and Wimborne and Belgian Ambassador were there. As usual, excellent dinner served by a butler and 3 footmen in livery. I had forgotten what such a sight looked like!

31 May
A long COS attended by Pownall at which we tried to disentangle some of that awful South East Asia, Chiang Kai-shek, American Long Range Bomber Commands. The whole show is an awful mess and must be disentangled. Mountbatten is quite irresponsible and tries to be loved by all, which won't work! He must face facts, Stilwell can't go on functioning in his present treble capacity and the sooner this is made clear to the Americans the better [see 15 June 1944]. I am afraid however that Mountbatten will be a constant source of trouble to us and will never really fit the bill as Supreme Commander.

News from Italy continues to be very good, I do so hope that Alex succeeds in breaking through on the Vilitri-Valtone front!

1 June
We had a long COS meeting at which we discussed the paper we are preparing to put over South East Asia and Pacific strategy to the American COS when they come over next week for the invasion. Not an easy paper when we have to steer clear between the rocks of Winston's ramblings in Sumatra, Curtin's sub-jugation to MacArthur, MacArthur's love of the limelight, King's desire to wrap all the laurels round his head, and last but not least real sound strategy! The latter may well get a bad position at the starting gate!! My God how difficult it is to run a war and to keep military considerations clear of all the vested interests and political foolery attached to it!!

We also discussed the future of Greece and then came across the usual desire of the Foreign Office to support some high brow ideas as to future governments entirely unacceptable to the local people, with utterly inadequate forces!!

I am tired to death of our whole method of running war, it is just futile and heart breaking.

In the afternoon, a long meeting with Pownall to discuss the heart breaking situation in Burma. I see disaster staring us in the face, with Mountbatten incapable of realizing it, Pownall clever enough but too lazy to appreciate the danger, and Giffard I am afraid lacking the adequate vision to see where he is going to. Oh! How I wish we had some more men with more vision. Or is it that I am very, very tired and becoming disheartened ? If so it is time I left this job!

Very refreshing dinner with Meinertzhagen, Bannerman, Bevan, Kennedy. We talked of birds and other subjects. Meinertzhagen most entertaining.

2 June

A COS of no great importance, but which was delayed by dear old Andrew Cunningham adopting the Admiralty attitude that a Supreme Commander 'co-ordinates' but does not 'command'!! It will take several more generations before this outlook can be thoroughly eliminated. Adam came to lunch and we went to a premiere film in the evening, taking Jane Lewin with us. The film had been given for benefit of SSAFA [Soldiers', Sailors' and Airmen's Families Association].

3 June

After finishing the COS I collected you at the flat and we drove down to Ferney Close.

4 June

Cross Channel operation [D-Day] was to have started on the night of the 4/5th but the weather was too bad, strong wind and low clouds. The operation has therefore had to be put off which is most regrettable. I had intended returning on Sunday evening, but stopped on as the operation was put off. Winston meanwhile has taken his train and is touring the Portsmouth area and making a thorough pest of himself!

It will be remembered by those who have read his Second World War *[vol. V, pp. 546 ff] that he had done his best to be on board a cruiser that night to participate in the operations. He never breathed a word about this plan to me, knowing full well that I would not encourage it! Thank heaven the King used his authority to stop him.*

This prolonged waiting period before the operation was shattering. I remember having all the same feelings as I used to get before starting in a point to point race – an empty feeling at the pit of one's stomach and a continual desire to yawn!

5 June

Left early, news having been received on previous evening that we were in Rome. Winston had returned on Sunday evening in a very highly strung condition. He invited the Chiefs of Staff to lunch, which was a bore. I found him over optimistic as regards prospects of the cross Channel operation and tried to damp him down. Similarly in Italy he now believes that Alex will wipe out the whole of the German forces!

A long Cabinet at which we were explained how troublesome de Gaulle was being now that he had been fetched back from Algiers! He is now refusing to broadcast unless Eisenhower alters the wording of his own broadcast!! I knew he would be a pest and recommended strongly that he should be left in Africa, but Anthony Eden would insist on bringing him over!

It is very hard to believe that in a few hours the cross Channel invasion starts! I am very uneasy about the whole operation. At the best it will fall so very very far short of the expectation of the bulk of the people, namely all those who know nothing of its difficulties. At the worst it may well be the most ghastly disaster of the whole war. I wish to God it were safely over.

I knew too well all the weak points in the plan of operations. First of all the weather, on which we were entirely dependent; a sudden storm might wreck it all. Then the complexity of an amphibious operation of this kind, when confusion may degenerate into chaos in such a short time. The difficulty of controlling the operation once launched, lack of elasticity in the handling of reserves, danger of leakage of information with consequent loss of that essential secrecy. Perhaps one of the most nerve wracking experiences when watching an operation like this unroll itself is the intimate knowledge of the various commanders engaged. Too good a knowledge of their various weaknesses makes one wonder whether in the moments of crisis facing them they will not shatter one's hopes.

To realize what it was like living through those agonizing hours, the background of the last 3 years must be remembered. All those early setbacks, the gradual checking of the onrush, the very gradual turn of the defensive to the offensive, then that series of Mediterranean offensives alternately leading up to this final all important operation which started in the early hours of the next morning.

6 June

By 7.30 I began to receive first news of the invasion. The airborne landings had been successful, the first waves were reported as going in, opposition not too serious, batteries firing from flanks, etc.

Throughout the day information has gone on coming in. On the British front the landing has gone well and the whole of 3 divisions are ashore. On the American front the western landing was a success, but the Eastern Corps (V) has failed practically along its whole front! They are now asking to land on our western beaches. This will probably have to be done, but must inevitably lead to confusion on the beaches.

Held our usual COS and meeting with Joint Intelligence Committee. Lunched with Maharaja of Kashmir, guests consisted of Mrs Churchill, Lady Cranborne, Lord and Lady Simon, the Lascelles and two more. Afternoon spent in Selection Board and meetings with Ted Morris, back from CGS job in

Delhi, and Horrocks who has just recovered from his wound and is very anxious to be given another Corps.

It has been very hard to realize all day that whilst London went on calmly with its job, a fierce conflict was being fought at a close distance on the French coast!

7 June

The invasion is a day older. I am not very happy about it. The American V Corps seems to be stuck. We are not gaining enough ground and German forces are assembling fast. I do wish to heaven that we were landing on a wider front.

During afternoon had interviews with Penney, returning to Italy to his 1st Division, [Willoughby] Norrie just back from mission with Duff Cooper having also visited Madagascar and Syria. Then General Béthouart who has come over with de Gaulle. He did not impress me much. A grey, putty faced, flabby sort of chap with a doleful countenance. However, de Gaulle is enough to depress anybody. Basil came to dine having come over for one of his usual visits.

News from Alexander continues to be excellent, he is all for dashing off to the Pisa-Rimini Line. And I have been trying to induce him to send something to Ancona as he moves up.

8 June

From 7.30 to 12 noon we had our usual COS with a meeting with Planners. We then went to meet Winston to discuss future plans. He had put forward a paper with much too early plans for operations on the west coast of France with troops from Italy. But we *must* first see what happens to our cross Channel operation, and what the final stages of Alex's offensive leads to. In any case we must go on smashing up the German forces in Italy up to the Pisa-Rimini line. After lunch interviews, and at 7 pm the new Army film at the Odeon followed by dinner with Lady Strathcona.

9 June

The news from France is better. The XXX British and V American Corps have now joined up together. However I am not yet entirely satisfied with the situation and wish the American front would join up and become a connected whole.

Béthouart, de Gaulle's Chief of Staff, came wishing to know situation. Money to report on return from India. George Clark, Wilson's Chief Administrative Officer, reported on situation in Italy and North Africa. At 7.30 pm went to Euston station to meet Marshall, King and Arnold, who had flown over from Washington. Then back to flat where Crerar had come to dine with me. We had an excellent talk prior to his going over to France with his Army HQ. Dill unable to come, unfortunately, owing to being unwell.

I missed Dill badly at this juncture; he had been so close to me during the last 3 years, and had always so well understood my strategy, I should have loved to have him with me as we reached the final stages.

10 June

American COS came to meet us at 11.30 and stopped till 1.30. We had a general review of the whole front. Before that the PM had called me up stating he proposed to visit Monty on Monday and wanted me to come with him, Smuts also coming. We are to leave by train on Sunday night and make an early start by destroyer on Monday. In afternoon slipped home for short weekend.

11 June

Left home at 12 noon to lunch with American Chiefs at Stanwell Place near Staines. After lunch we had a Combined Conference lasting till 5.30 pm. Decided Italian Campaign to stop at Apennines or Pisa-Rimini line, and an amphibious operation to be prepared to land either in southern France or in Bay of Biscay depending on situation prevailing at that time. Went back to flat for dinner and am now off to Ascot to get on the PM's train.

It was interesting to listen to Marshall explaining *now* why the Germans fought in Central Italy! He seemed to forget that I had given him all these arguments several months ago as a prediction of what I was convinced would happen. I do not believe that he has *any* strategic vision whatsoever!

Now at last we had put the South France operation in its right strategic position. By the time we reached the Pisa-Rimini line, the Italian theatre should have played its part in holding German reserves away from Northern France. We could then contemplate the landing in Southern France, to provide a front for French forces from North Africa, and to cooperate on southern flank of OVERLORD operations. The Bay of Biscay landings did not attract me.

12 June

At 10.15 pm I left the flat and drove to Ascot station where I picked up the PM's train. I found him with Smuts and the American COS finishing dinner. We got off to bed at a fairly reasonable time as we had to leave the train at 7.30 am to catch the destroyer *Kelvin* and leave Portsmouth at 8 am. The Americans had already started in a separate party. We had a very comfortable journey over and most interesting. We continually passed convoys of landing craft, minesweepers, bits of floating breakwater (Phoenix) being towed out, parts of the floating piers (Whales) etc. And overhead, a continuous flow of planes going to and coming from France. About 11 am we approached the French coast and the scene was beyond description. Everywhere the sea was covered with ships of all sizes and shapes, and a scene of continuous activity. We passed through rows of anchored LSTs and finally came to a 'Gooseberry', namely a row of ships sunk in a half crescent to form a sort of harbour and to provide protection from the sea. Here we were met by Admiral Vian (of Mediterranean fame) who took us in his Admiral's barge from which we changed into a DUKW (amphibious lorry). This ran us straight onto the beach and up onto the road.

It was a wonderful moment to find myself reentering France almost exactly 4 years after being thrown out for the second time, at St Nazaire. Floods of memories came back of my last trip of despair, and those long four years of work and anxiety at last crowned by the success of a reentry into France.

Monty met us on the beach with a team of jeeps which we got into and drove off on the Courseulles-Bayeux road, to about ½ way to the latter place. There we found Monty's HQ and he gave us an explanation on the map of his dispositions and plans. All as usual wonderfully clear and concise. We then had lunch with him and my thoughts wandered off to 4 years ago when I was at Le Mans and Laval waiting for Monty and his 3rd Division to join me. I knew then that it would not be long before I was kicked out of France if I was not killed or taken prisoner, but if anybody had told me then that in 4 years time I should return with Winston and Smuts to lunch with Monty commanding a new invasion force I should have found it hard to believe it.

After lunch we drove round to Bimbo Dempsey's HQ. I was astonished at how little affected the country had been by the German occupation and 5 years of war. All the crops were good, the country fairly clear of weeds, and plenty of fat cattle, horses, chickens etc. *(As usual Winston described the situation in his inimitable way when driving with me. He said, 'We are surrounded by fat cattle lying in luscious pastures with their paws crossed!' This is just the impression they gave one.)** And the French population did not seem in any way pleased to see us arrive as a victorious country to liberate France. They had been quite content as they were, and we were bringing war and desolation to the country. We then returned to Courseulles, having watched a raid by Hun bombers on the harbour which did no harm.

We reembarked on Vian's Admiral's Barge and did a trip right along the sea front watching the various activities. We saw 'Landing Crafts Tank' unloading lorries, tanks, guns etc onto the beaches in a remarkably short time. We then went to the new harbour being prepared west of Hamel. There we saw some of the large Phoenixes being sunk into place and working admirably. Also 'bombadores' to damp down waves, 'Whales' representing wonderful floating piers, all growing up fast. Close by was a monitor with a 14" gun firing away into France. Winston said he had never been on one of His Majesty's ships engaging the enemy and insisted on going aboard. Luckily we could not climb up as it would have been a very risky entertainment had we succeeded. Then we returned to our destroyer and went right back to the east end of the beach where several ships were bombarding the Germans. Winston wanted to take

---

*Italicized sentences not in manuscript diary, but in the 'Notes on my life' and in Bryant, *Turn*, p. 214.

part in the war, and was longing to draw some retaliation. However the Boche refused to take any notice of any of the rounds we fired. We therefore started back about 6.15 and by 9.15 were back at Portsmouth after having spent a wonderfully interesting day. We got on board the PM's train where we found Marshall and King. We dined on the way back to London where we arrived shortly after 1 am dog tired and very sleepy!

13 June

Last night Germans used their pilotless planes [V1s] for the first time, but did little damage. Cherwell and Duncan Sandys came to COS meeting where we discussed action to take and decided that we must not let defence interfere with the French battle! At 11.30 American Chiefs came and we had a Combined meeting where we drew up directives for Wilson and Eisenhower. We settled to limit advance in Italy to the Apennines and to prepare for amphibious operations of a 3 division lift for either Bay of Biscay, Western Mediterranean or Adriatic. Decision as to which to depend on course of events. American COS then lunched with us at the Savoy.

In afternoon Cabinet at 6 pm to discuss relaxation of various security measures which had been brought into force during the period prior to cross Channel invasion.

14 June

A very busy day!! Started with a long and difficult COS which included Joint Intelligence Committee and went on to lunch. Dashed back for lunch with you and our Mr Ti, Pongo also there. Had to leave in a hurry as we had a meeting with the American Chiefs of Staff in the afternoon which started at 2.30 and went on till 5 pm. We discussed the Pacific strategy and found that they were in agreement with a proposed strategy based on north western Australia and directed through Amboina towards Borneo.

Dashed back to WO to finish off work there, then on to 10 Downing Street for a dinner with PM attended by the King, Attlee, Lascelles, Marshall, King, Arnold, Cunningham, Portal, Ismay and self. The King I think enjoyed himself thoroughly and did not leave till 1.45 am!!! Winston began one of his long harangues stating that the Army was certain to crowd in 'dental chairs and YMCA institutions instead of bayonets' into the landing in France. What we wanted he said were combatants and fighting men instead of a mass of non combatants. We argued with him that fighting men without food, ammunition and petrol were useless, but he was in one of his foolish moods and not open to conviction. It is appalling the false conception of modern war that he has got.

15 June

Another busy day. Started COS at 10.30 with the Planners discussing difficult manpower problems. Then at 11.30 Mr Fraser (NZ Prime Minister) came to discuss future of New Zealand forces. He wasted a good ¾ hour to say what could have been fitted into 5 minutes. Anyhow he is all for joining us in the offensive from north Australia.

After lunch again the American COS, this time to discuss Burma. It is quite clear in listening to Marshall's arguments and questions that he has not even now grasped the true aspect of the Burma Campaign! After the meeting I approached him about the present Stilwell set up, suggesting that it was quite impossible for him to continue filling 3 jobs at the same time, necessitating him being in 3 different locations, namely: Deputy Supreme Commander, Commander Chinese Corps, and Chief of Staff to Chiang Kai-shek! Marshall flared up and said that Stilwell was a 'fighter' and that is why he wanted him there, as we had a set of commanders who had no fighting instincts! Namely Giffard, Peirse and Somerville, all of which according to him were soft and useless etc etc. I found it quite useless arguing with him.

Marshall had originally asked us to accept this mad Stilwell set up to do him a favour, apparently as he had no one else suitable to fill the gaps. I was therefore quite justified in asking him to terminate a set up which had proved itself as quite unsound. I had certainly not expected him to flare up in the way he did and to start accusing our commanders of lack of fighting qualities, and especially as he could not have had any opportunities of judging for himself and was basing his opinions on reports he had received from Stilwell. I was so enraged by his attitude that I had to break off the conversation to save myself from rounding on him and irreparably damaging our relationship.

Went out to dine with Birleys, came home to write up diary, and whilst writing a series of pilotless planes have come over. The second time we have this form of entertainment. Monty seems to be meeting with more serious opposition and to have suffered a series of heavy counter attacks, which so far he appears to have resisted.

16 June

CNS and CAS were away from COS having gone to France. Main topic was pilotless planes which have at last started their attacks on this country. At 11.45 Cabinet meeting to discuss same subject. This resulted in a Staff meeting with PM at 5 pm attended by Tedder, Hill (from Stanmore), Pile (from ADGB), 3 Chiefs of Staff. Again, very few real decisions were arrived at. In my mind it is pretty clear and 3 essentials stand out:

   a) attacks by what can be spared from Overlord on launching sites
   b) barriers of fighters, guns and balloons in succession south of London
   c) no sirens and no guns in London

We shall I hope eventually get these, but it will take time.

Dined with Bannerman in Hurlingham Club with you there, Bourdillons there also. Lovely evening.

17 June

I finished off the COS early, and after collecting you and Mary [Benita's sister] we drove off to Hartley Wintney. We had a noisy night of it with continual AA gunfire at the pilotless planes which were attacking London.

18 June

A quiet day at home.

19 June

Arrived up early to find that a pilotless plane had struck the Guards Chapel, Wellington Barracks during Sunday Service and had killed about 60 people!! Amongst them to my great grief Ivan Cobbold! And on my writing table was a letter from him written Saturday, sending me on a wire from the Duke de Luna who is fishing at Cairnton and asking me to lunch this week! It all gave me a very nasty turn, and I cannot get him and poor Blanche out of my mind. Hungerford Bridge had also been hit, and most of the windows of the WO blown in again.

News from France is good, the Cherbourg peninsula has been cut off by the Americans.

This afternoon at 5 pm conference with the PM attended by most of ADGB to decide how to attack the pilotless planes which are from now on to be called flying bombs. After that long Cabinet at which Winston was in very good form, quite 10 years younger, all due to the fact that the flying bombs have again put us into the front line!! We shall have to stop them and find some efficient counter or they will become troublesome.

The death of Ivan Cobbold was a ghastly blow to me. I had grown to know him very well in those weeks alone with him at Cairnton, and I had grown very fond of him. Both he and Blanche had been kindness itself to me. The blow was, I think, made all the worse by the fact that when Brian Boyle was telling me of his death, I was actually picking up Ivan's letter off my blotting pad. His invitation to lunch with him that week made a very large lump rise in my throat.

20 June

A careful review of the flying rockets at the COS. We are fitting up a row of butts for AA guns south of London, with balloons behind them and fighter aircraft in front. I think we shall be able to build up some form of protection. Fighting in Cherbourg goes well. In the afternoon had to inform Laurence Carr that his soldiering days had come to an end, I hated doing it and have a very special feeling for him. There is far more in him than the average person finds out. Then an interview with Sidney Clive who has taken over the Union Jack Club, and for him this is the most important matter at present! Finally dined with old Rollie, who was in great form.

21 June

We had a variety of points to consider at the COS, including petty squabbles between Mountbatten and Somerville on questions of command. It is astonishing how petty and small men can be in connection with questions of command.

A large bunch of flying bombs last night. I did not miss one by more than some 20 minutes on Constitution Hill last night, returning from dining at the Cav Club with Rollie Charrington. After lunch at 2.45 a meeting with the PM and Smuts. PM wanted Smuts to put before us his ideas for the prosecution of the war after clearing the Pisa-Rimini line in Italy. Were we to head for Italy, according to Alexander's dreams, or were we to launch another expedition into France? Although Smuts liked the idea of Vienna, he considered it would be better to remove a force from Italy and launch a new cross Channel expedition across the Calais narrows. He was evidently oblivious of the fact that the port capacity of this country will not support another expedition, that the shipping could not be found, and that if both these difficulties could be overcome we should arrive too late in the year to count on suitable weather. Then Winston, who had evidently been lunching very well, meandered for ¾ hours producing a lot of disconnected thoughts which had no military value. It is hard to keep one's patience on these occasions. We were kept till 4.45 pm.

Then back to WO for the unpleasant job of telling Martel that his soldiering days were over. He was followed by a series of interviews till 8 pm.

As soon as I sat down to dinner, PM called up asking me to come round to meet him and Eden and Macmillan, to discuss plans for the war in Italy! I knew the time would be utterly wasted and excused myself. We meet tomorrow evening instead.

22 June

Gammell (Wilson's Chief of Staff) attended our COS, together with the Planners and we examined Alexander's wild hopes of an advance on Vienna and all the other alternatives. The proposals he has made are not based on any real study of the problem, but rather the result of certain elated spirits after a rapid advance!

After lunch had an interview with Sykes, back from Washington, and Puttick (NZ Chief of Staff) who is just back from Italy and is now starting home. Discussed future of NZ Division with him, luckily they are to let it stop on for the present. Am now off for one of the PM's awful 10.30 meetings! Eden and Macmillan are to be present. We are to discuss Italian strategy and I know that as usual it will be a useless waffle round!

23 June

We had a long and painful evening of it listening to Winston's strategic ravings! I have seldom seen him more adrift in his strategic arguments. He had got Eden and Macmillan there and I think was trying to impress them. In the main he was for supporting Alexander's advance on Vienna. I pointed out that even on Alex's optimistic reckoning the advance beyond the Pisa-Rimini line would not start till after September. Namely we should embark on a campaign through the Alps in winter! It was hard to make him realize that if we took the season of the year and the topography of the country in league against us we should have 3 enemies instead of one. We were kept up till close on 1 am and accomplished nothing. As soon as I got to bed flying bombs came over in a constant shower for the next two hours. Finally the remnants of the night were spoilt by an early telephone call.

Cherbourg going rather slower, Alex's advance also slowed up. Lunched with Adam at the Carlton Grill. During afternoon Mr Fraser (PM of NZ) came to say goodbye.

24 June

Bannerman came to lunch with me after which we motored together to Camberley to see George Lodge (the artist) and his pictures. He is busy at present illustrating a new book of British birds which Bannerman is writing. We had a look round all his pictures and I finally bought one of a peregrine. Winston called me up after dinner to tell me that he had written a new paper on the policy to pursue in North Italy. He was very excited about it!

25 June

Spent quietly at home except for another long talk with Winston all about our future policy in Italy and not depriving Alex of the troops required for his victory! Had to sit up till 12.30 am awaiting Winston's new paper!

26 June

Arrived up at 9.15. Masses of telegrams and minutes in spite of having had a DR on previous evening. Then COS at which we had to draft a reply to Americans and deal with the PM's paper. We are up against the same trouble again, namely saving Alexander from being robbed of troops in order to land in Southern France!! We shall have great difficulties with Americans, especially as Alex keeps on talking about going to Vienna. We all had to lunch with Winston and talked shop all the time. Then again had another meeting with him at 6 which lasted till 8 pm to get him to pass our reply to the Americans. All went well and the reply has now gone, but will lead to lots of trouble with our American friends.

27 June

Rather a troublesome night with a series of flying bombs coming over between midnight and 3 am. One close one made me get out of bed and prepare to get under!

We had a long COS with Lord Cherwell and Duncan Sandys there discussing how to handle the flying bomb trouble. The danger really lies in the flying rocket with a 5 ton warhead starting. After lunch interviews, with Gammell before his departure and with Alan Cunningham over from Ireland who considers garrison might be reduced now. He is right and I must find some new home for him.

Cabinet at 6 pm which lasted till just on 9 pm!! Winston went on giving one strategic lecture after another. Finished up with a pathetic wail from Herbert Morrison who appears to be a real white-livered specimen! He was in a flat spin about the flying bombs and their effect on the population! After 5 years of war we could not ask them to stand such a strain etc etc!! In fact he did not mind if we lost the war much, provided we stopped the flying bombs! However, Winston certainly did not see eye to eye with him!

Herbert Morrison's performance was a poor one, he kept on repeating that the population of London could not be asked to stand this strain after 5 years of war. He suggested that our strategy in France should be altered and that our one and only objective should be to clear the north coast of France. It was a pathetic performance, there were no signs of London not being able to stand it, and if there had been it would only have been necessary to tell them that for the first time in history they could share the dangers their sons were running in France and that what fell on London was at any rate not falling on them. Thank heaven Winston very soon dealt with him.

28 June

This morning the American reply to our wire arrived, a rude one at that!! They still adhere to Anvil [Southern France] being carried out and want it at once. They produce a series of futile arguments. Amongst others they argue that we have derived benefit out of the Italian campaign, in spite of the fact that they were always opposed to it, but state that the reason for its success is attributable to Hitler's error in deciding to fight for Southern Italy. They forget that this is exactly what we kept on telling them would happen!! And now we have the most marvellous intercept message indicating the importance that Hitler attaches to Northern Italy, his determination to fight for it and his orders to hold a line south of the Pisa-Rimini line whilst this line is being developed! Kesselring's army is now a hostage to political interference with military direction of operations; it would be madness to fail to take advantage of it, and would delay the conclusion of the war. We spent most of the day drafting a reply refusing to withdraw forces at present for a landing in South France, with the opportunities that rest in front of us. Winston is also sending a wire to President backing up our message.

Meanwhile the war goes well. Cherbourg has definitely fallen, the attack for Caen has started well, the Russian attacks are a great success, and the Imphal-Kohima Road is open again!!

This is another example of the lack of elasticiy in the American method of running the war. We had now intercepted this all important message from Hitler to Kesselring giving him instructions to fight south of the Apennines to cover preparation of a line on Pisa-Rimini alignment. There could now be no argument that the Germans were about to retire in front of us in Italy. To my mind it was all important to keep them occupied there at this juncture, and prevent withdrawal of force from Italy to northern France. We had the forces deployed and ready for action, surely it was better to continue employing them there instead of losing a portion of them for a very problematical operation in Southern France, doubtful as to the successes it might achieve owing to the hazards connected with amphibious operations?

29 June

The PM has backed our telegram to the American Chiefs by one of his own to the President, which crossed ours from the President and necessitated a further one from the PM!!! We are in for an all out struggle with our American colleagues and I am frankly doubtful as to the outcome of it all!

This evening I collected Rollie at the Cav Club at 6 pm and went to Kew Gardens. It was lovely and peaceful there, I felt it was just what I wanted. Work, troubles, difficulties, differences of opinion, etc, etc had begun to make life jangle badly. Kew Gardens and contact with God through nature put all at rest again. There are times when I feel that I just can't stand one more day of this job and the burdens of responsibility which it means. On those occasions contact with nature has a wonderfully strengthening effect.

You came up today and we lunched with Sir Firoz Noon Khan at the Savoy, not a very exciting lunch.

30 June

The President's reply had arrived in the night. It is an interesting document as it is not till you get to the last para that you get to the basic reason for the opinions expressed. Then you find that owing to the coming Presidential election it is impossible to contemplate any action with a Balkan flavour irrespective of its strategic merits. The situation is full of difficulties, the Americans now begin to own the major strength on land, in the air and on the sea. They therefore consider that they are entitled to decide how their forces are to be employed. We shall be forced into carrying out an invasion of southern France, but I am not certain that this need cripple Alexander's power to finish crushing Kesselring. I am just off now to a 10 pm meeting with Winston to try and arrive at a final decision. He has ordered the Clipper and the York to stand by, so we may be flying off to Washington before we are much older, but I doubt it. I think Winston will realize there is nothing more to be gained by argument. It is very unfortunate that Alex and Winston ever started their wild schemes about going to Vienna. This has made our task with the Americans an impossible one.

After lunch went to Ivan Cobbold's memorial service. I do not remember going to a memorial service that upset me more, I miss him most awfully.

Later:
Just back from meeting with Winston. I thought at first we might have trouble with him, he looked like he wanted to fight the President. However in the end we got him to agree to our outlook which is: 'All right, if you insist on being damned fools, sooner than falling out with you, which would be fatal, we shall be damned fools with you, and we shall see that we perform the role of damned fools damned well'! We left Winston with Pug drafting a telegram which we are to see tomorrow morning and discuss with him at 11 am.

1 July
COS met at 10.30 to discuss PM's proposed wire to President deciding to accept their decision to do [Operation] Anvil. Not one of his best telegrams but it met the case fairly well. At 11 am we met the PM and told him of the minor amendments which were wanted. He was in a good mood and they all went through easily. Then finished off office work and started for home.

2 July
A wet but very happy Sunday at home with you. Wire came back from President agreeing and asking for a Directive to be sent to Wilson. Also sent wire yesterday for Alexander to come home.

3 July
Americans started attack from Cherbourg southwards. Flying bombs becoming more serious danger and likely to encroach on our war effort if we are not careful. Lunched with High Commissioner for India to say goodbye to Maharaja of Kashmir. Then at 5.30 record longest Cabinet meeting which lasted till 9.15 pm!!! Winston in one of his worst maudlin moods wasted hours and when we got onto flying bombs he ran short of time. Herbert Morrison as usual painting a gloomy picture of the state of London's morale, quite unjustified. However the threat is assuming dimensions which will require more drastic action.

4 July
A long COS, attended by Duncan Sandys and Cherwell, at which we discussed all the various measures for defeating flying bombs. The fighter aircraft are not proving fast enough, the guns are not hitting them, the balloons may have their cables cut, the launching sites are not worth attacking with bombers etc, etc. In fact rather a gloomy and unsatisfactory meeting.

Alexander had turned up early in the morning and I had two interviews with him. I told him that I felt he was missing his chances of smashing up Kesselring *before* he got back to the Pisa-Rimini line, and also that Oliver Leese was not providing the necessary hinge for the 8th Army which remained continually behind the Americans and the French! I am afraid Alex did not like this much, but it is very desirable to bring his feet to earth and to make him face the facts confronting him instead of his futurist dreams of an advance on Vienna.

PM sent for me at 6.30 pm. He was in a bad mood, with all his vindictive spirits aroused, wishing to continue his arguments with the President, and longing to have a good row with him! He has prepared an awful telegram and I only hope we succeed in stopping him from sending it!

5 July

Considerable excitement today preparing details for Winston's speech on flying bombs. We had to consider advisability of reprisals on small towns in Germany as a deterrent. Personally I am dead against it. The Germans fully realize that we are at present devoting nearly 50% of our air effort in trying to stop these beastly bombs, added to which about 25% of London's production is lost through the results of these bombs! They won't throw away these advantages easily. I am afraid however that Winston's vindictive nature may induce him to try reprisals. I hope we shall succeed in stopping him!

6 July

In the morning I drove down to Camberley to deliver a lecture on the world situation to the Staff College. Then lunched with you and drove back to London, arriving about 3.30. The afternoon was filled with office work and long visits from Alexander and Harding, discussing ways and means of furnishing the required forces for their offensive.

At 10 pm we had a frightful meeting with Winston which lasted till 2 am!! It was quite the worst we have had with him. He was very tired as a result of his speech in the House concerning the flying bombs, he had tried to recuperate with drink. As a result he was in a maudlin, bad tempered, drunken mood, ready to take offence at anything, suspicious of everybody, and in a highly vindictive mood against the Americans. In fact so vindictive that his whole outlook on strategy was warped. I began by having a bad row with him. He began to abuse Monty because operations were not going faster, and apparently Eisenhower had said that he was over cautious. I flared up and asked him if he could not trust his generals for 5 minutes instead of continuously abusing them and belittling them. He said that he never did such a thing. I then reminded him that during two whole Monday Cabinets in front of a large gathering of Ministers, he had torn Alexander to shreds for his lack of imagination and leadership in continually attacking at Cassino. He was furious with me, but I hope it may do some good in the future.

He then put forward a series of puerile proposals, such as raising a Home Guard in Egypt to provide a force to deal with disturbances in the Middle East. It was not till after midnight that we got onto the subject we had come to discuss, the war in the Far East! Here we came up against all the old arguments that we have had put up by him over and over again. Attlee, Eden and

Lyttelton were there, fortunately they were at last siding with us against him. This infuriated him more than ever and he became ruder and ruder. Fortunately he finished by falling out with Attlee and having a real good row with him concerning the future of India! We withdrew under cover of this smokescreen just on 2 am, having accomplished nothing beyond losing our tempers and valuable sleep!!*

I remember that ghastly evening as if it were yesterday. Winston had driven me to the verge of losing my temper in several Cabinet meetings when he had poured abuse on Alex's head in front of the whole Cabinet. Although I had explained to him the whole of the topography of the front on a raised model, he kept on attacking Alex's plans of attack, his lack of ideas, his continuing to bump his head on the same spot, the incurring of casualties for no results, his lack of vision and many more failings. As most of the Cabinet Ministers had little opportunity of judging for themselves, and took all he said for gospel, there was every danger of their opinion of Alex being seriously affected. When the whole process was starting again this evening with reference to Monty, although there were only 3 Cabinet Ministers, it was more than I could stand. I think what infuriated me most was that there had not been a single word of approval or gratitude for the excellent work Monty had done in the handling of the land forces in this very difficult amphibious operation. And now he was starting off again with a string of abuse. I lost my temper and started one of the heaviest thunderstorms that we had! He was infuriated, and throughout the evening kept shoving his chin out, looking at me, and fuming at the accusation that he ran down his generals.

*At one moment he turned to Eden to ask him if there was any foundation to such an accusation. I am glad to say that Eden agreed with me and said that he thought that what worried the CIGS was that Winston expressed views about his generals in Cabinet meetings that might be misinterpreted by some Cabinet ministers who were not fully acquainted with the facts. This did not calm Winston much, and the lightning and thunder continued to crash, and fortunately from my point of view finally settled on the unfortunate Attlee.***

7 July
Started COS at 10 so as to attend Cabinet at 11 am where Alexander gave an account of the operations in Italy. He did it very well. Lunched with the Portuguese Ambassador who I found very nice and an ornithologist which made the conversation much easier.

8 July
Had rather a longer COS than usual for a Saturday. After finishing work drove

---

*An entry heavily (but silently) censored by Bryant. Cf. *Triumph*, pp. 229–30.
**Cf. Eden's version of this 'deplorable evening', *The Reckoning* (London: Cassell, 1965), pp. 461–62; and Cunningham's: 'There is no doubt that the PM was in no state to discuss anything. Very tired and too much alcohol.' Cunningham diary, quoted in Martin Gilbert, *Road to Victory: Winston Churchill 1941–1945* (London: Heinemann, 1986), p. 844.

Alexander down to Virginia Water which gave us a good chance for a talk. He is the most delightful person and very attractive, but I am afraid very simple minded and entirely innocent of any understanding of the politician's under-hand methods! I am afraid Macmillan has him entirely fooled, he likes his company as he believes that he receives from him an insight into political affairs. He also reads Hansard religiously to keep him up to date 'in the political outlook' and I fear he has not even begun to understand what politics mean. It is just as well that he does not, a 'soldier must not be politically minded'; but why should not the converse hold good? It seems as reasonable to state that a 'politician must not be militarily minded'.

9 July
A quiet but wet Sunday at home. Received news that Monty had taken Caen.

10 July
A COS again seriously preoccupied with flying bombs. Also probable entry into the war of Turkey. Collins [Staff College] came to lunch with me. Cabinet at 5.30 with PM in good and affable mood. And now we are faced with another of those awful 10.30 pm meetings!! I only hope I shall not lose my temper with him this time.

Later: 1 am, we have now finished our meeting. He was in a pleasant mood. We wandered like a swarm of bees from flower to flower, but never remained long enough at any flower to admit of any honey being produced. It was a blank evening as far as the formulating of plans went. However he was less vin-dictive towards the Americans, and more easy to manage. But what waste of time it all is! He does not know the situation, has a false picture of the distribu-tion of forces and of their capabilities. A complete amateur of strategy, he swamps himself in details he should never look at and as a result fails ever to see a strategic problem in its true perspective.

11 July
We had a long COS with Lord Cherwell and Duncan Sandys attending to discuss flying bombs and rockets. The defence measures are making slow but steady progress. You came to lunch and we saw our first flying bomb together. During afternoon Halifax came round for a talk, spent about an hour discussing American conditions in Washington, the American Chiefs of Staff, Dill's illness etc. He was very nice and very helpful. In evening picked up Rollie Charrington at Cavalry Club and went to Kew gardens with him, finally dining with him.

12 July
The morning as usual filled with COS, this time settling some of occupation of

Germany after Armistice. The country to be divided into 3 zones, Eastern, North Western and South Western. The Russians take the Eastern, but we have a difference of opinion with the Americans as to the allocation of the two remaining ones.

The differences connected with zones in Germany lay in the fact that we wanted the North Western zone, being the zone nearest this country with all the ports facing us. The Americans also wanted this zone, and it took us some time before we discovered that this choice was due to the President refusing to let American lines of communication run through France ruled by de Gaulle. We solved this matter by offering the Americans lines of communications running through the North Western sector.

Pongo to lunch, then a war film of the African fighting and dinner with John Kennedy. Poor Bannerman was there, rather shaken after having been bombed twice in 3 days by doodlebugs [V1s] in the South Kensington Museum! He is now off to Cornwall for some well earned holiday. Apparently he saved himself from being blown to bits by diving under his oak table.

13 July

The capture of Amboina Island in the Pacific, and the military backing of Foreign Office policy in Greece, were the two topics of discussion at our COS meeting this morning. The former in anticipation of our meeting with the PM tomorrow on the Pacific strategy and the latter to try and preserve us against the wild schemes of the Foreign Office and their objectionable ambassador [to Greece] Mr Leeper! This combination, as I see it, is preparing to force on Greece a government of their own selection and to support this government with military power.* I can foresee a very serious military commitment very rapidly increasing.

Gave a lunch party to John Anderson and the Linlithgows, you and Diana [Charlesworth] came up for it. After lunch, interview with Cranborne asking for Willoughby Norrie for South Australian Governorship. Then Gort, who is leaving Malta for Palestine, followed by Beaumont Nesbitt who was very interesting on French, Polish and Greek situations in the Mediterranean. Finally, at 6 pm one of Winston's awful conferences to stimulate construction of synthetic ports in Normandy. The whole matter was settled before we met, but he did his best to confuse the issue.

---

*The resistance movement within Greece was split between political left and right, with the Communists forming a powerful and organized force. The tensions between them, and the inability of the government in exile or those foreign parties involved to broker a compromise, was eventually to lead to a bloody confrontation with the hallmarks of a civil war in December 1944, in which British forces became involved. The Foreign Office's policy was to create a post-war Greece which was pro-British, preferably a monarchy (despite the republican nature of most of the resistance), and definitely not Communist. They were willing to commit troops to obtain their ends. The military remained more concerned with the need to defeat the Axis, with much less regard for the post-war political consequences.

14 July

We had a rushed COS in order to meet the PM at 11.30 am to discuss Pacific strategy with a view of arriving at a final solution!!! Attlee, Eden, Lyttelton were there as usual, we were there from 11.30 to 2 pm and settled absolutely nothing!! We listened to all the PM's futile and empty arguments which we have listened to again and again. Both Attlee and Eden were against him, and yet on and on we meandered. In the end I said to him: 'We have examined the two alternatives [an attack on Japan based mainly on India or Australia] in great detail, we have repeatedly examined them for you, we have provided you with all possible information, and we are unanimous on our advice to you as to which course to select. They both have certain advantages, but in our minds we are quite clear as to which course we should select. However, we are even clearer still that one or other course must be selected at once, and that we cannot go on with this indecision. If the Government does not wish to accept our advice let them say so, but for heaven's sake let us have a decision!' He then stated that he must go on thinking about it and would give us a decision within a week! I doubt it!!

In the evening motored out to Chequers for the night, to meet Mr Stimson [US Secretary for War]. Stafford Cripps also there. I like him more each time I meet him. Stimson quite finished and hardly able to take notice of what is going on round him. After dinner we had a film and talk, and bed by 2 am.

15 July

Early rise and up to London for COS at 11 am, then escaped home.

16 July

Quiet Sunday at home.

17 July

A long COS attended by Woodhouse [Allied Military Mission to ELAS, Greek Communists] back from Greece. We were trying to decide policy as regards ELAS organization in Greece and whether time had come to denounce this organization. The whole future Greek policy is full of dangers, the Foreign Office with the Ambassador, Leeper, are likely to brew up a mass of future trouble for us, especially as they insist on retaining the King as their protégé hidden in rear, whilst the Greeks are determined not to have him back.

A desperate Cabinet this evening lasting from 5.30 to 9 pm! Winston wandering and meandering about, failing to grip his Cabinet and never coming to any decisions. I shudder to think where we are going with him as leader! Why cannot big men know when to close their career?

18 July

We had a long meeting with Cherwell and Duncan Sandys at the COS to discuss flying bombs and measures to meet them. The rocket is becoming a more likely starter. The tendency is of course to try and affect our strategy in France and to direct it definitely against rocket sites. This will want watching carefully.

Martin (*Telegraph* Mil Correspondent) came to lunch with me. He has been in trouble and has had a flying bomb on the roof of his flat. During afternoon Keightley, Commander 78th Division, came to see me, and after him Macready just over from Washington. He was very interesting concerning conditions in Washington and attitude of American Chiefs of Staff during the recent trouble about Anvil!

19 July
A nasty disturbed night with about a dozen flying bombs in the vicinity. The nearest landed about 150 yards away at about 3 am. It displaced the window frame of our sitting room, and blew a lot of glass out of the surrounding houses. I heard it coming, thought it was coming unpleasantly close, so slipped out of bed and took cover behind my bed on the floor to avoid glass splinters.

Got up intending to fly to see Monty, but could not make early start I had intended owing to heavy fog. Meanwhile at 9.30 PM sent for me. I found him in bed in a new blue and gold dressing gown, but in an unholy rage! What was Monty doing dictating to him, he had every right to visit France when he wanted. Who was Monty to stop him? As Defence Minister he had full right to visit any front he wanted! Haig had always allowed him in the last war when he was Minister of Munitions. He would not stand it. He would make it a matter of confidence etc etc. I found it hard to discover what the problem was, or to put in a word edgeways. At last I discovered that Eisenhower had told him that Monty had asked not to have any visitors during the next few days, and the PM had argued out that Monty had aimed this restriction mainly at him! Nothing that I could say would make him believe otherwise. I cannot help feeling that he is becoming more and more unbalanced! He is quite impossible to work with nowadays. I assured him that I could put the whole matter right in 5 minutes with Monty and left him.

I then went to COS till 11.30 when I left for Northolt, there Tedder had very kindly lent me his plane in which I had an excellent crossing to an improvised landing strip near Monty's HQ. We lunched on the plane and arrived about 2 pm. I had a long talk with Monty. First of all I put matter of PM's visit right by getting Monty to write a note to PM telling him he did not know that he wanted to come and inviting him. Then warned him of tendency in PM to listen to suggestions that Monty played for safety and was not prepared to take risks, mainly fostered by Tedder egged on by Coningham. Also warned him of PM's vindictiveness and desire to injure Monty by withdrawing Guards Tank Bde from him to give it to Alexander. I think these various backgrounds may assist Monty. I found him in grand form and delighted with his success east of Caen.

Harry Crerar also came over to see me and I had a long talk with him concerning the question of suitable Canadian higher commanders which seem very deficient.

Took away with me two Camembert cheeses and a bottle of brandy which had been captured from von Schlieffen in Cherbourg! On landing ground met Broadhurst who took me up in his Stork plane for a low flight over the coast and artificial harbour. Left at 6.30 pm and back in Northolt aerodrome by 7.30 pm. Drove round to leave Monty's letter with PM, could not see him as he was asleep. Got back to flat to find a letter from S of S showing that PM had been unbearable all day on the question of 'Monty trying to dictate to him'!! He had finally drafted a foul letter which he wanted to send to Eisenhower notifying him of the intended visit of the PM and of the fact that he would not see Monty, the whole most offensively worded. S of S called me up on telephone, I told him what I had done, and while we were talking he received a message from the PM stating that the letter to Eisenhower was not to be sent. Shortly afterwards PM called me up and said that he was delighted with Monty's letter and felt rather ashamed of himself for all he had said!! And well he might feel ashamed of himself! What a storm in a china cup! All for nothing!

When he sent for me that morning I at once realized that the situation was a dangerous one. He was literally frothing at the corners of his mouth with rage. He at once opened with a flow of abuse directed against Monty such as 'And who is your Monty that he should think he can dictate to me? Have I not got some position in this country as Prime Minister? Do you think I am going to be dictated to by a Monty? In the last war when I was only Minister of Munitions, I went to France whenever I wanted. Sir Douglas Haig always had a chateau and a staff officer at my disposal. And now as Prime Minister does your Monty think he is going to stop me?' As soon as I was able to get a word in edgeways I asked him how Monty was stopping him. He then told me that he was stopping visitors. I reminded him that as Defence Minister he was no visitor, it was all of no avail, nothing would pacify him. I therefore told him I was flying to see Monty and would enquire into the matter.

When I saw Monty I asked him what he was doing stopping the PM from coming to France. He assured me that he was doing nothing of the kind. I then told him that whether he was or not did not matter, but the important thing was that the PM was certain he was. Monty then told me that Stimson had visited Bradley's HQ and had remained with him so long that orders for an attack could not be got out, and the attack had to be postponed for 24 hours. Monty had therefore asked Ike to stop visitors for the present. This message had been passed on to the PM by Ike, and the PM had at once considered that it was directed at him. I therefore told Monty to go into his caravan and to write a letter to the PM on the following lines: 'The CIGS has just informed me that you are under the impression that I am trying to stop you from coming to France. This is the very last thing I should do, and I will always welcome your visits. I shall always have a caravan available for you, and if my duties prevent me from coming round with you personally I shall always have a staff officer at your disposal. I only hope you will pay me a visit soon.' Monty wrote practically these identical words, and this was the letter I brought back and which acted like oil on the troubled waters.

When I went to the Cabinet Offices to hand in the letter, the secretaries informed me that they had had a troubled day, being continually asked what Monty meant by trying to dictate to the PM. Finally P.J. Grigg also had a sad tale to tell of Winston's abuse of Monty. He read me out part of the letter drafted by Winston which P.J. was expected to sign; in it I remember, Ike was to be informed that the PM in his capacity of Defence Minister could visit France when he liked. That he would come on a certain date, but that he would not (repeat NOT) visit General Montgomery!

The letter worked like magic. I think Winston had forgotten that I had gone to France when he called up and said: 'I have had such a nice letter from Monty, he wants me to come to France whenever I like, he will meet me himself when he can, if not he will always have a staff officer at my disposal, and he will also always have a caravan at my disposal.' Peace had been restored temporarily, but it would not last very long.

20 July

We had our usual meeting with the Planners at 10.30. We then considered Winston's minute stating that he had decided that he could not give a decision on the Pacific strategy without discussing matters once more with Dickie Mountbatten!! We had sent him a minute stating that Supreme Commanders were not the people to decide world strategy, that these decisions must rest with the Combined Chiefs of Staff and governments concerned. However he cannot understand strategy and argues the relative advantages of an attack on North Sumatra as opposed to one on Amboina, instead of discussing relative merits of an attack on Japan based on India as opposed to one based on Australia. Now instead of arriving at a decision that is already months overdue he is going off skylarking in France where he can do nothing but disturb commanders who have got important battles to get on with.

At 12.15 Defence Committee meeting connected with our future Turkish policy, decided to urge Turkey to break off diplomatic and economic relations first, and to wait a bit before declaring war. You came up to lunch and the Robin Moneys lunched with us. After lunch had interview with Crawford who was back from France after watching heavy bombing put up by Air Force in support of Monty's attack east of Caen. The system proved most effective and was wonderfully efficiently carried out.

21 July

This morning when I turned on the 8 am news I was astounded to hear of the attempt on Hitler's life, although this was exactly what I had been expecting for some time. It is hard at present to tell how serious the business may be, and how it will ultimately turn out.

A bad night with buzz bombs, finishing off with one well within the ¼ mile radius of this flat. Macready came to COS meeting and gave us latest Washington news, which included Marshall's reaction to our wire trying to cancel the Southern France invasion. Apparently he put it all down to

Winston. A quiet interview with a long discussion with our Professor Ellis [Scientific Advisor] about the impending rocket attacks. He is pretty certain they are coming and works the rocket out at some 15 tons weight with a range of 160 miles.* Not a pleasant prospect.

22 July
The Kennedys came to lunch and I then drove them down to old Lodge's to see his studio, and from there home for Mrs Kennedy to have a talk with Crow who is going to take a holiday governess job with them. A very amusing afternoon.

23 July
My birthday at which I became 61 years old and felt like 71 as I started a heavy cold.

24 July
Poisonous cold with awful head which felt as if the top was going to blow off. Cabinet lasted from 6 pm to 8.45 pm and I did not think I could last it out and felt sick with headache. Just off to bed for a good night, but the buzz bomb alert is just starting!!

25 July
A very long and drawn out COS. First of all with the Joint Intelligence report, and secondly Duncan Sandys and the Professor (Cherwell) to discuss flying bombs and rockets. The large rocket is now taking very definite shape, and may be expected any day. Meanwhile flying bombs have greatly decreased during last 24 hours mainly due to our bombing of Courtrai. Adam came to lunch and we had a very useful talk. During the afternoon Boy Browning came in and we discussed airborne forces. Weather at last a little better and two new offensives started in Normandy.

26 July
We had a bad post war European policy paper which wasted a lot of our time this morning. Then Bertie, just back from Italy, and Hilda came to lunch. At 4 pm I was sent for by Winston and kept for an hour. Eisenhower had been lunching with him and had again run down Montgomery and described his stickiness and the reaction in the American papers! The old story again: 'He was sparing British forces at the expense of the Americans, who were having all the casualties.' However Winston was in a good mood and receptive to

---

*AB is referring to V2 rockets. The first of these hit Britain on 8 September 1944.

arguments. He even said that on all military matters I was his 'alter ego'!! The first time I had ever heard this, or had much reason to suspect it. In the end I was asked to dine tomorrow night to meet Eisenhower and Bedell Smith.

Then at 6 pm a long Cabinet on manpower which lasted till 8.45 pm and at which nothing whatsoever was settled! He cannot give decisions and fails to grip the Cabinet, just wanders on reminiscing! It is all heartbreaking.

27 July

I have earned my pay today! Started with a very rushed hour from 9.45 to 10.45 examining telegrams and being briefed for COS. At 10.30 COS attended by Planners at which we discussed many papers of importance. Back to WO to have an hour with S of S discussing post war policy and our policy in Europe. Should Germany be dismembered or gradually converted to an ally to meet Russian threat of 20 years hence? I suggested the latter and feel certain that we must from now onwards regard Germany in a very different light. Germany is no longer the dominating power of Europe, Russia is. Unfortunately Russia is not entirely European. She has however vast resources and cannot fail to become the main threat in 15 years from now. Therefore foster Germany, gradually build her up, and bring her into a federation of Western Europe. Unfortunately this must all be done under the cloak of a holy alliance between England, Russia and America. Not an easy policy and one requiring a super Foreign Secretary!

After lunch long manpower meeting with Weeks and Kennedy trying to organize post German war forces. At 6 pm Cabinet on the German rocket [V2s] and flying bombs [V1s] which lasted till 8 pm.

Then dinner with PM, Ike and Bedell Smith, intended to bring me closer to Ike and to assist in easy running between Ike and Monty. It did a lot of good. I have offered to go over with Ike if necessary to assist him in handling Monty. My God, what psychological complications war leads to!! The strategy of the Normandy landing is quite straight forward. The British must hold and draw Germans onto themselves off the western flank, whilst Americans swing up to open Brest Peninsula. But now comes the trouble, the press chip in and we hear that the British are doing nothing, and suffering no casualties, whilst the Americans are bearing all the brunt of the war!!

I am tired to death with and by humanity and all its pettiness! Will we ever learn to 'love our allies as ourselves'??!! I doubt it!

There is no doubt that Ike is all out to do all he can to maintain the best of relations between British and Americans, but it is equally clear that Ike knows nothing about strategy and is *quite* unsuited to the post of Supreme Commander as far as running the strategy of the war is concerned! Bedell Smith on the other hand has brains, no military education in the true sense, and unfortunately suffers from a swollen head. He is certainly one of the best American officers, but still falls far short when it comes to strategic outlook. With that Supreme Command set up it is no wonder that Monty's real high ability is not always realized. Especially so when 'national' spectacles pervert the perspective of the strategic landscape.

28 July
A COS as usual with all its variety of problems. Then an interview with S of S. At 3 pm another of those awful Cabinet meetings which lasted two hours, at which we spent all our time discussing the rocket and the flying bomb. All of this should have been finished yesterday, what a desperate waste of time! Winston gets more and more prosy relating all his old reminiscences when holding various Cabinet appointments, none of which have any bearing on the points under discussion. I remain very fond of him, but by heaven he does try one's patience!!

29 July
A fairly short Saturday COS followed by a get away by 1 pm and I was home for a late lunch.

30 July
Quiet Sunday at home.

31 July
A surprisingly short COS for a Monday morning. After lunch a long talk with Brocas Burrows [Head of British Military Mission] just back from Moscow and most interesting about his time there. Then Cabinet at 5.30 which dragged slowly on till 8.30 pm. At least an hour wasted in deciding what a bus driver should do when a buzz bomb was in the offing! Then another hour discussing whether we could possibly relax the blackout regulations! The more I see of Herbert Morrison, the more I despise him! If England is to be ruled by that type of man, then we are sunk for a certainty!

John Kennedy and his wife came to dinner to examine Elliot's [bird] books.

1 August
August! The month when wars usually start! I wonder whether this one will look like finishing instead!?

Our COS laboriously ploughed through the weekly report by the Joint Intelligence Committee, followed by the Flying Bomb Committee: Cherwell, Duncan Sandys, Bottomley, etc, etc. A great deal of talking, and from my point of view, great difficulty as chairman to keep discussion to the point. Portal loves showing his scientific knowledge, Cherwell must show his mathematical genius, and Duncan Sandys insists on letting one know that he has a great political future. All that takes up time and bores me to death. I feel dear old Andrew Cunningham sympathises with me!

After lunch a long Selection Board. Then Winston's next speech to be checked off. Finally a dinner party for S of S, Brocas Burrows just back from Moscow and P.J. Grigg. A great success, Brocas most interesting and confirmed all my views as to how the Russians should be handled.

2 August

Brocas Burrows attended our COS and we discussed the organization of some staff centre at Moscow, although I feel that it is highly unlikely that Stalin will ever agree to any such organization being established.

In the evening I picked up Rollie at 6 pm and we went down to Kew Gardens again, it was lovely down there. We sat on a seat and watched some young water hens being instructed by their mother as to how a bath should be taken! She gave a demonstration first, and then those tiny mites followed suit and copied her, a wonderful sight.

News tonight excellent! St Malo, Rennes, Vitré have all been captured, the latter being the last but one HQ that I occupied in France!!!

3 August

The war news goes on improving daily. In Normandy we have now broken [through] beyond Avranches towards St Malo and Rennes. If things go on as they are doing now we should be able to clear the Brest Peninsula fairly quickly. Beyond that it is rather hard to see what the Boche can do except retire to the line of the Seine, and it is also doubtful if he succeeds in doing this in view of our great preponderance in the air.

Had a lunch for the Portuguese Ambassador (Duke de Palmella). Had the Cranbornes, the Budget Loyds and a Mrs Palmer. After lunch had to have a coloured photograph taken for 'The Illustrated'. Buzz bombs very noisy last night, hope they behave better tonight!

4 August

Mountbatten is due to arrive tonight. On Monday (Bank Holiday!) we are to discuss his plans with him. Then Tuesday and Wednesday in the morning to discuss them with the PM with the object (we hope!) of getting a decision on the Pacific strategy by Wednesday so that Winston can start for Italy that night. Portal and I have said we could not go with him that night as we shall have to put his decision into effect. We intend to follow in about a week and just spend a week only in Italy.

Today Eisenhower has asked for the famous South of France landing to be cancelled and that same force to be transferred to Brittany instead. That is actually what we had suggested to the Americans and they had turned it down! It is far the best solution. Now Winston starts making work by first of all calling for a conference tonight at 10pm to discuss this change, and secondly by deciding to go to France tomorrow to discuss it with Montgomery. I cannot see what there is to discuss, it is a matter of taking a decision quickly, and the decision in this case is an easy one.

Later:

Winston did not keep us long. Told us that Eisenhower had lunched with him and read a paper to him with the suggestion that the South of France landing should be transferred to Brittany which Winston thoroughly agreed with. He gave us the impression that Ike had already sent a telegram about it to America. Winston had drafted a telegram to the President supporting this proposition strongly. I told him that although I entirely agreed with the proposal I was convinced that he was wrong in wiring to the President. This could only have the effect of swinging the Americans against us. He did not agree, decided to send his telegram, and asked us to send one to the American Chiefs supporting him!

5 August
Dickie Mountbatten turned up from India and we had a preliminary meeting with him to discuss his plans. Then slipped home.

6 August
Was called up on the telephone to be told that Eisenhower had never sent any telegram to America, and that he was strongly opposed to any change in the South of France attack plan!! Who has been 'double crossing' who? Has Ike fooled the PM, or has the PM fooled us!! In any case we have certainly not improved our relations with the Americans!

7 August
Bank Holiday, but a busy one! Back early. Dickie Mountbatten and Wedemeyer came to our COS and explained their Burma strategy. It is clear that now that Stilwell has led us down to Mitchinar [Myitkyina?] we shall have to go on operating in Burma. It is equally clear that the best way of doing so is to take the whole of Burma by an airborne attack on Rangoon. Furthermore it is clear that such an enterprise must reduce our effort in the Pacific. Finally as background to it all when will Germany be finished off and allow us to transfer our strength to the Far East? All these points we discussed repeatedly in a series of conferences all through the day. Now it remains to make up our minds, not the easiest part of the task!

8 August
Started with COS at 10.30 and at 11 am met PM and meeting lasted till 1.30 pm. Attended by Eden, Lyttelton, Attlee, Mountbatten and Chiefs of Staff, also Wedemeyer. Meeting resumed again from 6 pm to 8.30 pm and is due to meet once more from 10.30 pm to ? Up to the present we have settled absolutely nothing and as far as I can see we are unlikely to settle anything tonight. We have been discussing the Pacific strategy, recommending the capture of Burma by a landing at Rangoon combined with a Pacific strategy of naval, air and Dominion forces operating from Australia. Winston still hovers back to his tip of Sumatra and refuses to look at anything else.

1 am – Just back from our evening conference with the PM. It was if anything worse than any of the conferences of the day. I believe he has lost the power of giving a decision. He finds every possible excuse to avoid giving one. His arguments are becoming puerile, for instance he upheld this evening that an attack on the tip of Sumatra would force a withdrawal of Japanese forces in northern Burma and would liquidate our commitment in this area. We have conferred for 7 hours!!! with him today to settle absolutely nothing. Nor has he produced a single argument during the whole of that period that was worth listening to. I am at my wits' end and can't go on much longer!

9 August

Another very unpleasant day. Met COS at 10.30 when we discussed previous evening's work and as a result of it drafted our conclusions on South East Asia strategy. At 12.30 we met PM with Anthony, Oliver and Attlee. The PM produced a document of his own which he read out. It was not far off ours and I said so and suggested that Pug should draft a document combining our two papers. I told him privately that he was to draft it mainly on our paper with PM's phraseology.

After lunch meeting with Sosnkowski [C-in-C Polish Forces] who is very upset that we are not providing more assistance to the Underground Army fighting Germans in Warsaw. I had some difficulty in calming him.

Then Cabinet at 5.30 first of all to discuss despatch of force to Greece in event of German evacuation. Had discovered Paget was intending to use 5th Div for this purpose, whilst this division is intended for Italy. Cabinet lasted till 8.50 pm!! Had to dash back as I was dining with the Cranbornes. After dinner meeting with the PM at 10.30 pm which lasted till 1.30 am, at which we finally arrived at a policy for South East Asia. It is not what we started out for and not ideal but it saves as much as it can out of the wreck, whilst also meeting more rapid American advance, and the necessity for liquidating our Burma commitment by undertaking capture of Rangoon. On the other hand it still gives some scope for the use of our naval forces in the Pacific, and for the formation of a British Task Force in the Pacific.

10 August

This morning we drafted carefully our wire to America to put into effect last night's decision. A difficult wire to word as it had to remain acceptable to the Americans whilst remaining within the requirements of the PM. Two opposites very hard to reconcile!!

After lunch visit from Alan Cunningham, over from Ireland, to tell me results of his recent contacts with McKenna (Free State C-in-C). Apparently de Valera is contemplating introducing conscription! at any rate after the war. Must discuss effect of this on Northern Ireland with Basil.

Then visit from Archdale, who accompanied me on that momentous visit to Weygand in 1940. He is retiring. He was followed by Archie Nye, then S of S to inform him of my discussion with Winston. Finally Mountbatten looking for successor to Giffard and other points too. Then long discussion with D of Air, Crawford, on his last trip to France with the bombers supporting the Army. Finally rush home to change and got ready to dine with John Anderson at Claridges, official dinner for Morgenthau. Sat next to Herbert Morrison, dinner comprised Attlee, Eden, Lyttelton, Alexander, Sinclair, P.J., Brendan Bracken, Cherwell etc etc.

Winston started tonight by air for Italy. But not until he had redrafted our wire to the American COS and put it into a form and words in which it is unmistakable and bound to be recognized as emanating from him, and consequently crash any hope of getting it through!!!

11 August

We had to reconsider the PM's amendments and refuse to accept them with consequent delay. I then had a busy day with interviews, culminating with quite hopeless letters from Dickie Mountbatten to Marshall, which he sent me to look at!! I had to tell him that he could not send *any* of them and should attend COS on Monday with Wedemeyer and we could tell the latter what he should say to Marshall.

Finally left for home about 7 pm to take a long weekend. I was feeling absolutely cooked and dog tired after the last week's work and arguments with the PM!!

12 and 13 August

Spent quietly at home with you and resting peacefully. Just *heaven* after the previous week.

14 August

Back to WO by 9.30. News very good and every chance of rounding off Boche on Monty's front.

At COS Dickie and Wedemeyer attended, the latter most helpful and I hope he assists in putting the case to the Americans. Adam to lunch and long talks with him prior to my visit to Italy. Cabinet at 5.30 run by Attlee and finished in half the time. Then dinner at White's Club with Bertie and long talk with him. It is such a joy having him back and a chance of discussing matters with him again. Tonight landings in Southern France, near Toulon and St Raphael are to take place!!

15 August

Life has a quiet and peaceful atmosphere about it now that Winston is gone [to Italy]! Everything gets done twice as quickly, everybody is not on edge, one is not bombarded by a series of quite futile minutes and the whole machinery settles down to efficient smooth running. I feel that we have now reached the stage that for the good of the nation and for the good of his own reputation it would be a godsend if he could disappear out of public life. He has probably done more for this country than any other human being has ever done, his reputation has reached its climax, it would be a tragedy to blemish such a past by foolish actions during an inevitable decline which has set in during the last year. Personally I have found him almost impossible to work with of late, and I am filled with apprehension as to where he may lead us next.

A full morning at the COS studying with the Joint Intelligence Committee the German reactions to the Allied successes on all fronts. It is a wonderfully thrilling period. Apparently Germans contemplating holding the line of the Seine and Marne!

After lunch visit to Amery, who is very perturbed about the Indian grain situation. He is calling for our assistance and is very nervous lest Archie Wavell should resign the Viceroyship owing to the lack of support he is receiving from the Government. At 5 pm Cabinet run by Attlee on the rocket bomb and the desirability of giving Germans false reports through agents so as to move mean point of burst further south. Monty's great encircling move in France is making good progress and still holds out great hopes.

16 August

Most of the COS was taken up with problems as to how to support the Polish underground rising in Warsaw. The Russians appear to be purposely giving no assistance and the Poles here are naturally frantic. The landing near Toulon seems to be going well, whilst the operations in Normandy are working up towards a climax. There are great hopes of delivering a smashing blow which might go a long way towards clearing the road for the rest of France.

Gort came to lunch, he seemed very pleased with the idea of going as Governor of Palestine. He was in good form and looking much better than he has at times.

17 August

The Joint Planners came to attend the COS and we discussed all the difficulties facing us if we are to stage a Rangoon attack by next March! The War Office have been raising just one series of difficulties and delays. Their examination proved that it was impossible to do it by that date. I therefore had a 2 hours meeting this morning to prove to them that it is possible and must be done. It is extraordinary how exhausting it is having to drive a plan through against opposition. First on the part of the PM and now on the part of those responsible for it in the WO. There are moments when I would give anything just to get in a car and drive home, saying I was fed up with the whole show and they could look for someone else to fill my job! The making of plans is just child's play as compared to putting them into execution. I feel worn out and very glad at the thought of going to Italy for a change and rest.

18 August

We had a final interview with Dickie Mountbatten to discuss our plans for the capture of Rangoon which is based on our being able to start withdrawing the 6th Division from the European Theatre on Oct 1st. It is a gamble, but I believe one worth taking. During afternoon a Cabinet at 5 pm to discuss the underground rising in Warsaw and lack of support on behalf of the Russians. Then various interviews all in preparation for my departure tonight with Portal for Italy. We leave Northolt at midnight, hope to make Rabat about 7 am and Naples about 4 pm tomorrow.

19 August

2.30 pm – Over the sea between Tunis and Sicily. We left Northolt punctually at midnight. The party consisted of Portal with two of his assistants and myself with Boyle and Lockwood. We had a very good 8 hours flight to Rabat. The rising sun over a sea of clouds with a spotless pink sky above me was well worth flying 8 hours to see. At Rabat we motored to the hotel run by the RAF and had a shave bath and breakfast. At 10 am we were off again flying over Fez, Oujda, south of Oran and Algiers and out at Tunis. I had a good look from the air at the villa I was in last December with the PM when he was ill. Whilst flying over Africa we had a very good lunch and a specially smooth journey. We should now pass over the western end of Sicily and then fly straight on to Naples where we are due at about 4 pm. It is a wonderful feeling comparing this flight with my first journey down the Mediterranean before Alex and Monty were installed in Egypt. I then slunk along in a two engined Dakota under cover of darkness and very glad to get through safely.

Later: Caserta, 3000 miles
Punctually on the stroke of 4 pm we landed just north east of Naples having flown over 3000 miles in 14 hours and been 14 hours in the air out of the last 24 hours. We were met on the aerodrome by Wilson and Slessor and Gammell. We went up to Wilson's HQ and there discussed plans and prepared a programme for the next few days. I then had a long talk with Jumbo Wilson and finally came up to the hunting lodge above Caserta which he is living in. It has been a useful talk and many of my doubts as to the value of Oliver Leese are being confirmed. He is certainly not anything outstanding as a commander.

20 August   Caserta

Spent the whole morning in conferences with Jumbo Wilson, Portal, John Cunningham, Slessor, Gammell and the Americans Devers and [illegible], etc. We examined recent successes near Toulon, discussed future of the Southern France invasion, planned Mediterranean strategy, reoccupation of Greece when Germans collapse etc. For lunch Devers, [illegible], Portal and Slessor came to Jumbo's mess. After lunch more conferences to dinner. Paget turned up in the evening and I spent some time talking over some of his problems with him.

21 August   Alex's HQ south of Florence near Siena

A most interesting day. Left Naples aerodrome at 8.30 am and flew past Mount Camino where I established all my old contacts from my last visit and climbed up this hill, and then round Mount Cassino and Monastery Hill where we did two rings round and I had a most excellent view of the whole position. We then flew up the Liri valley, looking at all the ground I had looked at on my map and model time and time again. From there over Anzio bridgehead, which we examined carefully. Finally landed outside Rome. We did a 3 hour tour of Rome and had a very good view of some of the most important parts. At 1 pm we went to the British Embassy, to dine with Charles. I did not think much of either him or his wife as our ambassador in Rome at a critical moment such as the present one! To lunch: PM who had just arrived, Macmillan, Jumbo Wilson, Portal, Morland, Peck, Rowan and Tommy.

After lunch conference with PM on the question of Greece, got him to agree that the Greek Gov should be moved out to Italy. After meeting he kept me on to tell me that Jumbo Wilson was interfering too much with Alexander. This is not right, and I cannot believe that Alexander should have been guilty of suggesting such a thing, but I am not too certain. I also tackled him about Schreiber being appointed to Governor of Malta. Then I had a rush round Rome booksellers looking for bird books, but without success.

Embarked in plane at 6 pm and flew on up to Alex's HQ. He met me on the aerodrome and we had a lovely drive up to his small camp. Here I am very comfortable in one of his caravans.

22 August   Near Siena

At 9 am attended intelligence conference of Alex's to hear latest moves on all fronts. We then started off with a long tour of the front. First we visited Murray, who had just taken over command of 6th Armoured Division on right of XIII Corps. We had collected Kirkman, commander of XIII Corps, on the way. From there we visited Russell, commander 8th Ind Div, and then went on to an artillery medium HQ from which we had a very good view of Florence. We also had a shot at the Boche from there. Then we went to HQ 1st Div and visited Loewen, the commander. Tom was produced there and I found he was back in the 19th Regiment and apparently very happy. Came back about 7 pm and after a shower bath had a long discussion with Alex on questions of organization of the Mediterranean command. Found Alex very upset, evidently both Robertson and Harding had worked him up. I find that relations between Alex and Wilson are not of the best. This is troublesome and will require a good deal of working at. Dick McCreery came to dine, I was delighted at seeing him again.

23 August

Attended Alex's conference at 9 am and then started in a jeep for the landing strip near the camp. There we took off in 'Whizzers' for the Siena aerodrome where we changed into Alex's Dakota. We flew across Italy to Sesi, a landing ground just west of Ancona. There I met Anders of the Polish Corps and found him in great spirits in spite of all the Warsaw troubles with the Russians. His attitude being: 'We Poles have two deadly enemies, the Germans and the Russians. We are now engaged with the Germans – well, let us make a job of this enemy first.' We then drove up to Oliver Leese's HQ where we had lunch and discussed his forthcoming offensive. Met Walsh, his BGS, and Boillon, his Chief Q. After lunch Charles Keightley turned up, having just taken over V Corps. On way back I had interview with Burns, commanding the Canadian Corps.

Flew back to near Siena and on the way back to the camp visited Siena Cathedral which was most interesting. Finished up the day by dining with the PM in his villa where he had come back to for a few days to be near oncoming battle!

I think that it was during this visit that Alex told me that Harding had produced a very important paper that he would like me to go through. It was typical of Alex that he should ask me to discuss it with Harding [the Chief of Staff] instead of discussing it direct with him. I always found him very loath to discuss any strategic plans with me, as if he feared getting out of his depth. Anyway, I read Harding's paper and then talked it over with him. It was a fantastic scheme to create an all British front in Italy by removing all American forces from Italy to France and replacing them by British forces drawn from France. This all British force was then to proceed through northern Italy and through the Ljubljana Alps to the capture of Vienna. I had to draw his attention to the fact that with the shipping available such a move would take months, during which period a large force would take no part on either front. I then asked him if he thought it advisable that [in] the offensive on the main front, responsible for the final defeat of the Germans, we should leave the task entirely to the Americans and take an insignificant part? Finally, I asked him when he hoped to reach the line of the Apennines, when he would cross this line, when would he cross the River Po, and when did he hope to reach the Ljubljana Alps? At the present rate of advance I saw little hope of his reaching this line of mountains till the winter months when he would be faced with one single pass which would have to be kept open.

His scheme was fantastic mainly because he had not got the data to base it on. I quote this episode as an example of Alex's lack of appreciation of what he was faced with. He and Harding had been seeing a great deal of Winston during the last few days, and in their pipe dream had repeatedly captured Vienna, and expressed hopes that this could be accomplished by an all British force. Unfortunately in examining the winning post they were forgetting to devote enough attention to the fences immediately in front of them.

24 August

Freyberg came to have breakfast with me before my departure. He was in very good form. After listening to the morning's intelligence report I left for the aerodrome and by 10.45 we were off for Naples. We made good time and arrived at 12.15. There I found Gammell, who had various points he wanted to discuss. Portal was there also, and by 12.45 we had started for Gibraltar. We had lunch on board and after a very good run arrived at Gibraltar at 7 pm. We were met by Rusty Eastwood and went up to Government House for dinner. Had hoped to start again by 11 pm, but owing to foggy weather at home our departure was put off till 4 am. We went down to the plane shortly after midnight and put in some good sleep before taking off.

25 August   London

We crossed the coastline somewhere about 10 am, and by 11 am were landing at Northolt having flown just under 7000 miles in the 6 days we had been away. It has been a very useful trip and I have gathered a lot of information, but am somewhat troubled at the poor relations prevailing between Alex's and Wilson's HQs.

Spent most of the day getting into the picture and telling P.J. about my trip and the conditions in Italy. The news of German decay on all fronts continues to be almost unbelievable!

26 August

Attended COS again, but not much doing. Started for home early, calling on old Lodge in Camberley on the way home to leave some of his pictures with him. Found Hylda and Evelyn back from their long journey abroad.

27 August

Quiet Sunday at home.

28 August

Difficult COS where we considered Eisenhower's new plan to take command himself in Northern France on Sept 1st. This plan is likely to add another 3 to 6 months on to the war! He straight away wants to split his forces, sending an American contingent towards Nancy whilst the British army group moves along the coast. If the Germans were not as beat as they are, this would be a fatal move, as it is it may not do too much harm. In any case I am off to France tomorrow to see Monty and to discuss the situation with him. Meanwhile Paris is liberated, Rumania out of the war and Bulgaria tumbling out next. The Germans cannot last very much longer.

Attended Thanksgiving Service in the Crypt of St Paul's Cathedral for the liberation of Paris at 12 noon. Hearing the Marseillaise boom out gave me a deep thrill which stirred me inwardly. France seemed to wake again after being knocked out for 5 years.

Eisenhower's plans for change in the command were going to lead to a lot of discussion. Up to now he had been a Supreme Commander with separate commanders for naval, land and air forces. Now he proposed to assume the dual role of Supreme Commander and commander of the land forces. This change was brought about mainly by the American press resenting the fact that Monty was commanding all the land forces. Personally I consider it wrong for a Supreme Commander to attempt the role of the supreme task on one level and one of the services on the next level.

29 August

Left here at 9 am for Hendon where I took off in pouring rain with an escort of 3 fighters for Normandy. Arrived there 11 am and met by de Guingand who said that weather was too bad for flying on to Monty's HQ. I therefore had a 2¾ hours drive in pouring rain along muddy roads crammed with lorries and at times heavily scented with dead horses. We went through Caen, Falaise and Chambois. The latter was a regular shambles of broken tanks, lorries, carts and dead horses. Arrived Monty's HQ by 2 pm. Had lunch with him and long talk with him about recent crisis with Eisenhower. Apparently he has succeeded in arriving at a suitable compromise by which 1st US Army is to move on the right of 21st Army Group and head for area Charleroi, Namur, Liège, just north of Ardennes. Only unsatisfactory part is that this army is not under Monty's orders and he can only coordinate its actions in relation to 21st Army Group. This may work, it remains to be seen what political pressure is put on Eisenhower to move Americans on separate axis from the British.

Left at 3.30, had another 2¾ hours back to aerodrome and a murky fly home through clouds, reaching Hendon at 7.45 pm, having lost my escort of 3 fighters in the clouds. I hope they returned safely. Winston returned from Italy this evening with a temperature of 104!!

30 August

Apparently Winston has again got a minor attack of pneumonia. Not much, and they think they can get him right to start by sea in the *Queen Mary* for Quebec next week. I was sent for by him at 7 pm. Found him looking ill. I explained to him the difficulties that had been arising with Eisenhower taking control from Monty, and wanting to direct the American forces on Nancy and Frankfurt, leaving the British forces to deal with the German forces in northern France. He informed me that he wanted to make Monty a Field Marshal, the appointment to coincide (Sept 1st) with the date of Eisenhower assuming command of the land forces. He felt that such a move would mark the approval of the British people for the *British* effort that had led to the defeat of the Germans in France through the medium of Montgomery's leadership.

31 August

A long COS. Then Martin for lunch. In the evening a Cabinet at 6 pm connected with terms of release for personnel after defeat of Germany. A difficult and ticklish problem. Finally Rollie Charrington to dinner and a very pleasant evening with him.

1 September

Winston is improving rapidly and it looks as if we should all be starting for Quebec on Monday evening. Lunched with Adam today and we had a very useful talk about the Army generally. During morning and afternoon repeated telephone calls from Winston to find out whether Alex could reassume his senior position to Monty when he is made a Field Marshal at a later date!

2 September

Left early and after picking you up motored to Preshaw to shoot. Wild, windy and rainy day.

3 September

Quiet Sunday at home.

4 September

A lot of messages in, and many preparations all day for our departure. Lewin came to lunch. Cabinet at 5.40 attended by PM who was not looking at all well. I very much wonder whether he will be up to the strain of this trip. This evening our troops are reported in Brussels and advancing on Antwerp! It is very hard to believe it all!!

5 September   On board *Queen Mary*

Left the flat this morning shortly after 9 am for Addison Road [Station]. There I joined the PM's special train. The party on the train consisted of Winston, Clemmie, Moran, Portal, Cunningham, self, Tommy and Martin. Shortly after we had left the PM sent for us and we had a conference on Greece with him. He seems to be still very much of the opinion that we might be justified in dropping a parachute brigade (about 2,000–3,000 strong) near Athens with some 150,000 Germans still in Greece!! I had to convince him that such a plan was out of the question and that the dropping of this party was dependent on the Germans evacuating Greece or being prepared to surrender. He was looking much better and in very good form.

By about 7 pm we arrived on the Clyde and came straight on board the *Queen Mary*. I am again in the same cabin that I had on both my other trips to America. After dinner went up onto the bridge with Cunningham and Portal and watched the start of our journey.

I am not looking forward to this journey and conference. Winston is still always set on capturing the tip of Sumatra, he has agreed to our airborne campaign on lower Burma, but limits his sanction to the capture of Rangoon alone without the clearing of the rest of Burma. This makes the expedition practically useless and what is worse converts it into one which cannot appeal to the Americans since it fails to affect upper Burma where their air route is situated. I should have a difficult enough task to get the Americans to agree to the Burma plans, but with the PM in the background it becomes relatively impossible. Added to it all that I am feeling frightfully mentally tired and disinclined for a difficult conference!

It was probably just as well that I was not able to look into the future and see what was facing me. I was in for a series of the most difficult conferences with Winston on this journey. Conferences where he repudiated everything he had agreed to up to date. I do not think that he had thoroughly recovered from his go of pneumonia and he was still suffering from the after effects of the heavy doses of M and B [May and Baker, a sulphonamide] which he had been given. He was quite impossible to argue with. As for instance his idea of taking Rangoon and leaving the rest of Burma when the main idea of Burma campaign was to reopen communications through Burma to China.

During the conferences in Quebec, matters were even worse. He got it into his head that we were going to 'frame up' (he used those actual words to me) with the American Chiefs against him. As he knew that the American Chiefs could handle the President fairly easily, he feared that he would be faced with a military block of Chiefs of Staff plus the President against him. As matters stood we were very far from 'framing up' with our American colleagues even if we had wished to, which was unlikely as we were about to have a most difficult time to get any agreement at all with them. I could not get Winston to appreciate this, all his suspicions were aroused. Kept on sending for me to find out what we were settling, and trying to alter every decision. It was a ghastly time from which I have carried away the bitterest of memories.

6 September

Woke up to find the *Queen Mary* gliding down the Irish Channel with the Irish Coast in view. At 10.30 we held a COS conference to discuss our line of action with the Americans. We discussed possibility of beginning the withdrawal of forces from Europe for the war against Japan and came to the conclusion that as far as could be judged at the present moment we were justified, but should await events of the next few days before taking final decisions. We then discussed future of Italian campaign and came to the conclusion that it must soon become of secondary importance, namely as soon as the Pisa-Rimini line had been broken and Kesselring's forces defeated and driven back. Unfortunately it will not be easy to get Winston to see eye to eye with us on this matter. After lunch we had the COS [Planners?] in for a discussion. Finally, went to the 'pictures' and saw a very good film.

7 September

Started the day again with a Chiefs of Staff meeting which we got Leathers to attend in order to discuss the shipping situation which will arise when Germany is defeated. The call on personnel shipping will be enormous, what with move of forces to the Japanese war, repatriation of our prisoners, return of Americans to USA and on to Japanese war, Canadians to Canada, New Zealanders to their homes and South Africans to South Africa, and on top of it all certain civilian requirements which will have to be provided for. It is going to be a difficult problem to lay down priorities for all these moves.

Cunningham, Portal, Laycock and I went to lunch with Winston and Clemmie. He was not looking at all well and was most desperately flat. A good deal of it may be due to the M and B which he has been taking. A quiet afternoon finishing up with an evening at the cinema. Last night we passed close over a German submarine and intercepted his signal reporting having seen us! We are now level with Cape Finisterre and have just turned due west, making straight for Halifax. Destroyers have now left us and we have only one cruiser as escort, we are doing about 28 knots and the cruiser is having some difficulty keeping up with us.

8 September   Queen Mary

We have been travelling in the Gulf Stream all day and consequently living in a Turkish bath of hot clamminess. We began with a short COS and at 12 noon had a meeting lasting till 1.30 with the PM. He looked old, unwell and depressed. Evidently found it hard to concentrate and kept holding his head between his hands. He was quite impossible to work with, began by accusing us of framing up against him and of opposing him in his wishes. According to him we were coming to Quebec solely to obtain 20 landing ships out of the Americans to carry out an operation against Istria [coast of Slovenia] to seize Trieste; and there we were suggesting that with the rate at which events were moving Istria might be of no value. We also suggested moving troops from Europe for Burma and had never told him that the removal of these forces was dependent on the defeat of Hitler (a completely false accusation). He further said that we had told him only one division was required for Burma, and now we spoke of 5! (Here again a complete misstatement of facts.) It was hard to keep one's temper with him but I could not help feeling frightfully sorry for him. He gave me the feeling of a man who is finished, can no longer keep a grip of things, and is beginning to realize it. We made no progress and decided to go on tomorrow. He finished up by saying: 'Here we are within 72 hours of meeting the Americans and there is not a single point that we are in agreement over'!!

Spent the afternoon working up notes for tomorrow's meeting with him. In the evening went to see a film. I am feeling *very very* depressed at the thought of this meeting, unless Winston changes radically we shall be in hopeless situation.

9 September *Queen Mary*

We received 2 minutes from the PM today which show clearly that he is a sick man. His arguments are again centred on one point – Istria. We have come for one purpose only – to secure landing craft for an operation against Istria!! All else of importance fades into the shade of secondary considerations. But what is more serious he now repudiates an agreement which we secured with him weeks ago, and which we submitted to the Americans with his approval! Namely the possible formation of a British task force under MacArthur, a subject discussed with Curtin and Fraser during the Imperial Conference, and repeatedly thrashed out in the War Cabinet, is now repudiated, and disapproved as a matter of discussion with the Americans. The situation becomes quite impossible and I am at my wits' end as to what we are to do.

We were to have met him this evening but he had started another temperature and had to remain in bed cancelling an invitation for us to dine with him! I am afraid that he is very definitely ill and doubtful how much longer he will last. The tragedy is that in his present condition he may well do untold harm!

Went to see the film of Madam Curie's discovery of radium, I thought it was very good.

10 September

We had another meeting with Winston at 12 noon. He was again in a most unpleasant mood. Produced the most ridiculous arguments to prove that operations could be speeded up so as to leave us an option till December before having to withdraw any forces from Europe! He knows no details, has only got half the picture in his mind, talks absurdities and makes my blood boil to listen to his nonsense. I find it hard to remain civil. And the wonderful thing is that ¾ of the population of the world imagine that Winston Churchill is one of the Strategists of History, a second Marlborough, and the other ¼ have no conception what a public menace he is and has been throughout this war! It is far better that the world should never know, and never suspect the feet of clay of that otherwise superhuman being. Without him England was lost for a certainty, with him England has been on the verge of disaster time and again.

And with it all no recognition hardly at all for those who help him except the occasional crumb intended to prevent the dog from straying too far from the table. Never have I admired and despised a man simultaneously to the same extent. Never have such opposite extremes been combined in the same human being.

After our conference we lunched with him and Clemmie. During lunch we came alongside. [Malcolm] Macdonald [High Commissioner] came on board. Immediately after lunch we went ashore, and there I met Elkins, who was attached to 'N' Battery when I was a subaltern, and Goodeve who was with me in the Canadian Corps. By about 3 pm our special train had left for Quebec.

My criticism of Winston's wrath on that day was obviously unnecessarily hard, it should however be remembered that they were written at a moment of exasperation due to his attitude during the meetings we had held, and desperation as to how I was to handle the conference in front of me with his continuous obstruction.

11 September   Quebec

After a very comfortable journey we arrived here at 10 am to find President's train had arrived before us. Usual cheering, photographs etc, and we were off in cars to the Frontenac Hotel. Here again excellent accommodation. Conference after lunch and then several hours reading of messages. Finally dinner at the Citadel by the Athlones [Governor-General] for Winston and Roosevelt. All the rank, fashion and clergy of Quebec, plus all American Chiefs of Staff. Bad speeches by Athlone and President full of worthless platitudes lacking any sincerity. Am I getting soured against humanity as a whole, or am I right that such official banquets are the centres of the most ghastly hypocrisy!?

12 September

Today we started work and after a COS at 10 am we had our first [Combined] COS at 12 noon till lunch and again from 2.30 pm to 4.30 pm. It went off most satisfactorily and we found ourselves in complete agreement with American Chiefs of Staff. They were prepared to leave American divisions in Italy till Alex had finished his offensive. They were also prepared to leave LSTs for Istrian venture if required. At 4.30 pm we had an ordinary COS to discuss latest minute by PM on Pacific strategy. He is gradually coming round to sane strategy, but by heaven what labour we have had for it. He now accepts a naval contingent to the Pacific, a Dominion Task Force under MacArthur, etc, etc. At 6.30 pm we had to go up to the Citadel for a meeting with him. He was all smiles and friendliness for a change. How quickly he changes. An April day's moods would be put to shame by him!

   Lunched with Marshall, Leahy and Dill, the former as boring and as charming as usual. Dined at Citadel with Athlones, following were there, Roosevelt, Churchill, American Chiefs of Staff and British Chiefs of Staff. I sat on President's right and found him very pleasant and easy to talk to. King was on my right. After dinner Mackenzie King came in and I had a long talk with him. A tiring day, but a good deal accomplished.

13 September   Quebec

Started with a COS at 9 am as we were to meet the Americans at 10 am. However the PM sent for us and informed us it was essential for him to see us at 10 am. As a result we had to put off our meeting with the Americans. However, when we met him we found he had nothing special to see us about! I would have given a great deal to tell him what I thought of him.

   At 11.30 we had a Plenary meeting, which consisted of a long statement by the PM giving his views as to how the war should be run. According to him we had two main objectives, first an advance on Vienna, secondly the capture of

Singapore! However he did support the employment of naval forces in the Pacific. After lunch another meeting with American Chiefs followed by another COS at 4 pm which lasted till nearly 6 pm. Finally we had a reception by Mackenzie King, consisting of a supper for a vast assembly of Canadians plus the American and British Missions here.

It should be remembered that Winston was living in the Citadel whilst we were in the Frontenac Hotel. Every time we were sent for it entailed collecting cars and driving up and back from the Citadel, which wasted precious time.

It is worth noting that the two objectives he had named in the Plenary Meeting were neither of them in our plans. We had no plans for Vienna, nor did I ever look at this operation as becoming possible. Nor had we any plans for the capture of Singapore. However, by mentioning these objectives he was not assisting in our discussions with the American Chiefs.

14 September

I started the day by being called by Lockwood at 7.30 am and being told that the PM wanted to see me at 9 am and that Pug Ismay would like to see me before that! I hurried with breakfast and some office work and then saw Ismay. Found him very upset, having had a ghastly time on previous evening with Winston! PM had, on his own, wired to Dickie Mountbatten to find out how it was he was now wanting 6 divisions to capture Burma having originally said he only wanted 2 from outside. Dickie had wired back giving full details of the series of changes in plans that had occurred. As a result Winston had accused us all to Ismay of purposely concealing changes of plan from him to keep him in the dark. That we were all against him, and heaven knows what not! As a result Ismay had written out a letter handing in his resignation to him, and asked for my advice as to whether he should send it in!! I told him this decision must rest with him, but that I agreed it would probably bring Winston to his senses.

I then started off to see Winston at 9 am, wondering what awful row I should find myself mixed up in. To my surprise I found him in his bed and in a very good mood. Another wire from Dickie had arrived with new suggestions. He had now got over all his bad humour, he was now prepared to move 2nd Indian Div from Alexander, which he would not look at before! He was in such a good mood that I tackled him about the transfer of Oliver Leese from Alexander to replace Giffard with Dickie, and got him to agree!

I then dashed back for a COS at 9.30 am which was followed by a Combined meeting at 10 am lasting till 12 noon. A very successful meeting at which we got the Americans to accept the British fleet in Central Pacific, and also the Burma operation. We had great trouble with King who lost his temper entirely and was opposed by the whole of his own committee! He was determined if he could not to admit British naval forces into Nimitz's command in the Central Pacific. At 12.15 we had another short COS to decide how to deal with King's evident animosity towards the conclusions we had arrived at. We decided to get the PM at the final Plenary Meeting to 'cross the T's and dot the I's' in this respect. Bovey, a Canadian friend of mine, then came to lunch with me.

At 3 pm we attended a Canadian War Cabinet meeting in the Citadel. More of a politeness than anything else. At 4 pm we had a Chiefs of Staff meeting with the Canadian Chiefs of Staff. After that tea, some shopping, and 1½ hours office work. Finally went to dine with Colonel Clark (who provides all the wood pulp for the *Daily Mail*). He was giving dinner for American, Canadian and British Chiefs of Staff. He gave us an excellent dinner, exceptionally well served.

My mind is now much more at rest. We have nearly finished this meeting and they are the most awful strain. Things have gone well on the whole in spite of Winston's unbearable moods.

The fact that dear old patient Pug had at last reached the end of his tether and could stand Winston's moods no longer is some indication of what we had been through. Of course, poor old Pug always got the worst of it, but he was always so patient, and made so many allowances for all Winston's whims, that I felt it would take a climax to make him hand in his papers. I believe he did hand in his resignation and that Winston refused to take any notice of it. But for all that it relieved the tension.

15 September
A satisfactory day in everything except our contacts with the Prime Minister! Started with a COS at 9 am, followed by a Combined meeting at 10 am. There we succeeded in winding up the work of this meeting and produced our final report to President and Prime Minister. On the whole we have been very successful in getting the agreement which we have achieved, and the Americans have shown a wonderful spirit of co-operation. D. Taylor, a Canadian friend of mine of the last war, came to lunch with me.

In the evening we met the PM at 6 pm. A frightful interview!! He did his best to pull the whole of our final report to pieces, found a lot of petty criticisms and wanted to alter many points which we had secured agreement on with some difficulty. Anthony Eden was there, and he did his best to help us, but unfortunately Winston was in one of his worst tempers. Now Heaven only knows what will happen tomorrow at our final Plenary meeting. He may between now and tomorrow alter his outlook but I doubt it. The tragedy is that the Americans whilst admiring him as a man have little opinion of him as a strategist, they are intensely suspicious of him. All his alterations or amendments are likely to make them more suspicious than ever.

16 September   Oriskany Camp
The last day of the conference! We started the day with a COS at 9 am expecting to receive certain amendments by the PM to the final report. We did not know quite how we should deal with them as the final report was one which we had agreed to with the American Chiefs, it was therefore not possible for us

now to wish alterations to be brought in. These alterations should be done at the final Plenary meeting, but we had been unable to get Winston to see this last night. However, he must have thought better of it as those remarks never turned up, and instead we were told that he wanted to see us 10 minutes before the Plenary meeting.

At 11 am we had our final Combined meeting and then went up to the Citadel where we met Winston. The first thing he informed us was that he wanted us all for a meeting at 5 pm; we had previously made it quite clear that we proposed starting for our fishing trip at 2.30 pm! We told him that planes were ordered and all plans made. He said that we should not be seeing each other for 10 days and must have a meeting! We then found out that he had considerably reduced his remarks on our final report, and had decided to produce them himself at the meeting. He had also written a statement which could do little more than reduce the opinion that the Americans have of him as a strategist!! The meeting went off well and we returned full of gloom to the hotel to counter-order our planes. However, while we were at lunch we received a message from him saying that after all he would not have a meeting and would not want us!

We had a desperate rush and by 3 pm left the hotel for the aerodrome. Our party consisted of Portal, Cunningham, Leckie (Canadian CAS) and self. We took off in two amphibious planes and had an hour's very interesting flight north west from Quebec towards Hudson's Bay. Country mainly virgin forest and masses of lakes. After about 150 miles we reached the Oriskany Lake where the fishing camp is situated. The Camp covers a large area of lakes and lumber areas which supplies wood for paper pulping. The camp was beautifully laid out, 3 large log huts very well fitted up with electric lights, hot and cold water, showers, etc etc. Two of the huts were living ones and the third kitchen and dining room. De Carteret, one of the managers, acted as our host. We landed on the lake, taxied up to the landing stage, had tea, put up rods and started off in canoes to fish. Each one of us had a canoe and guide, we moved from lake to lake by 'portage', the guide carrying the canoe on his head.

We first of all went to Lake Deep with about ½ mile portage from the main lake. There we found some trout rising quite well and caught a good few small-ish ones. We then had a short portage to Lake Silver. As it was getting dark I caught a nice 2 pounder. Returned to camp by torchlight and an excellent dinner at about 9 pm. I had caught 14 trout, but only one good one.

I notice that in my diary I have made very little reference to Dill. This is not due to the fact that he was playing any lesser part than usual, on the contrary he continued to act as the most invaluable link between Marshall and me. I did, however, notice at this conference that he was very far from being his old self. He seemed to be wasting away, and both mentally and physically he was showing signs of slowing up. When walking down the passages of the hotel with him one had continually to check one's pace. When speaking to him one had frequently to repeat sentences to him as if his brain only slowly absorbed statements. I was very disturbed to see him in this state, but had no idea that this was the last occasion on which we should meet. Thank heaven I did not know – the parting would have been too hard.

17 September   Oriskany Camp

We got up at 6 am and after a cup of coffee started off with canoes and guides. We again went through Deep Lake and Silver Lake and from there on to Yate Lake and Spurey Lake and back to Silver Lake, having completed a circuit which brought us to a small log hut where breakfast had been sent out for us. After breakfast we set out again through Lakes Bladelrun, Zion, Sundance to Blue Lake. There we fished and trolled for some time and also had lunch which was brought out to us. Finally, into the evening we worked our way home by a series of 'portages' the way we came. How my little guide, who must have been nearly as old as I am, carried that 80 lb canoe all that distance is a marvel. We reached home after dark tired and hungry after a delightful day. I had caught 10 nice trout of about 1 to 1½ lbs.

18 September   Lac des Neiges

Up at 6 am and out to troll for grey trout in the main Oriskany Lake. We trolled a very large spoon about 2 inches long and one inch broad with two red eyes in it. I caught several small ones from 1½ to 2 lbs. We had breakfast at 9 am and then sallied out by car to fish another lake till lunch. This lake, called Harbison, was a long, narrow lake. Portal and I were on it whilst Leckie and Cunningham fished Lake Whaler. We came back to lunch and pack for our departure, and after lunch Cunningham took off for Quebec and New York, whilst Portal and I took off for Quebec hoping to be able to fly on to the Lac des Neiges. Unfortunately the latter is some 3000 feet up and was in the clouds, so we had to go by road. Our host, Colonel Clark, met us on the aerodrome and motored up with us. We stopped for tea at La Cabane, his river camp where Winston stayed last year. We hurried on to try and put some fishing in before dark, but we only had ½ hour before it became too dark to fish. We found the camp staff the same as last year with Rose the cook to welcome us and give us an excellent dinner.

19 September   Lac des Neiges

Up at 6 am and Portal and I, accompanied by Clark's son, set out for the bay opposite the camp where we found the trout rising well. We fished several other places returning for breakfast at 9.30 am. After a hurried breakfast we went out again till a late lunch at 2.30 pm and then out again till dark. I finished up the day having caught 62 trout, averaging a good 1½ lbs and with two of about 3 lbs. A most enjoyable day.

20 September

Up again at 6 am and fished hard till 2.30 pm when we had to leave. After the morning rise I concentrated on trying to catch a good grey trout and did a good deal of spinning with my tiny rod. I had great fun and succeeded in catching one of 12 lbs. It played very well and I had some difficulty in landing it with no gaff and only a landing net. I finished the day with 44 trout, which brought up my total for the two days to 106 trout averaging a good 1½ lbs and out of which 12 were grey trout. It is certainly the most wonderful lake for fish that I have ever seen. On the way down we stopped again at La Cabane. As we had a few minutes to spare whilst tea was being prepared we filled in the time fishing in the river opposite the long hut. During those few minutes Portal caught a trout of 5½ lbs!! The biggest ever caught in that pool. On returning to Quebec Clark gave us some coffee and sandwiches. He had also prepared a mass of food of all descriptions for us to take away with us. I have seldom met anybody kinder or more hospitable.

We returned to the Hotel to pack and prepare for an early start.

As we reached La Cabane we were handed an official looking telegram which had been sent up for us. It was from Winston and very typical of his better side. It ran as follows:

GUNFIRE (305)
Following for CIGS and CAS from Prime Minister.
Please let me know how many captives were taken by land and air forces respectively in Battle of Snow Lake.

Portal then worded the following excellent reply:

CORDITE (420)
Following for Prime Minister from CIGS and CAS.
Your gunfire 305 only just received. Battle of Snow Lake began at dawn 19th and finished 2.30 pm on 20th. Enemy forces were aggressive throughout and put up fierce resistance at all familiar strong points particularly Churchill Bay and Brooke Bay. Casualties inflicted by our land and air forces were approximately equal and totalled about 250 dead including the enemy general who surrendered to Land forces on Tuesday afternoon. In a short rearguard action at Cabane de Montmorency our air forces accounted for the largest submarine yet seen in these waters. We trust that you have had a comfortable journey.

21 September – In the Clipper

Got up at 5 am, left hotel at 5.30 and embarked on the clipper in the St Lawrence at 6 am. By 7 am we had taken off and were flying past the Frontenac Hotel looking into my bedroom window.

We had a comfortable journey over the clouds, reaching Botwood about 12 noon when we had lunch. At 2 pm we took off again for England. I went up to the pilot's seat to see the last of Newfoundland before we set out across the

Atlantic. We had with us a passenger, Lady Hartington [Duke of Devonshire's daughter-in-law], who has just lost her husband in France. By 8.30 am we were over Plymouth Bay nosing our way about in a very misty sky. However we made a beautiful landing.

22 September – London

We started the day by going to the RAF Mess for breakfast. While we were there we were informed that the mist had now cleared from Poole Harbour, where we were originally intended for, and where our special train was waiting for us. So we re-embarked and flew on to Poole, caught our train and were in London by 2.30 pm. I went to the office and worked till 7.30 pm including an interview with P.J. Grigg. Then motored home where I arrived shortly after 9 pm.

23 September

Very pleasant day's shooting with Rollie.

24 September

Quiet day at home.

25 September

Back to work with COS at 11 am when we worked out plans for recapture of Rangoon next March. Rosemary came to lunch prior to her departure for India. After lunch Anders (Polish Corps Commander) came to see me. He was very cheerful and in good form. At 5.30 usual Monday Cabinet which went very quickly owing to Winston's absence.

26 September

Went to Euston Station at 10 am to meet PM on his return from America. Large crowd as usual. He arrived looking very fit and cheerful. From there to Chiefs of Staff where we went into the question of next March's operations for recapture of Burma. After lunch Lascelles came to see me to fix up details of [the] King's visit to France which he hopes to do soon. Then had long interviews with Military Secretary settling future appointments and from there to S of S where we discussed the fact that Stalin wanted to get rid of Brocas Burrows and many other points.

27 September

This morning's COS was a short one, but mainly concerned with the set up of our Military Mission in Paris for Eisenhower and their relations with Duff Cooper the Ambassador. Not an easy matter to arrive at a tidy solution. In the afternoon had interviews with both Platt [GOC East Africa] and Nosworthy [GOC West Africa] to settle about the termination of their jobs at the end of this year. Then with Stewart to discuss the command of Canadian Army now that Crerar has gone sick.

Finally a Cabinet at 6 pm at which Winston wanted to discuss the desirability or otherwise of responding to German requests to send food for the British population in the Channel Islands. Decided not to send any in and to reply to Germans that it was their duty to keep population reasonably fed or to surrender if they were unable to do so.

28 September

A short COS attended by Planners when we discussed the manpower problem in relation to our future effort in the war against Japan. After lunch Lumsden, back from MacArthur's HQ, came to see me, and I had a long talk with him. He was followed by Roberts from Blamey's HQ so that I had a good insight into operations in the Pacific. In the evening went to see a premiere of *Hitler's Gangsters* – a poor film. Rollie Charrington came with me and we dined afterwards.

29 September

A short COS. Then Adam to lunch and a very useful talk with him on many important points. At 5 pm an Army Council meeting from which I was liberated as usual by P.J.'s thoughtfulness as soon as I had given my summary of the strategic situation. I am very lucky indeed to have P.J. as S of S. He is wonderfully considerate and very easy to work with. Lewin came to dine and I had a long talk with him. Thank Heaven this week is over, I am worn out!

30 September

There was little doing so we cancelled the COS and I made an early start for home, where I arrived for lunch.

1 October

Quiet day at home.

2 October

Left home early. A longish COS meeting where we discussed the Foreign Office attitude to our paper on dismemberment of Germany. We had considered the possible future and more distant threat to our security in the shape of an aggressive Russia. Apparently the FO could not admit that Russia might one day become unfriendly.

After lunch, called on Amery in India Office who wished to discuss his trip to

Italy from which he has just returned. Cabinet at 5.30 pm and at 10 pm meeting with PM to discuss Burma operation. Just before dinner had received message from Montgomery saying that he could not spare either 52nd , 3rd Divs or 6th Airborne Div, or 6th Guards Armoured Bde, or a Corps HQ, and drawing our attention to the fact that there is still heavy fighting in front of us before defeating Germany. Operations in Italy are also lagging behind and do not admit of the withdrawal of forces. I therefore advised against trying to stage Rangoon operation before next monsoon, and PM agreed. It is *very* disappointing, but I think the correct decision.

PM suddenly informed us that he and Anthony Eden were off to Moscow on Saturday next, and that he wanted me to come with him!! This is a bit of a surprise, and clashes with my plans to go to France on Wednesday till Sunday! I shall have to shorten the French trip. We were lucky to find the PM in a very reasonable and quiet mood. We might otherwise have failed to obtain any decision from him.

3 October

Plans for Moscow are taking shape, and we start on Saturday evening as far as I can see. (A large explosion has just gone off in the vicinity! Presumably a rocket!) The COS was attended by representatives of the Foreign Office whilst we discussed organization of control committees for Germany after defeat. You and the Pooks came to lunch and I took you shopping afterwards. In the afternoon first of all a Selection Board meeting and then interviews with Urquhart, the commander of the 1st Airborne Division just back from Arnhem. He was very interesting. Then Oliver Leese, back from Italy prior to going out to Burma to relieve Giffard.

4 October

Lunched with Merchant Taylors' Association where I was given an excellent lunch. After lunch started off for Heston aerodrome to visit Eisenhower at Versailles. He had sent me over his special Mitchell machine that cruises at 260 miles per hour! We had a somewhat bumpy journey through storms and arrived at Villecoutrai aerodrome where I had witnessed demonstrations some 10 years ago whilst attending a course at Versailles of 'Cycle d'Information'. It gave me a great thrill going through Versailles again. The last time had been in '39 when driving up from Laval to Lille. I had lunched at the Trianon Hotel. The previous occasion was when you and I had lunched there on our way back from Carcassonne, and before that of course the month I had spent there doing my course. We drove round to Ike's office in an annexe of the Hotel Trianon. I had a good talk with him and met Bedell Smith and de Guingand there. We then drove up to Ike's small chateau in St Germain, the one Rundstedt had occupied before he left Paris! Bertie Ramsay, Humfrey Gale, Leigh-Mallory, and Whiteley came to dine which gave me an excellent chance of having a talk with them. During the night I heard one of the rockets landing in Paris.

5 October

Comfortable morning leading up to a conference by Ike at 11.30 of his Army Group Commanders attended by Montgomery, Bradley, Devers, Tedder, Ramsay, Leigh-Mallory, Bedell Smith and de Guingand. Ike ran the conference very well. It consisted first of all of statements by Army Group Commanders, followed by the air and navy. Ike then explained his future strategy which consisted of the capture of Antwerp, and advance to the Rhine in the north and south, forcing the Rhine north and south of the Ruhr, capture of Ruhr followed by an advance on Berlin either from Ruhr or from Frankfurt depending on which proved most promising. Meanwhile Devers in the south to threaten Munich as a cover plan. During the whole discussion one fact stood out clearly, that Antwerp must be captured with the least possible delay. I feel that Monty's strategy for once is at fault, instead of carrying out the advance on Arnhem he ought to have made certain of Antwerp in the first place. Ramsay brought this out well in discussion and criticized Monty freely. Ike nobly took all blame on himself as he had approved Monty's suggestion to operate on Arnhem. [See footnote for 25 October 1944.]

I thought Ike ran the conference very well indeed, the atmosphere was good and friendly in spite of some candid criticisms of the administrative situation. After the meeting Ike asked Monty, Bradley and Devers to lunch which gave me a good chance of seeing them. After lunch flew back doing the journey Paris-London in 1 hour and 10 minutes!

Found Gammell in the office and had a long interview with him to discuss plans for Istrian operation. After dinner called up by PM to go round to him. All he wanted was to discuss with me my visit to Eisenhower and to hear the gossip. I found Portal there fixing up final details for the trip to Moscow, which are now settled.

6 October

A busy day, first of all catching up ground lost during visit to France, and secondly polishing off last bits before starting for Moscow. Adam came to lunch and I had a useful talk with him. In spite of all criticisms I have heard during the last year, and there have been many, I could not imagine anybody in the Army more capable than him to carry out duties of AG. Finally left London at 7 pm for home so as to have a clear day at home before starting for Russia.

7 October

A quiet day at home with early dinner so as to be ready for Boyle at 8.30 pm when he is to pick me up for Lyneham airfield where I am to meet Anthony Eden and depart at midnight.

Later: Boyle turned up and we had a good run through Basingstoke, Newbury, Hungerford, Marlborough etc. We arrived a little before Anthony who turned up after having dined with Queen Mary. At 12.10 am sharp we took off into the darkness.

8 October   Cairo

We had a good trip and arrived in Naples at 7.10 am after exactly 7 hours flying. We landed just in time as a very heavy rain thunderstorm broke as soon as we had landed and obscured everything, we should have had a job getting down in it. We landed just behind Winston's plane, and were met by Jumbo Wilson, Alexander, Macmillan, John Cunningham, etc, etc. We drove to a villa in Naples where we had a bath, shave and breakfast. We then had a conference with PM, Wilson, Alex, Eden, Pug and Jacob to discuss best plan to adopt to retain the American divisions and landing craft in Italy and to prevent them being withdrawn. Plans are difficult to make, Alex is getting stuck in the Apennines with tired forces and cannot spare any for amphibious operations. At same time Hungary is suing for peace, Russians advancing into Yugoslavia and Tito's partisans making ground. It is therefore hard to estimate what the situation will be when Alex can find forces, namely in Feb!

At 11.30 am we took off again, Eden having changed over into Winston's plane, who had asked me to come also, but I thought I had better remain in my plane and get on drafting wire to London with Ismay and Jacob on results of our conference in Naples. I am now in the air again writing this as we fly down the leg of Italy on our way to Cairo. It is hard to believe that I dined comfortably in England yesterday, had breakfast in Naples today, and may have my dinner in Cairo, and possibly breakfast in Crimea tomorrow with lunch in Moscow!!

Later:

We finished a very good flight to Cairo and arrived at 6.30 pm (8.30 local time) pitch dark, and did an excellent landing in the dark. Unfortunately the PM's machine did a bad landing and damaged the undercarriage and was unable to fly on. Paget met me and drove me to 'Casey Villa', where Moyne now lives and where we were to dine. After dinner we drove out at midnight for our departure for Moscow. We had to do a reshuffle as the PM's machine could not fly owing to the damage on its undercarriage. He therefore changed over into my plane, and we now consist of PM, Eden, Ismay, Moran, Martin (Sec), Thompson (Flag Lt), Lockwood and myself.

9 October   (In the air flying over Kharkov)

We took off at 1 am and flew out over the Aegean, round by the Dardanelles into the Black Sea, so as to avoid having to climb over the mountains of Turkey, as flying high is bad for the PM. We struck Russia over the Crimea, but it was still dark and also a cloud base. I got up at 8 am and just as I had finished dressing and shaving we passed over Dnieprovsk [Dnepropetrovsk?] and had a very good view of the famous dam over the River Dnieper. Beautiful clear day, and most interesting looking down on this country that has been so much fought over. PM seemed very tired last night. He is still asleep now which should do him good.

Later – Moscow

Had a very good breakfast in the air of shredded wheat, boiled egg and ham. Spent rest of journey looking at country and picking up all the old signs of the war such as derelict trenches, gun emplacements, demolished houses, anti-tank ditches, etc. From what I saw there is no doubt that the war has not left such deep scars on Russia as it has on the heavily fought over sectors of France and Italy. I was struck by the density of the population over the country we flew over, very much heavier than what I had met when flying up from Baku through Kuibyshev to Moscow. When we approached Moscow it became evident that the pilot was not quite clear as to where he was, and he started hawking around and finally found an aerodrome on which he came down and was told that the right aerodrome was some 30 kilometres further on. So we took off again and were very soon over Moscow. However, our next difficulty was that the undercarriage would not come down properly, and the emergency compressed air had to be used to get it fixed. Finally we landed, just before 12 noon (Moscow time), having done the trip from London in exactly 34 hours! We were met by Molotov, Maisky, a bevy of Russian Generals, Clark Kerr, Harriman, Brocas Burrows, etc, etc. A guard of honour to be inspected and marched past, the whole of God Save the King and the Russian National Anthem. Finally a broadcast speech by Winston.

I then drove off to the National Hotel where I have a sumptuous room, Pug, Jacob etc are all here with me. Winston is in a small house by himself and Eden is in the Embassy. I lunched with Brocas in his flat and discussed with him the Russian dislike for him which has resulted in our having to withdraw him. Then on to Embassy to see office arrangements that have been made for me. From there on to the British Mission buildings which I visited with Brocas, and had talks with a good few of the Mission personnel. Finally back to the hotel for dinner feeling somewhat weary.

10 October

I had a wonderful sleep, followed by a late breakfast and then went round to the office they have established for me in the Embassy. Beyond a few telegrams there was little work for me there, but I discovered we were all invited by Stalin to a large lunch for 2.30 pm. The party consisted of Winston, Stalin, Eden, Molotov, Gousev (over from London), Maisky, Harriman, Ismay, Burrows, Deane, Jacob, Peake and Calthorp, representatives from Dominions, Russian Generals and Foreign Office Staff. Great smartness all round and all foreign office staff, including interpreters, have now blossomed out into uniforms of a grey colour. Stalin greeted me with congratulations on my promotion and was in a most affable mood. The lunch was a complete banquet, starting with masses of hors d'oeuvres which included caviar, we passed on to sucking pig, then small scallops of mushrooms, followed by fish, then chicken and partridges, and finishing up with ices. We had as usual a series of speeches proposing everybody's health. Molotov started with the health of the PM, then Eden, then myself, then Ismay, then Harriman, etc, etc, and we all had to reply in turn. Finally Stalin himself got up and began a long speech. He referred to Winston's and Harriman's speeches in which they had mentioned the unreadiness for war of Britain and America. Stalin said this was the same in the case of the Russian forces. Why was this? The reason was easy to find, we were all three peace loving nations with no aggressive thoughts. Germany and Japan both aggressors were ready for war because they wanted war. How was this to be prevented in the future? Only by the cooperation of the three peace loving nations, provided they maintained the power to enforce peace when necessary, etc, etc. Finally Molotov said that he was in an aggressive mood and that he insisted that we all filled our glasses with champagne to drink an important toast he had to propose and one for which there must be no heel taps, and he himself would see that the glasses were emptied! He then proposed the health of the three great leaders, and we had to drain our glasses. Luckily up to then I had got off lightly and had only had one vodka and one glass of white wine!

It was 5.30 pm when we rose from the table, we had sat for 3 solid hours!! What had we done? Listening to half inebriated politicians and diplomats informing each other of their devotion and affection, and expressing sentiments very far detached from veracity. Are international friendships based on such frothy products of drunken orgies? If so God help the future!

We had not yet finished, but went into the next room for coffee, brandy, smoke and fruit. There I found myself at a small table with Winston, Stalin, Eden, Molotov, Maisky, Gousev, Balfour, Clark Kerr and Harriman. Finally at 6.15 pm we broke up and returned to the Embassy to read the latest telegrams. I finished by attending a sherry party given by Balfour at the Embassy. Then returned to the hotel for a quiet dinner and early bed.

11 October

Started with a visit to my office in the Embassy to read latest telegrams. At 11 am Brocas Burrows came to collect me to do some shopping. However the shopping though interesting was most unsuccessful and there is practically nothing worth buying although a lot of junk is changing hands even at very high prices. I then lunched at the American Embassy to discuss the lines on which we should work with the Americans when we come to discuss military questions. Harriman wants watching fairly carefully, he is all out for gathering laurels for his own brow at our expense!

In the afternoon drove out to a small height outside Moscow from which Napoleon watched the burning of the town. We had an excellent view of the town. Drove back through the 'Park of Culture' where they have got an excellent exhibition of captured German weapons of all types, from veterinary equipment to aeroplanes. A very well run show. At 6.30 pm proceeded to a cocktail party given by Molotov, found Maisky and Mme Maisky there, also Litvinov and Madame L, and all the rest of the people we have been meeting. Back to the office and the hotel for a bath and then to the Embassy at 9 pm for a dinner attended by Stalin and Winston. The speeches this time were kept till the end, but even then we only rose at midnight. During dinner a salute was fired for the capture of Cluj [Romania], a wonderful display of fireworks which were reflected in the Kremlin windows. After dinner a large reception of those who could not be fitted into the dinner. Finally the diplomatic heads with Stalin and Winston got into a huddle in a small room and remained on indefinitely. I escaped at 2 am and went off to bed, delighted to at last get some sleep.

12 October

There is some fable about some hunters going out to shoot a bear, who on the eve of the shoot became so busy arguing about the sale of the skin and the sharing of the proceeds, that they forgot to shoot the bear! I feel this is what we are doing here, ever since we arrived we have been busy discussing post war settlements, and as a result have completely neglected up to date the problem of how we are going to finish the war.

During the morning I went over to see Winston in bed, and settled various points about appointments with him, and the question of the withdrawal of Brocas Burrows. I also succeeded in riding him off any idea of trying to withdraw divisions from Italy to still try and carry out the Rangoon attack before the monsoon. He was mainly influenced by his desire to do something for Mountbatten. I also arranged with him some of the details of the military talks we are to have with Russians either Saturday or Sunday. He aims at leaving here on Monday and returning to London by Friday. I hope he keeps up to this plan.

In the afternoon I drove off with Moran to see the Monastery of the First Virgin's cemetery. It is just on the edge of Moscow. We visited the Greek church, walls covered with 16th century mural paintings in excellent condition, also lovely old ikons and clergy clothes. Outside was a large cemetery, and in it is buried Stalin's first wife, the tombstone is a stone pillar with a head carved out of the top. Well kept garden around it. Also in the cemetery there is a very large memorial to the big 6 engine Maxim Gorky aircraft which crashed in Moscow several years ago killing all its occupants, amounting to over 40.

In the evening I went to the opera to see *Prince Igor*. A vast theatre with the stage larger than the auditorium. Very fine music, singing, scenery and dresses; in fact far better staged than anything that could be done in London. It was a wonderful and most impressive performance. The theatre was packed, all stalls being reserved for commissars and officers. No sergeants allowed in them! And this in a country of supposed equality amongst all? (*We had tried to take stalls for some of our sergeant clerks, but were informed that they could not be admitted.*) Opera lasted from 7.30 till midnight.

Poles have now been fetched over from London, and today is to be devoted to discussions concerning the future of Poland. Weather turned much colder.

That morning whilst I was with Winston he suddenly looked up at me and asked: 'Why did not the King give Monty his [Field Marshal's] baton when he visited him in France?' I replied that I did not know, but that as batons were not Woolworth Stores they had to be made, and that probably one was not ready. 'No!' replied Winston, 'that is not it. Monty wants to fill the Mall when he gets his baton! And he will not fill the Mall!' I assured him that there was no reason for Monty to fill the Mall on that occasion. But he continued, 'Yes, he will fill the Mall because he is Monty, and I will not have him filling the Mall!'

Apparently he went on turning this matter over in his mind, for on the journey home he suddenly turned to me and said: 'Monty will <u>NOT</u> fill the Mall when he gets his baton!' I took the first opportunity I had to warn Monty to keep his visit to Buckingham Palace as quiet as possible.

It was a strange streak of almost unbelievable petty jealousy on his part. But I had frequently noticed that he liked the limelight to concentrate on him, and not to disperse on those that surrounded him. Those that got between him and the sun did not meet his approval. It was all a pretty human failing which somehow made him stand out all the greater, and the very flatness of the surround made the [missing word] stand out all the sharper.

13 October

Spent the morning preparing my notes for tomorrow's military meeting when I am to describe the situation on the French front, Italian front and Burmese front. It will not be an easy matter as I shall have to work through an interpreter which will not make it easy describing situation on the map. I lunched with Brocas Burrows in his Mission Mess, a huge building previously owned by a big textile merchant who had evidently been anxious to exhibit his wealth. (*This was I think the building in which the Mission discovered that 16 microphones had been established for listening in!*) After lunch went out with Brocas to visit the site of an old wooden castle owned by the Tsars and a special favourite of Ivan the Terrible. It used to overlook the Moskva River and vast forests, all cut down, on the far side. Nothing is left of the 16th century wooden castle as it decayed away, but in one of the subsequently built stone houses they have got a wonderful scale model in wood of the castle which gives one an excellent idea of the astounding work they carried out in wood. A woman guide took us round, she looked like an illiterate peasant woman, but was very far from it. She had made a special study of Russian history and it was quite impossible to stump her. Came back for a time to the office to read the latest telegrams, and then back to the hotel for tea and 2 boiled eggs, before going to the opera again. This simple meal was just heaven after all the orgies of food that we have been struggling through!

The opera we went to was *Eugene Onegin* and I think on the whole was better than last night. The scenery was again uncannily good, the duel scene was by half light in the snow amongst snow covered birch trees, with a cold mist rising up from the valley and a changing sky of pearl grey with a few occasional breaks of light. The singing was also quite beautiful. I could not help wondering what the effect of these wonderfully reproduced episodes of aristocratic life must have on the Communist audience. The state ball scenery and dresses were magnificent and I was interested to see that the audience was so impressed that it clapped spontaneously as the curtain was raised. The tendency towards better turn out, both in men and in women, is most noticeable since I was here last. The officers are competing against each other to turn out better and better. The women have not much chance of doing anything very great with the limited resources at their disposal, but they are certainly making the best of them, and are showing a tidiness which was totally absent the last time I was here.

It is very distressing to hear from the Mission here how impossible it is to build any sort of social relations with the local inhabitants. They will never come for meals, and never ask any of our representatives to come out. A vast gap exists which apparently cannot be bridged.

14 October

I spent the morning reading up notes in anticipation of our evening meeting with Stalin in the Kremlin. I then lunched with Admiral Archer who forms part of our military mission in Moscow. Then back to Embassy to read latest telegrams. At 5 pm I had a meeting with General Antonov, who represents Vasiliev (the CGS) who is up at the front. Burrows came with me and we were there for an hour. I found him most friendly and communicative. He explained how the Russian forces had been attacking on both flanks, ie Baltic and Balkans, where the going was softer, and how the surrender of Hungary might open up possibilities for attacks on Germany from the south. He said, however, that the Hungarian army was not conforming to the conditions of the surrender, that it contained many German officers and might yet give serious trouble. I then gave him a brief account of French and Italian fronts.

Rushed off at 6 pm for Gala ballet performance in main theatre. There we sat in the old Tsarist Royal box and our party consisted of Stalin, Winston, Eden, Molotov, Harriman, Maisky, Litvinov, Livenski, Ismay, Clark Kerr, Burrows and self. The ballet performance was perfect and was followed by a supper in an adjoining room where Stalin, Winston, Eden, Molotov, Harriman, Clark Kerr, Ismay, Maisky, Harriman's daughter and self were invited. Many toasts and speeches as usual.

Amongst the toasts Stalin made one which was not translated but which raised peals of laughter from all the Russians there. The toast had been for Maisky, and as he sat next to me and had not taken part in any of the laughter I asked him what all the laughter was about. With a glum look on his face he replied, 'The Marshal has referred to me as the Poet Diplomat because I have written a few verses at times, but our last poet-diplomat was liquidated – that is the joke!!'

Molotov again brought off one of his unpleasant toasts. This time it was so important that it could only be drunk with a tumbler of champagne! He said that he had ordered tumblers to be served all round. He could not complete his toast till he was satisfied that all tumblers were full, and he would also satisfy himself that all tumblers were empty when the toast had been drunk! He then proposed the toast of the Red Army!! I drained my tumbler and wondered what its effects would be on my strategic survey which was to follow on that evening!

Then back to the box for a fine performance by Red Army band, singers and dancers, including excellent Cossack dancers. Performance finished at 9.30 and we then rushed to the Kremlin for a military discussion in Molotov's study. Meeting attended by Stalin, Winston, Harriman, Antonov, Russian General Staff for Eastern front, Ismay, Jacob, Deane and self. I had brought maps of France, Italy and Burma and described military situations, through an interpreter, of all these fronts to Stalin. He asked several questions and expressed various views and opinions. Deane then described the Pacific War. Antonov then took up the running by describing the Russian front, and we asked him many questions. Stalin joined in the answers and we had a real satisfactory discussion on the whole of the German Eastern Front, including future moves. The whole was on a most open and free basis of discussion. We were given some tea and cakes about midnight, and finally broke up at 1.30 am well satisfied with our meeting. We have come a long way for it, and have had a long wait for it, but it has made up for these inconveniences. Tomorrow we continue the discussion at 6 pm at the Kremlin and shall then be dealing with Japan.

15 October

Brocas Burrows picked me up at 10 am and after going round to his flat to collect lunch and the Balfours we started off for Zagorsk Monastery. The monastery is situated about 40 miles north of Moscow and represents the Canterbury of Russia and one of the main religious centres. We had a lovely drive out in beautiful sunshine and spent the morning going round some of the churches and the Abbot's house, which has been retained with all its old furniture and was most interesting. We then started on the road back and stopped on the edge of a wood where we had an excellent picnic lunch provided by Brocas, sitting on rugs in the sun without our greatcoats on. We were back here about 3 pm and I then went through the telegrams.

At 6 pm we again met Stalin in the Kremlin, but this time a smaller party as Winston has got another go of fever! We discussed the war against Japan, and Antonov explained the situation as they saw it. They are allowing for a very large concentration of Japanese into Manchuria both from China and from Japan. Far more than the Japs will dare to withdraw. However they are certainly taking steps to concentrate adequate forces and consider they may require some 60 divs to deal with the 45 Jap divs they expect. I asked them whether they considered that they could maintain 60 divisions and their strategic air force over the trans-Siberian railway. Antonov replied in the affirmative but was corrected by Stalin who thought this was doubtful. The railway had a capacity of 36 pairs of trains per day, but of these only 26 could be counted on for military traffic, and the capacity of each train was from 600 to 700 tons. He considered that assistance from America across the Pacific would be required.

The meeting was most successful. There was never any doubt that the Russians were coming in [to the war against Japan] as soon as they could, and that they were prepared to discuss plans now. Stalin however drew attention to the fact that there was a political aspect to this problem that must also be tackled. What was Russia to get for her help?

The meeting finished at 8 pm and I dashed off to the Ballet to see *Snow [Swan] Lake*, which was quite excellent. Afterwards we went round to the American Embassy for supper and the Chief Ballerina was also invited to come, she was very nice and simple and not what one associates with film stars and such like. Bed at 1.30 am well satisfied with our military discussions. We have achieved far more than I expected that we should.

At our meeting with Stalin that day I was more than ever impressed by his military ability. When I asked Antonov that question as to whether he could maintain 60 divs and the strategic air offensive over the trans-Siberian railway, I felt fairly certain that he knew the answer but was not certain what Stalin might want him to say. He looked round at him for some guidance, but got no help, Stalin stood back with a complete poker face. Antonov, at a loss, said that they could, and was at once brushed aside by Stalin who then proceeded to explain technical matters such as the fact that the capacity of the trans-Siberian railway was limited to 36 pairs of trains per day. ... He displayed an astounding knowledge of technical railway details, had read past history of fighting in that theatre, and from this knowledge drew very sound deductions.

16 October

Luckily the reports of the PM's health are much better, his temperature has gone down and he is normal again. It was a gloomy prospect last night, the thought that he might be seriously laid up here! This morning we were allowed a visit to the Kremlin which was most interesting. We started with the old part of the palace, which used to be inhabited by Ivan the Terrible. This part is most Asiatic in appearance. All the original furniture is still there, and even his four poster bed. In the room next to his bedroom he murdered his boy of 16! We then saw his special church, and from there passed through various more modern parts of the castle till we got to the 18th century front with some marvellous reception rooms. Especially the hall of the Order of St George, where all the names of the recipients of this order are carved into the walls. There is also a hall of the Order of St Catherine which I recognized as the one [where] we had the banquet last time I was here, as I had noticed the small medallions of the Order which form part of the frieze near the ceiling. One vast room had been converted into a Chamber of Assembly for the two Soviet representative bodies. Every deputy had his own seat, desk, and a small loudspeaker on his desk! What would the Tsars have said if they had been told such a chamber would be established in the castle?!

Finished the castle and went out to look at the church from the outside, and also to see the largest bell in the world which crashed when they tried to hang it up in the 17th century. It was left where it fell, half buried in the ground, for over 100 years and then dug out and erected as a monument. We also saw a vast cannon, and what interested me even more, three great tits in the garden of the Kremlin! The first small birds I had seen up to date. We lunched with Admiral Archer, who gave a party for the military members of our mission. After lunch I worked in the Embassy till 6.30 pm and then came home for a bath and a quiet evening, a relief after all the gaieties of the last few days!

Our return journey has been put off for another 24 hours as Polish political discussions are hanging fire. It is a bore as now that our military work is over I am longing to get off. It gets very trying being followed everywhere and completely shadowed by 3 detectives and a major in the Red Army! They are quite nice and supposed to be there to watch over me, but it gets very trying. Their authority over the crowd is absolute. Whilst shopping the other day a crowd had collected round me. One of the detectives walked round saying quite quietly, 'It would be better for you not to be here' and they all dispersed and vanished at once! Weather continues glorious. I only hope that we are not missing our chance of good flying weather!

17 October

I despair! Our departure has again been put off for 24 hours! This time to give the Russians the opportunity of staging a Kremlin banquet. If we leave without such a banquet the impression will be created throughout Russia and reflected in Germany that our conferences have been a failure and that we are parting as a result of disagreement. It is lamentable! As a result we lose 24 hours and have to submit to one of those drunken orgies!!

Today, as there was no work to be done, I went off at 11 am to visit the offices of the newspaper called the *British Ally*. It is an excellent institution doing very good propaganda work. It publishes a paper weekly with articles showing British activities, photographs of interest, and extracts from out of the British press. In addition it runs a library of books to lend out to Russians. The whole institution being most popular. From there I went on to the Moscow equivalent of Selfridges, and walked round two floors. The building was crammed and every counter buried with purchasers in spite of the frightful prices, ie an eiderdown for £10 and a rug for £8 etc. And yet there were many articles which you could not find in an English shop. Children's toys for the small were far better than what you could raise in Hamleys. In the drug department there were rows of rubber hot water bottles! etc, etc.

For lunch we were taken out by Brocas Burrows to the house he has rented in the forest outside Moscow. We drove out about 30 miles and then took to four wheel drive vehicles to follow the track across the woods. Finally we arrived at a delightful wooden two storied house. There he gave us the most excellent lunch after which we had a walk through the woods. I hoped to see a black woodpecker there which I had not seen before, unfortunately he did not show up. After lunch we walked to the lake nearby and then drove back to the Embassy. Then I had a meeting with the Ambassador [Clark Kerr] at 6.30 pm to discuss the future of the mission and whether we should replace Brocas, which we decided not to do for the present. We then went to an evening show of Russian folk songs and dances, which was very good. Finally brought Brocas back to the hotel to dine. As all military and political discussions have been brought to an end I hope that we start early, as settled, the day after tomorrow.

18 October

This has been a day of filling in time as our departure had been put off 24 hours to admit of Kremlin dinner tonight! In the morning I visited the Red Army Club and Red Army Theatre. The former is a centre where the Red Army can meet, it contains a museum, small theatre or cinema, libraries, playing rooms and runs all out door sports grounds. There are similar centres in other towns, and the Moscow one acts as the parent organization. The museum was very interesting, containing masses of maps, diagrams etc, from the various fronts, but it would require hours to get full value out of it. The Army Theatre is a vast one, quite as large as the largest London theatre. It seats 1600 people, and could hold close on 2000 on the stage! It is run entirely by the Army and gives daily performances. After lunch I visited site of the castle started by Empress Catherine, but abandoned by her as she did not like it when half finished. Now I have the awful ordeal of the Kremlin dinner in front of me, and tomorrow we are by way of starting at 10.30.

Later:

The evening turned out to be quite a mild one. We met at 8 pm in the room of the Order of St Catherine. It was a very representative party from the Russian point of view. Stalin, Molotov, Maisky, Litvinov, Gousev, Voroshilov, Antonov, the heads of Artillery, Tanks, Aviation, Engineers, Railway, Supply, State Production, Navy etc, etc. On our side PM, Eden, Ismay, Jacob and self. Diplomatic – Clark Kerr, Balfour, 3 Dominion representatives, Americans Harriman and Deane. The dinner was good and less oriental than last time, consisting of caviar, hors d'oeuvres, soup, fish, chicken or beef, partridge and ice cream. The usual toasts and speeches went on continuously. To start with they were proposed by Molotov and later by Stalin himself. Molotov proposed my health with some very nice words and I had to reply. We rose at about 11.30 pm and went into the next room for coffee and fruit, and remained there till about midnight. We were then taken off to see two films which lasted till 2.15 am but were very good. After that we broke up and went home.

19 October

Left the hotel at 9.45 am for the aerodrome where I found that Eden and Clark Kerr had already arrived. It was drizzling very unpleasantly and cold. We then had to wait in the rain for the arrival of the PM. However the next arrival of importance was that of Stalin himself! A great honour that he should have come himself. We went on standing in the rain wondering how late Winston would be, and whether he was still possibly drying himself after his morning bath! However luckily he was not very late. We then had National Anthems, followed by inspection of the Guard of Honour, and march past by it. Small speeches in the microphones by Winston. Much hand shaking and at last the PM's plane slipped off to the runway followed closely by ours and the Liberator behind. By 11 am we were sailing over the top of Moscow, and seeing the Kremlin recede into the distance. We are now in the air heading for the Crimea in lovely sunshine, our work in Moscow finished and far more satisfactorily than I could ever have hoped for.

Later:

We had a cloudy flight down and did not see much of the ground till we crossed the sea leading into the Crimea. We landed at Sarabus aerodrome at 3.30 pm and were met by the Commissar for the Crimea and the Admiral commanding the local ground and air forces. We were given cars and driven off to Simferopol, about an hour's drive. There a house had been prepared for us to rest and feed in. PM remained there for a sleep, whilst Eden, Ismay and I and rest of party drove off into the mountains towards Yalta to see the country. Unfortunately there was not sufficient time to reach Sebastopol, but we were able to form a good general idea of the country. The main impression I gained is that the Crimea is far more prosperous than the rest of Russia that we saw. Houses better, clothes better, and general impression of more amenities of life. The Commissar told us that the population had been 1 million, but was reduced to 500,000 by the Boche, and they were forced at present to introduce additional population from Russia. We returned to our house at Simferopol by about 7 pm for a vast dinner, accompanied by a series of toasts as usual. Finally we returned to the aerodrome and took off at 1 am for Cairo. I wish we had had time to see Sebastopol and the country round it.

20 October

We had a good journey but I found it hard to sleep with a heavy cold and sore throat. At 8 am we landed outside Cairo (Cairo-West) and drove to breakfast with Moyne. Dickie Mountbatten also there. PM somewhat sour from lack of sleep! I am putting up at Mena Hotel as being more on the spot and in spite of Paget having very kindly asked me to put up with him. I feel certain that the PM will summon conferences at odd moments and Paget's home is in Cairo.

Later:

At 10.30 I ran a conference till 1 pm with Dickie Mountbatten, Wedemeyer, Ismay, and Jacob on the question of offensives from India. I discussed Dickie's new plan with him and all his various difficulties. Lunched at the hotel and then round to Moyne's villa to attend conference with PM on the question of Dickie's future plans. The conference went well and we got the PM to agree to plans connected with freeing Arakan of Japs. The plans require examining in much more detail, and many difficulties were as usual slurred over by Dickie's optimism.

Conference lasted till 5.30 and at 6.30 we had another with Paget attending to discuss the undesirability of letting French troops be sent to Syria and the

Lebanon. This conference lasted till 7.30 pm when I dashed back to Mena Hotel for a bath and change before dining with Moyne. Dinner consisted of PM, Eden, Moyne, Paget, Slessor, Wedemeyer, Moran, Kimmins etc. Towards end of dinner PM was in great form and produced several gems. He also informed me suddenly that we were to start at 11 am tomorrow instead of at midnight. Delighted, this should get us back 12 hours sooner. I had a very useful talk with both Paget and Dickie after dinner settling various difficulties of theirs.

21 October   In the air over the Mediterranean between Benghazi and Messina

I had an excellent night's sleep to make up for the bad previous one in the plane, and the throat much better. Left Mena Hotel at 9.45 am and drove to aerodrome with Paget. There we had Moyne, Paget, Mountbatten, Park etc accumulated to see us off. The PM had asked me to come with him in his plane where the party consisted of the two of us, Moran, Martin, typist and Tommy. By 11 am we were off and have so far had an excellent flight. We went straight from Cairo to Benghazi, and from there swung round to head for Naples. We could not go straight as it would have meant flying over Crete which is still held by the Germans. Whilst flying over Benghazi we were having an excellent lunch with hors d'oeuvres, soup, hot roast beef, beans, cheese, coffee and with it whisky soda, port and brandy! It is hard to believe that one is rushing through the air at 200 miles an hour and some 800 [8000?] feet above the ground! I have spent the whole morning reading all the PM's secret documents on the world situation [wireless intercepts] gathered by most secret methods which the PM has been passing on to me. PM very particular about the temperature of the aircraft, and walks about with a small thermometer. As the temperature was 72 during the whole of lunch I thought there was nothing much to complain about. He is complaining of feeling of a small cold, I pray to heaven that it does not develop into anything before we get home!

Later:

At 4 pm local time (2 pm Cairo time) we landed outside Naples having taken exactly 7 hours for the journey and averaged just under 200 miles per hour. We were met by Jumbo Wilson, Gammell, Macmillan and John Cunningham. Drove straight up to Wilson's guest house in Naples, had tea and sat down to a conference which lasted from 5.30 to 8.15 pm. PM was there for the beginning part and we discussed the possibilities of carrying out the Istria operation by landing on the Dalmatian coast. PM then left and I went on discussing a series of points connected with reinforcements, equipment, Polish forces and their expansion, raising of Italian forces etc, etc. I find it very weary work running conferences after a long flight, even though it is carried out in the greatest of comfort.

For dinner PM, Alex, Wilson, Cunningham, Macmillan, Ismay, Moran, Jacob, etc. PM in the very best of form, but unfortunately kept us up till 1 am local time, but 3 am Cairo time, which was the time we had got up by. Found out that Oliver Leese's departure was greeted with considerable joy, and I think Dick McCreery will be the successor in his place. I still feel quite certain that Harding (Alex's Chief of Staff) is not up to his appointment. Unfortunately Alex does not realize this fact, and wishes to stick to him.

22 October In the air over Southern France

We were told last night that the weather report was very bad, that it was highly unlikely that we should be able to fly by day, but that we might fly to Malta in the afternoon so as to make use of their night flying facilities and take off in the dark for home. I was to be told at 7 am if we could start. As I had been told nothing I was comfortably in bed at 8.30 am when I was suddenly informed that the weather had improved, and that we were due to leave the house at 9 am!! I had to rush my shave, dressing and breakfast and succeeded in being ready before the PM. At 10.10 am we took off and flew along Italian coast, across to north point of Corsica where we flew over Bastia and had a grand view of north Corsica silhouetted against a stormy sky. From there on to cross the French coast at Narbonne. We then headed inland, unfortunately we did not go near enough to Carcassonne for me to see it. I should have loved to look down on it from the air, in any case the fact of going near it brought back floods of memories of our week together there.

Later:

The weather turned nasty over France and we had to go up higher to get above the clouds, and from then on saw nothing of France till we were over the Cherbourg peninsula. We passed west of the Isle of Wight, over Andover, and swung in to Northolt which we reached at 5 pm, having done our journey in 6¾ hours. We found Clemmie on the aerodrome to welcome Winston and Archie Nye and Barney had come for me. We were not long in getting off and here I am back in the flat which I left only just over a fortnight, and have covered 10,500 miles since I left! It has been a remarkably successful trip with a great deal accomplished first in Russian meetings and in addition with the Cairo and Naples conferences. I have now got a lot to do to put the results of our conferences and talks into effect. Winston seemed none the worse for the journey and arrived back in great form. I am glad we have got him back safely and that he did not fall sick in Moscow! With this flight I have now passed the 100,000 miles in the air! since doing this job.

23 October

Started in again with the usual routine of COS meetings and Cabinet meetings! I am glad to have had a bit of a change from this form of life, and it is rather hard to step into it again. However, by this evening I felt as if I had never left London, and Moscow seemed as far away in the past as it is in miles from here.

I am very glad to have been back to Russia again, it is a country with much food for thought. One more of these vast experiments which humanity periodically carries out throughout the annals of history. Experiments which lead to much bloodshed, much upheaval, much suffering and finally when all is examined, some progress. In my mind Bolshevism, Nazism, Fascism etc all have their purpose; they all turn the wheel of destiny one or two more cogs forward. Forward towards the path of general progress. Humanity surges forward like the tide flowing. Successive waves of one or other 'ism' romp up the beach only to be sucked back almost to where they started from. But in that 'almost' lies the progress forward. It seems essential for humanity to subject itself to untold ordeals in order to achieve even slow progress towards perfection. The path of mankind in learning to 'love its neighbours as itself' is a thorny and rocky one. But for all that I have not the least doubt that mankind ultimately will reach the top rungs of this long and steep ladder.

24 October

A very usual day's work. First a long COS with the attendance of the Joint Intelligence Committee, then Duncan Sandys on the rocket and flying bomb. After lunch Charles Allfrey before taking over command in Egypt, and Oliver Leese on questions connected with Burma. Finally Harry Crerar to dinner. He has now recovered and is fit to go back to France again.

25 October

Our main problem at this morning's COS was how to procure sufficient reinforcements out of Canada without upsetting the equilibrium of Mr Mackenzie King's political position. There are plenty of trained men in Canada but they are only conscripted for service within Canada and have no intention of volunteering for service abroad. Lunched with John Anderson (Chancellor of the Exchequer) who had the Governor of the Bank of England and a Frenchman also there. As usual a most excellent lunch. In the afternoon I informed Kenneth Anderson that he was to take over East African Command. Then saw Boy Browning, who explained the action of his airborne forces at Arnhem.* At 6 pm meeting with the PM to discuss ammunition situation, which is not very healthy at present. Decided to increase production of medium artillery ammunition and reconsider 25 pdr at a later date. Finally dined with John Kennedy and saw his latest purchases [bird pictures] from Lodge.

---

*Operation Market Garden, an attempt to establish a bridgehead across the Rhine by the dropping of the 82nd and 101st US and 1st British Airborne divisions and the advance of the British 30th Corps, had been launched on 17 September 1944. It was commanded by a British officer, Lt-Gen. 'Boy' Browning. A combination of misfortune, poor intelligence and underestimates of German defensive strength meant that the British, dropped furthest away from the front line, were unable fully to capture their objectives – the bridges in the Dutch city of Arnhem – and were not reinforced by ground troops quickly enough. They withdrew on 25 September, effectively destroyed as a fighting unit.

26 October

We had the Planners in this morning and discussed with them the wonderful telegram from Marshall in which he seems to consider that if we really set our heart on it, and bank on its happening, irrespective of what happens in the future should we fail to do so, we ought to be able to finish the war before the end of the year!

After lunch saw Alan Cunningham to tell him of his appointment to Eastern Command. Then had a talk with our Military Attaché in Madrid and now have just had Rollie Charrington to dinner.

27 October

After the COS I had my usual lunch with Adam at the Carlton Grill and after a short afternoon's work started for home at 6 pm.

28 and 29 October

Two quiet and very happy days at home.

30 October

You came up with me in the morning. I had a long COS with many minutes by the PM. Lunched with you. Cabinet at 6 pm and finished up with a 10 pm meeting with the PM. He was in a good mood, and we got through surveys of the French front, Italian front and Burma front by midnight!!

31 October

We were concerned with the intended bombing of defences near Flushing. PM objecting with humanitarian reasons and Ike pressing for it to save casualties in the infantry attack. PM agreed.

We lunched together at flat, and then afterwards went to see Zargorski's book-binding establishment. At 4 pm I had an interview with the King which lasted till 5.15 pm. He was very full of his visit to France, and wanted to hear about our visit to Moscow. As usual he was perfectly charming. Back to WO to see Oliver Leese before his departure for India.

1 November

Nothing of special importance at COS. After lunch we went for a walk in Kew Gardens which was very refreshing. Returned to WO for interview with Lumsden before his return to MacArthur's HQ. Then long talk with P.J. Grigg on future of MI5 and of the dangers attending its future should it fall into the wrong hands. Then discussed with Nye and Crawford the future of the 1st Airborne Division which was so badly smashed up at Arnhem. Then had interview with Chatterton, who commands the Glider Pilot Regiment.

2 November

Started work as usual at 9.30 am. COS was not till 10 am and was a short one followed by many troubles! First an interview with Montague from Canada House. I had sent for him to discuss Alexander's wire in which he stated that Burns was unfit to command the Canadian Corps in Italy. I found out from him that a Canadian Cabinet crisis was on, resulting in Ralston being dismissed and McNaughton appointed as Defence Minister. Therefore desirability to damp down troubles in Canada for the present! Then interview with MS concerning unpleasant wire from Mountbatten about his future Chief of Staff to replace Pownall, when he wants Swayne or Nye and refuses Slim [Commander 1st Burma Corps].

Then lunch with PM at 10 Downing St to meet Bedell Smith. Found out that Ike's plan as usual entails attacking all along the front instead of selecting main strategic point. I fear that the November attack will consequently get no further than the Rhine at the most! PM not in his usual form and on the flat side. However, his fighting spirit the same as usual and he said that if he was a German he would get his small daughter to put a bomb under some British bed, he would instruct his wife to wait till some American was bending over his basin washing to strike him on the neck with a chopper, whilst he himself sniped at Americans and British indiscriminately!

Back to WO for interview with Noiret new French Military Attaché, quite a good type who had been old Gen Georges' Staff Officer in 1939. Then the Polish Chief of Staff who has succeeded Sosnkowski. Finally Lennox, who controls MI5, to discuss the future of this organization and the grave danger of its falling into the clutches of unscrupulous political hands, of which there are too many at present. Finally went with you to the premiere film for YMCA benefit, and had Cunningham to dine afterwards.

3 November

Not sufficient business for a COS so we had a rest for a change. I was however sent for by the PM at 10.45 am. He told me that he had been thinking over the desirability of replacing Dill now that he would be unable to carry on. (It was only yesterday at lunch that he stated that it was unnecessary to replace him and we had all remonstrated with him!) His suggestion now is to send Jumbo Wilson there, and to relieve him with Alexander, whilst Clark (the American) should relieve Alexander. It is probably the best solution to the problem, but will all depend on how Jumbo hits it off with Marshall. Last year in Cairo Marshall had a good opinion of him. I then tackled the PM on the question of making Jumbo a Field Marshal. He refused at first and said it was quite unnecessary, however by working away at him I got him to agree, and only hope he does not go back again. I feel Jumbo has certainly earned his baton as much as either Ironside or Gort!

We then had a large lunch party for the Amerys, Ismays, Alex's wife, Barney, you and I. In the evening I was again sent for by the PM, this time to discuss his proposed visit to France. He is to start on the 10th, attend Armistice

Ceremony in Paris, certain dinners etc, then fly to Besançon to visit French forces under de Lattre de Tassigny. From there to visit Ike and Monty. He wants me to come with him which will be great fun and very interesting. We are to send detachments of British forces to take part in the Nov 11ᵗʰ ceremony. The only bad part is the security side, the French have already announced his visit, and there might well be remnants of Germans representatives who would be only too ready to take advantage of a chance to have a shot at Winston.

4 November

After a short COS we started off together for home where we arrived in time for lunch and a peaceful afternoon.

5 November

A quiet Sunday at home.

On the wireless at 9 am the death of Jack Dill was announced, and I had the unpleasant feeling that another of the prominent landmarks of my life was gone, and with it one of my best friends and one to whom I owed more in my military career than to any other. His loss is quite irreparable and he is irreplaceable in Washington. Without him there I do not know how we should have got through the last 3 years.

In my mind we owe more to Dill than to any other general for our final victory in the war. If it had not been for the vital part he played in Washington we should never have been able to achieve the degree of agreement in our inter-Allied strategy. The war might indeed have taken a very different course. I had unbounded admiration for him combined with the deepest of devotion, whilst Marshall had grown to admire, respect and like him in no small measure. He was therefore in an ideal position to play the part of intermediary between us, and to bring us together when our view points were so divergent that I saw no hope of agreement. Any success that I may have had in getting Marshall to finally accept our Mediterranean and Italian strategy were entirely due to Dill's help. Repeatedly I heard him referred to as the best ambassador we had ever had in Washington.

The American opinion of him cannot be better exemplified than in his place of burial [Arlington National Cemetery]. And yet Winston would never recognize the services that Dill was rendering. Twice P.J. Grigg and I did our level best to secure him a peerage, this was never turned down by the PM but nothing ever came of it. I shall never be able to forgive Winston for his attitude towards Dill.

6 November

Usual early start from home and a difficult COS at which we discussed the problems of the partition of Palestine for the Jews. We are unanimously against any announcement before the end of the war, but our hand may well be forced.

After lunch Brocas Burrows came to see me, giving news of his last days in Moscow. Then Crerar to discuss new political situation in Canada with McNaughton as Defence Minister. The political outlook in Canada is not rosy.

5.30: our usual Cabinet, which turned out to be an exciting one. First of all the PM announced that Lord Moyne had been shot in the neck in Cairo by terrorists!* Then Winston and Amery had a set to on the India question. Winston had attacked the Viceroy, Amery flared up and told him he was 'talking damned nonsense'!! Winston said that if he had lost his temper to that extent he better withdraw from the Cabinet! Amery did not move and the situation calmed. Winston then had trouble with John Anderson and became even more sour. Finally we escaped at 8.15 but I came away with a feeling that Winston is losing his authority in the Cabinet and have not yet seen him with so little authority or control.

7 November

Started our COS with a wire Winston wished to send to the President in which he proposed that Wilson should take over Dill's place in Washington and that Alexander should take over from Wilson. So far so good, unfortunately he went on to suggest Alexander should combine the duties of Supreme Commander and his own at the same time. He went further to suggest that Greece should return to Middle East, where we have just taken it from, and in every possible way proposed upsetting the organization of Command in the Mediterranean. He had tried to bounce us with the telegram yesterday, and now again it must go off by 3 pm today! However we had to pull it to pieces badly and sent it back mutilated with our reasons. He has been unable to send it off, but has decided to have a 10.30 pm meeting with us which promises to be a fairly heated one!

Monty came to lunch with me in very good form, but pretty full of criticism of Ike and of his methods of running a war! After lunch I ran a Selection Board, and at 5.30 pm another Cabinet to finish off what we had left over yesterday. We spent hours discussing desirability of sending some food to Holland, Norway and Channel Islands, and never arrived at any very decisive results.

Later:
Just back (1 am) from our meeting with the PM. Anthony Eden attending, and just as I suspected he was responsible for the change in the PM's plans. He had just come back from Italy where he had been seeing Alexander who had as usual whined about being crushed by Wilson's HQ, the great duplication of work, etc, etc. As a result he had recommended combining the Supreme Commander and Group Commander into one, and wanted in fact to commit the error which Eisenhower has just made in France. We had a long discussion, luckily quite a pleasant one and not too heated. The problem was complicated

---

*Moyne, British Minister Resident in Middle East, was assassinated by the Stern gang on 6 November 1944.

by the First Sea Lord having a very small opinion of Alexander, and being convinced that he is incapable of doing the Supreme Commander's job in the Mediterranean. Personally I have also serious doubts and feel that he must be given the very best Chief of Staff. After much arguing I made my point, namely Wilson to replace Dill, Alex to replace Wilson, and Clark to replace Alex. It is not ideal, but it is the best that can be made of a very complicated situation with many personal factors (such as PM's admiration for Alex) impinging on it. Anthony Eden behaved well and seeing that he had messed things up did not press his point.

8 November

We discussed at the COS the telegram drafted by the secretariat as a result of our meeting last night and sent it on for the PM to despatch to the President. We also had our weekly meeting with Cherwell and Sandys on the flying bomb and the rocket. I am afraid that both of these are likely to interfere with the working of Antwerp harbour, a matter of the greatest importance in the future. You came up to lunch and we then went on to a concert at the Albert Hall for the first half of it. I then had an interview with Joubert de la Ferté, and he gave me some interesting sidelights on Mountbatten's HQ. He said that the Anglo-American relations continued to be bad. The Americans full of criticisms of our management of India, and expressing openly the opinion that if they had their way there would be no British Empire after the war! He was followed by Robertson and Lewis from Italy to discuss the administrative situation in Italy which is bad. Also had long discussion with Boy Browning and Crawford on the provision of glider pilots from the air force, and the necessity for training these pilots in ground fighting as well as in their glider training. Meanwhile the plans for our trip to Paris are materializing fast, and we are due to leave on Friday 10th.

This evening Cyril Falls, Military Correspondent of *The Times*, came to see me. He said that he was disturbed at the system of command in France with Eisenhower commanding in two planes, namely commanding the Army, Navy and Air Forces in his capacity as Supreme Commander and at the same time pretending to command the land forces, divided into 3 groups of armies directly.

He has hit the nail on the head and found the weakness of this set up which the Americans have forced onto Eisenhower. Unfortunately it becomes a political matter and the Americans, with preponderating strength of land and air forces, very naturally claim the privilege of deciding how the forces are to be organized and commanded. Falls had been seeing Monty and there is no doubt that Monty had been rubbing it in hard! It is however a very serious defect in our organization and one that may have evil repercussions on the strategy of the war. I do not like the layout of the coming offensive, and doubt whether we [will] even reach the Rhine, it is highly improbable that we should cross over before the end of the year.

9 November

We had the Planners in for our usual weekly talk, and to discuss further Mountbatten's plans for this spring. Then attended Mansion House lunch to install the new Mayor. Winston made his usual speech, I think it must be the fourth I have listened to there, but it was not quite as good as some of the previous ones. As there was no Archbishop of Canterbury Lord Simon took that job on. I sat next to Alexander (First Lord) and a Mrs Howard. During the afternoon I had a talk with Monty before he returns to France. He still goes on harping over the system of command in France and the fact that the war is being prolonged. He has got this on the brain as it affects his own personal position, and he cannot put up with not being the sole controller of land operations. I agree that the set up is bad but it is not one which can be easily altered, as the Americans have now the preponderating force in France, and naturally consider they should have a major say in the running of the war. Perhaps after they see the results of dispersing their strength all along the front it may become easier to convince them that some drastic change is desirable, leading to a concentration of force at the vital point. I also saw Lathbury during the afternoon, he was one of the Brigadiers of the 1st Airborne Division who was wounded in Arnhem, captured in hospital and escaped. The Dutch did marvels in looking after him, and finally assisted him and some 120 others to escape back to our lines. His story would make an excellent thriller. I finally had a long meeting with Weeks to consider whether we should cannibalize one or two divisions in the Mediterranean. He is inclined only to do one, personally I feel certain we shall have to do both ultimately and would sooner make one bite of the cherry. I expect P.J. will prefer to do one at a time, in the hope that he could get one division through easier than two with the PM! But the alternative will necessitate returning twice to the PM, which in my opinion will be worse still.

All the preparations for Paris are made, if fine we fly, if not we go by destroyer and I pray by heaven we may not have to go in the destroyer!! The Channel is very rough at present.

10 November   PARIS!!

After spending a usual morning and attending the COS I had an early lunch and left for Northolt Aerodrome where our party assembled, ready to embark in two Dakotas for Paris. The party consisted of PM, Anthony Eden, Mrs Churchill and Mary, Pug Ismay, Cadogan, two Foreign Office secretaries, Barney, Sawyers, Martin, detectives etc. We had an excellent flight over and arrived at 4.30 just south of Paris. Met on aerodrome by Guard of Honour of National Guard, de Gaulle, General Juin [Chief of General Staff], many members of cabinet and officials of all sorts. With long procession of cars we drove through Paris, with streets lined on either side. We went to Quai d'Orsay where Winston is stopping. There we deposited him and drove on to the Continental Hotel, Juin's HQ, where I am putting up. They have provided a comfortable suite of rooms with large double room, dressing room which

Barney is in, and a large drawing room. The hotel itself is closed. In my room I found a set of the most priceless bird books which had been drawn out of the Natural History Library for me to look at! Juin had asked Archdale of the Mission here if there was anything I might care for in my room to entertain me and he had suggested bird books, knowing me well! They are quite lovely and most of them original drawings.

In the evening I went to dine with the PM at the Quai d'Orsay. Party consisted of PM, Mrs C, Mary, Anthony and Beatrice Eden, the two Duff Coopers, Cadogan, Martin, and Tommy. PM in excellent form. Said last time he had been in the Quai d'Orsay building was 1940 when the French were busy burning the Archives preparing to depart. I was not able to escape before midnight.

11 November

At 10 am General Juin's ADC came to collect me, and we started off for the great function of the day. We drove to the Arc de Triomphe where we waited for the PM and de Gaulle. When he arrived, they went up together to lay a wreath on the unknown soldier's grave and for de Gaulle to relight the perpetual flame. De Gaulle then presented medals to a group of officers. After that we marched on foot down the Champs Élysées to a stand which had been put up and which we occupied. As no places had been marked, and half of them were already occupied, there was some scramble to get accommodated. I stood next to a French general who said, 'La foule, comme d'habitude, déborde la police!' [The crowd, as usual, overwhelms the police!] This was very much the case, there were the usual very futile 'agents' quite incapable of handling the crowd, especially press photographers, the security side was appalling and I had some uneasy feelings for Winston at times.

He had a wonderful reception and the Paris crowd went quite mad over him, with continuous cries of 'Churcheel! Churcheel!' After we had taken our places on the stand there was a parade of troops lasting an hour. Starting with the Garde Nationale and its band, and mounted troops (which have remained intact throughout the war) and passing onto bands and detachments of British, Canadian and American troops. We had an excellent band, a naval detachment, a grand composite Guards' Company and an RAF detachment. French forces followed, some Moroccan and Algerian detachments, some FFI [French Forces of the Interior] units transformed into Chasseurs Alpins, part of the new division being raised in Paris, and a fine detachment of the Airborne troops who worked with us in Normandy. After the review we drove off to Clemenceau's statue where we deposited wreaths, from there to Foch's grave where again wreaths were laid. Finally we went to the Hôtel de la Présidence, Rue St Dominique (where de Gaulle is installed) for our official lunch. It was a very large lunch with 68 guests including the whole of the Cabinet plus: Catroux, Giraud, Juin, Koenig [FFI], various admirals, ambassadors etc etc. De Gaulle made a short speech followed by Winston, after which we rose for coffee and cigarettes. I had a long conversation with old Giraud and discussed his recent wound, when his sentry shot him through the neck, the bullet coming out half way between the nose and the corner of his mouth without breaking his jaw! He told me that his wife, two daughters and seven grand children were still all held as hostages in Germany and he could not even obtain a word from them. After lunch I drove back to the hotel to look through papers delivered by airmail.

I must say that this morning's parade stirred me up very deeply. It was a wonderful feeling to be standing in Paris watching a review of French troops after the last four years of planning and struggling to get back again to France and to drive the Germans out of it. I even wondered at times whether I might be dreaming only and that we should wake to find ourselves back where we were a year ago.

In the evening we dined with General Juin who produced the most marvellous dinner of excellent soup, lobster, chicken, pâté de foie gras!, a marvellous ice with a soufflé around it! and beautiful fruits of pears, grapes and apples. With it excellent chablis, burgundy, sauternes and champagne in succession. The tragedy was that having been seriously upset intestinally for a week I had to deny myself most of it. He had as guests Giraud, Koenig, Tedder, Ramsay, Ismay, Barney and various other French generals and admirals. It was a very pleasant evening. I sat between Juin and Koenig and got practice for my French. At the end Juin made a very nice speech to which I replied in French with some difficulties and hunting for words.

This hotel during the war was the German civil investigation department, run by the Gestapo. Most of the Frenchmen that were in any way suspect were examined here. It was taken over by Juin in a very derelict condition.

12 November

I had a comfortable lazy morning and at 11.30 went to General Juin's office for a talk. He told me of all his designs to raise 8 French divisions as quickly as possible. He has got all the personnel for them and wishes at once to get these formations formed and in existence. Equipment is as usual the crux, what could we do to assist? I said we still had some 75 mms which the Americans had provided for us in our invasion danger period. He said these might be of use. He was very reasonable in all his requests and an easy individual to get on with. Later lunched with Juin 'en famille' with his wife, wife's friend, his boy of about 14, his ADC and Chief of Staff. Barney came too. We were given an excellent lunch.

Barney and I then went for a short walk before having to go for a meeting with de Gaulle. Ismay came with me. He received us in the same room that Clemenceau used to work in during the last war. He discussed the raising and arming of forces, very much on the same lines that Juin had in the morning. He was in one of his more pleasant moods and quite affable. We were with him for about an hour. Finished the day by dining with Koenig who had two generals dining who had taken a great part in the Resistance movement. They were most interesting about their experiences and lives led under a dozen different names and carried on from a dozen residence[s]. Four months was the most that the majority survived before getting caught by the Gestapo. Finally drove to the Gare de Lyon where we embarked into the presidential train for Besançon. Party consisting of PM, de Gaulle, Juin, self and a few others. A very comfortable train in which I have an excellent cabin, but the line is very rough, hence my bad writing!!

I was very interested to meet the Resistance Generals and to hear their views of de Gaulle. They did not think much of the part he had played. One of them said to me: 'De Gaulle! What did he do? Evacuated his family to London from the start, where he followed them. There he lived comfortably throughout the war, whilst we were risking our lives daily in contact with the Germans, living in the cellars with them overhead and expecting daily to be apprehended by the Gestapo. Meanwhile in his safe position he had the impertinence to say "Je suis la France"!' They were very bitter and had little use for him.

13 November
Woke to find the whole country we were travelling through covered with snow! And a grey morning with snow falling fast! We arrived in Besançon well up to schedule by 10 am. There we were met by General de Lattre [de Tassigny, 1st Army], the Prefect, the Mayor and a mass of other officials. It was snowing and very slushy under foot. Outside the station a band, a guard of honour and a large crowd. We solemnly stood in the snow whilst most of God Save the King, the Stars and Stripes and the la Marseillaise were played through.

As we arrived in the station … Winston was expected to alight from the train gracefully. However, at this moment Winston was still only half dressed, and as he completed his toilet, a process that lasted a full quarter of an hour, General de Lattre and his colleagues were rapidly being converted into Father Xmas! Finally Winston emerged in the dining carriage dressed as an airman. There Sawyers, his valet, proceeded to adjust his coat on him whilst he admired the general effect in the glass. At the correct moment Sawyers handed him from behind the two ends of the belt. This produced a thunderstorm of abuse: 'Sawyers you damned fool, why have you not removed that bastard!! You know I never want that bastard around me again! Cut off the damned thing!' Mary [Churchill] was standing beside me at the door that led into the corridor, and not knowing what further language the paternal anger might produce, withdrew gracefully down the corridor with a smile on her face. Finally and at last Winston was ready and out he stepped into the snow with a smile on his face, large cigar, and no longer adorned by that 'bastard thing'.

We then started off in cars, leading car PM, de Gaulle, de Lattre, and Mary, next car General Juin, Barney and self. We had a long drive of some 60 miles in the snow [east] to a place called Maîche, where de Lattre had his advanced HQ. He had hoped to take us forward to an observation post from which we could have seen the beginning of the battle which was to start today. But it was snowing far too heavily to see anything! There was already quite a foot of snow and the attack had had to be put off. The PM's car punctured twice and we got temporarily stuck in the rut at the side of the road, however, we finally arrived at Maîche. The PM was very cold and miserable looking and I hope will not be any the worse for it.

On arrival we were given a description, which was amplified by Béthouart, of the front held by the 1st French Army, and the plans for the attack. Considering that the divisions for the attack are on a 30 kilometre front each, have been fighting without rest for 2½ months, and also have just been reorganized by absorbing white personnel in lieu of the Senegalese who have to go back to Africa, the whole plan of attack struck me as being fantastic! It is another case of Eisenhower's complete inability to run the land battle as well as acting as Supreme Commander. Furthermore it is an example of the American doctrine of attacking all along the line. The American Army just north of de Lattre is attacking in an impossible country in the Vosges, all he will do there is lose men. He ought to establish a defensive front there and concentrate his forces on the Belfort gap. Any successful offensive there would turn the line of the Vosges and render this expensive attack unnecessary. The French realize these errors only too well and are fretting at being subjected to their results.

We were given lunch which finished off by a speech by Winston in French, followed by de Gaulle and de Lattre, and I was then ordered by the PM to make one in French also! There was nothing for it, but to make the best possible out of the situation. After lunch we started driving back in the snow with darkness coming on. But on the way home we had to visit a training camp where new Maquis recruits are being turned into reserves. We also saw a battalion of the Legion which marched past. A most impressive sight. Then some tanks loomed past in the semi-darkness, and to finish one of the new battalions did some community singing. Winston looked frozen, and I pray heaven that he will not be the worst for it. At 7 pm in the darkness and snow we rejoined the train, having been 9 hours on the go in the cold and snow and very glad to get back to the warmth of the train.

Throughout the day de Gaulle was most affable and pleasant, but I very much wonder if he has the personality to unite France for concerted action at this critical time. General Juin is a very pleasant type, easy to get on with, a proved good general in the field, but I doubt if he is a big enough man to act as Chief of Staff in Paris. De Lattre seems a fighting commander, with plenty of character and determination, but how good he really is would be hard to judge without seeing more of him. Béthouart does not impress me much. Finished off the day by dining with de Gaulle in his dining car on the train. Party consisting of PM, de Gaulle, Minister of War, Minister of Transport, General Juin, Chef de Cabinet, Mary C, Barney and various ADCs. I sat on de Gaulle's left, Mary C on his right. Winston had the two ministers on his left and right. He was in excellent form and even de Gaulle unbent a little. Now midnight and I am very sleepy. Train far too bumpy to write in!! The Presidential train though very comfortable was certainly not built for writing in, as exemplified in the above hand writing!

Of all the sights that we had seen that day the one that remained most rooted in my mind was the march past of the Foreign Legion battalion in the falling light and amongst fast falling snow flakes. We had just been inspecting units of Maquis personnel, good tough looking boys that promised well, when de Lattre said he would like to march past us a battalion of the Legion which he had in reserve. They had their own band and out of the darkness came the wildest strains of a march, played on some wind sort of pipes, which transported one to North Africa. Then out of the fast falling light and the falling snow flakes came a sight I shall never forget. The grandest assembly of real fighting men that I have ever seen, marching with their heads up as if they owned the world, lean, hard looking men, carrying their arms admirably and marching with perfect precision. They disappeared into the darkness leaving me with a thrill, and the desire for a division of such men.

One other incident that day that left a mark in my mind was Winston at lunch. He arrived completely frozen and almost rolled up on himself like a hedgehog. He was placed in a chair with a hot water bottle at his feet and one in the back of his chair. At the same time good brandy was poured down his throat to warm him internally. The results were wonderful, he thawed out rapidly and when the time came produced one of those indescribably funny French speeches which brought the house down.

14 November

The train left Besançon shortly after we got into it and travelled throughout the night to Paris where it arrived about 6 am. Then the coaches with de Gaulle, Juin and the ministers were cut off and we went on to Rheims. We arrived at 11 am and were met by Ike who drove us out to his camp situated on the golf links built by the big champagne merchants! He went over the dispositions of the front and seemed fairly vague as to what was really going on! We had lunch with him and then drove to the aerodrome where we took off for Northolt which we reached at 4.45 pm after a very comfortable flight.

It was a relief to get the PM safely back from this trip as the security in Paris was far from satisfactory. I thoroughly enjoyed the trip and now have a much clearer idea of the situation as regards developing French forces. We should most certainly get busy with giving them equipment as soon as port facilities admit.

When we lunched with Ike I was interested to see that Kay [Summersby], his chauffeur, had been promoted to hostess, and sat at the head of the table with Winston on her right. At Versailles she had been promoted to personal secretary and ran the lobby next to his office. Now she had moved one step up the ladder. In doing so Ike produced a lot of undesirable gossip that did him no good.

15 November

Started the old COS life again, and worried about PM's fantastic ideas as to what command implies, he has never yet understood the system of chain of command. This was all connected with the move of Wilson to replace Dill [in

Washington], and Alexander to replace Wilson [in the Mediterranean], whilst Clark is to take over from Alexander [in Italy]. Winston had wired to Alexander through secret channels without telling me. Alex who has got somewhat an inflated idea of his position has wired back a lot of very incomprehensible stuff, but what is far worse Alex has now started going behind Wilson's back and abusing what he does to politicians who visit him. I should have thought that Alex was above such disloyalty.

After lunch had a long meeting with Weeks to discuss supply of equipment to the French. Have also arranged for Weeks to visit Juin and the French minister of war.

16 November
Started our COS meeting with John Anderson (Chancellor of the Exchequer) on the question of the atomic bomb. He was very interesting and gave us an excellent account of what he knew about the research work going on in Germany and the likelihood of arriving at some conclusion in the near future, which does not seem to constitute a danger for the present.

We then met the planners to discuss the plans of Mountbatten, which are as usual half baked. Adam came to lunch with me and we had a most useful talk on the manpower situation, especially in India where the army is now some 30,000 below establishment. During the afternoon I had an interview with S of S, then Graham who has been commanding 50th Div, followed by Lord Templewood (former Sam Hoare), for news of Spain, and finally Willoughby Norrie, prior to his departure to take up governorship of South Australia. His tickets for himself, family, ADCs and servants cost him £1400!! and he has to pay out of his own pocket!

17 November
We found at the morning COS that Winston was still confused about the system of command in Italy and in the Mediterranean. Having tried hard to warp the whole organization while Wilson was Supreme Commander and Alex commanding the Group of Armies so as to try and put Wilson in the saddle for the benefit of Alexander, now that he places Alexander as Supreme Commander he is frightened lest his powers should be restricted in the manner he has endeavoured to reduce those of Wilson!! He is quite incapable of understanding the system and chain of command. We had to meet at 4 pm and after laborious explanations I at last got him to accept matters as they are. Finally the telegram was sent off to President with the new proposal, ie:

Wilson to replace Dill,
Alexander to replace Wilson,
Clark (USA) to replace Alexander,
Truscott (USA) to replace Clark.

I have grave doubts as to the efficiency of these new appointments! Wilson will, I am afraid, never be able to step into Dill's shoes, and I cannot imagine that Alex will ever make a Supreme Commander, he has just not got the brains for it.

18 November
Shot with Rollie Charrington.

19 November
Quiet Sunday at home

20 November
Early start. Fairly long COS with several post war problems. Also a discussion as to the unsatisfactory state of affairs in France, where Eisenhower completely fails as Supreme Commander and just does nothing. Bedell Smith lives back in Paris quite out of touch, as a result the war is drifting in a rudderless condition. Had a long and despondent letter about it from Montgomery over the weekend. Am preparing case as we shall have to take it up with the Americans before long.

After lunch Boy Browning came to see me to be informed that he is to go as Chief of Staff to Mountbatten. He took it well, but I doubt whether in his heart of hearts he was thrilled!

21 November
Received telegram this morning from President agreeing to Wilson replacing Dill, Alex-Wilson, and Clark-Alex, so we can now go ahead with the changes and hope for the best. Winston also announced that Alex and Wilson would be made Field Marshals so that part is fixed also, this was done during the evening Cabinet. American attacks round the Vosges have been doing better today, but I still feel certain that final results will fall far short of our hopes.

22 November
Duncan Sandys attended our COS for our fortnightly review of rockets and flying bombs. He does not improve on acquaintance, but no doubt possesses all the necessary qualities for a successful political career! Giffard came to lunch and poured his heart out to me about his treatment by Dickie Mountbatten, and as I thought he was given a very raw deal. I blame Henry Pownall for a great deal of it, he should have been able to control Dickie better than he did. In any case I feel certain that most of the credit for the Burma success is due to Giffard.

This evening dined at Claridges with Sir Alexander Livingstone, for his 150th dinner since the war started. The guests were the King of Greece, R.B. Rossetti, Winant, Chinese Ambassador, Stark, Vaughan, Doolittle, Cunningham, Portal,

Lord Simon, Lord [Illegible], Dalton, Lawrence, Hardy and Fox Williams. A good dinner followed by short speeches by Winant, King of Greece, and Chinese Ambassador.

23 November
Started with the American Thanksgiving Service in Westminster Abbey. A disappointing service on the whole. Then a COS meeting concerned with employment of French forces in the Pacific. You turned up for lunch and we went shopping at the Stores. In the evening we went to the Albert Hall for a concert in honour of Remembrance Day for the Americans. Trenchard had invited us to his box which contained PM, Mrs C, Attlee and his wife, Lord Simon and his wife, Cunningham and his wife, Portal and his wife, the two of us, and also Winant and Eden. A very disappointing performance with dull music.

24 November
At the end of this morning's COS meeting I cleared the secretaries out and retained only Pug. I then put before the meeting my views on the very unsatisfactory state of affairs in France, with no one running the land battle. Eisenhower, though supposed to be doing so, is detached and by himself with his lady chauffeur on the golf links at Rheims – entirely detached from the war and taking practically no part in the running of the war! Matters got so bad lately that a deputation of Whiteley, Bedell Smith and a few others went up to tell him that he must get down to it and RUN the war, which he said he would. Personally I think he is incapable of running the war even if he tries.*

We discussed advisability of getting Marshall to come out to discuss the matter, but we are doubtful if he would appreciate the situation. Finally decided that I am to see the PM to discuss the situation with him. It is one of the most difficult problems I have had to tackle. I know the only possible solution, but doubt whether we can bring it off. Bradley should be made commander of land forces, with Tedder as the air commander working closely with him. The front should then be divided into two groups of armies, one north of the Ardennes under Monty, one south under Patton, whilst Ike returns to the true duties of Supreme Commander.

Then we lunched with Andrew Cunningham, after which I went to Northolt to meet Jumbo Wilson, who has come back for a few days prior to taking up his appointment in Washington. In the evening P.J. came in for an account of his Cabinet in the morning and Winston's handling of the Palestine situation. Finally we both dined quietly and happily together.

---

*A passage which caused widespread offence in the US when first published there, during Eisenhower's presidency, even shorn of the last sentence (censored by Bryant). Cf., *Triumph*, p. 338.

25 November
No COS so finished off work early and drove off with you to take Mr Ti out for his birthday. We had a lovely sunny day and took him to the aerodrome south of Newbury where we had lunch.

26 November
Monty flew over from Belgium and landed at Hartford Bridge Flats at 11.30 am. I sent a car for him to drive him to Ferney Close where we had an hour together prior to his flying back. He came to discuss the situation in France and to try to arrive at the best way of putting it right. We decided that there are three fundamentals to be put right:

a) to counter the pernicious American strategy of attacking all along the line

b) to obviate splitting an army group with the Ardennes in the middle of it, by forming two groups (a northern and a southern) instead of three as at present

c) to appoint a commander for the land forces

The problem is how to get this carried out. What we want is Bradley as a Commander of Land Forces, Montgomery, Northern Group of Armies, with Patton's Army in his group – by substituting 3rd Army for 9th Army – and Devers commanding Southern Group. Monty is to see Eisenhower on Monday and if he opens the subject Monty is to begin putting forward the above proposals. Meanwhile I am to have a talk with the PM suggesting that Marshall should be asked to come over to discuss the matter. Without some such changes we shall just drift on and God knows when the war will end!

27 November
Returned early. Had a long COS, drawn out by a discussion between CAS and First Sea Lord involving inter-service rivalries liable to cause heated blood! Lewin and family came to lunch. Cabinet at 6.30 to 8.30 pm. PM evidently beginning to realize that all is not well in France, but incapable of really seeing where the trouble really lies! He is now pressing for clearing Holland during the next few months, which he thinks could be done 'in no time with 2 or 3 divisions'!

28 November
Jumbo Wilson came to attend our COS meeting and gave us his views on future operations in Italy and across to the Dalmatian coast. These are pretty well in accordance with the Directive we had prepared for him.

At 12.30 I went to see the PM, having asked for an interview with him. I told him I was very worried with the course operations were taking on the Western Front. I said that when we looked facts in the face this last offensive could only be classified as the first strategic reverse that we had suffered since landing in France. I said that in my mind two main factors were at fault, ie:

a) American strategy and b) American organization.

As regards the strategy the American conception of always attacking all along the front, irrespective of strength available, was sheer madness. In the present offensive we had attacked on 6 Army Fronts without any reserves anywhere. As regards organization, I said that I did not consider that Eisenhower could command both as Supreme Commander and as Commander of the Land Forces at the same time. I said that I considered Bradley should be made the commander of the Land Forces, and the front divided into two groups of armies instead of three, with the Ardennes between them. Montgomery to command the Northern, and Devers the Southern.

Winston said that he was also worried about the Western Front. He agreed with most of what I had said, but was doubtful as to the necessity for a land force commander. I think I succeeded in pointing out that we must take the control out of Eisenhower's hands, and the best plan was to repeat what we did in Tunisia when we brought in Alex as a deputy to Eisenhower to command the land forces for him. I told Winston that the only way of putting things right was to get Marshall to come over. He agreed, we decided to wait a few more days before doing so. Rushed back to lunch where Wainwright was waiting for me.

At 2 pm conference with P.J. and Weeks on the ammunition situation. At 5 pm conference with Jumbo Wilson, Weeks and Nye on the organization of command in Italy. Alex has the wildest ideas which I am certain will not work. Finally conference from 6 to 8 pm with Winston on the ammunition situation, and methods of boosting up production to meet possibility of war dragging on late into 1945.

29 November

Received telegram this morning from Monty. He had had a talk with Eisenhower. The latter had agreed that strategy was wrong, that results of offensive were strategic reverse, that front wanted reorganising, would not agree that commander of land forces was necessary. But prepared to put Bradley with a large group north of the Ardennes under Monty's orders, leaving Devers south of the Ardennes. This may be all right, but I still have grave doubts as Ike is incapable of running a land battle and it is all dependent on how well Monty can handle him.

The afternoon mainly taken up by a long visit of the King of Greece, full of suggestions as to how Greece should be run and how much firmer Papandreou should be with the EAMs and ELASs. King also desirous of having a British Military Mission to assist in raising new Greek army. At 6 pm meeting with PM to discuss Mediterranean and South East Asia. Resulted in a meandering meeting at which we did nothing for 2 hours! Winston getting more and more hopeless to work with! Dined with John Kennedy.

30 November

In the morning motored down to the Staff College to give one of my usual end of term talks. From there on to lunch with you and back to London for another talk with Jumbo Wilson before he goes back to Italy and sends Alex home for a spell. The more I look into the prospects of Alex acting as Supreme Commander the gloomier I feel about it! Dined with P.J. at the Savoy and Jumbo Wilson came for further talks. The important thing is to get Alexander to part with Harding as his Chief of Staff as he is quite unsuitable for the task.

1 December
Went to see Winston at 10 am to tell him about Monty's wires. Found him in bed having his breakfast, surrounded by birthday presents. 'This is diilicious [sic] butter given to me by my doctor, his wife makes it with her cow, she milks it and beats it up!! etc etc.' He was in a good mood and approved the steps that Monty had taken, including the latter's letter to Ike laying down in black and white results of their talk together. If only all Monty thinks he has settled materializes we shall be all right, but I have fears of Ike going back on us when he has discussed with Bedell Smith, Tedder etc!

Lunched with Adam at the Carlton Grill and had a very satisfactory talk with him. In the evening went to see a new film on America which we have prepared to educate the Army. I think it is good and should help in getting our soldiers to understand the Americans.

2 December
An early rise, a motor drive to Ferney Close to collect gun and then on to Turgis Green to shoot with Bertie Fisher. Weather kept fine, and we had a very pleasant day's shooting.

In the evening I was called up by the PM who had drafted a wire to Eisenhower that he wanted to send. It was a hopeless one referring to the conversations which Monty has been having with Ike, and which the latter does not even know that Monty has told me about! It also went on to give Ike advice as to how to run the war, and very bad advice at that! I tried to stop him, explaining to him the harm he would do, but he would not agree, stating that the interview had been much publicized by the Press, it was a matter for government decision and not a matter to be settled by military men on their own, etc etc! It was quite clear that his pride was offended that Monty and Ike had had some lime light turned on them which he had not shared! I got angry and told him that if he treated private wires that way it would make me very reluctant to show them to him again. However, I finally got him to hold his hand until Monday!

3 December
A quiet Sunday spoilt by a mass of correspondence sent down by DR and several telephone calls. Trouble brewing up in Greece, and all my worst forebodings coming true! Anthony Eden had originally asked for 5000 soldiers, I

had told him that he would end by wanting some 4 divisions, which he denied flatly. He has already absorbed over 40,000!! Also telephone call from Simpson [Commander US 9th Army], just back from visiting Monty and with Monty's latest news. Monty has now received Ike's reply and it does not look too good, he seems to be changing round since seeing Bradley!

4 December

A long COS followed by lunch with Budget Loyd at the Turf Club. At 3.15 pm I went off to complete my argument with Winston. I found him in a good humour and succeeded in getting him to withdraw an offensive minute he had written to me after our talk on Saturday. He also agreed not to send that wire to Eisenhower and not to do anything till Monty and Ike had had their talk next Thursday. He made some queer statements during our discussion! One was that he did not want anybody between Ike and the Army Groups as Ike was a good fellow who was amenable and whom he could influence! Bradley on the other hand was a sour faced blighter and might not listen to what he said. I replied that I could see little use in having an amenable Supreme Commander if he was totally unfit to win the war for him! Cabinet at 6 pm.

5 December

The Greek situation is getting more and more confused. Winston spent most of the early hours from 3 am onwards sending telegrams to Jumbo Wilson, Scobie [C-in-C] and Leeper [Ambassador]. Meanwhile, Wilson was sending me wires which did not fit in with the instructions Winston was sending him. It is fairly clear that Leeper has got the jitters, having originally asked for 5000 men as being ample to set the Greek government firmly on its feet, he has now got over 40,000 and considers that 'the military have badly underestimated the strength required' and should send more troops at once. This is *exactly* what I have been predicting from the very start! Winston had been trying to induce Wilson to leave the Parachute Brigade in Greece, whereas it is urgently required for operations in Italy! Added to which these operations are Anglo-American, and the approved directive to Wilson from the Combined Chiefs of Staff states that the operations in Greece must on no account be allowed to interfere with those in Italy. I asked for an interview with Winston, was told 12.15. He kept me waiting till 12.45 as he was in the House and having a bad time about the Greek situation! When he returned I put the whole case in front of him. I found him rather rattled about situation, however he agreed that the withdrawal of the Parachute Brigade should be proceeded with as settled. I do not see much daylight yet in that Greek situation. And I feel certain we shall have to send far more troops there!

Jack Collins came to lunch. He is now writing Archie Wavell's memoirs. Selection Board in the afternoon.

6 December

A very long COS which Alexander attended for a bit. I am afraid that it was an eye opener for him to find some of the problems and difficulties he is to be up against as Supreme Commander in Mediterranean!! He is a mere child at it and does not begin to grasp what his task is! God help him and may God help us! I have been doing my best to get him to shed Harding as his Chief of Staff, and take on someone of bigger calibre. I have offered him Monkey Morgan, Budget Loyd, Kirkman, Keightley or Scobie or anybody he likes to choose from. I have I think shaken him a little about Harding, at any rate I have appealed to his better feelings in so far as he is holding Harding back by retaining him. He has practically promised to change him, but wants to use Harding to settle him in!

Lunched with Franklyn and gave talk to Home Forces on the strategic situation. Drove Bulgy Thorne back and listened to his requirements [for Scotland]. Then had long interview with Alex in which I asked him to ensure that he did not 'over lie' Clark in the way he had accused Wilson of treating him! I have a great feeling of uneasiness about Alex filling this job adequately! Dined at Gray's Inn, John Anderson and Lord Simon there.

7 December

Another long COS during which we examined the American plans for the Pacific. They are based on the war in Europe ending before the end of this year, and do not bear any very direct relation to facts! They will have to slow up the estimates of their rates of advance. After lunch I had interview with Dick O'Connor, who is leaving a corps in France for an army in India and is sad about it. Then final interview with Boy Browning prior to his start[ing] to act as Chief of Staff to Mountbatten, and a difficult job he is going to have of it! Then interview with changing American military attachés. Finally talk with P.J. Grigg. Dinner party for Cunningham with Hylda and Evelyn there also.

8 December

Slipped home early in the evening in anticipation of shooting with Rollie next day.

After dinner called up by Winston to find that he wanted to send a wire to Wilson to reinforce Greece by two brigades. He is doing it without possibly being able to estimate what the situation is. However, one thing is certain, we must now get out of the mess that this Greek venture had led us in. Consequently I agreed to additional forces being sent, since the greater the force the quicker the job will be done. I warned him however that we shall be falling foul of the Americans, and that we shall have to have the Supreme Commander Mediterrancan's directive adjusted.

It may seem inconsistent that I insisted on the withdrawal of the parachute brigade and now consented to 2 brigades being sent, but it should be remembered that the parachute brigade were specialists and required for specific tasks.

9 December

Lovely day and shot with Rollie. Not many birds, but very jolly day.

10 December

Pouring all day, quiet Sunday at home.

11 December

Usual Monday rush rendered worse by Cabinet at 12 noon and a mass of telegrams. As I predicted the Americans in the shape of King turned sour about Greece, and ordered their LSTs not to be used for ferrying troops to Greece! However, Harry Hopkins put the matter right by reversing King's order.

12 December

I have just completed one of those days which should have been one of the key stones of the final days of the war and has turned out as utterly futile! I feel I have utterly failed to do what is required, and yet God knows how I could have done anything else. I started by going to the PM at 10 am to discuss with him Monty's letter. Found him in bed eating his breakfast and absorbed by the breakfast and by the last telegram from Alex on the situation in Greece!! He was quite incapable of concentrating on anything but his breakfast and the Greek situation! I remained till 10.30 am, found he had not even read Monty's letter, knew nothing about it. I tried to explain but he kept returning to Greece! 'How wonderful Alex was! What a grasp! What a quick appreciation of the situation! What a master mind!' How long will this last?

Disgusted I went to the COS which lasted till near 1 pm. Was informed during lunch that War Cabinet was to meet at 3 pm on Greece. We met and wasted 1½ hours deciding whether the Archbishop should be appointed as Regent. Finally Cabinet decided this should be done and drafted minute to that effect to King of Greece, who I understand refused! I then rushed back to WO but was summoned again to Cabinet at 5.30 pm which I refused to attend.

At 6 pm met Ike and Tedder with PM in the latter's map room, with whole COS. Ike explained his plan, which contemplates a double advance into Germany, north of Rhine and by Frankfurt. I disagreed flatly with it, accused Ike of violating principles of concentration of force, which had resulted in his previous failures. I criticized his future plans and pointed out impossibility of double invasion with limited forces he has got. I stressed the importance of concentrating on one thrust. I drew attention to the fact that with his limited forces any thought of attack on both fronts could only lead to dispersal of effort. Quite impossible to get the PM to even begin to understand the importance of the principles involved. Half the time his attention was concentrated on the possibility of floating mines down the Rhine!!! He *cannot* understand a large strategical concept and must get down to detail! Ike also *quite* incapable of understanding real strategy. To make it worse Tedder talks nothing but nonsense in support of Ike.

Finally dined at 10 Downing St with PM, Ike, Tedder, Cunningham, Portal and Ismay there. Conversation again returned to the same topic of the strategy but I got no further in getting either Winston or Ike to see that their strategy is fundamentally wrong. Amongst other things discovered that Ike now does not hope to cross the Rhine before May!!!

13 December

I was very depressed last night and seriously thought of resigning as Winston did not seem last night to attach any importance to my views. I found however today that the situation was far better than I thought. After the COS I went to see Winston at 1 pm. He told me that he had had to support Ike last night as he was one American against five of us with only Tedder to support him. And also he was his guest. I think he felt that I had been rather rough on Ike, but on the other hand I found that I had convinced him of the seriousness of the situation. What I had said last night had had far more effect on him than I had thought. He decided that the War Cabinet must assemble at 5.30 this evening and that I must put before them the whole strategic situation. In addition he wanted me to put in a paper on the whole matter.

At 5.30 pm we met at 10 Downing St, and I ran through the situation after the PM had given a general introduction. The date of May for the crossing of the Rhine had a profound effect on the Cabinet. However, it has cleared the air well, and the Cabinet now know what to expect, which is a good thing to counter the over optimistic attitude of the newspapers.

14 December

Jumbo Wilson came to attend our COS meeting to get into the problems we are dealing with prior to going to America. After lunch Teddy Schreiber came to see me, back from Malta for a few days. He seems to be fully absorbed in all the Malta problems and I should think doing a first class job. Tonight Ronnie Stanyforth and Prue came to dine.

15 December

A very short COS at which we discussed Dickie Mountbatten's troubles caused by the loss of his Chinese divisions. Adam came to lunch and told me about his various troubles. Then a visit by Duke of Gloucester prior to his departure for Australia. Followed by McConnel back from Palestine. Then Army Artillery Commanders from all fronts with Otto Lund for a short talk, and finally a meeting with S of S.

16 December

I had hoped to escape home for lunch, but at 11 am a message arrived from Chequers that the PM wanted a War Cabinet at 3 pm! As it took us two hours I did not escape till after 5 pm. It was about Greece. Leeper and Macmillan still shouting for the Archbishop as Regent, and the King of Greece refuses to have a Regent, and especially the Archbishop! After much talking it was decided to await results of the additional force that is being brought to Greece. Arrived home for a late tea.

17 December
Spent quietly at home.

18 December
A very quiet Monday. Short COS and Cabinet at 12 noon. In the afternoon Gammell came to see me. Germans are delivering strong counter offensive against Americans, who have no immediate reserves to stem the attack with. They ought ultimately to hold it all right, and to have an opportunity of delivering serious counter blow which might well finish off Germans. But I am not certain whether they have the skill required, I doubt it. It is a worrying situation, if I felt that the American Divisional, Corps, Army Commanders and Staff were more efficient than they are, there is no doubt that this might turn out to be a heaven sent opportunity. However, if mishandled it may well put the defeat of Germany back for another 6 months.

I feel that Rundstedt in launching this counter offensive feels that as 'a good officer' he is doing the right thing to put off defeat by means of a counter offensive destined to upset the Allied plans. I feel, however, that he must realize the great risks he is taking of achieving exactly the reverse results if the Americans can take advantage of the risks he takes. Perhaps as 'a good German' he considers that there may well be a definite advantage in bringing this war to an early conclusion, and consequently accepts all risks, great as they are, willingly?

Rundstedt had proved how faulty Ike's dispositions and organizations were. Spread out over a large front with no adequate reserves and no land force Commander to immediately take charge, we shall see that in his attempts to stop the Germans he was compelled to withdraw troops from Strasbourg and in doing so to almost create a crisis in the de Gaulle government. It was a bold stroke on the part of the Germans and had it not been for Monty's prompt action might well have scored a definite success. As it was Eisenhower was temporarily thrown off his balance. On the other hand there can be no doubt that, after having been keyed up for this offensive by Rundstedt, a definite reaction affected the German morale as a result of its failure.

19 December
Very little more news of the war in France, Eisenhower seems quite confident and so do his staff, that they can deal with this situation. I only hope that this confidence is not based on ignorance!

Situation in Greece improving also, but it seems pretty certain that we shall have to send additional reinforcements. Tommy Lindsell turned up this afternoon from India and gave me all the local news from that theatre.

20 December

Received telegram from Monty which showed clearly that the situation in France was serious. American front penetrated, Germans advancing on Namur with little in front of them, north flank of First American Army in state of flux and disorganisation, etc etc. Also suggesting that he should be given command of all forces north of the penetration. I sent copy to the PM who sent for me at 3.30 pm in the Map Room. I found him very much the worse for wear having evidently consumed several glasses of brandy at lunch. It was not very easy to ensure that he was absorbing the seriousness of the situation. We had many references to Marlborough and other irrelevant matters. However, I got him to telephone to Ike to put the proposal to him that Monty should take over the whole of the Northern Wing whilst Bradley ran the South. Ike agreed and had apparently already issued orders to that effect.

We were then summoned to the 6 pm Cabinet to discuss the French situation. Cabinet took it well on the whole. I rather doubt whether they realized all the possible implications!

21 December

Our COS did not take long. We examined the possibilities of outflanking the Rhine by landing on the Dutch, German, or Danish coasts. The prospects are not hopeful, but something might possibly be done through the canal to Antwerp and on into the Zuider Zee.

After lunch I had an interview with Hayes, who is going out as Military Attaché to Chungking.

Finally dined with Lord McGowan (ICI), who was giving a dinner for Mr Essington Lewis (Chief Manager of Broker Hill Proprietary Company Ltd in Australia). He had Anderson, Woolton, Alexander, Selborne, P.J., Sandys, Gowry etc. I sat between Woolton and Bain (Head of Chemical Dept of ICI) a man with one arm, but I should say great drive and energy.

News of the war in France much better. Provided the two 'gateposts' hold on either flank, there may be a chance of annihilating a great many of the sheep that have broken through. If only the Americans are up to it.

22 December

German offensive appears to be held in the north, but I am a little more doubtful about the south. Patton is reported to have put in a counter attack. This could only have been a half baked affair and I doubt it's doing much good. Alexander evidently worried about the Greek war and the instructions he is receiving from the Prime Minister! I predict he will be much more worried before he finishes with his present job!

23 to 30 December

Proceeded home on a week's leave.

Situation in France gradually improved and Rundstedt's offensive appears to be held, importance now rests in counter strokes to be delivered. Monty has had another interview with Ike. I do not like the account of it. It looks to me as if Monty, with his usual lack of tact, has been rubbing into Ike the results of not having listened to Monty's advice! Too much of 'I told you so' to assist in creating the required friendly relations between them. According to Monty, Ike agrees that the front should now be divided in two, and that only one major offensive is possible. But I expect that whoever meets Ike next may swing him to any other point of view! He is a hopeless commander.

Meanwhile Winston has done a spectacular rush to Greece, to try and disentangle the mess. He does not appear to have achieved much. The rest of the 46th Div is now off to Greece, this completes the 80,000 men I had originally predicted! And what are we to get out of it all? As far as I can see, absolutely nothing! We shall eventually have to withdraw out of Greece, and she will then become as communistic as her close neighbours consider desirable. Meanwhile the campaign in Italy stagnates.

1 January – 31 August 1945

1 January 1945

A new year started, and let us hope the last one of the war with Germany! I have now done 3 years of this job and am very very weary. I left home early this morning and after a dark, cold and slippery drive through fog, landed at the WO at 9.25 am. Not much trouble in getting into my stride, as I had had brown bags sent down daily with current news. During afternoon had interviews with Nosworthy, returning from West Africa, with Burrows, just starting for West Africa, and with Carton de Wiart, back from China. The latter was interesting about conditions prevailing in China, of Chiang Kai-shek's position which appears quite secure in spite of all gossip.

PM has sent in a regular flow of minutes throughout the afternoon, all of futile nature. *(This may have been the afternoon when I received 15!! such minutes.)* Either based on misconceptions due to faulty reading of documents placed in front of him, or concerned with details which he should not get himself mixed up with. As a result he causes a mass of unnecessary work, and clogs the wheels of the machine.

2 January

A poisonous day. Started COS at 10.30 with a meeting of Joint Intelligence Committee. This lasted till 12.15 pm when we adjourned to meet the PM in his Map Room. The first point was to discuss Alex's visit to Moscow. I told Winston I could see no object for this visit. Winston had himself expressed the wish that Alex was to run the battle in Italy and I asked him how he expected him to do so if he was to go to Athens twice, to Moscow once, then Belgrade, followed probably by going to the Crimea to attend our Combined meeting there? This defeated Winston temporarily but he is so mixed and confused in all his thoughts that in five minutes he was again pressing for him to go to Moscow!

He then propounded the wildest of strategy, which was purely based on ensuring that British troops were retained in the lime light if necessary at the expense of the Americans and quite irrespective of any strategic requirements! We wasted 1½ hours with him and only escaped at 1.45. I lunched with the St Clairs and at 3 pm was back for a Selection Board. Finally a ghastly Cabinet which lasted from 5.30 to 8.30 pm and might easily have been finished far more efficiently in one hour.

Little news from France today, but heard that Bertie Ramsay had been killed in a plane crash in Paris; his is a desperate loss.

3 January

Left Northolt by plane at 12.30 pm, with the PM for Paris. Rest of party: Tommy, Boyle, Mr Kimmins and Sawyers. Bumpy passage and dirty weather, took us 1¾ hours for the trip. Eisenhower met us on the aerodrome and drove us to his new house in Versailles. He has left Rundstedt's old house in St Germain and is now in the President's house just on the approach of Trianon. We found a very worried Ike as de Gaulle had taken exception to his proposed dispositions in Alsace and Lorraine: to withdraw front to the Vosges leaving only an outpost line. De Gaulle stated that such an abandonment of Strasbourg and of the Alsatians and Lorrainians would lead to an outcry throughout France, which could have no other results than to bring his government crashing to the ground! It had been arranged for de Gaulle to come to Versailles to see Ike this afternoon. So after lunch we went round to Ike's office and held a memorable conference consisting of PM, de Gaulle, Ike, Juin, Bedell Smith, and an interpreter and myself. De Gaulle painted a gloomy picture of the massacres that would ensue if the Germans returned to portions of Alsace or Lorraine. However, Ike had already decided to alter his dispositions so as to leave the divisions practically where they are and not to withdraw the 2 divisions that were to have moved up into Patton's reserve.

The PM then withdrew for a political talk with de Gaulle and I remained on for a discussion with Eisenhower about his front. He seemed worried about the turn of affairs, but I avoided returning to any questions of command organization or strategy as it is quite useless. Finally we returned to Ike's house before dinner, and had a longish talk with him there. To dinner Morgan, Whiteley, Eaker, Curtis, Strong and Gale turned up.

Long night: PM only moved off after 1.30 pm!! He then dragged me into his bedroom for a further talk. He said that he was beginning to see that any operation from Italy towards Vienna had little prospects! This is the result of many patient hours work winning him away from this venture! He agreed that any divisions rendered spare by a withdrawal of Kesselring to the Adige could better be employed on the main western front. This is most satisfactory. He then went on about Alex, saying that he could not leave him in Italy once this front had become a subsidiary one with only small forces there. He suggested that as Tedder was wanted back by the Air Ministry we might replace him with Alex. This also seems a sound move and one which might assist in keeping Ike on the rails in future. He asked me to try Ike about this suggestion and find out what his reactions would be.

4 January

Woke up to find it snowing hard! Impossible to fly up to Monty. Shall have to go by train instead. After breakfast went with Ike to his HQ, where we went through the situation with Whiteley, Strong and Robb [ACM]. On the whole the counterattacks appear to be making some progress towards narrowing the corridor at Bastogne. Unfortunately the air unable to function owing to this foul weather.

Later:

Duff Cooper turned up for lunch and at 4.30 pm we left for Versailles Station to get on board Ike's train which is to take us up to Monty's HQ through the night. After lunch, Winston put the move of Alex to replace Tedder forward to Ike, who said he would welcome him. We had a very comfortable dinner on the train, and a comfortable night, travelling up through Amiens, Arras, Lille, Brussels to Hasselt.

5 January

We arrived about 7.30 am. After breakfast Monty turned up at 9 am and I had about ¾ hours talk with him before the PM turned up. He seemed quite pleased with his attack which had started yesterday on Hodges's Army front and which was making good progress. I gathered from him that a large number of American divisions on his front were badly understrength, and had lost their offensive value temporarily. He seemed fairly confident that between him and Bradley they could deal with the Western end of the German salient, but said that the base of the salient would present a more difficult problem. I told him about the possibilities of obtaining later on reinforcements from Italy and of the possible scheme of Alex replacing Tedder. He said that he was all for such a plan which might go some way towards putting matters straight.

By 11.15 am we left by car for Brussels aerodrome. We passed through Louvain, which woke many memories of 1939 and of my discussions with Monty about the defence of Louvain. Of the retreat from Louvain to Brussels. How little did I expect, that last day when I drove back from Monty's HQ along that road, that over five years later I should be driving down that same road with Winston as Prime Minister!! Memories of that '39 period just surged through my brain.

About 12.30 pm we arrived at the aerodrome east of Brussels which the Boche used to bomb so heavily! There we found the plane and Mary Coningham. We lunched on the plane on the way back and in 1¾ hours we were back at Northolt aerodrome. Went straight to the WO where I had meetings with S of S, AG, QMG, VCIGS, DMO and DMI. Lewin came to dine.

6 January

Arrived home in time for lunch, and attended your lovely party for the children.

7 January

Quiet Sunday at home.

8 January

Very cold drive back to WO in the morning. Short COS followed at 12.30 by a memorial service at the Abbey for Bertie Ramsay. In the evening Cabinet at 6 pm. Except for an attack by PM on P.J. Grigg for not arranging better for reception for men returning on leave, a dull meeting.

Monty's offensive seems to be progressing very favourably, but I am not so certain that matters are all right in Alsace and Lorraine. Alexander is also worrying me by committing more and more troops in Greece without much hope of getting them out!

Later:

Had to go round to PM at 10.30 pm. He wanted first of all to gloat over the reply from Stalin, promising an offensive middle of Jan, which he had received to the wire he had sent asking for information and promising he would only divulge reply to Eisenhower and myself. By the way he had already told Anthony Eden and was contemplating telling the President!!! He was already in bed when I arrived, sipping coffee, drinking brandy and smoking his cigar. I was given coffee and brandy. We then discussed all the evils of Monty's press interview, which resulted in a call to Eisenhower and the sending for Brendan Bracken.* Shortly after Andrew Cunningham turned up, followed up by Pug Ismay. Then typist was sent for and wire was dictated to Roosevelt. Then the red stylo-pen was lost, Sawyers sent for, new pen was brought followed by old one being found inside bed etc, etc. Finally at 1.30 am we all withdrew, what had we accomplished beyond getting sleepy?! I know not.

9 January

COS at which I pointed out the necessity to draft a new directive to Alex telling him to finish off Greek enterprise at earliest possible moment, rest troops in Italy, prepare offensive, drive Kesselring back to Adige, and provide troops for France. We were told that Lumsden had been killed, a great loss. In afternoon interview with Wilson to try and induce him not to take his wife to Washington. Failed! He says he cannot afford to run a double establishment, and I am certain she will crash him in Washington! Then meeting with Pownall back from South East Asia. Finally dined with Ronnie Stanyforth.

10 January

Cold, snowy day again. A fairly long COS connected mainly with detailed points and some final considerations connected with our future trip to the Crimea. Jack Collins came to lunch and we had a long talk. Crerar came during the afternoon looking very well. Finished up the day with one of Barney's dinner parties.

---

*Montgomery had implied that it was he, not the Americans, who had defeated the Germans in the Ardennes.

11 January

Our COS was filled up in the first place trying to disentangle the plans for our next Combined meeting in the Crimea with a preliminary meeting in Malta. The latter place is too small to accommodate everybody and the former is very uncertain as to what accommodation exists! We then discussed with the Planners the next directive for Alexander based on early evacuation of Greece and transfer of forces from Italy to France. Finished the day with a delightful dinner with Rollie and Stella Charrington at Claridges. Bitterly cold day with periodic snow.

12 January

A very nice quiet day for a change, which gave me an opportunity to write a long letter to Alexander. He has now become completely lost in this damned Greek business, and has forgotten the whole war on the strength of it. He relies on Macmillan as his confidential advisor on all matters including military ones, and as a result loses all military perspective. The more I see of him the more I marvel at the smallness of the man. I do not believe that he has a single idea in his head of his own!

Adam came to lunch prior to starting off for a tour out to India, and we had a very useful talk.

13 January

After a short morning went home for the weekend.

14 January

A quiet Sunday at home.

15 January

Usual early start back for the WO. Plans for our journey to Malta and the Crimea are gradually taking shape. Cabinet at 5.30. Great deal of the time spent in listening to Herbert Morrison lamenting about the rockets. 'London had already suffered too much and could not be expected to suffer much more! Something must be done to lighten this burden! More energy must be displayed! It was all very well stating that the Army and the Battle required the support of our Air Force, London required such support and should not be denied it! etc, etc.' In fact, never mind if we have to put off defeating Germany but let us at any rate defeat the few rockets that land in London! If there are many like him in England we deserve to lose the war!

16 January

A very quiet day. Good news coming in from Russia, it looks as if they had started their winter offensive in earnest. I hope so, as it should make all the difference towards speeding up the end of the war. However, there is still a great deal to be done.

Boy Browning turned up from Ceylon this evening with message from Oliver Leese asking for additional aircraft for Burma operation.

17 January

We had a specially long COS as we had Boy Browning back from Kandy, having been sent by Dickie to plead his case for more transport aircraft for the Burma operations. There is no doubt that the operations there have taken quite a different turn, and there is now just a possibility of actually taking Rangoon from the north! This is due to the Japanese forces beginning to crumple up and to be demoralized. One of our difficulties arises through the fact that the transport aircraft belong to the Americans, and that the reconquest of lower Burma does not interest them at all. All they want is north Burma and the air route and pipe line and Ledo road into China. They have now practically got all of these, and the rest of Burma is of small interest to them. Lunched with the Navy League and sat between Lord Bennett and the First Lord. Afternoon filled up with a series of interviews.

18 January

A long meeting with COS preparing our directive for Alex in the Mediterranean and trying to clamp down his misplaced ardour in Greece! It is hard to tell at present who is Supreme Commander in the Mediterranean! Is it Macmillan or is it Alex? Surely it is Macmillan? It is too depressing to see how Alex's deficiency of brain allows him to be dominated by others!! He must have someone else to lean on! He has *no* personality of his own and lets anyone else climb into his skin!! In Africa, Sicily and South Italy he was carried by Montgomery. In central Italy by Oliver Leese and Harding and failed badly, and now he has selected Macmillan as his mount! His new charger may carry him over the political fences (perhaps), but will certainly crash him over the military ones!

My God how difficult war is to run owing to the personalities one has to handle, and how terribly dull it would be if they were all soulless cog wheels without any personal idiosyncrasies! But to handle them you must be young and full of vigour and enthusiasm, whereas every day I feel older, more tired, less inclined to face difficulties, less capable to face problems! What did Kipling say? 'If you can make your nerves and sinews serve you long after they are gone' or something of that kind, how difficult it is to carry out, how worthy of trial, but how dangerous of failure in view of its implications! Youth seems difficult enough to cope with when one is young, middle age is just one series of problems, but are not those of old age and decline the hardest to face bravely, and most important of all, with a balanced mind? Is not the inferiority complex of old age more difficult to size up and appreciate than that of youth?

At any rate the latter can only lead you into minor troubles, whilst the former may well have fatal results.

I think that in my criticism of Alex, I was certainly wrong in saying that 'he has no personality of his own'. He most certainly had a definite personality of exceptional charm, of outward calm which engendered confidence, of exceptional bravery and of great attractiveness. One could not help being fond of Alex and of enjoying being with him. I think, however, that it was just on account of all these outward qualities that on knowing him one realized the deficiency of brains and character. I have often described him as a beautiful Chippendale mirror, with the most attractive and pleasant frame, but when you look into the mirror you always find the reflection of some other person who temporarily dominates him, be it a Monty, an Oliver Leese or a Macmillan. I think that many of my criticisms of him are probably too hard, but on the one side I had so much affection and admiration for him that I was always angry that the other side of him did not live up to this charming exterior. There is no doubt that he may well be proud of what he achieved in the war.

19 January
The Canadian Mission attended our COS and I had to give them a short review of the situation on all fronts. In the afternoon Boy Browning came to say goodbye before returning to Ceylon.

Tedder on his way back from Moscow came to give results of his meeting with Stalin. He had not much to say beyond what had been developing in the wonderful Russian advance, which looks like speeding up the end of the war. Then attended dinner at the Savoy given by the Army Council for Somervell (USA) who was passing through London.

As I returned home found call from PM wanting to see me!! So off I started again. I found it was in connection with Greece and the fears he had that we should 'frame up' with the American Chiefs of Staff against him in an effort to pull out of Greece prematurely. I assured him that although strongly opposed to our original venture into Greece, now that we were committed, I fully realized the difficulty and impossibility of extracting forces out of Greece until such time as the Greek forces had been organized and trained to take on the job. It was a commitment which we had incurred against my military advice, no doubt based on excellent political reasons. But now that we were committed I fully realized all implications. He was in bed, looking very old, very meandering in his thoughts and watery about the eyes.

20 January
We had fairly full COS which completed our record week for the maximum number of items handled in one week since war started!!! It is a strange thing what a vast part the COS takes in the running of the war and how little it is known or its functions appreciated. The average man in the street has never heard of it. Any lime light for it could not fail to slightly diminish the PM's

halo! This may perhaps account for the fact that he has never yet given it the slightest word of credit in public!

Arrived home for late lunch, and spent afternoon gumming in book plates in my bird books. Wonderful news from Russia continues to come in. This may well be the beginning of the beginning of the end! However, I feel that this offensive may still fall short of final victory and necessitate another double offensive, East and West, in the Spring.

It is not astonishing that nobody knew much about the functions of the COS Committee in war, since this was the first war to be fought since this organization was brought into being between the wars. When war started it soon became the Central Battle Headquarters for all fronts, with the trinity of the 3 Chiefs of Staff acting in the capacity of a Supreme Commander of all fronts, and served by the Joint Planning Staff acting as an Operational Branch, and the Joint Intelligence Staff representing the Intelligence Branch. Both these staffs were integrated at all levels with various Ministries concerned such as Foreign Office, Home Office, Transport, Supply, etc, etc. This organization dealt with the day to day reports and messages. It was up to the Chiefs of Staff to think out what theatres of war were necessary, what the allocation of forces should be for them and to prepare the plans for the operations in that theatre. All this work had to be done in close consultation with the Government, and Government approval had to be obtained in all major issues. Finally it was up to the COS to issue the actual orders or directives to the Commanders in each theatre. Where Supreme Commanders were concerned on inter-allied fronts, then the matters were carried up to the Combined Chiefs of Staff for their decisions, which again had to obtain approval of their respective Governments. It will be seen, therefore, that the COS organization had grown into a very effective form of War HQ in close contact with the Government and in control of all operations and all theatres. Even now many years after the war, the country as a whole does not realize the value of this War HQ, which grew out of the COS Committee during the war.

21 January
Quiet Sunday at home.

22 January
Leathers attended our COS to discuss the shipping situation, he was as slippery as usual and we did not get very far with him. Eisenhower's appreciation was also in, it leaves us again with a most confused picture, still hankering after the Frankfurt line of advance, and in the end backing both, and being insufficiently strong for either. At 5.30 pm War Cabinet, drawn out by the usual endless statements by Winston. My God! How I loathe these Cabinet meetings! The waste of time is appalling.

Dined with Meinertzhagen who had the Director of the [London] Zoo dining there and his niece and daughter. An interesting evening.

23 January

I don't feel that I can stand another day working with Winston, it is quite hopeless, he is finished and gone, incapable of grasping any military situation and unable to give a decision. We met him this morning to try and get from him some decisions prior to our meeting with the American Chiefs of Staff. We wanted to get from him approval to our proposed Directives to the Supreme Commanders. The first was one to Alexander, laying down that forces should be withdrawn from Greece as soon as political situation admitted, and that some 6 divisions should be transferred from Italy to France. I had obtained full agreement from him before to these moves, now he began to hover and say we were crippling the Italian Front, yet he agreed that there was nothing now to be done in Italy or in Yugoslavia. He did not know what he wanted, but would not agree to anything. Then Eisenhower's directive, urging that only one offensive should be carried out, and that in the north, a much more debatable point, he took little interest in it, and it was the only point he expressed any sort of agreement with. Next, probable date of end of war, sufficiently vague to require little decision, yet refused to approve circulation of paper to Cabinet, Chiefs of Staff to make a statement instead. Next American suggestion of worn out bombers being flown empty into Germany. Again no definite decision although he had ridiculed the proposition in the Cabinet the previous day. Finally the conversion of the Long Range Penetration Groups to an Airborne Division for operations in Burma, a flat refusal to give decision after the whole case had been put before him, and a statement that he would send a decision in writing!! A matter of complete detail which he ought to have nothing to do with at all.

Finally dined at White's Club with Medlicott [21st Army Group], arriving at 8.45 pm, having been asked for 8 pm!! Gowrie [lately Governor-General of Australia] there to dine and very interesting on Australia, MacArthur, etc, etc.

24 January

This morning at the COS we tried to make some sense out of our meeting with Winston last night! It means sending a minute again asking for some decisions. This afternoon Anders (back from Italy) came to see me about the future of the Polish Forces. Apparently they are anxious to start planning for the eventual assembly of Polish Forces in France and to form them into an army with Anders at its head. They do not want to return from Italy to Poland via Vienna as they consider this likely to lead to a clash with the Russians! They would sooner join up in France, and swell their numbers with Poles from Germany, gradually returning through Germany, and if necessary carrying out a period of occupation of Germany. I foresee that this may well lead to many complications politically, and must discuss this matter with Anthony Eden.

25 January

We had a long meeting with the Planners to fix up final points for our meeting with the American Chiefs of Staff. Most points are now squared up, except that we have been unable to get agreement with PM over moves of divisions from Italy to France. He is basing his objections on the delays of the move. As we have cut down the times required for the move to 1½ instead of 2½ months, he should not now object any more. Unfortunately the whole matter is mixed up with the reduction of Alexander's command and the difficulty of finding another appointment for Alexander. In fact strategy is now being warped by personalities. I despair of ever being able to make him see straight! He has no alternative strategy for Italy and agrees that it must now become a secondary front and yet he cannot drive himself to taking a decision. It is hopeless trying to work with him and I have had quite enough of it.

From the continued abuse that I find on almost every page of my diary, I feel that I am perhaps conveying a false impression of my relations with him and of my feelings for him. Throughout all these troublesome times I always retained the same unbounded admiration, and gratitude for what he had done in the early years of the war. One could not help also being filled with the deepest admiration for such a genius and super man. And mixed with it all there were always feelings of real affection for the better side of him. In reading these diaries it must be remembered that I had a long and trying time with him and that the writing of this diary presented the only safety valve that I had to pent up feelings of irritation which I could share with no one else.

Monty was to fly over and come to lunch with me as he is again very depressed with the American strategy and Eisenhower's inability to retain a definite policy without waffling about. However, flying weather was too bad, and he is to come tomorrow instead. During afternoon Rusty Eastwood back from Gibraltar came to see me.

26 January

A pretty full day. Started with COS at 10 am and at 11 am met PM and Defence Committee to discuss Herbert Morrison's complaints about the [V2] rockets! He had the usual whines, that London was very tired and could not stand much more knocking about, etc, etc! He did not get much change. Then Monty came to lunch and I had a good talk with him. The old trouble keeps turning round and round in his head. Lack of organization of command on the part of the Americans and their failure to concentrate their efforts on the vital point. At 3 pm back to a Cabinet meeting to discuss the present overall shortage of shipping and to have approved the line of action to take with the Americans at the coming conference. Back to WO to meet Russian General on mission here, and also General Noiret, just back from seeing Juin in Paris. Finally dashed off home to have Saturday before starting for Crimea.

27 January

Quiet Saturday at home and a call in the evening stating that owing to bad weather departure had been put off.

28 January

Had a quiet Sunday at home, and motored up after dinner so as to complete final arrangements in anticipation of early departure tomorrow morning.

29 January   Malta

We left Northolt at 9 am! A poisonous cold morning, driving through a snow covered Hyde Park in half darkness. I loathed the idea of launching myself out into cold space and longed to be able to remain at home! However we had a wonderful trip mostly at 12,000 ft height over the clouds in brilliant sunshine. The little bits of France we saw were covered with snow till we got close to Toulouse, when the snow disappeared. We passed over Le Mans, Tours, Narbonne. Then over Sardinia, after which we descended into more bumpy going and by 2.45 after 5¾ hours were over Malta!! By 3 pm we had landed. Schreiber met us at the plane and took me off to 'The Palace'. There Jumbo Wilson and Bedell Smith are stopping. The rest are scattered throughout the island. All the American Chiefs are in the Artillery Mess, Andrew Cunningham with C-in-C Med, Portal with AOC-in-C, etc. There are rumours that PM was arriving tonight, but nothing certain about it.

30 January

Started our day with a COS at 10 am to decide on our line of action. At 12 noon we met the Americans to decide on the times of our meetings and the programme. I then lunched with Jumbo down at the Club, after which we again met the Americans at 2.30. We discussed the Western Front and Ike's Appreciation. Started with Bedell Smith and Bull [Assistant Chief of Staff] giving a description of Ike's plans. This description was very much in line with what we have always asked for, but not in line with what Ike had put down as his plan. This resulted in considerable discussion. Bedell Smith had to agree that Ike's paper did not entirely agree with what he (Bedell) had been propounding. As a result I said that we would probably be prepared to approve Bedell's statement as taken down in the minutes of the meeting but that we could not approve the appreciation by Eisenhower. I don't know how this will be received.

The PM arrived last night at 4 am and at once developed a temperature! However it dropped again later on and he moved out to his cruiser where he is now. I had to go out and see him there at 6.30 pm. Found Alex just coming away and Anthony Eden waiting to see him. Anthony and I went in and found him in bed. He asked me how we had got on today and I told him. I then asked him if he had talked matters over with Alex and whether he was now in agreement with us about the withdrawal of divisions from Italy. He said that he was now entirely with us and that I could now go ahead and discuss with the Americans. This is a Godsend as I was wondering how we should get through tomorrow's meeting with the Americans without having his agreement. He told me that he had also suggested to Alex that he should replace Tedder as

Deputy to Ike and that Alex was pleased with the idea. I shall have to see Alex tomorrow to find out his real reactions. This evening Teddy had a large dinner party for 22 with Marshall, King, Bedell Smith, Andrew Cunningham, Stark, Robb brothers, Somervell, Pug, Somerville, etc, etc. Weather unpleasantly cold!

31 January

We started the day with our COS meeting where we had some difficult points to consider. There was the question of the Western Front strategy, of Eisenhower's awful appreciation which points to no decisive action. Then there was Bedell Smith's interpretation which was very close to our own views and was recorded in the minutes of the previous day. We decided to adopt Bedell's statement and ignore Ike's appreciation. However when we met at 2.30 pm the situation was more confused than ever as Bedell Smith had sent another wire to Ike which was also impossible and Ike had wired back!! So we were again stuck. However we made good progress with the directive for Alexander withdrawing divisions from Italy for France, and also in getting the South East Asia directive approved, contemplating clearing of Burma and then proceeding with Malaya.

After the meeting I had a long and useful interview with Alex. Discussed withdrawal of forces from Italy, also his possible move to Deputy to Ike, which he is prepared to do. Finally told him that some of us had doubts as to whether Macmillan or Alexander was Supreme Commander of Mediterranean! This had I think the required effect. But, my God, how I loathe being unpleasant in this way.

I then attended a large dinner party with John Cunningham in the house of the C-in-C Mediterranean, Nelson's old headquarters. I must say that I felt swept off into the old ages imagining him here with his romance and his wars! Returned here and was just off to bed when Bedell Smith came in and we had at least an hour's talk trying to find some settlement to the difference that lies between us. I think that the talk did both of us good and may help in easing the work tomorrow. It has been a long day with much work, and I am feeling very tired, and old!

1 February

We have had a hard day of it. Rather a rush with telegrams etc before our COS at 10 am. This lasted till 1.15 pm and was long and difficult. We discussed shipping shortage, allocating shipping to liberated countries, stocks of oil in England, etc. All of them difficult. Leathers attended and certainly did not make the matter any easier! I then rushed off to lunch with Anthony Eden on his cruiser where he had Stettinius [Secretary of State], Harry Hopkins and Harriman were also there. I sat next to Stettinius and found him pleasant and easy to talk to. The only point that interested him was finally setting the zones of occupation of Germany.

I then rushed back to arrive in time for the CCS meeting at 2.30. There we had more difficulties about the Western Front. Marshall wished to go into 'closed session', he was opposed to cramping Eisenhower's style by issuing any directive to him! He wanted us to approve his quite unacceptable appreciation and plan. I refused to do this but said I would be prepared to 'take note' of it. Which we finally settled to do. However this allowed Marshall to express his full dislike and antipathy to Montgomery! Other points we settled were South East Asia, and Med strategy. PM sent for me at 6 pm on the cruiser *Orion*. I gave him an account of our proceedings which he seemed satisfied with. Finally dined with the Schreibers.

It had been an unsatisfactory meeting with the Americans which led us nowhere and resulted in the most washy conclusion. A decision to 'take note' certainly did not mean much, beyond the fact that although I did not approve of Ike's appreciation and plans, yet through force of circumstances I had to accept them. The 'force of circum-stances' was that we were dealing with a force that was predominantly American, and it was therefore natural that they should wish to have the major share in its han-dling. In addition there was the fact that Marshall clearly understood nothing of strategy and could not even argue out the relative merits of various alternatives. Being unable to judge for himself he trusted and backed Ike, and felt it his duty to guard him from interference. My talk with Bedell Smith on the previous evening had at any rate shown to me that Bedell was quite able to appreciate the dangers of Ike's strategy and I felt satisfied that he would use his influence to guide him.

To the above one further consideration weighed with me, namely the condition of the German forces. It was clear that after the failure of Rundstedt's offensive, German morale had deteriorated, and that we could from now on take greater liberties with him. Under these new circumstances, an advance on a wider front might present some advantages.

2 February

This morning when I went to my office Brian Boyle met me with the ghastly news that the plane Barney was travelling in had crashed last night in the sea near Pantelleria! Of the 20 passengers only 7 had been saved. In spite of several telegrams to try and obtain names of survivors it was not till just on 8 pm that I obtained the news that Barney was amongst those killed. It is a frightful blow as Barney had grown to be a most intimate companion, I always knew I could discuss anybody or anything with him without any fear of his ever repeating anything. He was always cheerful and in good humour no matter how unpleasant situations were. He had grown to know me well and was of the greatest help, I shall miss him most awfully, and feel so very very sorry for Diana. On top of that the day has been a very busy one and I have found it extremely difficult to concentrate my thoughts and not let them wander off to Barney.

We started our COS at 9.30 and had Leathers in for another discussion on the shipping. At 12 noon we met the Americans and finished off most of the items we wanted to do before leaving for the Crimea. We also produced an interim report for the President and PM on our work up to date. After lunch we had arranged a short tour for the Americans to the Palace, the Library and the Cathedral of the Knights of St John. This lasted till 4 pm and was most successful.

At 5.30 pm we all went to the President's battleship for an interim Plenary Meeting. Winston as usual had not read the paper although he had had it since this morning! He made [the] most foolish remarks about it which proved he had not read it, and altogether did not come out very well! However the paper was passed and agreed in its present form. After dinner just on midnight I drove to the aerodrome where we took off for the Crimea. The plane load consisted of Cunningham, Portal, Jacob, Boyle, and various others.

The loss of Barney Charlesworth was one of the worst blows I had during the war. He had come to me in France in 1940, we had been through Dunkirk together and since then had lived in the same flat, and during most of my time as CIGS we had most of our meals just the two of us together. I had consequently got to know him very well, and he knew me equally well. He was the most excellent companion, and it was always a relaxation to be with him.

The circumstances of the crash were also tragical. They had all embarked on one plane which developed engine trouble before they started. They were consequently taken to another plane, all members of the crew were individually excellent, but I believe had not flown as a crew together. Owing to some fault in the navigation the plane arrived over Pantelleria in the dark thinking they were over Malta. They kept calling up for the aerodrome to be lit up, but they were apparently incapable of receiving any messages. Finally, after flying round for some time, they sent a message saying that they were running out of fuel and would land on the sea. The pilot chose a small bay and, I believe, did an excellent landing on the sea. Unfortunately, at the point of landing there was a submerged wreck which ripped off the bottom of the plane and killed the occupants. That at any rate was the account that I was given after the disaster had been gone into.

3 February   Crimea

We had a good and smooth journey. Got up about 6 am to have a shave and breakfast. We were then flying over clouds over the Black Sea. At about 7.30 clouds cleared and we sighted Eupatoria on the west coast of the Crimea, we were heading for the aerodrome of Saki which is quite close, and shortly afterwards we made a safe landing, having taken a little over 7½ hours for the journey. Molotov, Gousev, Vyshinski and many others were on the aerodrome. We were given a cup of tea and then started off by car for Yalta. We drove by Simferopol, Alushta to Yalta and then on to near Alupka. Here we are lodged in one of the large Crimean houses of the Tsarist nobility days. Built by a Scottish architect in semi-Moorish, semi-Scotch style! The mixture is somewhat startling.

We have got here the PM, Anthony Eden, 3 Chiefs of Staff, Clark Kerr, Leathers, and a few others. The drive took us some 4½ hours over a fairly good road with a certain amount of snow. Here the snow is gone, but on the aerodrome and on the road through Simferopol there was a certain amount. The temperature is much milder than I had expected. We are also much more comfortably established than I had ever hoped for. This house was occupied by the German commander of the Crimean forces, and he had been promised the house as a gift after the war. He was consequently loath to carry out any destructions similar to those on other houses till the very last moment, and finally left it too late.

I forgot to write down yesterday that after the Plenary Meeting Winston asked me to stop on to discuss with him and the President and Marshall the proposal for Alexander and Tedder to change round. The President and Marshall considered that politically such a move might have repercussions in America if carried out just now. It might be considered that Alex was being put to support Ike after his Ardennes failure! However they were quite prepared to accept the change in about 6 weeks time after future offensive operations have been started by Ike, and the Ardennes operation more forgotten.

4 February

We had a COS meeting at 10 am to discuss our line of action during the next few days here. We finished by about 11 am and had nothing to do for the rest of the morning. I only wish we had a real full day to keep my thoughts from wandering off to poor old Barney.

After lunch Stalin came at 3 pm to call on Winston and we all met him in the hall. He then spent an hour with Winston, and Eden told me afterwards that he had raised the suggestion that we should send a force from Italy through Northern Yugoslavia to operate on their left flank. This is a bore as we had been killing that idea and banking on transferring troops from Italy to France instead and have got all agreed with Americans.

At 5 pm we met at the American Headquarters. They are living in the old Yalta Tsar's Palace. Marshall is in the Tsarina's bedroom and King in her boudoir, with the special staircase for Rasputin to visit her! We had a round table conference consisting of Stalin with Maisky interpreting for him (a new departure), Molotov, Antonov, their Admiral and Air Marshal, President, Leahy, Marshall, King, Stettinius, Harriman and Deane, PM, 3 Chiefs, Eden, Pug, Alex, and Clark Kerr. Meeting started with the usual compliments followed by an opening statement by Stalin calling in Antonov to give a statement of the war. He gave an excellent and very clear talk, but not much we did not know. Marshall then described the situation on the Western Front. This was followed by a rather general talk, the main item being the settling of a military meeting tomorrow for 12 noon at which we are to discuss the coordination of our military actions and offensives as Stalin considered the war might well go on till the summer and it was very desirable that our offensive actions should coincide. Weather again quite lovely and wonderfully mild.

5 February

We started our day with a COS at 10 am to decide the line on which we should run our meeting with the Americans and Russians. At 11.30 am we drove off to Antonov's HQ, halfway to Yalta. After many examinations by sentries we were admitted. Meanwhile the Americans had lost themselves and came down to this house! As a result they were ½ hour late, which was all to our advantage, as I got into a hug with Antonov whilst Portal and Cunningham got hold of their opposite numbers and proceeded to break the ice and make friends.

When Marshall, Leahy and King finally turned up we proceeded to our conference room and started work. The first point to settle was who should take the chair for the meeting! A duty I finally found myself stuck with!! I therefore opened up on the question of cooperation of theatres, pointing out that immediate coordination was covered by the Western Front February offensive. I then stated that as this offensive would continue during March and April at least, we hoped that the Russians would find it possible, in spite of the thaw and their long lines of communications, to continue their offensive through March and if possible April. Marshall then expanded this statement, and finally Antonov replied that it was their intention to continue as long as circumstances admitted. He then referred to the Italian Front and to the possibility of operating through the Ljubljana Gap towards Vienna. I replied pointing out difficulties of such action and our decision to reinforce the Western Front with 5 divisions from Italy.

From there we passed on to air action on both fronts and its coordination. This led to Leahy putting up proposals for Eisenhower having a mission in Moscow (a step we have always been against!). Before Antonov had time to reply, I stepped in saying that whilst we were in complete agreement with the Americans as to the desirability of liaison, we considered that this should be based on a sound organization. Namely a commission in Moscow whose duty it would be to settle all question of coordination of higher strategy with the American and British Chiefs of Staff, whilst on a lower level we established liaison with Theatre Commanders and Russian Army Group Commanders concerned. Antonov agreed to the former, but not to the latter without reference to Stalin. From the discussion it appeared that Marshall was also in agreement with us, but not Leahy who seemed to understand very little about the problem.

We finished up our meeting with a discussion on the coordination of strategic air bombing, a difficult matter. Antonov produced an arbitrary line running through Berlin, Leipzig, Vienna and Zagreb which did not suit us and which we reserved for our next discussion which was settled for the following day at the same time. Finally after 3 hours we broke up at 3 pm and drove home for lunch.

I then had a look at the birds on the sea front of our house. There I picked up a great northern diver, scoters, cormorants, many gulls and other diving ducks. Also dolphins feeding on shoals of fish.

At 6.30 we had a short COS to decide what action to take at tomorrow's meeting with Americans at 10.30 prior to meeting Russians. At dinner Winston came up to me and asked me to come round to his dinner table in his room as soon as I had finished to give him results of our meetings. I gave him a full account, and asked him how he had been getting on. The highlights of his remarks were that the President had said that the Americans would only remain in Germany for two years after the end of the war! France could assist in the army of occupation, but was not to be represented on the Inter-Allied Commission in Berlin! Last night Stalin showed great reluctance to propose the King's health stating that he was a republican, Americans failed to take our part in this connection! Stalin made excellent speech last night in proposing Winston's health, stating that he alone had stood up against the might of Germany at the critical moment and supported Russia when she was attacked, a thing he would never forget!!

Meanwhile Macmillan is donning the coat of Supreme Commander of the Mediterranean and submitting wild schemes for employing further forces in Greece, quite forgetting that we are fighting Germany!!! My God! how tired I am of it all!

6 February

At 10 am, the American Chiefs of Staff came here for a conference. We cleared up several minor points which had remained unsettled when we were in Malta, and we also settled our future line of action with the Russians. At 12 noon we went to Antonov's HQ and had a 3 hours conference.

I was again appointed as Chairman, and we had a very friendly meeting. Our discussion centred round the use of a bomber line of demarcation for strategic purposes. We solved this trouble by appointing a technical committee consisting of the Chiefs of the Air to settle the final details. From that we passed on to many questions as to the coordination of the Western offensive with the Russian operations. On the one side the crossing of the Rhine governs dates, on the other question of thaw conditions. But on the whole the coordination is fairly good. We then finished up with a run over of operations in the Pacific. Admiral King gave the Pacific fighting and I referred to the situation in Burma.

We were back here for a late lunch about 3.30 pm, after which I had a small walk through the park grounds down to the sea, looking for birds. I also had a good look round the castle we live in. It is the castle of Alupka, built by Prince Vorontsov in 1837 at the cost of 1½ million dollars, from the plans of an English architect, Blore, who combined Gothic and Moorish styles. Vorontsov was at various times Governor of Odessa, Viceroy of the Caucasus and Ambassador in London.

While we were at work the Foreign Secretaries met at 12 noon, and the High Ones again at 4 pm. I have not seen the PM this evening so do not know how they got on. Weather colder and inclined to rain. Sat next to Clark Kerr at dinner and had a long talk with him, I think he finds his life in Moscow a very lonely one!

7 February

I have had a most interesting day. We left at 9 am bound for Sebastopol and to see the British Crimea battlefields on the way! We had finished our military discussions, the political ones were still in full swing, so this was a good chance to break away and have a day off. We warned Winston and he agreed provided I trained some officer who could show him the Balaclava battlefields! So I took Peake along with me to show him what I had gathered from books lately and to relate it to the ground we should see. Our party consisted of Andrew Cunningham, Jumbo Wilson, Alex, Metcalfe, Moran, Peake, Boyle, Shaw etc. We had an excellent Russian guide, good cars with excellent drivers, which was good as our lives were in their hands at several points of the winding mountain road.

We left at 9 am and drove by what is known as Vorontsov's Road, namely the road constructed by the former owner of the house we are in, when he was Viceroy of the Crimea. This is a most lovely road winding high up on the mountains above the sea, with the most wonderful views. We drove within sight of the sea till we arrived at the Baidai Gate, a stone gate on top of the Phoros Pass, after which you drop down to the Tartar village of Baidai. There we saw fat, healthy children, full of fun and waving cheerfully to us, a good sign, and evidence that Russians are beginning to put the famine behind them. From there we drove on through Varmutka and then on through a long pass on the banks of the Black River tributary. This led us straight on to the battlefields of Balaclava. There was the port on our extreme left, on our immediate left the site of the Charge of the Heavy Cav Brigade, and on our right the site of the memorable Charge of the Light Cav Brigade!! And on top of it all confusion of recent tank battles connected with the last two sieges of Sebastopol!! I had luckily brought with me diagrammatic sketches of the battles, and also a copy of George Blackenbury's *Campaign in the Crimea* with its excellent sketches by William Simpson. With the help of these it was easy to reconstruct both the two memorable cavalry charges and the pictures made them live again. I was thrilled! While I was working it out with maps someone discovered a complete human skeleton within 5 yards of us, one of the victims of the last campaign. We could see Balaclava port quite clearly and could imagine its working organization as a base, the mud, the storms, the frightful difficulties, the awful sufferings, etc. And then on top of it all, as if this small corner of the world had not witnessed sufficient human suffering, there were ample signs of the vast recent conflicts to capture Sebastopol and then to free it! A grave beside a wrecked aeroplane here, a broken down tank there, rows upon rows of shell and bomb craters, twisted iron cheveaux-de-frise, tangled basket wire, odd graves, and the usual rubbish of a battlefield. It is very strange how history can repeat itself under a different guise.

From the Balaclava battlefields we drove over the approach saps to Sebastopol, with Inkerman on our right, and shortly the ghost of Sebastopol itself loomed up in front of us! Such a ghost!! Hardly a house standing, and those that stood had no roofs, but over the whole port rested that inexplicable atmosphere of pride such as one only feels on rare occasions. Verdun always gave me that feeling. I had it strongly today. If the Russians succeeded in holding out for 11 months* against double their number of Germans, favoured by overwhelming superiority in the air and in armour, whilst suffering great privations on the supply side, then there is no doubt in my mind that the Russian is very very great fighter.

We dropped into Sebastopol, drove between shattered houses to the Russian Admiral's HQ. There we were given a wonderful reception. First of all a ¾ hour lecture on the defence of Sebastopol, then a lunch with several toasts. After lunch we drove up to the old 'Flag Staff Hill' of the Crimean War, and from there studied the attack of the British in 1855, the Germans in 1941/2 and of the Russians in 1944 against Sebastopol. From there we drove to the site of the famous Malakov Redoubt, and had another wonderful view out towards the Inkerman Heights. We then dropped back into the port, said goodbye to our Russian admiral, and went out to see the *Franconia*, the large transatlantic transport that had been got ready for us in case we required a headquarters. They had certainly made a first class job of her.

Finally we started the journey home, but on the way out visited the old Crimean British war cemetery, it is in a bad way. Evidently it has acted as a strong point in the recent fighting and it has been heavily shelled. Nearly all the memorial chapels and graves have been badly smashed. A pathetic sight.

We had a lovely journey back with beautiful lights caused by the setting sun, and we reached home close on 7 pm in the dark. It has been an intensely interesting day, but one when the thought of dear old Barney still remained as a black cloud in the background. He would so much have loved to have been with us. I only hope that he may have been there in the spirit. This conference has been a nightmare with his loss hanging over me the whole time. I do so funk the thought of returning to the flat and realizing more than ever that he is gone!

8 February

We started with a COS at 10 am to examine the results of the Committee that had been sitting on oil and shipping during yesterday. These two troublesome matters had at last reached a stage of agreement. At 12 noon we drove over to meet the Americans for our final meeting with them, to pass the shipping, oil and equipment for Greek Forces. This all went through quite easily and now we are at liberty to draw up our final report which we are to consider tomorrow. We have, however, been invited to a banquet by Stalin tonight at 9 pm. This will mean one of those late nights with many toasts and much vodka. I am not looking forward to it!

Later:
Our dinner was as I expected a lengthy affair! We left here at 8.45 pm and

---

*From September 1941 to July 1942. AB is being generous in his assessment.

returned shortly after 1 am. The party consisted of Stalin, President, PM, Molotov, Eden, Stettinius, Leahy, 3 British Chiefs of Staff, 3 Russian Chiefs of Staff, Maisky, Gousev, Russian Ambassador in Washington, Clark Kerr, Harriman, Leathers, Byrnes, Roosevelt's daughter, Harriman's daughter and Sarah [Churchill]. *(In my diary I forgot to include the 3 American Chiefs of Staff who of course were there.)* The dinner as usual consisted of a series of toasts which went on continuously, with the result that most courses were cold before they reached one, or before one could settle down to try and eat them. Stalin was in the very best of form, and was full of fun and good humour apparently thoroughly enjoying himself. The standard of the speeches was remarkably low and most consisted of insincere slimy sort of slush! I became more and more bored, and more and more sleepy, and on and on it dragged. On my right I had General Antonov, who speaks just a little French, but not enough to be able to keep up a flowing conversation with him. On my left I had Harriman, whom I dislike and who annoys me intensely. Finally at about 12.45 am the party broke up and we rose from the table, shook hands with Stalin and departed for home and a welcome bed!

Amongst the various toasts that Stalin proposed was one which he dedicated to: 'those to whom we all look to in war for our security, those on whom our very security depends, the heroes of all the women, and the centre of all things as long as hostilities continue, only to be forgotten and lapse into oblivion as soon as hostilities cease – our soldiers'. I had an opportunity of reminding Stalin of this toast at a similar occasion in Potsdam [see 23 July 1945].

9 February

We had a short COS at 10 am to run through the final version of our Final Report. At 11 am we met the Americans for our final conference with them and to pass the Final Report. At 12 noon we had our Plenary Meeting with the PM and President and had our Final Report approved and received our usual reward of compliments on our good work! However after that we found our-selves stuck for some ¾ hour whilst the two great men meandered about amongst their thoughts and failed to produce any suggestions worthy of the long delay we were subjected to!

At last we escaped and drove back our ½ hour journey to our home for lunch. Barely was this finished when we had to start off again on our ½ hour drive to the American HQ for the usual photographs of this meeting. This took about half an hour and was a most disorganized procedure with no one getting the people in their places for the various military and political groups.

I then had a quiet afternoon writing letters and finally had to dine at 9 pm wltli Winston, who had invited Marshall and Alexander also to dine. It was a dull dinner party, Marshall's never ending accounts about details connected with his life and work, Winston's wanderings on useless strategy, and Alex dis-playing the smallness of his vision and conception of war in its more compli-cated aspects of higher direction. We never got up from the table till 12.30 am, and then only to go into the map room for ½ an hour. Finally Marshall left, Winston disappeared, and I was left alone with Alex. I took advantage of this occasion to give him more advice on how to carry on as a Supreme Commander without letting Macmillan function for him! I told him that at times I had grave doubts as to who was Supreme Commander, he or Macmillan! He took it very well, but it is not easy to give him advice as he is very 'naif' and unsuspecting of the ways of politicians! I hope our talk may be of use as it cost me one hour's sleep, and it was not until close on 2 am that I rolled into bed.

A satisfactory feeling that the conference is finished and has on the whole been as satisfactory as could be hoped for, and certainly a most friendly one.

10 February   In the air between Greece and Italy

We made an early start with breakfast at 7 am and off by 8 am after all the necessary goodbyes. At the last moment the Russians produced a parcel for each of us. We had a lovely drive of 4½ hours to the aerodrome where we landed at near Eupatoria. There we had more goodbyes, together with vodka and an egg! The Chief of the Air Staff had been sent down by Stalin to see us off. At 1 pm sharp we took off and made straight for the Turkish coast above Istanbul. We must have crossed at about Midye, but could not see anything as we were above the clouds. Shortly afterwards we saw the ground again and found ourselves at the point of the Gallipoli peninsula flying over Gulf of Saros with Suvla Bay on our left. The beaches of the landings of the last war were quite clear. We then had an excellent view of Imbros and Lemnos with Samothrace to the north of us. Shortly afterwards, clouds obliterated the ground and we saw nothing more till we found most beautiful snow covered mountains protruding above the clouds. We were flying north of and parallel to the Corinth Gulf, gradually the clouds broke and we had a glorious view of a series of snow covered peaks. We touched the sea again at the mouth of the Gulf of Corinth on the north side of it, and from there flew on over the island of Cephalonia. Now we are over the sea south of the foot of Italy, heading for Malta. We hope to arrive in Malta about dark.

Later: Malta

At 7 pm (Russian time, 5 pm Malta time) we landed in Malta having had an excellent trip. I went straight to the cemetery where Barney has been buried and laid a wreath on his grave, and also on the other three War Office officers who had been killed. My last words to Barney were haunting me, as I left Northolt ahead of him I had said 'Well we shall meet in Malta.' I then drove on to the Palace, where Schreiber had a dinner party for the three Chiefs of Staff and Leathers and Metcalfe. After dinner we drove down to the aerodrome at about 11 pm and got into bed to put in some sleep before our 2 am departure.

11 February

At 1.15 am Portal was woken up by the pilot, saying that last reports of weather over England were bad, that unless we started at once we might not get away for two days, that if we could not get into Northolt we should be certain of getting down in Norfolk. We decided to start at once. We had a very good night's journey and were called at 7 am and told that in an hour we should be in Northolt, and the weather good enough to get down. So I got up, shaved and had a cup of tea. Close on 8 am we began to occasionally see the ground through the clouds. I saw a river which I tried to fit in with the Thames. There was a large town, but it was certainly not Reading. Suddenly Portal came and said 'Do you know where we are? Over Paris!!' We were then again lost in heavy mist, the atmospherics were so bad that the wireless could not be used, and we wandered about over Northern France lost in the clouds! Luckily after some flying the pilot recognised Fécamp in a gap through the clouds. We then pushed on over the Channel, which was barely visible for fog, rain and mist. On crossing the English Coast, we soon found the weather slightly better and finally landed at Northolt at 9.30 am being 1½ hours over due. It was not a pleasant flight.

I went straight to the flat and was glad to be able to escape at once from the flood of Barney memories by driving home. I arrived home about 12 noon, some 23 hours only since I had left the Crimea, and this included a 7 hours visit to Malta. I am very glad this conference is over, it has been abominably trying with Barney's death hanging over me like a black cloud the whole time.

12 February

Spent quietly at home and very very happy to be back there.

13 February

Left home early again and started the usual work. Luckily the COS was a short one and the day's work not too hard. Rollie Charrington came to dinner and like the brick he is offered to take Barney's place as ADC. I should love to have him but wonder whether he would be happy at it. I shall have to think this over very very carefully.

14 February

We had a record COS for shortness and finished it in 30 minutes! You came up for lunch and we went shopping afterwards. I then had an interview with Platt who is retiring, having finished his East African Command. He was followed by the visit of a Greek general. Attlee then asked me to come round to 11 Downing St to see him and tell him results of Malta and Yalta conferences.

Finally home to a lonely dinner. This is a very trying week and the absence of dear old Barney just haunts me the whole time! This flat is all so very closely connected with him, that I miss him at every turn!

15 February

We had another record COS, which I finished off in ½ an hour!! I then went round after lunch to visit Mr Raphael King [book dealer] who had a new book for me. I felt I could have committed almost any extravagance, and very much 'up against all things and everything'. This week trying to get used to Barney's absence has been very very trying. I never realized how much I should miss him and what an awful void he would leave in my life.

This evening I had to go to Buckingham Palace to dine. It was a very small party, just the King, Queen, Portal and myself. The King and Queen were as usual quite extraordinary hosts and made one forget at once the regal atmosphere of the meeting. It was a most delightful easy dinner party.

The King thrilled about the new medal ribbons he has been devising, and had an envelope full of them in his pocket. The Queen quite charming and captivating, interested in everything, full of talk, and quite devoid of any regal stiffness. There is no doubt that they are a wonderful pair.

16 February

Again a fairly moderate COS without any bad controversial points. After the meeting I had poor Diana Charlesworth to lunch. It was a very heartbreaking lunch for both of us. She is wonderfully plucky outwardly but it was only too clear that inwardly she was torn in two with grief. I wish I could have done more to help her.

During the afternoon I had interviews with Hackett who had just returned from Holland, having been behind the German lines ever since the landing of the 1st Airborne Div. I also saw Foulkes just back from Italy where he has been commanding the Canadian Corps, and on his way to join up with Harry Crerar and the 1st Canadian Army.

Thank heaven this first week in the flat without Barney is over. It has been a very trying one.

17 February

No COS and an early start for home.

18 February

Quiet Sunday at home. Rollie Charrington came over and I fixed up with him to come and replace poor old Barney on the understanding that either of us can finish the agreement at any time.

19 February

Usual early start and very foggy drive up. Short COS. Then lunched with Duke de la Luna at Claridges, he very kindly offered me more fishing gut. Cabinet at 5.30 pm interrupted by Winston's return from the Mediterranean in tremendous form. Dined with Bertie at White's.

20 February

We had our usual weekly run round the world with the Joint Intelligence Committee. There are certainly a few small cracks that are beginning to appear in the German fighting machine, but no indications of a general cracking up. It is quite impossible to estimate how long it may last.

Hylda and Evelyn came to lunch, after which I had to go to Winston at 2.45 to discuss Eisenhower's last letter in which he proposes to employ Alex in the back areas if he comes to him as his Deputy! Winston had drafted quite a good letter which we ran through and made a few alterations in. In it he suggested coming out next Thursday with me on a visit.

Back to office for a visit from Kopanski (Polish Chief of Staff) and Ragowski. Kopanski adopting a wonderfully sober and quiet attitude on the Polish Question, but wanted to know what steps we proposed to take to regularise the position of the Polish Forces when the President resigned, and the present oath of allegiance was affected. He said the Poles wished to go on fighting with us, but were not prepared to return to Poland until they knew that it was entirely free and not a vassal of Russia in any shape or form. Anders has come back from Italy and Mackeck [Mikolajczyk?] from France, we are therefore likely to have a difficult and lively time during the next few days.*

21 February

Twice during the day I have received amendments of Winston's reply to Eisenhower, however they were not important alterations and all fitted in equallly well. Monty replied to my telegram that next week's visit was all right and welcome. Morgan came in the afternoon prior to going out to Alexander [as his Chief of Staff in place of Harding]. I had a long talk with him putting him into the picture and explaining to him what I required of him. Finally dined with the Oswald Birleys who were quite charming and could not possibly have been kinder and more sympathetic about the loss of Barney.

22 February

This afternoon the Dutch Ambassador came to see me about 2 additional ships for relief of Dutch in occupied Holland. Heaven knows they deserve it, but the difficulty is to find spare ships. Then Hawkesworth back from Greece and very interesting on conditions in Greece. Finally a very trying hour with General Anders, who is back from Italy. He had been to see the PM yesterday, but was still terribly distressed. According to him the root of the trouble lay in the fact that he could never trust the Russians after his experiences with them whilst Winston and Roosevelt were prepared to trust the Russians. After having been

---

*The Russian-backed 'Lublin Committee' had set itself up as the Provisional Government of Poland on 1 January 1945. It was to be formally recognized by the West in May of that year. The result was the dissolution of the government in exile, led by Mikolajczyk, in London. This caused a considerable problem for Polish servicemen fighting with the Allied armies in the West, who were unwilling to support such a Provisional Government.

a prisoner, and seeing how Russians could treat Poles, he considered that he was in a better position to judge what Russians were like than the President or PM. He said that he had never been more distressed since the war started. When in a Russian prison he was in the depth of gloom but he did then always have hope. Now he could see no hope anywhere. Personally his wife and children were in Poland and he could never see them again, that was bad enough. But what was infinitely worse was the fact that all the men under his orders relied on him to find a solution to this insoluble problem! They all said Oh! Anders will go to London and will put matters right for us, and he Anders saw no solution and this kept him awake at night. I felt most awfully sorry for him, he is a grand fellow and takes the whole matter terribly hard. He is to see Winston again next Wednesday and then he is to see me afterwards. I shudder at the thought of this next interview.

23 February

We had one of our usual monthly examinations of the [V2] rocket threat with Cherwell attending the COS, Duncan Sandys did not attend. It is pretty clear that no air action has much effect on this form of enemy attack. Our increased air measures have only resulted in additional bombs!! There is only one way of dealing with them and that is by clearing the area from which they come by ground action, and that for the present is not possible.

Adam came to lunch and we discussed our possible successors. Possibly Monty as CIGS, Nye or Swayne as AG, Robertson if he will take on QMG, Alex either Army Control in Germany or C-in-C in India, Dempsey C-in-C British troops in Austria, VCIGS Swayne or Browning. All C-in-Cs Home Command will also want changing with younger men. There will be one mass of post war problems which will require young and energetic men to solve them.

This evening I went to Soviet Embassy for Red Army Day. A very full reception.

A tale is connected with this last sentence. I mentioned that when we left the Crimea we were each of us presented with parcels. These contained vodka and caviar. All these parcels were put into the plane and shared out on our arrival. Apparently without warning us special consignments of vodka and caviar for the Soviet Embassy had been stowed in the plane, and were consequently also shared out amongst us! Within 48 hours the Foreign Office was called up by the Soviet Embassy asking where the consignment of vodka and caviar for Red Army Day Reception had got to! In vain the FO tried to reassemble this consignment, it was too late, certainly all the caviar was gone and not many drops of vodka remained. In an attempt to make up for this tragedy, I believe the FO presented several boxes of champagne to the Soviet Embassy.

24 February

No COS meeting so slipped off early. Called at old Lodge's house in Camberley to discuss the binding of his book. And then on home.

25 February
Quiet Sunday.

26 February
Came up with Rollie Charrington, his first day after replacing poor old Barney. Lewin came to lunch and was in very good form. In the afternoon I heard that Anders had been appointed Acting Commander-in-Chief of the Polish Forces. This will be just one more nail in the coffin of the Polish Army. I am disappointed as he had practically given me an undertaking that this would not occur when I met him before going to Russia. Short Cabinet, as thank heaven Winston did not attend. Basil came to dinner looking tired and depressed and not up to his usual form.

27 February
We had the Principal Administrative Officer Committee in with us this morning to discuss the oil reserve situation. In spite of putting the matter right with the Americans whilst in Malta, and deciding that our reserve should be of 6 million tons instead of 4 million, we now find that owing to shortage of tanker tonnage we may again be defeated. Morgan came to see me in the afternoon prior to departure for Italy to take over Chief of Staff to Alexander. I had to again ground him as to how he was to take charge of Alex and protect him against his lamentable lack of vision. Finished up by going to see the new American film taken in Technicolor of the carrier borne aircraft actions in the Pacific. A wonderful film.

28 February
Our COS was a short one. In the afternoon Dick McCreery from 8th Army came to see me, he was in very good form. Anders was to have come. Thank heaven, PM put off his meeting with him and I was able to put off my meeting with him. Dined with Bas (Admiral), Basil (Ulster PM) and Bertie. A very pleasant dinner.

1 March
We had a difficult problem at the COS in the shape of trying to work out the distribution of Personnel Shipping after the defeat of Germany. It is an almost insoluble problem as the available shipping cannot begin to cater for the multitude of moves, such as Americans and Canadians back to America and on to Japan, British home and on to Far East, New Zealanders home, South Africans home, prisoners to be repatriated, civil traffic, etc etc.

Lunched with Winston in the Annexe, you had also come up for it. Basil, Herbert Morrison, Moran and his wife, and the two of us. Winston in fairly good form, said that if he were Hitler he would have himself flown over to this country, hand himself to the Government stating that he alone was responsible for all the evils of Germany, and was prepared to stand the racket. According to Winston this would face us with a difficult problem.

All preparations are now ready for our visit to Monty and Ike tomorrow.

2 March   Geldrop near Eindhoven

We left WO, Rollie and I, at 9.45 for Northolt where we were to leave with the PM for France at 10.30 am. He was as usual late and it was just after 11 am when we left. We travelled by his new C54 machine – a beautiful and most comfortable machine, far quieter than the York. The journey to Brussels took us about 1¼ hours. The party consisted of Winston, Clemmie, Pug, Peck, Tommy, Rollie Charrington and I. We were met on the aerodrome by 'Mary' Coningham and Mary Churchill. Coningham took us off to his HQ in Brussels for lunch, where he gave us one of his usual sumptuous meals! After lunch we left Clemmie with Mary and flew on to Eindhoven aerodrome in 2 Dakotas. There Monty met us on the aerodrome and drove us to his HQ where he gave us tea. After that we went to the station and found Eisenhower's train which he had sent for us to live in. We changed and then went round to dine with Monty. After dinner we attended the interview which he holds every evening with his liaison officers. It was most interesting and most impressive. After completing this interview he dictates his daily wire to me based on his conception of the situation arrived at from the liaison officers' reports. The battle is going wonderfully well and there are signs from all sides of decay setting in in the German Army.

3 March   Train in siding at Geldrop

At 9.15 am, PM and I started off with Monty in his two Rolls cars. We motored straight to Maastricht (not badly damaged). Then we went to the 9th Army HQ and met Simpson, the USA Commander. He introduced us to his staff, and Winston and I had to make small speeches to them. We then drove on, Simpson with PM and Monty with me. We drove on towards Aachen, but stopped on the Siegfried Line to examine the dragon's teeth defences against tanks, and to look at some of the pillboxes which had been blown up by the Americans.

There is one episode connected with the Siegfried Line which I did not include in my diary, but which I must insert as it is typical of Winston's boyish humour. As we were leaving Simpson's HQ to get into the cars, Simpson asked Winston whether he wished to make use of the lavatory before starting. Without a moment's hesitation he asked 'How far is the Siegfried Line?' On being told about half an hour's run he replied that he would not visit the lavatory, but that we should halt on reaching the Siegfried Line! On arrival there the column of some 20 to 30 cars halted, we processed solemnly out and lined up along the line. As the photographers had all rushed up to secure good vantage points, he turned to them and said 'This is one of the operations connected with this great war which must not be reproduced graphically.' To give them credit they obeyed their orders, and in doing so missed a chance of publishing the greatest photographic catch of the war! I shall never forget the childish grin of intense satisfaction that spread all over his face as he looked down at the critical moment! [Cf. 26 March 1945.]

Aachen was very badly damaged and it was a relief to see at last German houses demolished instead of French, Italian, Belgian and British! There were a few Germans in the town but not many. We drove on through to Jülich on the River Roer where we met the American Corps Commander (Maclean) who carried out the crossing of the river on this front. It must have been a very formidable obstacle, especially when the river was in flood! The town was badly smashed.

We crossed by the Bailey Bridge and went to examine the Citadel, a Vauban brick fort with large moat which had been held by a company. The Americans took it by bringing a gun to blow open the door and stormed the entrance whilst covering their attack with flamethrowers directed onto the battlements. A very successful operation proving the value of flamethrowers. Here we were given lunch by the Americans, subsequently driving back to our train where we arrived about 4.30 pm after a very successful trip.

In the evening dined with Monty who had Bimbo Dempsey, Neil Ritchie and Bubbles Barker for dinner. It was a great joy seeing them again. After dinner we went with Monty to listen to the reports from his liaison officers. The day's fighting had been most successful and we ought to be able to close up to the Rhine on its full length to Cologne within the next few days I hope.

4 March

We left again at 10.15 am and drove through Eindhoven straight up to the Nijmegen road till we were short of that place. Then we stopped at Canadian Army HQ and met Crerar. We went into his map room and were given a very good short explanation of the fighting since the start of the operation to the present date. We then drove off through the Reichswald to a point on the far side where we ought to have been able to see the vast Rhine floods. Unfortunately it was raining and drizzling and we could see nothing. So we went to the Canadian Corps HQ where we found Symonds, the Corps Commander, who gave us an excellent lunch. We then drove to Goch, which we went through to reach an 8" gun which the PM was to fire. Surrounded by press photographers he pulled the lanyard and let her off. We then proceeded to Gennep to see the Bailey Bridges which had been put up over the Meuse, they were even longer than the ones I saw over the Sangro River last year.

We finished up with a visit to the 51st [Highland] Div who are out of the line and produced their pipes and drums. It was interesting to at last see this division on German soil. I first came in contact with them when I took over the remnants after St Valéry when I returned to France subsequently to Dunkirk. They were next under my orders when I commanded Home Forces, and I visited them twice in Scotland. Next I saw them immediately after their arrival in Egypt, and ready to move to the defence of Cairo against Rommel. Next in Tripoli after Rommel's defeat marching past the PM. Subsequently at Bougie in Algeria prior to invasion of Sicily, and now at last in Germany!

Tonight we dined in the train and Monty and de Guingand came to dinner. Winston fretted because he was not allowed nearer the front, and trying to make plans to come back for the operations connected with the crossing of the Rhine!

5 *March*   Rheims

Shortly after midnight our train started off and at 10 am we arrived at Rheims and were put into an outside siding. Ike's ADC came to collect us and drove Pug, Rollie and I up to Ike's HQ, a big agricultural college near the station. There I found Ike with Bradley and had a long talk with him about the war in general. He took me up to his map room and gave me the latest news about the situation on the front. We then went up to his mess which is in the Director's house of Heidsieck Monopole champagne. Bradley remained for lunch, and the PM showed up shortly before lunch. Whilst in the office I got Ike alone for a bit and told him that if he had strong feelings about Alex not coming as his deputy he should let the PM know. Apparently he is afraid that the introduction of Alexander would upset the outfit. Monty had also expressed the same opinion. After lunch I left Ike alone with the PM to give him a chance of expressing his views and went off with Rollie to visit the Heidsieck Champagne caves. I found it most interesting. The manager came round with us and explained the manufacture of champagne from the arrival of the grape juice to the departure of the boxes of champagne. The caves went down to 25 metres underground, and with 10 miles of underground passages! Each bottle has to be corked twice and the sediment removed before the second corking, a most elaborate process. The insertion of the large champagne cork was fascinating. We finished up by drinking half a bottle of '34 with the manager, and were taught how to taste champagne properly! We then tried to see the cathedral, but found it shut. For dinner Bedell Smith, Spaatz and Tedder came, I had a long discussion on fishing with Bedell Smith.

6 *March*   Back in London

Breakfast with Ike and another long talk with him. There is no doubt that he is a most attractive personality and at the same time a very very limited brain from a strategic point of view. This comes out the whole time in all conversations with him. His relations with Monty are quite insoluble, he only sees the worst side of Monty and cannot appreciate the better side. Things are running smoothly for the present, but this cannot last and I foresee trouble ahead before long. For all that, to insert Alex is only likely to lead to immediate trouble for all I gather! The war may not last long now and matters may run smoothly until the end. Therefore I feel now that it is best to leave Alex where he is. I think that Winston is now of the same opinion.

We left Ike's mess at 10.30 am and motored to the aerodrome outside where we took off shortly before 11 am. We had a good journey over, arriving back shortly after 12 noon. The C54 is certainly a much quieter machine than the old York. You met me at the aerodrome and we went off to the flat for lunch. The afternoon turned out to be a busy one with a Selection Board at 3.15 pm and a Cabinet at 5.30 pm which lasted till 8.15 pm and as far as I could see accomplished nothing! How ministers can afford to waste time in this way in times of war passes my understanding. What is more, Winston is by far the worst offender!

7 March

Herbert Morrison attended the COS to discuss what could be done to save London from rockets and buzz bombs. He painted a lurid picture of the awful 5 years London had suffered, and how wrong it was to expect her to go on suffering! He seemed to forget that theatres, cinemas, restaurants, night clubs, pubs, concerts etc have been in full swing for the last few years and very little affected by enemy action. We listened as sympathetically as we could and then explained to him our difficulties in trying to deal with this threat either by air or land action. (While I write I hear the rumble of one landing in the distance!)

Lunched with Franklyn at Home Forces and gave them a talk on the world situation afterwards. Back to the office for a flood of files, and then home to flat for dinner with Stella [Charrington] and Ted Morris dining.

8 March

We were back on the shipping troubles again this morning, and the worst of it is that I cannot quite get to the bottom of it. We were by way of having settled it all at Yalta and now PM wishes to establish further cuts! Jack Collins came to lunch. In the afternoon had a difficult and somewhat painful interview with Anders. On the whole he was I think a little repentant about his new post. He wanted to try and settle the many and varied problems that will arise if the London Polish Government goes!

9 March

This morning our main problem at the COS was the Dutch PM's lament to Winston concerning the starvation of the Dutch population and urging a reconsideration of our strategy so as to admit of an early liberation of Holland! One more of the continual repercussions of political considerations on strategical requirements. And many of them we have already had to compete with!! However it is pretty clear that our present plans for Monty's crossing of the Rhine cannot be changed. After the crossing of the Rhine again from a military point of view there is no doubt that we should work for the destruction of Germany and not let any clearing up of Holland delay our dispositions.

I had poor Diana Charlesworth to lunch, and did what I could for her to assist her in disentangling her life. I am so sorry for her. She would like to go to Brusssels, and I have asked Adam to find out if there is any opening for her there. Dined with Ronnie Weeks and Nancy Dill was there.

10 March

Just as I was rushing to make an early start home, a telegram turned up from Alex with certain underground peace proposals. These suggested the surrendering of the whole of Kesselring's army in Italy. However as Wolff [SS Commander in Italy] was the main instigator and he is a rabid SS follower of Himmler it does not seem very plausible. We are following it up for the present and sending representatives to Switzerland to the selected spot. I then slipped home where I arrived in time to lunch with you.

11 March

A quiet Sunday at home.

12.3.45!

It is sad that this date will not return for another 100 years! It looks so nice.

A rushed morning with COS and Cabinet, the latter luckily run by Attlee which shortened matters considerably. Long letter from Monty with all his plans for the attack across the Rhine on the 24th of this month. Also an invitation to the PM to come for it and stop with him. This is as a result of the letter I had written to him telling him the PM would get into another of his rages if he felt that Monty was again trying to dictate to him and stop him from coming out!

13 March

The day promised badly as we had been detailed for a conference at 6 pm on the feeding of the Dutch, and at 10 pm on the personnel shipping situation after defeat of Germany. I had a heavy cold and life seemed fairly black! However, both conferences have now been put off for the present and will come on again later in the week. This afternoon Jack Swayne [Chief of Staff to Auchinleck] came to see me and we had a long talk together about India. It is very satisfactory to hear that relations between the Auk and Dickie are good. But he confirms my fears that we may possibly have trouble later on between Oliver Leese and Dickie! If we do it will be Oliver's fault.

14 March

We again discussed the underground movements towards capitulation of German forces in Italy. Somehow the whole business looks pretty fishy and not very promising. You came up for lunch and old Bannerman came also. In the evening I had to go to see the King to explain to him the situation on the Western Front and the coming offensive. He was very interested in them. After dinner had to go round to No 11 Downing St for a meeting on distribution of personnel shipping after the defeat of Germany.

15 March

Our COS was again concerned with trying to extricate divisions out of Greece. I am afraid that Alexander, being now entirely in Macmillan's clutches, has forgotten the main object of this war, and no longer remembers that there are such people as the Germans! To him the situation in Greece is of paramount interest. This evening had Winant to dinner with Nancy Dill and Billy Gibbs to talk about America to him. Peter Portal and his wife also there. Thank heaven the evening is over; it weighed heavily on me, I felt it would be a sticky party.

16 March

I finished off COS and a few interviews and came home about 7 pm for the weekend.

17 and 18 March

Two quiet days at home.

19 March

Usual early start followed by rush of telephones and papers to be looked through, then COS at 11 am and Cabinet at 12 noon. This evening Crerar came to dine and I had a long and satisfactory talk with him after dinner. Thank heaven I have at last got the whole of the Canadian Army now assembled in France!

20 March

A drawn out and difficult COS owing to a certain amount of dissension amongst us on question of committee for research and developments. However Andrew Cunningham and Bob Laycock were with me and I think we got what we wanted. Pongo to lunch. In afternoon interview with Mr Mayne from the India Office on many questions connected with the Indian Army. Then Kimmins back from Oliver Leese, followed by an American cocktail party, and then the John Kennedys for dinner to discuss question of his taking on Governorship of South East Australia, which I advised him strongly to do if he gets a chance.

21 March

Adam came to lunch and told me about the arrangements that he had made for Diana Charlesworth to go to Rheims to start a hotel for inter-Allied soldiers. Also gave me details of his visit to France and Ike's HQ etc.

In the evening attended the British Ornithological Union Dinner and saw a most excellent bird film. Jack Whitaker took me there and Bannerman also came so that I should not feel too lost. Meinertzhagen was also there having healed up his broken rib.

22 March

A quiet day. Lunched with Ronnie and Stella at the Ritz. During afternoon saw S of S about John Kennedy taking on Governorship of South West [East?] Australia, and we both agreed that he would be good for the job. This evening Bertie and Budget Loyd came to dine. Tomorrow I start off with PM on this visit to France for him to see operation connected with the Rhine crossing. I am not happy about this trip, he will be difficult to manage, and has *no* business to be going on this trip. All he will do is to endanger his life unnecessarily and to get in everybody's way and be a damned nuisance to everybody. However nothing on earth will stop him!

23 March   Monty's HQ, Venlo

We had our usual COS after which I finished off some papers in the WO. I then lunched with Winston at the Annexe, a small lunch, only Clemmie, Brendan Bracken and Winston. Clemmie very full of all the preparations for her journey to Moscow next week and of all her visits there. After lunch I drove with Winston to Northolt. The road was up on the way and the driver was going to take the diversion, but this did not suit Winston, we had to go straight through! This meant shifting some of the barriers, driving on the footpath, etc, and on the whole probably took longer than going round! However Winston was delighted that he was exercising his authority and informed me that the King would not dream of taking such action, he was far more law abiding!

We left Northolt in a Dakota about 3 pm. Party consisting of PM, Tommy, Rollie, Sawyers and one Secretary. We had a very good 2 hours flight over Calais, Lille and Brussels. On arrival there we reduced the party to 4 (PM, Tommy, Sawyers and self) and drove on to Monty's HQ which is close to the aerodrome. We found Monty there, very proud to be able to pitch his camp in Germany at last!

We had tea, after which Monty described plan of attack for the crossing of the Rhine which starts tonight on a two army front. 9th American Army on right, 2nd British Army on left. Crossings take place throughout the night and the guns have already started and can be heard indistinctly in the distance. After dinner Monty went off to bed early and Winston took me off. First of all we walked up and down in the moonlight, it was a glorious night, and we discussed the situation we were in at the momentous moment of the crossing of the Rhine! We went back over some of our early struggles, back to Cairo when we had started Monty and Alex off. How he had had to trust my selection at that time. The part that the hand of God had taken in removing Gott at that critical moment etc etc. He was in one of his very nicest moods and showed appreciation for what I had done for him in a way in which he had never before.

We then went into his caravan and examined his box which had just arrived. It contained a telegram from Molotov which worried him a great [deal], connected with the Russian attitude to the peace negotiations which Wolff is trying to open in Berne. Russia's attitude worried him, their fear lest we should make a separate peace on the Western Front without them being in. He dictated a reply, let his secretary out of the caravan, called him back, reconsidered it, started writing another and finally very wisely left it till tomorrow to think over carefully.

I am now off to bed, it is hard to realize that within same 15 miles hundreds of men are engaged in death struggles along the banks of the Rhine, whilst hundreds more are keying themselves up to stand up to one of the greatest trials of their life! With that thought in one's mind it is not easy to lie down to try and sleep peacefully!

24 March   Venlo

At breakfast Monty told me that from all reports he had received the forcing of the Rhine was going well. At 8.45 the PM and I started off together with Monty's ADC. We had a ¾ hour drive to a view point about 2000 yards south of Xanten, from which an excellent view can be obtained when the weather is clear. Unfortunately it was rather hazy, but we could just make out the line of the Rhine from near Xanten to Wesel and could just see some of the boats ferrying across the Rhine where landings had taken place. We were in the middle of the battery positions supporting that portion of the front and there was a continual roar of guns as they were busy engaging German AA guns in anticipation of the arrival of the airborne divisions. The 6th British and 17th American were due to start arriving at 10 am to land in the area about two or three miles beyond the Rhine, the far side of the Dienfordter Wald. The 6th Division was starting from East Anglia and the 17th from the Paris area. They arrived punctually up to time and it was a wonderful sight! The whole sky was filled with large flights of transport aircraft. They flew straight over us and on over the Rhine. Unfortunately they disappeared into the haze before dropping their loads of parachutists. The flak artillery could be seen bursting amongst them before they disappeared. Shortly afterwards they began to stream back with doors open and parachute strings hanging under them. A few of them burst into flames on their way back, and shed their pilots who floated down in their parachutes. After about an hour's continuous stream the gliders began to arrive and sailed past flight after flight.

We remained at this view point for about 2 hours and then embarked in two armoured cars, one each. We went down into Xanten where we turned north and through Marienbaum at the NE corner of the Hochwald and on to a bit of high ground just south of Calcar. There we had a good view looking out onto the crossing place of the 51st Div (whose Div Commander was unfortunately killed this morning). We lunched there and then dropped down to 3rd Div HQ in an old castle. Whistler, the commander, met us and explained how his division had been responsible for preparing the front for attack. Winston then became a little troublesome and wanted to go messing about on the Rhine crossings and we had some difficulty in keeping him back. However in the end he behaved well and we came back in our armoured cars to where we had left our own car, and from there on back to this HQ. PM went off for a sleep which he wanted badly, he had been sleeping in the car nearly all the way home, gradually sliding onto my knee.

I washed dust away from my eyes and face, had tea, and then started off in Monty's plane for a fly round to look at the front. We flew very low over the Meuse from Venlo to Gennep, looking at the wonderful defences the Germans had built for this line. At Gennep we swung north east, right through the Reichswald to Cleves where we turned SE and flew along the main road Calcar-Xanten-Rheinberg. Finally we swung SW through Geldern and back to Venlo. Total trip about 100 miles and all of it most interesting. I was able to see most of the line of the Rhine beautifully.

Later:

I have now had dinner and attended Monty's conference with his liaison officers. From their reports there is no doubt that the operations have been an outstanding success. On the south each division has captured some 1000 odd prisoners with only one or two hundred casualties. On the north the 51st Div has had a tougher time. It has been up against those hard fighting Para divisions, and for some 600 prisoners has suffered over 600 casualties, including the Div Commander (Rennie). Added to that their ferry and bridging process is far behind the others. One of the outstanding successes of the day has been the employment of the airborne divisions in close proximity, and closely connected to the attack.

However, looking on the day as a whole, and connecting it with the successes of the American forces in recent weeks south of the Moselle, I am quite certain that the end of the Germans is very near indeed, and I would not be surprised to see them pack up at any moment. In a few days I feel that coordinated defence north of the Rhine will cease and that we shall be in a position to let Monty's 8th Armoured Division operate boldly through North Germany maintained by air supply. On top of it all we have these proposed negotiations of Wolff's suggesting Kesselring's surrender whilst still commanding forces in Northern Italy. Is it not likely that with the hopeless situation confronting him on the front he has just taken over that Kesselring may well be induced to surrender the whole of the Western front? If so what about the Russian front, it seems unlikely that the German soldier in the East will be induced to go on fighting when he hears the German soldier in the west has packed up.

25 March   Venlo

Palm Sunday. Started off by going to church with Monty at his small Headquarters service. Winston came along too. The hymns were good and the parson (a presbyterian) preached a good sermon. After church we motored off to Rheinberg where Anderson, commanding the 16th American Corps, had his headquarters. We were met there by Eisenhower, Bradley and Simpson (commander US 9th Army). I had a talk with Ike on the question of the surrender of Kesselring and all the other purely military surrenders. He also wanted to know whether I agreed with his present plans of pushing in the south for Frankfurt and Kassel. I told him that with the Germans crumbling as they are the whole situation is now altered from the time of our previous discussions. Evidently the Boche is cracking and what we want now is to push him relentlessly wherever we can until he crumples. In his present condition we certainly have the necessary strength for a double envelopment strategy which I did not consider as applicable when he was still in a position to resist seriously.

Anderson then explained his situation and the rapid progress they had made since they had crossed the Rhine. We then had a light lunch in the garden of German house which had been the colliery manager's house. After lunch we went down the Wesel road to Büderich where a house stands on the bank of the Rhine with a wonderful view across, and up to Wesel on one side and down to the bridge of boats further south which the Americans had established. We then got into a tank landing craft which was plying across the Rhine and crossed over! I remembered that the last time I had sailed on the Rhine was with Grasett, when we went by boat from Wiesbaden to Cologne, studying the country whilst at the Staff College. Little did I know then the conditions under which I should sail it the next time! It was a great thrill setting foot on the far bank. We spent a little time examining the German river defences and then recrossed the river. In doing so we attempted to work downstream towards the destroyed Wesel bridge but could not owing to a string of buoys across the river.

We got back into the car and motored to the main road bridge over the Rhine into Wesel. The bridge had been broken in several places but partly boarded over so that one could scramble about on it. Winston at once started scrambling along for some 40 yards. We found however that Wesel was still occupied and that considerable sniping was going on inside the town. About 200 yards lower down the bridging parties were getting ready to start a new bridge. They had apparently been spotted by the Germans as shells began to fall some 300 yards downstream; reports then came in that the Germans were shelling the road behind us, at the same time shells began to fall about 100 yards up stream of us. We decided that it was time to remove the PM who was thrilled with the situation and very reluctant to leave! However he came away more obediently than I had expected.

I must interrupt the diary here, as in it I failed to record a picture which is as vivid in my mind as it was on that day. It is the picture of the USA General Simpson, on whose front we were, coming up to Winston and saying 'Prime Minister, there are snipers in front of you, they are shelling both sides of the bridge, and now they have started shelling the road behind you. I cannot accept the responsibility of your being here, and must ask you to come away.' The look on Winston's face was just like that of a small boy being called away from his sandcastles on the beach by his nurse! He put both his arms round one of the twisted girders of the bridge, and looked over his shoulder at Simpson with pouting mouth and angry eyes! Thank heaven he came away quietly, it was a sad wrench for him, he was enjoying himself immensely!

We then returned home and after tea started off for another fly round in the small plane. This time I flew from Venlo up the Meuse to the junction of the Roer river. Then up the Roer river to just short of Jülich, there I turned north and went over Erkelenz, Gladbach and Krefeld. I wanted to go on via Mor, Rheinberg, Xanten and back, but we ran into dense smoke from the smoke screens that are being built up over the river and were lost in a few minutes. We turned northwest and after some flying found ourselves over Geldern and then came home.

This evening after dinner again attended Monty's evening séance with his liaison officers reporting results of their visits around the front. It is a most impressive scene, it is the modern form of the general and his gallopers and works admirably, but he has a very carefully selected team. Some commanders have objected to this system of his of collecting information as short circuiting them. Monty has however overruled any such objections.

The news of Patton's advance in the south is a clear indication that the Germans are cracking fast.

On page 372 of Eisenhower's Crusade in Europe *he refers to a conversation which took place between us on the day this diary entry was written. I feel certain that he did not write down at once the statement which he attributes to me, and I can only assume that when he came to write it down he did not remember clearly what I had said. According to him when we stood together on the bank of the Rhine on March 25th, I said to him: 'Thank God, Ike, you stuck by your plan. You were completely right, and I am sorry if my fear of dispersed efforts added to your burdens. The German is now licked. It is merely a question of when he chooses to quit. Thank God you stuck by your guns.' I think that when this statement is considered in connection with what I wrote in my diary that evening, it will be clear that I was misquoted. To the best of my memory I congratulated him heartily on his success, and said that as matters had turned out his policy was now the correct one, that with the German in his defeated condition no dangers now existed in a dispersal of effort. I am quite certain that I never said to him 'You were completely right', as I am still convinced that he was 'completely wrong', as proved by the temporary defeat inflicted on him by Rundstedt's counter stroke, which considerably retarded the defeat of Germany.*

26 March   Back in London
After packing up kit left camp at 10.15 am for Neil Ritchie (XII Corps) HQ. On the way we picked up Bimbo Dempsey. On meeting Neil we changed into jeeps

and I got in with him. We drove straight to Xanten and on to the river on the Bislich road. Here we found the new class 40 bridge which had just been completed and we drove over it and up into Bislich; there we turned north and drove along the bank of the Rhine to one of the 'landing craft tank' (known as Buffaloes) crossing places. On the way we passed a gang of newly captured prisoners, a weedy looking lot. We then got into the Buffaloes which had been used in the assault crossing and recrossed the Rhine. They are wonderful vehicles with tracks on both sides, swim like a boat and crawl up the far bank with their tracks. It was a strange feeling motoring along the east bank of the Rhine with old Ritchie, and looking back to our retreat to Dunkirk together! I reminded him of it and how little we then dreamed that 5 years later we should be on the Rhine together with Germany beat! I find it almost impossible to believe that after these 6 years of endless heartbreaking struggles, that we are now at last on the threshold of the end!

After recrossing the Rhine we motored further north to the site of the next bridge, a class 9, which was also busy pouring vehicles over onto the far bank. We then had an excellent lunch on the bank of the Rhine just where our front line had been up to now.

Just before lunch I saw Winston wandering off towards the Rhine, and wondered where he was off to. He had to cover a considerable distance to reach the bank of the Rhine, but this is where he was heading for and on arrival there he solemnly relieved himself in the Rhine! I could only see his back, but felt certain that on his face was that same boyish grin of contentment that I had seen at the Siegfried Line on a similar occasion! [Cf. 3 March 1945.]

After lunch we parted with Ritchie and drove back to Monty's HQ, then to the aerodrome at Venlo and by 3 pm were airborne and sailing off homewards. At 7 pm we landed at Northolt, drove back to flat and revelled in the first hot bath I had had since leaving! It has been a wonderful trip, and one which gave me a feeling of realization that all the last few years' toil and agony were at least producing results beyond my wildest hopes. Winston I think enjoyed the trip thoroughly, and received a wonderful reception wherever he went.

It was a relief to get Winston home safely, I knew that he longed to get into the most exposed position possible. I honestly believe that he would really have liked to be killed on the front at this moment of success. He had often told me that the way to die is to pass out fighting when your blood is up and you feel nothing.

27 March   London
Started COS work again and had one of our periodic meetings with Sandys and Cherwell to discuss rockets and flying bombs. Diana Charlesworth came to lunch to discuss her plans for going abroad. In the afternoon had an interview with Alex's [Chief of Staff] General Gruenther who had been sent over to prove how impossible it was for him to launch his offensive on April 10th if we took a

division away from him. However situation is such that one additional division on the Western Front won't make much difference, the Germans are breaking fast and we have sufficient force there now to deal with them without importing any further divisions.

Lovely spring weather and wonderful news of success pouring in continuously.

28 March

This afternoon Archie Wavell came round to my office and remained there about 1½ hours. He was in very good form and looked very well, but worried at the prospects of his meeting with Winston. I am afraid that he has good reason to be worried! From what he told me he is quite prepared to resign if he does not get what he wants, and I should not be surprised if he was eventually driven to take such a course. I received a copy of Monty's latest order, he is planning a bold drive to the Elbe with most of his armour, and judging by the general situation he has every chance of bringing it off.

29 March

A very long COS meeting with a series of annoying telegrams. The worst of all was one from Eisenhower direct to Stalin trying to coordinate his offensive with the Russians. To start with he has no business to address Stalin direct, his communications should be through the Combined Chiefs of Staff, secondly he produced a telegram which was unintelligible, and finally what was implied in it appeared to be entirely adrift and a change in all that had been previously agreed on.

Basil came to lunch having come over from Ireland for 24 hours. During the afternoon Anders came to see me, just back from Italy where he had been seeing his Polish forces. He was in the best of form, and determined to keep the Poles fighting the Germans and the rest to be settled later.

At 5.15 pm we were sent for by the PM to discuss Ike's telegram to Stalin and our proposed action. He was in a hopeless mood and kept us 2 hours to settle what we could have got through in 20 minutes! He drives me quite frantic and I can only just keep my temper nowadays. He meanders about, always grasping onto details and failing to see the leading points. Quite incapable to really grasp strategy and its implications. On those occasions I feel that I just can't stick another moment with him, and would give almost anything never to see him again! The last three years are beginning to tell, and the strain of dealing with him is taking effect!

This last paragraph hits the nail on the head. I had reached the end of my tether, and Winston had got so much on my nerves that all his difficult side was continually magnified in my mind. All my criticisms of him in these later days should consequently be read with this fact constantly in view.

30 March
Good Friday. Had a long COS in order to finish off all the work for the weekend. Matters however looked rather ominous owing to Eisenhower's ridiculous wire to Stalin, trying to coordinate matters with him. In fact the message was so badly worded that no one could understand it, and at the best he had no business to settle matters directly with Stalin. Especially as this short and unintelligible message indicated a change of policy! In the evening slipped off home, full of hope for a long weekend at home and away from worries.

31 March
Made an early start for Broadlands [salmon fishing on River Test] to fish No 1 beat with Andrew Cunningham. A windy day and unfortunately no fish up, but for all that a very pleasant day in the country. Returned home to find a message that the PM wanted a COS meeting at Chequers the next day, Easter Sunday, at 11.30 am!!!

1 April
Left home at 10.15 am for Chequers. We sat in conference with PM from 11.30 to 1.30 pm checking a wire he had drafted to the President. Not one of his best wires! We also discussed his wire to Ike, Ike's reply to him, and Ike's official reply to the CCS. Now that Ike has explained his plans it is quite clear that there is no very great change except for the fact that he directs his main axis of advance on Leipzig instead of on Berlin. He also transfers 9th [US] Army back to Bradley as soon as the Ruhr is surrounded, and delays further advance whilst sweeping up this place. Most of the changes are due to national aspirations and to ensure that the USA effort will not be lost under British command. It is all a pity and the straightforward strategy is being affected by the nationalistic outlook of allies. This is one of the handicaps of operating with allies. But as Winston says, 'There is only one thing worse than fighting with allies, and that is fighting without them!' We then had lunch at Chequers, party consisting of PM, Winant, Cherwell, Sandys and wife, Brendan Bracken, Sarah and 3 Chiefs of Staff. After lunch we had to go on drafting a reply to the American Chiefs' rather rude message. Finally returned home at 6.30 pm, the day having been completely spoilt by Winston!

2 April
A quiet day at home putting in book plates and pruning roses. Huxley came to tea with the Youngs, I was very interested meeting him and his wife.

3 April
Tedder attended COS and tried to explain that Ike was forced to take immediate action with Stalin as Monty had issued a directive Ike did not agree with! I

said that I was astonished that Ike found it necessary to call in Stalin in order to control Monty! Furthermore I could not accept this excuse as the boundaries of 21st Army Group and 9th Army still remained the same in Ike's order as in Monty's, the only difference being the transfer of the 9th Army from Monty to Bradley! Surely Stalin's help need not be called in for such a transfer!! The Cabinet this evening was attended by Smuts, Fraser, Forde and Evatt, Wavell and Firoz Khan Noon [Indian Representative, British Cabinet]. Many speeches were consequently necessary as greeting and signs of approval!

4 April

Nothing very special at the COS. You came up to lunch to meet the Wavells. When they left we dashed off to the Marble Arch Cinema to join Nanny and the children for *King Henry V*. A very happy time with you all, and then a dash back to WO to see Gairdner who is just off to MacArthur's HQ to replace Herbert Lumsden. He seems very pleased with this job. Then had a go with Gale, of the Airborne Division, who gave me further details about the 6th Airborne Div landing across the Rhine. He was full of praise for the Glider Pilot Regiment and the wonderful performance they had put up.

5 April

We started our COS sitting with a series of photos by the *Illustrated Post* photographer getting ready for the victory number of this paper!! I rather shudder as to what some of these may be like.

I had Adam to lunch again, and had an excellent talk with him about future changes in the Army Council which now become necessary. Then went off to Edwards's Bookshop in Marylebone High Street to look at a copy of Phillips's monograph on ducks. However, I arrived there at the same time as a telephone call for me saying PM wanted COS to meet him at 3 pm!! I looked at Phillips's book till 3.10 pm, then drove to the Annexe where I arrived at 3.15 pm, and was still kept waiting 5 minutes by the PM!! I felt rather like Drake going on with his game of bowls when the Armada had been sighted!

He wanted us to discuss his reply to Stalin's last wire in which he [Stalin] accuses us of faking up a surrender of Kesselring's forces on the Western Front without telling him about it!! He has accused the Americans of this also. To have all their glorious victories belittled in this way suits them ill, but to be accused of cheating hits them on the raw. In his letter he certainly draws the allies together if he does nothing else. We were kept for 1½ hours and nearly dragged on to the subsequent Cabinet. In the evening attended Cranborne's reception for Dominion Representatives in Claridges, and then dined at 10 Downing St for the same purpose. Speeches by PM, Fraser (NZ), Forde (Aust), Attlee and Sir Ramaswami Mudaliar [Governor General's Executive Council] replying for India. The latter quite one of the best speeches of the evening.

6 April

This morning during our COS we had a visit by General Hurley, the USA Ambassador in China. He is an outstanding personality, good looking, tall, clear cut features, well dressed and a very merry twinkle in his eye. He gave us the background of conditions in China and Indo-China. Touched on the likelihood or possibility of the various Chinese factions uniting, the possibility of making useful Chinese forces, etc. The only point he would not discuss was the political outlook of Indo-China. This was no doubt due to the President's determination not to return this colony to France. I afterwards dined with Eden at the Foreign Office to meet Hurley again. The lunch comprised Fraser (NZ), Winant, Selborne, Woolton, Dalton, Dixon, Ismay, Portal, Cunningham, etc. Hurley was in tremendous form towards the end of lunch, and most amusing. A born 'raconteur' with a great sense of humour and a good memory. After lunch to my great joy I collected a copy of Phillips's *A Natural History of the Ducks*. A book I had been looking for for a long time.

7 April

I had made all plans to escape early and was just starting off when a message came through from the PM that we were to report on Dickie Mountbatten's last wire! There was absolutely no hurry and absolutely no necessity for a Saturday meeting of the COS. He was told so, but insisted that we should meet, thereby again showing his complete lack of consideration for others and his masterly way of making work when not necessary to do so. On these occasions my feeling[s] for him are hard to describe! Had to wait up in town for lunch and come down in the afternoon.

8 April

A quiet Sunday at home recuperating from my cold.

9 April

A long COS at which I had a heated difference of opinion with CAS, refusing to support the RAF plan to send bombers to Luzon [Philippines] until we have more details about this plan. From the information I have at present it seems likely that the aerodromes will only be completed after they have ceased to be of any value. Hobo [Hobart] came to lunch in very good form. Long Cabinet at 5.30 pm attended by Smuts, Fraser (NZ), Forde, Evatt, Wavell, Firoz Khan Noon etc. Long discussion about possibility of feeding Holland, raised by Smuts.

10 April

Another long and very boring agenda for the COS. Amongst other items we appointed Monty as the 'Gauleiter' for the British occupied zone. May heaven help him with that job!! Lewis and Aitken came to lunch, and Rollie had a dinner for his cousin and Rollo and Elizabeth. The war has started another of its rather more sticky periods. We are not making very rapid progress just at present. The war looks like dragging on unless Stalin kicks off again which I have every reason to believe he will do before long!

11 April

Lunched at the Mansion House. The usual diplomatic lunch. Eden was called away and Amery had to propose the health of the Diplomatic Corps. French Ambassador replied. It was a dull lunch. During the afternoon [General] King, who has been looking after welfare in India, came to see me. Afterwards a representative from Arnold (American Air Chief) came to see me, and brought me a present of bananas, oranges and apples from him. A very kind thought.

12 April

We had to consider this morning at the COS one of Winston's worst minutes I have ever seen. I can only believe that he must have been quite tight when he dictated it.* It brought out all his worst qualities and was based on a complete misappreciation of existing organization. It went back to Ike's direct approach to Stalin, he abused Tedder for having allowed him to do so without referring to us, stated that Tedder failed entirely to realize that he was intended to act as the main link between Ike and us. Again forgetting that he himself had entirely undermined Tedder's position by continually communicating direct with Ike and cutting Tedder out! He then abused Whiteley, classifying him at one time as one of 'The Commission' and next as one of the 'Liaison Officers', forgetting that Morgan was the senior officer of the HQ and that in any case all these officers were part of Ike's own staff and, thank God, sufficiently loyal not to report matters behind his back!! But then matters such as 'chain of command' and 'loyalty to one's superiors' are unknown factors to him!! My God! how little the world at large knows what his failings and defects are! And thank heaven they don't or we should not be where we are now!

You came up and we lunched with the Crofts, the others being Duke of Devonshire, Humphrey Wyndham's wife, Oliver Leese's wife, and Stuart. This evening P.J. and his wife came to dine with us, and he asked me to stop on as CIGS with him if the Conservative Gov was returned, as Winston had asked him to come back as S of S. I told him I was quite ready to do if he wanted me, but that I did not feel that I should remain after the end of the year, which would complete 4 years, which I considered was already too long for a CIGS's tenure of office. He was very kind in things he said as regards my influence with Winston, and as to my being one of the few he had seen whom Winston would listen to. However you were there to hear what he said so I need not write about it!

---

*In the handwritten diary this sentence is struck through in different ink and does not appear elsewhere: neither in 'Notes on my life' nor in the bowdlerized Bryant, which reads: 'We had to consider this morning at the COS meeting one of Winston's minutes based on a complete misappreciation of the existing organization.' *Triumph*, p. 446.

13 April

You remained over for the day and we motored home together in the evening. A lovely evening with all the beautiful spring blossom quite at its best.

14 and 15 April

Spent quietly at home.

16 April

A busy morning with COS and War Cabinet. However PM did not attend the latter so it went reasonably fast, and I arrived home in good time for lunch. Glorious day and beginning to feel really warm.

17 April

A rushed and hurried COS at 10.15 as we had to attend the Roosevelt memorial service at St Paul's at 11 am.* Service was attended by King, Queen, PM, Kings of Greece, Yugoslavia, Norway etc etc. A very impressive service. You and children came for lunch and we went on to the Zoo. In the evening PM sent for me as Ike had come over and he wanted to discuss action to be taken when we joined forces with the Russians, prior to our withdrawing into our respective occupational areas. This evening received news from Alex that Henry [AB's grandnephew] had been killed! Poor old Basil and Cynthia!!

18 April

We had a rushed COS in order to meet PM and Eisenhower at 11 am. Orme Sargent and Strang came from the Foreign Office (two fairly typical FO products). Our main points of discussion were what arrangements should be made when we meet the Russians prior to returning to the zones of occupation. Secondly, what should be the zone given to the French? It should not separate the Americans from the British, it should not join up the French and the Russians, and it should not cut American communications to Bremerhaven. Tonight went to cinema with Rollie to see Sacha Guitry whom I always enjoy.

19 April

Went to Aldershot to inspect the passing out Company of OCTU [Officer Cadet Training Unit] at Mons Barracks. You and the children came to attend the parade. A glorious sunny day and a good parade. Lunched with you, and then drove back with Rollie to meet Mr Fraser (PM of NZ) who came to discuss future of NZ Div with me. Then had interview with Pownall to tell him there

---

*Roosevelt had died in office on 12 April 1945, and been replaced by Truman.

was no future employment for him. Finally long talk with S of S about Monty's deputy in his future job as Gauleiter of North Germany.

20 April

The Russians are now moving properly and it should not be long before we meet up with them on the Berlin-Dresden front. I feel that we shall still have several more weeks in front of us before we finish off the war. Several centres of resistance in Austria, Czechoslovakia, Denmark, Holland and Norway will have to be worked off and may give us considerable trouble. On the other hand Hitler's suicide might well bring the end on rapidly. Anyhow I am off on leave tomorrow morning early for a week on the Dee and I pray and hope that I may not be recalled!

21 to 30 April

Flew up to Inverness on the 21ˢᵗ and inspected a Brigade of Garrison Gunners turned into infantry. Bulgy met me on the aerodrome and drove me round, finally finishing up at Cairnton. There I stopped with Blanche Cobbold and the two boys. Bertie was there also. A whole week's fishing, unfortunately under poor conditions. Very few fish up. Caught 2 fish on my first morning, and no more fish after that!! The only other fish I caught the line broke! On 29ᵗʰ I flew down from Dyce to Odiham and arrived home for lunch. Two despatch riders with brown bags filled up the evening with work!

30 April

The usual early start and back to work again, refreshed by a week away, but with a great disinclination to start work again! A long COS and an unpleasant Cabinet with Winston in a bad mood. In spite of the fact that Alex had made the greatest advance he had yet brought off, he was abused for not having taken Trieste!! Dined with Archie Wavell at the Athenaeum. He was in good form, but worried by the reception his proposals were receiving from the PM.

1 May

A very long COS with three difficult subjects:

(a) Portal's desire to establish long range bomber groups on island near Formosa.

(b) Manpower paper on the redeployment for war against Japan.

(c) The transfer of South West Pacific area from the Americans' control to us.

In the afternoon a Selection Board and a long talk with S of S. The crumbling of Germany is fast. Forces in Italy may surrender to Alex tomorrow. At same time Bernadotte is carrying on negotiations with Himmler. The end must come soon.

2 May

Last night, on the midnight news, Hitler was reported as dead. After longing for this news for the last 6 years, and wondering whether I should ever be privileged to hear it, when I finally listened to it I remained completely unmoved. Why? I do not know. I fully realized that it was the real full stop to the many and long chapters of this war, but I think that I have become so war weary with the continual strain of the war that my brain is numbed, and incapable of feeling intensely.

The surrender of the German Army in Italy to Alex, expected at 2 pm, did not take place owing to Kesselring stepping in and sacking local commanders. However Kesselring is prepared to carry on but asks for 48 hours more. Meanwhile Monty reaches the Baltic, and it is possible that Boche will surrender Northern forces to him. I doubt whether Germany will last over the weekend! Meanwhile in Burma the landings south of Rangoon are going well.

This afternoon Anders again came to see me having returned from visiting his Corps of Poles in Italy. He says there are at least one million Poles in Western Europe which he can (and wishes to) get hold of to swell his forces. He wishes to take part in the occupation of Germany, and then has wild hopes of fighting his way home to Poland through the Russians! A pretty desperate problem the Polish Army is going to present us with!

3 May

In the middle of the crumbling of Germany suddenly wild rumours appear that Guatemala is going to attack our colony of Honduras! Much discussion at COS, much time wasted, only force available is Canadian Bn in Jamaica. Colonial Office must be approached, and Foreign Office informed owing to repercussions in America etc etc. In the end it turns out to be a bad forest fire in Guatemala which had necessitated employing most of their army to put it out, this had put Honduran nerves on edge, they saw ghosts everywhere and wasted our time unnecessarily.

Meanwhile Germany crumbles. The Italian front has surrendered, Monty takes 100,000 prisoners, Hamburg gives in and negotiations with Monty look like the rest of Northern Germany and Denmark giving in! Lunched with the Birleys. During afternoon Gammell came to see me prior to his going to Moscow. Then Victor Fortune back from his time as a prisoner, I had not seen him since 1939!! Tonight for dinner Stella, Main, Sinclair and Stanton.

4 May

A memorable day in so far as it will probably be one of the last ones of the second war with Germany! Monty met [Field Marshal] Keitel this morning, who surrendered unconditionally Holland, all North Germany, Schleswig Holstein, Denmark, Friesian Islands and Heligoland! Keitel then went on to Ike's HQ to discuss surrender of Norway. I had just got back to the flat when we were sent for for a COS meeting with PM in Cabinet room, 10 Downing Street.

We found him on the telephone busy telling the King about his conversation with Ike and Monty. He then told us all about it and he was evidently seriously affected by the fact that the war was to all intents and purposes over as far as Germany was concerned. He thanked us all very nicely and with tears in his eyes for all we had done in the war, and all the endless work we had put in 'from El Alamein to where we are now'. He then shook hands with all of us.

On the 9 pm news the announcement was made. Tomorrow we should hear the rest. The only part I am not clear about yet is whether Keitel has sufficient authority to stop the forces (some 50 divs) in Czechoslovakia. If they stop tomorrow then the war is over as they now form the only large force left.

5 May

Another flood of telegrams necessitated our having a Saturday COS meeting. The telegrams were mainly concerned with Alexander's difficulties with Tito about Trieste etc. Also masses about the negotiations for surrender. Envoys to come to Monty's HQ, and to be sent on to Ike, possibilities of final surrender today or on Sunday. Difficulty of carrying the Russians along with us, combined with great reluctance on the part of the Germans to surrender to the Russians, of whom they are terrified. Monty faced with difficult problem of surrender of Denmark occupational troops, over 1 million German soldiers, 400,000 Russian prisoners, 2 million excess German population in Schleswig Holstein etc etc.

6 May

A quiet Sunday, during the afternoon went over to meet Bertie Fisher and to put up hides for a nightingale, bullfinch, and black cap's nest.

7 May

Returned early as usual to find state of uncertainty about the announcement of the surrender of the Germans! Although all documents had been signed and hostilities were to cease from today, the Russians made difficulties saying that the negotiations should be signed in Berlin, and repudiating those documents which their representatives had accepted. PM had invited Chiefs of Staff with Pug Ismay and Hollis to lunch at 10 Downing St to celebrate the culmination of our efforts. It was a disturbed lunch, Winston was expecting a telephone call from the President [Truman] which only came after lunch. Meanwhile he received a telegram from Ike stating that it was likely he would have to fly to Berlin for the required Russian final negotiations. This necessitated a call being put through to Ike, which got through during the pudding period! During the interval Winston discussed the pros and cons of elections in June. We stressed the 'cons' from the military point of view, stating that it could lead only to dispersal of effort which would be better concentrated onto the war.

After lunch we went out into the Downing Street garden to be photographed with Winston to commemorate the years of work we had put in together in our effort to bring the war to its successful termination. There was no Cabinet meeting but we were warned for a visit to the Palace for 6.30 pm. However this did not materialize as after the PM's conversation with the President he decided to postpone his announcement till tomorrow afternoon at 3 pm. The King is also to speak at 9 pm.

So this is at last the end of the war!! It is hard to realize. I can't feel thrilled, my main sensation is one of infinite mental weariness! A sort of brain lethargy which refuses to register highlights, and remains on an even dull flat tone. And yet at the back of it all there is a feeling of only partially digested wonderful restfulness, a realization of something I have been striving endlessly for with hardly any hope of realization for month after month. The most acute feeling is one of deep depression such as I have experienced at the end of the strain of each Combined Chiefs of Staff Conference.

8 May   VE Day (Victory-Europe)

A day disorganized by victory! A form of disorganization that I can put up with. Started with usual COS meeting which took most of the morning. Then I had Auchinleck to lunch and a most satisfactory interview. He was in a charming mood, and we had a most satisfactory talk. I then had to go to 28 Museum St [bookshop] and had a difficult journey and found the place closed when I got there. At 4.10 pm left WO for Buckingham Palace where I was due at 4.30 pm. A meeting of War Cabinet and Chiefs of Staff with the King. I crossed Whitehall with difficulty, through Horse Guards, battled my way down the Mall and came into an impenetrable crowd outside the Palace. However, with much honking and patience we gradually got through and arrived in good time. PM was very late as he insisted on coming in an open car! At last PM, Bevin, Woolton, Lyttelton, Morrison, Sinclair and Anderson were gathered, in addition Cunningham, Portal, Ismay and Bridges. The King made very nice little speech of congratulation, finishing up with a reference to the Chiefs of Staff as that organization which probably only those present in the room had any idea what their real part had been in securing the success of this war. We were then photographed, first of all together, and then only the King, PM, and COS.

We then left for the Home Office where a balcony had been prepared on which the PM, Cabinet and COS were to come to see the crowd in Whitehall and to be cheered by them. A vast crowd stretching from near the WO to Parliament Square. Then back to the WO to finish off work. I had to go and see P.J. and on coming out Lady Grigg collared me and brought me into the passage. She said, 'I watched you getting into your car this morning from the window with a crowd looking at you, and none of them realizing that beside them was the man who had probably done most to win the war against Germany!' She said it was all wrong that they should not realize it, 'I do, and lots of people do, tell Lady Brookie from me.' It was very nice of her, she said it so nicely and I wish you had been able to hear her.

There is no doubt that the public has never understood what the Chiefs of

Staff have been doing in the running of this war. On the whole the PM has never enlightened them much, and has never once in all his speeches referred to the Chiefs of Staff or what they have been doing in the direction of the war on the highest plane. It may be inevitable, but I do feel that it is time that this country was educated as to how wars are run and how strategy is controlled. The whole world has now become one large theatre of war, and the Chiefs of Staff represent the Supreme Commanders, running the war in all its many theatres, regulating the allocation of forces, shipping, munitions, relating plans to resources available, approving or rejecting plans, issuing directives to the various theatres. And most difficult of all handling the political aspect of this military action, and coordinating with our American allies.

It is all far less spectacular than the winning of battles by commanders in the field, and yet if the COS make any errors the commanders in the field will never be in a position to win battles. Their actions are not in the limelight, indeed most of the time they are covered by secrecy. We therefore find the COS working and working incessantly, shouldering vast responsibilities, incurring great risks without the country ever realizing we were at work. It has been a wonderful experience, of never ending interest. At times the work and the difficulties to be faced have been almost beyond powers of endurance. The difficulties with Winston have been of almost unbearable proportions, at times I have felt that I could not possibly face a single other day. And yet I would not have missed the last 3½ years of struggle and endeavour for anything on earth.

I remember the night Winston offered me the job of CIGS in the large smoking room at Chequers, he went out of the room shortly afterwards. I was so overcome that my natural instinct was, when left alone in the room, to kneel on the sofa and pray to God for his assistance in my new task. I have often looked back, during the last 3½ years, to that prayer, and thanked God for the way he had listened to me and provided me with the help I had asked for, and without which I should have floundered in the first year. I am not a highly religious individual according to many people's outlook. I am however convinced that there is a God all powerful looking after the destiny of this world. I had little doubt about this before the war started, but this war has convinced me more than ever of this truth. Again and again during the last 6 years I have seen His guiding hand controlling and guiding the destiny of this world toward that final and definite destiny which He has ordained. The suffering and agony of war in my mind must exist to gradually educate us to the fundamental law of 'loving our neighbour as ourselves'. When that lesson has been learned, then war will cease to exist. We are however many centuries from such a state of affairs. Many more wars, and much suffering is required before we finally learn our lesson. However humanity in this world is still young, there are still many millions of years to run during which high perfection will be attained. For the present we can do no more than go on striving to improve more friendly relations towards those that surround us.

With these reflections I must leave behind the German war and now turn my energies during my few remaining days [as CIGS] towards the final defeat of Japan.

9 May

I started this diary well by taking a day off and going home! The day was VE2 day, namely the second day of victory in Europe, a national holiday. The majority of Englishmen apparently enjoy spending such a holiday by crowding together into the smallest possible space. Personally the less I see of the human species the more content I am! I went home, found you busy putting up wonderful flagstaffs and decorations, and incidentally cutting your hand badly! We had a happy and peaceful afternoon together looking after goats and chickens etc.

10 May

Returned to work early and on the whole had a fairly easy day of it. A short COS, a quiet lunch at home and a series of easy interviews. Only trouble connected with Syria and Lebanon which are brewing up for trouble. De Gaulle evidently determined to do all he can to lay his clutches again on this part of the world. The time has now come when we must decide whether friendship of France in Western Europe is of more importance than friendship of the Pan Arabic League in the Middle East. A difficult problem to decide, but one which requires a definite solution either one way or the other. I fear that we shall hover between the two.

11 May

Adam came to lunch and we had a long talk. In the evening I did an early get away, and arrived home before dinner.

12 May

Spent the morning in complete peace mending an old rabbit hutch! After lunch went to Turgis Green where I met Mussens [Fisher's gamekeeper] and Bertie Fisher. Mussens had nests of hawfinch, not ready to photograph, and nightingale, bullfinch, black cap. I spent 1½ hours photographing the bullfinches, light not very good and heat oppressive. Came home for late tea and more work at the rabbit hutch.

13 May

Had an early lunch and then motored up to London for the St Paul's Thanksgiving Victory Service. On the way we picked up Nancy Dill at the Berkeley. Service on the whole rather disappointing and did not do full justice to the occasion. After the service Winston had a War Cabinet to discuss the Yugoslav situation. He had received a telegram from Truman, full of bellicose views and ready to be rough with Tito. Winston delighted, he gives me the feeling of already longing for another war! Even if it entailed fighting Russia! He kept us till 6.15 listening to his meanderings. Then motored home again.

14 May

Early start, taking you up for the week. Fairly full COS with Tito and Russian troubles, plus de Gaulle brewing up mischief in Syria! For lunch Arthur Bryant came (the author), I found him very interesting. Monty came to see me in the afternoon and then a long and drawn out cabinet with Winston in one of his worst moods. Kept rambling on and on and failed ever to arrive at any conclusions. Escaped at 8 pm with the Cabinet still in full swing! I know few people better at wasting everybody's time than Winston.

15 May

A COS full of petty worries. Tito still refuses to withdraw out of Istria. Truman, after adopting a strong attitude towards turning out Yugoslavs out of Venezia Giulia last week, now states that he could not dream of asking America to start hostilities unless the Yugoslavs attacked us first.

Meanwhile de Gaulle insists on stirring up trouble in Syria by sending French reinforcements there. He also infuriates the Italians by refusing to withdraw his troops from north west Italy. In fact the vultures of Europe are now crowding round and quarrelling over bits of the Austro-German-Italian carcass which they are endeavouring to tear off. Meanwhile they gather round a table at San Francisco to discuss how to establish universal peace!*

16 May

A bad day! Started with a very rushed briefing for COS and long delayed by S of S for my COS meeting. I then had to run a very rushed COS meeting between 10.45 and 11.30 when we went for a meeting with the PM and Eisenhower. We were kept there from 11.30 to 1.30 pm and did absolutely nothing! Winston in one of his meandering moods wandered from the number of calories consumed by German prisoners, to Clemmie's experiences in Russia, back to Tito's aspirations in Venezia Giulia, to dash rapidly off into questions of Inter-Allied control of Germany, back to Clemmie's lunch party in Moscow where all the Moscow ladies had to be provided with dresses by the state, etc etc. A series of good catch words such as, 'When the eagles are silent the parrots begin to jabber' – Tito and de Gaulle being the latter! Or again, 'Let the Germans find all the mines they have buried, and dig them up. Why should they not? Pigs are used to find olives (!!!)'. We had to remind him that truffles were what pigs hunted for. We were then told that the children in Russia were taught a creed:

> I love Lenin
> Lenin was poor, and therefore I love poverty
> Lenin went hungry, therefore I can go hungry
> Lenin was often cold, therefore I shall not ask for warmth, etc etc.

---

*The United Nations Conference on International Organization – the inaugural meeting of the UN – was held in San Francisco 25 April to 26 June 1945.

'Christianity with a tomahawk' said Winston.

During the afternoon I had to see Croft, who is worried about the security of MI5 and 6, so am I!! Then Monty for a talk about his appointment as Gauleiter in Germany, and to warn him that Winston would press for Weeks as his deputy. I then collected you for the Russian Embassy victory party, then back to WO for meeting with S of S to tell him results of morning's meeting with Winston. Jack Collins came to dine with us. I was then pulled out at 11 pm to go to Winston who was dining Monty to discuss Weeks's appointment. Blackmail!! Winston ready to announce Monty and Weeks tomorrow provided we accept Weeks, and that I agree!! I saw through the blackmail and said I could not agree without his consulting P.J., which he has agreed to do. Got home by 1 am.

17 May
A very long and tiring day. COS lasted till 12.30. Then a talk with Basil whom I missed for dinner, Monty and S of S. The latter two meetings all concerned with Winston wishing to appoint Weeks as Monty's deputy in Germany. I then lunched at *The Times*, an excellent lunch, and Astor as usual quite charming. Back to WO for interview with Auk about appointment of Slim to Burma Command. Leese is going quite wild and doing mad things, prepared a fair rap on the knuckles for him! Delightful dinner with Budget.

18 May
A quiet Friday with an early start for home in the evening.

19 May
Saturday mainly occupied in trying to photograph hawfinches with Mussens.

20 May
In the afternoon joined up with the Andrew Cunninghams at Broadlands to take advantage of the last few days of the May Fly. Unfortunately the May Fly was over. Hooked good fish below the bridge and lost him.

21 May
Spent 3 hours in a hide photographing a pair of nightingales.

22 May
Back to work. Auchinleck came to lunch with me and we had a very useful talk together. In the evening the Birleys and the Whitakers came to dine.

23 May

A long and difficult COS meeting concerned with the Foreign Office proposals for starting the Allied Commission in Germany and for ultimately closing down Eisenhower's HQ. Meanwhile Winston insists on retaining that portion of the Russian zone which we have been able to occupy in our advance as a bargaining counter with the Russians. Considering that the only reason why we secured this ground was due to the fact that the Germans used their available forces to resist the Russians, thus facilitating our advance; and also considering that we have already agreed with the Russians as to the Zones of Occupation in Germany; I consider that Winston is fundamentally wrong in using this as a bargaining counter! But this is a political matter and politics are as crooked as rams' horns!

After COS collected you and we visited the captured German submarine at Westminster Bridge.

Wainwrights to lunch. In evening went to see Steer Webster's films of young flamingoes, which he took in Cutch [near Bombay], most interesting they were. Finally very delightful dinner with P.J. and Lady Grigg, with old Auchinleck dining also.

24 May

A long COS meeting with the Joint Planners in. We were discussing future operations in the Pacific after the capture of Singapore. We want if possible to participate with all 3 services in the attacks against Japan. It is however not easy to make plans as the Americans seem unable to decide between a policy of invasion as opposed to one of encirclement. It also remains to be seen what attitude Winston may take. I have no idea what his reaction will be. For the present he is absorbed in this mad election and for the next few months he will be unable to devote much attention to war plans!

This evening I went carefully through the Planners' report on the possibility of taking on Russia should trouble arise in our future discussions with her. We were instructed to carry out this investigation. The idea is of course fantastic and the chances of success quite impossible. There is no doubt that from now onwards Russia is all powerful in Europe.

It may be remembered that a few weeks earlier, when examining the desirability of dismembering Germany after her defeat, the COS had then looked upon Russia as our future potential enemy [see 2 October 1944]. This paper had created a considerable stir in the Foreign Office, who considered it very remiss of us to look upon our present ally as our probable future enemy. We might even have been asked to withdraw this paper had we not asked for an interview with Anthony Eden, who approved our outlook. Now only a few weeks later, Winston had come to us expressing his anxiety at seeing 'that Russian bear sprawled over Europe', and instructing us to examine from the military point of view the possibility of driving him back to Russia before the Americans and ourselves demobilized our forces! I asked him if he took charge of all the political aspects of launching a war on our ally! He said we could leave that aspect and concentrate on the military problem.

Here I was on the evening of May 24ᵗʰ, a few days after VE Day, examining the results of the Planners' work on this problem. The result of this study made it clear that the best we could hope for was to drive the Russians back to about the same line the Germans had reached. And then what? Were we to remain mobilized indefinitely to hold them there?

25 May
Made an early start and motored down to Broadlands with you where we met Andrew and Lady Cunningham. There we fished till the evening on all three beats till the evening and never saw a single fish!

26 May
Went to Turgis Green to photograph hawfinches, had a long spell with them, and am very doubtful as to results.

27 May
A quiet Sunday at home.

28 May
An early start. COS mainly concerned with the situation in the Levant which is getting daily worse. This in my mind is all due to the Foreign Office not taking a firm attitude with de Gaulle. Meanwhile Paget [C-in-C ME Force] is being left in a very difficult position. After lunch I was sent for by PM for an interview with him, Anthony Eden, Orme Sargent and one other. Evidently Eden wishes the military to step in once the French and Syrians have started a proper row! Winston holds different view and considers we should stand aside, watch our own interests and let the French and Syrians cut each other's throats. Personally I feel Winston is in this case right. If we step in now, we shall have to shoot up both sides to stop the fight, and shall increase our unpopularity with both. There is only one spot to stop the trouble and that is in Paris, by putting it across de Gaulle in no measured terms.

29 May
More discussion about Tito's activities in Venezia Giulia, and more disturbances in the Levant. Both of the above likely to lead to serious trouble before long. Lunched with the Military Attachés at Claridges, and spent long interval talking to them individually after lunch. Evidently part of the lobster I had was not quite as good as it might have been, and as a result I was violently sick during the afternoon, a thing I cannot ever remember happening to me before!

30 May

Situation in Syria is deteriorating rapidly, and will probably result in our having to settle the quarrel at the expense of the friendships of both sides. This evening I went off with Rollie for an evening's fishing north of London on a bit of water belonging to Barney's solicitor. No good with the trout but we had a pleasant dinner out of doors and saw three kingfishers which was a pleasant change from Whitehall. Meanwhile Paget has wired about situation in Syria deteriorating rapidly and Winston convened a Cabinet at 6.30 pm. I missed this treat by being out fishing! Decided to step in and stop the trouble, but first of all to ensure American participation, or at any rate approval of our actions.

31 May

We again discussed the 'unthinkable war' against Russia at this morning's COS, and became more convinced than ever that it is 'unthinkable'! Adam came to lunch with me and we discussed the departure and relief of all the Army Councillors during the next few months, and of the Commanders-in-Chief of the various Commands. After lunch a group [photo?] of all the Directors of the General Staff. Finally a discussion with S of S on future organization of the Army. Meanwhile Paget has been ordered to take action to stop any further bloodshed in Syria and Lebanon. Goodness knows where this may end if the Foreign Office does not unite with US State Department and set about de Gaulle in the way he deserves.

1 June

Lunched at the Ritz with Mr Marino, Brian Boyle's friend who is an expert on books. He returns to France shortly for a tour. In the evening we went together to Ronnie Weeks's cocktail party and then drove home.

2 June

Quiet Saturday at home whilst Jack, Madeline, Tom and Jane [Lees] went to Eton.

3 June

Lees family left for home in the morning.

4 June

COS concerned with de Gaulle's mad antics in Syria, Tito's aspirations in Venezia Giulia, and the Foreign Office's desire to withdraw troops from Persia in the hope of inducing the Russians to do the same! Both Lewin and Jumbo Goschen came to lunch and in the evening Lord Milne to discuss Cadet Movement and lack of drive displayed by the War Office in connection with it.

5 June

Another long COS with a meeting of the Joint Intelligence Committee to discuss the organization of a new Central Intelligence Board. The plan does not go far enough but is perhaps as far as it is possible to go for the present and until it is settled whether we are to have a Defence Ministry.

We were also puzzled as to how to deal with the *Jeanne d'Arc*, which has started with further reinforcements from Oran for Syria! If it arrives then it can only result in a flare up of all the trouble we have damped down with such difficulty. In addition, de Gaulle is also going mad in north-west Italy, issuing orders to General Doyen to fight sooner than retire! From Tito's side no answer yet.

Selection Board at 3.15 pm and a Cabinet at 6 pm. The first meeting I had attended with the new members. Winston looking very tired, but in quite good mood. Eden is now ill, so the load on Winston is heavier than ever.

6 June

Lunched with Home Forces and gave them a talk on world situation. This is probably the last talk I shall give them before they are dissolved and cease to exist as Home Forces. I kept going back in my mind to all the previous talks I had given them during some of the difficult days when I never hoped for such a situation as we are in now! But I feel very very weary.

7 June

A long and difficult survey of personnel shipping took up most of our time with the COS. What with redeployment of USA, Canadian, South African and New Zealand forces, together with the repatriation of prisoners and our movement of troops to the Far East, the claims of long overseas service men, leave, and civil travel, are very hard to fit in!! The whole matter becomes a bad headache! John Brooks on his way back to Alex came to lunch with me.

In the afternoon I had an interview with Scobie [GOC Greece], just back from Greece for a month's leave. He has had difficult times in his job there and was very interesting on the conditions in Greece. He was followed by Murchie, the Canadian Chief of Staff, who discussed a variety of problems connected with Canadian Forces and their return to Canada.

8 June

I had a difficult lunch with Anders at the Dorchester. He had just given up the appointment of Deputy Commander-in-Chief of the Polish Forces, and was about to return to the command of his old Corps in Italy. Just as fanatical as ever in his outlook on Russia, and determined if he can to increase the size of the Polish forces. He has no clear cut plans and just hopes for any further chance that may admit of his fighting his way back to Poland. In his present mood he is capable of doing dangerous things and will require watching carefully. Motored home in the evening.

9 and 10 June
Two quiet days at home.

11 June
Returned in the morning. Had a difficult time in the COS owing to P.J. Grigg's statement in the House last week in which he shortened the tour abroad before repatriation. This has raised an outcry from Dickie [Mountbatten], saying he cannot now stage his offensive on the fixed date owing to the loss of personnel this will produce. I am afraid there is something in what he says and that this may be a case of elections affecting operations. Both Portal and Cunningham are inclined to take Dickie's part, and I am not at all certain that they are not right.

You came up and we lunched with Montague [Canada House] at the Dorchester so as to meet Murchie the Canadian Chief of Staff.

At 5.30 pm a Cabinet in which Winston gave a long and very gloomy review of the situation in Europe. The Russians were further West in Europe than they had ever been except once. They were all powerful in Europe. At any time that it took their fancy they could march across the rest of Europe and drive us back into our island. They had a 2 to 1 land superiority over our forces, and the Americans were returning home. The quicker they went home, the sooner they would be required back here again, etc, etc. He finished up by saying that never in his life had he been more worried by the European situation than he was at present.

12 June
After COS rushed off to the Guildhall for Eisenhower's presentation of the freedom of the City. Ike made a *wonderful* speech and impressed all hearers in the Guildhall including all the Cabinet. He then made an equally good speech of a different kind outside the Mansion House, and a first class speech at the Mansion House lunch. I had never realized that Ike was as big a man until I heard his performance today! In the evening dined with the PM to meet Ike, Bedell [Smith], and Tedder. We remained sitting at the dining table till midnight, I then rushed off to catch a train at King's Cross.

13 June
Spent whole day inspecting 43rd Div.

14 June
Had a first class visit to the Farne Islands with lovely weather, accompanied by Ted Morris [C-in-C Northern Command], Naylor, Rollie Charrington.

15 June

Returned to London. Adam came to lunch. Army Council photo and finally dined with 'C' (Menzies) who wanted to extract old Sinclair [DMI] out of me. I am ready to let him go provided his health stands up to it.

16 June

After a morning's work motored down to Down House School to visit Pooks. A great afternoon with Physical Display, Ballet and Quick Play. Tom had turned up and also came, and Mr Ti was picked up on the way, so that it was a great family gathering.

17 June

Collected Pooks in the morning from her school and she stopped on for the night.

18 June

A remarkably quiet Monday! No Cabinet in the afternoon. Drafted letter to Mountbatten advising him to get rid of Oliver Leese who has proved to be a failure in South East Asia Command. It is very disappointing.

19 June

The elections continue to have a fatal effect on operations. The S of S's statement in the House reducing service abroad in India from 3 years and 8 months to 3 and 4 has had a most pernicious result on the prospect of our operations for the recapture of the Malay peninsula! We are now releasing more men than we have shipping to bring home! We therefore lose them from the fighting forces and disgruntle them by failing to bring them home! And all this just for some electioneering vote catching! Next Laski refuses to agree to Attlee going to the meeting of the Big Three, except in the quality of an onlooker! As a result the Big Three meeting is now to be put off from July 15th to August 15th, with all the incumbent disadvantages to the war by delaying the decisions of our badly wanted [Combined] Chiefs of Staff meeting! Had long and interesting talk with Slim [14th Army] this afternoon.

20 June

Slim attended our COS meeting and gave us an outline of the proposed operations for the capture of Malaya. I am still very worried about P.J.'s statement shortening period of service in South East Asia Command by 4 months. I do not see any daylight out of the muddle that this vote catching statement has got us into. Heaven help democracies if they must have elections in war!

Dined with Meinertzhagen to see the latest pictures Lodge has produced for his book, they were very attractive. Old Trenchard was also dining there, he gave me a feeling which I have had with a certain type of old soldier; that there is a very definite time in a man's life when it is best for him to go into retirement. I am approaching that age!

21 June

We had a long struggle this morning with the Planners trying to tidy up our policy for the prosecution of the war after the capture of Singapore. It is essential in my mind that we should provide some form of land force for operations against Japan proper, and yet the difficulties produced by the Principal Administrative Officers almost make it impossible. It is exhausting driving people on to make them overcome difficulties! During afternoon had a visit from Gen Bissell the American Director of Military Intelligence. He was very interesting about Japan, and evidently considers that the required results can only be obtained by invasion, and that encirclement is unlikely to achieve our object. I was next visited by General Sun, Chinese General from Burma, to whom I had to present a CB. Finally dined at Claridges with American Military Attaché to meet Bissell again. I sat next to Winant and had an interesting conversation with him on the desirability of retaining some hold on the Combined Chiefs of Staff organization after the end of the war. There is something quite exceptionally attractive about Winant and every time I see him I like him better.

22 June

A fairly quiet day on the whole. Left for home in the evening.

23 June

Spent working in the garden at home.

24 June

Mr Ti was fetched over for the day by you.

25 June

Adam came to lunch. More troubles in India due to Grigg's vote catching statement. Now settled that we go to Berlin on the 15th July.

26 June

Tom came up to lunch and I took him to the dentist and to the Service stores. S of S came back from Cardiff where he had been electioneering. I had a long talk with him concerning our troubles in India due to his statements concerning reduction of period of service abroad. I think he is beginning to see that we are in trouble, and will I think make a statement to help us out.

27 June

A long COS with meetings with Joubert [de la Ferté] and Wise on questions of organization of command in Burma. Dickie had put up a foolish scheme which we had to down. Then lunch at Lords to see Dempsey's 2ⁿᵈ Army team taking on the MCC. Long interview with P.J. in which I think we have got him to agree to make a further statement as regards the repatriation of men of 3 years and 4 months being held up owing to transport difficulties. Finally went to a very good film with Rollie and his two daughters.

28 June

We had both the Principal Administration Officers and the Planners in our COS to discuss our plans for operations after Singapore, and to go into questions of administrative matters with them. We are now putting up paper to PM for discussion next Monday in which we suggest that we should put up proposal to Americans for a small land force of some 3 to 5 divisions to participate in main attack against Japan. The composition and organization of this force to be decided after discussion with the Americans. I have no idea how Winston will receive this proposal.

Andrew Cunningham and Sinclair came to lunch after which we motored out to 'The Park' [Bletchley] where all the decoding and deciphering is carried out. I began by addressing some 400 of the workers who consist of all 3 services, both sexes, and civilians. They come from every sort of walk of life, professors, students, actors, dancers, mathematicians, electricians, signallers, etc etc. I thanked them on behalf of the Chiefs of Staff and congratulated them on the results of their work. We then toured round the establishment and had tea before returning.

When I got back I had an hour's interview with the King. He wanted to know whether it would be suitable for him to come to Berlin during our next meeting there. Apparently he had discussed this with Winston who had agreed, and wired to Truman who was also for it. However Stalin when approached apparently did not jump at the proposal! Monty also when written to about it was not much in favour of it from the security aspect. I think the King will abandon the project.

29 June

Alexander, home for a few days, attended this morning's COS meeting. We discussed the gradual reduction of forces in Italy, the arming of Greek army, the strength of this army, and also that of the proposed Italian army. After lunch I had to go to PM at 3 pm to tell him that we should have to withdraw Oliver Leese from South East Asia, and replace him by Slim. He kept me for an hour but agreed to all I wanted. We are now ordering Oliver home, appointing Slim in his place, and sending out Dempsey as the additional Army Commander. Came back to WO for a long talk with Alex whom I found in very good form.

Whilst I was with Winston and we were discussing the necessary changes in senior army officers, I told him that I considered I should go at the end of the year. He said that if as a result of the election he got in again he would not hear of my going, and that I was quite young (!!) and required to carry out the reorganization of the army! He said that he considered Alex should be brought into the WO in some form or other, 'Inspector General' or 'Commander-in-Chief' to assist in the work. I did not argue with him, but I cannot see how this is going to work. The only capacity in which he could come in is that of VCIGS and he is too senior for that. It would be far better for him to replace me.

30 June
I spent the morning in the office and during that time I got hold of Slim and informed him that he was to take over from Oliver Leese, and that Dempsey would be sent out to him. He seemed very pleased. I said that this change must not affect his leave in any way. After lunch we both motored on down to Hever Castle for the weekend. There amongst others we found the Barrington-Wards [*The Times*] and the Otleys [Director of Finance, WO].

1 July
Spent a comfortable and interesting weekend at Hever Castle, motoring back in the evening.

2 July
We are now faced with difficulties ahead concerning future of Polish Forces! In a few days we shall be recognizing the Warsaw government officially and liquidating the London one. The Polish forces then present a serious conundrum which the Foreign Office has done little to solve in spite of repeated applications for [a] ruling ever since May! Lunched with Pug Ismay, Lady Louis Mountbatten and Bridges [Cabinet Secretary] were there. Then went to see a new film of the invasion of the continent, I have seldom seen a worse film!

3 July
Started our COS with the Joint Intelligence Survey of the week and finished up with a visit by Professor Tizard on the scientific coordination and development of scientific research for war purposes. Sheilah [AB's niece] and Tom came to lunch after which I dropped Tom at a cinema and went back to WO for monthly Selection Board. More difficulties and problems to settle in connection with the liquidation of Polish Government in London, and recognition of Warsaw government. Very doubtful how the Polish Forces will take it and

whether any Poles will agree to go back to Poland. Thank heaven election is nearly over now!

4 July

We started with our usual COS and from there went on to a meeting with the PM at 12 noon to get him to approve our proposed policy for war after capture of Singapore. We are suggesting that we should send a force of some 5 divisions to take part in the direct attack against Japan. The exact composition of the force to depend on our conversations with the Americans when we meet them in Berlin. For the first half hour we rambled about every subject except the one we were after! Winston very tired after all his electioneering tours. He said he had never been so tired physically since the days of his escape during the Boer War! At last we got onto our problem and he confessed he had not even read the paper which we had prepared for him with such care! (And yet if the proposed strategy in the long run turns out successful, it will have originated in his futile brain!! This has happened so frequently now!) I therefore proposed to him that I should run over the suggestions on the map for him. He was delighted with this idea. How much he understood and really understood in his exhausted state it is hard to tell. However I got him to accept the plan in principle, to authorize our sending the plan to the Americans, and to pass the telegram to the Dominion PMs for their cooperation! A great triumph. I then approached him about awards of GCBs to the American Chiefs of Staff and their presentation by the King, which he also agreed to.

Got back to flat late for lunch with Hylda and Evelyn waiting for me. After lunch dropped Evelyn, bought some Thorburn originals, and returned to WO. There I interviewed Dempsey and told him he was for the Far East. I was very much disappointed at his attitude, he is suffering from a swollen head, and I took some pains to deflate it! I then had an interview with Duff Cooper who wanted a change in his military attaché [in Paris]. Had an interesting time with him discussing de Gaulle and the situation in France. He does not think de Gaulle will last very long. More troubles and letters fixing up the Polish situation.

Finally home for a dinner with John Kennedy and wife and Meinertzhagen. The former informed me of a rumour I had not yet heard that I was to be made the next Governor General of Canada!!! I had been told that Harry Crerar was to take that job on, and very well he would do it too.

5 July

Polling day, thank heaven we are getting on with the election, and I hope we shall soon have a sane government prepared to govern the country. Went down to Camberley to give one of my usual end of term talks. We then drove on to Ferney Close for lunch. You then voted and we motored back. In the evening we went to see Leslie Henson's show and took Tom and Junior Commander Wolf ATS out of the office. A disappointing play.

6 July

Started with a long COS in the morning with a series of interviews. Then after lunch had to attend a Cabinet at 3 pm to give details about Canadian riots in Aldershot during last two nights. Winston had already called me up at 9 am and been abusive on the telephone. At the Cabinet he again started being abusive: 'Why could we not keep better order? Had we no British troops to call in to restore order? Where was our military police? Were we going to let these wild Canadians break up the homes of these poor inoffensive shopkeepers?' etc, etc!!! In most of his suggestions he was drastically wrong! It is only as a very last resort that I should order British troops to rough handle Canadians who are giving trouble. It would be the very best way of starting real bad troubles. In such cases Canadians must deal with their own nationals. Even British Red Cap Police must be kept out of it. I was very annoyed and I hope he realized it from my answers.

At 6 pm we went to the South African reception where we met Smuts. Then home for the weekend.

7 and 8 July

A quiet weekend at home.

9 July

Most items connected with our impending visit to Berlin well advanced. Afternoon visit from Alex prior to his return to Italy. Then a long talk with the S of S on manpower, followed by visit from Montague on the Canadian Aldershot riots, and one from Ronnie Weeks connected with the situation in Berlin, namely lack of food and fuel.

10 July

A long COS with the Joint Intelligence Committee reporting on the ability of Japan to carry on with the war. Somewhat depressing report, but one which held out some hope of shortening the war if it were possible to find some more suitable definition for 'Unconditional Surrender'. One making it clear that we had no evil intentions on the Mikado [Emperor], the Japanese religion or Japanese society as a whole.

Pongo came to lunch, after which I dashed round to see Mr Wyatt at Lloyds Bank with reference to borrowing money for purchase of a house. Cabinet at 3 pm run by Anthony Eden not looking too well being only just back from his cure for his duodenal ulcer, and also having recently heard that his son is missing in Burma. At 6 pm poor Oliver Leese came to see me, having just arrived back [from SEAC]. Very sad and repentant. He took it all wonderfully well. Ready to go back to private life or any lower rank, or anything that might suit best. Shall have a difficult job to find employment for him.

11 July

Jumbo Wilson turned up at our COS having arrived from Washington. We had a very long meeting with the Planners in and discussing with them all the latest papers they had prepared for our Berlin meetings. You, your father and Tom came to lunch, after which I had a busy time. Long interview with S of S settling questions of future reliefs of QMG, AG, and LGA [?] India etc. Finally went to a play with the [Andrew] Cunninghams, Betty Stark and Alan Cunningham. Dined with them afterwards. A very pleasant evening.

12 July

Another long COS with Jumbo attending again. After lunch visit by Keightley and then long talk with Archie Nye just back from leave. Finally collected you and dined out with the John Kennedys to show them some [bird] films of the Farne Islands.

13 July

Jumbo Wilson again attended our morning COS and we finished off our preparations for Berlin. Then lunched with Lady Louis Mountbatten to meet the Crown Princess of Sweden. After which I dropped you at your father's flat and returned to WO to finish off work and prepare for run home in the evening taking your father with us.

14 July

Spent quietly at home.

... but there is much more to it than that which I must now add.

While I was at home on Saturday afternoon, I was told that there was a car with some gentlemen who wished to see me. When I went out I found I knew none of them except a boy from the village, who told me that these gentlemen wanted to put up a hide in the Hartley Wintney water-catchment area, and could I help them? He introduced me to Mr Eric Hosking, the great bird photographer, and Mr Wooton who was the head of a private school near Sandhurst. Apparently they had found a hobby's nest with young in a Scotch fir in the water catchment, and wanted to put up a hide. Benita called up Mr Lumley Cator, who was connected with the Water Board, and obtained the necessary authority. Meanwhile I was talking to Hosking who said that if he was successful perhaps I might care to make use of his hide? I told him that thought had certainly crossed my mind, but that I was off to Potsdam the next day for a conference that would last a fortnight. He replied that it would still be all right then and birds would not have left the nest. So I took his telephone number and arranged to call him up as soon as I returned from Potsdam.

This was the beginning of many happy days bird photographing with Eric Hosking, to whom I owe a great debt.

15 July   Potsdam

Left Ferney Close at 8.30 am with Rollie and motored to Northolt. There I met Andrew Cunningham and Peter Portal. At 9.45 am we set off in the old York for Berlin. We had an excellent trip flying down the Thames, across to near Ostend, along Scheldt, crossing it just above Antwerp, over Venlo to the Rhine at Duisberg. On over Essen, Hamm, Hamelin, Braunschweig, Magdeburg to an aerodrome close to Potsdam. There we were met by a Guard of Honour of Navy, Army and Air Force with a Marine Band. We all three took the salute and went round the Guard of Honour. After that a drive of some 20 minutes to our dwellings in Babelsberg! They consisted of a series of villas, all facing onto the lake, and very pleasant. We have a house for the three Chiefs of Staff, and have Jumbo with us. Attlee is next door on one side and Bridges [Cabinet Secretary] beyond him and PM beyond that. On the other side Pug. I spent the afternoon settling in and in the evening tried for a pike in the lake.

16 July

Started the day with a COS meeting attended by Jumbo Wilson at which we discussed our agenda for this afternoon's meeting with the Americans. At breakfast I was told that the PM had sent for me last night after I had gone to bed. In the morning he sent for me again before our COS meeting. This was to tell me that he had heard from Lascelles that the King wanted Alex to replace Athlone as Governor General of Canada. This is the job that John Kennedy had told me that Lascelles had said that they wanted me for [4 July]. A job I would have given a great deal for. However, I agree that Alex is ideally suited for it and told the PM so. Consequently it is pretty well settled that he goes there, and I remain with a few heartburns which I think Kipling's 'If' has taught me by now to overcome.

Monty came to see me at 12.30 and remained till after lunch. At 2.30 we had our first meeting with the Americans. Leahy, Marshall, King and Arnold were all there. An easy meeting with no controversial points! After the meeting Marshall and Arnold came to tea and we then went on to Berlin for a tour round. It was most interesting. I was very impressed by the degree of destruction. We went first to the heroes' gallery near the 1870 memorial. Then right over the Reichstag, from there on to the Chancellery which was even more interesting. It was possible to imagine the tragedies which had occurred there only some 2½ months ago. Hitler's study in ruins, with his marble top writing table upside down! The Gestapo HQ opposite and the scene of all their last struggles. In one part of the apartments masses of Iron Crosses on the floor and medal ribbons. On the way up I was handed a German decoration in its box by a Russian private soldier!! If I had been told a year ago that this would happen to me, I should have refused to believe it! In fact the whole afternoon seemed like a dream, and I found it hard to believe that after all these years' struggles I was driving through Berlin! The population did not look too thin but on the whole pathetic and surly. I saw many sights of refugees returning to Berlin which brought back to me vividly the picture of the French refugees rushing back to Lille as we arrived from Brussels.

In every way throughout this war the Germans have been made to suffer the same misery as they inflicted on others, but with 100% interest.

This last paragraph of course only refers to the miseries due to fighting and not those inflicted by the SS forces and in the concentration camps.

17 July
Started with usual work in the office. Then COS at which we discussed new papers received by the Secretariat from the Americans. The first was the American reply to our desire to participate in the direct attack on Japan. The reply was far better than we had hoped for, and the offer is accepted in principle. The second was a question of command in the Pacific. There I foresee more trouble ahead. We want a greater share in the control of the strategy in the Pacific and they are apparently reluctant to provide this share.

Alexander came to lunch and I had a chance of asking him afterwards how he liked the idea of the Canadian Governorship. He was delighted with the thought of it, and well he might be.

After lunch we met the Americans at 2.30 pm and had a very successful meeting with them. We discussed further the question of our participation in the attack on Japan and decided to accept the plan in principle and to appoint a Corps Commander and Staff as our representative to go out to discuss plans with MacArthur and Nimitz. After tea we drove to Potsdam and visited the old and new castles there (Sans Souci), most interesting. In each case an old retainer took us round and explained what the various rooms were, where Frederick the Great had died, including his actual chair, the dwellings of the last Kaiser, etc, etc.

18 July
Alexander attended our COS on a minor point connected with the appointment of Douglas, and one which should never have reached the COS. We then had a long discussion on Basic Agreements [among the occupying powers, on the occupation of Germany]. Leathers had been to the PM reporting that our paper did not adequately cover our import programme and the fat was in the fire! Abusive minutes from PM based on false facts and bearing no relation to realities. Ronnie Weeks came to lunch, not looking too well, and must be relieved without delay.

At 2.30 we had a Combined Chiefs of Staff meeting, and one that turned out more successful than I had hoped for. Our first few items were connected with Allied cooperation in the shape of Dutch and French requests to send contingents to Far East. These points were fairly easily disposed of. We then turned to questions of command in the Pacific and we were on much thinner ice! We had asked for a quarter share in the control of operations in the Pacific, and the Americans showed every sign of reluctance to afford us such facilities. However, Marshall made a very nice speech, pointing out the difficulties of control in the Pacific, and the desirability to simplify the control and avoid delays. They would be prepared to discuss strategy but final decisions must rest with them. If the plan for the invasion of the Tokyo Plain did not suit us we could withhold our forces but they would still carry on. On the whole I think that the discussion cleared the air a good deal and that the secretaries should now be able to draft out some form of agreement between us.

On conclusion of the meeting we were invited by Marshall to visit the 2nd American Armoured Division. The division was formed up on one of the big 'autobahns' facing inwards, with all tanks, armoured cars, self-propelled AA equipment, and infantry. A most impressive sight. The efficiency of the equipment left a greater mark on one than the physique or turn out of the men. Fished with Peter Portal in the lake in the evening.

19 July

Leathers attended our morning COS and was handled fairly roughly by the whole of the COS. He has been working into the Basic Agreements, which form the foundation of all our transactions with the Americans, certain clauses connected with our import programme. These clauses reduce to a minimum any chances of our ever getting any agreement with the Americans. Added to this fact he is so slippery that you can never tell when he is likely to let you down. However we finally suggested that the only way to get the matter settled was for him to interview the American General Somervell this afternoon. He agreed to do this but we do not know what the results may have been. After lunch we had another meeting with the American COS which went off well, and has considerably reduced the points remaining for discussion.

After tea we went back to Berlin to visit the stadium where Olympic Games were run, and also to see Hitler's dugout where he is supposed to have died. A sordid and unromantic spot. Absolute chaos outside of concrete mixers, iron reinforcing bars, timber, broken furniture, shell holes, clothes, etc, etc. Down below even worse chaos. It is however possible to make out one large sitting room probably used for meals, a study for Hitler, a bedroom of Hitler's opening into two separate bath and WC rooms, connecting through to Eva Braun's room. Beyond these an electric engine room, further bunks, galley and a well equipped surgery. Outside we were shown where Goebbels and his family were found, also where a body was found which was taken for Hitler. However, the Russian in charge said that he considered that Hitler was now in Argentina, and that Eva Braun had never died, but a mistress of Goebbels. I wonder if the truth will ever be known. We also had a look at the Air Ministry and had a drive round Berlin. The more one sees of it the more one realizes how completely destroyed it is. Weather warming up again. Apparently tripartite talks going strong and making some headway.

20 July

Another troublesome COS concerning Basic Agreements and sharing out of personnel shipping. It is not easy to reconcile the requirements of the Cabinet ministers and PM with the outlook of American Chiefs of Staff. We are expected at times to argue out impossibilities. Went to lunch with Monty, he had not got much to say, and was mainly concerned with his impending loss of Ronnie Weeks. Back for a 2.30 meeting with American Chiefs of Staff, which did not last very long. After which I went to visit the troops who had been preparing this camp, and thanked them for all their work. Finished up the evening by listening to RAF concert.

21 July

A fairly full day! Started from the PM's house in a convoy containing PM, Anthony Eden, Attlee, 3 American and 2 British Chiefs of Staff, Alex, Jumbo Wilson and of course Monty with the PM. We were off to Monty's victory parade with the 7th Armoured Div (Desert Rats) in the Charlottestrasse in Berlin. We arrived opposite the stand where we transferred to trucks to tour round the troops. In leading truck PM, Anthony, Lyne (commanding 7th Armoured Div) and myself. The RHA were formed up round the 1870 memorial, and beyond the 4th Hussars, 11th Hussars, RE etc. In other streets Navy, Infantry Bde and RAF. We returned to the stand and then the Division marched past. I suppose I ought to have been gripped by what this all meant. Here were British troops who had come from Egypt, through North Africa and Italy to France (a real example of the strategy I had been working for) parading where masses of German forces had goosestepped in the past! Somehow it left me cold.

We returned to Potsdam in time for lunch, after which COS at which we considered new bombshell by Americans on Lend-Lease [termination] and our suggested Basic Agreement. We then met the American COS at 3.30 and were unable to do much owing to this latest paper that they had tabled. At 4.15 pm we came out and Portal and I dashed to the aerodrome where we had a plane standing by for us. At 5 pm we were airborne and on a 450 mile flight through Magdeburg, Kassel, Frankfurt, to an aerodrome near Schongau (about 30 miles SW from Munich). We arrived there about 8.15 pm and were met by an officer detailed by Bedell Smith with cars. We drove off on the road to Oberammergau, a village about 6 miles short of this place called Altenau. There arrangements had been made for us in the local pub which was very comfortable. The scenery on the road was lovely and entirely untouched by the war. We changed hurriedly and went off fishing where we remained till 11pm. We caught a few trout but mostly small. By midnight we were glad to fall into bed!

22 July

Up at 5 am, hurried breakfast and off fishing till 12 noon. We again caught a small number of small fish, but the river was spoiled by countless American soldiers fishing with worms in every pool. As the German SS Division had also been fishing with hand grenades, the fishing had been badly spoilt but might be quite good. The surroundings were most attractive, nice brown coloured cattle with lovely sounding bells, very fine pine forests, and a feeling of wildness. The evening before we had seen a roe deer, and this morning I saw a stag crossing the river within 30 yards of me. We returned at 12 noon, had a bath, shave and clean up. We then went to a most attractive shooting lodge occupied by Bedell Smith where he gave us an excellent lunch. He is by way of recuperating there, but is not looking at all well. We left about 3 pm, returning to the pub where we found a message from the pilot saying he would like to start early as weather over Berlin were bad. We had a cup of coffee, followed by a very bumpy 20 miles at 40 miles per hour in a jeep! By 6.15 we were airborne and had started back on our 450 miles home. A very bumpy trip. On landing here at 9.15 pm we found they had had a minor tornado which had blown down masses of trees, lifted the roof off a hangar and killed a Russian!!

23 July

First of all a COS at 10.30 with some new amendments by American COS concerning allotment of captured shipping. Then we went on to a meeting with the American COS where we squared up most of our outstanding problems, and only left over the Basic Agreements which are dependent on the PM fixing up Lend-Lease and Support Programme for UK with the President.

At 1.30 pm we went round to lunch with the PM, just 3 Chiefs of Staff, Leathers, Ismay, and Anthony Eden, who came in later. I was completely shattered by the PM's outlook! He had seen the reports of the American results of the new TA ['Tube Alloys'] secret explosive experiments [the atomic bomb] which had just been carried out in the States. He had absorbed all the minor American exaggerations, and as a result was completely carried away! It was now no longer necessary for the Russians to come into the Japanese war, the new explosive alone was sufficient to settle the matter. Furthermore we now had something in our hands which would redress the balance with the Russians! The secret of this explosive, and the power to use it, would completely alter the diplomatic equilibrium which was adrift since the defeat of Germany! Now we had a new value which redressed our position (pushing his chin out and scowling), now we could say if you insist on doing this or that, well we can just blot out Moscow, then Stalingrad, then Kiev, then Kuibyshev, Karkhov, Stalingrad [sic], Sebastopol etc etc. And now where are the Russians!!!

I tried to crush his over-optimism based on the results of our experiment, and was asked with contempt what reason I had for minimizing the results of these discoveries. I was trying to dispel his dreams and as usual he did not like it. But I *shudder* to feel that he is allowing the half baked results of one experiment to warp the whole of his diplomatic perspective! During lunch Anthony Eden came in hot from his discussion with Molotov and Byrnes, I am afraid that he added to my gloom. Delightful as he is in my opinion he always seems to just miss the point.

Spent the afternoon reading over the minutes of the meetings of the big three and they are very interesting reading, the one fact that stands out more clearly than any other is that nothing is ever settled!!

Finally the day finished up with a big dinner by Winston attended by Stalin, Truman, Eden, Molotov, Byrnes, Marshall, King, Arnold, Leahy, Cunningham, Portal, AB, Ismay, Alexander, Montgomery, Attlee, Bridges, Zhukov, Antonov, Moran, etc, etc. It was a good dinner with RAF band, rather spoilt by continuous speeches. Truman proposed my health coupled with Antonov. I had to reply and in doing so reminded Stalin of his Yalta toast 'to those men who are always wanted in war and always forgotten in peace – the soldiers'. I said that I had studied Antonov's face with care to find whether he was forgotten and was glad to see that he was not. I reminded the politicians and diplomats that even in peace there might be a use for soldiers. And finally proposed the toast to the hope, perhaps a pious hope, that soldiers might not be forgotten in peace!! This went down well with Stalin, who replied at once that soldiers would never be forgotten. After dinner we had the menus signed up and I went round to ask Stalin for his signature, he turned round, looked at me, smiled very kindly and shook me warmly by the hand before signing. After the band playing all the national anthems we went off to bed.

It is interesting to note Winston's reaction, and my counter-reactions to the atomic bomb news. Winston's appreciation of its value in the future international balance of power was certainly far more accurate than mine. But what was worrying me was that with his usual enthusiasm for anything new, he was letting himself be carried away by the very first and rather scanty reports of the first atomic explosion. He was already seeing himself capable of eliminating all the Russian centres of industry and population, without taking into account any of the connected problems, such as delivery of the bomb, production of bombs, possibility of Russia also possessing such bombs, etc etc. He had at once painted a wonderful picture of himself as the sole possessor of these bombs and capable of dumping them where he wished, thus all powerful and capable of dictating to Stalin! This attitude brought out all my reactionary sentiments which led me into a failure to fully realize the importance of the new discovery.

24 July

Another full, but on the whole satisfactory day. Started with a COS at 10.30. Then a Plenary Meeting at 11.30 in the President's house with him and PM present. I was very interested in this first meeting with Truman after the many ones we had had with Roosevelt. On the whole I liked him, not the same personality as his predecessor, but a quick brain, a feeling of honesty, a good business man, and a pleasant personality. Last night in one of his quick remarks Stalin had said about him 'honesty adorns the man' and he was not far wrong. We went through our final report and got it all settled up. Leathers and Cherwell had mixed themselves up in the Basic Undertaking and had as a result made the Americans thoroughly suspicious, consequently the final terms secured by the PM were not as favourable as if we had been left to our own devices.

After lunch at 2.30 pm we had a meeting with the Russian Chiefs of Staff on a tripartite basis. The meeting was held in the Cecilienhof, the Crown Prince's House in Potsdam. Our meeting was quite cordial. Antonov informed us that the Russians were coming into the war in August. What could we do to hold Jap forces to prevent them from concentrating in Manchuria? Marshall and King replied from the American point of view, and I followed on with Cunningham and Portal as regards our operations. We then came back as Mountbatten had turned up and we had fixed up that he should give us a quick talk with the Americans at 5.30. It was a bad talk intended to show what marvels he had done in spite of being deprived of all the facilities of war! Finally dined with King to meet the American Chiefs of Staff and afterwards went to the new Potsdam Palace to listen to the Air Force Band. It played Handel's Largo for me by request quite beautifully.

Thus finished our Combined Chiefs of Staff Meeting, in Berlin!! where we had never hoped to meet in our wildest dreams in the early stages of this war. And now that we are here I feel too weary and cooked to even get a kick out of it. It all feels flat and empty. I am feeling very very tired and worn out.

It had been much the easiest of any of our meetings. The old battles were done and finished. No more battles to stop Americans from crossing the Channel too early. No more battles to lead them to North Africa and keep them there. No more battles to bring them along through Sicily to Italy, and no more battles to hold them in Italy till the critical moment. All that was by now past history.

There now only remained the Pacific problems to coordinate, and as in this theatre they had always been much more of a predominant partner, it was more a matter of conforming to their strategy. Looking back at the conference I remember only too well those feelings of unaccountable flatness that hung over me. I had a feeling that my mind was not registering properly the magnitude of the occasion. After all those years of relentless struggles, those hours of deep despondency, those shattering setbacks, those first signs of hope, that string of repeated successes, when the end came at last it seemed to fall flat and did not kindle that fire of enthusiasm which I should have expected. There is no doubt that I was suffering from extreme exhaustion by that time, and this fact in itself was probably sufficient to account for a grey outlook on our success.

25 July

By 10.30 am we were taking [to] the air in the 'York' for our journey home. Before flying off we did a couple of circles round Berlin to have a look at it from the air, and we were able to appreciate the degree of destruction. The flight back took us 3 hours and 10 mins, but as the clock went back 2 hours it left me still with plenty of time to put in some work in the War Office before lunch. I then spent the afternoon working up back papers and getting level with the work here. I find my brain quite exhausted nowadays and have to read each paper two or 3 times to make any sense of it.

26 July   London

Potsdam Conference is apparently over as far as we are concerned! The Conservative Government has had a complete landslide and is out for good and all!! If only Winston had followed my advice he would have been in at any rate till the end of the year! But what was my advice to him a mere soldier!!! Now he is gone, and P.J. Who shall I be dealing with in future, Attlee? as PM and who as S of S. I feel too old and weary to start off on any new experiments.

It is probably all for the good of England in the long run, any government in power during the next year is not going to last long. But what a ghastly mistake to start elections at this period in the World's History! May God forgive England for it.

27 July

A day of partings! First a COS to which Dickie came and did not contribute greatly to. After lunch I had a long interview with S of S. It was a sad one and I hate to see him go. We have worked wonderfully together, and I have grown to know him well and to appreciate his high qualities. I am genuinely fond of him, and very sad at our parting. Then at 5.30 pm had to go and see Winston at 10 Downing St, with other Chiefs of Staff. It was a very sad and very moving little meeting at which I found myself unable to say much for fear of breaking down. He was standing the blow wonderfully well.

Afterwards drove home, looking in on Alexander on the way back as he leaves for Italy on Monday. Arrived home for late dinner, and during dinner Eric Hosking turned up to fix details about my using his hide to photograph [the] hobby tomorrow.

The thought that my days of work with Winston had come to an end was a shattering one. There had been very difficult times, and times when I felt I could not stand a single more day with him, but running through all our difficulties a bond of steel had been formed uniting us together. We had been so closely linked together in this vast struggle that it would have been impossible for us to go on striving together unless a deep bond of friendship had existed; had this not been the case there would have been only one alternative, that of parting. No doubt Winston must frequently have felt that he could stand me no longer, and I marvel even now that as a result of some of our differences he did not replace me. There are few things that can bind two individuals more closely than to be intimately connected in a vast struggle against overwhelming odds and to emerge on top of all.

On reading these diaries I have repeatedly felt ashamed of the abuse I had poured on him, especially during the latter years. It must, however, be remembered that my diary was the safety valve and only outlet for all my pent up feelings. Feelings that had been engendered through friction generated from prolonged contacts of very tired individuals. During the last years Winston had been a very sick man, with repeated attacks of pneumonia, and very frequent attacks of temperature. This physical condition together with his mental fatigue accounted for many of the difficulties in dealing with him, a factor which I failed to make adequate allowance for in my diary. I shall always look back on the years I worked with him as some of the most difficult and trying ones in my life. For all that I thank God that I was given an opportunity of working alongside of such a man, and of having my eyes opened to the fact that occasionally such supermen exist on this earth.

The election was facing me with a double blow. On the one side the loss of Winston and on the other that of P.J. Grigg. Providence was indeed kind to me during the war to have placed P.J. at the helm in the WO. It would have been hard to find a man with whom I would sooner have worked. The position of a CIGS in war is a difficult one, he has to serve two masters. According to the Bible such a procedure is impossible. I should qualify this statement by stating that with exceptional masters this may be possible. If it was possible for me during the war this was thanks to the attitude of one of my masters, the S of S, and in spite of the fact that the other master, the PM, did not always contribute to the smooth running of this tripartite set up. In my early days I did sense some degree of suspicion on the part of P.J. concerning my activities on the COS committee and my direct contacts with the PM. However from the moment that I had gained his confidence, and assured him that he would always be kept informed of all my activities in the service of my second master, I received his unstinted help and invaluable advice in all my work. Gifted with one of the quickest brains I have met, it was an easy task to keep him in the picture even when time was short. I always knew when consulting him that I should get the most valuable advice. Above all I found that his nature was such that the more one saw of him the more one realized his sterling qualities of unflinching straightness. During the years I worked with him I grew to appreciate these qualities and developed a genuine deep affection for him which made our parting difficult.

The loss of these two old friends at this period of the war gave me a desolate and lonely feeling, and a disinclination to continue with the struggle.

28 July

Met Hosking at 8.30 at the White Lion and went on to the hide at once. A huge erection 26 feet high! but within 12 feet of the nest. There are 3 young birds. By 9 am I was established. At 10.45 the hen came for the first time and was at nest feeding for 10 minutes. At 12.15 she returned and was again there for close on 10 minutes. I took a lot of photographs and only hope that they may be good. It was a wonderful chance, and I believe the first time that a coloured cine picture of a hobby has been taken!

29 July

A quiet Sunday at home.

30 July

Usual early Monday start, left my priceless films with Kodak, I do pray that they may be good! A short COS followed by a visit to Akerman [probably Ackermann and Johnson, fine art dealers] to pick the rest of the pictures of

Thorburn's sketches. Finally a quiet afternoon. We still do not know who is to be our Secretary of State. I must say that I rather shudder starting in with a new man again!

31 July
We had a short COS, but interesting as we had the Combined [Joint?] Intelligence Committee in and they warned of the gathering clouds on the northern Greek frontier. Seven Yugoslav Divisions close to frontier, many more behind, 19 Bulgarian divisions, 350–400,000 Russians all in Bulgaria. It looks too much like power politics to be pleasant. Meanwhile Foreign Office as usual going adrift! We were originally told to send 10,000 troops to Greece to back the Government, I said it would require at least 80,000 to do what they wanted. I was informed politely that I knew nothing about it as it was a political matter and that 10,000 would be ample to give the necessary backing to the Government. We eventually sent about 90,000 into Greece!!!

Now having originally sent forces into Greece to restore law and order internally, we are informed that these self same forces are required to also defend the frontiers of Greece!! We are on a slippery slope, with one task leading into another all requiring more and more forces which we have not got. And at the same time we receive instructions to accelerate our own demobilization!

After lunch Freyberg came to see me, and I had a long discussion with him on the question of the New Zealand Div being made available for the Imperial Task Force destined for the invasion of Japan. It is hard to keep him on a high plane and he continually descends into detail.

1 August
An early start and by 7.30 am Rollie and I were off, heading for the hobby's nest! By 9.15 I was again up in the hide 22 feet above the ground and glad to have the climb up behind me! By 9.45 the hobby was back feeding and I exposed about 100ft of Kodachrome. I felt all was well and I must at least fit in another feed. But no luck – I remained till 2 pm and she never returned! At 2 pm Rollie with the whole family turned up, and we drove back to the flat where we had a large tea. I then went back to the WO and Rollie went off with you all to Sandgate to deposit you with Nancy [Dill]. Gibbon came to dine. Freyberg came to see me this evening to assure me that he was the one man to command the Corps for the invasion of Japan!

2 August
A remarkably short COS after which I collected my precious film of the hobby taken last Saturday. I am glad to say that it has turned out very good and I am delighted with it. During the afternoon, first an interview with Franklyn to say goodbye to him, and then one with Monkey Morgan just back from Italy. Finally long discussion with Simpson on plans for our Imperial Expedition for

the invasion of Japan with a corps of 1 British, 1 Canadian and 1 Australian Division.

3 August

Adam came to lunch and I had a long talk with him about appointments, he feels that Giffard as his successor would not be able to hold the job long enough owing to his age [nearly 60]. In the evening ran down to Sandgate to spend August Bank Holiday weekend with Nancy Dill, you and children.

4, 5 and 6 August

Lovely weather and several bathes. Finally returned evening of 6th as Monty was dining with me. I discussed with him WO appointments on the supposition that he might possibly replace me within the next few months.

7 August

I have had a long and somewhat weary day. First of all a Chiefs of Staff meeting with Mountbatten and Lloyd of the Australian Army. The latter was quite excellent and clear headed. The former was as usual quite impossible and wasted a lot of our time. Always fastening onto the irrelevant points, repeating himself, failing to recognize the vital points etc etc. Seldom has a Supreme Commander been more deficient of the main attributes of a Supreme Commander than Dickie Mountbatten. After lunch a Selection Board attended by Monty.

Then our first [Labour] Cabinet Meeting! We were asked to deal with the strategic situation! I had to start, and go all round the world starting with the occupied zone etc. I was asked many questions by Bevan, Miss Wilkinson etc, all of them mainly influenced by political as opposed to military motives. A wonderful transformation of the Cabinet with a lot of new faces, however some of the old ones are still there such as Attlee, Bevin, Stafford Cripps, Morrison, Alexander.

I remember being very impressed by the efficiency with which Attlee ran his cabinet. There was not the same touch of genius as with Winston, but there were more businesslike methods. We kept to the agenda, and he maintained complete order with a somewhat difficult crowd. Our work was quickly and efficiently completed.

8 August

A short COS, then a talk with our new S of S [Jack Lawson, MP for Chester-le-Street, ex-miner] to try and put him into the picture for a Defence Committee Meeting this afternoon. Gras[ett] came to lunch and was as delightful as ever, walked back to the WO with him. There I found Dickie Mountbatten waiting for me. As usual he wanted me to pull the chestnuts out of the fire for him, and expected me to tackle First Sea Lord to draw aircraft carrier from the Pacific Fleet for his purposes! I called his bluff and told him to do his own dirty work. We then went to our first Defence Committee meeting under Attlee. The party consisted of PM, Bevin, 3 Service Secretaries, Chiefs of Staff and Dickie Mountbatten. On the whole a successful meeting, at which we settled all we wanted. In the evening Army Council dinner at Claridges for Slim and Pownall. Then I met Bellenger [MP for Bassetlaw; S of S 1946–47] for the first time and also [Lord] Nathan [Parliamentary Under-Secretary for War].

9 August

Quite a long COS with the planners in discussing final actions necessary to put into action the preparation of the Corps for the invasion of Japan. Also getting the Greek frontier situation straightened out.

Lunched at the Aperitif with Rollie and Cynthia [his daughter]. After lunch went to see Mrs Archibald Thorburn, she was quite charming, showing me sketches by Thorburn and telling me all the old connections with him. She also insisted on giving me a Chillingham cow to go with the bull she had already given me! She also presented me with a sketch of red deer. The dear old lady was touchingly happy to discuss her husband's sketches with someone who was taking a real interest in them.

Back to the WO for a meeting with the CRAs which Otto Lund was running. Then a meeting with Slim prior to his departure for India [C-in-C Allied Land Forces, South East Asia]. I rubbed into him my dislike for 'prima donna generals' and 'film star generals', I hope he will take it to heart. Finally dined with Admiral Blake [Flag Officer Liaison US Navy] with you to say goodbye to old Stark who is leaving. Winant, Andrew Cunningham and wife were also there.

10 August

A memorable day as regards the war with Japan!* Started with a long COS attended by Mountbatten, I find it very hard to remain pleasant when he turns up! He is the most crashing bore I have met on a committee, is always fiddling about with unimportant matters and wasting other people's time.

Just before lunch BBC intercepts of Japanese peace offers were received in the shape of an acceptance of the Potsdam offer. There was however one rather obscure clause concerning the prerogatives of the Emperor being retained. PM convened a Cabinet for 3 pm when the message was examined. Stafford Cripps and Jowitt [former Attorney-General] expressed their legal opinions. Cabinet were unanimous that Americans must assume major share, but that if they were of the opinion that the clause affecting the Emperor was acceptable we should agree. I had to give a statement of the various measures that would become necessary in order to put the surrender into effect. Somewhat

---

*Atomic bombs had been dropped on Hiroshima and Nagasaki on 6 and 9 August respectively.

complicated problem! The Chiefs of Staff were liberated from the Cabinet at 4 and we convened a COS meeting for 5 pm to be attended by Joint Planners. I told them the general outline of what was required and instructed them to prepare a paper to be ready Sunday evening [12 August] and considered Monday morning covering the various actions required. Telegrams to Mountbatten, Dominions, information for Foreign Office, Dominion Office, etc. One of the main points of urgency is that of providing a force for the rapid occupation of Hong Kong. We finished about 6 pm.

I then returned to WO to deal with urgent papers, then picked up Nancy Dill at [the] Berkeley and you at the flat and off we started for a weekend at Sandgate.

11 and 12 August
Glorious weekend by the sea with 3 bathes and perfect rest and quiet! Returned London with you and children on Sunday evening arriving back in time for dinner.

Since then have been busy dealing with correspondence, telegrams and Planners' papers. All going well, reply has been sent to Japan, we now await their final acceptance. Meanwhile our plans for the Japanese surrender are progressing. MacArthur as Supreme Commander to work through the Emperor and Fraser [C-in-C Pacific Fleet] to be our representative with him. Force for Hong Kong progressing, also details for a Commonwealth occupational force. It is hard to realize that by the end of the coming week the war with Japan may be over!

13 August
We had a long COS meeting attended by the Foreign Office and representatives from South East Asia Command to discuss the dispositions necessary in the event of a Japanese surrender. Then lunched with you and the children and in the afternoon a Defence Committee on the same matter attended by Herbert Morrison, Bevin, 3 Secretaries of Services, Dominions, Colonies, Labour and Transport. I had to give a general account of all our recommendations.

Finally Hosking and his wife came to dine to see the coloured film of the hobby. Eric Hosking was delighted with it and very complimentary about it.

14 August
Announcement appeared this morning of the 3 Chiefs of Staff having been created Barons! When you look at some of the other Barons and Viscounts etc, one wonders whether it is such an honour and a distinction!

Joint Intelligence Committee attended the COS and we said goodbye to Cavendish-Bentinck of the Foreign Office who is now off as Ambassador to Moscow [Warsaw]. Pongo came to lunch. During the afternoon Halifax came to see me and we had a long talk. Finally dined with Stark who is returning to

Washington to say goodbye to him. Have just heard that midnight wireless announces Japan's final acceptance of the terms!! Can this really be the end of the war?

15 August

The end of this war for certain. Six very very long years of continuous struggle, nerve wracking anxiety, dashed hopes, hopeless bleak horizons, endless difficulties with Winston, etc etc finished with! When I look back at the blackest moments it becomes almost impossible to believe that we stand where we do. One thing above all others predominates all other thoughts, namely boundless gratitude to God, and to His guiding hand which has brought us where we are. Throughout the war his guiding influence has constantly made itself felt.

In the morning I had to attend the opening of Parliament in the capacity of ADC General to the King. I had never attended such a ceremony and found it interesting though not inspiring. After lunch I had to proceed to Storey's Gate to join up with PM, Bevin, Herbert Morrison and Greenly to proceed to the Palace. The other Chiefs of Staff, Pug Ismay and Bridges were also there. We were shown in to the King and had a short interview rather similar to the VE Day one, and subsequently had a photograph taken of the War Cabinet with the King and one of the King with the Chiefs of Staff. Back to WO where I had interviews with McCreery and the S of S [Lawson]. The latter again asked me to stop on for another year, I again pressed for situation to be reviewed at the end of this year. He also informed me that he wished to visit India shortly. Finally went home with you in anticipation of visit to Larkhill tomorrow.

16 August

Left home at 9.30 am with Rollie and motored to Larkhill to see one of Otto Lund's demonstrations. A lovely day and most interesting demonstration attended by the Master Gunner [Lord Milne], Copper Finlayson, Crocker and Alan Cunningham. Returned to War Office about 6 pm and put in 2 hours before dinner.

17 August

Gort came to lunch with me. I did not think that he was looking at all well. He was interesting about Palestine and all its problems. In the evening motored home dropping in on Lodge on way back to show him the new book of his pictures.

18 August

Spent quietly at home.

19 August

After an early lunch left home with you at 1 pm and motored to Buckingham Palace. There you took Lady Portal and Lady Cunningham into the car with you and drove on to St Paul's. Meanwhile Cunningham, Portal and I took our seats in a landau pulled by 4 bays in the King's procession to St Paul's. It was an interesting experience to go through and to look at the crowd instead of being one of them! On arrival at the Cathedral I rejoined you for the service. Subsequently again driving back in the procession which consisted of 3 landaus, one for the King and Queen, one for ladies in waiting and Lascelles, and one for us. On arrival at the Palace the King and Queen sent for us and were as usual kindness itself. Cunningham then drove me to the Ladies' Carlton Club where we joined up again and drove to Hartley Wintney.

20 August

Usual early start. Long COS. Afternoon filled with visits from Hobart, Ellis, our scientific advisor to discuss atomic bomb, MS, Eric Speed [PUS] and Archie Nye.

21 August

Hong Kong and its relief by British forces before the arrival of either Chinese or American forces filled most of our COS discussion and plans. However I think that the problem is gradually sorting itself out. This afternoon I attended for the first time the new Committee which I form part of under John Anderson to study the future of the Atomic Bomb. We have got a queer party of scientists, but it promises to be an intensely interesting committee. Finished up with a sherry party to meet Chennault who is on his way back from China.

22 August

A short COS in which we decided that Mountbatten must conform to MacArthur's wishes as regards the dates in the process of surrender. Namely to await the surrender in Tokyo before attempting surrenders in the outlying districts. [Gen] Martin came to lunch. After lunch had interviews with Jack Whitaker just back from his tour out to Burma and India. Then with King back from India on his Welfare trip. Fortescue, Stella and Stanton came to dinner.

23 August

We finished our COS with a private meeting discussing future of COS, our own successors and probable dates of our departures. We all favoured the period between January and March for the end of our tours. The following were possible successors:

CNS – Tovey too obstinate, John Cunningham the best, Fraser a little later after more experience.

CAS – Tedder best, Slessor possible but better to wait for couple of years.

CIGS – Monty very efficient from Army point of view, but very unpopular with large proportion of the Army. Archie Nye very capable but after 7 years in War Office must have some outside experience. Of these two both Portal and Cunningham strongly in favour of Monty.

Pug – Only two real alternatives. Jo Hollis or Ian Jacob. Pug favoured first, personally I feel certain Jacob is best. In any case Hollis may be required for the Marines.

We then discussed the cost of becoming a Baron. Apparently I can't get out of it under £200 which appals me.

Went out to lunch with Alba at the Spanish Embassy. Winston was to have been there but did not turn up. Portuguese Ambassador, Oliver Stanley, Bobbety Cranborne, Morton and several Spaniards. As usual one of the best lunches I have ever eaten. Long interview with MS trying to settle future moves in the Army Council and in senior commands. A very difficult matter! Finally out with Rollie and his wife to see *Me and My Girl* which was exceptionally amusing.

24 August
A very long COS as we could not agree on the question of command of Hong Kong after its liberation! Portal and I wanted to place [it] to start with under Dickie Mountbatten, and Cunningham wanted it under the COS. Finally we had to leave it for next Monday. Adam came to lunch, rather guilty as he had been releasing men from the Army faster than we can ship them home! Returned home in the evening.

25 and 26 August
A lovely weekend at home.

27 August
Early start. Another very busy sitting of the COS over the matter of Hong Kong and I do not think that we are any nearer a solution! During the afternoon visits from Schreiber and Paget back from Cairo. The latter with many difficult problems.

28 August
This morning I struggled with the COS trying to get the other two to realize the dangers of the Foreign Office policy in Greece, where they now suggest that we should take on frontier defence as well as our internal task of supporting the gov, maintaining law and order and distributing food. It is shattering how little sailors and airmen are able to understand the problems connected with land warfare! You and the children came up after lunch, and we had a wonderful party. Had another interview with Lawson [S of S], I fail to see how I am ever to get him to appreciate what his task really is!!

Lawson was a serious puzzle to me, he was one of the most charming of men. A religious man of high principles and of great charm, but completely ignorant of all military matters. He had not got the faintest idea what his job required of him and as far as I could see it was impossible to make him realize it. I found it quite beyond my powers to brief him on the various items for discussion on Cabinet Agendas. As far as I could see he never read any of the papers which were circulated to him, and I doubt if he would have been any the wiser even if he had read them. He was such a charming individual that I felt very distressed at not being able to help him more. On the other hand the contrast between him and P.J. Grigg was ghastly! With P.J. I had the best and most valuable advice on any matter I discussed with him. Now that was all gone. Luckily my furrow was now easier to plough, the war was over and work with Attlee was infinitely easier than work with Winston.

30 August

I have lost a day somewhere but can't make out where! This morning we had representatives from the Dominion Office in whilst we discussed Australia's latest claim to run an occupational force quite separate from ours in Japan. We were recommending another attempt to try and get Australia to join with our Commonwealth united force. They are trying to run out on their own. Dominion Office are not showing much guts in returning to the attack. Wavell came to lunch, I recommended to him that he should put up Auk for Field Marshal and he agreed with me. This afternoon attended one of Bevin's special Mediterranean Committees, we did not get very much further, but he was as usual very pleasant.

31 August

After our COS I had Paget to lunch, he was in excellent form and we had a most useful talk. In the evening I motored home.

ACKNOWLEDGEMENTS

We are grateful to the Trustees of Lord Alanbrooke's settlement for authorization to proceed with this project, and for unrestricted access to the Alanbrooke Papers in the Liddell Hart Centre for Military Archives at King's College, London. For sage advice at every stage we are indebted to the Director of Archive Services, Patricia J. Methven, and for efficient and friendly assistance to all of her staff. We applaud in particular Alan Kucia for his heroic work on the typescript. Documentary material in the care of the Centre is quoted by permission of its Trustees. The keepers of the keys to a number of other repositories have also been extremely helpful, notably Roderick Suddaby at the Imperial War Museum, and Effie Warr at the Natural History Museum, Tring.

We are grateful, also, to the British Academy, for the award of a Small Grant, which helped to defray the expenses of collation and computerization; to King's College, London, which elected Alex Danchev to a Visiting Senior Research Fellowship in War Studies for 1998–2000, and to Keele, which provided him with a much-needed period of research leave; and to Dr Jay Winter and Dr Peter Martland, at Cambridge, for their tolerance of Daniel Todman's work on this project.

We are grateful to the Estate of Anthony Powell and William Heinemann for permission to reproduce an extract from *The Military Philosophers* in our Introduction to this volume.

We would have got nowhere without the help of Bruce Hunter at David Higham Associates and Ion Trewin at Weidenfeld & Nicolson: we salute them both. Benjamin Buchan edited and Douglas Matthews indexed this little monster: we salute them too.

AD and DT
March 2001

INDEX